J(
Our Tr
Comp

`MW01503877`

We can help you ......

- Complete travel agency services, including expert travel planning and all travel reservations
- Passport Photos and International Driving Permits
- Fee-Free American Express® Travelers Cheques
- Discounts on Avis and Hertz Car Rentals
- Hotel Reservations
- Rail Tickets
- Individual and Escorted Tours

- Travel Insurance
- Tour Operator Default Protection Plan
- TripAssist, including 24-hour emergency access to legal, medical and travel related services worldwide
- AND Emergency Road Service Abroad — AAA maintains reciprocal agreements with auto clubs in 20 countries on five continents around the world

To Join AAA Today Just Call
1-800-336-4357

Discover the Benefits of Membership BEFORE You Take Your Next Trip.

Complete the postage-paid reply card TODAY.

£1
VOUCHER
May be redeemed in accordance with the conditions overleaf at any establishment whose entry displays the £1 symbol.

£1
VOUCHER
May be redeemed in accordance with the conditions overleaf at any establishment whose entry displays the £1 symbol.

£1
VOUCHER
May be redeemed in accordance with the conditions overleaf at any establishment whose entry displays the £1 symbol.

£1
VOUCHER
May be redeemed in accordance with the conditions overleaf at any establishment whose entry displays the £1 symbol.

£1
VOUCHER
May be redeemed in accordance with the conditions overleaf at any establishment whose entry displays the £1 symbol.

£1
VOUCHER
May be redeemed in accordance with the conditions overleaf at any establishment whose entry displays the £1 symbol.

£1
VOUCHER
May be redeemed in accordance with the conditions overleaf at any establishment whose entry displays the £1 symbol.

£1
VOUCHER
May be redeemed in accordance with the conditions overleaf at any establishment whose entry displays the £1 symbol.

CONDITIONS

Voucher and AA Bed & Breakfast 1995 Guide
must be shown on check in.
Only one voucher per person or party accepted.
Not redeemable for cash; no change given.
Valid until midnight 31 December 1995.
Only valid against a full-tariff
accommodation bill.
For full details, see page 9.

CONDITIONS

Voucher and AA Bed & Breakfast 1995 Guide
must be shown on check in.
Only one voucher per person or party accepted.
Not redeemable for cash; no change given.
Valid until midnight 31 December 1995.
Only valid against a full-tariff
accommodation bill.
For full details, see page 9.

CONDITIONS

Voucher and AA Bed & Breakfast 1995 Guide
must be shown on check in.
Only one voucher per person or party accepted.
Not redeemable for cash; no change given.
Valid until midnight 31 December 1995.
Only valid against a full-tariff
accommodation bill.
For full details, see page 9.

CONDITIONS

Voucher and AA Bed & Breakfast 1995 Guide
must be shown on check in.
Only one voucher per person or party accepted.
Not redeemable for cash; no change given.
Valid until midnight 31 December 1995.
Only valid against a full-tariff
accommodation bill.
For full details, see page 9.

CONDITIONS

Voucher and AA Bed & Breakfast 1995 Guide
must be shown on check in.
Only one voucher per person or party accepted.
Not redeemable for cash; no change given.
Valid until midnight 31 December 1995.
Only valid against a full-tariff
accommodation bill.
For full details, see page 9.

CONDITIONS

Voucher and AA Bed & Breakfast 1995 Guide
must be shown on check in.
Only one voucher per person or party accepted.
Not redeemable for cash; no change given.
Valid until midnight 31 December 1995.
Only valid against a full-tariff
accommodation bill.
For full details, see page 9.

CONDITIONS

Voucher and AA Bed & Breakfast 1995 Guide
must be shown on check in.
Only one voucher per person or party accepted.
Not redeemable for cash; no change given.
Valid until midnight 31 December 1995.
Only valid against a full-tariff
accommodation bill.
For full details, see page 9.

CONDITIONS

Voucher and AA Bed & Breakfast 1995 Guide
must be shown on check in.
Only one voucher per person or party accepted.
Not redeemable for cash; no change given.
Valid until midnight 31 December 1995.
Only valid against a full-tariff
accommodation bill.
For full details, see page 9.

AA

BED AND BREAKFAST GUIDE

Britain and Ireland

1995

Produced by AA Publishing
Atlas prepared by the AA's Cartographic Department
Maps © The Automobile Association 1994

Directory generated by the AA Establishment Database,
Information Research and Control, Hotel and Touring Services

The cover and title page show the
Thatched Cottage Hotel at Brockenhurst, Hampshire

Advertisements
Head of Advertisement Sales: Christopher Heard
Tel. 0256 20123 ext. 21544
Advertisement Production: Karen Weeks
Tel. 0256 20123 ext. 21545

Typeset by Avonset, Midsomer Norton, Bath
Printed and bound by Unwin Brothers Ltd.,

The contents of this publication are believed correct at the time of
printing. Nevertheless the Publisher cannot be held responsible for any errors or
omissions or for changes in the details given in this guide or for the
consequences of any reliance on the information provided in the same.
Although every effort has been made to ensure accuracy we always welcome
any information from readers to assist in such efforts and to keep the book
up to date.

Assessments of the establishments in this guide are based on the experience(s)
of the AA's professional hotel and restaurant inspectors on the occasion(s) of
their visit(s) and therefore the descriptions given in this guide may contain an
element of subjective opinion which may not dictate a reader's experience
on another occasion.

A CIP catalogue record for this book is available from
the British Library

Published by AA Publishing which is a trading name of
Automobile Association Developments Limited whose registered office is
Norfolk House, Basingstoke, Hampshire RG24 9NY,
Registered number 1878835

AA Ref 12250

ISBN 0 7495 0902 3

4

CONTENTS

AA
INSPECTION & CLASSIFICATION

HINTS FOR BOOKING YOUR STAY

The AA inspects and classifies more than 3000 small hotels, guest houses, farmhouse and inns for its 'AA recommended', 'AA Selected', and 'AA Premier Selected' categories. The precise number of places in the guide varies slightly from year to year, and we are happy this year to see a marked increase both in the total number of establishments in the guide, and in the top two categories.

Ⓠ Quality Awards (see also page 10)

All the establishments listed in the directory are given awards of between one and five Qs for quality. More details about the Q awards can be found in the section headed 'Quality Assessment' on page 10. Those places that have gained the two highest ratings - four Q and five Q awards - have their entries highlighted in the directory. Those with four Qs are in a tinted panel under the heading 'Selected' and those with five Qs, the very highest category, are headed 'Premier Selected' and have a photograph with their entry. For quick reference, you will find a list of the establishments awarded five Qs on page 11 and a list of establishments awarded four Qs on page 25.

Best Budget Bargains

Establishments that offer bed and breakfast for £15 or under are indicated by the symbol 🛏🍷 against their entry.

Staying at a Guest House

The term 'guest house' can lead to some confusion, particularly when many include the word 'hotel' in their name. For AA purposes, small and private hotels are included in this category when they cannot offer all the services required for our hotel star rating system.

The term does not imply that guest houses are infe rior to hotels, just that they are different. Many, indeed, offer a very high standard of accommodation. It is not unusual to be offered en suite bathrooms, for instance, or to find a direct-dial telephone and a colour television in your room. There is sometimes more than one lounge, and leisure facilities may include a swimming pool.

Some guest houses are only able to offer a set me in the evening, but many provide an interesting menu and a standard of service that one would expect in a good restaurant. You may have to arrange dinner in advance rather than just turning up in the dining room at the stated time. You should ask about the arrangements for evening meals when booking. Many places have a full licence, or at least a table licence and wine list.

Of course, some guest houses offer bed and break fast only, so guests must go out for the evening meal. It is also wise to check when booking if ther are any restrictions to your access to the house, particularly in the late morning and during the afternoon.

Guest houses in the London section of the book a all small hotels. London prices tend to be higher than those outside the capital, but those that we list offer cost-conscious accommodation, although normally only bed and breakfast is provided. To allow for all eventualities, we have also included a few which provide a full meal service and the charges for these will naturally be higher.

Staying at a Farmhouse

Farmhouse accommodation is particularly noted for being inexpensive and cosy, with a high standard of good home-cooking. Those listed in our book are generally working farms, and some farmers are happy to allow visitors to look around, or even to help feed the animals. However, we must stress that the modern farm is a potentially dangerous place, especially where machinery and chemicals are concerned, and visitors must be prepared to exercise care, particularly if they bring children. Never leave children unsupervised around the farm.

Sometimes, guest accommodation is run as a separate concern from the farm, and visitors are discouraged from venturing on to the working land. In other cases, the land has been sold off and only the house remains. Although the directory entry states the acreage and the type of farming carried out, you should check when booking to make sure that t matches your expectations.

As with guest houses, standards will vary considerably, and are often far above what one would expect. Some of our farmhouses are grand ex-manor houses furnished with antiques and offering a stylish way of life, whereas others offer more simply furnished accommodation, and in others guests may have to share the family bathroom and sitting/dining room.

All of the farmhouses are listed under town or village names, but obviously many will be some distance from any other habitation. The owners will, of course, give directions when you book, and we publish a six-figure map reference against the directory entry which can be used in conjunction with Ordnance Survey large-scale maps like the 1:50 000 Landranger series.

Staying at an Inn

We all know what we can expect to find in a traditional inn - a cosy bar, a convivial atmosphere, good beer and pub food. Nevertheless, there are a few extra criteria which must be met for the AA

classification. Breakfast is a must of course, in a suitable breakfast room, and the inn should also serve at least light meals during licensing hours. In this guide, a number of small, fully licensed hotels are classified as inns, and the character of the properties will vary according to whether they are traditional country inns or larger establishments in towns. Again it is important to check details before you book, and also remember to ask if you can arrive at any time of the day or only during opening hours.

Common to All

Whatever the type of establishment, there are certain requirements common to all, including a well-maintained exterior, clean and hygienic kitchens; good standards of furnishing; friendly and courteous service; access to the premises at reasonable times; the use of a telephone; and a full, cooked breakfast in the British or Irish tradition. Bedrooms should be equipped with comfortable beds, a wardrobe, a bedside cabinet, a washbasin (unless there is an en suite or private bath/shower room) with soap, towel, mirror and shaver socket and at least a carpet beside the bed. There should not be an extra charge for the use of baths or lavatories, and heating should not be metered.

NB. Where the entry for an establishment shows the central heating symbol, it does not necessarily mean that central heating will be available all year round. Some places only use it in winter, and then at their own discretion.

Booking

Book as early as possible, particularly for the peak holiday period which runs from the beginning of June to the end of September, and may also include Easter and other public holidays, In some parts of Scotland the skiing season is a peak holiday period.

Although it is possible for chance callers to find a night's accommodation, it is by no means a certainty, especially at peak holiday times and in popular areas, so it is always advisable to book as far in advance as possible. Some establishments will require a deposit on booking. Some may only accept weekly bookings from Saturday.

The AA regrets that it cannot undertake to make any reservations.

We have tried to provide as much information as possible about the establishments in our directory, but if you require further information, write to or telephone the establishment itself. Do remember to enclose a stamped addressed envelope, or an international reply-paid coupon if writing from overseas, and please quote this publication in any enquiry. Although we try to publish accurate and up to date information, please remember that any details, and particularly prices, are subject to change without notice and this may happen during the currency of the guide.

Smoking Regulations

The 'no-smoking' symbol when used by itself in the guide indicates a total ban on smoking throughout the premises. If only certain areas are designated no-smoking (eg bedrooms, dining room) the symbol is followed by the appropriate word.

Although we have tried to get accurate information on this question from the establishments, you must remember that the situation may change after the guide has gone to print and during the currency of this edition. If the freedom to smoke or to be in a smoke-free atmosphere is important to you, please make sure what the rule is before you book a room.

Cancellation

If you find that you must cancel a booking, let the proprietor know at once, because if the room you booked cannot be re-let, you may be held legally responsible for partial payment. Whether it is a matter of losing your deposit, or of being liable for compensation, you should seriously consider taking out cancellation insurance, such as AA Travelsure.

Complaints

Readers who have any cause to complain are urged to do so on the spot. This should provide an opportunity for the proprietor to correct matters. If a personal approach fails, readers should inform: AA Hotel Services, Basingstoke, Hants, RG21 2EA.

Fire Precautions

Many of the establishments listed in the Guide are subject to the requirements of the Fire Precautions Act of 1971. As far as we can discover, every establishment in this book has applied for, and not been refused, a fire certificate.

The Fire Precautions Act does not apply to Ireland (see the Contents page for the Irish Directory), the Channel Islands, or the Isle of Man, which exercise their own rules regarding fire precautions for hotels.

Food And Drink

If you intend to take dinner at an establishment, note that sometimes the meal must be ordered in advance of the actual meal time. In some cases, thi may be at breakfast time, or even on the previous evening. If you have booked on bed, breakfast and evening meal terms, you may find that the tariff includes only the set menu, but you can usually order from the à la carte menu, if there is one, and pay a supplement. On Sundays, many establishments serve the main meal at midday, and provide only a cold supper in the evening.

Some London establishments provide only a Continental breakfast. If a full English breakfast is available, this is indicated in their description.

In some parts of Britain, particularly in Scotland, high tea (i.e. a savoury dish followed by bread and butter, scones, cakes, etc.) is sometimes served instead of dinner, but dinner may be available as a alternative. The last time at which high tea or dinner may be ordered on weekdays is shown, but thi may vary at weekends.

Licences

The directory entry will show whether or not the establishment is licensed to serve alcohol. Many places in the guest house category hold a residential or restaurant license only, but all inns hold a fu licence. Licensed premises are not obliged to remain open throughout the permitted hours, and they may do so only when they expect reasonable trade.

Note that in establishments which have registered clubs, club membership does not come into effect, nor can a drink be bought, until 48 hours after joining.

Money-Off Voucher Scheme

In the front of this book you will find eight £1 vouchers which can be redeemed against your bill for accommodation at any of the establishments which show the £ symbol in the directory. You must tell the proprietor or receptionist that you wish to use the voucher when you check in at reception and show your copy of the 1995 Guide. If you do not mention the voucher until you are checking out, the proprietor is entitled to refuse to accept it because the bill may already have been made out.

Only one voucher may be presented for one room bill irrespective of the number of nights stayed. The vouchers are not valid if you are already benefiting from a discount under some other scheme, or from special off-peak rates.

The voucher scheme is not applicable in the Republic of Ireland.

Payment

Most proprietors will only accept cheques in payment of accounts if notice is given and some form of identification (preferably a cheque card) is produced. If a hotel accepts credit or charge cards, this is shown in its directory entry (see page 15 for details).

Prices

It should be noted that daily terms quoted throughout this publication show minimum and maximum prices for both one (sb&b) and two persons (db&b) and include a full breakfast. If dinner is also included this will be indicated in parenthesis (incl. dinner). Weekly terms, where available, show minimum and maximum prices per person, which take into account minimum double occupancy and maximum single occupancy, where appropriate, and may include the price of an evening meal (WBDi).

The Hotel Industry Voluntary Code of Booking Practice was revised in 1986, and the AA encourages its use in appropriate establishments. Its prime object is to ensure that the customer is clear about the precise services and facilities s/he is buying and what price will have to be paid, before entering into a contractually binding agreement. If the price has not been previously confirmed in writing, the guest should be handed a card at the time of registration, stipulating the total obligatory charge. The Tourism (Sleeping Accommodation Price Display) Order 1977 compels hotels, motels, guest houses, farmhouses, inns and self-catering accommodation with four or more letting bedrooms to display in entrance halls the minimum and maximum prices charged for each category of room. This order complements the Voluntary Code of Booking Practice. The tariffs quoted in the directory of this book may be affected in the coming year by inflation, variations in the rate of VAT and many other factors.

You should always confirm the current prices before making a booking. Those given in this book have been provided by proprietors in good faith, and must be accepted as indications rather than firm quotations.

In some cases, proprietors have been unable to provide us with their 1995 charges, but to give you a rough guide we publish the 1994 price, prefixed with an asterisk (*). It is also a good idea to ascertain all that is included in the price. Weekly terms can vary according to the meals that are included. We cannot indicate whether or not you are able to arrive mid-week, so if this is your intention, do check when making your reservation. Where information about 1995 prices is not given, you are requested to make enquiries direct.

VAT is payable, in the United Kingdom and in the Isle of Man, on both basic prices and any service. VAT does not apply in the Channel Islands. With this exception, prices quoted in the Guide are inclusive of VAT (and service where applicable).

Prices for the Republic of Ireland are shown in Irish punts. At the time of going to press (July 1994), the exchange rate is 1.01 Punts = £1.00 Sterling.

QUALITY ASSESSMENT

All establishments in the guide are assessed for the quality of what they provide. This assessment is made by our hotel inspectors on a subjective basis, following each inspection, and indicates the quality of the accommodation and services provided by each establishment.

Each establishment receives from one to five symbols in ascending order of merit. Those gaining from one to three Q awards are designated 'AA Recommended' and may display this on the AA sign outside their premises. This wording is not part of their entry in the directory, however.

Those gaining four or five Q awards are designated 'AA Selected' and 'AA Premier Selected' and may display this on their AA signs. 'Selected' and 'Premier Selected' establishments have this title over their entries in the directory, which are highlighted by a tinted panel and, in the case of 'Premier Selected', a photograph.

Q RECOMMENDED. This assessment indicates an establishment with simple accommodation and adequate bathroom facilities.

Q Q RECOMMENDED. This assessment indicates a sound standard of accommodation offering more in terms of decor and comfort and likely to have some bedrooms with en suite bath or shower rooms.

Q Q Q RECOMMENDED. This assessment indicates well appointed accommodation and a wider range of facilities than a one or two Q establishment. Bedrooms may have en suite bath/shower rooms.

Q Q Q Q SELECTED. This assessment indicates that the accommodation will be comfortable and well appointed, that hospitality and facilities will be of high quality, and that a reasonable proportion of bedrooms will have en suite bath or shower rooms

Q Q Q Q Q PREMIER❀SELECTED. Is the AA's highest assessment for guest houses, farmhouses or inns. It has been introduced in response to the rapidly growing number of really excellent establishments. It indicates an outstanding level of accommodation and service, with an emphasis on quality, good facilities for guests and an exceptionally friendly hospitable atmosphere. The majority of bedrooms will have en suite bath or shower rooms.

The quality assessment is shown in the directory entry as follows:

FALMOUTH Cornwall　　　　Map **2** SX25
GH Q Q **Ram Hotel** High Road XY21 1AB ☎(05036) 4321
FH Q Q Q Mr & Mrs J Smith **Homestead** DX8 1WY (SX261567) ☎ (05036) 3421

This year nearly 650 places have been awarded the distinction of a SELECTED assessment and nearly 150 places have the highest assessment of PREMIER SELECTED. Quick-reference lists of the Premier Selected and Selected establishments are given on pages 11 and 25.

PREMIER SELECTED

Category of establishments with a **QQQQQ** Rating for Quality - the AA's highest rating for guest houses, farmhouses and inns

Below is a quick-reference list in country and county order - England, Channel Islands, Scotland, Wales, Ireland - of all the Premier Selected establishments in this year's guide. The 'Premier Selected' establishments - those with the AA's highest award of five Qs - are highlighted in the directory with a tint panel and a photograph

11

SIDMOUTH
Broad Oak
SOUTH MOLTON
Kerscott Farm
TEIGNMOUTH
Thomas Luny House
TIVERTON
Hornhill Farm
TOTNES
Watermans Arms
WEST DOWN
Long House

DORSET
BEAMINSTER
Hams Plot
DORCHESTER
Yalbury Cottage
HORTON
Northill House

GLOUCESTERSHIRE
CHELTENHAM
Cleeve Hill
Lypiatt House
CLEARWELL
Tudor Farmhouse
TETBURY
Tavern House
WILLERSEY
Old Rectory

GREATER MANCHESTER
ALTRINCHAM
Ash Farm

HAMPSHIRE
BROCKENHURST
Thatched Cottage Hotel
HAYLING ISLAND
Cockle Warren
  Cottage Hotel
RINGWOOD
Little Forest Lodge
SWAY
Nurse's Cottage
WINCHESTER
Wykeham Arms

WOODFALLS
Woodfalls Inn

**HEREFORD &
WORCESTER**
BISHAMPTON
Nightingale Hotel
WHITNEY-ON-WYE
Rhydspence Inn

KENT
CANTERBURY
Old Rectory
Thruxted Oast
CRANBROOK
Hancocks Farmhouse
HAWKHURST
Conghurst Farm
PENSHURST
Swale Cottage
SITTINGBOURNE
Hampstead House
TONBRIDGE
Goldhill Mill

LANCASHIRE
CARNFORTH
New Capernwray Farm
HARROP FOLD
Harrop Fold
  Country Farmhouse
  Hotel
SLAIDBURN
Parrock Head
  Farm House Hotel
THORNTON
Victorian House

LONDON
Postal Districts
E11
Lakeside
W2
Pembridge Court

NOTTINGHAMSHIRE
NORTH WHEATLEY
Old Plough

OXFORDSHIRE
BURFORD
Andrews Hotel
KINGSTON BAGPUIZE
Fallowfields
OXFORD
Cotswold House
THAME
Upper Green Farm

SHROPSHIRE
CHURCH STRETTON
Rectory Farm

SOMERSET
BEERCROCOMBE
Frog Street Farm
Whittles Farm
CREWKERNE
Broadview
EAST COkER
Holywell House
KILVE
Hood Arms
LANGPORT
Hillards Farm
NORTON ST PHILIP
Monmouth Lodge
PORLOCK
Gable Thatch
RODE
Irondale
SOMERTON
Lynch Country House
SOUTH PETHERTON
Oaklands
WATCHET
Chidgley Hill Farm
WELLS
Littlewell Farm

STAFFORDSHIRE
OAKAMOOR
Bank House

SUSSEX (EAST)
ARLINGTON
Bates Green

FRANT
Old Parsonage
HASTINGS
Bryn-y-Mor
Parkside House
HOVE
Claremont House
RYE
Green Hedges
Jeakes House

SUSSEX (WEST)
BEPTON
Park House
BILLINGSHURST
Old Wharf
BOSHAM
Kenwood
ROGATE
Mizzards Farm
SUTTON
White Horse

WARWICKSHIRE
WARWICK
Shrewley House

WILTSHIRE
BRADFORD ON AVON
Bradford Old Windmill
Burghope Manor
BURBAGE
Old Vicarage
CALNE
Chilverster Hill House
LACOCK
At the Sign of the Angel
LECHLADE
Cottage-by-the-Church
LITTLE CHEVERELL
Little Cheverell House
MARLBOROUGH
Laurel Cottage
WEST GRAFTON
Mayfield

YORKSHIRE (NORTH)
REETH
Arkleside Hotel
RICHMOND
Whashton Springs Farm
STARBOTTON
Hilltop Country Guest House
WHITBY
Dunsley Hall
YORK
Arndale Hotel

CHANNEL ISLANDS

GUERNSEY
ST PETER PORT
Midhurst House

SCOTLAND

CENTRAL
BRIG O' TURK
Dundarroch
CALLANDER
Arran Lodge

FIFE
ANSTRUTHER
Hermitage Guest House
AUCHTERMUCHTY
Ardchoille

HIGHLAND
CONON BRIDGE
Kinkell House
FORT WILLIAM
The Grange
GRANTOWN-ON-SPEY
Ardconnel
Culdearn House
INVERNESS
Ballifeary
Culduthel Lodge
Moyness House
KINGUSSIE
The Cross
MUIR OF ORD
Dower House

LOTHIAN
EDINBURGH
Drummond House

STRATHCLYDE
BALLANTRAE
Cosses Country House
CONNEL
Ards House
TOBERMORY
Strongarbh House

WALES

GWYNEDD
BETWS-Y-COED
Tan-Y-Foel
BONTDDU
Borthwnog Hall
LLANFACHRETH
Ty Isaf Farmhouse
LLANWNDA
Pengwern Farm

POWYS
PENYBONT
Ffaldau Country House
  and Restaurant

NORTHERN IRELAND

CO. TYRONE
DUNGANNON
Grange Lodge

REPUBLIC OF IRELAND

KANTURK
Assolas Country House

CO. DUBLIN
DUBLIN
Aberdeen Lodge
Ariel House
Grey Door

HOW TO USE
THIS GUIDE

Place-names are listed alphabetically throughout the British mainland, but places on islands are listed under the appropriate island heading (e.g., Wight, Isle of, Channel Islands, Guernsey, Man, Isle of,) and there is a separate directory for Ireland that includes places both in Northern Ireland and in the Republic. Establishments are also listed alphabetically within their categories, first guest houses, then farmhouses, then inns.

The examples of entries below are intended to help you find your way through the directory. See also the explanation of abbreviations and symbols on pages 35-36

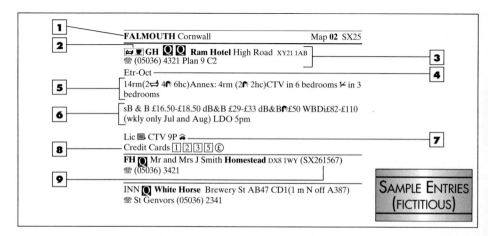

1. Towns (including London) are listed in strict alphabetical order followed by the county or region. This is the administrative county, or region, and not necessarily part of the correct postal address. Towns on islands are listed under the island name. With Scottish regions or islands, the old county name follows in italics.
The map reference shows first the location atlas page number, then the grid reference. To find the location on the atlas page, first find the appropriate square (indicated by two letters), then read the 1st figure across and the 2nd figure vertically.
The London street plans appear next to the London entries in the directory.

2. This symbol indicates that the establishment expects to provide bed and breakfast for under £15 per person, per night during 1995, but remember that circumstances and prices can change during the currency of the Guide.

3. Establishment name, address, postal code and telephone number. When an establishment's name is shown in italics the particulars have not been confirmed by the proprietor. Guest houses are identified by the letters GH, Farmhouses by FH, Inns by INN and Town and Country (Ireland only) by T&C- this is also the order in which they are listed beneath the town headings.
All establishments are now rated for quality on a scale of one to five, denoted by the letter Q. See page 10 for a full explanation.

The telephone exchange (STD code) is usually that of the town heading. Where it differs from the town heading the exchange name is given. In some areas, numbers are likely to be changed during currency of this book. In case of difficulty, check with the operator.Please also see the information about area dialling code changes, due to take place in April 1995, on page 34.

4. Opening details. Unless otherwise stated, the establishments are open all year, but where dates are shown they are inclusive: e.g.. 'Apr-Oct' indicates that the establishment is open from the beginning of April to the end of October. Some places are open all year, but offer a restricted service off season. The abbreviation 'rs' indicates this. It may mean either that evening meals are not served or that other facilities listed are not available. If the text does not say what the restricted services are, you should check before booking.

5. Accommodation details. The first figure shows the number of letting bedrooms. Where rooms have en suite bath or shower, the number precedes the appropriate symbol. Other bedrooms may have private bathrooms adjacent but these are not shown in the number of rooms with en suite facilities.

Annexe - bedrooms available in an annexe are shown. Their standard is acceptable, but facilities may not be the same as in the main building, and it is advisable to check the nature of the accommodation and tariff before making a reservation.

✗ no smoking establishment. If the establishment is not totally no-smoking, the areas where it is not permitted are shown after the symbol - e.g. '[symbol] restaurant

fb - family bedrooms.

CTV - colour television available in lounge. This may also mean televisions permanently in bedrooms or available on request. Check when making reservations.

✗ no dogs allowed in bedrooms. Some establishments may restrict the size and breed of dogs permitted and the rooms into which they may be taken. Establishments which do not normally accept dogs may accept guide dogs. Generally, dogs are not allowed in the dining room. Check when booking the conditions under which pets are accepted.

6. Prices Bed and breakfast per person/two persons, per night and per person, per week (inclusive of dinner at times). For a full explanation see page 9. Prices given have been provided by the owner in good faith, and are indications rather than firm quotations. Some establishments offer free accommodation to children provided they share the par-

ents' room. Check current prices before booking. See also page 9.

7. Facilities For key to symbols and abbreviations, see pages 35 and 36.

🚫 no coaches. This information is published in good faith from details supplied by the establishments concerned. Inns, however, have well-defined legal obligations towards travellers, and any member with cause for complaint should take this up with the proprietor or the local licensing authority.

nc - no children. A minimum age may qualify this restriction - e.g.. nc 4yrs means no children aged 4 or under. Although establishments may accept children of all ages they may not necessarily be able to provide special facilities. If you have very young children, check before booking about provisions like cots and high chairs, and any reductions made.

🧒 establishments with special facilities for children, which will include baby-sitting service or baby intercom system, playroom or playground, laundry facilities, drying and ironing facilities, cots, high chairs and special meals.

Note - if there are rooms adapted for or suitable for disabled people reference may be made in the description. Further details for disabled people will be found in the AA's Guide for the Disabled Traveller available from AA shops, free to members, £3.99 to non-members. Guests with any form of disability should notify proprietors, so that arrangements can be made to minimise difficulties, particularly in the event of an emergency.

8. Payment details (the following cards or discount vouchers may be accepted, but check current details when booking)

1 - Access/Eurocard/Mastercard
2 - American Express
3 - Barclaycard/Visa
5 - Diners
£ - Establishment accepts AA Money-Off Vouchers as detailed on page 9.

9. Ordnance Survey Map Reference This is shown for farmhouse entries only. As they are often in remote areas, we provide a six-figure map reference which can be used with Ordnance Survey maps.

GUEST HOUSE
OF THE
YEAR AWARDS
1995

The AA Inspected Bed & Breakfast in Britain guide is well respected for its recommendations of quality. It aims to lead its readers away from the discomforts and disappointments that can accompany a careless choice of holiday accommodation and towards the pleasures that a good small hotel, guest house, farmhouse or inn can bring. Any establishment that receives an AA rating falls into this latter category, but some are especially outstanding in the high standards they offer their guests. The best of these have been carefully assessed by our inspectors, and awarded the title of 'Guest House of the Year' for 1995.

ENGLAND

GOLDHILL MILL,
Tonbridge

Of the hundreds of guest houses visited by our inspectors in 1994, Goldhill Mill has been chosen as Guest House of the Year for England. The house is steeped in history - it was mentioned in the Domesday Book - and it retains its antiquity without seeming uncomfortable to the modern business or holiday guest. The bedrooms are individually furnished and feature anderson fabrics and such luxuries as a double spa bath in one bathroom. Outside the twenty acres of grounds include a flood-lit tennis court. It is not just the physical attractions of the house that set it apart, however. Our inspectors were particularly impressed by the friendly atmosphere that fills the building; resident proprietors offer natural, informal service and the guest is made to feel at ease as soon as he or she steps through the door. The quality of cooking is also of note, with breakfasts made to order from the freshest ingredients and featuring home-made preserves. There is no dinner at the Mill but a host of nearby restaurants offer a wide range of eating options. Finally, Goldhill Mill is three minutes from Tonbridge and 45 minutes from Gatwick airport. Together these factors make for an establishment that is hard to beat

WALES

TAN-Y-FOEL, Betws-y-Coed

A Roman lookout was stationed in what are now the grounds of Tan-y-Foel, such is the view from this delightful country house set high above the Conwy Valley. The building dates back in part to the 16th century and Tudor yeomen also erected the cruck-framed timber barn. Inside the house is attractively decorated and well furnished with fine antique pieces. There are two elegant sitting rooms in which guests can relax, but it is the bedrooms themselves that are the most impressive feature of the house. They feature four poster beds, some canopied with rich fabrics, and en suite modern bathrooms One room has a small private lounge area and two are reached externally. The house is not just beautiful, however; it is also friendly and has good facilities including an enclosed swimming pool for the summer months. Peter and Janet Pitman also offer a small but well balanced menu based on fresh local produce.

SCOTLAND

CULDEARN HOUSE, Grantown-on-Spey

Scotland is a country rich in Guest Houses, and Grantown on Spey has more than its fair share of these. This year one establishment stood out however, Culdearn House, winner of the 1995 Guest House of the Year award. The house is an impressive granite villa standing in its own well tended gardens at the Southern end of the town. It has been lovingly restored by the owners, Alasdair and Isobel Little, whose dedicated and genial hospitality has earned them a regularly returning clientele. Bedrooms are bright and airy with modern appointments and all the expected amenities. Public rooms include a spacious and comfortable lounge where guests can relax with a quiet drink in front of the cosy log fire. There is an elegant dining room in which Isobel serves her small, fixed price Taste of Scotland menu, carefully prepared using only the freshest of local produce.

IRELAND

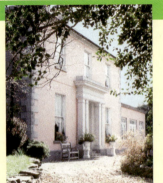

THE OLD RECTORY HOTEL AND RESTAURANT, Wicklow

The Irish are well known for their hospitality, and unsurprisingly the Guest House of the Year for Ireland is no exception. Paul and Linda Saunders have created a wonderful atmosphere at this charming Victorian Rectory and continue to work hard to ensure that their guests receive the best possible treatment. The bedrooms are equipped to a high standard and all individually styled with period furniture. The public rooms boast fine marbled fireplaces and high corniced ceilings. The Orangery restaurant is particularly attractive and forms the stage for Linda's innovative cuisine. Standing on the outskirts of Wicklow town, this a top quality establishment.

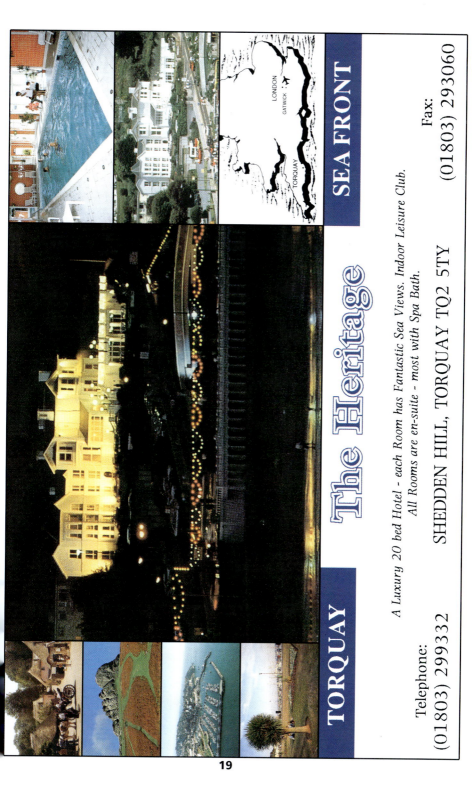

LANDLADY
OF THE
YEAR AWARDS
1994/95

BRITAIN'S LANDLADIES (and land-lords, of course) are out there at the sharp end of the country's tourist industry, welcoming tens of thousands of guests from all over the world in a season that runs from Easter until well into October. They cook endless breakfasts and evening meals, take a friendly interest in guests' likes and dislikes, offer information about sightseeing, keep their homes bright and immaculately clean at all times, ready to receive their new arrivals, and never have a day off until the long season is over, when they may well look forward to a winter of re-decorating and home improvements, all to get ready for the start of the next wave of holidaymakers the following year. Often, their thanks for all this is to see themselves caricatured as dragons who greet guests with a list of do's and don'ts - and mostly don'ts - as long as your arm, and generally acting like sergeant majors drilling raw recruits.

Knowing that this image is far from the truth and finally deserves to be banished, we decided this year to redress the balance just a little by asking all our inspectors to nominate the people they had encountered in the course of their travels and thousands of yearly visits, who offered guests an outstandingly warm welcome. Being on the road so many more days than anyone else, they are extremely receptive to even the smallest gesture of welcome. From this research base of some hundreds, we eventually arrived at a short list of 50, narrowed this down to 20, and after more hard work, emerged with three finalists well ahead on points ...

To make absolutely sure, we sent a family to stay at each place, complete with a child and one person who required a special diet, and at the end of their trips, they finally voted in favour of Mrs Moodie at Rovie Farm, Rogart, Sutherland in the far north-west of Scotland, as the outright winner of the AA's first Landlady of the Year Award.

Traditional Scottish Hospitality Gains the Top Award

CHRISTINE MOODIE and her husband, Stan, bought the farm, where they raise cattle, sheep and pigs, about 38 years ago and she began to take in guests shortly after their arrival. Some of the people who came to stay then, including her very first guest, a lady from Glasgow, are still regular visitors, and proof indeed that her hospitality has more than stood the test of time.

She came out to greet our anonymous family as soon as

Mrs Moodie welcomes guests to have a cup of tea and a chat in her kitchen or in the garden.
At the top of the page: her award came as a complete surprise and gave her her first visit to London.

they drove up, and, having shown them round the house and to their rooms, offered them tea either in the guests' sitting room, or in the kitchen 'for a wee chat'. They immediately felt comfortable and were very impressed by her ease of manner and the way in which she conveyed friendly interest without being intrusive or overwhelming.

For the husband of the family, who was on a wheat-free diet, she had obtained rye bread from Inverness, a mere 60 miles away, and organised suitable meals without making any fuss. For the 12-year-old daughter, she had invited her granddaughter to come over so that they could explore the farm and admire the lambs and calves.

Guests have their own dining room, and the home-cooked dinners are excellent, usually served at a set time, but arrangements were very flexible. Mrs Moodie generally comes in for a chat with the coffee at about 9 pm and shows a sense of humour and interest in her guests that hasn't faded in all her 38 years as a landlady.

CONGRATULATIONS TO THE TWO RUNNERS UP

The other two finalists, Mrs Orme of Bank House, at Oakamoor, within walking distance of Alton Towers in Staffordshire, and Mrs Knott at Ffaldau Country House at Llandegley near the charming mid-Wales town of Llandridnod Wells, Powys, were also very strong contenders. ▷

BANK HOUSE

Mrs Orme's house is absolutely splendid, with lovely furniture, china ornaments and interesting bric a brac, but she is not a bit proprietorial about it and soon made our family feel at ease. It is not, however, an ideal place to take very young children - the minimum age is 10 years old. She and her husband also have the knack of being interested and friendly but not inquisitive. Dinner is served in style, and again, Mrs Orme had gone to some trouble to keep wheat and flour off the menu, and to make sure that the 12-year-old was included in the conversation and enjoyed her meal.

FFALDAU COUNTRY HOUSE

This 16th-century Welsh longhouse was rescued by Mr and Mrs Knott from dereliction and planned as a guest house from the outset. Rooms are most attractive and the spacious first-floor landing is furnished as a TV lounge, with board games, including Trivial Pursuits and Backgammon.

Food is good here too, although catering for a wheat-free diet was more of a problem here, but breakfast is a particular strength, with more than 10 alternatives to choose from. Hospitality is certainly good here, and Mrs Knott is a very pleasant hostess.

Top Twenty. The final line up at The Lanesborough Hotel, London

BLENHEIM LODGE

Set amongst idyllic countryside yet close to the local attractions, our beautiful hotel makes a perfect base for a holiday in the Lakes, offering all the essential comforts – en suite, colour TV, tea/coffee making facilities and stunning views in every direction.

Visitors may expect an extra treat however, as we specialise in the best of traditional English cooking. So much so that our booklet "Recipes from the Past", featuring our most popular dishes, won a special mention in the "Lakeland Book of the Year" awards.

Write or telephone for our free hotel brochure (or our cook book on request, £1.80 inc p&p).

AA Selected. Les Routiers Casserole Award, Accommodation of the Year Award. Nominated, England for Excellence 1992. Ashley Courtenay Highly Recommended.

Jackie & Frank Sanderson, Blenheim Lodge, Brantfell Road, Bowness-on-Windermere, Cumbria LA23 3AE. Telephone: (0153 94) 43440

HAWKSMOOR

WINDERMERE

Ideally situated mid-way between Bowness and Windermere.
Easy walking distance both villages, backed by woodland.
Large private car park. Ground floor rooms, also level access
to lounge, dining areas. Off season breaks. Weekly rates
offered. Overnight stays welcome. Same resident proprietors
for last thirteen years. Traditional English home cooking.
Evening meal optional. Licensed. All rooms en suite
Four poster beds available for that special occasion.

Lake Road, Windermere, Cumbria LA23 2EQ
Telephone: 015394 42110

AA
Selected
Guest House

23

Abbey Lodge
Guest House

Newly built family run guest house which is all on ground level. Fully en suite rooms with sky TV, tea & coffee facilities, hair dryer, radio and telephone. Abbey Lodge is situated on the A772, the main bus route and just ten minutes from the city centre or two minutes from city bypass. Our establishment is furnished to a high standard. Competitive rates. Open all year. Private parking.

Proprietors: Sally & Terry Baigan

137 Drum Street, Gilmerton, Edinburgh, EH17 8RJ
Tel: 0131 664 9548 Fax: 0131 664 3965

Soulton Hall

Elizabethan Manor House with walled garden offering really relaxing holiday – Birdwatching, 50 acres oak woodland, fishing along 1½ miles of river and brook, free pony riding, good farm and country walks. Enjoy fresh food, super cooking, log fires, central heating, country life. Ironbridge, Country Market Towns, North Wales and castles easily reached.
Dinner, Bed & Breakfast. Restaurant open to non residents. Self catering cottages available on estate. Short Breaks.
Direct dial telephones.

Mrs A. Ashton	**2 miles east of Wem**
Soulton Hall	**on the B5065**
Nr. Wem, Shropshire	

Tel: (01939) 232786 Fax: (01939) 234097 ♛♛♛ **E.T.B.**

The Old Court House
CORSTON

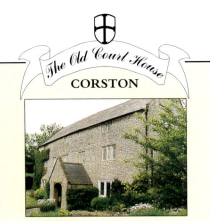

A magnificent 16th Century period residence situated in an attractive conservation village. Beautifully furnished accommodation, with breakfast in the Court Room once used by the infamous Judge Jeffries in the 1860's.

AA Premier Selected QQQQQ
ETB Highly Commended ♛♛

THE OLD COURT HOUSE, CORSTON
BATH, AVON BA2 9AP
TELEPHONE: BATH (01225) 874228

HENLEY HOUSE HOTEL

30 Barkston Gardens, Earls Court
London SW5 0EN
Tel: (0171) 370 4111/2
Fax: (0171) 370 0026

Overlooking a beautiful garden square in the Royal Borough of Kensington and Chelsea, this hotel offers 20 elegant and beautifully designed rooms, all with bathroom ensuite. Rooms have colour TV with satellite channels, direct dial telephone, hairdryer, and complimentary tea/coffee tray.

Knightsbridge, the West End and the exhibition halls are all within easy reach. **Please ask for brochure.**

Recommended by: AA QQQ

Prestigious Inter-Europe-Hotels / London's Best Bed & Breakfast Hotels / Small Hotels of London / Guide Routard

SELECTED CATEGORY

Establishments with a

◻◻◻◻
Rating for Quality

Last year the AA increased the steps in the Q for Quality Scheme from four to five. This does not mean that the AA relaxed its standards for the 4 Q establishments, which are still designated 'Selected' and have their entries highlighted by a tinted panel. On the contrary, establishments at the top end of the market have improved their standards greatly over the last few years.

Below is a quick-reference list in country and county order - England, Channel Islands, Scotland, Wales, Ireland - of all the Selected establishments in this year's guide. There is a separate list of 'Premier Selected' establishments on page 11.

ENGLAND

AVON
BATH
Arden House
Armstrong House
Badminton Villa
Bath Tasburgh
Bloomfield House
Cheriton House
Cranleigh
Kennard Hotel
Laura Place Hotel
Monkshill Guest House
Oakleigh House
Old Court House
Paradise House

Somerset House
 Hotel and Restaurant
KEYNSHAM
Grasmere Court Hotel
OLD SODBURY
Sodbury House
WESTON SUPER MARE
Ashcombe Court
Braeside
Milton Lodge

BERKSHIRE
LAMBOURN
Lodge Down
WINDSOR
Melrose

BUCKINGHAMSHIRE
HIGH WYCOMBE
Clifton Lodge
MARLOW
Holly Tree House
MILTON KEYNES
Old Bakery Hotel
CAMBRIDGESHIRE
CAMBRIDGE
Old School
 Guest House
ELY
Forge Cottage

CHESHIRE
CHESTER
Green Gables
Redland Private Hotel
CREWE
Clayhanger Hall Farm
HATTON HEATH
Golborne Manor
KNUTSFORD
Dog Inn
MACCLESFIELD
Hardingland Farm
 Country House
NANTWICH
Oakland House

CLEVELAND
STOCKTON-ON-TEES
Edwardian Hotel

CO DURHAM
DARLINGTON
Clow Beck House

CORNWALL & ISLES OF SCILLY
BODMIN
Treffry Farm
BOSCASTLE
Tolcarne House
Trerosewill Farmhouse
BUDE
Cliff Hotel
FALMOUTH
Penmere Guest House
Westcott Hotel
FOWEY
Carnethic House
HELSTON
Halzephron Inn
Nanplough Farm
LELANT
Badger Inn
LISKEARD
Tregondale Farm
LOOE
Coombe Farm
Harescombe Lodge
Panorama Hotel
Woodlands
MEVAGISSEY
Kerryanna
Mevagissey House
NEWQUAY
Degembris Farmhouse
Manuels Farm
Pendeen
Porth Enodoc
Priory Lodge
Towan Beach
Windward Hotel

25

PENZANCE
Chy-an-Mor
Rose Farm
Yacht Inn
POLPERRO
Landaviddy Manor
Lanhael House
PORT ISAAC
Archer Farm
PORTREATH
Benson's
SALTASH
Crooked Inn
ST AUSTELL
Poltarrow Farm
ST ERME
Trevispian Vean Farm
ST IVES
Dean Court
Kynance
Lyonesse
Monowai
Regent
ST JUST IN ROSELAND
Rose-da-Mar Hotel
ST MARTIN
Hotel La Michele
ST MARY'S
Carnwethers
   Country House
ST WENN
Wenn Manor
TRURO
Bissick Old Mill
Lands Vue
Rock Cottage
TYWARDREATH
Elmswood House

CUMBRIA
AMBLESIDE
Drunken Duck
Rothay Garth
Rowanfield Country House
BORROWDALE
Greenbank
Hazel Bank
BOWNESS-ON-WINDERMERE
Laurel Cottage
BRAMPTON
Cracrop Farm
Oakwood Park

CALDBECK
High Greenrigg House
COCKERMOUTH
New House Farm
CROSTHWAITE
Crosthwaite House
FAR SAWREY
West Vale Country
   Guest House
HAWSKHEAD
Rough Close Country House
KENDAL
Burrow Hall Country Guest
House
KESWICK
Abacourt House
Acorn House
Applethwaite Country House
Craglands
Dalegarth House Country Hotel
Greystones
Ravensworth
KIRKOSWALD
Prospect Hill
NEAR SAWREY
The Garth
NEWBY BRIDGE
Hill Crest
OAKFORD
Newhouse Farm
PENRUDDOCK
Highgate Farm
TROUTBECK
Broad Oak Country House
UNDERBARROW
Tranthwaite Hall
WINDERMERE
Applegarth
Archway Guest House
Beaumont
Blenheim Lodge
Fayrer Garden House
Fir Trees
Hawksmoor Guest House
Parson Wyke Country House
Woodlands

DERBYSHIRE
ALKMONKTON
Dairy House Farm
ASHBOURNE
Biggin Hill

Lichfield Guest House
BUXTON
Coningsby
Grosvenor House Hotel
Westminster Hotel
CARSINGTON
Henmore Grange
HOPE
Underleigh House
HOPTON
Henmore Grange
MATLOCK
Hodgkinsons Hotel
Lane End House
WINSTER
Dower House

DEVON
ASHBURTON
Gages Mill
AXMINSTER
Millbrook Farmhouse
BARNSTAPLE
Home Park Farm
BICKINGTON
East Burne Farm
BOVEY TRACEY
Willmead Farm
BRANSCOMBE
Masons Arms
BRATTON FLEMING
Bracken House
BUCKFASTLEIGH
Dartbridge Inn
BUDLEIGH SALTERTON
Long Range
CHAGFORD
Bly House
Glendarah
CROYDE
Moorsands House
CULLOMPTON
Rullands
DARTMOUTH
Boringdon House
Captains House
EXETER
Edwardian
HOLNE
Wellpritton Farm
HONITON
Colestocks House

26

Heathfield
ILFRACOMBE
Varley House
KINGSTON
Trebles Cottage
LYNMOUTH
Bonnicott House
Countisbury Lodge
Heatherville
LYNTON
Alford House
Hazeldene
Ingleside
Lynhurst
Waterloo House
MORETONHAMPSTEAD
Gate House
Great Sloncombe Farm
Slate Cottage
MORTEHOE
Sunnycliffe
NEWTON ABBOT
Barn Owl Inn
PLYMOUTH
Bowling Green
SHILLINGFORD
Old Mill
TAVISTOCK
Old Coach House
TEIGNMOUTH
Fonthill
TIVERTON
Lower Collipriest Farm
TORQUAY
Barn Hayes Country Hotel
Berburry
Glenorleigh Hotel
Kingston House
Olivia Court
Suite Dreams
TOTNES
Old Forge at Totnes
Red Slipper

DORSET
BLANDFORD FORUM
Home Farm
BOURNEMOUTH
Boltons
Cliff House Hotel
Silver Trees
Tudor Grange

BRIDPORT
Britmead House
CHARMOUTH
Newlands House
DAWLISH
Walton House
DORCHESTER
Westwood House
EVERSHOT
Rectory House
POOLE
Acorns
SHERBORNE
The Alders
SWANAGE
Fernlea
WAREHAM
Redcliffe Farm
WEYMOUTH
Bay Lodge
Channel View

ESSEX
CHELMSFORD
Snows Oaklands Hotel
MANNINGTREE
Dairy House Farm
THAXTED
Piggots Mill

GLOUCESTERSHIRE
BERKELEY
Greenacres Farm
BIBURY
Cotteswold House
BLOCKLEY
Lower Brook House
BOURTON-ON-THE-WATER
Coombe House
BOX
Hermitage
CHELTENHAM
Charlton House
Milton House Hotel
Stretton Lodge
CHIPPING CAMPDEN
Malt House
CIRENCESTER
Waterton Garden Cottage
LAVERTON
Leasow House
STOW-ON-THE-WOLD

Cotswold Cottage
Royalist Hotel
WINCHCOMBE
Wesley House

HAMPSHIRE
BARTON-ON-SEA
Bank Cottage
BASINGSTOKE
Fernbank Hotel
BRANSGORE
Tothill House
BROCKENHURST
Cottage Hotel
CADNAM
Kents Farm
Walnut Cottage
EMSWORTH
Crown Hotel
FAREHAM
Avenue House
FORDINGBRIDGE
Forest Cottage Farm
FRITHAM
Fritham Farm
LYMINGTON
Albany House
Efford Cottage
Our Bench
LYNDHURST
Ormonde House
RINGWOOD
The Nest
ROMSEY
Highfield House
SARISBURY GREEN
Dormy House
SOUTHAMPTON
Hunters Lodge
WARSASH
Solent View Private Hotel
WINCHESTER
Leckhampton
Shawlands

HEREFORD &
WORCESTER
BREDWARDINE
Bredwardine Hall
BROADWAY
Cusack's Glebe
Orchard Grove

HANLEY CASTLE
Old Parsonage Farm
HEREFORD
Grafton Villa Farm
Hermitage Manor
KIDDERMINSTER
Cedars Hotel
LEOMINSTER
Hills Farm
ROSS-ON-WYE
Edde Cross House
RUCKHALL
Ancient Camp Inn
WEOBLEY
Ye Olde Salutation Inn

HERTFORDSHIRE
ST ALBANS
Ardmore House

HUMBERSIDE
LOW CATTON
Derwent Lodge

KENT
CANTERBURY
Ebury
Ersham Lodge
Magnolia House
Pilgrim
Thanington Hotel
White House
CRANBROOK
The Oast
DOVER
Walletts Court
EYNSFORD
Home Farm
FAVERSHAM
Frith Farmhouse
GOUDHURST
Mill House
GRAVESEND
Overcliffe
HYDE
Needhams Farm
MARGATE
Greswolde
PETHAM
Old Poor House
PLUCKLEY
Elvey Farm

ROYAL
TUNBRIDGE WELLS
Danehurst House
St Martins's
SHIPBOURNE
Chaser Inn
SITTINGBOURNE
Saywell Farmhouse
WEST MALLING
Scott House
Woodgate

LANCASHIRE
BLACKPOOL
Sunray
CLAYTON-LE-WOODS
Brook House Hotel
CLITHEROE
Peter Barn
COLNE
Higher Wanless Farm
LONGRIDGE
Jenkinsons Farmhouse
SILVERDALE
Lindeth
YEALAND CONYERS
The Bower

LEICESTERSHIRE
CONISHOLME
Wickham House
SHEARSBY
Knaptoft House Farm
  & the Greenway
UPPINGHAM
Rutland House

LINCOLNSHIRE
HORNCASTLE
Greenfield Farm
LINCOLN
Carline
D'Isney Place Hotel
Minster Lodge
LOUTH
Masons Arms
SLEAFORD
Carre Arms
STAMFORD
Priory
STURTON-BY-STOW
Gallows Dale Farm

**LONDON
(Postal Districts)**
N4
Mount View
NW3
Langorf
Sandringham
SW3
Claverley House
Parkes Hotel
SW7
Five Sumner Place
Kensington Manor
W1
Bryanston Court
W2
Byron
Mornington
Norfolk Plaza
Norfolk Towers
W4
Chiswick
W7
Wellmeadow Lodge
W14
Aston Court
Russell Court

NORFOLK
COLTISHALL
The Hedges
HUNSTANTON
Claremont Guest House
KINGS LYNN
Russet House Hotel
SHERINGHAM
Fairlawns
SWAFFHAM
Corfield House
TIVETSHALL ST MARY
Old Ram Coaching Inn

NORTHAMPTONSHIRE
CHARLTON
Home Farmhouse

NORTHUMBERLAND
ALNMOUTH
High Buston Hall
Marine House
BERWICK-UPON-TWEED
Dervaig

HALTWHISTLE
Ald White Craig Farm
Broomshaw Hill Farm
HEXHAM
Middlemarch
KIRKWHELPINGTON
Shieldhall
ROTHBURY
Orchard

NOTTINGHAMSHIRE
NOTTINGHAM
Hall Farm House
Windsor Lodge

OXFORDSHIRE
BANBURY
La Madonette
 Country Guest House
BURFORD
Elm Farmhouse
CHISLEHAMPTON
Coach & Horses
EYNSHAM
ll Views
IDLINGTON
owood House
INGHAM
onygree Gate
EW
armhouse Hotel
 & Restaurant
MILTON-UNDER-WYCHWOOD
illborough Hotel
OXFORD
hestnuts Guest House
ial House
alaxie
Marlborough House
lbury Lodge Private Hotel
HENINGTON
otman House
WOODSTOCK
aurels
WOOLSTONE
White Horse

SHROPSHIRE
STON MUNSLOW
hadstone Guest House
BRIDGNORTH
aven Pasture

CHURCH STRETTON
Belvedere
Jinlye
CRAVEN ARMS
Keepers Cottage
DIDDLEBURY
The Glebe
IRONBRIDGE
Library House
LUDLOW
Number Twenty-eight
MARKET DRAYTON
Mickley House
Stoke Manor
MIDDLETON PRIORS
Middleton Lodge
SHREWSBURY
Fieldside
Mytton Hall
Sandford House
TELFORD
Church Farm
WEM
Soulton Hall

SOMERSET
DULVERTON
Dassels Country House
Highercombe
MINEHEAD
Gascony
Marston Lodge
NORTON ST PHILIP
Plaine Guest House
ROADWATER
Wood Advent Farm
SPAXTON
Gatesmoor
TAUNTON
Higher Dipford Farm
Meryan House Hotel
WASHFORD
Washford Inn
WELLINGTON
Pinksmoor
 Mill House
WELLS
Infield House
Southway Farm
Tor Guest House
WINCANTON
Lower Church Farm

STAFFORDSHIRE
AUDLEY
Domvilles Farm
CHEDDLETON
Choir Cottage and
 Choir House
STOKE-ON-TRENT
Old Dairy House
STONE
Whitgreave Manor

SUFFOLK
BEYTON
Manor House
BURY ST EDMUNDS
Six Bells Inn
Twelve Angel Hill
FRESSINGFIELD
Chippenhall Hall
GISLINGHAM
The Old Guildhall
HIGHAM
Old Vicarage
NEEDHAM MARKET
Pipp's Ford Farm
STOKE BY NAYLAND
Angel Inn

SURREY
HORLEY
High Trees Gatwick
Vulcan Lodge
REIGATE
Cranleigh

SUSSEX (EAST)
BRIGHTON
Adelaide Hotel
Amblecliff
EASTBOURNE
Beachy Rise
HARTFIELD
Bolebrook Watermill
HASTINGS
Filsham Farmhouse
Norton Villa
Tower
LEWES
Fairseat House
Nightingales
MAYFIELD
Rose & Crown

RYE
Holloway House
Mint Lodge
Old Borough Arms
Old Vicarage Guest House
Old Vicarage Hotel & Restaurant
Playden Cottage
SEAFORD
Avondale Hotel
UCKFIELD
Hooke Hall
South Paddock
WILMINGTON
Crossways
WINCHELSEA
Country House at Winchelsea
WORTHING
Aspen House
Moorings

SUSSEX (WEST)
FITTLEWORTH
Street Farm
RUSTINGTON
Kenmore Guest House
STEYNING
Springwells

TEESIDE
STOCKTON-ON-TEES
Edwardian Hotel

TYNE & WEAR
TYNEMOUTH
Hope House

WARWICKSHIRE
HASELEY KNOB
Croft
HATTON
Northleigh House
KENILWORTH
Victoria Lodge
OXHILL
Nolands Farm
STRATFORD-UPON-AVON
Gravelside Barn
Sequoia House
Twelfth Night
Victoria Spa Lodge
WARWICK
Old Rectory

WIGHT, ISLE OF
SANDOWN
St Catherine's
SHANKLIN
Bondi Hotel
Chine Lodge
Osborne House
VENTNOR
Madeira Hall
  Country House

WILTSHIRE
BRADFORD ON AVON
Widbrook Grange
CORSHAM
Manor Farm
DEVIZES
Potterne Park Farm
LONGLEAT
Sturford Mead Farm
MARLBOROUGH
Vines
MERE
Chetcombe House
NETTLETON
Fosse Farmhouse Country Hotel
SALISBURY
Grasmere House
Old House
Stratford Lodge
WINTERBOURNE STOKE
Scotland Lodge

YORKSHIRE (NORTH)
BEDALE
Blairgowrie Country House
BOROUGHBRIDGE
Crown Inn
GRASSINGTON
Ashfield House
HARROGATE
Acacia Lodge
Alexa House & Stable Cottages
Ashley House
Delaine
Ruskin
HUNTON
Countryman's Inn
INGLEBY GREENHOW
Manor House Farm
INGLETON
Oakroyd Old Rectory

KETTLEWELL
Langcliffe House
KIRBYMOORSIDE
Appletree Court
LOW ROW
Peat Gate Head
MASHAM
Bank Villa
PATRICK BROMPTON
Elmfield House
PICKERING
Rawcliffe House Farm
RASKELF
Old Farmhouse
  Country Hotel
SCARBOROUGH
Paragon
SCOTCH CORNER
Vintage
SKIPTON
Bridge House
  Restaurant & Hotel
WHITBY
Grantley House
Seacliffe
Waverley
YORK
Ashbourne House
Ashbury
Curzon Lodge and Stable
Cottages
Four Seasons
Grasmead House
The Heathers
Holmwood House
Midway House
Priory
St Denys

YORKSHIRE (SOUTH)
ROTHERHAM
Stonecroft Residential Hotel

YORKSHIRE (WEST)
BINGLEY
Hall Bank Private Hotel
HEBDEN BRIDGE
Redacre Mill
HOLMFIRTH
Holme Castle Country Hotel
WAKEFIELD
Stanley View

CHANNEL ISLANDS

GUERNSEY
ST PETER PORT
Les Ozouets
ST SAMPSON
Ann-Dawn Private Hotel

JERSEY
GROUVILLE
Lavender Villa
ST AUBIN
The Panorama
ST HELIER
Kaieteur Guest House

SARK
Hotel Petit Champ

SCOTLAND

BORDERS
COLDINGHAM
Dunlaverock House
EDBURGH
The Spinney
MELROSE
Dunfermline House
PEEBLES
Venlaw Farm
SELKIRE
Sunny Brae

CENTRAL
BALQUHIDDER
Stronvar House
CALLANDER
Arden House
Brook Linn
  Country House
DUNBLANE
Westwood
TRATHYRE
Creagan House
HORNHILL
Corshill

DUMFRIES
& GALLOWAY
EATTOCK
roomlands Farm

DALBEATTIE
Auchenskeoch Lodge
DUMFRIES
Orchard House
KIRKBEAN
Cavens House
KIRKCUDBRIGHT
Gladstone House
MOFFAT
Broomlands Farm
Gilbert House
TWYNHOLM
Fresh Fields

FIFE
ABERDOUR
Hawkcraig
ANSTRUTHER
Spindrift

GRAMPIAN
ABERDEEN
Cedars Private Hotel
Manorville
FORRES
Mayfield
Parkmount House
KEITH
Haughs Farm

HIGHLAND
ARDGAY
Ardgay House
BALLACHULISH
Fern Villa
Lyn-Leven
BOAT OF GARTEN
Heathbank the
  Victorian House
BRORA
Lynwood
CARRBRIDGE
Fairwinds Hotel
DORNOCH
Fourpenny Cottage Skelbo
DRUMBEG
Taigh Druimbeag
DRUMNADROCHIT
Borlum Farmhouse
Linne Dhuin
FORT WILLIAM
Ashburn House

Torbeag House
FOYERS
Foyers Bay House
GAIRLOCH
Birchwood
Horisdale House
GRANTOWN-ON-SPEY
Garden Park
Kinross House
INVERNESS
Ardmuir House
Dionard Guest House
Eden House
Taransay
  Lower Muckovie Farm
Old Rectory
KINGUSSIE
Avondale House
KYLESKU
Newton Lodge
NAIRN
Greenlawns
NETHY BRIDGE
Aultmore House
PORTREE
Quiraing
ROGART
Rovie Farm
SPEAN BRIDGE
Distant Hills
ULLAPOOL
Ardvreck
The Sheiling

LOTHIAN
GULLANE
Faussetthill House
EAST CALDER
Ashcroft Farmhouse
EDINBURGH
Ashgrove House
Brunswick
Classic
Dorstan Private Hotel
Ellesmere House
Elmview
Grosvenor Gardens
International
The Lodge
Roselea
Stuart House
Town House

STRATHCLYDE
AYR
Brenalder Lodge
Glenmore
Lagg Farm
BALLOCH
Gowanlea Guest House
BRODICK
Dunvegan
CARDROSS
Kirkton House
CONNEL
Loch Etive Hotel
Ronebhal
DUNOON
Anchorage
DUNURE
Dunduff Farm
GARTOCHARN
Ardoch Cottage
Mardella Farmhouse
Old School House
LARGS
Lea-Mar
Whin Park
OBAN
Rhumor
PRESTWICK
Fairways
Golf View Hotel
Redlands Bed & Breakfast
ST CATHERINE'S
Thisle House
TOBERMORY
Fairways Lodge

TAYSIDE
ARBROATH
Farmhouse Kitchen
BLAIR ATHOLL
Dalgreine
BRECHIN
Blibberhill Farm
DUNDEE
Beach House Hotel
KILLIN
Breadalbane House
FORFAR
Finavon Farmhouse
PERTH
Ardfern House

Lochiel House
PITLOCHRY
Craigroyston House
Dundarave House
Torrdarach
STANLEY
Tophead Farm
WESTERN ISLES
LEWIS
BREASCLETE
Corran View
Eshcol

WALES

CLWYD
CORWEN
Powys House Estate
RUTHIN
Eyarth Station
ST ASAPH
Bach-Y-Graig

DYFED
CAREW
Old Stable Cottage
CARMARTHEN
Farm Retreats
Pantgwyn Farm
GWAUN VALLEY
Tregynon Country
  Farmhouse Hotel
HAVERFORDWEST
Wilton House
LLANRHYSTUD
Pen-Y-Castell
NEW QUAY
Park Hall
PEMBROKE
Poyerston Farm
SOLVA
Lochmeyler Farm

GAMORGAN (MID)
MERTHYR TYDFIL
Llwyn On Guest Houe

GLAMORGAN (WEST)
NEATH
Cwmbach Cottages

SWANSEA
Cefn Bryn
Tredilion House

GWENT
ABERGAVENNY
Llanwenarth House

GWYNEDD
ABERDOVEY
Brodawel
Morlan Guest House
BALA
Abercelyn Country House
BANGOR
Country Bumpkin
BARMOUTH
Plas Bach Country House
BETWS-Y-COED
Tyn-Y-Celyn
CAERNARFON
Caer Menai
HARLECH
Castle Cottage Hotel
Gwrach Ynys Country
  Guest House
LLANDUDNO
Cornerways Hotel
Craiglands Private Hotel
Cranberry House
Hollybank
LLANEGRYN
Bryn Gwyn Country House
PENMACHNO
Penmachno Hall
ROEWEN
Gwern Borter Country Manor
TAL-Y-LLYN
Dolffanog Fawr

POWYS
BRECON
Coach Guest House
CHURCH STOKE
Drewin Farm
LLANDRINDOD WELLS
Three Wells
LLANGURIG
Old Vicarage
MONTGOMERY
Little Brompton Farm

NEWTOWN
Dyffryn Farmhouse
SENNYBRIDGE
Brynfedwen Farm
WELSHPOOL
Gungrog House
Lower Trelydan Farmhouse
Moat Farm

NORTHERN IRELAND

CO. ANTRIM
BUSHMILLS
White Gables
LISBURN
Brook Lodge Farmhouse

CO. LONDONDERRY
COLERAINE
Greenhill House

REPUBLIC OF IRELAND

CO. CARLOW
CARLOW
Barrowville Town House
MILFORD
Goleen Country House

CO. CLARE
BALLYVAUGHAN
Rusheen Lodge
ENNIS
Cill Eoin House

CO. CORK
BALLINADEE
Glebe House
KILLEAGH
Ballymakeigh House
KINSALE
Moorings
Old Bank House
SHANAGARRY
Ballymaloe House
YOUGHAL
Ahernes

CO. DONEGAL
CARRIGANS
Mount Royd
  Country Home

CO. DUBLIN
DUBLIN
Aaron
Glenogra
Merrion Hall
Mount Herbert Ltd
No 66
Northumberland Lodge
Ragkab Kidge

CO. GALWAY
CLIFDEN
Maldua
Mallmore House
CASHEL
Legends Restaurant
  & Town House
GALWAY
Ardawn House
Killeen House

CO. KERRY
DINGLE
Bambury's Guest House
Barnagh Bridge
  Country House
Doyles Town House
Green Mount House
Milltown House
TAHILLA
Tahilla Cove

CO. KILKENNY
KILKENNY
Shillogher House
KILLARNEY
Foleys Town House
Kathleen's Country House

CO. LIMERICK
ADARE
Adare Lodge
Coatesland House

CO. LOUTH
ARDEE
Gables House
DROGHEDA
Tullyesker House

CO. MAYO
ACHILL ISLAND
Gray's Guest House

CO. TIPPERARY
BANSHA
Bansha House

CO. WATERFORD
CAPPOQUIN
Richmond House
CHEEKPOINT
Three Rivers
DUNMORE EAST
Hillfield House
STRADBALLY
Carrigahilla House
  and Gardens

CO. WEXFORD
BALLYHACK
Marsh Mere Lodge
ENNISCORTHY
Ballinkeele House
FERNS
Clone House
GOREY
Woodlands Farmhouse
ROSSLARE
Churchtown House
WEXFORD
Ardruagh

CO. WICKLOW
GLENDALOUGH
Laragh Trekking Centre
RATHDRUM
Whaley Abbey
  Country House
WICKLOW
Old Rectory Country House
  & Restaurant

TELEPHONE NUMBERS

CHANGES TO NATIONAL AREA CODES

United Kingdom national area codes are due to change by 16th April 1995.
The digit 1 will be inserted after the first zero of the area code.

For example,
the code for Basingstoke is 0256
and will become 01256.

However, five UK cities will have completely new area codes and one extra digit will be added to subscriber telephone numbers in those cities only.

Leeds
0532, becomes 0113.
Callers should add 2 before the subscriber number

Bristol
0272 becomes 0117.
Callers should add 9 before the subscriber number

Sheffield
0742, becomes 0114.
Callers should add 2 before the subscriber number

Nottingham
0602, becomes 0115.
Callers should add 9 before the subscriber number

Leicester
0533, becomes 0116.
Callers should add 2 before the subscriber number

Some establishments have already given their new number in entries and advertisements. This is because British Telecom have informed them that the new number is already valid, in advance of the deadline of 16th April, although the old number will also continue in use until that date.

SYMBOLS AND ABBREVIATIONS

ENGLISH

- 🛏️ 🍴 Bed and breakfast for £15 or under
- Ⓠ Quality assessment (see p.10)
- ☎ Telephone number
- Private bath and WC
- Private shower and WC
- No smoking
- No dogs
- Ⓡ Tea/coffee-making facilities in bedrooms
- ✳ 1994 prices
- Full central heating
- No parking on premises
- Coach parties not accepted
- Special facilities for children (see p.15)
- Indoor swimming pool
- Outdoor swimming pool
- 9 18 9-hole or 18-hole golf course
- Tennis court(s)
- Fishing
- Riding stables on premises

- sB&B Single room including breakfast per person per night
- dB&B Double room (2 persons sharing a room) including breakfast per night
- WB&B Weekly terms, bed and breakfast, per person
- WBDi Weekly terms bed, breakfast and evening meal, per person
- alc A la carte
- CTV Colour television
- Etr Easter
- fb Family bedroom
- fr From
- hc Number of bedrooms with hot and cold water
- LDO Time last dinner can be ordered
- Lic Licensed
- mdnt Midnight
- nc No children, nc ... yrs, no children under ... years of age
- rm Letting bedrooms in main building
- rs Restricted service
- T Direct dial telephones in rooms
- TV Black and white television

- ▯ Credit cards (see p.15)
- £ Voucher scheme (see p.9)
- ► Entry continued overleaf

FRANCAIS

- 🛏️ 🍴 Chambre et petit déjeuner pour moins de £15
- Ⓠ Symbole AA d'évaluation qualitative (voir p.10)
- ☎ Numéro de téléphone
- Salle de bain privée avec WC
- Douche privée et WC
- Défense de fumer
- Chiens interdits
- Ⓡ Possibilité de faire le thé/le café dans les chambres
- ✳ Prix 1994
- Chauffage central intégral
- Pas de stationnement sur place
- Groupes en autocar pas reçus
- Facilités spéciales pour enfants - (voir p.15)
- Piscine à l'intérieur
- Piscine à l'extérieur
- 9 18 Terrain de golf à 9 ou 18 trous
- Court(s) de tennis
- Pêche
- Ecuries d'équitation sur les lieux

- sB&B Chambre à un lit et petit déjeuner par personne et par nuit
- dB&B Chambre à deux lits (2 personnes à une chambre) avec petit déjeuner par nuit
- WB&B Prix par semaine et par personne, chambre et petit déjeuner inclus
- WBDi Prix par semaine et par personne, chambre, petit déjeuner et diner inclus
- alc A la carte
- CTV TV en couleurs
- Etr Pâques
- fb Chambre de famille
- fr A partir de
- LDO Le dîner est à commander avant cette heure
- Lic Licence de boissons
- mdnt Minuit
- nc Enfants pas admis. nc ... ans, enfants au-dessous de ...ans pas admis
- rm Nombre de chambres dans le bâtiment principal
- rs Service réduit
- T Téléphone dans la chambre, direct avec l'exterieur
- TV

- ▯ Cartes de crédit (voir p.15)
- £ Bons (voir p.9)
- ► Suite au verso

DEUTSCH

- 🛏️ 🍴 Bett mit Frühstück für unter £15
- AA Katagorisierung der Qualität (siehe S.10)
- Ⓠ Telefonnummer
- ☎ Privatbadezimmer mit WC
- Privatdusche mit WC
- Rauchen verboten
- Hundeverbot
- Ⓡ Tee/Kaffeemöglichkeiten im Zimmer
- ✳ 1994 Preise
- Vollfernheizung
- Kein Parkplatz
- Reisebusgesellschaften nicht aufgenommen
- Sonderdienstleistungen für Kinder - (siehe S.15)
- Hallenbad
- Freibad
- 9 18 Golfplatz mit 9 oder 18 löcher
- Tennisplatz(Plätze)
- Angeln
- Reitstall an Ort und Stelle

- sB&B Übernachtung in einem Einzelzimmer mit Frühstück pro Person
- dB&B Doppelzimmer (2 Personer in einem Zimmer) mit Frühstück pro Nacht
- WB&B Wochenpreis pro Person, Übernachtung mit Frühstück
- WBDi Wochenpreis pro Person, Übernachtung mit Frühstück und Abendessen
- alc A la carte
- CTV Farbfernsehen
- Etr Ostern
- fb Familienzimmer
- fr Von
- LDO Letzte Bestellzeit für Abendessen
- Lic Ausschank alkoolischer Getränke
- mdnt Mitternacht
- nc Kinder nicht willkommen. nc .. Jahren, Kinder unter .. Jahren nicht willkommen
- rm Zimmeranzahl im Hauptgebäude
- rs Beschränkte Dienstleistungen
- T Zimmertelefon mit Aussenverbindung über Telefonzentrale
- TV

- ▯ Kreditkarten (seihe p.15)
- £ Gutschein (seihe p.9)
- ► Fortsetzung umseitig

35

SYMBOLS AND ABBREVIATIONS

ITALIANO

🛏💶	Camera e prima colazione a meno di 15 sterline
Ⓠ	Simbolo di valutazione qualitativa della AA (vedi p.10)
☎	Numero telefonica
🛁	Bagno e servizi privati
🚿	Doccia e servizi privati
🚭	Vietato fumare
🐕	Proibito ai cani
Ⓡ	Attrezzatura per fare il té o il caffé nelle camere
✳	Prezzi del 1994
♨	Riscaldemento centrale in tutte le camere
🅿	Senza parcheggio sul posto
🚌	Non si accettano comitive in gita turistica
oΔo	Attrezzature speciali per i bambini - (vedi p.15)
≋	Piscina coperta
⌇	Piscina scoperta
▶9▶18	Campo da golf a 9 o 18 buche
♞	Campo (i) da tennis
⌐	Pesca
℧	Scuola d'equitazione sul posto
sB&B	Prezzo di una camera singola con la colazione compresa (per notte)
dB&B	Prezzo di una camera doppia (2 persone per camera) con la colazione compresa (per notte)
WB&B	Tariffe settimanali per persona, camera e prima colazione
WBDi	Tariffe settimanali per persona, sono compresi la camera, la prima colazione e il pranzo
alc	Alla carta
CTV	Televisione a colori
Etr	Pasqua
fb	Camera familiare
fr	Da
LDO	Ora in cui si accettano le ultime ordinazioni
Lic	Autorizzato alla vendita alcolici
mdnt	Mezzanotte
nc	Proibito ai bambini. nc ... anni, proibito ai bambini sottoi ...anni
rm	Numero di camere nell'edificio principale
rs	Servizio limitato
T	Telefono in camera communicante direttamente con l'esterno
TV	
1	Carte di credito (vedi p.15)
£	Documento di riduzione (vedi p.9)
▶	La lista delle voci continua a tergo

ESPANOL

🛏💶	Cama y desaguno a menos 15 libras esterlinas
Ⓠ	Simbolo de evaluación calitativa de la AA (véase p.10)
☎	Numero de teléfono
🛁	Baño y servicios en cada habitación
🚿	Ducha y servicios en cada habitación
🚭	Prohibido fumar
🐕	Se prohibe a los porros
Ⓡ	Facilidades para hacer el té o el café en los habitaciones
✳	Precios de 1994
♨	Calafacción central
🅿	No poder estacionarse junto al establecimiento
🚌	No se aceptan los grupos de viajeros en coches de linea
oΔo	Facilidades especialies para los niños (véase p.15)
≋	Piscina cubierta
⌇	Piscina descubierta
▶9▶18	Campo de golf de 9 o 18 hoyos
♞	Cancha(s) de tenis
⌐	Pesca
℧	Escuela hípica
sB&B	Precio por noche de una habitación individual con desayuno incluido
dB&B	Precio por noche de una habitación para dos personas (2 personas compartiendo una habitación) con desayuno incluido
WB&B	Tarifas semanales cama y desayuno
WBDi	Tarifas semanales, el precio incluie a la cama, al desayuna y a la comida
alc	A la carte
CTV	Televisión en colores
Etr	Pascua de Resurrección
fb	Habitación familiar
fr	De
LDO	Ultimas ordenes
Lic	Con licencia para vender bebidas alcóholicas
mdnt	Medianoche
nc	Se prohibe le entrada a los niños. nc ...años, se prohibe la entrada a los niños de menos de ...años
rm	Número de habitaciones del edifico principal
rs	Servicio limitado
T	Teléfono en la habitación, comunicando con el exterior
1	Tarjetas de crédito (véase p.15)
£	Documento de rehaja (véase p.9)
▶	La lista continúa a la vuelta

BRITAIN, CHANNEL ISLES & ISLE OF MAN

ABBOTS BICKINGTON Devon   Map **02** SS31

FH Q Q Mrs E Bellew *Court Barton (SS384133)* EX22 7LQ
☎Milton Damerel(0409261) 214
May-Oct
A lovely old stone-built farmhouse standing in its own gardens commanding wonderful views over open countryside and 650 acres of mixed farmland. The cosy bedrooms are well furnished and decorated, and there is a pleasant lounge with an open fire. Farmhouse menus featuring home grown produce are offered to guests at separate tables in the large dining room.
4rm (1fb) Ⓡ ✸ LDO 5pm
▥ CTV nc3yrs ✔ rough shooting 640 acres arable beef sheep

ABBOTS BROMLEY Staffordshire   Map **07** SK02

FH Q Q Mrs M K Hollins *Marsh (SK069261)* WS15 3EJ
(1m N on B5013) ☎Burton-on-Trent(0283) 840323
Closed Xmas
A large modernised old farmhouse located on the B5103 road to Uttoxeter, one mile north of the village. There are two bedrooms: one quite spacious with modern furnishings and a shower cubicle, the other has exposed ceiling beams and is furnished with some antique pieces. Separate tables are provided in the large breakfast room, which also features exposed beams.
2rm (1fb) Ⓡ LDO 5pm
▥ CTV 87 acres mixed

ABERAERON Dyfed   Map **02** SN46

GH Q Q Q *Arosfa* 8 Cadwgan Place SA46 0BU ☎(0545) 570120
Close to the harbour in a Georgian preservation area, the main building and nearby cottage annexe provide quaint and cosy accommodation. The main building also provides meals and afternoon teas during the busier months.
3rm(1⇌2❢) Annexe 3rm (1fb) ✠ CTV in 3 bedrooms Ⓡ ✸ (ex guide dogs) dB&B£28-£32 dB&B⇌❢£36-£38 WB&B£98-£125 WBDi£153-£188 LDO 6pm
Lic ▥ CTV
£

GH Q Q Q *Fairview* Cadwgan Place SA46 0BU ☎(0545) 571472
Sympathetically restored, this delightful terraced house overlooks the pretty harbour. Cosy bedrooms with period furniture are made welcoming with personal mementoes, there is a congenial little lounge and a smart dining room where guests can enjoy Christine Wood's well cooked, plentiful food.
3rm(1⇌2❢) (2fb) CTV in all bedrooms Ⓡ LDO 4pm
▥ CTV

ABERDEEN Grampian *Aberdeenshire*   Map **15** NJ90

GH Q Q *Bimini* 69 Constitution Street AB2 1ET ☎(0224) 646912 FAX (0224) 646912
This friendly family run guesthouse is situated in the east end, near the beach. The bedrooms are modern in style and freshly cooked breakfasts are served at shared tables in the combined lounge/dining room.
7rm (1fb) ✠ CTV in all bedrooms Ⓡ ✸ (ex guide dogs) ✳ sB&B£17-£22 dB&B£32-£40
▥ CTV
Credit Cards ①③

SELECTED

GH Q Q Q Q **Cedars Private Hotel** 339 Great Western Road AB1 6NW ☎(0224) 583225 FAX (0224) 583225
This detached, granite-built house is located in the west end, about one mile from the city centre, and is a popular base for

business guests and tourists alike. The thirteen bedrooms vary in size but are comfortable and provide a good range of amenities, all with TV and tea trays. There is a small snooker table in the spacious lounge, and hearty breakfasts are served in the attractive dining room which features a beautiful ornate ceiling. Efficiently run by the friendly owners Mr and Mrs McBeath, a high standard of housekeeping is maintained. Car parking is provided at both the front and rear.
13rm(8⇌8❢) (2fb) CTV in all bedrooms Ⓡ ✸ (ex guide dogs)
▥ pool table
Credit Cards ①②③

GH Q Q Q **Corner House Hotel** 385 Great Western Road AB1 6NY (on A93) ☎(0224) 313063 FAX (0224) 313063
Two semidetached granite stone houses have been linked and extended to create this family run hotel, popular with business and holiday guests. Situated in the west end it has a friendly atmosphere and offers comfortable and well equipped accommodation.
17⇌❢ (3fb) ✠ in dining room CTV in all bedrooms Ⓡ T sB&B⇌❢£35-£48 dB&B⇌❢£46-£56 WB&B£160-£260 WBDi£230-£330 LDO 8pm
Lic ▥ CTV
Credit Cards ①②③£

GH Q Q Q *Fourways* 435 Great Western Road AB1 6NJ ☎(0224) 310218
This semidetached granite villa is conveniently situated in the west end, at the junction of the ring road and the A93. It has a relaxed and friendly atmosphere and offers good value bed and breakfast accommodation in bright, airy and well equipped bedrooms with tea making facilities. An excellent breakfast is served to guests in the combined lounge/dining room.
7rm(6⇌❢) (2fb) CTV in all bedrooms Ⓡ ✸ (ex guide dogs)
▥ CTV

GH Q Q **Klibreck** 410 Great Western Road AB1 6NR ☎(0224) 316115
Closed Xmas & New Year
Situated in a west end residential area, this friendly family-run guest house offers good value bed and breakfast accommodation. Well equipped, modern bedrooms vary in size. Good breakfasts are served, at shared tables on occasions, in the small rear dining room.
6rm (1fb) ✠ CTV in all bedrooms Ⓡ ✸ ✳ sB&Bfr£19 dB&Bfr£29
▥ CTV
£

SELECTED

GH Q Q Q Q *Manorville* 252 Gt Western Road AB1 6PJ ☎(0224) 594190
Norman and Mary Marshall's delightful semidetached, granite-built house is in the west end of the city with convenient access to both the ring road and central amenities. Recently refurbished to provide a high standard of bed and breakfast accommodation, the house is kept in immaculate condition and offers comfortable bedrooms with modern furnishings. There is an attractive lounge and a neat dining room where well cooked breakfasts are served.
3⇌❢ (2fb) CTV in all bedrooms Ⓡ
▥ CTV

GH 🇶🇶 **Open Hearth** 349 Holburn Street AB1 6DQ
☎(0224) 596888
Situated in the west end and convenient to the city centre, this
comfortable family-run guest house offers good-value bed and
breakfast accommodation. Bedrooms have modern appointments,
and there is a comfortable lounge. Nicely cooked breakfasts are
served at shared tables in the small dining room.
11rm (2fb) ⊁ in dining room CTV in all bedrooms ⓇR sB&B£22
dB&B£35
▥ CTV
£

GH 🇶🇶 **Strathboyne** 26 Abergeldie Terrace AB1 6EE (0.5m N
from bridge of Dee roundabout on A92) ☎(0224) 593400
Mrs Gillanders's semidetached granite-built house is situated in a
quiet residential area, just south of the city centre. Bedrooms are
modest but practical and well equipped: 2 rooms have en suite
facilities. Public areas include a pleasant lounge and small dining
room.
7rm(4🇷) (1fb) ⊁ in dining room CTV in all bedrooms ⓇR ✻
sB&B£18-£19 sB&B🇷£25-£26 dB&B£30-£32 dB&B🇷£36-£44
LDO 12.30pm
▥ CTV⊁
£

ABERDOUR Fife   Map **11** NT18

SELECTED
GH 🇶🇶🇶🇶 **Hawkcraig House** Hawkcraig Point KY3 0TZ
☎(0383) 860335
Mar-Oct
This is a small personally run guesthouse featuring fine views
and a good standard of cooking. It has no drinks licence, but
guests can bring their own alcohol, and smoking is permitted
in the conservatory.
2rm(1⇔1🇷) ⊁ ⋊ (ex guide dogs) sB&B⇔🇷£23-£25
dB&B⇔🇷£38-£40 LDO 24hr notice
▥ CTV nc10yrs
£

INN 🇶🇶🇶 **The Aberdour Hotel** 38 High Street KY3 0SW
(on A921) ☎(0383) 860325 FAX (0383) 860808
A cosy bar serving real ale and well equipped bedrooms with
satellite television are two of the attractions of this small hotel on
the main street. Its little restaurant features a regularly changing
menu, with high teas popular at weekends. During the quieter
winter months the bar does not open at lunch time from Monday
to Thursday.
11⇔🇷 (1fb)CTV in all bedrooms ⓇR T sB&B⇔🇷£32.50-£35
dB&B⇔🇷£47.50-£52 WB&B£150-£230 WBDi£220-£300 Lunch
£7-£10.50 High tea £5.50 Dinner £7-£10.50&alc LDO 9pm
▥
Credit Cards 1 2 3 £

ABERDOVEY Gwynedd   Map **06** SN69

SELECTED
GH 🇶🇶🇶🇶 **Brodawel** Tywyn Road, Brodawel LL35 0SA
(on A439) ☎(0654) 767347
Closed Jan-Feb
The Griffiths family offer a warm and friendly welcome to
their guests, many of whom return time after time. Brodawel
is set in its own grounds overlooking the golf course and
offers good quality accommodation. Bedrooms are bright and
cheerfully decorated, and are very well equipped with
thoughtful extras such as hair dryers. There is a cosy and
comfortable bar for residents.

6⇔🇷 (1fb) ⊁ CTV in all bedrooms ⓇR ✻ sB&B⇔🇷£20
dB&B⇔🇷£38 WB&B£126 WBDi£224 LDO 2pm
Lic ▥ nc10yrs
£

GH 🇶🇶 **Cartref** LL35 0NR (W on A493) ☎(0654) 767273
Just a stone's throw from a sandy beach, this friendly guesthouse
is run by the Williams family who ensure that it lives up to its
name - Cartref means 'home'. There is a traditional lounge, and
bedrooms are well equipped.
7rm(1⇔3🇷) (2fb) ⊁ in dining room CTV in 6 bedrooms ⓇR
sB&B£17-£18 dB&B£33-£34 dB&B⇔🇷£37-£38 WB&B£115-
£132 WBDi£175-£196 LDO 5pm
▥ CTV

SELECTED
GH 🇶🇶🇶🇶 **Morlan** LL35 0SE (W on A493)
☎(0654) 767706
Sue and Ron Coulter enjoy welcoming visitors to their home,
a fairly modern bungalow set in landscaped gardens
overlooking the estuary. The atmosphere is completely
informal and guests dine communally, unless privacy is
requested. The menu is set, but individual dislikes and
preferences are taken account of. There is a comfortable
lounge, a modern conservatory, and seats scattered throughout
the grounds. Bedrooms, which open on to the gardens, are
attractively decorated and thoughtfully equipped.
4rm(1⇔3🇷) CTV in all bedrooms ⓇR ⋊ (ex guide dogs)
LDO 3pm
Lic ▥ CTV nc16yrs

GH 🇶🇶 **Rossa** LL35 0NR (W on A493, establishment opposite
bowling green and tennis courts) ☎(0654) 767545
Closed Dec & Jan
Opposite the bowling greens, this small family-run guesthouse
offers accommodation in bright and pretty bedrooms. There is a
cosy lounge and a charming garden.
4rm(2🇷) (2fb) ⊁ in dining room CTV in 2 bedrooms ⓇR ✻
dB&B£28-£30 dB&B🇷£32-£34 WB&B£98-£115 WBDi£112-
£168 LDO 4pm
▥ CTV
£

ABERGAVENNY Gwent   Map **03** SO21

GH 🇶🇶 **Belchamps** 1 Holywell Road NP7 5LP (off A40)
☎(0873) 853204
A friendly, personally run little guest house overlooking the
Gavenny river from its setting at the edge of the town (but within
a short walk of the centre) offers accommodation in bright, well
equipped and maintained bedrooms. There is also a pleasant little
lounge and dining room downstairs. On site parking is limited, but
there is free parking nearby.
5rm (3fb) ⊁ in 2 bedrooms ⊁ in dining room ⊁ in lounges CTV
in all bedrooms ⓇR ⋊ (ex guide dogs) ✻ sB&B£18-£20
dB&B£36-£40 LDO 7pm
▥ CTV
£

SELECTED
GH 🇶🇶🇶🇶 **Llanwenarth House** Govilon NP7 9SF (3m W
on A465) ☎Gilwern(0873) 830289 FAX (0873) 832199
rs Jan
Run on personal, house-party lines by Bruce and Amanda
Weatherill, this imposing 16th-century house is in a fine
location in the Vale of Usk, with views of the Brecon Beacons.

Bedrooms are mostly spacious and offer a good range of modern comforts. Good home cooking is served, by candlelight, at an elegant communal table with wine from an excellent cellar. There is a large log-fired drawing room and the house is surrounded by mature gardens.
5rm(3⇌2♠) (1fb) ⚔ in dining room CTV in all bedrooms ® sB&B⇌♠£50-£60 dB&B⇌♠£64-£76 LDO 6.30pm
Lic ⪥ nc10yrs

FH Q Q Mrs D Miles *Great Lwynfranc (SO327193)*
Llanvihangel Crucorney NP7 8EN (off A465 3m N)
☎Crucorney(0873) 890418
Mar-Nov
Approached by a bumpy track off the A465 Abergavenny to Hereford road, this friendly little farmhouse offers traditional accommodation. From an elevated position it commands extensive views over the Llanthony Valley.
3rm (1fb) ®
⪥ CTV 154 acres mixed

FH Q Q Q Mrs J Nicholls *Newcourt (SO317165)* Mardy
NP7 8AU (2m N, on edge of village of Mardy) ☎(0873) 852300
Closed Xmas wk
Enthusiastically run by a young family, this 17th-century stone-built courthouse offers stylish accommodation in nicely furnished bedrooms. There is a comfortable lounge and dining room with handsome traditional furnishings. The house enjoys fine views of the Sugar Loaf mountain.
3⇌♠ ⚔ CTV in all bedrooms ® ★ (ex guide dogs) ✳
sB&B⇌♠£25 dB&B⇌♠£35-£40
⪥ CTV nc10yrs snooker 160 acres arable beef
£

ABERPORTH Dyfed   Map **02** SN25

GH Q Q Q *Ffynonwen Country* SA43 2HT ☎(0239) 810312
This pleasant family-run, converted farmhouse is in a lovely rural setting just east of the town. Bedrooms have been mostly modernised; there are several family suites and a ground-floor room adapted for disabled guests. Extensive public rooms include a pleasant lounge-style bar, a conservatory lounge and a small games room.
6rm(5⇌♠) (3fb)CTV in all bedrooms ® ✳ dB&B⇌♠£40 WBDi£170.10
Lic ⪥ ♪
£

ABERSOCH Gwynedd   Map **06** SH32

GH Q Q Q *Ty Draw* Lon Sarn Bach LL53 7EL (from village centre, take Sarn Bach road, guesthouse just beyond Abersoch Fire Station) ☎(0758) 712647
May-Sep
Mouth-watering home-made bread is the speciality of this house, made by Jean Collins who has been running the guesthouse with her husband, Peter, for several years. Bedrooms are bright and airy, with comfortable duvet-covered beds and modern white furniture. There is a cosy residents' lounge, and guests can relax on the shrub-sheltered lawns in fine weather. A secluded rear car park and the short walk to the sea and shops add to the attraction of this well maintained establishment.
7rm (2fb) ⚔ in bedrooms ⚔ in lounges ★ (ex guide dogs) ✳
sB&B£15-£19 dB&B£30-£38 WB&B£100-£130
CTV ♨
£

ABERYSTWYTH Dyfed   Map **06** SN58

GH Q Q Q *Glyn-Garth* South Road SY23 1JS ☎(0970) 615050
Closed 1 wk Xmas
A very soundly maintained guest house close to the harbour, castle

and South Promenade. Bedrooms have modern furnishings and there is one on the ground floor. There is a comfortable lounge and breakfast room with separate tables.
11rm(6⇌♠) (2fb) ⚔ in 8 bedrooms ⚔ in dining room ⚔ in lounges CTV in all bedrooms ® ★ sB&B£16-£17
sB&B⇌♠£28-£32 dB&B£32-£36 dB&B⇌♠£38-£44
Lic ⪥ CTV
£

GH Q Q *Llety Gwyn Hotel* Llanbadarn Fawr SY23 3SX (1m E A44) ☎(0970) 623965
rs 25-26 Dec
This is a family-run hotel has a comfortable lounge, a large bar and a gymnasium. Bedrooms vary in size, with a mix of older and modern furniture. It has family rooms on the ground floor and there are rooms in a separate annexe.
8rm(4♠) Annexe 6rm(1⇌3♠) (3fb) CTV in all bedrooms ® LDO 5pm
Lic ⪥ CTV snooker sauna solarium gymnasium
Credit Cards [1][3]

INN Q Q *Talbot Hotel* Market Street SY23 1DL ☎(0970) 612575
The Talbot, one of the oldest hotels in Aberystwyth, is centrally situated and close to the sea. It offers well equipped accommodation with modern facilities. In addition to the restaurant a good range of bar meals are available.
15rm(13⇌♠) (4fb) CTV in all bedrooms ® ★ (ex guide dogs) LDO 9.30pm
CTV
Credit Cards [1][3]

ABINGTON Strathclyde *Lanarkshire*   Map **11** NS92

FH Q Q Q Mrs M L Hodge *Craighead (NS914236)* ML12 6SQ
(N of village, 1m off B7078 (old A74)) ☎Crawford(08642) 356
due to change to (0864) 502356
May-Oct
Lying in an moorland valley with a small river winding past its garden, this clean, comfortable farmhouse has two good sized bedrooms, an attractive little dining room and a cosy guests' lounge.
2rm ⚔ in dining room ® ★ (ex guide dogs) ✳ sB&B£15-£16 dB&B£30-£32 LDO 5pm
⪥ CTV ♪ 600 acres mixed
£

ACASTER MALBIS North Yorkshire   Map **08** SE54

INN Q Q Q *Ship* YO2 1JH (2m S of A64 Bypass, accessible through villages of Copmanthorpe or Bishopthorpe)
☎York(0904) 705609 & 703888
On the banks of the River Ouse, this 17th-century coaching inn has a very inviting atmosphere with its oak-beamed bar and conservatory restaurant serving a range of good food. The bedrooms are delightfully furnished. There is a garden with a children's playground, and boats can moor at the quay.
8rm(2⇌6♠) CTV in all bedrooms ® sB&B⇌♠£37.50
dB&B⇌♠£39.50-£65 Bar Lunch £1.95-£8.95 Dinner £12.50&alc
LDO 9.30pm
⪥ CTV ♪
Credit Cards [1][3]
See advertisement under YORK

AIRDRIE Strathclyde *Lanarkshire*   Map **11** NS76

GH Q Q *Rosslee* 107 Forrest Street ML6 7AR (1m E on A89)
☎(0236) 765865
A detached period house, Rosslee sits well back from the main Bathgate road on the eastern side of town. It caters for both the commercial and tourist trade, offering neat bedrooms and a comfortable lounge with a residents' bar. A laundry and dry-cleaning service can be arranged.

▶

6rm(3♠) (2fb) ⚹ in dining room CTV in 5 bedrooms ®
sB&B£18-£22 sB&B♠£19-£23 dB&B£36-£44 dB&B♠£36-£46
LDO 11am
Lic ▥ CTV
£

AISLABY North Yorkshire   Map **08** SE78

GH Q Q **Blacksmiths Arms** Pickering YO18 8PE (on A170, 2m
W of Pickering) ☎Pickering(0751) 472182
Closed 4-12 Jan
An attractive roadside restaurant with pretty, pine furnished
bedrooms in the oldest part of the building, some showing the
original crook beams. Parts of the building date from Elizabethan
times, when it was a licensed public house. It was last used as a
Smithy during World War II and many of the original
Blacksmith's tools can be seen in the bar, where the old forge is
now used as an open fireplace. There are beams and stone walls
throughout the ground floor and the restaurant has the original
bread oven in its inglenook fire place.
5rm(1⇄2♠) (1fb) ⚹ in dining room CTV in all bedrooms ®
sB&B⇄B♠£22 dB&B£40 dB&B♠£44
WB&B£140-£154 WBDi£224-£238 LDO 9pm
Lic ▥
Credit Cards [1][3] £

ALBURY Surrey   Map **04** TQ04

INN Q Q Q **Drummond Arms** The Street GU5 9AG
☎Shere(0483) 202039
This appealing inn at the heart of a picturesque village has an
attractive garden with duck pond to its rear. Bedrooms were
recently brought up to an excellent standard, with good en suite
bathrooms and coordinating decor and fabrics setting off quality
pine furniture. A traditional bar menu augmented by some more
adventurous blackboard specials offers an alternative to the
elegant restaurant's à la carte meals and fondue evenings.
7⇄♠ CTV in all bedrooms ® ✻ (ex guide dogs) LDO 10pm
▥ nc10yrs
Credit Cards [1][3]

ALCONBURY Cambridgeshire   Map **04** TL17

INN Q Q **The Manor House Hotel** Chapel Street PE17 5DY
☎Huntingdon(0480) 890423 FAX (0480) 891663
Located in the centre of the village, this 16th-century former
manor farmhouse is now a popular inn. The accomodation is of a
good standard in comfortably equipped bedrooms. Public areas are
cosy with exposed beams and open fires. Guests have the option
of choosing from a bar menu with daily specials or from the
restaurant's à la carte menu at dinner from Tuesday to Saturday.
4⇄♠ in area of dining room CTV in all bedrooms ® ✻
sB&B⇄♠£35 dB&B⇄♠£39.25 Bar Lunch £5.90-£15 Dinner
£5.90-£15 LDO 9pm
▥
Credit Cards [1][3]

Telephone national area codes are due
to change by 16th April 1995. Please
see the note under 'How to Use this
Guide' at the front of the book.

ALDERTON Wiltshire   Map **03** ST88

P R E M I E R ❧ **S E L E C T E D**

FH Q Q Q Q Q Mrs V
Lippiatt **Manor Farm**
(ST840831) SN14 6NL
☎(0666) 840271
Apr-Oct

This impresive 17th-century
stone farmhouse sits in the
picturesque village of
Alderton, surrounded by pretty
Cotswold scenery and close to
all the attractions of Wiltshire
and Avon including the cities
of Bath and Bristol and the famous towns of Malmesbury and
Castle Combe. Three spacious bedrooms, two en suite and
one with a private bathroom next door, have been tastefully
decorated, comfortably furnished and nicely equipped with
CTV, tea/coffee making facilities and boxed toiletries.
Downstairs there is an attractive lounge and an elegant dining
room where a filling breakfast may be taken together or at
separate tables. Guests can choose from fresh fruit, cereals,
yogurt and warm rolls, all set out on a dresser, while bacon,
eggs, sausage, seasoned mushrooms and tomatoes are served
piping hot to the table. This is followed by toast and, on
occasion, by oatmeal pancakes. The house also offers the
experience of a busy working farm and has well tended,
relaxing gardens. The Lypiatt family are welcoming hosts and
a friendly atmosphere prevails.
3rm(2⇄♠) CTV in all bedrooms ® ✗
▥ CTV nc12yrs 600 acres arable beef
See advertisement under CHIPPENHAM

ALKMONTON Derbyshire   Map **07** SK13

S E L E C T E D

FH Q Q Q Q Mr A Harris **Dairy House** *(SK198367)*
DE6 3DG (3m up Woody Lane after turning off A50 at Foston)
☎Great Cubley(0335) 330359 FAX (0335) 330359
Mr and Mrs Harris encourage a friendly, relaxed environment
in this 16th-century red brick farmhouse on the outskirts of a
quiet village. There is a spacious and comfortable lounge, with
an inglenook fireplace and a delightful dining room, in which
guests enjoy freshly prepared farmhouse food at a communal
table. Bedrooms have been refurbished to offer neat
accommodation.
7rm(1⇄3♠) ⚹ ® ✗ (ex guide dogs) ✻ sB&Bfr£16
sB&B⇄♠£23 dB&Bfr£32 dB&B⇄♠£38 WB&B£105-£154
WBDi£187-£238 LDO 8pm
Lic ▥ CTV nc14yrs 82 acres stock

ALMONDSBURY Avon   Map **03** ST68

GH Q Q Q **Abbotts Way** Gloucester Road BS12 4JB (on A38, 2m
N of junct 16, M5) ☎(0454) 613134
This large modern house is set in 12 acres and has fine views of
the surrounding countryside. Bedrooms are comfortable and well
furnished, and the spacious conservatory/dining room is a
delightful setting in which to enjoy the delicious breakfasts.
6rm(3♠) (1fb) ⚹ in bedrooms ⚹ in dining room ✻ sB&B£18-£20
dB&B£36-£40 dB&B♠£38-£45 LDO breakfast
▥ CTV
Credit Cards [1][2][3][5] £

ALNMOUTH Northumberland   Map **12** NU21

SELECTED

GH Ⓠ Ⓠ Ⓠ Ⓠ Ⓠ **High Buston Hall** High Buston NE66 3QH (off A1068 between Alnmouth & Warkworth) ☎Alnwick(0665) 830341 FAX (0665) 830341
Feb-Dec
This delightful Grade II listed Georgian country house stands in five acres of grounds and is situated in an elevated position. It features two well proportioned public rooms, elegantly decorated and comfortably furnished with rugs, sofas, plants and games. The bright spacious bedrooms are more simply appointed but enjoy lovely views of the surrounding countryside and coastline. Meals are served house-party style around a large communal dining table.
3rm(2⇄↾) ⅟ CTV in all bedrooms Ⓡ ⅟ (ex guide dogs) ✳ dB&B£40-£55 dB&B⇄↾£40-£60 WB&B£140-£180 LDO 9am
Lic ▥

SELECTED

GH Ⓠ Ⓠ Ⓠ Ⓠ Ⓠ **Marine House Private Hotel** 1 Marine Drive NE66 2RW ☎Alnwick(0665) 830349
Sitting on the edge of the golf links with magnificent views across Alnmouth Bay, this 200-year-old former vicarage was originally built as a granary and is a listed building. It is now a well established family-run holiday hotel offering comfortable bedrooms with stylish fabrics and decor. On the first floor is the comfortable TV lounge and there is a cosy little bar on the landing. Enjoyable 5-course dinners are served in the small dining room. Children are welcome and there is a games room.
10⇄↾ (4fb) ⅟ in bedrooms ⅟ in dining room CTV in all bedrooms Ⓡ ✳ dB&B⇄↾£66-£78 (incl dinner) WBDi£230-£250 LDO 4pm
Lic ▥ CTV nc3yrs ⚭

Credit Cards ①③Ⓔ

GH Ⓠ Ⓠ Ⓠ **Westlea** 29 Riverside Road NE66 2SD
☎(0665) 830730
Closed 25-26 Dec
A family owned guest house by the River Aln, Westlea is conveniently located for the village centre and the sandy beaches. The house is beautifully maintained and guests can be sure of a warm welcome. Bedrooms are well equipped and there is a spacious lounge with plenty of books and tourist information. Good home cooking is provided.
7rm(6↾) (1fb) CTV in all bedrooms Ⓡ ⅟ LDO 6pm
▥ CTV nc2yrs

ALNWICK Northumberland   Map **12** NU11

GH Ⓠ Ⓠ Ⓠ **Aln House** South Road NE66 2NZ (on A1068)
☎(0665) 602265
Mar-Nov
Attractively decorated and well maintained, this Victorian house is set back from the main road in a well tended garden. Most of the bedrooms have views and there is a comfortable lounge.
7rm(5⇄↾) (2fb) ⅟ in dining room ⅟ in lounges CTV in all bedrooms Ⓡ sB&B⇄↾£17-£18 dB&B⇄↾£34-£36
Lic ▥ nc4yrs

GH Ⓠ **Aydon House** South Road NE66 2NT ☎(0665) 602218
This semidetached Victorian house is situated on the main road leading into town from the south. One of the bedrooms is spacious and comfortable, while the other is more compact and plainly furnished. There is a comfortable lounge and a neat dining room.

10rm(4⇄↾↾) (4fb) CTV in all bedrooms Ⓡ LDO 5pm
Lic ▥

GH Ⓠ Ⓠ Ⓠ **Bondgate House Hotel** Bondgate Without NE66 1PN
☎(0665) 602025 FAX (0665) 602554
Enthusiastic owners Ken and Julia Forbes continue to make improvements at their comfortable Georgian home near the town centre. Bedrooms are generally spacious, and there is a comfortable TV lounge and a pleasant dining room.
8rm(5↾) (3fb) ⅟ in dining room CTV in all bedrooms Ⓡ ⅟ (ex guide dogs) sB&B£17-£23 sB&B↾£23 dB&B↾£37 WB&B£154-£175 WBDi£231-£252 LDO 4.30pm
Lic ▥ CTV
Credit Cards ①③Ⓔ

GH Ⓠ Ⓠ Ⓠ **Charlton House** 2 Aydon Gardens, South Road NE66 2NT (from A1 pass Hardy's Fishing Museum on right and go straight over mini-roundabout for about 200yds) ☎(0665) 605185
Closed Dec-Feb
A semidetached house on the road leading into the town from the south has been carefully decorated and filled with antique and period pieces to emphasise its Victorian character. Bedrooms with their original fireplaces make effective use of quality fabrics and feature quilts made by owner Mrs Jones. The lounge and dining room echo the same theme, the uncovered natural floorboards of the latter giving a rustic authenticity.
3⇄↾ (1fb) ⅟ in bedrooms ⅟ in dining room CTV in all bedrooms Ⓡ ✳ dB&B⇄↾£32-£36 WB&B£112-£119 WBDi£182-£196 LDO 6pm
▥ CTV
Ⓔ

ALTON Hampshire   Map **04** SU73

INN Ⓠ Ⓠ **White Hart** London Road, Holybourne GU34 6EX
☎(0420) 87654 ▶

Marine House Private Hotel

AA
Selected
QQQQ

ALNMOUTH, NORTHUMBERLAND NE66 2RW
Telephone: Alnmouth (01665) 830349

RUNNERS-UP FOR AA Best Family Holiday in Britain 1984 and Northumbria Tourist Board. Holiday Hosts Award 1985.
Relax in the friendly atmosphere of this 200-year-old building of considerable charm, once a Granary. Overlooking the golf links and beautiful beaches. 10 comfortable bedrooms, all with en-suite facilities, colour TV and teasmade. Superb gourmet cuisine. Cocktail Bar and Games Room. Spacious lounge with colour TV. Children and pets welcome. Two adjacent self-catering cottages. Shiela and Gordon Inkster.
SPECIAL GOLFING BREAKS AND FAMILY HOLIDAY PRICES PLUS SPECIAL INTEREST WEEK-ENDS.

A sizeable pub with a garden, situated in the pretty village of Holybourne, north east of Alton, the White Hart has simply furnished bedrooms and a good local clientele who enjoy the weekly quiz night and occasional discos held in the Games Bar, which has a pool table, darts board and juke box. The garden is popular in the summer.

4rm CTV in all bedrooms [R] 🐕 (ex guide dogs) sB&Bfr£21 dB&Bfr£35 WB&Bfr£122 WBDifr£150 Lunch £1.95-£7.95alc Dinner £1.95-£7.95alc LDO 10pm

♨

Credit Cards [1] [3] [£]

ALTRINCHAM Greater Manchester — Map **07** SJ78

PREMIER SELECTED

GH [Q][Q][Q][Q][Q] Ash Farm Park Lane, Little Bollington WA14 4TJ (turn off A56 beside Stamford Arms) ☎061-929 9290

Closed Xmas

Peacefully situated in the pretty village of Little Bollington yet convenient for Manchester, this carefully restored 19th century farmhouse is the home of the famous snooker player David Taylor and his wife Janice. Janice's skills in the kitchen rival her husband's on the green baize; she offers a hearty breakfast and a generous dinner in the inviting lounge/dining room. The tastefully decorated bedrooms have high-quality, hand-made pine furniture, and compare favourably with some highly classified hotels. A third bedrooms has recently been added of the same standard as the original rooms. There is also a snooker room with a championship table which guests can use.

3rm(2🛁🚿) 🚭 in 1 bedrooms CTV in all bedrooms [R] T 🐕 (ex guide dogs) sB&B🛁🚿£40-£45 dB&B🛁🚿£50-£58 LDO 8pm

Lic ♨ nc9yrs snooker

Credit Cards [1] [2] [3] [5] [£]

GH [Q] *Bollin Hotel* 58 Manchester Road WA14 4PJ (beside A56) ☎061-928 2390

This large semidetached house with its own car park, set beside the Altrincham/Sale road, provides modest but soundly maintained bed and breakfast accommodation which includes some family rooms. The traditionally furnished breakfast room has separate tables, and there is a comfortable lounge.

10rm (2fb) CTV in all bedrooms [R]

♨ CTV

INN[Q][Q][Q] *The Old Packet House* Navigation Road, Broadheath WA14 1LW (on A56 Altrincham/Sale road at junct with Navigation Road) ☎061-929 1331

A pleasant old inn with car park at the rear. Attractively decorated bedrooms are equipped with such modern extras as trouser presses, while public areas retain the charm and character bestowed by exposed beams and open fires.

5rm(1🚿) CTV in all bedrooms [R] 🐕 (ex guide dogs) LDO 9pm

♨ CTV

ALYTH Tayside *Perthshire* — Map **15** NO25

INN[Q][Q] Losset Losset Road PH11 8BT ☎(08283) 2393

This friendly family run inn is close to the centre of the small town and offers a good all round standard of both accommodation and service. Bedrooms are bright and practical, and the snug lounge bar has a low ceiling and the original fireplace. There is a good range of food available.

3🚿 CTV in all bedrooms [R] LDO 9pm

♨

AMBLESIDE Cumbria — Map **07** NY30

GH [Q][Q][Q] Compston House Hotel Compston Road LA22 9DJ (in centre of village overlooking the park) ☎(05394) 32305

Ideally situated close to the town centre, this small family-owned hotel is worth seeking out. The carefully tended accommodation comprises fresh bedrooms and cosy public rooms, and the owners, Mr and Mrs Smith, provide a warm welcome and friendly service.

8🚿 (1fb) 🚭 in 1 bedrooms 🚭 in dining room CTV in all bedrooms [R] 🐕 (ex guide dogs) dB&B🚿£39-£53 LDO 10am

Lic ♨ P nc5yrs complimentary membership of leisure club

[£]

GH [Q][Q][Q] Easedale Compston Road LA22 9DJ (on one way system going north through Ambleside - bottom of Compston Road on corner overlooking bowling & putting greens) ☎(05394) 32112

Standing on a corner, this house is only a short walk from the village centre. It is being continually upgraded under the supervision of the resident owners Mr and Mrs Soar, who provide well maintained accommodation and friendly service. There is a small car park.

6rm(2🚿) (1fb) CTV in all bedrooms [R] 🐕 LDO 10am

♨

PREMIER SELECTED

GH [Q][Q][Q][Q][Q] Grey Friar Lodge Country House Hotel Brathay LA22 9NE (1.5m W off A593) ☎(05394) 33158

Mar-Oct

This delightful country house in lakeland stone sits at the foot of Loughrigg Fell on the Ambleside to Coniston and Langdale road, and its enthusiastic proprietors take great pride in creating a warm and welcoming atmosphere in which guests can relax and enjoy the lakes. Two comfortable lounges, like the pleasant dining room, are furnished in a style compatable with the character of the house, all of them having spectacular views of the Brathay River Valley and the encircling fells. Some mildly exotic touches transform traditional English home cooking, the result being a range of extremely tasty and satisfying dishes. Individually and attractively furnished bedrooms in a variety of sizes make good use of cheerful soft furnishings; all but one have en suite bathrooms, and this has its own private facilities.

8🛁🚿 🚭 in bedrooms 🚭 in dining room CTV in all bedrooms [R] 🐕 sB&B🛁🚿£27-£30 dB&B🛁🚿£40-£60 WB&B£140-£210 WBDi£215-£290 LDO 7.30pm

Lic ♨ nc12yrs

[£]

GH [Q][Q][Q] Lacet House Kelsick Road LA22 0BZ ☎(05394) 34342

3🚿 (1fb)CTV in all bedrooms [R] 🐕 (ex guide dogs) ✳ dB&B🚿£30-£33 WB&B£100-£120 WBDi£150-£170 LDO noon

♨

GH [Q][Q][Q] Lyndhurst Hotel Wansfell Road LA22 0EG (leave M6 at junct 36 onto A591) ☎(05394) 32421 FAX (05394) 32421

The Lyndhurst is a small family-run hotel set in secluded gardens within easy walking distance of the town centre. The prettily decorated bedrooms are all en suite, and one has a four-poster bed. Downstairs there is a cosy lounge and a small bar. The dining ▶

room, in a recently built conservatory, is an attractive setting for dinner, served at 6.45pm.

6🔑 Annexe 2🔑 ✗ in 1 bedrooms ✗ in area of dining room ✗ in 1 lounge CTV in all bedrooms Ⓡ 🍴 dB&B🔑£39-£50 WB&B£135-£165 WBDi£210-£230 LDO 4pm

Lic 🏧 nc
£

GH Ⓠ Ⓠ Ⓠ *Rydal Lodge Hotel* LA22 9LR (2m NW A591) ☎(05394) 33208

Closed 7 Jan-4 Feb

This small hotel, to which the assurance of warm hospitality, friendly service and home-cooked dinners brings guests back year after year, was originally Rydal's coaching inn, and parts of it date back to the early 1600s. Most of the individually decorated, traditionally furnished bedrooms are centrally heated, and both the comfortable first-floor lounge and attractive dining room look out over pretty gardens running down to the River Rothay. There is a car park behind the hotel.

8rm(2🔑) (1fb) LDO 7pm
Lic CTV ♪
Credit Cards ①③

GH Ⓠ Ⓠ Ⓠ **Smallwood Hotel** Compston Road LA22 9DJ ☎(05394) 32330

This spacious detached Lakeland stone building stands in the heart of the village and dates back to the early 19th century. Bedrooms are well equipped and have pretty decor, and there is a pleasant residents' lounge. The tea shop next door is also owned by the hotel.

13rm(11🔑) Annexe 1🔑 (4fb) ✗ in dining room CTV in 13 bedrooms Ⓡ LDO 8pm

Lic 🏧
£

ANCASTER Lincolnshire   Map **08 SK94**

🏠 FH Ⓠ Mrs F Mival **Woodlands** *(SK966437)* West Willoughby NG32 3SH (off the A153 between Sleaford and Grantham, 1m W of Ancaster) ☎Loveden(0400) 230340

Etr-Oct

Woodlands Farm is set well back from the road and offers peace, comfort, a warm greeting and limited facilities.

2rm (1fb)Ⓡ sB&B£15-£17 dB&B£28-£30 LDO previous day
🏧 CTV 12 acres mixed
£

ANDOVER Hampshire   Map **04 SU34**

GH Ⓠ Ⓠ Ⓠ **Virginia Lodge** Salisbury Road, Abbotts Ann SP11 7NX (on A343, 1m on right after Jet garage) ☎(0264) 710713

Brian and Helen Stuart's modern, comfortable bungalow is conveniently situated two miles from the town. There is a residents' lounge with TV and a separate breakfast room, where home-made marmalade, local honey and fresh farm eggs are served for breakfast. The local public house is within walking distance and usually serves evening meals. There is a large garden and parking area.

3rm(1🔑) ✗ CTV in all bedrooms Ⓡ 🍴 (ex guide dogs) sB&B£19-£22 sB&B🔑£24-£27 dB&B£32-£35 dB&B🔑£36-£40
🏧 CTV nc3yrs
£

ANGLESEY, ISLE OF Gwynedd   Map **06**

HOLYHEAD   Map **06 SH28**

🏠 🖥 GH Ⓠ Ⓠ **Offaly** 20 Walthew Avenue LL65 1AF ☎(0407) 762426

A small, cosy guest house situated just off the harbour and convenient for ferry travellers. The three bedrooms are modern and freshly decorated, and there is a comfortable lounge for residents. Car parking is easily available on the roadside.

3rm(1🔑) (2fb)Ⓡ 🍴 sB&B£13-£15 dB&B£26-£30 LDO 3pm
🏧 CTV

🏠 🖥 GH Ⓠ Ⓠ **Wavecrest** 93 Newry Street LL65 1HU ☎(0407) 763637

Situated just a short walk from the harbour, this cosy little guest house provides well equipped bedrooms with satellite TV. There is a particularly comfortable residents' lounge, and evening meals are available. There is no car park but street parking is easy. The property is situated near the ferry terminal and consequently is popular with travellers to Ireland.

4rm(2🚿) (3fb) CTV in all bedrooms [R] sB&B£14-£22 sB&B🚿£20-£25 dB&B£25-£30 dB&B🚿£28-£34 WB&B£90-£110 WBDi£140-£160 LDO 3pm
▥ CTV
[£]

RHOSCOLYN Map **06** SH27

GH [Q][Q][Q] The Old Rectory LL65 2DQ (take B4545 then follow signs Rhoscolyn just after Four Mile Bridge follow rd for 2 miles then rd alongside church) ☎Trearddur Bay(0407) 860214
Closed 21 Dec-19 Jan rs 1 wk Oct
This lovely old Georgian house stands in its own pleasant gardens, with both sea and rural views. The surrounding area has lots of footpaths, and is popular with bird-watchers. Accomodation is good; the bedrooms all have en suite facilities and are equipped with TV, radio and tea-making, and family rooms are also available. In addition to the cosy dining room, where guests sit around a large communal table, there is a choice of comfortable lounges, both having open fires in the cold weather.
5🛁🚿 (3fb) 🚭 in 2 bedrooms 🚭 in dining room 🚭 in lounges CTV in all bedrooms [R] sB&B🛁🚿£24-£31.50 dB&B🛁🚿£48-£51 WB&Bfr£160 WBDifr£260 LDO 10 am
Lic ▥ CTV
Credit Cards [1][3][£]

TREARDDUR BAY Map **06** SH27

🛏 📖 **GH [Q][Q] Moranedd** Trearddur Road LL65 2UE
☎(0407) 860324
This large detached house surrounded by attractive gardens is quietly situated in a residential cul-de-sac, within a short walk of the the beach. The accommodation is not luxurious, but the bedrooms are modern and most are quite spacious; family rooms are also available. Separate tables are provided in the breakfast room and there is a choice of two lounges, one a sun lounge.
6rm (1fb) 🚭 in dining room [R] 🐕 (ex guide dogs) sB&B£14-£15 dB&B£28-£30
Lic ▥ CTV
[£]

ANSTRUTHER Fife Map **12** NO50

PREMIER SELECTED

GH [Q][Q][Q][Q][Q] Hermitage Ladywalk KY10 3EX
☎(0333) 310909

Just a short stroll from the bustling harbour and Fisheries Museum, this interesting and historic house with its secluded walled garden, is a haven of peace and tranquillity. Tastefully and sympathetically restored by the current owners it offers a high standard of well appointed accommodation. There are two individually decorated bedrooms on each floor, and they share their own lounge and bathroom, a particularly good arrangement for a family or party of four. All enjoy delightful views. There is also a small, well stocked foyer library and an attractive dining room where breakfast is served. Home cooked evening meals are available on request and the establishment is licensed.
4rm (2fb) 🚭 in bedrooms 🚭 in dining room [R] T 🐕 (ex guide dogs) ✱ sB&B£25-£33 dB&B£40-£46 WB&B£126-£208 WBDi£196-£295 LDO 1pm
Lic ▥ CTV
Credit Cards [1][2][3][£]

SELECTED

GH [Q][Q][Q][Q] The Spindrift Pittenweem Road KY10 3DT (from W first building on left when entering town and from E last building on right when leaving) ☎(0333) 310573
Closed Xmas
Eric and Moyra McFarlane's stone-built Victorian home has been converted into a pleasant guest house. A number of original features have been retained including the attractive staircase and plasterwork. Bedrooms, though small, are neat and modern. The Captain's Room is particularly interesting with its fully wood-lined interior. Public rooms include an inviting lounge with a log fire and honesty bar and a bright dining room with bamboo tables and chairs.
8rm(7🛁1🚿) (3fb) 🚭 CTV in all bedrooms [R] 🐕 ✱ dB&B🛁🚿£50-£55 WB&B£171.50-£182 WBDi£238-£252 LDO 7pm
Lic ▥ CTV
Credit Cards [1][3]

INN[Q] ***The Royal Hotel*** 20 Rodger Street KY10 3DU
☎(0333) 310581 FAX (0333) 310270
A lively village inn close to the harbour, the Royal Hotel offers acceptable comfort in rooms which have recently been improved with the addition of bright new fabrics. A cosy residents' lounge is provided and a good range of meals is served in the bar.
11rm(2🛁7🚿) (1fb) CTV in 6 bedrooms [R] 🐕 (ex guide dogs) LDO 9pm
▥ CTV
Credit Cards [1][2][3][5]

APPLEBY-IN-WESTMORLAND Cumbria   Map **12** NY62

GH Ⓠ Ⓠ Ⓠ **Bongate House** Bongate CA16 6UE (0.5m from town centre on B6542 signposted Brough) ☎Appleby(07683) 51245
Closed Xmas & New Year
Bongate House is a Georgian residence set in one acre of landscaped gardens, which include a putting green and a croquet lawn. It provides comfortable accommodation in well equipped bedrooms, with a spacious lounge, cosy bar and separate dining room.
8rm(1⇦4ƒ) (4fb) ⊁ in dining room CTV in all bedrooms Ⓡ ⚟
(ex guide dogs) sB&B£16 dB&B£32 dB&B⇦ƒ£37 WB&B£105-£125 WBDi£150-£170 LDO 6pm
Lic ▥ nc7yrs croquet & putting lawn
£

ARBROATH Tayside *Angus*   Map **12** NO64

GH Ⓠ Ⓠ **Kingsley** 29 Market Gate DD11 1AU (close to harbour) ☎(0241) 73933 due to change to 873933
A family-run commercial guest house close to the town centre offers bedrooms with bright, cheerful fabrics, some modern in style of furnishing. For entertainment there is a games room with pool and darts and a residents' lounge. In summer evening meals are provided and a small residents' bar is opened.
14rm (8fb) ⊁ in dining room CTV in all bedrooms ✳ sB&Bfr£15 sB&Bfr£20 dB&Bfr£25 dB&Bfr£32 WB&Bfr£90 WBDifr£125 LDO 6pm
Lic ▥ CTV snooker childrens play ground
£

SELECTED

FH Ⓠ Ⓠ Ⓠ Ⓠ Mrs S A Caldwell *Farmhouse Kitchen*
(NO582447) Grange of Conon DD11 3SD (6m N, signposted from A933 just beyond Colliston) ☎(0241) 860202
Breakfasting arrangements, in a cosy alcove of the farm's kitchen, have given the bed and breakfast side of Grange of Conon farm its name. The bedrooms are pleasantly decorated and well equipped. A sun lounge looks onto the front garden, and there is a games and fitness room.
3rm (1fb) CTV in all bedrooms Ⓡ ⚟ (ex guide dogs)
▥ CTV nc3yrs ⟡ snooker solarium games room 560 acres arable

ARDBRECKNISH Strathclyde *Argyllshire*   Map **10** NN02

FH Ⓠ Ⓠ Ⓠ Mrs Whalley *Rockhill (NN072219)* PA33 1BH
☎Kilchrenan(08663) 218
May-Sep
Situated on the eastern side of Loch Awe and reached by a single stony track from the village, this farmhouse stands in peaceful isolation in its own grounds leading down to the lochside. Cosy and somewhat old fashioned, the house has a lounge with books and games and a neat little dining room with an honesty drinks counter. Bedrooms are simply decorated and furnished. Access to the two ground floor rooms is via the kitchen area, but privacy is ensured as there is a shared bathroom close by.
5rm(1⇦ƒ) (3fb) CTV in all bedrooms Ⓡ LDO 7pm
Lic nc8yrs ⟡ 200 acres horses sheep

ARDERSIER Highland *Inverness-shire*   Map **14** NH85

FH Ⓠ Ⓠ Ⓠ Mrs L E MacBean *Milton-of-Gollanfield*
(NH809534) Gollanfield IV1 2QT (just off A96 between Inverness & Nairn) ☎(0667) 462207
May-Nov
This substantial Victorian farmhouse, standing in its own garden, is an ideal base for the tourist, offering enjoyable home cooking and sound traditional comforts.
3rm Ⓡ ⚟ (ex guide dogs)
CTV 360 acres mixed arable beef sheep

ARDGAY Highland *Sutherland*   Map **14** NH58

SELECTED

GH Ⓠ Ⓠ Ⓠ Ⓠ **Ardgay House** IV24 3DH (on B9176 or via Tain on A836) ☎(0863) 766345
Apr-Oct rs Nov-Mar
Enthusiastic owners, Keith and Eileen Denton, have lovingly restored this grand old Victorian house which overlooks the Dornoch Firth. An ideal base for the tourist it offers a delightful, comfortable lounge with period furnishings, elegant dining room and well equipped, individually styled bedrooms where the current furnishings are being replaced by elegant Victorian pieces.
6rm(4⇦ƒ) (1fb) ⊁ in dining room ⊁ in lounges CTV in all bedrooms Ⓡ ⚟ (ex guide dogs) ✳ dB&B£32-£36 dB&B⇦ƒ£40-£48 LDO 7pm
Lic ▥ nc8yrs
£

ARLINGTON East Sussex   Map **05** TQ50

PREMIER ⚜ SELECTED

FH Ⓠ Ⓠ Ⓠ Ⓠ Ⓠ Mrs C McCutchan **Bates Green** *(TQ553077)* BN26 6SH (2.5m W of A22 towards Arlington turn right Old Oak Inn) ☎Polegate(0323) 482039
This charming brick-built, tile-hung farmhouse has been restored and enlarged since its beginnings as an 18th-century gamekeeper's cottage. Owner Carolyn McCutchan is a gardening enthusiast and the garden is regularly open for all to enjoy under the National Garden Scheme. The bedrooms, named after her daughters, are decorated and furnished in a cottagey style without being fussy, and all have smart en suite bathrooms. There is a choice of lounges, one on the first floor and another downstairs with a real log fire. Mrs McCutchan knows how to look after guests, with tea and home-made cake on arrival and a wonderful breakfast with freshly squeezed juice, locally cured bacon, old-fashioned sausages, free range eggs and a choice of excellent home-made preserves.
3⇦ƒ ⊁ Ⓡ ⚟ dB&B⇦ƒ£42-£45
▥ CTV nc10yrs ⚲(hard)150 acres sheep turkey

ARRAN, ISLE OF Strathclyde *Buteshire*   Map **10**

BRODICK   Map **10** NS03

GH Ⓠ Ⓠ Ⓠ *Allandale* KD27 8BJ ☎(0770) 302278
Closed Nov-Dec
Many guests return year after year to this comfortable detached house on the southern outskirts of the town. The practically furnished bedrooms vary in size, and there is an attractive lounge where guests can take an aperitif before sampling the enjoyable home cooking in the adjacent panelled dining room.
4rm(2⇦2ƒ) Annexe 2⇦ (1fb) CTV in all bedrooms Ⓡ LDO 6pm
Lic ▥

SELECTED

GH Ⓠ Ⓠ Ⓠ Ⓠ **Dunvegan House** Dunvegan Shore Road KA27 8AJ (Turn right from ferry terminal, 500yds along Shore Road) ☎(0770) 302811

This lovely island house stands on the seafront with views over the bay. Bedrooms, all no-smoking are comfortably furnished with modern and traditional pine units. There is a comfortable lounge where drinks are served.

10rm(6♠) (1fb) ⊁ in bedrooms CTV in all bedrooms ® ⊁ (ex guide dogs) ✳ sB&Bfr£18.50 dB&Bfr£37 dB&B♠fr£52 LDO 4pm
Lic ▥ CTV

LOCHRANZA
Map **10** NR95

GH Ⓠ Ⓠ *Kincardine Lodge* KA27 8HL ☎(0770) 830267
Apr-Oct
A sturdy Victorian house, Kincardine Lodge stands in its own well maintained garden overlooking the bay and castle, close to the Kintyre ferry terminal. It offers good value holiday accommodation and a choice of comfortable lounges, one no smoking.

7rm (4fb) ®
CTV

WHITING BAY
Map **10** NS02

GH Ⓠ Ⓠ Ⓠ *Invermay Hotel* Shore Rd KA27 8PZ
☎(0770) 700431
Apr-Oct
Built in the early part of the century, this fine detached house stands in its own garden beside the main road overlooking the sea to the Clyde coast beyond. Enthusiastic owners maintain high standards throughout, and public areas include a comfortable lounge with lots of books, a separate small dispense bar, and an attractive dining room where good home cooking is served.

7rm(5♠) ⊁ in bedrooms ⊁ in dining room ® ⊁ (ex guide dogs)
sB&Bfr£21 sB&B♠fr£30 dB&B♠fr£46 LDO 2pm
Lic ▥ CTV
£

ARROCHAR Strathclyde *Dunbartonshire*
Map **10** NN20

GH Ⓠ Ⓠ Ⓠ *Fascadail Country Guest House* Shore Road G83 7AB
☎(03012) 344
This fine period house overlooks Loch Long and, in good weather, has views of the Cobbler peak. It is set well back from the road in attractive gardens, and offers individually styled bedrooms, a stylish dining room and a comfortable lounge.

7rm(5⇔♠) (2fb) CTV in all bedrooms ® ⊁ (ex guide dogs)
LDO 6pm
▥ CTV nc8yrs

GH Ⓠ Ⓠ Ⓠ *Mansefield Country House* G83 7AG (on A814 near village store on Loch Long) ☎(03012) 282
This detached period house lies in its own gardens well back from the road, and has lovely views over Loch Long. Bedrooms vary in size, but the comfortable guests' lounge and a dining room with a fine fireplace are attractive features.

5rm(1♠) (2fb) CTV in all bedrooms ® LDO 6pm
▥ CTV

ARUNDEL West Sussex
Map **04** TQ00

GH Ⓠ Ⓠ Ⓠ *Arden* 4 Queens Lane BN18 9JN ☎(0903) 882544
This Victorian villa, dating back to 1840, is quietly situated off a small lane approaching the town centre, and is very neat and well maintained. Bedrooms are all furnished in the same basic modern style; there are also some on the ground floor. Full English breakfast is provided in the dining room; service is personally supervised by the resident proprietors Carol and Jeff Short.

8rm(3♠) CTV in all bedrooms ® ⊁ (ex guide dogs) ✳
sB&B£16-£19 sB&B♠£20-£25 dB&B£30-£34 dB&B♠£32-£38
▥ nc2yrs

GH Ⓠ Ⓠ *Bridge House* 18 Queen Street BN18 9JG
☎(0903) 882142 & 882779
Closed Xmas wk
As its name suggests, this small hotel is located by the bridge, and some rooms overlook the River Arun. The range of well equipped bedrooms includes those in the adjoining 16th-century cottage, standard ground floor rooms and larger family rooms. Some have recently been upgraded to a higher standard. There is a comfortable lounge, breakfast room and bar, and the evening meal is selected from a blackboard menu.

16rm(12⇔♠) Annexe 3⇔♠ (6fb) CTV in all bedrooms ® LDO 7.30pm
Lic ▥ CTV
Credit Cards ① ③

ASHBOURNE Derbyshire
Map **07** SK14

See also Waterhouses

SELECTED

GH Ⓠ Ⓠ Ⓠ Ⓠ *Biggin Mill Farm* Biggin-by-Hulland DE6 3FN (turn off A517 signposted Millington Green, after 1m take first turning on left after ford) ☎(0335) 370414
FAX (0335) 370414
2⇔♠ ⊁ CTV in all bedrooms ® ⊁ sB&B⇔♠fr£47.50 dB&B⇔♠fr£70 LDO 3pm
Lic ▥ nc
Credit Cards ① ② ③
See advertisement on p.49.

Rockhill Farm Country House

Ardbrecknish, By Dalmally, Argyll PA33 1BH
Tel: 0186 63 218

Rockhill is situated on the south-east shore of Lochawe and commands panoramic views of Cruachan Mountain. Breeding Hanoverian horses and sheep. Attractive modernised farmhouse. En-suite or private facilities. Peaceful holidays, beautiful surroundings, first class home cooking. Guests keep returning. Facilities include Loch fishing, and guests may bring their own boat, hill walking and pony trekking in the area. Residential licence. Fire certificate granted.

B&B from £16. D/B&B from £32.

SAE please for comprehensive brochure from
Helen & Brian Whalley.

SELECTED

GH Ⓠ Ⓠ Ⓠ **Lichfield** Bridge View, Mayfield DE6 2HN (from town take A52 for Leek, after 1.25m at Queens Arms turn left, 200yds up hill on left) ☎(0335) 344422
Closed 25 & 26 Dec
This attractive house is in an elevated position overlooking the River Dove. Decorated in pleasant cottage style throughout, the guest house has a comfortable lounge and separate dining room, where a good choice is offered at breakfast. Bedrooms are neat and fresh, with pretty fabrics.
4rm(2♠) (1fb) ⊁ CTV in all bedrooms Ⓡ ⴱ ✻
sB&B£18-£20 dB&B♠£34-£40
▥ CTV

FH Ⓠ Ⓠ Ⓠ Mrs M Hollingsworth *Collycroft (SK166434)*
Clifton DE6 2GN (2.5m S off A515) ☎(0335) 342187
A friendly welcome is assured at this quiet farmhouse just 5 minutes drive from the town centre. Bedrooms vary in sizes and styles, and recently an ensuite shower room has been added to one bedroom with the two remaining bedrooms sharing a modern bathroom. A hearty breakfast is served in the pleasant dining room and guests have the use of a comfortable lounge that looks out over gorgeous countryside.
3rm(1♠) CTV in all bedrooms Ⓡ

ASHBURTON Devon   Map **03** SX76
See also Bickington & Poundsgate

SELECTED

GH Ⓠ Ⓠ Ⓠ Ⓠ **Gages Mill** Buckfastleigh Road TQ13 7JW
☎(0364) 652391
Jan/Mar-Nov
Set in lovely gardens, this 14th-century stone mill house offers eight prettily decorated bedrooms, all en suite or with private facilities. The large sitting room has a small corner bar and leads into the dining room through stone arches. The food is freshly prepared by Chris Moore, and dishes might include beetroot and tomato soup, beef in Guinness with pickled walnuts, and oranges in caramel with Cointreau.
8⇆♠ (1fb) ⊁ in dining room CTV in 4 bedrooms Ⓡ ⴱ (ex guide dogs) ✻ sB&B⇆♠£21.50-£22.50 dB&B⇆♠£43-£45
WB&B£126-£136 WBDi£192.50-£203 LDO 3pm
Lic ▥ CTV nc5yrs croquet

ASHFORD Kent   Map **05** TR04
GH Ⓠ Ⓠ Ⓠ **Croft Hotel** Canterbury Road, Kennington TN25 4DU
☎(0233) 622140 FAX (0233) 622140
This well-maintained hotel stands in two acres of gardens, just over a mile from the centre of Ashford on the A28 Canterbury road and six miles from the Channel Tunnel. Some of the spacious bedrooms are large enough to provide the home comfort of lounge seating, and all, whether in the main house or garden annexes, are well furnished and equipped to modern standards. The small dining room offers à la carte and grill dishes with a small bar for pre-dinner drinks.
15⇆♠ Annexe 13⇆♠ (4fb) ⊁ in dining room CTV in all bedrooms Ⓡ T ✻ sB&B⇆♠£31.50-£37 dB&B⇆♠£41.50-£47 LDO 8pm
Lic ▥ CTV croquet
Credit Cards ①②③

GH Ⓠ Ⓠ Ⓠ **Warren Cottage** 136 The Street, Willsborough
TN24 0NB ☎(0233) 621905 & 632929 FAX (0233) 623400
4♠ CTV in all bedrooms Ⓡ ⴱ (ex guide dogs) ✻ sB&B♠£20-£25 dB&B♠£50 WB&B£175 WBDi£238 LDO 9.30pm
Lic ▥ CTV
Credit Cards ①

ASHOVER Derbyshire   Map **08** SK36
FH Ⓠ Ⓠ Ⓠ Mr J A Wootton **Old School** *(SK323654)* Uppertown
S45 0JF (off B5057, signposted left for Uppertown)
☎Chesterfield(0246) 590813
Mar-Oct
With all rooms on the ground floor, this modern stone-built farmhouse is ideal for young children and elderly guests.
4rm(2♠) (2fb) CTV in all bedrooms Ⓡ ⴱ ✻ sB&B£14-£16 dB&B£28-£32 WB&B£112 WBDi£154 LDO 9.30am
▥ CTV 45 acres poultry sheep beef

ASTHALL Oxfordshire   Map **04** SP21
INN Ⓠ Ⓠ Ⓠ **Maytime** OX8 4HW (0.25m N off A40)
☎(0993) 822068
Dating back to the 16th century, this traditional hostelry is in the centre of a Windrush Valley hamlet. An extensive range of meals and snacks is available from the menu, supplemented by daily specials written on the blackboard. Bedrooms, furnished with hand made elm furniture, are all on the ground floor convenient for the car park.
Annexe 6⇆ ⊁ in area of dining room CTV in all bedrooms Ⓡ T ✻ sB&B⇆£35-£43.60 dB&B⇆£48-£55 Lunch £4.75-£11.95alc Dinner £4.75-£11.95alc LDO 10pm
▥
Credit Cards ①②③

ASTON MUNSLOW Shropshire   Map **07** SO58

SELECTED

GH Ⓠ Ⓠ Ⓠ Ⓠ **Chadstone** SY7 9ER (8m N of Ludlow off the B4368) ☎Munslow(058476) 675 dut to change to (0584) 841675
This immaculate modern guest house enjoys delightful rural views across to the Clee Hills from its setting in two acres of attractive grounds some six miles east of Craven Arms. It offers a friendly welcome and caring service in a peaceful, relaxing atmosphere. Freshly decorated bedrooms (two of which have en suite facilities) are enhanced by pretty floral fabrics, there is a television lounge for residents on the first floor, and a patio at the rear of the building provides a popular sitting area on warmer days.
5rm(2⇆♠) ⊁ in bedrooms ⊁ in dining room CTV in 1 bedroom Ⓡ ⴱ sB&Bfr£30 dB&Bfr£40 dB&B⇆♠fr£44 LDO 7pm
Lic ▥ CTV nc12yrs
⊕

ASWARBY Lincolnshire   Map **08** TF03
INN Ⓠ Ⓠ Ⓠ **Tally Ho** NG34 8SA (3m S of Sleaford, on A15)
☎Culverthorpe(05295) 205
Located in pleasant open countryside, this stone 17th-century listed inn stands in neatly tended gardens, which include a barbecue and children's play area. It has become a popular venue for food, particularly bar meals, chosen from a menu or blackboard selections of interesting country dishes. Exposed beams and stone walls are prominent features in the attractive bar, which also boasts a log fire. The restored dining room has been decorated to reflect the original character of the inn, with polished wooden floors, attractive rich bold drapes, complementary cushion seating and copper pans displayed in the fireplace. All the neat, bright bedrooms are housed in an annexe building and are equipped with modern en suites, TV and tea-making facilities.
Annexe 6rm(2⇆4♠) CTV in all bedrooms Ⓡ ✻ sB&B⇆♠£30-£32 dB&B⇆♠£45-£47 Lunch £8.25-£10.50alc Dinner £11-£18alc LDO 10pm
▥
Credit Cards ①③⊕

AUCHTERMUCHTY Fife   Map **11** NO21

FH Ⓠ Ⓠ Ⓠ Ⓠ Ⓠ Mrs I
Steven **Ardchoille**
(NO248096) Dunshalt
KY14 7EY (on B936)
☎(0337) 828414
FAX (0337) 828414
Hospitality and food are
second to none at Donald and

Isobel Stevens' spotlessly
maintained farm guesthouse,
lying just outside the village
of Dunshalt. Guests are made
very much at home, and Isobel's imaginative four-course
dinner and hearty breakfasts, served around the one table,
have won universal praise. Bedrooms are neither large nor
ostentatious, but are pleasant, comfortable and thoughtfully
equipped. All give uninterrupted views across open farmland.
3rm(2♩) (1fb) ⠗ CTV in all bedrooms Ⓡ ⚲ (ex guide dogs)
sB&BⱤ£30-£40 dB&BⱤ£50-£70 LDO 6pm
▦ CTV 2 acres
Credit Cards ① ③

AUDLEM Cheshire   Map **07** SJ64

FH Ⓠ Ⓠ Mrs H M Bennion **Little Heath** *(SJ663455)* CW3 0HE
(take A529 from Nantwich for 5m, at 30mph sign turn right)
☎(0270) 811324
Apr-Nov
Set on a 50-acre dairy farm north of the village centre, this 200-
year-old brick-built house retains something of its original

character in the low beamed ceilings of a homely lounge and a
traditionally furnished dining room where guests share a single
large table. Spacious, well maintained bedrooms also have
predominantly traditional furniture, the two without en suite
facilities sharing a large modern bathroom and toilet.
3rm(1♩) ⠗ Ⓡ ⚲ (ex guide dogs) ✳ sB&B£15-£20 sB&BⱤ£15-
£23 dB&B£27-£32 dB&BⱤ£29-£36 LDO 10am
▦ CTV 50 acres dairy
ⓔ

AUDLEY Staffordshire   Map **07** SJ75

FH Ⓠ Ⓠ Ⓠ Ⓠ Mrs E E Oulton **Domvilles** *(SJ776516)*
Barthomley Road ST7 8HT (leave M6, junct 16, follow signs to
Barthomley) ☎Stoke-on-Trent(0782) 720378
Closed 25 Dec
Surrounded by open countryside yet only three minutes' drive
from junction 16 of the M6, this large and beautifully
preserved house dating back to 1730 is tastefully appointed
throughout in a style befitting its character; bedrooms have
antique furniture including a full or half tester bed, while the
elegant lounge features a very impressive period fireplace.
Guests share a table in the breakfast room and dinner can be
provided by prior arrangement. A former farm building is
being cleverly converted into a two-bedroomed self catering
unit which will also be available to bed and breakfast guests.
6rm(3♩) (2fb) CTV in all bedrooms Ⓡ ⚲ (ex guide dogs) ✳
sB&Bfr£22 sB&B⇆Ⱡ£26 dB&Bfr£34 dB&B⇆Ⱡ£36 LDO
6pm
CTV table tennis 225 acres dairy mixed

▶

AUSTWICK North Yorkshire   Map **07** SD76

FH Q Q Q Mrs M Hird **Rawlinshaw** *(SD781673)* LA2 8DD (on A65,3.5m NW of Settle) ☎Settle(0729) 823214

Etr-Sep

Mr and Mrs Hird run this charming 200-year-old farmhouse on a working farm and pony trekking centre at the northern end of the Settle by-pass. The accommodation is very comfortable and spotlessly clean. Guests have their own lounge downstairs and breakfast is served either here at a large table or in the dining room.

2rm(1⇨) ⊬ in dining room CTV in all bedrooms ⑧ 🏃 (ex guide dogs) dB&B£28-£32 dB&B⇨£32-£36

🛲 CTV ∪ 206 acres beef dairy horses sheep

AVETON GIFFORD Devon   Map **03** SX64

FH Q Q Q Mrs J Balkwill **Court Barton** *(SX695478)* TQ7 4LE ☎Kingsbridge(0548) 550312

Closed Xmas

A 16th-century manor house in a charming setting next to the parish church, surrounded by well kept gardens. Mr and Mrs Balkwill have renovated their home to provide large bedrooms, furnished with antiques and provided with thoughtful little extras. There is a comfortable sitting room and breakfast is served in the dining room, with the owners happy to offer several suggestions for places to dine.

7rm(6⇨🏠) (2fb) ⊬ in dining room ⑧ 🏃 (ex guide dogs) ✳ sB&B⇨🏠fr£25 dB&B fr£34 dB&B⇨🏠fr£36

🛲 CTV ↘table-tennis pool table croquet 40 acres mixed ⓔ

AVIEMORE Highland *Inverness-shire*   Map **14** NH81

⧫ ▼ **GH** Q **Craiglea** Grampian Road PH22 1RH (N of railway station) ☎(0479) 810210

Craiglea is a detached villa standing beside the main road close to the railway station and central amenities, and it offers reasonably priced practical accommodation. The simply decorated bedrooms have modern furnishings, and the public areas include a TV lounge and a dining room. Breakfast may occasionally be served at shared tables.

11rm(1🏠) (4fb) ⊬ in dining room ⑧ sB&B£14-£16 dB&B£28-£32 dB&B🏠£30-£34 WB&B£100-£110

CTV sauna skiing packages can be arranged in winter

Credit Cards ① ③ ⓔ

GH Q Q Q *Ravenscraig* Grampian Road PH22 1RP ☎(0479) 810278

Enthusiastic owners Robert and Christine Thompson are constantly making improvements to their comfortable house, which stands in its own grounds beside the main road at the north end of the village. Bedrooms, including those in the single-storey rear annexe, are smartly decorated and modern in style. Public areas include a lounge with comfortable seating, a TV and a good supply of books, and an attractive dining room where hearty breakfasts are served.

6🏠 Annexe 6🏠 (2fb) CTV in all bedrooms ⑧

🛲 CTV

Credit Cards ① ③

AXBRIDGE Somerset   Map **03** ST45

FH Q Mr L F Dimmock **Manor** *(ST420549)* Cross BS26 2ED (at junct of A38/A371) ☎(0934) 732577

Closed Xmas

Basic accommodation for a budget holiday is offered at this 400-year-old Mendip farmhouse, ideal for those with an interest in walking, touring or cycling. Pets are welcome and there are outside facilities for those who prefer to leave their dogs at the farm during the day. Family bedrooms are available and all rooms have tea-making facilities.

---

7 (2fb)⑧ ✳ sB&B£12.50-£13.75 dB&B£25-£27.50 WB&B£85-£93.50 WBDi£128.70-£141.30 LDO 5pm

CTV 250 acres beef sheep

AXMINSTER Devon   Map **03** SY29

SELECTED

FH Q Q Q Q Mrs S Gay **Millbrook Farmhouse** *(SY304987)* Chard Road EX13 5EG (on A358) ☎(0297) 35351

Closed Xmas, 2wks autumn & 3wks spring

A delightful thatched longhouse, with a history dating back to the 10th century, set in an acre of well tended gardens is conveniently located for both the town and coast. The bedrooms are furnished with antiques, set off by attractive fabrics, and provided with thoughtful extras such as fresh fruit and flowers. The sitting room features oak panelled walls and a huge inglenook fireplace. A charming conservatory is a recent addition, and guests may eat here or in the dining room, where local home-grown produce is served around a large communal table at dinner. An attractive collection of antique china is displayed throughout the house, and outside, guests can enjoy a game of croquet or badminton during the summer months.

3rm(1⇨🏠) (2fb) ⊬ CTV in all bedrooms ⑧ 🏃 (ex guide dogs) ✳ sB&Bfr£18 sB&B⇨🏠fr£20 dB&Bfr£31 dB&B⇨🏠fr£36 WB&B£108.50-£126 WBDi£178.50-£196 LDO 5pm

🛲 CTV putting croquet

AYR Strathclyde *Ayrshire*   Map **10** NS32

See also Dunure

GH Q Q Q *Arrandale Hotel* 2-4 Cassillis Street KA7 1DW ☎(0292) 289959

rs Winter

This small family-run hotel is within walking distance of the beach and promenade, and attracts business as well as tourist trade. Bedrooms vary in size, but most are nicely decorated and furnished. There is a comfortable lounge and a dining room with a small residents' bar and pool table.

13rm(1⇨2🏠) (6fb) CTV in all bedrooms 🏃 (ex guide dogs) Lic 🛲 CTV ✗nc6yrs

SELECTED

GH Q Q Q Q Q **Brenalder Lodge** 39 Dunure, Doonfoot KA7 4HR (2m S on A719) ☎(0292) 443939

rs during props holiday

This extended modern bungalow offers an ideal base for visitors who appreciate a warm welcome and high standards of appointment. Attractive fabrics have been used to good effect in bright, modern little bedrooms (all with private facilities) that include one family suite. The spacious lounge, with its comfortable leather settees and large natural stone fireplace, invites relaxation, while a smart dining room provides the ideal setting in which to enjoy delicious home-cooked meals - the four-course menu with choices at every stage is chalked up on a blackboard each evening.

3⇨🏠 (1fb) ⊬ in bedrooms ⊬ in dining room CTV in all bedrooms ⑧ ✳ dB&B⇨🏠£46-£60 WB&B£161-£196 LDO 24hrs prior

🛲 CTV nc7yrs

ⓔ

GH Q Q Q **Craggallan** 8 Queens Terrace KA7 1DU ☎(0292) 264998

Situated midway between the beach and the town centre, this attractive guest house has bright modern bedrooms, a small dining

room and a comfortable lounge.
6rm(2♠) (1fb) ⊁ in 2 bedrooms ⊁ in dining room CTV in all
bedrooms ℝ ✱ sB&B£15-£17 dB&B£30-£32 dB&B♠£36-£40
WB&B£105-£120 WBDi£140-£150 LDO 5pm
▥ CTV
£

GH Ｑ Ｑ Ｑ **Dargill** 7 Queens Terrace KA7 1DU ☎(0292) 261955
This small guest house is conveniently located between the town
centre and the sea. The accommodation is set on three levels,
offering cheerful modern bedrooms, a spacious lounge and cosy
dining room.
4rm(1♠) (2fb) ⊁ in 1 lounge CTV in all bedrooms ℝ ✱
sB&Bfr£18 dB&B£30-£32 dB&B♠£40-£42 LDO 2pm
▥ CTV nc3yrs

SELECTED

GH Ｑ Ｑ Ｑ Ｑ **Glenmore** 35 Bellevue Crescent KA7 2DP
☎(0292) 269830
This mid-terrace, two-storey house, with a small rose garden
at the front, is in a quiet residential crescent close to the town
centre. It has been extensively refurbished to provide a high
standard of decor, furnishings and fittings, with bold use of
colours and patterns. There is a separate spacious lounge and
a smaller dining room, both with fine fireplaces, and owner,
Mrs Reid, ensures that guests have the best of facilities. Street
parking is available, and while restrictions can apply, permits
are available. Bedrooms are very well equipped, all en suite,
with a good range of equipment.
5➪♠ (2fb)CTV in all bedrooms ℝ ⊁ ✱ sB&B➪♠£15-£30
dB&B➪♠£30-£45 WB&Bfr£105 WBDifr£160 LDO 5pm
▥ CTV ⊬

⊨ ☟ **GH** Ｑ Ｑ Ｑ **Langley Bank** 39 Carrick Road KA7 2RD
☎(0292) 264246 FAX (0292) 282628
This substantial semidetached period house is popular with business
guests as well as tourists. Bedrooms have high ceilings and elegant,
modern private bathrooms. The two upper-floor bedrooms have
the use of facilities on the first floor, and they all have telephones
and radio alarm clocks. There is no residents' lounge.
6rm(4♠) (1fb) ⊁ in dining room CTV in all bedrooms ℝ ⊁ (ex
guide dogs) sB&Bfr£15 sB&B♠£25-£40 dB&Bfr£30
dB&B♠£40-£60
▥
Credit Cards ① ② ③ £

GH Ｑ Ｑ **Windsor Hotel** 6 Alloway Place KA7 2AA (from the
centre of Ayr, take the A19 through Wellington Square and
establishment is the first guesthouse on the right)
☎(0292) 264689
Closed Xmas & New Year
Within walking distance of the town centre and the sea front, this
terraced house offers bedrooms of various sizes, including family
and ground-floor rooms. There is a comfortable lounge, and at
dinner a choice of courses and dishes is offered. Picnic lunches
can be provided.
10rm(7➪♠) (4fb) ⊁ in dining room CTV in all bedrooms ℝ ✱
sB&Bfr£20 sB&B➪♠fr£28 dB&B➪♠fr£44 WB&Bfr£140
WBDifr£195
▥ CTV ⊬
Credit Cards ① ③ £

FH Ｑ Ｑ Ｑ Mrs A Woodburn *Boreland (NS400139)* Hollybush
KA6 7ED (on the main A713, 6m S of Ayr) ☎Patna(0292) 531228
Jun-Sep
This well maintained farmhouse has two large comfortable
bedrooms and a spacious lounge where breakfasts are served.
3rm (2fb) ℝ ⊁
▥ CTV 190 acres dairy

SELECTED

FH Ｑ Ｑ Ｑ Ｑ Mrs R J Reid *Lagg (NS281166)* Dunure
KA7 4LE (5m S, on A719) ☎Dunure(0292) 500647
May-Oct
This modern farmhouse lies south of Ayr and has glorious
coastal views. The accommodation is tastefully decorated and
furnished throughout, and the bedrooms share a modern
bathroom. The lounge is an unusual shape and features a long
stone fireplace. There is an attractive little dining room and
everywhere is kept spotlessly clean.
2rm ℝ
▥ CTV 480 acres dairy sheep

AYTON, GREAT North Yorkshire   Map **08** NZ51

INN Ｑ Ｑ Ｑ *Royal Oak Hotel* High Green TS9 6BW
☎(0642) 722361 FAX (0642) 724047
Modern, attractively decorated bedrooms are a feature of this
18th-century former coaching inn. Bar meals are popular and a
very good three-course luncheon has been added to the varied
menus.
5➪♠ CTV in all bedrooms ℝ T LDO 9.15pm
▥ ⊬
Credit Cards ① ③

BAKEWELL Derbyshire   Map **08** SK26

GH Ｑ Ｑ Ｑ Castle Cliffe Private Hotel Monsal Head DE45 1NL
(3m NW) ☎Great Longstone(0629) 640258
A friendly guesthouse offers personal service, home-cooked
interesting regional British dishes and sound accommodation.
Some of the bedrooms have superb views over Monsal Dale.

▶

Castle Cliffe
Private Hotel
Monsal Head Bakewell Derbyshire DE45 1NL
Telephone: Gt Longstone 01629 640258

This could be the view from your bedroom
window as you enjoy a quiet break in the Peak
District. The Victorian house has a friendly
atmosphere with "real" fires in the Lounge and
Bar. British food is served including many less
well known regional dishes.
Special Breaks available including
Christmas & New Year.

9rm(2♠) (2fb) ⊁ in dining room CTV in 2 bedrooms ℝ ⋔ (ex guide dogs) sB&B£25-£35 dB&B£41-£45 dB&B♠£45-£47 WB&B£130-£150 WBDi£200-£230 LDO 5pm
Lic CTV
Credit Cards ① ③ ⓔ

GH ◎◎◎ Cliffe House Hotel Monsal Head DE45 1NL (3m NW off B6465) ☎Great Longstone(0629) 640376
Situated at the top of Monsal Dale, this house has some lovely panoramic views out across the Dale and surrounding Peak District. The proprietors are actively involved, which helps to create a friendly, relaxed environment. Guests can enjoy the traditional, freshly prepared home cooking, then adjourn to the relaxing TV lounge.
9rm(5⇔4♠) (3fb) ⊁ in dining room ⊁ in 1 lounge CTV in all bedrooms ℝ ⋔ (ex guide dogs) sB&B⇔♠£30 dB&B⇔♠£40-£42 WB&B£130-£136 WBDi£190-£203 LDO 10am
Lic ▥ CTV
Credit Cards ① ③ ⓔ

GH ◎◎◎ Merlin House Ashford Lane, Monsal Head DE45 1NL (1.5m NW, turn off A6 onto B6465 at Ashford-in-the-Water, follow signs to Monsal Head for a further 1.5m, entrance is 20yds from main rd) ☎Great Longstone(0629) 640475
Mar-Oct
A small, immaculately kept guesthouse lies in an lovely rural location. The friendly caring proprietors ensure high standards of housekeeping and the public areas have been recently changed, guests now having the use of a multi-purpose lounge cum breakfast room. The proprietors' local knowledge of the area and provision of maps and books on the Peak District is an added bonus.
2♠ ⊁ CTV in all bedrooms ℝ ⋔ sB&B♠£26-£28 dB&B♠£42-£46 WB&B£147
▥ nc

INN◎◎ Red Lion Rutland Square DE4 1BT
☎(0629) 812054 FAX (0629) 814345
6rm(1⇔2♠) CTV in 5 bedrooms ℝ ⋔ (ex guide dogs) LDO 8.45pm
▥
Credit Cards ① ③

BALA Gwynedd   Map **06** SH93

SELECTED

GH ◎◎◎◎ Abercelyn Country House Llanycil LL23 7YF (0.5m from outskirts of town on A494 towards Dolgellau) ☎(0678) 521109 FAX (0678) 520556
Closed 21 Dec-4 Jan
Dating back to 1729 and for many years the local rectory, this fine stone-built house is set in landscaped grounds overlooking Bala Lake in the Snowdonia National Park. It has smart guest rooms and a modern residents' lounge complete with TV and a good range of local tourist maps and guides. Only non-smokers are accommodated.
3rm(1⇔1♠) ℝ ⋔ (ex guide dogs)
▥ CTV

⋈ ▩ GH ◎◎ Erw Feurig Cefnddwysarn LL23 7LL (3m on A494 towards Corwen) ☎LLandderfel(06783) 262 due to change to (0678) 530262
Erw Feurig is a small farm guest house several miles east of the town near the village of Cefnddwysarn. It offers four rooms, some suitable for families and one with a single room adjacent. There is a small lounge in the older part of the house, which dates from the 17th century, and a modern dining room furnished in cottage style where good home cooking is served. The house is part of a large working farm with plenty of livestock on view and coarse fishing is available.

4rm(2♠) (2fb) ⊁ in 2 bedrooms ⊁ in dining room ⊁ in lounges ℝ ⋔ sB&B£14-£17 dB&Bfr£26 dB&B♠fr£32 WBDi£140-£160 LDO 5.30pm
▥ CTV ♪ snooker pool table
ⓔ

GH ◎◎ Frondderw Stryd-y-Fron LL23 7YD (travel down main street towards lake, at end of 30mph restriction take road right signposted to Bala golf course, 0.25m up hill take right fork)
☎(0678) 520301
Mar-Nov
Dating in part from 1540, this family-run hotel is situated above the town and has lovely views of the lake and the Berwyn mountains beyond. There is a TV lounge in addition to the large main lounge with its cheery wood burning stove. Several of the bedrooms are suitable for family use and one is reached by an exterior door.
8rm(1⇔3♠) (3fb) ⊁ in dining room ⊁ in 1 lounge ℝ ⋔ (ex guide dogs) sB&B⇔♠£19-£20 dB&B£28-£30 dB&B⇔♠£34-£40 WB&B£94.50-£136.50 WBDi£150.50-£192.50 LDO 5pm
Lic ▥ CTV
ⓔ

⋈ ▩ FH ◎◎ Mrs E Jones Eirianfa (SH967394) Sarnau LL23 7LH (4m N on A494) ☎Llandderfel(06783) 389
This modern bungalow is in an elevated position, with views over open countryside. Centrally heated bedrooms are attractively decorated and the combined dining room/lounge is furnished in cottage style. Guests enjoy a friendly family atmosphere.
3rm (1fb) ℝ ⋔ sB&B£15 dB&B£26 LDO 5pm
▥ CTV ♪ 150 acres mixed
ⓔ

FH ◎◎ Mrs M E Jones Penbryn (SH498723) Sarnau LL23 7LH (4m N on A494, outskirts of Sarnau village)
☎Llandderfel(06783) 297
This large stone-built 19th-century farmhouse has superb views over the Berwyn mountains. Owned by the friendly Jones family it offers attractively decorated compact bedrooms, a spacious dining room with lounge area and a TV lounge featuring a log fire and an interesting collection of personal memorabilia.
6rm (1fb) ⋔ ✳ sB&B£15-£16 dB&B£26-£30 WB&B£91-£105 LDO 6pm
▥ CTV ♪ 200 acres beef mixed sheep
ⓔ

BALINTORE Highland *Ross & Cromarty*   Map **14** NH87

FH ◎◎ Mr A Arthur Sycamores (NH870761) IV20 1XW (A9 N turn right for Balintore, 4.5m on left) ☎Fearn(0862) 832322
Good-value accommodation is offered at this friendly family-run farmhouse, situated west of the village in rolling countryside. The bedrooms, one with an en suite shower, are spacious and traditionally furnished. Public areas include a cosy TV lounge and a neat dining room, where enjoyable home cooking is served at individual tables. This is a no-smoking establishment.
2rm(1♠) (1fb) ℝ
⅙ 20 acres mixed livestock

BALLACHULISH Highland *Argyllshire*   Map **14** NN05

SELECTED

GH ◎◎◎◎ Fern Villa East Laroch PA39 4JE
☎(08552) 393 due to change to (01855) 811393
Closed Xmas & New Year
John and Beryl Clement's detached Victorian villa in the centre of the village provides bright accommodation ideal for holiday-makers. Enjoyable home-cooked dinners based on local produce are served at individual tables in the neat dining room. Refreshments are also available in the comfortable TV lounge.

5⇄𝄆 ⤙ Ⓡ 𝄇 (ex guide dogs) + dB&B⇄𝄆£54-£60 (incl dinner) WB&B£108-£126 WBDi£175-£196 LDO 6.30pm
Lic Ⓜ CTV nc16yrs

CLIFFE HOUSE HOTEL
Monsal Head, Bakewell, Derbyshire
Telephone: 01629 640376

SELECTED

GH 🅠🅠🅠🅠 *Lyn-Leven* White Street PA39 4JP (off A82)
☎(08552) 392
Closed Xmas
Lyn-Leven is a licensed family-run guest house with a superb outlook over Loch Leven and the Glencoe mountains. Bedrooms are small but bright and cheerful, and the annexe, with its own lounge, offers accommodation of a similar style and standard. There is a comfortable lounge in the main house, and an attractive dining room serving enjoyable traditional fare.
8rm(7𝄆) Annexe 5⇄𝄆 (1fb) CTV in 8 bedrooms Ⓡ LDO 7.30pm
Lic Ⓜ CTV
Credit Cards ① ③

BALLANTRAE Strathclyde *Ayrshire*   Map **10** NX08
GH 🅠🅠🅠 *Balkissock Lodge* KA26 0LP ☎(0465) 83537
FAX (0465) 83537
Closed Nov-15 Dec
Janet and Adrian Beale extend a warm welcome to guests at their peaceful country home. Bedrooms are all en suite, and public areas include a cosy lounge (the only room where smoking is permitted) with a live fire and a range of books.
3⇄𝄆 (1fb) CTV in all bedrooms Ⓡ 𝄇 (ex guide dogs) LDO 7pm

PREMIER 🏆 **SELECTED**

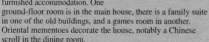

GH 🅠🅠🅠🅠🅠 *Cosses*
Country House Cosses
KA26 0LR (approach village on A77 and take turning for Laggan. Cosses is 2m after Laggan Caravan Park)
☎(0465) 83363 due to change to 831363 FAX (0465) 83598
Closed 24 Dec-5 Jan
This delightful farm has been converted to provide elegantly furnished accommodation. One ground-floor room is in the main house, there is a family suite in one of the out buildings, and a games room in another. Oriental mementos decorate the house, notably a Chinese scroll in the dining room.
1⇄ ⤙ in bedrooms CTV in all bedrooms Ⓡ ✳ sB&B⇄£40-£45 dB&B⇄£60-£70 LDO 7pm
Ⓜ games room (£)

BALLATER Grampian *Aberdeenshire*   Map **15** NO39
GH 🅠🅠🅠 *Moorside* Braemar Road AB35 5RL (on A93)
☎(03397) 55492 FAX (03397) 55492
Mar-Nov
This extended granite house lies in its own gardens in the centre of the village. It has a friendly atmosphere and the bright airy bedrooms offer good value accomodation. There is a comfortable lounge and hearty breakfasts are served in the dining room.
9rm(3⇄6𝄆) (3fb) ⤙ in dining room CTV in all bedrooms Ⓡ sB&B⇄𝄆fr£29 dB&B⇄𝄆fr£38 WB&Bfr£123
Lic Ⓜ
Credit Cards ① ③

Situated at the top of beautiful Monsal Dale, in the heart of the Peak District. The house has full central heating with all the bedrooms having full en-suite facilities, colour TV and tea making facilities. Guests can enjoy traditional home cooking and relax in the colour TV lounge. Ample car parking space. Sorry no pets allowed.

Under the personal supervision of Susan & Chris Harman.

Open all year except Christmas

Frondderw
Bala, Gwynedd LL23 7YD. N. Wales
Tel: Bala (01678) 520301

FRONDDERW is a seventeenth century mansion quietly situated in its own grounds on the hillside overlooking Bala town and lake, with magnificent views of the Berwyn Mountains.

All Bedrooms have hot/cold and tea/coffee making facilities. Full en-suite facilities are available in 50% of the bedrooms.

There is a large lounge and separate colour TV lounge for guests' use. No smoking allowed in the dining room.

An excellent evening meal is available on request. Vegetarian and other diets are catered for, advance notice required. Supper and residential licence. No garage accommodation. Outdoor parking free of charge. Sorry no guests' pets allowed in the house. Ideal centre for sightseeing, touring, walking and water sports.

Closed December, January and February.

GH 🇶🇶🇶 **Netherley** 2 Netherley Place AB35 5QE
☎(03397) 55792
Closed Nov-Jan rs Feb
Part of a terraced row just off the village green, this guest house is distinguished by its blue shutters and hanging flower baskets. Comfortable public rooms include a well proportioned dining room and a lounge with two separate areas. A table with tea and coffee-making equipment is available at all times, and bedrooms vary from large to small.
9rm(4⇄3🏫) (3fb) ⊁ in dining room ⊁ in 1 lounge CTV in 4 bedrooms ® ✱ sB&B£17-£19 dB&B£30-£34 dB&B⇄🏫£37 CTV ⊁nc4yrs
①

BALLOCH Strathclyde *Dumbartonshire*　　Map **10** NS38

GH 🇶🇶🇶 **Arbor Lodge** Old Luss Road G83 8QW (400yds from Glasgow to Loch Lomond road) ☎Alexandria(0389) 756233
FAX (0389) 78988
In a convenient position, this modern house has two large twins and two small double bedrooms, all nicely decorated. There is no lounge and the house is no-smoking.
4🏫 ⊁ CTV in all bedrooms ® 🏫 (ex guide dogs) ✱ dB&B🏫£40-£44
▥
Credit Cards ①③①

GH 🇶🇶🇶 **Beulah** Fisherwood Road G83 8SW
☎Alexandria(0389) 753022
Guests are warmly welcomed to this comfortable house which stands in a well tended garden between the railway station and River Leven. Its two en suite bedrooms are appointed in modern style, and hearty breakfasts are served at individual tables in the combined lounge/dining room.
2🏫 ⊁ CTV in all bedrooms ® ✱ sB&B🏫£18-£20 dB&B🏫£32-£34 WB&B£101-£108
▥ CTV nc12yrs
①

SELECTED

GH 🇶🇶🇶🇶 **Gowanlea** Drymen Road G83 8HS
☎Alexandria(0389) 752456
Closed 24-26 Dec
Many guests return year after year to this delightful semidetached villa situated in a quiet residential area within easy reach of central amenities. Reasonably spacious and attractively coordinated bedrooms are furnished in modern style, television is provided in the comfortable lounge and hearty breakfasts are served in a neat little dining room. Guests are assured of both a warm welcome and a relaxed, friendly atmosphere.
4⇄🏫 ⊁ CTV in 2 bedrooms ® 🏫 (ex guide dogs)
sB&B⇄🏫£19-£25 dB&B⇄🏫£36-£48 WB&B£136-£147
▥ CTV
①

BALQUHIDDER Central *Perthshire*　　Map **11** NN52

SELECTED

GH 🇶🇶🇶🇶 **Stronvar House** FK19 8PB
☎Strathyre(0877) 384688 FAX (0877) 384230
Mar-Oct
Dating from 1850, this laird's mansion sits in seclusion on the south side of Loch Voil - do not be deterred by the rough road! As well as offering accommodation, the house is the focal point for a heritage museum incorporating a craft shop and tea room (closing at 5pm). Bedrooms, most of which are massive,

are well equipped and have modern bathrooms. There is also a large lounge with an honesty bar for residents.
4⇄🏫 ⊁ in dining room CTV in all bedrooms ®
sB&B⇄🏫£39.50 dB&B⇄🏫£59 WB&B£185 WBDi£329 LDO 7.30pm
Lic ▥
Credit Cards ①③①

INN 🇶🇶🇶 **Monachyle Mhor** FK19 8PQ (4m SW)
☎Strathyre(0877) 384622 FAX (0877) 384305
Situated at the head of Loch Voil amid spectacular mountain scenery, this converted farmhouse is the ideal retreat. Rob Lewis is a welcoming host and his wife Jean prepares an interesting selection of tempting Taste of Scotland dishes, some of which are available throughout the day. Public areas are traditional, with a cosy bar, lounge, and attractive conservatory-style restaurant. The bedrooms are mostly spacious with simple decor. Fishing, stalking and grouse shooting can be arranged.
5⇄🏫 ® 🏫 (ex guide dogs) LDO 10pm
▥ CTV nc10yrs 🎣 grouse shooting
Credit Cards ①③

BALSALL COMMON West Midlands　　Map **04** SP27

GH 🇶🇶 **Blythe Paddocks** Barston Lane CV7 7BT
☎Berkswell(0676) 533050
Blythe Paddocks is a modern chalet-style bungalow on a smallholding surrounded by open countryside. The bedrooms are all well proportioned and share one good bathroom. Breakfast is served at a communal table, and Mrs Marshall's own Buff Orpington hens supply most of the eggs.
4rm CTV in all bedrooms ®
▥ CTV
Credit Cards ②

BAMFORD Derbyshire　　Map **08** SK28

INN 🇶🇶 **Ye Derwent Hotel** Main Road S30 2AY (BW)
☎Hope Valley(0433) 651395
There is a friendly, informal atmosphere at this traditional village inn, which offers freshly decorated accommodation. Competitively priced home-cooked bar meals are served in the bar-lounge or small dining room, along with a good range of ales. The proprietors have a boat and rod for hire on the nearby Ladybower Reservoir.
10rm(1⇄1🏫) (1fb) CTV in all bedrooms ® sB&Bfr£25 sB&B⇄🏫fr£30 dB&Bfr£40 dB&B⇄🏫fr£45 WB&B£140-£157.50 WBDi£185-£199 LDO 9.15pm
▥ boat for hire
Credit Cards ①③①

BAMPTON Devon

See **Shillingford**

BAMPTON Oxfordshire　　Map **04** SP30

INN 🇶🇶 **Talbot Hotel** Market Square OX8 2HA
☎Bampton Castle(0993) 850326
In the heart of the pretty Cotswold village, this inn offers modern, well equipped bedrooms, along with cosy traditional public areas. Extensive meal times and a varied choice of table d'hôte, à la carte and bar-snack menus ensure that guests do not go hungry.
6rm(5🏫) CTV in all bedrooms ® 🏫 (ex guide dogs) LDO 10pm
▥
Credit Cards ①③

BANBURY Oxfordshire　　Map **04** SP44

See also **Shenington**

GH Q Q **Belmont** 34 Crouch Street OX16 9PR ☎(0295) 262308
Bed and breakfast accommodation is provided by this Victorian town house standing a short walk from both the town centre and its famous Banbury Cross. All bedrooms have colour TV and the majority have en suite facilities; a small lounge adjoins the dining room where breakfast is served.
8rm(5♠) (1fb) ⊁ in dining room CTV in all bedrooms ® ✻ (ex guide dogs) sB&B£20-£25 sB&B♠£25 dB&B£30-£35 dB&B♠£40
▥. nc7-12yrs
Credit Cards ⊡ ⊡ ⓔ

GH Q Q Q **Calthorpe Lodge** 4 Calthorpe Road OX16 8HS
☎(0295) 252325
Quietly located a short walk from the famous Banbury Cross, this Victorian terraced guest house offers well equipped bedrooms. John and Eddie Blackwell provide a relaxed informal atmosphere, with reasonably priced accommodation. An evening meal can be provided by prior arrangement.
6rm(4⇌♠) (1fb) CTV in all bedrooms ®
▥. CTV
Credit Cards ⊡ ⊡ ⊡

SELECTED

GH Q Q Q Q **La Madonette Country** OX15 6AA (3m W off B4035) ☎(0295) 730212 FAX (0295) 730363
A 17th-century miller's house has been converted into a comfortable small hotel, with attractive well kept gardens bordered by a millstream. Owner Patti Ritter makes her guests very welcome, and the spacious bedrooms are exceptionally well equipped. The reception lounge has a bar, and conference facilities can be provided. Breakfast is served in the attractive dining room, where dinner can be provided by prior arrangement.
5⇌♠ (2fb)CTV in all bedrooms ® T ✻ (ex guide dogs) ✳ sB&B⇌♠£32-£34 dB&B⇌♠£42-£55
Lic ▥. CTV ⌇(heated)
Credit Cards ⊡ ⊡

INN Q Q *The Blinking Owl* Main Street, North Newington OX15 6AE ☎(0295) 730650
A range of meals and snacks is served in the atmospheric surroundings of this 16th-century stone-built inn in the village of North Newington, about two miles from the centre of Banbury. The en suite bedrooms located in an adjacent converted barn are comfortable, though compact, and below is a restaurant which serves weekend dinners and Sunday lunch.
3rm(1⇌2♠) CTV in all bedrooms ✻ LDO 9pm
▥. nc8yrs

BANGOR Gwynedd   Map **06** SH57

SELECTED

GH Q Q Q Q **Country Bumpkin** Cefn Coed, Llandegai LL57 4BG (Bangor side of A5/A55 junct, signposted off A522) ☎(0248) 370477 FAX (0248) 354166
Closed Xmas & Jan
An old farmhouse dating back over 200 years. Completely modernised over recent years, it is now a restaurant with rooms, and very popular with local diners, offering a fixed-price table d'hôte menu serving local fresh produce. There is also a breakfast room for guests and the comfortable lounge, also shared by diners, is the setting for pre-dinner drinks. The three bedrooms are excellent.
3⇌♠ ⊁ in dining room CTV in all bedrooms ® ✳ sB&B⇌♠fr£30 dB&B⇌♠fr£40 LDO 8.30pm
Lic ▥. nc12yrs
Credit Cards ⊡ ⊡

FH Q Q Q Mr & Mrs Whowell **Goetre Isaf Farmhouse** (*SH557697*) Caernarfon Road LL57 4DB (2m W on A4087)
☎(0248) 364541 FAX (0248) 364541
Goetre Isaf is a delightful farmhouse situated high above the A5, reached by its own private road. It is set in nine acres of bracken-covered hills with views of Snowdonia, Anglesea and the Lleyn Peninsula. The house dates from 1780 and there is an impressive inglenook fireplace in the cosy sitting room, complete with a wood burning stove. Bedrooms, one with a canopied bed, are freshly decorated .
3rm(1⇌♠) (1fb)T ✳ sB&B£15-£18 dB&Bfr£26 dB&B⇌♠fr£36
▥. CTV ⏦ 10 acres sheep horses bees
ⓔ

BANTHAM Devon   Map **03** SX64

INN Q Q Q **Sloop** TQ7 3AJ ☎Kingsbridge(0548) 560489 & 560215 FAX (0548) 560489
Dating back to the 16th century, this quaint inn was owned by a famous smuggler, and is situated in the village centre close to the beach. Bedrooms are comfortably furnished and have modern facilities; some enjoy fine views of sandy beaches, the estuary and Burgh Island. The bar and panelled dining room both feature the original beams, and lunch and supper are the high spots of the day, with an extensive range of imaginative home-cooked dishes displayed on blackboards, including a good choice of fish, shellfish and puddings.
5⇌♠ (2fb) CTV in all bedrooms ® dB&B⇌♠£53-£55 Lunch £7.50-£15.50alc Dinner £7.50-£15.50alc LDO 10pm
▥.

BARDON MILL Northumberland   Map **12** NY76

FH Q Q Q Mrs J Davidson **Crindledykes** (*NY787672*) Nr Housesteads NE47 7AF (on unclass rd, between A69 and B6318) ☎Haltwhistle(0434) 344316
A traditional old stone farmhouse in a wonderful rural situation offers accommodation which is full of character and spotlessly clean. Breakfast, and dinner by advance arrangement, are served around a communal table in the pleasant dining room which overlooks the attractive garden.
2rm ✻ ✳ dB&B£30-£34 LDO noon
▥. CTV 475 acres stock
ⓔ

BARMOUTH Gwynedd   Map **06** SH61

GH Q Q **Endeavour** Marine Parade LL42 1NA ☎(0341) 280271
Closed mid Dec-mid Jan
A cheerful little guest house on the promenade, a short walk from the shops, the Endeavour has many sea-facing bedrooms. The rooms are all spacious and several are suitable for families.
9rm(5♠) CTV in 8 bedrooms ® ✻ (ex guide dogs) LDO 4pm
Lic ▥. CTV
Credit Cards ⊡ ⊡

GH Q Q Q **Marwyn Hotel** 21 Marine Parade LL42 1NA
☎(0341) 280185 FAX (0341) 280228
Mar-1 Nov
The Marwyn is a small family-run guest house situated on the promenade with fine sea views from the lounge and many of the bedrooms. The rooms are well equipped and all have en suite bath or shower rooms. A cosy residents' bar is provided, and easy parking is available in the street.
5rm(1⇌4♠) Annexe 2⇌ (1fb) ⊁ in dining room CTV in all bedrooms ® ✻ (ex guide dogs) ✳ dB&B⇌♠fr£33 LDO 7.30pm
Lic ▥.
Credit Cards ⊡ ⊡ ⓔ

GH Q Q Q **Morwendon** LLanaber LL42 1RR (1.5m N on A496 coast road) ☎(0341) 280566
Closed Jan-Mar rs Nov-Dec

▶

John and Jan Timms offer a warm welcome at this small guest house, which is set in two acres of land to the north of the resort overlooking Cardigan Bay, with access to the sandy beach. Bedrooms all have en suite shower rooms and several have tower-shaped sitting areas. There is a cosy bar, a modern residents' lounge, and a pretty restaurant where honest home cooking is served.

6♠ (3fb) CTV in all bedrooms ⓡ 🐾 (ex guide dogs) LDO 5pm
Lic ▥ CTV

SELECTED

GH 𝗤𝗤𝗤𝗤 Plas Bach Country House Plas Bach, Glandwr, Bontddu LL42 1TG ☎(0341) 281234
FAX (0341) 281234
6⇄♠ ⚥ in bedrooms CTV in 10 bedrooms ⓡ
sB&B⇄♠£22.50-£28.50 dB&B⇄♠£45-£57 WB&B£145-£184 WBDi£217-£256

GH 𝗤𝗤𝗤 Wavecrest Hotel 8 Marine Parade LL42 1NA
☎(0341) 280330
Mar-20 Dec
10rm(7⇄♠) (4fb) CTV in all bedrooms ⓡ LDO 5pm
Lic ▥
Credit Cards ❑1 ❑3

BARNARD CASTLE Co Durham   Map **12** NZ01

GH 𝗤𝗤𝗤 The Homelands 85 Galgate DL12 8ES
☎Teesdale(0833) 38757
The Homelands is an attractive stone-built terraced house with some bedrooms located in separate houses in the same block. The lounge and dining room are elegantly furnished and the bedrooms are quite special, with thoughtful extras provided.

4rm(2♠) CTV in all bedrooms ⓡ 🐾 (ex guide dogs) LDO 8.15pm
Lic ▥
Credit Cards ❑1 ❑3

FH 𝗤 R & Mrs D M Lowson **West Roods** *(NZ022141)* Boldron DL12 9SW (off A66, 2.5m E of Bowes) ☎Teesdale(0833) 690116
Mar-Oct
A farmhouse set in very rural surroundings offers modest but well tended accommodation. There is a lounge for guests' use, and an abundance of touring information is provided for their convenience.

3rm(2♠) (1fb) ⚥ in bedrooms ⚥ in dining room CTV in all bedrooms ⓡ 🐾 (ex guide dogs) ✳ sB&Bfr£16 sB&B♠£20 dB&B♠£32-£40 WB&Bfr£100
▥ 54 acres dairy
Credit Cards ❑1 ❑2 ❑3 ❑5 £

INN𝗤𝗤𝗤 The Fox and Hounds Country Inn & Restaurant
Cotherstone DL12 9PF (4m W on B6277) ☎Teesdale(0833) 650241 & 650811
This charming and old inn with low ceilings and oak beams stands in the delightful village of Cotherstone, its warm welcome and very friendly service attracting a strong local following. An extensive range of skilfully produced dishes is served in the characterful dining room, and three well furnished bedrooms are provided with good facilities.

3⇄♠ ⚥ in bedrooms ⚥ in dining room CTV in all bedrooms ⓡ T 🐾 (ex guide dogs) ✳ sB&B⇄♠£47.50-£55 dB&B⇄♠£70-£85 (incl dinner) Lunch £11.40-£22.45alc Dinner £11.40-£22.45alc LDO 9pm
▥ nc9yrs
Credit Cards ❑1 ❑3 £

BARNEY Norfolk   Map **09** TF93

GH 𝗤𝗤𝗤 The Old Brick Kilns Little Barney NR21 0NL (NE of Fakenham, off A148 towards Barney) ☎(0328) 878305
FAX (0328) 878948

This well maintained house is very peaceful and offers well equipped, comfortable rooms. Breakfast is served round a large oval table, and dinner by prior arrangement. Mr and Mrs Greenhalgh are very welcoming hosts.

3⇄♠ (2fb) ⚥ CTV in all bedrooms ⓡ 🐾 (ex guide dogs)
sB&B⇄♠£18.50-£21 dB&B⇄♠£37-£42 WB&B£129.50 WBDi£220.50 LDO 7.30pm
Lic ▥ CTV table tennis boules croquet
Credit Cards ❑1 ❑3

BARNSTAPLE Devon   Map **02** SS53

See also Bratton Fleming

GH 𝗤𝗤 Cresta 26 Sticklepath Hill EX31 2BU ☎(0271) 74022
The Cresta is a detached pre-war house located at the top of Sticklepath Hill on the old road to Bideford. It offers simply appointed bedrooms, including en suite rooms on the ground floor, and a no smoking dining room where breakfast is served. Margaret Curtis is only too happy to arrange bridge games for her guests.

5rm(1♠) Annexe 1⇄ (1fb) ⚥ in dining room CTV in all bedrooms ⓡ ✳ sB&Bfr£15 sB&B⇄♠fr£20 dB&Bfr£28 dB&B⇄♠fr£32 WB&Bfr£84
▥ CTV

GH 𝗤 West View Pilton Causeway EX32 7AA ☎(0271) 42079
West View is an end of terrace red brick Edwardian house overlooking the park, a short walk from the centre of town. Bedrooms are brightly decorated and simply furnished, and a choice of dishes is offered at dinner in the small dining room.

7rm(1♠) (2fb) ⚥ in dining room CTV in all bedrooms ⓡ ✳ sB&B£15-£16 dB&B£30-£32 dB&B♠£33-£35 WB&B£105-£112 WBDi£147-£154 LDO 7pm
▥
Credit Cards ❑1 ❑3 £

GH 𝗤𝗤𝗤 Yeo Dale Hotel Pilton Bridge EX31 1PG (from A361 Barnstaple take A39 Lynton, hotel approx 0.25m from A361/A39 roundabout,on left past small park) ☎(0271) 42954
A listed 3-storey building with a 19th-century façade, the Yeo Dale has evidence of earlier architectural eras within. The features of each period have been carefully retained in the modernisation of the property, creating an individual hotel of some character. There are comfortably furnished bedrooms, a quiet sitting room and a separate bar-lounge, and a choice of home cooked dishes is offered in the attractive dining room.

10rm(6⇄♠) (3fb) ⚥ in dining room CTV in all bedrooms ⓡ sB&B£18 sB&B⇄♠£25 dB&B£35 dB&B⇄♠£48 WB&B£126-£175 WBDi£192.50-£231.50 LDO 5pm
Lic ▥ CTV ⚥
Credit Cards ❑1 ❑2 ❑3 ❑5 £

SELECTED

FH 𝗤𝗤𝗤𝗤 Mrs M Lethaby **Home Park** *(SS553360)*
Lower Blakewell, Muddiford EX31 4ET ☎(0271) 42955
Closed 25-26 Dec
This small, well modernised farmhouse is set in a quiet position with uninterrupted views of rolling countryside. Mrs Lethaby provides cheerful hospitality and an excellent home-cooked dinner using fresh local ingredients. Two modern bedrooms have en suite facilities and there are plenty of provisions for children.

Telephone national area codes are due to change by 16th April 1995. Please see the note under 'How to Use this Guide' at the front of the book.

3⇌ℱ (2fb) ⅄ in 2 bedrooms ⅄ in dining room ⅄ in lounges CTV in all bedrooms Ⓡ ✳ sB&B⇌ℱ£15-£18 dB&B⇌ℱ£30-£35 WB&B£110-£130 WBDi£150-£160 LDO 4pm
🅸 CTV ♨ 70 acres sheep
Ⓔ

FH Ⓠ Ⓠ Mrs J Dallyn **Rowden Barton** *(SS538306)* Roundswell EX31 3NP (2m SW B3232) ☎(0271) 44365
This rurally located modern farmhouse is reached by following the A3232 south of the Roundswell roundabout on the ring road. Bright, comfortable bedrooms share a bathroom and there are 2 spacious lounges downstairs, one with TV. Mrs Dallyn has excellent honey for sale.
2rm ⅄ in bedrooms Ⓡ 🐾 (ex guide dogs) ✳ sB&Bfr£14 dB&Bfr£28 LDO 5pm
🅸 CTV 90 acres beef sheep

BARTON-ON-SEA Hampshire   Map **04** SZ29

SELECTED
GH Ⓠ Ⓠ Ⓠ Ⓠ **Bank Cottage** Grove Road BH25 7DN
☎New Milton(0425) 613677
This attractive guest house is near the sea and the golf course. Mr and Mrs Neath are friendly hosts, and offer well equipped rooms, a spacious lounge well stocked with books and local information. There ae many restaurants nearby, but dinner may be available by prior arrangement.
3rm(2ℱ) ⅄ CTV in all bedrooms Ⓡ 🐾 sB&B£18-£20 sB&Bℱ£20-£22 dB&Bℱ£28-£37 WB&B£120-£200 WBDi£150-£280 LDO noon
🅸 CTV
Ⓔ

GH Ⓠ Ⓠ **Hotel Gainsborough** Marine Drive east BH25 7DX
☎New Milton(0425) 610541
Ideally located overlooking the sea and providing a delightfully old fashioned atmosphere, this small family-run hotel with ample forecourt parking space is gradually being upgraded by its new owner. Bedrooms are generally of a good size, all are provided with TV and tea-making facilities and most also have sea views.
5rm(2⇌2ℱ) (1fb) ⅄ in bedrooms ⅄ in dining room ⅄ in 1 lounge CTV in all bedrooms Ⓡ sB&B£17.50-£20 dB&B⇌ℱ£35-£45 WBDi£180-£200 LDO noon
Lic 🅸 nc12yrs

GH Ⓠ Ⓠ Ⓠ **Laurel Lodge** 48 Western Avenue BH25 7PZ (off A337, between Lymington & Christchurch, opposite Chewton Glen Hotel) ☎(0425) 618309
3ℱ ⅄ CTV in all bedrooms Ⓡ ✳ sB&Bℱ£18-£20 dB&Bℱ£32-£36 WB&B£101-£126 WBDi£158-£183 LDO am
🅸 CTV nc5yrs

BASINGSTOKE Hampshire   Map **04** SU65
See also Hook

SELECTED
GH Ⓠ Ⓠ Ⓠ Ⓠ **Fernbank Hotel** 4 Fairfields Road RG21 3DR
☎(0256) 21191 FAX (0256) 21191
Closed Xmas
This hotel is located off Cliddesden Road - follow signs to Fairfields. The accommodation has been extensively upgraded and bedrooms, some conveniently located on the ground floor, are well equipped; there are plans to install full en suite facilities for the remaining first-floor bedrooms. There is a comfortably furnished conservatory lounge and breakfasts are

served in a modern dining room, with personal service from the friendly and helpful proprietors Richard and Teresa White. Spanish and French are spoken, and there is a car park at the rear. .
16rm(13⇌ℱ) (1fb) ⅄ CTV in all bedrooms Ⓡ T 🐾 ✳ sB&B£25-£27 sB&B⇌ℱ£32-£38 dB&B£35-£37 dB&B⇌ℱ£40-£44
Lic 🅸 CTV
Credit Cards ①③Ⓔ

BASLOW Derbyshire   Map **08** SK27

INN Ⓠ Ⓠ **Rutland Arms** Calver Road DE4 1RP
☎Chesterfield(0246) 582276
This small village inn has a relaxed informal atmosphere, and a range of home-made bar snacks is available. The bedrooms are well equipped and pleasantly furnished in pine, with coordinanted soft furnishings. Public areas are scheduled for a major refurbishment during the coming year.
4rm (3fb) CTV in all bedrooms Ⓡ
🅸

INN Ⓠ Ⓠ Ⓠ **Wheatsheaf Hotel** Netherend DE4 1SR
☎(0246) 582240
This extensively refurbished village inn has inviting public areas and a friendly relaxed environment. A wide range of good, home-cooked food is served. The bedrooms are attractive, with good furnishings and colour-coordinated fabrics.
5rm(1⇌) (1fb) ⅄ in dining room ⅄ in lounges CTV in all bedrooms Ⓡ 🐾 (ex guide dogs) sB&Bfr£20 sB&B⇌fr£40 dB&Bfr£35 dB&B⇌fr£40 WB&Bfr£140 Lunch £8.50-£12.50&alc Dinner £8.50-£12.50 LDO 9.30pm
🅸
Credit Cards ①③Ⓔ

BASINGSTOKE
OAKLEA
London Road, Hook, Hampshire RG27 9LA

Oaklea is a fine Victorian house, only a mile from junction 5 of the M3. Beautifully furnished, it provides a full English breakfast and home cooked dinner comprising typically watercress soup, chicken cream tarragon, orange-rhubarb crumble, a good cheese board and fresh coffee. For a memorable & pleasurable stay.

Tel: 01256-762673 or Fax: 01256-762150

BATH Avon   Map **03** ST76

See also Keynsham, Rode and Timsbury

SELECTED

GH Q Q Q Q **Arden Hotel** 73 Great Pulteney Street
BA2 4DL ☎(0225) 466601 & 330039 FAX (0225) 465548
Feb-Nov
This very elegant Grade 1 listed building is set in a delightful
row of Georgian town houses, and only a short walk from the
city centre. The hotel is classically furnished throughout and
richly decorated, in keeping with the grandness and
architecture of the building. The bedrooms are well
proportioned with many original features retained. The
majority boast stylish French furniture, all with pretty Austrian
blinds and have a good range of modern facilities . During the
season Florizel's restaurant offers imaginative food.
10⇌🌂 (2fb)CTV in all bedrooms Ⓡ **T** 🏋 (ex guide dogs)
sB&B⇌🌂£35-£64 dB&B⇌🌂£50-£74
Lic ▥ ⅋
Credit Cards 1 3

SELECTED

GH Q Q Q Q **Armstrong House** 41 Crescent Gardens,
Upper Bristol Road BA1 2NB (on A4 in Central Bath)
☎(0225) 442211 FAX (0225) 334769
A carefully restored Victorian house a few minutes' level walk
from many of the city's tourist attractions offers
accommodation in warm, well equipped en suite bedrooms.
Breakfast is served in a charming dining room, and the
atmosphere throughout is relaxed and welcoming.
4🌂 (1fb) ⅍ in dining room CTV in all bedrooms Ⓡ **T** 🏋 (ex
guide dogs) dB&B🌂£46-£54 WB&B£144.99-£170
▥ nc6yrs
Credit Cards 1 3 £

GH Q *Arney* 99 Wells Road BA2 3AN (on A367)
☎(0225) 310020
Accommodation in simply furnished bedrooms is provided by this
Victorian terraced property on the Wells road; breakfast is served
at separate tables in the dining room.
7rm(1🌂) (3fb)
▥ CTV ⅋

GH Q Q Q **Ashley Villa Hotel** 26 Newbridge Road BA1 3TZ
(W on A4) ☎(0225) 421683 & 428887 FAX (0225) 313604
Closed 2 wks Xmas
Keen owners Mr and Mrs Kitcher continue to improve their
friendly small hotel. Bedrooms are well equipped and have
modern en suite facilities. There is a bright breakfast room, cosy
lounge, patio garden and outdoor swimming pool. The hotel is
conveniently positioned on the A4 within walking distance of the
city centre.
14rm(4⇌10🌂) (3fb) ⅍ in dining room CTV in all bedrooms Ⓡ
T 🏋 (ex guide dogs) sB&B⇌🌂£39-£45 dB&B⇌🌂£49-£59
WB&B£150-£245
Lic ▥ CTV ⅏
Credit Cards 1 3 £

GH Q Q **Astor House** 14 Oldfield Road BA2 3ND
☎(0225) 429134 FAX (0225) 429134
Closed Jan-10 Feb
Set in a pleasant residential area, not far from the centre, Astor
House offers simple but neat and well kept accommodation
designed for the budget end of the market. The relaxed, friendly
atmosphere attracts many foreign visitors.

8rm(2🌂) (2fb) ⅍ CTV in all bedrooms Ⓡ 🏋 (ex guide dogs)
dB&B£32-£36 dB&B🌂£40-£45 WB&B£102-£150
▥ CTV nc2yrs
Credit Cards 1 3 £

SELECTED

GH Q Q Q Q **Badminton Villa** 10 Upper Oldfield Park
BA2 3JZ ☎(0225) 426347 FAX (0225) 420393
Closed 24 Dec-1 Jan
This quality bed and breakfast establishment enjoys
magnificent views of Bath from its setting in a pretty terraced
garden on the city's southern slopes, only ten minutes from
the centre. A large Victorian house personally restored by its
enthusiastic owners, it offers only three bedrooms - each of
them individually styled and well decorated with rich
co-ordinating colours and fabrics. Attractively furnished in
pine, they also feature first class en suite facilities and are
equipped to satisfy today's discerning traveller.
3🌂 (1fb) ⅍ CTV in all bedrooms Ⓡ 🏋 (ex guide dogs) ✳
sB&B🌂£35 dB&B🌂£48-£55
▥ nc4yrs
Credit Cards 1 3 £

GH Q Q Q **Bailbrook Lodge** 35/37 London Road West BA1 7HZ
☎(0225) 859090 FAX (0225) 859090
Closed 25-26 Dec
Bailbrook Lodge is a double-fronted Georgian property built of
Bath stone. It stands in its own grounds set back from the A4, and
offers easy access to the city centre and the M4. There are en suite
bedrooms, a dining room offering a choice of dishes, and a
comfortable lounge with an honesty bar.
12rm(4⇌8🌂) (4fb) ⅍ in 4 bedrooms ⅍ in area of dining room
CTV in all bedrooms Ⓡ 🏋 (ex guide dogs) ✳ sB&B⇌🌂£32-£45
dB&B⇌🌂£50-£70 WBDi£168-£350 LDO 9pm
Lic ▥ CTV
Credit Cards 1 2 3 5 £

SELECTED

GH Q Q Q Q **The Bath Tasburgh** Warminster Road,
Bathampton BA2 6SH (on A36, 1 mile east of city centre,
signposted to Warminster) ☎(0225) 425096
FAX (0225) 463842
Set in two acres of well tended gardens and five acres of
pasture yet close to the city centre, this Victorian house enjoys
canal frontage and panoramic views over the Avon valley.
The bedrooms have been tastefully decorated and are well
equipped. There is a comfortable lounge leading into a
conservatory and breakfast is served in the dining room at
separate tables.
13rm(12⇌1🌂) (4fb) ⅍ in 7 bedrooms ⅍ in dining room CTV
in all bedrooms Ⓡ **T** 🏋 sB&B£36 sB&B⇌🌂£40-£50
dB&B£46-£48 dB&B⇌🌂£59-£72
Lic ▥ CTV ⚬Ø croquet
Credit Cards 1 2 3 5 £
See advertisement on p.60.

SELECTED

GH Q Q Q Q **Bloomfield House** 146 Bloomfield Road
BA2 2AS ☎(0225) 420105
Conscientious owners John Pascoe and Titos Argiris have
further improved their attractive Georgian house. The stylish
bedrooms, equipped for the discerning traveller, feature
canopied and half-tester beds, fine pieces of period furniture,
and modern brass-fitted mahogany panelled bathrooms. The
entrance hall has been imaginatively decorated with hand

---

painted murals and the comfortable breakfast room and adjacent lounge overlook the garden.
5⇌ʃ (1fb) ✗ CTV in all rooms ® T ⅋ (ex guide dogs) sB&B⇌ʃ£35-£45 dB&B⇌ʃ£45-£85
▥
Credit Cards ① ③ ⓔ
See advertisement on p.61.

GH Ⓠ Ⓠ Ⓠ **Brocks** 32 Brock Street BA1 2LN (MIN)
☎(0225) 338374 FAX (0225) 334245
Closed Xmas & 2 wks Jan
A little gem of a place, Marion Dodd's charming Georgian Grade II listed house offers individually styled bedrooms with a good range of modern facilities. There is a cosy lounge and breakfast room where a handsome English breakfast is served. The location, just off Bath's famous Circus, is ideal for both tourists and business guests. Pay and display parking is available during the day and there are local car parks close by.
8rm(4⇌ʃ) (2fb) ✗ in dining room CTV in all bedrooms ® ⅋ (ex guide dogs) ✳ sB&B£21-£22 sB&B⇌ʃ£36-£44 dB&B£42-£54 dB&B⇌ʃ£48-£54
▥
Credit Cards ① ③

SELECTED
GH Ⓠ Ⓠ Ⓠ Ⓠ **Brompton House Hotel** St John's Road BA2 6PT ☎(0225) 420972 FAX (0225) 420505
Closed Xmas & New Year
A fine Georgian building with Victorian additions and attractive walled gardens, this welcoming guest house within

▶

Bailbrook Lodge
QQQ

35/37 London Road West, Bath BA1 7HZ
Telephone & Fax: 01225 859090

A splendid Georgian residence designed by the famous architect John Everleigh is situated 1 mile east of Bath. The tastefully furnished accommodation has 12 en-suite bedrooms with TV and tea & coffee making facilities. Eight of the bedrooms overlook the garden, lawns and the magnificent Avon valley. The remainder overlook the grounds of Bailbrook House. Evening meals. Ample car parking.

Ashley Villa Hotel, Bath

AA
QQQ

ETB

26 Newbridge Road, Bath BA1 3JZ
Telephone: (01225) 421683 & 428887 Fax: (01225) 313604
Comfortably furnished licensed hotel with relaxing informal atmosphere, situated close to the city centre. All bedrooms have en suite facilities, colour television, direct dial telephone, tea and coffee making. Most Credit Cards welcome.
This small friendly hotel has recently been refurbished throughout. It has a **heated swimming pool** (summer only), with garden patio and car park.
You can be sure of a warm welcome from the resident owners,
Rod and Alex Kitcher, M.H.C.I.M.A.

the city centre is popular with business guest and tourist alike; the availabily of parking is no small bonus in this busy area. Painstaking renovation has upgraded the house whilst retaining much of its original charm. The pastel shades of the comfortable bedrooms are complemented by coordinating fabrics, and they offer a range of facilities normally associated with larger establishments. Both the traditional lounge and pretty dining room overlook the secluded garden.
18rm(2⇌16♠) (1fb) ⊁ in bedrooms ⊁ in dining room CTV in all bedrooms ® T ✻ (ex guide dogs) sB&B⇌♠£30-£40 dB&B⇌♠£56-£74
Lic ▥ nc7yrs
Credit Cards ①②③ ⓔ

PREMIER ⚜ SELECTED

GH ⓠⓠⓠⓠⓠ **Burghope Manor** Winsley BA15 2LA
☎(0225) 723557 FAX (0225) 723113
(For full entry see Bradford on Avon)

GH ⓠⓠⓠ **Carfax Hotel** Great Pulteney Street BA2 4BS
☎(0225) 462089 FAX (0225) 443257
Part of the elegant Georgian terrace that is Great Pulteney Street, this hotel offers mostly en suite bedrooms with views across Henrietta Park. Public rooms comprise a spacious reception area, a comfortable lounge, where hot drinks and buffet lunches are available, and a dining room where a fixed price menu is presented. The hotel is unlicensed.
39rm(34⇌♠) (3fb) ⊁ in dining room ⊁ in lounges CTV in all bedrooms ® T ✻ (ex guide dogs) ✳ sB&Bfr£25 sB&B⇌♠£35-

£46 dB&Bfr£45 dB&B⇌♠£55-£68 WB&B£154-£301 WBDi£196-£315 LDO 7.50pm
lift ▥ CTV games room
Credit Cards ①②③ ⓔ

SELECTED

GH ⓠⓠⓠⓠ **Cheriton House** 9 Upper Oldfield Park BA2 3JX (south of Bath, 0.5m along the A367)
☎(0225) 429862 FAX (0225) 428403
Closed Xmas & New Year
The conscientious owners of this characterful stone-built Victorian villa continue to upgrade it and their painstaking renovation has provided commendable standards of comfort. Set in an elevated position with views over the city and beyond, enclosed in well kept gardens, it offers accommodation in bright, appealing bedrooms with quality en suite facilities; intimate public areas are attractively furnished and styled to be equally pleasing.
9rm(2⇌7♠) ⊁ in 4 bedrooms ⊁ in dining room CTV in all bedrooms ® ✻ (ex guide dogs) ✳ sB&B⇌♠£35-£38 dB&B⇌♠£48-£58
▥ nc
Credit Cards ①③ ⓔ

GH ⓠⓠⓠ **Chesterfield Hotel** 11 Great Pulteney Street BA2 4BR
☎(0225) 460953 FAX (0225) 448770
This terraced Georgian building stands in a wide, elegant avenue close to tourist attractions and shops.
18⇌♠ (3fb)CTV in all bedrooms ® T ✻ (ex guide dogs) sB&B⇌♠£30-£40 dB&B⇌♠£45-£58
Lic ▥ CTV
Credit Cards ①②③

SELECTED

GH Q Q Q Q **Cranleigh** 159 Newbridge Hill BA1 3PX
☎(0225) 310197 FAX (0225) 423143

There have been further commendable improvements to this charming little bed and breakfast house, owned and run with enthusiasm by Arthur and Christine Webber. An attractive Victorian building of Bath stone in a convenient city location, it retains its original fireplaces and decorative plasterwork, the rooms enhanced by pastel decor and bold fabrics. American-style, vegetarian, continental and handsome traditional breakfasts feature daily.

5⇔ᚠ (2fb) ⊁ CTV in all bedrooms ® 乐 (ex guide dogs) sB&B⇔ᚠ£35-£45 dB&B⇔ᚠ£48-£63 WB&B£150-£250 ▥.

Credit Cards 1 3

GH Q Q Q **Devonshire House** 143 Wellsway BA2 4RZ
☎(0225) 312495

This friendly family-run guest house has comfortable, individually styled bedrooms furnished in stripped pine, set off with an abundance of Victorian trimmings, objets d'art and some antiques - the owners also run the adjacent antique shop. The brightly decorated rooms are well equipped with modern amenities. Meals are served in the small Victorian-style breakfast room. Positioned in Wellsway, on the outskirts of the city, Devonshire House has its own car park and an enclosed courtyard.

3⇔ᚠ (1fb) ⊁ CTV in all bedrooms ® sB&B⇔ᚠ£30-£35 dB&B⇔ᚠ£40-£45 WBDi£215-£230 LDO 4pm ▥.

Credit Cards 1 3 ⓔ

PREMIER 🏆 SELECTED

GH Q Q Q Q Q **Dorian House** 1 Upper Oldfield Park BA2 3JX (off A367)
☎(0225) 426336
FAX (0225) 444699

Every guest is made to feel personally welcome at this stone-built house which enjoys good views of the city and surrounding hills from a position just a short walk from the centre. All the attractive and individual bedrooms are extremely comfortable, each being equipped with en suite bathroom, television, telephone and tea-making facilities; two rooms even have four-poster beds. Full English breakfasts are served in a charming dining room, and the elegant lounge where residents relax in the evening has a small dispense bar.

8rm(5⇔3ᚠ) (2fb) ⊁ in dining room CTV in all bedrooms ® T 乐 (ex guide dogs) sB&B⇔ᚠ£39-£46 dB&B⇔ᚠ£49-£69 Lic ▥.

Credit Cards 1 2 3 5 ⓔ

GH Q Q **Dorset Villa** 14 Newbridge Road BA1 3JZ (W on A4)
☎(0225) 425975

Simply furnished bedrooms are enhanced by attractive soft furnishings at this early-Victorian property; dinner is served in a small restaurant which also has a residential licence, and some on site parking is available.

7rm(5ᚠ) (1fb) ⊁ in dining room CTV in all bedrooms ® ✳ sB&B£29-£35 dB&B£40-£42 dB&Bᚠ£42-£46 Lic ▥. CTV

Credit Cards 1 3 ⓔ

GH Q Q Q **Eagle House** Church Street, Bathford BA1 7RS (3m NE A363) ☎(0225) 859946 FAX (0225) 859069
Closed 23-30 Dec

This fine and meticulously restored Georgian house built by John Wood the Elder commands views over the nearby city from its attractive setting in 1.5 acres of mature grounds and gardens. Most of the bedrooms are both well proportioned and equipped in modern style, while public areas include a grand drawing room as well as a smaller sitting room and bright breakfast room. A supplement is charged for a full cooked breakfast. A cottage set in the old walled garden offers full use of the main building's facilities.

6⇔ᚠ Annexe 2⇔ᚠ (2fb) ⊁ in 1 bedrooms CTV in all bedrooms ® T sB&B⇔ᚠ£34-£39 dB&B⇔ᚠ£43-£66 WB&Bfr£140 Lic ▥. croquet lawn

Credit Cards 1 3 ⓔ

GH Q Q Q **Edgar Hotel** 64 Gt Pulteney Street BA2 4DN
☎(0225) 420619
Closed 25 Dec

Conveniently situated in the centre of Great Pulteney Street, this Regency town house provides comfortable bed and breakfast accommodation close to the city centre. Bedrooms are simply styled with compact modern en suites and a good range of facilities, and there is a modest breakfast room on the ground floor.

14ᚠ (1fb) ⊁ in dining room CTV in all bedrooms ® 乐 ✳ sB&Bᚠ£25-£35 dB&Bᚠ£35-£55 Lic ▥. CTV ⊁

Credit Cards 1 3 ⓔ

GH Q Q Q **Gainsborough Hotel** Weston Lane BA1 4AB
☎(0225) 311380 FAX (0225) 447411
Closed 1 wk Xmas

The Gainsborough is a large Victorian house set back in its own grounds and gardens, reasonably close to Victoria Park and city amenities. Bedrooms are well proportioned and soundly equipped, and there are spacious public rooms.

16rm(12⇔4ᚠ) (2fb)CTV in all bedrooms ® T 乐 sB&B⇔ᚠ£32-£42 dB&B⇔ᚠ£53-£63 Lic ▥.

Credit Cards 1 2 3 ⓔ

GH Q Q **Grove Lodge** 11 Lambridge, London Road BA1 6BJ (heading east from city centre on the A4, establishment 200yds before junction of A4 and A46) ☎(0225) 310860

Grove Lodge is a fine example of Regency architecture, and very much a family home, set in a walled garden with on-street parking close by. Bedrooms are clean and comfortable, and breakfast is served at separate tables in the breakfast room.

8rm (2fb) ⊁ CTV in all bedrooms ® 乐 (ex guide dogs) sB&B£18-£22 dB&B£35-£45 ⊁ ⓔ

GH Q Q Q **Haute Combe House** 174/176 Newbridge Road BA1 3LE ☎(0225) 420061 FAX (0225) 420061
11rm(10⇔ᚠ) (7fb) ⊁ in bedrooms ⊁ in dining room ⊁ in 1 lounge CTV in all bedrooms ® T sB&B£26-£32 sB&B⇔ᚠ£28-£36 dB&B⇔ᚠ£42-£52 LDO 6pm Lic ▥. CTV

Credit Cards 1 3 ⓔ
See advertisement on p.65.

Telephone national area codes are due to change by 16th April 1995. Please see the note under 'How to Use this Guide' at the front of the book.

PREMIER SELECTED

GH [Q][Q][Q][Q][Q] Haydon House 9 Bloomfield Park BA2 2BY ☎(0225) 444919 & 427351 FAX (0225) 444919

Initial impressions can mislead and this unassuming Edwardian house belies a wealth of elegance, charm and hospitality captured within very comfortable surroundings. Smoking is prohibited at Magdalene Ashman's enchanting house, tucked away in a quiet residential area and offering individually decorated bedrooms. Delightful little personal touches, such as a decanter of sherry, home-made biscuits and flowers, greet the guest on arrival. The public areas are snug, comfortable and richly furnished and a handsome breakfast, which may include porridge with whisky and scrambled egg with salmon, is served at the communal table in the breakfast room. There is an attractive, secluded garden and unrestricted street parking.

5🛁🚿 🚭 CTV in all bedrooms Ⓡ T 🐕 sB&B🛁🚿£35-£50 dB&B🛁🚿fr£55

▦ nc sun terrace

Credit Cards [1] [2] [3] [£]

GH [Q][Q] Henrietta Hotel Henrietta Street BA2 6LR

☎(0225) 447779

Closed 25 Dec

10🛁🚿 (3fb)CTV in all bedrooms Ⓡ 🐕 (ex guide dogs) * sB&B🛁🚿£25-£35 dB&B🛁🚿£35-£50

▦ CTV 🅿̸

Credit Cards [1] [2] [3] [£]

SELECTED

GH [Q][Q][Q][Q] Hermitage Bath Road SN14 9DT

☎(0225) 744187 FAX (0225) 744187

(For full entry see Box)

GH [Q][Q][Q] Highways House 143 Wells Road BA2 3AL (on the A367) ☎(0225) 421238 FAX (0225) 481169

Closed 24-27 Dec

Enthusiastically run by conscientious owners, this attractive Victorian house stands amid its own pretty terraced gardens in a residential area within easy reach of the city. Warm, personally finished bedrooms are well equipped for today's traveller, the residents' lounge is comfortable and there is a cosy breakfast room. Ample car parking space is provided.

7rm(6🛁🚿) 🚭 in 1 bedrooms 🚭 in dining room CTV in all bedrooms Ⓡ 🐕 (ex guide dogs) sB&B£33-£36 dB&B🛁🚿£48-£58 WB&B£154-£189

▦ nc5yrs

Credit Cards [1] [3] [£]

Telephone national area codes are due to change by 16th April 1995. Please see the note under 'How to Use this Guide' at the front of the book.

PREMIER SELECTED

GH [Q][Q][Q][Q][Q] Holly Lodge 8 Upper Oldfield Park BA2 3JZ (0.5m SW off A367) ☎(0225) 424042 FAX (0225) 481138

Carrolle Sellick's immaculately styled Victorian town house is a little gem. The bedrooms are exceptionally comfortable, beautifully decorated and furnished with pleasing colours and fabrics, and adorned with pictures and objets d'art. Two of the rooms have sumptuous marble-finished bathrooms, and all the en suites are equipped with fluffy towels and perfumed toiletries. The richly furnished lounge and bright conservatory dining room are equally attractive and offer views over the terrace to the city beyond. Carrolle and her partner George provide a warm hospitable welcome and personal but unobtrusive service. Neatly tucked away with useful car parking and a pretty garden, the house is well positioned for the city and for touring the region.

6🛁🚿 🚭 CTV in all bedrooms Ⓡ T 🐕 * sB&B🛁🚿£46-£48 dB&B🛁🚿£70-£85

▦

Credit Cards [1] [2] [3] [5]

SELECTED

GH [Q][Q][Q][Q] Kennard Hotel 11 Henrietta Street BA2 6LL ☎(0225) 310472 FAX (0225) 460054

Part of an attractive terrace close to Great Pulteney Bridge, this three-storey Georgian building is just a short walk from the town centre. Continued upgrading has resulted in well equipped, tastefully coordinated bedrooms, most of which have en suite shower rooms. There is a bright lower ground floor breakfast room where the friendly proprietors provide attentive service.

12rm(10🚿) (2fb) 🚭 in dining room CTV in all bedrooms Ⓡ T 🐕 (ex guide dogs) * sB&B£30-£35 dB&B🚿£48-£60

▦ 🅿̸

Credit Cards [1] [2] [3] [5] [£]

GH [Q][Q][Q] Lamp Post Villa 3 Crescent Gardens, Upper Bristol Road BA1 2NA (on A4, Bristol side of city) ☎(0225) 331221 FAX (0225) 426783

Closed 24-26 Dec

7rm(4🛁🚿) (1fb) 🚭 in bedrooms 🚭 in dining room CTV in all bedrooms Ⓡ T * sB&B£25-£30 dB&B🛁🚿£45-£50

▦ CTV

Credit Cards [1] [3]

SELECTED

GH [Q][Q][Q][Q] Laura Place Hotel 3 Laura Place, Great Pulteney Street BA2 4BH (turn left off A4 at 1st traffic lights over Cleveland Bridge, past fire station then turn right along Henrietta Rd into Laura Place) ☎(0225) 463815 FAX (0225) 310222

Mar-21 Dec

An elegant, beautifully preserved Georgian town house is conveniently situated for easy access on foot to the many places of interest in and around the city. The hotel also benefits from a small number of private parking places in a nearby yard. The spacious bedrooms are located on four floors, and have been decorated and furnished in keeping

with the building and equipped with a good range of
facilities. Breakfast is served at separate tables in the
attractive dining room and there is a small lounge area at
reception.
8rm(7⇨↑) (1fb) ⌘ in 4 bedrooms ⌘ in dining room CTV in
all bedrooms ® T ⌘ (ex guide dogs) ✻ sB&B⇨↑£50-£65
dB&B⇨↑£65-£85
⚌ nc11yrs
Credit Cards ① ② ③ ⓔ

PREMIER ❀ SELECTED

GH 🇶🇶🇶🇶🇶 *Leighton
House* 139 Wells Road
BA2 3AL (on A367 Exeter rd
out of Bath) ☎(0225) 314769
FAX (0225) 420210
This elegant Victorian family
home is set back from the
Wells road in beautifully kept
gardens with views over the
city and surrounding hills, and
is only a short walk from the
city centre. The spacious
bedrooms are all individually decorated and furnished, with the
emphasis on comfort. There is an attractive lounge where
drinks are served on request, and breakfast is served in a
bright split-level dining room. Resident proprietors Kathy and
David Slape are friendly and charming hosts.

▶

HAUTE COMBE

176 Newbridge Road, Bath BA1 3LE
👁👁👁 Tel: (01225) 420061 🇶🇶🇶
Fax: (01225) 420061
Mobile Phone: (0831) 379231
Proprietors: David and Jane Carnegie
A lovely old property with many original
features, close to both city sights, marina
and peaceful country walks along Cotswold
Way. From dinner or snacks to a trouser
press, service is our speciality, making sure
all our guest get the very best out of their
stay. Ample private parking. Take a
frequent shuttle bus to the centre or a stroll
along the river. *Open all year*

Holly Lodge

**8 Upper Oldfield Park,
Bath Avon BA2 3JZ**
Tel: 01225 339187 or 424042 Fax: 01225 481138
Holly Lodge is a large Victorian house set in its
own grounds and enjoys magnificent views over
the City. It is situated only 10 minutes from the
centre. Individually interior designed rooms, all
with bathrooms and some with four poster beds,
have TV and satellite movies, direct dial telephone
and hot drink facilities. Imaginative breakfasts are
enjoyed in the conservatory type breakfast room.
Beautiful lounge and well lit car park. Holly
Lodge features in many well known guide books
and is graded ETB de-luxe. For the comfort and
convenience of our guests Holly Lodge is strictly
no smoking. Well worth the extra splurge.

Irondale House
67 High Street, Rode, Bath, BA3 6PB
Tel: (01373) 830730

A very warm welcome is extended by Jayne
& Oliver Holder to this late 18th Century
village house 10 miles South of Bath, and
within easy reach of Longleat, Wells,
Salisbury and Lacock. The bedrooms are
recently decorated to the highest standards
and have private bathrooms. An excellent
breakfast is provided in the dining room,
and guests are welcomed to the imposing
drawing room which overlooks a pretty
walled garden, with a lovely view of the
countryside beyond. Parking is off street,
CTV in both bedrooms, and an excellent
pub (specialising in seafood) is only
5 mins walk.

8🛁🚿 (2fb) 🚭 in dining room CTV in all bedrooms Ⓡ T 🐕 (ex guide dogs)
Lic ▥
Credit Cards [1] [3] [£]

PREMIER SELECTED

GH [Q][Q][Q][Q][Q] ***Meadowland*** 36 Bloomfield Park BA2 2BX (turn off A367 at Bearflat into Bloomfield Rd Bloomfield Pk is second on right) ☎(0225) 311079

Set in its own mature grounds, on the outskirts of the city, this elegant residence has been personally restored by its conscientious owner, Catherine Andrew. The individually styled bedrooms are of distinct charm and equipped with a range of modern amenities. There is a comfortable lounge and a hearty breakfast, from an imaginative menu, provides a good start to the day. Special diets can be catered for with advance notice.
3🛁🚿 (1fb) CTV in all bedrooms Ⓡ 🐕
▥ CTV
Credit Cards [1] [3]

SELECTED

GH [Q][Q][Q][Q] Monkshill Shaft Road, Monkton Combe BA2 7HL ☎Combe Down(0225) 833028
Constructed of stone in 1902, this family home has a strong Victorian feel. It stands in an elevated rural position overlooking the village of Monkton Combe just a few minutes' drive from Bath. The comfortable bedrooms are tastefully furnished, and there is an attractive drawing room with chesterfields, a Victorian fireplace and a grand piano. Guests take breakfast at one large table in the elegant dining room.
3rm(2🛁🚿) (1fb) 🚭 in bedrooms 🚭 in dining room 🚭 in lounges CTV in all bedrooms 🐕 (ex guide dogs) * sB&B£30-£45 sB&B🛁🚿£40-£45 dB&B£45-£55 dB&B🛁🚿£55-£65 WB&B£150-£200
▥ nc2yrs croquet lawn
Credit Cards [1] [2] [3] [5] [£]

PREMIER SELECTED

GH [Q][Q][Q][Q][Q] Monmouth Lodge BA3 6LH ☎Frome(0373) 834367
(For full entry see Norton St Philip)

SELECTED

GH [Q][Q][Q][Q] Oakleigh House 19 Upper Oldfield Park BA2 3JX (off A367) ☎(0225) 315698 FAX (0225) 448223
4🛁🚿 🚭 in dining room 🚭 in lounges CTV in all bedrooms Ⓡ 🐕 (ex guide dogs) sB&B🛁🚿£35-£45 dB&B🛁🚿£45-£60
▥ nc14yrs
Credit Cards [1] [3] [£]

SELECTED

GH [Q][Q][Q][Q] Old Court House Corston BA2 9AP (A4 from Bath to roundabout at Globe Inn. Follow sign for Corston and on reaching village, church is on left and Old Court House on right) ☎(0225) 874228
Steeped in history - the infamous Judge Jeffreys is said to have stayed here in the 17th century–this charming house stands in a delightful village and offers an atmosphere of comfort and quality
3rm(1🛁2🚿) 🚭 CTV in all bedrooms Ⓡ 🐕 * sB&B🛁🚿£32-£40 dB&B🛁🚿£84-£100
▥ 🏊(heated)
See advertisement under Colour Section

GH [Q][Q][Q] Oldfields 102 Wells Road BA2 3AL (off A367) ☎(0225) 317984 FAX (0225) 444471
This hospitable guest house - a large Victorian family residence built from Bath stone and attractively set in its own gardens - looks out over the city from an elevated position just ten minutes from the centre, Roman Baths and Abbey. Bedrooms have been sympathetically restored, Laura Ashley furnishings and fabrics complementing the original style of the house. On-site parking is available.
14rm(1🛁9🚿) 🚭 in dining room CTV in all bedrooms Ⓡ 🐕 (ex guide dogs) * sB&B£25-£30 sB&B🛁🚿£40-£45 dB&B£40-£50 dB&B🛁🚿£55-£65 WB&B£126-£205
▥
Credit Cards [1] [3]

PREMIER SELECTED

GH [Q][Q][Q][Q][Q] Old School House Church Street, Bathford BA1 7RR (3m NE on A363, beyond St Swithuns Church) ☎(0225) 859593 FAX (0225) 859590

Built early in the19th century but now carefully modernised, this former school house in the village of Bathford (a few miles east of the city) offers comfortable bedrooms, each equipped with its own bathroom, a pay phone and such thoughtful extras as fresh flowers and boxed toiletries. Lounge and dining area are contained in a spacious reception room lavishly furnished with antique pieces and warmed by a log fire on winter evenings. Dinner is available by prior arrangement, the set main dish supplemented by a pleasing selection of starters and puddings. Guests are asked not to smoke.
4🛁🚿 (1fb) 🚭 CTV in all bedrooms Ⓡ T 🐕 * sB&B🛁🚿£45-£65 dB&B🛁🚿£60-£65 WB&B£200-£430 WBDi£335-£565 LDO noon
Lic ▥
Credit Cards [1] [3]

GH [Q][Q][Q] ***Orchard Lodge*** Warminster Road (A36), Bathampton BA2 6XG (MIN) ☎(0225) 466115
Conveniently situated two miles from the city centre, this small purpose-built establishment with its own large car park enjoys good views of the Avon Valley from an elevated position. It is comfortably furnished throughout, and en suite bedrooms are well equipped with a wide range of facilities. A sunbed, sauna and multi-gym are provided in the health area for guests' use.
14🛁🚿 (3fb) CTV in all bedrooms Ⓡ LDO 7.45pm
Lic ▥ sauna solarium
Credit Cards [1] [2] [3] [5]

SELECTED

GH Q Q Q Q **Paradise House Hotel** Holloway BA2 4PX
☎(0225) 317723 FAX (0225) 482005
Closed 20-28 Dec
This beautifully restored, elegant Georgian house boasts one of the finest views over the city and offers commendable bed and breakfast accommodation. The cosy public rooms are styled with rich colours, deep furnishings and complementary fabrics, and the building features a fine staircase, moulded ceilings and decorative cornices. The lounge overlooks the city and highlights the splendid walled garden, and a hearty breakfast is served in the bright attractive breakfast room every morning. The bedrooms are particularly comfortable, individually styled - again with good use of bold colours and fabrics. All are equipped to a high standard and the majority have bright en suite facilities.
9rm(6⇄1♠)(1fb) ⊁ in bedrooms ⊁ in dining room CTV in all bedrooms ® T ⊁ sB&B£34-£38 sB&B⇄♠£41-£50 dB&B£48-£55 dB&B⇄♠£60-£68 WB&B£140-£210
▥. nc10yrs croquet lawn boules pitch
Credit Cards 1 2 3 £

GH Q Q **Parkside** 11 Marlborough Lane BA1 2NQ (just past Queen Square and Charlotte St. car park, establishment on right before Park gates) ☎(0225) 429444
Closed Xmas wk
An Edwardian family home built in mellow Bath stone stands near the famous Royal Crescent, within walking distance of the city centre. Bedrooms are continually being upgraded, so that most now have their own shower rooms, and dinner is served in a comfortable dining room overlooking the well tended garden.
5rm(4♠) (2fb) ⊁ CTV in all bedrooms ® ✱ sB&B♠£25-£35 dB&B£39 dB&B♠£45-£49 WB&B£122.85-£154.35 WBDi£199.85-£231.35 LDO 6pm
▥. CTV nc5yrs

GH Q Q **Hotel St Clair** 1 Crescent Gdns, Upper Bristol Road BA1 2NA ☎(0225) 425543 FAX (0225) 425543
This family-owned and run guesthouse is conveniently positioned close to Victoria Park and the city centre. The bedrooms are well equipped with the usual modern amenities and are suitable for tourists or business people. There is an on-site car park to the rear of the premises.
9rm(6⇄♠) (2fb) ⊁ in dining room CTV in all bedrooms ® ⊁ (ex guide dogs) sB&B£22-£25 sB&B⇄♠£30-£38 dB&B£34-£38 dB&B⇄♠£38-£45 WB&B£110-£130
Lic ▥. ⊁nc3yrs
Credit Cards 1 3 £

SELECTED

GH Q Q Q Q **Somerset House Hotel & Restaurant** 35 Bathwick Hill BA2 6LD (Logis) ☎(0225) 466451 FAX (0225) 317188
Bedrooms occupy three floors of this classical Regency house which commands superb views of the city from an elevated setting and each has its own individual style. Guests have a choice of comfortable lounges, and the restaurant - like the rest of the house -operates a no-smoking policy. Ample parking space is available, and there is a well tended walled garden.
10⇄♠ (5fb) ⊁ ® T sB&B⇄♠£41.50-£49 dB&B⇄♠£83-£98 (incl dinner) WBDi£319 LDO 6.30pm
Lic ▥. CTV nc10yrs
Credit Cards 1 2 3 £

GH Q Q Q **Villa Magdala Hotel** Henrietta Road BA2 6LX
☎(0225) 466329 FAX (0225) 483207
A beautifully maintained, large Victorian house, overlooking

Henrietta Park, and close to Great Pulteney Street and the city centre, retains many interesting features, in particular a sweeping Italian-style staircase and moulded cornices. The house stands in its own well tended grounds, with the advantage of private parking. It has a pleasant breakfast room and its spacious bedrooms are immaculately maintained.
17⇄♠ (4fb)CTV in all bedrooms ® T T ⊁ (ex guide dogs) sB&B⇄♠£40-£49 dB&B⇄♠£50-£66
▥.
Credit Cards 1 3

GH Q Q Q **Wentworth House** 106 Bloomfield Road BA2 2AP (off A367) ☎(0225) 339193 FAX (0225) 310460
Closed Xmas
Personally run by keen owners Avril and Geoff Kitching, this attractive Victorian house is set in its own grounds complete with an outdoor swimming pool. Bedrooms are bright, well furnished and equipped, and the majority are en suite. Wholesome English breakfasts (and dinner by arrangement) are served in the stylish conservatory dining room, and there is a richly furnished and comfortable bar-lounge.
19rm(15⇄♠) (2fb) ⊁ in dining room CTV in all bedrooms ® T ✱ sB&B⇄♠£36-£40 dB&Bfr£40 dB&B⇄♠£45-£60 LDO 10.30am
Lic ▥. nc 5yrs ⋇(heated)
Credit Cards 1 3 £

INN Q **County Hotel** 18-19 Pulteney Road BA2 4EZ
☎(0225) 425003 & 466493 FAX (0225) 469845
Closed 25 & 26 Dec
The County is a large, conveniently positioned hotel close to the city centre. Compact but soundly equipped bedrooms are in the process of being upgraded. The public bars are popular, and bar snacks are available at lunchtime with more substantial meals offered in the evening.
22rm(1⇄11♠) (5fb) ⊁ in bedrooms ⊁ in dining room CTV in all bedrooms ® ✱ sB&B£22.50-£28.50 sB&B⇄♠£32.50-£37.50 dB&B£35-£40 dB&B⇄♠£45-£55 Lunch fr£3&alc LDO 7pm
▥. CTV
Credit Cards 1 3

BATTLE East Sussex   Map **05** TQ71

GH Q Q Q **Netherfield Hall** Netherfield TN33 9PQ (3m NW of B2096) ☎(0424) 774450
Closed Feb
Netherfield Hall is personally run by Jean and Tony Hawes, who provide light refreshments and cream teas throughout the day and sell a selection of gifts. There is a range of comfortable, individually furnished ground floor bedrooms, a shared family lounge and an attractive dining room with a real fire and lovely views over the verandah and garden. A self-catering apartment is now available.
3rm(2♠) Annexe 1♠ CTV in 3 bedrooms ® sB&B♠£25-£35 dB&B♠£45-£50 WB&B£150-£210 WBDi£220-£280
▥. CTV
£

FH Q Q Q Mr Mrs P Slater **Little Hemingfold Farmhouse Hotel** (TQ774149) Telham TN33 0TT (2.5m SE on N side of A2100) ☎(0424) 774338
Delightfully situated in woodland, overlooking a lake, this licensed farmhouse hotel is reached by a long bumpy track. The accommodation has been individually furnished to provide a range of bedrooms, all equipped to a high standard. There are two lounges with log fires, a small reception area and an attractive dining room. A daily four-course dinner is served as well as good farmhouse breakfasts.
3⇄ Annexe 9rm(7⇄♠) ⊁ in dining room ⊁ in 1 lounge CTV in all bedrooms ® T sB&B⇄£35 dB&B⇄£60-£65 WB&B£195-£210 WBDi£273-£294 LDO 7pm

Lic 🏠 ⚡(grass)🏊 boules swimming in lake croquet 40 acres
mixed
Credit Cards 1 2 3 £

BEAMINSTER Dorset   Map 03 ST40

PREMIER 🏆 SELECTED

GH QQQQQ *Hams Plot*
Bridport Road DT8 3LU
☎(0308) 862979
Apr-Oct
Owners Judy and Giles
Dearlove continue to maintain
the high standards of
accommodation and service
that guests have been
accustomed to expect when
staying at this charming house.
The spacious bedrooms are
comfortable and well-equipped. There are many added touches
that add to the warmth and atmosphere. Public areas include a
delightful library and lounge. A choice of breakfast is served in
the dining room.
3rm(2⇄1↑) ® ✗
Lic 🏠 nc10yrs ⚡(hard)croquet

VILLA MAGDALA HOTEL

Henrietta Road, Bath BA2 6LX
Telephone: (01225) 466329 Fax: (01225) 483207

An elegant Victorian town house hotel set in its own grounds, the Villa Magdala is situated in a quiet residential road overlooking Henrietta Park yet only a 5-minute level walk to the city centre. All 17 bedrooms have private bathroom, telephone, television and tea/coffee making facilities while some also have four poster beds. Private CAR PARK.

Widbrook Grange

Trowbridge Road, Bradford-on-Avon
Wiltshire BA15 1UH
Tel: 01225 864750 & 863173 Fax: 01225 862890

John and Pauline Price extend a warm welcome to their elegant, peaceful Georgian home in eleven secluded acres. The house and courtyard rooms, and the Manvers Suite for conferences and seminars, have been lovingly restored and exquisitely decorated and furnished with antiques. New indoor swimming pool. Evening Dinner is offered in the Dining Room with an interesting selection of wines.

Netherfield Hall

**NETHERFIELD, BATTLE,
EAST SUSSEX TN33 9PQ
Telephone: (01424) 774450**

A peaceful, happy house set in the heart of beautiful countryside and surrounded by woodlands. An ideal location to visit historical sites and other places of interest. Comfortable double rooms with en suite facilities. Full English breakfast. Ground floor bedrooms. Central heating. Parking on premises.

BEATTOCK Dumfries & Galloway *Dumfriesshire* Map **11** NT00

SELECTED

FH [Q][Q][Q][Q] Mrs K Miller **Broomlands** *(NT088015)* DG10 9PQ ☎(06833) 320
Etr-Oct
Attractively decorated, well equipped bedrooms are offered at this charming farmhouse. There is a comfortable lounge and an elegant dining room where hearty farmhouse breakfasts are served.
3🛁🚿 🚭 CTV in all bedrooms [R] 🐕 (ex guide dogs) sB&B🛁🚿£18 dB&B🛁🚿£32
♨ CTV nc12yrs 200 acres beef mixed sheep
[£]

FH [Q][Q][Q] Mr & Mrs Bell ***Cogrie's*** *(NY106974)* DG10 9PP (3m S off A74) ☎Johnstone Bridge(05764) 320
Mar-Nov
This 18th-century farmhouse is peacefully situated in rural surroundings and offers comfortable bed and breakfast accommodation. The traditionally furnished bedrooms are generally spacious and have modern coordinated fabrics and good beds. Public areas include a comfortable lounge and separate breakfast room.
4rm (3fb) [R] 🐕 LDO 6pm
♨ CTV 275 acres dairy mixed

BEAULY Highland *Inverness-shire* Map **14** NH54

GH [Q][Q] ***Arkton Hotel*** Westend IV4 7BT ☎(0463) 782388
This personally run, licensed guesthouse is conveniently situated at the south end of the village square and attracts both tourists and commercial visitors. It offers good value and practical accommodation in eight bedrooms . There is a dining room and TV lounge provided for guests, and the atmosphere is friendly throughout.
8rm (1fb) CTV in 3 bedrooms [R] LDO 8pm
Lic ♨ CTV nc6yrs

GH [Q][Q][Q] **Chrialdon Hotel** Station Road IV4 7EH
☎Inverness(0463) 782336
Enthusiastic owners Anthony and Jennifer Bond extend a warm welcome to all who visit their fine, turreted Victorian house, which stands in its own garden beside the main road. Drinks are provided in the comfort of the quiet lounge, and imaginative Scottish dishes, prepared from the best local produce, are served at the shared tables in the elegant dining room. Most bedrooms have en suite facilities.
8rm(2🛁4🚿) (2fb) 🚭 in dining room CTV in all bedrooms [R] ✻ sB&B£16-£18.50 dB&B£32-£37 dB&B🛁🚿£46-£55 WB&B£112-£192.50 WBDi£234.50-£315 LDO 7.30pm
Lic ♨
Credit Cards [1] [3]

GH [Q][Q][Q] **Heathmount** Station Road IV4 7EQ ☎(0463) 782411
Closed Xmas & New Year
Situated beside the main road close to the village square, this sturdy Victorian villa offers a friendly atmosphere and good-value bed and breakfast accommodation. Bedrooms are bright and airy with attractive decor and modern teak furnishings. Public areas include a spacious lounge and a neat dining room where hearty breakfasts are served at individual tables.
5rm (2fb) 🚭 in bedrooms 🚭 in dining room CTV in all bedrooms [R] sB&B£16-£17 dB&B£32-£34 WB&B£100-£110
♨ CTV

FH [Q][Q][Q] Mrs C Munro **Wester Moniack** *(NH551438)* IV5 7PQ (just off A862 between Inverness and Beauly, follow signs to Moniack Castle Wineries) ☎Drumchardine(0463831) 237
Many guests return year after year to Mrs Munro's comfortable, traditional farmhouse. A welcoming lounge complements the bright cheery bedrooms and enjoyable farmhouse fare is served at the communal table in the dining room.
2rm (1fb) 🚭 [R] ✻ sB&B£15-£16 dB&B£26-£28 WB&B£90-£95 WBDi£135-£145 LDO 8pm
♨ CTV 600 acres arable beef mixed sheep
[£]

BEDALE North Yorkshire Map **08** SE28

See also Hunton and Patrick Brompton

SELECTED

FH [Q][Q][Q][Q] Mrs D Knox **Blairgowrie Country House** *(SE241921)* Crakehall DL8 1JZ (1m N of Crakehall)
☎Richmond(0748) 811377
Closed Xmas & New Year
This delightful country house is surrounded by fields and meadows. Although it is not now part of a working farm, the owners farmed in the area for many years and the welcoming atmosphere of a traditional farmhouse still prevails. Bedrooms are beautifully decorated and there is a comfortable lounge and dining room, together with a sun lounge which leads out to a colourful garden.
2rm(1🚿) 🚭 CTV in all bedrooms [R] 🐕 ✻ sB&B🚿fr£25 dB&B🚿fr£34
♨ CTV nc10yrs 🎣 3 acres small holding

BEDDGELERT Gwynedd Map **06** SH54

GH [Q][Q] ***River Garden Restaurant*** LL55 4UY ☎(076686) 551
3🚿 CTV in all bedrooms [R] 🐕
♨ 🚫
Credit Cards [3]

BEDFORD Bedfordshire Map **04** TL04

GH [Q][Q] **Bedford Oak House** 33 Shakespeare Road MK40 2DX (NW on connecting road between A6/A428)
☎(0234) 266972 FAX (0234) 266972
This efficiently run family home offers, an attractive wood-panelled breakfast room and a spacious conference room; guests can help themselves to tea and coffee from the lounge at any time.
15rm(11🚿) (1fb) CTV in all bedrooms 🐕 (ex guide dogs) sB&B£20-£31 sB&B🚿£29.50-£32 dB&B£30-£32 dB&B🚿£35-£38
♨ CTV
Credit Cards [1] [2] [3] [5] [£]

GH [Q][Q] **Hertford House Hotel** 57 De Parys Avenue MK40 2TP
☎(0234) 350007 & 354470 FAX (0234) 353468
Closed 24 Dec-2 Jan
Most of the well kept bedrooms are spacious in this centrally located and family-run hotel; breakfast is served in a first-floor dining room which overlooks playing fields, and there is a combined reception, lounge and television room (with satellite TV) on the ground floor.
16rm (3fb) 🚭 in 4 bedrooms 🚭 in dining room CTV in all bedrooms [R] ✻ sB&B£20-£25 sB&B🛁🚿£30-£34.50 dB&B£37.50 dB&B🛁🚿£40-£45 WB&Bfr£140
♨ CTV
Credit Cards [1] [3] [5] [£]

BEER Devon Map **03** SY28

[🛏☕] **GH [Q]** **Bay View** Fore Street EX12 3EE
☎Seaton(0297) 20489
Mar-Nov rs Nov-Mar
Bay View is at the end of the village overlooking the beach and sea.
6rm(4🛁🚿) (1fb)CTV in 4 bedrooms [R] sB&B£14-£18 sB&B🛁🚿£18-£25 dB&B£28-£32 dB&B🛁🚿£32-£40 WB&B£92.50-£130
♨ CTV 🚫nc5yrs
[£]

BEERCROCOMBE Somerset Map **03** ST32

PREMIER SELECTED

FH QQQQQ Mrs V Cole **Frog Street Farm** *(ST317197)* Frog Street TA3 6AF ☎Hatch Beauchamp(0823) 480430

Mar-Nov

Still a working farm set in 160 acres, this attractive Somerset longhouse, clad in wisteria, dates back to 1436. The good sized bedrooms have pretty individual decor. One room - a converted cider house - has a separate lounge with TV. There is a comfortable residents' lounge with log-burning stove, but the heart of the farmhouse is undoubtedly in the kitchen and dining room, where Veronica Cole serves delicious home-cooked food. Outside, the swimming pool is in a sheltered spot and the well kept garden is very pretty. Run by the attentive Cole family, the whole house is extremely well presented and has a very friendly, cosy atmosphere.

3rm(2⇌1↱) ⊬ Ⓡ ✱ * dB&B⇌↱£44-£54 WB&Bfr£154 WBDifr£238 LDO 2pm

▥ CTV nc11yrs ⦬(heated) 160 acres dairy mixed stud

Ⓔ

PREMIER SELECTED

FH QQQQQ Mr & Mrs Mitchem **Whittles** *(ST324194)* TA3 6AH ☎Hatch Beauchamp (0823) 480301

Feb-Nov

Whittles Farm has 200 acres of dairy and beef farmland where Mr and Mrs Mitchem offer warm hospitality to their guests. The individually decorated bedrooms have a charm of their own while downstairs there is a snug rear dining room where Mrs Mitchem serves dinner by arrangement and breakfast at a large table. Guests have a choice of sitting rooms and wood-burning stoves create a relaxing atmosphere.

3⇌ ⊬ in bedrooms ⊬ in dining room ⊬ in 1 lounge CTV in all bedrooms Ⓡ ✱ * sB&B⇌£26-£28 dB&B⇌£42-£44 WB&B£140-£144 LDO 6.30pm(previous day)

Lic ▥ nc12yrs 200 acres beef dairy

BEESTON Nottinghamshire Map **08** SK53

GH QQ Fairhaven Private Hotel 19 Meadow Road NG9 1JP (200yds after railway station) ☎Nottingham(0602) 227509

Closed 25-26 Dec

A clean, modest hotel on the edge of the town. There is a really comfortable lounge in which to relax and watch TV.

10rm(4↱) (1fb) ⊬ in 5 bedrooms ⊬ in dining room ⊬ in 1 lounge CTV in 5 bedrooms Ⓡ ✱ sB&B£18-£21 sB&B↱£26-£30 dB&B£27-£32 dB&B↱£36-£40 LDO noon

Lic ▥ CTV

Ⓔ

BEITH Strathclyde *Renfrewshire* Map **10** NS35

FH QQ Mrs J Gillan **Shotts Farm** *(NS363500)* KA15 1LB ☎(0505) 502273

A 160-acre dairy farm surrounded by rolling countryside, Shotts Farm offers comfortable, compact, no smoking bedrooms with modern appointments. A combined lounge and dining room is also provided, where hearty farmhouse fare is served at a communal table. Friendly host Mrs Gillan maintains high standards of housekeeping.

3rm (1fb)CTV in all bedrooms Ⓡ ✱ * sB&Bfr£12 dB&Bfr£24 WB&Bfr£80 LDO 10am

▥ CTV 160 acres dairy

BELL BUSK North Yorkshire Map **07** SD95

GH QQQ Tudor House BD23 4DT ☎Airton(0729) 830301

mid Feb-mid Nov

Built in 1849, this well furnished guest house used to be the Bell Busk railway station. It is peacefully located and sees very few trains these days, though the occasional steam special still passes by. Two lounges and a small games area are provided for guests. The dining room was once the platform, and the smaller lounge was the booking office. It stands in well tended grounds and is also very much a family home.

4rm(1↱) (1fb) Ⓡ ✱ (ex guide dogs) sB&B£16-£20 dB&B£30-£32 dB&B↱fr£34 WB&B£90-£110 WBDi£153-£170

Lic ▥ CTV games room

Ⓔ

BELPER Derbyshire Map **08** SK34

See **Shottle**

Telephone national area codes are due to change by 16th April 1995. Please see the note under 'How to Use this Guide' at the front of the book.

SHOTTLE HALL GUEST HOUSE

Belper, Derby DE56 2EB

AA Guesthouse of the year 1982

Midlands Region

Country Guest House set in open countryside in the picturesque Ecclesbourne Valley. Ideally situated for overnight stays for visiting Derbyshire's many tourist attractions, or when seeking out of town locations and surrounding towns, either for business or pleasure.

Personal attention from proprietors:

Philip & Phyllis Matthews

Telephone: 01773 550203 or 550276

See gazetteer entry under Shottle

BEPTON (NEAR MIDHURST) West Sussex Map **04** SU81

PREMIER SELECTED

GH [Q][Q][Q][Q][Q] The Park House Hotel GU29 0JB (from centre of Midhurst take B2226 to Bepton) ☎Midhurst(0730) 812880 FAX (0730) 815643

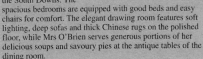

A small private country house hotel, parts of which date back to the 1600s, stands in a peaceful, rural setting close to Cowdray Park, Goodwood and the South Downs. The spacious bedrooms are equipped with good beds and easy chairs for comfort. The elegant drawing room features soft lighting, deep sofas and thick Chinese rugs on the polished floor, while Mrs O'Brien serves generous portions of her delicious soups and savoury pies at the antique tables of the dining room.

10rm(8🛁2🚿) Annexe 1🛁 (2fb)CTV in all bedrooms [R] T sB&B🛁🚿£47-£52 dB&B🛁🚿£81-£90 WBDi£378-£422 LDO noon

Lic ♨ CTV 🏊(heated) 🎾(grass)croquet pitch & putt

Credit Cards [1][2][3]

See advertisement under MIDHURST

BERE REGIS Dorset Map **03** SY89

GH [Q][Q][Q] *Culeaze* BH20 7NR ☎(0929) 471209

Apr-Oct

This fine manor house, in a peaceful setting, has some large bedrooms furnished in keeping with the character of the house, but facilities are limited. The comfortable sitting room has a conservatory extension and breakfast is served in the attractive dining room where guests share a large table.

4rm(1🛁) [R] 🐕

♨ nc10yrs 🎣

BERKELEY Gloucestershire Map **03** ST69

SELECTED

FH [Q][Q][Q][Q] Mrs B Evans ***Greenacres*** *(ST713008)* Breadstone GL13 9HF (2m W off A38, turn off A38 to Breadstone, in 0.75m on sharp left hand bend turn right up no through road, farm 300yds on right) ☎Dursley(0453) 810348

Closed 14 Dec-2 Jan

Well situated for touring the Cotswolds and visiting Bristol and Gloucester, this modern farmhouse sits in an elevated position. Rooms are attractively decorated with coordinated soft fabrics and pine furniture, and have modern en suite facilities. Generous breakfasts are served in the dining room overlooking the garden, and there is also a comfortable lounge with TV.

4rm(1🛁3🚿) CTV in all bedrooms [R] 🐕 (ex guide dogs)

♨ CTV nc10yrs sauna 47 acres horse breeding

BERRYNARBOR Devon Map **02** SS54

GH [Q][Q][Q] The Lodge Country House Hotel EX34 9SG (1.5m W of A399) ☎Combe Martin(0271) 883246

Closed Jan

Berrynarbor is renowned for being one of the best kept villages in the country. The house, an attractive family-run establishment, is on a slope, with an acre of well tended gardens. Most of the comfortable bedrooms have lovely country views. Traditionally furnished public areas and home-cooked evening meals are provided.

7rm(5🛁🚿) (2fb) 🚭 in dining room CTV in all bedrooms [R] LDO 6pm

Lic ♨ nc2yrs 9 hole putting

[£]

See advertisement under COMBE MARTIN

BERWICK-UPON-TWEED Northumberland Map **12** NT95

SELECTED

GH [Q][Q][Q][Q] Dervaig 1 North Road TD15 1PW (turn off A1 at A1167 (North Road) to town, last house on right before railway bridge) ☎Berwick(0289) 307378

5rm(3🛁🚿) (1fb)CTV in all bedrooms [R] dB&B£30-£40 dB&B🛁🚿£35-£50 WB&B£92-£137

♨

GH [Q][Q][Q] The Old Vicarage Church Road, Tweedmouth TD15 2AN ☎(0289) 306909

On the south side of the River Tweed stands the Old Vicarage, an attractive Victorian house offering good tourist accommodation. Bedrooms are mostly good-sized with cheery decor. There is a restful sitting room with plenty of reading material and an elegant dining room where breakfast may include Craster kippers.

7rm(4🚿) (1fb) 🚭 in dining room 🚭 in lounges CTV in all bedrooms [R] sB&B£14-£17 sB&B🚿£18-£35 dB&B£28-£34 dB&B🚿£36-£44 WB&B£88-£139

♨

[£]

BETTISCOMBE Dorset Map **03** SY39

GH [Q][Q][Q] Marshwood Manor DT6 5NS ☎Bridport(0308) 868442

Closed Dec-Jan

Marshwood Manor offers homely hospitality and well-appointed accomodation in a peaceful rural setting. Spacious bedrooms are thoughtfully decorated and furnished and have satisfactory equipment. Public rooms are light, airy and comfortable. Guests will enjoy the well-kept gardens and the good, honest English cooking.

6rm(2🛁3🚿) (3fb) 🚭 in dining room CTV in all bedrooms [R] ✳ sB&B£40 sB&B🛁🚿£44 dB&B£80 dB&B🛁🚿£88 (incl dinner) WB&B£186 WBDi£270

Lic ♨ 🏊(heated) croquet putting

Credit Cards [1][3][5]

See advertisement under BRIDPORT

BETWS-Y-COED Gwynedd Map **06** SH75

GH [Q] Bryn Llewelyn Holyhead Road LL24 0BN (on A5) ☎(0690) 710601

Good-value accommodation is offered at this stone-built guest house run by the friendly Naomi and Steve Parker. Bedrooms include several suitable for families, and these are much in demand in the tourist season. More en suite shower rooms are planned over the course of this year and next. A comfortable lounge is provided for guests.

7rm(2🚿) (3fb) 🚭 in 2 bedrooms 🚭 in dining room CTV in 2 bedrooms [R] ✳ sB&B£14-£17.50 dB&B£28-£34 dB&B🚿£34-£40 WB&B£90-£120

♨ CTV

GH [Q][Q][Q] The Ferns Holyhead Road LL24 0AN (on A5 close to Waterloo Bridge) ☎(0690) 710587

The Ferns is in the centre of the village with views of the River Conwy against a backdrop of wooded slopes. Keith and Teresa Roobottom are the friendly owners, and Teresa's touch is evident throughout the hotel in the pretty fabrics and attractive decor. All except two bedrooms have en suite showers and the other rooms can make up a family suite sharing a bathroom. A modern lounge

and a pine-furnished breakfast room are provided.
9rm(7♠) (2fb) ⊁ CTV in all bedrooms Ⓡ 🛠 (ex guide dogs)
sB&Bfr£18 sB&Bℝ£19 dB&B£32-£36 dB&Bℝ£36-£38
Lic ⬛ CTV nc4yrs
£

GH Ⓠ Summer Hill Non Smokers Guesthouse Coedcynhelier
Road LL24 0BL ☎(0690) 710306
Set in an elevated position with views of the River Llugwy and Fir
Tree Island, this family-run guest house is only a short walk from
the village, and is set in wooded grounds containing a car park.
Bedrooms are brightly decorated, and plans are well in hand to
modernise several and add en suite facilities. There is a
comfortable lounge, and evening meals are served on request.
7rm(3♠) (1fb) ⊁ Ⓡ ✳ sB&Bℝ£18-£20 dB&B£27-£30
dB&Bℝ£32-£36 LDO 5pm
Lic ⬛ CTV

Green Acres Farm
Breadstone, Berkley, Glos.
Tel: Dursley (01453) 810348

Beautifully situated in quiet surroundings between the River Severn and the Cotswolds. This Cotswold stone built house offers every convenience and a warm welcome. The bedrooms are delightfully furnished with either bathroom or shower en suite. You can relax and enjoy the lovely views from the large garden and the TV lounge or indulge in a sauna. The surrounding area is steeped in history and there are many places to visit.

P R E M I E R 🏅 S E L E C T E D

GH ⓆⓆⓆ Ⓠ Ⓠ Tan-y-Foel
Capel Garmon LL26 0RE (3m
SE) ☎(0690) 710507
FAX (0690) 710681
Closed Xmas rs Jan
Dating partly from the 16th
century, this delightful country
house lies high above the
Conwy Valley. There was once
a Roman lookout post in the
grounds and Tudor yeomen
erected the cruck-framed
timber barn. Bedrooms, including some four-poster rooms, are
attractively decorated and furnished with some fine antiques. ▶

Peter and Janet Pitman
Tan-y-Foel Country House
Capel Garmon, Nr. Betws-y-Coed, Gwynedd LL26 0RE
Telephone: 01690 710507 Fax: 01690 710681

WTB 👑 👑 👑 👑
DELUXE

The restful surroundings complement the personality of the hosts. Bedrooms, some four-posters, others with Victorian brass beds are all individually decorated. Fresh flowers are to be seen everywhere. Tan-y-Foel's location is another memorable feature. It stands in its own wooded grounds high on a hillside with wonderful views across the Conwy valley towards Snowdonia. This W.T.B. hospitality award "Best Small Hotel" 1992 and AA 5 Q Selected award winner 1994 hotel is further complemented by superb French style cuisine enhanced by a quality Welsh cheese board. Peace and tranquillity abound, no traffic or busy clamour, perfect place to unwind without the children (minimum age 7 years). Totally "no smoking" establishment.

An enclosed swimming pool is available for the summer months and there are two elegant sitting rooms. A small, well balanced menu is offered, based on fresh local produce. Tan-y-Foel has been selected as 'Guesthouse of the Year' 1995 for Wales.
7🛁🚿 🚭 CTV in all bedrooms [R] **T** 🐕 * dB&B🛁🚿£99-£110 WB&B£238-£329 WBDi£322-£430.50 LDO 6pm
Lic ♨ nc9yrs 🏊 (heated)
Credit Cards [1][2][3][5][£]

SELECTED

GH [Q][Q][Q][Q] Tyn-Y-Celyn Llanwrst Road LL24 0HD (N on A470) ☎(0690) 710202 FAX (0690) 710800
rs Jan-Feb
This large Victorian house is situated just north of the village, with lovely views of the Conwy and Llugwy valleys and the surrounding mountains. Maureen and Clive Muskus offer a warm welcome, and are constantly making improvements with guests' comfort in mind. Bedrooms are freshly decorated and furnished with good quality fitted units and several extra touches; most rooms enjoy magnificent views. There is a comfortable, modern lounge and pretty dining room, and a special feature is the large collection of paintings on display, many of which may be purchased.
8🛁🚿 (2fb) 🚭 in dining room CTV in all bedrooms [R] * sB&B🛁🚿£25-£35 dB&B🛁🚿£40-£45
Lic ♨ CTV
[£]

BEVERLEY Humberside — Map **08** TA03

See also Leven

GH [Q][Q] The Eastgate 7 Eastgate HU17 0DR
☎Hull(0482) 868464 FAX (0482) 871899
A friendly, family run guesthouse in the centre of this old town, offers cosy bedrooms that are individual in style, mostly with light cheerful decoration. Breakfast is served in an attractive dining room and light refreshments are available within the comfortable ground floor lounge.
18rm(7🚿) (5fb) 🚭 in bedrooms 🚭 in dining room * sB&B£15-£18.50 sB&B🚿£25-£30 dB&B£26-£32 dB&B🚿£34-£42
♨ CTV
[£]

BEXHILL East Sussex — Map **05** TQ70

GH [Q][Q] The Arosa 6 Albert Road TN40 1DG
☎(0424) 212574 & 732004
Situated in a quiet spot between the town centre and sea front, this small hotel offers bright modern bedrooms. There is a comfortable lounge at the front with a writing desk and a selection of games. Christine and Tony Bayliss create a caring atmosphere appreciated by a loyal clientele, including many elderly guests. A set evening meal is available in addition to breakfast.
9rm(3🛁🚿) (1fb) 🚭 in dining room CTV in all bedrooms [R] **T** 🐕 (ex guide dogs) sB&B£19 sB&B🛁🚿£25 dB&B£30 dB&B🛁🚿£40 WB&B£90-£150 WBDi£133-£193 LDO noon
♨ CTV 🚫
Credit Cards [1][2][3][£]

GH [Q][Q][Q] Park Lodge 16 Egerton Road TN39 3HH
☎(0424) 216547 & 215041
Ideally placed for all amenities, Park Lodge is an attractive corner house run by the Rogers family. Bedrooms are individually furnished in a pleasant mixture of styles. Breakfast and home cooked evening meals are served in the tastefully furnished dining room. There is also a cosy lounge and a residential licence.
10rm(6🛁🚿) (2fb) 🚭 in bedrooms 🚭 in dining room CTV in all bedrooms [R] **T** sB&B£17.50-£18.50 dB&B£39-£42 dB&B🛁🚿£42-£46 WB&B£127-£150 WBDi£175-£195 LDO 3pm
Lic ♨
Credit Cards [1][2][3][£]

BEYTON Suffolk — Map **05** TL96

SELECTED

GH [Q][Q][Q][Q] Manorhouse The Green IP30 9AF (4m E, turn off A45 at Beyton) ☎(0359) 270960 FAX (0284) 752561
Located on the north side of the village green, four miles east of Bury, this well preserved, late 15th-century house offers two large, attractively decorated bedrooms. Old beams and an inglenook fireplace have been preserved downstairs, and a welcome feature of the charming dining room where breakfast is served is the placing of armchairs in the wide windows.
2🛁🚿 🚭 CTV in all bedrooms [R] 🐕 * dB&B🛁🚿£36-£40
♨ nc8yrs

BIBURY Gloucestershire — Map **04** SP10

SELECTED

GH [Q][Q][Q][Q] Cotteswold House Arlington GL7 5ND
☎(0285) 740609
This attractive family house, constructed of Cotswold stone stands on the outskirts of this picturesque riverside village. Three spotless ensuite bedrooms have been tastefully decorated and furnished. Breakfast is served at separate tables and there is a comfortable lounge and small walled garden for guests' use.
3🛁🚿 (1fb) CTV in all bedrooms sB&B🛁🚿£22 dB&B🛁🚿£38 WB&B£115.50-£133
♨ ⛳

BICKINGTON (NEAR ASHBURTON) Devon — Map **03** SX77

SELECTED

FH [Q][Q][Q][Q] Mrs E A Ross **East Burne** *(SX799711)* TQ12 6PA (1m from A38) ☎Bickington(0626) 821496
Closed Xmas & New Year
A medieval hall house, East Burne Farm is reached along winding lanes in the depths of rural Devon. Mr and Mrs Ross offer a warm welcome and good value accommodation. The house has lots of character with oak beams and sloping floors and ceilings, and the simple bedrooms are freshly decorated and comfortable. In winter log fires blaze in the comfortable guests' lounge, and in summer guests can relax beside the pool.
3rm(2🚿) 🚭 [R] 🐕 (ex guide dogs) sB&B🚿£17.50 dB&B🚿£35 WB&B£105
CTV 🏊(heated) 40 acres cattle horses sheep
[£]

BIDEFORD Devon — Map **02** SS42

See also Parkham & Westward Ho!

GH [Q] *Kumba* Chudleigh Road, East-the-Water EX39 4AR (East-the-Water is E of Bideford, off A388) ☎(0237) 471526
This small guest house, set in a prominent position with views of the town, offers centrally heated no-smoking bedrooms (two with en suite facilities). Breakfast is served at separate tables in an informal dining room.
6rm(3🚿) (3fb) CTV in all bedrooms [R]
Lic CTV ⛳ putting green

GH Ⓠ Ⓠ Ⓠ **Mount Hotel** Northdown Road EX39 3LP (turn off A39 then right at Raleigh garage) ☎(0237) 473748
Closed Xmas
This small, interesting Georgian building in a partly-walled garden close to this historic riverside town offers comfortable, nicely decorated bedrooms. There is an attractive TV lounge and a small bar lounge, the only room where smoking is permitted. Resident proprietors Janet and Mike Taylor pride themselves on good home cooking and providing an establishment of character.
8rm(1⇌6🅵) (2fb) ⊁ in bedrooms ⊁ in dining room ⊁ in lounges Ⓡ 🏌 (ex guide dogs) ✳ sB&B🅵£19-£25 dB&B⇌🅵£37-£40 WB&B£125-£147 WBDi£170-£210 LDO 5pm
Lic 🖩 CTV
Credit Cards 1 3 £

GH Ⓠ Ⓠ Ⓠ **Pines at Eastleigh** Old Barnstaple Road, Eastleigh EX39 4PA (3m E off A39 at East-the-Water)
☎Instow(0271) 860561 FAX (0271) 860561
A small 18th-century country house hotel is set in seven acres of gardens and paddocks on the edge of the village of Eastleigh. The comfortable bedrooms have direct-dial telephones and the three new annexe rooms across the courtyard offer en suite facilities, as do several in the house. There is an attractive lounge and a bar lounge in the conservatory which is adjacent to a dining room serving a choice of home-cooked dishes.
1🅵 Annexe 3⇌🅵 (3fb) ⊁ CTV in all bedrooms Ⓡ T sB&B⇌🅵£17-£25.50 dB&B£46 dB&B⇌🅵£34-£51 WB&B£90-£132 LDO 12.30pm
Lic 🖩 o6 7.5 acre garden arrangements for golf
£

GH Ⓠ Ⓠ Ⓠ **Sunset Hotel** Landcross EX39 5JA ☎(0237) 472962
Mar-Oct
Overlooking picturesque Devon countryside, this small country hotel offers accommodation in individually furnished and decorated bedrooms. A comfortable lounge adjoins the dining room, where good home cooking is offered - everything is home made from fresh local produce, including locally caught fish. Smoking is not permitted anywhere in the hotel.
4🅵 (2fb) CTV in all bedrooms Ⓡ LDO 6pm
Lic 🖩 CTV
Credit Cards 1 3

BILLINGSHURST West Sussex
Map **04** TQ02

P R E M I E R ✦ S E L E C T E D

FH Ⓠ Ⓠ Ⓠ Ⓠ Ⓠ Mrs M Mitchell *Old Wharf* (TQ070256) Wharf Farm, Wisborough Green RH14 0JG
☎Horsham(0403) 784096
Closed 2 wks Xmas & New Year
Ideally situated for the ferry, being only five minutes from the terminal, this deceptively spacious Victorian property has been skilfully restored and refurbished in recent years by the pleasant owners, Mr and Mrs Mitchell. Standards throughout the hotel are high and housekeeping is excellent. Some bedrooms have en suite facilities, and all are well equipped and comfortable. Day rooms have a warm atmosphere. Breakfast is taken in an attractive dining room, and can be served early for guests needing to get away in good time for a morning ferry. For evening meals, there is a wide choice of restaurants in easy walking distance.
4⇌🅵 CTV in all bedrooms Ⓡ T 🏌
🖩 CTV nc12yrs 🏊 200 acres beef/sheep
Credit Cards 1 2 3 5

BINGLEY West Yorkshire
Map **07** SE13

S E L E C T E D

GH Ⓠ Ⓠ Ⓠ Ⓠ **Hall Bank Private Hotel** Beck Lane BD16 4DD ☎Bradford(0274) 565296 FAX (0274) 565296
Closed Xmas
Enthusiastic and attentive service is provided by the Wright family in this stone-built house standing in its own grounds. Bedrooms are well equipped, many with good views over the Aire Valley, and there is a large lounge, conservatory and games room. Evening meals offer a limited selection of carefully prepared dishes. Continental breakfast can be served in your room.
10rm(9⇌🅵) (2fb) ⊁ in dining room ⊁ in 1 lounge CTV in all bedrooms Ⓡ T 🏌 ✳ sB&B⇌🅵£25-£40 dB&B⇌🅵£40-£50 LDO 7.30pm
Lic 🖩 CTV nc4yrs games room
Credit Cards 2 £

BIRKENHEAD Merseyside
Map **07** SJ38

GH Ⓠ **Gronwen** 11 Willowbank Road, Devonshire Park L42 7JU
☎051-652 8306
Friendly and hospitable proprietors provide sound but dated accommodation at this large house close to the Glenda Jackson Theatre and Tranmere Rovers football ground. A cosy lounge and a small dining room with separate tables are provided.
5rm (1fb) CTV in all bedrooms Ⓡ ✳ sB&B£16 dB&B£30 WB&B£105 WBDi£140 LDO 7.30pm
🖩 CTV ✂

𝕿𝖄'𝕹-𝖄-𝕮𝕰𝕷𝖄𝕹 𝕳𝕺𝖀𝕾𝕰

S E L E C T E D

Betws-Y-Coed
Llanrwst Road (A470), Gwynedd, LL24 0HD
Tel: 01690 710202 Fax: 01690 710800
This spacious Victorian Guest House overlooks picturesque village of Betws-Y-Coed and has beautiful scenic views of the Llugwy Valley. There are eight bedrooms completely and tastefully refurnished. Each one has CTV, beverage makers, central heating, en-suite facilities, etc.
You are assured of a warm welcome by Maureen and Clive Muskus, comfortable accommodation and robust breakfast.

BIRMINGHAM West Midlands   Map **07** SP08

See also Blackheath

GH Q Q **Ashdale House Hotel** 39 Broad Road, Acock's Green B27 7UX (off A41, first on left after Acocks Green Centre)
☎021-706 3598 FAX 021-706 3598

Richard and Evelyn are friendly hosts concerned about the environment; they use eco-friendly products and serve breakfast made from organic produce. Their three-storey Victorian terrace house is furnished with stripped pine and Victoriana.

9rm(4🎇) (2fb) ⊁ in dining room CTV in all bedrooms ℝ ✳
sB&B£20 sB&B🎇£25 dB&B£32 dB&B🎇£37 WB&B£100-£125
▥, CTV
Credit Cards [1] [3] (£)

GH Q *Awentsbury Hotel* 21 Serpentine Road, Selly Park B29 7HU
☎021-472 1258 FAX 021-472 1258

Catering for a predominantly business clientele, the Awentsbury is in a quiet residential area close to the university and Pebble Mill. Bedrooms have all the usual facilities and public areas include a dining room and a small lounge.

16rm(6🎇) (2fb) CTV in all bedrooms ℝ T LDO 6pm
▥, ☖
Credit Cards [1] [2] [3]

GH Q Q Q **Bearwood Court Hotel** 360-366 Bearwood Road, Warley B66 4ET (on A4030, 3m from city centre) ☎021-429 9731 FAX 021-429 6175

A predominantly commercial hotel situated on a busy road within easy reach of the city centre. Bedrooms vary in size and style, but all are well equipped and have direct dial telephones. The extensive public areas include a formal reception and a bar.

24rm(23🎇) (3fb) ⊁ in 1 bedrooms ⊁ in dining room ⊁ in 1 lounge CTV in all bedrooms ℝ T ✻ (ex guide dogs) sB&B£25
sB&B🎇£32-£35 dB&B£42-£44 dB&B🎇£46-£48
WB&B£175-£224 WBDi£245-£294 LDO 8pm
Lic ▥, CTV ☖
Credit Cards [1] [3] (£)

GH Q Q **Beech House Hotel** 21 Gravelly Hill North, Erdington B23 6BT ☎021-373 0620

Closed 2wks Xmas & New Year

Personally run by the owner, Frank Westerman, Beech House is a small hotel, close to `spaghetti junction' on the M6, and convenient for the NEC. Bedrooms vary in size and style, en suite rooms have TV, and sets are available for hire in other rooms. There are two lounge areas downstairs.

9rm(4🎇🎇) (2fb) ⊁ in dining room ⊁ in 1 lounge CTV in 4 bedrooms ℝ sB&B£26 sB&B🎇🎇£33 dB&B£40 dB&B🎇🎇£47
WB&B£182-£231 WBDi£252-£301 LDO noon
▥, CTV nc5yrs
Credit Cards [1] [3]

GH Q Q Q **Bridge House Hotel** 49 Sherbourne Road, Acocks Green B27 6DX ☎021-706 5900 FAX 021-624 5900

Closed Xmas & New Year

A substantial private hotel with excellent facilities and professional standards. A lounge/dining room leads through into a conservatory and there are two bars furnished in deep red with button-back seating. This extremely clean, warm, security-conscious and well cared-for hotel, is convenient for the city centre and NEC.

30rm(2🎇28🎇) (1fb) ⊁ in 10 bedrooms CTV in all bedrooms ℝ
T ✻ ✳ sB&B🎇£32.90 dB&B🎇£47 LDO 8.30pm
Lic ▥, CTV
Credit Cards [1] [2] [3] [5] (£)

GH Q Q *Cape Race Hotel* 929 Chester Road, Erdington B24 OHJ (on A452, 2m from juncts 5 and 6 of M6) ☎021-373 3085
FAX 021-373 3085

A large detached house north of the city with its own garden, the Cape Race is convenient for access to the M6 and the city centre. The cleanly decorated bedrooms vary in size, but all have modern

furnishings and a good range of equipment. Drinks can be dispensed to the cottage-style dining room or the cosy lounge from a small bar.

9rm(8🎇) CTV in all bedrooms ℝ T ✻ (ex guide dogs) LDO 8.30pm
Lic ▥, CTV ☌(heated) ☓(hard)
Credit Cards [1] [2] [3]

GH Q Q *Elston* 751 Washwood Heath Road, Ward End B8 2JY
☎021-327 3338

rs Sat & Sun

A popular commercial guesthouse located on the A47, four miles from the city centre and close to 'spaghetti junction'. Rooms vary in size, style and furnishings and there is a comfortable guests' lounge and a tiny dining room overlooking the rear garden. A friendly, relaxed atmosphere created by proprietors Elsie and Tony Bennett is reciprocated by regular returning guests. Car parking is provided.

11rm(1🎇) CTV in all bedrooms ℝ LDO 8pm
▥, CTV

GH Q Q Q **Fountain Court Hotel** 339-343 Hagley Road, Edgbaston B17 8NH (on A456) ☎021-429 1754 FAX 021-429 1209
Made up of three houses, this hotel has a lounge, bar and dining room which are all bright, warm and clean despite the dark oak panelling. Bedrooms are modestly furnished but well equipped. The fixed-price menu for dinner has four or five choices for each course.

25🎇🎇 CTV in all bedrooms ℝ T ✳ sB&B🎇🎇£30-£39
dB&B🎇🎇£45-£55 WB&B£210-£273 WBDi£311.50-£374.50
LDO 8.30pm
Lic ▥, CTV nc
Credit Cards [1] [2] [3] [5] (£)

GH Q Q **Heath Lodge Hotel** Coleshill Road,Marston Green B37 7HT (1.5m from airport and NEC on edge of Marston Green village) ☎021-779 2218 FAX 021-779 2218

This hotel is in a quiet but convenient location. The bedrooms vary in size and standard, and public areas include a beamed gallery restaurant, a bar and comfortable lounge.

18rm(13🎇🎇) (1fb) ⊁ in dining room CTV in all bedrooms ℝ T
sB&B🎇🎇£23-£29.50 sB&B🎇🎇£25-£37.50 dB&B£30-£42
dB&B🎇🎇£32-£48 WB&B£140-£262.50 LDO 8.30pm
Lic ▥, CTV
Credit Cards [1] [2] [3] [5] (£)

GH Q **Homelea** 2399 Coventry Road, Sheldon B26 3PN (exit M42 junct 6 on to A45, 2.5m on left near Arden Oak public house) ☎021-742 0017

Closed Xmas

3rm(2🎇) ⊁ in 1 bedrooms ⊁ in dining room ⊁ in lounges CTV in all bedrooms ℝ ✳ sB&B£18 dB&B🎇£34-£36
▥, CTV
(£)

GH Q Q **Lyndhurst Hotel** 135 Kingsbury Road, Erdington B24 8QT ☎021-373 5695 FAX 021-373 5695

A large, considerably extended Victorian house, the Lyndhurst is conveniently located in the northern suburbs half a mile from junction 6 of the M6. The bedrooms, including those on the ground floor, have modern furnishings and equipment. There is a large dining room with an adjacent lounge bar, and a TV lounge.

14rm(1🎇12🎇) (3fb)CTV in all bedrooms ℝ ✻ (ex guide dogs)
sB&B£25-£30 sB&B🎇🎇£30-£40 dB&B🎇🎇£39.50-£49.50
WB&B£205-£235 WBDi£265-£295 LDO 8.15pm
Lic ▥, CTV
Credit Cards [1] [2] [3] [5] (£)

GH Q Q **Robin Hood Lodge Hotel** 142 Robin Hood Lane, Hall Green B28 0JX (on A4040, 5m from city centre) ☎021-778 5307 &
021-608 6622 FAX 021-604 8686

A commercial guesthouse with easy access to the city, NEC and airport. Rooms are located in the main hotel and two adjacent

▶

properties, offering functional but well equipped accommodation. There is a comfortable lounge with a bar and a small dining room.
7rm(1🛁2🚿) (1fb)CTV in all bedrooms [R] * sB&B£24-£29 sB&B🛁🚿£29 dB&B£38-£44 dB&B🛁🚿£42-£47
Lic ♨ CTV
Credit Cards [1] [3] [5] [£]

GH [Q] Rollason Wood Hotel 130 Wood End Road, Erdington B24 8BJ (NE Birmingham on A4040) ☎021-373 1230
FAX 021-382 2578
35rm(1🛁10🚿) (4fb)CTV in all bedrooms [R] sB&B£17.85-£24.50 sB&B🛁🚿£31-£36.25 dB&B£30-£43 dB&B🛁🚿£42-£52 WB&B£123-£212 LDO 8.30pm
Lic ♨ CTV games room
Credit Cards [1] [2] [3] [5] [£]

GH [Q] [Q] *Tri-Star Hotel* Coventry Road,Elmdon B26 3QR (on A45) ☎021-782 1010 & 021-782 6131
Convenient for the NEC and airport, this mainly commercial hotel offers simple, well maintained accommodation. Public areas include a games room, small bar and comfortable TV lounge with an archway to the dining area.
15rm(11🚿) (3fb) CTV in all bedrooms [R] 🐕 LDO 8pm
Lic ♨ CTV pool table
Credit Cards [1] [2] [3]

BIRTLEY Tyne & Wear — Map **12** NZ25

INN [Q] [Q] *Portobello Lodge* Durham Road DH3 2PF
☎091-410 2739
The William IV is a Victorian public house on the A6127 just as it approaches the town from the south. The accommodation is modern and there is an attractively decorated dining room adjoining a lounge bar. Bar meals are served at lunch time and in the evening.
12🛁🚿 (1fb) CTV in all bedrooms [R] 🐕 (ex guide dogs) LDO 9pm
♨
Credit Cards [1] [3]

BISHAMPTON Hereford & Worcester — Map **03** SO95

P R E M I E R SELECTED

FH [Q] [Q] [Q] [Q] [Q] Mrs H Robertson ***Nightingale Hotel*** *(SO988512)* WR10 2NH
☎Evesham(0386) 82521 & 82384

This mock-Tudor farmhouse offers comfortable accommodation in bright, fresh and well equipped bedrooms with pretty coordinating soft furnishings and modern en suite facilities. There are three lounge areas with excellent seating, fresh flowers, books and magazines. The dining room is in two parts and the small restaurant has gained a good local reputation, due to the high standard of cooking and imaginative menus. Proprietors Mr and Mrs Robertson are welcoming hosts whose concern for their guests' comfort ensures that visitors return regularly. The farmhouse is suitable for tourists and business guests alike, and small meetings can be accommodated.
4🛁🚿 (1fb) CTV in all bedrooms [R] 🐕 LDO 9pm
Lic ♨ ⛳18 🐎 snooker 200 acres beef arable
Credit Cards [1] [3]

BISHOP'S CASTLE Shropshire — Map **07** SO38

GH [Q] [Q] [Q] The Old Brick Guesthouse 7 Church Street SY9 5AA
☎(0588) 638471
Closed Xmas
Peter and Phyllis Hutton are the very capable owners of this little guest house situated in the main street. Exposed timbers and a fine original staircase reflect the age of the building, reputedly 17th or 18th century. Many of the bedrooms are furnished with pine, and the very comfortable lounge has an impressive inglenook fireplace. Dinner can be served with advance notice, and car parking is available.
5rm(2🛁🚿) (1fb) 🚭 in dining room [R] sB&B£19 sB&B🛁🚿£25 dB&B£35 dB&B🛁🚿£45 WB&B£120-£170 WBDi£190-£230 LDO 3pm
Lic ♨ CTV
[£]

INN [Q] [Q] [Q] The Boar's Head Church Street SY9 5AE (from A488 follow signs to livestock market, continue past market Inn is on the left at crossroads) ☎(0588) 638521
4🛁🚿 (1fb)CTV in all bedrooms [R] **T** sB&B🛁🚿£28-£32 dB&B🛁🚿£39-£48 WB&B£117-£130 WBDi£165-£180 Lunch £7-£10alc Dinner £8-£12alc LDO 9.30pm
♨ CTV pool
Credit Cards [1] [2] [3] [5] [£]

BISHOP'S STORTFORD Hertfordshire — Map **05** TL42

GH [Q] [Q] [Q] Cottage 71 Birchanger Lane, Birchanger CM23 5QA
☎(0279) 812349
A charming 17th-century Grade II listed cottage has been carefully modernised to retain its character. Set in a quiet rural location yet close to Bishop's Stortford, the accommodation is attractively decorated and furnished and well equipped. The panelled lounge is comfortable, and the delightful conservatory/dining room overlooks the garden.
15rm(2🛁11🚿) (1fb) 🚭 CTV in all bedrooms [R] 🐕 (ex guide dogs) sB&Bfr£28 sB&B🛁🚿fr£34 dB&B🛁🚿fr£44 WB&Bfr£146 WBDifr£216 LDO 9.30am
Lic ♨ croquet
Credit Cards [1] [3] [£]

BISHOPSTON West Glamorgan

See **Langland Bay & Mumbles**

BLACKFORD Tayside *Perthshire* — Map **11** NN80

GH [Q] [Q] Yarrow House Moray Street PH4 1PY ☎(0764) 682358
Attractive rooms are available at this guest house situated in the peaceful main street of the village, which has benefitted enormously from the by-pass of the A9. Meals are served at a communal table in the L-shaped lounge.
3rm(1🚿) (1fb) 🚭 in bedrooms 🚭 in dining room CTV in all bedrooms [R] * sB&B£13-£16 dB&B£26-£32 WB&B£70-£91 WBDi£105-£120
♨ CTV
[£]

BLACKHEATH West Midlands — Map **07** SO98

GH [Q] [Q] Highfield House Hotel Holly Road, Rowley Regis B65 0BH ☎021-559 1066
A popular commercial hotel located at Blackheath, which is also known as Rowley Regis, just 1.5 miles from junction 2 of the M5. The rooms, though modest with plain decor and functional furnishings, are well kept and standards of maintenance are good. Evening meals are served in the dining room, and there is a comfortable lounge with satellite TV.
14rm(2🛁🚿) CTV in all bedrooms [R] 🐕 (ex guide dogs) * sB&B£20-£25 sB&B🛁🚿£30-£35 dB&B£38-£40 dB&B🛁🚿£40-£45 LDO 6pm
Lic ♨ CTV
Credit Cards [1] [3]

BLACKPOOL Lancashire Map **07** SD33

GH [Q][Q] ***Arosa Hotel*** 18-20 Empress Drive FY2 9SD
☎(0253) 352555
A family-run private hotel situated just a short distance from Queens Promenade offers more spacious accommodation than many of the surrounding establishments. Practically furnished bedrooms are modern in style, while public areas include a cosy bar as well as a neatly appointed dining room.
20rm(3🛁16🚿) (7fb) CTV in all bedrooms [R] LDO 5pm
Lic ▦ CTV

🛏☕ **GH [Q][Q] Ashcroft Private Hotel** 42 King Edward Avenue FY2 9TA (turn off Queen Prom 2nd right after Savoy hotel)
☎(0253) 351538
This friendly little private hotel provides bright and cheerful, if rather compact, bedrooms; a cosy bar and small sun lounge augment the neat dining room.
9rm(5🚿) (3fb) 🚭 in dining room [R] sB&B£15-£18 sB&B🚿£17-£20 dB&B£30-£36 dB&B🚿£34-£40 WB&B£98-£119 WBDi£126-£153 LDO 2pm
Lic ▦ CTV
Credit Cards [1][3][£]

GH [Q][Q] Berwick Private Hotel 23 King Edward Avenue FY2 9TA ☎(0253) 351496
20 Mar-7 Nov
Fairly compact and simply appointed bedrooms are available at this small, family-run, private hotel set in a quiet side road off Queens Promenade; there is a cosy lounge, however, and the attractive dining room offers a choice of home-cooked dishes at dinner.
8rm(7🚿) 🚭 in dining room 🚭 in lounges [R] 🐕 dB&B£28-£32 dB&B🚿£30-£34 WB&B£101.50-£108.50 WBDi£112-£122.50 LDO 3pm
Lic ▦ CTV nc3yrs

GH [Q][Q] ***Brooklands Hotel*** 28-30 King Edward Avenue FY2 9TA
☎(0253) 351479
Improvements continue at this family run private hotel close to Queens Promenade, and several of its compact bedrooms now have smart modern en suite shower rooms. Public areas include a pleasant dining room and comfortable lounge bar.
18rm(12🚿) (3fb) CTV in all bedrooms [R] 🐕 (ex guide dogs) LDO 3.30pm
Lic ▦

GH [Q][Q][Q] Burlees Hotel 40 Knowle Avenue FY2 9TQ
☎(0253) 354535
Feb-Nov
Situated in a quiet residential area within easy reach of both the seafront and golf course, this double-fronted semidetached house continues to be improved by its welcoming owners. Particularly well maintained throughout, it offers pleasantly appointed and thoughtfully equipped bedrooms with modern en suite shower rooms; meals are taken in a neat dining room with matching pine tables, and guests can relax in either the comfortable lounge or a separate bar.
9🚿 (2fb) 🚭 in 6 bedrooms 🚭 in dining room CTV in all bedrooms [R] 🐕 sB&B🚿£20-£23 dB&B🚿£40-£46 WB&B£128-£145 WBDi£175-£198 LDO 4pm
Lic ▦ CTV ⌂
Credit Cards [1][3][£]

GH [Q][Q] Claytons 28 Northumberland Avenue, off Queens Promenade FY2 9SA ☎(0253) 355397 FAX (0253) 500142
Friendly owners Margaret and Gerry Clayton warmly welcome guests to their home situated in a quiet area of this popular resort, just off the Queens Promenade, near Uncle Tom's Cabin. Neat modern bedrooms with en suite shower rooms are equipped with Sky television as well as piped local radio, and a good-value dinner carte is available in the evening. Midweek excursions to local jazz clubs are organised for those so inclined.
6🚿 (1fb) 🚭 in 2 bedrooms 🚭 in dining room CTV in all bedrooms [R] 🐕 (ex guide dogs) sB&B🚿£16-£18 dB&B🚿£32-£36 LDO 4pm
▦ nc7yrs
Credit Cards [1][2][3][5][£]

GH [Q][Q] ***Cliff Head Hotel*** 174 Queens Promenade, Bispham FY2 9JN ☎(0253) 591086
This small, family-run private hotel occupies a corner site close to Bispham tram station on the northern promenade; its compact bedrooms are neatly tended and well equipped, the dining room incorporates a bar, and guests can relax in a cosy lounge.
7🛁🚿 (1fb) CTV in all bedrooms [R] LDO 5.30pm
Lic ▦ CTV

🛏☕ **GH [Q][Q] The Colby Hotel** 297 The Promenade FY1 6AL (om promenade midway between Blackpool Tower and Pleasure Beach) ☎(0253) 345845
Etr & May-Nov
A friendly, family-run hotel on a relatively quiet stretch of the promenade between the Golden Mile and Pleasure Beach provides bedrooms with en suite shower facilities, TV sets and tea trays; three large seafront rooms offer attractive four-poster beds and there are also two family rooms. As well as the dining room (which opens as a tea shop during the afternoons) there is a lounge containing a pool table. The hotel has no private car park, but promenade parking is usually possible and the Bloomfield car parks are nearby.
14🚿 (5fb)CTV in all bedrooms [R] 🐕 sB&B🚿£15-£25 dB&B🚿£26-£46 LDO 5pm
Lic ▦ CTV pool table
Credit Cards [1][3]

GH [Q][Q] Denely Private Hotel 15 King Edward Avenue FY2 9TA ☎(0253) 352757
Closed Xmas & New Year
▶

Burlees Hotel
40, Knowle Avenue, Blackpool FY2 9TQ
Tel: (01253) 354535
Proprietors: Mike and Linda Lawrence

Friendly, family run hotel situated off Queen's Promenade in peaceful residential area.

★ Ideal for holidays, business or conference delegates
★ Easy access to town centre and amenities
★ Unrestricted car parking, some on premises
★ Comfort and excellent cuisine assured
★ Central heating throughout
★ All rooms en-suite
★ All rooms with TV, clock radio, hair dryer and tea/coffee making facilities
★ Licensed to residents
★ Low seasons rates Feb to May.
Short Break Reductions,

A long-established private hotel in a quiet street off Queens Promenade provides accommodation in rooms varying in both size and comfort (though all are equipped with hairdryers); public areas include a large, plant-filled lounge and a neat dining room.
9rm(2♠) (2fb) ✁ in dining room Ⓡ ⚦ ✳ sB&B£15.75-£16.75 sB&B♠£17.75-£18.75 dB&B£31.50-£33.50 dB&B♠£35.50-£37.50 WB&Bfr£118.25 WBDi£140-£162.60 LDO 3.30pm
▥, CTV

GH Ⓠ Ⓠ *Derwent Private Hotel* 8 Gynn Avenue, North Shore FY1 2LD ☎(0253) 355194 FAX (0253) 596618
Bright and cheerful, this guest house is tucked away in a quiet street just off the promenade, near the Pembroke Hotel. Attractively decorated modern bedrooms include two suitable for family use, while public areas are made up of a large residents' lounge and a dining room which has been extended to provide a cosy bar. Limited parking is available.
12rm(4♠) (2fb) Ⓡ LDO 2pm
Lic ▥, CTV
Credit Cards ❶ ❸

GH Ⓠ Ⓠ *The Garville Hotel* 3 Beaufort Avenue, Bispham FY2 9HQ (2m N) ☎(0253) 351004
A small family-owned and run guest house situated in a quiet side road at Bispham, to the north of Blackpool. The best of the bedrooms have four-poster beds and private bathrooms; others are more compact but have good facilities and decor. There is a cosy lounge with a bar and a small breakfast room.
7rm(2⇄) (3fb) CTV in all bedrooms Ⓡ ✳ sB&B£13-£16 dB&B£24-£30 dB&B⇄£30-£36 WB&B£70-£95 WBDi£85-£115 LDO 2pm
Lic ▥, CTV
Ⓔ

GH Ⓠ Ⓠ Ⓠ *Hartshead Hotel* 17 King Edward Avenue FY2 9TA ☎(0253) 353133 & 357111
Closed 8 Nov-Feb rs Mar-Etr
Guests are assured of a friendly welcome at this small private hotel situated within easy reach of Queens Promenade. Though bedrooms are generally compact they are equipped with such extras as clock radios and telephones, while the pleasantly appointed public areas include a comfortable lounge bar and sun lounge.
10rm(1⇄9♠) (3fb) ✁ in bedrooms ✁ in dining room CTV in all bedrooms Ⓡ T sB&B♠£16-£24 dB&B⇄♠£32-£48 WB&B£100-£120 WBDi£122-£145 LDO 3pm
Lic ▥, CTV nc3yrs
Credit Cards ❶ ❷ ❸ Ⓔ

GH Ⓠ Ⓠ *Inglewood Hotel* 18 Holmfield Road FY2 9TB ☎(0253) 351668
Improvements have been made to this small private hotel situated in a quiet road running parallel to Queens Promenade; bedrooms remain fairly compact, but several have now been redecorated and their en suite shower rooms attractively retiled. Public areas include a cosy bar with separate sun lounge, and the daily-changing menu offers a choice of home-cooked dishes.
10♠ (2fb) CTV in all bedrooms Ⓡ ⚦ (ex guide dogs) LDO 10am
Lic ▥, CTV nc2yrs

GH Ⓠ Ⓠ Ⓠ *Lynstead Private Hotel* 40 King Edward Avenue FY2 9TA ☎(0253) 351050
Closed 1st 2 wks Jan
Under the same ownership for many years, this well maintained small private hotel is situated a short walk from the Queens Promenade. It offers interesting and inviting public areas which include a comfortable, well appointed lounge, a tramcar-themed bar and neat dining room featuring an extensive collection of teapots. Bedrooms, while well appointed, are generally very compact.
10♠ (4fb) Ⓡ ⚦ (ex guide dogs) LDO 3pm
Lic lift ▥, CTV ✗nc3yrs

⊨ ⚦ GH Ⓠ Ⓠ Ⓠ *Lynwood* 38 Osborne Road FY4 1HQ (adjoining promenade, opposite Sandcastle Centre) ☎(0253) 344628
Closed Xmas & New Year
This charming small guest house stands in a side street just off the promenade, opposite the South Pier and Sandcastle Centre. Run with care and dedication by proprietors of many years' standing, it offers meticulously cared for accommodation in compact but comfortably furnished bedrooms equipped with such thoughtful extras as quality toiletries, hairdryers and radios. There is a comfortable little lounge, and good value home-cooked meals are served in the neat dining room.
8rm(1♠) (2fb) ✁ in dining room CTV in all bedrooms Ⓡ ⚦ sB&B£13-£18 sB&B⇄♠£15-£22 dB&B£26-£36 dB&B⇄♠£30-£44 WB&B£80-£100 WBDi£110-£140 LDO breakfast
▥, ✗
Ⓔ

GH Ⓠ *Mimosa Motel* 24A Lonsdale Road FY1 6EE ☎(0253) 341906
A small, modern motel set in a side street not far from the promenade and central pier. Bedrooms all have private bathrooms and TV. Breakfast is delivered to the room each morning as there is no breakfast room. Parking is available at the rear.
15⇄♠ (3fb) CTV in all bedrooms Ⓡ ✳ sB&B⇄♠£16-£30 dB&B⇄♠£30-£40 WB&Bfr£112 LDO 8.30pm
▥, CTV
Credit Cards ❶ ❸ Ⓔ

⊨ ⚦ GH Ⓠ Ⓠ *North Mount Private Hotel* 22 King Edward Avenue FY2 9TD (off Queens Promenade, 1m N of North Pier) ☎(0253) 355937
This delightful semidetached house is situated in a quiet side road close to the seafront and the promenade. It provides a good standard of accommodation, with somewhat compact bedrooms having attractive soft furnishings. There is a comfortable lounge and a pleasant dining room.
8rm (1fb) ✁ in dining room Ⓡ sB&B£14-£16 dB&B£28-£32 WB&B£95-£105 WBDi£115-£125 LDO 3pm
Lic ▥, CTV

GH Ⓠ Ⓠ Ⓠ *The Old Coach House* 50 Dean Street FY4 1BP ☎(0253) 344330
This detached mock-Tudor house dating from 1851, set back from the road and fronted by an attractive garden, is conveniently situated for the South Pier and Sandcastle Centre. Family owned and run, it offers exceptionally well equipped bedrooms and public areas which include a pleasant small dining room and a conservatory lounge overlooking the garden.
5♠ (2fb) ✁ in dining room CTV in all bedrooms Ⓡ T ⚦ (ex guide dogs) ✳ sB&B♠£19.50-£22.50 dB&B♠£39-£45 WB&Bfr£136 WBDifr£178.15 LDO 9pm
Lic ▥,
Credit Cards ❶ ❷ ❸ Ⓔ

⊨ ⚦ GH Ⓠ Ⓠ *Sunny Cliff* 98 Queens Promenade, Northshore FY2 9NS (1.5m N of Tower on A584) ☎(0253) 351155
Etr-9 Nov & 4 days Xmas
Situated overlooking the sea front at the northern end of Queens Promenade, this long-established and friendly guest house is now adding en suite facilities to its compact bedrooms. Attractive public areas comprise a cosy bar, comfortable lounge and well appointed dining room where home-cooked meals are served.
9rm(8♠) (3fb) ✁ in dining room CTV in 8 bedrooms Ⓡ sB&B£15-£18 sB&B♠£17.50-£21 dB&B♠£35-£42 WB&Bfr£119 WBDi£137-£155 LDO 5pm
Lic CTV
Ⓔ

SELECTED

GH [Q][Q][Q][Q] Sunray 42 Knowle Avenue, Queens Promenade FY2 9TQ (from Tower, head N along Prom turning right at Uncle Toms Cabin, hotel 300yds on left)
☎(0253) 351937
Closed 15 Dec-5 Jan
This well maintained guest house, fronted by an attractive small garden and situated in a quiet residential area within walking distance of both seafront and golf course, has been extending a warm welcome to guests for many years. Bedrooms are comfortable and offer a host of extras which includes toiletries and biscuits; the cosy lounge provides books, magazines and games, and a set home-cooked meal is served at 5.30 each evening in the neatly appointed dining room.
9rm(1🛁8🚿) (2fb)CTV in all bedrooms Ⓡ **T** sB&B🛁🚿£24-£28 dB&B🛁🚿£48-£56 WB&B£144-£168 WBDi£204-£228 LDO 3pm
🅿 CTV
Credit Cards [1][2][3][£]

🛏☕ **GH [Q][Q] Surrey House Hotel** 9 Northumberland Avenue FY2 9SB (continue along Prom to Gynn Sq roundabout leading to Queens Prom, hotel is on fifth rd after roundabout)
☎(0253) 351743
Unpretentious accommodation is provided by this long-established guest house which stands in a side street close to the seafront to the north of the town. Bedrooms (all of which are equipped with hairdryers) vary in size, while public areas include a choice of lounges and a light, spacious dining room.
12rm(2🛁9🚿) (2fb) 🚭 in dining room Ⓡ sB&B£15-£22 sB&B🛁🚿£15-£22 dB&B£30-£44 dB&B🛁🚿£30-£44 WB&B£105-£154 WBDi£140-£189 LDO 4.30pm
🅿 CTV table tennis pool table

GH [Q][Q] ***The Windsor & Westmorland Hotel*** 256 Queens Promenade FY2 9HB ☎(0253) 354974
Located in a select area of the promenade, this canopied, licensed hotel is situated on the North Shore with many of its rooms overlooking the sea. The majority also have en suite facilities, and all have colour TV, radio and tea-making facilities. There is a lift to all floors.
32rm(26🛁🚿) (13fb) CTV in 31 bedrooms Ⓡ LDO 7pm
Lic lift 🅿 CTV
Credit Cards [1][3]

🛏☕ **GH [Q][Q][Q] Woodleigh Private Hotel** 32 King Edward Avenue, North Shore FY2 9TA ☎(0253) 593624
Mar-Oct
Friendly young owners continue to make improvements at this particularly well cared for private hotel which stands in a quiet area off Queens Promenade. Most bedrooms, though compact, are attractively decorated, well equipped and provided with modern en suite shower rooms, while public areas include an inviting lounge and small, neatly laid out dining room.
10🚿 (2fb) 🚭 in dining room CTV in all bedrooms Ⓡ 🚫🐕 sB&B🚿£15-£18 dB&B🚿£30-£36 WB&B£105-£126 WBDi£130-£140 LDO 2pm
🅿 CTV 🚫P
[£]

BLACKWOOD Gwent — Map 03 ST19

INN[Q][Q] ***Plas*** Gordon Road NP2 1D ☎(0495) 224674
Originally a farmhouse, this family-run inn stands above the town and has good views of the valley. Bedrooms are attractive and well equipped, and the bars are full of character, with stone walls and an inglenook fireplace.
6rm(4🚿) (1fb) CTV in 6 bedrooms Ⓡ LDO 9.45pm
🅿
Credit Cards [1][3][5]

BLAGDON Avon — Map 03 ST55

INN[Q][Q] ***Seymour Arms*** Bath Road BS18 6TH ☎(0761) 462279
This small, friendly Victorian inn is situated in the heart of the village on the main Bath road, in an elevated position overlooking Blagdon lake. The simply styled bedrooms are comfortable and well equipped and there is a welcoming bar with a good range of home-made bar food served in generous portions. The location alone makes this an ideal spot for a stop-over or pub meal.
4rm(3🚿) (1fb) CTV in all bedrooms Ⓡ 🚫🐕 (ex guide dogs) LDO 9.30pm
🅿

BLAIR ATHOLL Tayside *Perthshire* — Map 14 NN86

SELECTED

🛏☕ **GH [Q][Q][Q][Q] Dalgreine** Bridge of Tilt PH18 5SX
☎(0796) 481276
6rm(2🚿) (1fb) 🚭 Ⓡ sB&B£13.50-£15.50 sB&B🚿£15-£22 dB&B£27-£31 dB&B🚿£30-£34 LDO 3pm
CTV small snooker table

GH [Q][Q][Q] The Firs Saint Andrews Crescent PH18 5TA
☎(0796) 481256
Etr-late Oct
This substantial period house is set in its own gardens in a quiet residential area well off the main street in the centre of the village. Appealingly decorated and furnished to reflect the traditional character of the house, it provides pretty bedrooms, some with their original fireplaces, a cosy lounge with a log fire and a small dining room where smoking is prohibited, as it is in the bedrooms.

▶

4⇌♠ (2fb) ✗ in bedrooms ✗ in dining room CTV in all bedrooms ® ✳ dB&B⇌♠£35-£37 WB&B£115.50-£122.50 WBDi£182-£192.50 LDO 5pm
▥

BLAIRGOWRIE Tayside *Perthshire*   Map **15** NO14

GH Q|Q|Q **Duncraggan** Perth Road PH10 6EJ ☎(0250) 872082
Closed 26 Sep-Oct & 25 Dec
3rm(2♠) ✗ in bedrooms CTV in 1 bedroom ® 🔥 (ex guide dogs) ✳ sB&B£15.50-£16 sB&B♠fr£18 dB&Bfr£32 dB&B♠fr£36 WB&B£95-£109 WBDi£137-£143 LDO 5pm
▥ CTV ♨
£

GH Q|Q|Q **Ivybank House** Boat Brae, Rattray PH10 7BH
☎(0250) 873056
Ivybank lies in its own grounds, off the main road, and offers superior accommodation reflecting the Victorian character of the house. Some bedrooms retain beautiful Victorian fireplaces and there is a small lounge for guests to use.
5rm(3⇌♠) (2fb) CTV in 6 bedrooms ® LDO 6pm
▥ CTV ♨(hard)
Credit Cards 2

GH Q|Q|Q **The Laurels** Golf Course Road, Rosemount
PH10 6LH (S on A93) ☎(0250) 874920
Closed Dec
This modern stone house is well maintained throughout. The bright, airy bedrooms have white furniture, trouser presses and hair dryers, and thoughtful extras such as cotton wool balls and tissues are provided. Four of the bedrooms have top-quality en suites with power showers. There is a comfortable lounge and small dining room, offering a good range of dishes at both dinner and breakfast and a selection of wines, beers and spirits is available.
6rm(4♠) ® 🔥 ✳ sB&Bfr£17.50 dB&Bfr£30 dB&B♠fr£35 LDO 5.45pm
Lic ▥ CTV
Credit Cards 1 2 3 5

🚾 ▉ **GH** Q|Q|Q **Norwood House** Park Drive PH10 6PA
☎(0250) 874146
Louise and Bob Grant's late Victorian villa has been sympathetically modernised, while retaining lovely original features like the fine woodwork, ornate ceiling cornices and original fireplaces in the bedrooms. The attractive lounge is well supplied with books, magazines and games. The dining room has French windows opening on to the patio and garden. All the accommodation is beautifully maintained and there is space for car parking.
4rm (1fb) ✗ ® sB&B£14-£15 dB&B£28-£30 WB&B£87.50-£94.50 WBDi£126-£143.50 LDO 4.30pm
▥ CTV
£

GH Q|Q|Q **Rosebank House** Balmoral Road PH10 7AF (through town to traffic lights, cross bridge then take second turning on left)
☎(0250) 872912
last wk Jan-Oct
A detached Georgian house is set in its own gardens, well back from the A93 on the northern side of town. A commendable emphasis is put on housekeeping, hospitality and food by owners Charles and Sue Collings, and guests are nicely cosseted. The bright, airy bedrooms vary in size, and a large room downstairs serves as lounge and dining area. Sue Collings's cooking has won much praise.
7rm(5♠) (2fb) ® 🔥 (ex guide dogs) LDO 7pm
Lic ▥ CTV nc10yrs

BLAKENEY Gloucestershire

See **Lydney**

BLAKENEY Norfolk   Map **09** TG04

GH Q|Q **Flintstones** Wiveton NR25 7TL (off A148 at Letheringsett onto B1156 then 3m on left) ☎Cley(0263) 740337
Closed 25 & 26 Dec
Flintstones is a proudly maintained house located near the pub in the quiet village of Wiveton. A breakfast room is provided, where dinner is also served.
5♠ (3fb) ✗ CTV in all bedrooms ® ✳ dB&B♠£31-£36 WB&B£108.50 WBDi£178.50 LDO 5pm
Lic ▥

BLANDFORD FORUM Dorset   Map **03** ST80

GH Q|Q|Q **Fairfield House** Church Road DT11 8UB (in village of Pimperne, near A354) ☎(0258) 456756 FAX (0258) 480053
An attractive Georgian house is quietly located along a country lane, surrounded by its own well kept gardens. Bedrooms are freshly decorated, bright and well equipped with modern facilities. Two further rooms have been added, both spacious, with a shared bathroom just across the hall; one bedroom is well equipped for disabled guests and is located in the stable block. There is a cosy lounge complete with piano, games and books. A select à la carte menu is served in the restaurant, which is open to non-residents and is gaining a good local reputation.
5⇌♠ (1fb) ✗ in bedrooms ✗ in dining room CTV in all bedrooms ® (ex guide dogs) sB&B⇌♠£39.50-£42.50 dB&B⇌♠£64-£70 LDO 9pm
Lic ▥ U clay shooting instruction
Credit Cards 1 2 3 5 £

BLICKLING Norfolk   Map **09** TG12

INN Q|Q|Q **Buckinghamshire Arms Hotel** Blickling, Aylsham NR11 6NF ☎Aylsham(0263) 732133
Situated at the gates of Bickling Hall, this National Trust property offers well equipped guest rooms, all with trouser presses and hair dryers, four-poster or tester beds and comfortable leather armchairs. Originally an inn dating from the 17th century, it has a popular bar and restaurant.
3rm(1♠) (1fb) ✗ in dining room CTV in all bedrooms ® T 🔥 (ex guide dogs) ✳ sB&B♠£45 dB&B♠£60 WB&B£200-£315 Lunch £12.50-£15 Dinner £14-£20alc LDO 9.30pm
♪
Credit Cards 1 3 5 £

BLOCKLEY Gloucestershire   Map **04** SP13

BOAT OF GARTEN Highland *Inverness-shire*   Map **14** NH91

SELECTED

GH Q Q Q Q **Heathbank The Victorian House** PH24 3BD
☎(0479) 831234
Closed Nov & 1-25 Dec
Set in its own garden on the fringe of the village, Heathbank is a Victorian house of considerable character and charm. A genuine welcoming atmosphere prevails and everywhere you will find parts of a fascinating collection of bric-a-brac and objets d'art. Each bedroom has its own colour scheme, like the gold and blue room, with its lovely Edwardian open-work bedspread and collection of framed hats. Other rooms have a Victorian look and two rooms on the top floor are different again, decorated in pastel tones with views over the Abernethy Forest RSPB Reserve and the Cairngorms. The cosy lounge has books, magazines and board games. The set four-course menu is prepared from good local produce and dinner is served in the lovely Victorian dining room.
7rm(6⇌5♠) (1fb) ⍻ CTV in all bedrooms ® ♨ (ex guide dogs) sB&B£20-£40 sB&B⇌♠£22-£44 dB&B£40-£44 dB&B⇌♠£44-£68 WB&B£140-£238 WBDi£252-£350 LDO 6pm
Lic ▥ CTV

GH Q Q Q **Moorfield House Hotel** Deshar Road PH24 3BN
☎(0479) 831646
Dedicated owners Ron and Liz Gould continue to improve standards at their delightful detached Victorian house in the centre of the village. The lounge has had a face-lift, and guests can relax here with refreshments from the dispense bar. Enjoyable home cooking is served in the neat dining room adjacent. The bedrooms vary in size and have both modern and traditional appointments.
4rm(1⇌3♠) (1fb) ⍻ CTV in all bedrooms ® sB&B⇌♠£21 dB&B⇌♠£36 WB&B£126 WBDi£196 LDO 3pm
Lic ▥ CTV nc14yrs
£

BODENHAM Hereford & Worcester   Map **03** SO55

FH Q Q Q Mr & Mrs P J Edwards **Maund Court** *(SO561505)*
HR1 3JA (E of Leominster, just off A417) ☎(056884) 282
Closed Dec-Jan
An attractive and well maintained creeper-clad farmhouse dating from the 15th century and set in very pleasant gardens, complete with an outdoor swimming pool and croquet. Many old beams and exposed timbers are still to be seen in the house, where bedrooms are well equipped. There is a comfortable residents' lounge, which contains many maps and other tourist information, and owners Pauline and Raymond Edwards extend a warm welcome to their visitors.
4rm(3⇌1♠) ⍻ in dining room CTV in all bedrooms ® ✳
sB&B⇌♠fr£17 dB&B⇌♠fr£34 WB&B£110
▥ CTV ⚭(heated) croquet 130 acres mixed

BODLE STREET GREEN East Sussex   Map **05** TQ61

FH Q Q Mr & Mrs P Gentry **Stud** *(TQ652144)* BN27 4RJ (from Hailsham A271 turn left at Windmill Hill signposted Bodle Street, to White Horse Pub, take right fork signed Woods Corner, farm is 1.5m on left) ☎Herstmonceux(0323) 833201
Closed Xmas
Set in 70 acres of farmland, accommodation in this simply furnished farmhouse consists of three bedrooms, one with an en suite shower room, the others sharing an old-fashioned bathroom. There is a comfortable lounge with a TV, and breakfast is served in the sun lounge.
3rm(1♠) ⍻ in bedrooms CTV in all bedrooms ® ♨ sB&B£22-£25 dB&B£34-£38 WB&B£119-£154 WBDi£178.50-£213.50
▥ CTV 70 acres cattle sheep

BODMIN Cornwall & Isles of Scilly   Map **02** SX06

GH Q Q Q **Mount Pleasant Moorland Hotel** Mount PL30 4EX
(off A30) ☎Cardinham(01208) 821342
Apr-Sep
Five miles east of Bodmin, this 17th-century Cornish stone and slate farmhouse is situated on the edge of the moor. The majority of the light, airy bedrooms have en suite facilities. Full English breakfast, including home-produced, free-range eggs, is served in the dining room, and a traditional home-cooked set dinner is offered each evening.
7rm(1⇌5♠) (1fb) ⍻ in bedrooms ⍻ in dining room ⍻ in 1 lounge ® ✳ sB&B£16-£17.50 dB&B⇌♠£35-£38 WBDi£140-£169 LDO 5pm
Lic ▥ CTV nc5yrs
£

SELECTED

FH Q Q Q Q Mrs P A Smith **Treffry** Lanhydrock PL30 5AF (take B3268 from Bodmin towards Lostwithiel, after 2.5m at mini roundabout turn right and farm is 300yds on the right) ☎(0208) 74405 FAX (0208) 74405
Closed Xmas & New Year rs 20 Oct-Mar
Sixteenth-century granite-built Treffry was originally the home farm of the Lanhydrock Estate, which now belongs to the National Trust (the main house is just 300yds away). There are three bedrooms here, one of which has a four-poster bed, and all are very prettily decorated with coordinating soft furnishings and hand-made pine furniture. A comfortable drawing room has large sofas and wood-panelled walls, and meals are taken in the sunny restaurant. Home produced and locally grown food is used as much as possible. The farmhouse ▶

FAIRFIELD HOUSE

English Tourist Board
HIGHLY COMMENDED   En Suite Accommodation
&
Licensed à la carte Restaurant   **AA** QQQ

Full disabled facilities   All major credit cards accepted

Frances and Alan Bromley extend you a warm welcome to their distinctive, Grade II, Georgian Manor House set in 1.5 acres of gardens and a peaceful village. The bedrooms are tastefully furnished carefully retaining much antiquity whilst offering modern en-suite facilities. Accessible to all the fine Dorset coast/beaches/ countryside and the abundant Historical Heritage of Dorset. The 'Fairfield' restaurant serves cream teas, Sunday lunch and 'à la carte' evening dinner from 7pm (last order 9.00). Stables, Riding, Clay shooting and Golf arranged on request.

CHURCH ROAD, PIMPERNE,
(A354) BLANDFORD FORUM,
DORSET DT11 8UB
Telephone: 01258 456756 Fax: 01258 480053

stands in established gardens and play areas which it shares with eight self-catering cottages.

3rm(2♜) ⚹ CTV in all bedrooms Ⓡ ⋊ (ex guide dogs) dB&B♜£37-£38 WB&B£122-£125

▥ CTV nc6yrs nature trail woodland play area 200 acres dairy Ⓛ

BOLLINGTON Cheshire　　　Map **07** SJ97

INN|Q|Q| *Turners Arms Hotel* 1 Ingersley Road SK10 5RE
☎(0625) 573864

This small stone-built inn has a friendly, informal atmosphere and a choice of bars. It stands in a residential area on the Pott Shrigley/Whaley Bridge road at the edge of town. Bedrooms have modern furnishings and equipment, and good-value, wholesome food is served in the dining room.

8rm(2⇄3♜) (2fb) CTV in all bedrooms Ⓡ LDO 9.30pm

▥ pool darts

Credit Cards |1||2||3|

BOLTON Greater Manchester　　　Map **07** SD70

GH|Q|Q|Q| **Broomfield Hotel** 33-35 Wigan Road, Deane
BL3 5PX ☎(0204) 61570 FAX (0204) 650932

Considerable improvements have been made to this hotel, enhancing the quality throughout. Bedrooms, including ground floor rooms, are modern, and there is a small lounge, a lounge bar and an attractive cottage-style breakfast room.

15⇄♜ (1fb) ⚹ in 2 bedrooms ⚹ in dining room ⚹ in 1 lounge CTV in all bedrooms Ⓡ ⚹ sB&B♜£26-£28.50 dB&B♜£38-£40 WB&Bfr£175 LDO 9pm

Lic ▥

Credit Cards |1||2||3|

BOLTONGATE Cumbria　　　Map **11** NY24

P R E M I E R　❦　**S E L E C T E D**

GH|Q|Q|Q|Q|Q| **The Old
Rectory** CA5 1DA ☎Low
Ireby(06973) 71647
FAX (06973) 71798
Mar-Nov

This delightful house in a hamlet with rural views towards the Lakeland hills, is the home of Kathleen and Anthony Peacock. Part of the

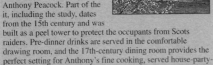

it, including the study, dates from the 15th century and was built as a peel tower to protect the occupants from Scots raiders. Pre-dinner drinks are served in the comfortable drawing room, and the 17th-century dining room provides the perfect setting for Anthony's fine cooking, served house-party-style at a large polished oak table. The bedrooms are decorated and furnished to the highest standard.

3rm(2♜) ⚹ Ⓡ ⋊ (ex guide dogs) ⚹ dB&B♜£68-£70 WB&B£238-£245 WBDi£377.65-£384.65 LDO 4pm

Lic ▥ CTV nc14yrs

Credit Cards |1||3|Ⓛ

BO'NESS Central *West Lothian*　　　Map **11** NS98

FH|Q|Q|Q| Mrs B Kirk *Kinglass (NT006803)* Borrowstoun Road
EH51 9RW (off B903) ☎(0506) 822861 & 824185
FAX (0506) 824433

A friendly farm guest house with splendid views across the Firth of Forth stands to the south of the town, convenient for junction 3 of the M9 and popular with regular business guests as well as tourists. Brightly decorated and well equipped bedrooms include

---

two which are in an adjacent private bungalow.

6rm(2♜) (1fb) CTV in all bedrooms Ⓡ T LDO 5.30pm

Lic ▥ CTV 750 acres arable

BONSALL Derbyshire　　　Map **08** SK25

GH|Q|Q|Q| **Sycamore** 76 High Street, Town Head DE4 2AR
☎Wirksworth(0629) 823903

Guests can relax on the front lawn of this 18th-century house which enjoys an elevated position overlooking the village. There is a choice of meals in the evening and prepared lunches are available.

5rm(3⇄1♜) (1fb) ⚹ in bedrooms ⚹ in dining room CTV in all bedrooms Ⓡ ⋊ (ex guide dogs) ⚹ sB&B£25-£30 dB&B♜£40-£44 LDO noon

Lic ▥ nc10yrs
Ⓛ

GH|Q|Q|Q| *Town Head Farmhouse* 70 High Street DE4 2AR
☎Wirksworth(0629) 823762

Tastefully converted and modernised in keeping with its 18th-century character, this house and its outbuildings are built around a small cottage garden and sited at the top of the town.

6♜ CTV in all bedrooms Ⓡ
▥ CTV nc6yrs

BONTDDU Gwynedd　　　Map **06** SH61

P R E M I E R　❦　**S E L E C T E D**

GH|Q|Q|Q|Q|Q| **Borthwnog
Hall Hotel** LL40 2TT (on A496)
☎(01341) 430271
FAX (01341) 430682
Closed Xmas

Beautifully situated overlooking the Mawddach estuary, this impressive Regency country house is perfectly preserved. Bedrooms are provided with many thoughtful extras and the public rooms are delightfully furnished and filled with antiques and excellent paintings. The comfortable lounge has an open fire on cooler evenings, and an extensive range of dishes is available in the elegant restaurant. A library art gallery is incorporated into the hotel.

3⇄♜ ⚹ in dining room ⚹ in lounges CTV in all bedrooms Ⓡ LDO 8.15pm

Lic ▥

Credit Cards |1||3|

BOROUGHBRIDGE North Yorkshire　　　Map **08** SE36

S E L E C T E D

INN|Q|Q|Q| *The Crown* Roecliffe YO5 9LY
☎(0423) 322578 FAX (0423) 324060

The Crown is a delightful country inn in an attractive village setting about a mile from Boroughbridge and the A1. All bedrooms are modern in style and facilities. An extensive range of meals is served in the beamed bar, or in the more formal restaurant from Tuesday to Saturday evenings. There are also facilities for weddings, conferences and other functions.

12⇄♜ CTV in all bedrooms Ⓡ T LDO 9.30pm
▥ ♨ ♪

Credit Cards |1||3|

BORROWDALE Cumbria   Map **11** NY21

SELECTED

GH Ⓠ Ⓠ Ⓠ Ⓠ **Greenbank** CA12 5UY (3m S of Keswick on B5289) ☎(07687) 77215
Closed 1 Jan-2 Feb & 4-31 Dec
This beautifully situated Lakeland house has excellent views over the Borrowdale Valley. The house stands in its own well kept grounds and gardens and is delightfully furnished, offering two comfortable lounges, one with colour TV, both with inviting log fires. Bedrooms have pine furniture and are prettily decorated and furnished with matching fabrics. All are en suite. A well produced five-course dinner prepared by Mrs Lorton is served each evening.
10rm(9⇉1♠) (1fb) ⊁ in bedrooms ⊁ in dining room Ⓡ 🍴
sB&B⇌♠£25 dB&B⇌♠£44-£50 WB&B£126-£147 WBDi£210-£231 LDO 5pm
Lic ▥ CTV
ⓔ

SELECTED

GH Ⓠ Ⓠ Ⓠ Ⓠ **Hazel Bank** Rosthwaite CA12 5XB (6m from Keswick on B5289 Seatoller road, turn left at sign just before Rosthwaite village) ☎(07687) 77248
Closed Dec-Feb rs Mar & Nov
This is a magical Victorian house standing in four acres of gardens and woodland overlooking Rosthwaite village and the Borrowdale Valley. With excellent good taste John and Gwen Nuttall have furnished and decorated their house, keeping the grace and character of the place. Bedrooms are very comfortable and one has a four-poster bed. The sitting room looks out over the garden and John Nuttall serves four-course set dinners in the elegant dining room.
6⇌♠ ⊁ CTV in all bedrooms Ⓡ sB&B⇌♠£43
dB&B⇌♠£86 (incl dinner) WBDi£265 LDO 7pm
Lic ▥ nc6yrs
Credit Cards ① ③ ⓔ

BORTH Dyfed   Map **06** SN68

GH Ⓠ Ⓠ Ⓠ **Glanmor Hotel** Princess Street SY24 5JP (turn off A487 onto B4353 signposted Borth, Glanhoe is situated at N end of sea front) ☎(0970) 871689
The Elliot family run this friendly guest house, just across the road from the sandy beach and close to the golf course. Four of the bedrooms have sea views. Separate tables are provided in the dining room and there is a bar in the lounge.
7rm(2♠) (3fb)CTV in 4 bedrooms Ⓡ sB&B£18.50 dB&B£37
dB&B♠£37 WB&B£129.50 WBDi£189 LDO 5pm
Lic CTV
ⓔ

BOSCASTLE Cornwall & Isles of Scilly   Map **02** SX09

GH Ⓠ Ⓠ Ⓠ *Melbourne House* New Road PL35 0DH
☎(0840) 250650
Within half a mile of the historic harbour, this fine Georgian house has excellent views of the Jordan Valley. The house is attractively furnished, retaining much of its original character, including a fine tiled entrance hall. Bedrooms are individually furnished and have colour TV, tea and coffee making equipment and en suite shower facilities or sole use of a bathroom with WC. There is a comfortable lounge and a well furnished dining room. The atmosphere is peaceful and relaxing, and there is plenty of car parking space.
6rm(3♠) CTV in all bedrooms Ⓡ LDO 6pm
Lic ▥ nc7yrs
Credit Cards ① ③

🖂 🛏 GH Ⓠ Ⓠ Ⓠ Ⓠ **Old Coach House** Tintagel Road PL35 0AS (at junct of B3266 and B3263) ☎(0840) 250398
Closed 23 Dec-2 Jan rs Nov-Mar
Situated on the Tintagel road at the top end of Boscastle village, this 300-year-old property has been carefully restored and converted to provide bedrooms with private baths or shower rooms. Two of these are on the ground floor and offer facilities for the disabled. The sunny conservatory to the rear of the house is used as a dining room, and there is a comfortable lounge with an open fire and lots of tourist information.
6rm(1⇌5♠) (1fb) ⊁ in dining room ⊁ in lounges CTV in all bedrooms Ⓡ 🍴 (ex guide dogs) sB&B⇌♠£15-£24
dB&B⇌♠£30-£48
▥ nc6yrs
Credit Cards ① ② ③ ⓔ

GH Ⓠ Ⓠ Ⓠ **St Christophers Country House Hotel** High St
PL35 0BD ☎(0840) 250412
Closed Jan & Feb
The warmest of welcomes awaits guests at St Christophers, and many return regularly for the home cooked food and relaxing atmosphere. All of the bedrooms have en suite or private facilities, and there is a comfortable lounge with jigsaw puzzles and reading materials in case the weather is unkind. Menus, based on local produce wherever possible, offer a choice at breakfast and dinner.
9rm(7♠) ⊁ in dining room CTV in all bedrooms Ⓡ ✳
sB&B♠£17.50-£18.50 dB&B♠£35-£37 WBDi£171-£178 LDO 8pm
Lic ▥ CTV nc12yrs
Credit Cards ① ③ ⓔ

SELECTED

GH Q Q Q Q **Tolcarne House Hotel & Restaurant**
Tintagel Road PL35 0AS (at junct of B3266/B3263)
☎(0840) 250654
Mar-Oct rs Nov & Feb
Tolcarne Hotel is a charming detached Victorian residence in
its own large garden looking down the valley to the sea. New
owners, the Crown family, are considerably upgrading the
property and are confidently expecting to improve their AA
'Q' rating. Bedrooms are decorated and furnished to a high
standard and offer many modern facilities. There is a
comfortable lounge with an open fire, and a separate bar ideal
for pre-dinner drinks. A choice of menus is offered at dinner.
9rm(8⇔7ℝ) (1fb) ⊁ in 4 bedrooms ⊁ in dining room CTV in
all bedrooms ℝ sB&B£17-£19 dB&B⇔ℝ£38-£54
WB&B£130-£160 WBDi£160-£220 LDO 9pm
Lic ▥ croquet
Credit Cards ① ③ ⓔ

SELECTED

✉ ▣ **FH** Q Q Q Q Mr & Mrs Nicholls **Trerosewill**
(SX095905) Paradise PL35 0DL ☎(0840) 250545
Closed 16 Dec-9 Jan
This recently built farmhouse is set in an elevated position
with glorious views across country to the sea. It offers a
winning combination of modern facilities and the warm
hospitality of Cheryl and Stephen Nicholls. The tastefully
decorated bedrooms are all en suite, and lots of thoughtful
extras are provided. There is a comfortable lounge with a
wood-burning stove and plenty of books and games. Cheryl is
an honest cook, using the best of fresh ingredients, and dinner
is available by arrangement. Guests are respectfully asked not
to smoke in the house.
7rm(6⇔9ℝ) (2fb) ⊁ CTV in all bedrooms ℝ T ⊀ (ex guide
dogs) sB&B£15-£19 dB&B⇔ℝ£32-£46 WB&B£100-£157.50
WBDi£195-£250 LDO 7pm
Lic ▥ CTV 92 acres dairy
ⓔ

BOSHAM West Sussex | **Map 04** SU80

P R E M I E R 🏵 S E L E C T E D

GH Q Q Q Q Q **Kenwood**
Off A259 PO18 8PH
☎(0243) 572727
FAX (0243) 572738
A mid-Victorian country house
set in three acres of mature
grounds. Individually
furnished spacious bedrooms
all have direct-dial telephone,
TV, clock radio and tea trays,
and two rooms are on the
ground floor. Some bedrooms

have distant harbour views, and one has a four-poster bed
dated 1760. The very comfortable lounge has a fine carved
log-burning fireplace, and there is a conservatory breakfast
room. Ample car parking is provided.
3⇔9ℝ (1fb) ⊁ in dining room CTV in all bedrooms ℝ T ⊀
(ex guide dogs) dB&B⇔ℝ£40-£45 WB&B£140-£160
▥ CTV ⚘ (heated) fitness equipment pool table

BOURNEMOUTH Dorset | **Map 04** SZ09
See also Christchurch and Poole

GH Q Q Q Q *Alum Grange Hotel* 1 Burnaby Road, Alum Chine
BH4 8JF ☎(0202) 761195
Closed Nov
This neat and well presented guesthouse is located in Alum Chine,
250 yards from the beach and promenade. The 14 bedrooms are
spacious and well equipped with TV, clock radio and tea trays; one
room has a four-posted bed together with a balcony and fine sea
views, and some rooms are reserved for non-smokers. Public areas
are nicely appointed and there is a well stocked bar and pool table.
Resident proprietor Mrs Hoath cooks the evening meal, offering a
daily varied table d'hôte menu together with a short à la carte
selection.
14rm(5⇔7ℝ) (7fb) CTV in all bedrooms ℝ LDO noon
Lic ▥ CTV
Credit Cards ③

✉ ▣ **GH** Q Q Q **Amitie** 1247 Christchurch Road BH7 6BP
☎(0202) 427255
A warm welcome is assured at this personally run and very well
presented establishment. Bedrooms are attractive with fresh decor
and modern facilities. Treasures from far and wide adorn the cosy
breakfast room where a hearty breakfast is served.
8rm(5⇔ℝ) CTV in all bedrooms ℝ ⊀ (ex guide dogs)
sB&B£13-£14 dB&B£26-£28 dB&B⇔ℝ£30-£34 WB&B90-
£98
▥
ⓔ

SELECTED

GH Q Q Q Q **The Boltons Hotel** 9 Durley Chine Road
South, West Cliff BH2 5JT ☎(0202) 751517
FAX (0202) 751629
Feb-Dec
In a convenient position, close to the West Cliff and only a
short distance from the town and the beaches, this personally
managed hotel offers a peaceful setting, a relaxed atmosphere
and very well appointed accommodation. Public areas include a
well appointed lounge area, a cosy bar with horse racing
memorabilia and a bright dining room.
12⇔ℝ (2fb) ⊁ in dining room CTV in all bedrooms ℝ T
sB&B⇔ℝ£24-£27 dB&B⇔ℝ£48-£54 WB&B£125-£155
WBDi£155-£190 LDO 7pm
Lic ▥ CTV nc3yrs ⚘(heated)
Credit Cards ① ③

GH Q Q Q **Cairnsmore Hotel** 37 Beaulieu Road, Alum Chine
BH4 8HY ☎(0202) 763705
Many guests return regularly to enjoy the warm atmosphere and
easy friendliness of this attractive, personally managed hotel.
Individually styled en suite bedrooms are well presented, and a
couple of them are furnished with four-poster beds. Comfortable
public areas are pleasantly appointed; the refurbished bar has a
cosy air, and a fine collection of teapots adorns the dining room.
Both forecourt and street parking are available.
10rm(9⇔ℝ) (1fb) ⊁ in dining room CTV in all bedrooms ℝ
dB&B⇔ℝ£30-£42 WB&B£92-£148 WBDi£127-£163 LDO 4pm
Lic ▥ nc5yrs
Credit Cards ① ③ ⓔ

GH Q Q Q **Carisbrooke Hotel** 42 Tregonwell Road BH2 5NT
☎(0202) 290432 FAX (0202) 310499
Enjoying a central location on the West Cliff and within walking
distance of the BIC, Winter Gardens, seafront and shops, this
private hotel is well presented and professionally managed.
Modern and bright in style, the bedrooms have fresh, bright decor,
and modern en suite facilities (mostly shower rooms). Public areas
include a cosy well stocked bar, pretty dining room where evening
meals are served, and a comfortable lounge. Some front forecourt
parking is provided.

22rm(19🛁🚿) (6fb)CTV in all bedrooms [R] **T** sB&B£17-£27 sB&B🛁🚿£20-£37 dB&B🛁🚿£33-£54 WB&B£100-£175 WBDi£135-£210 LDO 7pm
Lic ▦ CTV
Credit Cards [1][2][3][5][£]

GH [Q][Q][Q] Cherry View Hotel 66 Alum Chine Road BH4 8DZ
☎(0202) 760910
Comfortable and spotlessly maintained accommodation is offered at this family-owned hotel, which is fairly near Alum Chine and Westbourne. Each room has en suite facilities, mostly showers, and there is a tiny lounge, a smart bar, and a front-facing dining room where home-cooked evening meals are served.
11rm(1🛁10🚿) (1fb) 🚭 in 6 bedrooms 🚭 in dining room CTV in all bedrooms [R] 🐕 sB&B🛁🚿£22.50-£30 dB&B🛁🚿£30-£40 WB&B£108-£138 WBDi£150-£180 LDO 4pm
Lic ▦ nc7yrs
Credit Cards [1][2][3][5][£]

SELECTED

GH [Q][Q][Q][Q] Cliff House Hotel 113 Alumhurst Road BH4 8HS ☎(0202) 763003
Mar-Nov & Xmas
The friendly and warm welcome that proprietors Letty and Alex Clark extend to their guests ensure that many of them return year after year to stay at this attractive hotel. Cliff House occupies an elevated position on the clifftop at Alum Chine. The bedrooms are neat, bright and very well presented. Some of the bedrooms have balconies and many of them enjoy superb views far out to sea. The public areas are spacious and there is a warm friendly atmosphere about the place. The licensed restaurant serves home cooked meals with a choice at each course, which must be ordered in advance. Car parking is provided at the hotel.
12rm(2🛁10🚿) (4fb) 🚭 in dining room CTV in all bedrooms [R] 🐕 sB&B£25 sB&B🛁🚿£25-£29 dB&B🛁🚿£50-£60 WB&B£175-£210 WBDi£200-£235 LDO 6.30pm
Lic lift ▦ nc7yrs snooker

GH [Q][Q][Q] Cransley Private Hotel 11 Knyveton Road, East Cliff BH1 3QG (turn off A338 at St Paul's roundabout by ASDA Store, continue over first roundabout Knyveton Rd is the first on the left) ☎(0202) 290067
Etr-Oct
A small private hotel situated in a tree-lined avenue on the East Cliff, in a residential area. Well run by the charming proprietors Mr and Mrs Wilson, many improvements have been implemented and are planned to continue, ensuring that high standards are maintained. Bedrooms are nicely decorated and comfortable, all except one single room having private bathrooms. There is a well furnished lounge where a pot of tea is served on arrival, and a set home-cooked meal is served in the dining room, which overlooks the well tended gardens.
12rm(5🛁6🚿) 🚭 CTV in all bedrooms [R] 🐕 (ex guide dogs) sB&B£14-£15 sB&B🛁🚿£17-£21 dB&B🛁🚿£34-£42 WB&B£98-£145 WBDi£135-£175 LDO 5pm
Lic
[£]

GH [Q][Q][Q] *Croham Hurst Hotel* 9 Durley Road South BH2 5JH
☎(0202) 552353
Closed Jan rs Feb-Etr
This hotel situated on West Cliff, close to the town centre and theatre as well as beaches, has much to offer. Well presented and equipped bedrooms with modern facilities are complemented by public areas which are both comfortable and smart. Popular lunches are served in the convivial atmosphere of the bar, while dinner is chosen from the varied range of dishes featured on table d'hôte menus. Friendly proprietors are very much involved in the day-to-day running of the hotel.
40🛁🚿 (7fb) CTV in all bedrooms [R] **T** 🐕 LDO 7.15pm
Lic lift ▦
Credit Cards [1][3]

GH [Q][Q][Q] *Dene Court* 19 Boscombe Spa Road BH5 1AR
☎(0202) 394874
In a good location close to the centre of Boscombe and only a short distance from the pier, Dene Court offers bright, freshly decorated bedrooms. There is a comfortable lounge area and sunny dining room where wholesome home-cooked food is served, plus a small games room and a well stocked bar.
16rm(14🛁🚿) (7fb) CTV in all bedrooms [R] 🐕
▦ CTV snooker
Credit Cards [1]

GH [Q][Q][Q] Dorset House 225 Holdenhurst Road BH8 8DD
☎(0202) 397908
Closed 25 Dec
Smoking is now prohibited throughout this guest house which is conveniently located fairly near the railway station on the outskirts of the town centre. Neat, well presented and personally managed by proprietors who continue to make improvements year after year, it attracts regular clients among tourists as well as the commercial guests who provide the bulk of its trade. Parking space is provided.
6rm(2🛁🚿) CTV in all bedrooms [R] 🐕 ✳ sB&B£15-£19 sB&B🛁🚿£18-£20 dB&B£28-£30 dB&B🛁🚿£30-£32 WB&B£105-£126 WBDi£147-£168 LDO 6pm
▦ nc
[£]

GH [Q][Q] Hawaiian Hotel 4 Glen Road BH5 1HR
☎(0202) 393234
mid Apr-mid Oct

▶

Paradise,
Boscastle,
Cornwall
PL35 0DL
Tel/Fax: (01840) 250545

Come down on the farm in this modern farmhouse offering superior bed & breakfast on a working farm and watch milking and feeding of calves. Situated overlooking the picturesque village of Boscastle. All rooms are en suite and have unsurpassed panoramic views of Lundy and North Devon coast. Centrally heated with seasonal log fires. Large garden. Traditional farmhouse fayre, evening meal optional. Strictly no smoking. Special golf packages and Spring/Autumn Breaks.

A loyal clientele returns year after year to this small establishment near Boscombe's shopping area, the pier and beaches. Particularly popular with retired couples, it regularly wins the Saga Holiday award. Some of the bright, fresh and well presented bedrooms have en suite facilities, a comfortable lounge augments the cosy snug bar, and home-cooked meals are served in a neat dining room. Some forecourt car parking is provided.

12rm(8⇔5♠) (3fb) ⚞ in dining room CTV in all bedrooms ® ✹ (ex guide dogs) ✳ sB&B£16.50-£18.50 sB&B⇔♠£18.50-£20 dB&B£33-£36 dB&B⇔♠£37-£39 WB&B£96-£105 WBDi£130-£170 LDO 6pm
Lic ▥ CTV
£

GH Q Q Q Highclere Hotel 15 Burnaby Road BH4 8JF (follow signs for Westbourne then Alum Chine,Earle Rd, Beaulieu Rd or Crosby Rd lead of main road into Burnaby Rd) ☎(0202) 761350
Apr-Sep
A small late Victorian house located in quiet Alum Chine, with private parking, Highclere provides comfortable, adequate bedrooms some of which have sea views. The dining room includes a small bar in one corner and a choice of dishes is available for the evening meal.
9rm(4⇔5♠) (5fb) ⚞ in dining room CTV in all bedrooms ® T LDO 4pm
Lic ▥ CTV nc3yrs
Credit Cards 1 2 3 5 £

GH Q Q Q Q Holmcroft Hotel 5 Earle Road BH4 8JQ
☎(0202) 761289
In a good location, near to Alum Chine, and in a quiet residential area, this neat hotel is well run by its pleasant, caring proprietors. The bedrooms are bright, clean and well equipped. The public rooms are filled with plants, flowers and ornaments giving a warm homely feel to the place. A home cooked evening meal is offered and there is a cosy bar for pre and after dinner drinks.
19⇔♠ (2fb) ⚞ in dining room CTV in all bedrooms ® T sB&B⇔♠£29-£31.50 dB&B⇔♠£58-£63 (incl dinner) WB&B£126-£168 WBDi£167-£189 LDO 5pm
Lic ▥ CTV nc2yrs
Credit Cards 1 3 £

GH Q Q Q Linwood House Hotel 11 Wilfred Road BH5 1ND
☎(0202) 397818
Mar-Oct
In a quiet location between Boscombe, the shops and the sea, this detached house offers very comfortable public areas. The bedrooms are cosy and neat and some of them have sloping roofs and beams. There is an attractive rear garden, and the pleasant proprietors provide a warm and friendly welcome to their guests who return time and time again.
10rm(1⇔7♠) (2fb) ⚞ in dining room CTV in all bedrooms ® dB&B£34-£44 dB&B⇔♠£38-£48 (incl dinner) WB&B£87-£118 WBDi£129-£160 LDO 9.30am
Lic ▥ CTV nc6yrs

GH Q Q Q Lynthwaite Hotel 10 Owls Road BH5 1AF
☎(0202) 398015
A Victorian villa dating back to 1876, conveniently situated for the centre of Boscombe, the pier and seafront. Nicely furnished bedrooms have pretty, bright decor and are well equipped. Public areas are comfortable and include a first-floor lounge and balcony, an attractive dining room and well stocked bar.
14rm(10⇔1♠) (3fb) CTV in all bedrooms ® LDO 5pm
Lic ▥ CTV nc3yrs
Credit Cards 1 2 3

GH Q Q Mae-Mar Hotel 91/95 West Hill Road BH2 5PQ
☎(0202) 553167 FAX (0202) 311919
Convenient for the town, on the West Cliff side, this large guesthouse offers simply furnished en suite bedrooms at moderate prices.

39rm(4⇔25♠) (11fb) ⚞ in area of dining room ⚞ in 1 lounge CTV in all bedrooms ® ✹ sB&B£17.50-£21 sB&B⇔♠£20-£23.50 dB&B£35-£42 dB&B⇔♠£40-£47 WB&B£112.50-£135 WBDi£130-£180 LDO 5.30pm
Lic lift ▥ CTV ⚐
Credit Cards 1 2 3 5 £

▥ ⚑ GH Q Q Q Mayfield Private Hotel 46 Frances Road BH1 3SA ☎(0202) 551839
Closed Dec
A small cosy guesthouse located in a residential area overlooking Knyveton Gardens. It offers comfortable, neat accommodation with a welcoming atmosphere. Some bedrooms have private showers; all have TV and tea trays. Public areas include a bar/dining room, a snug TV lounge and small conservatory-style non-smoking area beyond, all of which feature an unusual collection of kettles, antique cameras and other bric-a-brac. A home-cooked four-course dinner is offered by the friendly proprietors, who enjoy welcoming guests into their home.
8rm(4♠) (1fb) ⚞ in dining room CTV in all bedrooms ® ✹ sB&B£13-£15 dB&B£26-£30 dB&B♠£31.50-£35.50 WB&B£84-£91 WBDi£105-£126 LDO 9am
Lic ▥ CTV nc7yrs
£

GH Q Q New Dorchester Hotel 64 Lansdowne Road North BH1 1RS ☎(0202) 551271
Closed 24 Dec-4 Jan
Accomodation is comfortable at this large detached Victorian villa on the Lansdowne road with modern, well maintained bedrooms, a small, cosy lounge and a nicely appointed dining room overlooking a pretty garden. Parking is ample.
8rm(3⇔2♠) CTV in all bedrooms ® ✹ LDO 6pm
Lic ▥ nc12yrs
Credit Cards 1 2 3 5

GH Q Q Q Newfield Private Hotel 29 Burnaby Road BH4 8JF ☎(0202) 762724
A neat, homely establishment located at Alum Chine, in the more residential part of the town, offers accommodation in brightly decorated, comfortable bedrooms; those at the top of the house have the most character, with their sloping ceilings and views across rooftops towards the sea. The lounge has a relaxed, informal atmosphere, and there is also a cosy bar area in one corner of the dining room where guests enjoy a home-cooked evening meal.
11rm(1⇔7♠) (4fb) ⚞ in dining room CTV in all bedrooms ® sB&B£17-£22 dB&B£34-£44 dB&B⇔♠£37-£47 WB&B£115-£145 WBDi£155-£190 LDO 2pm
Lic ▥ CTV
Credit Cards 1 2 3 £

GH Q Q Q Northover Private Hotel 10 Earle Road BH4 8JQ
☎(0202) 767349
In a quiet residential area close to Alum Chine, this personally managed establishment offers well presented bedrooms, the majority with en suite facilities. Traditionally styled public areas are filled with pretty plants and flowers, and the hotel has its own colourful garden.
10rm(6♠) (6fb) TV available ® LDO 5pm
Lic ▥ CTV nc3yrs

SELECTED

GH Q Q Q Q Silver Trees 57 Wimborne Road BH3 7AL (follow A338 into Bournemouth then A347 to Bournemouth University. Silvertrees is 1m from A338/A347 junct)
☎(0202) 556040 FAX (0202) 556040
This charming Victorian house with attractive well kept gardens is set back from the main road and offers a high standard of accommodation. Public areas include a cosy

lounge and pretty dining room, and the service is personally supervised by the proprietors, with snacks and light refreshments available during the day and evening.
5🚿 (1fb) 🚭 in 3 bedrooms 🚭 in area of dining room 🚭 in 1 lounge CTV in all bedrooms [R] 🐕 sB&B🚿£23-£25 dB&B🚿£38-£40
▦
Credit Cards [1][2][3]

🛏☕ **GH [Q][Q] Hotel Sorrento** 16 Owls Road BH5 1AG (turn left off A35 at St Johns Church then turn left at crossroads)
☎(0202) 394019
rs Xmas
This family run holiday guesthouse is located in a central residential area, close to Boscombe shops and pier. The accommodation varies in size, but rooms are fresh and bright, some being en suite. There is a comfortable TV lounge, well stocked bar and an attractive restaurant, where a four-course dinner is served; hot drinks and snacks are also provided in the evening. Another, quiet, lounge has a large selection of books and the hotel also has a solarium and mini-gym. Ample car parking is provided.
19rm(15🛁🚿) (5fb) 🚭 in dining room CTV in all bedrooms [R] sB&B£13.50-£16.50 sB&B🛁🚿£16-£21.50 dB&B£27-£33 dB&B🛁🚿£32-£43 WB&B£94.50-£140.50 WBDi£112.50-£182.50 LDO 4pm
Lic ▦ CTV solarium gymnasium
Credit Cards [1][3]

🛏☕ **GH [Q][Q][Q] Thanet Private Hotel** 2 Drury Road, Alum Chine BH4 8HA (follow signs for Alum Chine Beach hotel is on corner of Alemhurst Rd & Drury Rd) ☎(0202) 761135
FAX (0202) 761135
Apr-Oct
A mill house dating from 1884, this property stands in a quiet residential area. The accommodation is neat, fresh and bright, and while TV is not available in every room, there are sets available on request. Public areas have a traditional feel and include a lounge, tiny sun lounge and a dining room with a small but reasonably stocked dispense bar in one corner. A home cooked evening meal is offered.
8rm(5🚿) (1fb) 🚭 in dining room CTV in all bedrooms [R] 🐕 (ex guide dogs) sB&B£14.50-£18 dB&B£29-£36 dB&B🚿£33-£40 WB&B£99-£126 WBDi£126.50-£155 LDO 5pm
Lic ▦ CTV nc5yrs
[£]

SELECTED

🛏☕ **GH [Q][Q][Q][Q] Tudor Grange Hotel** BH1 3EE (follow signs for East Cliff) ☎(0202) 291472 & 291463
This very handsome Tudor house, dating back in parts to William and Mary, is set in its own secluded and well kept gardens. The public areas are very well presented and comfortable, with fine panelled walls and ornate ceilings; there is a spacious lounge, a cosy bar and home-cooked meals are provided in the dining room. Bedrooms are nicely decorated and offer a good range of modern, well maintained facilities. Mrs Heeley and her small, select team of staff ensure guests are well cared for, and they have a loyal following of regulars.
12rm(11🛁🚿) (4fb)CTV in all bedrooms [R] **T** sB&B£15-£19 sB&B🛁🚿£17.50-£30 dB&B🛁🚿£35-£60 WB&B£90-£190 WBDi£130-£240 LDO 7pm
Lic ▦ CTV
Credit Cards [1][3][£]

GH [Q][Q][Q] *Valberg Hotel* 1a Wollstonecraft Road BH5 1JQ
☎(0202) 394644
This privately owned, personally managed small hotel is situated in a quiet residential area, close to the promenade and sea. The building is Spanish in style, with whitewashed walls. Bedrooms are neat, clean and well furnished: two rooms have a balcony and they all have an suite showers. Public areas are comfortable, with a pleasant dining room and licensed bar. Ample car parking is provided at the front of the hotel.
10🚿 (2fb) CTV in all bedrooms [R] 🐕 LDO noon
Lic ▦ CTV nc4yrs

GH [Q][Q][Q] Weavers Hotel 14 Wilfred Road BH5 1ND
☎(0202) 397871
Apr-Oct
High standards of housekeeping are maintained at this well presented and good value establishment. Bedrooms are fresh and neat, and all but one has a smart en suite shower room. There is a well appointed bar, quiet lounge and pretty dining room where a home cooked evening meal is served.
7rm(6🚿) (1fb) 🚭 in dining room CTV in all bedrooms [R] 🐕 sB&B£22.50-£24.50 dB&B🚿£45-£49 (incl dinner) WB&B£129-£135 WBDi£140-£155 LDO 5pm
Lic ▦ nc7yrs
[£]

GH [Q][Q][Q] West Dene Private Hotel 117 Alumhurst Road BH4 8HS ☎(0202) 764843
14 Feb-5 Nov & 24-29 Dec rs 6 Nov-23 Dec & 30 Dec-13 Feb
Standing at the end of Alum Chine, this hotel has glorious views far out to sea. Personally managed by Mr and Mrs Merson for a number of years now, it offers neat and well presented accommodation. Public areas include a cosy bar, a comfortable lounge and a dining room where good home-cooked food is served.
17rm(5🛁7🚿) (4fb) 🚭 in dining room CTV in 15 bedrooms [R] 🐕 * dB&B£52-£68 dB&B🛁🚿£58-£74 (incl dinner) WB&B£132-£150 WBDi£168-£222 LDO 3.30pm
Lic ▦ CTV nc4yrs
Credit Cards [1][2][3][5]

GH [Q][Q] Woodford Court Hotel 19-21 Studland Road BH4 8HZ
☎(0202) 764907 FAX (0202) 761214
A family-run hotel stands in a residential area close to Alum Chine. Bedrooms are bright and fresh, with modern en suite facilities. Public areas include a comfortable lounge area and a modern, well stocked bar.
35rm(8🛁18🚿) (11fb) 🚭 in dining room 🚭 in 1 lounge CTV in all bedrooms [R] **T** sB&B£17-£22 sB&B🛁🚿£17-£22 dB&B£34-£44 dB&B🛁🚿£34-£44 WB&B£119-£152 WBDi£147-£195 LDO 6.15pm
Lic ▦ CTV nc2yrs golf holidays arranged
Credit Cards [1][2][3][£]

GH [Q][Q][Q] Wood Lodge Hotel 10 Manor Road BH1 3EY
☎(0202) 290891
Mar-Jan
A well run private hotel, Wood Lodge continues to be improved and upgraded. Bedrooms are comfortable and bright, with smart en suite facilities and pretty fabrics. There is a choice of lounges and a dining room overlooking the gardens. A putting green and bowls are available.
15rm(14🛁🚿) (5fb) CTV in all bedrooms [R] * sB&B🛁🚿£20-£28 dB&B🛁🚿£40-£56 WB&B£140-£196 WBDi£160-£208 LDO 7.30pm
Lic ▦ CTV 9 hole putting green 2 bowls rinks
Credit Cards [1][3][£]

BOURTON-ON-THE-WATER Gloucestershire Map **04** SP12

SELECTED

GH [Q][Q][Q][Q] Coombe House Rissington Road GL54 2DT
☎Cotswold(0451) 821966 FAX (0451) 810477
A substantial house stands in its own pretty lawned gardens, ▶

set well back from the Rissington road. It is family run by Graham and Diana Ellis, who are happy to help guests plan routes or to suggest local restaurants. The bedrooms are bright and fresh with plain, well maintained decor and pretty coordinating soft furnishings; all the rooms have private bathrooms and there are 2 ground floor rooms. Enjoyable breakfasts are served in the pleasant dining room, and there is also a comfortable sitting room. Smoking is not permitted.
7⇄ℝ (2fb) CTV in all bedrooms Ⓡ ⊀
Lic ▥
Credit Cards ①②③

BOVEY TRACEY Devon   Map **03** SX87

GH ◎◎ **Blenheim Hotel** Brimley Road TQ13 9DH
☎(0626) 832422
rs 25 & 26 Dec
A large Victorian house, the Blenheim has a large secluded garden leading onto open moorland. The owner, Mr Turpin, has a great interest in gardening, and he grows many unusual plants which are in evidence throughout the hotel. Accommodation is provided in large bedrooms with splendid views. Two guest lounges are provided, and meals cooked on the aga are served in the bright dining room.
5rm(1ℝ) (1fb) ⊁ in dining room ⊁ in 1 lounge CTV in 4 bedrooms sB&B£23.50-£25 dB&B£47-£50 dB&Bℝ£50-£53 WB&B£150-£160 WBDi£230-£240 LDO 7.30pm
Lic ▥ CTV
£

SELECTED

FH ◎◎◎◎ Mrs H Roberts **Willmead** *(SX795812)*
TQ13 9NP ☎Lustleigh(06477) 214
Closed Xmas & New Year
Guests at Willmead Farm are guaranteed a warm welcome from the charming hostess Mrs Roberts. Visitors from all parts of the world have trodden a path to her door for the past 20 years and have been rewarded by the total peace found at this picture postcard cottage. The house dates from 1437 and many of the original features have been lovingly restored. The simply whitewashed rooms feature beams and inglenook fireplaces, and in the dining room guests eat at a communal table. The hall, complete with a minstrels' gallery from which the bedrooms lead, completes the interior picture. Outside there are charming gardens with a duck pond.
3rm(1ℝ) ⊀ ⊁ sB&B£30 dB&B£43 dB&Bℝ£47
▥ CTV nc10yrs 32 acres beef & sheep
£

BOWNESS-ON-WINDERMERE Cumbria

See **Windermere**

BOX Wiltshire   Map **03** ST86

SELECTED

GH ◎◎◎◎ **Hermitage** Bath Road SN14 9DT (5m from Bath on A4 towards Chippenham, Hermitage is first drive on left after 30mph signs) ☎(0225) 744187 FAX (0225) 744187
5rm(1ℝ) (2fb) ⊁ in 3 bedrooms CTV in 2 bedrooms Ⓡ ⊀ (ex guide dogs) dB&B£38 dB&Bℝ£42-£48 WB&B£133-£168
▥ CTV ⤳(heated)
£

BRADFORD West Yorkshire   Map **07** SE13

GH ◎◎ **Maple Hill Hotel** 3 Park Drive, Heaton BD9 4DP (opposite Lister Park/Cartwright Hall) ☎(0274) 544061 FAX (0274) 481154

This spacious Victorian house stands in its own grounds and features some leaded stained glass windows and fine ornate ceilings. The bedrooms are very clean and tidy and some rooms have four-poster beds. There is a lounge bar and dining room with half-panelled walls.
12rm(2ℝ) (1fb) ⊁ in 2 bedrooms ⊁ in dining room CTV in all bedrooms Ⓡ sB&B£26 sB&Bℝ£31 dB&B£36 dB&Bℝ£41 WB&B£182-£217 WBDi£249-£284
Lic ▥ half size snooker table
£

BRADFORD ON AVON Wiltshire   Map **03** ST86

P R E M I E R   🏆   S E L E C T E D

GH ◎◎◎◎◎ **Bradford Old Windmill** 4 Masons Lane BA15 1QN ☎(0225) 866842

Hidden among trees on the steep hillside above the town, this stump of a windmill, lovingly restored by Peter and Priscilla Roberts, is an enchanting place to stay. The intriguing building, with its circular lounge, is furnished with character in mind. Distinctly different bedrooms might offer a round bed, a water bed or a minstrels' gallery. The Roberts are well travelled and a collection of artefacts acquired over the years adds further interest. Dinner may be ordered the previous day, and one might sample the delights of vegetarian recipes picked up in Mexico, Nepal, Gambia and Jamaica, to name a few.
4rm(1⇄2ℝ) (1fb) ⊁ CTV in all bedrooms Ⓡ ⊀ sB&B£35-£45 sB&Bⅎℝ£45-£59 dB&B£49-£55 dB&Bⅎℝ£59-£75 LDO previous day
▥ nc6yrs
£

P R E M I E R   🏆   S E L E C T E D

GH ◎◎◎◎◎ **Burghope Manor** Winsley BA15 2LA
☎(0225) 723557
FAX (0225) 723113
Closed Xmas week

This delightful medieval manor house has strong links with Henry VIII and is steeped in history and interest dating from the 13th century. Situated in its grounds and gardens, Burghope Manor is the family home of Elizabeth and John Denning who have lovingly restored the house to its former glory. Three ensuite bedrooms are equipped with modern facilities and tastefully decorated and furnished. Breakfast is served around a large table in an elegant dining room and dinner can be arranged. The atmosphere is relaxed and guests are encouraged to to enjoy the informal surroundings.
3⇄ℝ (1fb) ⊁ in bedrooms ⊁ in dining room ⊁ in lounges CTV in all bedrooms Ⓡ ⊀ ⊁ sB&Bⅎℝ£45-£55 dB&Bⅎℝ£60-£70
▥ CTV nc10yrs shooting and fishing by arrangement
Credit Cards ①②③ £

SELECTED

GH [Q][Q][Q][Q] Widbrook Grange Trowbridge Rd BA15 1UH (1m from town centre beyond the canal bridge on A363) ☎(0225) 863173 & 864750 FAX (0225) 862890

Just a mile from Bradford-on-Avon, this elegant property constructed of Bath stone is thought to have been built as a farmhouse. Several barns surrounding the main house have been converted into bedrooms, offering tastefully furnished accommodation equipped to a high standard. There is a choice of lounges and an evening meal is served at one large table in the dining room. An indoor swimming pool has recently been added.

4rm(3🛁🚿) Annexe 15🛁🚿 (2fb) 🚭 in dining room CTV in all bedrooms [R] **T** 🐕 * sB&B£30 sB&B🛁🚿£50 dB&B🛁🚿£69-£85 LDO 6.30pm

Lic ♨ 🏊 (heated) gymnasium

Credit Cards [1][2][3][5][£]

See advertisement under BATH

BRADING See **WIGHT, ISLE OF**

BRAEMAR Grampian *Aberdeenshire* Map **15** NO19

GH [Q][Q][Q] Callater Lodge Hotel 9 Glenshee Road AB35 5YQ (beside A93) ☎(03397) 41275 FAX (03397) 41275

Closed Nov-27 Dec

Peter and Mary Nelson are the charming hosts at this detached Victorian lodge, set in its own gardens on the southern side of the village. Mary's cooking has earned praise and Peter's carefully researched selection of malt whiskies deserves serious investigation. Public rooms are well proportioned and there is a welcoming open fire in the lounge. Bedrooms are comfortable and where space permits easy chairs are provided.

9rm(6🛁🚿) 🚭 CTV in all bedrooms [R] sB&B£19 sB&B🛁🚿£25 dB&B£38 dB&B🛁🚿£46-£50 WB&B£123-£162 WBDi£235-£274 LDO 7pm

Lic ♨

Credit Cards [1][3][£]

BRAITHWAITE Cumbria Map **11** NY22

GH [Q][Q][Q] Maple Bank CA12 5RY (just off A66 to N of Keswick) ☎(07687) 78229

s Nov-Feb

Maple Bank is an attractive Edwardian residence in an acre of garden two miles west of Keswick. Bedrooms are well equipped and tastefully decorated, and many have views of Skiddaw. There is a comfortable guests' lounge and an attractive dining room where well prepared evening meals are served.

🚿 (1fb) 🚭 in 1 bedrooms 🚭 in dining room CTV in all bedrooms [R] 🐕 dB&B🚿£42-£44 WB&B£142-£149 WBDi£200-£207 LDO pm

Lic ♨ CTV nc12yrs

Credit Cards [1][3][£]

BRAMPTON Cumbria Map **12** NY56

See also Castle Carrock

GH [Q][Q][Q] Courtyard Cottages Warren Bank, Station Road urn off A69 onto B6413 signed Castle Carrock and stablishment approx 300yds on right - concealed entrance gnposted) ☎(06977) 41818

losed Dec-9 Jan

ne luxurious ground-floor bedroom with a double bed is rovided at this attractive stone-built cottage in the courtyard of a ictorian mansion. The bedroom and bathroom have been ecially equipped for disabled guests, and there are wide oorways into the bathroom and at the entrance. There are no eps to negotiate and car parking facilities are provided mediately outside. Full breakfast is served in the room, and although there are no public rooms available to guests, they are welcome to enjoy the three acres of beautiful grounds.

🚭 CTV in all bedrooms [R] **T** 🐕 (ex guide dogs)

♨ nc15yrs

[£]

GH [Q][Q][Q] *Denton House* Low Row CA8 2LQ (4m E on A69) ☎Hallbankgate(06977) 46278 FAX (06977) 46278

An attractive Victorian house set in open countryside on the A69 to the east of Brampton, near Hadrian's Wall. Carefully refurbished by friendly proprietor Mrs Hamilton, the house is comfortable and very well furnished, with delightful bedrooms.

3 [R]

♨ CTV

SELECTED

GH [Q][Q][Q][Q] Oakwood Park Hotel Longtown Road CA8 2AP (from M6 take the A69 at junct 43, to Brampton) ☎(06977) 2436

An elegant Victorian residence standing in three acres of grounds, located just off the A6071 to the north of the village. The bedrooms are generally spacious, well furnished and comfortable, and there is a pleasant lounge with a log fire. A good range of home cooked food is available in the pleasant dining room, and service is friendly.

5rm(2🛁3🚿) (1fb) 🚭 in bedrooms CTV in all bedrooms [R] 🐕 (ex guide dogs) sB&B🛁🚿£26 dB&B🛁🚿£40 WB&B£135-£177 WBDi£212-£254 LDO 8pm

Lic ♨ CTV

Credit Cards [1][3][£]

See advertisement on p.93.

Callater Lodge

Braemar, Aberdeenshire, AB35 5YQ
Telephone: Braemar (013397) 41275

This comfortable, 9 bedroom Victorian lodge is set in its own spacious grounds surrounded by wonderful scenery. Informal, relaxing and friendly you can expect good food, an excellent wine list and an extensive selection of malt whiskies! There is ample parking. Callater Lodge is the ideal base for sampling the many delights and pursuits offered by Royal Deeside.

There is no smoking

Contact the resident proprietors —
Peter and Mary Nelson

SELECTED

FH ⓆⓆ Ⓠ Ⓠ Mrs M Stobart **Cracrop** *(NY521697)*
Kirkcambeck CA8 2BW (off B6318, 7m N of town)
☎(06977) 48245 FAX (06977) 48333
Jan-Nov
An early Victorian farmhouse, situated on a 400-acre working
farm raising pedigree Ayrshire cattle, offers four carefully
modernised en suite bedrooms which still retain much of their
original character. Public areas include a very comfortable
guests' lounge, a games room and the pleasant dining room in
which traditional country breakfasts are served. Marked trails
make it easy for visitors to explore the farm.
3🐾 (2fb) ⚓ CTV in all bedrooms Ⓡ 🏋 (ex guide dogs) ✻
sB&B🐾£20 dB&B🐾£36-£40 LDO 1pm
▥ CTV nc🗡 sauna 425 acres arable beef dairy mixed sheep
Credit Cards ②

FH ⓆⓆ Mrs Ann Thompson **Low Rigg** *(NY522651)* Walton
CA8 2DX ☎(06977) 3233
A typical stone-built Cumbrian farmhouse standing in a rural
location just outside the village of Walton (follow the sign for
Solmain from the village). The bedrooms are modern and there is
a pleasant lounge cum breakfast room.
2rm (1fb) Ⓡ ✻ sB&B£13-£16 dB&B£26-£32 WB&Bfr£90
WBDifr£150 LDO 1pm
CTV 70 acres dairy
Ⓔ

INNⓆⓆⓆ *The Blacksmiths Arms* Talkin Village CA8 1LE
(2m SE) ☎(06977) 3452
A typical Cumbrian inn situated in the village of Talkin, winner of
the best kept small village in the Carlisle area. Bedrooms are of a
very good standard, all with en suite facilities and TV. A good
range of bar food is provided, together with an extensive choice of
menu in the cosy retaurant.
5rm(3🔜2🐾) CTV in all bedrooms Ⓡ 🏋 (ex guide dogs) LDO
9pm
games room
Credit Cards ① ③

BRAMSHAW Hampshire   Map **04** SU21

INNⓆⓆⓆ **Bramble Hill Hotel** SO43 7JG
☎Southampton(0703) 813165
A former medieval hunting lodge set in mature grounds. Much of
the original character has been retained with features such as the
Billiard Room and lovely wood panelling which now forms part
of new restaurants. Bedrooms vary; several have fine Victorian
bathrooms, 4 have 4-poster beds and some antiques. Local game,
fresh fish and home-made puddings feature on the menu and a full
cooked or Continental breakfast is available at a supplementary
charge.
10rm(7🔜🐾) (3fb) ⚓ in dining room CTV in all bedrooms Ⓡ
sB&B🔜🐾£45-£60 dB&B£30-£40 dB&B🔜🐾£50-£70
WB&B£210-£255 WBDi£285-£315 Lunch £8.95-£12.95alc
Dinner £10-£15&alc LDO 9pm
▥ CTV snooker table clay shooting by arrangement
Credit Cards ① ③ Ⓔ

BRANDON Suffolk   Map **05** TL78

GH ⓆⓆⓆ *Riverside Lodge* 78 High Street IP27 0AU
☎Thetford(0842) 811236
A friendly old family home stands close to the town centre but in
14 acres of land which includes frontage to the river Ouse.
Accommodation comprises three good-sized bedrooms, a
breakfast room and a peaceful first-floor lounge.
3🔜🐾 (1fb) CTV in all bedrooms Ⓡ 🏋 (ex guide dogs)
▥ CTV ✺(grass)🗡

BRANSCOMBE Devon   Map **03** SY18

PREMIER 🏵 **SELECTED**

GH ⓆⓆⓆⓆⓆ **Coxes**
Barton EX12 3BJ
☎(0297) 80536
FAX (0297) 80531
Standing in its own grounds in
a village surrounded by
National Trust land, this
beautifully converted Tudor
barn is ideally placed for
exploring Devon's beauty
spots.
2🔜 ⚓ CTV in 1 bedroom
🏋 (ex guide dogs) ✻ dB&B🔜£40-£50 WB&B£130-£165
▥ Ⓔ

SELECTED

INNⓆⓆⓆ *The Masons Arms* EX12 3DJ (off A3052)
☎(029780) 300 due to change to (0297) 680300
FAX (029780) 500
8rm(5🔜) CTV in all bedrooms T sB&B£16-£24 dB&B£32-
£48 dB&B🔜£40-£90 WB&B£112-£302 WBDi£224-£414
Lunch frf9 Dinner fr£17.50&alc LDO 9.15pm
▥
Credit Cards ① ③

BRANSFORD Hereford & Worcester   Map **03** SO7?

GH Ⓠ **Croft** WR6 5JD ☎Leigh Sinton(0886) 832227
5rm(3🐾) (1fb) ⚓ in bedrooms Ⓡ ✻ sB&B£18-£20 sB&B🐾£22-
£24 dB&B£30-£37 dB&B🐾£33.60-£42 WB&B£105-£154
Lic ▥ CTV sauna jacuzzi
Credit Cards ① ③ Ⓔ

BRANSGORE Hampshire   Map **04** SZ1?

SELECTED

GH ⓆⓆⓆⓆ **Tothill House** Black Lane, off Forest Road
BH23 8DZ (from A35, turn right into Forest Road, left into
Black Lane and house is third gate on the right)
☎(0425) 674414 FAX (0425) 672235
In a remote New Forest location, this Edwardian gentleman's
residence is set in 12 acres of woodland. The spacious
bedrooms are individually furnished and provided with many
extras. There is a small library lounge and an impressive
breakfast room with a large communal table.
3rm(2🐾) ⚓ CTV in all bedrooms Ⓡ 🏋 (ex guide dogs)
sB&B🐾£25-£40 dB&B🐾£50 WB&Bfr£140
▥ nc16yrs

BRATTON FLEMING Devon   Map **03** SS6?

SELECTED

GH ⓆⓆⓆⓆ **Bracken House** EX31 4TG (off A399)
☎(0598) 710320
Apr-Oct rs Mar & Nov
8🔜🐾 CTV in all bedrooms Ⓡ sB&B🔜🐾£31-£47
dB&B🔜🐾£52-£64 WB&B£140-£182 WBDi£238-£280
LDO 6pm
Lic ▥ nc8yrs croquet library
Credit Cards ① ③

BRAUNTON Devon   Map **02** SS43

GH Q Q Q **Alexander Brookdale Hotel** 62 South Street
EX33 2AN ☎(0271) 812075
Mike and Wendy Sargeant's friendly guest house provides neat,
light and airy bedrooms. A spacious bar-lounge is provided as
well as a separate first floor lounge. Dinner is served by
arrangement in the simply furnished dining room.
3rm (2fb) ⊁ in bedrooms ⊁ in dining room CTV in all bedrooms
Ⓡ ⴕ (ex guide dogs) ✳ sB&B£17-£18 dB&B£34-£36
WB&B£180.50-£186.50 LDO 11am
Lic Ⅲ CTV nc8yrs
£

BREASCLETE See **LEWIS, ISLE OF**

BRECHIN Tayside *Angus*   Map **15** NO56

GH Q Q Q **The Station House** Farnell DD9 6UH (off A92 onto
A934 toward Forfar for 5m then turn right, proceed for 0.5m)
☎Farnell(0674) 820208
3rm(1ⴕ) ⊁ in dining room Ⓡ ⴕ (ex guide dogs) ✳ sB&Bfr£16
dB&Bⴕfr£30 dB&Bfr£25 dB&Bⴕfr£30 LDO noon
Ⅲ CTV

SELECTED

FH Q Q Q Q Mrs M Stewart **Blibberhill** *(NO553568)*
DD9 6TH (5m WSW off B9134) ☎Aberlemno(0307) 830225
A well maintained, lovely 18th-century farmhouse located, in
a very rural and peaceful setting with fine views of the Vale of
Strathmore. The house is very well furnished throughout, and
there is a pleasant lounge and a small conservatory
overlooking the attractive garden. Good home cooking is
served at the communal table in the cosy dining room.

3⇌ⴕ ⊁ CTV in all bedrooms Ⓡ ⴕ (ex guide dogs) ✳
sB&Bⴕfr£17.50 dB&Bⴕfr£35
Ⅲ CTV 300 acres arable beef mixed
£

BRECON Powys   Map **03** SO02

GH Q Q **Beacons** 16 Bridge Street LD3 8AH (W side of town
centre, just across the river) ☎(0874) 623339
Run by the friendly Cox family, this Georgian guest house is
situated just west of the town centre. Some of the bedrooms are in
a part of the building that used to be a row of weavers' cottages,
but all are now fully modernised and mostly furnished with pine.
One room has a four-poster bed, and there are several family
rooms. A comfortable lounge is available for residents as well as a
cosy bar in what used to be a meat cellar. During the summer the
restaurant is also used as an all-day coffee shop.
10rm(7⇌ⴕ) Annexe 1⇌ⴕ (2fb) ⊁ in bedrooms ⊁ in dining
room CTV in all bedrooms Ⓡ sB&B£16.50 sB&Bⴕⴕ£19.50
dB&B£33 dB&Bⴕⴕ£39 WB&B£99-£117 WBDi£153-£171
LDO 8.45pm
Lic Ⅲ CTV mountain bike hire
Credit Cards 1 2 3

GH Q Q **Borderers** 47 The Watton LD3 7EG (E on A40)
☎(0874) 623559
Originally a 17th-century drovers' inn, this cheerful little bed-and-
breakfast guest house stands on the Abergavenny side of town.
The courtyard is now used as a car park, and four of the bedrooms
are in annexe buildings surrounding it. These, like those in the
main building, are freshly decorated. The owners are friendly and
very welcoming.

▶

OAKWOOD PARK HOTEL
BRAMPTON, CUMBRIA
Tel: 016977 2436

Victorian built Hotel set in 10 acres of
secluded grounds. Convenient for the Lakes,
Hadrian's Wall, and the picturesque Border
Country. Traditional cuisine in a tranquil
atmosphere with open fires a feature. All
welcome for Morning Coffee, Afternoon Teas
and Evening Meals.

B&B	*£*	
Twin/Double	*20.00*	*per person*
Single	*26.00*	*per person*
Family Room	*56.00*	*per room*

The Blacksmiths Arms
TALKIN VILLAGE, BRAMPTON, CUMBRIA
Telephone: 0169 773452

*The Blacksmith's Arms offers all the hospitality
and comforts of a traditional Country Inn. Enjoy
tasty meals served in our bar lounges or linger over
dinner in our well-appointed restaurant.
We also have five lovely bedrooms all en suite and
offering every comfort.
We guarantee the hospitality you would expect
from a family concern and we can assure you of a
pleasant and comfortable stay.
Peacefully situated in the beautiful village of
Talkin, the Inn is convenient for the Borders,
Hadrian's Wall and the Lake District. Good Golf
course, pony trekking, walking and other country
pursuits nearby.
Personally managed by proprietors Pat and Tom
Bagshaw.*

5rm(3♠) Annexe 2rm(1⇌1♠) (2fb) ⊁ in 2 bedrooms ⊁ in dining room CTV in all bedrooms Ⓡ sB&B£18 sB&B⇌♠£20 dB&B£32 dB&B⇌♠£34-£36 WB&B£105-£120
Lic nc5yrs
£

SELECTED

GH ⚅⚅⚅⚅ **The Coach** Orchard Street, Llanfaes LD3 8AN (town one way system, turn left at traffic lights, over bridge then 300yds on right) ☎(0874) 623803
Closed 22 Dec-7 Jan
A very well maintained guest house stands on the western side of town. Bedrooms are smart and prettily decorated with floral fabrics and dark wood furniture, and have very good facilities. There is a residents' lounge with a fine Victorian fireplace and a small, attractive dining room where home cooking is served.
6⇌♠ (2fb) ⊁ CTV in all bedrooms Ⓡ T ⊀ ✳
dB&B⇌♠£36-£38 LDO 7pm
Lic ▥ nc

GH ⚅⚅ **Flag & Castle** 11 Orchard Street, Llanfaes LD3 8AN (on B460 .5m W) ☎(0874) 625860
A friendly, cosy little guest house opposite Christ College, west of the town centre. Guests dine together at a communal table in the open-plan lounge and dining room. Bedrooms are freshly decorated.
6rm(1♠) (1fb)CTV in 1 bedroom Ⓡ sB&B£16-£17 dB&B£30-£32 dB&B♠£34-£36 WB&B£90-£108
Lic ▥ CTV
Credit Cards ②£

FH ⚅⚅⚅ **Mrs H E Atkins Llandetty Hall** (SO124205) Talybont-on-Usk LD3 7YR (7m SE off B4558)
☎(0874) 87415 FAX (0874) 87415
This personally owned 17th-century farmhouse has glorious, unrestricted views over the River Usk and Brecon Beacons. The house itself is steeped in history, being associated with the signing of the death warrant for King Charles I, and was at one time the home of Disraeli's wife. Significant restoration has provided bright, comfortable modern bedrooms which still retain much of the original character and charm, with top marks given for first-class en suite bathrooms. There is a cosy lounge with an open fire and an attractive dining room adjacent. Guests have full access to the farm and gardens, and riding and stabling are available by arrangement.
3rm(2⇌1♠) ⊁ Ⓡ T ⊀ (ex guide dogs) sB&B⇌♠£21 dB&B⇌♠£34 WB&B£112 WBDi£175 LDO 6pm
▥ CTV nc10yrs 48 acres sheep
£

BREDWARDINE Hereford & Worcester   Map **03** SO34

SELECTED

GH ⚅⚅⚅⚅ **Bredwardine Hall** HR3 6DB
☎Moccas(0981) 500596
Mar-mid Nov
A warm welcome is assured from Wendy and Maurice Jancey at this 18th-century manor house with its magnificent reception hall and staircase. Set in its own wooded grounds with well kept lawns, most rooms have rural views. There is an elegant drawing room with several floor to ceiling windows, furnished with brown dralon seating, and the cosy dining room has an honesty bar. The majority of bedrooms are spacious, fitted with good quality furniture and all have en suite or private bathrooms, along with TV and tea making facilities.

5rm(3⇌1♠) ⊁ in bedrooms ⊁ in dining room CTV in all bedrooms Ⓡ ⊀ (ex guide dogs) ✳ sB&B♠fr£33 sB&B⇌♠£35 dB&Bfr£46 dB&B⇌♠£50 WB&B£156-£170 WBDi£240-£254 LDO 4.30pm
Lic ▥ nc10yrs
£

See advertisement under HEREFORD

BRENDON Devon Map **03** SS74

GH ⚅ **Brendon House Hotel** EX35 6PS ☎(05987) 206
Closed Xmas rs mid Nov-2 Mar
Brendon lies in one of the hidden valleys of Exmoor on the banks of the Lyn. Built in 1780 it is the haunt of walkers, fishermen and those who wish to explore north Devon. Bedrooms are cosy and the lounge has antique furniture and paintings.
5rm(1⇌3♠) (1fb) ⊁ in dining room CTV in 2 bedrooms Ⓡ ✳ dB&Bfr£35 dB&B⇌♠£37-£40 WB&Bfr£133 WBDifr£193 LDO 5pm
Lic ▥ CTV
£

BRENT ELEIGH Suffolk Map **05** TL94

FH ⚅⚅⚅ **Mrs J P Gage Street** (TL945476) CO10 9NU (access from A1141 Lavenham/Hadleigh road)
☎Lavenham(0787) 247271
Closed Dec-mid Feb
A 16th-century farmhouse with a well tended walled garden is situated in the centre of the village. The accommodation is of excellent quality and the lounge has a beautiful inglenook fireplace and log fire.
3rm(2⇌♠) ⊁ in bedrooms ⊁ in dining room Ⓡ ⊀ ✳ dB&Bfr£38 dB&B⇌♠£40
▥ CTV nc12yrs 143 acres arable
£

BRIDESTOWE Devon Map **02** SX58

FH ⚅⚅ **Mrs J E Down Little Bidlake** (SX494887) EX20 4NS (turn off A30 at the Sourton Cross exit and take old A30 road to Bridestowe) ☎(083786) 233
Etr-Oct
Home to the friendly Down family, this stone-built farmhouse is surrounded by farm buildings. There are two guest bedrooms, a comfortable lounge and an attractive dining room where an evening meal is available on request.
2rm Ⓡ ⊀ (ex guide dogs) dB&Bfr£28 WB&Bfr£85 WBDifr£130 LDO 7.30pm
▥ CTV ✔ 150 acres beef dairy mixed
£

FH ⚅⚅⚅ **Mrs M Hockridge Week** (SX519913) EX20 4HZ
☎(083786) 221
This 17th-century stone-built farmhouse with a rural setting on a working farm, is approached from the old A30, with easy access to both the north and south coasts of Devon. Bedrooms include a family room on the ground floor. The comfortable lounge has an open fireplace, and guests can enjoy home-cooked dinners served at separate tables in the dining room. Mrs Hockridge offers a warm welcome and a relaxed atmosphere.
5♠ (2fb) ⊁ in dining room ⊁ in lounges CTV in all bedrooms Ⓡ ✳ sB&B♠fr£19 dB&B♠fr£38 LDO 5pm
▥ CTV 180 acres dairy mixed sheep
£

See advertisement under OKEHAMPTON

BRIDGNORTH Shropshire Map **07** SO79

SELECTED

GH 🅠🅠🅠🅠 *Haven Pasture* Underton WV16 6TY (SW in village of Underton off B4364) ☎Middleton Scriven (074635) 632 FAX (074635) 632

Originally a farm cottage, this guesthouse has been extended over the years and high quality accommodation is now offered by welcoming owners Pat and David Perks. The bedrooms are pretty and well equipped and two have private patios. Guests dine at one table in the open-plan lounge/dining room.

3rm (1fb) CTV in all bedrooms ℝ LDO 8pm
🏖 CTV ⊀(heated)

GH 🅠🅠🅠 **Severn Arms Hotel** Underhill Street, Low Town WV16 4BB ☎(0746) 764616

2 Jan-Nov

This tall, terraced house is situated close to the cliff railway which links Low Town to High Town. The front rooms have lovely views of the old bridge across the river Severn at Low Town. Home-cooked meals are served in the dining room.

9rm(2⇌3rm) (5fb)CTV in 8 bedrooms ℝ T ✱ sB&B£22.50-£26 sB&B⇌m£34.50 dB&B£37 dB&B⇌m£44 WB&B£123-£143 WBDi£162-£182 LDO 4pm
Lic 🏖 CTV ✔
Credit Cards 1 2 3 £

INN🅠 *Kings Head Hotel* Whitburn Street WV16 4QN (off main street of High Town down narrow rd) ☎(0746) 762141

Dating back to 1603, this black and white timbered inn has been run for many years by Dave and Liz Broadley and offers good value accommodation. The inn is full of character, with an abundance of beams and exposed timbers in the cosy bars, where a

good range of bar food is served. There is a separate breakfast room.

5rm (3fb) CTV in all bedrooms ℝ ✱ (ex guide dogs) LDO 8pm
🏖

BRIDGWATER Somerset   Map **03** ST33

GH 🅠🅠 **Brookland Hotel** 56 North Street TA6 3PN
☎(0278) 423263

Closed 24 Dec-1 Jan

This Victorian villa is popular with business guests and tourists alike, and staff ensure that high standards are maintained. Bedrooms are comfortable, neat and include the usual modern comforts. The open-plan ground floor features leather chesterfields and there is a small bar. Dinner may be booked by prior arrangement.

8rm(3rm) (1fb)CTV in all bedrooms ℝ sB&B£25 sB&B⇌m£35 dB&B£40 dB&B⇌m£45 LDO 6pm
Lic 🏖 CTV
Credit Cards 1 2 3 £

GH 🅠🅠🅠 **Woodlands** 35 Durleigh Road TA6 7HX (from junc 24 of M5 head to Bridgwater,turn left at 2nd mini rdbt then left at traffic lights, in approx 0.75m narrow drive on left to Woodlands) ☎(0278) 423442

Resident proprietors Mr and Mrs Palmer have completely and carefully restored this Grade II listed, 17th-century family home, that stands quietly in two acres of gardens and grounds on the outskirts of the town. Its comfortable bedrooms are all equipped with modern facilities and thoughtful extras such as electric blankets. Breakfast (and dinner by arrangement) is served in an elegant dining room that also provides some lounge seating and a video player for guests' use.

4rm(1⇌2rm) ⊬ in bedrooms CTV in all bedrooms ℝ ✱ (ex

▶

Farmhouse – Bed & Breakfast
AA QQQ   ♨ ♨ Commended

"Maeswalter"
Heol Senni, Nr Brecon, Powys LD3 8SU
Telephone: 01874 636 629

Warm and friendly welcome in the 17th century non working farmhouse situated in the quiet and picturesque Heol Senni Valley. Tastefully decorated and comfortable en suite and basic bedrooms with H&C vanity units, remote control TV, tea/coffee facilities. All bedrooms have magnificent views accross the Senni Valley.
Excellent touring, fishing, walking, pony trekking, hang-gliding and bird watching area.

Maes-Y-Gwernen
Country Hotel AA ★
School Road, Abercraf, Swansea Valley
Tel: 01639 730218 Fax: 01639 730765

Maes-Y-Gwernen is a small but well appointed hotel set in its own grounds in the village of Abercraf. Our situation on the Southern edge of the Brecon Beacons National Park, close to Dan-Yr-Ogof showcaves, is convenient for both the Park and the Gower Coast. We offer good food, facilities, value and lovely surroundings.
Colour brochure available on request.

guide dogs) sB&B£18-£20 dB&B➪ℝ£37-£40 WB&B£112-£155
WBDi£160-£200 LDO 3pm
▥ CTV nc10yrs
Credit Cards ⨯1⨯ ⨯3⨯ ⨯£⨯

BRIDLINGTON Humberside   Map **08** TA16

GH ⓠⓠⓠ **Bay Ridge Hotel** Summerfield Road YO15 3LF
☎(0262) 673425
Caring hosts offer modestly appointed accommodation made
attractive by colour coordinated fabrics. Public rooms are inviting
and comfortable; the larger lounge with its chesterfield suite and
brass-inlaid teak coffee tables is augmented by a smaller, quieter
sitting room which is designated non-smoking and there is also a
central lounge bar with music and bar billiards. Interesting menus
of honest, home-cooked dishes draw regular visitors, and an
enclosed 'sun-trap' patio provides a pleasant place to eat on
warmer days.
14rm(6➪6ℝ) (5fb) ⊁ in dining room CTV in all bedrooms ⓡ ✳
sB&B£19-£20 dB&B➪ℝ£38-£40 WB&B£125-£128
WBDi£145-£155 LDO 5.45pm
Lic ▥ CTV bar billiards darts board games library
Credit Cards ⨯1⨯ ⨯3⨯ ⨯£⨯

GH ⓠⓠⓠ **Langdon Hotel** Pembroke Terrace YO15 3BX
☎(0262) 673065
Separated from the beach only by a road and a small, well tended
public garden, this hotel stands between the harbour and Spa
Theatre just a short walk from the town centre. The spacious
lounge and dining room have now been redecorated in attractive
light shades, and here, or on a small front patio, snacks are served
throughout the day; public areas also include a cosy little bar.
Bedrooms (the majority of them with cheerful floral decor and en
suite shower rooms) tend to be small, but fitted melamine
furniture makes the most of the space available.
20rm(11ℝ) (8fb) CTV in all bedrooms ⓡ ✻ (ex guide dogs)
LDO 5pm
Lic lift ▥

GH ⓠⓠⓠ **Marton Grange** Flamborough Road, Marton cum
Sewerby YO15 1DU ☎(0262) 602034
This Georgian house stands near an international-standard golf
course. It is particularly suitable for elderly or disabled guests,
providing a lift, emergency call system and specially equipped en
suite bathrooms. Home-cooked evening meals are served, and the
friendly proprietors will willingly cater for special diets (with
advance notice). Light refreshments are available as required and
packed lunches can be provided on request.
4➪ℝ ⊁ in 1 bedrooms ⊁ in dining room ⊁ in lounges CTV in
all bedrooms ⓡ ✳ sB&B➪ℝ£14-£16 dB&B➪ℝ£28-£32
WB&B£98-£112 WBDi£140-£154 LDO 5pm
lift ▥
⨯£⨯

GH ⓠⓠⓠ **Southdowne Hotel** South Marine Drive YO15 3NS
☎(0262) 673270
Genuine hospitality and immaculate standards of housekeeping
attract to this hotel a regular clientele of older guests who
appreciate its restful atmosphere. A large, comfortable sitting
room provides a quieter alternative to the television lounge, and
drinks can be obtained from a small dispense bar which doubles as
a reception desk in the hallway; the light, sunny dining room, like
the larger of the two lounges, looks out across the promenade and
sea. Car parking space is available on the hotel's frontage.
12rm(8ℝ) (2fb) CTV in 8 bedrooms ⓡ ✻ ✳ sB&B£17-£19
sB&Bℝ£19-£20 dB&B£34-£40 dB&Bℝ£40 LDO 5.30pm
Lic ▥ CTV
⨯£⨯

GH ⓠⓠⓠ **The Tennyson** 19 Tennyson Avenue YO15 2EU
☎(0262) 604382 FAX (0262) 604382
Holder of the Heart Beat award for healthy cuisine, and
recognized nationally in a recent competition, Linda Stalker prides

herself on her standards of service and cooking. Meals composed
of predominantly British dishes - enlivened by occasional flambé
specialities - are taken in a pleasant little dining room equipped
with separate tables; coffee is then served in the comfortable,
newly refurbished lounge. Attractively appointed bedrooms are
individual in style, a four-poster room furnished with antiques
proving particularly popular. All of them, however, are
thoughtfully equipped with a good range of facilities which
include TV, radio alarm clocks, trouser presses, hair dryers and tea
trays.
6rm(3➪2ℝ) ⊁ in bedrooms ⊁ in dining room CTV in all
bedrooms ⓡ ✳ sB&B➪ℝ£20-£24.95 dB&B£32-£34
dB&B➪ℝ£40-£44 LDO 8.30pm
Lic ▥ nc9yrs
Credit Cards ⨯1⨯ ⨯3⨯ ⨯5⨯ ⨯£⨯

BRIDPORT Dorset   Map **03** SY49

See also Bettiscombe & Chideock

GH ⓠⓠⓠⓠ **Britmead House** West Bay Road DT6 4EG
(approaching Bridport follow signs for West Bay.Britmead
House is 800yds S of the A35) ☎(0308) 422941
A very well presented property between West Bay and
Bridport provides accommodation in attractive, comfortable
bedrooms, some of which enjoy delightful rural views; all of
them are thoughtfully equipped and all but one offer modern
en suite facilities - that one having sole use of an adjacent
shower room. Excellent standards of housekeeping, the home-
cooked meal served each evening and the warm, friendly
atmosphere that pervades the whole house attract many regular
visitors. Car parking space is provided, and a self-catering
bungalow just across the road is proving very popular.
7rm(6➪ℝ) (1fb) ⊁ in dining room CTV in all bedrooms ⓡ
sB&B£24-£29 sB&B➪ℝ£28-£33 dB&B£38-£44
dB&B➪ℝ£46-£52 WB&B£105-£140 WBDi£189-£224 LDO
6pm
Lic ▥
Credit Cards ⨯1⨯ ⨯2⨯ ⨯3⨯ ⨯5⨯ ⨯£⨯

BRIGHTON & HOVE East Sussex   Map **04** TQ3

See also Rottingdean

GH ⓠⓠⓠⓠ **Adelaide Hotel** 51 Regency Square BN1 2FF
(Logis) ☎Brighton(0273) 205286 FAX (0273) 220904
Ideally positioned close to the conference centre, exhibition
halls, shops and sea front, this quality hotel has been lovingly
restored in keeping with its Grade II listed status while
providing every modern amenity. Lots of thoughtful extras are
provided in the bedrooms, and room service of light
refreshments and snacks is available. There is a comfortable
lounge with a writing desk, and dinner is served by
arrangement (except Sunday and Wednesday).
12➪ℝ (1fb) ⊁ in dining room CTV in all bedrooms ⓡ T ✻
sB&B➪ℝ£38-£60 dB&B➪ℝ£55-£75 LDO 5pm
Lic ▥ ✍
Credit Cards ⨯1⨯ ⨯2⨯ ⨯3⨯ ⨯5⨯ ⨯£⨯

GH ⓠⓠⓠ **Allendale Hotel** 3 New Steine BN2 1PB
☎Brighton(0273) 675436 FAX (0273) 602603
Closed 2 weeks over Christmas
Situated in one of Brighton's attractive seafront garden squares,
this converted Regency town house is conveniently located close
to the pier, conference centre, Royal Pavilion and shops. The
bedrooms are immaculate, tastefully decorated and comfortably
furnished; several are en suite, all are equipped with every

possible convenience and front rooms enjoy fine sea views. A small lounge area adjoins the breakfast room, where full English or continental breakfast is served, and the hotel is licensed.
13rm(6🚿) (5fb) 🚭 in dining room CTV in all bedrooms [R] **T** ✳ sB&B£27-£30 dB&B£36-£45 dB&B🚿£56-£66 LDO noon
Lic ♨ 🚫🅿
Credit Cards [1] [2] [3] [5] [£]

GH [Q][Q][Q] ***Alvia Hotel*** 36 Upper Rock Gardens BN2 1QF
☎Brighton(0273) 682939
Undergoing considerable upgrading, this family-run bed and breakfast establishment has a friendly and informal atmosphere, with the personal touch added by David Scourfield and his family. The room sizes vary but all are furnished in a modern style. Guests have a choice of cooked English breakfast dishes, and an enclosed car park at the rear of the building is provided.
9rm(6🚿) (1fb) CTV in all bedrooms [R] 🚫🐕 (ex guide dogs)
♨
Credit Cards [1] [2] [3] [5]

GH [Q][Q][Q] Ambassador Hotel 22 New Steine, Marine Parade BN2 1PD ☎Brighton(0273) 676869 FAX (0273) 689988
A smart Regency terrace house situated close to the Palace pier and seafront, the Ambassador is within walking distance of the town. It offers neat, well equipped, well maintained bedrooms. There is a TV lounge with a bar and a spacious new breakfast room.
10rm(2🛁8🚿) (3fb) 🚭 in dining room CTV in all bedrooms [R] **T** 🚫🐕 sB&B🛁🚿£23-£30 dB&B🛁🚿£38-£54
Lic ♨ CTV 🚫🅿
Credit Cards [1] [2] [3] [5] [£]

SELECTED

GH 🅠🅠🅠🅠 **Amblecliff Hotel** 35 Upper Rock Gardens
BN2 1QF ☎Brighton(0273) 681161 & 676945
FAX (0273) 676945
Bright and individually furnished in today's style, the
predominantly non-smoking bedrooms of this friendly and
personally-run guest house have been carefully designed to
combine good levels of comfort with every modern amenity.
A continental breakfast can either be delivered to the bedroom
or, like its English counterpart, served in a well appointed
breakfast/sitting room. Restricted pay-and-display car parking
is available, and private parking can usually be arranged.
8⇌🏲 (3fb) ⊁ in 6 bedrooms ⊁ in dining room CTV in 11
bedrooms ⓡ T 🏲 (ex guide dogs) dB&B⇌🏲£39-£54
WB&B£117-£162
Lic 🛲 CTV nc4yrs
Credit Cards 1️⃣ 2️⃣ 3️⃣ £

GH 🅠🅠🅠 **Arlanda Hotel** 20 New Steine BN2 1PD
☎Brighton(0273) 699300 FAX (0273) 600930
A pleasant garden square close to the sea front and amenities is the
setting for this attractive four-storey terraced house dating from
the 18th century. Bedrooms, though compact, are smartened by
coordinating soft furnishings and equipped with telephones and en
suite showers. Evening meals can be served, by arrangement, in
the combined lounge/dining room on the ground floor.
12rm(2⇌10🏲) (4fb) ⊁ in dining room CTV in all bedrooms ⓡ
T 🏲 (ex guide dogs) ✳ sB&B⇌🏲£18-£36 dB&B⇌🏲£34-£66
LDO 4pm
Lic 🛲
Credit Cards 1️⃣ 2️⃣ 3️⃣ 5️⃣ £

GH 🅠🅠🅠 **Ascott House Hotel** 21 New Steine, Marine Parade
BN2 1PD ☎Brighton(0273) 688085 FAX (0273) 623733
This small, friendly hotel is situated in a smart garden square
opposite the sea and personally run by proprietors Michael and Avril
Strong. Most of the bedrooms have en suite facilities, and although
they vary in size they are all attractively decorated, immaculately
maintained and exceptionally well equipped. Snacks are available
throughout the day, and there is a short but varied evening meal
menu. The dining room is tastefully appointed in period style, and
there is a cosy adjoining lounge as well as a foyer bar/reception area.
12rm(9🏲) (8fb) ⊁ in dining room CTV in all bedrooms ⓡ T 🏲
sB&B£18-£25 sB&B🏲£25-£36 dB&B£42-£46 dB&B🏲£44-£70
LDO 4pm
Lic 🛲 ⨍nc3yrs
Credit Cards 1️⃣ 2️⃣ 3️⃣ 5️⃣

GH 🅠🅠🅠 **At The Twenty One** 21 Charlotte Street, Marine
Parade BN2 1AG (turn off A23 onto A259 towards Newhaven
proceed for 0.5m) ☎Brighton(0273) 686450 FAX (0273) 607711
Situated close to the seafront in the Kemp Town area, this early
Victorian town house offers a choice of exceptionally well
equipped bedrooms, all but one being en suite. There is an
impressive four-poster bedroom with period furniture and in the
basement a charming double room with its own ivy-clad
courtyard. Breakfast (and evening meals by prior arrangement) is
enjoyed in the bright ground floor dining room and there is a
comfortable furnished lounge downstairs.
6rm(5🏲) CTV in all bedrooms ⓡ T 🏲 (ex guide dogs)
sB&B🏲£32-£45 dB&B🏲£46-£68 LDO 9am
Lic 🛲 nc9yrs
Credit Cards 1️⃣ 2️⃣ 3️⃣ £

GH 🅠🅠🅠 **Bannings** 14 Upper Rock Gardens, Kemptown
BN2 1QE ☎Brighton(0273) 681403
Bannings is an attractive part Georgian terraced guest house,
personally run by father and son Geoff and Steve Norris. Bedrooms
vary in size, and are gradually being upgraded. A traditional full
English breakfast is served, offering a good choice of dishes

including vegetarian. Pay and display parking is available.
6rm(3⇌🏲) (3fb) ⊁ in 2 bedrooms ⊁ in dining room CTV in all
bedrooms ⓡ 🏲 sB&B£19-£25 sB&B⇌🏲£25-£35 dB&B£34-
£48 dB&B⇌🏲£38-£50
🛲 nc12yrs
Credit Cards 1️⃣ 2️⃣ 3️⃣ 5️⃣ £

GH 🅠🅠🅠 **Brighton Marina House Hotel** 8 Charlotte Street,
Marine Parade BN2 1AG ☎Brighton(0273) 605349 & 679484
FAX (0273) 605349
A well maintined family-run guest house close to the seafront and
all local amenities offers accommodation in attractively furnished
bedrooms, each equipped with telephone, TV, hairdryer, clock
radio and tea tray. Both continental and English breakfasts are
served in the small dining room (where two sittings are usually
necessary) and dinner can be provided by prior arrangement.
Service is particularly friendly and helpful.
10rm(7🏲) (3fb)CTV in all bedrooms ⓡ 🏲 ✳ sB&B£13.50-£25
dB&B£27-£35 dB&B🏲£27-£45 WB&B£81-£150 WBDi£177-
£234 LDO 4pm
Lic 🛲 ⨍
Credit Cards 1️⃣ 2️⃣ 3️⃣ 5️⃣ £

GH 🅠🅠🅠 **Cavalaire House** 34 Upper Rock Gardens,
Kemptown BN2 1QF (follow A259 towards Newhaven, turn left at
second set of traffic lights) ☎Brighton(0273) 696899
FAX (0273) 600504
Closed Xmas & New Year
Easily recognised by its bright blue exterior, this small Victorian
terraced house is convenient for shops and sea. Proprietors Mr and
Mrs Jones continue to make improvements, particularly in the
decor and furnishing of the bedrooms. There is a bright breakfast
room with lace tablecloths and a pleasant small lounge with an
attractive marble fireplace.
9rm(3🏲) (2fb)CTV in all bedrooms ⓡ sB&B£17 dB&B£40-
£44 WB&B£120-£132
🛲 ⨍nc5yrs
Credit Cards 1️⃣ 2️⃣ 3️⃣ 5️⃣

PREMIER 🏵 SELECTED

GH 🅠🅠🅠🅠🅠 *Claremont
House* Second Avenue BN3 2LL
☎Brighton(0273) 735161
This elegant Victorian house
situated in a tree-lined street,
offers elegant accommodation
in spacious, well proportioned
rooms which have kept some
of their original features
including marble fireplaces
and moulded ceilings. The
bar and lounge have
comfortable cushioned cane furniture, chandeliers and coal-
effect gas fires. Dinner can be provided on request, and
although a fair amount of convenience food is used, it is a
useful standby if guests do not want to go out.
12⇌🏲 (2fb) CTV in all bedrooms ⓡ LDO 10pm
Lic 🛲 CTV ⨍ 🐾
Credit Cards 1️⃣ 2️⃣ 3️⃣ 5️⃣

GH 🅠🅠 **Cornerways Private Hotel** 18-20 Caburn Road
BN3 6EF ☎Brighton(0273) 731882
This large Victorian corner house offers a variety of
accommodation, mostly furnished in traditional style. There is a
small bar, a cosy TV lounge and a traditional dining room.
10rm(1🏲) (2fb)CTV in 4 bedrooms ⓡ ✳ sB&Bfr£16 dB&Bfr£32
dB&B🏲£35-£37 WB&Bfr£102 WBDifr£137 LDO 2pm
Lic 🛲 CTV ⨍
£

GH Q Q Dudley House 10 Madeira Place BN2 1TN
☎Brighton(0273) 676794
A smart terraced house close to the seafront and all amenities. The relatively simply furnished bedrooms are all kept spick and span; some of the rooms are more spacious and have en suite shower rooms. There is a small sitting room adjoining the dining room, where smoking is not permitted; both rooms have attractive marble fireplaces, plants and flowers.
6rm(3♠) (3fb) CTV in all bedrooms ® ★ (ex guide dogs) ✳
dB&B£29-£36 dB&B♠£35-£50 WB&B£95-£160
⊞ CTV nc5yrs

GH Q Q Q Gullivers 10 New Steine BN2 1PB
☎Brighton(0273) 695415 FAX (0252) 372774
This mid-terrace Regency residence is close to the seafront and all amenities. The attractively decorated bedrooms have floral duvets that coordinate with the curtains and all have direct-dial telephones, with the majority benefiting from en suite facilities. Breakfast is served in the bright dining room by the friendly owner, Sally Gannaway.
9rm(5♠) (3fb) CTV in all bedrooms ® T
⊞
Credit Cards 1 2 3 5

GH Q Q Q Kempton House Hotel 33/34 Marine Parade BN2 1TR
☎Brighton(0273) 570248 FAX (0273) 570248
This small hotel on the seafront, personally run in informal style by its proprietors, provides accommodation in attractive bedrooms which, though not large, are equipped with direct dial telephone, clock radio, TV, hairdryer, trouser press and tea tray. Public rooms comprise a combined dining room and bar reception area.
12♠ (4fb) CTV in all bedrooms ® T LDO 9am
Lic ⊞
Credit Cards 1 2 3 5

GH Q Q Kimberley Hotel 17 Atlingworth Street BN2 1PL
☎Brighton(0273) 603504 FAX (0273) 685373
Enjoying a central position just east of the Palace pier and close to the seafront, this hotel has been owned and managed by the Roland family for the past 30 years. The bedrooms are neat with traditional styles of decor and furnishings. There is a cosy lounge bar in addition to a comfortable front-facing lounge, equipped with books and magazines. Breakfast is served in the pretty dining room, and on-street parking is available, with a National Car Park nearby.
15rm(4⇨9♠) (3fb) ⊁ in dining room CTV in all bedrooms ® ★
(ex guide dogs) sB&B£18-£22 dB&B£30-£36 dB&B⇨♠£36-£40
WB&B£105-£120
Lic ⊞ CTV nc2yrs
Credit Cards 1 2 3 5

GH Q Q Malvern Hotel 33 Regency Square BN1 2GG
☎Brighton(0273) 324302 FAX (0273) 324302
Part of an attractive square, this small family-run hotel faces the sea and West Pier. The bedrooms are similarly furnished, though some have more recent decor and pretty duvets. All have en suite shower rooms and telephones. Public rooms comprise a lounge and a small bar.
12♠ CTV in all bedrooms ® T ★
Lic ⊞
Credit Cards 1 2 3 5

GH Q Q Melford Hall Hotel 41 Marine Parade BN2 1PE
☎Brighton(0273) 681435 FAX (0273) 624186
Closed 24 Dec-2 Jan
This small hotel enjoys a prime position overlooking the sea. Bedrooms are freshly decorated in a modern style with white furniture, floral duvets and coordinating curtains, and the majority are en suite. English breakfast is served in the dining room and there is a guests' lounge to the front. Car parking facilities, though limited, are an added bonus.

▶

25rm(23🛁🚿) (4fb) 🚭 in dining room CTV in all bedrooms [R] **T** 🚫🐕 (ex guide dogs) ✳ sB&B🛁🚿£28-£32 dB&B🛁🚿£44-£54 WB&B£150-£170
🛗 CTV
Credit Cards [1][2][3][5][£]

GH [Q][Q][Q] New Steine Hotel 12a New Steine, Marine Parade BN2 1PB ☎Brighton(0273) 681546
Mar-mid Dec rs Xmas & New Year
This delightful, long established hotel, personally run by its resident proprietors, offers a good range of bedrooms furnished in modern style. Public areas include a comfortable downstairs lounge as well as the well appointed breakfast room - which will serve a vegetarian meal by arrangement - and the atmosphere is very friendly and informal throughout. Restricted pay-and-display parking is usually available.
11rm(9🛁🚿) 🚭 in dining room CTV in all bedrooms [R] ✳ sB&Bfr£16 sB&B🛁🚿fr£25 dB&B🛁🚿£38-£42
🛗 CTV 🚫🅿 nc8yrs
[£]

GH [Q][Q] Paskins Hotel 19 Charlotte Street BN2 1AG ☎Brighton(0273) 601203 FAX (0273) 621973
This elegant Georgian mid-terrace house is situated in a peaceful street just a short distance from the seafront and the town centre. Bedrooms are very well equipped, most are attractively decorated in coordinated colour schemes and all but three are en suite. Public areas include a ground floor reception and lounge and the dining room and adjoining bar are furnished in a bright modern style.
19rm(16🛁🚿) (2fb) 🚭 in area of dining room CTV in all bedrooms [R] **T** ✳ sB&Bfr£15 sB&B🛁🚿£25-£30 dB&Bfr£25 dB&B🛁🚿£40-£55 LDO 5.30pm
Lic 🛗 nc5yrs
Credit Cards [1][2][3][£]

GH [Q][Q][Q] Pier View Hotel 28 New Steine BN2 1PD ☎Brighton(0273) 605310 FAX (0273) 688604
Closed 24-30 Dec
A smart Regency terraced house, Pier View is aptly named as it looks over the sea and Palace Pier. Bedrooms are freshly decorated and modern. The smartly appointed breakfast room combines with a small, comfortably furnished lounge. Proprietress Mrs King creates a welcoming and cheerful atmosphere.
11rm(8🚿) (3fb) 🚭 in dining room CTV in all bedrooms [R] **T** 🚫🐕 (ex guide dogs) sB&B£20-£24 sB&B🚿fr£29 dB&B🚿£44-£58 LDO 5pm
🛗 CTV
Credit Cards [1][2][3][5][£]

GH [Q][Q] *Prince Regent Hotel* 29 Regency Square BN1 2FH ☎Brighton(0273) 329962 FAX (0273) 748162
Situated at the top of the Square, this attractive Regency mid-terrace hotel offers a range of bedrooms to suit all tastes. Two have 19th-century four poster beds and ornate furnishings whilst others are simpler in style and more compact. All are en suite and well equipped, several have stocked mini bars. Continental breakfast can be served in the bedrooms or alternatively a full English breakfast is available in the dining room.
20🛁🚿 CTV in all bedrooms [R] **T** 🚫🐕 (ex guide dogs)
Lic 🛗 CTV nc12yrs
Credit Cards [1][2][3][5]

GH [Q][Q] Queensbury Hotel 58 Regency Square BN1 2GB ☎Brighton(0273) 325558 FAX (0273) 324800
Closed 3 days Xmas
One of several houses in an attractive square opposite the sea, the Queensberry is run by a friendly mother and daughter team. Rooms are comfortable and many have en suites or shower units. Breakfast is served in the bright dining room and there is a large traditionally furnished lounge.
16rm(6🛁🚿) (8fb) 🚭 in dining room CTV in all bedrooms [R] ✳ sB&B£18-£25 sB&B🛁🚿£20-£30 dB&B£30-£40 dB&B🛁🚿£40-£58 WB&B£140-£196
🛗 CTV
Credit Cards [1][3]

GH [Q][Q][Q] *Regency Hotel* 28 Regency Square BN1 2FH (opposite West Pier) ☎Brighton(0273) 202690 FAX (0273) 220438
Conveniently positioned for the conference centre, exhibition halls, shops and seafront, this well run small hotel offers a range of individually furnished bedrooms, all with modern equipment. Most rooms are en suite but those which are not provide good value for money. Evening meals are available by arrangement in the no-smoking dining room, and there is a cosy bar and traditional lounge.
14rm(1🛁10🚿) (1fb) CTV in all bedrooms [R] **T** 🚫🐕 (ex guide dogs) LDO noon
Lic 🛗 CTV 🏠
Credit Cards [1][2][3][5]

GH [Q][Q][Q] Trouville Hotel 11 New Steine, Marine Parade BN2 1PB ☎Brighton(0273) 697384
Closed Jan
Part of an attractive sea front square, the Trouville is a tastefully restored Grade II listed building run by proud owners Mr and Mrs Hansell. In recent years much improvement has taken place with co-ordinated decor and soft furnishings and there have been two more smart en suites added. The 4 poster room has its own balcony. A choice of breakfast is served in the ground floor dining room which opens out to a small lounge, both having original marble fireplaces.
9rm(4🚿) (1fb) 🚭 in dining room CTV in all bedrooms [R] 🚫🐕 ✳ sB&B£18 sB&B🚿£29 dB&B£30-£35 dB&B🚿£42-£46 WB&B£101.50-£150
Lic 🛗 CTV
Credit Cards [1][2][3][£]

GH [Q][Q] Westbourne Hotel 46 Upper Rock Gardens BN2 1QF ☎Brighton(0273) 686920
A Victorian terraced house in walking distance of all local amenities, Westbourne offers a range of bright comfortable bedrooms. There is a comfortable lounge, and the neat dining room has a small corner bar for residents.
10rm(6🚿) (4fb) 🚭 in 1 bedrooms 🚭 in dining room CTV in all bedrooms [R] 🚫🐕 ✳ sB&Bfr£17 sB&B🚿£25 dB&Bfr£32 dB&B🚿£44 WB&B£105-£140 WBDi£150-£190 LDO 6pm
Lic 🛗
Credit Cards [1][2][3][£]

BRIG O'TURK Central *Perthshire* Map **11** NN50

P R E M I E R S E L E C T E D

GH [Q][Q][Q][Q][Q]
Dundarroch Country House Trossachs FK17 8HT (on A821) ☎Trossachs(0877) 376200 FAX (0877) 376202
rs Nov-19 Dec

Morna Dalziel Williams' much-acclaimed small country guest house is set in some of Scotland's most attractive countryside. There are well appointed bedrooms and a small cosy lounge with a wood-burning stove. Only breakfast is provided here, but recommendations are made for some popular eating places in the area; for the more adventurous, a 20-minute drive over the 'Duke's Pass' to Aberfoyle and the award-winning Braeval Mill restaurant is especially recommended. The elegant breakfast room gives stunning views towards Ben Venue.
3🛁🚿 🚭 CTV in all bedrooms [R] **T** 🚫🐕 ✳ sB&B🛁🚿£42.75-

£49.75 dB&B⇔🛏️£55.50-£63.50 WB&Bfr£195 LDO 8.45pm
🔥, nc5yrs ✦
Credit Cards ①③ ©

BRIGSTEER (NEAR KENDAL) Cumbria — Map 07 SD48

FH QQQ Mrs B Gardner **Barrowfield** *(SD484908)* LA8 8BJ
☎Crosthwaite(05395) 68336
Apr-Oct
Dating back to the Elizabethan period, this charming farmhouse is set in peaceful lakeland scenery. A very pleasant standard of accommodation is maintained by Mrs Gardener. The house is on a long forest track leading from the Kendal road out of the village of Brigsteer and is signposted on a sharp bend.
3 (1fb) 🍴 dB&B£30-£34
🔥, CTV 180 acres dairy sheep
©

BRISTOL Avon — Map 03 ST57

In additon to the national changes to dialling codes on 16 April 1995 (ie the insertion of `1' after the first `0') the codes for certain cities are changing completely - The code for Bristol will be `0117' with each individual number prefixed by `9'.

GH QQQ Alandale Hotel 4 Tyndall's Park Road, Clifton BS8 1PG (adjacent to BBC studios) ☎(0272) 735407
Closed 2wks Xmas
This large, personally run, Victorian guest house stands next to the BBC studios and conveniently near the university, shops and business area. Bright, modern en suite bedrooms in a range of sizes are equipped with direct dial telephones and TV, while comfortable public areas include a bright breakfast room and spacious lounge with honesty bar. On-site car parking is limited.
17rm(5⇔12🐾) CTV in all bedrooms ® T sB&B⇔🛏️£28-£40 dB&B⇔🛏️£38-£48
Lic 🔥,
Credit Cards ①③©

GH QQ Alcove 508-510 Fishponds Road, Fishponds BS16 3DT (leave M32 junct2 follow signs into Fishponds & turn left into Fishponds Rd) ☎(0272) 653886 & 652436 FAX (0272) 653886
Small and friendly, this personally run guest house catering mainly for commercial business stands in a residential area just north of the city, with easy access to both the M4 and M32 motorways and the centre. Bedrooms offer adequate comfort and there is a cosy little breakfast room.
9rm(3🐾) (2fb) ⚔ in dining room CTV in all bedrooms ® 🍴 (ex guide dogs) sB&B£20-£25 sB&B🛏️£25-£30 dB&B£32-£36 dB&B🛏️£36-£40 LDO 4pm
🔥, CTV
©

GH QQ *Birkdale Hotel* 11 Ashgrove Road, Redland BS6 6LY (off Whiteladies road, 1m from city centre)
☎(0272) 733635 & 736332 FAX (0272) 739964
Closed Xmas wk
Conveniently positioned, the main building of this hotel houses the bar and restaurant while the majority of the bedrooms are situated in separate houses nearby. Most of these are modern and well equipped but those that are in the main house are scheduled for decoration.
42rm(34⇔8🐾) CTV in all bedrooms ® LDO 8pm
Lic 🔥,
Credit Cards ①③

GH QQQ Downlands 33 Henleaze Gardens, Henleaze BS9 4HH ☎(0272) 621639
A charming, tall, Victorian house set in a residential area near the Downs - yet within easy walking distance of the city centre - and personally run by conscientious owners offers accommodation in bright, individually styled bedrooms. There is a cosy breakfast

room and a comfortable lounge, the secluded garden is popular in summer, and unrestricted street parking is available.
10rm(2🐾) (1fb)CTV in all bedrooms ® ✳ sB&B£23-£27 sB&B🛏️£34 dB&Bfr£40 dB&B🛏️fr£46
🔥, ✗
Credit Cards ①③©

GH QQ Oakfield Hotel 52-54 Oakfield Road, Clifton BS8 2BG ☎(0272) 735556
Closed 23 Dec-1-Jan
Personally owned and run by Mrs Hurley since the 1940s, this well established hotel still deserves top marks for spotless housekeeping and refreshingly traditional standards, with classical silver and bone china in the breakfast room and service of early morning tea and hot drinks in the evening. Bedrooms have first-class beds and excellent linen. The Oakfield is in a convenient position close to Whiteladies Road, the BBC, Clifton and the university.
27rm (4fb) ⚔ in dining room CTV in all bedrooms ® sB&B£25-£27 dB&B£35-£37 WB&B£175 LDO 7pm
🔥, CTV

GH QQ Rowan Lodge 41 Gloucester Road North, Filton Park BS7 0SN (on junct of A38 with Bronksea road) ☎(0272) 312170
Closed Xmas & New Year
This large detached house with its own car park, is situated north of the city, close to the suburb of Filton and Bristol's business complex. Bedrooms are well equipped and there is a pleasant lounge/breakfast room.
6rm(3🐾) (2fb) ⚔ in dining room ⚔ in lounges CTV in all bedrooms ® ✳ sB&B£22-£30 sB&B🛏️fr£30 dB&Bfr£35 dB&B🛏️fr£40 WB&B£105-£210
🔥,
Credit Cards ①③©
See advertisement on p.103.

GH [Q][Q] Washington Hotel 11-15 St Pauls Road, Clifton BS8 1LX (follow A4018 into city, turn right at lights opposite BBC buildings, hotel is 200yds on left) ☎(0272) 733980
Telex no 449075 FAX (0272) 741082

Closed 23 Dec-3 Jan

This large, rambling, unlicensed hotel stands in a very convenient position for Clifton, the shops and the university. There is a range of well equipped bedrooms from the comfortable and well furnished to the more modest. The breakfast room is bright and cosy, and guests can also dine at the Racks restaurant located in the sister hotel, The Clifton. There is limited but unrestricted car parking in the opposite street.

46rm(34🛁🚿) (5fb) CTV in all bedrooms Ⓡ **T** sB&B£23-£27 sB&B🛁🚿£36-£45 dB&B£36-£45 dB&B🛁🚿£46-£59 LDO 11pm

Lic ♨

Credit Cards [1] [2] [3] [5] [£]

GH [Q][Q][Q] Westbury Park Hotel 37 Westbury Road, Westbury-on-Trym BS9 3AU (on A4018) ☎(0272) 620465
FAX (0272) 628607

Situated on the famous Durdham Downs, between Bristol city centre and junction 17 of the M5, this detached Victorian family house is ideal for holiday-makers and business guests. There is an attractive lounge adorned with fresh flowers, a bar where snacks are available and an elegant dining room where breakfast is served. Bedrooms have all the creature comforts, and most are en suite.

8rm(6🛁🚿) (2fb) 🚭 in dining room CTV in all bedrooms Ⓡ **T** ✱ sB&B£25 sB&B🛁🚿£33-£36 dB&B£38-£40 dB&B🛁🚿£43-£48 LDO 8.30pm

Lic ♨ CTV

Credit Cards [1] [2] [3] [5]

BRIXHAM Devon — Map **03** SX95

GH [Q][Q][Q] Harbour Side 65 Berry Head Road TQ5 9AA (follow signs for 'Marina') ☎(0803) 858899

This small friendly guest house is ideally situated, overlooking the outer harbour with views over the marina and Torbay beyond, yet within a few minutes' walk of the town. Proprietors Jenny and Peter Tomlins provide dinner by prior arrangement, and a choice of dishes is offered at breakfast. Bedrooms are neatly furnished and adequately equipped.

6rm(3🚿) (1fb) 🚭 in dining room CTV in all bedrooms Ⓡ 🐕 (ex guide dogs) sB&B£16-£20 dB&B£28-£32 dB&B🚿£32-£36 WB&B£98-£116 WBDi£154-£170 LDO 10am

CTV 🅿̸

[£]

GH [Q][Q] Harbour View Hotel 65 King St TQ5 9TH
☎(0803) 853052

Guests arriving by sea would have no trouble spotting this house as it directly overlooks the entrance to the inner harbour and was once the home of a harbour master. Bedrooms are simple but attractive with many facilities. Breakfast is served in the dining room/lounge.

9rm (1fb)CTV in all bedrooms Ⓡ 🐕 ✱ sB&B£18 dB&B£30-£36 LDO breakfast

♨

Credit Cards [1] [3]

GH [Q][Q] Raddicombe Lodge 105 Kingswear Road TQ5 0EX (on B3205) ☎(0803) 882125

14 Apr-14 Oct rs 15 Oct-19 Dec & 11 Jan-13 Apr

A mock-Tudor house stands in its own garden away from the town on the Kingswear road. The building is full of character and some of the bedrooms now have private bathrooms.

8rm(3🚿) (2fb) 🚭 in bedrooms CTV in all bedrooms Ⓡ 🐕 ✱ sB&B£15-£18.20 sB&B🚿£22.60-£26.60 dB&B£30-£36.40 dB&B🚿£42.60 WB&B£105-£137.20

Credit Cards [1] [3] [5] [£]

GH [Q][Q][Q] Ranscombe House Hotel Ranscombe Road TQ5 9UP ☎(0803) 882337

A little way from the town centre with views over the rooftops to the harbour, this 18th-century property stands in its own garden. Bedrooms are comfortable. Dinner and breakfast are served in a pleasant dining room and there is also a bar.

9🛁🚿 (2fb)CTV in all bedrooms Ⓡ **T** 🐕 (ex guide dogs) sB&B🛁🚿£20-£25 dB&B🛁🚿£40-£50 WB&B£126-£161 WBDi£199-£220 LDO 4pm

Lic ♨ CTV

Credit Cards [1] [2] [3] [5]

GH [Q][Q] Sampford House 59 King Street TQ5 9TH (foolw signs for harbour Sampford House overllooks inner harbour on south side just above Southern Quay) ☎(0803) 857761

Closed Dec & Jan rs Nov & Feb

Sampford House is a well maintained terraced property overlooking the inner harbour. Bedrooms are fairly compact, and there is a cosy lounge with tea-making facilities. The rear dining room overlooks a colourful courtyard and an evening meal can be provided by arrangement. Limited parking is available on the quay.

6rm(2🛁🚿) (1fb) 🚭 in dining room CTV in all bedrooms Ⓡ ✱ dB&B£30-£32 dB&B🛁🚿£36-£38 LDO 10am

♨ CTV

[£]

GH [Q][Q][Q] *Woodlands* Parkham Road TQ5 9BU ☎(0803) 852040

Mar-Oct

Walk a few yards from the town centre into a quiet road and you will find Woodlands - a Victorian house with well kept garden. There is no smoking. Bedrooms are up to hotel standards and breakfast is served in a sunny dining room with views to the outer harbour. There is a separate sitting room with open fire.

5🚿 (1fb) CTV in all bedrooms Ⓡ 🐕

♨

Credit Cards [1] [3]

BROADSTAIRS Kent — Map **05** TR36

GH [Q][Q][Q] *Bay Tree Hotel* 12 Eastern Esplanade CT10 1DR
☎Thanet(0843) 862502 FAX (0843) 860589

Situated in complete peace and quiet overlooking the sea, this small family hotel is within five minutes' walk of the town via a cliff-top footpath. The spacious bedrooms have bright and cheerful decor and four enjoy sea views. The dining room has large picture windows overlooking Stone Bay and the Channel, and there is a choice of menu at both breakfast and dinner. The cosy lounge also has sea views, and doubles as a small bar.

11🛁🚿 CTV in all bedrooms Ⓡ 🐕 (ex guide dogs) LDO 4pm

Lic ♨ nc10yrs

Credit Cards [1] [3]

GH [Q][Q] Devonhurst Hotel Eastern Esplanade CT10 1DR
☎Thanet(0843) 863010 FAX (0843) 868940

Margaret and David Payne offer a warm welcome to guests at their small hotel, which overlooks the sea and sandy bay. The pretty bedrooms are always being improved, with added facilities, fabric canopies, silk flowers and fresh floral decor. Four rooms have splendid views and two have their own balcony. Downstairs, the dining room combines with a fully stocked bar, and there is a small lounge with satellite TV. Early breakfasts and special diets can be catered for.

9🚿 (1fb) 🚭 in 4 bedrooms 🚭 in dining room CTV in all bedrooms Ⓡ 🐕 (ex guide dogs) ✱ sB&B🚿£20-£28 dB&B🚿£41-£48 WB&B£121-£135 WBDi£162-£179 LDO 5.30pm

Lic ♨ CTV nc5yrs

Credit Cards [1] [2] [3] [£]

GH [Q] *East Horndon Private Hotel* 4 Eastern Esplanade CT10 1DP
☎Thanet(0843) 868306

Mar-Nov

In a quiet position on the East Cliff seafront, this large Victorian house, now a small private hotel, offers a range of bedrooms varying from compact singles to spacious family rooms with en suite facilities, all modestly furnished. There is a traditionally styled lounge bar and a separate dining room where both breakfast and dinner are served.
10rm(4⇌🟋) (6fb) CTV in all bedrooms ® LDO noon
Lic 🎟 🎐
Credit Cards 1 3

GH Q Q Q **Gull Cottage** 5 Eastern Esplanade CT10 1DP
☎Thanet(0843) 861936
Closed Nov-Mar
A smart detached house dating from 1898, pleasantly situated overlooking the sea and sandy beach. Proprietors Joan and David Watling have completely refurbished the house and the rooms are most attractive, with striking fabrics and a mixture of old and modern furniture. There is a charming 1st floor lounge with panoramic views, and home-cooked evening meals are served in the licensed dining room, at separate tables. Home-made bread and marmalade is served at breakfast, together with a choice of cooked meal.
8rm(6🟋) (3fb) ⊬ CTV in 7 bedrooms ® 🟌 (ex guide dogs)
sB&B£20-£23 dB&B£40-£46 dB&B🟋£40-£46 WB&B£130-£135
Lic 🎟 CTV nc6yrs
Credit Cards 1 2 3 5

BROADWAY Hereford & Worcester   Map **04** SP03

SELECTED

GH Q Q Q Q **Cusack's Glebe** Cusack's Glebe, Saintbury WR12 7PX ☎(0386) 852210
Closed 15 Dec-15 Jan
2rm(1⇌1🟋) (1fb) ⊬ CTV in all bedrooms ® 🟌 (ex guide dogs) ✻ sB&B⇌🟋£38-£40 dB&B⇌🟋£49-£58 WB&B£173 nc8yrs

---

SELECTED

GH Q Q Q Q **Leasow House** WR12 7NA BROADWAY
☎Evesham(0386) 584526 FAX (0386) 584596
(For full entry see Laverton)

GH Q Q Q **Milestone House Hotel** 122 High Street WR12 7AJ
☎(0386) 853432
Closed 27 Dec-Jan
Milestone House offers comfortable individually furnished rooms well equipped with the usual modern amenities. The attractive conservatory restaurant, specialising in Italian dishes, is popular with residents and non-residents and has a good value table d'hôte menu in addition to the à la carte. There is a rear car park and a delightful area with hanging baskets, which become alive with colour in the summer.
4rm(2⇌2🟋) (1fb) ⊬ in bedrooms ⊬ in area of dining room CTV in all bedrooms ® 🟌 (ex guide dogs) ✻ dB&B⇌🟋£55-£57.50 LDO 9.30pm
Lic 🎟
Credit Cards 1 3
See advertisement on p.105.

Telephone national area codes are due to change by 16th April 1995. Please see the note under 'How to Use this Guide' at the front of the book.

Rowan Lodge Hotel
41 Gloucester Road North, Filton Park,
Bristol BS7 0SN
Telephone: (0117) 9312170

Comfortable & friendly family run hotel.
Situated on the A38 with easy access to the
M4 & M5. Tea/coffee making facilities, colour
TV in all rooms. Some rooms en-suite.
Free parking.

Hosts: Geraldine and Graham Champ

Leasow House
Laverton Meadows, Broadway,
Worcestershire WR12 7NA
Tel: Stanton (01386) 584 526 Fax: (01386) 584 596

Tranquilly situated approximately one mile off the B4632 (the
Wormington-Dumbleton Road) and some three miles south of
Broadway, making it ideally situated as a centre for touring
the Cotswolds and the Vale of Evesham.
We offer spacious accommodation with all the refinements of
the 20th century. All bedrooms have private shower/bathroom
en suite, colour television, tea and coffee making facilities.
Ground floor facilities for elderly and disabled people.
Leasow House is personally run by your hosts:
BARBARA & GORDON MEEKINGS
See gazetteer under Laverton

PREMIER 🏵 **SELECTED**

GH 🟦🟦🟦🟦🟦 **Old Rectory** Church Street WR12 7PN
BROADWAY ☎(0386) 853729
(For full entry see Willersey)

GH 🟦🟦 **Olive Branch Guest House** 78 High Street WR12 7AJ
☎(0386) 853440 FAX (0386) 853440
Constructed from Cotswold stone, just like the adjoining
properties, this small High-Street guest house dates back some
400 years. Bedrooms are neat and freshly decorated, and there is
one room in a converted outbuilding. The dining room has an
impressive slate floor and an inglenook fireplace, and many
original timbers can be seen.
8rm(6⇌🟥) (1fb) ⍋ in dining room CTV in all bedrooms ® ⅄
(ex guide dogs) ✳ sB&B£17-£19.50 dB&B⇌🟥£40-£45
WB&B£112 LDO 7.30pm
▥ CTV
Credit Cards ②£

SELECTED

GH 🟦🟦🟦🟦 **Orchard Grove** Station Road WR12 7DE
☎Evesham(0386) 853834
Closed Xmas & New Year
Set back off the Evesham road, a short walk from the village
centre, this immaculately kept house offers comfortable
modern accommodation in what is very much a family home.
It offers a cosy lounge, a breakfast room and well furnished
bedrooms, all nicely decorated, and there is a little terrace to
the rear overlooking the delightful garden. No smoking.
3rm(1⇌) (1fb) ⍋ CTV in 1 bedroom ® ⅄ (ex guide dogs)
✳ sB&B£20-£25 dB&B⇌£40-£45
▥ CTV nc10yrs
£

GH 🟦🟦🟦 **Small Talk Lodge** Keil Close, 32 High Street
WR12 7DP (on A44 in middle of High St next to Lygon Arms Hotel)
☎Evesham(0386) 858953
Situated behind a tea shop of the same name in the centre of the
High Street, this Cotswold stone lodge offers prettily decorated
bedrooms, including one family suite. Owner Lin Scrannage is a
proficient chef and many guests return regularly for the quality of
her food. Dinners are held by candlelight and the set meal is based
on seasonal produce.
8rm(6⇌🟥) (1fb) ⍋ in dining room ⍋ in lounges CTV in all
bedrooms ® ⅄ (ex guide dogs) ✳ sB&B£20-£30 dB&B£40-£44
dB&B⇌🟥£42-£50
Lic CTV
Credit Cards ①③£

BROCKENHURST Hampshire   Map **04** SU30

PREMIER 🏵 **SELECTED**

GH 🟦🟦🟦🟦🟦 **Thatched
Cottage Hotel** 16 Brookley
Road SO42 7RR (off A337)
☎(0590) 23090
FAX (0590) 23479
Closed 4-31 Jan rs Feb & Mar
5⇌🟥 CTV in all bedrooms
® T sB&B⇌🟥£55-£59
dB&B⇌🟥fr£78 LDO 9.30pm
Lic ▥ nc10yrs
Credit Cards ①③

SELECTED

GH 🟦🟦🟦🟦 **The Cottage** Sway Road SO42 7SH
☎Lymington(0590) 22296
Mr and Mrs Moore have a most comfortable, attractive hotel
in the village centre with many guests returning frequently.
Bedrooms are well furnished and the lounge is smart with
much character. In the summer cream teas are served in the
garden.
7rm(6⇌🟥) ⍋ in 2 bedrooms ⍋ in dining room CTV in all
bedrooms ® ⅄ sB&B£32-£34 sB&B⇌🟥£36-£40
dB&B⇌🟥£50-£64 WB&B£175-£195
Lic ▥ nc12yrs
Credit Cards ①③£

BRODICK See **ARRAN, ISLE OF**

BROMLEY Greater London   Map **05** TQ46

GH 🟦🟦 **Glendevon House** 80 Southborough Road, Bickley
BR1 2EN (turn off A222 at sign for railway station, hotel on fourth
side rd on right hand side) ☎081-467 2183
This detached period house is in a residential street near Bickley
station and Bromley shopping centre. Bedrooms vary in size and
are simply decorated and soundly equipped. Downstairs is a
comfortable lounge, and evening snacks are available.
11rm(3⇌🟥) (2fb)CTV in 10 bedrooms ® ✳ sB&B£23.50-£27
sB&B⇌🟥£29.50 dB&Bfr£37 dB&B⇌🟥£42 LDO 9pm
▥ CTV
Credit Cards ①③£

BROMPTON REGIS Somerset   Map **03** SS93

FH 🟦 Mrs G Payne **Lower Holworthy** *(SS978308)* TA22 9NY
☎(03987) 244
Closed Dec
Situated on the banks of Wimbleball Lake, popular for fishing and
water sports, this small farmhouse is in a secluded situation with
wonderful views across the lake and the rolling Exmoor
countryside. Set on a 200-acre livestock farm, it offers simple
bedroom accommodation and a cosy sitting room with a log fire.
Guests are given a hearty breakfast served in the attractive dining
room which has a wood burning stove.
3rm ® ⅄ (ex guide dogs)
▥ CTV 200 acres beef sheep
£

BROMSGROVE Hereford & Worcester   Map **07** SO97

FH 🟦🟦🟦 Mr & Mrs A Gibbs **Lower Bentley** *(SO662979)*
Lower Bentley B60 4JB ☎(0527) 821286
3rm(2⇌) (1fb)CTV in all bedrooms ® ✳ sB&Bfr£20
sB&B⇌fr£25 dB&Bfr£30 dB&B⇌£35 WB&B£90-£125
▥ CTV 346 acres dairy beef

BROMYARD Hereford & Worcester   Map **03** SO65

FH 🟦🟦🟦 Mrs P Morgan **Nether Court** *(SO619494)* Stoke
Lacy HR7 4HJ (on A465) ☎Hereford(0432) 820247
This Victorian farmhouse in the village of Stoke Lacy has
comfortable bedrooms furnished with some fine antique pieces.
The breakfast room is most impressive, with its old kitchen range
and original bread oven. There is a reading room for guests, and
the pleasant grounds include a tennis court and a lake.
3⇌ (1fb) CTV in all bedrooms ® ⅄ ✳ sB&Bfr£18 dB&Bfr£30
LDO 24hr notice
CTV ✔ 360 acres mixed

BRORA Highland *Sutherlandshire*   Map **14** NC90

SELECTED

GH 🅀🅀🅀🅀 **Lynwood** Golf Road KW9 6QS (turn off A9 by river bridge onto Golf Rd) ☎(0408) 621226

Closed Jan & Feb

Set in its own walled garden with views over the harbour and close to the golf course, this friendly, family-run guest house has a reputation for comfort and enjoyable home cooking. Excellent standards of housekeeping are maintained throughout, and the well decorated bedrooms are comfortably furnished in the modern style; one is suitable for disabled guests and has external access. There is a pleasant lounge and the attractive dining room has a conservatory extension overlooking the garden.

3rm(1⇄1ﰯ) Annexe 1ﰯ (1fb) ⊭ in bedrooms ⊭ in 1 lounge CTV in all bedrooms ® ✳ sB&B£19 sB&B⇄ﰯ£22 dB&B£32 dB&B⇄ﰯ£38 WB&B£105-£125 WBDi£169-£189 ▥ CTV

Credit Cards 1 3 £

BROUGH Cumbria   Map **12** NY71

FH 🅀🅀🅀 Mrs J M Atkinson **Augill House** *(NY814148)* CA17 4DX (400yds off A66) ☎(07683) 41305

Bedrooms and public areas are equally pleasant at this very attractive Georgian farmhouse just off the bypass on the eastern side of the village, and a particularly caring hostess provides good standards of home cooking.

3rm(2⇄1ﰯ) ⊭ CTV in all bedrooms ® ☈ (ex guide dogs) ✳ dB&B⇄ﰯ£38-£40 WB&B£120 WBDi£175 LDO 4pm ▥ CTV nc12yrs 40 acres mixed £

BROUGHTON-IN-FURNESS Cumbria Map **07** SD28

INN[Q][Q] Manor Arms The Square LA20 6HY (take A5092 signposted to Millom and then follow signs to Broughton-in-Furness) ☎(0229) 716286

3🚿 (1fb) 🚭 in bedrooms CTV in all bedrooms [R] 🐕 (ex guide dogs) ✻ sB&B🚿£21 dB&B🚿£36 Bar Lunch fr£1.20

🚫pool table

Credit Cards [1] [2] [3]

BUCKFAST Devon Map **03** SX76

GH [Q][Q][Q] ***Furzeleigh Mill Country Hotel*** Dart Bridge TQ11 0JP (beside A38 between Buckfast & Dartmoor) ☎Buckfastleigh(0364) 43476 FAX (0364) 643476

Its location on the edge of the National Park makes this old mill house a convenient stopover on the way to the West Country or base for exploring Dartmoor. Bedrooms are small but comfortably furnished and well equipped. Ample public areas include two dining rooms offering a wide variety of food from a choice of menus. There is a comfortable residents' lounge and a large bar where hosts Bob and Ann Sandford endeavour to make all their guests feel at home.

15rm(13🛁🚿) (2fb) CTV in all bedrooms [R] LDO 8.30pm

Lic ♨ CTV

Credit Cards [1] [2] [3] [5]

BUCKFASTLEIGH Devon Map **03** SX76

GH [Q][Q] ***Dartbridge Manor*** 20 Dartbridge Road TQ11 0DZ (beside A38 between Exeter & Plymouth) ☎(0364) 643575

A stone built 400-year-old manor house full of character with exposed beams and open fires. The bedrooms are well furnished and there is a comfortable lounge and breakfast room.

10🛁🚿 (2fb) 🐕

♨ CTV 🎣

SELECTED

INN[Q][Q][Q][Q] Dartbridge Totnes Road TQ11 0JR (turn off A38 onto A384) ☎(0364) 642214 FAX (0364) 643977

Situated on the banks of the Dart, this inn is owned and managed by the Evans family. Bedrooms are attractive, a wide choice of menus is available in the large oak panelled bar, and a function room has recently been added.

11🛁🚿 (1fb) 🚭 in dining room CTV in all bedrooms [R] T 🐕 (ex guide dogs) ✻ sB&B🛁🚿£35 dB&B🛁🚿£50-£55 WB&B£165-£190 WBDi£245-£265 LDO 9.30pm

♨

Credit Cards [1] [3]

BUDE Cornwall & Isles of Scilly Map **02** SS20

SELECTED

GH [Q][Q][Q][Q] Cliff Hotel Maer Down, Crooklets Beach EX23 8NG ☎(0288) 353110 FAX (0288) 353110

Apr-Oct

Situated near the cliff path, with extensive panoramic views, this hotel occupies an enviable position, with Crooklets Beach 200 yards away and the town centre within easy walking distance. Purpose-built, it provides well decorated and furnished bedrooms, several with sea views and some with balconies. The large well designed public areas include a bar and sun lounge where snacks are available all day, an attractive recently refurbished dining room and a games room with a pool table. There are extensive leisure facilities, with children well catered for in the large gardens.

15🛁🚿 (12fb) 🚭 in area of dining room 🚭 in 1 lounge CTV in all bedrooms [R] T ✻ sB&B🛁🚿£25-£40 dB&B🛁🚿£48-£64 WB&B£125-£200 WBDi£200-£250 LDO 6pm

Lic CTV 🏊 (heated) 🎾(hard)solarium indoor spa pool putting

[£]

GH [Q][Q] Links View 13 Morwenna Terrace EX23 8BU ☎(0288) 352561

Closed Dec

A popular terraced guesthouse overlooking the golf links and sea, within easy walking distance of the town centre. The bedrooms are comfortable and well decorated, some with en suite shower rooms. The dining room combines with the bar and there is a comfortable TV lounge.

7rm (2fb) 🚭 in dining room CTV in all bedrooms [R] 🐕 (ex guide dogs) ✻ sB&B£13-£15 dB&B£26-£30 WB&B£87-£91

Lic ♨ CTV

[£]

🛏☕ **GH [Q][Q] Pencarrol** 21 Downs View EX23 8RF (turn off A39 to town centre follow signs to Crooklets Beach, Downs View Road is ahead at Beach car park) ☎(0288) 352478

Closed Xmas rs Jan-Mar & Nov-Dec

This well established guesthouse sits in a quiet road overlooking the downs and golf links and is only a short stroll from sandy Crooklets Beach. The accommodation includes two convenient ground floor rooms, equipped with TV to avoid climbing the stairs to a first floor lounge which enjoys delightful views over the golf course to the sea. The bedrooms are all attractively decorated with coordinating wallpapers, fabrics and bed linen. The dining room is a large sunny room where a choice of breakfasts and light suppers are served.

8rm(2🚿) (1fb) 🚭 in dining room CTV in 7 bedrooms [R] 🐕 (ex guide dogs) sB&B£14-£15.50 dB&B£28-£31 dB&B🚿£32-£35 WB&B£85-£91.50 WBDi£140.50-£150.50 LDO 5pm

♨ CTV 🚫

[£]

FH [Q][Q][Q] Mrs S Trewin **Lower Northcott** *(SS215087)* Poughill EX23 7EL ☎(0288) 352350

This is a remote and secluded farmhouse, set in a valley with views of the coastline. It is ideal for children, who are particularly welcome to explore the farm and see the cows being milked. The bright, no-smoking bedrooms are simply furnished and bunk beds can be provided for children. There is a cosy TV lounge, plus a games room and the dining room has a communal table. The proprietors, Sally and William Trewin, create a very relaxed and informal atmosphere.

5rm(1🛁3🚿) (3fb) [R] 🐕 (ex guide dogs) ✻ dB&B🛁🚿fr£30 WB&Bfr£105 WBDifr£140 LDO 6.30pm

♨ CTV indoor playroom 470 acres arable beef dairy sheep

BUDLEIGH SALTERTON Devon Map **03** SY08

SELECTED

GH [Q][Q][Q][Q] Long Range Hotel 5 Vales Road EX9 6HS ☎(0395) 443321

Etr-Dec

Situated in a quiet residential area only 15 minutes' walk from the town centre, this attractive, modern detached building is the home of Sue and Paul Griffin who offer friendly and attentive service. Bedrooms are all soundly maintained and well equipped, and guests may choose to relax in the comfortable sitting room or the separate sun lounge. Menus offer a choice for each of the three courses at dinner, which is served at 7pm.

7rm(2🛁4🚿) (1fb) 🚭 in bedrooms CTV in all bedrooms [R] 🐕 sB&B£21.50 sB&B🛁🚿£21.50 dB&B£43 dB&B🛁🚿£43 WB&B£140 WBDi£212 LDO 8pm

Lic ♨

GH Q Q Q **Willowmead** 12 Little Knowle EX9 6QS
☎(0395) 443115
Comfortable, brightly decorated bedrooms are offered at this Victorian family house, which is about half a mile from the seafront and town centre. The resident proprietors welcome guests and provide a small choice of dishes on the dinner menu.
6rm(4ϝ) ⊁ in bedrooms ⊁ in dining room ® sB&B£16-£18 sB&Bϝ£17-£18 WB&B£110-£125 WBDi£150-£180
▥ CTV nc5yrs
£

BUNGAY Suffolk   Map **05** TM38

FH Q Q Q Mrs B Watchorn **Park Farm** *(TM304883)* Harleston Road, Earsham NR35 2AQ ☎(0986) 892180 FAX (0986) 892180
3⇄ϝ ⊁ CTV in all bedrooms ® ⴕ (ex guide dogs) ✳
sB&B⇄ϝ£22-£26 dB&B⇄ϝ£35-£39 LDO 24hrs prior
▥ 589 acres arable pigs poultry
Credit Cards 5 £

BURBAGE Wiltshire   Map **04** SU26

GH Q Q Q Q Q **The Old Vicarage** SN8 3AG
☎Marlborough(0672) 810495
FAX (0672) 810663
Closed Xmas & New Year

This fine brick and flint-built former Victorian vicarage dates from 1853 and is set in its own pretty gardens beside the church. Each of the 3 bedrooms has been tastefully decorated and furnished in the period of the house, with many thoughtful extra touches. The resident proprietors are charming and extend a warm welcome into their home, where the high standard of tasteful décor and furnishings is evident throughout. The drawing room is elegant and comfortable, stocked with a wealth of reading material and beautiful fresh flower arrangements, together with a log fire; drinks are served here before dinner. Guests dine together around a large antique table in the candlelit dining room; home cooked dinners showing imagination and flair are served, using top quality fresh produce. Breakfast is informal, with a good choice of cooked and continental dishes. Smoking is not permitted.
3⇄ ⊁ CTV in all bedrooms ® ⴕ (ex guide dogs) LDO noon
▥ CTV nc18yrs
Credit Cards 1 3

BURFORD Oxfordshire   Map **04** SP21

GH Q Q Q Q Q **Andrews Hotel** High Street OX18 4QA
☎(0993) 823151
FAX (0993) 823240
Closed 25 & 26 Dec
Conveniently situated in the high street of this famous Cotswold town, within walking distance of many pubs and restaurants, this attractive timbered building dates back to the 15th century.

Comfortable en suite bedrooms retain their characterful features and are prettily decorated with quality fabrics and furniture. The elegant lounges and breakfast room, together with a flower filled courtyard, set the scene for the splendid afternoon tea - a choice of blends accompanied by excellent home-made cakes, tarts and scones with thick Devonshire clotted cream - that is popular with residents and locals alike.
8⇄ϝ (1fb) ⊁ in dining room CTV in all bedrooms ⴕ (ex guide dogs) sB&B⇄ϝ£45-£69 dB&B⇄ϝ£59-£85
Lic ▥ CTV ⊬
Credit Cards 1 3

GH Q Q Q Q Q Q **Cottage-by-the-Church** Chapel Lane, Filkins GL7 3JG ☎(0367) 860613
(For full entry see Lechlade)

GH Q Q Q Q **Elm Farm House** Meadow Lane, Fulbrook OX18 4BW (A361 towards Chipping Norton for 0.5m)
☎(0993) 823611 FAX (0993) 823937
Quietly located in a village lane, this late-Victorian Cotswold-stone manor house has gables and mullion windows and is surrounded by well tended gardens with a croquet lawn. Bedrooms are comfortable and well equipped, several with private bathrooms. A choice of home-cooked dishes using fresh local produce is offered in the dining room, and there is a small bar. There are two lounges, the one with TV being

▶

THE CLIFF HOTEL

AA QQQQ Selected

CROOKLETS BEACH, BUDE EX23 8NG

Small quality family hotel, indoor swimming pool, all weather tennis and bowls. All rooms en suite with colour TV, phone, radio, drinks. Location is superb next to NT cliffwalk, a designated area of "outstanding natural beauty", 200 yards west Crooklets Beach, 200 yards east Maer Lake Reserve where peregine falcons hunt, 200 yards south Bude Golf Course. The excellent cuisine is freshly cooked and includes local fish, French and traditional dishes overseen by head chef Brian Sibley.

Phone FREE 0500 121273

reserved for non-smokers, the other has French windows opening on to the terrace.
7rm(4⇔↱) ⊬ in bedrooms ⊬ in dining room ⊬ in 1 lounge CTV in all bedrooms Ⓡ T Ħ (ex guide dogs) * sB&B£20-£29.50 dB&B£25-£40 dB&B⇔↱£40-£55 WB&B£140-£206.50 WBDi£245-£311.50 LDO 8pm
Lic ▥ CTV nc10yrs croquet lawn
Credit Cards [1][3] (£)

BURNLEY Lancashire — Map **07** SD83

GH QQQ Ormerod Hotel 121/123 Ormerod Road BB11 3QW
☎(0282) 423255
Situated opposite Queens Park, this is a charming end-of-terrace Victorian house. Bedrooms vary in size and the majority are comfortably furnished in contemporary style with effective use made of modern fabrics. There is an elegant lounge and breakfast is served in the pleasant mahogany-panelled dining room. Guests requiring dinner may visit the nearby Alexander Hotel which is under the same ownership.
9rm(3⇔6↱) (2fb) CTV in all bedrooms Ⓡ sB&B⇔↱£19-£24 dB&B⇔↱£33-£35
▥ CTV

BURNMOUTH Borders *Berwickshire* — Map **12** NT96

FH QQQ Mrs P Goff **Greystonelees** *(NT958604)* Greystonelees TD14 5SZ ☎Ayton(08907) 81709
Though this well proportioned house just south of the village is no longer part of the working farm that surrounds it, its collection of birds, animals and family pets are still an attraction. A folder in the attractively decorated, well equipped bedrooms contains an introduction to these - and you will find a cuddly toy on your pillow as well as thoughtful extras like tissues. The lounge is shared with the owners, and meals are usually served round one table in a dining room adorned with mounted birds and animals that have met their end on the A1.
3rm(1⇔1↱) ⊬ CTV in all bedrooms Ⓡ sB&B£15-£22 sB&B⇔↱£20-£25 dB&B£30-£32 dB&B⇔↱£34-£36 WB&B£90-£120 WBDi£135-£155 LDO 4pm
▥ CTV 140 acres mixed
Credit Cards [1][3] (£)

BURNSALL North Yorkshire — Map **07** SE06

GH Q Manor House BD23 6BW (on B6160, approaching from Grassington) ☎(0756) 720231
Closed Jan
A Victorian family-run hotel with traditionally styled bedrooms, several containing attractive antique furniture. There is a comfortable guests' lounge and a cosy bar. Meals in the dining room are served at individual tables.
7rm(3⇔↱) (2fb) ⊬ in bedrooms ⊬ in dining room Ⓡ Ħ dB&B£36-£40 dB&B⇔↱£43-£47 WB&B£126-£150 WBDi£175-£210 LDO 5pm
Lic ▥ CTV ⌡ U solarium

BURRELTON Tayside *Perthshire* — Map **11** NO23

INN QQQ Burrelton Park High Street PH13 9NX
☎(08287) 206 FAX (08287) 676
In the centre of the village, this popular roadside inn, with its bright modern bedrooms, enjoys a reputation for its hearty cooking and extensive menus. A wide range of mostly home-made dishes is available from 11am to 10pm, supported by a more up-market dinner menu in the restaurant. Real ale is on tap in the bar.
6⇔↱ (1fb) ⊬ in 1 bedrooms ⊬ in area of dining room CTV in all bedrooms Ⓡ sB&B⇔↱£30 dB&B⇔↱£45 WB&B£120-£157.50 WBDi£162-£213.50 Bar Lunch fr£4alc High tea fr£6alc Dinner £8-£16alc LDO 10.30pm
▥ CTV
Credit Cards [1][3] (£)

BURRY PORT Dyfed — Map **02** SN40

INN QQQ The George Stepney Road SA16 0BH
☎(0554) 832211
This very popular family-run inn and restaurant lies in the centre of the town. The 'Friendship' lounge is named after the seaplane flown by Amelia Erhardt when she arrived in the estuary after becoming the first woman to fly the Atlantic in 1928. A wide choice of food is available, staff are friendly, and the bedrooms, mostly spacious, are modern and comfortable.
5rm(4⇔↱) (2fb)CTV in all bedrooms Ⓡ Ħ (ex guide dogs) sB&B⇔↱£21-£30 dB&B⇔↱£36-£42 Lunch £6.05-£15.45alc Dinner £9.05-£20.25alc LDO 10.15pm
▥ nc6yrs

BURTON UPON TRENT Staffordshire — Map **08** SK22

GH QQQ Delter Hotel 5 Derby Road DE14 1RU
☎(0283) 535115
A fully modernised house situated on the edge of town, on the busy Derby road. The bedrooms are bright and clean, and in the small basement bar snacks are served in the evening.
5rm(1⇔4↱) CTV in all bedrooms Ⓡ Ħ (ex guide dogs) sB&B⇔↱£27 dB&B⇔↱£38 LDO 6pm
Lic ▥ CTV
Credit Cards [1][3] (£)

GH QQQ Edgecote Hotel 179 Ashby Road DE15 0LB (on A50, Leicester side of town) ☎Burton on Trent(0283) 568966
This large, well maintained Victorian house, now a privately-owned and personally-run hotel, stands only half a mile from the town centre. Bright, modern bedrooms include some suitable for family occupation, drinks can be dispensed in the comfortable lounge, and a dining room furnished in cottage style retains its original panelled walls. The hotel has its own private car park.
12rm(3↱) (3fb) ⊬ in bedrooms ⊬ in dining room CTV in all bedrooms Ⓡ sB&B£19.50-£25 sB&B↱£27-£33 dB&B£34-£38 dB&B↱£38-£46 LDO 7pm
Lic ▥ CTV
Credit Cards [1][2][3] (£)

BURWASH East Sussex — Map **05** TQ62

FH QQ Mrs E Sirrell **Woodlands** *(TQ656242)* TN19 7LA (1m W of Burwash on A265, on right side of road, house set back 0.33m off road) ☎(0435) 882794
Etr-Oct
Set in 55 acres of farmland, this 16th-century farmhouse is at the end of a private track. Three of the guest rooms are quite simply furnished and the fourth has a four-poster bed and en suite shower room. Breakfast is served at a communal table, and in the same room guests have a TV and can help themselves to hot drinks. Good value evening meals are available by prior arrangement.
4rm(1↱) Ħ sB&Bfr£17.50 dB&Bfr£30 dB&B↱fr£35 LDO am
▥ CTV 55 acres mixed

BURY ST EDMUNDS Suffolk — Map **05** TL86

GH QQQ The Chantry Hotel 8 Sparhawk Street IP33 1RY
☎(0284) 767427 FAX (0284) 760946
rs wknds
This large, listed Georgian house with a Tudor annexe is located near the town centre, next to the brewery. Bedrooms range from standard rooms to a private suite, furnished with antiques and prettily decorated with a small split-level lounge area. The cosy bar has a large blackboard dinner menu, and there is a spacious dining room.

14🛁🚿 Annexe 3🛁🚿 (1fb) 🚭 in dining room CTV in all bedrooms [R] T sB&B🛁🚿£32.50-£48 dB&B🛁🚿£49.50-£56 LDO 7pm
Lic 🅿
Credit Cards [1] [3] [5] [£]

GH [Q] [Q] [Q] ***Dunston Guest House/Hotel*** 8 Springfield Road IP33 3AN ☎(0284) 767981
A delightful, well maintained property situated in a quiet residential area. Good sized, well equipped bedrooms are located in the main building and the cottage extension, with ample parking between the two areas. There is an attractive dining room and a pleasant combined lounge and conservatory.
11rm(6🚿) Annexe 6rm(2🚿) (5fb) CTV in all bedrooms [R] 🐕
LDO 10pm previous day
Lic 🅿 CTV

GH [Q] [Q] [Q] The Olde White Hart Hotel 35 Southgate Street IP33 2AZ ☎(0284) 755547 FAX (0284) 724770
This former Tudor inn offers unique accommodation in four historic buildings dating from 1150 to 1680. Many of the original features have been retained, and bedrooms are immaculately maintained. There is a pleasant lounge and an informal eating area for breakfast, which is also available in bedrooms. Currently no other meals are provided, but the owners have a list of nearby eating places.
10🛁🚿 (2fb) 🚭 in 5 bedrooms 🚭 in dining room CTV in all bedrooms [R] T 🐕 (ex guide dogs) sB&B🛁🚿£39.50-£42.50 dB&B🛁🚿£49.50-£52.50
Lic 🅿
Credit Cards [1] [2] [3]

SELECTED

GH [Q] [Q] [Q] [Q] Twelve Angel Hill 12 Angel Hill IP33 1UZ ☎(0284) 704088 FAX (0284) 725549
6rm(2🛁4🚿) 🚭 CTV in all bedrooms [R] T 🐕 *
sB&B🛁🚿£45-£55 dB&B🛁🚿£60-£75
Lic 🅿 nc14yrs
Credit Cards [1] [2] [3] [5]

GH [Q] [Q] York 32 Springfield Road IP33 3AR ☎(0284) 753091
Closed Feb
7rm(1🛁1🚿) 🚭 in 2 bedrooms 🚭 in dining room 🚭 in lounges CTV in all bedrooms [R] * sB&B£16-£17 dB&B£32-£34 dB&B🛁🚿£40-£42 WB&B£112-£119
🅿
[£]

SELECTED

INN [Q] [Q] [Q] [Q] The Six Bells The Green, Bardwell IP31 1AW ☎(0359) 50820
Closed 25 Dec
This well maintained inn stands on the north-east fringe of the village and has a popular bar as well as a more formal restaurant. Eight bedrooms are housed in a barn conversion.
8🚿 (2fb)CTV in all bedrooms [R] T * sB&B🚿£35-£40 dB&B🚿£40-£55 WBDi£210-£235 Lunch fr£12.50&alc Dinner £5.95-£6.95&alc LDO 9.30pm
🅿
Credit Cards [1] [3] [£]

BUTTERMERE Cumbria Map 11 NY11

PREMIER SELECTED

GH [Q] [Q] [Q] [Q] [Q] Pickett Howe Buttermere Valley CA13 9UY ☎ Cockermouth(0900) 85444
end Mar-mid Nov

Pickett Howe, a Grade II listed building dating from 1650, is one of Lakeland's most charming and interesting farmhouses, with slate floors, oak beams, spice cupboards and mullioned windows.
Owners David and Dani Edwards have furnished the bedrooms in Victorian style and dinner in the candlelit dining room is served to the accompaniment of chamber music.
4🛁🚿 🚭 CTV in all bedrooms [R] T 🐕 dB&B🛁🚿£70 WB&B£245 WBDi£357 LDO noon
Lic 🅿 nc10yrs ♪
Credit Cards [1] [3]

Telephone national area codes are due to change by 16th April 1995. Please see the note under 'How to Use this Guide' at the front of the book.

Dunston Guest House/Hotel

8 Springfield Road,
BURY ST. EDMUNDS,
Suffolk IP33 3AN
Telephone: (01284) 767981

A 19th century house, full of character with a warm friendly atmosphere. 17 bedrooms, many with en suite facilities, all very comfortable with colour TV, tea/coffee etc. Car park, drinks licence, ironing, TV lounge, sun lounge, garden and play area. Ground floor rooms available. Situated in the centre of East Anglia it is the ideal base for touring the region with lovely towns and villages plus coastline. Nearest road A14 (previously A45).

BUXTON Derbyshire Map **07** SK07

PREMIER SELECTED

GH [Q][Q][Q][Q][Q] **Brookfield On Longhill** Brookfield Hall, Long Hill SK17 6SU (1.5m NW of Buxton off A5004)
☎(0298) 24151
FAX (0298) 24151

This Victorian retreat, just over a mile from Buxton, stands in ten acres of gardens and woodlands amid beautiful Peak District countryside. A quality small country hotel, it has period furnishings and antique pieces, yet modern facilities and hospitable service. The restaurant is fast becoming popular for its interesting, tasty menus and good wines.
7🛁🚿 🚭 in dining room CTV in all bedrooms [R] T
sB&B🛁🚿£35-£47.50 dB&B🛁🚿£55-£75 WB&Bfr£192.50
LDO 10.30pm
Lic ▦ CTV U
Credit Cards [1][2][3][5][£]

GH [Q][Q] ***Buxton Lodge Private Hotel*** 28 London Road SK17 9NX (on main rd out of Buxton towards Ashbourne) ☎(0298) 23522
Families are encouraged at this modern hotel close to the town centre, and a children's room is provided. On summer evenings barbecues are held in the garden.
7rm(3🚿) (1fb) CTV in all bedrooms [R] LDO 4pm
Lic ▦ CTV 🎲
Credit Cards [3]

GH [Q][Q][Q] **Buxton View** 74 Corbar Road SK17 6RJ
☎(0298) 79222 FAX (0298) 79222
Mar-Nov
A stone-built house stands in a quiet residential area on the north side of the town. Aptly named, it has well equipped accommodation, a neat colourful garden and private car parking.
5🛁🚿 (1fb) 🚭 in bedrooms 🚭 in dining room CTV in all bedrooms [R] * sB&B🛁🚿fr£20 dB&B🛁🚿fr£36 WB&Bfr£115 WBDifr£180 LDO 9am
▦
[£]

SELECTED

GH [Q][Q][Q][Q] **Coningsby** 6 Macclesfield Rd SK17 9AH (between A515 and A53 on B5059) ☎(0298) 26735
3🚿 🚭 CTV in all bedrooms [R] 🐕 sB&B🚿£32.50-£41.50 dB&B🚿£36-£45 WB&B£120-£150 WBDi£214.50-£244.50
LDO 4pm
Lic ▦ nc

GH [Q][Q] **Griff** 2 Compton Road SK17 9DN ☎(0298) 23628
Situated in a residential area convenient for the town centre, this guesthouse provides modest accommodation and car parking facilities.
5🚿 CTV in all bedrooms [R] 🐕 * dB&B🚿fr£30 WB&Bfr£105 WBDifr£130 LDO noon
▦ CTV nc

SELECTED

GH [Q][Q][Q][Q] **The Grosvenor House Hotel** 1 Broad Walk SK17 6JE ☎(0298) 72439 FAX (0298) 72439
This guesthouse is well situated in a quiet yet convenient location, overlooking the Pavilion Gardens and within two minutes' walk of the Opera House and town centre. The friendly proprietors provide cheerful service, with particular attention paid to both housekeeping and maintenance. Bedrooms are tastefully furnished and decorated, with pleasant light pastel colours, matching soft furnishings and Edwardian antique furniture; each room has a good modern en suite bathroom, TV and radio alarm. There is a nicely appointed lounge and a small dispense bar in the dining room. Dinner is available by arrangement, and there is a small coffee shop attached to the hotel which is a popular meeting place for locals and tourists.
8🛁🚿 (2fb) 🚭 in bedrooms 🚭 in dining room CTV in all bedrooms [R] 🐕 (ex guide dogs) sB&B🛁🚿£40-£45 dB&B🛁🚿£50-£70 WB&B£140-£192.50 WBDi£230-£275
LDO breakfast
Lic ▦ nc8yrs
Credit Cards [1][3][£]

GH [Q][Q] **Hawthorn Farm** Fairfield Road SK17 7ED (on A6 Manchester/Stockport rd) ☎(0298) 23230
Apr-Oct
Built in the 1600s and set in immaculate gardens, this charming listed farmhouse offers neat, fresh looking accommodation. Bedrooms in the main house are full of character, though some singles are small, and there are further rooms in a courtyard annexe. Guests have the use of an attractive lounge with a Tudor fireplace.
6rm(1🚿) Annexe 6rm(4🚿) (1fb)[R] * sB&B£19-£20 dB&B£38-£40 dB&B🚿£44-£45 WB&B£126-£154
▦ CTV
[£]

GH [Q][Q][Q] **Lakenham** 11 Burlington Road SK17 9AL
☎(0298) 79209
This guesthouse is located in a quiet residential avenue overlooking the Pavilion Gardens. Public rooms and bedrooms are Victorian in style, tastefully furnished with some lovely antiques, but providing modern facilities in comfortable and very clean surroundings.
6rm(1🛁5🚿) (3fb) 🚭 in dining room CTV in all bedrooms [R] * sB&B🛁🚿fr£25 dB&B🛁🚿fr£42 WB&Bfr£136.50 WBDifr£206.50 LDO 9am
[£]

GH [Q][Q][Q] **The Old Manse Private Hotel** 6 Clifton Road, Silverlands SK17 6QL ☎(0298) 25638
Closed Xmas & New Year
Located in a quiet residential road, this stone-built Victorian property is close to the Old Market Place and town centre. The enthusiastic owners have refurbished the house in recent years to provide neat bedrooms. Cosy public rooms include a small bar, TV lounge and cheerful dining room, where Mrs Whitaker presents honest, home-cooked evening meals.
8rm(4🚿) (2fb) 🚭 in dining room [R] * sB&B£17-£19.50 dB&B£34-£36 dB&B🚿£39-£40 WBDi£173-£189 LDO 5pm
Lic ▦ CTV nc2yrs
[£]

GH [Q][Q] **Roseleigh Private Hotel** 19 Broad Walk SK17 6JR
☎(0298) 24904
Closed Xmas-Jan rs Feb & Dec
In a pleasant location opposite the Pavilion Gardens and lake, this hotel looks out on a pedestrian walkway and cars can only gain access via Hartington Road. A good range of public rooms includes a quiet lounge, TV lounge, a small bar, and a dining room

where traditional home-cooked fare is served. Bedrooms are more simply furnished but offer en suite facilities.
13rm(9⇌↱) (1fb) ⊁ in dining room CTV in all bedrooms Ⓡ ✳ sB&B£20 dB&B⇌↱£40-£45 WB&B£140-£189 WBDi£195 LDO 5pm
Lic
Credit Cards [1] [3]

GH QQ Templeton 13 Compton Road SK17 9DN
☎(0298) 25275
Located in a predominantly residential road close to the town centre, this guest house offers freshly decorated bedrooms. Residents have the use of a comfortable ground floor lounge, and home-cooked evening meals are available with advance notice.
6rm(2↱) (2fb) ⊁ in dining room CTV in all bedrooms Ⓡ ✱ ✳ sB&B£23-£25 dB&B£30-£34 dB&B↱£34-£38 WB&B£101.50-£119 WBDi£154-£170 LDO noon
Lic ▥ CTV nc3yrs
Ⓔ

GH QQQ *Thorn Heyes Private Hotel* 137 London Road SK17 9NW (on A515) ☎(0298) 23539
Closed last 2 wks Nov & Jan
A Victorian house retaining much of its original character, Thorn Heyes provides a comfortable lounge with a bar and well equipped, individually decorated bedrooms. No evening meals are served; self-catering apartments are available in the grounds.
8↱ (2fb) CTV in all bedrooms Ⓡ
Lic ▥ nc14yrs
Credit Cards [1] [3]

SELECTED

GH QQQQ Westminster Hotel 21 Broadwalk SK17 6JT (approach via Hartington road) ☎(0298) 23929
FAX (0298) 71121
Feb-Nov rs mid Nov-Dec
Derek and Norma Stephens provide friendly service at this well established small hotel, which is in a pleasant location opposite the Pavilion Gardens (access for cars only by Hartington Road). Public rooms offer a cosy bar, a quiet lounge and a nicely appointed dining room. Bedroom sizes vary but each room has good en suite facilities.
12rm(6⇌6↱) ⊁ in dining room CTV in all bedrooms Ⓡ ✱ (ex guide dogs) sB&B⇌↱£25-£30 dB&B⇌↱£40-£45 WB&B£140-£210 WBDi£195-£215 LDO 3pm
Lic ▥
Credit Cards [1] [2] [3] Ⓔ

BYRNESS Northumberland — Map **12** NT70

FH QQ Mrs A Anderson ***Blakehope Burnhaugh*** *(NT783002)* Otterburn NE19 1SW (1.5m along A68 towards Rochester)
☎Otterburn(0830) 520267
Peace and quiet are assured in this well maintained, stone built farmhouse set in a pleasant garden. There is a comfortable lounge and breakfast is served in the conservatory sun lounge.
3rm (1fb) Ⓡ LDO 4pm
▥ CTV 150 acres beef

CADNAM Hampshire — Map **04** SU31

GH QQ The Old Well Restaurant Romsey Road, Copythorne SO4 2PE (on A31) ☎Southampton(0703) 812321 & 812700
A welcoming, family-owned and personally run restaurant on the edge of the New Forest, in the village of Copythorne, also offers accommodation. Three of the rooms are modern, with en suite facilities and attractive coordinated decor, while those in the older part of the building have a cosier, more traditional feel to them. Home-cooked lunches are served every day, but dinner is only available on Fridays and Saturdays; residents have the use of a small kitchen area where they can make tea or coffee and use the microwave if they do not wish to dine out on the other days. There is also a comfortable lounge. A private car park lies behind the building.
6rm(3⇌) (2fb)CTV in all bedrooms Ⓡ ✱ (ex guide dogs) ✳ sB&B£21-£25 sB&B⇌£25-£28 dB&B£32 dB&B⇌£40
Lic ▥ CTV nc3yrs
Credit Cards [3] Ⓔ

SELECTED

GH QQQQ Walnut Cottage Old Romsey Road SO40 2NP
☎Southampton(0703) 812275
Closed 24-26 Dec
The scenery of the New Forest makes a peaceful setting for this delightful Victorian cottage and its well kept garden. Tastefully decorated rooms offer a good standard of comfort and traditional English breakfast is served at a communal dining table in the elegant dining room. There is ample parking space.
3rm(2⇌1↱) ⊁ in dining room ⊁ in lounges CTV in all bedrooms Ⓡ ✱ (ex guide dogs) ✳ sB&B⇌↱£28-£30 dB&B⇌↱£40-£42 WB&B£133
▥ CTV nc14yrs free loan of bikes

FH QQQ Mrs A M Dawe **Budds** *(SU310139)* Winsor Road, Winsor SO4 2HN ☎Southampton(0703) 812381
Apr-Oct
With its very pretty front garden, this thatched farmhouse stands discreetly back from the road. The first floor bedrooms are a good size and very comfortable. Downstairs there is a TV lounge and the attractive dining room has a display of plates and bric-à-brac on the sideboards. The hostess, Mrs Dawe, is a cheerful, bustling lady who extends a warm welcome.
2rm(1⇌) (1fb) ⊁ Ⓡ ✱ (ex guide dogs) ✳ sB&B£16 dB&B£32
▥ CTV 200 acres beef dairy

SELECTED

FH QQQQ Mrs A Dawe **Kents** *(SU315139)* Winsor Road, Winsor SO4 2HN ☎Southampton(0703) 813497
Apr-Oct
A 16th-century thatched farmhouse has been renovated to provide attractive and comfortable bed and breakfast accommodation. Set in well tended cottage gardens and surrounded by its own pastureland, the farmhouse offers comfortable cottage-style decor, with oak beams and an inglenook fireplace. There is a pleasant lounge where guests are joined by the friendly owners, who can recommend one of the many New Forest pubs or restaurants.
2rm(1⇌1↱) (1fb) ⊁ ✱ dB&B⇌↱fr£34
▥ CTV nc2yrs 200 acres beef dairy

CAERNARFON Gwynedd — Map **06** SH46

See also Llanwnda

SELECTED

GH QQQQ Caer Menai 15 Church Street LL55 1SW
☎(0286) 672612
Apr-Dec
This small, personally run guesthouse is quietly situated, within a short walk of both the harbour and castle. The modern style accommodation is impeccably maintained, and family rooms are available. In addition to the attractive dining room, there is also a comfortable, cosy lounge.
7rm(3↱) (2fb) ⊁ in dining room ⊁ in lounges CTV in all bedrooms Ⓡ ✱ (ex guide dogs) sB&B£17.50-£18.50

▶

sB&B⚪£21-£25 dB&B£30-£32 dB&B⚪£36-£38
CTV ⅌ solarium
£

GH Ⓠ Ⓠ **Menai View Hotel** North Road LL55 1BD (N on A487)
☎(0286) 674602
A family run guest house with lovely views over the Menai Straits
from many bedrooms and from the first floor lounge bar. One
ground floor room is available for the less mobile guest. Evening
meals are served when required. The castle and shopping centre
are both within easy walking distance.
8rm(4⚫) (5fb)CTV in all bedrooms Ⓡ ⚬ ✱ sB&B£16
sB&B⚫£19-£24 dB&B£25-£28 dB&B⚫£31-£35 WB&B£85-
£115 LDO 6.30pm
Lic ⬛ CTV
£

CALDBECK Cumbria   Map **11** NY33

GH Ⓠ Ⓠ Ⓠ Ⓠ **High Greenrigg House** CA7 8HD (3m on
B5299) ☎(06974) 78430
Mar-Dec
Set in an ideal location for hiking enthusiasts, this delightful
17th-century farmhouse, situated at the foot of Caldbeck Fells,
is only half a mile from the Cumbria Way. Full of interest, the
house provides two lounges - one with stone flag flooring, a
superb old fireplace and a piano, the other equipped with a TV.
There are lots of books and games available, plus a separate
games room with a bar. A set dinner menu is served by Mrs
Jacobs in a bright dining room with pine tables. Old beams
and open stone walls feature in the attractive en suite
bedrooms. This is an ideal place to stay for peace and
tranquility.
7⇔⚫ (2fb) ⅊ in bedrooms ⅊ in area of dining room ⅊ in 1
lounge Ⓡ ✱ sB&B⇔⚫£19.50 dB&B⇔⚫£39 WB&B£117
LDO 5pm
Lic ⬛ CTV
Credit Cards ① ③ £

CALLANDER Central *Perthshire*   Map **11** NN60

GH Ⓠ Ⓠ Ⓠ **Abbotsford Lodge** Stirling Road FK17 8DA (off A84
eastern approach to town) ☎(0877) 330066
Set in its own grounds, well back from the main road on the
eastern side of the town, this large detached villa has extremely
attractive public areas which include a conservatory extension to
the dining room. Bedrooms are contained in both the original
house and a rear extension, the best of them having en suite
bathrooms.
18rm(4⇔5⚫) (7fb) ⅊ in dining room Ⓡ ✱ sB&B£16.50-£21.50
sB&B⇔⚫£20.50-£25.50 dB&B33-£35 dB&B⇔⚫£41-£44
WBDi£182-£208 LDO 7pm
Lic ⬛ CTV
£

GH Ⓠ Ⓠ Ⓠ **Annfield** 18 North Church Street FK17 8EG
☎(0877) 330204
This detached Victorian house, standing in its own gardens in a
side street only two minutes' walk from the town centre, offers
attractive public areas and bedrooms which are mainly of a
comfortable size.
8rm(2⚫) (2fb)Ⓡ sB&B£16 dB&B£32
⬛ CTV nc10yrs
£

GH Ⓠ Ⓠ Ⓠ Ⓠ **Arden House** Bracklinn Road FK17 8EQ
☎(0877) 330235
Mar-Oct
Arden House is a large stone property, set in its own grounds
high above the town and close to the golf course. Bedrooms
are comfortable, well proportioned and thoughtfully equipped.
There are two lounges, one with TV, and a small putting green
in the garden.
6⇔⚫ (2fb) ⅊ Ⓡ sB&B⇔⚫£18-£20 dB&B⇔⚫£36-£40
WBDi£170-£185 LDO 7pm
⬛ CTV ⚬ putting green
£

GH Ⓠ Ⓠ Ⓠ Ⓠ Ⓠ **Arran
Lodge** Leny Road FK17 8AJ (on
W outskirts, on A84)
☎(0877) 330976
Closed 15 Oct-16 Nov &
10 Jan-1 Mar
Pasqua and Robert Moore's
150-year-old bungalow is
situated at the west end of
town, with the River Leny
flowing past the rear garden.
The bedrooms, named after
local lochs, are individually styled and two have four-poster
beds. The spacious lounge opens onto the verandah, which is
a favourite spot for smokers as the house operates a no
smoking policy. The Victorian dining room, with period
furnishings and highly polished individual tables, is the setting
for Robert's carefully prepared dinners and hearty breakfasts.
4rm(2⇔2⚫) ⅊ CTV in all bedrooms Ⓡ ⚬ ✱
sB&B⇔⚫fr£38.40 dB&B⇔⚫fr£48 WB&B£178.50-£206.50
WBDi£276.50-£309.75 LDO 6pm
⬛ CTV nc12yrs ⤴

GH Ⓠ Ⓠ Ⓠ Ⓠ **Brook Linn Country House** Leny Feus
FK17 8AU ☎(0877) 330103
Etr-Oct
A fine country house set in two acres of terraced gardens with
magnificent views of the town. The solidly furnished
bedrooms are comfortable and well equipped. There is a
guests' lounge and an attractive dining room where the
emphasis is on fresh produce and wholefood. Vegetarians are
catered for; packed lunches are available, and confectionery is
sold.
7rm(5⚫) (2fb) ⅊ CTV in all bedrooms Ⓡ sB&B⚫£17-£20
dB&B⚫£42-£48 LDO 4pm
Lic ⬛

GH Ⓠ Ⓠ Ⓠ **Rock Villa** 1 Bracklinn Road FK17 8EH
☎(0877) 330331
31 Mar-1 Nov
Just off the main road at the eastern end of the town, this compact
Victorian villa with its own gardens is cheerfully decorated and
well looked after. Bedrooms are comfortable, and there is a
pleasant lounge.
6rm(3⚫) (1fb) CTV in 3 bedrooms Ⓡ ✱ sB&B£17-£18
dB&B£30-£32 dB&B⚫£36-£38
⬛ CTV

CALLINGTON Cornwall & Isles of Scilly Map **02** SX36

INN[Q][Q][Q] ***Manor House*** Rilla Mill PL17 7NT
☎Liskeard(0579) 62354

Peacefully situated in the village of Rilla Mill, the accommodation at this 300-year-old inn is contained in six modern chalet style cottages. All are named after Cornish rivers (2 enjoy a river frontage) and each chalet contains two bedrooms, an open-plan lounge/diner and facilities to enable self catering if required. Home-cooked bar meals and an extensive à la carte are available at the inn.

Annexe 6🛁🚿 (6fb) CTV in all bedrooms [R] LDO 9.30pm
🅿 CTV 🏠
Credit Cards [1][3]

CALNE Wiltshire Map **03** ST97

P R E M I E R S E L E C T E D

GH [Q][Q][Q][Q][Q] Chilvester Hill House Calne SN11 0LP (A4 from Calne towards Chippenham, after 0.5m take right turn marked Bremhill. Drive of house immediately on right) ☎(0249) 813981 & 815785 FAX (0249) 814217

Spacious, comfortable accommodation is offered at this stone-built house standing in its own grounds. Evening meals can be arranged.

3🛁 🚭 in dining room CTV in all bedrooms [R] 🐕 (ex guide dogs) ✱ sB&B🛁£40-£50 dB&B🛁£60-£75 LDO 11am
Lic 🅿 CTV nc12yrs 🏊(heated)
Credit Cards [1][2][3][5][£]

CAMBRIDGE Cambridgeshire Map **05** TL45

See also Little Gransden

GH [Q][Q][Q] ***Acorn*** 154 Chesterton Road CB4 1DA
☎(0223) 353888 FAX (0223) 350527

A small, family run establishment offering light, fresh accommodation and a friendly atmosphere. There are a couple of ground floor rooms, a family bedroom and cosy dining room where guests can have a hearty breakfast, vegetarian if desired. Evening meals must be booked in advance and there is car parking at the rear of the property.

5rm(3🚿) (1fb) CTV in all bedrooms [R] 🐕 (ex guide dogs) LDO 6pm
🅿

GH [Q][Q][Q] Assisi 193 Cherry Hinton Road CB1 4BX
☎(0223) 211466 & 246648 FAX (0223) 412900

Closed 15 Dec-10 Jan

Popular with students, this large house provides soundly furnished rooms with good en suite facilities. Its location is a 25-minute walk south-east from the city centre.

17🛁🚿 (2fb) 🚭 in dining room 🚭 in lounges CTV in all bedrooms [R] 🐕 (ex guide dogs) ✱ sB&Bfr£25 sB&B🛁🚿£29 dB&B🛁🚿£35-£39 LDO 7.30pm
🅿 CTV
Credit Cards [1][2][3]

See advertisement on p.114.

GH [Q][Q] Avimore 310 Cherry Hinton Road CB1 4AU (1.75m S of city centre just inside Cambridge Ring Rd) ☎(0223) 410956 FAX (0223) 576957

This small, family-run guesthouse is on the southern edge of Cambridge and offers accommodation in simple but well equipped bedrooms. There is a small television lounge occupying part of the breakfast room.

4rm(2🚿) (2fb) 🚭 in dining room CTV in all bedrooms [R] T 🐕 (ex guide dogs) ✱ sB&B£18-£26 sB&B🚿£26-£36 dB&B£30-£38 dB&B🚿£36-£40 WB&Bfr£120
🅿 CTV
Credit Cards [1][3][5][£]

GH [Q][Q] Benson House 24 Huntingdon Road CB3 0HH (on A604 near New Hall & Fitzwilliam House) ☎(0223) 311594

Benson House offers good accommodation in slightly compact rooms. Modest bedrooms are clean and two are on the ground floor. A bonus for this part of Cambridge is that some rear car parking spaces are provided.

5rm(2🚿) (3fb) 🚭 in dining room CTV in all bedrooms [R] ✱ sB&B£18-£21 dB&B£32-£40 dB&B🚿£35-£40
🅿
[£]

See advertisement on p.115.

GH [Q][Q] Bon Accord House 20 St Margarets Square CB1 4AP (in cul-de-sac just off Cherry Hinton road) ☎(0223) 411188 & 246568

Closed Xmas & New Year

To the south of the city centre in a quiet cul-de-sac is this well established, small, friendly family guesthouse. There is a small lounge and large dining room in which you can have a full choice of English breakfast. Bedrooms vary in size with some singles, compact but very clean.

9rm(1🚿) (1fb) 🚭 CTV in all bedrooms [R] 🐕 ✱ sB&Bfr£21 sB&B🚿fr£26 dB&Bfr£35 dB&B🚿fr£40
🅿
Credit Cards [1][3]

GH [Q][Q][Q] Brooklands 95 Cherry Hinton Road CB1 4BS
☎(0223) 242035 FAX (0223) 242035

Friendly owners ensure good levels of comfort at this modernised, attractively decorated guest house. It is located about 20 minutes' ▶

walk south-east of the centre, and has many amenities including a sauna.
5rm(1🛁4🚿) (1fb) CTV in all bedrooms [R] 🐕 (ex guide dogs) * sB&B🛁🚿£26-£28 dB&B🛁🚿£36-£40 LDO noon
♨ CTV sauna
Credit Cards [1] [2] [3] [5] [£]

GH [Q][Q][Q] Cristina's 47 St. Andrews Road CB4 1DL
☎(0223) 65855 & 327700
Closed 25-27 Dec
A friendly, small family guesthouse north of the city centre in a residential street. Guests have a lounge with colour TV but there is no smoking in the public rooms, just in the bedrooms. Rooms are spotlessly clean, light and well cared for, though some are small.
6rm(5🚿) (2fb) CTV in all bedrooms [R] 🐕 * sB&B£24-£25 dB&B🚿£35-£43
♨ CTV
[£]

GH [Q][Q] *Dresden Villa* 34 Cherryhinton Road CB1 4AA
☎(0223) 247539 & 215253
11rm(10🚿) (2fb) CTV in all bedrooms [R] LDO 8pm
♨ CTV

GH [Q][Q] Dykelands 157 Mowbray Road CB1 4SP
☎(0223) 244300
8rm(3🚿) (3fb) 🚭 in dining room 🚭 in lounges CTV in all bedrooms [R] sB&B£19.50-£22 sB&B🚿£24.50 dB&B£33-£36 dB&B🚿£39
Lic ♨ CTV
Credit Cards [1] [2] [3] [5]

GH [Q][Q][Q] Fairways 141-143 Cherry Hinton Road CB1 4BX (from city centre towards Addenbrookes Hospital turn off A1307 (after bridge) then left into Cherry Hinton Rd) ☎(0223) 246063 FAX (0223) 212093
Closed 24-26 Dec
This popular, family-run guest house catering predominantly for commercial guests continues to improve standards, and redecorated bedrooms now have direct dial telephones with integral radio alarms; most also have en suite showers. Public rooms include a pleasant, airy lounge which incorporates a well stocked bar and a pool table, and the comfortable dining room.
16rm(8🚿) (3fb) 🚭 in dining room CTV in all bedrooms [R] 🐕 (ex guide dogs) * sB&B£18.50-£20 sB&B🚿£25-£27 dB&B£32-£35 dB&B🚿£37-£40 LDO 7pm
Lic ♨ CTV pool table
Credit Cards [1] [3]

GH [Q][Q][Q] De Freville House 166 Chesterton Road CB4 1DA (at junc of Ring Road and Elizabeth Way) ☎(0223) 354993 FAX (0223) 321890
This attractively renovated and family-run Victorian house is located about a mile north-east of the city centre.
9rm(5🛁🚿) (1fb) 🚭 CTV in all bedrooms [R] 🐕 sB&B£18-£24 sB&B🛁🚿£30-£34 dB&B£32-£36 dB&B🛁🚿£40-£46
♨ CTV nc6yrs
[£]

GH [Q][Q] *Hamden* 89 High Street, Cherry Hinton CB1 4LU (2m E)
☎(0223) 413263
Friendly Italian proprietors maintain high standards of cleanliness and maintenance in this non-smoking guesthouse in Cherry Hinton. There is no lounge, but in warm weather guests may use the spacious rear garden.
4🚿 (1fb) CTV in all bedrooms [R] 🐕 (ex guide dogs)
♨ nc10yrs

GH [Q][Q][Q] Hamilton Hotel 156 Chesterton Road CB4 1DA (1m NE of city centre, off ring road A1134) ☎(0223) 65664 FAX (0223) 314866

▶

BENSON HOUSE

24 Huntingdon Road, Cambridge CB3 0HH

En suite and ground floor rooms available. Situated opposite the New Hall and Fitzwilliam College. Just 10 minutes from the town centre.

Telephone: 01223 311594 for enquiries and reservations.

Cristinas Guest House

47 St Andrews Road, Cambridge CB4 1DL
Telephone: (01223) 65855 & 327700

Guests are assured of a warm welcome at Cristinas Guest House, quietly located in the beautiful city of Cambridge, only 15 minutes walk from the City Centre and colleges. There are many places of cultural and historic interest to visit, as well as shops and leisure facilities. All rooms have colour TV and tea/coffee making facilities; some rooms are available with private shower and toilet. The house is centrally heated and there is a comfortable TV lounge. Private car park. Further details on application.
AA QQQ

FAIRWAYS GUEST HOUSE

This charming Victorian House, offers you a warm welcome. Full central heating. Colour TV, telephone, clock radio and tea/coffee making in all our bedrooms. Most rooms are en suite. Licensed Bar & Restaurant also open to non residents, pool table. Large car park. Near to golf course and Addenbrooke Hospital.

 Proprietors: 14 years Mr & Mrs M R Slatter **AA QQQ**

141-143 Cherryhinton Road Cambridge CB1 4BX
Tel: (01223) 246063 Fax: (01223) 212093

Hamden Guest House

Bed & Breakfast Accommodation

A purpose-built Guest House annexe to a family home, with its own separate entrance lobby and reception area.

All rooms en-suite, with colour TV and tea & coffee facilities.

Situated on the outskirts of Cambridge within short distance of city centre.

89 High Street, Cherry Hinton Cambridge CB1 4LU
Tel: (01223) 413263

This popular guest house is a mile to the north-east of the city centre and successfully manages to provide professional standards at a reasonable rate. Bedrooms offer a good range of facilities, and smart public areas include a spacious restaurant and a licensed bar offering snacks and bar meals.
18rm(13🚿) (3fb) 🚭 in area of dining room CTV in all bedrooms [R] **T** 🚫🐕 sB&B£20-£30 sB&B🚿£30-£35 dB&B£40 dB&B🚿£40-£50 LDO noon
Lic ♨ nc4yrs
Credit Cards [1][2][3][5]

GH [Q][Q][Q] Helen Hotel 167-169 Hills Road CB2 2RJ (1m E, follow signs to A604 Colchester) ☎(0223) 246465
FAX (0223) 214406
Closed 15 Dec-5 Jan
Hospitable owners work hard to maintain traditional values and good accommodation at this hotel about a mile east of the city. All bedrooms are equally well equipped, though sizes and styles do vary, while the comfortable lounge offers satellite TV and has a bar adjacent. Freshly home-cooked Italian and British dishes are served each evening, the day having begun with a hearty breakfast.
22🛁🚿 Annexe 5🚿 (4fb)CTV in all bedrooms [R] **T** * sB&B£34-£45 sB&B🛁🚿£40-£45 dB&Bfr£50 dB&B🛁🚿£55 WB&B£231-£280 WBDi£315-£371 LDO 7pm
Lic ♨ CTV
Credit Cards [1][2][3][5]

GH [Q][Q] Kirkwood House 172 Chesterton Road CB4 1DA (Exit junc13 M11) ☎(0223) 313874
Closed Jan
The cheerful and enthusiastic owner of this small Edwardian house provides sound bed and breakfast accommodation. Bedrooms are fresh and light, and there is one on the ground floor. Breakfast is taken in two sittings in a small dining room decorated with antique plates.
5rm(2🚿) 🚭 CTV in all bedrooms [R] 🚫🐕 * sB&B£21-£32 dB&B£38-£40 dB&B🚿£44-£46
♨ nc7yrs

GH [Q][Q][Q] Lensfield Hotel 53 Lensfield Road CB2 1EN (on SW side of city centre) ☎(0223) 355017 Telex no 818183
FAX (0223) 312022
Closed 2wks Xmas
A well established, friendly, family-run hotel situated a few minutes' walk from the city centre offers bedrooms which vary considerably in both size and style. Those recently refurbished provide modern en suite accommodation and all rooms are well equipped and maintained. The smart restaurant on the lower ground floor features carte and fixed-price menus of international dishes at competitive prices, and the small bar which stands next to it is very well stocked.
36rm(2🛁18🚿) (4fb) 🚭 in 4 bedrooms 🚭 in area of dining room 🚭 in lounges CTV in all bedrooms [R] **T** 🚫🐕 * sB&B🛁🚿£42-£45 dB&B🛁🚿£52-£58 WB&B£294-£315 WBDi£343-£364 LDO 8.45pm
Lic ♨ CTV
Credit Cards [1][2][3][5]

SELECTED

GH [Q][Q][Q][Q] Old School Hotel & Guest House 9 Greenside, Waterbeach CB5 9HW (0.50m from A10 in centre of Waterbeach village overlooking green) ☎(0223) 861609
FAX (0223) 441683
An attractively converted old school overlooking Waterbeach's village green offers a friendly and informal environment, resident owners making every effort to meet guests' needs. Modern bedrooms and shower rooms - though in some cases small - are immaculately maintained, and refreshments and drinks are served during the day in a pleasant conservatory lounge. An annexe building just off the rear car parking area contains a sauna and indoor swimming pool.
8🚿 CTV in all bedrooms [R] 🚫🐕 (ex guide dogs) *
sB&B🚿£28-£32 dB&B🚿£38-£40 LDO 8pm
Lic ♨ CTV 🏊 (heated) sauna
Credit Cards [1][2][3][5]

GH [Q][Q][Q] *Sorrento Hotel* 196 Cherry Hinton Road CB1 4AN ☎(0223) 243533 FAX (0223) 213463
Standing twenty-five minutes' walk away from the centre of the city, this family-run hotel offers a bar, TV lounge and large restaurant, with ample parking to the rear. The bedrooms are well equipped and most are furnished to a comfortable standard.
24rm(5🛁19🚿) (5fb) CTV in all bedrooms [R] LDO 8.30pm
Lic ♨ CTV petanque terraine
Credit Cards [1][2][3][5]

GH [Q][Q][Q] Suffolk House Private Hotel 69 Milton Road CB4 1XA (1.5m on A1309) ☎(0223) 352016 FAX (0223) 566816
This private hotel has fresh, attractive and tastefully furnished bedrooms, all with modern en suite facilities, TV, radios and tea trays, and most with showers. Hard working proprietors Mr and Mrs Cuthbert work hard to provide high standards of housekeeping and maintenance.
10rm(1🛁9🚿) (4fb) CTV in all bedrooms [R] 🚫🐕 sB&B🛁🚿£35-£45 dB&B🛁🚿£45-£60
Lic ♨ nc4yrs
Credit Cards [1][3][£]

CAMPBELTOWN Strathclyde *Argyllshire* Map **10** NR72

GH [Q][Q] Westbank Dell Road PA28 6JG ☎(0586) 553660
FAX (0586) 551121
Situated in a quiet side street off the Machrihanish road leading out of the town, this neat house is run by a friendly and enthusiastic couple. Most of the bedrooms are brightly decorated and have modern fitted units. A comfortable guests' lounge is provided.
8rm(2🚿) 🚭 in dining room CTV in 4 bedrooms [R] 🚫🐕 (ex guide dogs) sB&Bfr£20 sB&B🚿fr£24 dB&Bfr£32 dB&B🚿fr£40
Lic ♨ CTV 🚫🅿 nc3yrs
Credit Cards [1][3][£]

CANTERBURY Kent Map **05** TR15

See also Petham

GH [Q] Castle Court 8 Castle Street CT1 2QF ☎(0227) 463441
A simple, clean and well maintained guest house offering modest accommodation. There is a small dining room/lounge and a choice of English or Continental breakfast.
12rm (1fb) 🚭 in dining room CTV in 5 bedrooms sB&B£18-£22 dB&B£30-£34
♨ CTV
Credit Cards [1][3][£]

🛏 ☕ **GH [Q][Q] Cathedral Gate Hotel** 36 Burgate CT1 2HA (next to main gateway into cathedral precincts) ☎(0227) 464381
FAX (0227) 462800
This small family run private hotel is situated next to the cathedral. Low beam ceilings and sloping beams add to its character. Bedrooms are of various sizes, and a number have recently been redecorated. There is a comfortable lounge and a very small dining room, but guests can take breakfast in their rooms.
12rm(2🛁) (4fb) 🚭 in dining room CTV in all bedrooms [R] **T** sB&Bfr£15 sB&B🛁🚿£37.50-£45 dB&Bfr£45 dB&B🛁🚿£54-£68 LDO 9pm
Lic ♨
Credit Cards [1][2][3][5][£]

GH Q Q Q **Chaucer Lodge** 62 New Dover Road CT1 3DT (on A2 out of city centre to Dover, 0.25m S) ☎(0227) 459141 FAX (0227) 459141
This well kept guest house is within a 10-minute walk of the city centre. The neat, bright bedrooms provide good amenities and the cheerful hosts make certain their guests get a warm welcome.
6⇌↾ (2fb) ⊭ in 2 bedrooms ⊭ in dining room CTV in all bedrooms ® ➤ (ex guide dogs) dB&B⇌↾£36-£50 ⊞ ₤

SELECTED

GH Q Q Q Q **Ebury Hotel** New Dover Road CT1 3DX
☎(0227) 768433 FAX (0227) 459187
Closed 15 Dec-14 Jan
An imposing, double-fronted Victorian building, the Ebury Hotel is set back from the main road in two acres of well kept grounds. The spacious bedrooms are furnished to a high standard and many have original fireplaces. Reception is staffed throughout the day and evening, and guests dining in the hotel can enjoy pre-dinner drinks in the elegant lounge. The short menu offers individually priced dishes of traditional English cooking.
15⇌↾ (2fb) ⊭ in dining room CTV in all bedrooms ® T sB&B⇌↾£41-£44 dB&B⇌↾£59.50-£65 WB&Bfr£187 WBDi£235-£280 LDO 8.30pm
Lic ⊞ CTV ⚓ (heated) spa exercise equipment
Credit Cards ①②③ ₤

SELECTED

GH Q Q Q Q **Ersham Lodge** 12 New Dover Road CT1 3AP
☎(0227) 463174 FAX (0227) 455482
May-Oct
A large creeper-clad house, this hotel has been run by the Pellay family for over 15 years. Bedrooms are furnished in an ornate, traditional style, befitting the house. Smart public areas comprise a small lounge and spacious breakfast room leading on to the flower-filled patio and garden.
14rm(2⇌11↾) (1fb) ⊭ in bedrooms ⊭ in dining room CTV in all bedrooms ® T ➤ (ex guide dogs) ✳
sB&B⇌↾£32-£36 dB&B£38 dB&B⇌↾£44-£49
Lic ⊞.
Credit Cards ①②③ ₤

GH Q Q Q **Highfield Hotel** Summer Hill, Harbledown CT2 8NH
☎(0227) 462772
Closed Xmas & New Year
This impressive Victorian house has not lost any of its character through the provision of modern facilities. Mr and Mrs Smallwood continue to provide comfortable and well maintained accommodation and warm and friendly hospitality.
8rm(3↾) ® ➤ sB&B£27-£29 dB&B£38-£40 dB&B↾£48-£52
Lic ⊞ nc5yrs
Credit Cards ① ③

SELECTED

GH Q Q Q Q **Magnolia House** 36 St Dunstan's Terrace
CT2 8AX ☎(0227) 765121 FAX (0227) 765121
This well maintained Georgian house is set in a quiet residential area on the University side of town within ten minutes' walk of the main shopping area. It has a great deal of charm and an air of quality. Nearly all the bedrooms are small and slightly cramped, but they are well appointed; four have

▶

Helen Hotel

167/169 Hills Road, Cambridge CB2 2RJ
Tel: (01223) 246465 Fax: (01223) 214406

Gino and Helen Agodino welcome you to their family run hotel, situated one mile from city centre. Enjoy a high standard of Italian food, friendly and personal service. All rooms with en suite facilities, telephone, colour TV, tea/coffee facilities and hair dryer. Ample car park. Charming Italian garden.

Sorrento Hotel

196 CHERRY HINTON ROAD
CAMBRIDGE CB1 4AN
TELEPHONE: (01223) 243533
FAX: (01223) 213463

AA LISTED

Sorrento Hotel is a family managed establishment offering our guests a professional and comfortable standard of accommodation and service. Situated approximately 1.5 miles from the City centre in a quiet residential area of south Cambridge and close to the Addenbrookes Hospital. All bedrooms have en suite facilities, colour TV and direct dial telephone etc. Relax in our licensed bar or television lounge where coffee or afternoon tea is served. Our pleasant restaurant offers a variety of dishes on both our **à la carte** or **table d'hôte** menu.
We have a private car park at the rear with security lighting. We ensure you that your stay with us will be a pleasant one.

nicely tiled showers en suite and the other three have baths. A small, cosy tastefully appointed lounge with a TV is the only area in which smoking is allowed.
6🛁🚿 🚭 CTV in all bedrooms [R] 🐕 sB&B🛁🚿£36-£45 dB&B🛁🚿£50-£60
🅿 CTV
Credit Cards [1] [2] [3]

P R E M I E R SELECTED

GH QQQQQ The Old Rectory Ashford Road, Chartham CT4 7HS (on A28, 100yds E of turning for Chartham) ☎(0227) 730075

Closed 17 Dec-10 Jan

A lovely Georgian house has been tastefully and thoughtfully decorated and furnished to reflect the character of the building. The bedrooms are spacious, comfortable and well equipped, with all those little extra touches that help to make guests feel at home. There is a comfortable sitting room which has recently been redecorated, and in the dining room Mrs Creasy provides three-course dinners and excellent English breakfasts.
3🛁🚿 🚭 CTV in 1 bedroom [R] 🐕 (ex guide dogs) sB&B🛁🚿£25-£38 dB&B🛁🚿£42-£54 LDO noon
🅿 CTV nc14yrs
Credit Cards [1] [3]

GH QQQ Oriel Lodge 3 Queens Avenue (entering town on A2 from London, 400yds after first roundabout turn left into Queens Avenue) ☎(0227) 462845

An attractive detached Edwardian house in a residential area near the town centre has been completely renovated by proprietors Keith and Anthea Rishworth. The dining room combines with the lounge area where guests are welcomed on arrival with a cup of tea around the real log fire. The bedrooms are on the first floor and although two of them are compact, they are all bright and modern and two have smart en suite facilities. The gardens are available to guests and there is ample car parking.
6rm(2🚿) (1fb) 🚭 in bedrooms 🚭 in dining room CTV in all bedrooms [R] 🐕 sB&B£19-£24 dB&B£33-£40 dB&B🚿£42-£52
🅿 nc6yrs

GH QQQ Pointers Hotel 1 London Road CT2 8LR (follow signs for university & Whitstable, Hotel opposite St Dunstan's Church) (Logis) ☎(0227) 456846 FAX (0227) 831131

Closed 24 Dec-15 Jan

This large private hotel is well situated on a busy road some ten minutes' walk from the main shopping area. The condition of some of the showers could be improved, but there are plans for upgrading this winter; most rooms already have double-glazing and all have colour TV and central heating. There is a large entrance area with a dispense bar to one side and a lounge on the other, and the hotel enjoys the helpful hospitality of owner Mrs O'Brien.
14rm(10🛁🚿) (2fb)CTV in all bedrooms [R] T sB&B🛁🚿£35-£45 dB&B£42-£46 dB&B🛁🚿£55-£60 WB&Bfr£147 WBDifr£231 LDO 8.15pm
Lic 🅿
Credit Cards [1] [2] [3] [5] [£]

SELECTED

GH QQQQ Thanington Hotel 140 Wincheap CT1 3RY (on A28, just outside City Walls) ☎(0227) 453227 FAX (0227) 453225

This listed Grade II farmhouse was built around 1800 and extended in 1830. When it became an hotel in 1987, a new bedroom wing was built and in 1992 the games room and indoor heated swimming pool were added. The small lounge has comfortable modern seating, and there is a bar adjoining the well appointed dining room, where a generous breakfast is provided. Service is personally supervised by David and Jill Jenkins, and the atmosphere is friendly and relaxing.
10🛁 (2fb) 🚭 in dining room CTV in all bedrooms [R] T sB&B🛁£39-£48 dB&B🛁£55-£62
Lic 🅿 CTV 🏊 (heated) games room
Credit Cards [1] [2] [3] [5] [£]

P R E M I E R SELECTED

GH QQQQQ Thruxted Oast Mystole, Chartham CT4 7BX (4m SW on A28) ☎(0227) 730080

Closed Xmas

This is a charming 18th-century oast house and barn is set in an area surrounded by hop gardens and orchards. Guests are made to feel relaxed and welcome by the friendly staff whose attention to detail makes comfort assured. Spacious bedrooms are tastefully furnished and the welcoming sitting room houses many books and magazines. Typically English food is carefully prepared using good, fresh produce and is served in the characterful dining room. Ample parking facilities are available.
3🚿 🚭 in bedrooms CTV in all bedrooms [R] T 🐕 (ex guide dogs) sB&B🚿£65 dB&B🚿£75
🅿 nc8yrs croquet lawn
Credit Cards [1] [2] [3] [5]

SELECTED

GH QQQQ The White House 6 St Peters Lane CT1 2BP ☎(0227) 761836

There is a warm and friendly atmosphere within this attractive Regency house, which is personally run by the friendly owners, Mr and Mrs Blackman. Well maintained and attractive, The White House has good sized comfortable bedrooms, all very well-equipped. There is an elegant dining/sitting room, where guest take their breakfast at a large communal table.
9rm(7🛁2🚿) (2fb) 🚭 in dining room 🚭 in 1 lounge CTV in all bedrooms [R] 🐕 sB&B🛁🚿£25-£30 dB&B🛁🚿£35-£45
🅿 CTV
[£]

SELECTED

INN QQQQ The Pilgrims Hotel 18 The Friars CT1 2AS (from Canterbury follow signs for Marlowe Theatre,establishment situated opposite) ☎(0227) 464531 FAX (0227) 464531

Opposite the Marlowe Theatre you find this 350-year-old ▶

$\mathcal{M}$AGNOLIA $\mathcal{H}$OUSE

36 St Dunstan's Terrace, Canterbury, Kent CT2 8AX
Tel and Fax: (01227) 765121   HIGHLY COMMENDED

This friendly, family run Georgian house, set in a quiet street, just a few minutes walk from the Westgate Towers and the City centre with its magnificent Cathedral, is ideally situated for the University and touring the Kentish coast and countryside. Enjoy our en suite facilities or luxurious 4 poster suite, varied and delicious breakfast, and relax in the beautiful walled garden. Car parking.

THE OLD RECTORY

Vicarage Lane, Sherborne, Nr. Warwick CV35 8AB Tel: (01926) 624562
Fax: (01926) 624562

A licensed Georgian country house rich in beams, flagstones and inglenooks. Situated in a gem of an English village, one third of a mile from M40, junction 15.
14 elegantly appointed ensuite bedrooms thoughtfully provide all possible comforts; some antique brass beds and some wonderful Victorian style bathrooms. Choice of supper menu., hearty breakfasts. *Tasty Suppers*
Recommended by all major guides.

POINTERS HOTEL

1 London Road, Canterbury
Tel: 01227-456846 Fax: 01227 831131

Situated only a few minutes' walk from the City centre and Cathedral and close to the University.
Pointers is a family-run Georgian hotel offering home-produced English meals.
All bedrooms have either bath or shower and each is equipped with colour television, radio, direct-dial telephone and tea and coffee making facilities.

Private car park.   AA QQQ

THANINGTON HOTEL

140 Wincheap • Canterbury • Kent CT1 3RY
Telephone: 01227 453227
Fax: 01227 453225

10 minutes walk to the City Centre and Cathedral, Thanington Hotel offers 'up market' bed and breakfast accommodation together with a quiet, relaxed and friendly atmosphere. Ten pretty en-suite Bedrooms, Bar, Lounge, Snooker Room, Indoor Heated Swimming Pool and Private Car Park, it is the ideal base for exploring Canterbury and East Kent.
30 minutes drive to Channel Ports and Tunnel, 60 minutes to Gatwick, 90 to London.

building which is now a friendly, relaxed hotel in which the proprietors are personally involved. Bedrooms are smartly furnished and fitted and in the beamed bar a tempting range of meals and blackboard specials is available, as well as a number of real ales.

15⇔↑ (1fb)CTV in all bedrooms Ⓡ T ✻ (ex guide dogs) sB&B⇔↑£45-£50 dB&B⇔↑£55-£75 Lunch fr£10 Dinner fr£10 LDO 10.30pm
▥
Credit Cards 1 3

CARDIFF South Glamorgan   Map **03** ST17

GH Ⓠ Ⓠ **Albany** 191-193 Albany Road, Roath CF2 3NU
☎(0222) 494121
Closed Xmas wk
This is a small, personally run, friendly guesthouse in a convenient city location. It offers bright, well equipped bedrooms, a cosy breakfast room and a small lounge.
12rm(7⇔↑) (4fb) CTV in 7 bedrooms Ⓡ ✻ (ex guide dogs)
▥ CTV

GH Ⓠ **Balkan Hotel** 144 Newport Road CF2 1DJ
☎(0222) 463673
Conveniently located close to the city centre, this friendly guest house offers clean, modest accommodation for the budget end of the market.
14rm(5↑) (3fb) CTV in 13 bedrooms Ⓡ ✻ LDO 7pm
▥ CTV
Credit Cards 1 2

GH Ⓠ Ⓠ Ⓠ **Clare Court Hotel** 46/48 Clare Road CF1 7QP
☎(0222) 344839 FAX (0222) 665856
Closed 25-26 Dec
A small commercial-style hotel which is within walking distance of the city centre. The bedrooms are equipped with the usual modern comforts and guests can enjoy a drink in the popular bar-lounge.
8⇔↑ (2fb) ⊬ in dining room CTV in all bedrooms Ⓡ T ✻ (ex guide dogs) sB&B⇔↑£25 dB&B⇔↑£36 WB&B£90-£115 WBDi£115-£160 LDO 7.30pm
Lic ▥ CTV ⚡ ⚘
Credit Cards 1 2 3 ④

GH Ⓠ Ⓠ **Courtfield Hotel** 101 Cathedral Road CF1 9PH
☎(0222) 227701 FAX (0222) 227701
Closed 24-31 Dec
Well placed for the town centre, this friendly little hotel has bright public rooms and simply furnished but well equipped bedrooms. The licensed restaurant is open to non residents.
16rm(4↑) (3fb) ⊬ in lounges CTV in all bedrooms Ⓡ T ✻ sB&Bfr£20 sB&B↑£30 dB&Bfr£32 dB&B↑£45 LDO 8.30pm
Lic ▥ CTV ⚡
Credit Cards 1 2 3 5 ④

GH Ⓠ Ⓠ **Domus** 201 Newport Road CF2 1AJ ☎(0222) 495785
2 Jan-20 Dec
Well positioned for the city centre, this friendly, family-run guest house has small but well equipped bedrooms with telephones, TVs and tea-making facilities. There is a cosy bar, lounge and breakfast room, and useful parking to the rear.
10rm(2↑) (2fb) ⊬ in dining room CTV in all bedrooms Ⓡ T ✻ (ex guide dogs) sB&B£18-£23 sB&B↑£22-£25 dB&B↑£35-£40 LDO noon
Lic ▥ CTV
④

GH Ⓠ Ⓠ Ⓠ **Ferrier's (Alva) Hotel** 130/132 Cathedral Road CF1 9LQ ☎(0222) 383413 FAX (0222) 383413
Closed 2wks Xmas & New Year
Close to the Sophia Gardens stands a friendly and well established

family run hotel. Bright, clean bedrooms are equipped for business guests and tourists. There is a large lounge and congenial bar.
26rm(6⇔↑) (4fb)CTV in all bedrooms Ⓡ T sB&B£18-£20 sB&B⇔↑£28-£35 dB&B£30-£38 dB&B⇔↑£38-£48 LDO 7.45pm
Lic ▥ CTV
Credit Cards 1 2 3 5 ④

GH Ⓠ Ⓠ **Tane's Hotel** 148 Newport road CF2 1DJ
☎(0222) 491755 & 493898 FAX (0222) 491755
There is a bright, friendly atmosphere at this conveniently situated family-run guesthouse, which offers value-for-money, well maintained accommodation.
9rm (1fb) ⊬ in 5 bedrooms CTV in all bedrooms Ⓡ ✻ ✻ sB&Bfr£17 sB&Bfr£22 dB&Bfr£28 dB&Bfr£34 WB&Bfr£85 WBDifr£115 LDO 7pm
Lic ▥ CTV nc2yrs
Credit Cards 3 ④

CARDIGAN Dyfed   Map **02** SN14

⊨ ■ **GH** Ⓠ Ⓠ Ⓠ **Brynhyfryd** Gwbert Road SA43 1AE (on the B4548 in Cardigan town) ☎(0239) 612861
This long established, comfortable semidetached guesthouse standing opposite the King George V recreation ground is run by Nesta and Ieuan Davies who have offered their guests a genuine Welsh welcome for some 15 years. Bedrooms are all freshly decorated, there is a comfortable cottage-style lounge and enjoyable home cooking is served in the pretty dining room. Street parking is easy.
7rm(2↑) (1fb) ⊬ in dining room CTV in all bedrooms Ⓡ ✻ (ex guide dogs) sB&B£14.50-£15 sB&B↑fr£20 dB&B£29-£30 dB&B↑£32-£34 WBDi£140-£160 LDO 7.30pm
▥ CTV ⚡
④

CARDROSS Strathclyde *Dunbartonshire*   Map **10** NS37

SELECTED

GH Ⓠ Ⓠ Ⓠ Ⓠ **Kirkton House** Darleith Road G82 5EZ (0.5m N of village) (Logis) ☎(0389) 841951 FAX (0389) 841868
Closed 18 Dec-10 Jan
From its elevated position above the village, this delightful guest house offers fine views of the River Clyde and gentle rolling countryside. Enthusiastic owners Stewart and Gillian MacDonald have worked hard over the years to restore the farmhouse, which is built around a courtyard. The public areas have a rustic feel, and guests can relax with a drink in the lounge before sitting down in the dining room to sample Gillian's home cooking.
6⇔↑ (4fb)CTV in all bedrooms Ⓡ T sB&B⇔↑£31-£36 dB&B⇔↑£52-£57 WB&B£157.50-£175 WBDi£273-£290.50 LDO 7.30pm
Lic ▥ ⚘ ∪
Credit Cards 1 2 3
See advertisement under **HELENSBURGH**

CAREW Dyfed Map **02** SN00

SELECTED

GH Ⓠ Ⓠ Ⓠ Ⓠ *Old Stable Cottage* 3 Picton Terrace SA70 8SL
☎(0646) 651889
Closed 21 Dec-Jan
This delightful cottage was originally a stable and cart house for the nearby castle. Sympathetically restored by Lionel and Joyce Fielder, it is now a charming little retreat in a pretty location. The trap shed is now the entrance porch, leading into the spacious sitting room, furnished with deep sofas and

armchairs, with its inglenook fireplace, bread oven and wrought-iron spiral staircase. Bedrooms feature the original stable timbers but offer a range of modern creature comforts and a host of nice little personal touches such as reading material and dried flowers. Breakfasts, and evening meals by arrangement, are served at a communal table in the conservatory which opens onto the sheltered garden.
3rm(2⇆1ﬀ) (1fb) CTV in all bedrooms ® ✻ (ex guide dogs) LDO 7pm
⊞ nc5yrs

CARLISLE Cumbria   Map **11** NY45

See also Brampton, Castle Carrock, Longtown & Thursby

GH Q Q Q Angus Hotel 14 Scotland Road CA3 9DG (N on A7)
☎(0228) 23546
rs 24-31 Dec
A very pleasant family-owned small hotel providing a good standard of accommodation and service, is situated just to the north of the city centre, with adequate parking nearby. The menu offers a good choice of food, and there is also a small wine list.
12rm(7ﬀ) (4fb) ✔ in 7 bedrooms ✔ in dining room CTV in all bedrooms ® sB&Bﬀ£21-£34 dB&Bﬀ£34-£49 LDO 9pm
Lic ⊞
Credit Cards [1] [2] [3]

GH Q Q Q Crossroads House Brisco CA4 0QZ (0.75m from junct 42 of M6) ☎(0228) 28994
Closed Xmas & New Year
This modern house converted from two cottages has some interesting historical features including a Roman well in the hall and a carved oak beam from a nearby manor house in the dining room. Located on the Dalston road, it provides modern bedrooms and a comfortable sun lounge.
5rm (1fb) ✔ in bedrooms ✔ in dining room ✔ in 1 lounge ✳
sB&Bfr£17 dB&Bfr£32 LDO 10am
Lic ⊞ CTV
(£)

GH Q Q Q East View 110 Warwick Road CA1 1JU (on main rd into city from junct 43 of M6) ☎(0228) 22112
Attractively decorated bedrooms in a variety of shapes and sizes are offered at this Victorian guest house. There is an attractive breakfast room with individual tables, and a small car park to the side of the building.
9ﬀ (3fb) CTV in all bedrooms ® ✻

⊷ ▣ **GH Q Q Q Howard House** 27 Howard Place CA1 1HR
☎(0228) 29159
An elegant late-Victorian town house situated in a quiet conservation area close to the city centre offers four large, comfortable bedrooms equipped with radio alarm clocks and remote control TV; two of them have en suite facilities, one a four-poster bed. There is a fine Victorian fireplace in the homely lounge, and breakfast is served in an attractive rear dining room looking out over the small garden and patio.
5rm(2ﬀ) (2fb)CTV in all bedrooms ® ✻ sB&B£15-£16 dB&B£30-£32 dB&Bﬀ£34-£36 WB&B£100-£120 WBDi£149-£169 LDO 2.30pm
⊞ CTV
Credit Cards [1] [3]

⊷ ▣ **GH Q Q Q Kenilworth** 34 Lazonby Terrace CA1 2PZ
1.5m S, on A6) ☎(0228) 26179
A Victorian house situated south of the city. It provides very clean and well furnished bedrooms, together with a guests' lounge. Family-owned, the service is friendly.
5rm (2fb)CTV in all bedrooms ® sB&B£14-£16 dB&B£26-£28 WB&B£84-£98
⊞ CTV
(£)

___The Albany Hotel___
M4 junction 33

14 Victoria Road, Penarth, S Glamorgan CF6 2EF.
Tel: Cardiff (01222) 701242 Telefax: (01222) 701598

Ideally situated in quiet Victorian tree lined surroundings. Penarth, this attractive coastal resort, known as "garden by the sea" and home of the "Waverley" is located a mere 3 miles from Cardiff. The railway station, shopping centre, excellent restaurants, breathtaking cliff walks, an elegant promenade and pier are all close by to the Albany.
Reasonable rates from £17.50 pp.
You will find the Albany, well equipped, convenient, comfortable and inexpensive, combined with a friendly and relaxed atmosphere.

See gazetteer under Penarth

FERRIER'S HOTEL
132 Cathedral Road, Cardiff, CF1 9LQ
Tel: (01222) 383413

Ferrier's Hotel is a family-managed hotel set in a Victorian Conservation area and yet within walking distance of the city centre. 26 bedrooms, including 7 on the ground floor. All rooms tastefully furnished and have hot and cold water, central heating, radio, colour TV, tea & coffee making facilities and direct dial telephone. Many rooms with private shower and many en-suite. Bar meals are available Monday to Thursday. Light refreshments in the Cane Lounge and well stocked Bar. Resident's Lounge with colour TV. Full fire certificate. Car park, locked at night.

GH Q Q Q **Kingstown Hotel** 246 Kingstown Road CA3 0DE
☎(0228) 515292 FAX (0228) 515292
Closed Xmas
A pleasantly furnished and comfortable family-run hotel is
situated on the A7 north of the city centre and close to the M6.
Bedrooms are mainly modern with two rooms on the ground floor.
There is a small garden to the rear and ample parking is available.
6rm(4⇔1🐾) (1fb) ⊁ in dining room CTV in all bedrooms Ⓡ
sB&B£21 sB&B⇔♠£32 dB&B£34 dB&B⇔♠£39 LDO 9pm
Lic ▥ CTV
Credit Cards ①②③

GH Q Q Q **Parkland** 136 Petteril Street CA1 2AW
☎(0228) 48331
A pleasantly furnished and decorated guesthouse to the east of the
town centre. The bedrooms are pretty and are furnished to a high
standard. There is a cosy and comfortable lounge and an attractive
dining room. Service is friendly and helpful.
5rm(4🐾) (2fb) CTV in all bedrooms Ⓡ ✳ sB&B£15-£16.50
sB&B♠£18-£20 dB&B£26-£28 dB&B♠£32-£34 LDO 4pm
Lic ▥ CTV
£

GH Q Q **Wallsend** Church Lane, Bowness-on-Solway CA5 5AF
☎Kirkbride(06973) 51055
Previously the rectory, this spacious house is situated on the edge
of Bowness on Solway. The house contains thousands of books,
many of which are for sale.
3rm ⊁ Ⓡ ✳ sB&B£16-£20 dB&B£24-£30 LDO noon
▥ CTV nc10yrs
£

|⇔ ⚡| **GH** Q Q Q **The Warren** 368 Warwick Road CA1 2RU
(exit M6 junct 43 and proceed 0.5m down main road. Opposite
Esso petrol station) ☎(0228) 33663 & 512916
Built in 1839 and once known as the Star Inn, this guest house
offers prettily decorated and well equipped accommodation,
including two bedrooms at ground-floor level. Decorative antique
chamber pots are a feature of the lounge, and in addition to the
main lounge and dining room there are two conservatory lounges
at the front of the hotel.
6rm(5🐾) (1fb) ⊁ in bedrooms ⊁ in area of dining room CTV in
all bedrooms Ⓡ T 🐾 (ex guide dogs) sB&B£15 sB&B♠£20
dB&B♠£34-£36 WB&B£114-£116 WBDi£154-£156 LDO early
am
▥ CTV
£

|⇔ ⚡| **FH** Q Q Q Mrs A Westmorland **Blackwell** *(NY387512)*
Blackwell, Durdar CA2 4SH (2m S, close to race course)
☎(0228) 24073
This comfortable farmhouse is set around a cobbled yard with cow
sheds just outside the front door. It is situated on the edge of the
city next to the racecourse and is to some extent a town farm.
Bedrooms are attractively furnished, and though none of them
have wash basins, the bathroom is close by. A cosy lounge and
dining room are provided.
2rm (1fb) ⊁ in bedrooms sB&B£15-£16 dB&B£28-£30
WB&B£98-£105
▥ CTV ໓ 120 acres dairy mixed
£

CARMARTHEN Dyfed   Map **02** SN42

See also Cwmduad

FH Q Q Q Mrs J Willmott **Cwmtwrch Hotel & Four Seasons
Restaurant** *(SN497220)* Nantgaredig SA32 7NY (5m E, off A40)
☎Nantgaredig(0267) 290238 FAX (0267) 290808
This small guesthouse has its own very popular restaurant and bar
complex, where a wide choice of food is available. The bedrooms
are fully modernised; three pine furnished rooms are in converted
outbuildings, and three are in the original farmhouse, together

---

with the breakfast room, lounge and the new conservatory where
breakfast is served in the summer.
6rm(3⇔3🐾) (2fb) ⊁ in bedrooms CTV in 3 bedrooms Ⓡ
sB&B⇔♠£30-£36 dB&B⇔♠£42-£48 WB&B£160-£250
WBDi£255-£370 LDO 9pm
Lic ▥ CTV ໓ ♆ (heated) ▶9 gymnasium 30 acres sheep
£

SELECTED

FH Q Q Q Q Mrs F Burns **Farm Retreats** *(SN485203)*
Capel Dewi Uchaf Farm, Capel Dewi SA32 8AY (4m E)
☎Nantgaredig(0267) 290799 FAX (0267) 290003
Rustic elegance and modern comforts are the hallmarks of this
unassuming building which has been lovingly restored and is
set in an area of gentle scenic beauty. Guests are encouraged to
hand feed the nearby herd of deer. The three bedrooms are
welcoming and full of character, and there is a large dining
room where dinner is provided by the graceful hostess.
3rm(2⇔1🐾) ⊁ CTV in all bedrooms Ⓡ 🐾 LDO 10am
Lic ▥ CTV ♪ 34 acres non-working

SELECTED

FH Q Q Q Q Mr T Giles **Pantgwyn** SA32 7ES *(SN464216)*
☎Nantgaredig(0267) 290247
This beautifully restored house stands in a picturesque valley
and offers high quality accommodation in comfortable
surroundings.
3rm(2⇔🐾) (2fb) ⊁ CTV in all bedrooms Ⓡ 🐾 (ex guide
dogs) ✳ sB&B£23-£28 sB&B⇔♠£25-£30 dB&B£38-£46
dB&B⇔♠£42-£50 LDO 5pm
Lic ▥ ໓ pool table 12 acres beef sheep

INN Q Q Q **Cothi Bridge Hotel** Pontargothi SA32 7NG (6m E on
A40 towards Llandello) ☎(0267) 290251 FAX (0267) 290251
rs Oct-Mar
10rm(1⇔9🐾) (1fb) ⊁ in 5 bedrooms ⊁ in lounges CTV in all
bedrooms Ⓡ T ✳ sB&B⇔♠fr£30 dB&B⇔♠fr£45 WB&B£210
WBDi£200-£280 Lunch £15&alc Dinner £15&alc LDO 9pm
▥ CTV ♪
Credit Cards ①②③ £

CARNFORTH Lancashire   Map **07** SD47

PREMIER ♛ **SELECTED**

GH Q Q Q Q Q **New
Capernwray Farm**
Capernwray LA6 1AD (from
B6254, left at village green in
Over Kellet and continue for
2m)
☎(0524) 734284
FAX (0524) 734284
This stone-built former
farmhouse dates from 1697
and is situated in a delightful
rural location within easy
reach of Junction 35 of the M6. Carefully restored by the
owners Peter and Sally Townsend, it offers charming and
informal accommodation of a high standard. The three
bedrooms each have a private bathroom and are thoughtfully
furnished with many personal touches; they all enjoy views
over the surrounding countryside. The comfortable lounge is
full of character with exposed stone walls and oak beams, and
the dining room was originally the farm dairy. Enjoyable home

cooked dinners are served at the communal candlelit table. A house-party atmosphere prevails with guests congregating before dinner for a complimentary glass of sherry; there is no drinks licence but guests are welcome to bring their own.
3rm(1⇌1↟) ⊁ in bedrooms ⊁ in dining room CTV in all bedrooms ® ✳ sB&B⇌↟£30-£34 dB&B⇌↟£52-£58 LDO 5pm
▥ nc10yrs
Credit Cards ①③ⓔ

CARRADALE Strathclyde *Argyllshire*　　　Map **10** NR83

GH ◻◻◻ **Dunvalanree** Portrigh Bay PA28 6SE
☎(05833) 226 FAX (05833) 339
Etr-Oct
This fine Edwardian house has gardens almost stretching down to the shore and excellent views overlooking the bay. It is situated in the hamlet of Port Righ about half a mile from the village. The guesthouse is spotlessly maintained and has a lovely tranquil character about it, epitomised by its tasteful public rooms. The bedrooms are neat and vary in furnishings; some have modern units others have older furniture.
14rm (3fb) ⊁ in dining room ® ✳ sB&B£16.50 dB&B£33 WB&B£115.50 WBDi£175
Lic CTV ▶9 ⟋ squash

CARRBRIDGE Highland *Inverness-shire*　　　Map **14** NH92

GH ◻◻◻ **Carrmoor** Carr Road PH23 3AD (first right after bistro) ☎(0479) 841244
A comfortable, family-run licensed guesthouse, centrally located just off the main street. It has a relaxed atmosphere and the enthusiastic owners place much emphasis on welcoming hospitality. Bedrooms are bright and airy; en suite facilities are available. Good home cooking is provided in the smartly decorated dining room.
5↟ (1fb) ⊁ in bedrooms ⊁ in dining room ® sB&B↟£19-£23.50 dB&B↟£33-£37 WB&B£101.50-£115.50 WBDi£175-£189 LDO 8pm
Lic ▥ CTV mountain bikes for hire
Credit Cards ①③ⓔ

SELECTED

GH ◻◻◻◻ **Fairwinds Hotel** PH23 3AA ☎(0479) 841240
FAX (0479) 841240
Closed 5 Nov-16 Dec
This former Victorian manse has been sympathetically modernised and is set back from the main road, surrounded by seven acres of mature pine woods, with a small lochan in the grounds. Efficiently run by enthusiastic owners Mr and Mrs Reed, the house has a welcoming atmosphere, with high standards of housekeeping. Bedrooms are mostly spacious, with individual colour schemes and pine units and are equipped with thoughtful extras; they all have en suite shower or bathrooms, together with TV, clock radios and hairdryers. The lounge has an honesty bar and a log burner, and a varied menu of Scottish dishes is offered in the adjoining dining room. A selection of self-catering chalets are available, situated in the hotel grounds, and membership of the local Woodland Club enables guests to use facilities including a swimming pool, sauna, steam room, dry ski slope and tennis court for a reasonable cost.
5⇌↟ ⊁ in dining room ⊁ in 1 lounge CTV in all bedrooms ® **T** sB&B⇌↟£23-£25 dB&B⇌↟£44-£52 WB&B£140-£175 WBDi£215-£242 LDO 4pm
Lic ▥ nc12yrs
Credit Cards ①③ⓔ
See advertisement on p.125.

GH Ⓠ Ⓠ Ⓠ **Feith Mhor Country House** Station Road PH23 3AP (1.25m W) ☎(0479) 841621
Peacefully situated in its own grounds amid pleasant countryside, this substantial 19th-century house makes an ideal base for touring. The relaxing public areas include a spacious lounge and a dining room where wholesome Taste of Scotland dishes are prepared from the freshest local ingredients.
6rm(3➪3�) (1fb) ✗ in dining room ✗ in lounges CTV in all bedrooms Ⓡ sB&B➪♠£18-£21 dB&B➪♠£36-£42 WBDi£200-£214 LDO 6pm
Lic ▥ nc12yrs
Ⓔ

CARSINGTON Derbyshire　　　　　　　Map **08** SK25

SELECTED

GH Ⓠ Ⓠ Ⓠ Ⓠ **Henmore Grange** Hopton DE4 4DF (turn into Hopton from B5035 and take first left at Wirksworth end of bypass) ☎(0629) 540420
Set in lovely countryside overlooking Carsington Water, Henmore Grange offers attractive accommodation carefully converted from 17th-century farm buildings, which retain much of their original character with exposed beams and fireplaces. Guests have the use of a small TV lounge, a larger lounge with a bar counter, and a dining room, where hearty breakfasts, cream teas (in season) and dinner are served.
11rm(9➪♠) (2fb) ✗ in dining room Ⓡ ✳ sB&Bfr£20 sB&B➪♠£31 dB&B£36 dB&B➪♠£55 WB&B£120-£172.50 WBDi£190-£242.50 LDO 6pm
Lic ▥ CTV
Credit Cards 2 Ⓔ

CASTLE CARROCK Cumbria　　　　　　Map **12** NY55

▥✈ **FH** Ⓠ B W Robinson **Gelt Hall** (NY542554) CA4 9LT (B6413 to Castle Carrock) ☎Hayton(0228) 70260
Oak beams and low ceilings contribute to the charm and character of this typical Cumbrian farmhouse, dating back to 1818 and set at the centre of the village; bedrooms are fairly simple in appointment, but guests are assured of warm hospitality.
3rm(1➪) (1fb)✗ sB&B£13-£15 dB&B£26-£28 dB&B➪£28-£30 LDO 5pm
▥ CTV 250 acres beef dairy sheep
Ⓔ

CASTLE CARY Somerset　　　　　　　Map **03** ST63

INN Ⓠ Ⓠ Ⓠ **The George Hotel** Market Place BA7 7AH
☎(0963) 350761 FAX (0963) 350035
One of the oldest inns in Britain, this 15th-century, former coaching inn continues to be upgraded to a pleasing standard, while retaining the comfort and charm of an old-world establishment. The pretty oak-panelled dining room serves delicious dinners and Sunday lunches, while extensive, tasty bar meals are offered at lunchtimes Monday to Saturday. Chef Trevor Parsons has created a varied, interesting à la carte menu, with tempting dishes such as smooth duck liver and orange paté and a good selection of fish dishes, balanced with a range of meat and poultry, and his home-made puddings should not be missed. A well planned, sensibly priced wine list is provided, which gives good value for money, as does the à la carte menu. Modern comforts are supplied in the en suite bedrooms that are individually decorated and furnished. Service is charming and friendly, with a relaxed, easy atmosphere throughout.
12➪♠ Annexe 3➪♠ (1fb) ✗ in area of dining room CTV in all bedrooms Ⓡ T ✳ sB&B➪♠£40-£45 dB&B➪♠£65-£75 Lunch £8-£9.50 Dinner £12-£16alc LDO 9pm
▥
Credit Cards 1 3 Ⓔ

CASTLE DONINGTON Leicestershire　　　Map **08** SK42
For accommodation details see under **East Midlands Airport, Leicestershire**

CASTLE DOUGLAS Dumfries & Galloway *Kirkcudbrightshire* Map **11** NX76

GH Ⓠ Ⓠ Ⓠ **Rose Cottage** Gelston DG7 1SH (beside B727, 2m S) ☎(0556) 502513
Feb-Oct
Rose Cottage is an attractive whitewashed building offering cosy and attractive accommodation together with a friendly, welcoming atmosphere. The individually decorated bedrooms are neat and comfortable and there is a cosy lounge.
3rm(1➪♠) Annexe 2rm (1fb) ✗ in dining room Ⓡ ✳ sB&B£15-£18 dB&B£30 dB&B➪♠£35 WB&B£100-£135 WBDi£160-£195 LDO 5pm
▥ CTV
Ⓔ

CATLOWDY Cumbria　　　　　　　　Map **12** NY47

FH Ⓠ Ⓠ Ⓠ Mr & Mrs Lawson **Craigburn** (NY474761) CA6 5QP ☎Nicholforest(0228) 577214 FAX (0228) 577214
Poultry, pigs and goats, as well as various breeds of sheep and cattle - blackfaced ewes and suckler cows proving firm favourites with visitors - are kept on this 250-acre working farm situated in open country about 14 miles northeast of Carlisle; children are actively encouraged to touch the animals and to help with feeding. Accommodation is provided in modern en suite bedrooms and there are two lounges with books, games and TV as well as the spacious dining room and a residents' bar.
6rm(4➪2♠) (2fb) ✗ Ⓡ ✳ sB&B➪♠£18-£19 dB&B➪♠£36-£38 WB&B£113.40-£126 WBDi£176.40-£189 LDO 7pm
Lic ▥ CTV ♨ snooker 250 acres beef mixed sheep
Credit Cards 1 3 Ⓔ

CHAGFORD Devon　　　　　　　　　Map **03** SX78

SELECTED

GH Ⓠ Ⓠ Ⓠ Ⓠ **Bly House** Nattadon Hill TQ13 8BW
☎(0647) 432404
A granite-built former rectory, Bly House is set in five acres of well tended grounds surrounded by the dramatic scenery of the Dartmoor National Park. The spacious bedrooms have been redecorated, comfortably furnished and well equipped. Each has its own bathroom and some have four-poster or half-tester beds. There is an attractive lounge and a great hall with a wood-burning stove. Breakfast is served at separate tables in the elegant dining room.
6rm(5➪1♠) ✗ in dining room CTV in all bedrooms Ⓡ sB&B➪♠£30-£33 dB&B➪♠£50-£56
▥ CTV nc10yrs croquet

SELECTED

GH Ⓠ Ⓠ Ⓠ Ⓠ **Glendarah** TQ13 8BZ ☎(0647) 433270
This semidetached family home has recently been purchased by Allan and Pamela Simon, who have completely refurbished the accommodation. Each bedroom, now tastefully decorated and furnished, offers en suite facilities and modern equipment. Downstairs there is a cosy bar-lounge and an attractive dining room where breakfast is served.
6➪♠ Annexe 1➪ CTV in all bedrooms Ⓡ sB&B➪♠£22-£28 dB&B➪♠£44-£56
Lic ▥
Credit Cards 1 3 Ⓔ

CHANNEL ISLANDS	Map **16**
GUERNSEY	Map **16**

FOREST

GH Q Q Q **Mon Plaisir** Rue Des Landes GY8 0DY
☎Guernsey(0481) 64498 FAX (0481) 63493
Conveniently situated close to Petit Bot Valley and beautiful cliff
walks, this Guernsey farmhouse dates back to 1830. Spacious
modern bedrooms are freshly decorated and comfortably
furnished, each equipped with a smart en suite bathroom and small
fridge, in addition to other amenities. Mr Torode offers a hearty
English breakfast in the small dining room which adjoins the
guests' sitting room. A secluded garden and greenhouse can be
enjoyed on bright days.
4⇔🐾 CTV in all bedrooms ® 🦮 (ex guide dogs)
dB&B⇔🐾£30-£40
🏧
£

ST MARTIN

SELECTED

GH Q Q Q Q **Hotel La Michelle** Les Hubits GY4 6NB
☎Guernsey(0481) 38065 FAX (0481) 39492
Apr-Oct
Personally run by resident proprietors Susie and Roger
Edwards, this delightful hotel is situated in a quiet lane not far
from Fermain Bay. A new bar-lounge has been added and the
bedrooms have been tastefully furnished. In the attractive no-
smoking dining room a daily four-course dinner is available
with a choice of dishes. Desserts are particularly
recommended.
14⇔🐾 (5fb) ⊁ in dining room CTV in all bedrooms ® T 🦮
(ex guide dogs) ✳ sB&B⇔🐾£25-£34 dB&B⇔🐾£50-£68
(incl dinner) LDO 7.30pm
Lic 🏧 CTV nc8yrs ⚓(heated)
Credit Cards ① ② ③

ST PETER PORT

GH Q Q Q **Marine Hotel** Well Road (situated just off Glategny
Esplanade, opposite Queen Elizabeth II Marina)
☎Guernsey(0481) 724978
Situated only 30 yards from the seafront and the new marina, this
small hotel has a number of bedrooms suitable for families. There
is a comfortable lounge and a sunny summer terrace, with an old
red telephone box in working order (the only one on the island).
Smoking is not permitted in the public rooms.
11⇔🐾 (3fb) ⊁ in dining room ⊁ in lounges ® 🦮 (ex guide
dogs) ✳ sB&B⇔🐾£14.75-£23.50 dB&B⇔🐾£35-£44
🏧 CTV ⊁
Credit Cards ① ③

PREMIER 🏆 SELECTED

GH Q Q Q Q Q **Midhurst
House** Candie Road
☎Guernsey(0481) 724391
FAX (0481) 729451
mid Apr-mid Oct
This fine small private hotel
occupies a very smart location
next to Candie Gardens, and
the couple who have owned it
for the past 15 years have built
up an enviable reputation for
friendly personal service and

efficiently maintained accommodation - the latter including
some attractively furnished cottage-style garden rooms. The
comfortable open-plan lounge leads on to a well appointed
dining room where guests can choose from a daily-changing
menu featuring locally caught fish and some fine patisserie
and ice-creams; bread is home-made. The walled garden faces
south and limited private garaging is available in addition to
the free parking facilities adjacent to Cambridge Park.
5rm(2⇔3🐾) Annexe 3🐾 (1fb) ⊁ in dining room CTV in all
bedrooms ® T 🦮 sB&B⇔🐾£30-£38 dB&B⇔🐾£40-£62
WBDi£210-£294 LDO 6.45pm
Lic 🏧 nc8yrs
Credit Cards ① ③

SELECTED

GH Q Q Q Q **Les Ozouets Lodge** Ozouets Road
☎Guernsey(0481) 721288
Mar-Oct
Situated on the outskirts of town close to the Beau Sejour
Leisure Centre, this comfortable hotel was formerly a
Guernsey mansion house. Family-run with a friendly and
informal atmosphere, it has individually furnished and well
equipped bedrooms and an attractive restaurant where French
cooking can be enjoyed. Outside, the large secluded grounds
include a heated swimming pool, a grass tennis court, a
bowling green and a putting green.
13rm(5⇔8🐾) Annexe 1⇔🐾 (3fb) CTV in all bedrooms ®
🦮 LDO 7.45pm
Lic 🏧 nc5yrs ⚓(grass)bowling green putting green petanques
Credit Cards ① ③

Fairwinds Hotel

Carrbridge, PH23 3AA
Telephone & Fax: 01479 841240 AA
Selected

Experience a true Highland welcome. Dine on
Scotland's Finest Produce in our spacious Conservatory
Restaurant. Vegetarian dishes and packed lunches
available by arrangement. Relax in the Ptarmigan
Lounge Bar. Perhaps glimpse a shy Roe Deer from
your bedroom:- all our rooms are En-suite and
centrally heated.
Many activities locally:- Walking, Golf, Birdwatching
and many more, or just relax and enjoy the
beauty of the area. Allow us to make your
stay with us memorable.
Full details from Mrs E. Reed.

HIGHLY
COMMENDED

ST SAMPSON

SELECTED

GH 🅀🅀🅀🅀 **Ann-Dawn Private Hotel** Route des Capelles GY2 4GQ ☎Guernsey(0481) 725606 FAX (0481) 725930
Etr-Oct
Located in a quiet, residential street, some distance from the town and harbour, this guesthouse is surrounded by landscaped gardens. Bedrooms are freshly decorated, simply appointed and reasonably equipped, and housekeeping standards are good. In addition to breakfast, an evening meal is offered, and guests may also enjoy drinks from the residents' bar.
11⇌ ⊬ CTV in all bedrooms ® 🕇 ⁕ sB&B⇌£18.50-£24.50 dB&B⇌£33-£45 LDO 5pm
Lic ▥ nc12yrs
Credit Cards 1 3 £

JERSEY   Map 16

GREVE DE LECQ BAY

GH 🅀🅀🅀 **Des Pierres** JE3 2DT (on B65 near beach)
☎Jersey(0534) 481858 FAX (0534) 485273
Closed Xmas & New Year
Situated on top of a hill overlooking the bay and coastal countryside, this guesthouse offers modern, smartly decorated bedrooms, some of which have superb views; all rooms have good en suite facilities, double glazing, TVs, radios, hair dryers and tea trays and several are ideal for families. There is a basement bar and dining room, and the daily choice of fresh home-cooked dishes is displayed on a blackboard. Service is personally supervised by the resident proprietors Mr and Mrs Flath, who have owned the guesthouse for many years.
16rm(9⇌7♠) (4fb) ⊬ in lounges CTV in all bedrooms ® 🕇 ⁕ sB&B⇌£27-£33 dB&B⇌£54-£66 (incl dinner) WBDi£189-£231 LDO 8pm
Lic ▥ CTV gymnasium
Credit Cards 1 3

GROUVILLE

SELECTED

GH 🅀🅀🅀🅀 **Lavender Villa Hotel** Rue A Don JE3 9DA (approx 3m from St Helier on East Coast Road just off A3)
☎Jersey(0534) 854937 FAX (0534) 856147
Mar-Nov
Professionally managed by the charming proprietors Mr & Mrs Davies, this popular and busy hotel adjoins the Royal Jersey Golf Club at the 12th tee and is only a short stroll from the beach. Bedrooms are smart and bright with excellent en suite facilities whilst the traditional public areas are full of charm and character. The gardens and inviting outdoor pool are particularly enjoyed by guests.
21rm(10⇌11♠) (3fb) CTV in all bedrooms ® 🕇 LDO 7.45pm
Lic ▥ CTV nc3yrs ⛲
Credit Cards 1 3

ST AUBIN

GH 🅀🅀 **Bryn-y-Mor Private Hotel** Route de la Haule JE3 8BA (on A1) ☎Jersey(0534) 20295 FAX (0534) 24262
This small hotel overlooks St Aubin's Bay so many of the well equipped bedrooms have lovely sea views. Light refreshments are available throughout the day, either inside or on the garden terrace, and a daily changing set menu is provided in the dining room and

bar. Service here is particularly friendly and helpful.
14rm(11⇌♠) (4fb) ⊬ in dining room CTV in all bedrooms ® T sB&B£20-£27 sB&B⇌£23-£30 dB&B£40-£60 dB&B⇌£46-£70 (incl dinner) WB&B£119-£224 WBDi£140-£245 LDO 6.30pm
Lic
Credit Cards 1 2 3 5 £

SELECTED

GH 🅀🅀🅀🅀 **The Panorama** La Rue du Crocquet JE3 8BR ☎Jersey(0534) 42429 FAX (0534) 45940
Etr-Oct
Set high above the village and enjoying excellent sea views from most of the bedrooms, this delightful and very popular family-run guesthouse has a choice of individually decorated and well furnished bedrooms that are thoughtfully equipped with telephones, fridges and microwave ovens. In addition to the comfortable lounge, there is a new tea room, both with exquisite oak carved fireplaces, and a terraced tea garden, where many different varieties of tea are offered. As well as the full choice of afternoon teas, morning coffee and light refreshments are usually served throughout the day and are particularly recommended; this service is also offered to non residents. An excellent breakfast menu includes such dishes as a grand slam 'full house' or crumpets with bacon and maple syrup. A friendly service is personally provided by the enthusiastic proprietors John and Jill Squires. Car parking is limited and is located below the guesthouse at roadside level.
17⇌♠ (2fb) ⊬ in dining room ⊬ in lounges CTV in all bedrooms ® 🕇 sB&B⇌£20-£38 dB&B⇌£34-£66 ▥⁂nc10yrs tea garden
Credit Cards 1 2 3 5 £

ST HELIER

GH 🅀🅀🅀 **Cliff Court Hotel** St Andrews Road, First Tower ☎(0534) 34919
14 Apr-29 Oct
The Cliff Court Hotel has views across to St Aubins Bay. Bedrooms vary in size and design, and include a ground-floor room and two rooms with four-poster beds. Public rooms comprise a small TV lounge, a bar with a pool table, and a pleasant dining room where a home-cooked evening meal is served. The outdoor pool and terraced garden are popular in good weather.
16rm(15⇌) (4fb) ® 🕇 (ex guide dogs) LDO 7.30pm
Lic ▥ CTV ⛲(heated)
Credit Cards 3

SELECTED

GH 🅀🅀🅀🅀 **Kaieteur** 4 Ralegh Ave JE2 3ZG ☎(0534) 37004 FAX (0534) 67423
This elegant Victorian house is quietly yet centrally situated in a residential area above the centre of town. Bedrooms are fresh, bright and neatly appointed; all but one have smart modern shower rooms. The warm, relaxed and friendly atmosphere is appreciated by guests, many of whom return time and time again.
10rm(9♠) (1fb) ⊬ in dining room ⊬ in lounges CTV in all bedrooms ® 🕇 (ex guide dogs) sB&B♠£16-£24 dB&B♠£32-£29
▥ CTV
Credit Cards 1 3 £

GH 🅀🅀🅀 **Millbrook House** Rue de Trachy, Millbrook JE2 3JN (1.5m W on A1) ☎Jersey(0534) 33036 FAX (0534) 24317
Apr-Oct

This handsome Colonial and Georgian style property dates back over 200 years and stands in a quiet location close to the beach and town centre. Surrounded by 10 acres of mature grounds and gardens, the hotel has been restored and extended without altering the original character, and offers wonderful views over St Aubin's Bay. The 24 bedrooms are freshly decorated, comfortable and well equipped, each with a private bathroom. Public areas include comfortable lounges and a sunny conservatory extension to the well furnished dining room, where a home-cooked evening meal is offered. Ample car parking and a peaceful environment contribute towards making the hotel good value for money.
24rm(17⇌7↑) (2fb)CTV in all bedrooms ℝ T ✱ ✳ sB&B⇌↑£18-£28.50 dB&B⇌↑£36-£57 WB&B£126-£199.50 WBDi£168-£241.50 LDO 7pm
Lic lift CTV
Credit Cards 2

SARK

SELECTED
GH ℚℚℚℚ **Hotel Petit Champ** GY9 0SF
☎(0481) 832046 FAX (0481) 832469
Etr-Oct
16⇌↑ (2fb) ✗ in dining room ✗ in 1 lounge ✱ (ex guide dogs) sB&B⇌↑£42-£46 dB&B⇌↑£80-£96 (incl dinner) WBDi£280-£336 LDO 8.30pm
Lic ▥ CTV nc7yrs ⌇(heated) putting green
Credit Cards 1 2 3 5 ⓔ

CHARD Somerset   Map 03 ST30

GH ℚℚℚ **Watermead** 83 High Street TA20 1QT (on A30)
☎(0460) 62834
Situated at the top of the High Street and set back from the road, his small friendly guesthouse offers a high standard of housekeeping. All the comfortable bedrooms have colour TV and ome are fitted with en suite facilities. Public areas include a TV ounge and spacious dining room which has a view to the stables t the end of the garden.
)rm(6↑) ✗ in dining room CTV in all bedrooms ℝ ✳ sB&B£15 B&B↑£22.50 dB&B↑£35 WB&B£105-£157.50 WBDi£161-213.50 LDO noon
▥
ⓔ

CHARFIELD Gloucestershire   Map 03 ST79

NNℚℚ **Huntingford Mill Hotel** GL12 8EX
☎Dursley(0453) 843431
et in a gloriously peaceful location, yet only three miles from unction 14 of the M5, this old corn mill is full of character, ffering guests the use of over two miles of the Little Avon River or fishing. Bedrooms provide the overnight traveller with omfortable accommodation. There are several bar areas, log fires ive a cosy atmosphere and in the popular restaurant an extensive nenu includes such specialities as Texas size T-bone steaks.
rm (1fb) CTV in all bedrooms ℝ ✱ (ex guide dogs) LDO 10pm ▮ CTV ✔
'redit Cards 1 3

CHARING Kent   Map 05 TQ94

H ℚℚℚ Mrs P Pym **Barnfield** *(TQ924477)* TN27 0BN
☎(0233) 712421
ome 500 acres of arable and sheep-grazing land surround this ncient farmhouse which has all the comfort and individuality of a ell cared for home. It has low oak beams, open fires, an old tub the communal bathroom, plus numerous family mementoes and ooks dotted around. Bedrooms are comfortable and interestingly urnished. Meals are served in two rooms, one of which doubles as television lounge. Smoking is not permitted.

6rm ✗ ℝ ✱ sB&B£18.50 dB&B£37-£39 LDO 5pm
▥ CTV ⌇(hard)500 acres arable sheep
Credit Cards 3 ⓔ

CHARLTON Northamptonshire   Map 04 SP53

SELECTED
GH ℚℚℚℚ **Home Farmhouse** OX17 3DR
☎Banbury(0295) 811683 FAX (0295) 811683
A 16th-century village farmhouse set in half an acre of walled garden. The two bedrooms in the main house each have private bathrooms and are individually furnished; one on the top floor has the benefit of a small lounge and these rooms are reached by a winding staircase. A third room is up a stone stairway via the colourful courtyard, and this can also be let as a self-catering unit. There are two interconnecting sitting rooms and a stylishly furnished dining room.
2⇌↑ Annexe 1⇌↑ CTV in all bedrooms ℝ LDO 24hrs prior
▥ nc10yrs

CHARMOUTH Dorset   Map 03 SY39

SELECTED
GH ℚℚℚℚ **Newlands House** Stonebarrow Lane DT6 6RA (take eastern slip road from Charmouth Bypass caravan park to bottom of hill at bend turn left into Stonebarrow Lane)
☎(0297) 560212
Mar-Oct
This small private hotel in peaceful surroundings with an attractive garden, continues to provide comfortable and well appointed accommodation. The bedrooms, which vary in size, are well-equipped. There is a comfortable lounge and a dining room. A distinct feature is the excellent cooking of proprietor Clare Vear, and the menu changes daily.
12rm(11⇌↑) (2fb) ✗ in bedrooms ✗ in dining room ✗ in 1 lounge CTV in all bedrooms ℝ sB&B£20.50-£23 sB&B⇌↑£22.50-£25 dB&B⇌↑£45-£50 WB&B£142.50-£157.50 WBDi£228.70-£244.60 LDO noon
Lic ▥ CTV nc6yrs
ⓔ

CHEDDAR Somerset   Map 03 ST45

GH ℚℚ Market Cross Hotel Church Street BS27 3RA
☎(0934) 742264
Closed 7-29 Oct & 24 Dec-2 Jan
Personally run by Mr and Mrs Garland, this is an attractive Regency hotel in the middle of the village. Well equipped bedrooms are finished in soft colours, and there is a comfortable bar-cum-lounge overlooking the market cross. Children are welcome, and there is a toy area in the dining room where breakfast and dinner are served.
6rm(3↑) (2fb) CTV in all bedrooms ℝ ✱ (ex guide dogs) LDO 6pm
Lic ▥ CTV ✔
Credit Cards 1 3

SELECTED
FH ℚℚℚℚ Mrs C Ladd **Tor Farm** *(ST455534)* Nyland BS27 3UD (take A371 from Cheddar towards Wells, after 2m turn right towards Nyland, Tor Farm 1.5m on right)
☎(0934) 743710
A modern stone-built farmhouse stands in a rural location, with splendid views of the Levels and Mendip hills. Mr and

▶

Mrs Ladd offer traditional farmhouse holidays, and their house is a good base for visiting the local attractions. Bedrooms are not spacious, but they all have very pretty coordinating soft furnishings and comfortable beds, and many have smart modern private bathrooms. The lounge has an open fire and the dining room is light and spacious. A good choice is offered at dinner, including many home produced items such as beef, lamb and vegetables, together with local wines.

8rm(5⇌🏵) (1fb) ⊁ in bedrooms ⊁ in dining room ® 🏵 ⋇ sB&Bfr£17.50 dB&Bfr£30 dB&B⇌🏵£36-£43 WB&B£94.50-£135.45 LDO 6pm
Lic ⬛ CTV 33 acres beef
Credit Cards 1 3 ©

CHEDDLETON Staffordshire   Map **07** SJ95

SELECTED

GH Q Q Q Q **Choir Cottage and Choir House** Ostlers Lane ST13 7HS ☎Churnet Side(0538) 360561
Situated in a rather pretty village, this small delightful house offers an unsual choice of sleeping accommodation. Two bedrooms are housed in the separate cottage, which is over 300 years old and includes the 'Pine Room' which has a four-poster bed plus two small children's rooms, and the 'Roe Room' which has an attractively draped four-poster bed and a small patio area for summer use. The 'Green Room' is situated in the main house and has its own small conservatory lounge. All bedrooms are equipped with every modern comfort and good quality en suite facilities. Breakfast is served in the pine furnished dining room and dinner is available by prior arrangement. There is a pretty lounge with floral covered seating and for smokers a conservatory is provided, furnished with cane chairs.

2⇌🏵 Annexe 2⇌🏵 (1fb) ⊁ CTV in all bedrooms ® T 🏵 ⋇ sB&B⇌🏵£40-£45 dB&B⇌🏵£46-£54 LDO 24hrs notice ⬛ nc4yrs

---

CHELMSFORD Essex   Map **05** TL70

GH Q Q **Beechcroft Private Hotel** 211 New London Road CM2 0AJ (turn off A12 onto B10007 follow through Galleywood for 3m) ☎(0245) 352462 FAX (0245) 347933
Closed Xmas & New Year
Situated only a ten-minute walk from the centre of town, this small, family-run hotel benefits from the personal input of its cheery proprietors. Bedrooms are immaculately maintained and some have en suite bathrooms. Breakfast is served in a bright dining room and guests have a choice of lounges. Car parking is available at the rear.
20rm(9🏵) (2fb) ⊁ in dining room CTV in 19 bedrooms ®
sB&B£25.50-£28.56 sB&B🏵£33.70 dB&B£42.50-£42.95 dB&B🏵£52.50
⬛ CTV
Credit Cards 1 3 ©

GH Q Q Q **Boswell House Hotel** 118-120 Springfield Road CM2 6LF ☎(0245) 287587 FAX (0245) 287587
Closed 10 days Xmas
Boswell House is an attractive 19th-century town house, run as a small hotel by its hospitable owners for three years. The bedrooms have plain colour schemes, stripped pine furniture, modern facilities and lots of thoughtful extras. More than half are no-smoking. A home-cooked three-course meal is served each evening in the cottage-style dining room, and a range of snacks is available in the small licensed bar or in the comfort of your room.
13⇌🏵 (2fb) ⊁ in 9 bedrooms ⊁ in dining room ⊁ in 1 lounge CTV in all bedrooms ® T 🏵 (ex guide dogs) ⋇ sB&B⇌🏵£42-£45 dB&B⇌🏵£60 LDO 8.30pm
Lic ⬛ CTV
Credit Cards 1 2 3 5 ©

SELECTED

GH Q Q Q Q *Snows Oaklands Hotel* 240 Springfield Road CM2 6BP (near Essex Police HQ on A1113) ☎(0245) 352004
Snows Oaklands Hotel is an attractive neo-Georgian house set back from the road in a residential area. Bedrooms are a bit old fashioned, with floral fabrics and candlewick bedspreads, but they offer a good standard of comfort, as do the public areas. Guests have a choice of three lounges, including the recently added conservatory, overlooking the garden with its aviary and fishpond. The hotel has a residential license, and soup and sandwiches are available for a limited period in the evening.
14rm(13⇌🏵) (3fb) CTV in all bedrooms ® 🏵 (ex guide dogs) LDO 8pm
Lic ⬛ CTV

GH Q Q **Tanunda Hotel** 219 New London Road CM2 0AJ ☎(0245) 354295 FAX (0245) 345503
Closed 2 wks Xmas
This large modern house is in comfortable walking distance of the town centre and has its own car park. Bedrooms vary in size but are well equipped and some have en suite bathrooms. Breakfasts are served in a brightly decorated breakfast room, the guest house is licensed and there are two lounges - one for television and one overlooking the garden.
20rm(2⇌9🏵) CTV in all bedrooms ® T 🏵 (ex guide dogs) ⋇ sB&B£28 sB&B⇌🏵£33.70-£40 dB&B£42.50 dB&B⇌🏵£52.50
Lic ⬛ CTV
Credit Cards 1 3

CHELTENHAM Gloucestershire   Map **03** SO9?

GH Q Q Q **Abbey Hotel** 16 Bath Parade GL53 7HN ☎(0242) 516053 FAX (0242) 513034
An early Victorian terraced house, situated behind Sandford Park and close to the town centre, Abbey Hotel has been carefully modernised to provide compact but well equipped bedrooms and cosy public rooms.
11rm(7🏵) (1fb) ⊁ in dining room CTV in all bedrooms ® T ⋇ sB&B£28-£30 sB&B🏵£35 dB&B£52 dB&B🏵£58 WB&B£185-£235 WBDi£255-£305 LDO 6pm
Lic ⬛ ⨍
Credit Cards 1 2 3 ©

GH Q Q Q **Battledown Hotel** 125 Hales Road GL52 6ST (on B4075) ☎(0242) 233881 & (0374) 899734
An attractive Grade II listed Victorian villa built around 1880, conveniently positioned for access to the town centre. Owners Barbara and Ivor Austin have made significant improvements to provide comfortable accommodation, and most bedrooms are simply furnished but have a modern, tiled shower room. There is a cosy sitting room and a home-made set three-course evening meal is served in the dining room. On summer evenings a barbecue ma? be suggested, cooked and served in the gardens around the original Victorian fish pond.
7rm(5🏵) ⊁ in 5 bedrooms ⊁ in dining room ⊁ in lounges CTV in all bedrooms ® 🏵 ⋇ sB&B£20-£25 sB&B🏵£25-£29.50 dB&B£38-£42 dB&B🏵£44-£50 WB&B£175-£206.50 WBDi£252-£283.50 LDO 6pm
⬛,
©

GH Q Q Q *Beaumont House Hotel* 56 Shurdington Road GL53 0JE ☎(0242) 245986 FAX (0242) 245986
A large detached Victorian hotel with a distinctive white and gree? painted exterior, set back from the A46 in peaceful gardens, with ample private parking. Accommodation styles vary: most of the 18 rooms are spacious, whilst those on the lower ground floor are small but more modern; most have private bathrooms and facilities include TV, direct-dial telephones and radio alarms.

There is an elegant, comfortable lounge with a corner bar and a varied daily menu is served in the dining room on weekdays.
18rm(17⇶♠) (3fb) CTV in all bedrooms ⓡ T LDO 8pm
Lic ▥ CTV
Credit Cards ① ② ③

GH ⓠⓠⓠ **Beechworth Lawn Hotel** 133 Hales Road GL52 6ST (off the A40 London Rd) ☎(0242) 522583
An attractive Victorian house set back from the road in its own small garden, half a mile from the town centre. Modernised by hosts Mr and Mrs Brian Toombs, rooms have modern furnishings and an excellent range of facilities. Standards of maintainance and housekeeping are commendable, with comfortable, well equipped accommodation.
9rm(5♠) (2fb)CTV in all bedrooms ⓡ sB&B£22-£24 sB&B♠£28-£32 dB&B£38-£40 dB&B♠£44-£48 LDO 7pm
▥ CTV
ⓔ

SELECTED

GH ⓠⓠⓠⓠ **Charlton House** 18 Greenhills Road, Charlton Kings GL53 9EB ☎(0242) 238997
FAX (0242) 238997
Closed 22 Dec-3 Jan
3rm(1♠) ⌿ CTV in all bedrooms ⓡ ✝ sB&B£20-£24 sB&B♠£30 dB&B£40 dB&B♠£50 WB&B£120-£180 WBDif£180-£240 LDO early am
▥ CTV nc10yrs
Credit Cards ① ③

PREMIER ⚜ SELECTED

GH ⓠⓠⓠⓠⓠ **Cleeve Hill Hotel** Cleeve Hill GL52 3PR (on B4632 2.5m from town between Prestbury and Winchcome) ☎(0242) 672052

Located in an area of outstanding natural beauty and having direct access to the Cotswold Way, this personally run hotel offers thoughtfully equipped rooms with superb views - all of them looking either to Cleeve Common or across the valley to the Malvern Hills. The comfortable, elegantly furnished lounge provides a quiet place for guests to relax or enjoy a drink, and breakfast is served in a light, airy conservatory-style room. Dinner can be taken at one of the many good local restaurants which between them cater for all tastes, but a light meal of soup, omelette or sandwiches and salads can be taken at the hotel by arrangement.
10⇶♠ (1fb) ⌿ CTV in all bedrooms ⓡ T ✝ (ex guide dogs) ✳ sB&B⇶♠fr£45 dB&B⇶♠£60-£73
Lic ▥ nc8yrs
Credit Cards ① ② ③

GH ⓠⓠ **Crossways** Oriel Place, 57 Bath Road GL53 7LH ☎(0242) 527683
An attractive end-of-terrace listed Regency building stands conveniently close to the town centre. Bedrooms vary in size and shape but are all comfortably furnished, and there is a ground-floor room available. Generous breakfasts are served in the dining room at separate tables, with guests finding the puzzles left to entertain them at each table quite a talking point.
6rm(3♠) (3fb)CTV in all bedrooms ⓡ ✳ sB&B£16-£20 sB&B♠£25 dB&B£32-£34 dB&B♠£38-£40 WB&Bfr£105
▥ ⌿
Credit Cards ① ③ ⓔ

GH [Q][Q][Q] Hallery House 48 Shurdington Road GL53 0JE (directly adjacent to A46) (Logis) ☎(0242) 578450
FAX (0242) 529730

Set back from the road, this Victorian house is of architectural interest and not far from the centre. Bedrooms are individually furnished and well equipped. There is a small lounge overlooking the garden and in the dining room a good-value menu is available with choice of exciting and varied dishes.

16rm(10🛁🚿) (2fb) 🚭 in 3 bedrooms 🚭 in dining room 🚭 in lounges CTV in all bedrooms [R] **T** sB&B£25-£32 sB&B🛁🚿£35-£45 dB&B£40-£45 dB&B🛁🚿£50-£67 LDO 8.30pm
Lic ♨ 🚲 cycle hire
Credit Cards [1][2][3][5][£]

GH [Q][Q][Q] ***Hannaford's*** 20 Evesham Road GL52 2AB (N on A435 Evesham road) ☎(0242) 515181

The public rooms of this well maintained and welcoming terraced town house include the recent addition of a bright conservatory lounge bar and a comfortable sitting room. Bedrooms are modestly furnished but spacious and well equipped. Hannaford's is personally run by the Crowley family, who continue to make improvements.

10rm(9🛁🚿) (1fb) CTV in all bedrooms [R] **T** 🐕 LDO 9.30am
Lic ♨ CTV 🚫🅿
Credit Cards [1][3]

GH [Q][Q][Q] Hollington House Hotel 115 Hales Road GL52 6ST (0.5m from town on Prestbury road) ☎(0242) 519718
FAX (0242) 570280

This large detached Victorian house is built from Cotswold stone. The nine bedrooms vary in size and style, the majority having modern en suite shower facilities. There is a comfortable lounge with a corner bar, and a choice of good food is offered at dinner and breakfast.

9rm(8🚿) (2fb) 🚭 in bedrooms 🚭 in dining room CTV in all bedrooms [R] 🐕 ✱ sB&B£26-£30 sB&B🚿£32-£40 dB&B🚿£40-£60 WB&B£140-£210 WBDi£245-£315 LDO 5pm
Lic ♨ nc3yrs
Credit Cards [1][2][3][£]

GH [Q][Q] Ivy Dene 145 Hewlett Road GL52 6TS
☎(0242) 521726 & 521776

This comfortable detached house with an attractive garden stands in a good residential area within walking distance of the town centre. Guests are made to feel welcome and are accommodated in well modernised bedrooms equipped with colour TV and tea-making facilities; breakfast is served in a small dining room overlooking the garden.

9rm (2fb) 🚭 in dining room CTV in all bedrooms [R] ✱ sB&B£15-£16 dB&B£30-£32
♨ CTV 🚫🅿
[£]

GH [Q][Q] Lonsdale House Montpellier Drive GL50 1TX
☎(0242) 232379 FAX (0242) 232379
rs Xmas

An attractive period house, centrally located, with limited parking. Bedrooms are bright and airy and the blue and white breakfast room overlooks the garden. Guests may use the owners' lounge.

11rm(3🚿) (3fb) 🚭 in dining room CTV in all bedrooms [R] 🐕 (ex guide dogs) sB&B£18-£20 sB&B🚿£27 dB&B£36-£40 dB&B🚿£42-£48 WB&B£114-£170
♨ CTV
Credit Cards [1][3][£]

☎ Telephone national area codes are due to change by 16th April 1995. Please see the note under 'How to Use this Guide' at the front of the book.

P R E M I E R   S E L E C T E D

GH [Q][Q][Q][Q][Q] Lypiatt House Lypiatt Road GL50 2QW
☎(0242) 224994
FAX (0242) 224996

A charming Victorian villa set in its own grounds a short walk from the Montpelier area of the town, Lypiatt House is conveniently situated for easy access to the A40. Stylishly decorated throughout, it offers accommodation in attractively furnished and very well equipped bedrooms. An honesty bar is provided in the conservatory and the set dinner (served by arrangement) might include an avocado and hot bacon salad followed by rack of lamb or fresh salmon, with a spicy pear and walnut sponge for pudding; house wines are available to accompany the meal.

10rm(9🛁1🚿) 🚭 in dining room CTV in all bedrooms [R] **T** 🐕 (ex guide dogs) sB&B🛁🚿£48-£50 dB&B🛁🚿£65-£68 LDO 9am
Lic ♨
Credit Cards [1][3][£]

🛏 ☕ **GH [Q][Q][Q] Manor Barn** Cowley GL53 9NN (6m S, off A435 Cheltenham/Cirencester road) ☎(0242) 870229

Linda and Andrew Roff's little guest house is a clever barn conversion, combining rustic charm with modern comfort. The spotless bedrooms feature stone walls and are nicely furnished in cane and pine, with excellent divans and attractive decor. It is a no-smoking, bed and breakfast establishment set in rural surroundings five miles from Cheltenham.

3rm(1🚿) 🚭 sB&Bfr£15 dB&Bfr£30 dB&B🚿fr£35 LDO by arrangement
♨ CTV nc7yrs
[£]

SELECTED

GH [Q][Q][Q][Q] Milton House 12 Royal Parade, Bayshill Road GL50 3AY ☎(0242) 582601 FAX (0242) 222326

An imposing Regency house within the terrace of Royal Parade is benefiting from careful restoration by the owners Mr and Mrs Milton. Bedrooms are bright and comfortable, individually styled and decorated and furnished in pine, with a good selection of modern creature comforts and facilities. Public rooms are equally attractive, with many of the original features retained. This elegant house is also very conveniently located, with direct rear access to Montpellier, the heart of Cheltenham's excellent shopping area. There is also limited car parking available.

9🛁🚿 (4fb) 🚭 in 2 bedrooms 🚭 in dining room 🚭 in 1 lounge CTV in all bedrooms [R] **T** 🐕 ✱ sB&B🛁🚿£30-£45 dB&B🛁🚿£50-£70 LDO 9am
Lic ♨ CTV
Credit Cards [1][2][3][£]

GH [Q][Q] North Hall Hotel Pittville Circus Road GL52 2PZ (1m E of town centre) ☎(0242) 520589 FAX (0242) 216953
Closed Xmas & New Year

A substantial property located in a quiet tree-lined road a few minutes from the town centre. Accommodation incorporates a mixture of sizes, styles and furnishings: some rooms are quite modest, as are the en suite facilities. There is a large comfortable lounge overlooking the gardens at the rear, a small bar and a large dining room with a varied daily menu.

20rm(15⇔↱) (1fb) ⊬ in dining room CTV in all bedrooms Ⓡ T ✳ sB&Bfr£18 sB&B⇔↱£27.50-£30 dB&Bfr£31 dB&B⇔↱£43.50-£48 WB&B£126-£168 WBDi£189-£420 LDO 7.15pm
Lic 𝌆
Credit Cards [1] [3] (£)

SELECTED

GH QQQQ ***Stretton Lodge*** Western Road GL50 3RN
✆(0242) 528724 & 570771 FAX (0242) 570771
Initial impressions may be misleading for behind this fairly standard exterior lies a character residence with elegant public rooms and comfortable bedrooms. This large, Victorian semi has been carefully modernised by the owners, Mr and Mrs Price, to provide good accommodation, while retaining much of its charm. The en suite bedrooms are well proportioned, nicely decorated and softened with pleasing flowered drapes and fabrics, and have a range of facilities that include TV, direct-dial telephone, mini bar and trouser press with iron. There are various comfortable public areas, which are rich in attractive features, such as cornices and marbled fireplaces.
4⇔↱ (1fb) CTV in all bedrooms Ⓡ T ✗ (ex guide dogs)
LDO noon
Lic 𝌆
Credit Cards [1] [2] [3]

GH QQQ ***Willoughby Hotel*** 1 Suffolk Square GL50 2DR (150yds from A40) ✆(0242) 522798
Closed 2 wks Xmas & New Year
A very impressive late-Georgian Cotswold stone house enjoys a lovely position in the Montpellier district. Rooms have en suite facilites, yet retain many original features. There is a first floor dining room overlooking the bowling green, and a tiny guests' lounge.
9rm(7↱) (1fb) CTV in all bedrooms Ⓡ LDO 4pm
𝌆 CTV

GH QQ Wishmoor 147 Hales Road GL52 6TD (just off B4075)
✆(0242) 238504 FAX (0242) 226090
The atmosphere is relaxed and bedrooms are neatly furnished in this semidetached Victorian guest house which stands in its own gardens about a mile from the city centre. The ground floor contains a traditional lounge with massive cheeseplant and a separate dining room. Several rooms are designated non-smoking.
10rm(4↱) (1fb) ⊬ in 3 bedrooms ⊬ in dining room CTV in all bedrooms Ⓡ ✗ (ex guide dogs) ✳ sB&Bfr£18 sB&B↱fr£26 dB&Bfr£34 dB&B↱fr£44 LDO noon
𝌆
Credit Cards [1] [3] (£)

CHEPSTOW Gwent

See **Tintern**

CHERITON FITZPAINE Devon Map **03** SS80

▭ ▬ **FH QQ** Mrs D M Lock **Brindiwell** *(SS896079)* EX17 4HR (approach from Bickleigh Bridge on A396, take road signposted to Cadeleigh and after 3m a sign for farm on left)
✆(0363) 866357
This period, pink-painted Devonshire longhouse stands in a very secluded position two miles from the village, surrounded by a picturesque garden and with views of the Exe valley and Dartmoor. The bedrooms offer traditional comforts. Both the sitting room and dining room have open fireplaces, and breakfast is served at one large table.
4rm (1fb) ⊬ in 1 bedrooms ⊬ in 1 lounge CTV in 1 bedroom Ⓡ ✗ (ex guide dogs) sB&B£12-£15 dB&B£24-£30 WB&B£84-£105 WBDi£119-£140 LDO 5pm
CTV 120 acres sheep
(£)

CHESTER Cheshire Map **07** SJ46

GH QQ Arran House 52 Meadows Lane, Handbridge CH4 7BH
✆(0244) 677864
Closed Xmas week
2rm (1fb)CTV in all bedrooms Ⓡ sB&B£16 dB&B£27
𝌆 CTV

GH QQQ Bawnpark Hotel 10 Hoole Road, Hoole CH2 3NH
✆(0244) 324971 FAX (0244) 310951
The Bawn Park is a Victorian property on the A56 between the city centre and the M53. The bedrooms, all with compact en suite bathrooms, have modern furnishings and equipment. Lounge facilities include smoking and no-smoking areas, and separate tables are provided in the breakfast room. A laundry room has recently been added for guests' use. The accommodation at number 8, though owned by the same family, is not included in the AA classification scheme.
7rm(5⇔↱) (2fb) ⊬ in dining room ⊬ in 1 lounge CTV in all bedrooms Ⓡ ✳ sB&B£15-£20 sB&B⇔↱£25-£35 dB&B£28-£30 dB&B⇔↱£32-£38
𝌆 CTV
Credit Cards [1] [2] [3] (£)

GH QQ Dee House 67 Hoole Road, Hoole CH2 3NJ
✆(0244) 351532
Dee House is on the A56 between the city centre and the M53, and the car park is reached via Westminster Road. The bedrooms are furnished with a mixture of modern and older furniture, and though they are not luxurious they are soundly maintained. Separate tables are provided in the breakfast room and there is a small lounge area.
5rm(3⇔↱) (1fb) ⊬ in dining room CTV in all bedrooms Ⓡ ✗ ✳ sB&Bfr£19 sB&B⇔↱fr£23.50 dB&Bfr£30 dB&B⇔↱fr£32
𝌆 CTV
(£)

Hallery House

Logis of Great Britain

48 Shurdington Road, Cheltenham Spa,
Gloucestershire GL53 0JE
Tel: 01242-578450 Fax: 01242-549730

Steve and Angie welcome you to their lovely Victorian home offering:
- ★ Comfortable rooms with hospitality tray – majority en-suite
- ★ Colour TV with satellite in all rooms
- ★ Excellent traditional English or Continental breakfast
- ★ Imaginative and varied evening meals and we cater for all diets
- ★ Direct dial telephones ★ Licensed ★ Open to non-Residents
- ★ Large car park ★ Pets and children very welcome

Seven times winner of Spa award for customer comfort, excellent food and exceptional hygiene standards. Hallery House is of architectural interest and is situated on the main A46. It is a short walk from Cheltenham centre with all the attractions this beautiful town has to offer. Brochures available. Cycling holidays and short breaks a speciality
Amex, Visa and Mastercard accepted.

GH Ⓠ Devonia 33-35 Hoole Road CH2 3NH (on A56)
☎(0244) 322236
The Devonia is a terraced house north-east of the city centre,
convenient for the M53. It provides neatly furnished bedrooms of
differing sizes, a traditionally furnished dining room and a bar.
Family rooms are available.
10rm (6fb) ⊁ in dining room CTV in all bedrooms Ⓡ ✳
sB&B£20-£22.50 dB&B£30-£32.50 LDO 4pm
Lic ⊞ CTV
£

[⇔ ▣] GH Ⓠ Ⓠ Egerton Lodge 57 Hoole Road, Hoole CH2 3NJ
(on A56) ☎(0244) 320712
Closed 19 Dec-3 Jan
Part of an early Victorian terrace on the A56 between the city
centre and the M53, this small guest house provides soundly
maintained accommodation, including family rooms. There is a
ground-floor room, but occupants have to use the first-floor
shower and WC. There is no lounge, but an attractive breakfast
room with period furniture is provided.
7rm(4♠) (4fb)CTV in all bedrooms Ⓡ ✺ sB&B£15-£19
dB&B£25-£27 dB&B♠£29-£34
⊞ nc3yrs
Credit Cards ①②③ £

GH Ⓠ Ⓠ Eversley Hotel 9 Eversley Park CH2 2AJ (off A5116
signed to Ellesmere Port) ☎(0244) 373744
Closed 24 Dec-2 Jan
North of the city centre, off the A5116, this large house provides
modestly furnished but well equipped accommodation, including
some ground-floor rooms. There is a cosy lounge, a lounge bar
and a dining room with cottage-style furniture.
11rm(4⇔5♠) (3fb) CTV in all bedrooms Ⓡ ✺ ✳ sB&B£23
sB&B⇔♠£30 dB&B£39.50 dB&B⇔♠£43 WB&Bfr£140
WBDifr£178.50 LDO 6pm
Lic ⊞ CTV
Credit Cards ①③ £

GH Ⓠ Gables 5 Vicarage Road, Hoole CH2 3HZ (off A56)
☎(0244) 323969
Closed 23-27 Dec
The Gables is a small guest house north of the city centre,
conveniently located for the M53. The accommodation comprises
compact bedrooms, including family rooms, and a combined
lounge and breakfast room with individual tables. A small car park
is provided.
6rm (4fb) CTV in all bedrooms Ⓡ ✺
CTV

GH Ⓠ Ⓠ Ⓠ Gloster Lodge Hotel 44 Hoole Road, Hoole CH2 3NL
(on A56) ☎(0244) 348410 & 320231
Closed 24-31 Dec
A semidetached house with its own car park, Gloster Lodge stands
on the A56 between the city centre and the M53. It offers well
equipped bedrooms with modern furnishings, three of which are
on the ground floor in a purpose-built annexe. Breakfast is served
in a bright room at separate tables. Dinner is not usually provided.
5⇔♠ Annexe 3⇔♠ (2fb) CTV in all bedrooms Ⓡ T LDO 8pm
Lic ⊞
Credit Cards ①②③

2rm(1♠) (1fb) CTV in all bedrooms Ⓡ ✺ ✳ sB&Bfr£25
sB&B♠£28 dB&B♠£38-£40
⊞ table tennis three-quarter snooker table
£

GH Ⓠ Ⓠ Ⓠ Grove House Holme Street, Tarvin CH3 8EQ (5m E,
between A51/A54) ☎(0829) 740893
Closed 20 Dec-5 Jan
3rm(1⇔) ⊁ in bedrooms ⊁ in lounges Ⓡ ✺ ✳ sB&B£18.50-
£20 dB&Bfr£40 dB&B⇔£50 WB&B£130-£170
⊞ CTV nc12yrs

GH Ⓠ Ⓠ Ⓠ Vicarage Lodge 11 Vicarage Road, Hoole CH2 3HZ
(just off A56) ☎(0244) 319533
A small, well maintained guest house, Vicarage Lodge is situated
in a road off the A56, between the city centre and the M53. The
bedrooms are small but attractively decorated and have mainly
modern furniture. A small lounge area is provided, and a breakfast
room with individual tables.
4rm(1♠) CTV in all bedrooms Ⓡ ✺
⊞

CHESTER-LE-STREET Co Durham   Map **12** NZ25

GH Ⓠ Ⓠ Ⓠ Waldridge Fell Waldridge DH2 3RY ☎091-389 1908
5rm(1♠) (5fb) CTV in all bedrooms Ⓡ sB&Bfr£22 sB&B♠fr£27
dB&B£32-£36 dB&B♠£37-£40
⊞ CTV
£

CHEWTON MENDIP Somerset   Map **03** ST55

FH [Q][Q][Q] Mrs B Clothier **Franklyns** *(ST601522)* BA3 4NB (off A39) ☎(0761) 241372

Located in a rural position, this stone farmhouse offers mostly very spacious and extremely comfortable bedrooms, that share a bathroom on the same floor. There is a large lounge and a breakfast room that features picture windows overlooking the gardens. Outside, a tennis court is available along with parking facilities.

3rm CTV in all bedrooms ℝ ✻ (ex guide dogs)
▥ CTV ⚲(hard)400 acres arable dairy
£

CHIDEOCK Dorset   Map **03** SY49

GH [Q][Q][Q] **Betchworth House Hotel** DT6 6JW (on A35) ☎(0297) 89478

This pretty stone cottage standing at the top end of the village has been taken over by young and enthusiastic new proprietors who greet guests warmly. Parts of the building date back to the 17th century but all modern comforts are provided here, including a ground-floor bedroom. As well as breakfast and dinner, served in the dining room, morning coffee and very popular afternoon teas are served too. There is a cosy lounge and a pretty garden.

6rm(3♠) (1fb) ✼ in dining room ℝ ✻ (ex guide dogs) ✳
sB&Bfr£18 sB&B♠fr£20 dB&Bfr£36 dB&B♠£40-£44
▥ CTV
£

CHILHAM Kent   Map **05** TR05

INN [Q][Q][Q] **Woolpack** High Street CT4 8DL
☎Canterbury(0227) 730208 FAX (0227) 731053

Situated near the village's main square and imposing castle, this popular and welcoming inn dates back some 600 years. As well as a cosy, traditional bar there is an oak-beamed restaurant where home-produced meals are served. Well equipped bedrooms, including one with a four-poster bed and sizeable family rooms, are available in the main building and the nearby converted outbuildings.

5⇆ Annexe 10♠ (3fb) CTV in all bedrooms ℝ T
sB&B⇆♠fr£37.50 dB&B⇆♠fr£47.50 Bar Lunch fr£4.50alc
Dinner fr£12alc LDO 9.30pm
▥ CTV
Credit Cards [1][3]

CHIPPENHAM Wiltshire   Map **03** ST97

See also Calne

GH [Q][Q] *Oxford Hotel* 32/36 Langley Road SN15 1BX
☎(0249) 652542

The Oxford is a small family-run hotel within walking distance of the town centre and the railway station, and convenient for the M4. Bedrooms are well equipped and some have en suite shower rooms. There is an attractive bar-lounge and a choice of dishes is offered in the informal restaurant.

13rm(7♠) (1fb) CTV in all bedrooms ℝ LDO 5.30pm
Lic ▥
Credit Cards [1][2][3]

CHIPPING CAMPDEN Gloucestershire   Map **04** SP13

SELECTED

GH [Q][Q][Q][Q] **The Malt House** Broad Campden GL55 6UU
(1m S, signposted from B4081) ☎Evesham(0386) 840295
FAX (0386) 841334

Closed 23 Dec-1 Jan rs Mon

Just a mile from Chipping Campden in the picturesque village of Broad Campden, this quality, comfortable guesthouse was

▶

**9 Eversley Park,
Chester, CH2 2AJ
Telephone: (01244) 373744**

Attractive Victorian residence with all modern facilities, relaxing atmosphere and good food. ¾ mile north of city centre just off the A5116. Most rooms are en suite and have TV, telephone, tea/coffee. Hotel has its own Bar & Restaurant and car park.

Proprietors:
Bryn and Barbara Povey

MANOR FARM
Alderton, Chippenham, Wiltshire
SN14 6NL Telephone: (01666) 840271

This beautiful 17th century family home in picturesque Alderton, welcomes small numbers of guests to warm hospitality in large comfortable bedrooms each with private bathroom, colour TV, tea/coffee. The surrounding area is steeped with interest and boasts an excellent variety of places to wine and dine. Guests are welcome to enjoy the garden and interest of this busy working farm. **Prices from £22.50.**

once a row of cottages. The Malt House is lovingly cared for and very clean. Each bedrooms is unique, but with the same period character as the gorgeous lounge which overlooks a walled garden. Dinner is also available.
5rm(4🛁) 🚭 in dining room 🚭 in lounges CTV in all bedrooms [R] ✳ sB&B£42.50 dB&B🛁£69.50-£87.50 LDO noon
Lic ▥ croquet
Credit Cards [1][3]

GH [Q][Q][Q] Orchard Hill House Broad Campden GL55 6UU
☎Evesham(0386) 841473
rs Xmas & New Year
This 17th-century farmhouse in the centre of Broad Camden has been beautifully restored. Bedrooms have oak doors and beams and there is a family room in a converted hayloft across a courtryard. A room is being constructed as a lounge for guests and substantial breakfasts are served round a large refectory table in the flagstoned dining room.
2rm(1🛁1🚿) 🚭 CTV in all bedrooms [R] 🐕 (ex guide dogs) ✳ sB&B£35-£40 dB&B£40-£45 dB&B🛁🚿£43-£55 WB&B£140-£190
▥ nc8yrs
[£]

CHISELDON Wiltshire Map **04** SU17

FH [Q][Q][Q] M Hughes **Parsonage** *(SU185799)* SN4 0NJ
☎Swindon(0793) 740204
This attractive stone-built farmhouse is in a quiet position beside the church in the village of Chiseldon, which is only a mile from junction 15 of the M4 and four miles from the centre of Swindon. The bedrooms are comfortable and very traditional in style. The public areas are full of character with some tasteful personal touches, and guests share one large antique table in the dining room.
4rm(2🛁🚿) 🚭 in dining room [R] sB&B£22.50 sB&B🛁🚿£25 dB&B🛁🚿£40
▥ CTV 🐎 400 acres arable
[£]

CHISLEHAMPTON Oxfordshire Map **04** SU59

SELECTED

INN[Q][Q][Q][Q] ***Coach & Horses*** Stadhampton Road OX44 7UX (beside B480) ☎Stadhampton(0865) 890255
FAX (0865) 891995
Closed 26 Dec-30 Dec
This stone-built, listed 16th-century inn stands beside the B480 in the village centre, seven miles from Oxford. The chalet-style bedrooms are in an annexe round an attractively landscaped rear courtyard. The life of the inn revolves round its popular dining room, with both table d'hôte and à la carte menus offered and the bar, with its choice of real ales. Drinks and snacks are served outside in summer months. Mr and Mrs McPhillips offer guests a friendly and caring welcome.
9🛁🚿 CTV in all bedrooms [R] **T** 🐕 (ex guide dogs) LDO 10pm
Credit Cards [1][2][3][5]

CHOLMONDELEY Cheshire Map **07** SJ55

GH [Q][Q][Q] The Cholmondeley Arms SY14 8BT (on A49)
☎(0829) 720300 FAX (0829) 720300
This former school building, converted into a simple but pleasant bar/bistro, has retained much of its original character including the lofty ceilings and painted brick walls, now decorated with pictures and a variety of bric-à-brac. The furniture is a mixture of old, simple pieces including several original school desks. Meals can be selected from a comprehensive menu of hot and cold dishes, supplemented by a blackboard selection. Located in the old school house across the playground, the attractively decorated bedrooms are something of a contrast with their modern style and en suite facilities.
4🚿 (1fb)CTV in all bedrooms [R] ✳ sB&B🚿fr£34 dB&B🚿fr£46 LDO 10pm
Lic ▥ P̸
Credit Cards [1][3][£]

CHORLEY Lancashire Map **07** SD51

GH [Q][Q][Q] Astley House Hotel 3 Southport Road PR7 1LB (on A581) ☎(0257) 272315
This Victorian house, situated beside the A581 close to the town centre, has been renovated and decorated in a very attractive Laura Ashley style and provides bed and breakfast accommodation of character. The spacious double rooms are beautifully decorated. Breakfast is served at individual tables in the bright, attractive dining room which is furnished with antiques. There is a small private car park.
6rm(3🛁🚿) 🚭 in dining room 🚭 in lounges CTV in all bedrooms [R] 🐕 (ex guide dogs) ✳ sB&B£18-£20 sB&B🛁🚿£23 dB&B🛁🚿£40
▥
Credit Cards [1][2][3][5][£]

CHRISTCHURCH Dorset Map **04** SZ19

See also Bournemouth & Highcliffe-on-Sea

GH [Q] Belvedere Hotel 59 Barrack Road BH23 1PD
☎(0202) 485978
This spacious Victorian property on the main Christchurch-Bournemouth road - personally run by its proprietor for the last 40 years - provides a comfortable lounge, an attractive dining room and neat but simply furnished bedrooms with some modern facilities. Conveniently close to the county's rivers, it is particularly popular with fishermen, many of whom return year after year.
8rm (3fb)CTV in all bedrooms [R] ✳ sB&B£18-£20 LDO 4pm
Lic ▥ CTV

CHURCHINFORD Somerset Map **03** ST21

INN[Q][Q][Q] The York Inn Honiton Road TA3 7RF
☎Churchstanton(0823) 601333
This inn of character is centrally situated in the village of Churchinford, which is surrounded by the Blagdon Hills. The bedrooms are attractively decorated and comfortably furnished. The open-plan bars have been carefully split into three sections, one with a pool table, another, more comfortable with an inglenook fireplace, and the third a restaurant area where an extensive choice of dishes is offered from the à la carte or blackboard menu.
3🛁🚿 (1fb)CTV in all bedrooms [R] ✳ sB&B🛁🚿£25 dB&B🛁🚿£39 Lunch fr£14alc Dinner fr£14alc LDO 9.30pm
▥
Credit Cards [1][2][3]

CHURCH STOKE Powys Map **07** SO29

SELECTED

FH [Q][Q][Q][Q] Mrs C Richards **The Drewin** *(SO261905)* SY15 6TW ☎(0588) 620325
Apr-Nov rs Etr (if in Mar)
This 300-year-old farmhouse is part of a working farm, with splendid views of the surrounding countryside; Offa's Dyke footpath runs through the farm. Bedrooms are modern and well equipped, and there is a comfortable lounge with the original beams and inglenook fireplace.

2rm(1🐾) (2fb) ⚦ CTV in all bedrooms ® 🏋 dB&B£30-£32
dB&B🐾£32-£34 WB&B£100-£110 WBDi£155-£165 LDO
7pm
🎱 CTV games room 102 acres mixed
£

CHURCH STRETTON Shropshire — Map **07** SO49
See also Strefford

SELECTED

GH Ⓠ Ⓠ Ⓠ Ⓠ **Belvedere** Burway Road SY6 6DP (turn W off
A49 at Church Stretton and continue for 0.25m past war
memorial) ☎(0694) 722232 FAX (0694) 722232
This Victorian house on Burway road stands up above the
town, within easy walking distance of the shops. Many rooms
have superb views of the surrounding hills, and the dining
room overlooks the very well kept gardens and fish ponds. The
12 bedrooms are brightly decorated and spotlessly clean and
several have en suite shower rooms. There are two lounges,
one with TV and the other larger sitting room has a good
selection of books. Other facilities include a residents' licence
and ample off-road parking.
12rm(6🐾) (2fb)® ⚦ sB&B£21 sB&B🐾£26 dB&B£42
dB&B🐾£46 WB&B£132.30-£163.80 WBDi£189-£220.50
LDO 6pm
Lic 🎱 CTV ⚬
Credit Cards [1][3] £

GH Ⓠ Ⓠ Ⓠ **Brookfields** Watling St North SY6 7AR (NE edge of
village, close to A49) ☎(0694) 722314
This small family run guest house with a large car park is set
amongst trees, and overlooks the town, with fine views of the
Long Mynd and convenient for the town centre. To reach it you
take the Much Wenlock road off the by-pass then turn
immediately left. Bedrooms are bright and cheerful, with excellent
facilities. There is a small first floor sitting room with a collection
of books and local guides. The restaurant overlooks the
landscaped gardens.
4⇄🐾 (1fb) ⚦ in bedrooms CTV in 3 bedrooms ® T ⚦
sB&B⇄🐾£27-£35 dB&B⇄🐾£45-£55 LDO 9pm
Lic 🎱
£

GH Ⓠ Ⓠ Ⓠ **Hope Bowdler Hall** Hope Bowdler SY6 7DD (from
A49 take B4371) ☎(0694) 722041
Mar-Oct rs Nov
Set in 22 acres of extensive grounds this stone built manor house
is situated in the centre of Hope Bowdler village. There are
wooded slopes, wildfowl pools and a dove cote in the grounds and
also a tennis court for the more energetic guests. Bedrooms are
spacious and comfortable and there is a general feeling of
relaxation and peacefulness. The sitting room has a cheerful log
fire in colder weather.
2rm ⚦ 🏋 sB&B£17.50-£19 dB&B£35
🎱 nc12yrs ⚲(hard)

SELECTED

GH Ⓠ Ⓠ Ⓠ Ⓠ **Jinlye** Castle Hill, All Stretton SY6 6JP
☎(0694) 723243
Once a crofter's cottage dating back at least 200 years and
now extended to provide excellent accommodation, this stone-
built property lies in attractive lawns and gardens and the
front overlooking the Strettons and the rear set against the
sheep-filled mountains. Cream teas are served in the
conservatory and on the lawns in good weather, and there are
three superb sitting rooms, one with a log-burning stone

---

inglenook fireplace, a beamed ceiling and comfortable deep
sofas and easy chairs. Bedrooms sparkle with pretty decor and
matching fabrics. Family run, the house has a friendly
atmosphere and guests are assured of a warm welcome.
3🐾 ⚦ in bedrooms ⚦ in 1 lounge ® 🏋 ⚦
dB&B🐾£36-£48 WB&B£119-£140 WBDi£214-£235 LDO
2pm
🎱 CTV nc12yrs mountain bikes for hire

FH Ⓠ Ⓠ Ⓠ Mrs C J Hotchkiss *Olde Hall* (SO509926) Wall-
under-Heywood SY6 7DU (just off B4371 Much Wenlock to Church
Stretton road) ☎Longville(0694) 771253
Feb-Nov
This delightful Elizabethan farmhouse, owned by the Hotchkiss
family, has preserved a wealth of old timbers and a fine Jacobean
staircase. Bedrooms are attractively decorated and there is also a
lounge and traditionally furnished dining room.
3rm (1fb) CTV in all bedrooms ® 🏋
🎱 CTV 275 acres dairy

PREMIER ⚜ SELECTED

FH Ⓠ Ⓠ Ⓠ Ⓠ Ⓠ Mrs J
Davies *Rectory* (SO452985)
Woolstaston SY6 6NN (3.5m off
B4370 at All Stretton)
☎(0694) 751306
Closed Jan
This most attractive
half-timbered farm house
dates back to the 17th century
and, from its position on the
lower slopes of the Long
Mynd, commands magnificent
views over the countryside to the Wrekin, Shropshire's best
known landmark. Jeanette and John Davies enjoy sharing the
house with their guests, and many have become regulars over
the years. Bedrooms are full of character, and most have space
enough for sofas and armchairs, but the house also has a
spacious and comfortable sitting room. Guests share one of
two communal tables in the dining room at breakfast.
3⇄ ⚦ in bedrooms ⚦ in dining room CTV in all bedrooms
® 🏋 ⚦ sB&B⇄£25 dB&B⇄£38
🎱 CTV nc12yrs 170 acres beef

CIRENCESTER Gloucestershire — Map **04** SP00

GH Ⓠ Ⓠ **La Ronde Hotel** 52-54 Ashcroft Road GL7 1QX
☎(0285) 654611 & 652216
Personally run by Mr and Mrs Smales, this small, friendly hotel is
situated in the heart of the historic town, with car parking on site.
Bedrooms are soundly equipped, with cosy public areas including
a small restaurant offering a good range of nicely cooked,
imaginative dishes.
10⇄🐾 (2fb) ⚦ in dining room CTV in all bedrooms ® ⚦
sB&B⇄🐾£25-£40 dB&B⇄🐾£45-£48.50 WB&B£175-£245
WBDi£243.50-£265 LDO 7pm
Lic 🎱
Credit Cards [1][3] £

GH Ⓠ Ⓠ Ⓠ **Smerrill Barns** Kemble GL7 6BW (off A429)
☎(0285) 770907 FAX (0285) 770907
Recently converted from 18th century listed farm buildings, to
provide comfortable accommodation with modern facilities. The
individually furnished bedrooms are tastefully decorated and a
ground floor family room with two adjoining bedrooms and use of
a bathroom is available
7⇄🐾 (1fb) ⚦ CTV in all bedrooms ® 🏋 (ex guide dogs)

▶

sB&B⇔fr£25-£35 dB&B⇔fr£40-£55 WB&B£105-£140
IIII. nc3yrs
Credit Cards ① ③ ⓔ

SELECTED

GH ◨◨◨◨ Waterton Garden Cottage Ampney Crucis
GL7 5RX ☎(0285) 851303
Situated on the outskirts of Ampney Crucis, Waterton Garden
Cottage is part of a converted Victorian stables, set in a walled
garden with lawns, rose beds, espaliered fruit trees and an
outdoor swimming pool. With its high-ceilinged drawing room
and spacious reception, it is a peaceful retreat for business and
leisure guests alike. Rooms are brightly decorated and have all
the expected modern amenities as well as extras like books,
magazines and fresh flowers. In what was once the tack room
and is now an intimate restaurant, dinner can be served by
prior arrangement. Starters may include smoked trout mousse
or a white peach wrapped in bacon and cooked in a cheese
sauce. Rack of lamb glazed with redcurrant and flavoured with
rosemary, or pork fillet with wild mushrooms in a creamy
cider sauce, are typical main courses. Plum and soured cream
flan is a popular dessert.
3fr ✗ LDO 6pm
IIII. CTV nc7yrs ≋(heated)

GH ◨◨◨ Wimborne House 91 Victoria Road GL7 1ES
☎(0285) 653890
Handily placed for the town centre, this stone-built house has a
pretty garden and there is plenty of parking. Bedrooms are
comfortably furnished, each with an immaculate bathroom, and
there is a small lounge on the first floor where guests can relax.
5⇔fr ✗ CTV in all bedrooms ⓡ ✗ ✱ sB&B⇔fr£20-£30
dB&B⇔fr£30-£45 LDO 4pm
IIII. nc5yrs
ⓔ

INN ◨◨◨ Eliot Arms Clark's Hay, South Cerney GL7 5UA (off
A419) ☎(0285) 860215 FAX (0285) 860215
An attractive 16th-century gabled inn in the village of South
Cerney. The bar areas are cosy and welcoming with exposed beams,
brass and copper items and log fires. Upstairs, ten bedrooms are
immaculately furnished and there is a riverside garden.
12⇔fr (2fb) ✗ in 2 bedrooms ✗ in area of dining room ✗ in 1
lounge CTV in all bedrooms ⓡ T sB&B⇔fr£32.50-£35
dB&B⇔fr£48-£65 LDO 10pm
IIII.
Credit Cards ① ② ③ ⓔ

INN ◨◨◨ Masons Arms Meysey Hampton GL7 5JT (off A417)
☎(0285) 850164 FAX (0285) 850164
This small, personally run country inn, attractively positioned in a
pretty village just outside Cirencester, has recently been acquired
and renovated by enthusiastic owners. Bedrooms are spotless and
cosy, although some are compact, with a nice blend of antique
stripped pine furniture and a good range of modern facilities,
including en suite showers. Public rooms comprise a congenial bar
and an attractive breakfast room. A good range of home-cooked
food is served.
8fr (1fb) ✗ in dining room CTV in all bedrooms ⓡ ✱
sB&Bfr£24-£28 dB&Bfr£39-£45 Lunch £7.95-£13alc Dinner
£9.95-£12.95&alc LDO 9.30pm
IIII. nc4yrs
Credit Cards ① ③ ⓔ

CLACTON-ON-SEA Essex   Map **05** TM11

GH ◨◨◨ Sandrock Hotel 1 Penfold Road, Marine Parade
West CO15 1JN ☎(0255) 428215
An attractive Victorian house, 50 yards from the beach and pier,
with a small car park at the rear. Welcoming proprietors Henry and

Christine Jarvis are continuing to improve the property. Bedrooms
are nicely furnished and immaculately kept. The lounge has
books, games and a stereo, and there is a bar for residents in the
small dining room. The dinner menu changes daily, and a large
choice of dishes is offered for breakfast.
8rm(1⇔7fr) (3fb) ✗ in 1 bedroom ✗ in dining room CTV in all
bedrooms ⓡ ✱ sB&B⇔fr£22.50-£25.50 dB&B⇔fr£45
WB&B£140 WBDi£180 LDO 5pm
Lic IIII.
Credit Cards ① ② ③ ⓔ

CLAPHAM North Yorkshire   Map **07** SD76

INN ◨◨ The Flying Horseshoe LA2 8ES (1m W of A65 opposite
railway station) ☎(05242) 51229
Public areas of this inn have been considerably refurbished in
recent years and provide a pleasant environment in which to enjoy
well cooked and substantial bar meals as well as drinks. There is
also an attractive restaurant open for evening meals and four well
equipped modern bedrooms.
4rm(1⇔3fr) CTV in all bedrooms ⓡ ✱ sB&B⇔fr£25
dB&B⇔fr£40 LDO 9pm
IIII. ⌡

INN ◨◨◨ New Inn Hotel LA2 8HH ☎(05242) 51203
FAX (05242) 51496
A truly relaxed and friendly atmosphere pervades this eighteenth-
century country inn which stands near Clapham Beck in the
Yorkshire Dales National Park, both owners and staff working
hard to maintain the feeling of tranquillity. Bedrooms decorated to
a floral theme all have telephones, TV sets, controllable heating
and en suite bath or shower rooms, and there is a traditional first-
floor lounge available to those who wish to escape the bustle of
the popular bars and restaurant; bar food - detailed in a constantly
changing blackboard display - is also much in demand. The hotel
has its own car park.
13rm(7⇔6fr) ✗ in dining room CTV in all bedrooms ⓡ T
sB&B⇔fr£39 dB&B⇔£55-£58 WB&Bfr£180
WBDi£206.50-£241.50 Bar Lunch £1.65-£8.95alc High tea
fr£1.65alc LDO 9pm
IIII. ⌡ darts pool table
Credit Cards ① ② ③ ⓔ

CLAVERDON Warwickshire   Map **04** SP16

GH ◨◨ Woodside Country House Langley Road CV35 8PJ
(0.75m S of B4095) ☎(0926) 842446
Closed Xmas week
This small, pleasant guest house is situated on the Langley road,
about a mile from the village, and is surrounded by 17 acres of
woods and gardens. Bedrooms are traditionally furnished in
cottage style and there is one on the ground floor. Excellent home-
cooked dinners are available on request and Woodside has
convenient access to Warwick, Stratford-upon-Avon, the NEC and
the Midlands motorway network.
3rm (1fb) ✗ CTV in 2 bedrooms ⓡ ✱ sB&B£16-£20 dB&B£32-
£40 WB&B£108-£135 WBDi£164-£191 LDO 2pm
IIII. CTV ☌(hard)U croquet
ⓔ

FH ◨◨◨ Mrs L Smith Oaktree *(SP663192)* Buttermilk Lane,
Yarningdale Commonn CV35 8HW (take A4189 into Claverdon, turn
into Lye Green Rd, 1st left into Common Lane then 1st right to
Buttermilk Lane) ☎(0926) 842413
3⇔fr ✗ CTV in all bedrooms ⓡ ✗ (ex guide dogs)
sB&B⇔fr£25-£30 dB&B⇔fr£39 LDO 9pm
IIII. CTV private nature reserve 34 acres beef
ⓔ

CLAYTON-LE-WOODS Lancashire   Map **07** SD52

SELECTED

GH [Q][Q][Q][Q] **Brook House Hotel** 662 Preston Rd PR6 7EH
(on A6, 1m from junct 29 of M6) ☎Preston(0772) 36403
FAX (0772) 36403
rs Xmas
This well maintained 19th-century private hotel stands beside
the A6 half a mile to the south of Junction 29 of the M6.
Recently extended and continually being improved under the
present ownership, it provides a sound standard of comfort and
a friendly atmosphere. Bedrooms are well proportioned and
furnished, with modern amenities. There is a residents' lounge
bar and a beamed restaurant with a wide range of dishes
offered on the dinner menu.
21rm(19⇆🏠) (3fb) ⊁ in dining room ⊁ in 1 lounge CTV in
all bedrooms ⓡ **T** 🏋 (ex guide dogs) ✳ sB&B£26
sB&B⇆🏠£35 dB&B£36 dB&B⇆🏠£42 LDO 8.30pm
Lic 🛏.
Credit Cards [1][2][3]⑥

CLEARWELL Gloucestershire   Map **03** SO50

P R E M I E R ⚜ **S E L E C T E D**

GH [Q][Q][Q][Q][Q] **Tudor
Farmhouse Hotel &
Restaurant** GL16 8JS (turn off
A466 Monmouth/Chepstow
Road at Redbrook- follow
signs for Clearwell, turn left at
village cross, hotel on left)
☎Dean(0594) 833046
FAX (0594) 837093
rs Sun evening
This charming little retreat,
neatly tucked away in this
Forest of Dean village is very personally run by its hospitable
owners, Richard and Deborah Fletcher. The house dates back
to the 13th century and displays a wealth of exposed beams,
nooks and crannies, and fireplaces. A notable feature is the
ancient oak spiral staircase. Obviously, in a building of this
age, some bedrooms are more spacious than others, but all
offer a nice combination of charm and modern comforts. Less
mobile guests can be accommodated in the converted stable
adjoining the house. Chef Bill Denton offers a fine range of
imaginative dishes, based mainly on local produce, in the
intimate candle-lit restaurant.
6⇆🏠 Annexe 4⇆🏠 (3fb) ⊁ in 6 bedrooms CTV in all
bedrooms ⓡ **T** + sB&B⇆🏠£42.50-£47 dB&B⇆🏠£49-£59
WB&B£145-£175 WBDi£215-£245 LDO 9pm
Lic 🛏.
Credit Cards [1][2][3]

CLEETHORPES Humberside   Map **08** TA30

GH [Q][Q] *Mallow View* 9-11 Albert Road DN35 8LX
☎(0472) 691297
Situated between the town centre and steps from the seafront, this
long established guesthouse is in a Victorian terrace tucked away
behind the library. Well carpeted ground floor areas comprise a
pool room, bar with piano and small dining room. The ground
floor bedroom, which has its own bathroom, is the largest. Mrs
Meyers is the friendly proprietor.
16rm(1🏠) (1fb) CTV in 15 bedrooms ⓡ LDO 7pm
Lic 🛏. CTV ⊁

CLEVEDON Avon   Map **03** ST47

INN[Q][Q] **The Salthouse** Salthouse Road BS21 7TY
☎(0275) 871482
This is a very lively, popular seafront pub, with a garden play area
to the front and fine views across the bay. The two bedrooms are
quite compact, but are well equipped with modern facilities.
Sound bar meals are available.
2🏠 ⊁ in area of dining room CTV in all bedrooms ⓡ 🏋 ✳
sB&B🏠£28.50 dB&B🏠£57 Lunch £4.90-£6.90&alc Dinner
£4.90-£6.90&alc LDO 9pm
🛏. nc12yrs ⚿(hard)pool table darts skittles
Credit Cards [1][3]

CLIFTONVILLE Kent

See **Margate**

CLITHEROE Lancashire   Map **07** SD74

GH [Q][Q][Q] **Brooklyn** 32 Pimlico Road BB7 2AH ☎(0200) 28268
Pleasantly appointed and neatly maintained accommodation is
offered at this detached Victorian villa. Bedrooms vary in size but all
are well equipped and have smart en suite facilities. There is a
comfortable lounge with a small dispense bar, which overlooks the
patio garden. Evening meals are available between 6.30 and 7.30pm.
4🏠 ⊁ in bedrooms ⊁ in dining room CTV in all bedrooms ⓡ 🏋
(ex guide dogs) ✳ sB&B🏠£20-£23 dB&B🏠£32-£36 WB&B£105-
£140 WBDi£168-£199 LDO 5pm
Lic 🛏. CTV
Credit Cards [1][2][3]⑥

SELECTED

GH [Q][Q][Q][Q] **Peter Barn** Rabbit Lane, Cross Lane,
Waddington BB7 3JH ☎(0200) 28585
Closed 24 Dec-2 Jan
It is probably wise to ask for directions to this sympathetically
converted former tithe barn, set in delightful gardens in a rural
situation. The guest accommodation is all at first-floor level
and includes an inviting lounge, which is also the setting for
enjoyable breakfasts featuring home-made preserves and
muesli. Bedrooms are small but attractively decorated and
comfortably furnished.
3⇆🏠 ⊁ CTV in 1 bedroom ⓡ 🏋 (ex guide dogs)
dB&B⇆🏠£35-£39 WB&B£196-£218.40
🛏. CTV
⑥

CLOUGHTON North Yorkshire   Map **08** TA09

GH [Q][Q] *Cober Hill* Newlands Road YO13 0AR (just off A171, 6m
N of Scarborough) ☎Scarborough(0723) 870310
FAX (0723) 870271
Cober Hill is on the edge of the North Yorkshire Moors National
Park and stands in its own well-kept grounds. Used as a conference
and group centre in the winter, it is open to the general public in
summer. In addition to the excellent new bedrooms in a modern
wing there is more modest accommodation in the main house.
There are four comfortable lounges and two dining rooms serving
Yorkshire dishes - special diets can be catered for by arrangement.
44rm Annexe 31rm(17⇆14🏠) (13fb) ⓡ LDO 7pm
Lic 🛏. CTV ⚿(hard)bowling green croquet table-tennis putting
green

INN[Q][Q][Q] **Blacksmiths Arms** High Street YO13 0AE
☎(0723) 870244
6⇆🏠 (2fb) ⊁ in bedrooms CTV in all bedrooms ⓡ 🏋 (ex guide
dogs) ✳ sB&B⇆🏠fr£25 dB&B⇆🏠fr£40 Lunch £8-£12 Dinner
£8-£12&alc LDO 9.45pm
🛏.
Credit Cards [1][3]

CLOVELLY Devon Map **02** SS32

FH [Q][Q][Q] Mrs E Symons **Burnstone** *(SS325233)* Higher Clovelly EX39 5RX ☎(0237) 431219

Burnstone Farm is a white-painted, 16th-century long house set back from the A39 between Bideford and Bude. The bedrooms have been equipped with many thoughtful extras such as wrapped toiletries, and sweets and biscuits with the tea facilities. Each room has a wash basin but they share one bathroom. Breakfast is served at a large table in an attractive lounge/diner.

3rm (2fb)CTV in all bedrooms Ⓡ ✱ dB&Bfr£30 WB&Bfr£90 LDO 4pm

▥ 🎣 5 private lakes 500 acres arable dairy mixed

[£]

CLUN Shropshire Map **07** SO38

FH [Q][Q][Q] Mrs J Williams **Hurst Mill** *(SO318811)* SY7 0JA (just off B4368) ☎(0588) 640224

A more hospitable family than the Williams would be difficult to find. The house has an attractive setting beside the banks of the river. The rooms are simply furnished, but all the worries of the world evaporate when you unwind at this friendly working farm.

3rm(1🚿) (1fb) 🚭 in bedrooms 🚭 in dining room 🚭 in lounges CTV in 1 bedroom Ⓡ ✱ sB&B£15-£17 dB&B£30-£34 WB&Bfr£100 WBDifr£155 LDO 6.30pm

CTV 🐎 🎣 clay pigeon shooting 100 acres mixed

[£]

FH [Q][Q][Q] Mr & Mrs L Ellison **New House Farm** *(SO275863)* SY7 8NJ ☎Bishop's Castle(0588) 638314

Closed Xmas & New Year

This 18th-century farmhouse is set in over 200 acres of stock-rearing farmland, high in the Clun hills near the Welsh border. Bedrooms are large and furnished to a high standard, with pretty floral decor and fine views; a family room is also available. There are wood-burning stoves in the sitting room and dining room, and an evening meal is available by arrangement, with home produce from the garden used when possible. Three major walking routes are nearby including Offa's Dyke, and fishing and riding are both available locally: there is an abundance of reading material and local tourist information provided. Very much a working farm, there is an additional 110-acre sheep hill which includes an Iron Age Hill Fort. A telephone call for directions is recommended as the farm is rather difficult to locate.

3rm(2🛁🚿) (1fb) 🚭 CTV in all bedrooms Ⓡ dB&B£34-£37 dB&B🛁🚿£34-£37 WB&B£110-£120 WBDi£173-£183 LDO 2pm

CTV 325 acres mixed

COATBRIDGE Strathclyde *Lanarkshire* Map **11** NS76

GH [Q][Q][Q] ***Auchenlea*** 153 Langmuir Road, Bargeddie, Baillieston G69 7RS ☎041-771 6870

Good-value bed and breakfast accommodation is offered at this semidetached cottage on the A752, about a quarter of a mile south of the junction with the A79. Bedrooms vary in size but are all en suite. Hearty breakfasts are served in the combined lounge/dining room. This is a no-smoking establishment.

2🛁🚿 (1fb) CTV in all bedrooms Ⓡ 🐕 (ex guide dogs)

COCKERMOUTH Cumbria Map **11** NY13

GH [Q][Q][Q] ***Derwent Lodge Hotel*** Embelton CA13 9YA ☎(07687) 76606

An attractive stone building standing back from the A66 in the small hamlet of Embleton. It has recently been completely refurbished and now offers modern well-equipped bedrooms whilst an extensive range of food is available in the spacious restaurant.

8🚿 CTV in all bedrooms

▥

PREMIER SELECTED

GH [Q][Q][Q][Q][Q] ***Low Hall Country*** Brandlingill CA13 0RE (3m S on unclass off A5086) ☎(0900) 826654

Mar-Oct

Hugh and Enid Davies have furnished their 17th-century farmhouse to a very high standard, retaining its distinctive character. All the bedrooms have modern en suite facilities and coordinated fabrics are very much a feature. There is a log fire in the beamed lounge on chilly days, and another equally comfortable lounge offers TV, books and magazines. There is a new menu each evening in the dining room, and breakfast is a memorable meal.

6rm(1🛁5🚿) Ⓡ 🐕 (ex guide dogs) LDO 7.15pm

Lic ▥ CTV nc10yrs

Credit Cards [1][3]

SELECTED

GH [Q][Q][Q][Q] **New House** Lorton CA13 9UU (6m S, on B5289 between Lorton and Loweswater) ☎(0900) 85404

A beautifully restored 17th-century farmhouse standing about a mile outside Lorton. Old beams, stone fireplaces and flagged floors lend character to the rooms which include two comfortable lounges, three en suite bedrooms overlooking open country, and a candle-lit dining room where enjoyable four-course dinners are served. Smoking is not permitted in the house.

3🛁🚿 🚭 Ⓡ sB&B🛁🚿£40-£50 dB&B🛁🚿£60-£70 LDO 7pm

Lic ▥ nc12yrs

CODSALL Staffordshire Map **07** SJ80

FH [Q][Q][Q] Mrs D E Moreton **Moors Farm & Country Restaurant** *(SJ859048)* Chillington Lane WV8 1QF (between village of Codsall & Codsall Wood) ☎(0902) 842330 FAX (0902) 842330

A busy working farm in an isolated position five miles northwest of Wolverhampton. Many school parties have their first introduction to a variety of farm animals here, with over 100 acres of mixed farming. Bedrooms are attractively decorated, with TV and tea trays. There is a small cosy residents' lounge, an oak beamed bar, and a choice of menus.

6rm(3🚿) (3fb) 🚭 in dining room CTV in all bedrooms Ⓡ 🐕 ✱ sB&B£23-£24 sB&B🚿£28-£29 dB&B£38-£40 dB&B🚿£46-£48 LDO 5pm

Lic ▥ CTV nc4yrs 100 acres mixed

Credit Cards [5]

COLCHESTER Essex Map **05** TL92

GH [Q][Q] **Four Sevens** 28 Inglis Road CO3 3HU (down B1022 then 2nd right) ☎(0206) 46093

Vas and Calypso Demetri's comfortable family home is in a quiet residential area which is still close to the centre. Bedrooms are comfortable and dinner is available by arrangement. Traditional English cooking is a speciality.

6rm(2🚿) (1fb) 🚭 in dining room 🚭 in lounges CTV in all bedrooms Ⓡ 🐕 ✱ sB&B£20-£30 sB&B🚿£30 dB&B£30-£34 dB&B🚿£38-£40 LDO 8.30pm

▥

GH [Q][Q] **14 Roman Road** 14 Roman Road CO1 1UR ☎(0206) 577905

Closed 23-31 Dec

An attractive Victorian semidetached house stands in a peaceful residential road close to the castle and town centre. Bedrooms are immaculately kept and well furnished. Breakfast is cooked and served by charming proprietor Gill Nicholson.

2⇔fʳ ⊁ CTV in all bedrooms ® 🏃 sB&B⇔fʳ£26-£28 dB&B⇔fʳ£36-£38
Ⅲ. nc12yrs

GH |Q||Q| **Tarquins** 26 Inglis Road CO3 3HU ☎(0206) 579508 FAX (0206) 579508
A Victorian house in a quiet position has been run for many years by Mrs Hudson. There is a comfortable lounge with ornaments and plants and bedrooms are on the first and second floors. At busy times, guests may have to share a table at breakfast.
6rm(2fʳ) (4fb) ⊁ in dining room ⊁ in 1 lounge CTV in all bedrooms ® sB&B£20 sB&Bfʳ£30 dB&B£30 dB&Bfʳ£38 WB&B£120 WBDi£170 LDO 10am
Ⅲ. CTV nc5yrs
£

COLDINGHAM Borders *Berwickshire*   Map **12** NT96

SELECTED

GH |Q||Q||Q| **Dunlaverock House** TD14 5PA
☎(08907) 71450 FAX (08907) 71450
6⇔fʳ (1fb)CTV in all bedrooms ® ✳ sB&B⇔fʳ£32.50-£39.50 dB&B⇔fʳ£45-£59 WB&B£135-£177 WBDi£257.50-£299.50 LDO 7.30pm
Lic Ⅲ.
Credit Cards |1| |3|

COLEFORD Gloucestershire   Map **03** SO51

FH |Q||Q| Mrs S Davis **Lower Tump** *(SO588160)* Eastbach, English Bicknor GL16 7EU ☎Dean(0594) 860253
This farmhouse is part of a mixed stock farm and is set in a lovely position close to the beautiful Forest of Dean. The bedrooms are spacious, and there is a large lounge and a separate breakfast room. It is advisable to ask for directions.
2rm(1⇔1fʳ) (1fb)CTV in all bedrooms ® ✳ sB&B⇔fʳ£16-£16.50 dB&B⇔fʳ£26-£27 WB&B£91-£94.50
Ⅲ. CTV 150 acres mixed
£

COLESBOURNE Gloucestershire   Map **04** SP01

INN |Q||Q||Q| **Colesbourne** GL53 9NP (on A435 Cirencester to Cheltenham road) (Logis) ☎Cheltenham(0242) 870376 FAX (0242) 870397
This inn is over 200 years old and retains a traditional bar and beamed restaurant. The former stable block, with its rare lunette windows, has been converted to provide excellent guest rooms.
Annexe 10rm(6⇔4fʳ) CTV in all bedrooms ® T sB&B⇔fʳ£34 dB&B⇔fʳ£50 WB&B£160 WBDi£220-£250 Lunch £11.95 High tea fr£2.25 Dinner £11.95&alc LDO 10pm
Credit Cards |1||2||3||5| £

COLNE Lancashire   Map **07** SD84

SELECTED

FH |Q||Q||Q| Mrs C Mitson **Higher Wanless** *(SD873413)* Red Lane BB8 7JP ☎(0282) 865301
Closed Dec
Set in attractive rural countryside overlooking the canal, with leisurely narrowboats passing by, this quaint 250-year-old whitewashed farmhouse is an ideal base for touring. The house features a wealth of original oak beams and enormous fireplaces where a fire is lit in cooler weather. There is a cosy lounge, and a set dinner menu, offering honest, substantial

home-cooked food, is served in the comfortable dining room. Guests' approval of the planned dishes is very important to the friendly hosts and alternatives are available if necessary. The spacious bedrooms are attractively decorated and furnished, and very comfortably equipped with TV, radio alarm and beverage-making facilities, plus many little extras. There are several interesting walks nearby and fishing can be enjoyed from the canal bank.
2rm(1fʳ) (2fb) ⊁ CTV in 1 bedroom ® 🏃 ✳ sB&B£18-£24 sB&Bfʳ£20-£26 dB&B£34-£40 dB&Bfʳ£38-£40 LDO 9am
Ⅲ. CTV nc3yrs 25 acres shire horses sheep
£

COLTISHALL Norfolk   Map **09** TG21

SELECTED

GH |Q||Q||Q||Q| **The Hedges** Tunstead Road, Coltishall NR12 7AL (fron Norwich take B1150, turn right onto B1354, opposite river turn left into White Lion Rd at top take right fork) ☎Norwich(0603) 738361 FAX (0603) 738361
Closed 24 Dec-1 Jan
The Hedges is a friendly guest house with two acres of lawns located a short distance from the village and the River Bure. The bedrooms are all en suite and equipped in a clean modern manner. There is a large lounge with a log burning fire and a corner bar with a supply of spirits and beers, and a south facing breakfast room with garden views. The house has its own deep-bore well ensuring a supply of fresh drinking water.
6⇔fʳ (2fb) ⊁ in bedrooms ⊁ in dining room ⊁ in 1 lounge CTV in all bedrooms ® 🏃 (ex guide dogs) ✳ sB&B⇔fʳ£25 dB&B⇔fʳ£35-£40 WB&B£120-£150 LDO 2pm
Lic Ⅲ. CTV
Credit Cards |5| £

COLWYN BAY Clwyd   Map **06** SH87

GH |Q||Q| **Crossroads** 15 Coed Pella Road LL29 7AT
☎(0492) 530736
Closed 24 Dec-2 Jan
This large Victorian house is in a quiet part of the town, yet within easy walking distance of the centre and seafront. Bed and breakfast accommodation only is available, but there are numerous restaurants nearby. Bedrooms are bright and freshly decorated and all have TV and tea trays. A large residents' lounge features the original wooden fireplace. There is a public car park nearby, and Margaret Owens extends a genuine Welsh welcome to her guests.
6rm (2fb) CTV in all bedrooms ® ✳ sB&B£13-£15 dB&B£26-£30 WB&Bfr£85
Ⅲ. CTV ⊁
£

GH |Q| **Grosvenor Hotel** 106-108 Abergele road LL29 7PS
☎(0492) 530798 & 531586
A large double-fronted, stone-built hotel stands near the centre of the town. The bedrooms are neat, many are suitable for families and offer good value. There are two lounges, a games room and a snug cellar bar where snacks are served, as well as a pretty restaurant.
18rm(2⇔) (8fb)CTV in 15 bedrooms ® sB&Bfr£17.90 dB&Bfr£20.15 dB&B⇔fr£35.80 WB&Bfr£103.50 WBDifr£147 LDO 7pm
Lic CTV
Credit Cards |3|

GH |Q||Q||Q| **Northwood Hotel** 47 Rhos Road, Rhos-on-Sea LL28 4RS ☎(0492) 549931
A warm welcome awaits you at this friendly guest house just a short walk from the shops and the sea front. The bedrooms are ▶

fresh and bright. The restaurant looks out over the rear patio and there is a small bar next to it.
12rm(1➪10♠) (3fb) ⊬ in dining room CTV in all bedrooms ®
sB&B£16-£18 sB&B➪♠£18 dB&B£36 dB&B➪♠£36
WB&B£100-£120 WBDi£135-£149 LDO 6.15pm
Lic ⦿ CTV
Credit Cards [1][3] (£)

COMBE MARTIN Devon   Map **02** SS54
See also Berrynarbor

GH [Q][Q][Q] **Channel Vista** Woodlands EX34 0AT
☎(0271) 883514
26 Mar-Oct
Wilf and Dorothy Jackson took over this guest house in 1993, since when they have upgraded the bedrooms and landings, and installed a new rear door for easy access to the car park. A comfortable lounge and a small bar are available to guests, and in the dining room a set four-course dinner of home cooked dishes is offered. The house, which is no-smoking throughout, is well located for the beach and local amenities.
7rm(1➪6♠) (2fb) ⊬ CTV in all bedrooms ® sB&B➪♠£20-£25 dB&B➪♠£34-£38 WBDi£150-£165 LDO 4.30pm
Lic ⦿ nc8yrs
Credit Cards [1][3] (£)

GH [Q] *The Woodlands* 2 The Woodlands EX34 0AT
☎(0271) 882769
Mar-Oct
This modest little guest house offers accommodation in simply furnished and equipped bedrooms; public areas are made up of a homely lounge with bar and a dining room.
8rm (2fb) ♠ LDO 5pm
Lic CTV nc2yrs
Credit Cards [3]

COMRIE Tayside *Perthshire*   Map **11** NN72

[⇔][▼] **GH** [Q][Q] **Mossgiel** Burrell Street PH6 2JP (on A85)
☎(0764) 670567
Mossgiel is a neat roadside guest house with whitewashed walls and colourful window boxes. Bedrooms are thoughtfully equipped and the older furnishings are being replaced with new pine pieces. There is a small lounge and a cosy dining room.
6rm (1fb) ⊬ in bedrooms ⊬ in dining room ® sB&B£15-£18 dB&B£28-£32 WB&B£88-£101 WBDi£139-£151 LDO 6pm
Lic ⦿ CTV nc5yrs
Credit Cards [1][3]

CONGLETON Cheshire   Map **07** SJ86

INN [Q] **Egerton Arms Hotel** Astbury CW12 4RQ (off A34)
☎(02602) 73946
Good value for money and simple but well maintained accommodation is offered at this extended inn in the village of Astbury. A good selection of popular dishes is served in the separate dining room or in the lounge bar.
8rm ⊬ in 2 bedrooms ⊬ in area of dining room CTV in all bedrooms ® ✳ sB&B£24 dB&B£42 Lunch fr£6.95 High tea £4.95-£6.95 Dinner £9.50-£12.95alc LDO 9.30pm
⦿
Credit Cards [1][2][3][5]

CONISHOLME Lincolnshire   Map **09** TF39

> **SELECTED**
>
> **GH** [Q][Q][Q][Q] **Wickham House** Church Lane LN11 7LX (turn into Church Lane from the A1031 at telephone kiosk in Conisholme, Wickham House next to church)
> ☎North Somercotes(0507) 358465

Closed Xmas & New Year
Wickham House is set in a quiet lane amongst delightful rural countryside in the hamlet of Conisholme, off the A1031 and eight miles east of Louth. Originally a row of three 18th-century farm cottages, it has been transformed into a charming house which retains all its original character and interest, with a wealth of beams, open fires and leaded windows. Bedrooms are individual in style and furnished with comfort in mind; one room is on the ground floor. Guests have the use of a pleasant sitting room and cosy library.
4rm(2➪2♠) ⊬ CTV in all bedrooms ® ♠ (ex guide dogs) ✳ dB&B➪♠fr£36 LDO noon
⦿ nc8yrs
(£)

CONISTON Cumbria   Map **07** SD39

GH [Q][Q][Q] **Arrowfield** Little Arrow, Torver LA21 8AU (on A593)
☎(05394) 41741
Mar-Nov
A very attractive late Victorian house stands in well kept gardens on the main Coniston to Torver road. Bedrooms are modern in style and freshly decorated and furnished. There is a spacious and comfortable lounge with an open log fire and plenty of books. Dinner, available by arrangement, is served in the cosy dining room.
5rm(2♠) ⊬ in bedrooms ⊬ in dining room CTV in 4 bedrooms ® ♠ (ex guide dogs) ✳ sB&B£16.50-£20 dB&B£30-£39 dB&B♠£37-£44 WB&B£105-£129.50 WBDi£196-£220 LDO 9.30am
Lic ⦿ CTV nc3yrs
(£)

> **P R E M I E R**   ✿   **S E L E C T E D**
>
>
>
> **GH** [Q][Q][Q][Q][Q] **Coniston Lodge Hotel** Sunny Brow LA21 8HH (at crossroads on A593 close to filling station)
> ☎(05394) 41201
> rs Sun & Mon pm
> Family owned and run, this attractive, almost Swiss-style building offers a perfect place to relax and unwind, standing in a quiet side road close to the village. There are six modern en suite bedrooms with coordinated colour schemes and fabrics, equipped with thoughtful extras. There is a comfortable lounge, prettily decorated with matching seat covers and curtains. A set four-course dinner is served each evening in the pleasing dining room, except on Sunday and Monday. The menu is English in style and may include Coniston char (a fish native to the nearby lake).
> 6➪♠ ⊬ CTV in all bedrooms ® T ♠ (ex guide dogs) sB&B➪♠£29-£39 dB&B➪♠£52-£68 WB&B£182-£206.50 LDO 7.30pm
> Lic ⦿ nc10yrs
> Credit Cards [1][2][3] (£)

Telephone national area codes are due to change by 16th April 1995. Please see the note under 'How to Use this Guide' at the front of the book.

GH Ⓠ Ⓠ Ⓠ Ⓠ Ⓠ **Wheelgate**
Country House Hotel Little
Arrow LA21 8AU
☎(05394) 41418
Apr-Oct rs Feb-Mar
5♠ (3fb) CTV in all bedrooms
Ⓡ 🐾 (ex guide dogs)
sB&B♠£28-£32.50
dB&B♠£50-£65 WB&B£168-
£192.50 WBDi£260-£297.50
LDO 7pm
Lic ▥
Credit Cards ① ② ③

FH Ⓠ Mrs M Dutton **Knipe Ground** *(SD322977)* LA21 8AE
☎(05394) 41221
4rm ⧖ Ⓡ 🐾 ✳ sB&B£13-£15 dB&B£14-£16
nc6yrs 24 acres sheep horses

CONNEL Strathclyde *Argyllshire*   Map **10** NM93

GH Ⓠ Ⓠ Ⓠ Ⓠ Ⓠ **Ards**
House PA37 1PT (on A85, 4m
N of Oban) ☎(063171) 255
due to change to
(0631) 710255
Mar-Nov rs 1-23 Dec
Many guests return year after
year to Jean and John
Bowman's delightful house,
which is on the western edge
of the village with views over
the Firth of Lorn to Lismore
and the hills of Morvern beyond. Bedrooms are individually
decorated and vary in style, and the public areas include a
spacious drawing room with a real fire on cool evenings. The
high point of the day is John's carefully prepared five-course
dinner, featuring the best available fresh local produce. This is
a no-smoking establishment.
6rm(5⇔♠) ⧖ CTV in 1 bedroom Ⓡ 🐾 sB&B⇔♠£25-£35
dB&B⇔♠£42-£54 WB&B£157.50-£170 WBDi£262.50-£275
LDO 6pm
Lic ▥ CTV nc12yrs
Credit Cards ① ③ Ⓔ
See advertisement under OBAN

GH Ⓠ Ⓠ Ⓠ Ⓠ **Loch Etive Hotel** Main Street PA37 1PH
(200yds from A85 road) ☎(063171) 400 due to change to
(0631) 710400 FAX (063171) 680
Etr-28 Oct
Françoise Weber's and Bill Mossman's small private hotel has
a pretty garden and lies by a stream in the village some 200
yards from the main (A85) road. Bedrooms are comfortable
and deceptively spacious, the two top floor rooms having
particular character: one pine clad and the other with a natural
stone wall and beamed ceiling. The lounge is separated from
the neat dining room by a trellis, and Bill Mossman's good-
value three-course dinners are available May to mid-July.
6rm(4⇔♠) (2fb) ⧖ in 1 bedrooms ⧖ in dining room ⧖ in
lounges CTV in all bedrooms Ⓡ sB&B£19-£22
sB&B⇔♠£22-£26 dB&B£38 dB&B⇔♠£44-£48

WBDi£190-£220 LDO 6.30pm
Lic ▥
Credit Cards ① ③ Ⓔ

🖾 🖵 GH Ⓠ Ⓠ Ⓠ Ⓠ **Ronebhal** PA37 1PJ (on A85)
☎(0631) 71310
Apr-Oct
Ronebhal is a sturdy Victorian house on the A85 with a superb
outlook over Loch Etive. Bedrooms are well decorated, bright
and airy, and public rooms include an attractive TV lounge and
a smart dining room where hearty breakfasts are served at
individual tables. The house is maintained to a high standard,
the atmosphere is relaxed; smoking is prohibited.
6rm(3♠) (1fb) ⧖ CTV in all bedrooms Ⓡ 🐾 sB&Bfr£15
sB&B♠£23 dB&B£30-£38 dB&B♠£30-£45
WB&B£105-£154 LDO 8pm
▥ nc5yrs
Credit Cards ① ③ Ⓔ

Telephone national area codes are due to change by 16th April 1995. Please see the note under 'How to Use this Guide' at the front of the book.

CONON BRIDGE Highland *Ross & Cromarty* Map **14** NH55

P R E M I E R S E L E C T E D

GH [Q][Q][Q][Q][Q] Kinkell House Easter Kinkell IV7 8HY (on B9169)
☎Dingwall(0349) 861270

Enthusiastic owners, Steve and Marsha Fraser have sympathetically restored and refurbished this former 19th century farm house to create a very civilised small country house. Set in it's own peaceful grounds with panoramic views of Ben Wyvis, the Cromarty Firth and the Wester Ross hills, the house is an ideal base for exploring surrounding places of interest. The bedrooms are quite individual with attractive decor and are comfortably furnished in period style. Attractive public areas include two inviting lounges and, at the time of our visit, a new sun lounge was nearing completion. The elegant restaurant enjoys glorious views over the Conon Valley and is open to non-residents for both lunch and dinner. The changing small carte style menu offers a choice of interesting home cooked dishes based on fresh local ingredients.

3rm(1🛁2🚿) 🚭 in bedrooms 🚭 in dining room 🚭 in 1 lounge CTV in all bedrooms [R] ✱ sB&B🛁🚿£27-£42 dB&B🛁🚿£54-£64 WB&B£170-£265 WBDi£284-£378 LDO 9pm

Lic ♨

Credit Cards [1][3][£]

CONSETT Co Durham Map **12** NZ15

GH [Q][Q][Q] ***Greenhead*** Carterway Heads, (A68), Shotley Bridge DH8 9TP (just off A68, 2m from Shotley Bridge) ☎(0207) 55676

This charming guest house is set in a very rural location but is convenient to the A68 and only three miles from Shotley Bridge. Beams and exposed stone walls feature throughout, and bedrooms have good facilities.

3🛁🚿 (1fb) CTV in all bedrooms [R] LDO 5pm

Lic ♨ CTV

CONSTANTINE Cornwall & Isles of Scilly Map **02** SW72

INN[Q][Q][Q] Trengilly Wartha Nancenoy TR11 5RP (from Constantine follow signs to Nancenoy) (Logis)
☎Falmouth(0326) 40332 FAX (0326) 40332

The public bar of this inn is very much a Cornish local with a good range of real ales and imaginative bar meals. The intimate restaurant serves a fixed price menu. Bedrooms are individually furnished and well equipped. Other features of the inn are its international size petanque pitch, and special events such as the sausage festival and pudding week.

6rm(4🛁1🚿) CTV in all bedrooms [R] **T** sB&B£32-£38 sB&B🛁🚿£39-£42 dB&B£44-£48 dB&B🛁🚿£54-£59 WB&B£114-£165 WBDi£220-£270 Bar Lunch £8-£20 LDO 9.30pm

♨ ⛳ petanque

Credit Cards [1][2][3][5][£]

CONWY Gwynedd Map **06** SH77

See also Roewen

GH [Q][Q] Bryn Derwen Woodlands LL32 8LT (on B5106)
☎Aberconwy(0492) 596134

Closed 15 Dec-3 Jan rs 4 Jan-Feb

Bryn Derwen is a small family-run guest house within walking distance of the castle and town centre. The pretty bedrooms are individually furnished. A small TV lounge and an attractive pine-furnished breakfast room are provided.

5rm(1🛁🚿) (1fb) 🚭 in dining room 🚭 in lounges [R] ✱ sB&B£13.50-£23 dB&Bfr£27 dB&B🛁🚿fr£34 WB&B£81-£138 WBDi£123-£180 LDO noon

♨ CTV

[£]

🛏 ☕ **GH [Q][Q] Glan Heulog** Llanrwst Road LL32 8LT (on B5106) ☎Aberconwy(0492) 593845

This pleasant little guest house, the name of which means 'sunny banks', enjoys pleasant views extending as far as the castle from a setting above the town. Well maintained bedrooms equipped with TV sets and tea trays - and, in one instance, boasting a four-poster bed - are steadily being improved by the provision of en suite facilities; there is a modern lounge, and ample car parking space is available.

7rm(4🛁🚿) (1fb) 🚭 in dining room 🚭 in lounges CTV in all bedrooms [R] 🐕 (ex guide dogs) sB&B£13-£16 dB&Bfr£26 dB&B🛁🚿£29-£30 WB&B£82-£95 WBDi£131-£144 LDO 9.30am

Lic ♨

GH [Q][Q][Q] Pen-y-bryn Tearooms Lancaster Square LL32 8DE
☎Aberconwy(0492) 596445

Three small but well equipped bedrooms are provided at this popular tea shop which is housed in a building (known, until recently, as The Old Ship) dating back to the sixteenth century and located at the centre of the famous walled town; three car parking spaces are also available nearby. Several daily hot specials, snacks and teas are served between 11am and 5pm.

3rm(2🚿) (1fb) 🚭 CTV in all bedrooms [R] ✱ sB&Bfr£17.50 sB&B🚿fr£25 dB&Bfr£30 dB&B🚿fr£35

♨

[£]

COPMANTHORPE North Yorkshire Map **08** SE54

GH [Q][Q] ***Duke of Connaught Hotel*** Copmanthorpe Grange YO2 3TN (off Appleton Roebuck/Bishopthorpe road)
☎Appleton Roebuck(0904) 744318

Closed Xmas wk

In open countryside, this very skilfully converted group of farm buildings has well furnished bedrooms, a cosy lounge and a country-style dining room. The owners give friendly attention.

14rm(2🛁12🚿) Annexe 4rm (2fb) CTV in 14 bedrooms [R] 🐕 (ex guide dogs) LDO 6pm

Lic ♨

Credit Cards [1][2][3]

COPPULL Lancashire Map **07** SD51

FH [Q] Mrs Woodcock **Bridge Farm** *(SD569132)* Bridge Farm, Coppull Moor Lane PR7 4LL ☎(0257) 792390

3rm [R] 🐕 ✱ sB&Bfr£15 dB&Bfr£28

70 acres dairy

[£]

CORBRIDGE Northumberland Map **12** NY96

GH [Q][Q][Q] Morningside Riding Mill NE44 6HL
☎Hexham(0434) 682350 FAX (0434) 682350

Situated beside the A695 in the centre of the village of Riding Mill and conveniently placed for exploring the surrounding countryside, this stone-built blacksmith's house offers pleasant, well maintained accommodation. Individually decorated bedrooms are thoughtfully equipped, and public areas include a comfortable lounge and small breakfast room.

5rm(1🚿) (2fb) 🚭 CTV in all bedrooms [R] sB&B£17-£20 dB&Bfr£30 LDO breakfast

♨ CTV

[£]

GH Q Q Q **Priorfield** Priorfield, Hippingstones Lane NE45 5JA
☎Hexham(0434) 633179
Mar-Nov

Priorfield is a handsome Edwardian house in its own grounds just a short walk from the town centre. The two attractively decorated guest bedrooms have good facilities, including comfortable beds, colour TV and central heating. Breakfast is served in the combined lounge and dining room.
2rm (1fb) ⚑ in bedrooms CTV in all bedrooms ® ⚑ ✳
sB&B£20-£25 dB&B£30-£36
nc4yrs
£

FH Q Q Q Mr & Mrs T Jones **Low Barns** *(NY994644)*
Thornbrough NE45 5LX ☎(0434) 632408

Excellent bedrooms with attractive decor and good facilities are provided at Low Barns. There is also a cosy lounge for guests' use. The house stands in lovely countryside a short way from the town.
3⇨⚑ ⚑ in dining room CTV in all bedrooms ® ✳
dB&B⇨⚑fr£42 LDO 24hrs prior
2 acres non working
Credit Cards [1] [3]

CORSHAM Wiltshire   Map 03 ST87

FH Q Q Q Q Mrs C Barton **Manor Farm** *(ST846679)*
Wadswick SN14 9JB (take B3109 from Corsham, past mini-roundabout and turn left at Wadswick signpost. Second farmhouse on left) ☎(0225) 810700
Feb-Nov

This handsome 17th-century farmhouse overlooking beautifully tended gardens enjoys a quiet setting with rural views extending to the Box valley. Accommodation is offered in three spacious, quality bedrooms, and the gracious drawing room is an ideal place to relax after a day spent exploring the Roman ruins of Bath and picturesque Bradford-on-Avon. Breakfast - the only meal served in the large dining room - may be enjoyed en famille round a beautiful antique table.
3rm (2⚑) (1fb) ⚑ CTV in all bedrooms ® ⚑ (ex guide dogs)
✳ sB&B⚑£20-£25 dB&B⚑£37.50-£40 WB&B£125
riding arranged 500 acres arable sheep
Credit Cards [1] [3]

CORWEN Clwyd   Map 06 SJ04

GH Q Q **Coleg-y-Groes** LL21 0AU ☎(0490) 412169
Closed 24-27 Dec

Now run as a Christian retreat, this early 18th-century Grade II listed building was once a row of alms houses for clergy widows. It is set back off the A5 between the church and wooded hillside and has its own pretty lawns and gardens. Several rooms open directly on to the lawn, including one of the lounges which is set aside for reading and meditation. Another lounge has TV and a feature Welsh slate fireplace. The small bedrooms have recently been modernised.
6rm (2fb) ⚑ ® ⚑ (ex guide dogs) ✳ sB&B£15-£17 dB&B£30-£34 WB&Bfr£100 WBDifr£150.75 LDO previous evening
CTV
£

⚐ ⬛ **GH** Q Q **Corwen Court Private Hotel** London Road
LL21 0DP (on A5) ☎(0490) 412854
Closed Xmas-New Year rs Dec-Feb

Between 1871 and 1978 this stone-built house was the local police station and court house. The original cells still remain, and have been converted into six single bedrooms furnished with solid period furniture. Four double rooms have also been added and these have en suite bathrooms. Friendly owners Bob and Kit

Buckland have created a comfortable lounge and dining room in what was the old court house, and here Kit provides good value evening meals. The hotel lies alongside the A5 near the centre of the village.
10rm(4⇨⚑) ⚑ in dining room sB&B£13-£14 dB&B⇨⚑£28-£30 WB&B£91-£98 WBDi£140-£154 LDO 5pm
CTV ⚑
£

GH Q Q Q Q **Powys House Estate** Bonwm LL21 9EG
(on A5) ☎(0490) 412367

The Waite and Quinn families offer a warm welcome to their home, which is a delightful place to stay. Its mature grounds extend to several acres of well maintained lawns and gardens (complete with loungers), and the spacious bedrooms are bright and freshly decorated. Many original fireplaces remain and the panelled hall is particularly impressive. There is also a very comfortable lounge in which to relax.
3⚑ (1fb) ⚑ in bedrooms ⚑ in dining room ® ⚑ (ex guide dogs) sB&B⚑£21-£22 dB&B⚑£32-£34 WB&B£112 WBDi£196 LDO 6pm
CTV ⚑(grass)
£

COUNTISBURY (NEAR LYNTON) Devon   Map 03 SS74

FH Q Q Q Mrs R Pile **Coombe** *(SS766489)* EX35 6NF (0.5m off A39 on road to Brendon) ☎Brendon(05987) 236
Apr-Oct rs Nov & Dec

Nestling on the north Devon coastline and within the boundary of Exmoor National Park lies Coombe Farm with 365 acres of hills and field, where Exmoor horned sheep and Devon cattle are reared. This early 17th-century house has a dining room with inglenook fireplace, old beams and seats people at individual tables. A four-course dinner is served and there is a cosy sitting room with TV where guests can relax. Bedrooms are warm and comfortable.
5rm(2⚑) (2fb) ⚑ ® ⚑ (ex guide dogs) dB&B£33-£42 dB&B⚑£39-£47 WB&B£110-£130 LDO 5pm
Lic CTV 365 acres sheep

COUPAR ANGUS Tayside *Perthshire*   Map 11 NO23

GH Q Q **Eastwood** Forfar Road PH13 9AN ☎(0828) 27485

This house stands on the main road on the north-eastern edge of town. Bedrooms are neat if unpretentious, and there is a family room with a connecting single room. Attractive public rooms include a pleasant lounge and small dining room where breakfast is taken at two communal tables.
3rm (1fb) ⚑ in 3 bedrooms ⚑ in dining room ® ✳ sB&B£14-£15 dB&B£28-£30 WB&B£98-£105
CTV

COVENTRY West Midlands   Map 04 SP37

GH Q **Ashleigh House** 17 Park Road CV1 2LH ☎(0203) 223804
Closed Xmas

In a cul-de-sac close to the town centre and convenient for the railway station, Ashleigh House offers en suite bedrooms some of which are compact. There is a small guests' lounge with TV and video and an attractive restaurant decorated in Laura Ashley fabrics with a small bar. Car parking is available at the rear.
10rm(8⚑) (5fb) CTV in all bedrooms ® ⚑ ✳ sB&B£16-£20 sB&B⚑£20-£23.50 dB&B£28-£32 dB&B⚑£32-£34 WB&B£105-£126 WBDi£140-£161 LDO 8.45pm
Lic CTV

GH [Q][Q] ***Croft Hotel*** 23 Stoke Green, Off Binley Road CV3 1FP (second turning on right after Humber Road traffic lights on A427/428) ☎(0203) 457846

The Croft is situated in an established residential area overlooking the green. Simple, clean and bright bedrooms are offered along with varied public areas. The bar, complete with pool table, serves draught beer and lager, and there is a set-price menu with grills and a range of bar snacks.

12rm(4🚿) (1fb) CTV in 6 bedrooms [R] LDO 8.30pm

Lic ♨ CTV pool table

Credit Cards [1] [3]

GH [Q][Q][Q] ***Hearsall Lodge Hotel*** 1 Broad Lane CV5 7AA ☎(0203) 674543

This comfortable guesthouse is conveniently located close to the A45 with easy access to the city centre. It is professionally run by Mr & Mrs Entwhistle who offer rooms which are well equipped with modern facilities, including direct dial telephones; most rooms have private showers, but are not fully en suite. The cosy dining room has a corner bar.

13rm (2fb) CTV in all bedrooms [R] LDO 7.30pm

Lic ♨ CTV

Credit Cards [1] [3]

COWDENBEATH Fife — Map 11 NT19

GH [Q][Q] Struan Bank Hotel 74 Perth Road KY4 9BG ☎(0383) 511057

Situated in an elevated position on the northern approach to the town, this family run commercial hotel continues to be gradually improved. Bedrooms are generally rather compact and modest. Public areas include a pleasant dining room with individual tables and a comfortable lounge with small bar area.

8rm (1fb) 🚭 in dining room [R] * sB&Bfr£17 dB&Bfr£31 LDO 6pm

Lic ♨ CTV

Credit Cards [1] [2] [3] [£]

CRACKINGTON HAVEN Cornwall & Isles of Scilly — Map 02 SX19

PREMIER SELECTED

FH [Q][Q][Q][Q][Q] Mrs M Knight **Manor** *(SX159962)* EX23 0JW ☎St Gennys(0840) 230304

Manor Farm is surrounded by 25 acres of farmland, just a mile from the beach at Crackington Haven. Dating back to the Doomsday list, it has been tastefully restored to provide luxurious accomodation, and the bedrooms are beautifully furnished incorporating many antiques; all have en suite or private bathrooms. There is a cosy sitting room with a log burner, a more formal drawing room and a small TV lounge. Guests gather at the honesty bar before dinner, which is taken at the huge dining room table. Interesting menus are offered using as much local produce as possible, and breakfast is served in a separate sunny room. Guests are requested not to smoke in the house.

3rm(2🛁) Annexe 2🚿 🚭 🐕 sB&B🛁🚿£28-£30 dB&B🛁🚿£56-£60 LDO 5pm

Lic ♨ CTV nc18yrs snooker table tennis 30 acres beef

PREMIER SELECTED

FH [Q][Q][Q][Q][Q] Mrs J Crocker ***Trevigue (SX136951)*** EX23 0LQ ☎St Gennys(0840) 230418

Mar-Sep

Trevigue is a National Trust farmhouse nestled in a hollow on the exposed north Cornish coast, just a few yards from the coastal path, close to the isolated Strangles Beach. The 16th-century granite-built house, set in an enclosed cobbled courtyard, offers an ideal combination of historic character and modern comfort. There are three bedrooms in the main house and two in the Mediterranean-style villa a short distance away, all attractively furnished with many fine antique pieces. The two cosy sitting rooms have flagstone floors and log burning stoves in inglenook fireplaces. In the height of summer guests may choose between eating in the intimate dining room or the converted barn.

4rm(2🛁2🚿) CTV in 2 bedrooms [R] 🐕 LDO 5pm

Lic CTV nc12yrs 500 acres dairy mixed

PREMIER SELECTED

FH [Q][Q][Q][Q][Q] Mrs P Mount **Treworgie Barton** *(SX178968)* EX23 0NL ☎St Gennys(0840) 230233

Apr-Sep rs Feb-Mar & Nov

Treworgie Barton is a 16th-century farmhouse peacefully situated at the head of the Millook valley, affording glorious views across open country and the rugged coastline to the sea. Five tastefully decorated bedrooms are offered, two in a converted barn. There is a comfortable lounge, where a log fire burns on cooler evenings, and here guests are given tea and home-made biscuits on arrival. Dinner is served in the elegant dining room. It is a set meal but careful account is taken of guests' preferences. Food is freshly cooked and good use is made of local produce. The farmhouse is not licensed but wine can be brought in at no extra charge.

3rm(2🛁1🚿) Annexe 2🛁🚿 (1fb) 🚭 CTV in all bedrooms [R] 🐕 (ex guide dogs) * dB&B🛁🚿£34-£46 WB&B£99-£141 WBDi£190-£240 LDO 4pm

106 acres beef sheep

INN[Q][Q][Q] Coombe Barton EX23 0JG ☎St Gennys(0840) 230345 FAX (0840) 230788

Mar-Oct rs Nov-Feb

Originally built as a residence for the 'captain' of the local slate quarry, this attractive inn has an unrivalled position on the beach and is popular with locals and tourists alike. Most bedrooms have en suite facilities and some offer stunning sea views. There are three lively bars, including a friendly children's room, and a separate dining room where breakfast is served. A wide choice of food is available from blackboard, snack and à la carte menus, including plenty of fresh fish.

7rm(3🛁) (1fb)CTV in 3 bedrooms [R] * sB&B£17.50-£19.50 dB&B£35-£40 dB&B🛁£45-£55 WB&B£110-£125 Bar Lunch

▶

Hearsall Lodge Hotel

**1 BROAD LANE,
COVENTRY CV5 7AA
Telephone: (01203) 674543**

Family run hotel situated close to town centre in select residential area. Eighteen bedrooms with colour TV, tea and coffee making facilities and showers. Full central heating – Residents' TV lounge. Licensed bar. Ample parking space. Easy access to A45/M6 for National Exhibition Centre, Birmingham International Airport and Royal Showground at Stoneleigh.

TREVIGUE FARM
Crackington Haven

A superb 16th century farmhouse on a 500-acre dairy and beef farm with 2½ miles of spectacular coast-line. All bedrooms en-suite with tea-making facilities, two with colour TV. Beautifully appointed, tranquil sitting rooms with great emphasis placed on imaginative cuisine. An ideal location for touring Cornwall and Devon. Children over 12 years most welcome. Licensed.

**Janet Crocker, Trevigue, Crackington Haven,
Bude, Cornwall EX23 0LQ
Phone: St. Gennys (01840) 230418**

Premier Selected

Manor Farm   Crackington Haven N. Cornwall

Welcome to our beautiful, secluded Domesday listed Manor House one mile from sea. Once held by the Earl of Montain, half brother to William the Conqueror, the Manor has since been tastefully restored and adapted to provide an elegant peaceful setting, surrounded by landscaped gardens and rolling hills. We offer charming accommodation with private facilities. Dining here is considered the highlight of the day. The games room includes a full sized snooker table. Regret no children and no smoking in the house.

Mrs M. Knight   Tel: St Gennys (01840) 230304

£5-£12.50alc Dinner £7.50-£15alc LDO 9.30pm
ᴪ, CTV
Credit Cards ① ② ③ ⓔ

CRAIL Fife   Map **12** NO60

GH Ⓠ Ⓠ Ⓠ *Caiplie* 51-53 High Street KY10 3RA
☎(0333) 450564
Mar-Oct Closed Dec-Jan rs Nov & Feb-1 Mar
A warm welcome is assured at this popular licensed guesthouse situated in the centre of this picturesque coastal village, within easy walking distance of the attractive harbour. Bedrooms vary in shape and size and all are clean and comfortably furnished, with colourful fabrics and thoughtful extras. There is a cosy lounge on the first floor, and the bright, cheerful dining room overlooks the main road and offers daily changing menus which include a choice of Scottish and continental dishes.
7rm (1fb) Ⓡ LDO 4pm
Lic ᴪ, CTV ⤶

GH Ⓠ Ⓠ **Selcraig House** 47 Nethergate KY10 3TX
☎(0333) 450697
In a quiet street between the village centre and the harbour, this stone built house dates from the 1700's and the welcoming owner, Margaret Carstairs, has furnished the public areas in appropriate style. There is an inviting first floor lounge and attractive dining room, the recent conservatory extension providing space for separate tables for all guests. Bedrooms vary in size, those on the top floor being most compact.
5rm (2fb) ⤶ CTV in all bedrooms Ⓡ sB&Bfr£22 dB&Bfr£32 WB&Bfr£100 WBDifr£184 LDO noon
CTV
ⓔ

INN Ⓠ Ⓠ Ⓠ **Golf Hotel** 4 High Street KY10 3TB
☎(0333) 450206 & 450500 FAX (0333) 450795
rs 26 Dec & 1 Jan
Dating from the 14th century, this centrally situated former coaching inn has been modernised to provide a sound standard of accommodation. Bedrooms are pleasant and in contemporary style, with pine furniture and cheerful coordinated fabrics. There is a comfortable first floor lounge, and an extensive range of meals is served in either the dining room or bars.
5ᐟⓇ (1fb)CTV in all bedrooms Ⓡ sB&BᐟⓇ£26-£28 dB&BᐟⓇ£44-£48 Lunch £1.25-£6.25 High tea £4.95-£9.50 Dinner £1.45-£9.75 LDO 9pm
ᴪ, CTV
Credit Cards ① ③

CRANBROOK Kent   Map **05** TQ73

PREMIER 🌺 **SELECTED**

GH Ⓠ Ⓠ Ⓠ Ⓠ Ⓠ **Hancocks**
Tilsden Lane TN17 3PH
☎(0580) 714645
Further improvements have been made to this charming house and a small suite with its own sitting room is now available. Comfort and furnishings remains at a very high level, and the well appointed bedrooms have special touches such as a bowl of fruit and mineral water. An open fire in the spacious and comfortable lounge adds to the relaxation, particularly after a good, well prepared evening meal. Breakfasts are hearty and enjoyable.

3ᐠⓇ ⤶ CTV in all bedrooms Ⓡ dB&BᐠⓇ£45-£54 WB&B£150 WBDi£255-£272.50 LDO 2pm
ᴪ, nc9yrs
ⓔ

SELECTED

FH Ⓠ Ⓠ Ⓠ Ⓠ Mrs S Wickham **The Oast** *(TQ755345)* Hallwood Farm TN17 2SP (A229 1m S) ☎(0580) 712416
Mar-Oct rs Nov-Feb
A long drive from the main road leads to this delightful farmhouse set in peaceful rural surroundings. The furnishings are in keeping with the style of the house, bedrooms are spacious and there is a comfortable sitting room. At breakfast, for which there is a choice of English or Continental, guests share one large table.
2ᐠⓇ ⤶ CTV in all bedrooms Ⓡ 🐾 sB&BᐠⓇfr£22 dB&BᐠⓇ£34-£35 WB&B£119-£154
ᴪ, 200 acres arable fruit sheep
ⓔ

CRANFORD Greater London
For accommodation details see **Heathrow Airport**

CRASTER Northumberland   Map **12** NU22

INN Ⓠ Ⓠ Ⓠ *Cottage* Dunstan Village NE66 3SZ (NW, off Howick to Embleton road) ☎Embleton(0665) 576658
A privately owned inn situated in the village of Dunstan, just a few minutes' drive from the coast, the Cottage provides practical, modern accommodation in well equipped ground-floor bedrooms. A good range of menus is offered in either the characterful bar, or the attractive restaurant. A charming conservatory leads on to the patio and secluded gardens.
10ᐠⓇ CTV in all bedrooms Ⓡ T 🐾 (ex guide dogs) LDO 9.30pm
ᴪ,
Credit Cards ① ③

CRAVEN ARMS Shropshire   Map **07** SO48

SELECTED

GH Ⓠ Ⓠ Ⓠ Ⓠ **Keepers Cottage** Clungunford SY7 0PL
☎Little Brampton(05887) 419
Closed mid Dec-mid Jan
Standing in 43 acres of woodland, this large, newly built house is available for shooting parties. The bedrooms are well proportioned with thoughtful extras, and there is an oak-panelled lounge with bar and snooker table. Breakfast is served at one long pine table in the huge, quarry-tiled kitchen.
3ᐠⓇ (3fb) ⤶ CTV in all bedrooms Ⓡ 🐾 * sB&BᐠⓇ£17 dB&BᐠⓇ£34
ᴪ, 🐕
ⓔ

CRAWFORD Strathclyde *Lanarkshire*   Map **11** NS92

GH Ⓠ Ⓠ **Field End** ML12 6TN ☎(08642) 276
Closed Xmas & New Year
This guest house is reached by way of a narrow, steep track from the village main street, and looks out across open pastureland. There is a spacious bedroom upstairs, and a small one off the rear corridor leading to the kitchen on the ground floor. Smoking is not permitted.
3rm(2ᐠⓇ) (1fb) ⤶ CTV in all bedrooms Ⓡ 🐾 (ex guide dogs)

sB&B£18-£22 dB&B£30-£34 WB&B£105-£130 WBDi£155-£180 LDO 5pm
CTV
Credit Cards 1 3 £

CRAWLEY West Sussex

For accommodation details see **Gatwick Airport**

CREDITON Devon   Map **03** SS80

FH Q Q Mr & Mrs M Pennington *Woolsgrove (SS793028)*
Sandford EX17 4PJ (3m NW on unclassified road, 1m N of A377)
☎Copplestone(0363) 84246
Feb-Nov
This peaceful 17th-century farm sits in the fold of a hill looking down over the well tended garden to the fields beyond. The large double bedrooms are individually furnished and there is a large comfortable sitting room with a log burning stove. Breakfast and the optional four-course evening meal are taken in the dining room, which has an open fire when the weather dictates.
3rm (2fb) ® LDO 6pm
CTV 150 acres mixed

CREWE Cheshire   Map **07** SJ75

FH Q Q Q Mrs Diana Edwards **Balterley Hall** *(SJ765499)*
Balterley CW2 5QG (4m SE) ☎(0270) 820206
Closed Xmas
Situated in the lane opposite Balterley's village church, this is a large and imposing Grade II listed house dating back to the mid-17th century. Two of the three bedrooms are very large, one being a family room, and all are well equipped and furnished with a mixture of antique and modern pieces. Breakfast, and dinner by prior arrangement only, are taken at one large table in the cosy breakfast room-cum-lounge.
3rm(2↑) (1fb) ⊁ in 1 bedrooms ⊁ in dining room ⊁ in lounges CTV in all bedrooms ® ⊁ (ex guide dogs) sB&B£17-£22 sB&B£22-£25 dB&Bfr£28 dB&Bfr£34 LDO noon
CTV 240 acres arable mixed pigs sheep
£

SELECTED

FH Q Q Q Q Ms M Hughes *Clayhanger Hall Farm*
(SJ728574) Maw Lane, Haslington CW1 1SH ☎(0270) 583952
The accommodation on this large dairy and sheep farm has been created from disused farm buildings. There are four well equipped bedrooms, all individually styled with pretty coordinating colour schemes and modern furnishings. Breakfast is taken at one large table in the pleasant lounge/breakfast room and there is a pretty garden.
4↑ CTV in all bedrooms ® ⊁ LDO 4.30pm
CTV ✈ 250 acres dairy/sheep

CREWKERNE Somerset   Map **03** ST40

PREMIER SELECTED

GH Q Q Q Q Q **Broadview**
43 East Street TA18 7AG (on the Yeovil road) ☎(0460) 73424
The easiest access to this small colonial-style bungalow is from the Yeovil direction, due to a hairpin bend on the drive. Bedrooms are well presented and the comfortable lounge area is adorned with many ornaments, an array of indoor plants and a few colourful

caged birds. Dinner is available by arrangement and is served around a large antique table. Guests are requested not to smoke in the public rooms.
3⇥↑ ⊁ CTV in all bedrooms ® sB&B⇥↑£30-£35 dB&B⇥↑£46 WB&B£161 WBDi£245 LDO 9am

---

CRIANLARICH Central *Perthshire*   Map **10** NN32

GH Q Q Q **Glenardran Guest House** FK20 8QS (beside A85 on eastern approach to village) ☎(01838) 300236
Lying on the A85 to the east of the village, this spotlessly clean and well maintained guest house offers well proportioned accommodation in bright, fresh bedrooms. The attractive public rooms are adorned with interesting items collected by the owners.
6rm(1↑) (1fb) ⊁ CTV in all bedrooms ® ✳ sB&B£17.50 dB&B£35 dB&B£40 WB&B£122.50 WBDi£192.50 LDO 6pm
Lic
Credit Cards 1 3 £

GH Q Q Q **The Lodge House** FK20 8RU ☎(08383) 300276
Apr-Dec
This secluded Highland house is in an elevated position with fine views over the valley to the hills beyond. Particularly well maintained, it offers attractive bedrooms, including one in a pine chalet. There are two lounges, one with a dispense bar, and an appealing little dining room where home cooked meals are served. Smoking is only allowed in the bar lounge.
6rm(5↑) ⊁ in bedrooms ⊁ in dining room ⊁ in lounges CTV in all bedrooms ® ⊁ (ex guide dogs) sB&B£26-£34 dB&B£52-£62 WBDi£245-£280 LDO 8pm
Lic CTV ♨ ✈
Credit Cards 1 3 £

CRICCIETH Gwynedd Map **06** SH43

GH [Q][Q][Q] Glyn-Y-Coed Private Hotel Portmadoc Road LL52 0HL (E on A497) ☎(0766) 522870 FAX (0766) 523341
Closed Xmas & New Year
Glyn-Y-Coed is a friendly family-run hotel situated above the main road into the resort, with fine views over the castle and sea. Bedrooms are fresh and pretty and several have canopied beds. Family rooms are available and one suite. A lounge and small bar is provided for residents, along with a garden and car park.
10rm(3🛁7🚿) (5fb) 🚭 in 2 bedrooms 🚭 in area of dining room 🚭 in 1 lounge CTV in all bedrooms [R] sB&B🛁🚿£18-£22 dB&B🛁🚿£36-£44 WB&B£125-£145 WBDi£190-£210 LDO 4pm
Lic ♨ CTV
Credit Cards [1][3][£]

GH [Q][Q][Q] Min y Gaer Private Hotel Porthmadog Road LL52 0HP (on A497 400yds E of jct with B4411) ☎(0766) 522151 FAX (0766) 522151
Mar-Oct
Situated back off the main road with ample parking, there are superb views of the castle from this well-maintained family hotel. Bedrooms are bright and airy, well equipped and many are suitable for families. Residents have a comfortable lounge and a separate bar.
10rm(9🚿) (3fb) 🚭 in dining room CTV in all bedrooms [R] sB&B🚿£17-£20 dB&B🚿£34-£40 WB&B£119-£126 WBDi£175-£182 LDO 4pm
Lic ♨ CTV ⛳
Credit Cards [1][2][3][£]

GH [Q] *Neptune Hotel* Marine Terrace LL52 0EF ☎(0766) 522794
Apr-Sep
These sister establishments offer simple but soundly maintained accommodation, some of the bedrooms overlooking Cardigan Bay. They provide good value for money and are popular with holidaymakers.
8rm(1🛁3🚿) (2fb) CTV in 4 bedrooms LDO 5pm
Lic CTV P̸

CRICKHOWELL Powys Map **03** SO21

GH [Q][Q][Q] Dragon House Hotel High Street NP8 1BE ☎(0873) 810362 FAX (0873) 811868
This small town-centre hotel has been sympathetically converted and extended to provide a comfortable retreat, full of character. Bedrooms in the main house have pleasing decor and bold colours. Rooms in the rear courtyard are not quite so opulent but are also comfortable and well equipped. The bar and lounge are both cosy and the menu also caters for vegetarians.
13rm(8🛁🚿) Annexe 3🛁🚿 (3fb) 🚭 in 5 bedrooms 🚭 in dining room CTV in all bedrooms [R] **T** * sB&Bfr£23 sB&B🛁🚿fr£33 dB&Bfr£38 dB&B🛁🚿fr£48 LDO 8.30pm
Lic ♨ CTV
Credit Cards [1][2][3][£]

GH [Q][Q] The Fir's Tretower NP8 1RF ☎Bwlch(0874) 730780
Mary Eckley extends a warm welcome to her 300-year-old house, set in attractive lawns and gardens just off the A479 near the mediaeval Tretower Court and Castle. One of the four neat, cosy bedrooms is contained in a converted outbuilding and the dining room occupies the space where the barn once was; a spacious sitting room, warmed by a wood-burning stove in winter, features some fine exposed timbers.
3rm(1🛁🚿) Annexe 1🛁🚿 🚭 in bedrooms CTV in 1 bedroom [R] * dB&B£34 dB&B🛁🚿£42
♨ CTV
[£]

CRICKLADE Wiltshire Map **04** SU09

GH [Q][Q][Q] Chelworth Hotel Upper Chelworth SN6 6HD ☎Swindon(0793) 750440
Closed mid Dec-mid Jan
This family home constructed of mellow stone has been modernised and extended into a small hotel. Set in its own well tended gardens in the Cotswold village of Chelworth, it offers easy access to Swindon, Malmesbury and the M4. Bedrooms are modern and well equipped, and the comfortable lounge leads into the dining room.
7rm(6🚿) (1fb) CTV in 6 bedrooms [R] 🐕 (ex guide dogs) * sB&B£20-£30 sB&B🚿£25-£30 dB&B£40 WB&B£180-£210 LDO 7pm
Lic ♨ CTV

CRIEFF Tayside *Perthshire* Map **11** NN82

GH [Q][Q][Q] Comeley Bank 32 Burrell St PH7 4DT (on A822) ☎(0764) 653409
This tastefully decorated little guesthouse is located on the southern outskirts of the town. The attractive lounge and dining room reflect the house's Victorian character, whilst the simple bedrooms are bright and cheerful.
5rm(2🚿) (2fb) 🚭 in bedrooms 🚭 in dining room CTV in all bedrooms [R] * sB&B£15 dB&B£30 dB&B🚿£36 LDO 5pm
Lic ♨ CTV
[£]

CROESGOCH Dyfed Map **02** SM83

FH [Q][Q] Mrs A Charles ***Torbant** (SM845307)* SA62 5JN (just off A487 between Fishguard & St David's) ☎(0348) 831276
rs Nov-Etr
This 17th-century farmhouse is part of a busy working farm. Bedrooms are neat and bright, and public rooms are spacious and comfortable and include a function suite.
6rm(2🛁1🚿) (2fb) [R] 🐕 (ex guide dogs) LDO 6pm
Lic ♨ CTV 110 acres dairy

CROMER Norfolk Map **09** TG24

GH [Q][Q][Q] Beachcomber 17 Macdonald Road NR27 9AP (leaving Cromer via Runton Road, first left after the Cliftonville Hotel) ☎(0263) 513398
Closed 25-26 Dec
7rm(5🚿) (1fb) 🚭 in bedrooms CTV in all bedrooms [R] 🐕 * sB&B£14-£16 dB&B£30-£32 dB&B🚿£30-£35 WB&B£98-£112 WBDi£130-£136.50 LDO 4pm
lift ♨ CTV

GH [Q][Q] Birch House 34 Cabbell Road NR27 9HX ☎(0263) 512521
Great pride is taken in the maintenance of this no-smoking guest house, which is located a short distance west of the town centre. All the bedrooms have colour and satellite TV, and dinner is readily provided on request.
8rm(1🛁2🚿) (1fb) 🚭 CTV in all bedrooms [R] * sB&B£16 sB&B🛁🚿£19 dB&B£32 dB&B🛁🚿£38 WB&B£98-£112 WBDi£126-£140 LDO 4pm
Lic P̸
Credit Cards [1][3]

GH [Q][Q] Chellow Dene 23 MacDonald Road NR27 9AP ☎(0263) 513251
Mar-Nov
Some of the more spacious bedrooms at this cheerful, family-run guest house have had en suite showers installed. Good standards are maintained, and a lounge with a fish tank and a bright breakfast room are provided.
7rm(4🚿) (1fb)CTV in all bedrooms [R] sB&Bfr£17 dB&B🚿fr£34 LDO 5pm
Lic ♨ CTV

GH Q Q Q **Morden House** 20 Cliff Avenue NR27 0AN (off A140)
☎(0263) 513396

Morden House is a large late Victorian property south of the centre. The friendly owners offer old-fashioned hospitality and few modern trappings. A TV lounge is provided, and a dining room where a home-cooked dinner is served.

6rm(4⇨1♠) (1fb) ⚹ in dining room ⚹ in lounges ℝ ♒ (ex guide dogs) sB&B£20 sB&B⇨♠£21.50 dB&B£40 dB&B⇨♠£43 WB&B£133 WBDi£175-£182 LDO 5pm
Lic ⊪ CTV
Credit Cards 5

GH Q Q *Sandcliff Private Hotel* Runton Road NR27 9AS
☎(0263) 512888

Closed 21 Dec-4 Jan

A cheerful atmosphere and simple standards are maintained at this large Victorian property on the seafront to the west of the centre. There is a large bar-lounge and a breakfast room where dinner is also served.

24rm(9⇨10♠) (10fb) CTV in all bedrooms ℝ LDO 6pm
Lic

GH Q Q Q **Westgate Lodge Private Hotel** 10 MacDonald Road NR27 9AP ☎(0263) 512840

Mar-29 Nov

Westgate Lodge is a smartly kept guest house run in a friendly and relaxed manner by Mr and Mrs Robson. There is a recently refurbished restaurant and bar area, and hairdryers and radio clock alarms have been added to all the bedrooms.

11♠ (4fb) ⚹ in bedrooms ⚹ in dining room CTV in all bedrooms ℝ ♒ ⚹ dB&B♠fr£47 WBDi£197.40 LDO 6.30pm
Lic ⊪ nc3yrs

CROMHALL Avon   Map **03** ST69

FH Q Q Mrs S Scolding **Kimber's Lea** *(ST699905)* Talbots End GL12 8AJ (2m from junct 14 M5)
☎Chipping Sodbury(0454) 294065

Etr-Sep

A farmhouse with views across farmland in a peaceful location. Bedrooms are attractive and there is a large lounge.

3rm ⚹ ⚹ ⚹ sB&Bfr£16 dB&Bfr£32 WB&Bfr£112
⊪ CTV nc5yrs 175 acres dairy

CROSTHWAITE Cumbria   Map **07** SD49

SELECTED

GH Q Q Q Q **Crosthwaite House** LA8 8BP
☎(05395) 68264

mid Mar-mid Nov

The Dawson family ensure that guests are well looked after at this charming 18th-century house. Bedrooms are bright and fresh and there are lovely views from the front of the house. Public rooms are well furnished and home cooking is a feature of the meals.

6♠ CTV in 3 bedrooms ℝ ⚹ sB&B♠£20-£22 dB&B♠£40-£44 WBDi£210-£220 LDO 5pm
Lic ⊪ CTV

CROYDE Devon   Map **02** SS43

SELECTED

GH Q Q Q Q **Moorsands House Hotel** Moor Lane EX33 1NP
☎(0271) 890781

Apr-Oct

In a residential area between the village and the beach is this white, semidetached Victorian villa. Stained glass panels in the

front door and a fireplace in the comfortable lounge are some of the original features. There is a second lounge with a bar. The bright, well kept bedrooms have matching floral fabrics and compact en suite shower rooms. The Daltons offer a cheerful welcome to their guests.

8♠ (3fb) CTV in all bedrooms ℝ
Lic ⊪ CTV nc2yrs
Credit Cards 1 3

GH Q Q Q **West Winds** Moor Lane EX33 1PA (at village centre turn left and first left again following signs to Croyde Bay)
☎(0271) 890489 FAX (0271) 890489

Apr-Nov

4rm(3⇨♠) CTV in all bedrooms ℝ ⚹ dB&Bfr£38 dB&B⇨♠£42 WB&B£133-£147 WBDi£196-£210 LDO 7.30pm
Lic ⊪
Credit Cards 1 3

P R E M I E R ❀ S E L E C T E D

GH Q Q Q Q Q **Whiteleaf At Croyde** EX33 1PN (turn off A361 at Braunton for Croyde, Whiteleaf is on left at `Road Narrows' sign)
☎(0271) 890266

Closed Dec, Jan, Feb & 2weeks Apr, Jul & Oct

Set back from Croyde Bay's golden sands and away from the centre of the village, a 1930s detached house surrounded by colourful gardens offers accommodation in well equipped, individually furnished and decorated bedrooms. Dinner is served at 8.15pm, and guests are asked to make their choice two hours earlier from the varied and imaginative range of dishes available - salmon quenelles with a vermouth and pink peppercorn sauce, for example, might be followed by soup and a honeyed leg of Lunesdale duck served with fresh vegetables. Breakfast is equally interesting, the house speciality being baked eggs with smoked salmon, and a choice of freshly made breads is also provided.

3⇨♠ (1fb) ⚹ in dining room ⚹ in 1 lounge CTV in all bedrooms ℝ T sB&B⇨♠£37 dB&B⇨♠£54 WB&Bfr£189 WBDifr£294 LDO 6.30pm
Lic ⊪
Credit Cards 1 3

FH Q Q Q Mr & Mrs Barnes **Denham Farm & Country House** *(SS480404)* North Buckland EX33 1HY
☎(0271) 890297 FAX (0271) 890297

Closed 18-28 Dec

Jean and Tony Barnes' delightful farmhouse is in a village setting some two miles from the breathtaking coastline at Croyde. The bedrooms are bright, well furnished, and equipped with modern en suite facilities. Jean offers good home cooked meals in the informal restaurant, and a comfortable bar-lounge is provided with a separate quiet lounge.

10⇨♠ (2fb) ⚹ in dining room ⚹ in 1 lounge CTV in all bedrooms ℝ ♒ dB&B⇨♠£40-£50 WB&B£140-£147 WBDi£190-£217 LDO 6pm
Lic ⊪ CTV ⚙ games room table tennis skittle alley 160 acres beef sheep
£

CROYDON Greater London Map **04** TQ36

GH [Q][Q][Q] Kirkdale Hotel 22 St Peter's Road CR0 1HD
☎081-688 5898 FAX 081-680 6001
Closed 2 days Xmas
The Wallingfords are the welcoming hosts at this Victorian house, situated in a residential area not far from the town centre. They continue to make improvements and nearly all the rooms now have en suite facilities. Bedrooms vary in size, but are bright, pretty and very well kept, and direct dial telephones have recently been installed. The house has some period features including stained glass on the staircase, ceiling mouldings and a mahogany fire surround in the reception/lounge, where plants and ornaments create a friendly atmosphere. On sunny days guests can sit outside on the patio.
19🛁🚿 🚭 in bedrooms 🚭 in dining room CTV in all bedrooms Ⓡ **T** 🐕 (ex guide dogs) ✱ sB&B🛁🚿£20-£35 dB&B🛁🚿£40-£55 WB&B£139-£180
Lic 🅿 CTV
Credit Cards [1][2][3][£]

GH [Q][Q][Q] Markington Hotel 9 Haling Park Road CR2 6NG (turn off A235 between the Swan & Sugar Loaf Pub and the Red Deer Pub) ☎081-681 6494 FAX 081-688 6530
rs Xmas
Well cared for accommodation is provided at this personally run guest house located to the south of Croydon. Public rooms include a popular bar, a snooker room and a dining room where simple evening meals are served. There is a car park with security lighting to the rear.
21rm(20🛁🚿) (2fb) 🚭 in 4 bedrooms CTV in all bedrooms Ⓡ **T** 🐕 ✱ sB&B🛁🚿£30-£45 dB&B£40 dB&B🛁🚿£45-£50 LDO 8.30pm
Lic 🅿 CTV
Credit Cards [1][2][3][£]

GH [Q][Q] *Oakwood Hotel* 69 Outram Road CR0 6XJ
☎081-654 2835
rs 25 & 26 Dec
This Victorian house, in a quiet residential side street, has been run for many years by Mrs Delve. Bedrooms vary in size but all are clean and bright and have en suite facilities. There is a lounge with a pool table and a combined bar and breakfast room.
17rm(10🛁7🚿) (3fb) CTV in all bedrooms Ⓡ LDO 8pm
Lic 🅿 CTV sauna solarium
Credit Cards [1][2][3][5]

CRUDEN BAY Grampian *Aberdeenshire* Map **15** NK03

INN[Q][Q][Q] Red House Hotel Aulton Road AB42 7NJ
☎Peterhead(0779) 812215 FAX (0779) 812320
6rm(3🛁🚿) (1fb)CTV in all bedrooms Ⓡ **T** ✱ sB&B£30-£45 dB&B£60-£80 dB&B🛁🚿£70-£90 (incl dinner) LDO 9pm
🅿 ⛳18 snooker
Credit Cards [1][2][3][£]

CULLODEN MOOR Highland *Inverness-shire* Map **14** NH74

FH [Q][Q] Mrs E M C Alexander **Culdoich** *(NH755435)* IV1 2EP
☎Inverness(0463) 790268
May-Oct
A small traditional farmhouse overlooking the Culloden Battlefield, situated just off the Davicot-Cawdor road. It has two spacious bedrooms which are comfortably furnished, and there is a cosy TV lounge and a separate dining room where guests are served a hearty breakfast around a communal table.
2rm (1fb) 🚭 in dining room Ⓡ 🐕 ✱ dB&B£30-£32 LDO 5pm
CTV 200 acres mixed
[£]

CULLOMPTON Devon Map **03** ST00

See also Uffculme

SELECTED

GH [Q][Q][Q][Q] Rullands Rull Lane EX15 1NQ
☎(0884) 33356 FAX (0884) 35890
A 15th-century longhouse, Rullands is set in beautiful rolling countryside. It provides modern facilities while retaining original features such as a circular stairway and old cruck beams on the landing. Public areas are shared with non-resident diners when the restaurant is open (from Tuesday to Saturday).
6rm(4🛁🚿) (1fb) 🚭 in bedrooms 🚭 in dining room CTV in all bedrooms Ⓡ ✱ sB&B£29 sB&B🛁🚿£32-£35 dB&B🛁🚿£45-£50 LDO 9.45pm
Lic 🅿 nc12yrs 🎾(hard)
Credit Cards [1][3]

CWMDUAD Dyfed Map **02** SN33

🛏 🍺 **GH [Q][Q][Q] Neuadd-Wen** SA33 6XJ (alongside A484, 9m N of Carmarthen) ☎Cynwyl Elfed(0267) 281438
This family-run guesthouse and restaurant lies in a peaceful wooded valley. There are two lounges available for residents.
7rm(5🛁🚿) (1fb) 🚭 in dining room 🚭 in 1 lounge CTV in all bedrooms Ⓡ sB&B£13-£14.50 sB&B🛁🚿£15-£16.50 dB&B£26-£29 dB&B🛁🚿£30-£33 WB&B£86-£95 WBDi£122-£140 LDO 7.30pm
Lic 🅿 CTV
Credit Cards [1][3][£]

DALBEATTIE Dumfries & Galloway *Kirkcudbrightshire* Map **11** NX86

SELECTED

GH [Q][Q][Q][Q] Auchenskeoch Lodge DG5 4PG (5m E off B793) ☎Southwick(038778) 277 due to change to (0387) 780277 FAX (0387) 780277
Etr-Oct
5🛁🚿 🚭 in dining room Ⓡ ✱ sB&B🛁🚿£30-£32 dB&B🛁🚿£46-£50 LDO 8pm
Lic CTV 🎾(grass)🎣 snooker croquet lawn
Credit Cards [1][3]

🛏 🍺 **INN[Q][Q] Pheasant Hotel** 1 Maxwell Street DG5 4AH
☎(0556) 610345
A feature of this town centre hotel is its 'all you can eat' buffet lunch, available Monday to Saturday in the pleasant restaurant. A special children's menu is also available. The bar is open all day and at least two real ales are on offer. Bedrooms are functional and clean and most have en suite facilities.
7rm(6🛁🚿) (3fb)CTV in all bedrooms Ⓡ **T** 🐕 (ex guide dogs) sB&B£14-£19 sB&B🛁🚿£19-£25 dB&B£28 dB&B🛁🚿£38-£45 Lunch £3.75-£5.50&alc Dinner £6.75-£7.50&alc LDO 9pm
🅿
[£]

DALCROSS Highland *Iverness-shire* Map **14** NH75

FH [Q][Q][Q] Mrs M Pottie **Easter Dalziel Farmhouse** *(NH755509)* Easter Dalziel Farm IV1 2JL
☎Ardersier(0667) 462213 FAX (0667) 462213
Closed 20 Dec-20 Jan rs 1-20 Dec & 20 Jan-28 Feb
Many visitors return year after year to this delightful early Victorian farmhouse, which is set amid gentle wooded countryside, and is convenient for Inverness Airport. The spacious bedrooms are tastefully decorated and comfortably furnished with both traditional and period pieces, though they lack facilities such as en suite bathrooms and telephones. There is a cosy lounge and a dining room furnished with antiques where hearty breakfasts are served at a sturdy oak table. Evening meals are available by arrangement.

3rm ® dB&B£30-£34 WB&B£105-£112 WBDi£175-£182 LDO 10am
CTV 210 acres arable/beef/sheep
Credit Cards 1 3 £

DALKEITH Lothian *Midlothian* Map **11** NT36

INNQQ *Barley Bree Motel* 3 Easthouses Road EH22 4DH (0.5m on B6482, off A68) ☎031-663 3105
This unusual operation combines a comfortable Indian restaurant, that also offers European menus, a public bar, a function room and bright, cheerful bedrooms that are nicely equipped. The Barley Bree is on the southern outskirts of Dalkeith.
4⇄ſ\ CTV in all bedrooms ® LDO 11.30pm
Ⅲ. snooker skittles
Credit Cards 1 2 3

DALMALLY Strathclyde *Argyllshire*

See **Ardbrecknish**

DARLINGTON Co Durham Map **08** NZ21

GHQQQ **Woodland** 63 Woodland Road DL3 7BQ (on A68) ☎(0325) 461908
Family owned and run, this guest house is part of a Victorian terrace beside the A68 just south of the centre of the town. Attractively furnished throughout, it offers well equipped bedrooms and a comfortable lounge.
8rm(1⇄ſ\) (2fb) ⊁ in dining room CTV in all bedrooms ® ✳
sB&B£20-£24 sB&B⇄ſ£29 dB&B£34 dB&B⇄ſ£40
Ⅲ. CTV
£

SELECTED

FHQQQQ Mr & Mrs D & A Armstrong **Clow Beck House** *(NZ281100)* Monk End Farm, Croft on Tees DL2 2SW ☎(0325) 721075
Clow Beck is a modern-style farmhouse set in open countryside on the edge of the village of Croft-on-Tees. There are two lovely bedrooms in the main house and some spacious rooms in a nearby annexe. The lounge is decorated in blue and has a delightful Chinese carpet and comfortable deep seating. Breakfast is served at one large table.
2rm(1ſ\) Annexe 3⇄ſ\ ⊁ in dining room CTV in all bedrooms ® ⊁ ✳ sB&B£25-£34 sB&B⇄ſ£30-£34
dB&B£38 dB&B⇄ſ£42-£47
Ⅲ. CTV ✔ 90 acres mixed
£

DARTMOUTH Devon Map **03** SX85

SELECTED

GHQQQQ **Boringdon House** 1 Church Road TQ6 9HQ ☎(0803) 832235
Mar-Dec
3⇄ ⊁ CTV in all bedrooms ® ⊁ sB&B⇄£30-£49 dB&B⇄£45-£49 WB&B£275-£315
Ⅲ.

SELECTED

GHQQQQ **Captains House** 18 Clarence Street TQ6 9NW ☎(0803) 832133
A charming small Georgian Grade II listed house built about 1730 and conveniently situated in a quiet street close to the shops, harbour and River Dart. Personally run by the

---

enthusiastic owners Ann and Nigel Jestico, bed and breakfast is provided with good standards of housekeeping throughout. Bedrooms are individually furnished and decorated with character and charm, with modern facilities and several extra touches. Superb English breakfasts using fresh local produce are served in the dining room or bedrooms. There are local car parks nearby, and the guesthouse is within walking distance of the ferry and quayside.
5rm(3⇄2ſ\) ⊁ in 1 bedrooms ⊁ in dining room CTV in all bedrooms ® sB&B⇄ſ£24-£28 dB&B⇄ſ£34-£48
WB&B£105-£140
Ⅲ. nc5yrs
Credit Cards 2 £

P R E M I E R ⚜ **S E L E C T E D**

GHQQQQQ **Ford House** 44 Victoria Road TQ6 9DX ☎(0803) 834047
Mar-Dec

A detached Regency town house is situated 500 yards from the harbour and quayside. Two of the three bedrooms are on the lower ground floor level and all of them are individually furnished and decorated with flair, featuring a selection of antiques and objets d'art. The rooms are well equipped and have spacious private bathrooms. Dinner is taken around a large mahogany table, with a daily changing set Cordon Bleu menu using fresh local produce, especially fish; a range of vegetarian dishes is also available. An à la carte breakfast is served until midday, and there is an open log fire in the drawing room. Tea is served in the sheltered garden on sunny days, and car parking is available at the rear. The hotel is unlicensed, but will arrange local delivery of alcohol and allow guests to bring their own drinks.
3⇄ſ\ in dining room CTV in all bedrooms ® T sB&B⇄ſ£35-£50 dB&B⇄ſ£46-£60 WB&B£161-£322
LDO noon
Ⅲ.
Credit Cards 1 2 3 £

GHQQQ *Sunny Banks* 1 Vicarage Hill TQ6 9EN (centre of town, 200yds from post office, behind bowling green) ☎(0803) 832766
Friendly owners Rosemary and Shaun Pound welcome guests to their guest house situated in a residential area two minutes' walk from the town centre and quay. The bedrooms are bright, attractively decorated and well equipped, and there is a small comfortable lounge. A set dinner using the best of local produce is available in the dining room if ordered in advance.
10rm(2⇄4ſ\) (2fb) CTV in all bedrooms ® LDO 7.30pm
Lic Ⅲ. CTV

DATCHET Berkshire Map **04** SU97

GHQQQ *The Beeches* 19 The Avenue SL3 9DQ ☎Slough(0753) 580722
The Beeches is a large Victorian house, close to the station and village, which is naturally well furnished and comfortable. Bedrooms on two upper floors are spacious and decorative, and facilities include satellite TV. Public areas are restricted to a sunny breakfast room.
7rm(6⇄ſ\) (2fb) CTV in all bedrooms ® ⊁
Ⅲ.
Credit Cards 1 3

DAWLISH Devon   Map **03** SX97

GH Ⓠ *Mimosa* 11 Barton Terrace EX7 9QH (on entering Dawlish follow signs to Museum, Mimosa is directly opposite)
☎(0626) 863283
Close to the town centre and beaches, this holiday guesthouse is family run.
9rm(1🏠) (4fb) 🗙 (ex guide dogs) LDO 3pm
Lic ⊞ CTV nc3yrs

SELECTED

GH Ⓠ Ⓠ Ⓠ Ⓠ **Walton House** Plantation Terrace EX7 9DR (off A379) ☎(0626) 862760
Quietly located but within walking distance of the town centre, Walton House is a grade II listed Georgian property, now run by the welcoming owners, John and Doreen Newton. It has comfortable, well equipped bedrooms and a high standard of cleanliness throughout. Hearty breakfasts are served by Mr Newton.
6⇄🏠 (1fb) ⊁ in dining room CTV in all bedrooms Ⓡ 🗙 (ex guide dogs) dB&B⇄🏠£28-£38
⊞
Credit Cards [1] [3]

DEBDEN GREEN Essex   Map **05** TL53

FH Ⓠ Mrs K M Low **Wychbars** *(TL579320)* CB11 3NA (at end of long unclassified lane off B1051) ☎Bishops Stortford(0279) 850362
Remotely situated, this 200-year-old moated, whitewashed farmhouse stands in 3.5 acres and offers 2 simply furnished bedrooms with a shared shower room.
2rm CTV in all bedrooms Ⓡ sB&B£18 dB&B£34
lift ⊞ CTV 600 acres arable non-working
£

DENBIGH Clwyd   Map **06** SJ06

GH Ⓠ Ⓠ **Cayo** 74 Vale Street LL16 3BW ☎(0745) 812686
Closed Xmas
A red-brick town house close to the town centre has been run by the MacCormack family for nearly 20 years. The bedrooms are pleasantly decorated and there is a television lounge. The dining room offers good home cooking. This is a very friendly place and street parking is easy.
6rm(1⇄3🏠) ✳ sB&B£15-£16 dB&Bfr£30 dB&B⇄🏠£32 LDO 2pm
Lic ⊞ CTV ⸙
Credit Cards [1] [2] [3] £

DENNY Central *Stirlingshire*   Map **11** NS88

FH Ⓠ Ⓠ Ⓠ Mr & Mrs Steel **The Topps** *(NS757843)* Fintry Road FK6 5JF (just off B818, 4m W) ☎(0324) 822471
A popular base for visiting businessmen and tourists alike, this modern chalet-style farmhouse enjoys a peaceful rural setting on a slope beside the B818 some four miles west of Denny. Efficiently run, it offers a relaxed, friendly atmosphere and Taste of Scotland fare based on the best fresh produce available; dinner is now served to non-residents. Bedrooms, though variable in size, are comfortable, and the cosy little lounge provides both a dispense bar and plenty of reading material.
8rm(1⇄7🏠) (1fb) CTV in all bedrooms Ⓡ LDO 5pm
Lic ⊞ CTV ⸙ 300 acres cashmere goats sheep
Credit Cards [1] [3]

DERBY Derbyshire   Map **08** SK33

See also Shottle

GH Ⓠ Ⓠ **Dalby House Hotel** 100 Radbourne Street, off Windmill Hill Lane DE22 3BU (turn off A52 into Windmill Hill Lane near A52/A38 junct) ☎(0332) 342353

This large detached house provides accommodation in a quiet residential area, and has ample enclosed car parking. The public rooms include a comfortable ground floor lounge and a light appealing dining room which looks out over the pleasant walled garden. Bedrooms are of variable sizes and offer fresh sound accommodation.
9rm (2fb) ⊁ in dining room CTV in all bedrooms Ⓡ sB&B£16-£18 dB&B£28-£32 LDO 4pm
⊞ CTV
£

GH Ⓠ Ⓠ Ⓠ *Georgian House Hotel* 32/34 Ashbourne Road DE22 3AD ☎(0332) 349806
Georgian House is a smart little hotel in a conservation area of the city's west end. Public rooms, dominated by the restaurant, retain much of their original character, and a further lounge area is being created. A new style of food operation was being launched at the time of our visit, with a good choice offered from market and à la carte menus, now also served to non-residents. Bedrooms are pleasantly furnished with dark wood fittings and floral fabrics. Four-poster and ground floor rooms are available.
21rm(14⇄🏠) (5fb) CTV in all bedrooms Ⓡ T LDO 9.30pm
Lic ⊞ CTV ⸙

GH Ⓠ Ⓠ Ⓠ **Rangemoor Park Hotel** 67 Macklin Street DE1 1LF ☎(0332) 347252 FAX (0332) 369319
Simple accommodation in a terraced house near town centre.
24rm(13⇄🏠) (3fb) ⊁ in dining room CTV in all bedrooms Ⓡ T sB&B£23-£25 sB&B⇄🏠£35-£36 dB&B£35-£37 dB&B⇄🏠£48-£50
⊞ CTV
Credit Cards [1] [2] [3] [5] £

GH Ⓠ Ⓠ *Rollz Hotel* 684-8 Osmaston Road DE2 8GT (on A514 2m S) ☎(0332) 341026
Light, clean and modestly appointed accommodation is offered at this predominantly business establishment on the A514 about two miles south of the city centre. Colour TVs with satellite channels have been installed in the bedrooms. A comfortable lounge bar is readily available to guests and a set evening meal is provided on request.
14rm (1fb) Ⓡ 🗙 (ex guide dogs) LDO 9pm
Lic ⊞ CTV

DERVAIG See **MULL, ISLE OF**

DEVIL'S BRIDGE Dyfed   Map **06** SN77

GH Ⓠ Ⓠ **Mount Hazel** Pontrhydygroes SY25 6DQ (turn off B4343 at Pontrhydygroes Post Office/General stores, establishment approx 600yds on left) ☎Pontrhydygroes(0974) 282289
This large building is just 500 yards from the village post office, up a steep private road, and yet it enjoys a tranquil setting overlooking a wooded valley. There is a spacious lounge and a dining room where both lunch and dinner are served on request. The accommodation is simple.
3rm(2🏠) (1fb) CTV in all bedrooms Ⓡ ✳ dB&Bfr£30 dB&B🏠£34-£38 WB&B£96-£118 WBDi£150-£171 LDO any time
Lic ⊞
£
See advertisement on p.155.

DEVIZES Wiltshire   Map **04** SU06

GH Ⓠ Ⓠ Ⓠ **Pinecroft** Potterne Road SN10 5DA (0.25m S of town square on A360 to Salisbury opposite 'Southgate' public house) ☎(0380) 721433 FAX (0380) 728368
A part-Georgian, part-Edwardian family home within easy walking distance of the town centre offers comfortable, clean bedrooms. Breakfast is served at one large table.
5⇄🏠 (1fb) ⊁ in 4 bedrooms ⊁ in dining room ⊁ in lounges CTV in all bedrooms Ⓡ 🗙 sB&B£20-£24 sB&B⇄🏠£24

▶

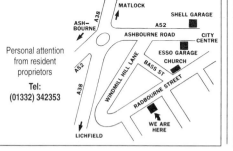

dB&B£30-£32 dB&B🛁🚿£38 WB&B£100-£150 WBDi£150-£200

▥ 🚗 mountain bikes for hire badminton

Credit Cards [1][2][3][£]

GH [Q][Q][Q] ***Rathlin*** Wick Lane SN10 5DP (off A360 on outskirts of town) ☎(0380) 721999

Rathlin is a family home situated in a residential area close to the town centre. All the rooms have en suite showers, colour TV and hospitality trays. There is a comfortable lounge with a tranquil Edwardian atmosphere, and dinner is served in the cosy dining room.

4🚿 CTV in all bedrooms [R] 🐕 LDO 6pm

▥

SELECTED

FH [Q][Q][Q][Q] Mrs O Webster ***Potterne Park Farm*** *(SU006573)* Potterne SN10 5QT ☎(0380) 724257

Closed Dec

3rm(1🛁1🚿) [R] 🐕 LDO 10am

▥ CTV nc12yrs 492 acres arable

DIBDEN Hampshire — Map **04** SU40

GH [Q][Q] **Dale Farm** Manor Road, Applemore Hill SO45 5TJ (A326 towards Fawley 1st rdbt sign to Applemore then 1st right after rdbt into Manor Rd after 200yds turn right) ☎Southampton(0703) 849632

Closed Xmas

This attractive 18th-century former farmhouse lies half hidden behind a riding stables down an unmade road. Modern bedrooms are bright and cosy, some overlooking the forest, and breakfast is served in a pine-furnished lounge/dining room.

6rm (2fb)[R] 🐕 (ex guide dogs) ✱ sB&B£18-£19 dB&B£31-£34 WB&B£85-£100 WBDi£160 LDO 11am

▥ CTV ⛳ U

[£]

DIDDLEBURY Shropshire — Map **07** SO58

SELECTED

GH [Q][Q][Q][Q] **The Glebe** SY7 9DH (4m NE of Craven Arms on B4368) ☎Munslow(01584) 841221

Situated near Diddlesbury village stream, the pleasant lawns and garden of this impressive 400-year-old Elizabethan farmhouse are overlooked by the church's Norman tower. Three bedrooms are housed in a converted outbuilding and two share the character of the house with exposed wall timbers. The panelled sitting room has a welcoming wood burning stove, and an adjacent bar offers similar comfort. Evening meals are available by arrangement only in the flag-stoned dining room, which is furnished with fine period pieces. For many years the Wilkes family have offered their guests warm hospitality and are now assisted by son Adrian.

3🛁🚿 🚭 in bedrooms 🚭 in dining room CTV in all bedrooms [R] 🐕 (ex guide dogs) dB&B🛁🚿£45-£52

Lic ▥ nc8yrs

DINTON Buckinghamshire — Map **04** SP71

FH [Q][Q][Q] Mrs J M W Cook **Wallace** *(SP770110)* HP17 8UF (from A418 take the turning marked Dinton/Ford, then 1st left signed Upton, where farm can be found on the right) ☎Aylesbury(0296) 748660 FAX (0296) 748851

This delightful 16th-century farmhouse is situated in the heart of the countryside. The comfortable bedrooms are spacious and equipped with en suites or private bathrooms. There is a beamed sitting room with an open fire and TV, leading onto the patio. Breakfast is served at a communal table in the kitchen, beside an inglenook fireplace and bread ovens. A further highlight of a stay here is the range of animals at the farm: rare breeds of sheep, an aviary and heavy horses. The lovely grounds include a pond and pleasant walks.

3rm(2🛁🚿) (1fb) 🚭 in bedrooms 🚭 in dining room [R] 🐕 (ex guide dogs) sB&Bfr£28 dB&B🛁🚿£38-£40

▥ CTV ⛳ 70 acres beef cattle sheep

Credit Cards [1][3][£]

DIRLETON Lothian *East Lothian* — Map **12** NT58

INN[Q] **Castle** EH39 5EP (off A198) ☎(0620) 850221

Closed 21 Dec-5 Jan rs Nov-Apr

Overlooking the ruins of Dirleton Castle, this small family-run inn beside the village green is a popular base for golfers. There is a choice of bars, accommodation offers good value, and the atmosphere is friendly.

4rm(3🛁1🚿) Annexe 4rm CTV in 4 bedrooms [R] ✱ sB&Bfr£20 sB&B🛁🚿£25 dB&Bfr£40 dB&B🛁🚿£50 LDO 8.30pm

▥ CTV pool table

Credit Cards [1][3]

DOLGELLAU Gwynedd — Map **06** SH71

FH [Q][Q][Q] Mr & Mrs D I Jones **Fronolau Farm Restaurant** *(SH747176)* Tabor LL40 2PS (2m SE) ☎(0341) 422361

Situated under Cader Idris with views over the Mawddach Estuary, an old stone farmhouse has been converted to create this popular restaurant with rooms. A cosy bar is provided, and a spacious lounge with an inglenook fireplace and exposed timbers. By the end of 1994 there should be a further six en suite bedrooms and a large function room.

10rm(6🛁🚿) (4fb) 🚭 in 4 bedrooms 🚭 in area of dining room CTV in all bedrooms [R] ✱ sB&Bfr£17.50 sB&B🛁🚿fr£30 dB&B£29-£32 dB&B🛁🚿£39-£43 WB&B£91.35-£122.85 LDO 10pm

Lic 🚗 40 acres sheep

[£]

🛏☕ **FH [Q][Q]** Mrs E W Price **Glyn** *(SH704178)* LL40 1YA (1m W, via A493) ☎(0341) 422286

Mar-Nov

This 300-year-old farmhouse is part of a working farm set in the wooded hillside high above the town. The bedrooms are neat and well decorated and one has recently been fitted with an en suite shower. There is a cosy lounge and a dining room with an open fire and a fine Welsh dresser. Trout fishing is available nearby.

4rm(1🚿) (1fb) 🚭 in dining room CTV in 2 bedrooms [R] sB&Bfr£12.50 dB&B£27-£29 dB&B🚿£32 WB&Bfr£80

▥ ⛳ 150 acres mixed

[£]

DONCASTER South Yorkshire — Map **08** SE50

GH [Q][Q] **Almel Hotel** 20 Christchurch Road DN1 2QL ☎(0302) 365230 FAX (0302) 341434

A double-fronted Victorian property with bay windows and decorative herring-bone brickwork, situated quite close to the town centre. Public areas are neat and fresh-looking, offering guests a lounge, a well stocked bar and a dining room. Evening meals are served from 5-8 pm. Bedrooms have fitted furniture and a good range of facilities. Guests should note that they are expected to settle the bill when they arrive, and to pay a deposit if they require a front-door key.

30rm(24🛁🚿) (1fb)CTV in all bedrooms [R] ✱ sB&B£21-£27.50 sB&B🛁🚿£27.50-£31 dB&B£36-£40 dB&B🛁🚿fr£40 LDO 8pm

Lic ▥ CTV

Credit Cards [1][2][3][5]

INN[Q][Q] ***Nelsons Hotel*** Cleveland Street DN1 1TR ☎(0302) 344550 FAX (0302) 341596

This small privately owned hotel is situated in the town centre, close to the main shopping areas and within easy walking distance of the railway station. The bright and pleasant bar is busy and popular, and a good range of hot and cold bar meals are served. The bedrooms are soundly decorated and have modern furnishings. There is no car park, but plenty of public facilities are located in the area.

9rm (2fb) CTV in all bedrooms ® LDO 8pm

▥

Credit Cards ③

DORCHESTER Dorset   Map 03 SY69

See also Evershot & Winterbourne Abbas

GH ⓠⓠⓠ **The Creek** Ringstead DT2 8NG (take A352 Wareham rd,turn right after approx 4m onto A353 towards Weymouth. After 1m turn left to Ringsted Beach) ☎Warmwell(0305) 852251
A very comfortable family home located down a private toll road; much of the surrounding land is owned by the National Trust, although the beach is privately owned by the Fisher family. There are two bedrooms, in addition to self-catering accommodation, each having pretty, coordinating decor and reasonable facilities. Guests are offered tea on arrival in the sunny lounge which is comfortable, well furnished and faces the sea. Evening meals are taken around a shared dining table, and the family are cheerful and welcoming. Telephone reservations are advised, and smoking is not allowed in the bedrooms.

2rm(1👣) ⌘ in bedrooms ® 🐾 (ex guide dogs) LDO 10am
▥ CTV nc10yrs ⏃(heated)
ⓔ

Telephone national area codes are due to change by 16th April 1995. Please see the note under 'How to Use this Guide' at the front of the book.

The Castle Inn

Dirleton, East Lothian
Telephone: (01620) 850221

Overlooking the green of one of Scotland's most beautiful 'heirloom' villages and situated in an area surrounded by many well known golf courses — North Berwick, Muirfield, Gullane and Luffness.
The Castle Inn offers golfing parties of up to 14 accommodation in a *warm*, friendly atmosphere. *There are 4 en suite rooms in the hotel and four rooms sharing a bathroom in the annexe.* All rooms are centrally heated. Relax in the small lounge in front of the television or enjoy a glass of real ale with a bar lunch or supper.

For further information please contact Robin Stewart

MOUNT HAZEL
Guest House
Pontrhydygroes
Dyfed SY25 6DQ
AA QQ

Situated 4 miles south of Devils Bridge just off B4343. Offering remarkable bird life, wonderful walks and unspoiled picturesque countryside.
★ En suite rooms with tea/coffee facilities and colour TV.
★ Superb candlelit dinners
★ Traditional Welsh teas
★ Full English breakfast
★ Residential Licence
★ Log fires in lounge
★ Ample parking

For brochure Tel: 01974-282289

CHURCHVIEW
GUEST HOUSE
WINTERBOURNE ABBAS, DORCHESTER, DORSET DT2 9LS

QQQ

This 300-year-old Guesthouse, noted for its warm, friendly hospitality and delicious home cooking is located in a small village 5 miles west of Dorchester. Set in a designated area of outstanding natural beauty, Church-view makes an ideal touring base. All our comfortable rooms have tea making facilities and central heating, most en-suite. There are two lounges, one set aside for non-smokers, an attractive period dining room and well-stocked bar. Evening meal, bed and breakfast from £26.00 per person.

For further details please contact
Michael and Jane Deller. ☎ **(01305) 889296**

SELECTED

GH QQQQ Westwood House Hotel 29 High West Street DT1 1UP (Logis) ☎(0305) 268018 FAX (0305) 250282

Originally built as a coaching house for Lord Ilchester in 1815, this handsome Georgian town house stands at the top end of town. Personally managed by the proprietors, it offers individually styled bedrooms with good facilities and thoughtful extras such as bathrobes. Two of the en-suite bathrooms have spa baths. A good breakfast is served in the bright and airy conservatory breakfast room and there is an attractive lounge. Parking can be difficult during the day although there is a public car park near by.

7rm(5⇌⌐) (1fb)CTV in all bedrooms Ⓡ **T** sB&B£25-£38 dB&B£39.50-£45 dB&B⇌⌐£49.50-£59.50

Lic ▥ CTV

Credit Cards [1] [3] (£)

PREMIER SELECTED

GH QQQQQ Yalbury Cottage Country Lower Bockhampton DT2 8PZ (2.5m E off A35) ☎(0305) 262382

Closed Jan-mid Feb

This thatched cottage is set in a quiet rural area on the east side of the town, and has been restored and extended to provide comfortable accommodation. Bedrooms are individually furnished in modern styles and provide every convenience imaginable. Public areas are elegantly furnished and feature original oak beams and inglenook fireplaces. There is a stylish drawing room with comfortable seating, a log fire and plenty of books and magazines. A set price menu is offered in the candlelit dining room, with a limited but changing menu reflecting the individual style of Pauline Voss who uses only fresh, good quality produce. Her husband Rolf Voss has compiled a varied and informative wine list, and is happy to make suggestions.

8⇌⌐ ⊬ in 6 bedrooms CTV in all bedrooms Ⓡ ⊁ * sB&B⇌⌐£30.50-£34.50 dB&B⇌⌐£41-£55 WB&B£143.50-£161 WBDi£248.50-£266 LDO 7.30pm

Lic ▥ nc12yrs

Credit Cards [1] [3]

FH QQ Mrs M Tomblin **Lower Lewell** *(SY744897)* West Stafford DT2 8AP ☎(0305) 267169

3rm (2fb)Ⓡ * sB&B£16-£20 dB&B£30-£35

▥ CTV 250 acres mixed

DORNOCH Highland *Sutherland* Map **14** NH78

SELECTED

GH QQQQ Fourpenny Cottage Skelbo IV25 3QF ☎(0862) 810727

20 Feb-20 Dec

2⇌⌐ Annexe 2⌐ (1fb) ⊬ CTV in all bedrooms Ⓡ ⊁ (ex guide dogs) dB&B⇌⌐£45-£50 WB&B£157.50-£175 WBDi£241.50-£259 LDO 7pm

▥ CTV

DORRINGTON Shropshire Map **07** SJ40

GH QQQ Ashton Lees Ashton Lees SY5 7JW (6m S on A49) ☎(0743) 718378

Closed Feb

A very pleasant creeper-clad house offers clean, brightly decorated bedrooms equipped with TV and video. There is a comfortable lounge with a good supply of books and local guides. In the large rear gardens, shaded by ornamental trees, afternoon teas are served in good weather by Doreen Woodall, who also provides evening meals if advance warning is given.

3rm(1⇌⌐) ⊬ in bedrooms ⊬ in 1 lounge CTV in all bedrooms Ⓡ ⊁ sB&Bfr£17 sB&B⇌⌐fr£20 dB&Bfr£34 dB&B⇌⌐fr£40 WB&B£107-£125 LDO 9am

Lic CTV

(£)

DORSINGTON Warwickshire Map **04** SP14

FH QQQ Mrs M J Walters **Church** *(SP132495)* CV37 8AX ☎Stratford-on-Avon(0789) 720471 & (0831) 504194 FAX (0789) 720830

A large Georgian farmhouse situated in the centre of this small picturesque village, seven miles from Stratford. A single-storey stable block has been cleverly converted into modern bedrooms, with private bathrooms and attractive pink furniture; one room is especially designed for disabled guests. Three more spacious and traditionally furnished rooms are located in the main house. There is an open fire in the comfortable lounge, and the breakfast room is furnished with several antique pieces, together with a variety of bric-à-brac. The 127 acre farm is arable, with beef and horses, which guests are welcome to explore, with riding and fishing available.

3rm Annexe 4⇌⌐ (2fb) CTV in 4 bedrooms Ⓡ ⊁ (ex guide dogs) * dB&B£28-£31 dB&B⇌⌐£33-£36

▥ CTV ✓ stabling available 127 acres mixed

DOUGLAS See **MAN, ISLE OF**

DOVER Kent Map **05** TR34

GH QQQ Ardmore Private Hotel 18 Castle Hill Road CT16 1QW (on A258 adjct Dover Castle) ☎(0304) 205895 FAX (0304) 208229

Closed Xmas

4⌐ (1fb) ⊬ CTV in all bedrooms Ⓡ ⊁ dB&B⌐£30-£45

▥ ✗

GH QQ Beulah House 94 Crabble Hill, London Road CT17 0SA (on A256) ☎(0304) 824615

This is a late 19th-Century double fronted house with attractive, well-kept gardens. Bedroom furnishings and equipment are simple but adequate. The sitting room is comfortable and there is a well-decorated dining room offering a choice of breakfast.

8rm (3fb) ⊬ in dining room ⊬ in 1 lounge CTV in 1 bedroom ⊁ (ex guide dogs) * sB&B£20-£22 dB&B£38-£40 WB&Bfr£105

▥ CTV

(£)

GH QQQ Castle House 10 Castle Hill Road CT16 1QW ☎(0304) 201656 FAX (0304) 210197

Castle House is conveniently situated near to the castle, docks and town centre. Attractively decorated bedrooms are thoughtfully furnished and well-equipped, but public areas are limited to a very small lounge and a bright, fresh dining room serving a set price dinner menu and a choice of breakfast.

6⌐ (1fb) ⊬ CTV in all bedrooms Ⓡ ⊁ (ex guide dogs) * sB&B⌐£18-£28 dB&B⌐£28-£40 WB&B£90-£126 WBDi£140-£180 LDO 6pm

Lic ▥

Credit Cards [1] [2] [3] (£)

GH QQ Dell 233 Folkestone Road CT17 9SL ☎(0304) 202422

This brick-built Victorian terrace house is situated on the busy Folkestone road and has been run by proprietors Mr and Mrs Robbins for many years. Bedrooms are bright, simply furnished and immacuately maintained; they all use shared facilities. A small lounge area with TV adjoins the dining room, where a set breakfast is served from 7am; a continental breakfast tray is available for guests catching an early ferry.

5rm(1♠) (3fb)Ⓡ 🐾 (ex guide dogs) sB&B£16-£20 dB&B£28-£37 dB&B🌲£32-£42
▥ CTV
ⓛ

GH ⓆⓆ **Gateway Hovertel** Snargate Street CT17 9BZ (between East & West Ferry Terminals) ☎(0304) 205479
FAX (0304) 211504
Closed 23 Dec-6 Jan
This modern hotel overlooks the marina. It is designed, as its name suggests, to cater for ferry passengers, and there is ample private car parking. Bedrooms are adequately equipped, and there are several family rooms with travel cots and bunk beds. There is a small TV lounge, a large dining room and a small bar. Owners Mr and Mrs Peters personally supervise the running of the hotel, and a continental breakfast buffet is included in the room price, but full English breakfast is available for an extra charge.

27rm🌲🏠 (7fb)CTV in all bedrooms 🐾 (ex guide dogs)
sB&B🌲🏠£30-£35 dB&B🌲🏠£45-£50 LDO 7pm
Lic ▥ CTV
Credit Cards ① ③ ⓛ

GH ⓆⓆⓆ **Number One** 1 Castle Street CT16 1QH
☎(0304) 202007
Overlooked by the castle, this appealing Georgian end-of-terrace house is conveniently situated a few minutes' drive from the ferries and hoverport. The individually decorated bedrooms offer plenty of charm, being furnished with period pieces and several thoughtful extra touches. Garden rooms have their own entrance and are popular in the summer. There is an elegant lounge furnished with antiques. A set breakfast is served in bedrooms, or for early risers a light breakfast tray can be prepared the previous

▶

FOURPENNY COTTAGE

Dornoch Sutherland IV25 3QF
Telephone: 01862 810727
AA QQQQ Selected

Originally a highland croft which has been enlarged and modernised, stands in 2½ acres and overlooks the sandy beach of Dornoch Firth and Scottish Wild Life Nature Reserve at Loch Fleet. The cottage has four bedrooms all en suite and with colour TV and tea/coffee facilities. Delicious traditional cooked meals are a speciality and are served in the large dining room which overlooks the sea and open countryside. Ideally situated for touring and walking with golf, tennis and bowling all found locally.

𝕽𝖊𝖈𝖙𝖔𝖗𝖞 𝕳𝖔𝖚𝖘𝖊

Fore Street, Evershot, Dorset DT2 0JW
Telephone: (0193583) 273

An 18th century listed building of great charm, situated in this quiet and unspoilt Dorset village in an area of outstanding natural beauty made famous by Thomas Hardy's 'Tess of the D'Urbevilles'. Utmost comfort, with lovely centrally heated bedrooms each with en suite bathroom, colour TV, tea & coffee making facilities. The home cooking is superb with some exotic dishes to enjoy together with more traditional fare, including freshly baked bread from the Village Bakery and locally made sausages for your breakfast. Relax in the separate lounges with log fire during the winter months. Nearby many beautiful walks and places of interest to visit. Open all year except Christmas and New Year. Sorry no pets.

GATEWAY HOVERTEL

SNARGATE STREET **01304**
DOVER 205479

Tel: 205479
THE PETERS FAMILY
MEMBERS OF DOVER HOTELIERS GROUP

• **Overnight Guests Welcome**
• **27 rooms with bath or shower, WC and TV**
• **Family rooms**
• **Residents' Bar and Nightporter**
• **Breakfast from 3.00 a.m.!!**
• **Close to Hoverport, shops, restaurants and 'Takeaways'**
• **Between East and West Ferry Terminals**
• **Coach and Car Park alarmed, secure**
• **Group Rates**

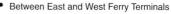

SAVE £10 by staying two nights – or stay three nights and only pay for two (not July/August)

night. Long term parking may be arranged, and some lock up garage space is available.
5rm(3🚿) (3fb) 🚭 in dining room 🚭 in lounges CTV in all bedrooms [R] 🐕 dB&B£34-£38 dB&B🚿£36-£42
♨
[£]

GH [Q][Q][Q] ***Peverall House Hotel*** 28 Park Avenue CT16 1HD
☎(0304) 202573 & 205088
This fine Victorian corner house is quietly situated in a residential area. Bedrooms are modestly furnished, well decorated and comfortable, and a relaxing sitting room leads to a dining room that serves a set menu of basic English dishes. Snacks are also available, as is a choice of breakfast.
6rm(2🛁) (2fb) CTV in all bedrooms [R] 🐕 LDO noon
Lic ♨ CTV

GH [Q][Q] St Brelades 80/82 Buckland Avenue CT16 2NW
☎(0304) 206126 FAX (0304) 211486
Set in a residential area on the fringe of the town centre, St Brelades offers clean but basic accommodation, some en suite. The dinner menu offers a choice of Indian and English dishes. There is also a small sitting room.
6rm(3🚿) (4fb) 🚭 in dining room 🚭 in lounges CTV in all bedrooms [R] 🐕 * sB&B£20-£24 dB&B£30-£38 dB&B🚿£34-£42
Lic ♨ CTV
Credit Cards [1] [3] [£]

GH [Q][Q][Q] St Martins 17 Castle Hill Road CT16 1QW
☎(0304) 205938 FAX (0304) 208229
Closed Xmas
Further improvements have taken place at this friendly guest house. There are now a number of spacious family rooms - clean comfortable and nicely decorated. There is also a relaxing lounge and a small dining room serving a choice of breakfast.
6🚿 (3fb) 🚭 CTV in all bedrooms [R] 🐕 dB&B🚿£30-£40
Lic ♨ P̸

SELECTED

GH [Q][Q][Q][Q] Wallett's Court West Cliffe, St Margarets-at-Cliffe CT15 6EW (1.5m NE of A2/A258 junct, off B2058)
☎(0304) 852424 FAX (0304) 853430
Closed 24-27 Dec rs Sun
Further upgrading has made this attractive, friendly house an even more pleasant place to stay. Spacious bedrooms are tastefully and comfortably furnished and have many modern facilities. The welcoming sitting room has lots of character as does the well-appointed restaurant where the chef/patron prepares dishes of high quality. Breakfast is served in the newly-built, bright conservatory overlooking the well-kept gardens.
3🛁🚿 Annexe 6🛁🚿 (1fb) 🚭 in dining room CTV in all bedrooms [R] T 🐕 (ex guide dogs) * sB&B🛁🚿£40-£60 dB&B🛁🚿£50-£70 LDO 8.30pm
Lic ♨ CTV 🏊 🎾(hard)games room
Credit Cards [1] [3]

DOWNHAM MARKET Norfolk Map **05** TF60

GH [Q][Q][Q] The Dial House 12 Railway Road PE38 9EB
☎(0366) 388358 FAX (0366) 382198
rs 24-31 Dec
Built of Carr stone, this pleasing 17th-century house stands on a relatively quiet road. The friendly proprietors make every effort to cater for personal requests, particularly dietary needs. The main drawing room serves also as a dining room and there is another quiet lounge. Smoking is not permitted in the cheerfully decorated bedrooms.
3rm(2🛁🚿) 🚭 [R] 🐕 (ex guide dogs) * sB&B£18 sB&B🛁🚿£25 dB&B£29 dB&B🛁🚿£35 WB&B£91-£110 WBDi£154-£173 LDO noon
♨ CTV

DOWNTON Wiltshire Map **04** SU12

GH [Q][Q][Q] Warren 15 High Street SP5 3PG ☎(0725) 510263
Closed 15 Dec-15 Jan
A charming house set at the heart of the village, opposite the Post Office, dates back to 1450, and retains its period character in antique-furnished rooms with exposed beams. One of the two lounges is warmed by a real fire, and the French windows of a pretty dining room open onto the patio and garden. A delightfully lived-in, cared-for and relaxing atmosphere pervades the entire house.
6rm(2🛁🚿) (1fb) 🚭 in dining room [R] sB&B£25-£28 sB&B🛁🚿£30-£32 dB&B£38-£40 dB&B🛁🚿£40-£42
♨ CTV nc5yrs
[£]
See advertisement under SALISBURY

DREWSTEIGNTON Devon Map **03** SX79

GH [Q][Q] The Old Rectory EX6 6QT ☎(0647) 281269
FAX (0647) 21269
Closed 21-31 Dec
3rm(1🛁🚿) 🚭 [R] 🐕 * sB&Bfr£18 sB&B🛁🚿fr£21 dB&Bfr£30 dB&B🛁🚿fr£36
♨
[£]

DROITWICH Hereford & Worcester Map **03** SO86

GH [Q][Q] The Larches 46 Worcester Road WR9 8AJ (on A38 by Highfields Hospital) ☎(0905) 773441
A fine old house dating back to 1729, set in wooded grounds on the Worcester road just a short distance from the town centre, offers accommodation in four modern bedrooms equipped with television sets and thoughtful extras like hot water bottles. Smoking is not permitted anywhere in the house. Car parking facilities are available.
4rm CTV in all bedrooms [R] 🐕 (ex guide dogs) LDO 10am
♨

DROXFORD Hampshire Map **04** SU61

GH [Q][Q] ***Coach House Motel*** Brockbridge SO3 1QT
☎(0489) 877812
This converted coach house is situated on the outskirts of this quiet village in the picturesque Meon valley. The motel-style bedrooms are on two levels and the reception office is combined with a small breakfast room. Full cooked breakfast is included in the room tariff. There is a pub nearby with licensed restaurant facilities.
8rm(6🛁2🚿) CTV in all bedrooms [R] 🐕 (ex guide dogs)
♨
Credit Cards [1] [2] [3] [5]

DRUMBEG Highland *Sutherland* Map **14** NC1

SELECTED

GH [Q][Q][Q][Q] Taigh Druimbeg IV27 4NW ☎(0571) 833209
In a peaceful setting of three acres of grounds on the fringe of a picturesque village, this attractive Victorian house has been sympathetically restored to provide comfortable accommodation. Warmly welcoming, it offers a choice of cosy lounges, and enjoyable home cooking is served at the communal dining table. The individually decorated bedrooms are well kept and furnished in various styles, all en suite and with tea making facilities. Smoking is not permitted.

3♠ ✕ Ⓡ ✖ (ex guide dogs) ✳ sB&B♠fr£22.50
dB&B♠fr£45 WB&Bfr£135 WBDifr£195 LDO 7pm
▥ CTV nc14yrs

DRUMNADROCHIT Highland *Inverness-shire*   Map **14** NH52

GH ⓆⓆⓆ **Enrick Cottage** Lower Milton IV3 6TZ (on A813)
☎(0456) 450423 FAX (0456) 450423
Mar-Oct
A warm friendly atmosphere prevails at this homely cottage where
good value bed and breakfast accommodation is offered.
Bedrooms, with ensuite showers, are comfortable, and many of the
furnishings have been made personally by Mr Raper in his
workshop behind the house. Hearty breakfasts are served in the
combined lounge/dining room and ample secure parking is
available.
2♠ ✕ Ⓡ ✳ dB&B♠£32-£34
▥ CTV nc15yrs chair making course (windsor chairs)
Credit Cards ①③ⓔ

SELECTED

▤▨ **GH** ⓆⓆⓆⓆ **Linne Dhuinn** Lewiston IV3 6UW (with
Lewiston Garage on right, turn right pass Lewiston Arms,
hotel approx 0.50m on left) ☎(0456) 450244
Hospitable owners Jim and Audrey Forrester extend a warm
welcome to guests at their comfortable modern house in the
village centre. Efficient underfloor heating makes the place
cosy; bedrooms have good facilities and attractive fabrics, and
hearty breakfasts are served at pine tables in the lounge/dining
room. There is a no-smoking rule.
3⇄♠ (2fb) ✕ CTV in all bedrooms Ⓡ ✖ (ex guide dogs)
sB&B⇄♠£15-£20 dB&B⇄♠£27-£36 WB&B£85-£135
▥ CTV
ⓔ

SELECTED

FH ⓆⓆⓆⓆ Mr A D MacDonald-Hair *Borlum*
Farmhouse (NH518291) IV3 6XN ☎(0456) 450358
From its position on the hill a mile south of the village, this
delightful early 18th-century farmhouse enjoys commanding
views over Loch Ness and the surrounding hills. The spacious
bedrooms are individually decorated and comfortably
furnished, for the most part, with antiques. This is a
no-smoking establishment and the only TV is in the annexe
room. Public rooms comprise a sun lounge and an attractive
breakfast room with individual tables, books and a log-burning
stove. Riding is available, including facilities for disabled
riders.
5rm

DUDDINGTON Northamptonshire   Map **04** SK90

NNⓆⓆⓆ **Royal Oak Hotel** High Street PE9 3QE
☎Stamford(0780) 83267
A delightful 17th-century stone-built inn where the open plan
public areas have a lively atmosphere, whether it be in the dining
area - skilfully decorated in shades of pink and green - or the cosy
bar where a good selection of meals are available. The charming
bedrooms are attractively decorated in cottage style and all are
equipped with a good range of modern amenities.
✖⇄♠ (2fb) CTV in all bedrooms Ⓡ LDO 9.30pm
▥
Credit Cards ①③

DULVERTON Somerset   Map **03** SS92
See also Oakford

St Brelades Guest House

80/82 Buckland Avenue, Dover, Kent CT16 2NW
Tele: 01304 206126
Fax: 01304 211486

This charming and
very comfortable
establishment is run
by proprietors with a
reputation for
friendly and reliable
service.
The bedrooms have
either full en-suite
facilities or private
showers and all
have CTV and tea
making facilities.
Downstairs, there is a full bar service and
residents lounge. In the dining room, where
excellent evening meals are served every
evening, there are personal touches, fresh
flowers and displays of photographs which
add to the pleasant atmosphere.
Off-street parking is available and early
starts are catered for.

Wallett's Court Hotel & Restaurant

West Cliffe, St Margarets-at-Cliffe
Dover, Kent CT15 6EW
Tel: (01304) 852424 Fax: (01304) 853430

Chris & Lea Oakley invite you to stay at Wallett's Court a
manor house restored in the 17th Century but with cellars
dating back to Domesday. Reception rooms are large with
carved oak beams, ornate fire places and antique furniture.
All bedrooms have bathrooms en suite and are tastefully
furnished. They have tea-making facilities, telephone and
colour television.

Wine and dine in the Jacobean restaurant, with 2 AA
Rosettes. Take a trip across the Channel or within an hour's
drive visit Leeds Castle and the many lovely houses,
gardens and beauty spots of Kent. Wallett's
Court is only a short drive from
championship golf courses.

SELECTED

GH QQQQ *Dassels Country House* TA22 9RZ
☎Anstey Mills(03984) 203 FAX (03984) 561
A superb Georgian style country house set in nine acres of grounds is surrounded by beautiful lawns and gardens, two miles off the B3227, with panoramic views of the lovely countryside. Family run, accommodation is offered in individually furnished, comfortable bedrooms, including some on the ground floor and in a garden annexe. Mrs Spencer is renowned for her delicious dinners featuring a range of dishes using fresh farm produce and home-grown vegetables. Local pursuits include walking, pony trekking, fishing and clay-pigeon shooting.
7⇌ Annexe 3 (3fb) CTV in all bedrooms Ⓡ
Lic CTV

SELECTED

GH QQQQ Highercombe TA22 9PT ☎(0398) 23451
A large, imposing Grade II listed country house set in eight acres of lovely gardens and grounds with an abundance of shrubs. Originally built as a hunting lodge, this 14th-century property has delightful bedrooms and superlative views across the rolling landscape of Exmoor. A generous English breakfast is served at separate tables in the spacious lounge/breakfast room. The area abounds with footpaths and bridlepaths, with open moorland only half a mile or so away.
3rm(2) (1fb) Ⓡ sB&B£16-£22 sB&B£18-£24 dB&B£32-£34 dB&B£36-£38
CTV
£

DUMBARTON Strathclyde

See **Cardross**

DUMFRIES Dumfries & Galloway *Dumfriesshire* Map **11** NX97

SELECTED

GH QQQQ Orchard House 298 Annan Road DG1 3JE
☎(0387) 55099
(1fb) CTV in all bedrooms Ⓡ ✱ sB&B£25 dB&B£34-£37 WB&B£119
CTV

DUNBAR Lothian *East Lothian* Map **12** NT67

GH QQ *Marine* 7 Marine Road EH42 1AR ☎(0368) 863315
Mar-Oct
An enthusiastic Italian couple are the new owners of this guest house, part of a terrace, but close to the sea. It offers bright, clean, good value accommodation and a first floor lounge with baby snooker table.
10rm (3fb)
CTV

GH QQQ Overcliffe 11 Bayswell Park EH42 1AE (off A1, opposite Lauderdale Park) ☎(0368) 864004
The red, sandstone semi-detached villa is within reach of the seafront and the town centre. Although compact, it is nicely decorated and has an attractive lounge. All bedrooms have a mini-bar selection.
6rm(3) (3fb) in dining room CTV in all bedrooms Ⓡ ✱ dB&B£32 dB&B£37 WB&B£112-£129.50 WBDi£182-£199.50 LDO 5pm
Lic CTV
£

GH QQ *St Beys* 2 Bayswell Road EH42 1AB ☎(0368) 863571
Feb-Dec
Just off the High Street, this traditional guest house has fine sea views from the first floor lounge. Bedrooms are thoughtfully appointed.
6rm (3fb) CTV in all bedrooms Ⓡ LDO 6pm
CTV
Credit Cards 3

GH QQ St Helens Queens Road EH42 1LN ☎(0368) 863716
Closed Nov-Feb
A red sandstone house lying on the main road leading into the town. Bedrooms vary in size with the larger ones being particularly comfortable. St Helens is a totally no-smoking establishment.
7rm(2⇌) (1fb) Ⓡ ✱ sB&B£15 dB&B£28 dB&B⇌£32 WB&B£90-£104
CTV
£

GH QQQ Springfield Edinburgh Road EH42 1NH (turn off A1 onto Dunbar Loop, establishment is on main road west side of Dunbar near Belhven Church) ☎(0368) 862502
Feb-Nov
This well built detached Victorian villa, standing in a residential area to the west of the town, is a popular base for visiting golfers. The establishment is licensed and a warm friendly atmosphere prevails. The spacious bedrooms are comfortably furnished and there is an attractive lounge on the first floor. Delicious home-cooked food is served in the pine-furnished dining room.
5rm(1⇌) (2fb)CTV in all bedrooms Ⓡ sB&B£17.50 dB&B£33 dB&B⇌£36 WB&B£122.50 WBDi£173.25 LDO 5pm
Lic CTV
Credit Cards 1 3

DUNBLANE Central *Perthshire* Map **11** NN70

SELECTED

GH QQQQ Westwood Doune Road FK15 9ND (leave A9 on A820, turn towards Doune 0.5m on left) ☎(0786) 822579
Mar-Nov
Bob and Liz Duncan's charming modern house stands in an acre of attractive gardens in a select development beside the A824 Doune road. High standards of housekeeping are maintained throughout, and the comfortable bedrooms offer thoughtful extras. A spacious lounge is provided, and hearty Scottish breakfasts are served at individual tables in the dining room. This is a no smoking establishment.
3rm(2⇌) Ⓡ (ex guide dogs) dB&B⇌£34-£37
CTV nc
£

DUNDEE Tayside *Angus* Map **11** NO43

SELECTED

GH QQQQ Beach House Hotel 22 Esplanade, Broughty Ferry DD5 2EN ☎(0382) 76614 due to change to 776614
FAX (0382) 480241
A small private hotel combining the cosiness of a guest house with the benefits of a larger establishment -part of a quiet terraced row looking out on to the Tay estuary - attracts business guests as well as tourists. Bedrooms vary in size but are all thoughtfully equipped, providing clock radios and hair dryers. Popular dinners offer a wide choice, and drinks and coffee are served in a delightful bar; room service of drinks, snacks and continental breakfast is also available.

5⇌♪ (1fb) ⊁ in dining room CTV in all bedrooms ⑧ T ⊁* ⊁
sB&B⇌♪£32-£38 dB&B⇌♪£40-£45 LDO 6pm
Lic ▥.
Credit Cards ①③

GH Ⓠ Ⓠ Ⓠ **Invermark Hotel** 23 Monifeith Road, Broughty
Ferry DD5 2RN (3m E A930) ☎(0382) 739430
Invermark is a large detached house set in its own gardens.
Bedrooms are spacious and sensibly furnished, and there is a
comfortable lounge in which to relax. This establishment is totally
no smoking.
4rm(3♪) (1fb) ⊁ CTV in all bedrooms ⑧ ⊁ (ex guide dogs)
sB&B♪£25-£30 dB&B♪£40 LDO by arrangement
Lic ▥. pool table
Credit Cards ③

DUNFERMLINE Fife   Map **11** NT08

SELECTED

GH Ⓠ Ⓠ Ⓠ Ⓠ **Clarke Cottage** 139 Halbeath Road KY11 4LA
☎(0383) 735935
4♪ ⊁ CTV in all bedrooms ⑧ ⊁ (ex guide dogs)
sB&B♪£21-£25 dB&B♪£38-£46 WB&B£130-£150
▥.
Ⓔ

[↤ ▆] **GH** Ⓠ Ⓠ Ⓠ **Hopetoun Lodge** 141 Halbeath Road KY11
4LA (exit M90 at junct 3 and travel 1.5m through Halbeath, past
retail park on right, over the roundabout and two sets of lights. On
left after garage) ☎(0383)620906
There are good-sized ground-floor bedrooms in this detached
house between the M90 and the town. Breakfast is served around a
communal table in the lounge.
3rm (1fb) ⊁ CTV in all bedrooms ⑧ ⊁ (ex guide dogs)
sB&B£15-£18.50 dB&B£30-£39 WB&B£105-£129.50
▥. CTV

DUNKELD Tayside *Perthshire*   Map **11** NO04

GH Ⓠ Ⓠ Ⓠ **Bheinne Mhor** Perth Road, Birnam PH8 0DH (off A9,
loop rd through Birnam village, opposite post office)
☎(0350) 727779
Closed 19 Dec-16 Jan
This attractive, turreted Victorian house stands on the main road of
the village, which lies on the south-west side of the River Tay
from Dunkeld. Bedrooms are pleasant, with extra little touches
such as fruit, books and radio alarm clocks, and there is a
comfortable lounge. Smoking is not permitted.
3rm(2♪) ⊁ ⑧ ⊁ (ex guide dogs) * sB&Bfr£18 dB&Bfr£36
dB&B♪£38.00 WB&B£114-£120 WBDi£198-£204 LDO day
before
▥. CTV nc12yrs
Ⓔ

GH Ⓠ Ⓠ Ⓠ **Waterbury** Murthly Terrace PH8 0BG (next to church
and post office) ☎(0350) 727324
Traditionally furnished and offering very clean standards, this
three-storey guesthouse is in the main street and all but one of the
bedrooms are on the second floor. They are well proportioned and
four have retained their Victorian fireplaces. There is a lounge and
a dining room with sensible sized, well spaced tables.
5rm (1fb) ⊁ in bedrooms ⊁ in dining room ⑧ sB&B£15.50-£16
dB&B£31-£32 WB&B£101.50-£105 LDO 5.30pm
Lic ▥. CTV
Credit Cards ① ② ③ Ⓔ

DUNLOP Strathclyde *Ayrshire*   Map **10** NS44

GH Ⓠ Ⓠ Ⓠ **Struther Farmhouse** Newmill Road KA3 4BA (within
village approx 200yds from railway station)
☎Stewarton(0560) 484946
Closed 2wks spring & autumn rs Sun & Mon
A sturdy stone-built house, Struther Farm stands in its own grounds
on the edge of the village. The spacious bedrooms are mostly
traditional in style, and public rooms offer a cosy TV lounge and
two dining areas. The house has a good reputation for enjoyable
home cooking, and the dinner menu presents a choice of dishes at
each of four courses. Meals are also available to non-residents.
4rm (2fb) ⑧ LDO 8.30pm
▥. CTV

DUNMOW, GREAT Essex   Map **05** TL62

GH Ⓠ Ⓠ **Cowels Cottage** Cowels Farm Lane, Lindsell CM6 3QG
(take unclass road heading west, off B1057, 4m N of town)
☎Great Easton(0371) 870454
This is a friendly, quiet farmhouse in which each bedroom has its
own private facilities. There is a TV lounge which also serves as a
breakfast room.
3rm(1⇌♪) (1fb) ⊁ in bedrooms ⊁ in dining room ⊁ in 1 lounge
⑧ ⊁ * sB&B£16-£20 sB&B⇌♪fr£20 dB&Bfr£40
WB&Bfr£126
▥. CTV

DUNOON Strathclyde *Argyllshire*   Map **10** NS17

SELECTED

GH Ⓠ Ⓠ Ⓠ Ⓠ **The Anchorage** Lazaretto Point, Shore Road,
Ardnadam, Holy Loch PA23 8QG (3m N on A815)
☎(0369) 5108 due to change to 705108 FAX (0369) 5108
▶

Dassels
Dulverton, Somerset TA22 9RZ
Tel: (013984) 203 Fax: (013984) 561

A superb Georgian style country house,
magnificently situated in nine acres of
tranquil surroundings on the
Devon/Somerset border. Home cooking a
speciality – home grown vegetables, fresh
baked rolls, mouth watering sweets
served with clotted cream. Licensed. All
the tastefully decorated bedrooms are en
suite and include colour TV and tea
making facilities. There are many places
to go and things to do in the area.

North of Dunoon, this detached period house overlooks the Holy Loch. It has been completely renovated to provide pretty pine-furnished bedrooms, one with a four-poster bed. There is a large lounge where a coal fire burns in cool weather.
5🛁 (1fb) 🚭 CTV in all bedrooms [R] 🐕 (ex guide dogs) ✳ dB&B🛁£35-£47 WB&B£122.50-£164.50 WBDi£210-£252 LDO 9pm
Lic ♨ discount on membership of country club
Credit Cards [1][3][£]

GH [Q][Q][Q] The Cedars 51 Alexandra Parade, East Bay PA23 8AF ☎(0369) 2425 due to change to (0369) 702425 FAX (0369) 6964
Good value bed and breakfast accommodation is offered at this friendly family run hotel which enjoys a lovely outlook over the Firth of Clyde from its position on the seafront. The tastefully decorated bedrooms are bright and cheerful with modern amenities; the larger rooms have tables and comfortable chairs, and non smoking rooms are available on the top floor. There is a small lounge with sea views , and an attractive dining room where hearty breakfasts are served.
11🛁 (1fb) 🚭 in 4 bedrooms 🚭 in dining room 🚭 in lounges CTV in all bedrooms [R] **T** 🐕 ✳ sB&B🛁£19-£25 dB&B🛁£38-£50
Lic ♨ ✗
Credit Cards [1][2][3][5][£]

DUNSTER Somerset

See **Minehead & Roadwater**

DUNURE Strathclyde *Ayrshire* Map **10** NS21

SELECTED

FH [Q][Q][Q][Q] Mrs A Gemmell **Dunduff** Dunure KA7 4LH (on A719, 400yds past village school on left) ☎(0292) 500222 FAX (0292) 500222
Mar-Oct
3rm(2🚿) (2fb) 🚭 CTV in 2 bedrooms [R] 🐕 (ex guide dogs) ✳ sB&B£20-£25 sB&B🚿fr£25 dB&B🚿fr£40 WB&Bfr£128
♨ CTV 600 acres beef sheep

DUNVEGAN See **SKYE, ISLE OF**

DURHAM Co Durham Map **12** NZ24

GH [Q][Q][Q] Lothlorien 48/49 Front Street, Witton Gilbert DH7 6SY ☎091-371 0067
A quaint roadside cottage in the village of Witton Gilbert some three miles from Durham. Mrs Milne provides delightful accommodation and service. There is a cosy lounge featuring an old cooking range from a miner's house.
3rm 🚭 in dining room [R] 🐕 ✳ sB&B£17 dB&B£34 WB&B£119
♨ CTV

INN[Q][Q][Q] Bay Horse Brandon DH7 8ST (take A690 2.5m W) ☎091-378 0498
Recently been extended to provide very well furnished bedrooms and a restaurant, this charming stone-built inn stands in the village of Brandon. Family-owned, it provides warm, friendly service, with a good range of food available either in the bar or the restaurant.
Annexe 10🛁 (1fb) CTV in all bedrooms [R] **T** ✳ sB&B🛁£28 dB&B🛁£37 Lunch £2.50-£7 Dinner £2.50-£7.50 LDO 9.30pm
♨
Credit Cards [1][3][£]

INN[Q][Q][Q] *Rosie O'Gradys* 80 Gilesgate ☎091-386 4370
8🚿 (2fb) CTV in all bedrooms [R] 🐕 (ex guide dogs) LDO 9.30pm
♨

DYLIFE Powys Map **06** SN89

INN[Q][Q] Star SY19 7BW (off B4518 9m NW of Llanidloes) ☎Llanbrynmair(0650) 521345
The Star is a remote inn set amid wild and rugged scenery. It offers fairly simple but neat accommodation and a good range of food in the character bar or dining room. Service is friendly and a cosy lounge is provided for guests.
7rm(2🛁) (1fb) 🚭 in dining room 🚭 in 1 lounge [R] sB&Bfr£17 dB&B£34 dB&B🛁£36 WB&B£119 WBDi£165 Lunch £3.25-£7.95 High tea £3.25-£7.95 Dinner £3.25-£7.95 LDO 10.30pm
♨ CTV U boat hire pony trekking
Credit Cards [1][3][£]

DYMCHURCH Kent Map **05** TR12

GH [Q][Q] Chantry Hotel Sycamore Gardens TN29 0LA (200yds E of Dymchurch village on coast side of A259) ☎(0303) 873137
This part-timbered house stands in a private road with direct access to the sea. Most of the bedrooms are of a good size, some with adjoing bunk bedded rooms perfect for children; there are plans to upgrade the rooms over the winter. A wide range of home cooking is available and a separate TV lounge leads to a nice lawn. There is car parking at the front of the house.
6rm(5🛁) (5fb) 🚭 in dining room CTV in all bedrooms [R] ✳ sB&B£19.95-£30.50 sB&B🛁£19.95-£30.50 dB&B£35-£39 dB&B🛁£39.90-£45 WB&B£112.50-£142.50 WBDi£150-£190 LDO 8.30pm
Lic ♨ CTV table tennis boules
Credit Cards [1][2][3][£]

GH [Q][Q] Waterside 15 Hythe Road TN29 0LN (on A259 5m W of Hythe) ☎(0303) 872253
Improvements continue at an extended house which stands by the side of the A259 bordering a dyke and with views of the marsh to the rear. Most bedrooms are small and quite simple in style though three now have private facilities. A useful car park is available.
7rm(3🚿) (1fb) 🚭 in dining room CTV in all bedrooms [R] 🐕 sB&B£14-£16 sB&B🚿£16-£17 dB&B£26-£28 dB&B🚿£33-£35 WB&B£88-£120 WBDi£126-£157.50 LDO 8pm
Lic ♨ CTV
[£]

EARDISLAND Hereford & Worcester Map **03** SO45

FH [Q][Q][Q] Mary Johnson **The Elms** *(SO418584)* HR6 9BN ☎Pembridge(0544) 388405
This small, renovated farmhouse is set in the centre of the village. Guests are reminded that no smoking is permitted in the house.
4rm 🚭 🐕 ✳ sB&Bfr£17 dB&Bfr£32 WB&Bfr£102
nc12yrs 32 acres stock rearing
[£]

EARLS COLNE Essex Map **05** TL82

INN[Q][Q] Riverside Inn Motel 40/42 Lower Holt Street CO6 2PH (on A604) ☎(0787) 223487 FAX (0787) 222034
On the banks of the River Colne, this part-timbered, purpose-built motel occupies the site of old farm buildings. The modern chalet-style rooms are plainly furnished but comfortable. Breakfast, charged separately, is cooked and served by the chatty owner, Mr Collyer, and guests may have to share tables. The adjacent freehold pub serves drinks and meals, and there is a garden with a children's play area.
11🚿 (3fb) CTV in all bedrooms [R] ✳ sB&B🚿£27.50-£29.50 dB&B🚿£40-£44 Lunch fr£3.50&alc Dinner £6-£15alc LDO 9.45pm
♨
[£]

EASINGWOLD North Yorkshire Map **08** SE56

GH QQQ ***Roseberry View*** Easingwold Road, Stillington YO6 1LR ☎(0347) 810795

Closed 22-30 Dec

This bungalow is situated half a mile from Stillington village and is set in open countryside, with an attractive large garden. There are comfortable, good-sized bedrooms, and a guests' lounge which doubles as a breakfast room.

3rm(1🚿) CTV in all bedrooms ® ✗ (ex guide dogs)
▥

EASTBOURNE East Sussex Map **05** TV69

See also Wilmington

GH QQQ Bay Lodge Hotel 61 & 62 Royal Parade BN22 7AQ ☎(0323) 732515 FAX (0323) 735009

Mar-Oct

This attractive double-fronted gabled house overlooking the sea offers accommodation in smart, mostly en suite bedrooms where new soft furnishings have been used to good effect. A set four-course dinner is produced by the cheerful proprietor each evening, and afterwards guests can relax in the bar or one of the sun lounges.

12rm(9🛁🚿) ⊬ in dining room ⊬ in 1 lounge CTV in all bedrooms ® ✗ (ex guide dogs) ✳ sB&B£17-£21 dB&B🛁🚿£36-£44 WB&B£95-£145 WBDi£158-£197 LDO 6pm
Lic ▥ CTV ⊬nc7yrs
Credit Cards 1 3 £

SELECTED

GH QQQQ ***Beachy Rise*** 20 Beachy Head Road BN20 7QN ☎(0323) 639171

This attractive house built towards the end of the 19th century and set in the conservation area of Meads village, between the town centre and Beachy Head, offers charmingly decorated bedrooms furnished with some antiques. Freshly prepared set dinners are served each evening in an elegant dining room overlooking the small south-facing garden, and a vegetarian alternative can be provided. A comfortable lounge invites relaxation, and ample street parking is available.

6rm(2🛁4🚿) CTV in all bedrooms ® ✗ (ex guide dogs) LDO noon
Lic ▥ ⊬
Credit Cards 1 3

GH QQQ Camelot Lodge 35 Lewes Road BN21 2BU (on A2021) ☎(0323) 725207

Personally supervised by the proprietor, Mr Smart, Camelot Lodge is a period 1920s house in Tudor style, set in a residential area. Well appointed throughout, it has comfortable bedrooms, a pleasant sitting room and a cosy little bar where drinks are served before the set dinner.

9rm(1🛁8🚿) (1fb) ⊬ in dining room CTV in all bedrooms ® ✗ (ex guide dogs) sB&B🛁🚿£21-£27 dB&B🛁🚿£42-£48 WB&B£126-£140 WBDi£175-£189 LDO 4pm
Lic ▥ CTV nc5yrs
Credit Cards 1 3 £

GH QQQ Far End Hotel 139 Royal Parade BN22 7LH ☎(0323) 725666

Apr-Oct

A small, friendly guesthouse stands on the seafront beside Princes Park. Bedrooms are bright and modern and public areas include a comfortable first-floor lounge, a small bar and an attractive dining room where both breakfast and dinner are served.

10rm(4🚿) ⊬ in dining room ⊬ in lounges CTV in all bedrooms ® ✳ sB&B£17-£20 dB&B£34-£40 dB&B🚿£46-£50
WB&B£110-£120 WBDi£150-£180 LDO 1pm
Lic ▥ CTV nc4yrs
£

GH QQQ Flamingo Private Hotel 20 Enys Road BN21 2DN ☎(0323) 721654

A detached Victorian house in a residential area with unrestricted street parking. The spacious bedrooms are freshly decorated and comfortable. Many of the building's original features have been retained including the elegant staircase and a notable stained glass window. Public areas include a TV lounge overlooking the gardens, a cosy bar lounge and a spacious dining room with separate tables.

12rm(5🛁7🚿) (1fb) ⊬ in dining room ⊬ in 1 lounge CTV in all bedrooms ® ✗ (ex guide dogs) ✳ sB&B🛁🚿£21-£22.50 dB&B🛁🚿£42-£45 WB&B£133-£140 WBDi£175-£185.50 LDO 4.30pm
Lic ▥ CTV ⊬nc5yrs
Credit Cards 1 2 3 £

GH QQ ***Mowbray Hotel*** Lascelles Tce BN21 4BJ ☎(0323) 720012

Apr-Dec

This immaculately kept building is convenient for the Grand Parade and Devonshire Theatre. There is a lift to the bright, neatly kept bedrooms, and guests have use of a comfortable lounge and dining room.

15rm(6🚿) CTV in all bedrooms ® LDO 5.30pm
lift CTV nc6yrs
Credit Cards 1 3

GH QQ ***Stirling House Hotel*** 5-7 Cavendish Place BN21 3EJ ☎(0323) 732263

Closed 1st wk Nov,last wk Jan & 1st wk Feb

This is a terraced house, with a smart pink exterior and is situated ▶

THE Bay Horse
RESIDENTIAL

Brandon Village, County Durham DH7 8ST
Telephone: (0191) 378 0498

Stone built accommodation, 3 double, 6 twin and 1 family room all en suite, centrally heated, attractively furnished, TV, tea/coffee making facilities, telephone and hair dryer. 50 cover restaurant and bar meals served in the Inn. Ample car parking. Beer garden. 3 golf courses and sports centre within 3 mile radius. Many places of interest, 3 mile from historic Durham City. Ideal for the business person or holiday maker. Children welcome.

close to the seafront. The bedrooms are dated in style with mixed furnishings and fabrics, but many benefit from en suite facilities. There is a comfortable bar with floral sofas and a dining room, split into sections - one of which has an impressive display of Toby jugs. A separate lounge is also available for non smoking guests. The guesthouse is run by the proprietors, who always offer a friendly welcome.

20rm(11🚿) (1fb) CTV in all bedrooms Ⓡ 🐕 (ex guide dogs) LDO 9am

Lic CTV nc10yrs

GH [Q][Q][Q] St Omer Hotel 13 Royal Parade BN22 7AR ☎(0323) 722152

Apr-Sep rs Oct-Nov & Mar

13rm(4🛁6🚿) (1fb)CTV in all bedrooms Ⓡ 🐕 (ex guide dogs) sB&B£24-£28.50 dB&B£52-£57 dB&B🛁🚿£62 (incl dinner) WB&B£115.50-£168 WBDi£147-£194 LDO 5pm

Lic ▥ CTV

Credit Cards [1][3]

EAST CALDER Lothian *Midlothian* Map **11** NT06

SELECTED

FH [Q][Q][Q][Q] Mr & Mrs Scott **Ashcroft Farmhouse** *(NT095682)* EH53 0ET (on B7015, off A71) ☎Midcalder(0506) 881810 FAX (0506) 884327

6🚿 (2fb) 🚭 CTV in all bedrooms Ⓡ 🐕 (ex guide dogs) dB&B🚿fr£44 WB&Bfr£154

▥ 5 acres cattle sheep

Credit Cards [1] [£]

See advertisement under EDINBURGH

FH [Q][Q][Q] Mrs J Dick **Overshiel** *(NT099689)* EH53 0HT (0.5m NE off B7015) ☎(0506) 880469 FAX (0506) 883006

1rm Annexe 2🚿(1fb) 🚭 CTV in all bedrooms Ⓡ 🐕 (ex guide dogs) ✱ sB&B£20 sB&B🚿£22-£25 dB&B£32 dB&B🚿£36

▥ CTV 340 acres mixed

[£]

EAST COKER Somerset Map **03** ST51

PREMIER SELECTED

GH [Q][Q][Q][Q][Q] Holywell House Holywell BA22 9NQ (Leave Yeovil on A30 towards Crewkerne, turn left after 2m at signpost to East Coker, continue down lane Holywell House is on right). ☎West Coker(0935) 862612 FAX (0935) 863035

Closed Xmas

Proprietors Jackie and Ronnie Somerville spent two years restoring this beautifully proportioned period house. Originally a miller's house built of local Ham stone, it stands in three acres of grounds with two streams meandering in front. The guest rooms are thoughtfully equipped and spacious. Guests taking dinner make their choice earlier in the day, and breakfasts are chosen from an extensive list on the day before. Meals are normally served at one large table, though individual tables can be provided.

3rm(2🛁🚿) (1fb) 🚭 in bedrooms 🚭 in dining room 🚭 in lounges CTV in all bedrooms Ⓡ 🐕 (ex guide dogs) ✱ sB&B🛁🚿£40-£45 dB&B🛁🚿£55-£65 LDO 24hrs prior

▥ 🏠 🎾(hard)croquet & garden games

[£]

EAST DEREHAM Norfolk Map **09** TF91

GH [Q][Q][Q] Clinton House Well Hill, Clint Green, Yaxham NR19 1RX (leave A47 & join B1135 towards Wymondham, at Yaxham take rd towards Mattishall after 1m is Clint Green, turn right at school) ☎(0362) 692079

Clinton House offers spacious bedrooms. Guests are encouraged to use the lounge, too, with its comfortable seating, colour TV and video recorder. Breakfast is served in a large, bright conservatory overlooking the attractive lawns and tennis court. Smoking is not permitted in the house.

3rm Annexe 1🛁🚿 (2fb) 🚭 CTV in 1 bedroom Ⓡ 🐕 (ex guide dogs) sB&B£18-£20 sB&B🛁🚿£22-£30 dB&B£28-£32 dB&B🛁🚿£35-£40 WB&B£91-£105

▥ CTV 🎾(grass)croquet

[£]

EAST MIDLANDS AIRPORT Leicestershire Map **08** SK42

GH [Q][Q] The Four Poster 73 Clapgun Street DE7 2LF ☎Derby(0332) 810335 & 812418

Ample parking is provided at this colourful establishment close to the town centre. The owners strive to maintain standards in a warm and friendly atmosphere.

7rm(3🛁🚿) Annexe 4rm CTV in all bedrooms Ⓡ

▥ CTV

[£]

GH [Q][Q][Q] Park Farmhouse Hotel Melbourne Road, Isley Walton DE74 2RN ☎Derby(0332) 862409 FAX (0332) 862364

Closed Xmas & New Year

A rambling farm complex, close to the race track, this hotel offers spacious accommodation with excellent facilities for both business and leisure users.

9rm(4🛁4🚿) (2fb) 🚭 in 2 bedrooms 🚭 in dining room CTV in all bedrooms Ⓡ **T** sB&B£37-£42 sB&B🛁🚿£39.50-£46 dB&B£50-£60 dB&B🛁🚿£56-£66 LDO 8.30pm

Lic ▥

Credit Cards [1][2][3][5] [£]

INN [Q][Q] ***Le Chevalier Bistro Restaurant*** 2 Borough Street DE74 2LA ☎Derby(0332) 812005 & 812106 FAX (0322) 811372

This small popular bistro set in a narrow side street in the town centre offers four cheerful, well appointed bedrooms. In the attractive bar and restaurant area competently cooked meals are served.

4🛁🚿 (1fb) CTV in all bedrooms Ⓡ 🐕 (ex guide dogs) LDO 10.30pm

▥ CTV pool table

Credit Cards [1][3]

EBBERSTON North Yorkshire Map **08** SE88

INN [Q][Q] The Foxholm YO13 9NJ (on B1258) ☎Scarborough(0723) 859550

The stone-built farmhouse has now become a licensed Free House. It has en suite bedrooms with a snug dining room and modern bar, and a good range of food is available.

7🛁🚿 🚭 in dining room CTV in all bedrooms Ⓡ sB&B🛁🚿£25.50-£28.50 dB&B🛁🚿£47-£53 WB&B£144-£190 Lunch £1.75-£8.95alc Dinner £3.95-£15alc LDO 9pm

▥

EDENBRIDGE Kent Map **05** TQ44

GH [Q][Q][Q] Knowlands Five Fields Lane TN8 6NA ☎Four Elms(0732) 700314

An attractive guest house in a peaceful rural setting. The spacious bedrooms provide comfortable accommodation and are adequately equipped. The owners Mr and Mrs Haviland personally supervise and provide a high standard of hospitality.

2rm 🚭 CTV in all bedrooms Ⓡ ✱ dB&B£50

▥ 🎾(hard)

EDINBURGH Lothian *Midlothian* Map **11** NT27

GH [Q][Q][Q] Abbey Lodge 137 Drum Street, Gilmorton EH17 8RJ
☎031-664 9548 FAX 031-664 3965

Situated beside the A7 on the southern outskirts of the city, just a couple of minutes from the bypass, this purpose-built guest house will appeal to business guests as well as tourists. Bedrooms (all of them on the ground floor) are practically furnished and well equipped, providing radio, hair dryer, satellite TV and plug for direct dial telephone. Guests have the use of a small sun lounge off the owners' lounge and there is a cheerful dining room which shares the friendly and informal atmosphere of the whole establishment.

5🛁🚿 (5fb) CTV in all bedrooms Ⓡ sB&B🛁🚿£25 dB&B🛁🚿£35-£50 LDO noon
Lic ♨ CTV
Credit Cards [1][2][3][5][£]
See advertisement under Colour Section

GH [Q][Q] Adam Hotel 19 Lansdowne Crescent EH12 5EH
☎031-337 1148
Closed 24 Dec-2 Jan

Forming part of a terraced row in a Georgian crescent, this family-run licensed guest house offers mostly spacious bedrooms with lofty ceilings. The rooms have recently been redecorated but the furnishings remain modest and traditional. A lounge is provided and hearty breakfasts are served in the attractive dining room.

9rm (2fb)CTV in all bedrooms 🐕 (ex guide dogs) sB&B£22-£22.50 dB&B£44
Lic ♨ CTV ⊘
[£]

GH [Q][Q][Q] The Adria Hotel 11-12 Royal Terrace EH7 5AB
☎031-556 7875
Closed Nov-Dec

This friendly family-run guesthouse forms part of a Georgian terrace overlooking the Carlton Hill gardens. Bedrooms vary in size and some are fitted with attractive period furniture. The original character of the house has been skilfully retained in the comfortable lounge and restored breakfast room.

24rm(6🛁🚿) (7fb)Ⓡ 🐕 ✱ sB&B£20-£26 sB&B🛁🚿£30-£35 dB&B£40-£47 dB&B🛁🚿£50-£58
♨ CTV ⊘
[£]

GH [Q][Q] Ailsa Craig Hotel 24 Royal Terrace EH7 5AH
☎031-556 1022 FAX 031-556 6055
18rm(15🛁🚿) (6fb)CTV in all bedrooms Ⓡ sB&B£22.50-£35 sB&B🛁🚿£25-£40 dB&B🛁🚿£45-£70 WB&B£175-£280 WBDi£238.65-£342 LDO 4pm
Lic ♨ CTV ⊘
Credit Cards [1][2][3][5][£]

GH [Q][Q][Q] Allison House 15/17 Mayfield Gardens EH9 2AX (on A701) ☎031-667 8049 FAX 031-667 5001

This well run private hotel - created from two adjoining properties on the south side of the city - offers bedrooms in a variety of sizes, all made attractive by an effective use of fabrics and well equipped to include trouser presses. The lounge incorporates an honesty bar, and good-value dinners are served in a cheerful dining room.

24rm(22🚿) (10fb) 🚭 in area of dining room CTV in all bedrooms Ⓡ **T** ✱ sB&B🚿£25-£35 dB&B🚿£42-£70 LDO 9.30pm
Lic ♨ CTV
Credit Cards [1][2][3][5][£]

GH [Q][Q] Anvilla 1a Granville Terrace EH10 4PG ☎031-228 3381

This detached Victorian house lies in a residential area just south-west of the city centre. Nicely decorated and comfortably furnished, the attractive first-floor lounge features a beautiful ornate ceiling, and the original fireplace can be seen in the small breakfast room.

6rm (2fb) 🚭 in dining room CTV in all bedrooms Ⓡ sB&B£18-£20 dB&B£34-£38
♨ CTV

GH [Q][Q][Q] Ashdene House 23 Fountainhall Road EH9 2LN
☎031-667 6026
Closed 2 wks in winter

High standards of housekeeping and maintenance are assured at this family-run holiday and business guest house, situated in a desirable conservation area on the south side of the city. The comfortable bedrooms vary in size and provide a good range of amenities. Breakfast is served at individual tables in the attractive dining room which also has a small lounge area. This is a no-smoking establishment.

5rm(4🚿) (2fb) 🚭 CTV in all bedrooms Ⓡ **T** 🐕 (ex guide dogs) ✱ dB&B🚿£36-£50 WB&B£126-£175
♨

SELECTED

GH [Q][Q][Q][Q] ***Ashgrove House*** 12 Osborne Terrace EH12 5HG
☎031-337 5014

Ashgrove is a detached period house on the Glasgow road to the west of the city centre. The en suite bedrooms are tastefully furnished and equipped with radios, trouser presses and hairdryers. The lounge with its sun-lounge extension is shared with the owners, and there is a spacious and well appointed breakfast room.

7🚿 (2fb) CTV in all bedrooms Ⓡ 🐕 (ex guide dogs)
♨ CTV
See advertisement on p.167.

GH [Q][Q] Ben Doran 11 Mayfield Gardens EH9 2AX
☎031-667 8488
Closed 20-27 Dec
Good-value bed and breakfast accommodation is offered at this friendly, family-run guest house which caters for both business and tourist guests in a south-side residential area. Bedrooms with lofty ceilings are mostly spacious and well equipped. Breakfast is served at individual tables in the large dining room.
9rm(1🛁3🚿) (5fb)CTV in all bedrooms [R] * sB&B£18-£25 dB&B£36-£42 dB&B🛁🚿£40-£50
♨
[£]

GH [Q][Q] Boisdale Hotel 9 Coates Gardens EH12 5LG
☎031-337 1134 FAX 031-313 0048
Forming part of a terraced row in a west-end residential area, this friendly, family-run guesthouse caters for both business and holiday visitors. Hearty breakfasts are served.
11rm(5🛁6🚿) (6fb) CTV in all bedrooms [R] * sB&B🛁🚿£20-£35 dB&B🛁🚿£40-£70 LDO 7pm
Lic ♨ CTV 🅿̸

GH [Q][Q][Q] Bonnington 202 Ferry Road EH6 4NW
☎031-554 7610
This is a semidetached Victorian house in a residential area in the north side. Attractive fabrics brighten the pleasant bedrooms. There is a comfortably furnished lounge and breakfast is served in traditional style by the kilted owner, Mr Watt.
6rm(2🛁2🚿) (3fb) 🚭 in dining room CTV in all bedrooms [R] dB&B£38-£44 dB&B🛁🚿£46-£52 LDO 10am
♨ CTV
[£]

SELECTED

GH [Q][Q][Q][Q] Brunswick Hotel 7 Brunswick Street EH7 5JB
☎031-556 1238 FAX 031-556 1238
Closed Xmas & New Year
Bedrooms at this terraced guest house are enhanced by attractive decor and quality coordinated fabrics. The larger rooms have sitting areas with comfortable chairs. A small lounge is provided and a cheery breakfast room.
11🚿 (1fb) 🚭 CTV in all bedrooms [R] 🐕 sB&B🚿£25-£45 dB&B🚿£50-£90
♨ nc2yrs
Credit Cards [1][2][3][£]

GH [Q][Q][Q] Buchan Hotel 3 Coates Gardens EH12 5LG (W along A8) ☎031-337 1045 FAX 031-538 7055
Good value bed and breakfast accommodation is offered at this friendly family-run hotel, which is in a terraced row close to Haymarket railway station. Single bedrooms are rather small but others are spacious, and public areas include a comfortable lounge and a dining room with a beautiful plaster ceiling.
12🚿 (5fb) CTV in all bedrooms [R] sB&B🚿£25-£35 dB&B🚿£40-£60
♨ CTV 🅿̸
Credit Cards [1][2][3][£]

SELECTED

GH [Q][Q][Q][Q] Classic 50 Mayfield Road EH9 2NH
☎031-667 5847
Quality and style are features of this small guest house on the south side of the city. Tastefully decorated and thoughtfully equipped bedrooms include one family room.
4rm(3🛁🚿) 🚭 CTV in all bedrooms [R] 🐕 * sB&B£18-£22 sB&B🛁🚿£25-£35 dB&B£36-£44 dB&B🛁🚿£36-£50 LDO 8pm
♨ CTV 🅿̸
Credit Cards [1][3][5]

GH [Q][Q] Clifton Private Hotel 1 Clifton Terrace, Haymarket EH12 5DR ☎031-337 1002 FAX 031-337 1002
Good value bed and breakfast accommodation is offered at this friendly private hotel situated in the west end close to Haymarket railway station. Bedrooms vary in size, and public areas include a spacious first-floor lounge, due for refurbishment at the time of our visit. There is a pleasant, ground-floor breakfast room.
11rm(4🚿) 🚭 in dining room CTV in all bedrooms [R] sB&B£21-£28 sB&B🚿£25-£28 dB&B£38 dB&B🚿£40-£50 WB&B£147-£196
♨ CTV 🅿̸
Credit Cards [1][3][£]

GH [Q][Q][Q] Crion 33 Minto Street EH9 2BT ☎031-667 2708 FAX 031-662 1946
Constant improvements are being made to this delightful Victorian house, which is in a desirable south-side residential area, a short drive from the city centre and bypass. The well decorated bedrooms, though compact, are tastefully furnished and comfortable. Well cooked breakfasts are served in the attractive lounge/dining room.
6rm(3🚿) (1fb) 🚭 in dining room 🚭 in lounges CTV in all bedrooms [R] 🐕 (ex guide dogs) sB&B£18-£23 dB&B🚿£38-£56
♨ CTV

GH [Q][Q] Daisy Park 41 Abercorn Terrace, Joppa EH15 2DG
☎031-669 2503 FAX 031-669 0189
6rm(3🚿) (2fb) 🚭 in dining room 🚭 in lounges CTV in all bedrooms [R] 🐕 (ex guide dogs) * sB&B£19-£25 dB&B£36-£42 dB&B🚿£36-£50
♨ CTV 🅿̸

GH [Q][Q] Dalwin Lodge & Restaurant 75 Mayfield Road EH9 3AA ☎031-667 2294 FAX 031-667 2294
Closed 24-27 Dec rs Sun
This small, family-run guest house and restaurant forms part of a terraced row and is on the city's south side, within a short drive of the centre. Bedrooms are adequately equipped. The small restaurant, open to non-residents, offers an excellent-value, fixed-price lunch menu, with a more extensive choice available in the evening.
5rm (1fb)CTV in all bedrooms [R] 🐕 (ex guide dogs) * sB&B£15-£18 dB&B£30-£36 LDO 8pm
Lic ♨ 🅿̸
[£]

SELECTED

GH [Q][Q][Q][Q] Dorstan Private Hotel 7 Priestfield Road EH16 5HJ ☎031-667 6721 & 031-667 5138 FAX 031-668 4644
The high level of regular custom at this large Victorian house justifies Mairae Campbell's reputation for hospitality. The bedrooms vary in size and most are furnished with quality fitted units. The smaller rooms have pine furniture and all have telephones. There is an elegant lounge and a small dining room with booth seating.
14rm(12🛁🚿) (2fb) 🚭 in dining room 🚭 in lounges CTV in all bedrooms [R] T 🐕 (ex guide dogs) * sB&B£22-£40 sB&B🛁🚿£35-£45 dB&B£50-£60 dB&B🛁🚿£55-£70 LDO 3pm
♨
Credit Cards [1][3][£]

GH 🔘🔘🔘🔘🔘 **Drummond House** 17 Drummond Place
EH3 6PL ☎031-557 9189
FAX 031-557 9189

This establishment is totally no smoking.
Here is an opportunity to savour the delight of staying in a historic New Town house, in elegantly furnished, well equipped accommodation. Mr and Mrs Dougall create a house-party atmosphere and the food is of cordon bleu standard.
3rm(2⇔🏠) ✖ 🏠 dB&B⇔🏠£70 LDO 24hrs notice
🏢 CTV ✗nc12yrs
Credit Cards 1 3

GH 🔘🔘 **Dunstane House** 4 West Coates EH12 5JQ ☎031-337 6169
Good value bed and breakfast accommodation is offered at Mrs Hunter's comfortable Victorian mansion in the west end beside the A8. Bedrooms are mostly spacious, and shower cabinets are provided in all rooms without private bathrooms. There is a dispense bar in the lounge, and nicely cooked breakfasts are served in the adjacent dining room.
15rm(4🏠) (5fb) ✖ in dining room CTV in all bedrooms ®
sB&B£32-£35 dB&B£52-£62 dB&B🏠£62-£72
Lic 🏢 CTV
Credit Cards 1 2 3 £

GH 🔘🔘 **Edinburgh House** 11 McDonald Road EH7 4LX
☎031-556 3443
Situated in the east of the city, this family-run guest house ▶

Ashgrove House
12 Osborne Terrace (on A8) • Edinburgh • EH12 5HG
Telephone: 0131 337 5017 • Fax: 0131 313 5043

Magid & Heather welcome you to our family run Victorian Guest House, just a few minutes walk to Edinburgh's famous Princes Street and Castle. You can park your car in our car park and explore this historic city with peace of mind. Our rooms are very comfortable and have shower en suite, hair dryer, trouser press, TV and welcome tray. Evening meals can be prepared by arrangement.

Boisdale Hotel

9 Coats Gardens, Edinburgh EH12 5LG
Telephone: 0131 337 1134
Fax: 0131 313 0048
Situated 5 minutes from the City centre, just off the main road and 2 minutes from Haymarket Station. All rooms are pleasantly decorated and have TV, tea/coffee making facilities and central heating. Full Scottish breakfast is served with dinner 6pm on request. Residents licence. Colour TV and Bar. Personal supervision by proprietors:
Mrs A. J. T. Cook

EDINBURGH
DORSTAN
PRIVATE HOTEL

7 Priestfield Road, Edinburgh, EH16 5HJ
Tel: 0131-667 6721/5138 Fax: 0131-668 4644
A tastefully furnished Victorian house,
The Dorstan offers a warm welcome & comfortable accommodation. Situated in a quiet southside residential area conveniently located for bypass & city centre. Come & enjoy the friendly personal service of this family run hotel. **AA** Selected
Proprietor: Mairae Campbell. Send for colour brochure

occupies 2 floors of a tall building just off Leith Walk and offers good value bed and breakfast accommodation in bright, cheerful bedrooms. Some are on the small side.
5rm(2🚿) (1fb) CTV in 2 bedrooms [R] LDO 8pm
♨

GH [Q][Q] Elder York 38 Elder Street EH1 3OX ☎031-556 1926
In this city centre guest house near the bus station, the third and fourth floors of a Victorian tenement have been transformed into bright, airy bedrooms - some with full en suite facilities and several with shower units - and an attractive breakfast room with well spaced tables. There is no lounge.
13rm(3🚿) (3fb) CTV in all bedrooms [R] 🐕 (ex guide dogs) ✳ sB&B£20-£22 dB&B£36-£40 dB&B🚿£44-£48
♨

SELECTED

GH [Q][Q][Q][Q] Ellesmere House 11 Glengyle Terrace EH3 9LN ☎031-229 4823 FAX 031-229 5285
Celia and Tommy Leishman offer warm hospitality at their terraced guesthouse overlooking Bruntsfield Links. The bedrooms are well proportioned and comfortable, with bathrooms fitted to a high standard. The lounge also doubles as a breakfast room, where guests are under no obligation to share tables.
6rm(4🛁🚿) (2fb) 🚭 in bedrooms 🚭 in dining room CTV in all bedrooms [R] 🐕 (ex guide dogs) sB&B£18-£28 dB&B🛁🚿£36-£56
♨ CTV 🚫🅿
[£]

SELECTED

GH [Q][Q][Q][Q] Elmview 15 Glengyle Terrace EH3 9LN ☎031-228 1973 FAX 031-228 1973
Comprising the lower floor of a terraced house, Elmview offers a relaxing town house atmosphere. The three well proportioned bedrooms are furnished in dark pine and have smart modern en suite bathrooms with shower cubicles; they are well stocked with thoughtful extras including a fridge. There is no lounge, and breakfast is taken around a large table in the dining room.
3🛁🚿 🚭 CTV in all bedrooms [R] T 🐕 dB&B🛁🚿£50-£60
♨ 🚫🅿 nc8yrs
Credit Cards [1][3] [£]

GH [Q][Q][Q] Galloway 22 Dean Park Crescent EH4 1PH (W on A9) ☎031-332 3672
Forming part of a Victorian terrace, this guest house lies little more than a stroll from the west end of Princes Street. Bedrooms are mostly a good size. Guests will share tables at breakfast unless they request otherwise.
10rm(6🛁🚿) (6fb)CTV in all bedrooms [R] ✳ sB&B£22-£30 sB&B🛁🚿£30-£45 dB&B£34-£40 dB&B🛁🚿£40-£50 WB&Bfr£102
♨
[£]

GH [Q][Q][Q] *Glendale Hotel* 5 Lady Road EH16 5PA ☎031-667 6588
A friendly, family-run sandstone guesthouse on the south side beside the Cameron Toll shopping centre, with easy access to both the city centre and by-pass. Bedrooms, though varying in size, are comfortable and well equipped. There is a first-floor lounge which is equipped with TV and, surprisingly, an exercise bicycle. Enjoyable home cooking is offered in the adjacent dining room.
8rm(4🚿) (3fb) CTV in 7 bedrooms [R] 🐕 (ex guide dogs) LDO noon
♨ CTV
Credit Cards [1][3]

GH [Q][Q] *Glenisla Hotel* 12 Lygon Road EH16 5QB ☎031-667 4877 FAX 031-667 4098
This attractive semidetached sandstone house is situated in a quiet residential area on the south side of the city, and is gradually being improved by the friendly owners. There is a spacious and comfortable first floor TV lounge, and good home cooking is served in the dining room. Bedrooms vary in size.
7rm(4🚿) (2fb) [R] LDO 8.15pm
Lic ♨ CTV
Credit Cards [1][3]

GH [Q][Q][Q] Glenora Hotel 14 Rosebery Crescent EH12 5JY ☎031-337 1186 FAX 031-337 1186
Personally run by the resident proprietors, this comfortable private hotel is situated in the west end close to Haymarket station. The spotlessly clean bedrooms are mostly spacious and offer modern appointments. Public areas include a comfortable TV lounge and spacious breakfast room. Smoking is not allowed in any of the bedrooms or in the breakfast room.
10🚿 (2fb) CTV in all bedrooms [R] 🐕
Lic ♨ CTV 🚫🅿
Credit Cards [1][3]

GH [Q][Q] Glenorchy Hotel 22 Glenorchy Terrace EH9 2DH ☎031-667 5708
Good value commercial and tourist accommodation is offered at this family run guesthouse quietly situated in a south side residential area, only ten minutes from the city centre. Bedrooms are well equipped and spacious, and there is a pleasant first floor lounge with TV. Enjoyable home cooking is available by arrangement, and snacks are served in the lounge.
9🛁🚿 (2fb)CTV in all bedrooms [R] sB&Bfr£20 sB&B🛁🚿fr£25 dB&Bfr£40 dB&B🛁🚿fr£45
♨ CTV 🚫🅿
Credit Cards [1][2][3]

GH [Q][Q][Q] Greenside Hotel 9 Royal Terrace EH7 5AB ☎031-557 0022 FAX 031-557 0022
This friendly, family-run house forms part of a fine Georgian terrace overlooking Calton Hill, near the east end of Princes Street. It offers good value bed and breakfast accommodation in spotlessly maintained bedrooms, each of which is individually decorated and comfortably furnished; the original master rooms are particularly spacious. There is a quiet terraced garden to the rear.
14🛁🚿 (5fb) 🚭 in dining room CTV in all bedrooms [R] sB&B🛁🚿£22.50-£35 dB&B🛁🚿£45-£70 WB&B£157.50-£245 WBDi£220.15-£307.65 LDO 4pm
♨ CTV 🚫🅿
Credit Cards [1][2][3][5] [£]

SELECTED

GH [Q][Q][Q][Q] Grosvenor Gardens Hotel 1 Grosvenor Gardens EH12 5JU ☎031-313 3415 FAX 031-346 8732
Situated in a quiet cul-de-sac in the West End, this delightful Victorian town house has been refurbished throughout to provide excellent-value accommodation. Some of the bedrooms are very spacious, and all are individually furnished and decorated. Hearty breakfasts are served at shared tables in the attractive dining room.
8🛁🚿 (3fb) 🚭 in dining room 🚭 in lounges CTV in all bedrooms [R] 🐕 (ex guide dogs) ✳ sB&B🛁🚿£28-£38 dB&B🛁🚿£56-£80
♨ CTV 🚫🅿 nc5yrs
Credit Cards [1][2][3]

GH [Q] *Halcyon Hotel* 8 Royal Terrace EH7 5AB ☎031-556 1033 & 031-556 1032
Forming part of a Georgian terrace, just east of the city centre, this

family-run guesthouse offers good value, practical accommodation. Bedrooms are simply furnished and the standard of housekeeping is high. There is a comfortable TV lounge on the first floor and generous breakfasts are served in the pleasant dining room.

16rm (6fb) ®
▥ CTV ✗✗(hard)

GH Q Q **A Haven** 180 Ferry Road EH6 4NS (Logis)
☎031-554 6559 FAX 031-554 6559
This detached Victorian house situated on the northern side of the city attracts business guests as well as tourists. Bedrooms vary in size, most being furnished with fitted units. There is a small lounge area off the dining room.
11rm(2➪9♠) (4fb) CTV in all bedrooms ® T ✗ (ex guide dogs)
sB&B➪♠£25-£40 dB&B➪♠£45-£65 LDO 8pm
Lic ▥ CTV
Credit Cards ① ③

GH Q Q **Heriott Park** 256 Ferry Road EH5 3AN ☎031-552 6628
Situated on the North side, this friendly family run guesthouse forms part of a terraced row and enjoys an outlook over the city to the castle. Bedrooms vary in size but are comfortable; some have en suite facilities and they all have TV. There is a pleasant first floor lounge and spacious breakfast room: dinner is available during weekdays on request. Smoking is not permitted in public areas.
6rm(2♠) (4fb) ✗ in dining room ✗ in lounges CTV in all bedrooms ® ✳ sB&B£18-£20 sB&B♠£30 dB&B£30-£34 dB&B♠£40-£45
▥ CTV

SELECTED

GH ◙◙◙◙ **International** 37 Mayfield Gardens EH9 2BX
☎031-667 2511 FAX 031-667 1109
Martha Miller is the enthusiastic hostess at this attractively
decorated terraced house on the southern side of the city.
Bedrooms are solidly furnished and, apart from two small
singles, spacious; a huge family room is available. Breakfast is
taken at individual tables in the lounge/dining room.
7⇥❡ (3fb) ✗ in dining room ✗ in lounges CTV in all
bedrooms ® 🏃 (ex guide dogs) ✳ sB&B⇥❡£25-£32
dB&B⇥❡£36-£64
🛏,
£

GH ◙◙ **Kariba** 10 Granville Terrace EH10 4PQ ☎031-229 3773
A friendly, family-run terraced guest house located in a residential
area within five minutes' drive of the city centre. Bedrooms are
compact but well maintained. Sharing a table may sometimes be
necessary in the lounge/dining room, which also has a TV.
9rm(8⇥❡) (3fb) ✗ in dining room ✗ in lounges CTV in all
bedrooms ® ✳ sB&Bfr£18 sB&B⇥❡£26 dB&B£36-£40
dB&B⇥❡£38-£44
🛏, CTV

GH ◙◙◙◙ **Kew** 1 Kew Terrace, Murrayfield EH12 5JE
☎031-313 0700 & 031-313 4407
Totally renovated in 1993, this period house offers modern
bedrooms and a small but cheerfully decorated breakfast room. It
is located about a mile and a half west of the city on the main A8
Glasgow road.
5rm(3❡) (2fb) ✗ in dining room ✗ in lounges CTV in all
bedrooms ® sB&B£22-£26 dB&B£44-£50 dB&B❡£50-£60
🛏,
Credit Cards 1 3 £

GH ◙◙◙ **Kilmaurs** 9 Kilmaurs Rd EH16 5DA ☎031-667 8315
Situated in a south side residential area, this family-run guesthouse
offers good value bed and breakfast accommodation. Bedrooms
vary in size and have light modern furnishings and all the
expected amenities. The lounge and dining room are combined
and at peak times it may be necessary to share a table with other
guests for breakfast.
5❡ (3fb) CTV in all bedrooms ® dB&B❡£34-£44 WB&B£105
🛏,✗nc3yrs
£

GH ◙◙ **Kingsley** 30 Craigmillar Park, Newington EH16 5PS (S
on A701) ☎031-667 8439
Situated on the south side of town in a terraced row, this friendly,
family-run guesthouse offers good value, modern facilities and
family bedrooms. There is a lounge and an airy dining room where
breakfast is served.
6rm(4❡) (3fb) ✗ in bedrooms ✗ in dining room CTV in all
bedrooms ® 🏃 ✳ dB&B£30-£34 dB&B❡£34-£44
🛏, CTV nc6yrs
Credit Cards 1 3 £

GH ◙◙ **Kirklea** 11 Harrison Road EH11 1EG (off A70, behind St
Michael's church, at junct with A71) ☎031-337 1129
FAX 031-337 1129
This guesthouse stands in a terraced row on the west side of the
city, and has accommodation of mixed size. There is no lounge,
but the dining room has two armchairs and a TV.
6rm(1❡) (1fb) ✗ in dining room ✗ in lounges CTV in all
bedrooms ® ✳ sB&B£18-£23 dB&B£30-£42 dB&B❡£38-£46
🛏,
Credit Cards 1 2 3 £

GH ◙◙ **The Lairg** 11 Coates Gardens EH12 5LG
☎031-337 1050 FAX 031-346 2167
The bright modern bedrooms (several very large with good en

suites) contrast with the more subdued style of the lounge and
dining room at this family guest house. The house is part of a
terraced row just off the Glasgow road on the western side of the
city.
10❡ (3fb) ✗ in dining room ✗ in lounges CTV in all bedrooms
® sB&B❡£19-£28 dB&B❡£38-£56
Lic 🛏, CTV ✗
Credit Cards 1 2 3 £

GH ◙◙ **Lindsay** 108 Polwarth Terrace EH11 1NN
☎031-337 1580 FAX 031-337 9174
The Lindsay Guest House is situated on the western side of the
city with the Union Canal close to its back garden. The house is
continually being upgraded, and all the bathrooms have been
modernised. Most of the bedrooms are a good size and all have
comfortable chairs.
8rm(3❡) (2fb) ✗ in dining room ✗ in lounges CTV in all
bedrooms ® ✳ sB&B£20-£35 dB&B£40 dB&B❡£50
🛏,
Credit Cards 1 2 3

SELECTED

GH ◙◙◙◙ **The Lodge Hotel** 6 Hampton Terrace, West
Coates EH12 5JD (on main A8, 1 mile west of city centre)
☎031-337 3682 FAX 031-313 1700
Dedicated hosts Linda and George Jarron have created an
attractive small hotel from this semidetached Georgian house
on the A8 Glasgow road, west of the city centre. Bedrooms
come in various sizes and have splendid modern bathrooms,
as well as welcoming touches such as fresh fruit and flowers.
Home cooked three-course set dinners are served, and there is
an elegant lounge and residents' bar.
10❡ in 8 bedrooms ✗ in dining room CTV in all bedrooms
® T 🏃 ✳ sB&B❡£38-£50 dB&B❡£50-£80 LDO 7.30pm
Lic 🛏,
Credit Cards 1 3 £

GH ◙◙ **Lugton** 29 Leamington Terrace EH10 4JS
☎031-229 7033 FAX 031-228 9483
4❡ (1fb)CTV in all bedrooms ® 🏃 sB&B❡£20-£28
dB&B❡£40-£56
🛏,

GH ◙◙ *Maple Leaf* 23 Pilrig Street EH6 5AN ☎031-554 7692
The cheery and outgoing personalities of the owners make for a
friendly and informal atmosphere at this 'home from home' in a
terraced row on the northern side of the city. The accommodation
is bright and reasonably sized, and includes two good family
rooms. Table sharing may be necessary at breakfast.
11rm(4❡) (2fb) CTV in all bedrooms ®
🛏, CTV ✗

GH ◙◙ *Marchhall Hotel* 14-16 Marchhall Crescent EH16 5HL
☎031-667 2743 FAX 031-662 0777
Good value accommodation is offered at this friendly family-run
business and tourist establishment in a quiet south side residential
area. Bedrooms vary in size but provide a good range of
amenities. Public areas include a tiny bar, a fully licensed timber
clad bar and a bright restaurant with an à la carte menu.
13rm(6⇥❡) (3fb) CTV in all bedrooms ® LDO 3pm
Lic 🛏, CTV ✗
Credit Cards 1 3

GH ◙◙ **Mardale** 11 Hartington Place EH10 4LF ☎031-229 2693
Good-value bed and breakfast accommodation is offered at this
friendly family-run guest house in a residential cul-de-sac on the
south side. Bedrooms, though compact, are well decorated and
attractive fabrics have been used to good effect. Nicely cooked
breakfasts are served in the attractive first-floor dining room,
which incorporates a lounge area.
▶

6rm(3➪) (2fb) ⊁ in dining room ⊁ in lounges CTV in all bedrooms ⓡ T sB&B£17-£20 dB&B£34-£40 dB&B✿£40-£56 ▥
Credit Cards ①③ⓔ

GH ⓠⓠⓠ **Meadows** 17 Glengyle Terrace EH3 9LN (E of A702, between the Kings Theatre and Bruntsfield Links)
☎031-229 9559 FAX 031-229 2226
Closed 18-28 Dec
Comfortable, well proportioned bedrooms are offered at this efficiently run guest house overlooking the links. The rooms are sensibly furnished to meet the needs of both the tourist and the business traveller. A useful map of local amenities is given to each guest, and breakfast is served refectory-style at two tables.
6rm(4➪) (3fb) ⊁ in dining room CTV in all bedrooms ⓡ sB&Bfr£23 sB&B✿£43 dB&Bfr£44 dB&B✿fr£54 ▥,⊬
Credit Cards ①②③ⓔ

GH ⓠⓠⓠ *The Newington* 18 Newington Road EH9 1QS
☎031-667 3356
Bedrooms vary in size and character at this solidly traditional guest house on the south side of the city, but most have a country house flavour. A Colonial theme prevails throughout: mementos from the Far East abound, and massive pot plants dominate both the dining room and upstairs lounge.
8rm(3➪) (1fb) CTV in all bedrooms ⓡ
Lic ▥

GH ⓠⓠⓠ **Parklands** 20 Mayfield Gardens EH9 2BZ (.5m S)
☎031-667 7184
Forming part of a terraced-row in a south-side residential area, this spotlessly maintained guest house offers good value bed and breakfast accommodation. The spacious bedrooms are bright and airy and furnished in modern teak. Well cooked breakfasts are served in the combined lounge/dining room.
6rm(5➪) (1fb) ⊁ in 1 bedrooms ⊁ in dining room ⊁ in lounges CTV in all bedrooms ⓡ ✱ (ex guide dogs) dB&B£36-£42 dB&B✿£36-£50
▥,
ⓔ

GH ⓠⓠ **Park View Villa** 254 Ferry Road EH5 3AN
☎031-552 3456
Part of a terraced block on the north side, this family-run guesthouse offers good value bed and breakfast accommodation. Bedrooms are neatly furnished and comfortable. Views of the castle are enjoyed from the lounge, and breakfast is served, occasionally at shared tables, in the smart dining room.
7rm(4➪) (3fb) ⊁ in dining room CTV in all bedrooms ⓡ ✱ (ex guide dogs) ✳ sB&B£20 sB&B✿£26 dB&B£30 dB&B✿£40 ▥, CTV ⊬
Credit Cards ①③

GH ⓠⓠ **Ravensdown** 248 Ferry Road EH5 3AN ☎031-552 5438
This friendly, family-run guest house is situated on the north side and enjoys a fine outlook over the city. Bedrooms, some non-smoking, are tastefully decorated and comfortably furnished. Public areas include a cosy TV lounge and a bright, spacious dining room where hearty breakfasts are served.
7rm (5fb) ⊁ CTV in all bedrooms ⓡ ✱ sB&B£20-£36 dB&B£30-£36
Lic ▥, CTV

GH ⓠⓠⓠ **Ravensnuek** 11 Blacket Avenue EH9 1RR
☎031-667 5347
Ravensnuek is a lovingly restored Victorian semi in a quiet lane just off the A68 on the south side of the city. It has been tastefully furnished throughout and most of the bedrooms still have their original fireplaces. There is a fine period lounge where breakfast is also served.

6rm (1fb) ⊁ in 4 bedrooms ⊁ in dining room ⓡ ✱ ✳ dB&B£34-£44 dB&B£50
▥, CTV

GH ⓠ *Rosebery Private Hotel* 13 Rosebery Crescent, West End EH12 5JY ☎031-337 1085
A Victorian terraced house situated in the city's west end convenient to the Haymarket, offering practical bed and breakfast accommodation for tourists. Freshly cooked breakfasts are served in the spacious dining room at individual tables.
10rm(6➪) (1fb) CTV in all bedrooms ⓡ
▥,⊬

SELECTED

GH ⓠⓠⓠⓠ **Roselea** 11 Mayfield Road EH9 2NG
☎031-667 3556
Maureen Invernizzi's flair for interior design is evident in her delightful terraced guest house on the south side of the city. Tasteful decor and elegant fabrics enhance the period style, while the luxurious bathrooms would grace a top hotel. Each of the bedrooms without en suites has its own bathroom, and bathrobes are thoughtfully provided. There is a small but comfortable lounge and a well proportioned dining room.
7rm(5➪) (3fb) CTV in all bedrooms ⓡ LDO N
▥,
Credit Cards ①②③

GH ⓠⓠ **Rowan** 13 Glenorchy Terrace EH9 2DQ ☎031-667 2463
This sturdy, stone-built Victorian house is situated in a quiet residential area on the south side of the city close to Cameron Toll. Efficiently run by a friendly owner, it offers good-value accommodation in well maintained bedrooms. Breakfast is served in the lounge/dining room.
9rm(2➪) (2fb) ⊁ in dining room ⊁ in lounges CTV in all bedrooms ⓡ ✳ sB&B£18-£21 dB&B£32-£42 dB&B✿£36-£50 ▥, CTV
Credit Cards ①③ⓔ

GH ⓠⓠⓠ **St Margaret's** 18 Craigmillar Park EH16 5PS
☎031-667 2202
Feb-Dec
Some of the bedrooms at St Margaret's are very large and all are enhanced by tasteful soft furnishings and coordinated fabrics; there is also an attractive lounge. The guesthouse is on the A701/A772 on the south side of the city centre.
7rm(4➪) (3fb) ⊁ CTV in all bedrooms ⓡ ✱ ✳ dB&B£30-£36 dB&B✿£36-£48
▥, CTV
Credit Cards ①③ⓔ

GH ⓠⓠⓠ **Salisbury Hotel** 45 Salisbury Road EH16 5AA (left off A7) ☎031-667 1264 FAX 031-667 1264
Closed Xmas-New Year
A fine property converted from two Georgian houses, this hotel is quietly situated between two of the main roads leading into the city from the south. The bedrooms are sensibly furnished with comfortable seating, and all but the two single rooms are well proportioned.
12rm(9⇄➪) (3fb) ⊁ in dining room CTV in all bedrooms ⓡ sB&B⇄✿£20-£30 dB&B⇄✿£40-£50 WB&B£130-£200
Lic ▥, CTV
ⓔ

GH ⓠⓠⓠ **Salisbury View Hotel** 64 Dalkeith Road EH16 5AE
☎031-667 1133 FAX 031-667 1133
rs 23-28 Dec
Salisbury View is a detached sandstone house by the A68 on the south side of the city, close to the Commonwealth Swimming Pool. Attractively decorated throughout, its well equipped bedrooms are popular with business guests and tourists alike.

There is a tasteful lounge with a residents' bar and a spacious dining room.
8🚿 (1fb) 🚭 in dining room CTV in all bedrooms [R] ✱ sB&B🚿£26-£37 dB&B🚿£50-£60 WB&B£175-£210 WBDi£267-£302 LDO noon
Lic 🅿
Credit Cards [1] [3] [5] [£]

GH [Q] Sherwood 42 Minto Street EH9 2BR ☎031-667 1200
FAX 031-667 1200
Closed Xmas & New Year
This modest guesthouse, south of the city, caters for the budget bed and breakfast market and offers good value for money. The accommodation is functional and kept spotlessly clean. It has a combined lounge and dining room. The bedrooms are bright, clean and well equipped.
6rm (3fb)CTV in all bedrooms [R] dB&B£26-£40
🅿
[£]

GH [Q][Q] Southdown 20 Craigmillar Park EH16 5PS (off A701)
☎031-667 2410
Feb-Nov
Good-value accommodation is offered at this friendly family-run guest house on the south side of Edinburgh, close to Cameron Toll. John and Muriel Hamilton are welcoming hosts and enjoy caring for their guests. There is a comfortable lounge with books and board games, and hearty breakfasts are served at individual tables in the dining room.
6rm(4🚿) (2fb) 🚭 in bedrooms 🚭 in dining room CTV in all bedrooms [R] T 🐕 (ex guide dogs) sB&B🚿£20-£35 dB&B🚿£36-£50
🅿 CTV

GH Ⓠ Ⓠ Ⓠ **Strathmohr** 23 Mayfield Gardens EH9 2BX ☎031-667 8475
Strathmohr is a family-run guest house with mainly spacious bedrooms equipped with radios and hairdryers. Smoking is prohibited throughout the house.
7🛏 (4fb) ✗ CTV in all bedrooms Ⓡ 🐾 (ex guide dogs) sB&Bſ£25-£35 dB&Bſ£32-£56
💷 CTV
£

GH Ⓠ Ⓠ Ⓠ **Stra'ven** 3 Brunstane Road North, Joppa EH15 2DL ☎031-669 5580
This well maintained semidetached Victorian house is situated three miles east of the city in a quiet cul-de-sac, close to the seafront and with easy access to the A1. The spacious bedrooms all have private bathrooms, and there is an attractive first floor lounge with sea views. Smoking is not permitted.
7🛏⇨🛏 ✗ CTV in all bedrooms Ⓡ 🐾 (ex guide dogs)
💷 CTV ⅌

SELECTED

GH Ⓠ Ⓠ Ⓠ Ⓠ **Stuart House** 12 East Claremont Street EH7 4JP ☎031-557 9030 FAX 031-557 0563
Closed 18-27 Dec
Discreet but attentive service is provided at this attractively appointed Georgian-style terraced house north of the city centre. Stylishly decorated bedrooms are thoughtfully equipped with such extras as books and magazines, hair dryers, tissues and toiletries; several showers have now been upgraded, as has the spacious master bedroom with its two double beds and writing bureau. There is a cosy little lounge, and breakfast is taken at two long tables in an elegant dining room.
7rm(6⇨🛏) (1fb) ✗ CTV in all bedrooms Ⓡ T 🐾 sB&B£28-£34 dB&B⇨ſ£60-£70
💷 nc2yrs
Credit Cards ①②③ £

GH Ⓠ Ⓠ Ⓠ **Terrace Hotel** 37 Royal Terrace EH7 5AH ☎031-556 3423 FAX 031-556 2520
Fine views of the River Forth are enjoyed from the upper floors of this comfortable town house, which forms part of a fashionable Georgian terrace within easy reach of the east end of Princes Street. Bedrooms are mostly spacious with lofty ceilings, and the public rooms comprise an elegant lounge and a neat dining room where hearty breakfasts are served.
14rm(11⇨🛏) (7fb) CTV in 12 bedrooms Ⓡ 🐾 ✳ sB&B£22-£25 sB&B⇨ſ£24-£35 dB&B£39-£44 dB&B⇨ſ£49-£64
CTV ⅌
Credit Cards ① ③

GH Ⓠ Ⓠ **Tiree** 26 Craigmillar Park EH16 5PS ☎031-667 7477 FAX 031-662 1608
This stone-built family run guesthouse forms part of a terraced row in the Southside and offers good value, practical accommodation. Bedrooms vary in size but provide adequate facilities, and hearty breakfasts are served at individual tables in the rear dining room. This is a no-smoking establishment.
7rm(5🛏) (2fb) ✗ in dining room ✗ in lounges CTV in all bedrooms Ⓡ ✳ sB&B£16-£18 dB&B£32-£36 dB&Bſ£34-£50
💷

SELECTED

GH Ⓠ Ⓠ Ⓠ Ⓠ **The Town House** 65 Gilmore Place EN3 9NV ☎031-229 1985
5⇨ſ🛏 (1fb) ✗ CTV in all bedrooms Ⓡ 🐾 (ex guide dogs)
💷 CTV

GH Ⓠ Ⓠ **Varis Villa** 17 Viewforth Terrace, Merchiston EH10 4LJ ☎031-229 8454
Apr-Oct
3rm CTV in all bedrooms Ⓡ ✳ dB&B£28-£36
💷
£

GH Ⓠ Ⓠ **Villa Nina** 39 Leamington Terrace EH10 4JS ☎031-229 2644 FAX 031-229 2644
4🛏 (1fb) CTV in all bedrooms 🐾 ✳ dB&B£29-£34 WB&B£98-£105
💷 nc12yrs

ELIE Fife · Map **12** NO40

GH Ⓠ Ⓠ Ⓠ **The Elms** 14 Park Place KY9 1DH ☎(0333) 330404
Apr-Sep
An attractive detached house dating from 1880, situated in this picturesque coastal village; it sits back from the main road and there is a well tended walled garden to the rear. Bedrooms vary in size and style and some of them have private bathrooms. There is a comfortable first floor lounge and the pleasant dining room has a fine plaster frieze.
7rm(1⇨3🛏) (2fb) ✗ in dining room CTV in 4 bedrooms Ⓡ sB&Bfr£23.50 sB&B⇨ſ£45 dB&B£36 dB&B⇨ſ£49 WB&B£126-£171.50 WBDi£185-£228 LDO 6.30pm
Lic 💷 CTV ⅌ nc 8yrs
£

ELTERWATER Cumbria · · · · · · · · · · · · · Map **07** NY30

INN Ⓠ Ⓠ Ⓠ **Britannia** LA22 9HP ☎Langdale(05394) 37210 FAX (05394) 37311
Closed 25 & 26 Dec
The Britannia is a traditional British inn, painted black and white, in a delightful village setting. The bedrooms are attractively furnished and have many modern features, while retaining much of their original charm. The bars are small but atmospheric with open fires and oak beams. An extensive range of bar food is served at lunchtime and in the evening, and on sunny days one can eat on the patio. The afternoon menu offers light snacks and cream teas. An attractive dining room and lounge are provided for residents.
9rm(6🛏) Annexe 4rm(1🛏) CTV in all bedrooms Ⓡ T sB&B£18.50-£23.50 dB&B£37-£56 dB&Bſ£43-£62 WB&B£112-£206.50 WBDi£229-£346.50 Bar Lunch £5-£8alc Dinner £16.75 LDO 7.30pm
💷
Credit Cards ① ③ £

ELY Cambridgeshire · · · · · · · · · · · · · · · Map **05** TL58

GH Ⓠ **Castle Lodge Hotel** 50 New Barns Road CB7 4PW ☎(0353) 662276
This family-owned and run hotel is situated in a residential area, yet is within walking distance of the cathedral and town centre. The public areas are quite comfortable, clean and well maintained, and there is a well stocked bar. Rooms on the first floor are simply furnished, some with private bathrooms; the second-floor rooms are quite basic.
10rm(1⇨2🛏) (1fb) CTV in all bedrooms Ⓡ 🐾 (ex guide dogs) LDO 7.30pm
Lic 💷
Credit Cards ① ③

SELECTED

FH Ⓠ Ⓠ Ⓠ Ⓠ Mrs A Morbey **Forge Cottage** *(TL554784)*
Lower Road, Stuntney CB7 5TN (off A142) ☎(0353) 663275 FAX (0353) 662260
Located in the small village of Stuntney, this 18th-century

farmhouse sits in a peaceful part of the village with 2.5 acres of landscaped gardens and grounds. During the summer months, guests are welcome to view the Shire horses put out to graze, and the hard tennis court is available for guests to use. The quality bedrooms are all no smoking, are colour coordinated throughout and are furnished with a nice mixture of antiques and superior, chintz style soft furnishings. There is a dining room and lounge that interchange with the seasons, so visitors can enjoy the comfort of the large open log fire in winter months. Both rooms are nicely decorated with rich colours that complement the oak beams and antique furniture. Guests dine communally at a highly polished table and dinners are only available by prior arrangement; alternatively the family has good connections with a local restaurant and can generally make bookings for guests.

2rm(1⇌1🌊) ✗ in bedrooms ✗ in lounges CTV in all bedrooms Ⓡ ✗ (ex guide dogs) ♦ sB&B⇌🌊£30 dB&B⇌🌊£45

▥ nc10yrs ⚘(hard)U 3000 acres arable vegetables ⓔ

FH QQQ Mrs H Nix **Hill House** *(TL819487)* 9 Main Street, Coveney CB6 2DJ (off A142) ☎(0353) 778369 2🌊 ✗ CTV in all bedrooms Ⓡ ✗ dB&B🌊£36-£40 ▥ nc10yrs 240 acres arable Credit Cards 5

EMBLETON Northumberland Map **12** NU22

FH QQ A D Turnbull **Doxford** *(NU183233)* Doxford Farm NE6 7SDY (signposted from B6347) ☎Charlton Mires(0665) 579235 FAX (0665) 579215 Closed Xmas & New Year

▶

Situated four miles from the sea and set in 600 acres of rolling countryside, the farmhouse offers comfortable bedrooms including one in an adjacent outbuilding suitable for a family or smokers - there is no smoking in the house. On cold evenings a log fire burns in the sitting room, and enjoyable farmhouse cooking is served in the dining room. On Sundays, interested guests can have a guided tour around the farm. Outdoor activities include tennis, squash, fishing. There are also five terraced cottages to let.

4rm (1fb) ✗ in 3 bedrooms ✗ in dining room CTV in 1 bedroom Ⓡ ✻ sB&B£16-£24 dB&B£32-£36 dB&B🚿£34-£38 LDO noon

CTV 🎾(grass)🎣 squash 400 acres arable/beef/sheep

Credit Cards [3] [£]

EMSWORTH Hampshire Map **04** SU70

GH [Q][Q][Q] Jingles Hotel 77 Horndean Road PO10 7PU (turn off A259 towards Rowlands Castle and continue for approx 1m) ☎(0243) 373755 FAX (0243) 373755

Standing in a quiet location north of the village centre, this licensed, family-run hotel is in a rural setting with a small garden and sunny patio. One room has a four-poster bed and there are ground-floor rooms. Public areas include a TV lounge, cosy bar and a no-smoking dining room. Resident proprietors Angela and Christopher Chapman share the cooking and produce a daily 4-course menu. Vegetarians are particularly well catered for. Facilities including in-house laundry, iron and board can all be provided.

13rm(7🛁🚿) ✗ in 3 bedrooms ✗ in dining room CTV in all bedrooms Ⓡ ✻ sB&B£23 sB&B🛁🚿£31 dB&B£40 dB&B🛁🚿£52 LDO 7pm

Lic 🅿 CTV

Credit Cards [1] [3] [£]

GH [Q][Q][Q] ***Merry Hall Hotel*** 73 Horndean Road PO10 7PU ☎(0243) 372424

Closed 25 Dec-3 Jan

Situated north of the village centre, this popular licensed hotel, personally run by Trevor and Barbara Bartley, is much in demand for receptions, functions and parties, besides being well known for a very good value Sunday lunch. The modern bedrooms are all well equipped and the atmosphere is friendly and informal. Dinner, cooked by Barbara Bartley, offers a full choice of dishes, but the restaurant is closed on Sunday evenings. There is ample car parking, and a 48-hour laundry service, ironing facilities and newspapers can all be provided.

10rm(7🛁3🚿) (2fb) CTV in all bedrooms Ⓡ **T** 🐕 LDO 7.30pm

Lic 🅿 CTV putting green

Credit Cards [1] [3]

SELECTED

INN[Q][Q][Q][Q] ***The Crown Hotel*** 8 High Street PO10 7TW ☎(0243) 372806 FAX (0243) 370082

9rm(7🛁🚿) (1fb) CTV in all bedrooms Ⓡ **T** LDO 9.30pm

🅿

Credit Cards [1] [2] [3]

EPSOM Surrey Map **04** TQ26

GH [Q][Q] ***Epsom Downs Hotel*** 9 Longdown Road KT17 3PT ☎(0372) 740643 FAX (0372) 723259

A friendly hotel quietly situated in a residential road close to the town centre and benefiting from ample forecourt parking. Bedrooms are generally on the small side and modestly furnished, but most have private bathrooms and they all have direct dial telephones and TV. Public areas are open plan, and include a bar and pleasant restaurant open to non-residents, and a small lounge area with satellite TV. Evening meals and bar snacks are available, and service is informal. Small speciality conference and business facilities are available, with wedding receptions and buffets catered for.

14rm(3🛁9🚿) CTV in all bedrooms Ⓡ **T** 🐕 LDO 9pm

Lic 🅿 CTV

Credit Cards [1] [2] [3] [5]

GH [Q][Q][Q] The White House Downs Hill Road KT18 5HW ☎(0372) 722472 FAX (0372) 744447

A late Victorian house with ample car parking and attractive gardens to the front. Bedrooms upstairs are generally spacious and well furnished, with private bathrooms, whilst ground floor rooms are more modest, with showers only; all rooms have telephones and TV. Breakfast and evening meals are served in the dining room, and the willing proprietors Mr and Mrs Stupple also offer light snacks and continental breakfast trays in bedrooms. The hotel has a residential licence, and there is a small comfortable lounge.

15rm(4🛁3🚿) (1fb) CTV in all bedrooms Ⓡ 🐕 (ex guide dogs) ✻ sB&B£32.50-£49.50 sB&B🛁🚿£45.50-£49.50 dB&B£55.50-£59.50 dB&B🛁🚿£59.50 WB&B£227.50 WBDi£237.50 LDO 8.30pm

Lic 🅿 CTV

Credit Cards [1] [3] [£]

ERLESTOKE Wiltshire Map **03** ST95

FH [Q][Q][Q] Mrs P Hampton **Longwater Park** *(ST966541)* Lower Road SN10 5UE (turn off A360 at West Lavington onto B3908 for 3m, in Erlestoke village turn right by post office signed Marston/Worton,Longwater is 400yds on right) ☎Devizes(0380) 830095 FAX (0380) 830095

Closed Xmas & New Year

Detached from the organically managed farm, this modern brick farmhouse overlooks parkland and lakes. The larger lake can be fished, while the smaller is set aside for waterfowl. Rooms are split between the main house and a separate building: all are comfortably furnished. There is an attractive lounge and conservatory. Organically produced ingredients are used wherever possible in the preparation of meals. Mr and Mrs Hampton encourage guests to be part of the family, which includes four cats.

3🛁🚿 Annexe 2🛁🚿 (1fb) ✗ in bedrooms ✗ in dining room ✗ in 1 lounge CTV in all bedrooms Ⓡ sB&B£25 sB&B🛁🚿£25 dB&B🛁🚿£40 WB&B£135-£160 WBDi£205-£230 LDO 5pm

Lic 🅿 CTV nc12yrs 🎣 166 acres beef waterfowl organic

[£]

ESCRICK North Yorkshire Map **08** SE64

GH [Q][Q][Q] Church Cottage YO4 6EX ☎York(0904) 728462 FAX (0904) 728462

An attractive house is surrounded by gardens and woodland. Bedrooms have been recently decorated and there is a large dining room where breakfast is served.

7rm(6🚿) (3fb) CTV in all bedrooms Ⓡ 🐕 (ex guide dogs) ✻ sB&B🚿£25-£35 dB&B🚿£35-£45 WB&B£122.50-£157.50 LDO 8pm

Lic 🅿 9 hole garden putting

Credit Cards [1] [3] [£]

See advertisement under YORK

INN[Q][Q][Q] Black Bull Inn Main Street YO4 6JP ☎(0904) 728245 & 728154

8🛁🚿 (1fb) CTV in all bedrooms Ⓡ sB&B🛁🚿£35-£40 dB&B🛁🚿£48-£58 Lunch £4.95-£15.95&alc Dinner £4.95-£15.95&alc LDO 10pm

🅿 🐴

Credit Cards [1] [3] [£]

See advertisement under YORK

ETTINGTON Warwickshire Map **04** SP24

[🏠 🍴] **FH [Q][Q]** Mrs B J Wakeham **Whitfield** *(SP265506)* CV37 7PN (on A429, 1m from Ettington) ☎Stratford on Avon(0789) 740260

Closed Dec

A spacious farmhouse seven miles from Stratford-upon-Avon. Accommodation is comfortable, and the newly created ground floor bedroom is particularly attractive. The Wakeham family are friendly, welcoming hosts.

3rm(2🚿) (1fb) 🚭 in dining room [R] 🐕 (ex guide dogs) sB&B£14-£20 dB&B£28-£29 dB&B🚿£31-£32

♨ CTV 220 acres mixed

[£]

EVERSHOT Dorset Map **03** ST50

SELECTED

GH [Q][Q][Q][Q] Rectory House Fore Street DT2 0JW

☎(0935) 83273 FAX (0935) 83273

Closed Xmas

The picture-postcard village of Evershot, immortalised by Thomas Hardy as 'Evershead' in 'Tess of the D' Urbervilles', provides the setting for Rectory House. It is a handsome stone building dating back to the 18th century and offers spacious accommodation – the bathrooms are huge – in the main house and four smaller but equally well equipped and nicely decorated bedrooms in the converted stable block. There are two comfortable lounges to choose from, one charmingly cosy, the other more formal and elegant, and a pretty dining room faces the village street. A set evening meal using fresh local produce is served here. There is also a pretty garden.

6🛁🚿 🚭 in bedrooms 🚭 in dining room 🚭 in 1 lounge CTV in all bedrooms [R] 🐕 (ex guide dogs) sB&B🛁🚿£30-£50 dB&B🛁🚿£50-£60 WBDi£245-£270 LDO 7pm

Lic ♨ TV nc10yrs

Credit Cards [1] [3] [£]

See advertisement under DORCHESTER

EVESHAM Hereford & Worcester Map **04** SP04

GH [Q][Q][Q] Church House Greenhill Park Road WR11 4NL

☎(0386) 40498

Antiques and family mementoes add to the friendly, country house atmosphere provided by Veronica and Michael Shaw, in this large semidetached house set back from the A435 in a residential area close to the town centre. Bedrooms are furnished with good quality fabrics and interesting antique pieces, including Victorian dressing tables and wardrobes. Guests are well prepared for the day with a substantial breakfast served at the large ornate table in the dining room. For dinner, the proprietors have a good knowledge of local restaurants and pubs.

3🛁🚿 (1fb) 🚭 in dining room CTV in all bedrooms [R] sB&B🛁🚿£25-£32 dB&B🛁🚿£35-£42

♨

[£]

GH [Q][Q][Q] The Croft 54 Greenhill WR11 4NF (0.5m on A435)

☎(0386) 446035

This large white Georgian house is set in pleasant gardens on the outskirts of the town, off the A435. The bedrooms are very well furnished, some being remarkably spacious and filled with extra welcoming touches. There are two comfortable lounges, and breakfast is served around a large table by the friendly owner, Mrs Sheila Larne.

3rm(2🛁🚿) (1fb) 🚭 in dining room CTV in all bedrooms [R] sB&B£25-£28 sB&B🛁🚿£28-£32 dB&B£36-£40 dB&B🛁🚿£38-£42

♨ CTV

[£]

GH [Q][Q] Park View Waterside WR11 6BS (0.25m SE on B4035)

☎(0386) 442639

Closed 25 Dec-1 Jan

26rm (2fb) 🚭 in dining room sB&B£18.50-£23 dB&B£34-£39 LDO 7pm

Lic CTV

Credit Cards [1] [2] [3] [5] [£]

EXETER Devon Map **03** SX99

GH [Q] *Braeside* 21 New North Road EX4 4HF ☎(0392) 56875

Closed 25-26 Dec

Braeside is close to both the university and the city centre. The seven bedrooms are spread over three floors and several have shower cubicles. Breakfast is served in the attractive pine-furnished dining room. Parking is limited to public car parks or the road outside.

7rm(3🚿) (1fb) CTV in all bedrooms [R] LDO 4pm

♨ 🚫🅿

SELECTED

GH [Q][Q][Q][Q] The Edwardian 30/32 Heavitree Road EX1 2LQ ☎(0392) 76102 & 54699

Closed Xmas & New Year

Two Edwardian terraced houses have formed a friendly guesthouse run by resident proprietors Michael and Kay Rattenbury. Several of the bedrooms have antique furnishings in the Edwardian style whilst others are more modern. Books and games are provided in the cosy lounge and there are two attractive dining rooms.

14rm(11🛁🚿) (1fb) 🚭 in dining room 🚭 in lounges CTV in all bedrooms [R] T sB&B£22 sB&B🛁🚿£30-£32 dB&B🛁🚿£40-£46 WB&B£126-£140

♨ CTV

Credit Cards [1] [2] [3] [5] [£]

GH [Q][Q][Q] Hotel Gledhills 32 Alphington Road EX2 8HN

☎(0392) 430469 & 71439 FAX (0392) 430469

Closed 2 wks Xmas/New Year

▶

The White House Hotel

Downs Hill Road, Epsom, Surrey KT18 5HW

Tel: (01372) 722472 Fax: (01372) 744447

ETB 👑👑👑

* Situated ½ mile from Epsom Downs, 3 miles from M25

* Single & double rooms — most en suite

* Full English breakfast

* Weekend rates

The Gledhills is an attractive red brick Victorian house on the edge of the city close to the quay. Almost all the comfortable bedrooms have en suite shower rooms as well as a range of modern equipment. Charming hosts David and Suzanne Greening maintain high standards and are rewarded by a large number of returning guests. There is a sunny breakfast room and a cosy bar where a wide variety of home cooked snacks is served.
12rm(11🚿) (4fb) 🚭 in dining room CTV in all bedrooms [R] 🐕 sB&B£20-£22 sB&B🚿£25-£27.50 dB&B🚿£39-£43 WB&B£132-£165 LDO 8.30pm
Lic ♨ CTV
Credit Cards [1][3]

GH [Q][Q] Park View Hotel 8 Howell Road EX4 4LG (from M5 follow signs B3183 City Centre until you reach the clock tower roundabout, 3rd exit Elm Grove at end of road T junct, turn left Howell Road) ☎(0392) 71772 FAX (0392) 53047
Closed Xmas
The Park View Hotel is located in a particularly quiet and attractive residential area of town, yet close to the city centre, station and university. It is a Grade II listed house with bright accommodation on three floors. There is a comfortable lounge with floor to ceiling windows, and an attractive breakfast room leading out to the rear garden and patio area.
10rm(2🛁2🚿) Annexe 5🚿 (2fb) 🚭 in 1 bedrooms 🚭 in dining room CTV in all bedrooms [R] **T** * sB&B£20-£22 sB&B🛁🚿£28-£32 dB&B£35 dB&B🛁🚿£43-£45 WB&Bfr£92
♨ CTV
Credit Cards [1][3][£]

GH [Q][Q] Sunnymede 24 New North Road EX4 4HF ☎(0392) 73844
Closed 24 Dec-1 Jan
A city-centre guest house, Sunnymead is close to the university and the main shopping area. The bedroooms are on three floors and all have either en suite shower rooms or shower cubicles in the rooms. Breakfast is served at separate tables in the dining room, which is part conservatory. Parking is limited to public car parks or to the road outside.
9rm(5🚿) (1fb) 🚭 in dining room CTV in all bedrooms [R] 🐕 * sB&B£19-£21 sB&B🚿£21 dB&B£29 dB&B🚿£32 LDO 9pm
♨ CTV P̸

GH [Q] Telstar Hotel 77 St Davids Hill EX4 4DW ☎(0392) 72466
A small, family-run guesthouse stands in a terrace of small hotels, close to the university, station and city centre. Bedrooms are clean and comfortable, and the friendly proprietors serve breakfast in the attractive dining room.
9rm (1fb) 🚭 in dining room [R] * sB&B£13-£16 dB&B£25-£30 dB&B£28-£32 WB&B£90-£110
♨ CTV
[£]

GH [Q][Q] *Trees Mini Hotel* 2 Queen's Crescent, York Road EX4 6AY ☎(0392) 59531
A family-run guesthouse, close to all the amenities and just a short walk from the city centre, offers simple bedrooms which are spotlessly clean and comfortable. There is a quiet lounge and a set evening meal is now available in the dining room. Devonshire hospitality comes naturally to the resident proprietors.
10rm(1🛁) (1fb) CTV in all bedrooms [R] 🐕 LDO 10am
♨ CTV
Credit Cards [1][3]

EYE Suffolk — Map 05 TM17

INN[Q][Q][Q] Four Horseshoes Wickham Road, Thornham Magna IP23 7HD ☎(0379) 678777
10rm(2🛁7🚿) (1fb)CTV in 8 bedrooms [R] **T** * sB&Bfr£37.50 sB&B🛁🚿£45 dB&Bfr£55 dB&B🛁🚿£65 Lunch £20-£25alc High tea £7-£8 Dinner £20-£25alc LDO 10pm
♨ CTV
Credit Cards [1][2][3][5][£]

INN[Q][Q][Q] The White Horse Stoke Ash IP23 7ET (on the A140 between Ipswich/Norwich) ☎(0379) 678222 FAX (0379) 678557
A 17th-century coaching inn is set alongside the main road. Seven good-sized bedrooms are in a modern annexe and two are in the main building. The bars and restaurant are spread over two floors and there are plenty of exposed timbers and an inglenook fireplace.
2🛁 Annexe 7🛁 CTV in all bedrooms [R] **T** 🐕 (ex guide dogs) LDO 9.30pm
♨
Credit Cards [1][3][£]

EYNSFORD Kent — Map 05 TQ56

SELECTED

FH [Q][Q][Q][Q] Mrs Sarah Alexander **Home Farm** *(TQ537656)* Riverside DA4 0AE ☎Farningham(0322) 866193 FAX (0322) 868600
Mar-Nov
Set on the edge of the village, this is a charming farmhouse offering tasteful accomodation. There are three large en suite bedrooms with fine period furniture and good facilities. The comfortable sitting room is similarly spacious with a brick fireplace and a good piano. An evening meal and a choice of breakfast are served at the communal table of the low-beamed dining room.
3rm(1🛁2🚿) 🚭 [R] 🐕 (ex guide dogs) sB&B🛁🚿£27-£29 dB&B🛁🚿£36-£38
♨ CTV nc12yrs 850 acres arable
[£]

EYNSHAM Oxfordshire — Map 04 SP40

SELECTED

GH [Q][Q][Q][Q] All Views Main A40 OX8 1PU ☎Oxford(0865) 880891
All Views is an attractive Cotswold stone chalet bungalow run in conjuction with a nursery/farm shop. Gerry and Joan Thomas welcome guests to their home and offer comfortable, well equipped bedrooms, all on the ground floor with good modern bathrooms. Breakfast is taken in the open plan kitchen/breakfast room, and there is a lounge available to guests.
4🛁🚿 🚭 in dining room 🚭 in lounges CTV in all bedrooms [R] **T** 🐕 (ex guide dogs) * sB&B🛁🚿£30 dB&B🛁🚿£40
♨ CTV nc10yrs
[£]

FAKENHAM Norfolk — Map 09 TF92

See also Barney

INN[Q][Q][Q] Sculthorpe Mill Lynn Road, Sculthorpe NR21 9QG (2m SW, off A148, signposted) ☎(0328) 856161 & 862675 FAX (0328) 856651
6🛁🚿 (1fb) 🚭 in 2 bedrooms CTV in all bedrooms [R] **T** * sB&B🛁🚿£30 dB&B🛁🚿£50-£75 Lunch £8.50-£14.95&alc Dinner £8.50-£14.95&alc LDO 9.30pm
♨ 🏌 🎣
Credit Cards [1][2][3]

FALFIELD Avon — Map 03 ST69

GH [Q][Q] Green Farm GL12 8DL ☎(0454) 260319
Situated on the A38, just half a mile north of junction 14 on the M5, this large house is set back in its own pleasant grounds which include a tennis court and outdoor swimming pool. Parts of the house date back to the 16th century, and it was formerly the principal house of a large farm; some of the original character has

been retained, with flagstone floors, exposed beams and open fires. Bedrooms vary in size and are simple, bright and soundly appointed.
8rm(1⇌) ⅍ in bedrooms CTV in 1 bedroom ⓡ ✳ sB&Bfr£20 sB&B⇌£30 dB&Bfr£30 dB&B⇌£40 LDO 8.30pm
▥ CTV ⅋ℝ(hard)

FALMOUTH Cornwall & Isles of Scilly   Map **02** SW83

GH Ⓠ Ⓠ Ⓠ **Cotswold House Hotel** Melvill Road TR11 4DF
☎(0326) 312077
Pamela and Graham Cain's small hotel is conveniently located just a few minutes' walk from the town centre, harbour and beach. It has limited on-site parking and a small sunny garden. Bedrooms are attractively coordinated and well equipped. A cosy bar and a comfortable lounge are provided for guests, and at dinner a choice of traditional dishes and salads is offered.
10rm(9⇌♠) (2fb) ⅍ in dining room CTV in all bedrooms ⓡ ✻ ✳ sB&B⇌♠£18 dB&B⇌♠£36 WB&B£125 WBDi£170 LDO 7pm
Lic nc4yrs
Ⓔ

▨ ▆ **GH** Ⓠ Ⓠ **Dolvean Hotel** 50 Melvill Road TR11 4DQ
☎(0326) 313658
14rm(5⇌♠) (1fb)CTV in all bedrooms ⓡ ✻ (ex guide dogs) sB&B£13.50-£16.50 sB&B⇌♠£15.50-£18.50 dB&B£27-£33 dB&B⇌♠£31-£37 WB&B£90-£120 WBDi£152.50-£177.50 LDO 6pm
Lic CTV nc5yrs
Credit Cards ① ② ③

GH Ⓠ Ⓠ Ⓠ **Ivanhoe** 7 Melvill Road TR11 4AS ☎(0326) 319083
This family run guesthouse stands in an Edwardian terrace between the town centre and beaches. There is a comfortable lounge downstairs, and well kept bedrooms on the two floors ▶

above vary in size and headroom, but all are brightly decorated with colourful duvets.
7rm(4🚿) (2fb) 🚭 in dining room CTV in all bedrooms [R] 🐕 ✱ sB&B£16-£18 dB&B🚿fr£32
♨ CTV
Credit Cards [1][2][3][5][£]

GH [Q][Q][Q] Melvill House Hotel 52 Melvill Road TR11 4DQ
☎(0326) 316645 FAX (0326) 211608
Closed 23 Dec-1 Jan
Situated between the shops and the sea, this attractive pink painted semi-detached Victorian villa provides well equipped accommodation, including one ground-floor room. A set four-course dinner, described by owner Gail Jones as basic home cooking, is served in the dining room and a comfortable lounge is provided for guests' use.
7rm(5🛁2🚿) (3fb) CTV in all bedrooms [R] 🐕 ✱ sB&B🛁🚿£17.50-£19.50 dB&B🛁🚿£31-£37 WBDi£145-£152 LDO 5.30pm
Lic ♨ CTV nc7yrs
[£]

SELECTED

GH [Q][Q][Q][Q] Penmere "Rosehill", Mylor Bridge TR11 5LZ
☎(0326) 374470
Aptly named from the Cornish for 'head of the water', this detached traditional stone house dating from 1862 has views over Mylor Creek and the surrounding countryside. Lovingly restored by its owners, it provides individually furnished and decorated bedrooms - each of them named after a local area - with coordinated fabrics and pine furniture. A varied choice is offered at breakfast, but this is the only meal served; a selection of menus from local eating places is available for guests' guidance. The open-plan dining room/lounge is a no smoking area.
6rm(4🛁🚿) (2fb) 🚭 in dining room 🚭 in lounges CTV in all bedrooms [R] 🐕 (ex guide dogs) sB&Bfr£22 sB&B🛁🚿fr£25 dB&Bfr£40 dB&B🛁🚿fr£47
♨
[£]

GH [Q][Q][Q] *Penty Bryn Hotel* 10 Melvill Road TR11 4AS
☎(0326) 314988 FAX (0326) 378130
Nov-Dec
A small, terraced, family-run hotel conveniently situated for the town centre and seafront. Bedrooms are well maintained and equipped, with modern facilities and some have fine sea views. There is a comfortable lounge together with a cosy bar and breakfast room. The hotel is personally run by the friendly resident proprietor Mrs Jane Wearne.
7rm(5🚿) (3fb) CTV in all bedrooms [R]
Lic ♨ CTV
Credit Cards [1][3][5]

GH [Q][Q][Q] San Remo Hotel Gyllyngvase Hill TR11 4DN
☎(0326) 312076
Etr-mid Oct
10rm(8🛁🚿) (1fb) CTV in all bedrooms [R] 🐕 (ex guide dogs) LDO 6pm
nc5yrs
Credit Cards [1]

🛏☕ **GH [Q][Q] Treggenna** 28 Melvill Road TR11 4AR (A39 for Falmouth docks) ☎(0326) 313881
6rm(4🚿) (2fb) 🚭 in 2 bedrooms CTV in all bedrooms [R] sB&B£14-£14.50 sB&B🚿£15-£16 dB&B£28-£30 dB&B🚿£30-£32 WB&B£100-£135 WBDi£140-£150 LDO 10am
Lic ♨ CTV
Credit Cards [1][3]

🛏☕ **GH [Q][Q][Q] Trelawney** 6 Melvill Road TR11 4AS
☎(0326) 311858
Closed Xmas
Conveniently situated midway between the town centre and the beaches, this guesthouse is personally run by Ann and Colin Mackenzie. Bedrooms are well equipped and maintained to a high standard of cleanliness. Breakfast is served in the attractively decorated dining room.
6rm(4🚿) (2fb) CTV in all bedrooms [R] sB&B£14-£16 dB&B🚿£30-£34 WB&B£110
♨
Credit Cards [1][3][£]

SELECTED

GH [Q][Q][Q][Q] Westcott Hotel Gyllyngvase Hill TR11 4DN (follow signs to beach) ☎(0326) 311309
3 Jan-Oct rs Jan-Mar
This agreeable and well maintained family-run house is located close to the beach. Bedrooms are clean and comfortable, and several have sea views. Public areas include a welcoming lounge and a reception hall with an interesting collection of plates.
10rm(6🛁4🚿) Annexe 1🛁 (2fb) 🚭 in bedrooms 🚭 in dining room CTV in all bedrooms [R] 🐕 ✱ WB&B£133-£175 WBDi£155-£189 LDO 6pm
Lic ♨ CTV nc5yrs
[£]

FALSTONE Northumberland — Map 12 NY78

INN[Q][Q][Q] Pheasant Stannersburn NE48 1DD
☎Bellingham(0434) 240382 FAX (0434) 240024
Closed 25-26 Dec rs Jan-Feb
Situated in the beautiful Northumberland National Park, just a mile from the Keilder Water reservoir, this delightful family-run country inn was originally a seventeenth-century farm; much of its earlier character is still retained in low beams, stone walls and open fires. The two bars serve meals both at lunchtime and in the evening, but freshly prepared home-cooked dinners, are also available in the very attractive pine-furnished dining room. Bedrooms (all of which have modern en suite facilities) are housed in converted outbuildings built of mellow stone.
Annexe 8🚿 (1fb) 🚭 in bedrooms 🚭 in dining room 🚭 in lounges CTV in all bedrooms [R] ✱ sB&B🚿fr£30 dB&B🚿fr£52 Bar Lunch £3-£6 Dinner £10-£12.50&alc LDO 8.50pm
♨ pool room darts
[£]

FAREHAM Hampshire — Map 04 SU50

SELECTED

GH [Q][Q][Q][Q] Avenue House Hotel 22 The Avenue PO14 1NS
☎(0329) 232175 FAX (0329) 232196
A very smart and sophisticated hotel conveniently located on the A27 west of the town centre. The accommodation has been extensively upgraded to provide a high standard of comfort. Bedrooms are all well equipped and include a room with a four-poster bed and a convenient ground-floor room for disabled guests. A new, well furnished conservatory lounge is a recent addition. Small meetings can be accommodated, but dinner is not served. There are, however, plenty of restaurants nearby.
17🛁🚿 (3fb) 🚭 in 4 bedrooms CTV in all bedrooms [R] **T** sB&B🛁🚿£29.50-£43 dB&B🛁🚿£39.50-£53
♨
Credit Cards [1][2][3][£]

FARINGDON Oxfordshire — Map **04** SU29

GH [Q][Q][Q] **Faringdon Hotel** Market Place SN7 7HL
☎(0367) 240536 FAX (0367) 243250
A large building in the centre of town near the church, the Faringdon's rooms, some in an annexe overlooking a small courtyard, have excellent facilities, including satellite TV. There is a fully licensed bar and the restaurant offers a short menu of appetising dishes.
15rm(9🛁6🚿) Annexe 5rm(1🛁4🚿) (3fb)CTV in all bedrooms Ⓡ **T** ✱ sB&B🛁🚿£40-£46.50 dB&B🛁🚿£40-£56.50 LDO 9pm
Lic ▥
Credit Cards [1][2][3][5][£]

FARMBOROUGH Avon — Map **03** ST66

GH [Q][Q][Q] ***Streets Hotel*** The Street BA3 1AR
☎Mendip(0761) 471452 FAX (0761) 471452
Closed 23 Dec-1 Jan
Personally owned and run, this small private hotel is in a picturesque village between Bath and Wells. It comprises a 17th-century house with some accommodation in a converted coach house. Rooms are bright and individually furnished. There is a choice of lounges, a bar and pleasant conservatory, plus almost an acre of gardens.
3🛁🚿 Annexe 5🛁🚿 CTV in all bedrooms Ⓡ **T** 🐕 LDO 8.50pm
Lic ▥ CTV nc6yrs ⤷(heated) solarium
Credit Cards [1][2][3]

FAR SAWREY Cumbria — Map **07** SD39

SELECTED

GH [Q][Q][Q][Q] **West Vale Country** LA22 0LQ (2.75m from Hawkshead on B5285) ☎Windermere(05394) 42817
Mar-Oct
A very well furnished family run guesthouse on the edge of this village which is famous for its associations with Beatrix Potter. Built of lakeland stone, it stands in its own delightful garden and has superb open views towards Grizedale Forest and the mountains beyond. Bedrooms are comfortably furnished and spotlessly clean: most have private showers. There is a very comfortable lounge with an open log fire, and service is friendly.
8🛁🚿 (3fb) 🚭 in dining room Ⓡ 🐕 (ex guide dogs) sB&B🛁🚿£21.50 dB&B🛁🚿£43 WB&B£150.50 WBDi£206.50 LDO 4pm
Lic ▥ CTV nc7yrs coarse & trout fishing
[£]

FAVERSHAM Kent — Map **05** TR06

GH [Q][Q][Q] **Porch House** The Street, Eastling ME13 0AY
☎(0795) 890229 FAX (0795) 890150
Closed 23 Dec-2 Jan
3🛁🚿 🚭 in bedrooms CTV in all bedrooms Ⓡ 🐕 ✱ sB&B🛁🚿fr£30 dB&B🛁🚿fr£38 WB&Bfr£100
▥ nc14yrs

SELECTED

FH [Q][Q][Q][Q] Mrs S Chesterfield **Frith** *(TQ944555)* Otterden ME13 0DD ☎(0795) 890701 FAX (0795) 890009
A delightful late-Georgian farmhouse set in two acres of attractive gardens and four acres of orchard has been carefully furnished and decorated to retain its original charm. The three spacious en suite bedrooms are well-equipped and furnished with period furniture. Fine pictures and ornaments adorn the comfortable sitting room which is filled with books and magazines. A traditional English evening meal prepared using fresh produce is served on a large wooden communal table, as is a choice of breakfast.
3🚿 🚭 CTV in all bedrooms Ⓡ 🐕 sB&B🚿£27.50-£32 dB&B🚿£47-£52
▥ nc10yrs U carriage rides 6 acres non-working
Credit Cards [1][3]

INN [Q][Q][Q] **White Horse** The Street, Boughton ME13 9AX
☎Canterbury(0227) 751343 FAX (0227) 751090
Dating back to the 15th-century, this inn provides a good standard of accommodation in reasonably sized rooms which are furnished in keeping with the style of the building. There are two bars and a restaurant, where a menu of home made pies and grills is served. A reasonable choice of popular, inexpensive wines is also available.
13rm(7🛁6🚿) (2fb) CTV in all bedrooms Ⓡ **T** sB&B🛁🚿fr£37.50 dB&B🛁🚿fr£47.50 Bar Lunch fr£4.50alc Dinner fr£12.20alc LDO 9.30pm
▥ CTV
Credit Cards [1][3]

FAZELEY Staffordshire — Map **04** SK20

GH [Q][Q] ***Buxton Hotel*** 65 Coleshill Street B78 3RG
☎Tamworth(0827) 285805 & 284842 FAX (0827) 285805
Closed 25-26 Dec rs 1 Jan
Originally a doctor's residence on the Peel Estate, the house is situated alongside the A4091 just south of its junction with the A5. Bedrooms are modestly appointed but all have TV and telephones. There is an oak panelled bar, the dining room features an ornately carved wooden fireplace, and the spacious lounge includes a full size snooker table.
15rm(4🛁9🚿) (4fb) CTV in all bedrooms Ⓡ **T** LDO 8.15pm
Lic ▥ CTV
Credit Cards [1][3]

FECKENHAM Hereford & Worcester — Map **04** SP06

GH [Q][Q][Q] **The Steps** 6 High Street B96 6HS
☎Astwood Bank(0527) 892678
3rm(1🚿) 🚭 in bedrooms 🚭 in dining room Ⓡ sB&B£18-£20 sB&B🚿£22-£24 dB&B£30-£34 dB&B🚿£34-£38 WB&B£126-£154 WBDi£182-£210
▥ CTV
[£]

FELINDRE (NEAR SWANSEA) West Glamorgan — Map **03** SN60

FH [Q][Q] Mr F Jones **Coynant Farm** *(SN648070)* SA5 7PU (4m N of Felindre off unclass rd linking M4 junct 46 and Ammanford)
☎Ammanford(0269) 595640 & 592064
Rather isolated and reached by a gated concrete road, this comfortably appointed and family-run farmhouse is well worth the journey. It is set in spectacular countryside, with pursuits such as fishing and pony riding available to guests. Children particularly may enjoy feeding the farm pets.
5rm(3🛁🚿) (2fb) 🚭 in bedrooms 🚭 in dining room CTV in all bedrooms Ⓡ 🐕 (ex guide dogs) ✱ sB&Bfr£18 sB&B🛁🚿fr£18 dB&Bfr£36 dB&B🛁🚿fr£36 WB&B£126 WBDi£154.50-£164.50 LDO 7pm
Lic ▥ 🎣 U games room 200 acres mixed
[£]

FELIXSTOWE Suffolk — Map **05** TM33

INN [Q][Q][Q] **Fludyer Arms Hotel** Undercliff Road East IP11 7LU
☎(0394) 283279 FAX (0394) 670754
This small family-run inn sits on the quieter end of the seafront, just ten yards from the beach. Bedroom styles differ, the first floor rooms are furnished to a good modern standard, with nicely ▶

coordinating decor and soft furnishings, all with private bathrooms. Second floor rooms are more modestly appointed, most having comfortable armchairs, with price differentials providing reasonable value for money. Public areas have a pleasant informal atmosphere, and a range of home-cooked bar food is served at lunch and dinner.

8rm(6⇔♠) (1fb) ⚹ in area of dining room ⚹ in 1 lounge CTV in all bedrooms ⓡ ✳ sB&B£24 sB&B⇔♠£32 dB&B£38 dB&B⇔♠£46 Bar Lunch £3-£8 Dinner £3-£8 LDO 9pm
Credit Cards ① ② ③ ⓔ

FELTHAM Greater London

For accommodation details see **Heathrow Airport**

FILEY North Yorkshire   Map **08** TA18

GH ❑❑❑ **Abbots Leigh** 7 Rutland Street YO14 9JA (from A170 follow signs for town centre, then turn right at church clock tower, then second left) ☎Scarborough(0723) 513334

Conveniently situated close to the town centre, seafront and gardens, this attractive small hotel is comfortable and tastefully furnished. All bedrooms have modern en suite facilities and colour TV, but smoking is not allowed in the bedrooms nor the dining room. A five-course meal is served from 5.30pm to 6.30pm each evening with a varied choice of dishes.

6⇔♠ (3fb) ⚹ in bedrooms ⚹ in dining room CTV in all bedrooms ⓡ ✹ (ex guide dogs) sB&B⇔♠£20-£30 dB&B⇔♠£36 WB&B£113-£210 WBDi£169-£266 LDO 4pm
Lic ⬛ nc3yrs
Credit Cards ① ③ ⓔ

GH ❑❑❑ **Downcliffe Hotel** The Beach YO14 9LA
☎Scarborough(0723) 513310 FAX (0723) 516141
Mar-Nov

A stone-built Victorian house, the Downcliffe Hotel is in a unique position on the seafront. All the bedrooms are well equipped and comfortable and many have sea views. There is a residents' bar, lounge and spacious dining room where evening meals are served.

15rm(4⇔6♠) (9fb) ⚹ in dining room CTV in all bedrooms ⓡ ✳ sB&B£20-£27 sB&B⇔♠£21-£27 dB&B£40-£46 dB&B⇔♠£42-£54 LDO 6.30pm
Lic ⬛ CTV pool table
Credit Cards ① ③ ⓔ

GH ❑❑❑ **Seafield Hotel** 9/11 Rutland Street YO14 9JA
☎Scarborough(0723) 513715

The Seafield is a friendly family-run hotel close to Crescent Gardens and the beach. Bedrooms are modern though compact, and most have en suite facilities. There is a particularly large and comfortable guests' lounge and a small bar where pre-dinner drinks can be taken. A 4-course Yorkshire dinner is served at 6pm each evening.

13rm(3⇔7♠) (7fb) ⚹ in bedrooms ⚹ in dining room CTV in all bedrooms ⓡ ✹ sB&B£16.50-£18.50 sB&B⇔♠£18.50-£20.50 dB&B£33-£37 dB&B⇔♠£37-£41 WB&B£110-£138 WBDi£146-£174 LDO 4pm
Lic ⬛ CTV
Credit Cards ① ② ③ ⓔ

Telephone national area codes are due to change by 16th April 1995. Please see the note under 'How to Use this Guide' at the front of the book.

FIR TREE Co Durham   Map **12** NZ13

GH ❑❑❑❑❑ **Greenhead Country House Hotel**
DL15 8BL (on A68, turn right at Fir Tree Inn) ☎Bishop Auckland(0388) 763143

This delightful little hotel stands just off the A68, its location making it popular with businessmen and holiday-makers alike. Friendly proprietors greet guests with tea and biscuits on arrival and offer spacious, well furnished and decorated accommodation with modern facilities. One of the bedrooms features a four-poster bed and another opens directly onto the well tended garden, but some rooms can only be reached by way of a spiral staircase. There is a comfortable beamed TV lounge downstairs which includes a small bar, and though dinner is not served there are plenty of restaurants in the area.

8⇔♠ (1fb) ⚹ in 2 bedrooms ⚹ in dining room ⚹ in 1 lounge CTV in 7 bedrooms ⓡ ✹ (ex guide dogs) ✳ sB&B⇔♠£35 dB&B⇔♠£40-£45 LDO 5pm
Lic ⬛ CTV nc13yrs
Credit Cards ① ③

FISHGUARD Dyfed   Map **02** SM93

FH ❑❑❑ Mrs Lilwen McAllister *Erw-Lon (SN028325)*
Pontfaen SA65 9TS (on B4313 between Fishguard and Maenclochog) ☎(0348) 881297

An impeccably maintained farmhouse with rear views over the Gwaun Valley and handy for the Irish ferry. Mrs McAllister provides a warm welcome and comfortable bedrooms for her guests. There is a lounge and pleasant dining room.

3rm(1♠) ⓡ ✹ (ex guide dogs)
⬛ CTV nc10yrs 128 acres beef sheep

FITTLEWORTH West Sussex   Map **04** TQ0

FH ❑❑❑❑ Mrs M Kemp **Street Farm** *(SU142185)*
Lower Street RH20 1EN (turn off A283 from Petworth at Bury Arundel, onto B2138 and farm 0.25m on left opposite Swan Inn) ☎(0798) 865885
Feb-Nov

Mrs Kemp's attractive house stands in peaceful countryside in a charming village. Rooms are individually furnished to a high standard and there is also self-catering accommodation.

3⇔♠ ⚹ CTV in 2 bedrooms ⓡ ✹ ✳ sB&B⇔♠£28 dB&B⇔♠£48
⬛ nc11yrs 6 acres non-working

FLAX BOURTON Avon   Map **03** ST5

INN❑❑❑ **Jubilee** Main Road BS19 3QX ☎(0275) 462741
Closed 25 Dec evening

A most attractive and very popular roadside inn on the outskirts of Bristol, with ample car parking space on site. The bedrooms offer neat accommodation with some nice extra touches, and there is a spacious guests' lounge on the first floor. Public areas are full of character, with pleasant bars, a log fire and a good range of home-cooked meals.

3rm ⓡ sB&Bfr£25 dB&Bfr£50 LDO 10pm
⬛ CTV nc14yrs
Credit Cards ① ③

FLAXTON North Yorkshire   Map **08** SE66

FH Q Q Mrs M J Robinson **The Grange Farm** *(SE684632)* Oak Busk Lane YO6 7RL ☎Flaxton Moor(0904) 468219
Adjoining a working arable and sheep farm, this farmhouse offers three large and comfortable rooms. There is a good-sized lounge with TV and a separate breakfast room.
3rm(1🛏) (1fb) ⊁ in dining room ® 🍴 (ex guide dogs) ✳ dB&B£28-£32 dB&Bℜ£32
▥ CTV 100 acres arable sheep
ⓔ

FORDINGBRIDGE Hampshire   Map **04** SU11

GH Q Q Q **Colt Green** Damerham SP6 3HA
☎Rockbourne(0725) 240 due to change to (01725) 518240
Closed Jan & Dec
Set in an acre of walled riverside garden, Colt Green offers a tranquil country house environment. The ground-floor rooms are furnished with antiques but provide modern standards of comfort, and the no-smoking bedrooms are all well equipped. A cosy fire warms the lounge, and breakfast and high tea are served in the dining room. A four-course dinner prepared from fresh local ingredients is served at 8pm.
3rm(1🛏) ⊁ ® 🍴 (ex guide dogs) dB&B£36-£38 dB&Bℜ£40-£42 WB&B£108-£226 WBDi£192-£310 LDO 10am
▥ CTV nc8yrs
ⓔ

SELECTED

FH Q Q Q Q Mr & Mrs I Dollery **Forest Cottage** *(SU178150)* Godshill SP6 2LH ☎(0425) 652106
FAX (0425) 652106
Closed 23 Dec-1 Jan
2🛏 CTV in all bedrooms ® 🍴 (ex guide dogs) ✳ sB&Bℜ£35 dB&Bℜ£50-£60
▥ nc13yrs 🌡(heated) ʊ sauna solarium gymnasium mountain bikes aromatherapy

---

FOREST See **GUERNSEY under CHANNEL ISLANDS**

FORFAR Tayside *Angus*   Map **15** NO45

SELECTED

GH Q Q Q Q **Finavon Farmhouse** Finavon DD8 3PX (turn off A 90 at Milton of Finavon exit, approximately 5m N of Forfar) ☎(0307) 850269
This modern house is set in three acres of secluded grounds. The en-suite bedrooms have thoughtful touches such as hair dryer, radio/clock/alarm, tissues and good toiletries. There is a comfortable lounge and meals are taken round one table in the cosy dining room, the proprietors being very flexible about meal times.
3🛏 CTV in all bedrooms ® ✳ dB&Bℜ£30-£40 WB&B£100-£130 WBDi£156-£190 LDO 6.30pm
▥ CTV mini pitch & putt
ⓔ

FORGANDENNY Tayside *Perthshire*   Map **11** NO01

FH Q Q Mrs M Fotheringham **Craighall** *(NO081176)* PH2 9DF 0.5m W off B935 Bridge of Earn-Forteviot Rd)
☎Bridge of Earn(0738) 812415 FAX (0738) 812415
This bungalow is on the farm driveway amid peaceful countryside, but only 15 minutes by car to Perth. Accommodation is compact but equipped to meet modern standards, and there is a comfortable lounge.

3rm(2🛏) (1fb) ® 🍴 LDO 9pm
▥ CTV ✦ 1000 acres beef mixed sheep

FORRES Grampian *Morayshire*   Map **14** NJ05

SELECTED

GH Q Q Q Q **Mayfield** Victoria Road IV36 0RN (opposite Grant Park car park on main road through town)
☎(0309) 676931
Secluded in its own gardens just off the main road on the eastern side of town, this fine Victorian house has been tastefully furbished to retain its character, in a bright, modern style. Bedrooms are comfortable and very well proportioned, and there is a small lounge with tourist information and a wall map of the area. Breakfast is taken around a communal table in the stylishly decorated dining room.
3rm(2🛏) (1fb) ⊁ in bedrooms ⊁ in dining room CTV in all bedrooms ® 🍴 ✳ dB&B£30-£37 dB&Bℜ£37-£50 WBDi£126-£175
▥ CTV
ⓔ

SELECTED

GH Q Q Q Q **Parkmount House** St Leonards Road IV36 0DW ☎(0309) 673312 FAX (0309) 673312
Mar-Oct
This impressive town house was built in 1868 and is set in its own grounds in a quiet residential area just south of the town centre. The high ceilinged bedrooms, with individual colour schemes, are furnished in modern and traditional style and fitted with the usual amenities. A feature of the spacious lounge is its ornate plasterwork, and well prepared Scottish and Continental dishes are served in the attractive dining room. A no smoking policy has now been introduced.
6🛏 (2fb) ⊁ CTV in all bedrooms ® T ✳ sB&B⇋ℜ£35-£40 dB&B⇋ℜ£55-£60 WB&Bfr£210 WBDifr£300 LDO 5pm
Lic ▥ ⌾
Credit Cards ① ③ ⓔ

FORT WILLIAM Highland *Inverness-shire*   Map **14** NN17

SELECTED

GH Q Q Q Q Q **Ashburn House** Achintore Road PH33 6RQ (junc A82 and Ashburn Ln 500yds from large rbt at south end of Fort William High St) ☎(0397) 706000
FAX (0397) 706000
Jan-Oct
Smoking is not permitted in this detached Victorian house standing in its own grounds overlooking Loch Linnhe. It has been recently modernised and refurbished throughout to offer a sound standard of accommodation. Bedrooms are decorated in soft pastel shades which tone in with the attractive fabrics and comfortable modern furnishings; binoculars are provided in those which overlook the loch. Enjoyable home-cooked meals are served at individual tables in the dining room, and the adjoining conservatory lounge enjoys stunning views of the Ardgour hills.
6🛏 ⊁ CTV in all bedrooms ® 🍴 (ex guide dogs) ✳ sB&B⇋ℜ£25-£30 dB&B⇋ℜ£40-£60 WB&B£130-£400 ▥ ⌾
Credit Cards ① ③ ⓔ

🖈 ☎ **GH** Q Q Q **Benview** Belford Road PH33 6ER
☎(0397) 702966
Mar-Nov

▶

This friendly, family-run guesthouse is situated beside the A82 just north of the town centre. Several of the bedrooms have en suite facilities and TV, and there are two comfortable lounges, one with TV.
12rm(8🛁🚿) 🚭 in bedrooms 🚭 in dining room CTV in all bedrooms [R] 🚫🐕 (ex guide dogs) sB&B£15-£17 dB&B£30-£34 dB&B🛁🚿£32-£40 WB&B£100-£270
♨ CTV
[£]

GH [Q][Q][Q] Glenlochy Nevis Bridge PH33 6PF (0.5m N on A82) ☎(0397) 702909
Good-value bed and breakfast accommodation is offered at this friendly family-run guest house which stands in its own grounds opposite the Distillery, beside the A82, close to the entrance to Glen Nevis. Bedrooms, though compact, are well decorated, and public areas include a cosy first floor lounge and a small neat ground floor breakfast room.
10rm(8🚿) (2fb) 🚭 in 4 bedrooms CTV in all bedrooms [R] 🚫🐕 (ex guide dogs) * sB&B£16-£21 sB&B🚿£18-£22 dB&B£28-£37 dB&B🚿£31-£44 WB&B£105-£147
♨ CTV
Credit Cards [3] [£]

P R E M I E R S E L E C T E D

GH [Q][Q][Q][Q][Q] The Grange Grange Road PH33 6JF ☎(0397) 705516
Etr-Oct

Enthusiastic owners Joan and John Campbell have done a splendid job of renovating and refurbishing their late-Victorian home, standing in its own well tended grounds south of the town centre off the A82. Attractive bedrooms are individual in style, enhanced by use of modern decor and fabrics. All expected facilities and comforts are provided, including a welcoming glass of sherry. The lounge is spacious and relaxing with views over Loch Linnhe. Joan's hearty breakfasts are served at individual tables in the small, rear dining room.
3rm(1🛁2🚿) 🚭 CTV in all bedrooms 🚫🐕 (ex guide dogs) dB&B🛁🚿£44-£62 WB&B£154-£210
nc13yrs

GH [Q][Q][Q] *Guisachan House* Alma Road PH33 6HA (off A82, 100yds past St Marys Church) ☎(0397) 703797
FAX (0397) 703797
Closed 16 Dec-4 Jan
A detached house which sits in an elevated position overlooking the town, with fine views of Loch Linnhe. Bedrooms are bright, cheerful and well maintained; there is a comfortable lounge and an attractive dining room.
13rm(2🛁11🚿) (3fb) CTV in all bedrooms [R] 🚫🐕 LDO 5.30pm
Lic ♨ CTV nc8yrs
Credit Cards [1] [3]

GH [Q][Q][Q] Lochview Heathercroft, Argyll Road PH33 6RE ☎(0397) 703149
Etr-Oct
Extended and completely modernised, this former croft house has a lovely outlook to Loch Linnhe from its hillside above the town. The large lounge window takes full advantage of the view. Substantial breakfasts are served at individual tables in the adjacent dining room. This is a no-smoking establishment.
8🛁🚿 🚭 CTV in all bedrooms [R] 🚫🐕 sB&B🛁🚿£25-£30 dB&B🛁🚿£36-£42 WB&B£120-£130
♨

GH [Q] Rhu Mhor Alma Road PH33 6BP (N on A82, after hospital turn first right then first left) ☎(0397) 702213
Etr-Sep
A substantial Victorian dwelling, now a friendly holiday guesthouse which is family run in traditional style, overlooks Loch Linnhe from its position high above the town. Charming bedrooms vary in size, while public areas have lots of character. There is a choice of lounges (with smoking banned in the television room) and a dining room where enjoyable home-cooked meals are served at shared tables.
7rm (2fb) 🚭 in dining room 🚭 in 1 lounge [R] sB&B£16-£17 dB&B£32-£34 WB&B£105-£107 WBDi£165-£167 LDO 5pm
♨ CTV
[£]

SELECTED

GH [Q][Q][Q][Q] Torbeag House Muirshearlich, Banavie PH33 7PB (5m N, from the A830 take the B8004 going north from Banavie) ☎Corpach(0397) 772412
Closed Nov-Dec
Overlooking magnificent countryside, this spacious house stands in extensive gardens. Rooms are comfortably furnished and the owners offer a friendly welcome.
2🛁🚿 🚭 in bedrooms 🚭 in dining room CTV in all bedrooms [R] dB&B🛁🚿£35-£50 WB&B£104-£148 WBDi£191.50-£253 LDO 10am
♨ 🎾(grass)
[£]

FOWEY Cornwall & Isles of Scilly Map **02** SX15

GH [Q][Q] *Ashley House Hotel* 14 Esplanade PL23 1HY ☎(0726) 832310
Quietly situated, this well managed hotel has been considerably upgraded in recent years. The restaurant and bar, with its feature stone wall and open fireplace, adds a new dimension, and there is a similarly well furnished traditional lounge. Bedrooms are generally spacious.
6rm(3🛁1🚿) (6fb) CTV in all bedrooms [R] 🚫🐕 (ex guide dogs) LDO 6pm
Lic ♨ CTV
Credit Cards [1] [3]

SELECTED

GH [Q][Q][Q][Q] Carnethic House Lambs Barn PL23 1HQ (off A3082, directly opposite "Welcome to Fowey " sign) ☎(0726) 833336
Closed Dec-Jan
This elegant Regency manor house is set in beautiful, award-winning gardens on the outskirts of a pretty village. The charming owners, David and Trisha Hogg, have modernised the house over the last six years, and bedrooms are comfortable and attractive. The four-course dinner offers a wide choice of fresh, home-cooked dishes, and the house-party atmosphere is relaxed and friendly, with many guests returning year after year. The gardens offer a sheltered, heated swimming pool, putting, croquet, bowls and tennis. Private winter house parties for small groups are proving very popular: a minimum of ten guests ensures the exclusive use of the hotel but early booking is essential.
8rm(5🚿) (2fb) 🚭 in 2 bedrooms 🚭 in dining room CTV in all bedrooms [R] sB&B£30-£40 sB&B🚿£40 dB&B£44-£48 dB&B🚿£52-£60 WB&B£147-£200 WBDi£232-£285 LDO 8pm
Lic ♨ 🚗 🏊(heated) 🎾(grass)badminton putting bowls golf practice net
Credit Cards [1] [2] [3] [5] [£]

GH Q Q Q **Wheelhouse** 60 Esplanade PL23 1JA
☎(0726) 832452
Mar-Oct rs Nov-Feb
There are wonderful views across the estuary to Polruan from this
terraced Victorian house and they can be enjoyed from the front
bedrooms, the small terrace and the dining room. A pleasant
sitting room with a collection of houseplants has a small honesty
bar, and the dining room is decorated with a pretty collection of
china. Parking is difficult in Fowey and it is best to park in the car
parks above the village.
6rm(2♠) (1fb) CTV in 4 bedrooms ® ⅍ ✱ sB&B£16.50-£22.50
sB&B♠£22.50 dB&B£33-£37 dB&B♠£45 WB&B£115.50-£140
WBDi£175.50-£200 LDO noon
Lic Ⅲ CTV ⅍
£

INN Q Q Q **King of Prussia** Town Quay PL23 1AT (St Austell
Brewery) ☎St Austell(0726) 832450
This pink, quayside inn is named after a local clergyman-cum-
smuggler who operated around Prussia Cove. All six bedrooms,
which have lovely views across the estuary, have pine furniture
and an apricot colour scheme. The main public bar is on first-floor
level and here a good selection of home-cooked meals and snacks
s available. Breakfast and dinner are served in the downstairs
dining room.
⅍♠ (4fb) CTV in all bedrooms ® ⅍ (ex guide dogs) LDO
9.30pm
Ⅲ
Credit Cards ①②③

FOWNHOPE Hereford & Worcester   Map 03 SO53
GH Q Q Q **Bowens Country House** HR1 4PS (6m SE of
Hereford on B4224) ☎(0432) 860430 FAX (0432) 860430
A substantial creeper clad house set back from the road in its own

colourful gardens. The rooms vary in size; some are very spacious
and all are very attractive with their coordinating decor and
furnishings. Ground floor rooms are also available in a separate
building. There is a very comfortable lounge with pink armchairs
and sofas and its own, small honesty bar. There is a half wood
panelled dining room. At the front of the house, the rooms have a
pleasant outlook across the putting green to the pretty village
church.
8rm(3⅍♠) Annexe 4⅍♠ (2fb) ⅍ in dining room CTV in all
bedrooms ® ✱ sB&Bfr£20 sB&B⅍♠fr£25 dB&Bfr£40
dB&B⅍♠fr£50 WB&B£140-£175 WBDi£202-£228 LDO 8pm
Lic Ⅲ nc10yrs ♀(grass)9 hole putting
Credit Cards ①③£

FOYERS Highland *Invernesshire*   Map 14 NH42

SELECTED

GH Q Q Q Q **Foyers Bay House** Lochness IV1 2YB
☎Gorthleck(0456) 486624 FAX (0456) 486337
This splendid Victorian villa peacefully set in four acres of
beautiful grounds has been sympathetically converted and
renovated to provide good quality holiday accommodation.
Bedrooms vary in size but are comfortable and well equipped,
with private bathrooms, TV and telephones. There is an
attractive conservatory café/restaurant overlooking Loch Ness
where snacks and meals are available all day. The hotel also
offers eight self-catering lodges.
3⅍♠ ⅍ in bedrooms CTV in all bedrooms ® T ⅍ (ex
guide dogs) ✱ sB&B⅍♠fr£22-£28 dB&B⅍♠fr£34-£46
WBDi£154-£190 LDO 7.30pm
Ⅲ CTV
Credit Cards ①②③£

TORBEAG HOUSE

This spacious modern country house must
surely occupy one of the most stunning
locations in the Highlands with magnificent
views of Ben Nevis, Aonach Mor and the
Great Glen. Here you will find a warm
welcome, peace and tranquility, superb
food (all home made), elegant
accommodation and our personal
attention all in beautiful surroundings.
For further details contact:

**Ken or Gladys Whyte, Torbeag House,
Muirshearlich, Banavie by Fort William,
Inverness-shire PH33 7PB
Telephone: (01397) 772412**

CARNETHIC

H·O·U·S·E

Lambs Barn • Fowey • Cornwall
Tel: (01726) 833336
David & Trisha Hogg

This delightful Regency house, situated
in tranquil countryside close to the sea
at Fowey, provides gracious
accommodation and excellent food.
Licensed bar & heated outdoor
swimming pool.
1½ acres mature gardens
AA selected in 1992
For FREE brochure write or telephone

              QQQQ

AA SELECTED

FRAMLINGHAM Suffolk   Map **05** TM26

FH Ⓠ Ⓠ Ⓠ Mrs A Bater **Church Farm** *(TM605267)* Church Road, Kettleburgh IP13 7LF ☎(0728) 723532
The purpose of this delightful rural setting is 'people and pigs' according to the friendly owner, Mrs Bater. The 70 acres involve pig farming at a suitable distance from the house and a caring approach towards guests. The spacious bedrooms are comfortably functional, and there is a lounge with a wood burning stove. Dinner is readily provided on request.
3rm(1♠) ⊬ in bedrooms ⊬ in dining room Ⓡ 🗙 ⁎ dB&B£34-£36 dB&Bℱ£36-£38 WB&B£119-£126 WBDi£175-£182 LDO 6.30pm
CTV clay pigeon shooting 70 acres arable pigs

FRANT East Sussex   Map **05** TQ53

P R E M I E R 🏆 **S E L E C T E D**

GH Ⓠ Ⓠ Ⓠ Ⓠ Ⓠ **The Old Parsonage** TN3 9DX
☎Tunbridge Wells (0892) 750773
FAX (0892) 750773
Charming proprietors Tony and Mary Dakin are the first non-clerics to live at this delightful Georgian rectory. They offer luxurious accommodation, and some rooms with four-poster or canopied beds. There is an elegant lounge and a conservatory leading to a ballustraded terrace overlooking the secluded three-acre garden, and breakfast is served at a large oak refectory table.
3⇔♠ ⊬ in dining room ⊬ in lounges CTV in all bedrooms ⁎ sB&Bℱ£32-£42 dB&Bℱ£50-£56 WB&B£150-£170
▥ CTV
Credit Cards ①ⓔ

FRESHWATER See **WIGHT, ISLE OF**

FRESSINGFIELD Suffolk   Map **05** TM27

S E L E C T E D

GH Ⓠ Ⓠ Ⓠ Ⓠ **Chippenhall Hall** IP21 5TD (8m E of Diss on B1116) ☎(0379) 586733 & 588180 FAX (0379) 586272
This historic house traces its history back to Saxon times. Old beams and fireplaces are natural features of the interior, and the installation of modern comforts has respected the character of the building.
3⇔♠ ⊬ in bedrooms Ⓡ 🗙 (ex guide dogs) dB&Bℱ£54-£60 WB&B£180-£200 WBDi£341-£361 LDO 6pm
Lic ▥ CTV nc13yrs ◷(heated) ♪ ⊶ squash ♾ snooker sauna solarium gymnasium croquet lawn clay pigeon shooting
Credit Cards ①③

FRINTON-ON-SEA Essex   Map **05** TM21

GH Ⓠ **Forde** 18 Queens Road CO13 9BL ☎(0255) 674758
Closed Dec
Quietly situated in a residential area close to the sea, this long-established family-run guest house offers neat bedrooms, a cosy TV lounge and a separate dining room. Unrestricted street parking is available.
6rm (1fb) ⊬ in dining room sB&B£19.50 dB&B£30 WB&B£105
▥ CTV nc5yrs
ⓔ

FRITHAM Hampshire   Map **04** SU21

S E L E C T E D

FH Ⓠ Ⓠ Ⓠ Ⓠ Mrs P Hankinson **Fritham** *(SU243144)* SO43 7HH (leave M27 at junct 1 and follow signs to Fritham) ☎(0703) 812333 FAX (0703) 812333
Closed 24 Dec-28 Dec rs mid July-mid Sept & BH's
3⇔♠ Ⓡ ⁎ sB&Bℱ£20-£22 dB&Bℱ£33-£36 LDO 24hrs
▥ CTV nc10yrs forest walks 51 acres mixed grass

FROGMORE Devon   Map **03** SX74

INN Ⓠ Ⓠ **Globe** TQ7 2NR (3.75m of Kingsbridge on A379)
☎Kingsbridge(0548) 531351
Situated between Dartmouth and Kingsbridge, the Globe is an ideal base from which to explore the beautiful South Devon countryside. It offers comfortable bedrooms, a cosy lounge bar, and the lively Sportsman Bar with pool, darts and satellite TV. The informal Barn Restaurant offers a good choice of meals including a children's menu, and hosts Duncan and Sheila Johnston provide a warm welcome.
6rm(3♠) (1fb)CTV in all bedrooms Ⓡ ⁎ sB&B£17.50-£20 sB&Bℱ£17.50-£25 dB&B£27-£35 dB&Bℱ£30-£40 WB&B£90-£120 Lunch £6-£10alc Dinner £6-£20alc LDO 10pm
▥ CTV pool darts cycle hire canoe hire
Credit Cards ①③ⓔ

FROME Somerset   Map **03** ST74

GH Ⓠ Ⓠ Ⓠ **Wheelbrook Mill** Laverton BA3 6QY
☎(0373) 830263
This charming country home is a 200-year-old stone-built mill just off the A36 within easy reach of Bath. The mill is set well back from a quiet lane overlooking the brook and open fields, with only the ducks to disturb the peace. A spacious double room is offered to guests, providing a good range of facilities, and a more modest single room is also available in conjunction with the double. Owners Andrew and Shelley Weeks and their two young sons treat guests as friends of the family; breakfast is taken around a long communal table in the cluttered country kitchen and Andrew and Shelley are likely to join their guests. An informal and relaxed atmosphere prevails.
4rm(2⇔) CTV in 2 bedrooms Ⓡ 🗙 LDO 24hr notice
▥ CTV ⚬

FYLINGDALES North Yorkshire   Map **08** NZ90

INN Ⓠ Ⓠ Ⓠ **Flask** YO22 4QH (on A121)
☎Whitby(0947) 880305 FAX (0947) 880592
6⇔♠ (2fb) ⊬ in dining room CTV in all bedrooms Ⓡ 🗙 sB&Bℱ£25 dB&Bℱ£40 WB&B£130 Bar Lunch £3.95-£7.95 LDO 9.30pm
▥ CTV
ⓔ

GAIRLOCH Highland *Ross & Cromarty*   Map **14** NG87

GH Ⓠ Ⓠ **Bain's House** Strath IV21 2BZ ☎(0445) 2472
Good value bed and breakfast accommodation is offered at this friendly family-run guesthouse, with its white walls, ornamental shutters and flowering window boxes. The compact bedrooms are fitted with a mixture of modern and traditional furnishings and guests are welcome to share the owners' comfortable lounge.
5rm (1fb) ⊬ in lounges CTV in all bedrooms Ⓡ ⁎ sB&B£15 dB&B£27-£28
▥ CTV

SELECTED

GH Ⓠ Ⓠ Ⓠ Ⓠ **Birchwood** IV21 2AH (overlooks harbour)
☎(0445) 2011
Apr-mid Oct
Mrs Elsie Ramsay is a welcoming host to this well maintained guesthouse which overlooks Old Gairloch harbour and the Isle of Skye beyond. Bedrooms are bright and airy with comfortable modern furniture. There is a pleasant TV lounge, small sun porch giving superb views of the harbour, garden patio and tastefully appointed dining room where guests can enjoy hearty breakfasts, occasionally served at shared tables.
6↑ (1fb) ⅒ in bedrooms ⅒ in dining room Ⓡ
dB&B↑£38-£48 WB&B£133-£168
▥ CTV

SELECTED

GH Ⓠ Ⓠ Ⓠ Ⓠ **Horisdale House** Strath IV21 2DA (turn off A832 onto B8021, establishment 0.9m on right just beyond Strathburn House) ☎(0445) 712151
May-Sep
This modern, detached villa standing in its own gardens commands breathtaking views across the bay to the distant mountains. Run by Amelia Windsor and Patricia Strack for the past 13 years, the dedication and enthusiasm of these charming American ladies have encouraged guests to return year after year. Bedrooms vary in size, but all are brightly decorated, soundly furnished and spotlessly clean. Public rooms are spacious and have superb views, and dinners are also of note, for the ladies are as enthusiastic about food as they are about the care of their guests.
6rm(1⇌) (1fb) ⅒ Ⓡ ✗ sB&B£19 dB&B£36 dB&B⇌£42
LDO 9am
▥ nc7yrs

GALSTON Strathclyde *Ayrshire*　　　Map 11 NS53

FH Ⓠ Ⓠ Ⓠ Mrs J Bone **Auchencloigh** *(NS535320)* KA4 8NP (5m S off B7037-Scorn Rd) ☎(0563) 820567
Apr-Oct
There is a no smoking policy at this farmhouse set in rolling countryside, from which both the Ayrshire coast and the Island of Arran can be seen on clear days. The three good sized bedrooms are served by a modern bathroom with a bath and separate shower, and downstairs is a comfortable guests' lounge.
3rm Ⓡ ✗ ✱ sB&Bfr£15 dB&Bfr£30 WB&Bfr£105 LDO 4pm
▥ CTV sauna 240 acres beef mixed sheep
£

GARBOLDISHAM Norfolk　　　Map 05 TM08

GH Ⓠ Ⓠ Ⓠ **Ingleneuk Lodge** Hopton Road IP22 2RQ (turn S off A1066 on to B1111. 1m on right) ☎(01953) 681541
Xmas and Sun
Ingleneuk Lodge is a modern bungalow set in ten acres of woodland. It has well equipped bedrooms, ample sitting and dining rooms, and dinner is served on request.
rm(8⇌↑) (2fb) ⅒ in 4 bedrooms ⅒ in dining room CTV in all bedrooms Ⓡ T sB&B£22 sB&B⇌↑£31.50 dB&B£36 dB&B⇌↑£49 WB&B£119-£164.50 WBDif£210-£252 LDO 1pm ic ▥
Credit Cards 1 2 3 £

GARGRAVE North Yorkshire　　　Map 07 SD95

GH Ⓠ Ⓠ **Kirk Syke Hotel** 19 High Street BD23 3RA (on A65 4m W of Skipton) ☎Skipton(0756) 749356
Closed 16-28 Dec
This comfortable Victorian house in the village centre maintains

very acceptable standards throughout; a relaxing lounge and pleasant dining room are provided, and all the bedrooms (some of them contained in a rear annexe) have colour TV.
4rm(3⇌) Annexe 6⇌↑ ⅒ in dining room CTV in all bedrooms Ⓡ ✗ sB&B£22 sB&B⇌↑£30 dB&B⇌↑£42-£44 LDO 10am
Lic ▥. CTV nc5yrs
Credit Cards 1 3

GARSTANG Lancashire　　　Map 07 SD44

FH Ⓠ Ⓠ Ⓠ Mrs J Higginson **Clay Lane Head** *(SD490474)* Cabus, Preston PR3 1WL (1m N on A6) ☎(0995) 603132
Mar-23 Dec
This ivy clad former dairy farmhouse dates from the 18th century and much of its former character has been retained, particularly in the breakfast room with its exposed stone walls and beamed ceiling. There is also a cosy lounge.
3rm(2⇌↑) (1fb) ⅒ in bedrooms CTV in 2 bedrooms Ⓡ ✗ (ex guide dogs) sB&B£17-£18 sB&B⇌↑£22-£23 dB&B£28-£30 dB&B⇌↑£34-£36 WB&B£88-£112
▥. CTV 30 acres beef
£

GARTOCHARN Strathclyde *Dunbartonshire*　　　Map 10 NS48

SELECTED

GH Ⓠ Ⓠ Ⓠ Ⓠ **Ardoch Cottage** Main Street G83 8NE (on A811) ☎(0389) 830452
Mabel and Paul Lindsay's delightful 200-year-old cottage has been sympathetically restored and modernised to provide an ideal base for touring. The bedrooms are attractively decorated and fabrics have been used to good effect. Mabel Lindsay offers enjoyable home-cooked fare at a communal table in the ▶

Birchwood

Gairloch, Ross-Shire IV21 2AH

Telephone: (01445) 2011

Beautifully situated in its own grounds amongst mature woodland and enjoying magnificent vistas. Recently refurbished to a very high standard, all six comfortable bedrooms are en suite. Birchwood provides the perfect base from which to explore the many and varied places of interest in the Gairloch area. Close to Inverewe Gardens and the beautiful Loch Maree. Sandy beaches and a 9 hole golf course are within walking distance.

lounge/dining room, and guests can relax in the comfortable sun lounge. Standards of housekeeping are impeccable throughout.
3🛁🚿 🚭 in bedrooms 🚭 in dining room Ⓡ ✱
sB&B🛁🚿£27.50-£30 dB&B🛁🚿£35-£42 LDO 5pm
🌡 CTV
[£]

SELECTED

GH [Q][Q][Q][Q] ***The Old School House*** G83 8SB
☎(0389) 830373
Efficiently run by enthusiastic owners Judy and John Harbour, this sympathetically converted 18th-century school house stands beside the A811 about a mile north of the village and enjoys fine views of the surrounding countryside. Judy is a charming host and her interest in food is reflected in her imaginative cordon bleu cooking, which is served at a communal table in the attractive dining room. New en suite bedrooms have been created, and though small they are comfortable and very individual in style. A spacious lounge is also provided.
3rm(1🛁) (1fb) CTV in all bedrooms Ⓡ 🐕 (ex guide dogs)
LDO noon
Lic 🌡

SELECTED

FH [Q][Q][Q][Q] Mrs S Macdonnell **Mardella** *(NS442866)*
Old School Road G83 8SD ☎(0389) 830428
3rm(1🛁🚿) (2fb) 🚭 Ⓡ ✱ sB&B£24-£26 dB&Bfr£35
dB&B🛁🚿fr£40 WB&B£165-£179 WBDi£228-£242 LDO 9am
🌡 CTV 9 acres sheep poultry

GATEHOUSE OF FLEET Dumfries & Galloway
Kirkcudbrightshire Map **11** NX55

GH [Q][Q] Bobbin 36 High Street DG7 2HP (signposted from A75 close to clocktower) ☎(0557) 814229
The Bobbin, a neat guest house on the main street, doubles as a coffee shop, offering home baking at morning coffee time, lunch and afternoon tea. The comfortably furnished bedrooms vary in size and a lounge is provided for guests' use.
6rm(2🚿) (3fb) 🚭 in dining room 🚭 in lounges CTV in all bedrooms Ⓡ sB&B£20-£23 sB&B🚿£23-£25 dB&B£37-£39 dB&B🚿£44-£52 WB&B£122-£133 WBDi£158-£188 LDO 5pm
🌡 CTV
Credit Cards [1][3]

GATWICK AIRPORT (LONDON) West Sussex Map **04** TQ24

GH [Q][Q][Q] Barnwood Hotel Balcombe Road, Pound Hill RH10 7RU ☎Crawley(0293) 882709 FAX (0293) 886041
Closed Xmas-1 Jan
This fully licensed hotel situated in a residential area offers a range of bedrooms, all well equipped and some upgraded to a very high standard. Bar and lounge open out on to the rear gardens, and the restaurant adjoining them features both fixed-price and à la carte menus; snacks are also served in the bar. Two conference/function rooms are available and there is plenty of parking space. Breakfast is provided at a supplementary charge.
35🛁🚿 (3fb) CTV in all bedrooms Ⓡ **T** 🐕 (ex guide dogs)
sB&B🛁🚿£30-£34 dB&B🛁🚿£34-£41 LDO 9pm
Lic 🌡
Credit Cards [1][2][3][5]

GH [Q][Q][Q] Chalet 77 Massetts Road RH6 7EB (from M23 junct 9 follow A23 signed Redhill/London. At large rbt turn rt past Texaco Garage then 2nd rt, signed Horley Town Centre into Massetts rd) ☎Horley(0293) 821666 FAX (0293) 821619
Close to the airport and offering good parking facilities, this small, newly established guesthouse is kept in excellent condition throughout. All bedrooms are similarly furnished in modern style, there is a compact breakfast room and television lounge, and guests have the freedom of the kitchen to make tea and coffee as required.
6rm(4🚿) (1fb) 🚭 CTV in all bedrooms Ⓡ 🐕 (ex guide dogs) ✱
sB&Bfr£24 sB&B🚿fr£32 dB&B🚿fr£42
🌡 CTV
Credit Cards [1][3][£]

GH [Q][Q] Copperwood Massetts Road RH6 7DJ
☎Crawley(0293) 783388 FAX (0293) 820155
Named after the surrounding copper beech trees, this appealing house dates back to 1904. It provides overnight guest accommodation; each of the five bedrooms has an individual colour scheme, with pretty fabrics and decor, and although compact, they are ideal for short stays. A full English breakfast is served in the bright dining room, and light snacks are available until 9pm. Courtesy transport and parking are available by arrangement.
5rm(1🚿) (1fb) 🚭 in dining room CTV in all bedrooms Ⓡ ✱
sB&Bfr£24 sB&B🚿fr£32 dB&Bfr£35 dB&B🚿fr£42
🌡
Credit Cards [1][3][5][£]

GH [Q][Q] Gainsborough Lodge 39 Massetts Road RH6 7DT (2m NE of airport adjacent A23) ☎Horley(0293) 783982
FAX (0293) 785365
The bedrooms of this detached Edwardian house are furnished in different styles. A generous English breakfast is served in the dining room which opens onto the garden. Guests catching early flights can help themselves to cereal, juice and toast. Long-term parking is available at a reasonable price.
12🛁🚿 (2fb) 🚭 in dining room CTV in all bedrooms Ⓡ 🐕 (ex guide dogs) ✱ sB&B🛁🚿£29-£32.50 dB&B🛁🚿£40-£42.50
🌡 CTV
Credit Cards [1][2][3][5][£]

GH [Q][Q][Q] Gatwick Skylodge London Road, County Oak RH11 0PF (2m S of airport on A23) ☎Crawley(0293) 544511
Telex no 878307 FAX (0293) 611762
Closed 25-29 Dec
Long-term car parking is available by arrangement at this good-value modern hotel, and courtesy transport is provided to and from the airport terminals. Bedrooms - some of them conveniently located on the ground floor - are double-glazed and well equipped while the very popular bar/dining area offers bar food at lunch time and a daily fixed-price menu in the evening; breakfast is not included in the room tariff.
51🛁 (7fb) CTV in all bedrooms Ⓡ 🐕 (ex guide dogs) ✱
sB&B🛁£44.50-£54.50 dB&B🛁£44.50-£54.50 LDO 9.15pm
Lic 🌡
Credit Cards [1][2][3][£]

SELECTED

GH [Q][Q][Q][Q] High Trees Gatwick Oldfield Road RH6 7EP (follow signs for A23 London passing airport on left, turn right at next roundabout to Horley/Redhill. First right into Woodroyd Av and Oldfield Rd) ☎(0293) 776397
FAX (0293) 785693
Closed 24-26 & 31 Dec
A new and conveniently situated non-smoking guest house located in an established residential area, within walking distance of the town centre, shops and restaurants. Bedrooms are modern, bright and furnished in pine, with thoughtful little

extras. There is a very comfortable TV lounge, and a sitting/writing room on the first floor. The breakfast room overlooks the lawned rear garden, and reception and the kitchen are open plan. Continental breakfast is included in the room tariff, and cooked full English breakfast is subject to an additional charge. Light refreshments are usually available throughout the day.
8🛁🚿 (2fb) 🚭 CTV in all bedrooms [R] 🐕 * sB&B🛁🚿£33 dB&B🛁🚿£44
🅿 CTV
Credit Cards [1] [3] [£]

;H [Q][Q][Q] **The Lawn** 30 Massetts Road RH6 7DE
☎Horley(0293) 775751 FAX (0293) 821803
:losed Xmas
\ most attractive Victorian house which has been carefully reserved and tastefully furnished by friendly owners Ken and anet Stocks. Bedrooms all have pretty, coordinating fabrics and lecor, good comfortable seating and TV; some rooms have private athrooms. The dining room has been decorated in the Victorian tyle, and photographs throughout the house remind guests of its rigins as a girls' school. A small lounge/reception room has ecently been added. The guesthouse is conveniently situated 1.5 niles from Gatwick airport and within two minutes' walk of the own centre.
rm(4🚿) 🚭 CTV in all bedrooms [R] dB&B£35 dB&B🚿£42
🅿 nc12yrs
'redit Cards [1] [2] [3] [5] [£]

;H [Q][Q][Q] *Little Foxes* Ifield Woods, Ifield Road RH11 0JY
☎Crawley(0293) 552430 FAX (0293) 562607
et in five acres of grounds in Ifield Wood, this small hotel is only en minutes' drive from Gatwick Airport and two miles from ▶

Crawley town centre. It has a licensed bar open throughout the day for residents, serving light refreshments and snacks, and a small restaurant area for hot, freshly prepared meals, including vegetarian specialities. Bedrooms, some on the ground floor, are well furnished and double glazed. Stay-park-fly packages can be arranged, and there is a 24-hour courtesy bus service to and from the airport.
9🛁🚿 (2fb) CTV in all bedrooms [R] 🚫 LDO 9pm
Lic ▥
Credit Cards [1] [2] [3]

GH [Q][Q] Massetts Lodge 28 Massetts Road RH6 7DE
☎Horley(0293) 782738 FAX (0293) 782738
This pleasant Victorian guesthouse is a popular overnight stopover for people with early flights from Gatwick airport. Most of the cheerfully decorated bedrooms are now en suite, and they all have TV and tea trays. A continental breakfast is served before 7am, otherwise a full English breakfast is available, as well as competitively-priced evening meals cooked by the owner Paula Gatley.
8rm(5🛁🚿) (2fb) 🚭 in dining room CTV in all bedrooms [R] 🚫 (ex guide dogs) ✱ sB&B£23 sB&B🛁🚿£32 dB&B£34 dB&B🛁🚿£39 LDO 7.45pm
▥
Credit Cards [1] [2] [3] [5] [£]

GH [Q][Q] Rosemead 19 Church Road RH6 7EY
☎Horley(0293) 784965 FAX (0293) 820438
This small, family run guesthouse offers nicely kept but modestly furnished bedrooms with shared bathrooms. A substantial English breakfast is served in the cheerful dining room, and a sound standard of housekeeping is maintained by Mrs Wood. Adequate car parking is available.
6rm(2🚿) (2fb) 🚭 in dining room 🚭 in lounges CTV in all bedrooms [R] ✱ sB&B£23 sB&B🚿£29 dB&B£35 dB&B🚿£42
▥
Credit Cards [1] [3] [5] [£]

SELECTED

GH [Q][Q][Q][Q] Vulcan Lodge 27 Massetts Road RH6 7DQ
☎Horley(0293) 771522
Dating from the late 17th century and originally a farm house, this attractive property is set back from the main road in a secluded position whilst still being convenient for both town centre and airport. Four individually decorated bedrooms show a wealth of feminine touches, the pretty breakfast room is furnished in pine, and guests have their own lounge with chintzy armchairs. Smoking is not permitted downstairs.
4rm(3🚿) 🚭 in dining room CTV in all bedrooms [R] 🚫 sB&Bfr£24.50 sB&B🚿fr£31 dB&B🚿fr£42
▥
Credit Cards [1] [3]

GH [Q][Q] Woodlands 42 Massetts Road RH6 7DS (off A23 1m N of Gatwick Airport) ☎Horley(0293) 782994 & 776358
FAX (0293) 776358
An attractive detached house provides good parking facilities and transport to the airport. Bedrooms are bright and freshly decorated, and all have en suite shower rooms. Smoking is not permitted.
5🚿 (2fb) 🚭 CTV in all bedrooms [R] 🚫 ✱ sB&B🚿£25-£27.50 dB&B🚿£36-£40
▥
[£]

GAYHURST Buckinghamshire Map **04** SP84

FH [Q][Q] Mrs K Adams **Mill** *(SP852454)* MK16 8LT (1m S off B526 unclass rd to Haversham) ☎Newport Pagnell(0908) 611489 FAX (0908) 611489
Fresh-air pursuits such as tennis, fishing and riding are encourage by the rural setting of this popular 17th-century farm house; it offers simple bedrooms in keeping with the original character of the building and an inviting open lounge/breakfast room overlooking fields.
3rm(1🛁🚿) (1fb) 🚭 in 2 bedrooms 🚭 in dining room 🚭 in 1 lounge CTV in all bedrooms [R] ✱ sB&B£17.50-£20 sB&B🛁🚿£17.50-£20 dB&B£35 dB&B🛁🚿£35 LDO 4pm
▥ CTV 🎾(hard)🎣 🐎 rough shooting trout fishing 550 acres mixed
[£]

GIGGLESWICK North Yorkshire Map **07** SD8

INN[Q][Q][Q] Black Horse Hotel Church Street BD24 0BE
☎Settle(0729) 822506
The origins of this small village inn, in a quiet location next to the church, can be traced back to 1663. The bedrooms all have modern facilities and pine furniture. There is also a small television lounge on the first floor for the sole use of residents, while downstairs traditional hand-pulled ales are available in the intimate and comfortable bars. Meals are served in the bars at lunchtime and in the restaurant during the evening.
3rm(1🛁2🚿) 🚭 in lounges [R] ✱ dB&B🛁🚿fr£40 WB&Bfr£129.50 WBDifr£185.50 Bar Lunch £6.35-£9alc Dinner £7.40-£11.75alc LDO 8.45pm
▥ CTV
Credit Cards [1] [3] [5]

GILWERN Gwent Map **03** SO2

FH [Q][Q][Q] Mr B L Harris **The Wenallt** *(SO245138)* NP7 0HP (0.75m S of A465 Gilwern by pass) ☎(0873) 830694
This 16th-century Welsh longhouse has lovely views of the Usk Valley. Spacious comfortable bedrooms are provided together wit good public rooms.
3rm(1🛁) Annexe 4rm(1🛁3🚿) 🚭 in 3 bedrooms 🚭 in dining room [R] sB&B£18-£22 sB&B🛁🚿£22 dB&Bfr£30 dB&B🛁🚿fr£36 LDO 6pm
Lic ▥ CTV 50 acres sheep

GISLINGHAM Suffolk Map **05** TM

SELECTED

GH [Q][Q][Q][Q] The Old Guildhall Mill Street IP23 8JT
☎Mellis(0379) 783361
Closed Jan
This immaculately maintained, thatched 15th-century Guildhall lies in the centre of the village. Original features include beams, timbers and fireplaces. Bedrooms are full of character, three having very low ceilings and the fourth room is reached by a spiral staircase; they all have modern en suite bathrooms. The comfortable lounge has a small but well equipped bar, and a snooker room is also available for meetings. Ray and Ethel Tranter ensure that their guests have a warm welcome, with a family atmosphere prevailing.
4🛁 CTV in all bedrooms [R] dB&B🛁£50 WB&B£150 WBDi£200 LDO 6pm
Lic ▥
[£]

GLAN-YR-AFON (NEAR CORWEN) Gwynedd Map **06** SJ

FH [Q] Mr & Mrs D M Jones **Llawr-Bettws** *(SJ016424)* Bala Road LL21 0HD (A5 from Corwen to Betws-y-Coed, at 2nd traffic lights turn onto A494, pass Thomas Motor Mart. Take 1st right after village) ☎(049081) 224
A friendly farmhouse dating from 1918 situated just off the A49 a few miles west of its junction with the A5. Very much a workir farm, it offers freshly decorated, comfortable bedrooms lacking modern refinements. The lounge has an open fire, and there is a

trout lake in the grounds.
2rm (1fb)🌂 (ex guide dogs) ✳ sB&Bfr£12.50 dB&Bfr£25
WB&Bfr£87.50 WBDifr£122.50 LDO 7.30pm
CTV table tennis swings climbing frame 20 acres non working

GLASBURY Powys   Map **03** SO13

FH Q Q Q Mrs B Eckley **Fforddfawr** *(SO192398)* HR3 5PT
☎(0497) 847332
Mar-Nov
This friendly, personally run 17th-century farmhouse is bordered
by the river Wye, just two miles west of Hay-on-Wye on the
B4350. Set back in a pretty garden, it is very much a working farm
with bright, recently decorated, comfortable bedrooms and
spacious lounges.
3rm(1🌂) ⌘ CTV in all bedrooms ® 🌂 ✳ sB&B£18-£20
dB&B£32-£36 dB&Bfr£26-£40 WB&B£100-£112
⊞ CTV 280 acres mixed
£

GLASGOW Strathclyde *Lanarkshire*   Map **11** NS56

GH Q Q Q **Botanic Hotel** 1 Alfred Terrace, Great Western Road
G12 8RF (off M8 at junct 17, turn right for hotel in 0.75m on left,
directly above A625 Great Western Road) ☎041-339 6955
FAX 041-339 6955
This substantial house sits high above the Great Western Road on
the right-hand side entering the city, and offers comfortable, well
proportioned bedrooms. There is no lounge, and parking in this
restricted area may be difficult.
11rm(3🌂) (4fb) CTV in all bedrooms ®
⊞
Credit Cards 1 2 3
see advertisement on p.193.

Massetts Lodge
28 Massetts Road, Horley, Surrey

GH Q Q Q **Dalmeny Hotel** 62 St Andrews Drive, Nithsdale Cross G41 5EZ ☎041-427 1106 & 6288
The bedrooms are comfortable and thoughfully equipped at this small, family-run hotel, situated in a residential area on the city's southern side. The attractive public rooms, including a restaurant open to non-residents, highlight the house's period features.
8rm(2⇔1🟥) CTV in all bedrooms ⓡ ✳ sB&B£27 sB&B⇔🟥£45 dB&B£42 dB&B⇔🟥£52 LDO 10.30pm
Lic ⬛ CTV
Credit Cards ①②③ ⓔ

GH Q Q Q **Hotel Enterprise** 144 Renfrew Street G3 6RF
☎041-332 8095 FAX 041-332 8095
The Enterprise is a small terraced hotel in the heart of the city. The smart, well equipped bedrooms are attractive to both business guests and tourists. The hotel is ostensibly B&B only, but one can choose a meal from menus provided by nearby take-away restaurants and it will be brought in and served in the dining room. Parking is metered but there is a multi-storey five minutes' walk away.
6⇔🟥 (2fb) ⊬ in 1 bedrooms ⊬ in dining room CTV in all bedrooms ⓡ T ✳ sB&B⇔🟥£30-£45 dB&B⇔🟥£50-£75 WB&B£210-£315 WBDi£274-£379 LDO 7.30pm
Lic ⬛ CTV ⊬
Credit Cards ①②③ ⓔ

GH Q Q **Kelvin Private Hotel** 15 Buckingham Terrace, Great Western Road, Hillhead G12 8EB (leave M8 at junct 17 follow A82 Kelvinside/Dumbarton 1m from motorway on right before Botanic Gardens) ☎041-339 7143 FAX 041-339 5215
Two Grade A Victorian terraced houses have been linked to create this popular guest house which stands in a narrow lane fronting Great Western Road on the north-west side of the city. Most bedrooms are well proportioned (though singles tend to be compact), while public areas include a quiet lounge and separate breakfast room on the first floor.
21rm(1⇔8🟥) (5fb) CTV in all bedrooms ⓡ
⬛
Credit Cards ①③

GH Q Q **Lomond Hotel** 6 Buckingham Terrace, Great Western Road G12 8EB (on A82, right hand side before Botanic Gardens) ☎041-339 2339 FAX 041-339 5215
17rm(6⇔🟥) (6fb)CTV in all bedrooms ⓡ sB&B£23-£28 sB&B⇔🟥£28-£35 dB&B£36-£40 dB&B⇔🟥£46-£52 WB&B£147-£180
⬛ ⊬
Credit Cards ①②③

GH Q Q **The Victorian House** 212 Renfrew Street G3 6TX
☎041-332 0129 FAX 041-353 3155
Several terraced buildings have been converted into a four-storey property providing bed and breakfast accommodation right in the centre of the city. Bedrooms are bright, modern and practical, although much of the original character has been retained. 24-hour reception is provided, and the guesthouse is best approached by Sauchiehall Street and turning left up Garnet Street. Parking meter restrictions apply.
45rm(33🟥) (3fb) ⊬ in dining room CTV in all bedrooms ⓡ T ✴ (ex guide dogs) sB&B£21-£25 sB&B🟥£25-£28 dB&B£36 dB&B🟥£40
⬛ ⊬
Credit Cards ①③

GLASTONBURY Somerset   Map **03** ST53

FH Q Q Q Mrs J Tinney **Cradlebridge** *(ST477385)* BA16 9SD (take A39 from Glastonbury heading south, after Morlands factory take 2nd right signposted Meare/Wedmore farm is signposted on left after 1m) ☎(0458) 831827
Closed Xmas
This 200-acre dairy farm is situated one mile west of Glastonbury on the fringe of the Somerset Levels. The spacious ground floor

bedrooms are located in a delightful barn conversion, with a patio area outside each offering extensive views to the Mendip Hills. A traditionally cooked farmhouse breakfast is served in the compact dining room where guests eat at a large communal table.
Annexe 2🟥 (2fb) ⊬ in dining room CTV in all bedrooms ⓡ ✴ sB&B🟥£25 dB&B🟥£35 WB&B£105
⬛ 200 acres dairy
ⓔ

GLENCOE Highland *Argyllshire*   Map **14** NN15

GH Q Q Q **Scorrybreac** PA39 4HT (off A82 just outside village, 500 metres from Bridge of Coe) ☎Ballachulish(08552) 354 due to change to (01855) 811354
Closed Nov
A family-run holiday guest house, Scorrybreac enjoys fine views over Loch Leven from its hillside position above the village. It is popular with both tourists and outdoor enthusiasts, offering good value accommodation in compact modern bedrooms. Public areas include a lounge and a neat dining room where hearty dinners are available by prior arrangement.
6rm(4🟥) ⊬ CTV in all bedrooms ⓡ sB&B🟥£16-£20 dB&B🟥£28-£36 WB&B£90-£110 WBDi£163.50-£183.50 LDO 10am
⬛ CTV

GLENMAVIS Strathclyde *Lanarkshire*   Map **11** NS7●

FH Q Mrs M Dunbar **Braidenhill** *(NS742673)* ML6 0PJ
☎Glenboig(0236) 872319
Mrs Dunbar's cheerful hospitality more than compensates for the lack of frills at this unassuming working farm, which lies on the Coatbridge side of the B803 in a semi-rural area with good views to the north. The accommodation offers reasonable comfort and there is a pleasant lounge and separate dining room.
3rm (1fb) ⓡ ⊬
⬛ CTV 50 acres arable mixed

GLOUCESTER Gloucestershire   Map **03** SO8

GH Q **Claremont** 135 Stroud Road GL1 5JL
☎(0452) 529540 & 529270
Conveniently situated on the Stroud road, this spotlessly clean guest house has been run by Mrs Powell for many years and is a welcoming, hospitable place to stay. Accommodation is offered in six immaculate bedrooms, and the cosy lounge/dining room is pleasantly furnished. Off road parking is provided at the rear of the house.
6rm (2fb) ⊬ in dining room CTV in all bedrooms ⓡ T✴ sB&B£15.50-£16 dB&B£30-£31 WB&Bfr£89.50
⬛ CTV

GOATHLAND North Yorkshire   Map **08** NZ8●

GH Q Q **Fairhaven Country Hotel** The Common YO22 5AN
☎Whitby(0947) 896361
Set in the heart of a delightful moorland village, with beautiful views all around, this house offers comfortable public rooms and neat bedrooms. Service is friendly, and a log fire burns in the lounge on cooler evenings.
9rm(4⇔9🟥) (3fb) ⊬ in dining room CTV in 5 bedrooms ⓡ sB&B£18.50 sB&B⇔🟥£27.50 dB&B£37 dB&B⇔🟥£45 WB&B£129.50-£157.50 WBDi£185-£210 LDO 5pm
Lic ⬛ CTV garden putting green games room
Credit Cards ①③ ⓔ

GH Q Q Q **Heatherdene Hotel** YO22 5AN
☎Whitby(0947) 86334
Commanding beautiful views over the surrounding countryside, and situated in the moorland village of Goathland, this delightful country house was once the local vicarage. Spacious, comfortable and tastefully decorated bedrooms are very much a feature, modern in many respects yet retaining much of the character of

the house. The large lounge, with a small bar in one corner, provides fine views of the moors and valleys, and the attractive dining room, with individual tables, is an ideal setting for the traditional home-cooked meals provided by proprietors Lisa and John Pearson-Smith.
8rm(2🛁4🚿) (3fb) 🚭 in 1 bedrooms CTV in all bedrooms [R] LDO 8pm
Lic ♨ solarium

GODALMING Surrey Map **04** SU94

GH [Q][Q][Q] Fairfields The Green, Elstead GU8 6DF
☎Farnham(0252) 702345
Closed 18 Dec-1 Jan
A modern detached house is situated in the centre of the village of Elstead with ample car parking and a garden to the rear. The bedrooms are pleasantly furnished with fresh pastel colours and are very well equipped. Breakfast is served by owner Janet Pryce at individual tables in the copy dining room. Smoking is not permitted.
3rm(2🛁🚿) (1fb) 🚭 CTV in all bedrooms [R] 🐕 dB&B🛁🚿£35-£40
♨ nc3yrs
[£]

GOLSPIE Highland *Sutherland* Map **14** NC80

FH [Q][Q] Mrs G Murray **Kirkton Farm** *(NE799989)* KW10 6TA
☎(0408) 633267
20 May-Sep
2rm 🚭 🐕 (ex guide dogs) sB&B£20 dB&B£28 WB&B£98
900 acres arable beef sheep
[£]

GORRAN HAVEN Cornwall & Isles of Scilly Map **02** SX04

INN[Q] Llawnroc PL26 6NU ☎Mevagissey(0726) 843461
The accomodation at this village inn is basic but comfortable. Bedrooms vary in size but are well-equipped and there is a small first floor sitting room. The dining room is of typical inn style and offers simple English cooking on a choice of menus.
6rm(2🛁3🚿) (2fb) 🚭 in dining room CTV in all bedrooms [R] 🐕 (ex guide dogs) sB&B🛁🚿£18-£24 dB&B🛁🚿£30-£44 WB&B£105-£154 LDO 9.30pm
♨ CTV
Credit Cards [1][2][3][5][£]
See advertisement under MEVAGISSEY

GOUDHURST Kent Map **05** TQ73

SELECTED

GH [Q][Q][Q][Q] Mill House Church Road TN17 1BN (on A262 from Sissinghurst Castle, opposite St Marys church)
☎(0580) 211703
2rm(1🛁1🚿) (1fb) 🚭 CTV in all bedrooms [R] 🐕 sB&B🛁🚿£25-£30 dB&B🛁🚿£35-£40 WB&B£122.50-£140
♨ CTV

GRAMPOUND Cornwall & Isles of Scilly Map **02** SW94

🛏☕ **GH [Q][Q] Perran House** Fore Street TR2 4RS (on the A390 between St Austell and Truro) ☎St Austell(0726) 882066
A delightful listed cottage with its own rear car park, Perran House has been carefully modernised, and offers well equipped bedrooms. The pine-furnished breakfast room also serves home-made cream teas and light snacks every afternoon in summer, and full English breakfast is included in the room tariff. Smoking is discouraged. ▶

•Botanic Hotel•

1 ALFRED TERRACE, by GREAT WESTERN ROAD, GLASGOW G12 8RF
Phone: 0141 339 6955 / 6802 Fax: 0141 339 6955

Situated in the heart of the fashionable West-End close by the Botanic Gardens. Ideal for all destinations. Lots of amenities within walking distance, to name but a few: Art Galleries and Museums, Glasgow University, S.E.C.C. 25 minute walking distance. Glasgow Airport 10 miles / 20 minute drive. Bedrooms very spacious and comfortable. All have colour television, tea/coffee making facilities and central heating throughout. Italian and French also spoken by the resident proprietor, Franco Soldani.

Dalmeny Hotel

62 St Andrews Drive, Nithsdale Cross, Glasgow G41 5EZ
Telephone: 0141-427 1106 & 6288

Situated in a conservation area in the city's southern side and near to the famous Burrell Collection in the Pollok Country Park. The 120 year old building has many period features and modern amenities for your comfort, with the majority of the bedrooms en suite. Private car park.

5rm(2⇌1♠) (1fb) ✗ in dining room ✗ in lounges CTV in all bedrooms ⓡ ♏ (ex guide dogs) sB&B£13-£14.50 dB&B£26-£29 dB&B⇌♠£28-£34 WB&B£85-£120
▥.
Credit Cards ①③ⓔ

GRANGE-OVER-SANDS Cumbria — Map 07 SD47

GH Ⓠ Ⓠ Birchleigh Kents Bank Road LA11 7EY
☎(05395) 32592
Closed Jan
The Birchleigh is a small, friendly guesthouse offering a good standard of accommodation and service. The house is conveniently situated for the town centre and the bay is just a short walk away.
5rm(1⇌4♠) (2fb) ✗ CTV in 4 bedrooms ⓡ ✱ sB&B⇌♠fr£18 dB&B⇌♠fr£36 WBDifr£182
▥. ⋏
Credit Cards ②

P R E M I E R 🌑 **S E L E C T E D**

GH Ⓠ Ⓠ Ⓠ Ⓠ Greenacres
Lindale LA11 6LP (2m N)
☎(05395) 34578
Closed 5-19 Nov, Dec & New Year
This charming white painted 19th-century cottage is situated in the centre of Lindale village about two miles from Grange-over-Sands. Mr and Mrs Danson are attentive hosts, and guests can

be sure of a well produced home-cooked dinner. The colour coordinated bedrooms are all en suite, each has colour TV, and lots of thoughtful extras are provided. The comfortable lounges have open log fires in the winter months, and the establishment has a residential licence. Greenacres offers excellent value for money and is well situated for exploring southern Lakeland and the beautiful Morecambe Bay area.
5⇌♠ (1fb) ✗ CTV in all bedrooms ⓡ ♏ ✱ sB&B⇌♠fr£30 dB&B⇌♠£50-£56 WB&Bfr£170 WBDifr£250 LDO noon
Lic ▥.
Credit Cards ①③ⓔ

GRANTOWN-ON-SPEY Highland *Morayshire* — Map 14 NJ02

P R E M I E R 🌑 **S E L E C T E D**

GH Ⓠ Ⓠ Ⓠ Ⓠ Ⓠ Ardconnel House Woodlands Terrace
PH26 3JU ☎(0479) 872104
FAX (0479) 872104
Closed Nov-Dec
Enthusiastic owners have made major improvements to this fine Victorian house set in its own gardens at the south end of the town. Upgraded bedrooms are all comfortably furnished and attractively decorated - some traditional and others in modern style. On cooler evenings a welcoming log fire burns in the spacious lounge, and enjoyable home-cooked meals are served in a bright airy dining room. This is a no smoking establishment.

6♠ (2fb) ✗ CTV in all bedrooms ⓡ ♏ sB&B♠£28.50-£30 dB&B♠£46-£60 LDO 4.30pm
Lic ▥. CTV nc10yrs
Credit Cards ①②③

GH Ⓠ Ⓠ Ⓠ Ardlarig Woodlands Terrace PH26 3JU (just off A95)
☎(0479) 873245
Closed 22-27 Dec
Efficiently run by Sue and Mike Greer, this solid Victorian house stands in its own garden at the south end of the town. The bedrooms are spacious and well decorated, and although they lack en suite facilities they have all the other usual amenities. The lounge is well supplied with books and board games, and in the refurbished dining room interesting Taste of Scotland dishes are served at individual tables.
7rm (3fb) ✗ in 3 bedrooms ✗ in dining room CTV in all bedrooms ⓡ ✱ sB&Bfr£17.50 dB&Bfr£35 WB&B£112.50-£115 WBDi£165-£175 LDO 4.30pm
Lic ▥. CTV golf shooting & fishing can be arranged
ⓔ

✉🖴 **GH Ⓠ Ⓠ Brooklynn** Grant Road PH26 3LA
☎(0479) 873113
Apr-Oct
A detached Victorian villa is situated in a quiet residential area within easy reach of the town centre. Bedrooms are individually decorated and furnished in modern and traditional styles, the TV lounge is comfortable, and dinner is served by prior arrangement in the separate dining room.
6rm(2♠) ✗ in dining room ⓡ ♏ sB&B£14.50-£15.50 dB&B£29-£31 dB&B♠£35-£37 WB&B£100-£108 WBDi£163-£171 LDO by arrangement
▥. CTV
ⓔ

GH Ⓠ Bydand Dulnain Bridge PH26 3LU (3m S on A95)
☎(0479) 851278
2rm ✱ dB&B£28-£30 WB&B£91-£97.50 WBDi£140-£146.50 LDO 8.30pm
CTV
Credit Cards ①③

P R E M I E R 🌑 **S E L E C T E D**

GH Ⓠ Ⓠ Ⓠ Ⓠ Ⓠ Culdearn House Woodlands Terrace
PH26 3JU (off A95 turn left at 30mph sign) (Logis)
☎(0479) 872106
FAX (0479) 873641
Mar-Oct
Many guests return year after year to Alasdair and Isobel Little's delightful granite-built villa which stands in its own landscaped garden on the

southern fringe of the town easily recognised at night by the glow from the small table lamps in every front window. Guests can relax with a quiet drink in front of a log fire in the attractive lounge. Isobel competently prepares the evening meals with local produce like venison, beef, lamb and salmon and offers three choices at each course, served in the elegant dining room. Bedrooms are spotless with mixed appointments and the expected amenities. Special golf, angling and riding packages can be arranged. Culdearn has been chosen as 'Guesthouse of the Year' 1995 for Scotland.
9rm(2⇌7♠) ✗ in 6 bedrooms ✗ in dining room CTV in all

bedrooms ℝ ✝ (ex guide dogs) sB&B⇌✿£48
dB&B⇌✿£96 (incl dinner) WBDi£295 LDO 6pm
Lic ▥ nc5yrs
Credit Cards 1 3 5 £

SELECTED

GH Ⓠ Ⓠ Ⓠ Garden Park Woodside Avenue PH26 3JN
(turn off High St at Forest Rd, Garden Park is at junc of
Forest Rd & Woodside Av) ☎(0479) 873235
Mar-Oct
A comfortable, modernised Victorian house built in 1863,
quietly situated in pretty gardens in a residential area, next to
the golf course and pine forests. The six individually furnished
bedrooms are mostly compact but all have private bath or
shower and tea trays. There is a cosy TV lounge and a quiet
writing room, with enjoyable home cooking served at
individual tables in the smart dining room.
5⇌✿ ⊁ in dining room CTV in 4 bedrooms ℝ ✝ (ex guide
dogs) sB&B⇌✿£18.50-£23.80 dB&B⇌✿£37-£46
WB&B£122-£145 WBDi£180-£212 LDO 5pm
Lic ▥ CTV nc12yrs

SELECTED

GH Ⓠ Ⓠ Ⓠ Ⓠ Kinross House Woodside Avenue PH26 3JR
☎(0479) 872042 FAX (0479) 873504
Etr-Oct
An attractive Victorian house is situated in a quiet residential
area convenient for the town centre and River Spey. It has a
relaxed, friendly atmosphere and offers comfortable
accommodation, with well equipped, bright and cheerful
bedrooms, some of which have private bathrooms. The cosy
lounge has a log fire, and enjoyable home cooking is served in
the dining room. Smoking is not permitted.
6rm(5✿) (1fb) ⊁ CTV in all bedrooms ℝ ✝ (ex guide dogs)
⊁ sB&B£20-£22 sB&B✿£25-£27 dB&B✿£42-£48
WB&B£147-£168 WBDi£217-£266 LDO 4pm
Lic ▥ nc7yrs
Credit Cards 1 3 £

GH Ⓠ Ⓠ Ⓠ Pines Woodside Avenue PH26 3JR ☎(0479) 872092
FAX (0479) 872092
Jan-Oct
Good-value family accommodation is offered at this friendly
family-run guest house - a sturdy Victorian property in its own
large garden beside a pine wood. The bedrooms are spacious and
public areas comprise a comfortable lounge and a smart dining
room with a sun-lounge extension.
9rm(5✿) (3fb) ⊁ in dining room CTV in all bedrooms ℝ
sB&Bfr£17 dB&Bfr£34 dB&B✿fr£44 WB&B£108.50-£135
WBDi£165.50-£195 LDO 3pm
Lic ▥
£

GRASMERE Cumbria   Map **11** NY30

GH Ⓠ Ⓠ Ⓠ Bridge House Hotel Stock Lane LA22 9SN (turn off
A591, establishment 1/4 mile on left immediately before St
Oswalds church and bridge) ☎(05394) 35425
Apr-6 Nov rs 6 Nov-Mar
Formerly a private residence, this hotel is set in secluded gardens
in the centre of the village, close to the River Rothay. The
bedrooms have been thoughtfully furnished and equipped with
modern facilities. Public rooms include a comfortable lounge with
an adjoining bar, and an attractive dining room in which five-
course evening meals are served.

12⇌✿ ⊁ in dining room CTV in all bedrooms ℝ T ✝
sB&B⇌✿£30-£35 dB&B⇌✿£60-£70 WB&B£190-£205
WBDi£260-£275 LDO 7pm
Lic ▥ nc8yrs
Credit Cards 1 3

GH Ⓠ Ⓠ Ⓠ Lake View Country House Lake View Drive
LA22 9TD (turn off A591 after Prince of Wales then left at Wild
Daffodil Tea Shop) ☎(05394) 35384
Mar-Nov rs Dec-Feb
An attractive stone house stands in its own well kept gardens in a
quiet side road in the village centre, with a view of the lake. The
house is comfortably furnished throughout and there are two cosy
lounges. Service is very friendly.
6rm(3✿) ⊁ in dining room CTV in all bedrooms ℝ ✳
sB&Bfr£22.50 dB&Bfr£45 dB&B✿fr£53 WB&B£150-£178
WBDi£214-£242 LDO noon
nc12yrs
£

GH Ⓠ Ⓠ Ⓠ Raise View White Bridge LA22 9RQ
☎(05394) 35215 FAX (05394) 35215
Closed Dec-Jan
A Lakeland stone cottage situated just a short walk from the
village centre and offers pleasant accommodation. The bedrooms
are prettily decorated, there is a cosy lounge and friendly service is
provided by the resident owners.
6rm(4✿) (1fb) ⊁ CTV in all bedrooms ℝ ✝ dB&B£34-£36
dB&B✿£38-£42
▥ nc5yrs

GRASSINGTON North Yorkshire   Map **07** SE06

SELECTED

GH 🔲🔲🔲🔲 **Ashfield House Hotel** BD23 5AE
☎(0756) 752584
Closed Jan rs Nov-Dec
Lovingly owned and run by Keith and Linda Harrison, this
attractive stone-built 17th-century house nestles in a quiet corner
of the village. The comfortable bedrooms are pretty, and the two
delightful lounges both feature log fires, beams and plenty of
books. A set four-course dinner using the best produce available
is provided by Linda in the cottage-style dining room, furnished
with polished wooden tables and fresh flowers. Afternoon tea in
front of the fire is not to be missed, and service is caring and
friendly at all times. Smoking is not permitted.
7rm(6♠) ⊁ CTV in all bedrooms ® ⊁ (ex guide dogs)
sB&Bfr£22 sB&B♠£29.50 dB&B♠£44-£55 WBDi£215-£250
LDO 5.30pm
Lic ⅏ nc5yrs
Credit Cards ❙1❙ ❙3❙ £

GH 🔲🔲🔲 *Greenways* Wharfeside Avenue BD23 5BS
☎Skipton(0756) 752598
Apr-Oct
Situated on the banks of the River Wharfe, this charming detached
house has sizeable bedrooms which are brightly decorated and
furnished in a modern style yet retaining the character of the
property. The comfortable lounge has a TV and there are fine
views of the river and the surrounding hills from the dining room.
When entering the village from the Skipton direction, turn left at
the school and follow the road to the bottom.
4rm(3♠) (1fb) CTV in all bedrooms ® LDO 5pm
Lic ⅏ CTV nc7yrs

GH 🔲🔲🔲 **The Lodge** 8 Wood Lane BD23 5LU ☎(0756) 752518
Mar-Oct rs Dec
An attractive, detached, grey-stone Victorian house standing on
the edge of the village and providing a good all round standard of
both accommodation and service. There is a cosy lounge for
guests and the bedrooms are pleasantly furnished and decorated,
most having views of the surrounding countryside.
8rm(1⇄2♠) ⊁ in dining room ® ⊁ sB&Bfr£24 dB&B£32
dB&B♠£42 LDO 2pm
⅏ CTV
£

GRAVESEND Kent   Map **05** TQ67

GH 🔲🔲 *The Cromer* 194 Parrock Street DA12 1EW
☎(0474) 361935
Closed 24 Dec-2 Jan
Dating back to the 1830s, this attractive guest house is in a
convenient location in the town centre and has its own car park.
Bedrooms are traditional in style and have changed little over the
years. There is an ornate breakfast room and a small TV lounge.
11rm(1⇄) (3fb) CTV in all bedrooms ⊁
⅏ CTV nc9yrs

SELECTED

GH 🔲🔲🔲🔲 **Overcliffe Hotel** 15-16 The Overcliffe
DA11 0EF (W side of town on A226) ☎(0474) 322131
FAX (0474) 536737
This is a well-appointed family run hotel. All bedrooms,
whether in the main building or the annexe below, are sensibly
furnished in a modern style and boast many modern facilities.
The attractive dining room adjacent to the lounge bar serves a
short à la carte menu at dinner accompanied by a reasonably

---

priced wine list. Ample car parking is available.
19♠ Annexe 10⇄♠ CTV in all bedrooms ® **T** ✳
sB&B♠£50-£55 dB&B♠£60-£65 WB&B£350-£385
WBDi£455-£525 LDO 9.30pm
Lic ⅏ ⌖
Credit Cards ❙1❙ ❙2❙ ❙3❙ ❙5❙ £

GREAT

Placenames incorporating the word 'Great', such as Gt Yarmouth,
will be found under the actual placename, ie Yarmouth.

GREEN HAMMERTON North Yorkshire   Map **08** SE45

INN 🔲🔲🔲 **Bay Horse** York Road YO5 8BN
☎Boroughbridge(0423) 330338 & 331113 FAX (0423) 331279
An attractive former coaching inn stands just off the A59 between
York and Harrogate, three miles east of its junction with the A1.
Modern bedrooms are in a sympathetically designed building at
the rear; all are equipped with every modern facility including
showers, and most are on the ground floor. The bars are full of
character, featuring beams, stone walls, horse brasses, prints and
other bric-à-brac. A varied à la carte menu is provided in the
attractive restaurant adjoining the bar areas, where an extensive
choice of bar meals is offered at lunchtime.
Annexe 10⇄♠ (1fb)CTV in all bedrooms ® **T** ✳ sB&B♠£30
dB&B♠£45 WB&B£122.50 Bar Lunch £1.50-£7.50 Dinner
£4.95-£11.50alc LDO 9.30pm
⅏
Credit Cards ❙1❙ ❙3❙ ❙5❙ £
See advertisement under YORK

GREENHEAD Northumberland   Map **12** NY66

FH 🔲🔲🔲 Mr B & Mrs P Staff **Holmhead** *(NY659661)*
Hadrians Wall CA6 7HY ☎Brampton(06977) 47402
FAX (06977) 47402
Closed 19 Dec-9 Jan
This characterful farmhouse is built of stone from Hadrian's Wall,
on which it stands. Although no longer a working farm, the
atmosphere remains with the sight of sheep grazing in the fields.
Bedrooms are cheery, if compact, and guests are encouraged to
relax in the comfortable lounge with an honesty bar, television,
books and games. Mrs Staff is a mine of information on local
attractions and is also responsible for producing reputedly the
longest breakfast menu in the world at 127 items. Meals are served
around a large communal table in the spacious dining-room.
4♠ Annexe 1rm (1fb) ⊁ ® ⊁ dB&B♠£43-£44 WB&B£132-
£136 WBDi£244-£248 LDO 3pm
Lic ⅏ CTV ⊿ table tennis 300 acres breeding sheep cattle
Credit Cards ❙1❙ ❙2❙ ❙3❙ £

GRETNA (WITH GRETNA GREEN) Dumfries & Galloway
Dumfriesshire   Map **11** NY36

GH 🔲🔲🔲 **The Beeches** Loanwath Road DG16 5EP (turn left off
B7076 at Crossways Garage and follow road for a qaurter of a
mile) ☎Gretna(0461) 337448
Closed 8 Dec-14 Jan
A 19th-century former farmhouse, the Beeches looks out over
open countryside towards the Solway Firth and the Lakeland hills.
There are two comfortable bedrooms, both with en suite facilities,
and a lounge with TV that doubles as a breakfast room. This is a
no-smoking establishment.
2♠ (1fb) ⊁ CTV in all bedrooms ® ⊁ dB&B♠£33-£35
⅏ CTV nc10yrs

GH 🔲🔲 **Greenlaw** DG16 5DU (off A74) ☎Gretna(0461) 338361
Greenlaw is a detached red brick house situated within walking
distance of the famous old smithy. Some of the bedrooms are
small but one has a four-poster bed and en suite facilities. A
breakfast room and a comfortable guests' lounge are provided,

along with good parking facilities.
8rm(1♠) (1fb) ✗ in dining room CTV in all bedrooms ®
sB&B£16-£18 dB&B£26-£28 dB&B♠£34-£36
▥ CTV
£

GH Q Q Q **Surrone House** Annan Road DG16 5DL
☎(0461) 338341
Set back from the main road, in the romantic border town of
Gretna, this one-time farmhouse, with connections dating back to
Viking times, now offers modern accommodation. The bedrooms
are generally spacious, nicely equipped and have good bathrooms,
while the public areas include two small but comfortable lounges
and a steak bar style room open to non residents.
7rm(6⇔3♠) (4fb)CTV in all bedrooms ® ✻ (ex guide dogs)
sB&B⇔♠£32 dB&B⇔♠£46 LDO 8pm
Lic ▥ CTV
Credit Cards [1] [2] [3] £

GREVE DE LECQ BAY See **JERSEY** under
CHANNEL ISLANDS

GRINDON Staffordshire   Map **07** SK05

FH Q Q Q Mrs P Simpson **Summerhill Farm** (*SJ083532*)
ST13 7TT ☎(0538) 304264
3rm(2♠) ✗ CTV in 2 bedrooms ® ✻ sB&B£15-£18
sB&B♠£18-£20 dB&B♠£33-£38
▥ CTV 52 acres dairy

GROUVILLE See **JERSEY** under **CHANNEL ISLANDS**

GUERNSEY See **CHANNEL ISLANDS**

GUILDFORD Surrey   Map **04** SU94

GH Q Q **Blanes Court Hotel** Albury Road GU1 2BT
☎(0483) 573171 FAX (0483) 32780
Closed 1wk Xmas
An imposing Edwardian house set in a quiet residential area offers
freshly decorated but modestly furnished bedrooms (some of
which are compact); a buffet breakfast is served in the
conservatory which overlooks an attractive garden, and the same
room doubles as a bar in the evening, when snacks are available.
20rm(4⇔10♠) (3fb) CTV in all bedrooms ® LDO 6pm
Lic ▥ CTV
Credit Cards [1] [2] [3]

GUISBOROUGH Cleveland   Map **08** NZ61

INN Q Q Q **Fox & Hounds** Slapewath TS14 6PX (2m on A171)
☎(0287) 632964 & 635280 FAX (0287) 610778
Modern bedrooms are a feature of this popular hotel on the road to
Whitby. The original building was once a railway station on the
Saltburn to Guisborough line, but has now been extended and
refurbished to include two restaurants, a traditional bar and a
conservatory as well as the well appointed bedrooms. Meals are
good value and a wide range of dishes is available. There is also a
well equipped children's play area.
15⇔♠ (2fb) CTV in all bedrooms ® T LDO 9.45pm
▥
Credit Cards [1] [2] [3] [5]

GULLANE Lothian *East Lothian*   Map **12** NT48

SELECTED

GH Q Q Q Q **Faussetthill House** 20 Main Street EH31 2DR
(on A198) ☎(0620) 842396
Mar-Dec
A detached Edwardian house in its own gardens offers good

quality accommodation, a relaxing sitting room and attractive
dining room.
3rm(2♠) ✗ ® ✟ sB&B£25-£26 sB&B♠£28-£32
dB&B£38-£40 dB&B♠£44-£46 WB&B£126-£154
▥ CTV nc10yrs
Credit Cards [1] [3] £

GUNNISLAKE Cornwall & Isles of Scilly   Map **02** SX47

GH Q Q Q **Hingston House Country Hotel** St Anns Chapel
PL18 9HB ☎Tavistock(0822) 832468
Standing in an elevated position in the centre of the village, this
late-Georgian property enjoys splendid wide views out across to
Plymouth and the Tamar Valley. The freshly decorated bedrooms,
most of which are en suite, are reasonably equipped and all are
comfortable but simply furnished. There is a very comfortable
lounge filled with books, flowers and plants, which has open fires,
as does the characterful, cosy bar. A set meal, using fresh
ingredients, is cooked and served by Mrs Shelvey, and a relaxed,
friendly atmosphere prevails throughout.
10rm(8♠) (1fb) CTV in all bedrooms ® ✻ sB&Bfr£25
sB&B♠fr£31 dB&Bfr£42 dB&B♠fr£50 WB&B£138-£166
WBDi£220-£248 LDO 7pm
Lic ▥ CTV croquet putting green
Credit Cards [1] [3] £

GWAUN VALLEY Dyfed   Map **02** SN03

SELECTED

FH Q Q Q Q Mr P Heard & Mrs M J Heard **Tregynon
Country Farmhouse Hotel** (*SN054345*) SA65 9TU (4m E of
Pontfaen, at intersection of B4313/B4329) (Welsh Rarebits)

▶

Surrone House

**ANNAN ROAD, GRETNA
TEL: 01461 338341**
Situated in the country village of Gretna.
All bedrooms have their own private
bathroom and TV and are very comfortable and QUIET. Catering for breakfast
and evening meals, all our produce is
home grown and freshly prepared. Many
facilities available locally, while the
English Lakes – South West Scotland –
The Borders – Kielder Forest and Dam
make excellent day visits.

☎Newport(0239) 820531 FAX (0239) 820808
Closed 2wks winter
This 16th-century farmhouse is situated in the scenic Gwaun Valley, in the heart of Pembrokeshire. It has a very attractive lounge with an inglenook fireplace, and features authentic wooden settles in addition to comfortable modern seating. The restaurant is in two parts and wholesome food plus vegetarian dishes are highlighted on the menu. There are a few bedrooms in the main house, which are rather on the small side, although the five bedrooms in the converted outbuilding are larger. All are very well decorated and furnished with mainly pine furniture. Each room has modern en suite facilities and is equipped with a TV and telephone.
3🚿 Annexe 5🛁 (4fb) 🚭 in bedrooms 🚭 in dining room CTV in all bedrooms [R] **T** 🐕 dB&B🛁🚿£46-£65 WBDi£248.75-£316 LDO 6pm
Lic 📺 10 acres sheep
Credit Cards [1] [3]

HADDINGTON Lothian *East Lothian* Map **12** NT57

FH [Q][Q] Mrs K Kerr **Barney Mains Farmhouse** *(NT524764)* Barney Mains EH41 3SA (off A1, 1m S of Haddington) ☎Athelstaneford(0620) 880310 FAX (0620) 880639
Mar-Nov
This 18th-century Georgian house enjoys a fine outlook over the surrounding countryside. The individually decorated bedrooms are spacious and comfortably furnished in a traditional style. There is also a comfortable lounge and hearty farmhouse breakfasts are served at the communal table in the dining room.
3rm 🚭 in bedrooms 🚭 in dining room [R] 🐕 (ex guide dogs) ✱ sB&B£16-£22 dB&B£30-£38
📺 CTV 580 acres arable beef sheep

HADLEIGH Suffolk Map **05** TM04

GH [Q][Q][Q] **Odds & Ends** 131 High Street IP7 5EJ (turn off A12 onto B1070 house at end of High St) ☎Ipswich(0473) 822032
A delightful 16th-century town house on the main thoroughfare has a walled rear garden. A private dwelling until recent years, Ann Stephenson has successfully converted the public areas into a busy restaurant, the decor and furnishings accentuating the period charm. The garden rooms are popular with disabled people.
6rm(2🛁) Annexe 3🚿 🚭 in dining room 🚭 in lounges CTV in all bedrooms [R] sB&B£20-£30 sB&B🛁🚿£25-£35 dB&Bfr£36 dB&B🛁🚿fr£40 LDO 5.30pm
Lic 📺 nc8yrs
[£]

INN[Q][Q] **The Marquis of Cornwallis** Upper Layham IP7 5JZ (on B1070 between Hadleigh & A12) ☎(0473) 822051
FAX (0473) 822051
Situated a mile from the town at Upper Layham, this charming old inn dates back to the 16th century. Exposed beams and sloping floors are features of the comfortable, spacious bedrooms. Downstairs there are convivial bars and a cosy restaurant serving home-cooked dishes including vegetarian meals. The large rear lawn runs down to the River Brett.
3rm(1🛁🚿) 🚭 in 1 bedrooms CTV in all bedrooms [R] 🐕 (ex guide dogs) ✱ sB&Bfr£25 sB&B🛁🚿fr£27 dB&Bfr£35 dB&B🛁🚿fr£39 Lunch £1.95-£15alc Dinner £1.95-£15alc LDO 9.30pm
🎣 riding & coarse fishing can be arranged
Credit Cards [1] [2] [3] [5] [£]

HAINTON Lincolnshire Map **08** TF18

[🛏] **GH** [Q][Q][Q] **The Old Vicarage** School Lane LN3 6LW (off A157) ☎Burgh-On-Bain(0507) 313660
The Old Vicarage stands in its own gardens in a peaceful Wolds village just off the A157. It is an attractive mixture of Georgian and Victorian architecture, with spacious, comfortable rooms, all furnished in keeping with the style of the house.
3rm 🚭 CTV in all bedrooms [R] 🐕 sB&B£15 dB&B£30 WB&B£96 WBDi£140 LDO 3pm
📺 nc12yrs
[£]

HALFORD Warwickshire Map **04** SP24

INN[Q] ***Halford Bridge*** Fosse Way CV36 5BN
☎Stratford on Avon(0789) 740382
This listed Cotswold stone coaching inn on the A429 has pretty, individually decorated, well maintained bedrooms. A wide choice of meals is served either in the lounge bar with its welcoming open fire, or in the cottage-style dining room.
6rm (1fb) CTV in all bedrooms [R] 🐕 (ex guide dogs) LDO 9pm
Credit Cards [1] [3]

HALSTOCK Dorset Map **03** ST50

See also Yeovil

GH [Q][Q][Q] **Halstock Mill** BA22 9SJ (signposted from the Cheddington road) ☎Corscombe(0935) 891278
Closed Xmas
This cosy guest house, in a peaceful setting, is full of character. The bedrooms are well equipped and comfortable and there is a sitting room and a small dining room.
4🛁 CTV in all bedrooms [R] 🐕 (ex guide dogs) sB&B🛁£27-£30 dB&B🛁£44-£50 WB&B£140-£189 WBDi£238-£287 LDO am
Lic 📺 nc5yrs stabling available
Credit Cards [1] [2] [3] [£]

HALTWHISTLE Northumberland Map **12** NY76

SELECTED

FH [Q][Q][Q][Q] Mrs J Laidlow **Ald White Craig** *(NY713649)* Shield Hill NE49 9NW (from B6318 turn off at Milecastle Inn, 0.75m on right) ☎(0434) 320565 & 321175
Closed 15 Dec-6 Jan
A modernised 17th-century croft which overlooks small neat gardens and part of the South Tyne valley. There are three very attractive ground floor bedrooms all with immaculate, modern en suite facilities. The dining room, with one large table, adjoins a very comfortable beamed lounge with a coal fire. The bungalow is part of the owner's sheep farm which is some distance away, although 14 acres adjoin the property. Smoking is not permitted.
3🛁🚿 🚭 CTV in all bedrooms [R] 🐕 (ex guide dogs) ✱ dB&B🛁🚿£37-£44 WB&Bfr£125
📺 nc12yrs 80 acres stock rearing rare breeds
[£]

SELECTED

FH [Q][Q][Q][Q] Mrs J Brown **Broomshaw Hill** *(NY706654)* Willia Road NE49 9NP ☎(0434) 320866
Mar-Nov
It is worth asking for directions to this impressive 18th-century farmhouse which is situated in a rural setting on the northern fringe of the town. Bedrooms are both spacious and comfortable, and the tastefully decorated public areas have polished wood floors with good quality rugs, chunky stone walls, antique furniture and delightful pictures and bric-à-brac. A bridleway and footpath lead from the house to Hadrian's Wall which is less than two miles away.
3rm (1fb) 🚭 in area of dining room CTV in all bedrooms [R] dB&B£32-£34 WB&B£110-£115 LDO 10am
📺 CTV 7 acres livestock horses
[£]

HAMPSTHWAITE North Yorkshire Map **08** SE25

GH [Q][Q][Q] ***Lonsdale House*** Village Green HG3 2EU
☎Harrogate(0423) 771311
A late Victorian house which overlooks the green of this attractive village, situated in the beautiful Nidderdale countryside is only five miles from Harrogate. Most of the bedrooms have private bathrooms and are individually furnished and decorated, some having fine views. The restaurant specialises in wholesome English food using local produce, and there is a comfortable, spacious lounge.
5rm(3🛁🚿) [R] LDO noon
Lic ▦ CTV

HAMPTON-IN-ARDEN West Midlands Map **04** SP28

GH [Q][Q][Q] Cottage Kenilworth Road B92 0LW (on A452)
☎(0675) 442323 FAX (0675) 443323
Beside the A452, and handy for the NEC, this white cottage has gabled leaded windows. Space is at a premium, but the rooms are beautifully decorated and furnished. Owner Roger Howler is a popular, outgoing character who makes a stay here memorable.
9rm(5🚿) (2fb)CTV in all bedrooms [R] sB&B£20 sB&B🚿£25 dB&B£34-£36 dB&B🚿£39 WB&B£140-£175
▦ CTV
[£]

HANLEY CASTLE Hereford & Worcester Map **03** SO84

SELECTED

GH [Q][Q][Q][Q] Old Parsonage Farm WR8 0BU (turn off B4211 onto B4209, 150yds on right)
☎Hanley Swan(0684) 310124
Closed 21 Dec-2 Feb
An 18th-century country residence, finished with mellow brick, stands on the outskirts of the village affording beautiful views of the castle and the Malvern Hills. Genuine hospitality is provided by Ann and Tony Addison: Ann is responsible for the imaginative cooking and Tony is an accredited wine expert. Over 100 wines are available and wine tasting sessions are often held in the old cider mill next to the house. Bedrooms are spacious and well furnished and there are two comfortable sitting rooms for residents.
3🛁 (1fb) 🚭 🐕 * dB&B🛁£41-£47 WB&B£145-£160 WBDi£245-£260 LDO day before
Lic ▦ CTV nc10yrs
[£]

HARLECH Gwynedd Map **06** SH53

SELECTED

GH [Q][Q][Q][Q] Castle Cottage Hotel Pen Llech LL46 2YL
☎(0766) 780479
Believed to date from 1585, this delightful property stands a few yards from the famous castle. Beams and exposed timbers are evident in many bedrooms, the bar and the restaurant. The latter has been extended over the years and offers a regularly changing fixed price two-or three-course menu based on fresh and local produce. There is a choice of lounges, and the bedrooms are attractively furnished in pine with floral decor and fabrics.
6rm(4🛁🚿) 🚭 in dining room [R] * sB&Bfr£23 sB&B🛁🚿fr£38 dB&B🛁🚿fr£50 LDO 9pm
Lic ▦ CTV
Credit Cards [1] [2] [3] [£]

SELECTED

GH [Q][Q][Q][Q] Gwrach Ynys Country Ynys, Talsarnau LL47 6TS (2 miles N of Harlech on the A496)
☎(0766) 780742 FAX (0766)780742
Closed Xmas
Situated in a lowland area on what was an island when the sea washed the walls of Harlech Castle, this Edwardian house with an acre of attractive lawns and gardens offers genuine Welsh hospitality. Smart bedrooms are equipped with all modern facilities; only one does not have en suite amenities, and it has private use of a nearby bathroom. Honest, home-cooked meals make use of local farm produce wherever possible, guests have a choice of two comfortable lounges, and ample car parking space is available.
7rm(1🛁5🚿) (2fb) 🚭 in dining room 🚭 in lounges CTV in all bedrooms [R] **T** sB&B£16-£19 dB&B🛁🚿£32-£38 LDO noon
▦ CTV
[£]

FH [Q] Mrs E Jones **Tyddyn Gwynt** *(SH601302)* LL46 2TH (2.5m off B4573 (A496)) ☎(0766) 780298
Most of this small friendly farmhouse was built about 100 years ago, but some parts are considerably older. It is set in a remote location some 1.5 miles southeast of Harlech, surrounded by spectacular mountain scenery. The modest bedrooms are simply furnished, and the small cosy lounge has TV and a welcoming log fire in the winter. A variety of bric-à-brac enhances the historic ambience of the house, which provides an ideal base for walkers.
2rm (1fb) [R] * dB&Bfr£27 WBDifr£140 LDO 7pm
CTV 3 acres small holding
[£]

HARLESTON Norfolk Map **05** TM28

INN[Q][Q] ***Swan Hotel*** 19 The Thoroughfare IP20 9DQ
☎(0379) 852221 FAX (0379) 854817
Located in the centre of the busy market town, this traditional inn offers simply furnished accommodation. The ground floor comprises a busy operation of two bars, a restaurant and weekend carvery. There is also a small meeting room.
13rm(10🛁) (1fb) CTV in all bedrooms [R] **T** LDO 9pm
▦ CTV
Credit Cards [1] [3] [5]
See advertisement on p.201.

HARPFORD Devon Map **03** SY09

GH [Q][Q] Otter House EX10 0NH (turn off A3052 into village, 0.25m on right after church) ☎(0395) 568330
2rm 🚭 [R] 🐕 (ex guide dogs) dB&B£35 LDO 24hrs
▦

GH [Q][Q][Q] Peeks House EX10 0NH (off A3052)
☎Colaton Raleigh(0395) 567664
An elegant Grade II listed building dating back to the 16th century stands in this small village on the East Devon Way, with the coastal resort of Sidmouth just over three miles away. Carefully restored by owners Derek and Brenda Somerfield, the house now provides modern accommodation with attractive fabrics used to good effect in the bedrooms. The main public rooms feature comfortable sofas and window seats in the drawing room and well polished individual tables in the dining room. Meals can also be served outside on the terrace when the weather permits.
5🛁🚿 🚭 in bedrooms 🚭 in dining room CTV in all bedrooms [R] * sB&B🛁🚿£21-£26 dB&B🛁🚿£42-£52 WB&B£140-£175 WBDi£200-£235 LDO 1pm
Lic ▦ CTV
[£]

HARROGATE North Yorkshire   Map **08** SE35

SELECTED

GH 🅠🅠🅠🅠 **Acacia Lodge** 21 Ripon Road HG1 2JL (on A61 600yds N town centre) ☎(0423) 560752

Just a short walk from the town centre, this mellow, stone-built semidetached Victorian house is set back from the A61. Bedrooms, with a happy blend of modern and antique furniture, are well equipped and attractively decorated. The charming lounge is particularly inviting and has lots of reading matter, and there is a pretty dining room.

5⇌🈯 (1fb) ⊬ CTV in all bedrooms ® 🅷 (ex guide dogs) dB&B⇌🈯£48
🈴 CTV nc5yrs
£

SELECTED

GH 🅠🅠🅠🅠 **Alexa House & Stable Cottages** 26 Ripon Road HG1 2JJ (on A61) ☎(0423) 501988 FAX (0423) 504086

This attractive stone house, dating from 1830, is situated just a short walk from the town centre on the Ripon road. The well furnished accommodation includes a comfortable lounge and dining room, where Yorkshire home cooking is served each evening, as well as the prettily decorated and thoughtfully equipped bedrooms. Some rooms are located in a converted stable block to the rear.

9rm(3⇌6🈯) Annexe 4🈯 (1fb) ⊬ in dining room CTV in all bedrooms ® T sB&B⇌🈯£32-£35 dB&B⇌🈯£50-£55 WB&B£160-£175 WBDi£220-£240 LDO 6.30pm
Lic 🈴 CTV
Credit Cards ①③£

GH 🅠🅠🅠 **Anro** 90 Kings Road HG1 5JX ☎(0423) 503087

Closed 25-26 Dec

Conveniently situated close to the conference centre and the main shopping area, this friendly guesthouse offers traditionally furnished bedrooms, in addition to a comfortable guests' lounge and a spacious dining room where four-course dinners are served.

7rm(3🈯) (1fb) CTV in all bedrooms ® 🅷 LDO 4.30pm
🈴 CTV nc7yrs

SELECTED

GH 🅠🅠🅠🅠 **Ashley House Hotel** 36-40 Franklin Road HG1 5EE ☎(0423) 507474 FAX (0423) 560858

Closed 20 Dec-2 Jan rs 9-19 Dec

Three converted town houses make up this hotel, which is set in a tree-lined road close to the International Conference Centre. Bedrooms are attractively decorated and most have en suite facilities and other modern features. There are two lounges, a bar and a pretty dining room where breakfast and evening meals are served.

16rm(13⇌🈯) (3fb) ⊬ in dining room ⊬ in 1 lounge CTV in all bedrooms ® T * sB&B£24.75-£26.50
sB&B⇌🈯£29-£34 dB&B£42-£47 dB&B⇌🈯£48.50-£61 WB&B£165-£225 WBDi£240-£300 LDO noon
Lic 🈴 CTV
Credit Cards ①②③£

GH 🅠🅠🅠 **Ashwood House** 7 Spring Grove HG1 2HS (off A61) ☎(0423) 560081 FAX (0423) 527928

Closed 24 Dec-1 Jan

Ashwood House is a handsome Edwardian property, carefully furnished by charming hosts Gill and Kristian Bendtson. It offers a comfortable lounge and a dining room decorated and furnished in

---

Wedgwood blue. Bedrooms are equally attractive and thoughtfully equipped.

9rm(7⇌9🈯) (1fb) ⊬ in 4 bedrooms ⊬ in dining room CTV in all bedrooms ® 🅷 sB&Bfr£21 sB&B⇌🈯fr£26 dB&B⇌🈯£44-£48 WB&B£133-£152
Lic 🈴 CTV
£

GH 🅠🅠🅠 **Cavendish Hotel** 3 Valley Drive HG2 0JJ ☎(0423) 509637

Overlooking the Valley Gardens and convenient for the town centre, this large, family owned and run sandstone house offers a friendly welcome and caring service; attractively furnished bedrooms are well equipped, and there is a pleasant, very comfortable lounge.

10rm(3⇌7🈯) CTV in all bedrooms ® T LDO 8.30pm
Lic 🈴
Credit Cards ①③

GH 🅠🅠🅠 **The Dales Hotel** 101 Valley Drive HG2 0JP ☎(0423) 507248 FAX (0423) 507248

Overlooking the delightful Valley Gardens, this well furnished house has attractively coordinated bedrooms with a good range of facilities. An elegant lounge with an honesty bar is also provided, and there is a neat dining room to the rear. The house is enthusiastically run by resident owners.

8rm(6⇌🈯) (2fb) ⊬ in dining room CTV in all bedrooms ® sB&B£25 sB&B⇌🈯£34-£36 dB&B⇌🈯£44-£50 LDO 9am
Lic 🈴 CTV
Credit Cards ①②③£

SELECTED

GH 🅠🅠🅠🅠 **Delaine Hotel** 17 Ripon Road HG1 2JL ☎(0423) 567974 FAX (0423) 561723

Rupert and Marian Viner are the friendly hosts at the Delaine, an attractive house in lovely gardens, well worthy of its 'selected' award. It offers a comfortable lounge, pretty bedrooms and good home cooking.

8rm(2⇌6🈯) Annexe 2rm(1⇌1🈯) (2fb) ⊬ in bedrooms ⊬ in dining room CTV in all bedrooms ® T 🅷 * sB&B⇌🈯fr£35 dB&B⇌🈯£50-£52 LDO 3pm
Lic 🈴 CTV
Credit Cards ①②③£

GH 🅠🅠 **Gillmore Hotel** 98 Kings Road HG1 5HH ☎(0423) 503699 FAX (0423) 503699

Within walking distance of the Conference Centre, this privately owned guest house provides modern bedrooms, including family rooms, and there is a comfortable lounge with a large-screen TV.

22rm(2⇌4🈯) (8fb)CTV in 9 bedrooms ® * sB&B£20-£22.50 sB&B⇌🈯£35 dB&B£37-£40 dB&B⇌🈯£42-£45 WB&B£129.50-£245 WBDi£189-£305 LDO 4pm
Lic 🈴 CTV snooker
£

GH 🅠🅠🅠 **Glenayr** 19 Franklin Mount HG1 5EJ ☎(0423) 504259

Glenayr is a comfortable, well furnished guest house in a quiet tree-lined road not far from the conference centre. It offers a cosy lounge and attractively decorated bedrooms. Mrs Webb, the charming hostess, provides excellent home cooking.

6rm(5🈯) CTV in all bedrooms ® 🅷 (ex guide dogs) * sB&B£18.50-£19 dB&B🈯£40-£45 WB&B£135 WBDi£225 LDO 4.30pm
Lic 🈴
Credit Cards ①②③£

GH 🅠🅠🅠 **Knox Mill House** Knox Mill Lane, Killinghall HG3 2AE ☎(0423) 560650

Built around 1785, this former mill owner's house is in a lovely location on the banks of a mill stream by the original waterwheel.

All the attractively decorated bedrooms face south with views over the meadows and stream beyond. There is a comfortable lounge with colour TV and a single dining table in a vaulted alcove (once a dairy), with a small library adjoining.
3rm(2🛏) ⓡ ⚔
▥ CTV nc10yrs

GH ⓠⓠⓠ Lamont House 12 St Mary's Walk HG2 0LW
☎(0423) 567143
Closed Xmas
A family-run late Victorian property, Lamont House is situated in a quiet side road within walking distance of the town centre. It has a tastefully furnished lounge, pleasant dining room and neatly decorated bedrooms.
9rm(3🛏) (2fb) CTV in all bedrooms ⓡ ✱ sB&B£20
sB&B🛏£27.50 dB&B£35 dB&B🛏£50
Lic ▥
Credit Cards ①ⓔ

GH ⓠⓠ Prince's Hotel 7 Granby Road HG1 4ST (off A59)
☎(0423) 883469
This impressive late Victorian terraced house is situated just off the A59 as it enters The Stray from the Knaresborough direction. The spacious double and family rooms feature very comfortable chairs, central heating, double glazing and some antique pieces. One room has a king sized four-poster bed with fully closing drapes. There is a very comfortable Victorian-style lounge with ample armchairs and sofas, and although there is no bar there is a table licence. The proprietors pride themselves on the standard of their traditional home cooking, prepared without the use of convenience foods. Dinner is served in the elegant dining room at 6.30pm and the price includes three courses and coffee. Special diets can also be catered for.
6rm(2⇔2🛏) (1fb) ✗ in dining room CTV in all bedrooms ⓡ ⚔ sB&B⇔🛏£19 dB&B⇔🛏£38 LDO 9am
▥ CTV ⚘nc3yrs

GH QQ The Richmond 56 Dragon View, Skipton Road
HG1 4DG ☎(0423) 530612
A terraced house conveniently situated off the A59 east of the town and at the end of the famous Stray, this friendly, family-run guest house provides comfortable accommodation including a lounge and a good-sized dining room. It is equally suitable for leisure and business guests.
6rm(5🏠) ⚲ in dining room CTV in all bedrooms ® ⋎ (ex guide dogs) sB&B🏠£20 dB&B🏠£40 WB&B£140
▥ CTV
Credit Cards ①②③ Ⓔ

GH QQ Roxanne 12 Franklin Mount HG1 5EJ ☎(0423) 569930
Closed 24 Dec-2 Jan
A small, Victorian house in a quiet side road conveniently placed for the Conference Centre. Bright, pleasant bedrooms and a combined lounge and dining room where there is a TV are provided.
5rm (1fb)CTV in 3 bedrooms ® ⋎ (ex guide dogs) ✶ sB&B£15-£17.50 dB&B£30-£35 WB&B£105-£122.50 WBDi£150.50-£168 LDO 4pm
▥ CTV
Credit Cards ①③ Ⓔ

SELECTED

GH QQQQ Ruskin Hotel 1 Swan Street HG1 2SS
☎(0423) 502045 FAX (0423) 506131
Closed 19 Dec-2 Jan
An excellent hotel in its own gardens stands just off the A61. Bedrooms are furnished to a high standard, and the dining room offers a choice of dishes on its table d'hôte menus.
7⇔🏠 (2fb) ⚲ in bedrooms ⚲ in dining room CTV in all bedrooms ® ⋎ (ex guide dogs) sB&B⇔🏠£34-£45 dB&B⇔🏠£50-£69 LDO 8.45pm
Lic ▥ nc2yrs
Credit Cards ①③ Ⓔ

GH QQQ Scotia House Hotel 66/68 Kings Road HG1 5JR
☎(0423) 504361 FAX (0423) 526578
Closed Xmas/New Year
A well run and friendly small hotel, conveniently situated for the conference centre, Scotia House offers a very good standard of accommodation, with attractively decorated bedrooms and a comfortable lounge. Small buffet lunches and private dinners can be arranged.
14rm(1⇔10🏠) (1fb) ⚲ in 7 bedrooms ⚲ in dining room CTV in all bedrooms ® T ✶ sB&Bfr£24 sB&B⇔🏠fr£26 dB&B⇔🏠fr£50 LDO 7pm
Lic ▥ CTV nc7yrs
Credit Cards ①③ Ⓔ

GH Q Shelbourne 78 Kings Road HG1 5JX ☎(0423) 504390
Situated close to the conference centre, this small guest house offers an adequate standard of accommodation together with friendly service. Public rooms comprise a cosy lounge and breakfast room/bar.
8rm (3fb) ⚲ in dining room CTV in all bedrooms ® ✶ sB&B£16 dB&B£30 WB&B£100-£105 LDO noon
Lic ▥ CTV
Credit Cards ①③ Ⓔ

GH QQQ Stoney Lea 13 Spring Grove HG1 2HS
☎(0423) 501524
Closed Xmas & New Year
A good all-round standard of accommodation is provided at this pleasant Victorian house situated close to the Conference Centre. Bedrooms are thoughtfully equipped and there is a comfortable lounge. Mrs Cargill, the resident owner, gives very friendly service.
7⇔🏠 ⚲ in dining room CTV in all bedrooms ® ⋎ (ex guide dogs) sB&B⇔🏠fr£28 dB&B⇔🏠fr£40

▥ CTV nc4yrs
Ⓔ

GH QQQ Wharfedale House 28 Harlow Moor Drive HG2 0JY
☎(0423) 522233
In a pleasant location overlooking Valley Gardens, this immaculately kept hotel is also convenient for the town centre and various conference facilities. The bedrooms are well appointed, and there is an attractive dining room and a comfortable lounge where drinks are served. The owners are both trained chefs and meals are often prepared to individual requirements.
8rm(1⇔7🏠) (2fb) CTV in all bedrooms ® T sB&B⇔🏠fr£26 dB&B⇔🏠fr£46 LDO 4pm
Lic ▥
Ⓔ

GH QQQ Wynnstay House 60 Franklin Road HG1 5EE
☎(0423) 560476
A comfortable and meticulously maintained Victorian house conveniently situated for the town centre and exhibition halls provides accommodation in attractively decorated, well equipped, en suite bedrooms.
5🏠 (2fb) ⚲ in dining room CTV in all bedrooms ® ✶ sB&B🏠£20-£23 dB&B🏠£40-£46 WB&B£140 WBDi£210 LDO 2pm
▥
Credit Cards ①③

HARROP FOLD Lancashire   Map 07 SD74

PREMIER 🏅 SELECTED

FH QQQQQ Mr & Mrs P Wood **Harrop Fold Country Farmhouse Hotel** *(SD746492)*
BBY 4PJ ☎Bolton-by-Bowland (0200) 447600
Closed Jan
Set in 280 acres of a beef and sheep farm, this delightful 16th-century farmhouse offers pretty bedrooms, named after flowers, with canopied beds and many thoughtful extras. There is a cosy bar and a first-floor lounge with an interesting nautical collection. Food is fresh and cooked with great care.

5⇔ Annexe 2rm(1⇔1🏠) ⚲ in bedrooms ⚲ in dining room ⚲ in 1 lounge CTV in all bedrooms ® T ⋎ (ex guide dogs) sB&B⇔🏠£39.50-£45 dB&B⇔🏠£60-£65 WBDifr£281 LDO 8pm
Lic ▥ 280 acres sheep beef
Credit Cards ①③ Ⓔ

HARROW Greater London   Map 04 TQ18

GH Q Central Hotel 6 Hindes Road HA1 1SJ
☎081-427 0893 FAX 081-427 0893
Long established and personally run, this guest house offers extensive free car parking and easy access to central London as well as good-value accommodation in neat, well presented bedrooms; a cooked English breakfast is included in the room tariff.
10rm(3🏠) (3fb)CTV in all bedrooms ® ⋎ sB&B£20-£28 sB&B🏠£28-£36 dB&B£38-£48 dB&B🏠£36-£48
▥ CTV
Credit Cards ①③

GH QQQ Crescent Lodge Hotel 58/62 Welldon Crescent
HA1 1QR ☎081-863 5491 & 081-863 5163 FAX 081-427 5965
A small family run hotel in a quiet residential crescent, this hotel is only a short drive from Wembley, Heathrow and central London. Bedrooms are tastefully decorated and well equipped. There is a cosy lounge and bar, and a choice of dishes is available

from the menu in the informal restaurant. The resident proprietors are welcoming and friendly.
21rm(13♠) (2fb) CTV in all bedrooms ⑧ T ✠ LDO 7.30pm
Lic ▥ CTV ⚲
Credit Cards ①②③

GH ◖Q◗◖Q◗ Hindes Hotel 8 Hindes Road HA1 1SJ
☎081-427 7468 FAX 081-424 0673
Free fore-court car parking and a relaxed, friendly atmosphere are provided by this long established, value-for-money guest house with good access to central London; accommodation is gradually being upgraded and will soon include new en suite rooms on the ground floor. Guests can start the day with a cooked English breakfast and later take their ease in the traditional TV lounge.
14rm(7♠) (2fb) ⚹ in dining room CTV in all bedrooms ⑧ ✠ (ex guide dogs) ✳ sB&B£25-£29 sB&B♠£34-£37 dB&B£35-£39 dB&B♠£45-£49 LDO 4.30pm
▥ CTV ⚲
Credit Cards ①②③ ⓔ

HARTFIELD East Sussex   Map 05 TQ43

SELECTED

FH ◖Q◗◖Q◗◖Q◗ Mrs C Cooper *Bolebroke Watermill (TQ481373)* Perry Hill, Edenbridge Road TN7 4JP (off B2026 1m N of Hartfield) ☎(0892) 770425
Mar-Oct rs Nov
A delightful old mill and barn has been converted into this unique and charming guest house. The barn has three bedrooms, two of which have four poster beds, and all are tastefully furnished and well-equipped. These rooms share a spacious comfortable lounge with lots of books and magazines. A narrow, steep staircase leads to the two compact bedrooms in the Mill, which also has its own lounge. Thoughtful touches such as a decanter of sherry and a bowl of fruit are welcome extras. Breakfast is served in the main house and Mrs Cooper has established a well deserved reputation for her breakfasts. Dinner is no longer served, but a light, cold snack can be served to guests in their bedrooms.
2⇄♠ Annexe 2⇄♠ CTV in all bedrooms ⑧ ✠ LDO 10am
▥ CTV nc7yrs 6 acres smallholding
Credit Cards ①②③

HARTLAND Devon   Map 02 SS22

GH ◖Q◗◖Q◗ Fosfelle EX39 6EF (off A39 onto B3248 for 2.5m)
☎(0237) 441273
A 17th-century former manor house stands in well kept gardens and lovely countryside, a short drive from the sea. Two lakes provide trout and coarse fishing, which are both popular. The bedrooms have comfortable beds and are furnished in country style with some antiques, and has modern facilities including telephones and tea making equipment. The bar supports a local darts team, and sometimes entertainment is provided in the barn, or a barbecue on the patio. The spacious dining room offers both à la carte and table d'hôte menus.
7rm(1⇄1♠) (2fb) ⚹ in bedrooms CTV in 3 bedrooms ⑧ ✠
sB&B£17.50-£21.50 dB&B£35-£43 dB&B⇄♠£35-£45
WB&B£120-£130 WBDi£160-£190 LDO 9pm
Lic ▥ CTV ⚲ ♪ snooker
Credit Cards ①③ ⓔ

HASELEY KNOB Warwickshire   Map 04 SP27

SELECTED

GH ◖Q◗◖Q◗◖Q◗ Croft CV35 7NL ☎(0926) 484447
FAX (0926) 484447
Situated in the small village of Haseley Knob, five miles north

---

west of Warwick. The Croft is equally suitable for tourists and business guests, being close to Stratford as well as the NAC, NEC, M6, M40, and M42. Two interconnecting ground floor rooms are available, one of which opens into the garden at the rear of the building. Public areas include two lounges and an attractive conservatory dining room, where dinner is usually served at a communal table. Guests are not permitted to smoke in the house.
5♠ (2fb) ⚹ CTV in all bedrooms ⑧ sB&Bfr£20 sB&B♠fr£22.50 dB&B♠fr£40 LDO 2pm
▥ CTV
ⓔ

See advertisement under WARWICK

HASTINGS & ST LEONARDS East Sussex Map 05 TQ80

GH ◖Q◗◖Q◗ Argyle 32 Cambridge Gardens TN34 1EN
☎(0424) 421294
This mid-terrace house is close to the railway station and town centre, and has a ground floor TV lounge and a basement breakfast room. Three of the simply furnished bedrooms have en suite facilities.
8rm(3♠) (3fb) ⚹ in dining room CTV in all bedrooms ⑧ ✠ ✳
sB&B£16-£20 sB&B♠£22-£26 dB&B£28-£36 dB&B♠£32-£40
WB&B£91-£112
▥ CTV ✗nc4yrs

Telephone national area codes are due to change by 16th April 1995. Please see the note under 'How to Use this Guide' at the front of the book.

PREMIER SELECTED

GH [Q][Q][Q][Q][Q]
Bryn-y-Mor 12 Godwin Road TN35 5JR (A259 coast road keeping sea on right bear left at Old Town & follow road up hill, at the Convent turn right into Ashburton Rd then 2nd right) ☎Hastings(0424) 722744 FAX (0424) 445933

The Victorians knew how to make themselves comfortable, and their standards are recreated at this hotel, together with modern facilities. The Bryn-y-Mor overlooks the town with its own lovely terraced garden and outdoor swimming pool. The bedrooms are ornately furnished to include a four-poster or quarter tester bed and a sofa or chaise longue. There is a choice of lounges, one with an honesty bar, and a candlelit dining room with a fine display of silver; dinner is by arrangementonly. Two self-catering apartments are also available.

4rm(3🚿) 🚭 in 1 lounge CTV in all bedrooms [R] 🐕 (ex guide dogs) sB&B🚿£35-£45 dB&B🚿£46-£70 WB&B£161-£245
Lic ▦ CTV 🏊(heated)
Credit Cards [1][2][3]

GH [Q][Q] Caspers 8 Tackleway TN34 3DE ☎(0424)712880
Caspers, an 18th-century Grade II listed terraced house, provides a friendly home from home with two letting rooms on the top floor, and excellent views overlooking the harbour and town. The house is personally run by proprietors Derek and Elaine Caspar, and families are made particularly welcome. Meals are served by arrangement in the attractive breakfast room, and special vegetarian breakfasts are a feature. Street parking is usually available.

2rm (1fb) 🚭 in dining room 🚭 in lounges CTV in all bedrooms [R] 🐕 * sB&B£14 dB&B£28
[£]

GH [Q][Q][Q] Eagle House Pevensey Road TN38 0JZ ☎(0424) 430535 & 441273 FAX (0424) 437771
Peacefully located in a residential area within walking distance of Warrior Square railway station, this detached Victorian house benefits from a car park and a rear garden where the proprietors' hens wander freely. Bedrooms have been furnished in a traditional style with mostly reproduction furniture, candlewick bedspreads and flock decor - all are very well equipped, and all but three more simply furnished rooms are en suite. Public areas are similar in style and decor, recreating something like the Victorian elegance with crystal chandeliers, original cornices and a marble fireplace in the lounge bar. Dinners are available or the proprietors will bring a supper tray to your room.

20🛁🚿 (2fb) 🚭 in dining room CTV in 23 bedrooms [R] T 🐕 (ex guide dogs) * sB&B🛁🚿£31.60 dB&B🛁🚿£49 WB&B£199 WBDi£331.65 LDO 8.30pm
Lic ▦
Credit Cards [1][2][3][5][£]

SELECTED

GH [Q][Q][Q][Q] Norton Villa Hill Street, Old Town TN34 3HU ☎Hastings(0424) 428168
Home to Peter and Janice Marshall, this attractive Victorian villa is in a good position for views of the harbour, old town and sea. The bedrooms provide every modern comfort and the lounge can be used if required. There is a sunny breakfast room with lace table cloths and blue Italian crockery, where a traditional cooked breakfast is served. The house, which is no smoking throughout, is usually closed between 10.30am and 2.30pm.

4🛁🚿 🚭 CTV in all bedrooms [R] 🐕 * sB&B🛁🚿£20-£22 dB&B£34-£38 dB&B🛁🚿£35-£40 WB&B£125-£150
CTV nc15yrs
[£]

PREMIER SELECTED

GH [Q][Q][Q][Q][Q] Parkside House 59 Lower Park Road TN34 2LD (follow town centre signs turn right at first traffic lights then first right into Lower Park Rd) ☎(0424) 433096 FAX (0424) 421431

An elegant Victorian house overlooking Alexandra Park, Parkside has very comfortable bedrooms, individually decorated, and furnished with a mixture of modern and antique furniture. The comfortable lounge has kept its original marble fireplace, and there is a separate sun lounge and an attractive dining room where Mrs Kent will serve a three-course set dinner by prior arrangement; guests are welcome to bring their own wine.

5rm(4🚿) (1fb) CTV in all bedrooms [R] T 🐕 (ex guide dogs) LDO 3pm
Lic ▦ CTV P̸

GH [Q][Q] The Ridge Guest House & Restaurant 361 The Ridge TN34 2RD ☎Hastings(0424) 754240
A popular, family run bed and breakfast establishment, The Ridge offers functional modern bedrooms, some located on the ground floor. Evening meals are available by prior arrangement, and served in the spacious restaurant. A bar and TV lounge are provided for guests.

11🚿 (2fb) CTV in all bedrooms [R] 🐕 * sB&B🚿£18-£20 dB&B🚿£30-£34 WB&B£90-£120 LDO 9.15pm
Lic ▦ CTV
Credit Cards [1][£]

SELECTED

GH [Q][Q][Q][Q] Tower Hotel 26-28 Tower Road West TN38 0RG ☎(0424) 427217 & 423771
Quietly located above St Leonards-on-Sea, this Victorian house has been skilfully extended to provide a choice of bedrooms, some of which are on the ground floor. The rooms are individually decorated, some with private bathrooms, and all have TV and tea trays. A freshly prepared set menu is provided in the attractive, well furnished dining room, and other public rooms include a conservatory breakfast room, small well stocked bar, and a spacious comfortable lounge. Service is particularly helpful, available throughout the day from resident proprietors Roy and Joan Richards. There is no car park, but unrestricted street parking is readily available.

12rm(10🛁🚿) (2fb) 🚭 in bedrooms 🚭 in dining room CTV in all bedrooms [R] 🐕 sB&B🛁🚿£25-£30 dB&B🛁🚿£42-£47.50 WB&B£126-£142.50 WBDi£199.50-£253.35 LDO 4pm
Lic ▦ CTV P̸
Credit Cards [1][2][3][5][£]

GH [Q][Q] Waldorf Hotel 4 Carlisle Parade TN34 1JG (located on the main coastal road A259 from Folkestone to Brighton, between Hastings Old Town and the pier) ☎(0424) 422185
A long-established seafront hotel, the Waldorf offers a range of modern bedrooms, some with good sea views. There is an

attractive restaurant and a cosy lounge, and a freshly prepared three-course evening meal is provided. Service, by the Harding family, is friendly and helpful.

12rm(3⇌2↿) (3fb) CTV in all bedrooms ⓡ ⚑ (ex guide dogs) ✳ sB&B£20-£24 sB&B⇌↿£24 dB&B£32 dB&B⇌↿£42 WB&B£108-£140 WBDi£160-£190 LDO 11.30am
Lic CTV ✗
£

Situated on the western fringe of St Leonards within easy reach of the seafront, this former gentleman's residence has been converted to provide comfortable well furnished accommodation. The cosy bar serves freshly prepared home cooked pub food and Harvey's real ale. Breakfast is taken in a separate room.

9🚿 (1fb)CTV in all bedrooms [R] 🐕 (ex guide dogs) * sB&B🚿fr£28 dB&B🚿fr£46 WB&Bfr£175 WBDifr£231 LDO 9.30pm

♨ CTV

Credit Cards [1][3][£]

HATHERSAGE Derbyshire — Map **08** SK28

FH [Q][Q][Q] Mr & Mrs P S Wain **Highlow Hall** *(SK219802)* S30 1AX (off B6001 between Hathersage & Grindleford, turn towards Abney & Gliding Club for 1.5m)

☎Hope Valley(0433) 650393

A 16th-century manor house farmhouse set in picturesque and peaceful rural surroundings, with enthusiastic young owners. Bright bedrooms are all cheerfully decorated in attractive individual styles and are generally of good proportions. Guests have the use of a comfortable lounge which has views over the surrounding hills and dales. A set price evening meal is available in the small dining room; smoking is not permitted here or in the bedrooms.

6rm(3🚿) (2fb) 🚭 in bedrooms 🚭 in dining room [R] * sB&B£18 sB&B🚿£40 dB&B£40-£50 dB&B🚿£46-£66 WB&B£120-£198 WBDi£195-£273

Lic CTV 900 acres mixed sheep

INN[Q][Q][Q] Scotsman's Pack School Lane S30 1BZ (off A625)

☎(0433) 650253

Closed 22 Dec-2 Jan

4🛁🚿 🚭 in area of dining room CTV in all bedrooms [R] 🐕 (ex guide dogs) * sB&B🛁🚿£27.50-£35 dB&B🛁🚿£47-£55 Bar Lunch £4-£11 High tea £2.50-£3 Dinner £10-£15 LDO 9.30pm

♨ nc14yrs

[£]

HATTON Warwickshire — Map **04** SP26

SELECTED

GH [Q][Q][Q][Q] Northleigh House Five Ways Road CV35 7HZ (off A4177) ☎Warwick(0926) 484203

Closed 15 Dec-30 Jan

A large detached house, its attractive gardens surrounded by agricultural land, offers impeccably maintained accommodation, the majority of the individually styled bedrooms being quite spacious and including fridges among their good array of modern equipment. The attractive dining room is furnished in period style, as is the spacious lounge with its comfortable seating and wealth of reading material; evening meals can be provided (by prior arrangement) for parties of four or more. There is a total ban on smoking throughout the house.

7🛁🚿 🚭 CTV in all bedrooms [R] sB&B🛁🚿£28-£38 dB&B🛁🚿£38-£55 LDO previous day

♨ CTV

Credit Cards [1][3][£]

See advertisement under WARWICK

HAVANT Hampshire — Map **04** SU70

See also Emsworth

HAVERFORDWEST Dyfed — Map **02** SM91

SELECTED

GH [Q][Q][Q][Q] Wilton House 6 Quay Street SA61 1BG

☎(0437) 760033 FAX (0437) 760297

Originally a saddler's and harness-maker's, this charming guest house and tea shop stands in the heart of the town next to the quay. Sympathetically restored, it provides spacious bedrooms with attractive Victorian pine furniture and modern facilities. Refreshments can be taken in the small patio garden in summer.

6rm(1🛁5🚿) 🚭 in bedrooms 🚭 in dining room CTV in all bedrooms [R] 🐕 (ex guide dogs) sB&B🛁🚿£25-£30 dB&B🛁🚿£40-£45 LDO 10pm

Lic ♨

Credit Cards [1][2][3]

HAVERIGG Cumbria — Map **07** SD17

GH [Q][Q][Q] Dunelm Cottage Main Street LA18 4EX

☎Millom(0229) 770097

Closed Jan

A delightful little cottage situated in the centre of the village, with a very convenient car park just over the road. The bedrooms are pretty and well furnished and good home cooking is served round a long table in the cosy dining room. There is a pleasant lounge, and resident owner Mrs Fairless provides attentive and friendly service.

3rm [R] dB&Bfr£40 LDO 6.30pm

♨ CTV P̸ nc10yrs

HAWES North Yorkshire — Map **07** SD88

GH [Q][Q][Q] Steppe Haugh Town Head DL8 3RJ (on A684)

☎Wensleydale(0969) 667645

Dating back to 1643, this charming cottage-style house is said to be the oldest in Hawes, and is only a few minutes' walk from the centre. Bedrooms are small but comfortable and there is a large lounge with a log fire and TV. Guests eat in the pretty dining room at individual lace-clothed tables.

6rm(2🚿) CTV in 2 bedrooms [R] 🐕 * sB&B£15-£20 sB&B🚿£30 dB&B£28 dB&B🚿£36 WB&B£98-£126 WBDi£203-£231 LDO 5pm

Lic ♨ CTV nc10yrs

HAWICK Borders *Roxburghshire* — Map **12** NT51

GH [Q][Q][Q] Oakwood House Buccleuch Road TD9 0EH

☎(0450) 372896 & 372814

Closed 24 Dec-5 Jan

Set back from the A7 on the southern approach to the town centre and pleasantly situated overlooking the bowling green and park, this solid Victorian villa offers a comfortable standard of bed and breakfast accommodation. Individually decorated bedrooms are well equpped and there is a comfortable lounge in which to relax. The whole property is neatly maintained and the resident owners extend a warm welcome to all their guests.

3rm(1🚿) 🚭 CTV in all bedrooms [R] 🐕 sB&B£18-£25 dB&B£30-£35 dB&B🚿£35-£40

♨ CTV nc5yrs

Credit Cards [5][£]

Telephone national area codes are due to change by 16th April 1995. Please see the note under 'How to Use this Guide' at the front of the book.

HAWKHURST Kent   Map **05** TQ73

P R E M I E R 🕊️ **S E L E C T E D**

FH 🔾🔾🔾🔾🔾 Mrs
Rosemary Piper **Conghurst
Farm** *(TQ768283)* TN18 4RW
(1.5m E on A268)
☎(0580) 753331
FAX (0580) 754579
Mar-Oct rs Nov & Feb
This delightful farmhouse is
set in 500 acres and is
surrounded by unspoilt
countryside. It has been home
to generations of the Piper
family since 1760 and the oldest part dates back over 300
years. Each of the bedrooms is spacious, comfortable and
individually decorated and furnished. There is an elegant
drawing room where guests can enjoy tea on arrival or pre-
dinner sherry and the log fire in cold weather. Rosemary Piper
specialises in traditional English cookery including home-
made soups, pies and desserts, and dinner is served family-
style in the grand dining room. The farmhouse breakfast
includes home-made preserves and fresh fruit. Smoking is not
permitted in the house.
3⇌ ⊬ ® 🏵 (ex guide dogs) ✳ dB&B⇌£39-£42
WB&B£122.50-£133 WBDi£199.50-£210 LDO 10am
🖳 CTV nc12yrs ⚘500 acres mixed
ⓔ

HAWKSHEAD Cumbria   Map **07** SD39

GH 🔾🔾🔾 Ivy House LA22 0NS ☎(05394) 36204
20 Mar-7 Nov
This attractive Georgian house stands on the edge of the village
and has the benefit of its own car park. Rooms are either in the
main house or the annexe next door; they are all modern with
good facilities. There is a comfortable lounge, and a good standard
of home cooking is offered.
6rm(3⇌3🏵) Annexe 5rm(3⇌2🏵) (2fb) ⊬ in dining room CTV in
5 bedrooms ® ✳ sB&B⇌🏵£27.50 dB&B⇌🏵£51-£55
WBDi£220.50-£234.50 LDO 6pm
Lic 🖳 CTV ♪
ⓔ

S E L E C T E D

GH 🔾🔾🔾🔾 **Rough Close Country House** LA22 0QF
(1.25m S on Newby Bridge rd) ☎(05394) 36370
Apr-Oct rs Mar
Anthony and Marylin Gibson offer a warm and friendly
welcome to their guesthouse which overlooks Esthwaite Water
to the south of Hawkshead village. The bedrooms are well
equipped and offer the usual facilities. There is a spacious
lounge with TV and a small bar. Dinner is served in the
charming dining room.
5⇌🏵 ⊬ in bedrooms ⊬ in dining room ® 🏵 (ex guide
dogs) dB&B⇌🏵£70-£75 (incl dinner) WBDi£234.50-£252
LDO 7pm
Lic 🖳 CTV nc12yrs
Credit Cards 1 3 ⓔ

INN🔾🔾 *Kings Arms Hotel* LA22 0NZ ☎(05394) 36372
A famous old Lakeland pub in the centre of the village, the Kings
Arms has a delightful character, with oak beams and an open log
fire features of the bar. Bedrooms are compact but well furnished,
and good facilities are provided. An extensive range of food is
available either in the bar or dining room.
▶

CONGHURST FARM

Conghurst is a Georgian farmhouse set in totally
peaceful, unspoilt countryside. Accommodation is
in three delightfully spacious bedrooms, all with
private facilities. There is an elegant drawing
room and separate television room. Excellent
evening meals available by prior arrangement.
**Conghurst was voted the Best Newcomer to
the guide in the South East in 1993.**

**Mrs Piper, Conghurst Farm, Hawkhurst,
Kent TN18 4RW**
Telephone: 01580 753331 Fax: 01580 754579

• COUNTRY HOUSE •

Blessed with a beautiful, tranquil setting
amidst rolling hills and overlooking the
peaceful, Esthwaite Water, this impressive
Georgian house has uninterrupted views
from all bedrooms of the lake, mountains,
forest and fells.
Once the holiday home of Beatrix Potter,
and only 5 mins walk from "Hill Top", her
Lakeland farmhouse, Ees Wyke now offers
accommodation of a high standard, a
growing reputation for first class cuisine, and
welcoming hospitality.
An ideal base for touring, walking or just
relaxing surrounded by the beauty of
Cumbria.
**Near Sawrey, Hawkshead,
Cumbria LA22 0JZ**
Telephone: Hawkshead (015394) 36393

9rm(4♠) (2fb) CTV in all bedrooms ® T LDO 9pm
▥.
Credit Cards 1 3

INN◖Q◗◖Q◗◖Q◗ *Red Lion* The Square LA22 0MV
☎(05394) 36213 FAX (05394) 36747
A 15th-century coaching inn stands in the centre of this popular
village, with the benefit of its own car park. Bedrooms are prettily
furnished, with good facilities. There is a convivial bar offering a
selection of real ales and Scottish malts, and a good range of food
is available either here or in the cosy beamed restaurant to the rear.
13rm(8♠) (2fb) CTV in all bedrooms ® ✹ LDO 9pm
▥.
Credit Cards 1 3

INN◖Q◗◖Q◗◖Q◗ **Sun** Main Street LA22 0NT ☎(05394) 36236
6rm(1➡5♠) (1fb) ✗ in bedrooms ✗ in area of dining room CTV
in all bedrooms ® ✹ ✱ dB&B➡♠fr52 Lunch £5-£8 Dinner
£7-£12 LDO 9.30pm
▥, ✗
Credit Cards 1 3 £

HAWORTH West Yorkshire   Map **07** SE03

GH ◖Q◗◖Q◗◖Q◗ **Ferncliffe Hotel** Hebden Road BD22 8RS (on A6033
near junct with B6144) ☎(0535) 643405
The Ferncliffe is a modern bungalow in an elevated position on
the Hebden Bridge road, enjoying good views over the valley. The
bedrooms are prettily furnished and offer good facilities, and there
is a cosy bar at the side of the restaurant, and a further small
lounge upstairs.
6♠ (1fb) ✗ in area of dining room ✗ in lounges CTV in all
bedrooms ®   ✱ sB&B♠£19.50-£22 dB&B♠£39 WB&B£136.50-
£154 WBDi£204.75-£222.25 LDO 8.30pm
Lic ▥. CTV
Credit Cards 1 3

HAYES Greater London   Map **04** TQ08

GH ◖Q◗ **Shepiston Lodge** 31 Shepiston Lane UB3 1LJ
☎081-573 0266 & 081-569 2536 FAX 081-569 2536
This small guest house is close to Heathrow airport and offers
adequately equipped rooms. There is a comfortable TV lounge and
an evening meal is available in the small dining room. The house
has a garden and a large car park is available for guests wishing to
leave cars while on holiday.
13rm (3fb)CTV in all bedrooms ® ✹ (ex guide dogs) ✱
sB&B£27.50-£30.50 dB&B£40.50-£43.50 LDO 9pm
Lic ▥. CTV
Credit Cards 1 2 3 5 £
See advertisement under HEATHROW AIRPORT

HAYLING ISLAND Hampshire   Map **04** SZ79

GH ◖Q◗◖Q◗◖Q◗◖Q◗◖Q◗ **Cockle
Warren Cottage Hotel** 36
Seafront PO11 9HL (take A3023
continue S to seafront then
turn left & continue for 1m
hotel on left) (Logis)
☎(0705) 464961
A small tile-hung farmhouse
located at the eastern end of
the seafront, with a large
colourful garden. Personally
run by the charming, very
welcoming Skelton family, the accommodation is extremely
well presented, with many extra touches. The standards of
both maintenance and housekeeping are excellent, and each of

the appealing bedrooms has its own individual style. The
comfortable lounge area leads into the very pretty
conservatory dining room, where Diane Skelton serves a set
four-course dinner using fresh fish, seafood, poultry and game
in dishes based on English and French provincial cuisine.
Organically grown vegetables, home-baked bread and freshly
made soups also feature, together with delicious rock cakes
offered with tea on arrival.
4➡♠ Annexe 1♠ ✗ in bedrooms ✗ in dining room ✗ in 1
lounge CTV in all bedrooms T ✹ (ex guide dogs) ✱
sB&B➡♠£45-£64 dB&B➡♠£64-£84 LDO 6pm
Lic ▥. nc12yrs ☇(heated)
Credit Cards 1 2 3

HAY-ON-WYE Powys   Map **03** SO24

See also Glasbury

GH ◖Q◗◖Q◗◖Q◗ **York House** Hardwick Road, Cusop HR3 5QX (on
B4348) ☎(0497) 820705
rs Xmas
This late Victorian residence on the edge of the town (off the
B4348 Hereford road) boasts a collection of white doves and
fantails in addition to beautiful lawns and gardens. The house is
furnished throughout in keeping with its origins and surroundings,
and the atmosphere is friendly, peaceful and relaxing; most of the
bedrooms look out across the gardens to the mountains beyond,
and all are well equipped with such extra facilities as television
sets, clock radios and even books and magazines. Ample secluded
car parking is available.
5rm(3➡♠) (2fb) ✗ CTV in all bedrooms ® sB&B£17.50-£22
sB&B➡♠£26.50 dB&B£35-£37 dB&B➡♠£40-£44
WB&B£110.25-£138.60 WBDi£185.85-£214.20 LDO 5pm
▥. nc8yrs
Credit Cards 1 2 3 £

HEASLEY MILL Devon   Map **03** SS73

GH ◖Q◗◖Q◗◖Q◗ **Heasley House** EX36 3LE (4m from A361, through N
Molton signposted Simons Bath & Heasley Mill)
☎North Molton(05984) 213
Closed Feb
This small family run hotel is set in a peaceful village with easy
access to Exmoor and the coast. The accommodation is
comfortable and the atmosphere relaxed. There is a cosy lounge
and the dining room is full of character. Home-cooked dishes
make up the predominantly set menus and are served around a
large table in the dining room.
8rm(2➡3♠) ®   ✱ sB&B➡♠fr22.50 dB&B➡♠£45-£40
WB&B£150 WBDi£240 LDO 5pm
Lic ▥. CTV
Credit Cards 1 3 £

HEATHROW AIRPORT Greater London   Map **04** TQ07

See also Slough

GH ◖Q◗◖Q◗ **The Cottage** 150 High Street, Cranford TW5 9PD
☎081-897 1815
Set in a quiet cul-de-sac off Cranford High Street, this guesthouse
offers clean, comfortable and well maintained accommodation on
the ground and first floors. There is an informal and relaxed
atmosphere under the proprietor Mrs Parry's personal supervision.
6rm (1fb) CTV in all bedrooms ✹ (ex guide dogs) LDO 10pm
Lic ▥.

GH ◖Q◗◖Q◗ **The Hounslow Hotel** 41 Hounslow Road, Feltham
TW14 0AU ☎081-890 2358 FAX 081-751 6103
23➡♠ CTV in all bedrooms ® T LDO 8.45pm
Lic ▥. CTV
Credit Cards 1 2 3 5

GH Ⓠ Ⓠ Ⓠ **Longford** 550 Bath Road, Longford UB7 0EE (approx 1.5m from junct 14 of M25) ☎Slough(0753) 682969
FAX (0753) 794189
Closed Xmas week
Situated in Longford village, opposite the Kings Arms pub, this 17th-century house retains its period character with beams, fine wood panelling and antique furniture. Bedrooms are a good size and a lounge and breakfast room are provided. The Kings Arms, under the same management, is open all day serving bar meals and real ales.
5rm ⊁ in bedrooms ⊁ in dining room CTV in all bedrooms Ⓡ
✴ sB&Bfr£26 dB&Bfr£38
▥ CTV nc10yrs
Credit Cards ①③Ⓛ

HEBDEN BRIDGE West Yorkshire   Map **07** SD92

SELECTED

GH Ⓠ Ⓠ Ⓠ Ⓠ **Redacre Mill** Redacre, Mytholmroyd HX7 5DQ (on A646 towards Hebden Bridge) ☎Halifax(0422) 885563
Mar-Oct rs Nov-17 Dec & 10 Jan-Feb
A converted Victorian warehouse charmingly situated overlooking the Rochdale canal at Mytholmroyd, within half an hour of Junctions 20 and 26 of the M62. A high standard of accommodation is offered, with five individually decorated and comfortably furnished bedrooms all thoughtfully equipped and spotlessly maintained and each with a private bathroom. Public areas include an L-shaped lounge/dining room where home-cooked meals are served, and outside there is a waterside terrace where guests may enjoy a drink watching the sun set over the canal. Surrounding the mill are two acres of attractive gardens and lawns, and there is ample parking. This

▶

Sun Inn

**Main Street, Hawkshead,
Cumbria LA22 0NT
Telephone: (015394) 36236**

The Sun Inn is situated in the unspoilt village of Hawkshead which is rich in history and magnificent surroundings. The 17th century building contains original beamed ceilings and open fires. The Sun is proud of its excellent home made food with all dishes prepared using the finest quality local produce. A wide range of beers including real ales and an extensive range of wines and spirits are also available all served by friendly, welcoming staff.

Hounslow Hotel

♣♣♣ English Tourist Board

VISA
MASTERCARD
ACCESS
EUROCARD
DINERS
AMERICAN
EXPRESS

EASY ACCESS
M3, M4, M25 – HEATHROW AIRPORT
CENTRAL LONDON & TOURIST ATTRACTIONS
COURTESY TRANSPORT HEATHROW
PRIVATE PARKING – LOCK-UP GARAGES
MODERATE PRICES
COMFORTABLE ROOMS ALL EN SUITE WITH
COLOUR TV, PRIVATE TELEPHONE,
WELCOME TRAY
WEEKEND BREAKS
SPECIAL RATES – COSY RESTAURANT
BAR & LOUNGE

**41 Hounslow Road, Feltham, Middx. TW14 0AU
Tel: 0181-890 2358 Fax: 0181-751 6103**

AA
Q

English Tourist Board
COMMENDED

SHEPISTON LODGE

**31 SHEPISTON LANE, HAYES, MIDDX. UB3 1LJ
Tel: 0181-573 0266 Tel/Fax: 0181-569 2536
Fax: 0181-569 2279**

Only ten minutes from Heathrow (not on flight path), Shepiston Lodge is a character house, where emphasis is on comfort and friendliness.
All bedrooms have colour TV; tea/coffee facility and central heating. New Bar. Spacious garden. Evening meals available. Ample parking, even for holidays. Easy access from A/M4, A/M40 and M25

establishment is totally no smoking.
5rm(2⇔3♠) (1fb) ⌧ CTV in all bedrooms ® ⅍ (ex guide dogs) sB&B⇔♪♠£30-£35 dB&B⇔♪♠£45-£55 WB&B£160-£210 WBDi£210-£280 LDO 8pm
Lic ▥.
Credit Cards ①③£

HELENSBURGH Strathclyde *Dunbartonshire*　　Map **10** NS28

See also Cardross

GH Ｑ Ｑ **Thorndean House** 64 Colquhoun Street G84 9JP (W off B832 at Stafford Street and take first right) ☎(0436) 674922
FAX (0436) 674922
Good-value accommodation is offered in this sturdy Victorian villa north of the town centre. Bedrooms are bright and airy and a hearty breakfast is served at a large table in the lounge/dining room. By arrangement, guests can be taken for a trip on the owners' yacht. The house is no-smoking.
3rm(2♠) (1fb) ⌧ ® sB&B£18-£20 sB&B♠£25-£27 dB&B£32-£36 dB&B♠£37-£42 WB&B£135
▥ CTV sailing in yacht
£

HELMSLEY North Yorkshire　　Map **08** SE68

FH Ｑ Ｑ Mrs M E Skilbeck **Middle Heads** *(SE584869)* Rievaulx YO6 5LU (From Helmsley take B1257 Stokesley road, and in approx 2.75m turn right sign posted Midddle Heads Farm follow road for 1m) ☎Bilsdale(0439) 798251
Mar-Nov
A very secluded farmhouse at the end of a long farm lane to the north of Helmsley providing friendly service and comfortable accommodation. There is a cosy lounge and a beamed dining room. Bedrooms, while not ensuite, nevertheless, have private bathrooms and shower rooms.
3rm ⌧ in bedrooms ⌧ in dining room ® ⅍ ✳ dB&Bfr£30
▥ CTV nc5yrs 170 acres arable beef mixed sheep

HELSTON Cornwall & Isles of Scilly　　Map **02** SW62

GH Ｑ Ｑ Ｑ **Helston Golf & Leisure** Wendron TR13 0LX (1m N on B3297) ☎(0326) 572518
This recently-restored farmhouse, in conjunction with a developing 9-hole golf course, is run by a friendly family. Smoking is discouraged.
3rm ⌧ ® ⅍ (ex guide dogs) ✳ sB&B£20 dB&B£30
Lic ▥ CTV ▶18 ✎(hard)pool table amusement parlour

FH Ｑ Ｑ Ｑ Mrs I White *Little Pengwedna (SW638318)* Little Pengwedna Farm TR13 0BA ☎Leedstown(0736) 850649
Cattle breeding has made this friendly farmhouse well known nationally. Its rooms retain the charm and character of the building, and are enhanced by many pretty ornaments, pictures and flowers from the well tended front lawn. Mrs White is a most welcoming hostess. Little Pengwedna is four miles north-west of Helston, on the Hayle road (B3302).
3rm(1♠) ® ⅍ (ex guide dogs) LDO 6pm
▥ CTV 74 acres cattle

FH Ｑ Ｑ Mrs G Lawrance **Longstone** *(SW662319)* Trenear TR13 0HG (take B3297 from Helston towards Redruth for 2m, turn left to Coverack Bridges, then first right and continue left to farm) ☎(0326) 572483
Mar-Nov
A simple but comfortable farmhouse is part of a working farm in a peaceful, remote setting amidst beautiful countryside. There is ample space both inside and out for families, and facilities include a playroom and sun lounge.
5rm(2⇔♠) (2fb) ⌧ in bedrooms ⌧ in dining room sB&B£16-£18

---

dB&B£28-£32 dB&B⇔♪♠£31-£36 WB&B£95-£110 WBDi£130-£150 LDO 4pm
▥ CTV 62 acres dairy
£

FH Ｑ Ｑ Ｑ Ｑ Mrs J Makin **Nanplough** *(SW682214)* Cury Whitecross TR12 7BQ ☎(0326) 241088
Guests can expect a friendly welcome from Jan and John Makin at their Victorian farmhouse located about five miles from Helston. The bedrooms have the usual modern comforts plus hair dryers and magazines. Dinner is provided by arrangement and guests can enjoy traditional English cooking with seasonal home-grown vegetables and fruit. There is a spacious lounge and outdoor amenities include a heated outdoor pool and, if weather permits, a weekly barbecue. Three self-catering cottages are available and there is a riding stable on the adjacent farm.
3♠ ⌧ in dining room CTV in all bedrooms ® ⅍ (ex guide dogs) dB&B♠£28-£40 WB&B£98-£140 WBDi£157.50-£199.50 LDO 24hrs
▥ CTV ✎(heated) games room 26 acres
Credit Cards ①③£

INN Ｑ Ｑ Ｑ Ｑ **Halzephron Inn** Gunwalloe TR12 7QB (3m S of Helston on A3083 turn right sigposted Gunwalloe,proceed through village Inn is on the left) ☎(0326) 240406
Closed 24-31 Dec
2rm(1⇔1♠) ⌧ in dining room CTV in all bedrooms ® ⅍ (ex guide dogs) sB&B⇔♠£35 dB&B⇔♠£50 WBDi£175-£245 Lunch £7.95-£11.95alc Dinner £7.95-£17.75alc LDO 9.30pm
nc14yrs
Credit Cards ①③£

HENLEY-ON-THAMES Oxfordshire　　Map **04** SU78

GH Ｑ **Flohr's Hotel & Restaurant** Northfield End RG9 2JG
☎(0491) 573412 FAX (0491) 579721
A listed Georgian town house situated a short walk from the town centre with simply furnished, individually decorated bedrooms. A choice of imaginative dishes from the set-price menu is offered in the formal beamed restaurant.
9rm(1⇔2♠) (4fb)CTV in all bedrooms ® T ✳ sB&B£39.50-£54 sB&B⇔♠fr£54 dB&Bfr£69 dB&B⇔♠fr£79 LDO 10pm
Lic ▥ CTV
Credit Cards ①②③£

GH Ｑ Ｑ Ｑ **Slater's Farm** Peppard Common RG9 5JL
☎Rotherfield Greys(0491) 628675
Situated four miles west of Henley on the B481 at Peppard, it is best to ring for detailed directions to Slaters Farm as it is not easy to find. Though no longer a farmhouse, it is a charming detached property, 270 years old in parts, with a pretty garden offering tennis and croquet in a conservation area. Very much a home which is open to guests, the house has a gracious breakfast room and lounge with a feature fireplace, together with smart new bathrooms and cosy bedrooms. It is a good base for touring, and direct, high-speed trains to London from nearby Reading take only half an hour. The area has many good pubs for dinner.
3rm ⌧ in bedrooms CTV in 1 bedroom ⅍ (ex guide dogs) sB&B£20-£25 dB&B£40-£50
▥ CTV ✎(hard)
£

HENSTRIDGE Somerset   Map **03** ST71

FH ◖◗◖◗◖◗ Mrs P Doggrell *Toomer (ST708192)* Templecombe
BA8 0PH (entrance to farm on A30 between Milborne Port and
Henstridge traffic lights) ☎Templecombe(0963) 250237
Amidst 400 acres of mixed farmland, this 300-year-old farmhouse
is surrounded by neat gardens. The good sized bedrooms are on
the first floor and provide pleasant accommodation. Breakfast is
taken around a communal table in a lovely dining room, and there
is a separate lounge with a TV and deep comfortable sofas.
3rm(1♠) (2fb) CTV in all bedrooms ® ✝ (ex guide dogs)
▥ CTV ✔ 400 acres arable dairy

HEREFORD Hereford & Worcester   Map **03** SO54
See also Bodenham & Little Dewchurch

SELECTED
GH ◖◗◖◗◖◗◖◗ *Hermitage Manor* Canon Pyon HR4 8NR (3.5m
NW off A4110 towards Canon Pyon) ☎(0432) 760317
Mar-mid Dec
With eleven acres of grounds, sheltered by extensive deer
woodlands, this impressive manor house is set in an elevated
position overlooking rural Hertfordshire. It has a magnificent
oak panelled lounge, a hall with polished floorboards and a
cheerful wood burning stove, plus a second no smoking
lounge, featuring an interesting carved wooded fireplace, and
a small TV lounge, all furnished with modern comfortable
seating. Most bedrooms are exceptionally large, well furnished
in mixed styles, and equipped with en suite bathrooms and
TV.
3rm(2⇔1♠) CTV in all bedrooms ® ✝
▥ CTV nc9yrs bowling croquet

GH ◖◗◖◗ Hopbine Hotel Roman Road HR1 1LE (on A4103,
beyond the race course) ☎(0432) 268722
A small, friendly hotel situated on the outskirts of the town with
modest but well equipped bedrooms. There are two lounge areas
and a small bar, and the hotel is particularly popular with business
guests. A set evening meal is served in the cosy dining room,
which is run on informal lines by owners Mr and Mrs Horne.
20rm(14⇔) (4fb) ⍏ in dining room ⍏ in lounges CTV in all
bedrooms ® ✳ sB&Bfr£17 sB&B⇔fr£21 dB&Bfr£30
dB&B⇔fr£34 LDO before noon
Lic ▥ CTV
£

SELECTED
FH ◖◗◖◗◖◗◖◗ Mrs J Layton **Grafton Villa Farm**
(SO500361) Grafton HR2 8ED (2m S off A49) ☎(0432) 268689
Closed 23-28 Dec
This early 18th-century farmhouse is at the heart of a working
farm and pretty lawns and gardens surround the house. Jennie
Layton is the very friendly owner, offering a warm welcome
and good home cooking. Bedrooms are named after the local
woodlands viewed from their windows and are fresh and
bright, with some fine antique pieces. Each has a hair dryer,
television and hot water bottle, and the refreshments tray
includes Earl Grey and herbal teas. There is a comfortable
lounge with log fire in colder weather.
3rm(2⇔♠) (1fb) ⍏ in bedrooms ⍏ in dining room CTV in all
bedrooms ® sB&Bfr£19 sB&B⇔♠£20 dB&B£32-£35
dB&B⇔♠£38-£40 LDO 3pm
▥ CTV 200 acres mixed
£

FH Ⓠ Ⓠ Ⓠ Mr D E Jones **Sink Green** *(SO542377)* Rotherwas HR2 6LE (on B4399) ☎Holme Lacy(0432) 870223
Closed Xmas
This delightful 16th-century ivy-clad farmhouse is three miles from the city centre. The bedrooms include one with a four-poster bed, and are attractively decorated with a good range of facilities; all the rooms have modern neat en suite showers or baths and are furnished with antiques. There is a large comfortable lounge with a log-burning stove and piano. Breakfast is taken in the dining room which features a flagstone floor. This establishment is totally no smoking.
3rm(2⇌1♠) ✗ CTV in all bedrooms Ⓡ ♉ (ex guide dogs) sB&B⇌♠£20-£24 dB&B⇌♠£36-£46
🏛 CTV 180 acres beef sheep
£

HEVERSHAM Cumbria　　　　Map **07** SD48

GH Ⓠ Ⓠ Ⓠ **Springlea** LA7 7EE (on A6 1m N of Milnthorpe traffic lights) ☎(05395) 64026
2⇌♠ (1fb)CTV in all bedrooms Ⓡ ✳ sB&B⇌♠£15-£25 dB&B⇌♠£26-£37 WB&B£80-£120 WBDi£122-£162 LDO 4pm
🏛 sun lounge

HEXHAM Northumberland　　　　Map **12** NY96

SELECTED

GH Ⓠ Ⓠ Ⓠ Ⓠ **Middlemarch** Hencotes NE46 2EB (on main street, next to St Mary's church and overlooking Abbey and park) ☎(0434) 605003
This listed Georgian house at the centre of the town has the advantage of its own car park. Spacious premises offer a delightful lounge with a wealth of magazines and tourist information, whilst large bedrooms with good facilities are furnished to a high standard. The charming owner and her family provide warm, friendly service.
3rm(1♠) (1fb) ✗ in bedrooms ✗ in dining room CTV in all bedrooms Ⓡ sB&B£26-£36 sB&B♠£36 dB&B£40-£41 dB&B♠£48-£50
🏛 nc10yrs
£

FH Ⓠ Ⓠ Ⓠ E A Courage **Rye Hill** *(NY958580)* Slaley NE47 0AH (5m S, off B6306) ☎Slaley(0434) 673259 FAX (0434) 673259
In a rural location, close to the village of Slaley, this attractive farmhouse provides comfortably furnished bedrooms, a well equipped games room and a cosy lounge. Meals are taken around two pine tables in the dining room which overlooks the garden.
6⇌♠ (2fb) ✗ in bedrooms ✗ in dining room CTV in all bedrooms Ⓡ sB&B⇌♠£20 dB&B⇌♠£36 WB&B£113.40-£126 WBDi£183.40-£196 LDO 6pm
Lic 🏛 CTV snooker games room 30 acres sheep
£

INN Ⓠ Ⓠ Ⓠ **Rose & Crown** Main Street, Slaley NE47 0AA ☎(0434) 673263
An attractive inn set in the centre of the village of Slaley, some five miles from Hexham, the Rose and Crown has two pleasant bars, one with an interesting collection of mugs adorning the ceiling. There are three well furnished guest rooms, and a good selection of food is available in either the bar or cosy dining room.
3⇌♠ ✗ CTV in all bedrooms Ⓡ ♉ (ex guide dogs) sB&B⇌♠£17.50-£25 dB&B⇌♠£35-£50 WB&B£20-£160 WBDi£170-£210 Lunch £3.50-£6.95 Dinner £1.50-£9.95&alc LDO 10pm
🏛
£

HEYSHAM Lancashire　　　　Map **07** SD46

GH Ⓠ Ⓠ *Carr-Garth* Bailey Lane LA3 2PS ☎(0524) 851175
Etr-mid Oct
An attractive 17th-century residence situated in neat gardens close to Heysham village. Bedrooms are nicely decorated and very well maintained and there are two lounges (one with colour TV), and a dining room with separate tables.
8rm (2fb) Ⓡ LDO 4pm
CTV

HIGHAM Suffolk　　　　Map **05** TM03

SELECTED

GH Ⓠ Ⓠ Ⓠ Ⓠ **The Bauble** Higham CO7 6LA (on B1068, near the bridge at the foot of the hill) ☎Colchester(0206) 337254 FAX (0206) 337263
Set on the edge of this very pretty village in the heart of Constable country, The Bauble is converted from two 16th-century cottages. It is surrounded by a lovely garden, rich in colour in the summer months, with patio doors leading from the lounge. The dining room has a communal mahogany table with brass inlaid period chairs, and all around the house there are gleaming, polished antiques and other fine items, such as Dalton figures, and Indian paintings on rice paper on the staircase to the bedrooms. Each of the bedrooms is colour themed, with soft furnishings in either Laura Ashley or Sanderson prints, and Mrs Watkins has exercised her considerable talent for combining practicality with style.
3rm(1⇌2♠) ✗ in 1 bedrooms ✗ in dining room CTV in all bedrooms Ⓡ ♉ ✳ sB&B⇌♠£20-£25 dB&B⇌♠£40-£45
🏛 nc12yrs ♉(heated) ♖(hard)
£

SELECTED

GH Ⓠ Ⓠ Ⓠ Ⓠ **The Old Vicarage** CO7 6JY ☎(0206) 337248
Approaching the village from the A12 (1.5 miles), turn left at the green and the Old Vicarage is the distinctive ochre washed and timbered house on the right with leaded windows. The dignified, high-ceilinged rooms look out onto lovely gardens with manicured lawns and colourful shrubberies tended by Mrs Parker. The same talented green fingers are evident in the lounge where, on our last visit, an orange tree was in fruit and the most glorious orchids were in bloom among the fine antiques. Despite the finery, the house has a lived in and welcoming atmosphere. The bedrooms are similar, really comfortable and colour coordinated, but include curious combinations such as raffia matting covered in rugs, and came next to an antique dresser. The Parkers are renowned for their hospitality and it is a pleasure to stay with them.
3rm(2⇌) (1fb) ✗ in dining room ✗ in lounges CTV in all bedrooms Ⓡ ✳ sB&B£25-£38 dB&B£40-£48 dB&B⇌£50-£54
🏛 CTV ♖♖(hard)♪ boats
£

HIGH CATTON Humberside　　　　Map **08** SE75

FH Ⓠ Ⓠ Ⓠ Mr & Mrs Foster **High Catton Grange** *(SE128541)* YO4 1EP (leave A166 in Stamford Bridge opposite `Corn Mill' left at church for approx 1.5m take first turning right to High & Low Catton,first farm on left) ☎Stamford Bridge(0759) 371374
Closed early Dec-mid Jan
Standing in open countryside a mile from the village crossroads, this 18th-century farmhouse provides prettily decorated bedrooms with several thoughtful touches. There is a cosy guests' lounge and a pleasant dining room overlooking the garden.

3rm(1🛁🚿) (1fb) 🚭 in dining room 🚭 in lounges CTV in 1 bedroom [R] ✱ dB&B£29-£32 dB&B🛁🚿£36-£40
▦ CTV 300 acres arable beef dairy
[£]

HIGHCLIFFE-ON-SEA Dorset Map **04** SZ29

GH [Q][Q][Q] ***The Beech Tree*** 2 Stuart Road BH23 5JS (from Christchurch take A337 to New Milton, after 2m take 1st turning right past traffic lights into village) ☎Highcliffe(0425) 272038

A small guest house has a warm and friendly atmosphere. The bedrooms, although not large, are attractively decorated and furnished. There is a compact dining room where a set price dinner and choice of breakfasts is offered. The lounge is small but cosy.

7rm(5🚿) CTV in all bedrooms [R] 🐕 (ex guide dogs) LDO 6pm
▦ CTV nc

HIGH WYCOMBE Buckinghamshire Map **04** SU89

GH [Q][Q] ***Amersham Hill*** 52 Amersham Hill HP13 6PQ (300yds from High Wycombe Railway Station on the A404)
☎(0494) 520635

Closed Xmas & New Year

A simple guest house on three floors, with comfortable bedrooms, lies close to the town centre and the railway station.

8rm(1🚿) CTV in all bedrooms [R] 🐕 (ex guide dogs)
▦

SELECTED

GH [Q][Q][Q][Q] **Clifton Lodge Hotel** 210 West Wycombe Road HP12 3AR ☎(0494) 440095 & 529062
FAX (0494) 536322

West of the town centre this well cared for hotel has its bedrooms distributed among a maze of corridors. They are of various shapes but are all well equipped and include a four-poster room with a large whirlpool bath. The ground floor has a restaurant with conservatory, a bar and a lounge with satellite TV.

32rm(12🛁8🚿) (2fb) 🚭 in dining room CTV in all bedrooms [R] **T** 🐕 (ex guide dogs) ✱ sB&B£30-£47 sB&B🛁🚿£47 dB&B£52-£67 dB&B🛁🚿£67 LDO 8.45pm
Lic ▦ CTV sauna jacuzzi
Credit Cards [1] [2] [3] [5] [£]

HILTON Cambridgeshire Map **04** TL26

INN[Q][Q][Q] **Prince of Wales** Potton Road PE18 9NG (follow B1040 to Biggleswade from A604/A14 and B1040 to St Ives from A45) ☎Huntingdon(0480) 830257 FAX (0480) 830257

Closed 24-25 Dec

This small public house has a friendly atmosphere in the limited public rooms. Bedrooms, though compact, are well fitted out. Guests are welcome to use the comfortable lounge bar in the afternoons and have breakfast and bar meals in the open-plan dining area. A good choice of bar meals is on offer with daily blackboard specials including 'healthy eating' and vegetarian dishes.

4🚿 CTV in all bedrooms [R] sB&B🚿£22.50-£33 dB&B🚿£45-£48 Lunch £5.35-£12.95alc Dinner £5.35-£12.95alc LDO 9.15pm
▦ CTV nc5yrs pool table darts
Credit Cards [1] [2] [3] [£]

HIMBLETON Hereford & Worcester Map **03** SO95

FH [Q][Q][Q] Mrs P Havard **Phepson** *(SO941599)* WR9 7JZ (from Droitwich take B4090 for 2m then turn right & proceed for 2m)
☎(0905) 391205

Closed Xmas & New Year

Popular with business travellers and tourists alike, this traditional 17th-century rambling farmhouse is set in the heart of the country, yet is only five miles from the M5. There is a very comfortable lounge with a good selection of games. Bedrooms are cosy and simple, and both rooms in the Granary annexe have good en suite facilities.

2🛁🚿 Annexe 2🛁 (1fb) CTV in all bedrooms [R] ✱ sB&B🛁🚿fr£19.50 dB&B🛁🚿fr£34 WB&Bfr£107
▦ CTV 170 acres beef sheep
[£]

HINCKLEY Leicestershire Map **04** SP49

GH [Q][Q][Q] **Ambion Court Hotel** The Green, Dadlington CV13 6JB ☎(0455) 212292 FAX (0455) 213141

A pleasant conversion of a red-brick farm building, this hotel overlooks the village green in Dadlington. It offers good public rooms, including a comfortable lounge bar and a lounge with exposed brickwork, a piano, books and board games. At dinner English cooking with international influences is served. The bedrooms, all equally well equipped, are split between the modern annexe and the main house.

2🚿 Annexe 5rm(1🛁4🚿) (1fb) 🚭 in 7 bedrooms 🚭 in dining room CTV in all bedrooms [R] **T** sB&B🛁🚿£30-£45 dB&B🛁🚿£45-£60 WB&B£200-£250 WBDi£275-£310 LDO 8.30pm
Lic ▦ CTV
Credit Cards [1] [3] [£]
See advertisement on p.215.

GH [Q][Q][Q] **Woodside Farm** Ashby Road, Stapleton LE9 8JE (on A447, 3m N of Hinckley, just beyond Woodlands Nurseries)
☎Market Bosworth(0455) 291929 FAX (0455) 291929

Major changes have taken place at this Georgian farmhouse over the last year with the addition of several new bedrooms, another lounge and a reception office. These enhance the original lounge, dining room/conservatory and small bar. Bedroom styles are now divided between the more traditional old rooms and those with

▶

Clifton Lodge Hotel

210 West Wycombe Road,
High Wycombe, Bucks HP12 3AR
Tel: 01494 440095 & 529062
Fax: 01494 536322

Situated on the A40 West Wycombe approximately one mile from the M40 London to Oxford motorway and close to the centre of historic High Wycombe, the principal town of the Chilterns. Ideal for touring the Thames Valley, Oxford, Cotswold etc. There are ample car parking facilities and pleasant gardens. Good English breakfast, lunches and dinner available. All rooms have central heating, colour TV and direct dial telephone. Small functions catered for. Licensed.

Under the personal supervision of the resident proprietors Jane & Brian Taylor

light modern fitted furnishings in the new wing. The bedrooms are all no-smoking. The house is set in a 16-acre smallholding, and it offers a good range of home cooked meals.

10rm(8🛁🚿) (1fb) 🚭 in bedrooms 🚭 in area of dining room 🚭 in 1 lounge CTV in all bedrooms Ⓡ 🐕 sB&B🛁🚿£28.50-£35 dB&B🛁🚿£40-£50 LDO 9.30pm

Lic ♨ CTV

Credit Cards [1][3]

HINTON CHARTERHOUSE Avon — Map **03** ST75

GH [Q][Q][Q] Green Lane House Green Lane BA3 6BL (turn off B3110 in village by the Rose & Crown Inn) ☎Bath(0225) 723631

Two 18th-century cottages have been well converted to create this attractive, welcoming little guesthouse. The individually decorated bedrooms are bright and well equipped, and there is a cosy lounge with an open fire in addition to the breakfast room.

4rm(2🚿) 🚭 in dining room Ⓡ 🐕 (ex guide dogs) ✳ sB&B£24-£32 sB&B🚿£31-£37 dB&B£36-£43 dB&B🚿£42-£49

♨ CTV

Credit Cards [1][2][3][£]

HITCHAM Suffolk — Map **05** TL95

FH [Q] Mrs B Elsden ***Wetherden Hall*** *(TL971509)* IP7 7PZ ☎Bildeston(0449) 740412

Feb-Nov

This attractive farmhouse is set on a working farm on the outskirts of the village on the road to Kettlebaston and offers comfortable, well kept accommodation. Downstairs there is a combined lounge/dining room where hearty breakfasts are served.

2rm (1fb) 🐕

♨ CTV nc9yrs 🌾 300 acres mixed

HITCHIN Hertfordshire — Map **04** TL12

GH [Q][Q][Q] Firs Hotel 83 Bedford Road SG5 2TY ☎(0462) 422322 FAX (0462) 432051

rs 25 Dec-2 Jan

Originally a manor house, this roadside hotel close to the town centre has varied accommodation, including some in modern extensions. There is a fully licensed bar and the Classico Restaurant offers an à la carte menu specialising in Italian cooking.

30rm(24🛁🚿) (2fb)CTV in all bedrooms Ⓡ **T** ✳ sB&B£31 sB&B🛁🚿£37-£49 dB&B£48 dB&B🛁🚿£54-£59 LDO 9.30pm

Lic ♨ CTV

Credit Cards [1][2][3][5][£]

HOARWITHY Hereford & Worcester — Map **03** SO52

FH [Q][Q] Mrs C Probert **The Old Mill** *(SO546294)* HR2 6QH ☎Carey(0432840) 602

Dating from the 18th century and now converted into a small country guest house, the Old Mill stands at the centre of the village; the owners farm land elsewhere, but horses and sometimes sheep are kept here. Guest rooms in cottage style are attractively decorated and furnished, the comfortable television lounge is warmed by a log fire in winter, and meals are taken in a beamed dining room.

6rm(2🚿) 🚭 ✳ sB&Bfr£15 sB&B🚿£17 dB&Bfr£30 dB&B🚿£34 WB&B£95-£110 WBDi£140-£160 LDO 7pm

♨ CTV

HOLBEACH Lincolnshire — Map **08** TF32

GH [Q][Q][Q] Pipwell Manor Washway Road, Saracens Head PE12 8AL (off A17) ☎(0406) 423119

This period farmhouse is set amid arable farmland. Lesley Honnor greets her guests warmly, and invites each of them on arrival to tea and cake in a sunny lounge furnished with highly polished tables and with book-lined walls surrounding the pine mantle and leaded fireplace. The dining room is dominated by a central oak table, and original Georgian panelling is accentuated by candy stripe wallpaper, while greenery and dried flower arrangements in huge baskets add further appeal. The bedrooms, two of which are really roomy, all have an armchair or sofa; the soft furnishings and decor are totally coordinated and quite lavish in either Laura Ashley or Sanderson fabrics. The house is immaculate and lovely to look at but, more important, very comfortable and welcoming.

4rm(3🛁🚿) 🚭 Ⓡ 🐕 sB&B£20 dB&B🛁🚿£34-£38

♨ CTV

HOLMBURY ST MARY Surrey — Map **04** TQ14

INN[Q][Q][Q] Royal Oak The Glade RH5 6PF (turn off A25 onto B2126 at Abinger Hammer, inn is 2.50m on right overlooking village green) ☎(0306) 730120

2🚿 🚭 in bedrooms CTV in all bedrooms Ⓡ 🐕 (ex guide dogs) ✳ sB&B🚿£25 dB&B🚿£38 Lunch £4.50-£10 High tea £3.50-£6.50 Dinner £4.50-£15 LDO 9.30pm

♨

Credit Cards [3]

HOLMFIRTH West Yorkshire — Map **07** SE10

SELECTED

GH [Q][Q][Q][Q] Holme Castle Country Hotel Holme Village HD7 1QG (2m S on A6024) ☎(0484) 686764 FAX (0484) 687775

A conversion of three period houses, Holme Castle looks out over beautiful countryside. Rooms have preserved a period atmosphere but provide modern comfort.

8rm(5🛁🚿) (3fb) 🚭 CTV in all bedrooms 🐕 (ex guide dogs) sB&B£20-£40 sB&B🛁🚿£35-£50 dB&B£40-£50 dB&B🛁🚿£45-£65 WB&B£133-£259 WBDi£183-£354 LDO noon

Lic ♨ CTV 🎠 childrens playground

Credit Cards [1][2][3][£]

INN[Q][Q][Q] White Horse Scholes Road, Jackson Bridge HD7 7HF (off A616, 1m from New Mill) ☎(0484) 683940

Closed 24-25 Dec & 31 Jan

Renowned for its appearances in 'Last of the Summer Wine', this traditional Yorkshire inn has a friendly atmosphere. Bedrooms, though on the compact side, are attractive, and there is a good choice of meals served in the distinctive bar.

5🛁🚿 (3fb)CTV in all bedrooms Ⓡ 🐕 (ex guide dogs) ✳ sB&B🛁🚿£25 dB&B🛁🚿£37 Lunch £2.45-£5.95alc LDO 9.30pm

♨

[£]

HOLNE Devon — Map **03** SX76

SELECTED

FH [Q][Q][Q][Q] Mrs S Townsend **Wellpritton** *(SX716704)* TQ13 7RX ☎Poundsgate(0364) 631273

Closed 25-26 Dec

Wellpritten Farm is on the fringe of Dartmoor National Park some 1.5 miles from the village, in an area ideal for walkers. There are four attractive bedrooms, two of them family suites, with many useful extras. Guests are invited to enjoy Sue Townsend's home cooked fare in the dining room and relax in the comfortable sitting room.

4rm(1🛁2🚿) (2fb) 🚭 in bedrooms 🚭 in dining room Ⓡ 🐕 (ex guide dogs) ✳ sB&Bfr£16 sB&B🛁🚿£18 dB&Bfr£32 dB&B🛁🚿£36 WB&B£112 WBDi£154 LDO 4pm

♨ CTV 🎯games room snooker table-tennis skittles 15 acres mixed

[£]

HOLSWORTHY Devon Map **02** SS30

[🛏🍴] **GH** [Q][Q][Q] **Woodlands** Dunsland Cross EX22 7YQ (4.5m E, junct A3072/A3079) ☎(0409) 221627

Closed 25 Dec

2🚿 CTV in all bedrooms Ⓡ 🐕 sB&B🚿£15-£17.50 dB&B🚿£31 WB&B£95-£98

🅿

FH [Q][Q] Mr & Mrs E Cornish **Leworthy** *(SS323012)* EX22 6SJ (leave Holsworthy via Bodmin St, past the Chapel in the direction of North Tamerton, Leworthy is signposted left after 3m) ☎(0409) 253488 FAX (0409) 254671

Home cooking is a feature at this farmhouse, in a peaceful, rural setting. The accommodation provided is clean and comfortable, and children are made very welcome. Tours of the farm and hay rides are available as well as other leisure pursuits.

10rm(3🚿) (5fb) 🚭 in dining room 🚭 in 1 lounge Ⓡ 🐕 (ex guide dogs) ✳ sB&B£16.50-£19.50 sB&B🚿£18.50-£21.50 WB&B£108-£125 WBDi£171-£186 LDO 6pm

Lic CTV 👶 🎾(hard)U 235 acres mixed

[£]

HOLT Norfolk Map **09** TG03

GH [Q][Q][Q] **Lawns Private Hotel** Station Road NR25 6BS ☎(0263) 713390 FAX (0263) 713390

The Lawns is a Victorian red brick property offering well proportioned bedrooms with many modern amenities. Fresh home-cooked food is served for all meals and real ale is available in the bar.

11🛁🚿 (2fb) 🚭 in dining room 🚭 in lounges CTV in all bedrooms Ⓡ **T** ✳ sB&B🛁🚿£35 dB&B🛁🚿£58 WB&B£165 WBDi£250 LDO 8.30pm

Lic 🅿

Credit Cards [1] [2] [3] [5] [£]

HOLYHEAD See **ANGLESEY, ISLE OF**

HOLYWELL Clwyd Map **07** SJ17

FH [Q][Q] Mrs M L Williams **Bryn Glas** *(SJ155737)* Babell CH8 7PZ (turn off A55 for Holywell, proceed to traffic lights, turn left uphill to Brynford village pass church to next crossroads turn right for Babell) ☎Caerwys(0352) 720493

Apr-Oct

A farm enjoys panoramic views of the Clwydian mountains. Guests are made to feel very much at home by the Williams family. Two bedrooms suitable for families are available, and there is a television in the lounge.

2rm (1fb) 🚭 Ⓡ ✳ dB&B£25-£30

🅿 CTV pony trekking 40 acres beef mixed sheep horses

[£]

FH [Q][Q][Q] Mrs M Jones **Greenhill Farm** *(SJ186776)* CH8 7QF (from Holywell follow sign to St Winefrid's Well, 200yds on turn left opposite the Royal Oak and follow road uphill to end) ☎(0352) 713270

Mar-Nov

Visitors are warmly welcomed to this farmhouse overlooking the sea and are free to explore the 120 acres of land that it works. The seventeenth-century origin of the building is evident in the many exposed timbers and beams which still exist in bedrooms, lounge and dining room.

3rm(1🛁) (1fb)CTV in 1 bedroom Ⓡ 🐕 sB&Bfr£17 dB&Bfr£34 dB&B🛁fr£38 LDO 9am

CTV 👶 snooker table childrens play area 120 acres dairy mixed

[£]

ambion court hotel

The Green, Dadlington, Nuneaton CV13 6JB

English Tourist Board COMMENDED

Telephone: (01455) 212292

Fax: (01455) 213141

Charming, modernised Victorian farmhouse overlooking Dadlington's tranquil village green, 2 miles north of Hinckley, convenient for Birmingham, Coventry, Leicester, NEC, M1 and M6. All rooms are en-suite and extremely comfortably appointed, particularly the imposing Pine Room honeymoon suite. There is a delightful lounge, cocktail bar and a restaurant offering creative International fare and extensive function menus. Conference facilities are also available. Ambion Court offers comfort, hospitality and exceptional tranquillity for tourists and business people alike.

Resident proprietors John & Wendy Walliker

See gazetteer under Hinckley

Greenhill Farm Guesthouse

Holywell, Clwyd. Tel: Holywell (01352) 713270

A 16th century working dairy farm overlooking the Dee Estuary with beamed and panelled interior retaining old world charm.

Tastefully furnished interior with some bedrooms having bathroom/shower en-suite. We have a childrens play area and utility/games room including washing machine, tumble dryer, snooker table and darts board.

Relax and enjoy typical farmhouse food, within easy reach of both the coastal and mountain areas of N. Wales.

Proprietors: Mary and John Jones

HONITON Devon   Map **03** ST10

SELECTED

GH 🅀🅀🅀🅀 *Colestocks House* Feniton, Payhembury
EX14 0JR (1m N unclass rd) ☎(0404) 850633
FAX (0404) 850901
Mar-Oct
Lying in two acres of tranquil walled gardens, this
16th-century thatched cottage offers spacious en suite
bedrooms, equipped with good facilities and Laura Ashley soft
furnishings. The lounge and bar promote a cosy atmosphere,
where a range of reading material is provided, along with
comfortable seating and access to the garden during summer.
A choice of home-cooked dishes, with a French influence, is
served in the relaxed surroundings of the dining room, which
boasts a large and attractive inglenook fireplace.
9rm (2fb) CTV in all bedrooms ® ⊁ LDO 7pm
Lic ⅏
Credit Cards [1] [3]

GH 🅀🅀🅀 **The Crest** Moorcox Lane, Wilmington, Honiton
EX14 9JU (on A35 at eastern end of Wilmington village)
☎(0404) 831419
3rm(2⇆1ℝ) (1fb)CTV in all bedrooms ® ✳ sB&B⇆ℝ£20-£32
dB&B⇆ℝ£32 WB&Bfr£112 WBDifr£147 LDO 8pm
⅏ CTV

📖 💻 FH 🅀🅀 Mrs I Underdown **Roebuck** *(ST147001)*
EX14 0PB (western end of Honiton-by-pass) ☎(0404) 42225
This farmhouse offers comfortable accommodation and is situated
in a prominent position on the A30 just outside the town centre,
which is famous for its lace and numerous antique shops.
Breakfast is served at individual tables in the dining room, and
there is a comfortable lounge. Smoking is not permitted in the
bedrooms or dining room.
4 (1fb) ⊁ in bedrooms ⊁ in dining room CTV in 1 bedroom ®
sB&B£14 dB&B£28
⅏ CTV 180 acres dairy mixed

SELECTED

INN🅀🅀🅀 **The Heathfield** Walnut Road EX14 8UG
☎(0404) 45321 & 45322 FAX (0404) 45321
Closed 25-26 Dec & 1 Jan rs Sun
This beautifully restored thatched 16th-century longhouse is
approached through a modern housing estate. There are
spacious lounge bar areas where an interesting selection of bar
meals is offered from a blackboard menu, and a separate à la
carte restaurant featuring local specialities. Bedrooms are large
and particularly well equipped, including the bridal suite with
its locally hand-crafted pine four-poster bed.
5⇆ℝ CTV in all bedrooms ® T ⊁ (ex guide dogs) ✳
sB&B⇆ℝ£29.38 dB&B⇆ℝ£41.13 LDO 10pm
⅏ nc14yrs skittle alley
Credit Cards [1] [2] [3]

HOOK Hampshire   Map **04** SU75

GH 🅀🅀 **Cedar Court Country** Reading Road RG27 9DB (1m N
of Hook on B3349) ☎Basingstoke(0256) 762178
This long established bungalow offering bed and breakfast
accommodation is quietly situated at the end of a shared private
drive. Bedrooms are basic but well presented and there is a
comfortable lounge and small breakfast room. Ample car parking
is provided.
6rm(3ℝ) (1fb) ⊁ in dining room CTV in all bedrooms ® ⊁ (ex

guide dogs) ✳ sB&B£17-£19 sB&Bℝ£23-£25 dB&B£28-£32
dB&Bℝ£33-£35
⅏ CTV
Credit Cards [1] [2] [3] [5] £

GH 🅀🅀 **Cherry Lodge** Reading Road RG27 9DB (on B3349)
☎Basingstoke(0256) 762532 FAX (0256) 762532
Closed Xmas
Cherry Lodge is a small, extended bungalow on the northern edge
of the village. Being completely family run and lacking any
pretentions, it has become a home from home for travelling
business people. The modern bedrooms all have en suite facilities
and direct dial telephones. There is a comfortable TV lounge with
deep armchairs and a simple conservatory-type dining room where
the set two-course dinner is of the hearty British `meat and two
veg' variety.
6⇆ℝ (1fb) ⊁ in dining room ® T ✳ sB&B⇆ℝ£24-£26
dB&B⇆ℝ£35-£37.50 LDO midnight
⅏ CTV
Credit Cards [1] [2] [3]

GH 🅀🅀 **Oaklea** London Road RG27 9LA (on A30, 200yds from
centre of Hook) ☎(0256) 762673 FAX (0256) 762150
A detached Victorian family-run guest house offers good value for
money, in a convenient location on the A30, with a delightful
large walled garden. Personally managed for many years by Mr
and Mrs Swinhoe, it offers a warm welcome and caters well for
both leisure and business guests, many of whom return frequently.
Bedrooms vary in size but are neat and nicely presented in an old
fashioned style. There is a licensed bar area and a pleasant lounge,
and a four-course evening meal is offered.
10rm(4ℝ) (1fb) ⊁ in 4 bedrooms ⊁ in dining room CTV in 5
bedrooms ® ✳ sB&Bfr£23 sB&Bℝ£36 dB&B£32 dB&Bℝ£40
WB&B£161-£252 WBDi£234.50-£325.50 LDO noon
Lic CTV ⚲
Credit Cards [2] £
See advertisement under BASINGSTOKE

HOPE Derbyshire   Map **07** SK18

SELECTED

GH 🅀🅀🅀🅀 **Underleigh House** Off Edale Road S30 2RF
☎(0433) 621372 FAX (0433) 621372
6rm(2⇆4ℝ) CTV in all bedrooms ® ⊁ (ex guide dogs)
sB&B⇆ℝ£28-£32 dB&B⇆ℝ£46-£48 WBDi£245-£250
LDO noon
Lic ⅏ nc12yrs

HORLEY Surrey

For accommodation details see under **Gatwick Airport, London**

HORNCASTLE Lincolnshire   Map **08** TF26

SELECTED

FH 🅀🅀🅀🅀 Mrs J Bankes Price **Greenfield Farm**
(TF175745) Minting LN9 5RX (take A158 eastward, through
Wragby and after 3m turn right at Midge pub, farm 1m on
right) ☎(0507) 578457
Closed Xmas & New Year
3rm(2ℝ) ⊁ ® ⊁ (ex guide dogs) ✳ sB&Bℝ£18-£20
dB&Bℝ£36-£38 WB&B£119
⅏ CTV 387 acres arable
£

HORNCHURCH Greater London   Map **05** TQ58

INN🅀🅀🅀 **The Railway Hotel** Station Lane RM12 6SB (adjacent
to railway station) ☎(0708) 476415 FAX (0708) 437315

This 1930s purpose-built inn retains much of that period's character with a large open-plan public area offering pleasant seating areas, soft lighting and polished woodwork. The bedrooms are fully modernised and equipped with the extras sought by the business or leisure traveller of today.
11🛁🚿 CTV in all bedrooms Ⓡ T 🐕 (ex guide dogs)
sB&B🛁🚿£39 dB&B🛁🚿£39 Lunch £6.50-£12.75 Dinner £6.50-£12.75 LDO 9pm
♨
Credit Cards [1][2][3][5]

HORN'S CROSS Devon Map **02** SS32

P R E M I E R SELECTED

GH [Q][Q][Q][Q][Q] Lower Waytown EX39 5DN
☎Horns Cross(0237) 451787
Etr-Oct

A beautiful conversion of a barn and roundhouse has created this delightfully spacious and comfortable home, where Caroline and Chris May are the welcoming hosts. The unique round sitting room with beams and an inglenook adjoins the spacious dining room where the excellent breakfasts are served. The bedrooms, one of which is on the ground floor, are tastefully decorated and furnished (smoking in the bedrooms is not permitted). There are five acres of gardens and grounds with stream-fed ponds and ornamental waterfowl.
3🛁🚿 🚭 in bedrooms 🚭 in dining room CTV in all bedrooms Ⓡ 🐕 * sB&B🛁🚿£30-£32 dB&B🛁🚿£40-£45 WB&B£126-£200
♨ CTV nc8yrs

HORSFORD Norfolk Map **09** TG11

GH [Q][Q][Q] Church Farm Church Street NR10 3DB
☎Norwich(0603) 898020 & 898582 FAX (0603) 891649
A well-kept property in a rural setting south of the village, this guest house offers a dining room, lounge and five spacious bedrooms, each with its own shower.
5🚿 (3fb) 🚭 in dining room CTV in all bedrooms Ⓡ 🐕 (ex guide dogs) * sB&B🚿£17-£20 dB&B🚿£32-£36
♨ CTV
Credit Cards [5]

HORSHAM West Sussex Map **04** TQ13

GH [Q][Q][Q] *Blatchford House* 52 Kings Road RH13 5PR
☎(0403) 265317 FAX (0403) 211592
Closed Xmas
An impressive, listed Grade II Georgian house built in 1852 and located in a residential area, within a short drive of Gatwick. The modern bedrooms are all freshly decorated and comfortable, the rest being on the first floor, with some also on the ground floor. A spacious and comfortable TV lounge augments the attractive conservatory dining room, where set dinners are available.
11🚿 CTV in all bedrooms Ⓡ T
♨ CTV
Credit Cards [1][3]

HORSHAM ST FAITH Norfolk Map **09** TG21

GH [Q][Q][Q] Elm Farm Chalet Hotel Norwich Road NR10 3HH
(on A140 Cromer road from Norwich, pass airport, take right hand turning into village) ☎Norwich(0603) 898366
FAX (0603) 897129
rs 25-26 Dec
A delightful hotel set in spacious grounds near the centre of the village, Elm Farm provides comfortable accommodation in modern brick annexes, which are equipped to a high standard. The main building has a large reception area, plenty of lounge space and a dining room where both lunch and dinner are served.
Annexe 18rm(16🛁🚿) (2fb) 🚭 in 10 bedrooms 🚭 in dining room 🚭 in 1 lounge CTV in all bedrooms Ⓡ T 🐕 (ex guide dogs)
sB&B🛁🚿£29.50-£35 dB&B£48 dB&B🛁🚿£54 WB&B£147.50-£245 WBDi£276.50-£315 LDO 6.30pm
Lic ♨ CTV
Credit Cards [1][2][3][£]

HORTON Dorset Map **04** SU00

P R E M I E R SELECTED

GH [Q][Q][Q][Q][Q] Northill House BH21 7HL
☎Witchampton(0258) 840407
Closed 20 Dec-mid Feb

Just off the edge of a small village, this delightful country house offers a warm welcome and a cosy, relaxing atmosphere. The spacious public rooms are light, airy and comfortable, and the dining room has a conservatory extension which is very popular with guests during the summer months. The bedrooms are well equipped and maintained. The Garnsworth family continue to offer hospitality of the highest standard. A selection of books and magazines are provided for

▶

Brookfield Farm Hotel

Where the welcome is always warm

Situated amidst the beautiful and peaceful countryside of West Sussex, with its own lake for boating, fishing and swimming and adjoining golf course. Just 20 miles from the South Downs and the South Coast. Originally a Sussex farm house that has become a hotel of distinction. The restaurant is renowned for good country food.
All bedrooms are well equipped with the majority en suite. Open throughout the year for long or short stays, with personal attention and service at all times. Amenities include ample car park, licensed bars, games room, sauna, golf driving range, six hole course, putting green together with lovely, quiet walking country. Children and well behaved animals welcome.
Winterpit Lane, Plummer Plain, Horsham, West Sussex RH13 6LU
Tel: 01403 891568 Fax: 01403 891499

guests in the lounge, where winter guests can warm themselves by the log fire.
9rm(7🛁2🚿) (1fb) 🚭 in dining room CTV in all bedrooms [R] **T** 🐕 (ex guide dogs) sB&B🛁🚿£37 dB&B🛁🚿£65 WB&B£204.75 WBDi£286.65 LDO 7pm
Lic ♨ nc8yrs
Credit Cards [1] [2] [3] [£]
See advertisement under WIMBORNE MINSTER

INN[Q][Q][Q] Horton Cranborne Road BH21 5AD (on B3078 between Wimborne and Cranbourne)
☎Witchampton(0258) 840252 FAX (0258) 841400
Further improvements have taken place at this popular country inn. The comfortable bedrooms are well-equipped, and the redecorated, refurnished dining room offers simple English dishes. Service is friendly and attentive.
6rm(2🛁) CTV in all bedrooms [R] * sB&B£17.50-£20 dB&B£40-£45 dB&B🛁£50-£55 Bar Lunch £8.50-£15.50alc Dinner £13.95-£18alc LDO 9pm
♨ CTV
Credit Cards [1] [3]

HORTON IN RIBBLESDALE North Yorkshire Map **07** SD87

INN[Q][Q] Crown Hotel BD24 0HF (take B6479 from Settle)
☎(0729) 860209 FAX (0729) 860327
This family-run village inn is said to date back to the 17th century and stands right on the Pennine Way as it passes through the Ribble Valley. Bedrooms are sizeable but simply decorated. Tasty home-made meals are a feature of the two bars, where beams and open fires create a traditional atmosphere. There are also a dining room, two guests' lounges with television, and a spacious beer garden behind the inn.
9rm(2🚿) (4fb)[R] sB&B£18.30-£20.60 sB&B🚿£22.60-£25.20 dB&B£36.60-£41.20 dB&B🚿£45.20-£50.40 WB&B£122.80-£141 LDO 6.30pm
♨ CTV

HOUNSLOW Greater London Map **04** TQ17

GH [Q][Q] Omar 97 Hanworth Road TW3 1TT (on A314)
☎081-577 9969
This recently redecorated and refurbished guesthouse offers spacious bedrooms, most of them sharing shower and WC facilities. A traditional English breakfast is not available but a Continental breakfast, with the addition of eggs if required, is provided.
16rm(1🛁🚿) (1fb) 🚭 in dining room 🚭 in lounges CTV in 6 bedrooms 🐕 (ex guide dogs) * sB&B£25-£30 dB&B£40-£45 dB&B🛁🚿£45-£50 WB&B£140-£175
♨ CTV

GH [Q][Q] Shalimar Hotel 215-221 Staines Road TW3 3JJ
☎081-577 7070 & 081-572 2816 FAX 081-569 6789
This small hotel is situated within walking distance of the town centre and has recently benefited from alterations and refurbishment of its attractively decorated, well equipped bedrooms. The open-plan TV lounge with adjacent bar, and the dining room overlook the landscaped garden.
31rm(22🚿) (7fb) 🚭 in 2 bedrooms 🚭 in area of dining room CTV in all bedrooms [R] **T** 🐕 * sB&B🚿£34-£38 dB&B🚿£44-£48 LDO noon
Lic ♨ CTV
Credit Cards [1] [2] [3] [5] [£]

HOVE East Sussex

See **Brighton & Hove**

HUBY North Yorkshire Map **08** SE56

GH [Q][Q] The New Inn Motel Main Street YO6 1HQ (between A19 & B1363) ☎Easingwold(0347) 810219
This modern brick built motel offering chalet style accommodation with functional bedrooms, is situated behind an inn of the same name (but not connected), in the main street of this small Yorkshire village. There is a small breakfast room, and convenient parking is available outside the chalets.
8🚿 (2fb) 🚭 in dining room 🚭 in lounges CTV in all bedrooms [R] sB&B🚿£25-£30 dB&B🚿£40-£38 WB&B£175-£200
Lic ♨ CTV 🎣
[£]

HUCKNALL Nottinghamshire Map **08** SK54

INN[Q][Q] ***Station Hotel*** Station Road NG15 7TQ ☎(0602) 632588
This large, early Victorian public house is situated approximately a quarter of a mile from the high street. It has been considerably modernised and restored to provide pleasant bar facilities and spacious bedrooms, all with central heating and colour TV.
6rm (2fb) CTV in all bedrooms [R] 🐕 (ex guide dogs) LDO 9.30pm
♨
Credit Cards [1] [3]

HUDDERSFIELD West Yorkshire Map **07** SE11

GH [Q][Q][Q] Elm Crest 2 Queens Road, Edgerton HD2 2AG (A629 signed Halifax, 100yds on right after traffic lights)
☎(0484) 530990 FAX (0484) 516227
A friendly style of service is provided at this attractive Victorian house a mile from the town centre. Bedrooms are well furnished and equipped, and there is a comfortable guests' lounge. This establishment is totally no smoking.
8rm(5🚿) (2fb) 🚭 CTV in all bedrooms [R] **T** 🐕 * sB&B£22-£25 sB&B🚿£32-£35 dB&B£42-£45 dB&B🚿£57-£60 WB&B£154-£200 WBDi£238-£250 LDO 9pm
Lic ♨ CTV nc5yrs
Credit Cards [1] [2] [3] [£]

HULL Humberside Map **08** TA0[illegible]

GH [Q][Q][Q] Earlesmere Hotel 76/78 Sunny Bank, Spring Bank West HU3 1LQ ☎(0482) 41977 FAX (0482) 473714
Closed Xmas rs wknds
The proprietors provide a personal and friendly service at this hotel, which is in a residential area just off Spring Bank West Road. There is a ground-floor lounge with cable TV, a small dispense bar and modestly appointed bedrooms. Ample on-street parking is available.
15rm(7🚿) (4fb) 🚭 in dining room CTV in all bedrooms [R] * sB&B£18.80 sB&B🚿£27.02 dB&B🚿£41.12-£47 WB&Bfr£131.60 WBDifr£230 LDO 6pm
Lic ♨ CTV 🅿
Credit Cards [1] [3] [£]

HUNGERFORD Berkshire Map **04** SU3

GH [Q][Q][Q] Marshgate Cottage Hotel Marsh Lane RG17 0QX (from A338 turn right beside railway bridge into Church St, 0.5m cross stream & turn sharp right) ☎(0488) 682307
FAX (0488) 685475
Closed 25 Dec-17 Jan
This pretty, early 17th-century thatched cottage has been sympathetically extended to provide well equipped, mostly ground-floor bedrooms in a modern wing around a walled courtyard. There is a cosy residents' lounge and breakfast is served in an attractive dining room. Family-run, the hotel is tucke[d] away at the end of a quiet country lane overlooking fields and the canal, but is less than a mile from the centre of Hungerford.
9rm(1🛁6🚿) (1fb) 🚭 in 3 bedrooms 🚭 in area of dining room 🚭 in 1 lounge CTV in all bedrooms [R] **T** 🐕 (ex guide dogs)

sB&Bfr£25.50 sB&B⇄ſ£35.50 dB&Bfr£39.50
dB&B⇄ſ£48.50 LDO 7.30pm
Lic ⪢ nc5yrs
Credit Cards [1] [2] [3] (£)

HUNSTANTON Norfolk   Map **09** TF64

SELECTED

GH [Q][Q][Q][Q] *Claremont* 35 Greevegate PE36 6AF
☎(0485) 533171
This large, white detached house is convenient for both the
shops and the seafront. The energetic owners have been
making improvements, resulting in tastefully refurbished
bedrooms with a few extra personal touches. Public rooms
include a breakfast room, a bar and a lounge with a display of
assorted ornaments.
7⇄ſ (1fb) CTV in all bedrooms (R)
Lic ⪢ CTV nc5yrs
Credit Cards [1] [3]

GH [Q][Q][Q] **Pinewood Hotel** 26 Northgate PE36 6AP (turn off
A149 into Greevegate, 2nd right by bank, 200yds on right)
☎(0485) 533068
Closed Xmas & New Year
This Victorian building is near the seafront and is popular with
both commercial and leisure guests. Rooms are being redecorated
to feature a country theme. Public areas include a quiet lounge, bar
and restaurant where a simple à la carte menu, supplemented by
specials of the day, offers fresh home-cooked meals.
8rm(4ſ) (4fb) ⥾ in bedrooms ⥾ in dining room CTV in all
bedrooms (R) ⚹ sB&B£17.50-£36 sB&Bſ£25-£40 dB&B£37-
£40 dB&Bſ£45-£50 LDO 6pm
Lic ⪢
Credit Cards [1] [2] [3] (£)

GH [Q][Q][Q] *Rosstyn House* 3 Lincoln Square North PE36 6DW
☎(0485) 532065
3rm(1ſ) CTV in all bedrooms (R) ⋇
⪢ CTV

GH [Q][Q][Q] **Sutton House Hotel** 24 Northgate PE36 6AP
☎(0485) 532552
This large, well maintained stone building stands above the
seafront, with fine sea views from most of the bedrooms and the
first-floor lounge. Bedrooms are bright and well kept and the
lounge has an enclosed patio. There is also a cosy bar and a
breakfast room where evening meals are served.
7rm(6⇄ſ) (2fb) ⥾ in bedrooms ⥾ in dining room CTV in all
bedrooms (R) sB&B£18-£26 sB&Bſ£20-£28 dB&B£36-£40
dB&B⇄ſ£40-£52 WB&B£140-£175 WBDi£195-£240 LDO
4pm
Lic ⪢ CTV
Credit Cards [1] [3] (£)

HUNTLY Grampian *Aberdeenshire*   Map **15** NJ53

GH [Q][Q][Q] **Dunedin** 17 Bogie Street AB54 5DX (opposite fish and
chip shop) ☎(0466) 794162
This family run holiday and commercial guesthouse is situated at
the east end of the town, a short walk from the town square. The
bedrooms are furnished in a modern style and have good facilities.
There is a cosy top floor lounge and hearty breakfasts are served
in the bright dining room, where tables may have to be shared
with other guests on occasions.
5ſ (1fb) CTV in all bedrooms (R) ⋇ ⋇ sB&B£20.50-£21
dB&Bſ£33-£34
⪢ CTV

FH [Q][Q][Q] Mrs M Grant **Faich-Hill Farm** *(NJ532347)* Faich-
Hill, Gartly AB54 4RR (adjacent to Gartly church) ☎(046688) 240
Many guests return year after year to Faich-Hill, where the Grant
family have been farming since 1884. The house has a friendly
welcoming atmosphere with well decorated bedrooms comfortably
furnished in traditional style. Public areas include a relaxing TV
lounge and a small sun lounge, the latter being the only place in
the house where smoking is permitted. Hearty home cooking is
served at the communal table in the attractive dining room.
2rm(1ſ) (1fb) (R) ⋇ ⋇ dB&Bſfr£35 LDO 6pm
⪢ CTV 500 acres livestock arable

HUNTON North Yorkshire   Map **07** SE19

SELECTED

INN [Q][Q][Q][Q] **The Countryman's** DL8 1PY (just off A684
Bedale/Leyburn Road between Patrick Brompton and
Constable Burton) ☎Bedale(0677) 450554
Beams, log fires, and good home cooking characterise this
delightful old inn. The bars are full of character and resident
owners David and Pauline Robinson provide warm and
friendly service. Bedrooms are individually decorated and
particularly well furnished.
7⇄ſ ⥾ in bedrooms ⥾ in dining room CTV in all bedrooms
(R) ⚹ sB&B⇄ſ£27-£30 dB&B⇄ſ£44-£46 Lunch £4-£6alc
Dinner £5.50-£12alc LDO 9.30pm
⪢ nc14yrs pool table
Credit Cards [1] [2] [3] (£)

HUTTON-LE-HOLE North Yorkshire   Map **08** SE79

GH [Q][Q] **The Barn Hotel & Tearooms** YO6 6UA
☎Lastingham(0751) 417311

▶

CLAREMONT
GUEST HOUSE
EXCLUSIVELY FOR NON-SMOKERS

35 GREEVEGATE, HUNSTANTON,
NORFOLK PE36 6AF
Telephone: (01485) 533171

Spacious Victorian guest house, central position near
shops, beach and gardens. All rooms en suite and
furnished with our guests comfort in mind, some
with sea views.
For your well being we are a **NO SMOKING**
establishment and offer a superb full English breakfast
with healthy options. Off street car parking.
Clean safe beach, easy coastal walks, enjoyable all
year round.

AA
Selected
QQQQ

Closed Xmas
This attractive stone-built guesthouse and tea room was, as its name suggest, once a barn and its pretty inner courtyard and rough stone walls are well known to tourists from all over the world. It is at the centre of the village in which sheep roam at will, on the edge of the North Yorkshire Moors. Bedrooms are mostly compact each individually and attractively decorated with modern features. The guests' lounge is warm and relaxing with an open fire in winter. Meals are served in an attractive dining area separated from the tea rooms. A private car park at the rear leads to the guests' entrance and reception.
8rm(3🛁🚿) (1fb) 🚭 Ⓡ 🐕 (ex guide dogs) sB&Bfr£21 sB&B🛁🚿fr£26 dB&Bfr£42 dB&B🛁🚿fr£52 WB&Bfr£132 WBDifr£202
Lic ♨ CTV
Credit Cards [1][3][£]

HYDE Greater Manchester — Map **07** SJ99

SELECTED

FH [Q][Q][Q][Q] Mr & Mrs I Walsh **Needhams** *(SJ968925)* Uplands Road, Werneth Low, Gee Cross SK14 3AQ
☎061-368 4610 FAX 061-367 9106
This delightful stone-built house dates back to 1662 and is situated in a remote location between two country parks, reached by way of a long and very rough road. The farmhouse is close to the golf course and enjoys spectacular views from its elevated position. Many of the house's original features remain, including low beamed ceilings. The bedrooms are cosy, modern and very well equipped, with TV, radio alarm and direct dial telephones; most have en suite showers, and family accommodation is also available; all the rooms enjoy panoramic views over two counties. The combined dining room/bar is small and cosy, with cottage style furniture and an open fire. Evening meals are served nightly, with orders taken in advance for the speciality menu. A courtesy service to and from the airport and railway stations is available for a small charge.
7rm(6🚿) (1fb)CTV in all bedrooms Ⓡ **T** sB&B🚿fr£19 dB&Bfr£30 dB&B🚿fr£32 LDO 9.30pm
Lic ♨ CTV ⛳12 🐎 30 acres beef
Credit Cards [1][2][3][£]

HYTHE Kent — Map **05** TR13

GH [Q][Q] Sunny Bank House 3 Station Road CT21 5PN
☎Shepway(0303) 267087
3rm (1fb) 🚭 in bedrooms CTV in 1 bedroom * sB&Bfr£20 dB&Bfr£32 WB&Bfr£110
♨ CTV
[£]

GH [Q][Q][Q] The White House 27 Napier Gardens CT21 6DD
☎(0303) 266252
This large house is situated at the end of a cul-de-sac overlooking the cricket ground and about half a mile from the sea. Bedrooms are large and all have en suite facilities. An attractive garden with tables and chairs provides a quiet place to relax, and the upstairs breakfast room and balcony is an agreeable venue for Kennet's excellent breakfast. There is no lounge, but a conservatory housing a three piece suite is about to be built.
3rm(2🚿) (1fb) CTV in all bedrooms Ⓡ 🐕 (ex guide dogs) * sB&B£20-£25 sB&B🚿fr£25 dB&Bfr£34 dB&B🚿fr£36
♨ CTV
[£]

ILFORD Greater London — Map **05** TQ48

GH [Q][Q][Q] ***Cranbrook Hotel*** 24 Coventry Road IG1 4QR
☎081-554 6544 & 4765 FAX 081-518 1463
Conveniently situated in a residential area close to the town centre, this hotel offers modern, comfortable bedrooms - some with spa baths - and a well stocked bar lounge and cosy dining room. Friendly and attentive service is provided by the Perry family who have greatly improved this hotel during their 18 years of ownership.
16rm(13🚿) (7fb) CTV in all bedrooms Ⓡ LDO 7.30pm
Lic ♨ CTV
Credit Cards [1][2][3][5]
See advertisement under LONDON

GH [Q][Q] Park Hotel 327 Cranbrook Road IG1 4UE
☎081-554 9616 & 081-554 7187 FAX 081-518 2700
Opposite Valentine's Park, and close to the town centre, this hotel is being continually upgraded by the owners, Mr and Mrs Witmore, and offers modern bedrooms and pleasant public areas. A good public transport system passes the establishment and makes it an ideal base for touring the immediate area and central London.
20rm(7🛁10🚿) (3fb)CTV in all bedrooms Ⓡ sB&B£28 sB&B🛁🚿£36.50-£39.50 dB&B£38 dB&B🛁🚿£42.50-£46.50 LDO 8pm
Lic ♨ CTV
Credit Cards [1][3][£]

ILFRACOMBE Devon — Map **02** SS54

See also West Down

GH [Q][Q][Q] ***Collingdale Hotel*** Larkstone Terrace EX34 9NU
☎(0271) 863770
Mar-Oct
Enjoying a good location, this hotel offers bedrooms on three floors. Those at the back enjoy fine views across the golf course to the sea. Golfers and cricketers are among the regular guests here and advance booking is advisable. The hotel has been upgraded and the en suite bedrooms have been redecorated and furnished with coordinating soft fabrics. Further improvements have also taken place in the bar and dining room.
9rm(3🚿) (6fb) Ⓡ 🐕 LDO 5.30pm
Lic CTV 🅿̸
Credit Cards [1][3]

GH [Q][Q][Q] ***Cresta Private Hotel*** Torrs Park EX34 8AY
☎(0271) 863742
mid May-Sep
A well established hotel, the Cresta has been in the Seddon family for many years. The current generation continue to make improvements and, overall, the bedrooms are bright, well furnished and comfortable. Some ground-floor rooms are available, and a lift serves all floors. There is a cosy lounge area, a bar with a dance floor, and a bright dining room.
24rm(15🚿) (10fb) TV available Ⓡ LDO 6.30pm
Lic lift ♨ CTV putting green
Credit Cards [1]

GH [Q][Q] Dedes Hotel 1-3 The Promenade EX34 9BD
☎(0271) 862545 FAX (0271) 862234
Closed 23-26 Dec
Dedes is in a central location directly opposite the beach and the Pavilion Theatre, the front facing rooms enjoying good views. Bedrooms, all but a few en suite, tend to be small but are nicely furnished and have good quality beds. There is a residents' lounge and lounge bar, in addition to the public bar, and for meals there is a choice between a café and more formal restaurant. The hotel specialises in clay-pigeon shooting holidays.
17rm(10🛁2🚿) (6fb) 🚭 in area of dining room CTV in all bedrooms Ⓡ * sB&B£18.50-£19.50 sB&B🛁🚿£21.50-£27.50 dB&B£35-£37 dB&B🛁🚿£41-£45 WB&B£122.50-£157.50 WBDi£185.50-£213.50 LDO 9.45pm
Lic CTV clay pigeon shooting
Credit Cards [1][2][3][5][£]

GH Q Q **Lympstone Private Hotel** Cross Park EX34 8BJ (off Promenade (Wilder Road) ☎(0271) 863038
Mar-Oct rs Mar-May
The resident proprietors of this well established guesthouse provide a friendly welcome and individually designed bedrooms that are comfortably old-fashioned in style, as is the guests' lounge. A pleasant dining room offers bright and cheerful surroundings.
15rm(9♠) (4fb) ⊁ in dining room CTV in all bedrooms Ⓡ ✳ sB&B£13-£15 dB&B£26-£30 dB&B♠£30-£32 WB&B£84-£105 Lic CTV
£

GH Q Q Q **Merlin Court Hotel** Torrs Park EX34 8AY
☎(0271) 862697
A fine example of late Victorian architecture, the Merlin Court looks out across the rooftops to the town beyond. It is a friendly place with many regular guests. Bedrooms are bright and fresh and there is a cosy lounge area, dining room and bar. The bar and skittle alley is a great attraction.
14rm(2⇌9♠) (5fb) CTV in all bedrooms Ⓡ ⊁ (ex guide dogs) LDO 5pm
Lic ▥ CTV skittle alley
Credit Cards ⊡ ⊡

⇆ ▼ **GH** Q Q **Southcliffe Hotel** Torrs Park EX34 8AZ
☎(0271) 862958
Spring BH-17 Sep rs Mar-Apr
A substantial brick-built Victorian property set in its own lawned garden just a short hilly walk from the town centre and beaches caters very well for families, most rooms having bunks or adjacent children's rooms. The lower ground floor contains extensive games and play rooms, there is a "Mums' kitchen", and a separate sitting room provides a quiet alternative to the bar lounge.
30♠ (8fb) ⊁ in dining room ⊁ in lounges Ⓡ ✗ sB&B£15-£17 dB&B♠£30-£34 WB&B£105-£119 WBDi£145-£159 LDO 6pm Lic CTV ⚬⚬ games room
Credit Cards ⊡ ⊡

GH Q Q **Strathmore Private Hotel** 57 St Brannocks Road X34 8EQ (on A361 approach into Ilfracombe, 0.25 from Mullacot Cross roundabout) ☎(0271) 862248
Apr-Oct
A rather handsome Victorian semidetached property, the Strathmore has cosy public areas and a recently refurbished bar. There is a short menu of home cooked fare, and snacks and refreshments are available throughout the evening. Bedrooms are fresh and bright, all but a couple offering small en suite facilities.
rm(8⇌♠) (3fb) ⊁ in dining room ⊁ in lounges CTV in all bedrooms Ⓡ sB&B£16 sB&B⇌♠£18 dB&B⇌♠£36 WB&B£110.80 WBDi£160 LDO 5pm
Lic ▥
Credit Cards ⊡ ⊡ ⊡ ⊡ £

GH Q Q Q Q **Varley House** 13 Chambercombe Park Terrace, Chambercombe Park EX34 9QW ☎(0271) 863927
FAX (0271) 863927
mid Mar-Oct
At Varley House Roy and Barbara Gable offer a warm welcome and well equipped accommodation in tastefully decorated bedrooms, including one ground-floor room. The bar is the social centre, but there is a beautifully proportioned lounge with a good selection of books and magazines. Barbara Gable prepares imaginative dinners with a choice of dishes, including home-made soups, pâtés and traditional steak and kidney pie. Guests are asked to smoke only in the lounge and bar.
9rm(8⇌♠) (3fb) ⊁ in bedrooms ⊁ in dining room CTV in all bedrooms Ⓡ sB&B£19.50-£20.50 dB&B⇌♠£42-£45

WBDi£180-£200 LDO 5.30pm
Lic ▥ CTV nc5yrs
Credit Cards ⊡ ⊡ ⊡ £

GH Q Q Q **Westwell Hall Hotel** Torrs Park EX34 8AZ
☎(0271) 862792
Standing in its own grounds in an elevated position, Westwell Hall has good views of the harbour and out across the town. The well proportioned bedrooms have fresh decor and en suite facilities, and there is a warm, cosy feel to the public areas, which include a games room where children may play. Home cooked fare is served in the dining room, and gourmet weekends in March and October are very popular.
9⇌♠ (1fb) ⊁ in dining room CTV in all bedrooms Ⓡ ✳ sB&B⇌♠£23-£25 dB&B⇌♠£46-£50 WB&B£161-£175 WBDi£210 LDO 7pm
Lic ▥ snooker croquet table tennis
Credit Cards ⊡ ⊡ £

INGLEBY GREENHOW North Yorkshire   Map **08** NZ50

FH Q Q Q Q **Mrs M Bloom Manor House** (*NZ586056*)
TS9 6RB ☎Great Ayton(0642) 722384
Closed 21-29 Dec
Standing at the foot of the Cleveland Hills, this is an 18th-century farmhouse built of Yorkshire stone, offering spacious and comfortable accommodation. Bedrooms are full of character, with interior stonework and wooden beams as well as every modern comfort. There is an attractive dining room, and a cosy lounge with a wood-burning stove and a view of

▶

the lawns and the woodland where wildlife includes rabbits, partridges, pheasants, wild ducks and the occasional deer. To find the house, take the B1257 Stokesley - Helmsley road, turning east at the Great Broughton crossroads, and continuing for 2.5 miles before taking the Manor road by the church.
3rm(1🛁) 🚭 Ⓡ 🐕 dB&B🛁£70-£76 (incl dinner) WBDi£230-£250 LDO 5pm
Lic ♨ CTV nc12yrs 🎣 rough shooting & stabling for guests horses 164 acres mixed
[£]

INGLETON North Yorkshire Map **07** SD67

GH [Q][Q][Q] Ferncliffe Main Street LA6 3HJ ☎(05242) 42405
Closed Nov
4🚿 🚭 in dining room CTV in all bedrooms Ⓡ dB&B🚿fr£38 WB&Bfr£126 WBDifr£193
♨ CTV
[£]

GH [Q][Q] Langber Country Tatterthorne Road LA6 3DT
☎(05242) 41587
Closed 24 Dec-3 Jan
Set in open countryside, this modern house offers adequate accommodation together with friendly service. The bedrooms are basic but comfortable and all have views. There is a large lounge with TV.
7rm(2🛁1🚿) (3fb) 🚭 in bedrooms 🚭 in dining room Ⓡ sB&B£15.50-£19.50 dB&B£29.90-£34 dB&B🛁🚿£32-£39 WB&B£98-£121 WBDi£133-£152 LDO 5pm
♨ CTV
[£]

SELECTED

GH [Q][Q][Q][Q] Oakroyd Old Rectory Main Street LA6 3HJ
☎(05242) 41258
A former rectory is now a family hotel conveniently situated just off the A65, on the edge of the village. Bedrooms are furnished in contemporary style; many have fine views of the surrounding countryside. There is a comfortable guests' lounge with TV, books, magazines and board games. The dining room is very attractively furnished and decorated, enhanced by a collection of paintings and prints; excellent home-cooked food is served, with a set evening menu offering an extensive choice. The cosy bar is the only area where smoking is allowed. Resident owners Peter and Ann Hudson are genial hosts, and Peter Hudson's cooking has been highly praised.
6🚿 (2fb) 🚭 in bedrooms 🚭 in dining room 🚭 in lounges CTV in all bedrooms Ⓡ 🐕 (ex guide dogs) dB&B🚿£40-£50 WBDi£210-£249 LDO 5.30pm
Lic ♨ CTV nc11yrs
[£]

GH [Q][Q][Q] Pines Country House Hotel LA6 3HN (on A65)
☎(05242) 41252
Standing in an elevated position on the A65 just north of the town, this charming hotel in country house style combines warm, friendly service with good all round standards of accommodation. Double-glazed bedrooms are attractively furnished, there is a very comfortable lounge, and meals are served in a delightful conservatory featuring an 80-year-old grape vine.
5rm(4🛁🚿) (2fb) 🚭 in bedrooms 🚭 in dining room 🚭 in 1 lounge CTV in all bedrooms Ⓡ * sB&B£26-£28 sB&B🛁🚿£26-£28 dB&B£34-£36 dB&B🛁🚿£36-£40 WB&B£125-£150 WBDi£175-£187 LDO 6pm
Lic ♨ CTV
Credit Cards [1] [3]

GH [Q][Q][Q] Springfield Private Hotel Main Street LA6 3HJ
☎(05242) 41280
Closed Xmas
A stone-built late Victorian property, the Springfield Hotel has its original conservatory still in situ. Bedrooms are well furnished and service is warm and friendly. There are fine views to the rear and the house now has its own private fishing on the River Greta.
5🚿 (1fb) 🚭 in dining room 🚭 in 1 lounge CTV in all bedrooms Ⓡ sB&B🚿£20-£21 dB&B🚿£36-£38 WB&B£115-£120 WBDi£175-£185 LDO 5pm
Lic ♨ CTV 🎣
[£]

GH [Q][Q] Stacksteads Tatterthornm Road LA6 3HS (from A65 towards Settle, turn right at Masons Arms public house into Tamerthorn Road, farm 300 yds on right) ☎(05242) 41386
3rm(2🚿) 🐕 * sB&B🚿£14 dB&B🚿£28 LDO 8.30am
♨ CTV

INNERLEITHEN Borders *Peebleshire* Map **11** NT33

INN[Q][Q][Q] Traquair Arms Hotel Traquair Road EH44 6PD (from A72 Peebles to Galashiels road take B709 for St Mary's Loch & Traquair) ☎(0896) 830229 FAX (0896) 830260
Lying just off the main street, this small hotel is personally run by the owners and has a deserved reputation for its enjoyable, good-value meals served either in the bar or dining room. Real ale is on tap, including one brewed at famous Traquair House nearby. Bedrooms are nicely decorated and very well equipped.
10🛁🚿 (2fb) 🚭 in dining room CTV in all bedrooms Ⓡ **T** * sB&B🛁🚿£37 dB&B🛁🚿£58 WB&B£180 WBDi£282 Lunch £11-£15alc High tea £6.50 Dinner £14-£19 LDO 9pm
♨ 🎣
Credit Cards [1] [2] [3] [5] [£]

INSTOW Devon Map **02** SS4

GH [Q][Q][Q] Anchorage Hotel The Quay EX39 4HX
☎(0271) 860655 & 860475
Closed Feb
Standing on the quay, only a few minutes' walk from a sandy beach, this well presented Victorian guesthouse offers easy access to the North Devon Link and M5. Bedrooms with en suite shower are centrally heated and equipped with telephones, colour televisions and tea-making facilities. There is a choice of comfortable, well furnished lounges on the first floor, with an attractive restaurant and bar lounge at ground level.
17rm(2🛁15🚿) (6fb) 🚭 in area of dining room CTV in 2 bedrooms Ⓡ **T** * sB&B🛁🚿£21-£25 dB&B🛁🚿£42-£50 WB&B£147-£175 WBDi£198-£225 LDO 9.30pm
Lic ♨ CTV
Credit Cards [1] [3]

INVERGARRY Highland *Inverness-shire* Map **14** NH3

GH [Q][Q][Q] Craigard PH35 4HG ☎(0809) 501258
Closed Xmas & New Year
A warm welcome awaits visitors to this sturdy Victorian house on the Road to the Isles just west of the village. Spacious bedrooms are comfortably furnished in both modern and traditional styles, and the provision of some en suite facilities took place at the beginning of the 1994 season. Relaxing public rooms include a choice of lounges - one for non smokers - and a smart dining room offering a daily changing five-course menu of carefully prepared dishes.
7rm(2🛁1🚿) 🚭 in bedrooms 🚭 in dining room CTV in 2 bedrooms Ⓡ 🐕 (ex guide dogs) * sB&B🛁🚿fr£20 dB&Bfr£32 dB&B🛁🚿fr£40 WB&B£112-£140 WBDi£196-£224 LDO 11am
Lic CTV nc8yrs
[£]

GH Q Q Q **Forest Lodge** South Laggan PH34 4EA (3m SW on A82) ☎(0809) 501219

Efficiently run by Janet and Ian Shearer, this purpose built guesthouse offers good-value accommodation in bright, airy bedrooms. The comfortable TV lounge also has a range of books and board games, and enjoyable home cooking is served in the neat dining room.

7♠ (2fb) ✗ in dining room ✗ in lounges ® dB&B♠£30-£34 WB&B£100-£110 WBDi£163-£180 LDO 6.30pm

▥ CTV

£

INVERGORDON Highland *Ross & Cromarty*   Map **14** NH76

GH Q Q Q **Craigaron** 17 Saltburn IV18 0JX (1.25m N on B817, 200yds beyond traffic lights at Saltburn Pier) ☎(0349) 853640

Closed Xmas & New Year

4rm(2♠) ✗ in dining room CTV in all bedrooms ® ✱ sB&B£18-£22 sB&B♠£25 dB&B£29-£31 dB&B♠£34-£36 WB&B£90-£105 WBDi£140-£160 LDO 4pm

▥ CTV nc10yrs

£

INVERKEITHING Fife   Map **11** NT18

GH Q Q Q **Forth Craig Private Hotel** 90 Hope Street KY11 1LL ☎(0383) 418440

Situated on the southern approach to the town, close to the Forth bridges, this small, purpose-built private hotel offers practical accommodation popular with both business people and tourists. Bedrooms are not large, but they are very neatly maintained and comfortable. There is a small, cosy lounge and a pleasant dining room with views of the Firth of Forth.

5♠ ✗ in bedrooms ✗ in dining room CTV in all bedrooms ® sB&B♠£22-£24 dB&B♠£36-£38 LDO 6pm

Lic ▥

Credit Cards 1 3 £

INVERNESS Highland *Inverness-shire*   Map **14** NH64

See also Ardersier

GH Q Q Q **Aberfeldy Lodge** 11 Southside Road IV2 3BG ☎(0463) 231120

Situated in a quiet residential area close to the town centre, this sturdy detached stone-built house has a welcoming atmosphere and provides comfortable accommodation. Bedrooms upstairs vary in size but have modern facilities and offer the expected amenities. Ground floor accommodation includes a choice of lounges, a dining room and 2 further bedrooms; smoking is not permitted on this floor.

♠ (4fb) ✗ in 3 bedrooms ✗ in dining room ✗ in lounges CTV in all bedrooms ® ✱ dB&B♠£38-£50 WB&B£133-£175 WBDi£217-£259 LDO 4pm

▥

£

SELECTED

GH Q Q Q Q **Ardmuir House** 16 Ness Bank IV2 4SF (on E bank of river, opposite the cathedral) ☎(0463) 231151

Attractive decor and coordinated fabrics have been used to good effect in the bedrooms at Ardmuir House. Drinks are available in the ground-floor lounge overlooking the river, and enjoyable home cooking is served in the tastefully appointed dining room.

11♠ (2fb) ✗ in dining room CTV in all bedrooms ® sB&B♠£29.50-£32 dB&B♠£47-£52 WB&B£151-£172 WBDi£214-£240 LDO 7pm

Lic ▥

Credit Cards 1 3 £

PREMIER SELECTED

GH Q Q Q Q Q **Ballifeary House Hotel** 10 Ballifeary Road IV3 5PJ (off A82) ☎(0463) 235572 FAX (0463) 235572

Etr-mid Oct

Margaret and Danny Luscombe have created a friendly atmosphere at their detached Victorian villa, which lies in its own mature gardens in a quiet residential area convenient for Eden Court theatre and within walking distance of the town centre and the river Ness. Spotlessly maintained throughout, it offers comfortable attractive bedrooms. The set four-course dinner offers enjoyable home cooking, with a choice for the starter and main course, but these require to be ordered by noon. Pre-dinner drinks and after dinner coffee are served in the pleasant lounge, but smoking is not permitted.

8⇔♠ ✗ CTV in all bedrooms ® ✶ (ex guide dogs) sB&B⇔♠£30-£32 dB&B⇔♠£60-£64 WB&B£203-£217 WBDi£303-£317 LDO 6pm

Lic ▥ nc12yrs

Credit Cards 1 3 £

See advertisement on p.225.

GH Q Q Q **Brae Ness Hotel** 17 Ness Bank IV2 4SF (0.25m along river bank below Inverness Castle in direction of Dores (B862) from town centre) ☎(0463) 712266

Etr-Oct

▶

ARDMUIR HOUSE, INVERNESS

A family run hotel beside the River Ness: close to the town centre.

Our licensed, non-smoking dining-room features home cooking with fresh local produce. All rooms have a private bathroom, colour TV, tea/coffee making and hair dryers.

Special discounts are available for stays of 3 days or more. We will be pleased to send our brochure and tariff on request.

Jean and Tony Gatcombe
16 Ness Bank, Inverness IV2 4SF
Tel: (01463) 231151

A Georgian house on the riverfront has been converted to create this comfortable family-run private hotel. The bedrooms are gradually being upgraded to offer modern comforts and amenities, and enjoyble home cooking is served in the river-facing dining room.
10rm(9⇨↑®) (2fb) ⚹ in 5 bedrooms CTV in all bedrooms ⓡ ⚹
(ex guide dogs) sB&B⇨↑®£25-£33 dB&B⇨↑®£44-£58
WB&B£140-£189 WBDi£220-£269 LDO 7pm
Lic ▥
Credit Cards ①③

GH ◖Q◗◖Q◗◖Q◗ **Clach Mhuilinn** 7 Harris Rd IV2 3LS
☎(0463) 237059
Closed Dec-Jan
Jacqi and Iain Elmslie's delightful modern detached home stands in an attractive garden in a quiet residential area close to the town centre. It has a relaxed friendly atmosphere and there are high standards of housekeeping throughout. Bedrooms are variable in size with mixed modern appointments while public areas include a spacious and comfortable lounge which opens on to the small dining area where hearty breakfasts are served at the communal table overlooking the secluded garden.
3rm(1®) ⚹ ⓡ ⚹ sB&B£19-£21 dB&B£36-£40 dB&B↑®£38-£42
▥ CTV nc10yrs
Credit Cards ①③ ⓔ

GH ◖Q◗◖Q◗◖Q◗ **Craigside** 4 Gordon Terrace IV2 3HD
☎(0463) 231576 FAX (0463) 713409
Efficiently run by Janette and Wilf Skinner, this Victorian lodge is situated in a residential area overlooking the castle and offers good-value bed and breakfast accommodation. The bedrooms, where smoking is not encouraged, vary in size and provide a wide range of amenities, and there is a comfortable lounge with well filled book shelves. Freshly cooked breakfasts are served in the dining room, where at peak times it may be necessary to share a table.
6rm(5⇨↑®) ⚹ in dining room CTV in all bedrooms ⓡ ⚹ (ex guide dogs) ⚹ sB&B£20 sB&B⇨↑®£20 dB&B£36
dB&B⇨↑®£36 WB&B£110
▥
ⓔ

GH ◖Q◗◖Q◗◖Q◗◖Q◗◖Q◗ **Culduthel Lodge** 14 Culduthel Road IV2 4AG ☎(0463) 240089 FAX (0463) 240089
Dedicated owners David and Marion Bonsor have carefully restored this fine Grade II Georgian residence. The comfortable and mostly spacious bedrooms have been decorated to a high standard and attractive fabrics have been used to good effect with the highly polished dark wood furniture. Fresh flowers and complimentary sherry add a welcoming touch. Day rooms are elegant, and light refreshments are willingly served in the drawing room. A good choice of dishes prepared from fresh local produce is served in the dining room.
12⇨↑® (1fb) ⚹ in 9 bedrooms ⚹ in dining room CTV in all bedrooms ⓡ T ⚹ (ex guide dogs) sB&B⇨↑®£40
dB&B⇨↑®£64-£66 WB&B£220-£225 WBDi£320-£330 LDO 8pm
Lic ▥ nc5yrs
Credit Cards ①③

SELECTED

GH ◖Q◗◖Q◗◖Q◗◖Q◗ **Dionard** 39 Old Edinburgh Road IV2 3HJ
☎(0463) 233557
Pleasant, immaculately kept accommodation is a feature of this detached house standing in its own gardens. The owners offer a friendly welcome.
3® ⚹ in 1 bedrooms ⚹ in dining room ⚹ in 1 lounge CTV in all bedrooms ⓡ ⚹ sB&B↑®£20-£28 dB&B↑®£36-£44
▥ CTV

SELECTED

GH ◖Q◗◖Q◗◖Q◗◖Q◗ **Eden House Hotel** 8 Ballifeary Road IV3 5PJ (cross Ness Bridge from High St in town centre. First left and first left again and then second left 200mtrs from Eden Court Theatre) ☎(0463) 230278
A warm welcome and comfortable, attractively decorated rooms are assured at this pleasant sandstone house. Meals are enjoyable, and smoking is confined to the front porch.
5rm(4®) (2fb)CTV in all bedrooms ⓡ ⚹ (ex guide dogs) sB&Bfr£25 sB&B↑®£30 dB&B↑®£40-£50 WB&B£126-£157.50 WBDi£231-£262.50 LDO 4pm
▥ nc3yrs

GH ◖Q◗◖Q◗ **Four Winds** 42 Old Edinburgh Road IV2 3PG
☎(0463) 230397
Closed Xmas wk & New Year
A sturdy mid 19th-century villa, this guesthouse offers good-value bed and breakfast accommodation. Public areas include a comfortable lounge, stocked with a variety of books, and a traditional dining room with individual tables.
5® (2fb)CTV in all bedrooms ⓡ ⚹ sB&B↑®fr£18 dB&B↑®fr£36 WB&Bfr£103
▥ CTV

GH ◖Q◗◖Q◗◖Q◗ **Hebrides** 120a Glenurquhart Road IV3 5TD (on A82 Fort William road) ☎(0463) 220062
Situated at the south end of town close to the Caledonian canal, this family-run guesthouse offers good value bed and breakfast accommodation. The two bedrooms are comfortably furnished and well equipped, one with an en suite shower, the other with exclusive use of a bathroom. Enjoyable breakfasts are served at individual tables in the neat dining room. High standards of housekeeping are maintained throughout the guesthouse, and smoking is not permitted.
2rm(1®) (1fb) ⚹ CTV in all bedrooms ⓡ ⚹ sB&B↑®£19-£25 dB&B£36-£44 dB&B↑®£36-£44 WB&B£119-£140
▥
Credit Cards ①③ ⓔ

GH ◖Q◗◖Q◗◖Q◗ **Laggan View** Ness Castle Fishings, Dores Road IV1 2DH (3m from town centre on B862) ☎(0463) 235996 FAX (0463) 711552
3® (1fb)CTV in all bedrooms ⓡ sB&B↑®fr£20 dB&B↑®£36-£40 WB&B£126-£140 WBDi£175-£200 LDO 7.30pm
▥ CTV
Credit Cards ①③

GH ◖Q◗◖Q◗ **Leinster Lodge** 27 Southside Road IV2 4XA
☎(0463) 233311
Closed Xmas & New Year
Leinster Lodge is a friendly family-run house offering good-value bed and breakfast accommodation ten minutes' walk from the central amenities. There are mostly spacious bedrooms, a comfortable lounge and a traditional dining room where substantial breakfasts are served at individual tables.
6rm(2®) (2fb)CTV in 5 bedrooms ⓡ ⚹ sB&B£16 dB&B£32 dB&B↑®£36

⬚ CTV
£

PREMIER ⚜ SELECTED

GH 🅀🅀🅀🅀🅀 **Moyness House** 6 Bruce Gardens
IV3 5EN ☎(0463) 233836
FAX (0463) 233836
Closed 24 Dec-3 Jan

Once the home of writer Neil M Gunn, this late 19th-century house is in a residential area ten minutes walk from the town centre. It has been Nonna and Michael Jones' home for 11 years and they have built it up into a first-class small hotel. Nonna is an excellent cook, offering a choice of dishes at dinner, and though the house is not licensed you are welcome to bring your own wine. The pine-furnished bedrooms are compact but comfortable.
7rm(2⇄5🏠) ✖ in dining room CTV in all bedrooms ®
sB&B⇄🏠£25-£29 dB&B⇄🏠£50-£58 WB&B£175-£203 WBDi£265-£293
Lic ⬚
Credit Cards ① ② ③ £

SELECTED

GH 🅀🅀🅀🅀 **The Old Rectory** 9 Southside Road IV2 3BG
☎(0463) 220969
Closed 21 Dec-5 Jan

▶

BRAE NESS HOTEL

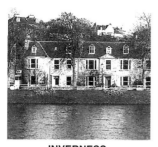

INVERNESS
Ideally situated beside the River Ness. 5 minutes walk from the town centre. Excellent home cooking with fresh produce served in our non-smoking dining room with table licence. All rooms have private bathroom, TV, tea making facilities and most are reserved for non smokers.
**John & Margaret Hill,
Ness Bank, Inverness IV2 4SF
Telephone (01463) 712266**

Ballifeary House Hotel

**10 Ballifeary Road, Inverness IV3 5PJ
Telephone: 01463 235572 Fax: 01463 235572**

The Hotel with an enviable reputation recommended in many leading guides.
Situated in own spacious grounds in a most desirable area of Inverness, offering a quiet, relaxing atmosphere. 10 minute picturesque walk to town. All rooms en suite bathrooms, TV etc. Excellent home cooking. Residents licence. Car park. No smoking throughout.
*Brochure/reservations:
Margaret & Danny Luscombe*

Where every Prospect Pleases

Craigside Lodge

*4 Gordon Terrace, Inverness IV2 3HD
Tel: (01463) 231576*

Comfortable detached and spacious Victorian House in residential area yet only few minutes walk to town centre. Beautiful views of town, river. Castle and countryside from lounge. All six bedrooms are en suite and fitted to please the discerning visitor. Craigside assures its guest of good food, comfort and experienced, courteous service. Central heating. Parking. Fire Certificate.

Brochure with pleasure from Wilf & Janette Skinner.

There is much style and charm to John and Neina Lister's detached period house, which lies close to the church in a residential area a short drive from the town centre. The attractive bedrooms are individually decorated, with cheerful fabrics and modern furniture. There is a quiet lounge with an ample supply of books and board games, and the little dining room features lace-covered circular tables. Smoking is not permitted.

4rm(3♠) (1fb) ⊬ CTV in all bedrooms ® ⅋ (ex guide dogs) dB&B♠£32-£38
⠿ CTV nc7yrs

SELECTED

FH Ⓠ Ⓠ Ⓠ Ⓠ Mrs A Munro **Taransay** Lower Muckovie *(NH707436)* IV1 2BB ☎(0463) 231880
This modern bungalow looks out over the Moray Firth. Accommodation is comfortable and breakfast is served at one large table.

2rm(1♠) ⊬ CTV in 1 bedroom ® dB&B♠£32-£36 WB&B£110-£120
CTV 170 acres dairy
£

GH Ⓠ Ⓠ Ⓠ *Riverside House Hotel* 8 Ness Bank IV2 4SF
☎(0463) 231052
Situated on the south bank of the River Ness, convenient for the town centre, this friendly guesthouse offers good value bed and breakfast accommodation. Bedrooms vary in size. The attractive dining room and small lounge overlook the river.
11rm(5⇋5♠) (3fb) CTV in all bedrooms ® LDO 7pm
Lic ⠿ CTV ⅌

GH Ⓠ Ⓠ *Roseneath* 39 Greig Street IV3 5PX ☎(0463) 220201
Excellent-value bed and breakfast accommodation is provided at this sturdy sandstone house south of the river. The spotlessly clean bedrooms are bright and cheery, and hearty breakfasts are served at individual tables in the combined lounge and dining room.
4rm(2♠) (2fb) CTV in all bedrooms ® T
⠿ CTV

GH Ⓠ Ⓠ Ⓠ *St Ann's Hotel* 37 Harrowden Road IV3 5QN
☎(0463) 236157 FAX (0463) 236157
Situated in a west end residential area, ten minutes' walk from the town centre, this friendly family-run house is now under the ownership of Jim and Betty Gardiner. The bedrooms are bright and airy with modern furniture, and there is a comfortable lounge where guests can relax with a drink from the dispense bar. Evening meals are available with advance notice.
6rm(5⇋9♠) (3fb) ⊬ in dining room CTV in all bedrooms ® ✳ sB&Bfr£16 sB&B⇋♠£18 dB&B⇋♠£37-£40 WB&B£110-£135 WBDi£195-£225 LDO 9pm
Lic ⠿ CTV
£

GH Ⓠ Ⓠ Ⓠ *Sunnyholm* 12 Mayfield Road IV2 4AE
☎(0463) 231336
This modern guest house lies in a residential area near the town centre and provides compact but bright, well equipped bedrooms in a modern ground-floor extension. There is a comfortable lounge and neat dining room in the main house, access to which is through a porch overlooking the secluded rear garden.
4♠ CTV in all bedrooms ® ⅋ (ex guide dogs)
⠿ CTV

GH Ⓠ Ⓠ Ⓠ *Windsor House Hotel* 22 Ness Bank IV2 4SF (from town centre follow signs to Dores/Holme Mills on A862)
☎(0463) 715535 FAX (0463) 713262
Closed 20 Dec-5 Jan
Improvements continue at this well run business and tourist hotel, which is situated beside the River Ness convenient for central amenities. The conservatory has been converted to create an L-shaped dining room and there are two comfortable lounges as well as an honesty bar. Bedrooms are small but well equipped, and have practical modern furnishings.
18⇋3♠ (6fb) CTV in all bedrooms ® T ⅋ (ex guide dogs) LDO 6pm
Lic ⠿
Credit Cards ①③

INN Ⓠ Ⓠ Ⓠ **Heathmount** Kingsmills Road IV2 3JU
☎(0463) 235877 FAX (0463) 715749
Closed 31 Dec-2 Jan
Built in 1868, this friendly family run Highland inn is situated in a residential area within easy reach of the town centre, castle and railway station. The well equipped bedrooms have private bathrooms, trouser presses, direct-dial telephones and tea trays; there is also a four-poster bedroom suite. The characterful bars are popular with the locals, and the restaurant offers a good range of home cooking and char-grills.
5⇋♠ (1fb)CTV in all bedrooms ® T sB&B⇋♠£37.50 dB&B⇋♠£49.50 LDO 9.15pm
⠿
Credit Cards ①③

IPSWICH Suffolk   Map **05** TM14

GH Ⓠ Ⓠ Ⓠ *Bentley Tower Hotel* 172 Norwich Road IP1 2PY (turn right off A12 at Chevalier roundabout)
☎(0473) 212142 FAX (0473) 212142
Closed 24 Dec-4 Jan
This large family run guest house is well established and has a welcoming atmosphere. The comfortable bedrooms have good proportions and are well appointed. Elegant public rooms feature high ceilings, and include a sitting room with satellite TV, an inviting bar and pleasant dining room.
11♠ (2fb) ⊬ in 2 bedrooms CTV in 13 bedrooms ® ⅋ (ex guide dogs) ✳ sB&Bfr£25 sB&B♠fr£38 dB&Bfr£35 dB&B♠fr£48 WB&Bfr£175 WBDifr£235 LDO 8.45pm
Lic ⠿
Credit Cards ①③£

GH Ⓠ *Cliffden* 21 London Road IP1 2EZ ☎(0473) 252689 FAX (0473) 252689
15rm(7♠) (3fb) ⊬ in 1 bedrooms CTV in all bedrooms ® ⅋ (ex guide dogs) ✳ sB&Bfr£15 sB&B♠£18 dB&Bfr£25 dB&B♠£30 WB&B£105
⠿

GH Ⓠ Ⓠ Ⓠ *Highview House Hotel* 56 Belstead Road IP2 8BE
☎(0473) 601620 & 688659
A commercial, family-owned guesthouse is situated in a quiet area of the city above the railway station. Bedrooms are very well equipped and a high standard of cleanliness is maintained. Dinner is provided with a small simple à la carte menu in a pleasant dining room, which leads into a sitting area with a full-sized metered snooker table.
11rm(7⇋9♠) (1fb) CTV in all bedrooms ® T LDO 7.30pm
Lic ⠿ CTV
Credit Cards ①③

IRONBRIDGE Shropshire   Map **07** SJ6●

GH Ⓠ Ⓠ Ⓠ *Broseley* The Square, Broseley TF12 5EW
☎Telford(0952) 882043
Closed 22-27 Dec
A comfortable guesthouse stands in the centre of the town with an adjacent public car park. The rooms are well equipped and have all the facilities required by the business or tourist visitor.

6⇄🟊 (3fb) ⌘ in dining room ⌘ in lounges CTV in all bedrooms
Ⓡ T sB&B⇄🟊£25-£29 dB&B⇄🟊£40-£45 LDO by arrangement
Lic ▥,⨯
Credit Cards [1] [3]

SELECTED

GH Ⓠ Ⓠ Ⓠ Ⓠ Ⓠ **The Library House** 11 Severn Bank TF8 7AN
☎Telford(0952) 432299
Situated just 100yds from the famous landmark, this small
family-run guesthouse was until 1960 the local library. The
lounge now occupies this spot and is furnished with deep
modern easy chairs and settees, with a drinks table for diners.
The quarry tiled dining room is pine furnished and dates from
1750, and was once a doctor's surgery. Bedrooms are
individually decorated with coordinated fabrics and have
comfortable armchairs. There are terraced gardens to the rear
with fine views of the local church, and free car parking is
available nearby. George and Chris Maddocks are a very
friendly couple and offer warm hospitality at their totally no
smoking establishment.
3⇄🟊 (1fb) ⌘ CTV in all bedrooms Ⓡ sB&B⇄🟊£35
dB&B⇄🟊£44 LDO 4pm
Lic ▥ CTV⨯

GH Ⓠ Ⓠ Ⓠ *Wharfage Cottage* 17 The Wharfage TF8 7AW
☎Telford(0952) 432721
Feb-Nov
2🟊 (1fb) CTV in all bedrooms Ⓡ ⊁

ISLE OF

Placenames incorporating the words 'Isle of' or 'Isle' will be found
under the actual name, eg Isle of Wight is under Wight, Isle of.

IVER HEATH Buckinghamshire   Map **04** TQ08

GH Ⓠ Ⓠ Ⓠ **Bridgettine Convent** Fulmer Common Road SL0
0NR (from Iver Heath roundabout take Pinewood Road pass Film
Studios to cross roads and turn left into Fulmer Common Road)
☎Fulmer(0753) 662073 & 662645 FAX (0753) 662172
A peaceful stay is assured at this Tudor building, set back from a
country lane, which is run as a guest house by sisters of the order
of St Bridget of Rome. Bedrooms are all simply furnished,
spotlessly clean and no-smoking. Public areas include a library, TV
lounge and a quiet lounge. Dinner can be served by the nuns, but it
is generally breakfasts only. Guests are welcome to use the chapel.
13rm(3🟊) (3fb) ⌘ ⊁ LDO 2pm
▥ CTV
Ⓔ

JACOBSTOWE Devon   Map **02** SS50

FH Ⓠ Ⓠ Mrs J King **Higher Cadham** *(SS585026)* EX20 3RB
(from Jacobstowe village take A3072 towards Hatherleigh/Bude, a
few yards after church turn sharp right in front of Cottage Farm
continue for 0.5m) ☎(0837) 85647
Closed Xmas
A Devon longhouse with a farm which is part of the Tarka Trail
scheme, allowing the public to walk part or all of the 180 miles of
river and countryside path. The charming bedrooms are named
after four of the rivers mentioned in Tarka The Otter; one room
has a four-poster bed. The lounge and dining room have beamed
ceilings and log burners, and traditional farmhouse fare is
provided at the large dining room table. Conversion of barns into a
restaurant and 5 additional ensuite bedrooms should be completed
by the 1995 season.
4rm (1fb) ⌘ in dining room Ⓡ ⊁ (ex guide dogs) ✳ sB&B£14.50
dB&B£29 WB&Bfr£95 WBDifr£125 LDO 7pm
Lic ▥ CTV nc3yrs games room nature trail 139 acres beef sheep
Ⓔ

JEDBURGH Borders *Roxburghshire*   Map **12** NT62

GH Ⓠ Ⓠ **Ferniehirst Mill Lodge** TD8 6PQ (2.5m S on A68, at the
end of a private track directly off A68) ☎(0835) 863279
Situated south of the town in a secluded valley beside the River Jed
and surrounded by 25 acres of land, this purpose built chalet-style
lodge and riding centre offers compact, plainly furnished rooms with
good beds. Drinks are taken in the spacious lounge overlooking the
river, and home cooking is served at shared tables in the dining room.
11rm(5⇄3🟊) ⌘ in dining room Ⓡ T ✳ sB&B⇄🟊£21
dB&B⇄🟊£42 WB&B£140 WBDi£224 LDO 6pm
Lic ▥ CTV ⨯ ♨
Credit Cards [1] [3]

GH Ⓠ Ⓠ Ⓠ **'Froylehurst'** Friars TD8 6BN ☎(0835) 862477
FAX (0835) 862477
Mar-Nov
This late Victorian house stands in its own grounds in an elevated
position enjoying fine views over the town and offers comfortable,
good value bed and breakfast accommodation. Bedrooms are well
maintained, spacious and individually decorated with coordinating
fabrics and easy chairs. There is an inviting, well furnished
lounge, and hearty Scottish breakfasts are served around a
communal table in the small dining room. Guests should note that
the approach road to the guesthouse is very steep.
5rm (3fb) ⌘ in bedrooms ⌘ in dining room CTV in all bedrooms
Ⓡ ⊁ dB&B£30-£32 WB&Bfr£100
▥ CTV nc5yrs
Ⓔ

GH Ⓠ Ⓠ Ⓠ **Kenmore Bank Hotel** Oxnam Road TD8 6JJ (off A68
entering town from S) ☎(0835) 862369
With views over the town and abbey, this family-run guesthouse
offers a sound standard of accommodation. Bedrooms vary in size,
but all are attractively decorated. The proprietor's paintings
decorate the dining room and lounge, and many are for sale. ►

RIVERSIDE
HOUSE HOTEL
8 Ness Bank, Inverness IV2 4SF
Telephone: (01463) 231052

The Hotel occupies the most picturesque spot on the
banks of the River Ness. Opposite St. Andrews
Cathedral and Eden Court Theatre. 3 minutes walk
from town centre. Very convenient for day trips to
Loch Ness, Skye and North Coast. All 11 bedrooms
have H & C, colour TV, tea & coffee tray, duvets and
central heating. Double, twin, or triple rooms with
private facilities. Cosy single rooms. Residential licence.
Bed and Breakfast £24 – £28

6⇄🐾 (2fb) ⊁ in dining room CTV in all bedrooms Ⓡ ✳
sB&B⇄🐾£27-£42 dB&B⇄🐾£36-£44 WB&B£126-£154
WBDi£231-£259 LDO 6.30pm
Lic ⭄ ♪
Credit Cards ① ③ £

SELECTED

GH ⬛⬛⬛⬛ The Spinney Langlee TD8 6PB (2m S on A68)
☎(0835) 863525 FAX (0835) 863525
Mar-2nd wk Nov
This delightful modern house stands in several acres of
pleasant, well maintained grounds beside the A68, two miles
south of the town. Well proportioned bedrooms are
comfortably furnished and immaculately maintained. There is
a comfortable lounge on the ground floor equipped with books
and TV, and a good choice of breakfast is served at individual
tables in the dining room. Friendly service is provided by the
owner Mrs Sandra Fry.
3rm(2🐾) ⊁ in bedrooms ⊁ in dining room Ⓡ 🐾 (ex guide
dogs) dB&B🐾£36-£42
⭄ CTV

GH ⬛⬛⬛ Willow Court The Friars TD8 6BN (from Market Sq
take Exchange St, Friars 50yds along on the right)
☎(0835) 863702
Standing in two acres of gardens with panoramic views over the
town, this modern chalet bungalow is reached up a steep drive.
Although situated in a quiet residential area, it is within easy
walking distance of the market square. Attractively maintained
throughout, bedrooms are on the ground floor, with a family room
upstairs. There are two lounges, one leading to the small
conservatory dining room where good home cooking using fresh
garden and local produce is served.
4rm(3⇄🐾) (1fb) ⊁ in dining room ⊁ in 1 lounge
CTV in all bedrooms Ⓡ ✳ sB&B£18-£30 sB&B⇄🐾£18-£30
dB&B⇄🐾£30-£36 WB&B£105-£126 WBDi£189-£210 LDO 6pm
Lic ⭄ CTV
£

JERSEY See **CHANNEL ISLANDS**

KEIGHLEY West Yorkshire   Map **07** SE04

GH ⬛⬛⬛ Bankfield 1 Station Road, Cross Hills BD20 7EH (turn
off A650/A629 Aire Valley trunk road at Kildwick roundabout
and take weight limit restriction road towards Cross Hills. 0.5m
on right) ☎Cross Hills(0535) 632971
Comfortable and spotless accommodation is offered in the stone-
built house. There is a comfortable lounge and a small garden
where guests can sit out on fine days.
3rm(1🐾) (1fb) ⊁ in bedrooms CTV in 1 bedroom Ⓡ ✳
sB&Bfr£16 sB&B🐾£18 dB&Bfr£32 dB&B🐾£36 WB&Bfr£112
⭄ CTV
£

KEITH Grampian *Banffshire*   Map **15** NJ45

SELECTED

FH ⬛⬛⬛⬛ Mrs J Jackson The Haughs *(NJ416515)*
AB55 3QN (1m from Keith off A96) ☎(0542) 882238
Apr-Oct
This traditional farmhouse is ideally placed for touring and
Mrs Jackson is a most welcoming hostess. Bedrooms are
bright and cheery, with all modern comforts; smoking is
discouraged. There is an attractive sitting room and a sunny,
south-facing dining room where good home cooked meals are
served at separate tables.

4rm(3⇄🐾) (1fb) ⊁ in bedrooms ⊁ in dining room CTV in all
bedrooms Ⓡ 🐾 (ex guide dogs) ✳ dB&B⇄🐾£32-£34 LDO
3pm
⭄ 165 acres beef mixed sheep
£

FH ⬛⬛⬛ Mrs Bain *Saughwells Farm (NJ384552)* Forgie
AB55 3RJ ☎Fochabers(0343) 820409
Excellent-value holiday accommodation is offered at this fully
modernised farmhouse set amid gently rolling countryside west of
Keith. The well equipped bedrooms are comfortable and there is a
cosy lounge where guests can relax. Mrs Bains' delightful home
cooking is served at the communal table in the small, neat dining
room.
2rm

KENDAL Cumbria   Map **07** SD59

See also Brigsteer

SELECTED

GH ⬛⬛⬛⬛ Burrow Hall Country Guest House
Plantation Bridge LA8 9JR (on A591) ☎Staveley(0539) 821711
Burrow Hall was built in 1648 and has been carefully
extended and modernised. There are two delightful lounges
with oak beams and log fires, and a cosy dining room where a
well prepared dinner is served. Paul and Honor Brind provide
friendly service.
3🐾 ⊁ in bedrooms ⊁ in dining room 🐾 dB&B🐾£45
WB&B£157.50 WBDi£220 LDO 7pm
Lic ⭄ CTV nc16yrs
Credit Cards ① ③

GH ⬛⬛⬛ Higher House Farm Oxenholme Lane, Natland
LA9 7QH ☎Sedgewick(05395) 61177 FAX (05395) 61177
Higher House is a 17th-century beamed farmhouse situated in the
village of Natland, a mile south of Kendal. It has charming
bedrooms with en suite facilities, and one has a four-poster bed.
There is a guest lounge with a log fire, and a dining room with one
large table and attractive place settings. On fine days guests can sit
outside and enjoy the surrounding fells or wander through the
grassy orchard.
3rm(1⇄2🐾) (1fb) ⊁ CTV in 1 bedroom Ⓡ ✳
sB&B⇄🐾£22.50-£24.50 dB&B⇄🐾£35-£39 LDO 1pm
⭄ CTV 🐾9

PREMIER 🏵 SELECTED

**GH ⬛⬛⬛⬛⬛ Lane
Head Country House Hotel**
Helsington LA9 5RJ (0.5m S off
A6) ☎(0539) 731283 &
721023
Closed Nov
An attractive 17th-century
house situated in an acre of
well tended gardens
overlooking Kendal and the
surrounding hills. It is reached
by a country lane off the A6
south of the town, and is only a 10 minute drive from junction
36 of the M6. Bedrooms are particularly well appointed, many
having panoramic views over the countryside. There is an
elegant, spacious lounge with a log fire and an ample supply
of books. A set menu offering a good choice of excellent
home-cooked food is served in the pleasant dining room which
overlooks the garden.

7rm(4⇄3♠) (1fb) ⊬ in dining room CTV in all bedrooms ®
T ✠ (ex guide dogs) sB&B⇄♠£35-£40 dB&B⇄♠£55-£60
LDO 5pm
Lic ▥.
Credit Cards ① ② ③ £

P R E M I E R 🏆 S E L E C T E D

GH Q q q q q Low Jock
Scar Selside LA9 9LE (6m N on
A6) ☎(0539) 823259
FAX (0539) 823645
Mar-Oct
Philip and Alison Midwinter
welcome guests to their
charming small country
guesthouse, which was
featured as the Best Newcomer
in Northern England in the
1994 Guide. The house is built
of traditional Lakeland stone and has been tastefully restored
by the owners to provide many modern facilities. It is four
miles from Kendal in secluded gardens surrounded by
woodland with a stream running by. Dinners are provided by
arrangement, and smoking is prohibited throughout.
5rm(3♠) ⊬ ® sB&B£27 sB&B⇄♠£32 dB&B£40
dB&B⇄♠£50 LDO 10am
Lic ▥ CTV nc12yrs

GH q q q Martindales 9-11 Sandes Avenue LA9 4LL (N on A6,
before Victoria Bridge) ☎(0539) 724028
A good standard of accommodation and service is provided at this
mid-terrace guest house to the north of the town centre. The
bedrooms are prettily decorated and have good facilities, and the
comfortable bar-lounge has an open fire in the Victorian fireplace.
8♠ (1fb) ⊬ in dining room CTV in all bedrooms ® ✠ (ex guide
dogs) ✳ sB&B♠£25-£28 dB&B♠£40-£42 WB&B£175-£196
LDO 1pm
Lic ▥ nc8yrs
Credit Cards ① ③

FH q q Mrs S Beaty Garnett House (SD500959) Burneside
LA9 5SF (0.5m from the A591 Kendal/Windermere road, 2m from
Kendal) ☎(0539) 724542
Closed Xmas & New Year
This charming Cumbrian farmhouse dates back to the 15th century
and is full of character. It offers a good standard of
accommodation, with well furnished bedrooms and a comfortable
wood-panelled lounge. Very much a working farm, it is situated
close to the village of Burneside to the north of Kendal, and
service is warm and friendly.
5rm(3♠) (2fb) ⊬ in dining room CTV in all bedrooms ® ✠ ✳
dB&Bfr£26 dB&B♠fr£30 LDO 5pm
CTV 750 acres dairy sheep
£

FH q q q Mrs J Ellis Gateside (NY494955) Windermere Road
LA9 5SE (2m from the A591 Kendal travelling towards Windermere on
A591) ☎(0539) 722036
Closed Xmas & New Year
An attractive white painted farmhouse situated on a working farm on
the A591 Windermere road, with easy access to junction 36 of the
M6. Bedrooms are prettily decorated and full of character, some
featuring beams. There is a cosy guests' lounge and a spacious
dining room, with friendly service provided by owner Mrs June Ellis.
5rm(2♠) (1fb) ⊬ in dining room CTV in all bedrooms ® ✳
sB&B♠fr£20 dB&B£30-£32 dB&B♠£35-£38 LDO 4.30pm
▥ 280 acres dairy sheep
£

KENMORE BANK HOTEL JEDBURGH

Oxnam Road, Jedburgh TD8 6JJ
Tel: (01835) 862369
Open all year

A charming, family-run hotel just off the A68
to/from Edinburgh. Situated beside the Jed
Water, it enjoys panoramic views of the Abbey
and town. Just five minutes' away from shops,
restaurants, and pubs. All bedrooms en-suite with
colour TV. Central heating. Choice of menu,
wines and snacks. Prices from £18.00 B&B.

Proprietors: Charles and Joanne Muller

LANE HEAD HOUSE Country Hotel

The Property: *A delightful 17th Century
country house in an elevated location on the
southern edge of Kendal.*
The View: *Magnificent panoramic views of
surrounding fells.*
The Gardens: *An acre of private grounds
featuring a unique knot garden.*
The Interior: *Tastefully combined interior decor
& furnishings.*
The Total: *"Commendable"*
Helsington, Kendal, Cumbria LA9 5RJ
Tel: (01539) 731283

FH Q Q Q Mrs E M Gardner **Natland Mill Beck** *(SD520907)*
LA9 7LH (1m from Kendal on A65) ☎(0539) 721122
Mar-Oct
This lovely Cumbrian farmhouse is steeped in history and
provides a delightful place to stay. It is just outside Kendal close
to the A65. Guests are made to feel most welcome by Mrs
Gardener, who really does enjoy running the bed and breakfast
side of the farmhouse. There is a lovely walled garden, and guests
are welcome to wander around the farm.
3rm(1ffl) ⓡ ⅍ ✳ dB&Bffl£30-£32
🏬 CTV 100 acres dairy
ⓔ

KENILWORTH Warwickshire   Map **04** SP27

GH Q Q Q **Abbey** 41 Station Road CV8 1JD ☎(0926) 512707
FAX (0926) 59148
A short walk from the town centre, this large house is impeccably
maintained by proprietors Angela and Trevor Jefferies, who
provide a delightful hospitality. Some bedrooms are on the small side,
but all have modern furniture and equipment. There is a
comfortable lounge as well as a pine-furnished dining room.
7rm(2ffl) (1fb) ⅍ in dining room CTV in all bedrooms ⓡ ⅍ (ex
guide dogs) sB&B£19-£21 sB&Bfffr£24 dB&Bfr£34
dB&Bfffr£40 LDO 5pm
Lic 🏬 CTV
ⓔ

GH Q Q Q **Castle Laurels Hotel** 22 Castle Road CV8 1NG (on
A452) ☎(0926) 56179 FAX (0926) 54954
Closed 24 Dec-2 Jan
Castle Laurels is an impeccably maintained Victorian house close
to the castle. The bedrooms are traditionally furnished and vary in
size, though all have modern equipment. One is furnished for
family occupancy. There is a comfortable lounge and a dining
room with separate tables.
12ffl (1fb) ⅍ in bedrooms ⅍ in dining room ⅍ in lounges CTV in
all bedrooms ⓡ **T** ⅍ (ex guide dogs) ✳ sB&Bfffr£29.50
dB&Bfffr£47 LDO 7pm
Lic 🏬
Credit Cards ① ③ ⓔ

GH Q Q Q **Ferndale** 45 Priory Road CV8 1LL ☎(0926) 53214
Ferndale is a soundly maintained, friendly guest house, in a
residential road close to Abbey Fields Park. It provides attractively
decorated bedrooms with modern furnishings and equipment.
Family bedded rooms, including one at ground floor level, are
available. Separate tables are provided in the breakfast room, and
there is a comfortable lounge. Car parking is at the side of the
house.
7⇌ffl (2fb) ⅍ in dining room CTV in all bedrooms ⓡ ✳
sB&Bⅾffl£18-£20 dB&Bⅾffl£32-£36
Lic 🏬 CTV
ⓔ

GH Q Q Q **Hollyhurst** 47 Priory Road CV8 1LL (on A452)
☎(0926) 53882 FAX (0926) 864283
The brightly decorated and soundly maintained modern
accommodation available at this semidetached house just a short
walk from Abbeyfields Park, conveniently close to the town
centre, includes some family rooms. Residents have the use of a
comfortable lounge and bar, evening meals are provided by prior
arrangement, and there are car parking facilities on site.
8rm(3ffl) (2fb) CTV in all bedrooms ⓡ sB&B£16 sB&Bffl£18
dB&Bfr£32 dB&Bffl£36 WB&Bfr£110 LDO noon
Lic 🏬 CTV
ⓔ

GH Q Q Q Q **Victoria Lodge Hotel** 180 Warwick Road
CV8 1HU (0.25m S on A452, opposite St Johns Church)
☎(0926) 512020 FAX (0926) 58703
Closed 25 Dec-1 Jan
This early Victorian house was virtually derelict when bought
by Malcolm and Joyce Chilvers in 1990. They subsequently
carried out extensive restoration and modernisation work,
ensuring that none of the original character was lost. The
comfortable, modern bedrooms are tastefully decorated and
furnished to a high standard; all the rooms are en suite, with
direct dial telephones, TV and tea trays, supplemented by
many thoughtful extra touches. One room, on the ground
floor, comprises a double suite, with a separate lounge and
private terrace overlooking the garden. Three other rooms, at
the front, have their own balconies. A good choice of home-
cooked dishes is served in the pleasant dining room, featuring
period style furniture. There is also a cosy lounge and small
bar. Conference facilities are available, and private parties for
up to 24 can be catered for. Outside, there is a delightful
walled garden and private parking.
7⇌ffl ⅍ CTV in all bedrooms ⓡ **T** ⅍ (ex guide dogs) ✳
sB&B⇌ffl£32-£33 dB&B⇌ffl£39.50-£47 LDO 7.30pm
Lic 🏬 CTV nc14yrs
Credit Cards ① ② ③ ⓔ

KENTALLEN Highland *Argyllshire*   Map **14** NN05

FH Q Q Mrs D A MacArthur *Ardsheal Home Farm*
(NN996574) PA38 4BZ ☎Duror(063174) 229
Apr-Oct
This cottage style farmhouse, peacefully set near the shore of
Loch Linnhe, offers a friendly atmosphere and good bed and
breakfast accommodation. Upper floor bedrooms are comfortably
furnished in traditional style, while the ground floor room is more
modern and has exclusive use of a bathroom. Hearty breakfasts
are served round the dining room's communal table, and a
comfortable TV lounge invites relaxtion - though guests are also
welcome to take an interest in farm activities.
3 (1fb) ⓡ ⅍ (ex guide dogs)
🏬 CTV 1000 acres beef sheep

KESWICK Cumbria   Map **11** NY22

GH Q Q Q Q **Abacourt House** 26 Stanger Street CA12 5JU
☎(07687) 72967
A charming Victorian house standing in a quiet side road, only
a short way from the town centre has been tastefully
refurbished to a very high standard. Bill and Sheila Newman
are good hosts, and there is a very pleasant atmosphere, with
convenient car parking to the rear.
4ffl ⅍ CTV in all bedrooms ⓡ ⅍ dB&Bffl£40
🏬 nc

GH Q Q Q Q **Acorn House Hotel** Ambleside Road
CA12 4DL (500yds from town centre opposite St John Church)
☎(07687) 72553
Feb-Nov
A well furnished family-run Georgian property which offers
guests individually styled bedrooms equipped with the usual
modern comforts, including colour TV and radio alarms.
There is a comfortable lounge and the house is close to the
town centre where there are several restaurants and pubs
serving good food.

10rm(9⇒3ʰ) (3fb) ⤢ in bedrooms ⤢ in dining room CTV in all bedrooms ® ⅋ (ex guide dogs) dB&B⇒ʰ£44-£55 Lic ⊞, nc5yrs
Credit Cards 1 3

GH Q Q Q **Allerdale House** 1 Eskin Street CA12 4DH
☎(07687) 73891
Personally run by its resident owners, this attractive house has a fountain in the well kept front garden and is set in a quiet side road not far from the town centre. Bedrooms are well equipped and there is a delightful lounge. The dining room has an interesting collection of plates around the walls.
6⇒ʰ (2fb) CTV in all bedrooms ® T LDO 4.30pm
Lic ⊞, nc5yrs

SELECTED

GH Q Q Q Q **Applethwaite Country House Hotel**
Applethwaite CA12 4PL (off A591) ☎(07687) 72413
A splendid Victorian house standing in 2 acres of beautiful grounds and gardens overlooking Keswick, Derwentwater and the Borrowdale Valley. A cosy bar adjoins a very comfortable and elegant drawing room which leads to a conservatory with a tented ceiling. The attractively appointed dining room looks out over the lawn and gardens. A 4 course dinner is provided each evening offering a choice of dishes at each course. All bedrooms are individually furnished and decorated.
14rm(7⇒5ʰ) (4fb) ⤢ in 7 bedrooms ⤢ in dining room ⤢ in 1 lounge CTV in all bedrooms ® ⅋ (ex guide dogs) ✳ sB&B⇒ʰ£25-£28 dB&B⇒ʰ£50-£56 WB&B£175-£196 WBDi£265-£286 LDO 6.45pm
Lic ⊞, CTV bowling green putting croquet lawn
Credit Cards 1 3 £

⼤ ▰ **GH** Q Q Q **Avondale** 20 Southey Street CA12 4EF (take first left at Cenotaph into Southey St Avondale 100yds on right)
☎(07687) 72735
Situated in a quiet side road close to the town centre, this attractive terraced guest house is family run and offers well furnished accommodation. Smoking is not permitted.
6rm(4ʰ) ⤢ CTV in all bedrooms ® ⅋ (ex guide dogs) sB&B£14-£15 dB&B£28-£30 dB&Bʰ£34-£36 WB&B£96-£117 WBDi£162-£183 LDO breakfast
Lic ⊞, nc12yrs
Credit Cards 1 3 £

GH Q Q Q **Beckside** 5 Wordsworth Street CA12 4HU (turn off A66 onto A5271, Wordsworth St just beyond Shell Petrol Station next to Fitz Park) ☎(07687) 73093
This charming stone-built, terrace cottage in a quiet side road convenient for the town centre offers bright, pretty bedrooms. There is a small cosy lounge on the top floor and a pleasant dining room. Smoking is not permitted.
3ʰ ⤢ CTV in all bedrooms ® ⅋ (ex guide dogs) dB&Bʰ£32-£36 WB&B£110-£115 WBDi£170-£185 LDO 4pm
⊞, ⼳nc12yrs
£

GH Q Q **Brierholme** 21 Bank Street CA12 5JZ (on A591, 100yds from post office) ☎(07687) 72938
Brierholme is a small family-run guesthouse in the centre of town with its own car park. The well equipped bedrooms have a cheerful atmosphere, and the comfortable lounge has a selection of board games.
6⇒ʰ (2fb) ⤢ in bedrooms ⤢ in dining room CTV in all bedrooms ® dB&B£35-£40 dB&B⇒ʰ£38-£44 LDO 3pm
Lic ⊞,

GH Q Q Q **Charnwood** 6 Eskin Street CA12 4DH (0.5m S off A6)
☎(07687) 74111
rs Nov-Mar wknds only
Steve and Kath Johnson are the friendly hosts at this well maintained guest house in a quiet side road not far from the town centre. Bedrooms are freshly decorated and offer good facilities, and a comfortable lounge is provided.
6ʰ (2fb) CTV in all bedrooms ® ⅋ LDO 4pm
Lic ⊞, nc10yrs

GH Q Q Q **Claremont House** Chestnut Hill CA12 4LT (SE on A591) ☎(07687) 72089
The first guesthouse you reach when entering the town from the Windermere road, Claremont stands in its own garden. Bedrooms are attractively decorated and there is a guests' lounge and a small dining room.
5⇒ʰ ⤢ in bedrooms ⤢ in dining room ® ⅋ sB&B£22-£23 dB&B⇒ʰ£44-£46 LDO 4pm
Lic ⊞, CTV nc3yrs
£

See advertisement on p.233.

GH Q Q Q **Clarence House** 14 Eskin Street CA12 4DQ (second turning on left after Shell garage Greta St leads to Eskin St)
☎(07687) 73186
Closed 25th & 26th Dec
This family-owned detached, stone-built guest house is set in a quiet side road close to the town centre. The plainly decorated bedrooms are fresh, bright and fitted with modern style furniture, there is a comfortable lounge, and enjoyable home cooking is served in the pleasant dining room. The rule of the house is 'no smoking'.

▶

Applethwaite

Country House Hotel

Telephone: (017687) 72413

Characterful family run Victorian country residence in idyllic and peaceful location. Stunning views over Derwentwater and Borrowdale. 2½ acres woodland gardens. Excellent home cooked food with vegetarian specialities always available. Charming period lounge with log fire. Keswick 1½ miles. Open all year.

Resident proprietors: Tom & Gail Ryan.

9rm(8⇨↑⬥) (3fb) ⤬ CTV in all bedrooms ⓡ ↑⬥ (ex guide dogs) sB&B£17-£19 dB&B⇨↑⬥£36-£42
▥, ⅊nc5yrs
£

SELECTED

GH ⬛⬛⬛⬛⬛ Craglands Penrith Road CA12 4LJ (guesthouse at the foot of Chestnut Hill on right entering Keswick) ☎(07687) 74406
Closed Xmas
Craglands is an appealing Lakeland house, with white pebble dash exterior, where guests can be assured of a warm welcome from the owners, Mr and Mrs Dolton. The attractively decorated bedrooms have coordinating fabrics and good quality duvets, with many little extras including colour TV and hair dryer. Well prepared meals are served in the pleasant dining room and there is a comfortable lounge.
5rm(1⇨2↑⬥) CTV in all bedrooms ⓡ ↑⬥ (ex guide dogs) LDO 4pm
▥, nc8yrs

SELECTED

GH ⬛⬛⬛⬛ Dalegarth House Country Hotel Portinscale CA12 5RQ (approach Portinscale from A66 pass Farmers Arms approx 100yds on left to hotel) ☎(07687) 72817
This delightful house stands in lovely grounds in the village of Portinscale, not far from Keswick. Bright, freshly decorated bedrooms offer good facilities, there are two very well furnished lounges, and tempting home-cooked meals are served in the newly extended dining room. Friendly hosts provide warm, caring service throughout.
10⇨↑⬥ (1fb) CTV in all bedrooms ⓡ ↑⬥ (ex guide dogs) ⁂ sB&B⇨↑⬥£25-£26.50 dB&B⇨↑⬥£50-£53 WB&B£165-£175 WBDi£235-£245 LDO 5.30pm
Lic ▥ CTV nc5yrs
Credit Cards ①③£

GH ⬛⬛⬛ Edwardene 26 Southey Street CA12 4EF
☎(07687) 73586 FAX (07687) 73824
A well maintained and attractively decorated conversion of two similar adjoining houses in a terrace. There are two nice lounges and dinner is served from 6.30 to 7.30pm.
11rm(3↑⬥) (3fb) ⤬ in bedrooms ⤬ in dining room ⓡ ↑⬥ (ex guide dogs) sB&B£16-£17 dB&B£32-£34 dB&B↑⬥£36-£40 WB&B£100-£120 WBDi£160-£200 LDO 6pm
Lic ▥ CTV
Credit Cards ①③£

GH ⬛⬛⬛ Fell House 28 Stanger Street CA12 5JU
☎(07687) 72669
Closed 25 Dec
This pleasant Victorian house in a side road close to the town centre offers bright, fresh bedrooms and a cosy lounge, standards of both accommodation and service being very satisfactory.
6rm(2↑⬥) (1fb)CTV in all bedrooms ⓡ ↑⬥ sB&B£15.50-£16.50 dB&B£31-£33 dB&B↑⬥£36-£38
▥, CTV

GH ⬛⬛ *Foye House* 23 Eskin Street CA12 4DQ ☎(07687) 73288
This Victorian house is set in a quiet side road not far from the town centre. It provides pleasant accommodation and service is friendly and attentive. Smoking is not permitted.
7rm(4↑⬥) (2fb) CTV in all bedrooms ⓡ LDO 4pm
Lic ▥ CTV ⅊

GH ⬛⬛⬛⬛ Goodwin House 29 Southey Street CA12 4EE
☎(07687) 74634
An attractive Victorian house situated on the corner of a quiet side road close to the town centre, with unrestricted parking outside. Bedrooms are spacious and well furnished, each with TV and tea trays.
5rm(2↑⬥) (2fb) ⤬ in dining room CTV in all bedrooms ⓡ ↑⬥ (ex guide dogs) sB&B£12-£15 dB&B↑⬥£26-£36 LDO midday
Lic ▥

SELECTED

GH ⬛⬛⬛⬛ Greystones Ambleside Road CA12 4DP (opposite St John's Church) ☎(07687) 73108
Closed 1 Dec-31 Jan
This spacious end-of-terrace guesthouse is situated in a quiet location convenient for the town centre. The well equipped bedrooms are decorated with coordinating fabrics and the accommodation is stylish and comfortable. There is a cosy lounge and good home cooking is served in the attractive dining room.
8rm(2⇨6↑⬥) ⤬ CTV in all bedrooms ⓡ ↑⬥ (ex guide dogs) sB&B⇨↑⬥£21-£23 dB&B⇨↑⬥£42-£46 LDO 2pm
Lic ▥ nc8yrs
£

GH ⬛⬛⬛ Heatherlea 26 Blencathra Street CA12 4HP
☎(07687) 72430
Closed Xmas
4↑⬥ (2fb) ⤬ CTV in all bedrooms ⓡ ↑⬥ (ex guide dogs) dB&B↑⬥£34-£35 LDO 10am
Lic ▥ ⅊
£

GH ⬛⬛⬛ Leonards Field 3 Leonards Street CA12 4EJ
☎(07687) 74170
Closed 23 Dec-Jan rs Feb
This small guesthouse, run by friendly and caring owners, is situated in a quiet side road. The attractive bedrooms are furnished with soft matching fabrics and all have colour TV. In summer a well tended front garden offers a kaleidoscope of colour. Smoking is not permitted in this establishment.
8rm(3↑⬥) (1fb) ⤬ CTV in all bedrooms ⓡ ⁂ sB&B£14-£15.50 dB&B£28-£30 dB&B↑⬥£30-£34 WB&B£98-£119 WBDi£150-£170 LDO 4.30pm
Lic ▥, ⅊nc5yrs

GH ⬛⬛⬛ Lynwood 12 Ambleside Road CA12 4DL
☎(07687) 72081 FAX (07687) 75021
Closed Xmas
Lynwood is a commodious and comfortable Victorian house set in a quiet side road convenient for the town centre. The bedrooms are prettily decorated and well equipped, and the proprietors are friendly and caring. This is a no-smoking establishment.
7rm(6↑⬥) (1fb) ⤬ CTV in all bedrooms ⓡ ↑⬥ sB&B£17.50 dB&B↑⬥£40-£50 WB&B£140-£175 WBDi£215.25-£250.25 LDO 2pm
Lic ▥,
Credit Cards ①③£

GH ⬛⬛ *Melbreak House* 29 Church Street CA12 4DX
☎(07687) 73398
Built on a corner site in a quiet road this guesthouse is convenient for the town centre. Smoking is not allowed in the bedrooms, which are bright and fresh with various styles of furnishings. There is a comfortable lounge and the dining room displays an

interesting collection of memorabilia. Some Scandinavian languages are spoken.
12rm(7♠) (3fb) CTV in all bedrooms ® LDO 4pm
Lic ▥ CTV ✗

SELECTED

GH ◯◯◯◯ **Ravensworth Hotel** 29 Station Street CA12 5HH (turn off A591 into Station Street at War Memorial, hotel is on right) ☎(07687) 72476
Closed 1 Dec-Jan
Part of a small terrace of substantial Victorian houses in the town centre, this private hotel provides a high standard of accommodation together with friendly personal service by proprietors John and Linda Lowrey. Bedrooms are prettily decorated and have every modern facility. There is an excellent residents' lounge and an attractive dining room with a small bar.
8rm(1⇌7♠) (1fb) ✗ in 2 bedrooms ✗ in dining room CTV in all bedrooms ® ✗ ✳ sB&B⇌♠£20-£33 dB&B⇌♠£26-£50 WB&B£91-£150
Lic ▥ CTV nc6yrs
Credit Cards ①③

GH ◯◯ **Richmond House** 37-39 Eskin Street CA12 4DG (enter Keswick on main road take second left after Shell petrol station into Greta St continue into Eskin St) ☎(07687) 73965
Closed Xmas
No-smoking accommodation is provided in this double-fronted, stone-built house which stands in a quiet side road close to the town centre. Fresh, brightly decorated bedrooms make good use of coordinated fabrics, and guests have the use of both a cosy lounge and a small bar at one end of the pleasant dining room.
9rm(7♠) (1fb) ✗ CTV in all bedrooms ® ✗ (ex guide dogs) ✳ sB&B£14.50-£20 sB&B♠£18-£20 dB&B£29-£31 dB&B♠£33-£35 WB&B£90-£115 WBDi£150-£170 LDO 5pm
Lic ▥ CTV ✗ nc5yrs
Credit Cards ①②③ ⓔ

GH ◯◯◯ **Rickerby Grange Country House Hotel** Portinscale CA12 5RH (by-pass Keswick on A66 Cockermouth road turn left at Portinscale sign, pass Farmer Arms Inn on left & turn down second lane to the right) ☎(07687) 72344
Closed Dec-Jan
Attractive and family-owned, this small hotel in the delightful village of Portinscale features a very spacious dining room where five-course dinners are served; a comfortable lounge is also provided for guests' use. Modern bedrooms with good facilities include some ground-floor rooms, one of which has a four-poster bed.
13rm(11⇌♠) (3fb) ✗ in dining room ✗ in 1 lounge CTV in all bedrooms ® T sB&Bfr£22 dB&Bfr£44 dB&B⇌♠£48-£50 WB&B£145-£165 WBDi£215-£235 LDO 5pm
Lic ▥ nc5yrs
ⓔ

GH ◯◯◯ **Skiddaw Grove Hotel** Vicarage Hill CA12 5QB (turn off at Keswick rbt, junc A591, into Keswick, turn right into Vicarage Hill hotel 20 yds on left) ☎(07687) 73324
Closed 20-28 Dec
An early Victorian house stands in its own grounds in a quiet part of the town between Bassenthwaite and Derwentwater, with extensive views of Skiddaw. Bedrooms are modern and well equipped, all with private bathrooms, clock radios and tea trays; TVs are also available. Public areas include a bar lounge, residents' lounge and dining room, with magnificent views over Bassenthwaite Lake and Skiddaw. Home-cooked food is prepared from fresh local produce, and special diets can be catered for by prior arrangement. An outdoor heated pool is available in summer months, and the hotel has a private garden with a sun terrace and a car park. Smoking is only permitted in the bar lounge. ▶

THE MILL INN
MUNGRISDALE
Nr. Penrith, Cumbria CA11 0XR
Telephone: 017687 79 632

A fine 16th century Inn in a peaceful village setting by the River Glendermackin nestling under the Skiddaw range of fells and close to Blencathra. 2 miles off the A66, 10 miles from Keswick and 8 miles from Ullswater. Old fashioned hospitality, modern facilities, real ale and imaginative home cooked food.

Claremont House
Chestnut Hill, Keswick, Cumbria CA12 4LT
Telephone: (017687) 72089

Claremont House is a 150 year old, former lodge house offering very pretty bedrooms with lace canopied beds and en suite facilities. Food here is our priority with a reputation over the years for consistently high quality. Vegetarians are also catered for and very welcome.

10⇄♠ (1fb) ✂ in bedrooms ✂ in dining room CTV in all bedrooms Ⓡ 🐾 (ex guide dogs) sB&B⇄♠£22-£24 dB&B⇄♠£44-£48 WB&B£154-£168 WBDi£231 LDO 7pm Lic ▥ ⅃(heated) table tennis ⓔ

GH Ⓠ Ⓠ Ⓠ Stonegarth 2 Eskin Street CA12 4DH
☎(07687) 72436
Family owned and run, this small hotel offers a good all round standard of accommodation and service. The bedrooms have recently been upgraded, there is a cosy lounge, and home cooking is provided in the pleasant dining room.
9⇄♠ (3fb) ✂ in 5 bedrooms ✂ in dining room ✂ in lounges CTV in all bedrooms Ⓡ T sB&B⇄♠£17-£23 dB&B⇄♠£34-£46 WBDi£185-£225 LDO 6pm
Lic ▥ nc5yrs
Credit Cards ①③ⓔ

GH Ⓠ Ⓠ Sunnyside 25 Southey Street CA12 4EF
☎(07687) 72446
Closed 15 Dec-15 Feb rs 15 Nov-15 Dec
A pleasant and well run guest house, Sunnyside is in a quiet side road not far from the town centre, and has the benefit of its own car park. The accommodation comprises modern bedrooms with good facilities and a comfortable first-floor lounge.
8rm (2fb) ✂ in dining room CTV in all bedrooms Ⓡ 🐾 (ex guide dogs) ▥.
Credit Cards ①③

GH Ⓠ Ⓠ Swiss Court 25 Bank Street CA12 5JZ ☎(07687) 72637
Situated in a short terrace in the town centre, this guesthouse has bedrooms which, although modestly decorated and furnished, are neat, clean and well equipped.
7rm 🐾
▥ CTV nc6yrs

GH Ⓠ Ⓠ Ⓠ Thornleigh 23 Bank Street CA12 5JZ (on A591 opposite Bell Close Car Park) ☎(07687) 72863
Feb-Nov
This friendly, town centre, family run guesthouse has been upgraded to a very high standard with much thought being given to guests' comfort. Bedrooms have all been tastefully redecorated and recarpeted and the ensuite shower units upgraded. There is a comfortable lounge on the first floor and an attractive dining room on a lower floor. Colourful flower baskets outside enhance the inviting appearance.
6⇄♠ ✂ in 4 bedrooms ✂ in dining room CTV in all bedrooms Ⓡ 🐾 dB&B⇄♠£38-£45 WB&B£126-£136.50
▥, nc16yrs
Credit Cards ①③ⓔ

GH Ⓠ Ⓠ Yew Tree House 28 Eskin Street CA12 4DG (turn left off A591 opposite Fitz Park straight across two junctions into Eskin St, Yew Tree third GH on left) ☎(07687) 74323
Yew Tree House is a small, pleasantly furnished house in a quiet side road near the town centre. Bedrooms are prettily decorated and there is a cosy residents' lounge.
5rm(2♠) (1fb) ✂ in dining room ✂ in lounges CTV in all bedrooms Ⓡ ✽ sB&B£13-£13.75 dB&B£26-£27.50 dB&B♠£30-£32 WB&Bfr£90 WBDifr£140 LDO 1pm
▥ CTV ✂

KETTERING Northamptonshire   Map 04 SP87

GH Ⓠ Ⓠ Headlands Private Hotel 49-51 Headlands NN15 7ET
☎(0536) 524624 FAX (0536) 83367
A large Victorian house, located in a quiet conservation area close to the town centre offers a sound standard of accommodation. The neat, tidy bedrooms vary in size from compact singles to more spacious doubles. The dining room features an interesting display of period china and foot warmers.
13rm(7⇄♠) (3fb) ✂ in dining room CTV in all bedrooms Ⓡ ✽

sB&B£17.50-£19.50 sB&B⇄♠£28-£30.50 dB&B£30-£35 dB&B⇄♠£34-£40 WB&B£122.50-£133 WBDi£185-£196 LDO 5pm
▥ CTV
Credit Cards ①③ⓔ

KETTLEWELL North Yorkshire   Map 07 SD97
See also Starbotton

SELECTED

GH Ⓠ Ⓠ Ⓠ Ⓠ Langcliffe Country BD23 5RJ (off B6160, at 'Kings Head' take road marked 'Access Only')
☎(0756) 760243 & 760896
A charming double-fronted detached house quietly situated in this attractive Dales village with a southern aspect down Wharfedale and splendid views of the surrounding fells. The house stands in well tended gardens, and all rooms have fine views. Bedrooms are spacious and comfortable, tastefully furnished and particularly well equipped, most with private bathrooms. There is also a self-contained cottage annexe adjacent which has been equipped for elderly and disabled guests; one room on the ground floor has also been adapted for similar use, with wheelchair access from the car park. Home-cooked four-course dinners are served in the conservatory dining room overlooking the gardens, or in an adjacent room with a large oak table, ideal for families or parties. There is a log fire in the cosy sitting room, and a private car park adjacent to the house.
6rm(4⇄♠) CTV in all bedrooms Ⓡ T sB&B⇄♠fr£36 dB&B⇄♠£55 WB&B£165-£182 WBDi£267-£294 LDO 9am
Lic ▥ CTV
Credit Cards ①③

KEXBY North Yorkshire   Map 08 SE75

FH Ⓠ Ⓠ Ⓠ Mrs K R Daniel Ivy House (SE691511) YO4 5LQ
☎York(0904) 489368
A late Victorian farmhouse with a dairy and mixed farm. Bedrooms are comfortable and of a good size. The lounge and the breakfast room both look out onto the garden. This is a cheerful and friendly house in pleasant countryside.
3rm (1fb) CTV in all bedrooms Ⓡ 🐾 ✽ sB&B£16-£18 dB&B£28-£30
▥ CTV 132 acres mixed
ⓔ

KEYNSHAM Avon   Map 03 ST66

SELECTED

GH Ⓠ Ⓠ Ⓠ Ⓠ Grasmere Court Hotel 22/24 Bath Road BS18 1SN (on A4 between Boliston and Bath)
☎Bristol(0272) 862662 FAX (0272) 862762
Equidistant from Bristol and Bath, this small family-run hotel offers immaculate accommodation and high standards throughout. Bedrooms are tastefully furnished in warm colour coordinating fabrics, and there is a congenial bar/lounge. Dinner and breakfast are served in the pleasant dining room, with home-grown vegetables used whenever possible. An outdoor swimming pool is available for guests during warmer months.
16⇄♠ (3fb) ✂ in bedrooms ✂ in dining room CTV in all bedrooms Ⓡ T 🐾 ✽ sB&B⇄♠£34-£43 dB&B⇄♠£46-£64 LDO 7.30pm
Lic ▥ CTV
Credit Cards ①②③ⓔ

🛏 🍴 **FH** [Q] Mrs L Sparkes **Uplands** *(ST663664)* Wellsway BS18 2SY (off B3116) ☎Bristol(0272) 865764 & 865159
Closed Dec
This large, rambling, creeper-clad farmhouse dating back over 200 years occupies a convenient position near Keynsham and close to both Bath and Bristol. Bedrooms are spacious enough to be used for families. Breakfast is served at separate tables in the dining room.
7rm(3🚿) (4fb) 🚭 in 2 bedrooms 🚭 in dining room 🚭 in lounges CTV in all bedrooms [R] 🐕 (ex guide dogs) sB&B£15-£25 dB&B£30-£40 dB&B🚿£35-£40 WB&B£80-£120
▦ CTV 200 acres dairy

KIDDERMINSTER Hereford & Worcester Map **07** SO87

SELECTED

GH [Q][Q][Q][Q] **Cedars Hotel** Mason Road DY11 6AL (turn off ring rd onto A442 to Bridgenorth then 1st left, hotel opposite police station) (MIN) ☎(0562) 515595 FAX (0562) 751103
Closed 25-31 Dec
Just north of the town centre, this well maintained private hotel provides good quality, well equipped accommodation. Small conferences can be accommodated. Breakfast is available at a supplementary charge.
20🚿 (6fb) 🚭 in 7 bedrooms CTV in 22 bedrooms [R] **T** sB&B🛁🚿£22.50-£43.80 dB&B🛁🚿£25.70-£48 LDO 8.30pm
Lic ▦
Credit Cards [1][2][3][5] [£]

GH [Q][Q] **Collingdale Hotel** 197 Comberton Road DY10 1UE ☎(0562) 515460 & 862839
A friendly small hotel just half a mile from the town centre. Bedrooms are pretty, with floral wallpaper and fabrics, and many are pine furnished. Evening meals are available.
9rm(1🛁3🚿) (2fb) 🚭 in area of dining room CTV in all bedrooms [R] LDO 2pm
Lic ▦ 🏡
[£]

GH [Q][Q] **Gordonhouse Hotel** 194 Comberton Road DY10 1UE (100yds from jct A449/A448) ☎(0562) 822900 FAX (0562) 865626
Bedrooms are neat and clean in this busy hotel near the railway station. The breakfast room and lounge look out onto a pleasant garden. There is a bar for residents.
15rm(1🚿) Annexe 3rm (2fb) 🚭 in dining room CTV in all bedrooms [R] ✱ sB&B£19-£22 sB&B🚿£26-£28 dB&B£32-£38 dB&B🚿£38-£44 LDO 7pm
Lic ▦ CTV
Credit Cards [1][2][3][5] [£]

KIDLINGTON Oxfordshire Map **04** SP41

SELECTED

GH [Q][Q][Q][Q] **Bowood House** 238 Oxford Road OX5 1EB (on the A4260, 4m N of Oxford, opposite Thames Valley Police H.Q.) ☎Oxford(0865) 842288 FAX (0865) 841858
Closed 24 Dec-1 Jan
A modern detached red brick property situated in this large village, only four miles from the centre of Oxford. Ten of the twenty bedrooms are located in the main house, the others are approached by a covered walkway: rooms in the garden wing are all on the ground floor. Bedrooms are well decorated and equipped, with TV, direct-dial telephone, radio alarm, trouser press and hair dryers; the majority have private bathrooms. There is a cosy lounge and well stocked bar, and a wide choice of dishes is offered in the terrace dining room, with a realistically priced à la carte menu; the restaurant is closed on Sundays. There is ample parking at the rear of the property.
10rm(8🛁🚿) Annexe 12🛁🚿 (4fb)CTV in all bedrooms [R] **T** 🐕 (ex guide dogs) ✱ sB&B£32 sB&B🛁🚿£37-£50 dB&B🛁🚿£52-£62 LDO 8.30pm
Lic ▦
Credit Cards [1][3]
See advertisement also under OXFORD

KILBARCHAN Strathclyde *Renfrewshire* Map **10** NS46

GH [Q][Q] **Ashburn** Milliken Park Rd PA10 2DB (follow signs for Johnstone onto B787 and turn right opposite bus garage) ☎(0505) 705477 FAX (0505) 705477
A popular stopover for travellers using Glasgow Airport, this large detached house stands in its own gardens overlooking surrounding farmland. It has a spacious lounge with an honesty bar, and enjoyable home cooking is served at shared tables in the adjacent dining room. Bedrooms are mostly well proportioned.
6rm(2🚿) (3fb)CTV in all bedrooms [R] sB&B£20-£22 sB&B🚿£27-£31 dB&B£34-£38 dB&B🚿£50-£53 WB&Bfr£115 WBDifr£185 LDO 11am
Lic ▦ CTV
Credit Cards [1][3] [£]

KILBURN North Yorkshire Map **08** SE57

INN [Q][Q][Q] **Forresters Arms Hotel** YO6 4AH ☎Coxwold(0347) 868386 & 868550 FAX (0347) 868386
This attractive village inn is situated beneath the famous Kilburn White Horse, next to the parish church, which, together with the

▶

inn was built by the Normans in the 12th century. Bedrooms are modern in style, and although rather compact, are all individually furnished and decorated, with a mixture of pine and mahogany furniture; two rooms have four-poster beds. There are two bars serving a wide range of bar meals at lunchtime and in the evenings. There is also an attractive dining room for evening meals.

10⇄🏠 (2fb) ⊬ in dining room CTV in all bedrooms ® T ✻ sB&B⇄🏠£38 dB&B⇄🏠£56-£66 WB&B£196-£231 WBDi£230-£265 Lunch £3-£6 Dinner £5-£10&alc LDO 9.30pm ▥

Credit Cards 1 3 ⓔ

KILLIECRANKIE Tayside *Perthshire*   Map **14** NN96

GH Ⓠ Ⓠ Ⓠ *Dalnasgadh House* PH16 5LN
☎Pitlochry(0796) 473237
Etr-Oct
Set in its own grounds off the old A9 (B8079) half a mile north of the village, this fine detached period house is spotlessly maintained. Furnishings and decor are traditional, and, together with some fine woodwork, exemplify the character of the house.
5rm ® 🐾 (ex guide dogs)
▥ CTV
See advertisement under PITLOCHRY

KILLIN Central *Perthshire*   Map **11** NN53

SELECTED
GH Ⓠ Ⓠ Ⓠ Ⓠ **Breadalbane House** Main Street FK21 8UT
☎(0567) 820386 FAX (0567) 820386
This detached village-centre house has been tastefully modernised throughout, and is well maintained and spotlessly clean. There is a comfortable lounge and an attractive dining room adorned with ornaments and paintings. Both the dinner and breakfast menus offer a good choice, and the home cooking has been much praised by guests. Whilst some of the bedrooms are compact, all are thoughtfully equipped with extras such as fresh fruit, radios and hair dryers.
5rm(1⇄4🏠) (2fb) ⊬ in bedrooms ⊬ in dining room CTV in all bedrooms ® ✻ sB&B⇄🏠£25-£30 dB&B⇄🏠£34-£40 WB&Bfr£113.40 WBDifr£183.40 LDO 6pm
▥ CTV
Credit Cards 1 3

KILMARNOCK Strathclyde *Ayrshire*   Map **10** NS43

GH Ⓠ Ⓠ Ⓠ **Burnside Hotel** 18 London Road KA3 7AQ
☎(0563) 22952 due to change to 522952 FAX (0563) 73381
Enthusiastic owners Judith and David Dye continue to make improvements at their detached sandstone house, including the provision of more en suite bathrooms to the bright bedrooms. Public areas comprise a spacious lounge and a neat dining room where enjoyable home cooking is served. The house has a relaxed atmosphere and high standards of housekeeping are maintained.
10rm(5⇄3🏠) (4fb) ⊬ in dining room CTV in all bedrooms ®
sB&B⇄🏠£18-£26 dB&B⇄🏠£30-£40 LDO noon
▥ CTV
Credit Cards 1 2 3

🖛 ▼ **GH** Ⓠ Ⓠ **Eriskay** 2 Dean Terrace KA3 1RJ
☎(0563) 32061 due to change to 532061
Eriskay is a detached stone-built house, located north of the town centre, efficiently run by friendly owners Angus and Cathy MacDonald. Bedrooms are bright and airy with modern furnishings, though some of the singles are limited in size. Hearty breakfasts are served at individual tables in the neat dining room, which also has a small lounge area.
6rm(2🏠) (3fb) ⊬ in dining room CTV in all bedrooms ®
sB&B£15-£20 sB&B🏠£19-£20 dB&B£28-£30 dB&B🏠£34-£36

WB&B£95
▥ CTV
ⓔ

KILVE Somerset   Map **03** ST14

P R E M I E R ✺ S E L E C T E D

INN Ⓠ Ⓠ Ⓠ Ⓠ Ⓠ **Hood Arms** TA5 1EA (12m W of Bridgwater on the A39)
☎Holford(0278741) 210
Closed 25 Dec

The busy village in which this seventeenth-century coaching inn stands is an ideal spot from which to explore the beauty of the Quantocks and Somerset coast. Comfortable, well equipped bedrooms offer such thoughtful extras as fresh flowers and iced water, while delicious meals served in a cosy bar offer an alternative to the good choice of dishes featured on the restaurant carte.
5⇄🏠 ⊬ in dining room CTV in all bedrooms ® T
sB&B⇄🏠£36-£38 dB&B⇄🏠£60-£65 WB&B£185-£195 WBDi£280-£300 Bar Lunch £2.25-£3.50alc Dinner £8-£16alc LDO 10pm
▥ nc7yrs
Credit Cards 1 3 ⓔ

KINGHAM Oxfordshire   Map **04** SP22

SELECTED
GH Ⓠ Ⓠ Ⓠ Ⓠ **Conygree Gate** Church Street OX7 6YA (centre of village off A429 & A361) ☎(0608) 658389
Closed 25 Dec-1 Jan
A weathered Cotswold stone farmhouse in the village centre with leaded windows and stone fireplaces, dating back to 1648. There are four bedrooms on the ground floor decorated in original style by Kathryn Sykes. The cosy lounge has an inviting inglenook log fire and leads into a tiny well stocked bar. Meals are served in the country-style dining room.
10rm(1⇄7🏠) (3fb) ⊬ in dining room CTV in all bedrooms ® ✻ sB&B£27 dB&B£50 dB&B⇄🏠£52 WB&Bfr£182 WBDifr£259 LDO 5pm
Lic ▥
Credit Cards 1 3 ⓔ

KINGHORN Fife   Map **11** NT28

INN Ⓠ Ⓠ Ⓠ *Longboat* 107 Pettycur Road KY3 9RU (turn off at the 'Scottish Soldier' memorial on A921) ☎(0592) 890625
Enjoying wonderful views of the Firth of Forth to Edinburgh and the Lothian hills, this friendly family owned and run inn is popular with locals and visitors alike. Bedrooms are all similarly equipped and furnished and two have a balcony and sea view. There are also good views from the restaurant and lounge bar which are open each evening. Light meals are available throughout the day in the Hideaway wine bar situated almost on the water's edge. A fine function suite has been built to resemble the inside of an old sailing ship.
6⇄🏠 CTV in all bedrooms ® LDO 9.30pm
▥
Credit Cards 1 2 3 5

KINGSBRIDGE Devon   Map **03** SX74

GH Ⓠ Ⓠ Ⓠ **Ashleigh House** Ashleigh Road, Westville TQ7 1HB
☎(0548) 852893 FAX (0548) 852893

rs Nov-Mar

This friendly guesthouse is situated on the edge of the town off the Salcombe road, and is an ideal base for touring the South Hams. The first-floor bedrooms feature patchwork quilts, all have tea-making facilities, and colour TV is available by prior arrangement. Home-cooked dishes are served daily in the spacious dining room, and Mike and Jenny Taylor are always on hand to assist guests.

8rm(3🚿) (1fb) 🚭 in bedrooms 🚭 in dining room CTV in 4 bedrooms Ⓡ sB&B£20-£21 sB&B🚿£22-£23 dB&B£30-£32 dB&B🚿£34-£36 WB&B£98-£119 WBDi£164-£185 LDO 4pm

Lic CTV

Credit Cards [1] [3]

GH [Q][Q][Q] South Allington House Chivelstone TQ7 2NB ☎Chivelstone(0548) 511272 FAX (0548) 511272

The Baker family farm locally and Barbara Baker welcomes guests to their charming listed period house, where a no-smoking policy is in force and morning coffees and afternoon teas are served. Bedrooms are attractively decorated and comfortable, and electric blankets are supplied for the colder months.

11rm(5🛁🚿) (2fb) 🚭 CTV in 1 bedroom Ⓡ 🐕 (ex guide dogs) sB&B£18-£19 dB&B£32-£34 dB&B🛁🚿£37-£48

♨ CTV 🎣 croquet bowls

[£]

KINGS CAPLE Hereford & Worcester — Map **03** SO52

INN[Q] *British Lion* Fawley HR1 4UQ ☎Carey(0432) 840280

One of only three inns of this name in Great Britain, this remotely situated establishment lies in a quiet backwater south of Hereford. Accommodation is adequate and there is a cosy bar with a friendly atmosphere where regulars meet.

3 Ⓡ LDO 9pm

♨ CTV

KINGSDOWN Kent — Map **05** TR34

GH [Q][Q][Q] Blencathra Country Kingsdown Hill CT14 8EA ☎Deal(0304) 373725

An attractive modern detached country guest house, surrounded by a pleasant garden and close to the sea, is quietly situated in a peaceful side road of this sleepy village. Rooms are attractively decorated and of a good size. There is a well appointed, comfortable lounge, a small honesty bar and a smart dining room which overlooks the garden.

7rm(4🚿) (3fb) 🚭 in bedrooms 🚭 in dining room CTV in all bedrooms Ⓡ 🐕 (ex guide dogs) ✱ sB&B£17-£20 sB&B🚿£20-£25 dB&B£34-£38 dB&B🚿£36-£38 WB&B£108-£140

Lic CTV croquet lawn

KINGSEY Buckinghamshire — Map **04** SP70

FH [Q][Q][Q] Mr & Mrs N M D Hooper **Foxhill** *(SP748066)* HP17 8LZ (from Thame take A4129 to Kingsey, farm is last house on right) ☎Haddenham(0844) 291650

Feb-Nov

The Hoopers offer a friendly welcome at their white-painted, listed farmhouse, which is set back in lovely grounds complete with duck pond. An added bonus is the swimming pool, which is available for use during warmer weather. The first floor bedrooms are spacious with oak-beamed ceilings, and pleasantly furnished. Downstairs there is an entrance hall with polished quarry tiles and a cheerful lounge/breakfast room.

3rm 🚭 CTV in all bedrooms Ⓡ 🐕 (ex guide dogs) sB&B£20-£22 dB&B£38-£40 WB&B£133-£154

♨ CTV nc5yrs 🏊(heated) 4 acres non-working

[£]

KINGSLEY Cheshire — Map **07** SJ57

GH [Q][Q][Q] Charnwood Hollow Lane WA6 8EF ☎(0928) 787097 FAX (0928) 788566

2rm(1🛁🚿) (1fb) 🚭 CTV in 1 bedroom Ⓡ **T** 🐕 sB&B£18-£20 sB&B🛁🚿£25 dB&B£36-£40 dB&B🛁🚿£45

♨ CTV

KING'S LYNN Norfolk — Map **09** TF62

See also Tottenhill

GH [Q][Q] Beeches 2 Guannock Terrace PE30 5QT ☎(0553) 766577 FAX (0553) 776664

A family-run Victorian house, the Beeches is located in a quiet residential area to the south-east of the town. Freshly cooked meals are served in the dining room which overlooks a well tended garden. Most of the bedrooms are spacious and each one has a direct-dial telephone.

7rm(4🛁🚿) (2fb) CTV in all bedrooms Ⓡ **T** ✱ sB&Bfr£20 sB&B🛁🚿fr£26 dB&Bfr£32 dB&B🛁🚿fr£38 LDO 4.30pm

Lic ♨ CTV

Credit Cards [1] [3]

GH [Q][Q][Q] Fairlight Lodge 79 Goodwins Road PE30 5PE ☎(0553) 762234 FAX (0553) 770280

Closed 24-26 Dec

A tastefully furnished Victorian house, Fairlight Lodge is set in neat gardens with ample private parking. There is a comfortable lounge with an open fire, books and a music system, and a dining room where a good choice of hearty breakfasts is served. Main house and garden rooms offer a range of en suite and ground-floor bedrooms, all pleasantly decorated.

7rm(4🚿) (1fb) 🚭 in 2 bedrooms 🚭 in dining room 🚭 in lounges CTV in all bedrooms Ⓡ sB&B£16 sB&B🚿£20-£25 dB&B£30 dB&B🚿£38

♨

[£]

GH [Q][Q] Guanock Hotel South Gate PE30 5JG (Follow signs to town centre. Establishment immediately on right of South Gates) ☎(0553) 772959

A predominantly business establishment, the Guanock is located south of the centre just inside the town gate. The bedrooms tend to be small, but are neat in appearance and spotlessly clean. An evening meal is served in the cheerful dining room, and bar meals and light refreshments are available in either the pool lounge or small bar.

17rm (5fb) 🚭 in 8 bedrooms 🚭 in dining room CTV in all bedrooms Ⓡ 🐕 (ex guide dogs) sB&B£22-£23 dB&B£32-£34 LDO 5pm

Lic ♨ pool room

Credit Cards [1] [2] [3] [5] [£]

GH [Q][Q][Q] *Havana* 117 Gaywood Road PE30 2PU ☎(0553) 772331

Closed Xmas

To find the Havana, from the A17 to the town centre, take the last exit at the mini roundabout to Gaywood and continue to the very end, turn right at the T-junction and the guesthouse is a few yards along on the left. It is a small terraced property continually improved by proprietors Mr and Mrs Breed. All the bedrooms have now been redecorated using the Country Diary wild flowers scheme with matching fabrics and décor, together with pastel painted chairs and marble effect vanity shelves. The dining room and lounge is combined, the tables set with colourful waxed cloths.

7rm(2🚿) (1fb) CTV in all bedrooms Ⓡ 🐕

♨ CTV

GH [Q] Maranatha 115 Gaywood Road PE30 2PU ☎(0553) 774596

Competitively priced accommodation is offered at this guest house catering mainly for the business traveller. Bedrooms, although on the small side, are generally fresh looking. The strikingly decorated lounge has a good gas fire, colour TV and organ for guests' use. Evening meals and snacks are readily available.

▶

6rm(1🚿) (2fb) 🚭 in dining room CTV in all bedrooms [R] ✳ sB&B£15-£17 dB&Bfr£26 dB&B🚿fr£30 LDO 6pm
♨ CTV
[£]

SELECTED

GH [Q][Q][Q][Q] Russet House Hotel 53 Goodwins Road PE30 5PE ☎(0553) 773098 FAX (0553) 773098
Closed Xmas & New Year

A warm welcome is provided by owners Rae and Barry Muddle at this extended Victorian house. There are twelve well-kept bedrooms of varying size, all with private facilities and many additional personal touches. Cosy public rooms include a bar, lounge and dining room where home-cooked food is served. In addition there is a garden and plenty of parking.

12rm(8🛁4🚿) (1fb) 🚭 in 1 bedrooms 🚭 in dining room CTV in all bedrooms [R] **T** 🐕 (ex guide dogs) ✳ sB&B🛁🚿£29.50-£42.50 dB&B🛁🚿fr£46.50 LDO 7.45pm
Lic ♨
Credit Cards [1][2][3][5]

KINGSTON Devon Map **03** SX64

SELECTED

GH [Q][Q][Q][Q] Trebles Cottage Hotel TQ7 4PT
☎Bigbury-on-Sea(0548) 810268 FAX (0548) 810268

This pretty cottage stands at the top of a tranquil village, only a mile from a sandy beach and 12 miles from Plymouth. The bedrooms vary in size and furnishings but all are well equipped. The comfortable sitting room with large sofas is partly wood-panelled and has an open log fire on cooler evenings. A small cocktail bar leads into the dining room, where breakfast and an optional four-course evening meal using local fresh produce are served. There is a delightful sunny terrace and garden and ample private parking.

5🛁🚿 🚭 in 3 bedrooms 🚭 in dining room CTV in all bedrooms [R] ✳ sB&B🛁🚿£30-£36 dB&B🛁🚿£45-£60 WB&B£157.50-£210 WBDi£230-£277.50 LDO 4pm
Lic ♨ nc12yrs
Credit Cards [1][2][3] [£]

KINGSTON BAGPUIZE Oxfordshire Map **04** SU49

PREMIER SELECTED

GH [Q][Q][Q][Q][Q]
Fallowfields OX13 5BH
☎Longworth(0865) 820416
Telex no 83388
FAX (0865) 820629

A stone-built house going back 300 years, once the home of the Begum Aga Khan, today in the capable hands of Anthony and Peta Lloyd. It is surrounded by its own land including croquet lawn, swimming pool and productive kitchen garden. In one field, a copse and a large pond are being nurtured to create a wildlife sanctuary. Peta Lloyd is an accomplished cook.

4🛁🚿 🚭 CTV in all bedrooms [R] **T** ✳ sB&B🛁🚿£40-£64 dB&B🛁🚿£55-£73 WB&B£178-£249 WBDi£358-£429 LDO 6.30pm
Lic ♨ CTV nc10yrs 🏊(heated) 🎾(hard)croquet lawn
Credit Cards [1][2][3] [£]

KINGUSSIE Highland *Inverness-shire* Map **14** NH70

SELECTED

GH [Q][Q][Q][Q] *Avondale House* Newtonmore Road PH21 1HF
☎(0540) 66173
7rm(3🛁🚿) (1fb) CTV in all bedrooms [R] LDO 5pm
♨

GH [Q][Q] *Craig An Darach* High Street PH21 1JE
☎(0540) 661235
Closed Nov-Dec

From its elevated position, this imposing Victorian house overlooks the Spey Valley and the Grampians. Bedrooms vary in size and offer a mixture of modern and traditional furnishings. There is an impressive panelled entrance hall and a lounge/dining room, where breakfast may be served at shared tables at busy times. This is a no smoking establishment.

3🚿 (1fb) [R]
♨ CTV

GH [Q][Q][Q] Homewood Lodge Newtonmore Road PH21 1HD
☎(0540) 661507

Fine views over the Spey Valley are enjoyed from this sturdy Victorian house which stands in an elevated position at the south side of the town. The spacious bedrooms are decorated in soft pastel shades and offer mixed styles of furnishings. There is a quiet lounge with TV and books, and imaginative home cooking is served in the attractive pine-furnished dining room. Smoking is not permitted.

4🚿 (2fb) 🚭 [R] 🐕 (ex guide dogs) sB&B🚿£19.50-£21.50 dB&B🚿£39-£43 WB&B£130-£150 WBDi£203.50-£223.50 LDO 3pm
♨ CTV nc5yrs

GH [Q][Q] *Sonnhalde* East Terrace PH21 1JS ☎(0540) 661266
Closed Nov & Dec

A solid detached Victorian house is set on a hillside above the town, with fine views over the Spey Valley and Cairngorms. Accommodation is offered in bedrooms which vary in size and appointments; smoking is not permitted. There is a pleasant lounge and enjoyable home cooking is offered in the dining room. Special wildlife, fishing and photography packages are available on application.

8rm (3fb) CTV in 1 bedroom LDO 2pm
♨ CTV

KINROSS Tayside *Kinross-shire* Map **11** NO10

INN[Q][Q][Q] The Muirs Inn 49 Muirs KY13 7AU
☎(0577) 862270 FAX (0577) 862270

With its entrance just off the main road on the northern side of the town, this inn has been tastefully modernised whilst retaining much of its cottage style character. The bedrooms lie above the bars and are reached by means of an outside door. Whilst compact, they are nicely decorated and very well equipped to include radios and trouser presses. The inn has a popular restaurant and the bar lunch menu is particularly impressive. It is also renowned for its real ales.

5🛁🚿 CTV in all bedrooms [R] 🐕 (ex guide dogs) sB&B🛁🚿£35 dB&B🛁🚿£55 WB&B£164.50 WBDi£234.50 Lunch £9.50-£12.95&alc High tea £4.75-£6.95&alc Dinner £10.95-£14.95&alc LDO 9pm
♨ nc11yrs
Credit Cards [1][3] [£]

KINVER Staffordshire Map **07** SO88

INN[Q][Q][Q] Kinfayre Restaurant 41 High Street DY7 6HF
☎(0384) 872565 FAX (0384) 877724

A fully modernised inn situated in the heart of the village, with

well equipped bedrooms in a separate building. Evenings are busy here with the skittle alley, but peace and quiet can be found in the private gardens which have a heated pool for residents' use only.
11🐾 (1fb) ⌇ in dining room ⌇ in lounges CTV in all bedrooms Ⓡ 🏠 (ex guide dogs) ✳ sB&B🐾fr£30 dB&B🐾fr£50 WB&Bfr£175 Lunch £3.95-£7.35&alc Dinner £4.95-£9.95&alc LDO 10pm
🏧 CTV ⌇(heated) skittle alley
Credit Cards ①③

KIPPFORD Dumfries & Galloway *Kirkcudbright* Map **11** NX85

GH ⓠⓠⓠ **Boundary Cottage** Barnbarroch DG5 4QS (from Dalbeattie take A710, Solway coast rd, for 2m. Boundary Cottage on left) ☎(0556) 620247
Closed Xmas
This lovingly cared for cottage, surrounded by beautiful countryside offers a good standard of accommodation. There is a delightful garden where Mrs Williams keeps hens and geese, and a comfortable lounge with garden views.
3rm (1fb) ⌇ in dining room ⌇ in lounges CTV in all bedrooms Ⓡ ✳ dB&B£30-£33 dB&B£32-£35 WB&B£95-£104 WBDi£147.50-£156.50
🏧 CTV

KIRKBEAN Dumfries & Galloway *Dumfriesshire* Map **11** NX95

SELECTED

GH ⓠⓠⓠⓠ **Cavens House** DG2 8AA (on A710)
☎(038788) 234
A delightful country mansion with many historical connections, Cavens House is set in eleven acres of mature gardens and woodland close to the Solway coast. Bedrooms are spacious and well furnished; two are located on the ground floor. The large lounge has a piano, TV, board games and an honesty bar. A games room and a putting green are also provided. The four-course evening meal is very much a feature, served in the attractive dining room overlooking the gardens.
6rm(4⇄2🐾) (1fb) ⌇ in dining room CTV in all bedrooms Ⓡ ✳ sB&B⇄🐾£25-£35 dB&B⇄🐾£48-£56 WBDi£239-£289 LDO 7pm
Lic 🏧 CTV ♨
Credit Cards ①③Ⓔ

KIRKBY LONSDALE Cumbria   Map **07** SD67

PREMIER ❀ SELECTED

GH ⓠⓠⓠⓠⓠ **Cobwebs**
Country House Leck, Cowan
Bridge LA6 2HZ
☎(05242) 72141
FAX (05242) 72141
Mar-Dec rs Sun
This charming 17th-century farmhouse is peacefully located just off the A65 at Cowan Bridge, two miles southeast of the town. The house has been carefully furnished, with great success, to create a country house atmosphere, with the friendly young owners Paul Kelly and Yvonne Thompson devoting much attention to their guests' well being. The five delightful bedrooms are superbly furnished, with every modern facility and several thoughtful extras. There are two charming lounges, one with an open log fire, with plenty of books, magazines and fresh flowers

▶

Russet House Hotel

Tel: King's Lynn (01553) 773098 👑 👑 👑

One of the nicest old houses in one of the most historic Towns in England. Set in beautiful secluded gardens a short walk from Town Centre and River Ouse. Four poster suite. Pretty en suite rooms with TV and courtesy Tea/Coffee.

Cosy little bar – roaring fire in winter!

Elegant Dining Room – good food. Ample room to park your car.

Rae & Barry Muddle (we try not to live up to our name!)

Vancouver Ave/Goodwins Road, King's Lynn Norfolk PE30 5PE

THE MUIRS INN KINROSS

A TRADITIONAL SCOTTISH COUNTRY INN
– That's Simply Something Special
Appointed by Taste of Scotland and listed as "One of Scotland's Best Pubs" recommended by CAMRA in their Good Beer Guide, approved by Les Routier and awarded 3 crowns with Commendation by the Scottish Tourist Board and 3Q's by the AA, it is full of character and offers comfort and ambience throughout including its 5 en-suite bedrooms. Award nominated, home cooked Fresh Country Fayre at sensible prices is served from Breakfast to Supper (including Traditional Scottish High Teas) every day of the year in its own popular Maltings & Cellar Restaurant rooms. The Mash Tun & Wee Still Bars serve a connoisseurs choice of a Rare Range of Scottish Fruit Wines & Real Ales plus a superb selection of Malt Whiskies as well as an amazing array of Beers, Wines & Spirits from all over the world. This charming Inn hosts intimate parties of up to 30 guests for all occasions. The ideal venue for business or pleasure and a superb holiday centre with 130 golf courses and all major cities within driving distance. **Write or Ring for Brochure, Tariff & Details to:**
THE INNKEEPER
49 MUIRS, KINROSS, SCOTLAND. Tel: 01577 862270

everywhere. Tempting four-course dinners with a choice of starter are served in the attractive conservatory restaurant, with top quality fresh produce a feature.
5⇌↿ CTV in all bedrooms Ⓡ ⫟ LDO 7.30pm
Lic ▥ nc12yrs ⤴
Credit Cards ①③

P R E M I E R 🏵 S E L E C T E D

GH ⓆⓆⓆⓆⓆ Hipping Hall Hotel Cowan Bridge
LA6 2JJ (on A65)
☎(05242) 71187
FAX (05242) 72452
Closed Jan

This handsome country house in beautiful, secluded gardens stands back from the A65 two miles southeast of Kirkby Lonsdale, on the Cumbrian/ Yorkshire border; the remains of a hamlet dating back to the fifteenth century, it gains great character and charm from retained features reminiscent of a very early age. Attractively decorated and very comfortable bedrooms furnished with antiques offer en suite facilities, telephones and television sets, the two in an adjacent converted coach house also being equipped for self catering. A five-course evening meal is served, dinner party style, in the Great Hall (complete with minstrels' gallery), the price including a different wine to complement each dish. This delightful hotel will please not only the holiday-maker but also any business person looking for peace and seclusion.
7rm(6⇌1↿) ⊬ in dining room CTV in all bedrooms Ⓡ T ✳ sB&B⇌↿£62 dB&B⇌↿£78 LDO 6.30pm
Lic ▥ CTV nc12yrs
Credit Cards ①③ⓔ

KIRKBYMOORSIDE North Yorkshire   Map 08 SE68

S E L E C T E D

GH ⓆⓆⓆⓆ Appletree Court Town Farm, 9 High Market Place YO6 6AT ☎(0751) 431536
This mellow grey stone cottage was once part of a working farm, and original timbers from the old hayloft are still visible. Now the home of Jean and Fred Adamson, it is situated at the top end of the town and is easy to find. The bedrooms are named after varieties of apples, and are charmingly furnished and decorated with Laura Ashley fabrics, books, magazines and several extra touches. Downstairs there is a combined dining room/lounge which is comfortable and tastefully furnished and decorated. Smoking is not permitted.
4⇌↿ ⊬ CTV in all bedrooms ⫟ ✳ sB&B⇌↿£27 dB&B⇌↿£42 LDO noon
▥ nc12yrs

KIRKCUDBRIGHT Dumfries & Galloway
Kirkcudbrightshire   Map 11 NX65

S E L E C T E D

GH ⓆⓆⓆⓆ Gladstone House 48 High Street DG6 4JX
☎(0557) 331734
Situated in the High Street, opposite the historic tolbooth, this beautifully restored Georgian town house offers just three bedrooms of an exemplary standard, all with modern en suite facilities. The spacious lounge runs along the entire width of

the building and offers views of the garden to the rear. Breakfast is served in the attractively appointed little dining room.
3⇌↿ ⊬ CTV in all bedrooms Ⓡ ⫟ (ex guide dogs)
dB&B⇌↿£50
▥ nc14yrs
Credit Cards ①③ⓔ

KIRK IRETON Derbyshire   Map 08 SK25

INNⓆⓆ *Barley Mow* Main Street, Kirk Ireton DE6 3JP
☎Ashbourne(0335) 370306
Closed Xmas wk
An inn full of character and charm is situated in the small, hilltop village of Kirk Ireton. Built in 1683, the imposing building offers a more modern bedroom annexe that is decorated and furnished to a country style in keeping with the character of the inn, and all rooms are equipped with TV and tea-making facilities. The beamed cottage parlour, with its solid fuel fire and piano, forms a small, cosy bar area. Evening meals are served by arrangement and special diets along with vegetarians can be catered for. Outside, the large walled garden is available for guests to use and there is ample off-street parking.
5rm(4⇌1↿) (1fb) CTV in all bedrooms Ⓡ LDO noon
▥

KIRKMUIRHILL Strathclyde *Lanarkshire*   Map 11 NS74

FH Ⓠ Mrs I H McInally **Dykecroft** *(NS776419)* ML11 0JQ (on A726, 1.5m towards Strathaven) ☎Lesmahagow(0555) 892226
Good-value bed and breakfast accommodation is offered at this modern bungalow-style farmhouse, which is set amid gentle rolling countryside beside the Strathaven road. Bedrooms are small with neat decor and traditional furnishings, and there is a comfortable lounge/dining room where hearty breakfasts are served, occasionally at shared tables. Smoking is not encouraged in the rooms.
3rm ⊬ in bedrooms ⊬ in dining room Ⓡ ✳ sB&B£16-£18 dB&B£29-£31 WB&B£100-£115
▥ CTV 60 acres sheep
ⓔ

KIRKOSWALD Cumbria   Map 12 NY54

S E L E C T E D

GH ⓆⓆⓆⓆ **Prospect Hill Hotel** CA10 1ER
☎Lazonby(0768) 898500 FAX (0768) 898088
Closed 24-26 Dec
Sympathetically developed from an interesting collection of 18th-century farm buildings several years ago, this delightful hotel set in open countryside a mile north of the village provides an excellent base from which to explore the area. Bedrooms - many of them retaining their stone walls - are individually decorated and furnished; some feature brass bedsteads while others have patchwork quilts, homespun curtains and thick carpets. Guests can relax over a drink in the former byre, now a charming and characterful bar with beamed ceiling, flagged floor and an abundance of old farm implements.
9rm(4⇌↿) Annexe 2⇌↿ (1fb) ⊬ in area of dining room CTV in 2 bedrooms Ⓡ ⫟ ✳ sB&B⇌↿£40 dB&B£46 dB&B⇌↿£60 LDO 8.45pm
Lic ▥ CTV croquet clock golf barbecue patio
Credit Cards ①②③ⓔ

KIRKWHELPINGTON Northumberland Map **12** NY98

SELECTED

GH [Q][Q][Q][Q] Shieldhall Wallington, Cambo NE61 4AQ (towards Wallington Hall & Rothbury 0.25m E of crossroads A696/B6342) ☎Otterburn(0830) 40387 FAX (0830) 40387

Though this charming guest house stands in delightful rural surroundings it is only a short distance from the A696. Developed from eighteenth-century farm buildings, it provides accommodation in bedrooms set around three sides of a large courtyard with lawns and flower borders in the centre; antique pieces are very much in evidence in the two comfortably furnished lounges (one with television, the other containing a hidden bar) and in a dining room featuring an inglenook fireplace and a wealth of objets d'art. A four-course dinner menu is firmly based on fresh, seasonal produce.

6rm(5🛁🚿) (1fb) CTV in 4 bedrooms [R] 🐕 (ex guide dogs) * dB&Bfr£38 dB&B🛁🚿£44 LDO noon

Lic 🅿 CTV nc13yrs

KIRTLING Cambridgeshire Map **05** TL65

FH [Q][Q] Mrs C A Bailey **Hill** *(TL685585)* CB8 9HQ ☎Newmarket(0638) 730253

Situated midway between Saxon Street and the village of Kirtling, this is a traditional 16th-century farmhouse with a modern exterior, surrounded by arable and pasture farmland. Accommodation is comfortable and clean and the public rooms include a lounge and dining room with open log fires and a games room.

3rm(2🚿) CTV in 1 bedroom [R] * sB&B£22 sB&B🚿£22 dB&B£40 dB&B🚿£40 LDO 8.30pm

Lic 🅿 CTV games room 500 acres arable

[£]

See advertisement under NEWMARKET

KIRTON Nottinghamshire Map **08** SK66

GH [Q][Q][Q] ***Old Rectory*** Main Street NG22 9LP ☎Mansfield(0623) 860083 Telex no 378505 FAX (0623) 860751

Closed Xmas & New Year

A former Georgian rectory, set back from the village High Street in neatly tended grounds, offers fresh, inviting bedrooms and a choice of eating styles - informal meals in the lounge bar or a more substantial choice in the dining room.

10rm(5🚿) (1fb) [R] 🐕 (ex guide dogs) LDO 7pm

Lic CTV

Credit Cards [1][3]

KNARESBOROUGH North Yorkshire Map **08** SE35

GH [Q][Q][Q] ***Newton House Hotel*** 5/7 York Place HG5 0AD ☎Harrogate(0423) 863539 FAX (0423) 869748

Friendly service is provided by the resident owners of this guest house. It is a very attractive Grade II Georgian building and offers easy access to the town centre from its position on the A59 York road. Particularly spacious bedrooms are attractively decorated and thoughtfully equipped, a good-sized lounge has very comfortable seating and the elegant dining room is newly furnished. There is on site parking.

10rm(9🛁🚿) Annexe 2rm(1🛁1🚿) (3fb) CTV in all bedrooms [R] LDO 7pm

Lic 🅿 CTV

Credit Cards [1][3]

See advertisement under HARROGATE

GH [Q][Q][Q] The Villa The Villa Hotel, 47 Kirkgate HG5 8BZ ☎Harrogate(0423) 865370 FAX (0423) 867740

This charming character house standing next to the railway station, near the town centre, offers accommodation in attractively furnished bars equipped with telephones and mini-bars. A delightful breakfast lounge overlooks the River Nidd, and there is also a comfortable lounge; service is attentive and the atmosphere warm and friendly throughout.

6rm(4🚿) (1fb) 🚭 in dining room CTV in all bedrooms [R] **T** sB&B£16.50 dB&B🚿£40 WB&B£140

Lic 🅿 CTV ⊘

[£]

KNOWLE West Midlands Map **07** SP17

GH [Q][Q][Q] Ivy House Warwick Road, Heronfield B93 0EB (3m from junct 5 of M42, on A4141) ☎(0564) 770247 FAX (0564) 770247

A 250-year-old property, rendered white and attractively covered in virginia creeper, Ivy House is situated a mile and a half out of Knowle. Guest accommodation is separate from that of the owners, and the bedrooms are improving all the time. Bathrooms are modern and all of a good size. There is a combined lounge and dining room where light evening snacks can be provided.

8🚿 (1fb) 🚭 CTV in all bedrooms [R] sB&B🚿£25-£28 dB&B🚿£40-£46

🅿 CTV 🎣

[£]

KNUTSFORD Cheshire Map **07** SJ77

GH [Q][Q][Q] The Hinton Town Lane, Mobberley WA16 7HH ☎Mobberley(0565) 873484 FAX (0565) 873484

This large house stands on the B5085 in the village of Mobberley, three miles north-east of Knutsford, and has a pleasant garden. The modern bedrooms are all attractively decorated and equipped with a telephone point, for which a portable pay phone can be provided. Two of the bedrooms and the adjacent bathroom can be let as a family suite. Separate tables are provided in the brightly decorated dining room, and the hotel is licensed.

4rm(2🛁🚿) (1fb) 🚭 CTV in all bedrooms [R] 🐕 (ex guide dogs) * sB&Bfr£27 sB&B🛁🚿fr£30 dB&Bfr£39 dB&B🛁🚿fr£48 WB&Bfr£182 WBDifr£245 LDO 4.30pm

Lic 🅿

Credit Cards [1][2][3][5]

GH [Q][Q] ***Pickmere House*** Park Lane, Pickmere WA16 0JX ☎(0565) 733433

Closed Xmas

Dating from 1772, this imposing house stands in the village of Pickmere. Its mainly spacious bedrooms are traditionally furnished but equipped with modern facilities. There is a comfortable lounge extending into two rooms, and dinner is served by prior arrangement in the beamed dining room. The house is no-smoking throughout.

9rm(5🚿) (3fb) CTV in all bedrooms [R]

🅿 CTV

See advertisement on p.243.

SELECTED

INN[Q][Q][Q][Q] ***The Dog Inn*** Well Bank Lane, Over Peover WA16 8UP ☎Chelford(0625) 861421

This popular and very well maintained inn stands in the village of Over Peover. Traditionally furnished bedrooms have modern facilities plus thoughtful extras such as fresh fruit, biscuits etc. A good selection of home-cooked dishes is displayed on a blackboard menu and can be served either in the pleasant lounge bar or adjacent dining room.

3🛁🚿 CTV in all bedrooms [R] 🐕 (ex guide dogs) LDO 9.30pm

🅿 pool table

KYLESKU Highland *Sutherland*   Map **14** NC23

SELECTED

GH ▢▢▢▢ **Newton Lodge** IV27 4HW (1.5m S on A894)
☎(0971) 502070
Etr-mid Oct
8rm(2⇄6↑) ⊁ in bedrooms CTV in 6 bedrooms ® ✳
sB&B⇄↑£23.50-£25 dB&B⇄↑£47-£50 LDO 7.30pm
Lic Ⅷ CTV nc13yrs
Credit Cards ① ③

INN▢▢▢ **Kylesku Hotel** IV27 4HW ☎Scourie(0971) 502231
FAX (0971) 502313
Mar-Oct
7⇄↑ (1fb) ⊁ in dining room CTV in all bedrooms ® ✳
sB&B⇄↑£16.50-£25 dB&B⇄↑£35-£48 Lunch £9.95-£20
Dinner £9.95-£20 LDO 9pm
Ⅷ CTV ✔ pool table
Credit Cards ① ③ ⓔ

LACOCK Wiltshire   Map **03** ST96

P R E M I E R 🖑 **S E L E C T E D**

GH ▢▢▢▢▢ **At the
Sign of the Angel** 6 Church
Street SN15 2LA
☎Chippenham(0249) 730230
FAX (0249) 730527
Closed 23 Dec-30 Dec

This ancient property of
enormous character is in the
centre of the National Trust
village of Lacock, which is in
itself steeped in history.
Access to the M4 is easy via
Chippenham, and Bath is only a short drive away. The Sign of
the Angel dates back to the 15th century and has been run
since 1953 by the Levis family, who are always on hand to
offer a friendly welcome to guests. The two dining rooms and
the first-floor lounge have log fires during the winter months,
and the guesthouse has gained a reputation for good traditional
English cooking. The set-price menu is good value; a
vegetarian or fish dish may be ordered instead of the daily
roast, complemented by a wide selection of starters and
desserts. Each bedroom has been individually decorated and
lavishly furnished with beautiful antique pieces in keeping
with the style of the building. There are four bedrooms in a
cottage annexe, and all the rooms have modern facilities and
many thoughtful extras such as fresh flowers and mineral
water.
6⇄ Annexe 3⇄ (1fb)CTV in all bedrooms ® T
sB&B⇄£55-£75 dB&B⇄£75-£95 LDO 9pm
Lic Ⅷ nc10yrs
Credit Cards ① ② ③

LADYBANK Fife   Map **11** NO30

GH ▢▢▢ **Redlands Country Lodge** KY7 7SH ☎(0337) 31091
Closed 2wks Mar
This converted gamekeeper's cottage about half a mile to the east
of the village offers accommodation in a Norwegian-style pine
lodge. Well equipped bedrooms each have their own entrance, and
there is a comfortable lounge. The dining room is in the orginal
cottage.
4↑ (1fb) CTV in all bedrooms ® ✗ (ex guide dogs) LDO 2pm
Lic Ⅷ CTV

LAMBERHURST Kent   Map **05** TQ63

INN▢▢ **George & Dragon** School Hill TN3 8DQ
☎(0892) 890277
Set in the centre of this small village on the main A21, the George
and Dragon offers basic accomodation in good-sized bedrooms,
attractively decorated and well-equipped. The main bar has some
comfortable seating and a good selection of bar snacks, while an à
la carte menu is seved in the well-appointed dining room.
6rm(4⇄↑) (1fb) CTV in all bedrooms ® ✗ (ex guide dogs)
LDO 9.30pm
Ⅷ pool table
Credit Cards ① ③

LAMBOURN Berkshire   Map **04** SU37

SELECTED

FH ▢▢▢▢ Mr & Mrs Cook **Lodge Down** *(SU302777)*
The Woodlands RG16 7BJ (take B3400 from Lambourn, then
follow signs for Baydon, farm 1m E of Baydon)
☎Marlborough(0672) 40304 FAX (0672) 40304
This attractive farmhouse lies in tranquil countryside with
splendid views across the gallops of Lambourn Downs. Its
own grounds include a swimming pool (for summer use) and a
training course for horses. The spacious sitting room has a
television and a real fire in winter. Breakfast is served round
a large mahogany table. Bedrooms are all on the first floor,
are of a good size and decorated and furnished in period; all
have en suite bathrooms. Owners John and Sally Cook offer
their guests a friendly and informal welcome which puts them
at their ease.
3⇄↑ (1fb) ⊁ in bedrooms ® ✗ (ex guide dogs) sB&B£18-
£25 dB&Bfr£40
Ⅷ CTV ✎ ⚲(hard)75 acres
ⓔ
See advertisement under NEWBURY

LANCASTER Lancashire   Map **07** SD46

GH ▢▢▢ **Lancaster Town House** 11/12 Newton Terrace,
Caton Road LA1 3PB (1m from exit 34 of M6) ☎(0524) 65527
Neat bedrooms and comfortable public areas are offered at this
well furnished guesthouse, which caters for business guests and
tourists alike. Service is friendly and helpful.
5rm(2⇄3↑) (2fb) ⊁ in dining room ⊁ in lounges CTV in all
bedrooms ® ✗ (ex guide dogs) ✳ sB&B⇄↑£22-£25
dB&B⇄↑£34.50-£40
Ⅷ ✎ nc4yrs

LANGHOLM Dumfries & Galloway
Dumfriesshire   Map **11** NY38

GH ▢▢ **Langholm Guest House & Restaurant** 81 High Street
DG13 0DJ ☎(03873) 81343
Enthusiastic young owners are steadily improving this small
guesthouse in the centre of town. The bedrooms towards the back
of the house offer the best facilities. There is a cosy lounge, and a
good range of meals in the restaurant, which is open all day.
4rm(1↑) (2fb) ⊁ in bedrooms ⊁ in area of dining room CTV in
all bedrooms ® ✳ sB&B£17.50 dB&B£35 dB&B↑£42 LDO
9pm
Lic Ⅷ ✎9
ⓔ

LANGLAND BAY West Glamorgan   Map **02** SS68

See also Bishopston and Mumbles

GH ▢▢▢ **Wittemberg Hotel** SA3 4QN
☎Swansea(0792) 369696 FAX (0792) 366995
Closed 5-30 Jan

In a quiet spot just a short walk from the beach, this comfortable hotel has seen improvements with the new owners, the Thomas family, embarking on a refurbishment programme at the beginning of 1994. Bedrooms are well equipped, with pleasant decor and fabrics, and there is a comfortable lounge and bar. On-site car parking is provided.

11rm(10♠) (3fb) ⚤ in dining room CTV in all bedrooms ® ✻ (ex guide dogs) ✱ sB&B♠£26-£32 dB&B£30-£36 dB&B♠£40-£52 WB&B£100-£150 WBDi£130-£195 LDO 7pm
Lic ⬛ CTV
Credit Cards [1] [2] [3]

LANGPORT Somerset   Map **03** ST42

PREMIER 🦌 **SELECTED**

GH QQQQQ *Hillards*
High Street, Curry Rivel
TA10 0EY ☎(0458) 251737

A delightful Grade II listed building, once a working farm dating back to the 17th century is still full of old world charm, with a wealth of oak and elm panelled walls, beamed ceilings and large open fireplaces. The bedrooms display a style and charm in keeping with the period, with the emphasis on guests' comfort. A hearty breakfast is served in the dining room at a large oak table, and the courtyard is a pleasant place to sit and relax on warm evenings. An attractive outbuilding conversion now provides some self-catering accommodation. Smoking is not permitted. Situated on the A378, it is very convenient for the A303 or junction 25 of the M5.
4rm(1⇨♠) Annexe 2⇨♠ ✻ (ex guide dogs)
⬛ CTV nc

LARGS Strathclyde *Ayrshire*   Map **10** NS25

SELECTED

GH QQQQ **Lea-Mar** 20 Douglas Street KA30 8PS (take A78, on reaching town turn left at sign for Brisbane Glen/Inverclyde Sports Centre. Lea-mar 100yds on right)
☎(0475) 672447
4♠ ⚤ CTV in all bedrooms ® ✻ (ex guide dogs) ✱ dB&B♠fr£40
⬛ CTV nc12yrs

SELECTED

GH QQQQ **Whin Park** 16 Douglas Street KA30 8PS
☎(0475) 673437
Closed Feb
Whin Park is a well maintained detached house in a residential street. All the bedrooms have good quality en suite shower rooms and modern furnishings. There is a comfortable lounge and an attractive dining room with lace covered tables. The house is closed between 12.30 and 2.30pm each day.
4♠ (1fb) ⚤ in dining room CTV in all bedrooms ® ✻ (ex guide dogs) sB&B♠fr£21 dB&B♠fr£42
Credit Cards [1] [3] ⓔ

FH QQQ Mrs M Watson **South Whittlieburn** *(NS218632)*
Brisbane Glen KA30 8SN ☎(0475) 675881
Quietly located on a country road, this farmhouse has attractively decorated bedrooms with extras such as tissues and toiletries. ▶

PICKMERE HOUSE

AA
QQ

Park Lane, Pickmere, Knutsford, Cheshire WA16 0JX
Tel: & Fax: 01565 733433

A listed Georgian farmhouse built in 1772. Conveniently located in a rural hamlet with views over farmlands, yet swift, easy access to motorway network. Two miles west of M6 junction 19, on B5391. Ideal for airport, Manchester, Chester, Warrington, Runcorn and Liverpool. Spacious en suite rooms with colour TV, tea/coffee, hair dryer etc. Parking at the rear. **No smoking policy.**

THE WITTEMBERG
Private Hotel
2 Rotherslade Road, Langland, Mumbles, Swansea SA3 4QN
Telephone: (01792) 369696 Fax: (01792) 366995

Family run licensed hotel with relaxed, informal atmosphere. Located 100 yards from Langland beach, 1 mile Mumbles and 6 miles from Swansea. Ideally located to explore the Gower Peninsula. All rooms have TV, tea/coffee making facilities, most have toilet and shower en suite. Ample parking.

Resident owners: Andrew and June Thomas.

There is also a comfortable lounge.
3rm(1🛁🚿) (1fb) 🚭 in bedrooms 🚭 in dining room CTV in all bedrooms Ⓡ 🐕 (ex guide dogs) * sB&Bfr£15.50 sB&B🛁🚿fr£18.50 dB&Bfr£30 dB&B🛁🚿fr£36
♨ CTV 155 acres sheep
[£]

LATHERON Highland *Caithness* Map **15** ND13

FH [Q][Q][Q] Mrs C B Sinclair **Upper Latheron** *(ND195352)* KW5 6DT (2m N of Dunbeath off A9) ☎(05934) 224
May-Sep
From its elevated position south of the village and off the A9, this traditional farmhouse enjoys a fine outlook over the North Sea. No smoking is allowed in the bedrooms which are well decorated and furnished in a mixture of modern and traditional styles. Hearty breakfasts are served at a communal table in the comfortable lounge/dining room. It offers good value bed and breakfast accommodation. Pony trekking is available.
3rm (1fb) 🚭 🐕 (ex guide dogs) sB&B£16-£18 dB&B£28-£30 LDO 6pm
♨ CTV U 200 acres cattle ponies sheep
[£]

LAUNCESTON Cornwall & Isles of Scilly Map **02** SX38

FH [Q][Q][Q] Mrs M Smith **Hurdon** *(SX333828)* PL15 9LS (leave A30 at first Launceston exit (A388) and continue towards Industrial Estate. Then follow signs for 'Trebullet')
☎(0566) 772955
May-Oct
This handsome 18th-century stone-built farmhouse is situated at the end of a tree-lined drive, south of the town of Launceston, on a 400-acre working farm. Much of the original character of the house has been retained and is now combined with modern facilities to provide six spacious bedrooms. There is an attractive lounge, and dinner is served at separate tables in the elegant dining room. The Smith family welcome guests, but respectfully request them not to smoke in the house.
6rm(4🛁) (1fb) 🚭 Ⓡ 🐕 (ex guide dogs) * sB&B£14.50-£15 sB&B🛁£17-£17.50 dB&B£29-£30 dB&B🛁£34-£35 WB&B£84-£105 WBDi£138-£159 LDO 4.30pm
♨ CTV 400 acres mixed

FH [Q][Q] Mrs K Broad **Lower Dutson** *(SX340859)* PL15 9SP (on A388) ☎(0566) 776456
Neatly furnished and decorated bedrooms are offered in a farmhouse which has been the home of the Broad family since 1897; the original building on the same site dated back to the seventeenth century. Guests have the use of a spacious lounge/dining room, and a three-bedroomed self-catering cottage attached to the house is also available. The mixed farm of 180 acres includes a coarse fishing lake as well as fishing on a stretch of the River Tamar where in September 1993 a salmon weighing 20.5 lbs. was caught.
3 (1fb) 🚭 Ⓡ 🐕 (ex guide dogs) * sB&Bfr£15 dB&Bfr£26 WB&Bfr£91 WBDifr£140
♨ CTV 🎣

LAVERTON Gloucestershire Map **04** SP03

SELECTED

GH [Q][Q][Q][Q] **Leasow House** WR12 7NA (take B4632 from town to Cheltenham for 2m & turn right to Wormington then 1st on right) ☎Evesham(0386) 584526 FAX (0386) 584596
This early 17th-century Cotswold stone farmhouse is situated southwest of Broadway off the A4632 (signposted Worminston and Dumbleton, it is the first farm on the right). Bedrooms are very modern and well equipped, all with en suite facilities, yet the character of the farmhouse has been retained. The comfortable library has a wide range of books and guides. Two new bedrooms have recently been added, and these share a mini kitchen and comfortable lounge.
5🛁🚿 Annexe 2🛁 (2fb) 🚭 in dining room CTV in all bedrooms Ⓡ **T** sB&B🛁🚿£30-£45 dB&B🛁🚿£48-£60
♨
Credit Cards [1][2][3]
See advertisement under BROADWAY

LEAMINGTON SPA (ROYAL) Warwickshire Map **04** SP36

🛏 ☕ **GH** [Q][Q] **Charnwood** 47 Avenue Road CV31 3PF
☎(0926) 831074
Soundly maintained accommodation is offered at this semidetached Victorian house, and family bedded rooms are available. Separate tables are provided in the dining room, which also doubles as a lounge. The guest house is conveniently located for the town centre and railway station.
6rm(1🛁1🚿) (1fb) 🚭 in dining room 🚭 in lounges CTV in all bedrooms Ⓡ sB&B£15 dB&B£30 dB&B🛁🚿£35 WB&B£105 WBDi£154 LDO noon
♨
Credit Cards [1][3][5]

GH [Q][Q][Q] **Coverdale Private Hotel** 8 Portland Street CV32 5HE
☎(0926) 330400 FAX (0926) 833388
This attractive Regency house is centrally located and convenient for most of the town's amenities. Carefully modernised, the bedrooms are well equipped with direct-dial telephones, radios, TV and trouser presses; two rooms are located at ground floor level and family rooms are also available, most with en suite facilities. Breakfast is served in the pleasant dining room, and there is also a lounge. A small car park is available for guests and there is on-street parking nearby.
8rm(2🛁4🚿) (2fb) 🚭 in 2 bedrooms CTV in all bedrooms Ⓡ **T** * sB&Bfr£28 sB&B🛁🚿£31 dB&Bfr£38 dB&B🛁🚿£42
♨
Credit Cards [1][3][£]

GH [Q][Q][Q] ***Flowerdale House*** 58 Warwick New Road CV32 6AA
☎(0926) 426002 FAX (0926) 883699
A delightful Victorian house situated on the Warwick road on the outskirts of Leamington. Accommodation is attractively decorated, with bedrooms varying in size and style. The comfortable lounge has a small adjoining residents' bar, and the attractive dining area leads through to a conservatory extension, where breakfast may be taken in the summer. Dinner is available by arrangement only.
6rm(4🛁2🚿) (1fb) CTV in all bedrooms Ⓡ 🐕 (ex guide dogs)
Lic ♨
Credit Cards [1][3]

GH [Q][Q] **Glendower** 8 Warwick Place CV32 5BJ (300yds W of Fire Station) ☎(0926) 422784
This semidetached Victorian house is situated on the B4099 west of the town centre. It provides simple but soundly maintained modern accommodation suitable for commercial visitors and tourists alike; family rooms are also available. The spacious public rooms retain many original features, and the guesthouse has a bar license. Street parking nearby is usually available.
9rm(2🛁) (3fb) 🚭 in dining room CTV in all bedrooms Ⓡ sB&Bfr£17 dB&Bfr£34 dB&B🛁fr£39.50 LDO 7pm
Lic ♨ CTV
[£]

FH [Q][Q][Q] Mrs R Gibbs **Hill** *(SP343637)* Lewis Road, Radford Semele CV31 1UX (2m from Leamington Spa on the A425)
☎(0926) 337571
Closed Xmas & New Year
Located on a mixed farm, and popular with both business people and tourists, this well maintained mid-Victorian house lies east of Leamington Spa. Bedrooms vary in size and their furnishings

range from modern to period style. Public areas in this no smoking accommodation include a comfortable TV lounge and conservatory/breakfast room with solid pine furniture.

5rm(3♨) (1fb) ⠀ CTV in 2 bedrooms ® ⠀ ⠀ sB&Bfr£17 sB&B♪£20 dB&Bfr£30 dB&B♪£38 ⠀, CTV 350 acres arable beef mixed sheep ⠀

LECHLADE Gloucestershire   Map **04** SU29

GH Ⓠ Ⓠ Ⓠ Ⓠ Ⓠ **Cottage-by-the-Church** Chapel Lane, Filkins GL7 3JG
☎(0367) 860613
2⇨♨ ® ✳ dB&B⇨♪£36-£40 WB&B£110-£120
⠀, CTV nc10yrs

LEDBURY Hereford & Worcester   Map **03** SO73

GH Ⓠ Ⓠ Ⓠ **Wall Hills Country Guesthouse** Hereford Road HR8 2PR (off A438) ☎(0531) 632833
Closed 24-31 Dec
An impressive Georgian mansion set well back from the A438, overlooking the town. Bedrooms are generally spacious and comfortable: two have modern en suite facilities and the third has a private bathroom. The lounge has a piano, an open fire and honesty bar, and chef/proprietor David Slaughter serves fresh seasonal produce in the pleasant dining room.
3rm(1⇨1♨) (1fb) ⠀ in bedrooms ⠀ in dining room ® ⠀ sB&B£30-£35 sB&B⇨♪£32-£38 dB&B⇨♪£45-£50 LDO 8.30pm
Lic ⠀, CTV
Credit Cards ⟦1⟧⟦3⟧ Ⓔ

LEEDS West Yorkshire   Map **08** SE33

In addition to the national changes to dialling codes on 16 April 1995 (ie the insertion of `1' after the first `0') the codes for certain cities are changing completely - the code for Leeds will be `0113' with each individual number prefixed by `2'.

GH Ⓠ Ⓠ Ⓠ **Ash Mount Hotel** 22 Wetherby Road, Oakwood LS8 2QD ☎(0532) 658164 FAX (0532) 658164
Located in a pleasant residential area at Oakwood, close to Roundhay Park, this large Victorian house is set back from the road, with a large front garden and ample car parking. Bedrooms vary in size and decor is light and fresh. Public areas include a quiet comfortable lounge and neat dining room with a bar.
11rm(7⇨♪) (1fb) ⠀ in dining room ⠀ in lounges CTV in all bedrooms ® T ✳ sB&B£20-£21 sB&B⇨♪£29-£30 dB&B£36-£38 dB&B⇨♪£44-£46
Lic ⠀, CTV
Credit Cards ⟦1⟧⟦3⟧

GH Ⓠ Ⓠ Ⓠ **Merevale Hotel** 16 Wetherby Road, Oakwood LS8 2QD ☎(0532) 658933 & 737985
Closed Xmas
There have been many changes to this pleasantly furnished and comfortable house since Mr and Mrs Jeynes took over. The well cared for bedrooms have coordinated fabrics, and a good lounge is provided.
14rm(6⇨♨) (1fb) ⠀ in dining room ⠀ in lounges CTV in all bedrooms ® ⠀ ✳ sB&B£20 sB&B⇨♪£29 dB&B£34 dB&B⇨♪£44

Lic ⠀, CTV
Credit Cards ⟦1⟧⟦3⟧ Ⓔ

GH Ⓠ Ⓠ Ⓠ *Trafford House Hotel* 18 Cardigan Road, Headingley LS6 3AG ☎(0532) 752034 FAX (0532) 742422
Closed Xmas
The Trafford House and Budapest Hotel is formed by bedroom annexes grouped around the original house and its bar, lounge and dining room. Bedroom sizes and styles vary considerably, with the n ost recent building offering the most attractive rooms. Resident owners and local staff provide friendly service.
18rm(4♨) (4fb) CTV in all bedrooms ® T ⠀ (ex guide dogs) LDO noon
Lic ⠀, CTV
Credit Cards ⟦1⟧⟦3⟧

LEEK Staffordshire   Map **07** SJ95

GH Ⓠ **Peak Weavers Hotel** King Street ST13 5NW (in town centre behind St Mary's Church) ☎(0538) 383729
Built at the end of the last century and extended more recently, this detached house lies behind the Catholic church just off the centre of this attractive moorland town, which is an ideal centre for exploring the Peak District. Bedrooms are neat and well tended and there are extensive lounge areas.
11rm(3⇨1♨) (2fb)CTV in 2 bedrooms ® ⠀ (ex guide dogs) ✳ sB&B£16-£25 sB&B⇨♪£25 dB&B£30 dB&B⇨♪£32-£34 LDO 8.30pm
Lic ⠀, CTV

INN Ⓠ Ⓠ **Abbey** Abbey Green Road ST13 8SA (off A523, 0.5m outside Leek on the Macclesfield road) ☎(0538) 382865
Popular locally for its substantial, good-value bar food, the inn lies in the countryside just outside Leek. It has an annexe with modern, comfortable, well equipped bedrooms.
Annexe 7♨ CTV in all bedrooms ® T ⠀ (ex guide dogs) sB&B♪£27 dB&B♪£42 LDO 8pm
⠀, nc14yrs
Credit Cards ⟦1⟧⟦2⟧⟦3⟧⟦5⟧ Ⓔ

LEICESTER Leicestershire   Map **04** SK50

In addition to the national changes to dialling codes on 16 April 1995 (ie the insertion of `1' after the first `0') the codes for certain cities are changing completely - the code for Leicester will be `0116' with each individual number prefixed by `2'.

GH Ⓠ Ⓠ **Alexandra House** 342 London Road, Stoneygate LE2 2PJ (1m S, near University) ☎(0533) 703056
FAX (0533) 705464
Freshly decorated bedrooms with slightly older en suite shower facilities are available at this friendly guesthouse south of the city centre. There is plenty of off-street parking.
4♨ ⠀ in bedrooms ⠀ in dining room ® T ⠀ ✳ sB&B♪£28 dB&B♪£40
⠀,
Credit Cards ⟦1⟧⟦3⟧

GH Ⓠ Ⓠ Ⓠ **Burlington Hotel** Elmfield Avenue LE2 1RB (just off A6, 0.75m from railway station) (MIN) ☎(0533) 705112
FAX (0533) 704207
Closed Xmas & New Year
Much of the original character of this house is retained in the airy dining room and lounge areas with their Victorian panelling and ceiling features. Bedrooms are light and modern, and most have en suite facilities or shower cubicles. Ample private parking is provided.
16rm(11♨) (1fb)CTV in all bedrooms ® ⠀ (ex guide dogs) sB&B£27-£29 sB&B♪£34-£36 dB&B£35-£39 dB&B⇨♪£38-£44 LDO 8.30pm
Lic ⠀, CTV
Credit Cards ⟦1⟧⟦2⟧⟦3⟧ Ⓔ

GH [Q][Q] ***Croft Hotel*** 3 Stanley Road LE2 1RF ☎(0533) 703220 FAX (0533) 703220

A large detached red brick Victorian house which stands about a mile from the city centre, just off the A6. Some of the centrally heated bedrooms have en suite facilities and many have shower cubicles; all are supplied with TV and tea-making equipment. There is a modern lounge with bar and an attractive restaurant where breakfast is served and evening meals, by arrangement.

26rm(6🛁🚿) (1fb) CTV in all bedrooms [R] 🐕 (ex guide dogs) LDO 5pm

Lic ♨ CTV

Credit Cards [1] [3]

GH [Q][Q] Scotia Hotel 10 Westcotes Drive LE3 0QR (take 3rd turning on the right after A46 leaves the A47 west end of Leicester) ☎(0533) 549200

Well maintained accommodation is offered at this private hotel just off the A46 Narborough Road. The bedrooms are cheerfully decorated in floral designs, and include some ground-floor rooms and some in a nearby annexe. The dining room has pleasant views of the rear garden, and guests can choose an evening meal from a daily or à la carte menu between 7.30 and 9pm.

11rm(4🛁🚿) (1fb)CTV in all bedrooms [R] * sB&B£20-£22 sB&B🛁🚿£25-£27 dB&B£36-£38 dB&B🛁🚿£40-£44 LDO 8pm

Lic ♨

GH [Q][Q] The Stanfre House Hotel 265 London Road LE2 3BE (turn left at roundabout on A6) ☎(0533) 704294

Closed 24 Dec-2 Jan

Mrs Bond is the friendly hostess at Stanfre House, where sound standards are maintained. Guests have the use of a comfortable lounge which, along with the dining room, is decorated with a collection of brass and plates. There is also an electric organ which guests are welcome to play. Bedrooms are at the rear of the house away from traffic noise.

12rm (1fb) 🚭 in dining room CTV in 6 bedrooms * sB&B£20 dB&B£32

Lic ♨ CTV

[£]

GH [Q][Q][Q] Stoneycroft Hotel 5/7 Elmfield Avenue LE2 1RB ☎(0533) 707605 FAX (0533) 706067

This large well maintained building is located in a quiet residential area on a road off the A6 London road, about one mile south of the city centre. Bedrooms are equipped with wooden open plan fitted furniture, and colour coordinated soft furnishings. Public rooms now feature good colour schemes and decor throughout, and include an informal lounge area, a pool and TV room, a breakfast room and a fully licensed bar and restaurant serving simple meals in the evening.

44rm(25🛁🚿) (4fb) CTV in all bedrooms [R] 🐕 (ex guide dogs) sB&B£20-£25 sB&B🛁🚿£28-£32 dB&B£30-£35 dB&B🛁🚿£38-£42 WB&B£140-£200 WBDi£200-£250 LDO 9pm

Lic ♨ CTV pool table

Credit Cards [1] [3] [5] [£]

LELANT Cornwall & Isles of Scilly — Map **02** SW53

SELECTED

INN[Q][Q][Q][Q] Badger TR26 3JT ☎Hayle(0736) 752181

This village inn is situated just off the A30, convenient for St Ives and close to the Hayle Estuary. Bedrooms are comfortable, attractive, and well equipped. The spacious bars retain their character and there is a no-smoking conservatory restaurant where a hot carvery is offered on Saturday nights and Sunday lunch time. The good daily selection of bar meals includes popular home-made puddings.

6🛁🚿 🚭 in dining room 🚭 in lounges CTV in all bedrooms [R] T 🐕 (ex guide dogs) * sB&B🛁🚿£25-£28 dB&B🛁🚿£39-£45 Lunch £3.50-£8&alc Dinner £3.50-£12&alc LDO 10.15pm

♨ nc6yrs

Credit Cards [1]

LEOMINSTER Hereford & Worcester — Map **03** SO45

See also Bodenham

GH [Q][Q] ***Knapp House*** Luston HR6 0DB (2.5m N on B4361) ☎(0568) 615705

Dating back to the 16th century, this black and white timbered house has a pleasant garden. Bedrooms are smart and brightly decorated, and the impressive panelled lounge has a cheerful log fire burning in the colder weather.

2rm (1fb) [R] LDO 5pm

♨ CTV

SELECTED

FH [Q][Q][Q][Q] Mrs J Conolly **The Hills** *(SO564638)* Leysters HR6 0HP ☎Leysters(056887) 205 due to change to (01568) 750205

Feb-Oct

At this attractive creeper-clad farmhouse dating back to the 15th century, Jane and Peter Conolly offer a warm welcome to their guests, many of whom return regularly. Two bedrooms are in the main house (one was used as a chapel in the 1920s) and the third, called The Tigeen (Irish for Little House), has been converted from an old barn a few yards away. The timbered lounge, with its wood-burning stove, has a cheerful atmosphere, and good home-cooked meals are served in the adjoining flag-floored dining room.

3rm(2🛁1🚿) 🚭 CTV in all bedrooms [R] sB&B🛁🚿£25-£27 dB&B🛁🚿£40-£44 WB&Bfr£140 WBDifr£245 LDO 5pm

♨ nc12yrs 120 acres arable

Credit Cards [1] [3] [£]

FH [Q] Mrs E Thomas **Woonton Court** *(SO548624)* Leysters HR6 0HL (take A39, 2.5m from town onto A4112 and pass through Kimbolton, turning right for Woonton before Leysters village. Farm 0.5m down lane.) ☎(0568) 87232 due to change to (0568) 750232

Closed 22-27 Dec

2rm(1🛁) CTV in all bedrooms [R] * sB&B£16-£18 dB&B£29 dB&B🛁£30-£32 WB&B£95-£105 LDO previous day

♨ CTV 250 acres mixed

[£]

LERWICK See **SHETLAND**

LEVEN Humberside — Map **08** TA14

INN[Q][Q] ***The New Inn*** 44 South Street HU17 5NZ ☎Hornsea(0964) 542223

4rm(3🚿) (1fb) CTV in 3 bedrooms 🐕 (ex guide dogs)

♨

LEVENS Cumbria — Map **07** SD48

INN[Q][Q][Q] Gilpin Bridge Hotel & Restaurant Bridge End LA8 8EP (on A5074, 100mtrs from junct with A590) ☎Witherslack(05395) 52206

An attractive inn with a beamed bar and restaurant, the Gilpin Bridge serves real ale and a wide choice of bar meals. The restaurant is open for dinner and table reservations are advisable, especially at weekends. Bedrooms are modern in style and very well equipped. One room has a four-poster bed and another an impressive brass bedstead.

10rm(6🛁4🚿) 🚭 in 2 bedrooms CTV in all bedrooms [R] 🐕 (ex

guide dogs) ✳ sB&B⇄🛏£29.50 dB&B⇄🛏£46-£55 Lunch £5-
£10alc Dinner £7-£15alc LDO 9pm
🛏,
Credit Cards [1] [3]

LEW Oxfordshire　　　　　　　　Map **04** SP30

SELECTED

FH [Q][Q][Q][Q] Mrs M Rouse **The Farmhouse Hotel**
(SP322059) University Farm OX18 2AU (on the A4095, 3m
SW of Witney on the Bampton Road)
☎Bampton Castle(0993) 850297 & 851480
FAX (0993) 850965
Closed Xmas & New Year rs Sun
This 17th-century Cotswold stone farmhouse situated in the
tiny village is part of the Rouse family's working farm; the
attractive gardens and terraces have peaceful country views.
Bedrooms are individually furnished and decorated and retain
many of the original features, including oak-beamed ceilings,
inglenook fireplaces and a Victorian bath: they all have private
bathrooms, TV, direct-dial telephone and radio alarm; one
room on the ground floor has been designed for disabled
guests. The comfortable sitting room has a splendid inglenook
fireplace, and a cosy bar adjoins the beamed restaurant with
an attractive conservatory, used mostly as a breakfast room.
The restaurant is open to non-residents, and simple farmhouse
food is offered, with a daily-changing menu offering a variety
of seasonal choices. Smoking is not permitted in the restaurant
and bedrooms.
6⇄🛏 (2fb) ⊬ in bedrooms ⊬ in dining room ⊬ in 1 lounge
CTV in all bedrooms Ⓡ T 🛏 (ex guide dogs) ✳
dB&B⇄🛏£50-£70 LDO 6pm
Lic 🛏, nc5yrs 216 acres dairy
Credit Cards [1] [3]

LEWDOWN Devon　　　　　　　　Map **02** SX48

FH [Q][Q] Mrs M E Horn **Venn Mill** *(SX484885)* EX20 4EB (from
A386 follow signs for Lewdown continue for 4m to Combebow
turn sharp right just past cottages & phone box)
☎Bridestowe(083786) 288
Etr-Oct
Attractive, colour-coordinated and double-glazed guest rooms
open onto a well tended garden at this farm bungalow. There is a
comfortable lounge, and meals are served at separate tables in the
dining room.
3rm (1fb) CTV in 1 bedroom Ⓡ 🛏 ✳ sB&B£16 dB&B£32 LDO
4pm
CTV ♪ 160 acres beef dairy sheep
ⓔ

LEWES East Sussex　　　　　　　　Map **05** TQ41

SELECTED

GH [Q][Q][Q][Q] **Fairseat House** Newick BN8 4PJ (on A272
between Haywards Heath and Uckfield) ☎(0825) 722263
An elegant Edwardian house, furnished throughout with
antiques, provides accommodation in three large bedrooms
with much to commend them; each has its own private
facilities - which in one case include a fine old bathtub with
claw feet. Two drawing rooms feature open fires and ancestral
portraits, while the gardens include ample parking space as
well as a covered heated swimming pool and south-facing
terrace. The eggs served at breakfast will have been laid by the
hotel's own hens, and a skilfully prepared four-course dinner
will offer home-grown vegetables.
3⇄🛏 ⊬ in bedrooms ⊬ in dining room 🛏

sB&B⇄🛏£23-£27 dB&B⇄🛏£42-£60
🛏. CTV nc🛏(heated)
Credit Cards [3]

SELECTED

GH [Q][Q][Q][Q] **Nightingales** The Avenue, Kingston BN7 3LL
☎(0273) 475673
Nightingales is a modern family bungalow with a splendid
garden in the village of Kingston just outside Lewes. Hosts
Geoff and Jean Hudson clearly enjoy catering for guests. The
bedrooms are well furnished and the lounge is shared with the
Hudsons. Breakfast is a feast, with juice, Greek yoghurt and
apricots, cereals, free-range eggs and organic produce among
the goodies. A self-catering flat is available.
2rm(1⇄🛏) ⊬ CTV in all bedrooms Ⓡ 🛏 (ex guide dogs)
sB&Bfr£23 sB&B⇄🛏fr£30 dB&Bfr£38 dB&B⇄🛏fr£45
WB&B£140-£280
🛏. CTV

LEWIS, ISLE OF Western Isles *Ross & Cromarty*　　Map **13**

BREASCLETE　　　　　　　　Map **13** NB23

SELECTED

GH [Q][Q][Q][Q] **Corran View** 22a Breasclete PA86 9EF
☎(0851) 621300
Situated 18 miles west of Stornoway in a quiet village
overlooking East Loch Roag, a former croft house has been
extended and modernised to create this friendly, family-run
holiday guesthouse. Bedrooms, though compact, are
comfortably furnished in the modern style. There is a small
dining room and a welcoming lounge.
3🛏 ⊬ in bedrooms ⊬ in dining room CTV in all
bedrooms Ⓡ dB&B🛏£73 (incl dinner) WB&B£150
WBDif£240.50 LDO 7pm
🛏. CTV
Credit Cards [1] [3]

SELECTED

GH [Q][Q][Q][Q] **Eshcol** PA86 9ED ☎(0851) 621357
mid Mar-mid Oct
This modern house enjoys a fine outlook over Loch Roag to
the hills beyond. Bedrooms are attractive, the lounge has a
relaxed, friendly atmosphere and meals are enjoyable.
3⇄🛏 ⊬ in bedrooms CTV in all bedrooms Ⓡ
sB&B⇄🛏fr£25 dB&B⇄🛏fr£40 WBDif£240-£270 LDO
6.30pm
🛏. nc8yrs

STORNOWAY　　　　　　　　Map **13** NB43

GH [Q][Q][Q] **Ardlonan** 29 Francis Street PA87 2NF
☎(0851) 703482
Closed Xmas & New Year
Situated at the end of a terrace in a residential area close to the
town centre, this personally run guesthouse offers comfortable,
good value accommodation. The breakfast menu offers a good
choice of dishes, while tasty home baking is served to guests in
the lounge in the evening.
5rm (1fb) ⊬ in bedrooms ⊬ in dining room ⊬ in 1 lounge CTV
in 3 bedrooms Ⓡ 🛏 sB&B£19 dB&B£36
🛏. CTV
ⓔ

LEYBURN North Yorkshire Map **07** SE19

GH [Q][Q][Q] ***Eastfield Lodge Private Hotel*** 1 St Matthews Terrace DL8 5EL (on A684, near St Matthews Church) ☎Wensleydale(0969) 23196

An unpretentious guesthouse on the outskirts of this Dales town provides spacious bedrooms, a comfortable lounge with a bar for guests and an attractive dining room.

9rm(4🚿) (2fb) CTV in all bedrooms Ⓡ

Lic ♨

Credit Cards [1] [3]

INN[Q][Q][Q] **Foresters Arms** Carlton-in-Coverdale DL8 2BB (5m SW) ☎(0969) 40272

Located amid beautiful scenery in the peaceful village of Carlton in Coverdale, this delightful Dales inn with beamed ceilings and open log fires is full of charm. Attractively decorated bedrooms are well equipped, guests have the use of a small lounge, and an extensive range of bar meals provides an alternative to those served in the restaurant. Service is very friendly.

3rm(2🚿) (1fb) 🚭 in area of dining room CTV in all bedrooms Ⓡ **T** ✳ sB&B🚿£30 dB&B🚿£55 WB&B£150 WBDi£241.25 Bar Lunch £8-£20&alc Dinner £8-£20&alc LDO 9.30pm

♨

Credit Cards [1] [3]

LICHFIELD Staffordshire Map **07** SK10

GH [Q][Q] **Coppers End** Walsall Road, Muckley Corner WS14 0BG (on A461, 100yds from Muckley Corner rbt off the A5) ☎Brownhills(0543) 372910

This detached property built in 1935 as a police station and cell (hence the name) is now a personally run guesthouse, located three miles southwest of Lichfield. It provides bedrooms with modern furnishings and equipment, two of which are located on the ground floor; smoking is not permitted in bedrooms. There is a pleasant comfortable lounge, and a small cosy dining room where tables are shared.

6rm(1🚿) 🚭 in bedrooms 🚭 in area of dining room CTV in all bedrooms Ⓡ ✳ sB&B£21-£23 sB&B🚿fr£28 dB&Bfr£34 dB&B🚿fr£40 LDO noon

Lic ♨ CTV

Credit Cards [1] [2] [3] [5] [£]

GH [Q][Q][Q] ***The Oakleigh House Hotel*** 25 St Chads Road WS13 7LZ ☎(0543) 262688 & 255573

Closed 27 Dec-1 Jan rs Sun evening & Mon

A nicely preserved, charming house dating back to 1909, set in attractive gardens next to Stowe Pool, less than half a mile from the cathedral. Bedrooms in the main house have mainly period style furniture, and those in the single-storey annexe are furnished in modern style; they are all well equipped. There is a cosy lounge, a small pleasant bar and an attractive conservatory restaurant.

5rm(3🛁🚿) Annexe 5rm(1🛁4🚿) CTV in all bedrooms Ⓡ **T** LDO 9.30pm

Lic ♨ nc

Credit Cards [1] [3]

LIFTON Devon Map **02** SX38

GH [Q][Q] **Mayfield House** PL16 0AN ☎(0566) 784401

A spacious, detached, family-run guest house is set back off the A30, in the village. Smoking is not permitted in the attractively decorated bedrooms. There is a cosy bar lounge downstairs.

3rm (1fb) 🚭 in bedrooms CTV in all bedrooms Ⓡ 🐕 (ex guide dogs) ✳ sB&B£17 dB&B£31.50

Lic

Credit Cards [2] [£]

LIGHTHORNE Warwickshire Map **04** SP35

FH [Q][Q][Q] Mrs J Stanton **Redlands** *(SP334570)* Banbury Road CV35 0AH (off B4100, 5m S of Warwick) ☎Warwick(0926) 651241

Closed Xmas

This is a carefully preserved 16th-century stone-built house. The bedrooms are spacious and attractively decorated: two have modern furnishings whilst the third has traditional furniture and an antique bed, together with a private bathroom; there is also a family room. The comfortable lounge features exposed beams which indicate its age. The house is surrounded by 100 acres of land, two of which are pleasant lawned gardens including an unheated open-air swimming pool.

3rm(1🛁) (1fb) 🚭 in bedrooms Ⓡ 🐕 (ex guide dogs) ✳ sB&B£15-£17.50 dB&B£30-£34 dB&B🛁£32-£36

♨ CTV 🏊100 acres arable

[£]

LINCOLN Lincolnshire Map **08** SK97

GH [Q][Q] **Brierley House Hotel** 54 South Park LN5 8ER ☎(0522) 526945 & 522945

Located on a quiet avenue overlooking South Common Golf Course, Brierley House is about half a mile from the city centre. Modest but sound accommodation is offered and guests have the use of a comfortable lounge. There is a dining room with a small bar, and evening meals are available by prior arrangement.

7rm(2🛁4🚿) CTV in all bedrooms Ⓡ 🐕 ✳ sB&B£20-£25 sB&B🛁🚿£25 dB&Bfr£36 dB&B🛁🚿£39.50 LDO breakfast

Lic ♨ CTV ⛳adjacent 18 hole golf course

[£]

SELECTED

GH [Q][Q][Q][Q] **Carline** 1-3 Carline Road LN1 1HL ☎(0522) 530422

Closed Xmas & New Year

Enthusiastic owners offer a warm welcome at this popular guest house in a quiet residential area below the castle. The bedrooms vary in size and are individually furnished and attractively decorated in cheerfully coordinated colour schemes. Annexe rooms have their own comfortable lounge, and there is an additional lounge in the main house. This is a no-smoking establishment.

9🛁🚿 Annexe 3rm(1🚿) (2fb) 🚭 CTV in all bedrooms Ⓡ 🐕 (ex guide dogs) sB&Bfr£20 sB&B🛁🚿£29 dB&B£32 dB&B🛁🚿£38

♨ nc2yrs

[£]

SELECTED

GH [Q][Q][Q][Q] **D'Isney Place Hotel** Eastgate LN2 4AA ☎(0522) 538881 FAX (0522) 511321

D'Isney Place is an unusual establishment, close to the cathedral, offering quality accommodation in bedrooms of varying size. Each room is individually furnished, with en suite facilities and personal touches such as fresh milk and good towelling bathrobes. Deluxe rooms have even more comforts, perhaps a four-poster bed and a jacuzzi bathroom. There is no lounge or dining room, and breakfast is served to the bedroom in fine Minton china.

18rm(15🛁3🚿) (2fb) 🚭 in 4 bedrooms CTV in all bedrooms Ⓡ **T** ✳ sB&B🛁🚿£51 dB&B🛁🚿£64

♨

Credit Cards [1] [2] [3] [5]

SELECTED

GH [Q][Q][Q][Q] Minster Lodge Hotel 3 Church Lane LN2 1QJ ☎(0522) 513220 FAX (0522) 513220

Minster Lodge is a pleasant red brick house with a colourful garden frontage situated within 500yds of the historic Newport Arch and a short walk from the cathedral. The house is beautifully kept and provides light, fresh accommodation in well equipped rooms with double glazing and modern bathrooms. Guests have sole use of a comfortable lounge, with a chesterfield suite, writing desk and small corner bar. A good choice is offered at breakfast, which is served in the bright dining room.

6🛁🚿 (2fb) 🚭 in dining room CTV in all bedrooms [R] **T** ✱ sB&B🛁🚿£35-£43.50 dB&B🛁🚿£40-£49
Lic ▥ CTV
Credit Cards [1][2][3][5][£]

GH [Q][Q][Q] Tennyson Hotel 7 South Park LN5 8EN (S of city centre on A15, nr South Park Common) ☎(0522) 521624 FAX (0522) 521624

An immaculately maintained house with friendly owners, the Tennyson is situated on the southern inner ring road. The bedrooms, which vary in size, are fresh and light in appearance, and where space permits comfortable armchairs are provided. A good choice of dishes is available at dinner; light refreshments are served in the small lounge area during the day.

8rm(2🛁6🚿) (1fb) 🚭 in dining room CTV in all bedrooms [R] **T** 🐕 ✱ sB&B🛁🚿£26-£28 dB&B🛁🚿£38-£42 LDO 7.45pm
Lic ▥
Credit Cards [1][2][3][5][£]

LINLITHGOW Lothian *West Lothian* Map **11** NS97

FH [Q][Q][Q] Mrs A Hay **Belsyde House** *(NS976755)* Lanark Road EH49 6QE (1.5m W on A706, first left after crossing Union Canal) ☎(0506) 842098

Closed Xmas

A large period farmhouse with fine views to the north stands in extensive grounds two miles southwest of the town. Well proportioned double and family bedrooms are available as well as two singles, and public areas are made up of a pleasant lounge and a dining room with separate tables.

4rm(1🚿) (1fb) CTV in all bedrooms [R] 🐕 (ex guide dogs) ✱ sB&Bfr£17 dB&Bfr£34 dB&B🚿fr£40 LDO noon
▥ CTV 106 acres beef sheep
[£]

FH [Q] Mrs W Erskine **Woodcockdale** *(NS974761)* Lanark Road EH49 6QE (on A706) ☎(0506) 842088
5rm(1🚿) (3fb) 🚭 CTV in all bedrooms [R] sB&Bfr£18 dB&Bfr£32 dB&B🚿fr£38 WB&Bfr£108
▥ CTV 700 acres dairy sheep cattle

LISKEARD Cornwall & Isles of Scilly Map **02** SX26

GH [Q][Q][Q] Elnor 1 Russell Street PL14 4BP (between town centre & railway station) ☎(0579) 342472 FAX (0579) 345673

Closed Xmas

This neat guesthouse has recently been extended to provide an additional three en suite bedrooms. Public areas are cosy and simply styled and a good home-cooked breakfast is served, but now there are more restaurants in the town an evening meal is only available on request. The small rear car park is an added bonus here.

9rm(4🚿) (1fb) 🚭 in dining room CTV in 4 bedrooms [R] **T** 🐕 sB&B£16.50 sB&B🚿£19.50 dB&B£33 dB&B🚿£39 LDO 5pm
Lic ▥ CTV
[£]

Halfway Farm, Motel and Guest House
Swinderby, Lincoln LN6 9HN
Telephone: Swinderby 01522 868749
Fax: 01522 868082

This elegant Georgian farmhouse and farm building provides excellent accommodation in 17 rooms within the main house and the single-storey outbuildings, modernised to a high standard providing character rooms at a reasonable price. Car parking is unlimited. Full English Breakfast is served in the farmhouse.

Tennyson Hotel
7 South Park, South Park Avenue, Lincoln,
Telephone: (01522) 521624 Fax: (01522) 521624

A first class hotel 1 mile from City Centre near South Park Common and golf courses. All rooms en-suite, direct dial telephones in all bedrooms, radio, colour TV, hair dryer, tea making facilities, licensed restaurant, lounge, car park. Good Food. Bargain breaks. A perfect base for visiting picturesque Lincolnshire. Access/Visa/Amex/Diners Club accepted.

Personally supervised by Resident Proprietors Lino and Maybelle Saggiorato

SELECTED

FH [Q][Q][Q][Q] Mrs S Rowe **Tregondale** *(SX294643)* Menheniot PL14 3RG (E of Liskeard 1.5m N of A38)
☎(0579) 342407

Ring and ask for directions to this well modernised farmhouse, where the Rowe family tend 200 acres of mixed farmland including a herd of pedigree South Devon cattle and long wool sheep. The house has a friendly atmosphere, and guests sit around a communal table for meals. Traditional farmhouse fare is served, using as much home grown produce as possible. Bedrooms are pretty with tasteful coordinating soft furnishings, and a self catering cottage is available.

3🛁🚿 (1fb) CTV in all bedrooms [R] 🐕 ✱ sB&B£18-£20 dB&B🛁🚿£35-£36 WB&B£112-£122.50 WBDi£168-£175 LDO 6pm

CTV 🎾(hard)180 acres arable beef mixed sheep

[£]

LITTLEBOURNE Kent Map **05** TR25

INN[Q][Q][Q] King William IV 4 High Street CT3 1ST (turn off M2 at the Howletts Zoo junct, proceed to Littlebourne, when you join A257 establishment is directly opposite)
☎Canterbury(0227) 721244 FAX (0227) 721244

Lying in the centre of the village, this is a country inn of some character. A good local clientele enjoys simple wholesome cooking, lunch and dinner being served seven days a week and the blackboard menu changing daily. A sample meal consisted of flavoursome home-smoked salmon with scrambled egg, a braised rabbit with leeks and ale, and a well-prepared caramel and almond pudding with sauce anglaise. A short wine list features inexpensive wines and service is friendly.

4🛁🚿 (1fb)CTV in all bedrooms [R] 🐕 (ex guide dogs) sB&B🛁🚿£25-£30 dB&B🛁🚿£35-£40 Lunch £9.50-£21alc Dinner £9.50-£21alc LDO 9.20pm

♨ nc10yrs traditional pub games

Credit Cards [1] [3]

LITTLE CHEVERELL Wiltshire Map **03** ST95

PREMIER SELECTED

GH [Q][Q][Q][Q][Q] Little Cheverell House Little Cheverell SN10 4JJ
☎Devizes(0380) 813322
FAX (0380) 813322

White gates at the bottom of the hill in the village are the only sign to this splendid stone-built Georgian rectory standing in well tended gardens which has been sympathetically extended over the years. Very much the home of Sir Donald and Lady Ruth Hawley, the house contains a fascinating collection of pictures, books and ornaments, evidence of years of travel around the world. Bedrooms are spacious, well equipped with comforts and furnished in keeping with the style of the house. Dinner is taken at the family dining table, and Lady Ruth Hawley produces delicious meals, drawing on an interesting repertoire of international dishes and using her own fresh garden produce.

2🛁🚿 🚭 [R] 🐕 (ex guide dogs) sB&B🛁🚿£33-£38 dB&B🛁🚿£48-£52 LDO 9am

♨ CTV nc12yrs 🎾(hard)

[£]

LITTLE DEWCHURCH Hereford & Worcester Map **03** SO53

FH [Q][Q] Mrs G Lee **Cwm Craig** *(SO535322)* HR2 6PS
☎Carey(0432) 840250

This attractive Georgian farmhouse is run with pride by Mrs Lee. Although it is close to the village centre, it is advisable to ask for directions. The spacious bedrooms are furnished with some interesting antique pieces, and there are several very comfortable sitting areas, as well as a snooker room. Between December and Easter on this working farm young calves are hand-fed, to the delight of any children who are staying.

3rm (1fb) 🚭 in dining room [R] 🐕 (ex guide dogs) ✱ dB&B£28-£32 dB&B🚿£32-£36 WB&B£91-£105

♨ CTV snooker/pool table darts 190 acres arable beef

[£]

LITTLE GRANSDEN Cambridgeshire Map **04** TL25

FH [Q][Q][Q] Mrs M Cox **Gransden Lodge** *(TL288537)* Longstowe Road SG19 3EB (2m off A1198)
☎Great Gransden(0767) 677365 FAX (0767) 677647

Gransden Lodge is a proudly kept farmhouse on the B1046 between Little Gransden and Longstowe. Animal lovers will be interested to know that the owners have two bulldog mastiffs and there are some pedigree Gelbwieh cattle on the predominantly arable holding. Smoking is not permitted in the house.

3🛁🚿 🚭 CTV in all bedrooms [R] 🐕 ✱ sB&B£16-£18 dB&B🛁🚿£32 WB&Bfr£100

♨ CTV 860 acres arable beef mixed

[£]

LITTLE PETHERICK Cornwall & Isles of Scilly Map **02** SW97

GH [Q][Q][Q] The Old Mill Country House PL27 7QT (off A30 onto A389) ☎Rumford(0841) 540388

Mar-Oct rs Nov-Etr

A listed 16th-century converted corn mill, this hotel enjoys a village setting, by a stream, in its own carefully tended gardens. There is a choice of lounges where drinks are available, and dinner is served at separate tables in the Mill Room.

6rm(1🛁4🚿) 🚭 in 1 bedrooms 🚭 in dining room 🚭 in 1 lounge [R] 🐕 (ex guide dogs) dB&B£40.70-£42.30 dB&B🛁🚿£48-£53.20 WBDi£195-£241 LDO 6pm

Lic ♨ CTV nc14yrs

Credit Cards [1] [3] [£]

LIVERPOOL Merseyside Map **07** SJ39

GH [Q][Q][Q] Aachen Hotel 91 Mount Pleasant L3 5TB
☎051-709 3477 & 1126 FAX 051-709 1126

Closed 25 Dec-7 Jan

Situated close to the Roman Catholic cathedral and convenient for the city centre, this long established and popular private hotel is run in a friendly and efficient manner. Although accommodation is fairly compact, bedrooms are attractively furnished and offer several extras such as hair dryers, trouser presses and satellite TV. There is a neat breakfast room, and a small lounge bar where a small range of snacks is offered in the evening.

17rm(11🛁🚿) (6fb) 🚭 in 10 bedrooms 🚭 in dining room CTV in all bedrooms [R] T 🐕 (ex guide dogs) ✱ sB&B£22-£30 sB&B🛁🚿£28-£30 dB&B£30-£36 dB&B🛁🚿£38-£44 WB&B£154-£210 WBDifr£194.28 LDO 8.30pm

Lic ♨ CTV 🅿 snooker

Credit Cards [1] [2] [3] [5] [£]

GH [Q][Q][Q] The Blenheim 37 Aigburth Drive, Sefton Park L17 4JE ☎051-727 7380

Virtually derelict when the present owner acquired it, this very large Victorian house has been fully restored to provide brightly decorated accommodation with modern furnishings. There is a pleasant dining room with separate tables and a comfortable lounge with lots of maritime pictures.

17rm(3♠) (4fb) ⚲ in dining room CTV in all bedrooms ® ✠ ✳
sB&B£17.50-£21 sB&B♠£21-£24 dB&B£29 dB&B♠£35
WB&Bfr£122.50 WBDifr£164 LDO 7pm
▥ CTV
Credit Cards [1] [3] £

LIZARD Cornwall & Isles of Scilly   Map **02** SW71

P R E M I E R 🏆 S E L E C T E D

GH Q Q Q Q Q

Landewednack House Church
Cove TR12 7PQ
☎The Lizard(0326) 290909
FAX (0326) 290909

Once a rectory, this
17th-century house is located
in the grounds of the church, in
attractive walled gardens well
away from the main tourist
areas. Bedrooms are
individually furnished and
decorated with style and flair, and two rooms share a spacious
jacussi bathroom. Set menus based on local ingredients are
served at a communal table. There are two comfortable sitting
rooms, and a self catering apartment is also available.
Smoking is not permitted.
4rm(1⇌1♠) ⚲ CTV in all bedrooms ® T✠ (ex guide
dogs) ✳ sB&B£18.50-£20.50 dB&B£40-£44 dB&B⇌♠£50-
£60 LDO 8pm
Lic ▥ nc11yrs boule croquet jacuzzi

GH Q Q Q **Penmenner House Hotel** Penmenner Road TR12 7NR
☎(0326) 290370
Located in its own grounds, with spectacular views of the
lighthouse and magnificent coastal scenery, this small hotel is run
by Muriel and Ray Timporley in friendly relaxed style. Bedrooms
on the first floor are all well equipped, and there is a comfortable
lounge with a small bar. Evening meals are available by prior
arrangement, served in the elegant dining room.
8rm(5♠) ⚲ CTV in all bedrooms ® ✠ (ex guide dogs) ✳
sB&B£21-£22 sB&B♠£23-£24 dB&B£38-£40 dB&B♠£42-£44
WB&B£122-£158 WBDi£192-£230 LDO 5pm
Lic ▥ CTV nc3yrs table tennis pool table
Credit Cards [1] [3] £

LLANBEDR Gwynedd   Map **06** SH52

INN Q Q Q **Victoria** LL45 2LD ☎(034123) 213
Situated alongside the River Artro, this old stone-built coaching
inn offers modern pine furnished bedrooms and a choice of bars.
The original Settle Bar with it flagstone floor, black stove and old
furniture contrasts with the large lounge bar and restaurant which
opens out onto the pleasant gardens. A wide range of meals is on
offer and local beaches and the lovely Cwm Nantcol are within
easy reach.
5⇌♠ CTV in all bedrooms ® LDO 9.30pm
▥ CTV
Credit Cards [1] [3]

LLANBERIS Gwynedd   Map **06** SH56

GH Q Q Q **Alpine Lodge Hotel** 1 High Street LL55 4EN
☎(0286) 870294
Apr-10 Oct
Situated at the northern edge of the mountain resort village, this
large stone-built house offers well decorated bedrooms, including
two family rooms, several with lake and mountain views. There is
a comfortable lounge and the restaurant includes a small bar.

6rm(4⇌3♠) (2fb) CTV in all bedrooms ® ✠ (ex guide dogs)
sB&B⇌♠£25-£33 dB&B⇌♠£35-£43 LDO 6pm
Lic ▥
£

GH Q Q Q **Lake View Hotel** Tan-y-Pant LL55 4EL
☎(0286) 870422 FAX (0286) 872591
Lake View is a small, friendly hotel overlooking Llyn Padarn. The
central part of the building is believed to be about 250 years old and
features a beamed bar with inglenook fireplace and a comfortably
furnished lounge. The restaurant, which is popular locally, has good
views over the lake and mountains. Bedrooms are neat and modern.
10rm(9♠) (3fb)CTV in all bedrooms ® ✠ (ex guide dogs) ✳
sB&B♠fr£27 dB&B♠fr£40 LDO 9.30pm
Lic ▥ CTV
Credit Cards [1] [3] [5] £

LLANDEILO Dyfed   Map **03** SN62

GH Q Q Q **Brynawel** 19 New Road SA19 6DD ☎(0558) 822925
rs 25 & 26 Dec
Situated on the main road close to the town centre, this small, mid-
terrace, family-run hotel provides a cheerful and friendly service. It
has a popular café-style restaurant, which serves a selection of hot
and cold food throughout the day. The prettily decorated bedrooms
are furnished with modern laminated furniture and all have a TV.
There is a quiet, modern lounge available for guests.
5rm(2⇌1♠) (1fb) CTV in all bedrooms ® ✠ (ex guide dogs) ✳
sB&B£19-£24 sB&B⇌♠£24 dB&B£29 dB&B⇌♠£35
Lic ▥
Credit Cards [1] [3] £

LLANDOGO Gwent   Map **03** SO50

GH Q **Brown's Hotel & Restaurant** NP5 4TW
☎Dean(0594) 530262
Feb-Nov
Positioned in the centre of the village and close to the river, this
guesthouse is popular with fishermen. The en-suite bedrooms are
modest in furnishings and style. A small café, also run by the
owners of the guesthouse, provides refreshments all day.
7rm(1♠) LDO 7.30pm
Lic CTV nc

INN Q Q Q **The Sloop** NP5 4TW (A466) ☎Dean(0594) 530291
FAX (0594) 530935
With lovely views of the Wye valley from its riverside position,
this former mill is now a road-side inn offering well equipped
modern bedrooms. Its bar is popular, not least for the wide range
of food available.
4⇌♠ CTV in all bedrooms ® ✳ sB&B⇌♠£25.50
dB&B⇌♠£39-£47 Lunch £9-£13alc Dinner £9-£13alc LDO 10pm
▥ nc9yrs
Credit Cards [1] [2] [3] £

LLANDOVERY Dyfed   Map **03** SN73

GH Q Q Q **Llwyncelyn** SA20 0EP (on A40, follow signs for
Llandeilo, cross railway and river bridge, guest house on left)
☎(0550) 20566 due to change to (01550) 720566
Closed Xmas
Run by the friendly Griffiths family, this large detached house has
a lovely garden which runs down to the river Towy. The pretty
bedrooms are equipped with solid furniture and duvets can be
supplied on request. There is a pleasant lounge furnished with old-
fashioned, comfortable suites. Good home cooking is served in the
dining room.
6rm (3fb) ⚲ in dining room ® ✠ (ex guide dogs) sB&B£18-£22
dB&B£32-£34 WB&B£89.60-£128.80 WBDi£171.85-£211 LDO
7.30pm
Lic ▥ CTV ⌘
£

LLANDRINDOD WELLS Powys   Map **03** SO06

See also Penybont

GH Ⓠ Ⓠ **Griffin Lodge Hotel** Temple Street LD1 5HF (on A483 in town centre) ☎(0597) 822432

A large Victorian, town-centre house lying alongside the A483 trunk road. Bedrooms have recently been improved and freshly decorated. The lounge and bar adjoin each other and there is a pine furnished restaurant where a wide range of snacks is available, as well as more substantial à la carte meals.

8rm(5♠) ⊁ in dining room CTV in all bedrooms Ⓡ sB&B£18-£20 sB&B♠£21.50-£23.50 dB&B£36 dB&B♠£43 WB&B£108-£129 WBDi£179.50-£200.75 LDO 7.30pm

Lic ▥ CTV

Credit Cards ① ② ③ ⓔ

GH Ⓠ Ⓠ Ⓠ **Guidfa House** Crossgates LD1 6RF (3m N, at jct of A483/A44) (Logis) ☎Penybont(0597) 851241 FAX (0597) 851875

This very comfortable, family-run guest house -conveniently situated at the A44/A483 junction just three miles north of Llandrindod Wells - has its own car park as well as well maintained lawns and gardens. Bright, freshly decorated bedrooms are well equipped in modern style, most of them having en suite bath or shower rooms, and there is a comfortable residents' lounge. Small business meetings can now be catered for.

7rm(5⇔♠) ⊁ in dining room CTV in all bedrooms Ⓡ ⊁ (ex guide dogs) ✳ sB&Bfr£21 sB&B♠fr£31 dB&B⇔♠fr£44 WB&B£126-£186 WBDi£200-£260 LDO 7pm

Lic ▥ nc10yrs

Credit Cards ① ③

⇔ ➍ GH Ⓠ Ⓠ **The Kincoed** Temple Street LD1 5HF (on A483 50yds beyond the hospital) ☎(0597) 822656 FAX (0597) 824660

Positioned in the centre of the spa town and run by very experienced proprietors, a popular little hotel which provides good family accommodation has recently installed telephones in all its rooms. A small residents' bar leads off a restaurant offering two fixed-price menus; food is all freshly cooked on the premises - and entries in the visitors' book would seem to suggest that breakfasts are particularly noteworthy! Off-street car parking is available.

10rm(5⇔♠) (3fb) ⊁ in 2 bedrooms CTV in all bedrooms Ⓡ sB&B£15-£17.50 dB&B£28-£36 dB&B⇔♠£32-£40 WB&B£90-£125 WBDi£155-£199 LDO 9.30pm

Lic ▥ nc2yrs

Credit Cards ① ③ ⓔ

FH Ⓠ Ⓠ Mrs R Jones **Holly** *(SJ045593)* Howey LD1 5PP (Howey 2m S A483) ☎(0597) 822402

Apr-Nov

Well furnished bedrooms are offered at this comfortable, spotlessly bright and clean family farmhouse. It is set in its own pretty gardens, and a traditional dining room and lounge are also provided.

3⇔♠ (1fb) Ⓡ ⊁ ✳ dB&B⇔♠£32-£36 WB&B£112-£126 WBDi£155-£160 LDO 5pm

▥ CTV 70 acres beef sheep

SELECTED

FH Ⓠ Ⓠ Ⓠ Ⓠ Mr & Mrs R Bufton **Three Wells** *(SO062586)* Chapel Road, Howey LD1 5PB (Howey 2m S A483 then unclass rd, E 1m) ☎(0597) 824427 FAX (0597) 822484

This delightful farmhouse, run by the Bufton family, offers a very high standard of accommodation on a working farm. Bedrooms are well proportioned, have excellent beds, and the many little personal touches include a generous supply of reading material. Some rooms have their own sitting room, and are thus ideal for families. There is a choice of lounge, and all public areas have a view over the farm's own lake and the surrounding countryside. Fishing and riding can be arranged, food is plentiful, and for the less mobile there is a stair chair lift.

14⇔♠ ⊁ in dining room ⊁ in 1 lounge CTV in all bedrooms Ⓡ T 🏃 sB&B⇔♠£17-£18 dB&B⇔♠£34-£44 WB&B£110-£145 WBDi£165-£200 LDO 6pm

Lic lift ▥ CTV nc8yrs ➔ 50 acres beef mixed sheep

ⓔ

LLANDUDNO Gwynedd   Map **06** SH78

GH Ⓠ Ⓠ Ⓠ **Beach Cove** 8 Church Walks LL30 2HD (last road on left before pier) ☎(0492) 879638

Closed Xmas

Just off the promenade and a short walk from the pier, this immaculate little guest house offers attractive bedrooms with richly coloured decor and fabrics. One room has recently been fitted with a four-poster bed, and another room is located on the ground floor. The dining room has an unusual collection of nostalgic film and film star pictures on display. A residents' lounge and solarium are provided.

7rm(5♠) (2fb) ⊁ in 2 bedrooms ⊁ in dining room ⊁ in lounges CTV in all bedrooms Ⓡ 🏃 (ex guide dogs) dB&Bfr£24 dB&B♠fr£34 WB&Bfr£110 WBDifr£160 LDO 5.30pm

▥ CTV solarium

ⓔ

GH Ⓠ Ⓠ Ⓠ **Bodnant** 39 St Marys Road LL30 2UE ☎(0492) 876936

This small Edwardian guest house is situated in a quiet residential area within easy walking distance of the shops and seafront. Owners Peter and Anna Ankers offer guests a truly Welsh welcome, including lessons on the language and its history, and traditional Welsh dishes and folk music. Bedrooms are bright and well maintained, and there is a residents' lounge. Smoking is not permitted.

5⇔♠ CTV in all bedrooms Ⓡ 🏃 ✳ dB&Bfr£28 dB&B⇔♠fr£32 WB&Bfr£112 WBDifr£164.50

Lic ▥ nc12yrs

GH Ⓠ Ⓠ Ⓠ **Brannock Private Hotel** 36 St Davids Road LL30 2UH (enter town via A470, turn left prior to Holy Trinity church, through traffic lights then turn right off Trinity avenue) ☎(0492) 877483

Closed Xmas & New Year

Run for many years by the friendly Conyers family, the Brannock is situated in a quiet part of town, but within walking distance of the promenade and shops. Bedrooms are fresh and well equipped, many having en suite shower rooms. There is a pretty cottage-style dining room and a small foyer lounge for residents.

7rm(4♠) (1fb) CTV in all bedrooms Ⓡ LDO 5pm

▥ nc3yrs

Credit Cards ① ③

GH Ⓠ Ⓠ Ⓠ **Britannia Hotel** Promenade, 15 Craig-y-Don Parade LL30 1BG (close to North Wales Theatre & 100yds from Texaco garage) ☎(0492) 877185

Closed Dec

Run by the friendly Williams family for over 20 years, this well maintained guest house is situated on the promenade at Craig-y-Don. Traditional cooking is offered and Mrs Williams is well known for her mouth-watering sweets. Bedrooms are bright and cheerful and there are two rooms on the ground floor.

9rm(7⇔♠) (5fb) ⊁ in dining room ⊁ in lounges CTV in all bedrooms Ⓡ 🏃 (ex guide dogs) ✳ dB&Bfr£27 dB&B⇔♠fr£33 WBDi£129-£149 LDO 5pm

▥

⇔ ➍ GH Ⓠ Ⓠ **Bryn Rosa** 16 Abbey Road LL30 2EA ☎(0492) 878215

Though this end terraced house fronted by a small garden area stands in the shadow of the Great Orme, it is located in a residential area not far from the promenade and shops. Pretty public areas provide a contrast to modest, mainly compact bedrooms.

8rm(4♪) (2fb) ⊁ in dining room CTV in all bedrooms ®
sB&Bfr£13 sB&B♪fr£15 dB&Bfr£26 dB&B♪fr£30 WB&Bfr£90
WBDi£132-£142 LDO 4.30pm
▥ CTV nc2yrs
Credit Cards ①③⑥

GH ⓠⓠⓠ **Buile Hill Private Hotel** 46 St Mary's Road LL30 2UE
☎(0492) 876972
Mar-Nov
A short walk from the town centre and railway station, this
pleasant corner property is set in a quiet residential area. Friendly
proprietors, the Ward family, create a relaxed atmosphere and
provide freshly decorated accommodation. There is a small
residents' bar, a modern lounge and pretty gardens with a car park.
13rm(3⇥4♪) CTV in 2 bedrooms ® LDO 4pm
Lic ▥ CTV nc5yrs

GH ⓠⓠⓠ **Carmel Private Hotel** 17 Craig-y-Don Parade,
Promenade LL30 1BG (on main promenade between the Great and
Little Ormes) ☎(0492) 877643
Etr-Oct rs Apr
A private hotel situated in end-of-terrace position on the eastern
side of the promenade, with the added advantage of its own rear
car park, offers accommodation in bright, cheerful bedrooms - the
front-facing ones enjoying fine views of the bay. Public areas
include an attractive foyer lounge and dining room.
9rm(6♪) (2fb) ⊁ in lounges CTV in 10
bedrooms ® ✳ sB&Bfr£13.50-£18.50 dB&Bfr£27-£28 dB&B♪£32-
£33 WB&Bfr£91-£94.50 WBDi£129.50-£136.50 LDO noon
▥ CTV nc4yrs

GH ⓠⓠⓠ **Hotel Carmen** Carmen Sylva Road, Craig-y-Don
LL30 1LZ ☎(0492) 876361
Mar-Nov rs Xmas
Conveniently located a few yards from the promenade at Craig-y-
Don this large double-fronted hotel offers sound accommodation.
The friendly and enthusiastic owners, Mr and Mrs Newberry, have
added en suite facilities to most of the rooms, along with new beds
fitted with attractive duvets. Public areas include a spacious
residents' lounge furnished with comfortable, modern suites and a
separate bar featuring an electic organ and regular entertainment
during the season. There is no car park but street parking is readily
available.
8⇥♪ (4fb) ⊁ in 12 bedrooms ⊁ in dining room ⊁ in 1 lounge
CTV in all bedrooms ® ✠ (ex guide dogs) ✳ sB&B⇥♪£26
dB&B⇥♪£48-£52 WB&B£150-£180 LDO 5.30pm
Lic ▥ CTV ⊀nc10yrs
①

GH ⓠⓠⓠⓠ **Cornerways Hotel** 2 St Davids Place
LL30 2UG ☎(0492) 877334
Apr-1 Nov
Run by the friendly Rumbold family, this pleasant little hotel
is situated in a quiet residential area, within a short walk of the
promenade and shopping centre. Bedrooms are well equipped
with modern facilities and most have Stag or modern pine
furniture. There are several canopied beds, and one room has
its own sitting room. A comfortable lounge is provided and
honest home cooking is on offer.
7⇥♪ ✠ in dining room ⊁ in dining room CTV in all bedrooms
® ✠ (ex guide dogs) ✳ sB&B⇥♪£20 dB&B⇥♪£40-£44
WB&Bfr£140 WBDifr£200 LDO 3pm
Lic ▥ nc

GH ⓠⓠⓠⓠ **Craiglands Private Hotel** 7 Carmen Sylva
Road, Craig-y-Don LL30 1LZ ☎(0492) 875090

Mar-Nov
Run for over 25 years by the Mullin family, this small and
immaculately kept hotel is situated just off the promenade at
Craig-y-Don. Blodwen Mullin does all the cooking herself
using only fresh produce. Her baking has gained quite a
reputation, and she even makes her own bread. The fresh
bedrooms all have en suite bath or shower rooms, and a
comfortable residents' lounge is provided. Easy street parking
is available.
6⇥♪♪ (1fb) ⊁ in dining room CTV in all bedrooms ® ✳
sB&B⇥♪£18.50 dB&B⇥♪£34 WB&B£129.50 WBDi£196
LDO 4pm
▥ CTV nc4yrs

GH ⓠⓠⓠⓠⓠ **Cranberry House** 12 Abbey Road LL30 2EA
☎(0492) 879760
Mar-Oct
Named after a very attractive collection of Cranberry
glassware, this is a delightful family-run guesthouse, strictly
for non-smoking guests. The bedrooms have been attractively
decorated with coordinating fabrics and wallpaper, and
furnished with pine and some fine antiques. The pleasant
sitting room has deep sofas and fresh flowers, and meals are
served at round lace-covered tables in the dining room. This
Victorian house is conveniently situated in a quiet residential
area of the town, within easy walking distance of local
amenities, with the advantage of its own car park.
6⇥♪ ⊁ CTV in all bedrooms ® ✠ (ex guide dogs)
dB&B⇥♪£34-£40 WB&Bfr£120 WBDifr£175 LDO noon
▥ CTV nc
Credit Cards ①②③⑥

GH ⓠⓠ **Granby** Deganwy Avenue LL30 2DD (turn left by
cenotaph on beach near pier, continue down dual carriageway 2
blocks on left hand side) ☎(0492) 876095
Centrally situated, this guest house is just a short walk from the
seafront and shopping centre. It has a a cosy residents' bar, a small
lounge and a pretty dining room. Bedrooms include several
suitable for families and many have en suite shower rooms.
9rm(5♪) (4fb) CTV in all bedrooms ® LDO 4pm
Lic CTV
Credit Cards ①③

GH ⓠⓠⓠⓠ **Hollybank** 9 St Davids Place LL30 2UG
☎(0492) 878521
Etr-Nov
Hollybank is a spotlessly maintained guest house situated in a
quiet part of town, with its own enclosed rear car park.
Bedrooms are brightly decorated and all have a good range of
facilities, including en suite bath or shower rooms. A modern
lounge and pretty dining room are provided and a liquor
licence is held. Only non smokers are accommodated.
7⇥♪ (2fb) ⊁ CTV in all bedrooms ® sB&B⇥♪£20-£22
dB&B⇥♪£36-£40 WB&B£119-£126 WBDi£168-£175 LDO
4pm
Lic ▥
Credit Cards ①③⑥

GH ⓠⓠⓠ **Hotel Messina** Hill Terrace LL30 2LS
☎(0492) 875260 FAX (0492) 875260
The Messina is a small family-run hotel situated under the wooded
slopes of the Great Orme with excellent views over the

▶

promenade. Bedrooms include several suitable for families, and all are attractively decorated and well equipped. A comfortable residents' lounge is provided and the restaurant takes full advantage of the views. The cosy bar features an unusual display of pop records collected by the Astle family over the years.
10rm(4⇨3🅵) (5fb) ⊱ in dining room CTV in all bedrooms Ⓡ ✳ sB&B£17-£20 dB&B£32-£34 dB&B⇨🅵£37-£39 WB&B£110-£125 WBDi£158-£173 LDO 6.30pm
Lic 🛏
Credit Cards ① ② ③ ⓔ

GH ⓠⓠ *Minion Private Hotel* 21-23 Carmen Sylva Road LL30 1EQ ☎(0492) 877740
Etr-mid Oct
A large corner property with pretty gardens and its own car park, this hotel stands in a quiet residential area within easy reach of both the seafront and the Craig-y-don shopping area. Bedrooms - two of them on the ground floor - all have en suite bath or shower rooms, and guests can relax in the cosy bar or a comfortable TV lounge.
12rm(5⇨7🅵) (1fb) Ⓡ LDO 4pm
Lic CTV

GH ⓠⓠⓠ **Montclare Hotel** North Parade LL30 2LP
☎(0492) 877061
Mar-Oct
A tall, terraced guesthouse stands almost on the seafront at the pier end of the promenade, conveniently close to the main shopping area. Bedrooms are all neat and modern, with coordinating fabrics and colour schemes; they all have en suite facilities. The comfortable lounge has deep upholstered cane seating and there is a small bar. Enjoyable home cooking using fresh produce is served in the pretty dining room.
15rm(2⇨13🅵) (6fb) ⊱ in 6 bedrooms ⊱ in dining room CTV in all bedrooms Ⓡ ✻ (ex guide dogs) ✳ sB&B⇨🅵fr£17 dB&B⇨🅵fr£34 WB&Bfr£110 WBDifr£150 LDO 3pm
Lic 🛏 ⅌

ⓔ

GH ⓠⓠⓠ **Orotava Private Hotel** 105 Glan-y-Mor Road, Penrhyn Bay LL30 3PH ☎(0492) 549780
The Orotava Hotel is superbly situated at Penrhyn Bay just east of Llandudno. The lounge and many of the bedrooms look out over the bay, and the pretty lawns and gardens give access to the sea wall. The front restaurant is very popular locally at lunch times.
6rm(4⇨2🅵) CTV in all bedrooms Ⓡ ✻ ✳ sB&B⇨🅵£16.50 dB&B⇨🅵£33 LDO 6pm
Lic 🛏 CTV nc15yrs
Credit Cards ① ③

🖼 💺 GH ⓠⓠ **Rosaire Private Hotel** 2 St Seiriols Road LL30 2YY ☎(0492) 877677
Mar-Oct
The Rosaire is in a peaceful location in easy walking distance of both shores and the town centre, and many bedrooms have good views over the area including the Great Orme. There is a comfortable residents' lounge, pretty gardens, ample parking and a warm welcome extended by the friendly Evans family.
10rm(2⇨6🅵) ⊱ in dining room CTV in 9 bedrooms Ⓡ sB&B£13.50-£14.50 dB&B⇨🅵£30-£32 WB&B£105-£112 WBDi£139-£150 LDO 4pm
Lic 🛏 nc3yrs
ⓔ

GH ⓠⓠⓠ **St Hilary Hotel** 16 Craig-y-Don Parade, Promenade LL30 1BG (on main promenade close to New Theatre & Conference Centre) ☎(0492) 875551
Feb-Oct
Stylishly decorated throughout, this private hotel at the eastern end of the promenade offers sweeping views of the bay from the window seating of some of its front-facing bedrooms. The welcoming foyer lounge area is augmented by another comfortable sitting room.

11rm(8🅵) (8fb) ⊱ in dining room CTV in all bedrooms Ⓡ ✻ (ex guide dogs) ✳ sB&B£13.50-£27 sB&B🅵£16.50-£33 dB&B£27 dB&B🅵£33-£36 WB&B£94.50-£115.50 WBDi£129-£149 LDO 5.30pm
Lic 🛏 ⅌
Credit Cards ① ③ ⓔ

GH ⓠⓠ *Sunnyside Private Hotel* Llewelyn Avenue LL30 2ER
☎(0492) 877150
Etr-Oct & Xmas
Run by the friendly Bryson family, this large detached house has a patio garden in the front and is only a short walk from the town centre and seafront. The majority of the bedrooms have en suite facilities, and there are some bedrooms on the ground floor. There is a comfortable lounge for residents and a bar complete with its own dance floor where entertainment is provided several times a week. The property has access to the sandy beaches.
26rm(5⇨8🅵) (4fb) CTV in all bedrooms Ⓡ LDO 7.30pm
Lic 🛏 CTV

GH ⓠⓠⓠ **Thorpe House** 3 St Davids Road LL30 2UL
☎(0492) 877089 FAX (0492) 876627
Mar-Oct
Thorpe House is a well maintained hotel in a quiet residential area of the town, convenient for both shores and the town centre. Bedrooms, including some family rooms, are freshly decorated and bright, and many have en suite facilities. A spacious residents' lounge is provided, along with a modern restaurant and a cosy bar. Easy street parking is available.
10rm(1⇨7🅵) (4fb) ⊱ in dining room CTV in 8 bedrooms Ⓡ ✳ sB&B£15.50 sB&B⇨🅵£18 dB&B£31 dB&B⇨🅵£36 WB&B£108-£129.50 WBDi£164.50 LDO 4pm
Lic 🛏 CTV ⅌
ⓔ

GH ⓠⓠⓠ **Warwick Hotel** 56 Church Walks LL30 2HL
☎(0492) 876823
Set on the lower slopes of the Great Orme this large, detached Victorian house has good views of the town and beyond. The majority of the bedrooms have en suite facilities and satellite television is available. Public areas include a residents' bar, spacious lounge and an attractive restaurant which overlooks lawns where guests can relax in good weather.
16rm(8⇨5🅵) (9fb) CTV in all bedrooms Ⓡ ✳ sB&B£18-£20 sB&B⇨🅵£21-£23 dB&B£36-£40 dB&B⇨🅵£42-£46 WB&B£90-£138 WBDi£125-£180 LDO 6.45pm
Lic 🛏 CTV ⅌
Credit Cards ① ② ③ ⓔ

GH ⓠⓠ *Wedgwood Hotel* 6 Deganwy Avenue LL30 2YB
☎(0492) 878016
Etr-Dec
Centrally situated and within walking distance of the seafront, this hotel has attractively decorated bedrooms which, although not large, are equipped with such useful items as clock radios and hair dryers. The relaxing lounge, cosy bar and dining room are Victorian in style.
11rm(2⇨7🅵) (1fb) CTV in all bedrooms Ⓡ LDO 3pm
Lic 🛏 CTV

GH ⓠⓠ *Winston* 5 Church Walks LL30 2HD (guesthouse at the bottom of Church Walks which is opposite the pier on the North Shore) ☎(0492) 876144
Situated 80 yards from the seafront and pier, this well kept guest house has been run by the Healeys for more than 20 years. Bedrooms are attractive with matching floral drapes and wallpapers - many have canopied beds. The lounge is modern and comfortable. Good home-cooked meals are available in the dining room. Unrestricted street parking is available.
7rm(6🅵) (1fb) CTV in all bedrooms Ⓡ ✻ LDO 4pm
🛏 CTV nc2yrs
Credit Cards ① ③

LLANEGRYN Gwynedd   Map **06** SH50

SELECTED

FH 🅀🅀🅀🅀 Mrs Griffiths **Bryn Gwyn Country Farm House** *(SH610060)* LL36 9UF (im inland from A493)
☎Tywyn(0654) 711771
Mar-Oct

Set in four-acres of gardens and paddocks and situated within the Snowdonia National Park, this delightful old house dates back to 1730. The bedrooms may not be luxurious but are well maintained. Public rooms include a lovely dining room with antique furniture, where guests can eat off Minton China, and a choice of lounges. A simple games room has been created from a converted garage.

3rm(1⇦1🏿) (2fb) ✗ in bedrooms ✗ in dining room ✗ in 1 lounge CTV in 1 bedroom ® 🏿 (ex guide dogs) ✳ dB&B£29-£37 dB&B⇦🏿£42 WB&B£88-£126 WBDi£176-£214 LDO 2pm
🎟 CTV bicycles 4 acres non-working
£

LLANELLI Dyfed   Map **02** SN50

GH 🅀 Awel Y Mor 86 Queen Victoria Road SA15 2TH
☎(0554) 755357

Awel Y Mor is a small guesthouse just a short walk from the town centre, with neat bedrooms and a comfortable open plan lounge/breakfast room.

▌1rm(4⇦3🏿) (2fb) CTV in 7 bedrooms 🏿 (ex guide dogs) ✳ sB&B£15 sB&B⇦🏿£15 dB&B£26 dB&B⇦🏿£26 WBDi£133 LDO 4.30pm
🎟 CTV

LLANFACHRETH Gwynedd   Map **06** SH72

PREMIER 🏆 **SELECTED**

GH 🅀🅀🅀🅀🅀 Ty Isaf
LL40 2EA (opposite the church)
☎Dolgellau(0341) 423261

Beautifully situated on the edge of the village and offering superb views, this traditional Welsh longhouse has been lovingly decorated and furnished by present owners Graham and Diana Silverton. There are three guests' lounges, one with an open fire and old beams. An excellent evening meal with some choice is available.

3⇦🏿 ✗ in bedrooms ✗ in dining room ® sB&B⇦🏿£23-£33 dB&B⇦🏿£46 WB&B£161 WBDi£238 LDO 6pm
🎟 CTV nc13yrs
£

LANFAIR CAEREINION Powys   Map **06** SJ10

H 🅀🅀🅀 Mrs J Cornes **Cwmllwynog** *(SJ071065)* SY21 0HF
▌urn left off A458 into village pass the church through Milin y ▌dol farm 1m on left) ☎(0938) 810791
▌n-Nov

▌his 17th-century farmhouse with its exposed beams and inglenook ▌replace is just off the B4385. It offers a warm welcome and ▌dditional home cooking using local produce wherever possible.
▌m(1🏿) CTV in all bedrooms ® 🏿 ✳ dB&B🏿fr£32
▌BDifr£150 LDO 4pm
▌ CTV 105 acres dairy
▌

INN🅀🅀 **Goat Hotel** High Street SY21 0QS (leave A458 just after light railway station through town hotel opposite church)
☎(0938) 810428

An historic 17th-century village inn stands almost opposite the church, and has a roaring fire in the timbered bar where visitors can enjoy the local atmosphere. There is a small dining room for evening meals and breakfast. The bedrooms have ceiling beams and uneven floors, but are modern otherwise.

6rm(4⇦🏿) (1fb)® T sB&B£20 sB&B⇦🏿£25 dB&B£30 dB&B⇦🏿£40 Lunch £5-£7.50 Dinner £7-£12.50alc LDO 9pm
🎟
Credit Cards 1 3 £

LLANGOLLEN Clwyd   Map **07** SJ24

GH 🅀🅀🅀 Hillcrest Hill Street LL20 8EU (leave A5 at traffic lights up the hill at the side of the Grapes Hotel, Hillcrest 200 metres on left) ☎Wrexham(0978) 860208

An immaculate Victorian house set in extensive grounds a short walk from the centre of this popular tourist town. Attractively decorated bedrooms feature many original fireplaces and are well equipped with modern facilities; family rooms are also available. There is a comfortable residents' lounge, and good value home cooking is offered, with only non smokers accommodated.

7🏿 (2fb) ✗ CTV in 1 bedroom ® 🏿 (ex guide dogs) ✳ dB&B🏿£38-£40 WB&B£266 WBDi£325.50 LDO noon
Lic 🎟 CTV
£

FH 🅀 Mrs A Kenrick **Rhydonnen Ucha Rhewl** *(SJ174429)* Rhewl LL20 7AJ ☎(0978) 860153
Etr-Nov

The Kenrick family, who have run this farm for many years, provide a warm, welcoming atmosphere. The accommodation is clean and well decorated, and there is a traditionally furnished lounge and dining room for guests. Shooting and fishing are available.

4rm (2fb) LDO 3pm
🎟 CTV 125 acres dairy

LLANGURIG Powys   Map **06** SN98

SELECTED

🍴 🎀 GH 🅀🅀🅀🅀 **Old Vicarage** SY18 6RN (off A470/A44 trunk road) ☎(05515) 280 due to change to (0686) 440280 FAX (05515) 280
Mar-Oct

A comfortable home-from-home, this attractive Victorian vicarage is set back in a quiet cul-de-sac near the centre of the village. Excellent standards of housekeeping are maintained throughout and all bedrooms have good quality furnishings. There are two lounges, one designated no-smoking, and both stacked with books and local information. Afternoon teas are a feature, and the house also promotes a range of local food and craft goods.

5rm(2⇦2🏿) (2fb) ✗ in bedrooms ✗ in dining room ✗ in 1 lounge CTV in 4 bedrooms ® sB&B£15 dB&B⇦🏿£40 WB&B£140 WBDi£200 LDO 6.30pm
Lic 🎟 CTV nc5yrs
£

LLANIDLOES Powys   Map **06** SN98

INN🅀🅀 **Mount** China Street SY18 6AB (off A470)
☎(0686) 412247

A fourteenth-century listed building, this inn at the centre of the busy market town offers smart bars divided into several parts - one of them suitable for children; particularly impressive is what appears to the original bar, with its polished cobbled floor, wooden

▶

settles and black fireplace. Externally accessed bedrooms all have modern en suite shower rooms and are equipped with TV and tea trays. The inn is popular for its wide range of food, and meals are served on the patio in fine weather. On site parking is available.
3♠ (1fb)CTV in all bedrooms ® 🏃 (ex guide dogs) ✳ sB&B♠£25 dB&B♠£35 WB&B£105-£150 WBDi£180-£225 LDO 8.45pm
🎱 CTV play area for children

LLANON Dyfed   Map 06 SN56

INN[Q][Q][Q] *Plas Morfa Hotel & Restaurant* Plas Morfa SY23 5LX ☎(0974) 202415
At one time this building was a brewery, which accounts for its distinctive character. The accommodation is bright and spacious and most rooms face the sea. There is a welcoming bar and restaurant as well as a further bar/disco in a converted warehouse.
8⇆♠ (2fb) CTV in all bedrooms ® LDO 9.30pm
🎱
Credit Cards [3]

LLANRHYSTUD Dyfed   Map 06 SN56

SELECTED

FH [Q][Q][Q][Q] Mrs T T Mizen **Pen-Y-Castell** *(SN539684)* SY23 5BZ (take B4337 for about 1m climbing steep hill then follow guesthouse signs) ☎Nebo(0974) 272622
High above Cardigan Bay, just 2.5 miles from the village, and commanding beautiful views, this modernised guesthouse sits in pleasant grounds and boasts its own trout lake. Run by the friendly Mizen family, it offers pretty bedrooms with coordinating colour schemes, and a family unit with a separate bunk-bedded room. The cosy lounge has a cheerful wood-burning stove, and there is also a sun lounge with comfortable cushioned cane seating.
6⇆♠ (1fb) ⠗ in bedrooms ⠗ in dining room ⠗ in 1 lounge CTV in 3 bedrooms ® 🏃 (ex guide dogs) ✳ sB&B⇆♠£25 dB&B⇆♠£50 WB&B£170 WBDi£250 LDO 6pm
Lic 🎱 CTV ⚓ boating lake 35 acres beef sheep
£

LLANSANTFFRAID-YM-MECHAIN Powys   Map 07 SJ22

FH [Q][Q][Q] Mrs M E Jones *Glanvyrnwy (SJ229202)* SY22 6SU ☎Llansantffraid(0691) 828258
This stone-built farmhouse, situated on the edge of the village, dates back some 300 years, and three windows are still bricked up from the time of the window tax. The two neat bedrooms have a pretty decor, and there is a choice of comfortable lounges. Guests also enjoy the well tended gardens and lawns. Mrs Jones has long extended warm Welsh hospitality, and some guests have been returning regularly for 20 years.
2rm ® 🏃 (ex guide dogs)
CTV nc3yrs 42 acres beef

LLANWDDYN Powys   Map 06 SJ01

FH [Q][Q] H A Parry **Tynymaes** *(SJ048183)* SY10 0NN ☎(069173) 216
May-Sep
Situated just a few miles from Lake Vyrnwy this cosy farmhouse, run by the Parry family offers a warm welcome. The lounge is spacious and comfortable and the bedrooms are bright and cheerful.
3rm (1fb) ⠗ in bedrooms ⠗ in dining room ® 🏃 ✳ sB&B£15 dB&B£28-£30 WB&B£98-£105
🎱 CTV 420 acres beef sheep
£

LLANWNDA Gwynedd   Map 06 SH45

P R E M I E R 🦢 S E L E C T E D

FH [Q][Q][Q][Q][Q] Mr & Mrs G Rowlands **Pengwern** *(SH459587)* Saron LL54 5UH ☎(0286) 830717
Closed Dec & Jan
Peacefully situated between the mountains and the sea, this beautifully preserved and impeccably maintained large Victorian house commands wonderful views of Snowdon and the 130 acres of land on which it stands. There are three period furnished but modern and well equipped bedrooms in the main house, two of which have enormous and luxurious en suite bathrooms and the third has exclusive use of a modern bathroom and toilet. A fourth self-contained unit, located in a single storey cottage to the rear of the house, comprises a large double room plus a small twin and has its own spacious lounge, bathroom and kitchen. This is a no smoking establishment.
3rm(2⇆♠) Annexe 1⇆♠ CTV in all bedrooms ® 🏃
🎱 130 acres beef sheep

LLANWRTYD WELLS Powys   Map 03 SN84

GH [Q][Q][Q] **Lasswade Country House Hotel** LD5 4RW (turn off A483 signposted Llangammarch Wells hotel 200yds on right) ☎(05913) 515 FAX (05913) 611
A handsome Edwardian house is set in a prime position with commanding views of the surrounding countryside. Owners Jack and Beryl Udall provide a welcoming environment, with spacious well equipped bedrooms, a comfortable traditional lounge and attractive dining room. A choice of plentiful, fresh, home-cooked dishes is offered, making good use of local produce. The hotel also features a sunken garden and south-facing terrace. Many birdwatchers are drawn to the area for the Red Kite, famous in this vicinity.
8⇆♠ ⠗ in bedrooms ⠗ in dining room CTV in all bedrooms ® T sB&B⇆♠£27.50 dB&B⇆♠£55 WB&B£175 WBDi£252 Lic 🎱 CTV nc12yrs sauna solarium
Credit Cards [1][3]£

LOCHINVER Highland *Sutherland*   Map 14 NC02

GH [Q][Q] **Ardglas** IV27 4LI ☎(05714) 257
Feb-Nov
Built on the hill overlooking the bay and harbour this friendly family-run guesthouse offers good value bed and breakfast accommodation. The well maintained non-smoking bedrooms, which vary in size, are equipped with mixed modern appointments and there is a comfortable TV lounge. Hearty breakfasts, occasionally at shared tables, are served in the small dining room overlooking the bay.
8rm (2fb) CTV in 1 bedroom ®
🎱 CTV

LOCHRANZA See ARRAN, ISLE OF

LOCHWINNOCH Strathclyde *Renfrewshire*   Map 10 NS3

FH [Q][Q] Mrs A Mackie **High Belltrees** *(NS377584)* PA12 4JN (situated 1m off the A737 to Largs road) ☎(0505) 842376
Over the years Mrs MacKie has built up a long list of regular visitors to her welcoming farmhouse, which stands in an elevated position amid gentle rolling countryside. The accommodation comprises comfortable bedrooms, a combined lounge/dining room and a cosy sun lounge.

4 (2fb)CTV in all bedrooms ® ✝ (ex guide dogs) ✳ sB&B£15-£17 dB&B£30-£32 WB&B£95-£100
⊞ CTV 220 acres dairy mixed sheep

LOCKERBIE Dumfries & Galloway *Dumfriesshire*
Map 11 NY18
GH Q Q **Kirkside of Middlebie** DG11 3JW (off A74 onto B722, first left at Middlebie) ☎Ecclefechan(0576) 300204
Rurally situated but within two miles of the A74(M) in the hamlet of Middlebie, this 19th-century country house is very much the home of Captain and Mrs Milne-Home and has a comfortable lived-in atmosphere. A drawing room is provided for guests' use and home-cooked meals are served in the cheerfully decorated dining room.
2rm ® ✳ sB&Bfr£20 dB&Bfr£40 LDO noon
⊞ CTV

GH Q Q Q **Rosehill** Carlisle Road DG11 2DR (south end of town)
☎(0576) 202378
Dating from 1871, this sandstone house set in an attractive garden stands beside the B723 just to the south of the town centre. It offers pleasant bed and breakfast accommodation and the well proportioned public rooms include a lounge and separate breakfast room.
5rm(2f❜) (2fb) CTV in all bedrooms ® sB&B£17-£20 dB&B£32-£34 dB&Bf❜£36-£38
⊞ CTV
£

LONDON Greater London

Places within the London postal area are listed below in postal district order commencing East then North, South and West, with a brief indication of the area covered. Other places within the county of London are listed under their respective placenames.

E11 LEYTONSTONE

P R E M I E R 🏆 **S E L E C T E D**

GH Q Q Q Q Q **Lakeside**
51 Snaresbrook Road,
Wanstead E11 1PQ (half mile from end of M11 close to Snaresbrook Underground Station) ☎081-989 6100
Mar-Nov
Within two minutes of Snaresbrook Underground Station on the Central Line, this light, airy and well maintained house can offer convenient access to central London. It stands in a residential road, with colourful gardens front and rear, with the bonus of views to a lake with swans and to a part of Epping Forest. The house has many attractive 1930s features including a white-panelled hall, high ceilings and continental stained glass. The bedrooms are a good size, spotlessly clean and attractive. A freshly cooked breakfast is served and guests will enjoy an informal, friendly welcome from owners Mr and Mrs Seal.
3❜f❜ ✘ CTV in all bedrooms ® ✝ ✳ dB&B❜f❜£35-£39.50
⊞ nc12yrs

E18 SOUTH WOODFORD

GH Q Q Q **Grove Hill Hotel** 38 Grove Hill, South Woodford E18 2JG (off A11 London Rd, close to South Woodford tube station) ☎081-989 3344 FAX 081-530 5286
A small private, hotel in a residential area. The accommodation is modest in style with clean and nicely maintained bedrooms. A ▶

THE CRANBROOK HOTEL
22-24 COVENTRY ROAD, ILFORD, ESSEX IG1 4QR

Telephone: 0181-554 6544 or 554 4765
or 518 2964 or 554 5814
Fax: 0181-518 1463
Licensed Restaurant
Most rooms have bathroom and telephone, some with jacuzzi. All rooms colour TV satellite – Tea & coffee – Radio. 20 minutes by train to London, 2 minutes town centre and station, 5 minutes Gants Hill underground,
7 miles City and 10 miles West End.
Easy reach of M11, M25 & A406.
Access, Visa & American Express accepted.

AA QQQ

LAKESIDE
51 Snaresbrook Road, London E11 1PQ

VISITING LONDON? BE OUR GUESTS!
Have a comfortable night in a superior en-suite room, with all facilities.
Take a full English breakfast in our elegant dining room, or on the flower decked garden terrace.
Then walk 2 min. Central Line Tube to see the sights of London

Access all airports, pickups arranged
(Free parking)

0181-989-6100

choice of English or Continental breakfast is available.
21rm(10🛁2🚿) (2fb) CTV in all bedrooms [R] **T** LDO 9pm
Lic ♨ CTV
Credit Cards [1] [2] [3]

N4 FINSBURY PARK

SELECTED

GH [Q] [Q] [Q] [Q] Mount View 31 Mount View Road N4 4SS
☎081-340 9222 FAX 081-342 8494
A delightful Victorian terraced house in a quiet well situated location, with a pleasant rear garden and unrestricted roadside parking. The bedrooms are generally spacious, and individually furnished in an elegant English style with good quality coordinating fabrics and decor, together with thoughtful little extra touches. A choice of breakfast, including health food, is served at two sittings around a communal table in the open plan dining room downstairs, which opens out on to the patio. Direct access to London is good, being fairly close to Finsbury Park underground; new arrivals should take the 'Wells Terrace' exit: prior arrangements can be made for collection from the station.
3rm(2🛁🚿) 🚭 CTV in all bedrooms 🐕 * sB&B£18-£26 dB&B£36 dB&B🛁🚿£40 WB&B£105-£182
♨ 🅿

N8 HORNSEY

GH [Q] [Q] Aber Hotel 89 Crouch Hill N8 9EG ☎081-340 2847
FAX 081-340 2847
Situated in a residential area and within easy reach of the city centre, this hotel offers compact but well furnished bedrooms. It has a comfortable sitting room and a small dining room.
9rm (4fb) 🚭 in 2 bedrooms 🚭 in dining room 🐕 sB&B£20-£26 dB&B£36-£38 WB&B£112-£140
♨ CTV
Credit Cards [1] [3] [£]

GH [Q] [Q] [Q] White Lodge Hotel 1 Church Lane, Hornsey N8 7BU
☎081-348 9765 FAX 081-340 7851
A well maintained bed and breakfast establishment in a busy residential area, it offers well equipped bedrooms and an attractive and comfortable sitting room. Breakfast is served in the small dining room.
16rm(8🚿) (5fb) CTV in all bedrooms [R] 🐕 (ex guide dogs) * sB&B£24-£26 dB&B£34-£36 dB&B🚿£40-£42 LDO at breakfast
♨ CTV 🅿
Credit Cards [1] [3]

N19 UPPER HOLLOWAY

GH [Q] [Q] [Q] Parkland Walk 12 Hornsey Rise Gardens N19 3PR
☎071-263 3228 & 071-404 5011 FAX 071-831 9489
Built about 1880 this house has been beautifully restored by Lawrence and Penny Solomons who have made good use of period and antique furniture throughout. Bedrooms are sympathetic to the English Town House style and guests (six max) share two general bathrooms. There is a comfortable lounge and guests have unrestricted access to the house where a no smoking policy is strictly observed. A full English breakfast is cooked to order and the helpful and friendly owners are happy to recommend local restaurants for other meals.
4rm (1fb) 🚭 CTV in all bedrooms [R] 🐕 * sB&B£20-£28 dB&B£40-£46 WB&B£138-£168
♨ CTV
Credit Cards [2] [£]

NW1 REGENT'S PARK

GH [Q] [Q] [Q] ***Four Seasons Hotel*** 173 Gloucester Place, Regents Park NW1 6DX ☎071-724 3461 & 071-723 9471
FAX 071-402 5594
A relaxing and comfortable atmosphere is created by the resident proprietors of this friendly hotel. Bedrooms furnished in modern style are being slowly upgraded, but all are double-glazed and have direct dial telephones and TV; two of them are conveniently situated on the ground floor. Breakfast - cooked by request, otherwise continental - is served in a conservatory which looks on to the roof garden, and light refeshments can usually be provided. Laundry, dry cleaning, ironing and fax services are also available, and there is meter car parking round the corner in Ivor Place.
16rm(14🛁🚿) (2fb) CTV in all bedrooms 🐕
♨
Credit Cards [1] [2] [3] [5]

NW2 CRICKLEWOOD

GH [Q] Clearview House 161 Fordwych Road NW2 3NG
☎081-452 9773
In a quiet residential area, this small guest house has clean and well maintained accommodation. The bedrooms are neatly furnished and equipped. There is a good size dining/lounge on the ground floor.
6rm (1fb) CTV in 1 bedroom 🐕 (ex guide dogs) * sB&Bfr£14 dB&Bfr£28 WB&Bfr£85
♨ CTV nc5yrs
[£]

GH [Q] [Q] [Q] ***The Garth Hotel*** 64-76 Hendon Way NW2 2NL
☎081-455 4742
Situated on the southbound carriageway of the A41 Hendon Way, this family-run hotel has been extensively redeveloped, and offers a wide range of accommodation. The 53 bedrooms are furnished in bright, modern style, each with a private bathroom and equipped with TV, direct-dial telephone and tea trays. The impressive marble foyer leads to the Tivoli restaurant and bar which specialises in Italian cuisine. Extensive conference and banqueting facilities are available, and there is a large car park at the rear. The hotel is conveniently located five minutes' drive from the M1 and 4.5 miles from Oxford Circus.
53rm(30🛁10🚿) (9fb) CTV in all bedrooms [R] LDO 11pm
Lic ♨ CTV
Credit Cards [1] [2] [3] [5]

NW3 HAMPSTEAD

GH [Q] [Q] La Gaffe 107-111 Heath Street NW3 6SS (located at the top end of Heath St 200yds from Hampstead Underground)
☎071-435 4941 & 071-435 8965 FAX 071-794 7592
Annexe 18🚿 🚭 in bedrooms CTV in all bedrooms 🐕 (ex guide dogs) * sB&B🚿£42.50-£50 dB&B🚿£60-£65 LDO 11.30pm
Lic ♨
Credit Cards [1] [2] [3] [5] [£]

SELECTED

GH [Q] [Q] [Q] [Q] The Langorf Hotel 20 Frognal, Hampstead NW3 6AG ☎071-794 4483 FAX 071-435 9055
In a quiet residential area, this guest house offers accommodation of a high standard. As well as a dining room/bar where guests can choose from either English or Continental breakfast, there is a small but comfortable foyer/lounge. Light meals and snacks are available 24 hours a day. All the bedrooms are well-equipped.
31🛁🚿 (2fb)CTV in all bedrooms [R] **T** 🐕 sB&B🛁🚿£45-£61 dB&B🛁🚿£50-£90 WB&B£360 LDO 10.30pm
Lic lift ♨ CTV
Credit Cards [1] [2] [3] [5] [£]
See advertisement on p.261.

SELECTED

GH [Q][Q][Q][Q] ***Sandringham Hotel*** 3 Holford Road, Hampstead NW3 1AD ☎071-435 1569 FAX 071-431 5932

A delightful period house in a very elegant village neighbourhood, within walking distance of the underground station and all the local attractions. The accommodation which is still being upgraded is furnished with antiques, enhancing the English country house atmosphere. Personally run by the resident proprietors Michael and Jill von Grey, the hotel's reputation lies in the personal attention to customer care. Bedrooms are non smoking and individually furnished with thoughtful little extras. There is a formal sitting room and an attractive, well appointed breakfast room, where traditional cooked breakfast usually includes fresh baked muffins, choice of teas and coffees, and fresh fruit. Service of light meals is available throughout the day, and local restaurants can be recommended.

17rm(11🛁🚿) (4fb) CTV in all bedrooms T 🚫🐕

Lic ♨

Credit Cards [1][3]

NW4 HENDON

GH [Q][Q] Peacehaven Hotel 94 Audley Road, Hendon Central NW4 3HB (turn off A41 at Hendon Central, turn right into Vivian Avenue then 5th left into Audley Road) ☎081-202 9758 & 081-202 1225

The bedrooms at this guest house are neatly furnished and equipped. Guests take their meals in the small dining room which overlooks the garden and a choice of either English or Continental breakfast is available.

13rm(7🛁🚿) CTV in all bedrooms [R] 🚫🐕 (ex guide dogs) * sB&B£38 sB&B🛁🚿£48 dB&B£50 dB&B🛁🚿£60

♨

Credit Cards [1][2][3][5] [£]

NW11 GOLDERS GREEN

GH [Q][Q][Q] ***Anchor Hotel*** 10 West Heath Drive, Golders Green NW11 7QH ☎081-458 8764 FAX 081-455 3204

12rm(9🚿) (2fb) CTV in all bedrooms [R] T 🚫🐕 (ex guide dogs)

♨ CTV

Credit Cards [1][3]

GH [Q][Q] Central Hotel 35 Hoop Lane, Golders Green NW11 8BS ☎081-458 5636 FAX 081-455 4792

13🛁🚿 CTV in all bedrooms T 🚫🐕 * sB&B🛁🚿£30-£40 dB&B🛁🚿£50-£60

♨

Credit Cards [1][2][3][5]

GH [Q][Q][Q] Croft Court Hotel 44 Ravenscroft Avenue, Golders Green NW11 8AY ☎081-458 3331 FAX 081-455 9175

An attractive detached house in a residential area within walking distance of Golders Green tube station. This Kosher hotel offers modern and well equipped bedrooms with en suite facilities. A cooked breakfast is served in the large dining room.

19rm(14🛁5🚿) (4fb)CTV in all bedrooms [R] T 🚫🐕 * sB&B🛁🚿£54 dB&B🛁🚿£60-£69 LDO 12hrs notice

♨ CTV

Credit Cards [1][2][3]

SE9 ELTHAM

GH [Q][Q][Q] ***Yardley Court Private Hotel*** 18 Court Road SE9 5PZ ☎081-850 1850

Comfortable accommodation at a reasonable price is offered at this private hotel. The bedrooms are well-equipped. Guests have a choice of either English or Continental breakfast which is served in the attractive conservatory area which overlooks the garden.

9rm(8🚿) (1fb) CTV in all bedrooms [R] 🚫🐕 (ex guide dogs)

♨

Credit Cards [1][3]

SE10 GREENWICH

INN[Q][Q] The Pilot Inn 68 Riverway, Greenwich SE10 0BE ☎081-858 5910

Pleasantly situated on the Riverside Walk close to the river and the Thames Barrier, this modern and very popular pub features real ale and home cooked food. The tastefully furnished bedrooms are located in an annexe to the side, and are served by two general showers and a bathroom. Full English breakfast is included in the room tariff and unrestricted street parking is available.

7rm (1fb)CTV in all bedrooms 🚫🐕 * sB&Bfr£25 dB&Bfr£40 Bar Lunch £1.50-£4 Dinner £3.50-£8 LDO 8.45pm

♨

[£]

SE19 NORWOOD

GH [Q][Q] Crystal Palace Tower Hotel 114 Church Road, Crystal Palace SE19 2UB ☎081-653 0176

This privately owned bed and breakfast establishment offers clean and well maintained bedrooms. Among the public areas are a lounge and dining room where guests take their meals at separate tables.

11rm(4🛁4🚿) (4fb) 🚭 in dining room CTV in 8 bedrooms [R] * sB&B£21-£27.50 sB&B🛁🚿£25-£27.50 dB&Bfr£32 dB&B🛁🚿£36-£39

♨ CTV

Credit Cards [1][3] [£]

SE22 EAST DULWICH

GH [Q][Q][Q] Bedknobs 58 Glengarry Road, East Dulwich SE22 8QD (opposite Dulwich Hospital) ☎081-299 2004

A terraced Victorian house, where great care has been taken to ensure that the furnishings are in keeping with the style of the building. The bedrooms are cosy and comfortable with modern bath and shower rooms. Breakfast is served in the small dining room where guests share one large table and both English and Continental breakfast is offered.

3rm (1fb) 🚭 in dining room CTV in all bedrooms [R] 🚫🐕 sB&B£19.50-£25 dB&B£37-£45 WB&B£125-£150

♨

[£]

SW1 WESTMINSTER

GH [Q][Q][Q] The Executive Hotel 57 Pont Street, Knightsbridge SW1X 0BD ☎071-581 2424 FAX 071-589 9456

This elegant Victorian town house is situated just a stone's throw from fashionable Knightsbridge and several museums. The bedrooms may be compact but all are en suite and are equipped with every modern facility. A self-service hot and cold breakfast buffet is served in the air-conditioned basement dining room.

27🛁🚿 (3fb) 🚭 in 9 bedrooms 🚭 in dining room CTV in all bedrooms [R] T 🚫🐕 (ex guide dogs) * sB&B🛁🚿£55-£70 dB&B🛁🚿£75-£99

Lic lift ♨

Credit Cards [1][2][3][5] [£]

GH [Q][Q] ***Willett Hotel*** 32 Sloane Gardens, Sloane Square SW1W 8DJ ☎071-824 8415 Telex no 926678 FAX 071-730 4830

This elegant London town house is situated in a quiet, tree-lined street leading off Sloane Square and offers a range of comfortable, attractively furnished bedrooms, mostly with en suite facilities. Guests have a wide choice of dishes from the buffet-style breakfast served in the brightly decorated dining room.

18rm(15🛁🚿) (6fb) CTV in all bedrooms [R] T 🚫🐕

♨

Credit Cards [1][2][3][5]

GH Ⓠ Ⓠ *Winchester Hotel* 17 Belgrave Road SW1V 1RB
☎071-828 2972 Telex no 269674 FAX 071-828 5191
The bedrooms at this well maintained hotel have recently been refurbished. All of them have been re-carpeted and some have been completely redecorated. Public areas are limited to the dining room which offers both Continental and English breakfast.
18⇆ꜰ (2fb) CTV in all bedrooms ⅋
▥ nc10yrs
See advertisement on p.263.

GH Ⓠ Ⓠ Ⓠ **Windermere Hotel** 142/144 Warwick Way, Victoria
SW1V 4JE ☎071-834 5163 & 071-834 5480 FAX 071-630 8831
The owners of this private hotel continue to upgrade the facilities offered to guests. The bedrooms vary in size, but all are comfortable and well-equipped. There is a small lounge and an attractive dining room, which offers a small à la carte dinner menu, light snacks and a choice of breakfasts.
23rm(19⇆ꜰ) (7fb) ⅋ in dining room ⅋ in lounges CTV in all bedrooms Ⓡ T ⅋ (ex guide dogs) sB&B£34-£46 sB&B⇆ꜰ£49-£55 dB&B£48-£54 dB&B⇆ꜰ£59-£79 LDO 9.30pm
Lic ▥ CTV ⅌
Credit Cards ①②③
See advertisement on p.263.

SW3 CHELSEA

▶

mostly with smart, modern en suite facilities. There is a reading-room lounge well supplied with chesterfields, books and magazines, and a good English breakfast is served in the dining room. Tea, coffee and hot chocolate are available all day.
32rm(28⇌⚑) (5fb) CTV in all bedrooms T ✗ (ex guide dogs)
lift ▥ ✗
Credit Cards [1] [2] [3]

SELECTED

GH [Q] [Q] [Q] [Q] ***The Parkes Hotel*** 41-43 Beaufort Gardens, Knightsbridge SW3 1PW ☎071-581 9944 FAX 071-225 3447
Situated in a quiet leafy cul-de-sac only minutes away from Harrods and the rest of Knightsbridge and Hyde Park, this elegant Edwardian house has been recently refurbished. It offers a high standard of accommodation, mostly consisting of tastefully appointed suites of various sizes, although there are a few standard double bedrooms. A good buffet breakfast is provided in an elegant breakfast room. There is a lift to all floors, and a uniformed porter on duty day and evening.
33⇌⚑ (15fb) CTV in all bedrooms [R] T ✗
lift ▥
Credit Cards [1] [2] [3]

SW5 EARLS COURT

GH [Q] [Q] [Q] Henley House Hotel 30 Barkston Gardens, Earls Court SW5 0EN ☎071-370 4111 FAX 071-370 0026
One of a row of similar Victorian houses near the heart of Earl's Court, Henley House has recently been completely renovated to create a charming small hotel. From the book-lined reception area to the very comfortable bedrooms, the emphasis is on informal elegance; patterned rugs and matching floral curtains and bedspreads feature throughout. A continental breakfast is served, but cooked meals can be arranged if ordered in advance.
20⚑ (2fb) ⊬ in dining room CTV in all bedrooms [R] T ✗ (ex guide dogs) ✻ sB&B⚑£45-£60 dB&B⚑£68-£81 WB&B£238-£283.50 LDO 6.45pm
▥ ✗
Credit Cards [1] [2] [3] [5] [£]
See advertisement under Colour Section

GH [Q] [Q] Swiss House Hotel 171 Old Brompton Road, South Kensington SW5 0AN ☎071-373 2769 & 071-373 9383 FAX 071-373 4983
This small, proprietor-run hotel offers comfortable well maintained accommodation. A buffet continental breakfast is included in the room price, with a proper cooked breakfast available at a small extra cost. A selection of snacks is available from midday.
16rm(14⇌⚑) (7fb) ⊬ in 4 bedrooms ⊬ in dining room CTV in all bedrooms T ✻ sB&B£34 sB&B⇌⚑£48 dB&B£50 dB&B⇌⚑£64 LDO 9.30pm
▥ CTV ✗
Credit Cards [1] [2] [3] [5]

SW7 SOUTH KENSINGTON

SELECTED

GH [Q] [Q] [Q] [Q] Five Sumner Place Hotel 5 Sumner Place, South Kensington SW7 3EE ☎071-584 7586
FAX 071-823 9962
This small South Kensington hotel is part of an impressive stucco-fronted Victorian terrace. Attractively decorated, comfortably sized bedrooms have those extra little touches like mineral water, irons and trouser presses that show thought for a guest's needs. In the bright conservatory dining room afternoon tea is served as well as breakfast.
13⇌⚑ (4fb) CTV in all bedrooms T ✗ ✻ sB&B⇌⚑£62-£79 dB&B⇌⚑£85-£116
lift ▥ CTV ✗
Credit Cards [1] [2] [3] [5] [£]

SELECTED

GH [Q] [Q] [Q] [Q] Kensington Manor Hotel 8 Emperors Gate SW7 4HH ☎071-370 7516 FAX 071-373 3163
Kensington Manor is situated a short distance from the museums and shops, and is about a four-minute walk from Gloucester Road underground station. It offers tastefully furnished accommodation with every modern amenity. Full English and Continental breakfasts are provided in the pretty breakfast room.
14rm(13⇌⚑) (4fb) CTV in all bedrooms [R] ✗ (ex guide dogs) ✻ sB&B£40-£50 sB&B⇌⚑£45-£69.32 dB&B£70-£89 dB&B⇌⚑£75.20-£94
Lic ▥ ✗
Credit Cards [1] [2] [3] [5] [£]

SW19 WIMBLEDON

GH [Q] [Q] [Q] Kings Lodge Hotel 5 Kings Road SW19 8PL ☎081-545 0191 FAX 081-545 0381
rs Xmas
This small, privately owned hotel offers a good standard of accommodation. The bedrooms which are modern in style, are well-equipped, although some of them are a little compact. Breakfast and dinner is served in the bright, new dining room. There is also a small sitting room.
7rm(6⇌⚑) (4fb)CTV in all bedrooms [R] T ✗ (ex guide dogs) sB&B⇌⚑£39-£55 dB&B⇌⚑£49-£69 WB&B£313-£355 LDO 8pm
▥ CTV
Credit Cards [1] [2] [3] [5] [£]

GH [Q] [Q] Trochee Hotel 21 Malcolm Road SW19 4AS ☎081-946 1579 & 3924 FAX 081-785 4058
Further improvements have been made to this small, family run hotel. There are now additional bedrooms with en suite facilities, which although simple and functional, are comfortable. Public areas include a lounge and dining room.
17rm (2fb)CTV in all bedrooms [R] ✗ (ex guide dogs) sB&B£32-£35 dB&B£46-£49
▥ CTV
Credit Cards [1] [2] [3] [£]

GH [Q] [Q] Wimbledon Hotel 78 Worple Road SW19 4HZ ☎081-946 9265 081-946 1581 FAX 081-946 9265
This detached Victorian house, situated on the corner of Elm Grove, offers a choice to suit everyone. The bedrooms are simply furnished to the same standard, with some compact family rooms available. All rooms are equipped with TV, clock alarm radios and tea making facilities and some offer en suite showers. A small lounge and a non smoking breakfast room - offering inclusive, full English breakfast - add to the overall comfort.
14rm(5⇌⚑) (6fb) CTV in all bedrooms [R] T ✗ ✻ sB&B£40-£45 sB&B⇌⚑£45-£50 dB&B£45-£50 dB&B⇌⚑£50-£55
▥ CTV
Credit Cards [1] [3] [5]

GH [Q] [Q] [Q] Worcester House 38 Alwyne Road SW19 7AE ☎081-946 1300 FAX 081-785 4058
A small but comfortable guest house with a friendly and warm atmosphere. The bedrooms are well-equipped. Public areas are limited with a small dining room.

263

9♠ (1fb)CTV in all bedrooms ® T ✾ (ex guide dogs) ✳
sB&B♠£45.50-£49.50 dB&B♠£59.50-£62.50
Ⅲ. CTV
Credit Cards 1 2 3 5 £

W1 WEST END

GH Q Q Blandford Hotel 80 Chiltern Street W1M 1PS
☎071-486 3103 FAX 071-487 2786
This large bed and breakfast hotel is handy for Baker Street station
and offers a sound standard of accommodation in nicely appointed
and well equipped bedrooms. There is a small bar lounge on the
ground floor for drinks and breakfast, serving both English and
Continental styles in a pleasant dining room.
33⇆♠ (3fb) ⊬ in dining room ⊬ in 1 lounge CTV in all
bedrooms ® T ✾ (ex guide dogs) sB&B⇆♠£55-£60
dB&B⇆♠£70-£75
Lic lift Ⅲ. CTV⊬
Credit Cards 1 2 3 5 £

SELECTED
GH Q Q Q Q Bryanston Court 60 Great Cumberland
Place W1 (BW) ☎071-262 3141 Telex no 262076
Bryanston Court is ideally located just a minute from Marble
Arch and Oxford Street. Bedrooms on four floors can be
reached by lift and are furnished in a practical modern style.
There is a charming bar, separate lounge and bright dining
room for the continental breakfast buffet (English available at
an extra charge). There is also room service.
54rm(4⇆50♠) (3fb) CTV in all bedrooms ® T ✾
sB&B⇆♠£55-£65 dB&B⇆♠£65-£90 LDO 10pm
Lic lift Ⅲ. ⊬
Credit Cards 1 2 3 5

GH Q Q Q Hotel Concorde 50 Great Cumberland Place
W1H 7FD ☎071-402 6169 Telex no 262076
Closed 23 Dec-1 Jan
Adjoining the Bryanston Court hotel which the Theodore family
also own, this well managed hotel has been recently renovated.
Bedrooms are all furnished to the same standard, with good
quality modern showers, direct-dial telephone, radio, TV, hair
dryer and tea making facilities. There is a lift to all levels, and a
small basement breakfast room; a supplementary charge is made
for full English breakfast. The Theodore family have managed the
hotel for over two family generations, and it enjoys a loyal
international clientele. There is a very attractively furnished club-
style foyer sitting area, but no car park: parking meters can usually
be found nearby and there is a local NCP car park.
28rm(5⇆23♠) (1fb)CTV in all bedrooms ® T ✾ (ex guide
dogs) ✳ sB&B⇆♠£62-£65 dB&B⇆♠£72-£75
Lic lift Ⅲ. CTV
Credit Cards 1 2 3 5 £

GH Q Edward Lear Hotel 28-30 Seymour Street W1
☎071-402 5401 FAX 071-706 3766
Close to Oxford Street, this former home of artist and writer Edward
Lear offers bed and breakfast accommodation at prices that represent
good value for the West End. The bedrooms, though simply
furnished, are well equipped and well maintained. The dining room
is nicely appointed and serves a choice of breakfasts. Parking is
difficult in this area so nearby multi-storeys are the best solution.
31rm(12⇆♠) (2fb) ⊬ in dining room ⊬ in 1 lounge CTV in all
bedrooms ® T ✾ sB&Bfr£39.50 sB&B⇆♠fr£55
dB&Bfr£49.50 dB&B⇆♠fr£67.50
Ⅲ. CTV⊬
Credit Cards 1 3 £

GH Q Q Q Georgian House Hotel 87 Gloucester Place, Baker
Street W1H 3PG ☎071-935 2211 & 071-486 3151
FAX 071-486 7535

Conveniently situated near Baker Street, ideal for the Planetarium
and Madam Tussaud's, this privately owned hotel retains much of
its period character and has a choice of modern bedrooms.
Continental breakfast (English on request) is served in the
breakfast room, and there is a lift to all levels. Car parking can be
difficult.
19rm(14⇆5♠) (3fb) ⊬ in dining room CTV in all bedrooms ®
T ✾ sB&B⇆♠£50-£55 dB&B⇆♠£65-£70
Lic lift Ⅲ. nc5yrs
Credit Cards 1 2 3 £

GH Q Q Q Hart House Hotel 51 Gloucester Place, Portman Sq
W1H 3PE ☎071-935 2288 FAX 071-935 8516
This Georgian town house offers well equipped, attractively styled
bedrooms and there is a small, pleasant dining room which, with
its oak furniture and lace cloths, is reminiscent of an English
tearoom. It is situated close to Oxford Street and the West End and
has been steadily upgraded by the resident owner, Andrew
Bowden.
16rm(11⇆♠) (4fb) CTV in all bedrooms ® ✾ sB&B£40-£45
sB&B⇆♠£40-£50 dB&B£55-£60 dB&B⇆♠£60-£75
Ⅲ. CTV⊬
Credit Cards 1 2 3 £

GH Q Q Q The Regency Hotel 19 Nottingham Place W1M 3FF
☎071-486 5347 FAX 071-224 6057
This friendly, elegant and personally run hotel is located close to
Oxford Circus and Madame Tussaud's. Bedrooms are well
furnished and equipped with many extras, including mini bars. A
choice of hot and cold buffet breakfast is served in the breakfast
room on the lower-ground floor and room service is available
between 7.00am and 11.00pm, including hot meals and light
refreshments. Other services include laundry, and facilities for
small meetings.
20⇆♠ (2fb) ⊬ in 2 bedrooms ⊬ in area of dining room ⊬ in 1
lounge CTV in all bedrooms ® T ✾ (ex guide dogs) ✳
sB&B⇆♠£40-£55 dB&B⇆♠£60-£75 WB&B£225-£325
WBDi£295-£395 LDO 9pm
Lic lift Ⅲ. ⊬
Credit Cards 1 2 3 5 £

W2 BAYSWATER, PADDINGTON, NOTTING HILL GATE

SELECTED
GH Q Q Q Q Byron Hotel 36-38 Queensborough Terrace
W2 3SH (just off the Bayswater Rd close to Queensway)
☎071-243 0987 Telex no 263431 FAX 071-792 1957
Situated near Bayswater Road only a few yards from Hyde
Park, this elegant Victorian house with five floors and a lift
has beautifully designed public areas. Bedrooms, too, are
richly furnished and well equipped. There is an attractively
appointed dining room where guests can choose between
English and Continental breakfasts. Standards of housekeeping
throughout are commendably high.
42⇆♠ (3fb) ⊬ in all bedrooms ® T ✾ (ex guide dogs)
sB&B⇆♠£75.50 dB&B⇆♠£89 LDO 8pm
Lic lift Ⅲ. CTV⊬
Credit Cards 1 2 3 5 £

GH Q Q Q Camelot Hotel 45-47 Norfolk Square W2 1RX
☎071-723 9118 & 071-262 1980 Telex no 268312
FAX 071-402 3412
This well appointed and comfortable private hotel is close to
Paddington Station and well situated in a quiet square. Bedrooms
are particularly well equipped and a modern automatic lift serves
all floors except the 6th. Car parking can be difficult.
44rm(36⇆♠) (8fb) CTV in all bedrooms ® T ✾ (ex guide dogs)
lift Ⅲ. CTV⊬
Credit Cards 1 3

GH [Q][Q][Q] ***Kingsway Hotel*** 27 Norfolk Square, Hyde Park W2 1RX ☎071-723 7784 & 071-723 5569 Telex no 885299 FAX 071-723 7317

This small family-run hotel overlooks the gardens of an attractive square a few minutes' walk from Paddington Station. Bedrooms are equipped to a good standard with all modern conveniences. Public areas are somewhat limited but there is a small foyer lounge and a breakfast room.

33rm(30🛁🚿) (4fb) CTV in all bedrooms Ⓡ 🐕 (ex guide dogs)
lift ♨ CTV
Credit Cards [1] [2] [3] [5]

GH [Q][Q][Q] Mitre House Hotel 178-184 Sussex Gardens, Hyde Park W2 1TU ☎071-723 8040 Telex no 914113 FAX 071-402 0990

A popular, family run hotel has been modernised over the last few years to provide comfortable and well-equipped bedrooms. There is a small bar and a comfortable lounge, as well as a spacious dining room where a choice of breakfasts is offered.

70rm(64🛁🚿) (3fb) 🚭 in 10 bedrooms 🚭 in area of dining room CTV in all bedrooms **T** 🐕 (ex guide dogs) ✻ sB&B🛁🚿£50-£60 dB&B🛁🚿£65-£70
Lic lift ♨ CTV jacuzzi
Credit Cards [1] [2] [3] [5]

SELECTED

GH [Q][Q][Q][Q] Mornington Hotel 12 Lancaster Gate W2 3LG (BW) ☎071-262 7361 FAX 071-706 1028

Scandinavian-owned and styled, this hotel offers comfortable, clean and well equipped bedrooms. Breakfast is from a buffet offering continental items though a cooked breakfast can be arranged on request. There is a library bar offering snacks and a lounge. This is altogether a pleasant hotel to use as a base to explore London.

68🛁🚿 (6fb)CTV in all bedrooms Ⓡ **T** sB&B🛁🚿fr£80 dB&B🛁🚿£90-£100
Lic lift ♨ 🅿̸ sauna
Credit Cards [1] [2] [3] [5]

SELECTED

GH [Q][Q][Q][Q] Norfolk Plaza Hotel 29/33 Norfolk Square, Paddington W2 1RX ☎071-723 0792 Telex no 266977 FAX 071-224 8770

Situated close to Paddington station this large refurbished terraced hotel offers professional room and breakfast service with a high degree of quality and comfort. Bedrooms, equipped with modern fitted furniture, are of a good size, and public rooms include an open plan reception/lounge/bar and breakfast room with cool tiled floors and pastel decor.

87🛁🚿 (25fb) 🚭 in 5 bedrooms 🚭 in dining room CTV in all bedrooms Ⓡ **T** 🐕 (ex guide dogs) sB&B🛁🚿£69-£75 dB&B🛁🚿£88-£98
Lic lift ♨ 🅿̸
Credit Cards [1] [2] [3] [5] [£]

SELECTED

GH [Q][Q][Q][Q] Norfolk Towers Hotel 34 Norfolk Place W2 1QW (close to Paddington Station & St Mary's Hospital) ☎071-262 3123 Telex no 268583 FAX 071-224 8687

The Norfolk Towers is a popular establishment located in Bayswater near Paddington Station. Public areas are spacious and well furnished. There is a smart lounge bar, Cads Wine Bar where tasty bar snacks are served, and an attractive dining room. A lift serves all floors, and bedrooms are modern with good en suite facilities. The hotel has recently acquired some car-parking spaces a short distance away.

85🛁🚿 (3fb)CTV in all bedrooms **T** 🐕 (ex guide dogs) sB&B🛁🚿fr£60 dB&B🛁🚿fr£90 LDO 10pm
Lic lift ♨ 🅿̸
Credit Cards [1] [2] [3] [5] [£]

GH [Q][Q] ***Park Lodge Hotel*** 73 Queensborough Terrace, Bayswater W2 3SU ☎071-229 6424 FAX 071-221 4772

This tall terraced house in Bayswater near Queensway and Bayswater Tube stations offers well maintained bed and breakfast accommodation. Public areas are limited but there is a nicely appointed dining room. All bedrooms have en suite facilities.

29rm(2🛁27🚿) (2fb) CTV in all bedrooms Ⓡ **T** 🐕 (ex guide dogs) LDO noon
♨
Credit Cards [1] [2] [3] [5]

GH [Q][Q] Parkwood Hotel 4 Stanhope Place, Marble Arch W2 2HB ☎071-402 2241 FAX 071-402 1574

This terraced house situated close to Marble Arch offers modest B&B accomodation. Bedrooms are compact but adequately furnished and equipped. There is a comfortable reception lounge and breakfast is served in the lower ground floor dining room.

18rm(13🛁🚿) (4fb) 🚭 in dining room 🚭 in lounges CTV in all bedrooms Ⓡ **T** 🐕 (ex guide dogs) sB&Bfr£39.75 sB&B🛁🚿fr£55 dB&Bfr£54.50 dB&B🛁🚿fr£67.50 WB&Bfr£175
♨ CTV 🅿̸
Credit Cards [1] [3] [£]

GH [Q][Q][Q] Rhodes Hotel 195 Sussex Gardens W2 2RJ ☎071-262 5617 & 071-262 0537 FAX 071-723 4054

Part of an attractive period terrace, this small hotel is close to Lancaster Gate tube and Hyde Park. Considerable sums have been invested to improve the accommodation. Bedrooms, from the basement to the fourth floor, have a good range of equipment (including fridges), fresh decor and fitted furniture. Continental breakfast (or English at a small extra charge) is served in a dining room decorated with elaborate stencils. The lounge and reception area will also soon have been redecorated.

18rm(15🛁🚿) (5fb)CTV in all bedrooms Ⓡ **T** 🐕 sB&B🛁🚿£40-£50 dB&B🛁🚿£52-£65
♨ CTV
Credit Cards [1] [3]

GH [Q][Q] Slavia Hotel 2 Pembridge Square W2 4EW ☎071-727 1316 FAX 071-229 0803

Away from the main road, this well maintained hotel offers a good standard of accommodation. The bedrooms are neatly furnished and adequately equipped. Guests have a choice of either English or Continental breakfast, taken in the spacious and bright dining room. There is also a comfortable lounge.

31🚿 (8fb)CTV in 12 bedrooms **T** ✻ sB&B🚿£33-£49 dB&B🚿£42-£66
Lic lift ♨ CTV
Credit Cards [1] [2] [3] [5] [£]

W4 CHISWICK

SELECTED

GH [Q][Q][Q][Q] Chiswick Hotel 73 Chiswick High Road W4 2LS ☎081-994 1712 FAX 081-742 2585

A busy, private hotel where the owner Mr Drew and his pleasant staff extend a warm welcome to all their guests. The bedrooms vary in size but all are comfortable and well-equipped.

33🛁🚿 (5fb)CTV in all bedrooms Ⓡ **T** ✻ sB&B🛁🚿fr£62.50 dB&B🛁🚿fr£85 WB&B£269-£415

WBDi£374-£520 LDO 8.30pm
Lic ▦ CTV
Credit Cards [1][2][3][5][£]

W5 EALING

GH [Q][Q] Creffield Lodge 2-4 Creffield Road, Ealing W5 3HN (CON) ☎081-993 2284 Telex no 935114

This is the budget annexe of the three-star Carnarvon, with comfortable, basic, standard bedrooms simply furnished in the old-fashioned style. There is no breakfast room, but guests can use all the facilities of the Carnarvon. There is good public transport access to central London.

19rm(5🛁🚿) (1fb) 🚭 in area of dining room 🚭 in 1 lounge CTV in all bedrooms [R] T 🐕 (ex guide dogs) sB&B£30-£35 sB&B🛁🚿£40-£45 dB&B🛁🚿£50-£55 LDO 9.15pm
Lic ▦
Credit Cards [1][2][3][5][£]

W6 HAMMERSMITH

GH [Q][Q][Q] *Premier West Hotel* 28-34 Glenthorne Road, Hammersmith W6 OLS ☎081-748 6181

This family run hotel is in a convenient location, close to the River Thames and within walking distance of Hammersmith tube station. The bedrooms are well-equipped. There is a bar/lounge on the ground floor and dinner is served from Monday to Friday in the attractive dining room.

26🛁🚿 Annexe 15🛁🚿 (5fb) CTV in all bedrooms [R] 🐕 (ex guide dogs)
Lic ▦ CTV
Credit Cards [1][2][3][5]

W7 HANWELL

SELECTED

GH [Q][Q][Q][Q] Wellmeadow Lodge 24 Wellmeadow Road W7 2AL ☎081-567 7294 FAX 081-566 3468

This charming individual guest house is tucked quietly away in a residential area close to Boston Manor underground station, giving excellent access to South Kensington's shops and museums, Heathrow Airport and Earls Court Exhibition Centre. Bedrooms have recently been upgraded and there are now two with marble bathrooms and separate large showers. The comfortable lounge has an honesty bar and service of light refreshments throughout the day, and on warm days the garden patio, add a further dimension. Personally run by the resident proprietors, Francis Hornak and Kennie Davey, the atmosphere is relaxing, with fine English breakfasts served in the kitchen at an antique table. Free on-street parking is a major benefit.

6🛁🚿 🚭 CTV in all bedrooms [R] T 🐕 (ex guide dogs) sB&B🛁🚿£47-£53 dB&B🛁🚿£64.63-£84.60 WB&B£226.21-£452.41 WBDi£324.91-£575.79 LDO noon

🅿 ⊘

Credit Cards [1][2][3][£]

W8 KENSINGTON

GH [Q][Q] Apollo Hotel 18-22 Lexham Gardens W8 5JE (first turning on left after Cromwell Hospital continue for 100yds hotel on right) ☎071-835 1133 Telex no 264189 FAX 071-370 4853

Closed 24 Dec-1 Jan

Sister hotel to the next-door Atlas, the Apollo has continued to improve its facilities and its sizeable, comfortable bedrooms have been given a more modern air. English and continental-style breakfasts are served in the dining room and although there is only a small lounge here, guests may use the bar in the Atlas Hotel. There is a lift and a night porter to add to the advantage of being in a good area.

52rm(35🛁11🚿) (4fb)CTV in all bedrooms T 🐕 (ex guide dogs) * sB&B£30 sB&B🛁🚿£50-£55 dB&B🛁🚿£60-£65

Lic lift 🅿 ⊘

Credit Cards [1][2][3][5]

GH [Q][Q] Atlas Hotel 24-30 Lexham Gardens W8 5JE ☎071-835 1155 Telex no 264189 FAX 071-370 4853

Closed 24 Dec-1 Jan

Benefitting from a bright modern reception and bar, the Atlas, like the Apollo next door, which is owned by the same family, has well equipped, recently refurbished rooms of a good size. Public areas include a small lounge, a comfortable bar and a pleasant dining room. A lift and a night porter add to the advantage of a good location and the friendly staff are supervised by Keith Fenton, son of the owner of the two hotels.

57rm(14🛁31🚿) (6fb)CTV in all bedrooms T 🐕 (ex guide dogs) * sB&B£30 sB&B🛁🚿£50-£55 dB&B🛁🚿£60-£65

Lic lift 🅿 ⊘

Credit Cards [1][2][3][5]

W14 WEST KENSINGTON

SELECTED

GH [Q][Q][Q][Q] Aston Court Hotel 25/27 Matheson Road W14 8SN ☎071-602 9954 Telex no 919208 FAX 071-371 1338

A well-appointed private hotel which has recently undergone a change of ownership. Bedrooms vary in size but are all modern and equipped to a good standard. Comfortable public areas including a small bar are attractively decorated and furnished. The conservatory dining room is compact but guests can take English or Continental breakfasts in ther rooms if they prefer.

29rm(10🛁19🚿) (3fb) CTV in all bedrooms [R] T 🐕 (ex guide dogs)

Lic lift 🅿 CTV ⊘

Credit Cards [1][2][3][5][£]

GH [Q][Q][Q] Avonmore Hotel 66 Avonmore Road W14 8RS ☎071-603 4296 & 3121 FAX 071-603 4035

Close to Olympia and within easy reach of Kensington High Street, this delightful little hotel is personally run by Mrs McKenzie. Bedrooms are attractive and very well equipped. There is a small bar, a light and airy dining room and a friendly atmosphere. Car parking in this area is limited but public transport is good.

9rm(7🛁🚿) (3fb)CTV in all bedrooms [R] T 🐕 * sB&B£41-£45 sB&B🛁🚿£55-£58 dB&B£56-£60 dB&B🛁🚿£65-£68

Lic 🅿 CTV ⊘

Credit Cards [1][2][3]

GH [Q] *Centaur Hotel* 21 Avonmore Road W14 8RP ☎071-602 3857 & 071-603 5973

Its friendly atmosphere is the most important feature of this well kept, family-run guest house which stands in a quiet, residential area, convenient for Olympia and Earls Court. Bedrooms are nicely decorated and there are a small lounge and dining room with shared tables. Car parking is metered in the immediate vicinity.

12rm(3🚿) (5fb) CTV in all bedrooms T 🐕

🅿 CTV

SELECTED

GH [Q][Q][Q][Q] Russell Court Hotel 9 Russell Road, Kensington W14 8JA ☎071-603 1222 FAX 071-371 2286

Situated in a leafy road, adjacent to the Olympia Centre, and within easy reach of Kensington High Street, the Russell Court provides comfortable, well equipped bedrooms, all with double-glazing and en suite bath or shower rooms. There is lift service to all floors. The residents' bar serves drinks and snacks and there is an attractive lounge with conservatory as well as a dining room where breakfast is served. For business guests there are fax and telex services.

18🛁🚿 CTV in all bedrooms [R] T 🐕 (ex guide dogs) sB&B🛁🚿£39.50-£59.50 dB&B🛁🚿£49.50-£69.50 WB&B£140-£175

Lic lift 🅿 CTV ⊘nc2yrs

Credit Cards [1][2][3][5][£]

WC1 BLOOMSBURY, HOLBORN

GH [Q][Q] Mentone Hotel 54-55 Cartwright Gardens WC1H 9EL ☎071-387 3927 & 071-388 4671 FAX 071-388 4671

A striking feature of this small, private hotel is the attractive floral display outside the building. The bedrooms are well-equipped and there is an attractive dining room where both English and Continental breakfast is offered.

27rm(15🚿) (10fb) 🚭 in dining room CTV in all bedrooms [R] 🐕 * sB&B£32-£35 sB&B🚿£35-£45 dB&B£38-£45 dB&B🚿£45-£56 WB&Bfr£175

🅿 🎾(hard)

Credit Cards [1][3][£]

LONGLEAT Wiltshire — Map **03** ST84

FH [Q][Q][Q] Mrs J Crossman **Stalls** *(ST806439)* BA12 7NE (turn off A362 at Corsley beside the White Hart, follow road for 2m towards Longleat House farmhouse is on right hand side) ☎Maiden Bradley(0985) 844323

This 120-year-old farmhouse, once the home farm of the Longleat estate, is still a working farm surrounded by open countryside.

Bedrooms are comfortable and guests are invited to share the relaxed family atmosphere.
3rm ✂ in bedrooms ✂ in 1 lounge CTV in all bedrooms 🐾 ✳
sB&B£15-£16 dB&B£30-£32
▥ CTV table tennis table childrens play area 350 acres dairy
£

SELECTED

FH Q Q Q Q Mrs L N Corp **Sturford Mead** *(ST834456)*
BA12 7QU (on A362 half way between Warminster & Frome)
☎Westbury(0373) 832213
A welcoming farmhouse overlooking National Trust land close to Longleat House offers accommodation in attractively decorated bedrooms with coordinated colour schemes; two have their own showers and the other sole use of a bathroom across the landing. Breakfast is served at separate tables in a pleasant dining room, and there is a comfortable lounge.
3rm(1↩2🐾) ✂ CTV in all bedrooms Ⓡ 🐾 (ex guide dogs)
sB&Bfr£25 dB&B£32-£35 dB&B↩🐾£32-£35
▥ CTV 🐷 5 acres pig

LONGRIDGE Lancashire   Map 07 SD63

SELECTED

FH Q Q Q Q Mrs E J Ibison **Jenkinsons** *(SD611348)*
Alston Lane PR3 3BD (off B6243 Preston to Longridge road - follow signs to Alston Hall College) ☎(0772) 782624
rs Xmas
Over 200 years old, this delightful farmhouse has been carefully renovated to offer accommodation of great character, with flagstones, beams, oak furniture, exposed stone walls and an inglenook fireplace. Quality appointments are evident in the bedrooms. Home cooked dinners are available on request.
6rm ✂ Ⓡ 🐾 (ex guide dogs) ✳ sB&B£20 dB&B£40
WB&Bfr£140 WBDifr£227.50 LDO 4pm
▥ CTV nc12yrs 100 acres dairy sheep

LONGTOWN Cumbria   Map 11 NY36

PREMIER 🏵 **SELECTED**

FH Q Q Q Q Q Mr & Mrs
J Sisson **Bessiestown**
(NY457768) Catlowdy CA6 5QP
(take B6318 one and a half
miles to Catlowdy farm first
on left)
☎Nicholforest(0228) 577219
FAX (0228) 577219
This delightful farmhouse
stands on a small sheep and
beef farm in a tiny village

close to the Scottish border.
Six spacious and very attractively decorated bedrooms with modern en suite facilities offer TV, radio alarms and beverage-making equipment, while downstairs there are two lounges (one with an honesty bar) and a very pleasant dining room where hearty breakfasts and home-cooked dinners are served at individual lace-covered tables. An indoor heated swimming pool is open from mid-May to mid-September, and one of the old farm buildings has been converted into a games room.
4↩✂ (1fb) ✂ in dining room ✂ in 1 lounge
CTV in all bedrooms Ⓡ 🐾 (ex guide dogs) sB&B↩🐾£24-£27
dB&B↩🐾£38-£43 WB&Bfr£130 WBDifr£190 LDO 4pm
Lic ▥ CTV ❣ (heated) games room 80 acres beef sheep
Credit Cards ① ② ③ £

LOOE Cornwall & Isles of Scilly   Map 02 SX25

SELECTED

GH Q Q Q Q **Coombe Farm** Widegates PL13 1QN (on B3253 just S of Widegates village, 3.5m east of Looe)
☎Widegates(0503) 240223
Mar-Oct
There are 10.5 acres of grounds and gardens surrounding this agreeable 1920s house with views down the valley to the sea. Bedrooms are furnished to a high standard; three are in the attractive annexe and are suitable for families. The dining room and sitting room both have open fires for cooler days while french windows open to the garden for balmy summer evenings. Sally and Alexander Low offer a four-course candlelit dinner to their guests. Guests are asked not to smoke.
7🐾 Annexe 3🐾 (6fb) ✂ CTV in all bedrooms Ⓡ T ✳
sB&Bfr£18 dB&Bfr£36 WB&Bfr£126 WBDifr£200
LDO 7pm
Lic ▥ CTV nc5yrs ❣(heated) table tennis snooker croquet
£
See advertisement on p.271.

GH Q Q **Gulls Hotel** Hannafore Road PL13 2DE ☎(0503) 262531
Etr-Oct & Xmas
This hotel features a sun lounge and a patio which look down on the beach, the village and out to sea. Many bedrooms have the same view and there is also a bar and dining room where supper is served.
11rm(2🐾) ✂ CTV in 5 bedrooms Ⓡ ✳ sB&B£12-£16
dB&B£24-£32 dB&Bfr£30-£38 WB&Bfr£72-£96 WBDif£135-£159
LDO at breakfast
Lic ▥ CTV
£

SELECTED

GH [Q][Q][Q][Q] Harescombe Lodge Watergate PL13 2NE ☎(0503) 263158

It would be advisable to ask for directions to this former shooting lodge dating from 1760, set in delightful surroundings alongside the tidal creek of the West Looe river. Barry and Jane Wynn are charming proprietors and provide a friendly, relaxed atmosphere, to which guests return time and again. Tastefully restored, the house is in an ideal spot for nature lovers, as the nearby estuaries of the East and West Looe rivers provide an abundance of interesting wildlife. Bedrooms are beautifully furnished, and a hearty breakfast is served.

3rm(2🛁1🚿) [R] 🐕 (ex guide dogs) dB&B🛁🚿£32-£38

♨ nc12yrs

[£]

GH [Q][Q] 'Kantara' 7 Trelawney Terrace PL13 2AG (on main Looe/Polperro road, 120yds above Looe Bridge opposite car park) ☎(0503) 262093

At this hillside house overlooking the river, John and Hazel Storer make everyone feel at home, especially families. The bar/lounge is an obvious meeting point and breakfast is served in the sunny dining room.

5rm (3fb) 🚭 in dining room CTV in all bedrooms [R] ✱ sB&B£12.50-£15 dB&B£25-£30 WB&B£83-£100 WBDi£142.50-£159.50 LDO 4pm

Lic CTV D.O.T registered boat available for fishing

Credit Cards [1][2][3][£]

SELECTED

GH [Q][Q][Q][Q] Panorama Hotel Hannafore Road PL13 2DE (in West Looe overlooking pier & beach) ☎(0503) 262123 FAX (0503) 265654

With fantastic views of the sea, beach and village this hotel is well named. All the rooms are pretty, some have balconies and there is a four-poster bed. The lounge bar and sun lounge is where guests gather in the evening and the dining room has starched white linen cloths. There is also a lounge with comfy sofas and a warm fire on chilly evenings.

10rm(1🛁9🚿) (4fb) 🚭 in dining room 🚭 in lounges CTV in all bedrooms [R] 🐕 sB&B🛁🚿£22-£32 dB&B🛁🚿£44-£64 WB&B£132-£192 WBDi£195-£250 LDO 6.30pm

Lic CTV

Credit Cards [1][2][3][5][£]

GH [Q][Q][Q] Polraen Country House Hotel Sandplace PL13 1PJ (2m N, at jct of A387/B3254) ☎(0503) 263956

Dating back to 1742, this attractive granite country house is set in two acres of pretty, well kept gardens. The spacious bedrooms are well appointed, freshly decorated and comfortable. Public areas are well furnished and cosy, and the proprietress is a warm and welcoming hostess.

5rm(1🛁4🚿) (2fb) 🚭 in dining room CTV in all bedrooms [R] ✱ sB&B🛁🚿£27.50 dB&B🛁🚿£44-£48 WB&B£140-£154 WBDi£234-£248 LDO 8pm

Lic ♨

Credit Cards [1][3][£]

GH [Q][Q][Q] St Aubyns Marine Drive, Hannafore,West Looe PL13 2DH ☎(0503) 264351

Etr-end Oct

Built in 1894, this fine Victorian former gentleman's residence stands only 50 yards from the beach in West Looe. The house retains many of its original features and public rooms are furnished in keeping, with tapestries, paintings and some antiques. Bedrooms have modern facilities and are equipped to a high standard.

8rm(4🛁🚿) (5fb) 🚭 in dining room 🚭 in lounges CTV in 4 bedrooms [R] 🐕 sB&B🛁🚿fr£20 dB&B£34-£40 dB&B🛁🚿£44-£54

CTV

Credit Cards [1][3][£]

SELECTED

GH [Q][Q][Q][Q] Woodlands St Martins Road PL13 1LP ☎(0503) 264405

You will find this pleasant Victorian house on the edge of woodlands overlooking the river and only a short walk from the village. All bedrooms are agreeably furnished and the sitting room with its open fire and the dining room have a warm, country house feel, with stripped pine doors. Home cooking is the thing, using local, home-grown and organic produce.

5rm(4🚿) (2fb) 🚭 in 3 bedrooms 🚭 in dining room CTV in all bedrooms [R] 🐕 (ex guide dogs) sB&B£18-£20 dB&B🚿£36-£42 WB&B£122-£140 WBDi£210-£224 LDO 6.30pm

Lic ♨

[£]

LOUGHBOROUGH Leicestershire Map **08** SK51

GH [Q][Q] De Montfort Hotel 88 Leicester Road LE11 2AQ (on A6 Leicester rd) ☎(0509) 216061 FAX (0509) 233667

Dramatically improved by new owners, this previously simple establishment near the town centre now offers an improved range of facilities in cheerfully decorated bedrooms - many of them with en suite shower rooms. An upgrading of public areas is planned for late 1994. Set-price and short à la carte dinner menus offer a range of home-cooked dishes.

9rm(7🛁🚿) (3fb) 🚭 in 3 bedrooms 🚭 in dining room CTV in all bedrooms [R] sB&B£20-£21.50 sB&B🛁🚿£25 dB&B£35-£38 LDO 6pm

Lic ♨ CTV

Credit Cards [1][2][3][£]

GH [Q][Q][Q] Garendon Park Hotel 92 Leicester Road LE11 2AQ ☎(0509) 236557

Friendly and enthusiastic owners continue to improve accommodation at this small hotel near the town centre. Recently upgraded bedrooms are colourfully decorated and well equipped, while a comfortable lounge provides both satellite television and video films. A short à la carte menu supplements the pleasant dining room's table d'hôte. Cars can be parked opposite the hotel.

9rm(5🛁🚿) (2fb) 🚭 in 1 bedrooms 🚭 in dining room CTV in all bedrooms [R] ✱ sB&B£21.50 sB&B🛁🚿£25-£30 dB&B🛁🚿£35-£40 WB&B£150.50-£175 WBDifr£189 LDO 8pm

Lic ♨ CTV 🅿

Credit Cards [1][2][3][£]

LOUTH Lincolnshire Map **08** TF38

SELECTED

GH [Q][Q][Q][Q] Wickham House Church Lane LN11 7LX ☎North Somercotes(0507) 358465

(For full entry see Conisholme)

SELECTED

INN[Q][Q][Q][Q] Masons Arms Cornmarket LN11 9PY ☎(0507) 609525

An 18th-century posting inn, the Masons Arms has been refurbished throughout to provide modern amenities while retaining its historic character. The public rooms are popular with the townsfolk, for real ales and bar snacks or more formal

dining in the Pentalpha Room restaurant. The light and inviting bedrooms are generally of a good size, and pleasantly furnished in pine. Some have en suite facilities and the remainder share a renovated Victorian bathroom.
10rm(5⇌f) ⚹ in area of dining room CTV in all bedrooms ® ♄ (ex guide dogs) ✳ sB&Bfr£20 sB&B⇌f£30-£35 dB&B£35-£45 dB&B⇌f£40-£45 WB&B£175-£200 WBDi£200-£250 Lunch fr£6.50 Dinner £10-£17.50alc LDO 9.30pm
📖 ♪
Credit Cards ① ③ ⓔ

LOW CATTON Humberside   Map **08** SE75

SELECTED

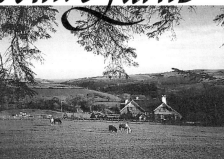

while ensuring modern comforts for its guests. In the evenings a five-course dinner is served, for which prior arrangement is appreciated.
5rm(1🛁4🚿) 🚭 CTV in all bedrooms Ⓡ dB&B🛁🚿£47 WB&B£164.50 WBDi£224 LDO 4pm
Lic ♨ nc8yrs
[£]
See advertisement under YORK

LOWER BEEDING West Sussex Map **04** TQ22

FH [Q][Q][Q] Mr J Christian Brookfield Farm Hotel *(TQ214285)* Winterpit Lane, Plummers Plain RH13 6LU
☎(0403) 891568 FAX (0403) 891499
Quietly located in rural surroundings, this friendly hotel offers a choice of bedrooms all furnished in the modern style. There is a cosy beamed lounge, bar and a restaurant, which overlooks the lake and golf course. Other facilities include a golf driving range, boating lake, putting green, six-hole practice golf course with PGA pro-tuition, sauna, and children's play area.
20🛁🚿 (2fb) 🚭 in area of dining room 🚭 in lounges CTV in all bedrooms Ⓡ **T** ✱ sB&B🛁🚿£35.15-£42 dB&B🛁🚿£47-£52.88 LDO 9.30pm
Lic ♨ CTV ⛳7 🎣 snooker sauna games room putting 300 acres mixed
Credit Cards [1][2][3][5][£]
See advertisement under HORSHAM

LOWESTOFT Suffolk Map **05** TM59

GH [Q][Q][Q] ***Albany Hotel*** 400 London Road South NR33 0BQ
☎(0502) 574394
This popular, small hotel is near the seafront and the town centre. There is a lounge bar and breakfast room. Bedrooms are generally of a good size.
7rm(3🛁🚿) (3fb) CTV in all bedrooms Ⓡ 🐕 (ex guide dogs) LDO 1pm
Lic ♨ CTV
Credit Cards [1][3]

GH [Q][Q] ***Fairways*** 398 London Road South NR33 0BQ
☎(0502) 572659
Set back from the seafront at the southern end of the town, this well run guest house offers bright bedrooms, a comfortable lounge with colour TV and a video recorder, and a dining room with a dispense bar.
7rm(3🛁🚿) (4fb) CTV in all bedrooms Ⓡ LDO 4pm
Lic ♨ CTV
Credit Cards [1][2][3]

GH [Q][Q] Kingsleigh 44 Marine Parade NR33 0QN (on the A12 overlooking the seafront) ☎(0502) 572513
Closed Xmas
Central to the town and on the seafront, this is a nicely kept guesthouse with good sea views from the front rooms. The car park is on London Road South near to the building.
6rm (2fb) 🚭 in dining room CTV in all bedrooms Ⓡ ✱ sB&B£17-£20 dB&B£30-£32 WB&Bfr£102
♨ nc3yrs
[£]

GH [Q][Q][Q] Rockville House 6 Pakefield Road NR33 0HS (A12 1m past water tower take sharpe turning right)
☎(0502) 581011 & 574891
rs Oct-Apr
In a quiet road near the seafront, this tidy guesthouse has a welcoming lounge with games and books and a dining room where dinner or supper trays are served by arrangement. Bedrooms are thoughtfully arranged.
7rm(2🛁1🚿) 🚭 in dining room CTV in all bedrooms Ⓡ 🐕 (ex guide dogs) sB&Bfr£22 sB&B🛁🚿fr£33.50 dB&Bfr£37.50 dB&B🛁🚿fr£43.50 WB&Bfr£112.50 WBDifr£177.50 LDO 10am
Lic ♨ ✗ nc12yrs beach hut
Credit Cards [1][3][£]

GH [Q][Q][Q] Somerton House 7 Kirkley Cliff NR33 0BY
☎(0502) 565665
This is a distinctive blue and white house on the seafront. The bedrooms, one with a four-poster, one with a half tester, all have individual character and thoughtful extras.
8rm(4🚿) (4fb) 🚭 in 2 bedrooms 🚭 in dining room CTV in all bedrooms Ⓡ ✱ sB&B£22-£27 sB&B🚿£27-£30 dB&B£38 dB&B🚿£43 WB&Bfr£120 WBDifr£183 LDO 5pm
Lic ♨ CTV
Credit Cards [1][2][3][5][£]

LOW ROW North Yorkshire Map **07** SD99

SELECTED

GH [Q][Q][Q][Q] ***Peat Gate Head*** DL11 6PP
☎Richmond(0748) 86388
Set in the midst of one of Yorkshire's most beautiful dales, this 400-year-old house is full of charm and character, with low ceilings, beams and exposed stone walls. The hospitable owner, Alan Earl, is a very capable cook producing excellent Yorkshire dinners. The accommodation includes warm, cosy bedrooms and two lounges.
6rm(3🚿) Ⓡ 🐕 LDO 5.30pm
Lic ♨ CTV ✗ nc5yrs

LUDGVAN Cornwall & Isles of Scilly Map **02** SW53

FH [Q] Mrs A R Blewett **Menwidden** *(SW502337)* TR20 8BN
☎Penzance(0736) 740415
Closed Dec-Jan
First-time visitors would be well advised to ask for directions to this small market garden and dairy farm within easy reach of Land's End, Penzance, St Ives and the Lizard Peninsula. The pebble-dashed family house has extensive views, and accommodation is sound (though most of the bedrooms lack wash basins). Well cooked, wholesome meals are served in the dining room, and guests can take their ease in a cosy lounge with TV.
6rm (2fb) ✱ sB&Bfr£14 dB&Bfr£28 LDO 1pm
CTV 40 acres dairy/market gardening
[£]

LUDLOW Shropshire Map **07** SO57

GH [Q][Q][Q] Cecil Sheet Road SY8 1LR ☎(0584) 872442
Closed 20 Dec-6 Jan
A small, immaculately maintained, family-run guest house with easy access to or from the by-pass, the Cecil has cheerful and brightly decorated bedrooms, a cosy modern lounge, a separate bar with TV and a pretty rear garden. Gillian and Maurice Phillips offer a friendly welcome; Gillian will provide a good evening meal and also cater for vegetarians and special diets if she has advance warning. Off-road car parking is available.
10rm(3🚿) (1fb) 🚭 in bedrooms 🚭 in dining room 🚭 in 1 lounge CTV in all bedrooms Ⓡ sB&Bfr£17.50 dB&B£35-£41 dB&B🚿fr£41 WB&B£116-£136 WBDi£176-£196 LDO 9am
Lic ♨ CTV
Credit Cards [1][3][£]

SELECTED

GH [Q][Q][Q][Q] 28 Lower Broad Street SY8 1PQ
☎(0584) 876996 FAX (0584) 876996
This delightful half-timbered town house is situated close to Ludford Bridge and the River Teme. It has pretty, well equipped bedrooms and there is a cosy lounge with plenty of

books that opens out onto a small walled garden where guests may sit in good weather. The Ross family are friendly and efficient. They provide a fixed-price dinner menu and a good range of wines. Street parking is easy.
2rm(1🛁1🚿) Annexe 2🛁🚿 🚭 in bedrooms 🚭 in dining room CTV in all bedrooms Ⓡ sB&B🛁🚿£35-£50 dB&B🛁🚿£45-£50 WB&B£146-£160 WBDi£235-£250 LDO 8.30pm
Lic 🅿 🚫
Credit Cards [1] [2] [3] [£]

INN [Q] [Q] [Q] The Church The Buttercross SY8 1AW (in town centre) ☎(0584) 872174 FAX (0584) 877146
Closed Xmas Day
Dating from 1740, this delightful inn stands on an ancient site next to St Laurence's church, opposite the famous butter cross. Stuart and Brenda Copland are genial, energetic hosts and they have a loyal following of regularly returning guests. Bedrooms are brightly decorated with pretty drapes and matching bed covers. The bars are cosy and full of character, with a good range of bar food always available. There is a public car park nearby.
8rm(5🛁3🚿) (1fb) 🚭 in dining room 🚭 in lounges CTV in all bedrooms Ⓡ 🐕 (ex guide dogs) sB&B🛁🚿£28-£40 dB&B🛁🚿£40 Dinner £4.50-£7.95alc LDO 9pm
🅿
Credit Cards [1] [3]

LUNCARTY Tayside *Perthshire* Map **11** NO02

GH [Q] [Q] Ordie House PH1 4PR ☎Perth(0738) 828471
Two crofts have been converted to make a well-kept guest house. All rooms are on the ground floor, including a large lounge where the owners serve tea and biscuits on arrival.
4rm(2🚿) 🚭 in dining room Ⓡ ✳ sB&B£18-£20 dB&B£28-£30 dB&B🚿£32 WB&B£100 WBDi£150 LDO 6pm
🅿 CTV
[£]

LUTON Bedfordshire Map **04** TL02

GH [Q] [Q] Arlington Hotel 137 New Bedford Road LU3 1LF (on A6) ☎(0582) 419614 FAX (0582) 459047
Set back from the A6, towards Bedford, this detached commercial hotel is convenient for Luton airport and the M1. The bedrooms are well equipped, with en suite facilities and direct dial telephones being standard. There is a small traditionally styled bar and large dining room where simple evening meals are served.
19rm(2🛁17🚿) (3fb)CTV in all bedrooms Ⓡ **T** 🐕 (ex guide dogs) sB&B🛁🚿£35-£40 dB&B🛁🚿£40-£52 WB&B£225-£250 WBDi£295-£325 LDO 8.30pm
Lic 🅿
Credit Cards [1] [2] [3] [5]

GH [Q] [Q] Leaside Hotel 72 New Bedford Street LU3 1BT ☎(0582) 417643 FAX (0582) 34961
A large Victorian hotel, the Leaside is popular for its comfortable bar and elegant restaurant. Bedrooms are well equipped but do not match the style of the public areas. The hotel can be difficult to find so it is worth asking for directions.
11rm(1🛁10🚿) (1fb)CTV in all bedrooms Ⓡ **T** 🐕 (ex guide dogs) ✳ sB&B🛁🚿£35-£37.50 dB&B🛁🚿£45-£50 LDO 9.30pm
Lic 🅿 CTV threequarter size snooker table
Credit Cards [1] [2] [3] [5]

LUTTERWORTH Leicestershire

See **Shearsby**

LYDFORD Devon   Map **02** SX58

PREMIER ⚜ SELECTED

GH 🅠🅠🅠🅠🅠 **Moor View Hotel** Vale Down EX20 4BB (turn off A30 at Sourton Cross onto A386 Tavistock road, hotel is approx 4m on right) ☎(0822) 82220

Built as a farmhouse in 1869, Moor View became a small hotel and restaurant in the early 1980s. David and Wendy Sharples took over three years ago. There is a stylishly decorated drawing room, a separate bar (the only room in which smoking is allowed) and a dining room named Crockers, after the previous owners, where a table d'hôte dinner menu is offered. Sunday lunches and cream teas are also served. In cool weather, open fires are lit in the public rooms.

6rm(4⇄4♠) (1fb) ⚲ in bedrooms ⚲ in dining room CTV in all bedrooms ⑧ sB&B£30 sB&B⇄♠£35 dB&B£40 dB&B⇄♠£50 WB&B£160 WBDi£275 LDO 10am Lic ▥ CTV nc12yrs croquet lawn
£

LYDNEY Gloucestershire   Map **03** SO60

GH 🅠🅠🅠 **Lower Viney Country** Viney Hill GL15 4LT (2.5m from Lydney off A48 on unclassed road) ☎Dean(0594) 516000 FAX (0594) 516018

This charming, cottage-style guest house is well maintained and professionally run by a friendly and helpful couple. Located just outside the village of Blakeney, off the A48, it has been sympathetically extended and the rooms are quite spacious, comfortable and full of personal touches; many have lovely views of the surrounding countryside. There are two lounges and dinner can be provided. Smoking is not permitted.

6♠ ⚲ CTV in all bedrooms ⑧ ⊁ (ex guide dogs) dB&B♠fr£40 LDO 1pm
Lic ▥ CTV
Credit Cards ① ③ £
See advertisement under BLAKENEY

LYME REGIS Dorset   Map **03** SY39

GH 🅠🅠 **Coverdale** Woodmead Road DT7 3AB ☎(0297) 442882 Feb-Nov rs Dec-Jan

Situated high above the town, yet within five minutes' walk of the centre, this neat guest house makes the ideal base from which to explore this beautiful coastal area. The no-smoking bedrooms are simply furnished and well maintained, some enjoying superb views to West Bay and Portland, with Lyme Regis Bay in the foreground. There is a comfortable lounge area and a dining room where Mrs Harding offers a home cooked dinner.

8rm(5♠) (2fb) ⚲ ⑧ ⊛ sB&B£13-£17 dB&B£24-£30 dB&B♠£28-£36 WB&B£84-£125 WBDi£118.65-£165 LDO 4pm ▥ CTV nc18mths

GH 🅠🅠🅠 **St Michael's Hotel** Pound Street DT7 3HZ ☎(0297) 442503

A pleasant family run guesthouse situated just a short way from the centre of this popular seaside town. Accommodation is offered in large well maintained bedrooms, some enjoying super sea views. The dining room and lounge are most attractive, and facilities include a hairdressing salon and sunbed room. Breakfast is the only meal served, but there is a small bar area.

12rm(4⇄6♠) (1fb) ⚲ in dining room ⚲ in 1 lounge CTV in all bedrooms ⑧ ⊛ sB&B£20 sB&B⇄♠£21-£25 dB&B£40

---

dB&B⇄♠£42-£50 Lic ▥ nc3yrs solarium Credit Cards ① ③

GH 🅠🅠🅠 **The White House** 47 Silver Street DT7 3HR (on A3070 Axminster-Lyme Regis rd approx 50mtrs from jct with A3052) ☎(0297) 443420 Apr-Oct

A friendly, relaxing atmosphere pervades this charming house. Bedrooms are well-decorated, furnished and equipped with en suite facilities, and the dining room is bright and airy. Guests are well looked after throughout their stay.

7♠ ⚲ in bedrooms ⚲ in dining room CTV in all bedrooms ⑧ dB&B♠£40 WB&B£112-£126 ▥ nc10yrs
£

LYMINGTON Hampshire   Map **04** SZ39

SELECTED

GH 🅠🅠🅠🅠 **Albany House** Highfield SO41 9GB ☎(0590) 671900 Closed 2wks in winter

With views over the Solent and the Isle of Wight, this Regency house has accommodation that has been tastefully and individually furnished. Mrs Wendy Gallagher, the owner, provides a friendly welcome, and a four-course evening meal from fresh local produce. There is a comfortable sitting room and a walled garden.

3⇄♠ (1fb) ⚲ in dining room CTV in all bedrooms ⑧ sB&Bfr£26 sB&B⇄♠£39 dB&B⇄♠£48-£56 WB&B£151-£176 WBDi£225-£245 LDO noon ▥ CTV
£

GH 🅠🅠🅠 **Cedars** 2 Linden Way, Highfield SO41 9JU ☎(0590) 676468

3rm(2♠) ⚲ CTV in all bedrooms ⑧ ⊁ ⊛ dB&Bfr£34 dB&B♠£38 WB&Bfr£119 ▥ nc

GH 🅠🅠🅠 **Durlston House** Gosport Street SO41 9EG ☎(0590) 676908

This family-run bed and breakfast establishment stands within walking distance of the town centre and is ideally placed for access to the Isle of Wight ferry. In its friendly, relaxed and informal atmosphere guests have a choice of well equipped no-smoking bedrooms in modern style and the use of both a smart breakfast room and comfortable lounge. Ample forecourt parking is available.

4♠ (1fb) ⚲ CTV in all bedrooms ⑧ ⊁ ⊛ sB&B♠£15-£20 dB&B♠£30-£38 WB&B£105-£140 ▥ CTV
£

SELECTED

GH 🅠🅠🅠🅠 **Efford Cottage** Milford Road, Everton SO41 0JD ☎(0590) 642315 & (0374) 703075 FAX (0590) 642315

This attractive property surrounded by pretty, well tended gardens is set back from the Milford road between Everton village and the yachting town of Lymington. Guests are warmly welcomed here, and a happy, friendly atmosphere pervades the house. Three bright, fresh bedrooms (two of them with en suite facilities) offer good firm beds and a wealth of extra facilities which includes telephones, trouser presses and mini fridges; all the enjoyable fare - including immensely

---

popular marmalades and jams - is home-cooked, and many visitors make this a regular base for their exploration of the beautiful surrounding area.
3rm(2♠) (1fb) ⊁ in dining room CTV in all bedrooms ⓇＲ sB&B£18-£25 dB&B£30-£35 dB&Bℐ£35-£40 WB&B£100-£130 WBDi£148.50-£205.50 LDO 1.5 hrs prior
⊞ CTV nc5yrs

P R E M I E R ❦ **S E L E C T E D**

GH ⓆⓆⓆⓆⓆ **The Nurse's Cottage** Station Road SO41 6BA
☎(0590) 683402 FAX (0590) 683402
(For full entry see SWAY)

S E L E C T E D

GH ⓆⓆⓆⓆ **Our Bench** Lodge Road, Pennington
SO41 8HH (from A337 turn right signposted Pennington Village, pass the church, then 2nd right guesthouse on left)
☎(0590) 673141 FAX (0590) 673141
Situated in a residential street in the village of Pennington, this modern, chalet-style bungalow offers comfortable and very well maintained accommodation. In addition to the dining room, where breakfast and evening meals are served, there is a cosy, conservatory-style lounge which overlooks the well tended gardens. A separate building houses a heated swimming pool, a Jacuzzi and a sauna. Smoking is not permitted.
3♠ ⊁ ⓇＲ ✹ sB&Bℐ£17-£22 dB&Bℐ£37-£39 WB&B£119-£154 WBDi£161-£200 LDO 8pm
⊞ CTV nc16yrs ⌖ (heated) sauna jacuzzi mountain bikes Ⓔ

LYNDHURST Hampshire   Map **04** SU30
See also Fritham

S E L E C T E D

GH ⓆⓆⓆⓆ **Ormonde House** Southampton Road
SO43 7BT ☎(0703) 282806 FAX (0703) 283775
Closed 20-27 Dec
This fine Victorian house with a pretty front garden and good parking facilities is set back from the main road opposite open forest within walking distance of the town centre, and offers accommodation which continues to be upgraded by its resident proprietors. All bedrooms have TV, direct dial telephones and facilities for making hot drinks, but the best also offer sofa seating, a table and a trouser press; one of the two ground-floor rooms is equipped for disabled guests. Home-cooked evening meals are served from Monday to Thursday and the hotel is licensed. Good-value midweek and winter breaks are available.
15rm(11ℐ4♠) (1fb) ⊁ in 6 bedrooms ⊁ in dining room CTV in all bedrooms ⓇＲ T ✳ sB&Bℐℐ£28-£30 dB&Bℐℐ£40-£60 WB&B£140-£180 WBDi£205-£245 LDO 6.30pm
Lic ⊞
Credit Cards ①②③Ⓔ

GH ⓆⓆⓆ **Penny Farthing Hotel** Romsey Road SO43 7AA
☎Southampton(0703) 284422 FAX (0703) 284488
Ideally situated, only yards from the village centre and High Street, this attractive, personally run hotel stands on one of the main routes into Lyndhurst. Recently refurbished, it offers nicely equipped bedrooms with smart en suite facilities. The spacious day rooms include lounges and a dining room at the front of the house for breakfast. There is a wide choice of restaurants in

walking distance for evening meals. There is ample parking space at the rear of the hotel, and the friendly owners create a welcoming atmosphere.
11rm(10ℐ♠) (2fb) ⊁ in bedrooms ⊁ in dining room ⊁ in 1 lounge CTV in all bedrooms ⓇＲ sB&Bℐℐ£25-£35 dB&Bℐℐ£45-£70 WB&B£140-£195
Lic ⊞ CTV
Credit Cards ①③

GH ⓆⓆⓆ **Whitemoor House Hotel** Southampton Road
SO43 7BU ☎(0703) 282186
Closed Xmas
This long-established and popular little hotel - personally run by the resident proprietors for more than 15 years, and offering a friendly 'home from home' atmosphere - overlooks the New Forest from an ideal setting on the Southampton-Lyndhurst road. Bright, traditionally styled, no-smoking bedrooms are very well presented and maintained, the windows at the front of the building having secondary glazing. Guests can relax in a comfortable lounge (or in the attractive rear garden in summer), and there is a sunny breakfast room. Light refreshments and snacks can be served throughout the day and parking is available.
8rm(1ℐ6♠) (2fb) ⊁ in bedrooms ⊁ in dining room CTV in all bedrooms ⓇＲ ✹ (ex guide dogs) sB&B£25-£30 sB&Bℐℐ£30-£40 dB&B£44-£50 dB&Bℐℐ£44-£50 WB&Bfr£155
Lic ⊞ CTV
Credit Cards ①③Ⓔ
See advertisement on p.277.

LYNMOUTH Devon   Map **03** SS74
Lynmouth telephone numbers are due to be prefixed by 7 during the currency of this guide. See also Lynton

THE PENNY FARTHING HOTEL
Romsey Road, Lyndhurst, Hampshire SO43 7AA
Telephone: 01703 284422 Facsimile: 01703 284488

Ideally situated a moments walk from Lyndhurst High Street this smart family run Hotel offers centrally heated rooms with ensuite, colour TV and tea coffee facilities. There is a comfortable residents lounge/Bar with Satellite TV and large private car park to the rear. Lyndhurst is the centre of the New Forest and provides the main visitor information centre as well as a fine selection of shops, cafes, restaurants and inns.

SELECTED

GH 🔍🔍🔍🔍 **Bonnicott House** Watersmeet Road EX35 6EP
(opposite Anglican church) ☎Lynton(0598) 53346
Mar-Nov
A small, privately owned hotel has been recently upgraded to
exceptionally high standard. Comfortable public rooms are
thoughtfully appointed and attractively decorated while well-
equipped bedrooms enjoy coordinated soft furnishings and
some fine period furniture. The bright, colourful dining room
overlooking the sea offers a set menu at dinner and a wide
choice of English breakfasts.
8🏳 (2fb) ⊁ in 6 bedrooms ⊁ in dining room ⊁ in lounges
CTV in all bedrooms ® sB&B➪🏳£20-£25 dB&B➪🏳£40-
£50 WB&B£130-£160
Lic 🛲 nc5yrs

GH 🔍🔍🔍 **Corner House** Riverside Road EX35 6EH
☎(0598) 53300
Mar-Oct
The spacious bedrooms of this guesthouse have been completely
refurbished to a high standard. They are all attractively decorated,
thoughtfully furnished and well-equipped with comfortable sofas,
colour TVs and tea-making facilities. There is no sitting room but
the large restaurant is open all day serving coffee.
3🏳 ⊁ in bedrooms CTV in all bedrooms ® 🏋 dB&B🏳£40-£46
WB&B£120-£138 LDO 9pm
Lic 🛲 nc8yrs
Credit Cards 1️⃣ 3️⃣

SELECTED

GH 🔍🔍🔍🔍 **Countisbury Lodge Hotel** Tors Park
EX35 6NB ☎Lynton(0598) 52388
Mar-Dec
Commanding an elevated position overlooking the bay, this is
a small guesthouse with a friendly, informal atmosphere. It is
well-appointed throughout. The bedrooms, all en suite, are
thoughtfully decorated, furnished and equipped while the
public rooms, though compact, are very comfortable. The
menu is set price with a choice at dinner and at breakfast.
6rm(3➪3🏳) (1fb) ⊁ in dining room ⊁ in lounges ® ✳
dB&B➪🏳£52 WB&B£164 WBDi£227 LDO 5pm
Lic 🛲 CTV
Credit Cards 1️⃣ 3️⃣

SELECTED

GH 🔍🔍🔍🔍 **The Heatherville** Tors Park EX35 6NB
☎Lynton(0598) 52327
Mar-Oct
Built over 100 years ago, the Heatherville, run by Roy and
Pauline Davis, enjoys a wonderful location, overlooking the
River Lyn and the beautifully wooded Summerhouse Hill, yet
is in easy walking distance of the attractive town of Lynmouth.
Bedrooms, some of which have en suite bathrooms, are
warmly furnished, and Mr and Mrs Davis are hospitable hosts.
Delicious home cooking is a priority, and there is a good
choice of dishes to suit all tastes. Guests may relax in a cosy
sitting room, and perhaps enjoy a drink before dinner. This is
an ideal base for exploring an area that includes Exmoor and
Doone Country and the famous Valley of the Rocks.
9rm(1➪4🏳) (2fb) CTV in 5 bedrooms ® ✳ sB&Bfr£22
dB&Bfr£44 dB&B➪🏳fr£48 WB&Bfr£154 WBDifr£212
LDO 5.30pm
Lic 🛲 CTV nc7yrs

LYNTON Devon   Map **03** SS74
See also Lynmouth

SELECTED

GH 🔍🔍🔍🔍 **Alford House Hotel** Alford Terrace EX35 6AT
(Logis) ☎(0598) 52359 due to change to 752359
Set high on a hillside overlooking the bay, this charming
Georgian house offers accomodation of the highest standard.
The lounge is comfortable and thoughtfully appointed and
some of the attractively decorated, well-furnished bedrooms
have four-poster beds. The elegant dining room offers a
choice of breakfast and a set dinner menu and displays the
same warm, friendly atmosphere as the rest of the hotel.
8rm(1➪6🏳) ⊁ in bedrooms ⊁ in dining room CTV in all
bedrooms ® 🏋 (ex guide dogs) ✳ sB&Bfr£22
dB&B➪🏳£48-£52 WBDi£200-£230 LDO 8pm
Lic 🛲 CTV ⊁nc9yrs
Credit Cards 1️⃣ 3️⃣ £

GH 🔍🔍🔍 **Castle Hill House** Castle Hill EX35 6JA
☎(0598) 52291
9➪🏳 (3fb) ⊁ in 2 bedrooms CTV in all bedrooms ®
sB&B➪🏳£26-£30 dB&B➪🏳£38-£44 WB&B£115-£125
WBDi£185-£195 LDO 9.45pm
Lic 🛲 CTV ⊁🐾

Credit Cards 1️⃣ 3️⃣

SELECTED

GH 🔍🔍🔍🔍 **Hazeldene** 27 Lee Road EX35 6BP
☎(0598) 52364 due to change to 752364
Closed mid Nov-28 Dec
A high standard of accomodation is offered at this well-
established guest house. Bedrooms vary in size but all are
attractively decorated and thoughtfully furnished. There are
two small, comfortable lounges, one for non-smokers, and a
pleasant dining room where an evening meal is available.
9➪🏳 (2fb) ⊁ in 2 bedrooms ⊁ in dining room ⊁ in 1 lounge
CTV in all bedrooms ® ✳ dB&B➪🏳£35-£42 WB&B£119-
£140 WBDi£196-£215 LDO 5pm
Lic 🛲 CTV nc5yrs
Credit Cards 1️⃣ 2️⃣ 3️⃣ 5️⃣ £

SELECTED

GH 🔍🔍🔍🔍 **Ingleside Hotel** Lee Road EX35 6HW (on
private rd between Town Hall & Methodist church)
☎(0598) 52223 due to change to 752223
Mar-Oct
This attractive Victorian house is set above the village with
views across the Watersmeet Valley to Lynton Bay and the
hills of Exmoor. Built in 1895 as a gentleman's residence, it
now makes a very comfortable hotel. Bedrooms are warm and
pleasantly furnished and the dining room is light and bright.
Guests are asked not to smoke in the large sitting room where
a fire burns on cold evenings.
7rm(4➪3🏳) (2fb) ⊁ in dining room ⊁ in lounges CTV in all
bedrooms ® 🏋 sB&B➪🏳£25-£28 dB&B➪🏳£44-£48
WB&B£140-£154 WBDi£224-£238 LDO 5.30pm
Lic 🛲 nc12yrs
Credit Cards 1️⃣ 3️⃣ £

SELECTED

GH Ⓠ Ⓠ Ⓠ Ⓠ **Lynhurst Hotel** Lyn Way EX35 6AX
☎(0598) 52241 due to change to 752241 FAX (0598) 52241
Mar-Oct

There is a cheery atmosphere at this most attractive Victorian property, which is personally run by the proprietors. The house is filled with pretty fabrics, ornaments and dried flowers. It is so cosy and comfortable that it is no surprise that many guests return frequently. Home-cooked meals are available.

7rm(2⇌2ʀ) (1fb) ⊬ CTV in all bedrooms Ⓡ ✳ dB&B£38-£44 dB&B⇌ʀ£38-£48 WB&B£105-£140 WBDi£175-£230 LDO noon
Lic CTV ⅌
Ⓔ

GH Ⓠ Ⓠ Ⓠ *Mayfair Hotel* Lynway EX35 6AY ☎(0598) 53227
due to change to 753227

A recent change of ownership has seen improvements to this character house, now with a comfy lounge and brightly styled dining room, both with Victorian marble fireplaces and assorted antiques and period pieces. The house itself is set high above the town and enjoys splendid views out to sea and of an expanse of National Trust headland.

9rm(6⇌ʀ) (1fb) CTV in all bedrooms Ⓡ LDO 5pm
Lic ⬛
Credit Cards ①②③

|⇌ ☞| GH Ⓠ Ⓠ **Retreat** 1 Park Gardens, Lydiate Lane EX35 6DF
(top end of Lydiate Rd which runs parallel to main town road (Lee Rd)) ☎(0598) 53526 due to change to 753526
A well-maintained, clean guest house has basic but adequate accomodation. Reasonably sized bedrooms are thaughtfully

▶

The Heatherville
Tors Park, Lynmouth, Devon.
Telephone: (01598) 52327

★ Beautiful house, situated in sunny, quiet, secluded position overlooking the River Lyn.
★ Excellent home cooking of Traditional English Cuisine.
★ Full central heating.
★ Comfortable colour TV lounge.
★ Separate charming bar lounge.
★ Tea & Coffee making facilities in all rooms.
★ 4 minutes from village and harbour.
★ Private car park.
★ Some rooms with private shower, toilet and colour TV
★ Lovely Honeymoon Suite with colour TV and tea/coffee making facilities.
★ Brochure, sample menu and tariff on request from resident proprietors Roy and Pauline Davis.

WHITEMOOR
HOUSE HOTEL

AA
LISTED
Southampton Road,
Lyndhurst, New Forest
Hampshire SO43 7BU
Telephone: Lyndhurst (01703) 282186

A beautiful country house hotel, overlooking the New Forest, where a personal service awaits you from this family run hotel.

☐ Comfortable colour TV lounge with residential licence.

☐ Tea/coffee facilities in all rooms & colour TV.

☐ All rooms en-suite and fully central heated.

☐ Ample private car parking.

☐ Ideal for business, holidays, golfers and walkers.

☐ Brochure/tariff on request. All major credit cards accepted.

INGLESIDE HOTEL
Lee Road, Lynton. Tel: (01598) 752223

Since 1972 Clive and Lesley Horn have been offering a warm welcome to their guests at Ingleside, which is set high in its own grounds overlooking the village. The standards are very high which you'd probably expect from a family who pride themselves on their accommodation and cuisine. Enjoy good food and wine from the imaginative menu.
All bedrooms have a bath or shower and w.c. en-suite, colour TV and beverage facilities. Ample safe car parking is always available in hotel grounds.
Send for free brochure with sample menus or telephone for personal service.

decorated and comfortable as is the small lounge. Breakfast and the evening meal are served in the bright dining room.
6rm (2fb) ⊁ in dining room ⓡ sB&B£15-£16 dB&B£30-£32 WB&B£100-£106 WBDi£160-£173 LDO 4pm
▥ CTV
£

GH ⓠⓠⓠ **St Vincent** Castle Hill EX35 6JA (adjacent to Exmoor Museum) ☎(0598) 52244 due to change to 752244
Closed mid Dec-mid Jan
Situated close to the village centre, this attractive Georgian house has many period features, in particular a splendid Regency spiral staircase. The bedrooms are well maintained and spotlessly clean. There is a cosy lounge and a separate bar in the flagstoned basement. The Buckleys offer a freindly welcome to their guests.
6rm(1⇄2ℝ) (1fb) ⊁ CTV in all bedrooms ⓡ ⴕ (ex guide dogs) sB&B£16-£17 dB&B£32-£34 db&B⇄ℝ£37-£39 WB&B£102-£125 WBDi£170-£195 LDO 11.30am
Lic nc8yrs
£

PREMIER ✿ SELECTED

GH ⓠⓠⓠⓠⓠ **Victoria Lodge** Lee Road EX35 6BS
☎(0598) 53203 due to change to 753203
Feb-Dec
This double-fronted Victorian house is furnished in Victorian style with the original fireplaces and mantlepieces. Bedrooms are all of a high standard. Dinner is prepared by the owners, Mr and Mrs Bennett, and the four-course meal can be enjoyed in a charming dining room. Smoking is not allowed anywhere in the hotel.
10⇄ℝ (1fb) ⊁ CTV in all bedrooms ⓡ ⴕ dB&B⇄ℝ£36-£60 WB&B£112-£185 WBDi£200-£283 LDO 4pm
Lic ▥
Credit Cards ①③

SELECTED
GH ⓠⓠⓠⓠ **Waterloo House Hotel** Lydiate Lane EX35 6AJ
☎(0598) 53391 due to change to 753391
Waterloo House is an attractive Georgian hotel run in a friendly and relaxed style by its owners Sheila and Roger Mountis. The individually furnished bedrooms are comfortable and well equipped, and the choice of lounges includes a no-smoking room with a log fire and a TV lounge with a dispense bar. The elegant dining room features imaginative menus of home cooked dishes, and with notice vegetarian and other special diets can be catered for.
9rm(8⇄ℝ) (2fb) ⊁ in 4 bedrooms ⊁ in dining room ⊁ in 1 lounge CTV in all bedrooms ⓡ sB&Bfr£17.50 sB&B⇄ℝfr£23.50 dB&B⇄ℝfr£36 WB&Bfr£110 WBDifr£180 LDO 7pm
Lic ▥ CTV
£

LYTHAM ST ANNES Lancashire   Map **07** SD32

GH ⓠⓠ **Cullerne Hotel** 55 Lightburne Avenue, St Annes on Sea FY8 1JE ☎St Annes(0253) 721753
This well maintained house from the late Victorian period stands in a quiet side road just off the Promenade and is run by friendly, caring owners. Bedrooms have good facilities (though none are en

suite), and guests have the use of both a cosy bar and a very comfortable lounge. Forecourt parking is available.
5rm (2fb) ⊁ in dining room CTV in all bedrooms ⓡ ⴕ ✳ sB&B£14 dB&B£28 WB&B£98 WBDi£112 LDO noon
Lic ▥ CTV
£

GH ⓠⓠⓠ **Endsleigh Private Hotel** 315 Clifton Drive South FY8 1HN ☎St Annes(0253) 725622
This welcoming and very well maintained private hotel near the shopping centre - just two minutes' walk from the seafront and other amenities - offers accommodation in neat, modern bedrooms with en suite bath or shower rooms; these include several family units with separate children's rooms and two externally accessed rooms on the ground floor. Meals are served in a two-part restaurant, there is a comfortable residents' lounge, and the hotel has its own forecourt car park.
15⇄ℝ (3fb) ⊁ in 6 bedrooms ⊁ in dining room ⊁ in lounges CTV in all bedrooms ⓡ ⴕ ✳ dB&B⇄ℝ£39-£41 WB&B£120-£127 WBDi£159-£169 LDO 4pm
Lic ▥

GH ⓠ **Lyndhurst Private Hotel** 338 Clifton Drive North FY8 2PB ☎St Annes(0253) 724343
This tall gabled Victorian semidetached house is situated close to the town centre opposite Ashton Gardens and offers modestly appointed accommodation. Bedrooms vary in size with those at the front enjoying views of the park. There is a spacious comfortable lounge with TV and the dining room is adjacent. Car parking is provided at the front of the house.
12rm(1⇄3ℝ) (4fb) CTV in 4 bedrooms ⓡ LDO noon
CTV

GH ⓠⓠⓠ **Strathmore Hotel** 305 Clifton Drive South FY8 1HN ☎St Annes(0253) 725478
Well cared for and friendly, with the added advantage of its own car park, this guest house stands only a few minutes' walk from town centre and beach. Bright, fresh bedrooms have been well equipped, meals are taken in a pleasant rear dining room, and there is an elegant lounge.
10rm(2⇄3ℝ) ⊁ in dining room CTV in all bedrooms ⓡ ⴕ ✳ sB&B£17-£19 sB&B⇄ℝ£19-£21 dB&B£34-£38 dB&B⇄ℝ£38-£42 WB&B£119-£133 WBDi£147-£168 LDO 5pm
Lic ▥ nc9yrs

MACCLESFIELD Cheshire   Map **07** SJ97

SELECTED
FH ⓠⓠⓠⓠ Mrs Anne Read **Hardingland Farm Country House** (SJ958725) Macclesfield Forest SK11 0ND
☎(0625) 425759
Mar-Nov
This beautifully preserved stone-built Georgian farmhouse enjoys a remote and peaceful location overlooking spectacular scenery to the east of the town; it is reached from the A537 by turning in to a long, narrow and winding lane immediately opposite the millstone which serves as a Peak National Park boundary marker. Both the spacious lounge and the dining room - where guests gather round one table to share an excellent meal - have period furnishings, and bedrooms also reflect the original character of the house.
3rm(1⇄) ⊁ ⓡ ⴕ dB&B£36 dB&B⇄£40-£44 WB&B£126-£154 WBDi£217-£245 LDO 9am
▥ CTV nc16yrs 17 acres smallholding beef sheep
£

MACHRIHANISH Strathclyde Argyllshire   Map **10** NR62

GH ⓠⓠⓠ **Ardell House** PA28 6PT (opposite golf course)
☎(0586) 810235
Closed Xmas & New Year rs Nov-Feb

Popular with golfers, this detached Victorian house offers fine views across the golf course and out to sea to the distant islands of Islay and Jura. The accommodation ranges from solid, well proportioned rooms, to some simpler top-floor rooms and those in a chalet-style annexe. There is a comfortable lounge with an honesty bar.
7rm(1🛁5🚿) Annexe 3🚿 (1fb) 🚭 in bedrooms 🚭 in dining room CTV in all bedrooms Ⓡ * sB&B🛁🚿£22-£30 dB&B🛁🚿£44-£50
Lic 🔥
[£]

MACHYNLLETH Powys — Map **06** SH70

GH [Q][Q][Q] Maenllwyd Newtown Road SY20 8EY (on A489 opposite the hospital) ☎(0654) 702928 FAX (0654) 702928
Closed 25 & 26 Dec
Situated opposite the cottage hospital, this large detached Victorian house was once a manse. Now a family-run guesthouse, it provides good, comfortable accommodation, together with ample car parking and a pleasant lawn area at the rear.
7rm(4🛁🚿) (2fb) 🚭 in 4 bedrooms CTV in all bedrooms Ⓡ * sB&B£16-£20 sB&B🛁🚿£20 dB&B£28 dB&B🛁🚿£34 WB&B£89-£108 WBDi£139-£158 LDO 1pm
Lic 🔥 CTV
Credit Cards [1][2][3][5] [£]

FH [Q][Q] Mr & Mrs D Timms **Rhiwlwyfen** *(SH761983)* Forge SY20 8RP ☎(0654) 702683
Apr-Oct rs Oct-Apr
This secluded, remote 17th-century farmhouse lies in the hills above the nearby hamlet of Forge, and is reached across the golf course. There are three smart, comfortable bedrooms, and a relaxing lounge with an inglenook log fire.
2rm (2fb) 🚭 in dining room 🚭 in 1 lounge Ⓡ 🐕 (ex guide dogs) * sB&B£15 dB&B£30 LDO 8pm
🔥 CTV 100 acres beef sheep
[£]

MAIDENHEAD Berkshire — Map **04** SU88

P R E M I E R S E L E C T E D

GH [Q][Q][Q][Q][Q] Beehive Manor Cox Green Lane SL6 3ET ☎(0628) 20980
Closed Xmas
Do not be put off by the carved gargoyles on the wooden lintel of this splendid Elizabethan house, which lies in the quiet and leafy fringes of Maidenhead, for there is the warmest welcome within from the two owners. Shortly after arrival, you will find yourself in their spacious lounge, enjoying tea and cakes. All the rooms have period features, with latticed windows and stained glass, moulded ceilings and panelled walls. The bedrooms are a good size, comfortably appointed and prettily decorated, some with garden views. If the generous hospitality was not reason enough for a stay here, the breakfast comes a close second. Freshly squeezed orange juice, warm newly baked bread, a choice of fine home-made preserves and a selection of hot dishes are all on offer. This is a most friendly and relaxing home from home.
3rm(2🛁1🚿) 🚭 in bedrooms 🚭 in dining room 🚭 in lounges 🐕 sB&B🛁🚿£35 dB&B🛁🚿£55
🔥 CTV nc12yrs
[£]

MAIDSTONE Kent — Map **05** TQ75

GH [Q][Q] Rock House Hotel 102 Tonbridge Road ME16 8SL (on A26) ☎(0622) 751616 FAX (0622) 756119
Closed 24 Dec-1 Jan
More en suite facilities have been added and the decor upgraded at this guesthouse west of the town centre. There is a lounge and a cheery breakfast room.
11rm(5🛁🚿) (3fb) 🚭 in dining room CTV in all bedrooms Ⓡ 🐕 sB&B£24-£30 sB&B🛁🚿£30-£36 dB&B🛁🚿£35-£44 WB&B£140-£210
🔥 CTV
Credit Cards [1][3] [£]

GH [Q][Q][Q] Willington Court Willington Street ME15 8JW (1.5m E, at junct of A20 Asford Rd & Willington St) ☎(0622) 738885
This small, family-run guesthouse has been further upgraded to provide more modern facilities. The bedrooms are well-appointed and equipped with trouser press, TV, tea-making and a number of extra touches including sewing kit and free toiletries. There is a cosy lounge, a second, no-smoking lounge, and a conservatory. The dining room has also been refurbished in keeping with the style of the house.
4🛁🚿 🚭 in bedrooms 🚭 in dining room 🚭 in 1 lounge CTV in all bedrooms Ⓡ 🐕 (ex guide dogs) sB&B🛁🚿£25-£33 dB&B🛁🚿£38-£46 WB&B£119-£217
🔥 CTV nc16yrs
Credit Cards [1][2][3][5] [£]

MALDON Essex — Map **05** TL80

INN [Q][Q] Swan Hotel Maldon High Street CM9 7EP ☎(0621) 853170 FAX (0621) 854490
This freshly kept inn close to the centre of the attractive town offers public areas neatly divided into a bar/eating area and a separate breakfast room occasionally used for conferences; bedrooms are located above these.
6🛁🚿 (2fb) 🚭 in 2 bedrooms CTV in all bedrooms Ⓡ 🐕 * sB&B£25-£35 sB&B🛁🚿£35 dB&B£40 dB&B🛁🚿£48 WB&B£175-£245 WBDifr£205 Lunch £3.50-£6.50 Dinner £4-£8 LDO 9pm
🔥
Credit Cards [1][2][3][5] [£]

MALHAM North Yorkshire — Map **07** SD96

GH [Q][Q][Q] Sparth House Hotel BD23 4DA (in centre of village) ☎Airton(0729) 830315
Parts of this spacious house date from 1664, making it one of the oldest in Malham. Some of the bedrooms are situated in a more modern wing at the rear, and have lovely views of the surrounding hills; although rather compact, they are very functional. The bedrooms in the older part of the house are a good, comfortable size and nicely decorated with modern fabrics. All the bedrooms are no smoking. Downstairs, there is a spacious dining room with a cosy bar area and an adjoining games room. Sensible forethought has been given by providing two comfortable lounges, one for smokers and one for non smokers and both are equipped with TV.
10rm(7🛁🚿) 🚭 in bedrooms 🚭 in dining room 🚭 in 1 lounge CTV in 7 bedrooms Ⓡ 🐕 (ex guide dogs) sB&B£20.50 dB&B£37 dB&B🛁🚿£50 WBDi£131.25-£210 LDO 5pm
Lic 🔥 CTV table-tennis darts
[£]

MALMESBURY Wiltshire — Map **03** ST98

FH [Q][Q][Q] Mrs R Eavis **Manor** *(ST922837)* Corston SN16 0HF (on A429, 3m from junct 17 of M4) ☎(0666) 822148
This attractive stone-built farmhouse dates back to the 18th century and is part of a working farm in the village of Corston, and ideally placed for exploring nearby Malmesbury and the

►

Cotswolds. Bedrooms are comfortable and tastefully decorated; there is an elegant lounge with an open fireplace and an adjacent breakfast room. For evening meals, there is a good choice of places within walking distance.
6rm(3🛁🚿) (2fb) 🚭 CTV in all bedrooms [R] 🐕 * sB&B£16-£22 sB&B🛁🚿£20-£24 dB&B£32-£38 dB&B🛁🚿£36-£40
▥ CTV 436 acres arable dairy
Credit Cards [1][3][£]

🛏 ▪ **FH** [Q][Q] Mrs E G Edwards **Stonehill** *(SU986894)* Charlton SN16 9DY (3.5m from town on B4040) ☎(0666) 823310
This 15th-century Cotswold stone farmhouse is surrounded by a working dairy farm, just a short drive from England's oldest borough, Malmesbury. The neatly appointed bedrooms are comfortable. There is a combined lounge/breakfast room where guests share a large table. Animal lovers are welcome to bring their own dogs who can enjoy the company of the family's cats and dogs.
3rm(1🚿) (1fb) 🚭 in bedrooms CTV in 1 bedroom [R] sB&B£14-£18 sB&B🚿fr£20 dB&B£28-£30 dB&B🚿£36-£40 WB&B£98-£122.50
▥ CTV 🌳 180 acres dairy
[£]

MALPAS Cheshire — Map **07** SJ44

GH [Q][Q][Q] **Laurel Farm** Chorlton Lane SY14 7ES
☎(0948) 860291 FAX (0948) 860291
3rm(2🛁1🚿) (1fb) 🚭 CTV in all bedrooms [R] dB&B🛁🚿£46-£50 LDO on arrival
▥ CTV nc12yrs

P R E M I E R S E L E C T E D

FH [Q][Q][Q][Q][Q] Mrs K M Ritchie **Tilston Lodge** *(SJ463511)* Tilston SY14 7DR (3m N of Malpas)
☎Tilston(0829) 250223

This beautifully preserved Victorian property with spacious and attractive gardens was originally a shooting lodge, which was enlarged in 1878 and further extended in Edwardian times.
It stands on the edge of the small village of Tilston, north of Malpas, and is part of a 12-acre holding where rare breeds of sheep, cattle, fowl and poultry are reared. The house is tastefully decorated and furnished throughout. The bedrooms have numerous thoughtful extra touches; one room has a four-poster bed. There are two comfortable lounges and an attractive breakfast room with two tables, where dinner can be provided with advance notice. Smoking is discouraged in the house.
3🛁🚿 (1fb) 🚭 CTV in all bedrooms [R] 🐕 (ex guide dogs) * dB&B🛁🚿£50-£56
▥ CTV croquet table tennis 16 acres rare breeds poultry sheep
[£]

MALVERN Hereford & Worcester — Map **03** SO74

GH [Q][Q][Q] **Pembridge Hotel** Graham Road WR14 2HX
☎(0684) 574813 FAX (0684) 574813
8rm(6🛁2🚿) CTV in all bedrooms [R] **T** 🐕 (ex guide dogs) sB&B🛁🚿£32-£40 dB&B🛁🚿£50-£60 LDO 8pm
Lic ▥ nc
Credit Cards [1][3]

GH [Q][Q][Q] **Sidney House Hotel** 40 Worcester Road WR14 4AA
☎(0684) 574994
rs Xmas & New Year
A Grade II listed house dating from 1823 stands in an elevated position alongside the A449 just west of the town centre with extensive views over the Severn valley towards the Vale of Evesham and the Cotswolds. Bedrooms are attractively decorated and mostly furnished with stripped pine; an excellent range of facilities is provided including hair dryers, together with some thoughtful extra touches. There is a comfortable lounge with an honesty bar, and a pleasant dining room. Proprietors Tom and Margaret Haggett are friendly, welcoming hosts.
8rm(5🚿) (2fb) 🚭 in dining room CTV in all bedrooms [R] sB&B£20-£27 sB&B🚿£30-£35 dB&B£39 dB&B🚿£49 LDO 3pm
Lic ▥ CTV
Credit Cards [1][2][3][£]

MAN, ISLE OF — Map **06**

DOUGLAS — Map **06** SC37

GH [Q][Q][Q] **Ainsdale Guest House** 2 Empire Terrace, Central Prom ☎(0624) 676695 FAX (0624) 676695
Apr-Sep rs Etr & Spring bank holiday
This Victorian terraced property is set back from the Promenade and is soundly maintained, with proprietors Les and Margaret Whitehouse continuing to make improvements. Bedrooms vary in size but all have modern furniture and equipment, and family rooms are also available. There is a bright, pleasant lounge and an attractive dining room, both decorated to a good standard.
14rm(8🛁🚿) (2fb) 🚭 in 8 bedrooms 🚭 in dining room 🚭 in 1 lounge CTV in 6 bedrooms [R] sB&B£17.50 sB&B🛁🚿£21 dB&B£30-£32 dB&B🛁🚿£37-£36 WB&B£105-£129.50 WBDi£147-£171.50 LDO 6pm
▥ CTV ⊘
[£]

GH [Q][Q] **All Seasons** 11 Clifton Terrace, Broadway
☎(0624) 676323 FAX (0624) 676323
A small guesthouse with friendly young owners occupying part of a Victorian terrace, situated a few hundred yards up from the promenade. Bedrooms vary in size but all have modern equipment, and a two-bedroom suite for families is available. There is a pleasant dining room furnished with pine tables, an adjacent bar and a cosy lounge on the first floor, where smoking is not permitted.
8rm(6🚿) 🚭 in dining room 🚭 in lounges CTV in all bedrooms [R] sB&B🚿£19 dB&B🚿£35 WB&B£105-£133 LDO 9pm
Lic ▥
[£]

GH [Q][Q] ***Hydro Hotel*** Queen's Promanade ☎(0624) 676870
A large family run Edwardian hotel sits on the Promenade, at the end of a row of terraced properties. Bedrooms vary in size and shape but they all have modern equipment and many have sea views; family rooms are also available and a lift serves all floors. Public areas are spacious and include a choice of bars, two lounges and a large restaurant, which is also available for functions.
60rm(11🛁20🚿) (17fb) CTV in all bedrooms [R] 🐕 (ex guide dogs) LDO 7pm
Lic lift ▥ solarium pool table darts
Credit Cards [1][3][5]

GH [Q][Q] ***The Laurels*** 2 Mona Drive, Central Promenade
☎(0624) 674884 FAX (0624) 674884
Mar-Oct
An attractive, well maintained terraced property conveniently situated close to the promenade. It provides compact but pleasantly furnished bedrooms featuring cheerful coordinating fabrics. There is a comfortable lounge, a neat dining room and a cosy bar.
14rm(8🛁🚿) (1fb) [R] 🐕 (ex guide dogs)
Lic CTV

GH Ⓠ Ⓠ **Rosslyn Guest House** 3 Empire Terrace, Central Promenade ☎(0624) 676056 FAX (0624) 674122
Closed 29 Nov-2 Jan
This friendly guest house is situated in a row of terraced properties, just back from the Promenade. Bedrooms vary in size and style and are modestly appointed; family rooms are available. There is a small cosy bar, and an attractively decorated comfortable lounge on the first floor. Separate tables are provided in the dining room.
16rm(4⇨🟊) (3fb) ⊁ in 4 bedrooms ⊁ in dining room ⊁ in lounges CTV in 5 bedrooms Ⓡ 🅷 (ex guide dogs) ✻ sB&B£15 sB&B⇨🟊£25 dB&B£30 dB&B⇨🟊£40 WB&B£105 WBDi£175 Lic ⊞ CTV ⨍nc5yrs
£

GH Ⓠ Ⓠ Ⓠ **Ebor Hotel** 402 Wilbraham Road, Chorlton Cum Hardy M21 0UH ☎061-881 1911 & 061-881 4855
Closed Xmas
Some three miles south of the city centre, in the suburb of Chorlton-cum-Hardy, this large Victorian house is conveniently situated for the motorway network and the airport. The traditional-style public areas include a bar, a lounge and a dining room with individual tables. The bedrooms, which vary in size, all have modern furnishings.
16rm(8🟊) (3fb) CTV in all bedrooms Ⓡ 🅷 ✻ sB&B£22 sB&B🟊£27 dB&B£32 dB&B🟊£37 WB&B£147-£182 LDO 5pm Lic ⊞ CTV nc4yrs darts
Credit Cards 1 3 £

GH Ⓠ Ⓠ **Kempton House Hotel** 400 Wilbraham Road, Chorlton-Cum-Hardy M21 0UH (on A6010) ☎061-881 8766
Closed 24-26 Dec
Situated in the suburb of Chorlton-cum-Hardy, three miles south of the city centre, this large Victorian house is within easy reach of the airport and motorway network. The bedrooms, while not luxurious, have modern furnishings and equipment. Other facilities include a lounge, a small bar and a car park.
14rm(4🟊) CTV in all bedrooms Ⓡ 🅷 (ex guide dogs) ✻ B&B£20.50-£22 sB&B🟊£25-£27 dB&B£29.50-£31 dB&B🟊£33.50-£36.50 LDO 5pm Lic ⊞ CTV
Credit Cards 1 3 £

GH Ⓠ Ⓠ Ⓠ **New Central Hotel** 144-146 Heywood Street, Cheetham M8 7PD ☎061-205 2169 FAX 061-205 2169
Situated in a quiet residential area at Cheetham, yet only a mile from the city centre and Victoria Station, this double-fronted, detached house offers neatly maintained rooms and the resident owners create a friendly, relaxed atmosphere.
10rm(5🟊) CTV in all bedrooms Ⓡ sB&B£20.50-£21.50 dB&B🟊fr£21.50 dB&B£30-£33 dB&B🟊£35 LDO 7.30pm Lic ⊞ CTV
£

SELECTED

FH Ⓠ Ⓠ Ⓠ Ⓠ Mrs B Whitworth **Dairy House** *(TM148293)* Bradfield Road, Wix CO11 2SR (between Colchester and Harwich, turn off A120 into Wix village. At crossroads take road signposted Bradfield and farm is 1m on left) ☎(0255) 870322
(1fb) ⊁ in bedrooms CTV in 2 bedrooms Ⓡ 🅷 (ex guide dogs) sB&B£16 sB&B🟊£18 dB&B£30 dB&B🟊£33 WB&B£100-£105
⊞ CTV games room pool table croquet 700 acres arable fruit

▶◀ ■ **GH** Ⓠ Ⓠ Ⓠ **Brackenwood** 67 Wynnstay Lane LL12 8LH (turn off B5445 by Red Lion pub) ☎Wrexham(0978) 852866 FAX (0978) 852065
This family-run guest house stands amid well maintained lawns which back on to 13 acres of woodland where visitors may wander at will. The comfortable television lounge opens out onto a patio and gardens, while a modern conservatory serves as the dining room. Bright, cheerful bedrooms are centrally heated and equipped with tea-making equipment.
7rm(1⇨1🟊) (1fb) ⊁ in bedrooms CTV in dining room CTV in 1 bedroom Ⓡ sB&B£15-£17 sB&B⇨🟊£17-£20 dB&B£27-£30 dB&B⇨🟊£29-£32 WB&B£190-£204 WBDi£315-£329 LDO at breakfast time
⊞ CTV
£

FH Ⓠ Ⓠ Mr & Mrs J Matthews **Greys** *(TL604112)* Ongar Road CM6 1QR (in Margaret Roding village turn off A1060 by telephone kiosk, second house on left approx 0.5m)
☎Good Easter(0245) 231509
The guest bedrooms at Greys Farm are neat and tidy, and have shared use of a bathroom. Guests are greeted with hot drinks, which are provided at all reasonable hours. Full English breakfast is served at separate pine tables in the small dining room, and there is a comfortable beamed lounge for relaxing and reading up on local information.
3 ⊁ 🅷 dB&Bfr£32
⊞ CTV nc10yrs 340 acres arable beef sheep

Ebor Hotel

**402 Wilbraham Road,
Chorlton-cum-Hardy,
Manchester M21 0UH
Telephone: 0161-881 1911/4855**

Welcome to the Ebor Hotel. Ideally situated 3 miles from the City Centre. Close to Manchester Airport and convenient to the motorway network. All rooms have colour TV, shaver points, tea & coffee making equipment and central heating, and many rooms are en-suite. The Hotel has a licensed bar lounge, a pleasant dining room, colour TV lounge and car park. Evening meal is available upon request. Discount available for long term stay.

MARGATE Kent   Map **05** TR37

GH Q Q **Beachcomber Hotel** 3-4 Royal Esplanade, Westbrook CT9 5DL ☎Thanet(0843) 221616
Some of the bedrooms at this well kept guest house have views over the sands of Westbrook Bay. There is a well stocked bar and a cosy lounge area, as well as the TV lounge and dining room where freshly prepared meals are served.
15rm (3fb) ⚹ in dining room Ⓡ ⋔ sB&B£16.50-£17 dB&B£33-£35 WB&Bfr£105 WBDifr£150 LDO 10am
Lic ▥ CTV
£

SELECTED

GH Q Q Q Q **The Greswolde Hotel** 20 Surrey Road, Cliftonville CT9 2LA ☎Thanet(0843) 223956
This comfortable house has a warm, friendly atmosphere and a high level of hospitality. Lounge and dining room are well-furnished and decorated in period victorian style as are the spacious bedrooms which are equipped with most of the essentials.
6rm(1⇌5♠) (2fb) ⚹ in dining room CTV in all bedrooms ⓇsB&B⇌♠£21 dB&B⇌♠£35
Lic ▥
Credit Cards 1 3 £

GH Q Q **Westbrook Bay House** 12 Royal Esplanade, Westbrook CT9 5DW ☎Thanet(0843) 292700
This is an improving small guest house providing clean, comfortable accomodation. Bedrooms are well equipped, all have tea and coffee making facilities and some are en suite. A welcoming lounge is available to guests and breakfast is served in the well-appointed dining room.
11rm(4♠) (4fb)CTV in 10 bedrooms ⓇⓍ⋔ (ex guide dogs) ⚹ sB&Bfr£14 dB&B♠fr£32 WB&Bfr£94 WBDifr£120 LDO 4.30pm
Lic ▥ CTV
£

MARKET DRAYTON Shropshire   Map **07** SJ63

SELECTED

FH Q Q Q Q Mrs P Williamson **Mickley House** *(SJ615325)* Faulsgreen, Tern Hill TF9 3QW (A41 to Tern Hill roundabout, then A53 towards Shrewsbury, first right for Faulsgreen, 4th house on right) ☎(0630) 638505
Closed Xmas
This charming Victorian house offers a high standard of accommodation, including spacious, ground-floor rooms.
3⇌♠ (1fb) ⚹ CTV in all bedrooms ⓇⓍ⋔ sB&B⇌♠£25-£28 dB&B⇌♠£40-£52 WB&B£140-£175
▥ CTV 125 acres beef

SELECTED

FH Q Q Q Q Mr J M Thomas **Stoke Manor** *(SJ646278)* Stoke-on-Tern TF9 2DU (in village of Stoke-on-Tern midway between A41 & A53) ☎Hodnet(0630) 685222 (0630) 685666
Closed Dec
An 18th-century farmhouse set in 250 acres of arable land, is situated in the village of Stoke-on-Tern, reached off the A53 at Hodnet. The three bedrooms all have en suite bathrooms, and are furnished with stripped pine, TV and tea making facilities. There are lovely views of the Shropshire Plain from the comfortable, modern sitting room. No evening meal is served, but there are ample local restaurants nearby. Artefacts

---

and pottery dating from the 12th century are displayed in the house, and the unusual cellar bar features a collection of old farm implements. The grounds include a lake stocked with crayfish and tench, and there are fishing rights on a stretch of the River Tern.
3⇌♠ (1fb) ⚹ in bedrooms ⚹ in dining room CTV in all bedrooms ⓇⓍ⋔ (ex guide dogs) ⚹ sB&B⇌♠£25-£27.50 dB&B⇌♠£40-£50
Lic ▥ nc5yrs ♪ vintage tractor collection farm trail 250 acres arable
£

MARKINCH Fife   Map **11** NO20

INN Q Q Q **Town House Hotel** 1 High Street KY7 6OQ ☎Glenrothes(0592) 758459 FAX (0592) 741238
Situated on the main street close to the station, this family owned former coaching inn is popular for its award winning bar food, served in the pleasant Provost restaurant and lounge. Bedrooms have been attractively refurbished with pine units and colourful co-ordinated fabrics and are well equipped, most having smart modern en-suite bathrooms.
4rm(3⇌♠) (1fb) CTV in all bedrooms ⓇsB&Bfr£35 sB&B⇌♠£40 dB&B£50 Lunch fr£3.95&alc High tea fr£4.95 Dinner fr£11.45 LDO 9pm
▥
Credit Cards 1 2 3 5 £

MARKSBURY Avon   Map **03** ST66

GH Q Q *Wansdyke Cottage* Crosspost Lane BA2 9HE ☎Bath(0225) 873674
Wansdyke Cottage is a stone-built 18th-century property conveniently situated on the A39/B3116 crossroads south of Bath. The reception rooms, with coal fires in cooler weather, offer views to Stantonbury hill and the surrounding farmland. The guest bedrooms, including one ground-floor room, are individually furnished and there is access to bathrooms close by. An extensive dinner menu is offered.
4rm(1⇌) ⓇLDO 6pm
▥ CTV

MARLBOROUGH Wiltshire   Map **04** SU16

See also Burbage

PREMIER 🏆 **SELECTED**

GH Q Q Q Q Q **Laurel Cottage** Southend, Ogbourne St George SN8 1SG (on A346) ☎Ogbourne St George(0672) 841288
Apr-Oct rs Mar
A very pretty thatched, brick and flint cottage, this guest house nestles in a fold of the Marlborough Downs three miles from the town. Rooms vary in style, the most spacious is the Ridgeway Suite above the garage. Breakfast is taken round one large table, and guests can relax in a cosy lounge. Tea, coffee, sandwiches, filled rolls and home-made cake are available on request. This is a no-smoking establishment.
3rm(1⇌) (1fb) ⚹ CTV in all bedrooms ⓇⓍ⋔ sB&Bfr£26 sB&B⇌fr£34 dB&B£33-£38 dB&B⇌£40-£47
▥ CTV
£

SELECTED

GH [Q][Q][Q][Q] **The Vines** High Street SN8 1HJ
☎(0672) 516583 & 515333 FAX (0672) 515338
6🛁🚿 (2fb)CTV in all bedrooms [R] sB&B🛁🚿£19-£25 dB&B🛁🚿£40-£50 LDO 9.30pm
Lic 🅿
Credit Cards [1][2][3][5]

MARLOW Buckinghamshire — Map **04** SU88

SELECTED

GH [Q][Q][Q][Q] **Holly Tree House** Burford Close, Marlow Bottom SL7 3NF ☎(0628) 891110 FAX (0628) 481278

This modern property is situated in a quiet residential area overlooking a wooded valley and convenient for the M4 and M40. The attractively furnished bedrooms vary in size and are equipped with the usual modern comforts including TV, direct-dial telephone and ironing boards; the carpeted bathrooms all have shower attachments. The informal breakfast room is adjacent to a small comfortable lounge with TV and video, which overlooks the sun patio. Guests have the use of an outdoor heated pool and are assured of a friendly welcome from Tina Wood.
5🛁🚿 CTV in all bedrooms [R] **T** 🐕 (ex guide dogs) sB&B🛁🚿fr£54.50 dB&B🛁🚿£62.50-£72.50
🅿 CTV 🏊(heated)
Credit Cards [1][2][3][£]

MARTOCK Somerset — Map **03** ST41

GH [Q][Q][Q] ***Wychwood*** 7 Bearley Road TA12 6PG
☎(0935) 825601

Wychwood is a tastefully decorated family home in a quiet cul-de-sac of a modern housing estate. Bedrooms are comfortable, there is an elegant lounge and dinner is served by prior arrangement at separate tables in the dining room.
3rm 🛁🚿

MARTON Warwickshire — Map **04** SP46

FH [Q][Q] Mrs P Dronfield **Marton Fields** *(SP402680)* CV23 9RS (1m off A423 take left bend at church through village then take left fork in road farm on right) ☎(0926) 632410
Closed Xmas

Marton Fields, an attractive red brick house, set in mixed farmland, is located about one mile down a lane leading from the village church. The spacious bedrooms are mainly furnished in traditional style, and modern comforts include electric blankets when necessary. There are two lounges, one of which has a wood-burning stove. Breakfast is served in a traditionally furnished room and there is seating for six people at one table. Mrs Dronfield is a talented artist and examples of her work can be seen throughout the house.
3rm(1🚿) 🚭 [R] 🐕 (ex guide dogs) sB&B£20-£22 sB&B🚿fr£26 dB&B£36-£40 dB&B🚿£38-£40 LDO 6pm
🅿 CTV ⛳ croquet lawn painting holidays 240 acres arable mixed sheep

MARY TAVY Devon — Map **02** SX57

GH [Q][Q][Q] **The Stannary** PL19 9QB (4m N of Tavistock on A386) ☎(0822) 810897 FAX (0822) 810898

This attractive 16th-century property with a Victorian extension is in the village of Mary Tavy on Dartmoor, close to Tavistock. Run as a vegetarian restaurant and guesthouse by resident proprietors Alison Fife, chef, and Michael Cook who is responsible for service, the welcome is warm and the food is creative. There is a lot of choice and Michael produces many of his own wines, liqueurs and spirits for sale in the restaurant. The public areas have a Victorian theme, many of the proprietors' personal pieces have been used to give an individuality to the house and comfort is emphasised throughout. Four bedrooms have been tastefully decorated in a style of simple elegance and there is a garden.
3rm 🚭 in bedrooms 🚭 in dining room 🚭 in 1 lounge CTV in all bedrooms [R] 🐕 (ex guide dogs) sB&B£70 dB&B£120 (incl dinner) WBDi£330-£390 LDO 9pm
Lic 🅿 nc12yrs
Credit Cards [1][2][3]

🛏 ☕ **FH** [Q][Q][Q] Mrs B Anning **Wringworthy** *(SX500773)* PL19 9LT (take A386 farm signed 2 miles after Mary Tavy)
☎(0822) 810434
Mar-Oct

Though a large portion of this Devon farmhouse is Jacobean it actually dates back to the Domesday Book. The dining room is particularly fine with its flagstone floor, linenfold panelling and large dining table, where traditional farmhouse breakfasts are served. The simple bedrooms have the modern comforts of colour TV and tea-making facilities, and a lounge with a huge fireplace and cosy log-burner is available.
3rm 🚭 in bedrooms CTV in all bedrooms [R] 🐕 (ex guide dogs) sB&B£15-£16 dB&B£30-£32
🅿 CTV 80 acres beef sheep
[£]

MASHAM North Yorkshire — Map **08** SE28

SELECTED

GH [Q][Q][Q][Q] **Bank Villa** HG4 4DB ☎Ripon(0765) 689605
Etr-Oct

Set in its own gardens on the A6108 as it approaches the village from Ripon, this charming stone-built Georgian house ▶

provides attractively decorated bedrooms, with antique pine furniture and dark beams featuring in several. There are two comfortable lounges and a spacious dining room, where breakfast and three-course dinners are served and a small wine list is offered.

7rm ⊁ in bedrooms ⊁ in dining room ⊁ in 1 lounge sB&Bfr£26 dB&B£36 WB&Bfr£112.50 WBDifr£200 LDO noon

Lic ▥ CTV nc5yrs
£

MATLOCK Derbyshire   Map **08** SK36

GH Q Q **Bradvilla** 26 Chesterfield Road DE4 3DQ (on A632 towards Chesterfield, below convent school) ☎(0629) 57147
Closed 22-28 Dec
2rm(1⇘) (1fb) ⊁ in bedrooms ⊁ in dining room ⊁ in lounges CTV in 1 bedroom ⓡ ✳ dB&Bfr£15 dB&B⇘£16.50 WB&B£90 ▥.

S E L E C T E D

GH Q Q Q Q **Hodgkinsons Hotel** 150 South Parade DE4 3NR ☎(0629) 582170
Closed Xmas
7ⁿ CTV in all bedrooms ⓡ T sB&Bⁿ£30-£35 dB&Bⁿ£50-£80 WB&B£175-£280 WBDi£280-£420 LDO 8pm
Lic ▥ hairdressing salon within hotel
Credit Cards ① ② ③

S E L E C T E D

GH Q Q Q Q **Lane End House** Green Lane, Tansley DE4 5FJ (opposite Gate Inn public house) ☎(0629) 583981
Mr and Mrs Smith extend a warm welcome to guests at their lovely home in the small village of Tansley. Bedrooms are pleasantly decorated and individually furnished. One has an en suite bathroom and the rest are served by their own private bathrooms. A comfortable lounge is provided, and carefully produced evening meals are taken at a communal table in the small dining area. Special diets can be catered for with advance notice.
3rm(1⇘ⁿ) ⊁ CTV in all bedrooms ⓡ sB&B£29-£32.50 sB&B⇘ⁿ£30-£35 dB&B£38-£46 dB&B⇘ⁿ£46-£50 WB&B£130-£170 WBDi£209-£239 LDO 6pm
Lic ▥ CTV nc12yrs croquet
Credit Cards ① ③ £

FH Q Q Mrs M Brailsford *Farley (SK294622)* Farley DE4 5LR (1.5m to the NW of Matlock) ☎(0629) 582533
Closed Xmas & New Year
This busy working farm, set high in the Derbyshire hills, has bright warm bedrooms, and a cheery welcome awaits guests from Mrs Brailsford and her dogs!
3rm (2fb) CTV in 1 bedroom ⓡ ✳ sB&B£16-£17 dB&B£30-£32 WB&B£105 WBDi£147 LDO 5pm
▥ CTV ∪ 275 acres arable beef dairy
£

FH Q Q Q M Haynes *Packhorse (SK323617)* Tansley DE4 5LF (2m NE of Matlock off A632 at Tansley) ☎(0629) 582781
Mrs Haynes offers a warm welcome at this delightful farmhouse, set in open countryside high above Matlock, close to the village of Tansley. Bedrooms are neat and pretty with coordinated decor and fabrics. The comfortable lounge, with views of the extensive gardens, is kept cosy by an open log fire.
4rm (2fb) ⓡ ✝
▥ CTV nc3yrs 40 acres mixed

FH Q Q Mrs Janet Hole *Wayside (SK324630)* Matlock Moor DE4 5LF ☎(0629) 582967
Closed Xmas & New Year
Fresh-looking accommodation is offered at this 17th-century farmhouse, set high on Matlock moor two miles out of Matlock on the A632. There is a comfortable lounge with an open fire and TV, and breakfast is taken in the light, airy conservatory. Newly converted self-catering cottages with modern facilities are now also available.
6rm (2fb) ✝ (ex guide dogs)
▥ CTV 60 acres dairy

MAWGAN PORTH Cornwall & Isles of Scilly   Map **02** SW86

GH Q Q Q **White Lodge Hotel** TR8 4BN (on coast road between Newquay & Padstow opposite Mawgan Porth pitch & putt) ☎St Mawgan(0637) 860512
Mar-Nov & Xmas
Especially popular with golfers and dog owners, this family-run hotel is generally busy with many regular guests. There are bright bedrooms and comfortable public areas, including a lounge, an attractive bar and a dining room where a good variety of meals is served.
16rm(11⇘ⁿ) (7fb) CTV in 17 bedrooms ⓡ ✳ sB&B£20-£23 sB&B⇘ⁿ£23.50-£26.50 dB&B£40-£46 dB&B⇘ⁿ£47-£53 WB&B£140-£161 WBDi£165-£195 LDO 7.30pm
Lic CTV games room
Credit Cards ① ② ③ £

MAXEY Cambridgeshire   Map **04** TF10

GH Q Q Q **Abbey House** West End Road PE6 9EJ ☎Market Deeping(0778) 344642
In a peaceful village location, this delightful Georgian house offers accommodation in both the main building and the converted coach house. All bedrooms are simply furnished and decorated in pastel colours. There is a comfortable lounge, an elegant breakfast room and gardens which contain what is claimed to be the oldest yew tree in the county.
3rm(1ⁿ) Annexe 6ⁿ (1fb) ⊁ in 6 bedrooms ⊁ in dining room CTV in all bedrooms ⓡ ✝ (ex guide dogs) ✳ sB&B£24.50 sB&B⇘ⁿ£28.50 dB&B£38 dB&B⇘ⁿ£40-£43
▥ CTV ✔
£
See advertisement under STAMFORD

MAYFIELD East Sussex   Map **05** TQ52

S E L E C T E D

INN Q Q Q Q **Rose & Crown** Fletching Street TN20 6TE (off A267) ☎(0435) 872200 FAX (0435) 872200
A delightful, family-run free house with oak beamed bars and log burning fires, this village inn has been welcoming guests since the early 16th century. It has recently been refurbished to provide comfortable, individually furnished bedrooms with access from the outside. There is a wide selection of bar meals and light snacks, including the recommended Chef's Specials, and an à la carte menu is offered in the informal restaurant. A range of enjoyable dishes is served such as smoked salmon quenelles, home-made steak and ale pie and a number of salads. The dessert menu is also popular and the interesting wine list includes some quality wines.
4⇘ⁿ CTV in all bedrooms ⓡ ✝ (ex guide dogs)
sB&B⇘ⁿ£48 dB&B⇘ⁿ£55 Lunch £3.95-£6.95alc Dinner £11-£16alc LDO 9.30pm
▥ nc5yrs
Credit Cards ① ③ £

MELROSE Borders *Roxburghshire* Map **12** NT53

SELECTED

GH [Q][Q][Q][Q] Dunfermline House Buccleuch Street TD6 9LB (opposite Abbey car park) ☎(0896) 822148

In the centre of town close to the abbey, this delightful Victorian house has been carefully restored to provide agreeable accommodation. All bedrooms are provided with thoughtful extras. There is a cosy sitting room, and hearty breakfasts including home-made preserves are served in the attractive dining room. Smoking is not allowed in this establishment.

5🚿 🚭 CTV in all bedrooms Ⓡ 🐕 ✻ sB&B🚿£20-£22 dB&B🚿£40-£44 WB&B£130-£140

▥

[£]

ᴊH [Q][Q][Q] **Little Fordel** Abbey St TD6 9PX (close to Melrose ᴬbbey) ☎(0896) 822206

)uietly located but still in the centre of the town, this attractively enovated former school house has the advantage of its own arking facilities. Comfortable accommodation comprises one win and one huge family room, and breakfast is taken at ndividual tables in the pleasant lounge.

:rm(1🛁1🚿) 🚭 CTV in all bedrooms 🐕 dB&B🛁🚿£40 VB&B£126

▥ CTV

IELVICH Highland *Sutherland* Map **14** NC86

;H [Q][Q][Q] Tigh-na-Clash Tigh-na-Clash KW14 7YJ (on A836 pposite the Croft Inn) ☎(06413) 262

ᴊar-Sep

'his comfortable detached modern house situated at the east side f the village offers good-value tourist accommodation. The no-moking bedrooms vary in size and offer a mixture of modern and aditional furnishings. Hearty breakfasts are served at shared ables in the dining room, which forms part of the owner's ersonal lounge; a separate small lounge is available for guests. ther meals are available at the small inn directly opposite which owned and run by the same family.

rm(4🚿) 🚭 in bedrooms 🚭 in area of dining room CTV in all edrooms Ⓡ 🐕 (ex guide dogs) sB&B£16-£16.50 sB&B🚿£20-21 dB&B£32-£33 dB&B🚿£40-£42 WB&B£108.50-£143.50 DO 8pm

▥ nc8yrs

redit Cards [1] [3]

IENDHAM Suffolk Map **05** TM28

H [Q][Q] Mrs J E Holden **Weston House** *(TM292828)* IP20 0PB rom A143 or B1123 follow signs for Mendham then follow signs om centre of village) ☎St Cross(0986) 782206

ᴊar-Nov

Irs Holden maintains a good clean standard throughout her iendly home, which is on a 300-acre mixed farm. The three acious bedrooms are simply furnished, and the large omfortable lounge has TV and an upright piano.

m(2🚿) (1fb) 🚭 in bedrooms 🚭 in dining room 🚭 in lounges Ⓡ ;&B£17 sB&B🚿£19.50 dB&B£29 dB&B🚿£34 WB&B£87.50-01.50 WBDi£154-£168 LDO 2pm

▥ CTV 300 acres arable beef mixed

edit Cards [2] [£]

IENDLESHAM GREEN Suffolk Map **05** TM06

H [Q][Q][Q] ***Cherry Tree Farm*** IP14 5RQ

'Stowmarket(0449) 766376

b-Nov

artin and Diana Ridsdale provide immaculately kept bedrooms and a willingness to make your stay comfortable in this timbered farmhouse. Guests are encouraged to sample home produced meals with a choice of East Anglian wines. Smoking is only allowed in the lounge.

3rm(2🛁🚿) 🐕 (ex guide dogs) LDO 2pm

Lic ▥ CTV nc

MERE Wiltshire Map **03** ST83

SELECTED

GH [Q][Q][Q][Q] ***Chetcombe House Hotel*** Chetcombe Road BA12 6AZ (off A303) ☎(0747) 860219

An elegant detached property on the edge of the village offers comfortable and spotlessly clean bedrooms. A small bar is available at reception and access to the beautifully kept gardens is through the attractive lounge. Home-cooked dinners, making use of home-grown vegetables in season, are offered in the informal dining room.

5🛁🚿 (1fb) CTV in all bedrooms Ⓡ LDO 5pm

Lic ▥

Credit Cards [1] [2] [3]

MERIDEN West Midlands Map **04** SP28

GH [Q][Q][Q] Meriden Hotel Main Road CV7 7NH (on B4104) ☎(0676) 522005 FAX (0676) 523744

Well placed for the NEC, this licensed guest house offers mostly spacious rooms which are well equipped for its commercial trade, and a small dark bar leading into the breakfast room.

13🛁🚿 (1fb) 🚭 in area of dining room CTV in all bedrooms Ⓡ **T** sB&B🛁🚿£38.80-£50.80 dB&B🛁🚿£64.65 LDO 6.30pm

Lic ▥ CTV 🚗

Credit Cards [1] [2] [3] [5]

MERTHYR TYDFIL Mid Glamorgan Map **03** SO00

SELECTED

GH [Q][Q][Q][Q] Llwyn Onn Cwmtaf CF48 2HS (4m N off A470, overlooking reservoir) ☎(0685) 384384

This sparkling and personally run little guesthouse is perched high up with unrestricted views across the expanse of the Llwyn reservoir. Owners Moyra & Robert Evans continue to make improvements with every season and the standard of maintenance is quite faultless. Comfortable, bright and prettily decorated bedrooms are furnished in pine and have excellent beds, linen and nice little personal touches as well as a good range of modern equipment. Excellent breakfasts are taken in the comfortable dining room which overlooks the little sun terrace and garden. There is also a cosy lounge.

4rm(2🛁🚿) CTV in all bedrooms Ⓡ 🐕 (ex guide dogs)

▥

Credit Cards [1] [3] [£]

INN[Q][Q][Q] Tredegar Arms Hotel 66 High Street, Dowlais Top CF48 2YE (off junct of A465 & A470 on the old Merthyr Tydfil road) ☎(0685) 377467

Conveniently positioned just north of the town close to the junction of the A465/A470, this character inn (under the same ownership as The Little Diner at Dowlais Top) has recently been upgraded to offer accommodation in comfortable, brightly decorated bedrooms well equipped to meet the needs of today's traveller. Popular, friendly bars and a cosily attractive little restaurant make up the public areas, and useful car parking is provided on site.

5rm(2🛁3🚿) (1fb) CTV in all bedrooms Ⓡ

▥

Credit Cards [1] [2] [3]

MEVAGISSEY Cornwall & Isles of Scilly   Map **02** SX04

GH Q Q Q **Headlands Hotel** Polkirt Hill PL26 6UX (follow one way system through village & ascend towards Port Mellon, hotel 0.25m on right) ☎(0726) 843453

Feb-Nov & Xmas/New Year

There are panoramic views over the sea from the terrace, lounge bar and dining room of this popular and well run small hotel. Patrick and Maureen Grist create an informal and relaxing atmosphere and Maureen offers good home cooking, using local produce and some local recipes. Patisserie, ice creams and sorbets are all home made, the herbs are home grown and a four-course dinner might consist of home-made soup, roast duck with black cherry sauce, baked fillet of Megrim sole and desserts from the trolley.

14rm(9♠) (3fb) ⊁ in dining room ⊁ in 1 lounge CTV in 9 bedrooms sB&B£18-£22 sB&B♠£22-£26 dB&B£36-£44 dB&B♠£44-£52 WB&B£111-£167 WBDi£198.50-£254.50 LDO 7.30pm

Lic ⅏ CTV

ⓔ

SELECTED

GH Q Q Q Q **Mevagissey House** Vicarage Hill PL26 6SZ ☎(0726) 842427

Mar-Oct

In four acres of lovely mature gardens, this delightful Georgian house enjoys views right across the valley, yet is only a few minutes' walk from the village. The individually furnished bedrooms are well equipped and day rooms include a spacious and comfortable lounge (where smoking is discouraged), a sun lounge, garden terrace and small bar. The dining room features a daily set four-course menu as well as a carte, and a well chosen wine list. Light refreshments and cream teas are also available.

6rm(1➡3♠) (2fb) ⊁ in 4 bedrooms ⊁ in dining room ⊁ in lounges CTV in all bedrooms ⓡ ⋇ (ex guide dogs) sB&B£16-£21 dB&B➡♠£36-£48 WB&B£126-£168 WBDi£210-£252 LDO 5pm

Lic ⅏ nc7yrs

Credit Cards 1 3

GH Q Q Q **Spa Hotel** Polkirt Hill PL26 6UY

☎St Austell(0726) 842244 FAX (0726) 842244

Now under the ownership of Eric and Lesley Bailey, this hotel is peacefully situated in an acre of mature grounds. There is a choice of bedrooms, all overlooking the garden, and the best have access to the terrace. The comfortable bar is in Tudor style, and there is a cosy, traditional lounge and a dining room where Eric offers a very good value four-course dinner, featuring local seafood when available.

12rm(11➡♠) (3fb) CTV in all bedrooms ⓡ sB&Bfr£18 sB&B➡♠£21 dB&B➡♠£36-£42 WB&B£126-£147 WBDi£182-£203 LDO 7pm

Lic ⅏ CTV pool table pitch & putt darts putting green

Credit Cards 1 3 5

GH Q Q Q **Tremarne Hotel** Polkirt Hill PL26 6UY

☎(0726) 842213 FAX (0726) 843420

Mar-Oct

Quietly situated up a private road away from the bustle of the village centre, this small, family-run hotel enjoys a relaxed and friendly atmosphere and good views across the bay. The young and enthusiastic owners are steadily upgrading the rooms, which now have a fresh, bright decor. All bedrooms are en suite and most now have pretty and coordinated decor and furnishings; those not yet upgraded are still neat and comfortable. Public areas are comfortable and nicely appointed.

14➡♠ (2fb) ⊁ in dining room ⊁ in 1 lounge CTV in all bedrooms ⓡ ⋇ sB&B➡♠£24-£28 dB&B➡♠£38-£50

WB&B£125-£168 WBDi£210-£250 LDO 7pm

Lic ⅏ ⅂(heated)

Credit Cards 1 2 3 5 ⓔ

SELECTED

FH Q Q Q Q Q Mrs L Hennah **Kerryanna** *(SX008453)* Treleaven Farm PL26 6RZ ☎(0726) 843558

Mar-Oct

Percy and Linda Henneh's well furnished modern farmhouse, enjoys lovely views of the village and sea below, specially from the lounge. Bedrooms have recently been upgraded with pine and pretty fabrics. The daily four-course dinner is excellent value, orders for the main course usually taken in advance. Vegetarian and children's menus are provided.

6➡♠ (2fb) CTV in all bedrooms ⓡ ⋇ ⋇ dB&B➡♠£36-£46 WBDi£182-£230 LDO 5pm

Lic ⅏ nc5yrs ⅂(heated) games room putting green 200 acres arable beef

---

FH Q Q Q Mrs A Hennah **Treleaven** *(SX008454)* PL26 6RZ (turn right at foot of hill when entering Mevagissey) ☎(0726) 842413

Closed 15 Dec-7 Jan

The farmhouse looks down over the rooftops of Mevagissey and is only a short stroll from the sea. Bedrooms are all attractive and the large dining room is also open to non residents. There is a good choice of fixed-price menu and à la carte, including a 'carve your own joint', and the restaurant is open for lunch and cream teas as well, so guests are in danger of over-indulging. There is a heated swimming pool and an 18-hole putting course.

6♠ (1fb) ⊁ in dining room CTV in all bedrooms ⓡ ⋇ dB&B♠£32-£50 WB&B£105-£160 WBDi£165-£240 LDO 8pm

Lic ⅏ ⅂(heated) games room, putting green 200 acres mixed

Credit Cards 1 3 ⓔ

INN Q Q *The Ship* Fore Street PL26 6UQ (St Austell Brewery) ☎(0726) 843324

Built in the reign of Elizabeth I, the public bar of this historic inn retains its beamed and flagstoned interior. The modern bedrooms are furnished in pine, and there is a separate breakfast room on the first floor. Real ales and popular bar meals are served, and the locally caught fish dishes on the blackboard menu should not be overlooked. Charged car parking is usually available at the harbour.

6rm (2fb) CTV in all bedrooms ⓡ LDO 8.30pm

⅏ ⁄

MIDDLEHAM North Yorkshire   Map **07** SE1

INN Q Q Q **The Black Swan Hotel** Market Place DL8 4NP (CON) ☎Wensleydale(0969) 22221

rs 24-27 Dec

Beamed ceilings and gleaming horse brasses abound in this listed 17th-century inn situated in the market place of a town which is renowned as the northern centre for racehorse training. The attractively decorated bedrooms are full of character: two have four-poster beds, several are beamed and those in the older part of the hotel very much reflect the age of the building. A wide variety of bar meals is served and there is a full menu in the main dining room. The beer garden backing onto the castle is floodlit for summer evenings.

7➡♠ (1fb)CTV in all bedrooms ⓡ ⋇ sB&B➡♠£26-£30 dB&B➡♠£42-£60 Lunch £8-£12alc Dinner £10-£16alc LDO 9pm

⅏,

Credit Cards 1 3 ⓔ

MIDDLETON-IN-TEESDALE Co Durham   Map **12** NY9

GH Q Q Q **Brunswick House** 55 Market Place DL12 0QH (opposite St Mary's church) ☎Teesdale(0833) 640393

This attractive little guest house in the market place dates back to 1760 and offers prettily decorated bedrooms with pine furniture. A small lounge adjoins the dining room which doubles as a tea shop during the summer months.
4rm(3🚿) (1fb) 🚭 in bedrooms 🚭 in dining room CTV in all bedrooms [R] 🐕 (ex guide dogs) sB&B🚿£20-£27.50 dB&B🚿£40 WBDi£195 LDO 7pm
Lic ♨
Credit Cards [1] [5] [£]

MIDDLETON PRIORS Shropshire Map **07** SO69

SELECTED

GH [Q] [Q] [Q] [Q] Middleton Lodge WV16 6UR (1m NE on unclass rd) ☎Ditton Priors(074634) 228 or 675
Closed Xmas
Set in 20 acres of Shropshire countryside overlooking Brown Clee hill, this 17th century property with its pebble dash frontage, was once a hunting and shooting lodge. Three bedrooms are available, one of which can be made en suite. One of the bedrooms has a four poster bed, the other two have brass beds, all of them are well furnished and comfortable with period pieces and coordinated fabrics. There is a choice of two sitting rooms, one of which has an original Knowle settee. The slab floored dining room, featuring a log fire and original bread oven, is furnished with solid oak tables and breakfast only is served. Middleton lodge is a no smoking establishment.
3rm(2🛁1🚿) CTV in all bedrooms [R] 🐕 (ex guide dogs) *
sB&B🛁🚿£25-£30 dB&B🛁🚿£40-£45
♨ CTV nc5yrs

MIDDLEWICH Cheshire Map **07** SJ76

FH [Q] [Q] Mrs S Moss **Forge Mill** *(SJ704624)* Warmingham CW10 0HQ ☎Warmingham(027077) 204 due to change to (0270) 526204
The oldest part of this house dates back to the early 18th century but it was enlarged in mid-Victorian times. Original features, such as the tiled entrance hall, have been preserved and the house is furnished throughout in a style befitting its age and character. There are two spacious bedrooms, both no-smoking, a comfortable lounge and a boldly decorated breakfast room where separate tables are provided. Dinner is available by prior arrangement only.
2rm 🐕 (ex guide dogs) * dB&Bfr£30
♨ CTV 🎾(grass)150 acres mixed
[£]

MIDHURST West Sussex

See **Rogate**

MILTON COMMON Oxfordshire Map **04** SP60

INN [Q] [Q] ***Three Pigeons*** OX9 2NS ☎Great Milton(0844) 279247
This small and popular country inn offers a choice of bars, a good variety of bar meals at lunchtime and in the evening, and comfortable bedrooms, reached by an external staircase. It is handy for the motorway network - junction 7 of the M40 coming from London, junction 8 coming from the Midlands.
🛁🚿 (1fb) CTV in all bedrooms [R] 🐕 LDO 10pm
♨ CTV
Credit Cards [1] [2] [3] [5]

MILTON KEYNES Buckinghamshire Map **04** SP83

See also Gayhurst and Whaddon

Llawnroc Inn

A family run hotel & village pub overlooking the picturesque harbour & fishing village of Gorran Haven. Enjoy the friendly atmosphere & breathtaking views from our large terraced lawns.
★ Sample good beers including real ales
★ Delight in our varied home cooked meals & bar snacks
★ Restaurant
All rooms are en-suite, have colour TV, coffee/tea making & face the sea. Large private car park.
A warm welcome awaits you from licensees John & Janet Gregory
Gorran Haven, St Austell, Cornwall PL26 6NU
Ring Mevagissey (01726) 843461
Send S.A.E. for brochure

Park House

Bepton, Midhurst, West Sussex GU29 0JB
Tel: (0173081) 2880 Fax: (0173081) 5643

Park House is fully equipped to give maximum comfort with the atmosphere and amenities of an English Country House. Private bathrooms – television and telephone in all bedrooms. Large garden. Grass tennis courts, putting lawn. Croquet. Heated swimming pool. 9 hole pitch & putt. Under the personal supervision of the resident owner. Licensed.
Barclay, Visa and Access accepted

SELECTED

GH ◉◉◉◉ **Old Bakery** Main Street, Cosgrove Village MK19 7JL (off A508 towards Northampton. Take first right for Cosgrove, hotel on left after the bridge over Grand Union Canal) ☎(0908) 263103 262255 FAX (0908) 263620
A full cooked or Continental breakfast is available at a supplementary charge.
8⇌ᚦ (1fb) ⊬ in 2 bedrooms ⊬ in dining room CTV in all bedrooms Ⓡ **T** 𝕏 (ex guide dogs) ✳ sB&B⇌ᚦ£33.50-£41.50 dB&B⇌ᚦ£41.50 LDO 9pm
Lic 🎟
Credit Cards [1][2][3]

GH ◉◉◉ **Thurstons Private Hotel** 90 High Street, Newport Pagnell MK16 8EH ☎Newport Pagnell(0908) 611377
This establishment is part of a subtantial town house on the High Street of Newport Pagnell. Bedrooms are on three floors and are simply appointed with en suite facilities. There is a small lounge area adjoining the breakfast room, and a large car park.
8rm(2⇌6ᚦ) CTV in all bedrooms Ⓡ 𝕏 (ex guide dogs)
Lic 🎟
Credit Cards [1][2][3]

MILTON-UNDER-WYCHWOOD Oxfordshire   Map **04** SP21

SELECTED

GH ◉◉◉◉ **Hillborough Hotel** The Green OX7 6JH (off A424 Burford-Stow village centre) ☎Shipton-under-Wychwood(0993) 830501 FAX (0993) 832005
Situated at the heart of the Cotswolds, within easy driving distance of such places of interest as Burford and Stow-on-the-Wold, this small family-run hotel opens its restaurant to non-residents. A three-storey stone-built property, it stands in its own garden overlooking the village green; attractively decorated and furnished bedrooms are equipped to maximise guests' comfort, while public areas include a pleasant bar with open fireplace and flagstone floors and a relaxing conservatory lounge as well as the spacious restaurant with its wide selection of dishes.
6rm(5⇌1ᚦ) Annexe 4⇌ (3fb) ⊬ in dining room CTV in all bedrooms Ⓡ **T** sB&B⇌ᚦ£40-£48 dB&B⇌ᚦ£58-£74 WB&Bfr£182 WBDifr£259 LDO 9.15pm
Lic 🎟 ♨ croquet
Credit Cards [1][2][3] ⓔ

MINEHEAD Somerset   Map **03** SS94

🛏 ♨ **GH** ◉◉◉ **Avill House** 12 Townsend Road TA24 5RG
☎(0643) 704370
This Victorian semidetached three-storey house with a brightly painted façade and colourful flower beds, is conveniently located a short walk from the town and seafront. The accommodation is being steadily improved, and bedrooms have smart, functional furniture, pretty coordinating décor and interesting paintings of local attractions; they are all comfortable and kept spick and span. The bar has recently been extended and is cosy and comfortable, and a new sitting room is currently being built. The front-facing dining room is simple in décor, and a small choice for an evening meal is offered, along with a huge breakfast served by Mrs Wood. There is ample forecourt parking.
9rm(3ᚦ) (4fb) ⊬ in dining room ⊬ in 1 lounge CTV in all bedrooms Ⓡ sB&Bfr£15 sB&Bᚦfr£20.50 dB&Bfr£28 dB&Bᚦfr£34 WB&Bfr£91 WBDifr£147 LDO 4pm
Lic CTV
ⓔ

GH ◉◉◉ **Bactonleigh** 20 Tregonwell Road TA24 5DU
☎(0643) 702147
Mar-1 Dec
An informal atmosphere and attentive service is provided at this small family-run hotel, which is only a three-minute, level walk from the beach and the town centre. Additional en suite facilities have been installed in the bedrooms, where guests are requested to refrain from smoking. The table d'hôte dinner menu offers good value for money.
8rm(4ᚦ) (1fb) CTV in all bedrooms Ⓡ ✳ sB&Bfr£15 dB&Bfr£30 dB&Bᚦfr£35 WB&B£101.50-£119 WBDi£147-£164.50 LDO 5pm
Lic 🎟 CTV

SELECTED

GH ◉◉◉◉ **Gascony Hotel** The Avenue TA24 5BB
☎(0643) 705939
Mar-Oct
In a good location in the centre of the town, and only 200 yards from the seafront, this Victorian property has been transformed over the years by its owners Kay and John Luckett into a most attractive and comfortable hotel. The accommodation is maintained to a high standard and it offers good sized bedrooms, bright and modern with smartly tiled en suite bathrooms. The open plan lounge and bar are welcoming and have recently been redecorated. There is a pretty pink and green dining room which has a Welsh dresser with a collection of pewter on display.
13⇌ᚦ (2fb) ⊬ in dining room CTV in all bedrooms Ⓡ sB&B⇌ᚦ£23-£25 dB&B⇌ᚦ£44-£48 LDO 5.30pm
Lic 🎟 nc5yrs
Credit Cards [1][3] ⓔ

SELECTED

GH ◉◉◉◉ **Marston Lodge Hotel** St Michaels Road TA24 5JP (situated just before St Michaels church off North Hill)
☎(0643) 702510
1 Mar-31 Oct
A substantial detached town house dating back to 1905 standing in delightful gardens high above the town, beach and harbour. Many of the spacious, well equipped and immaculately maintained bedrooms enjoy superb views across Minehead Bay, the Quantocks, Dunster and the rolling landscape of Exmoor. The cocktail bar has pleasantly coordinating soft furnishings, and dinner is served in the tastefully decorated dining room, prepared by Mr and Mrs Allen, using fresh produce and home-grown vegetables.
12rm(5⇌7ᚦ) ⊬ CTV in all bedrooms Ⓡ 𝕏 sB&B⇌ᚦ£25-£29 dB&B⇌ᚦ£50-£56 (incl dinner) WB&B£159-£179 WBDi£225-£250 LDO 7pm
Lic 🎟 nc10yrs
ⓔ

GH ◉◉◉ **Mayfair Hotel** 25 The Avenue TA24 5AY
☎(0643) 702719
Mar-Nov
A small private hotel located in the town centre, yet within walking distance of the seafront, offers old fashioned standards of comfort and hospitality. Well equipped bedrooms are clean and bright and stocked with thoughtful extra touches. The comfortabl lounge is prettily furnished, and a good home-cooked meal in traditional English style is prepared and served by Mr and Mrs Segenhour. There is a separate bar lounge, a small garden and ample parking at the rear of the hotel.
16rm(5⇌11ᚦ) Annexe 9rm(4⇌5ᚦ) (10fb) ⊬ in dining room CTV in all bedrooms Ⓡ 𝕏 (ex guide dogs) ✳ sB&B⇌ᚦ£24-£2

dB&B⇌ℙ£46-£50 WB&B£130-£140 WBDi£157-£170 LDO
6pm
Lic ⠿.
Credit Cards ☐1 ☐3

INN ℚℚℚ Kildare Lodge Townsend Rd TA24 5RQ
☎(0643) 702009 FAX (0643) 706516
Conveniently sited for direct access to the town centre, with ample
forecourt parking, this listed Free House, designed by Edwin
Lutyens, has been attractively furnished to provide comfortable
modern rooms. Bedrooms in a variety of sizes are all well
equipped. A bar lounge renowned for its real ale provides a
popular local rendez-vous, and there is a children's room. The
restaurant augments its à la carte menu with a weekend carvery.
4⇌ℙ Annexe 5rm(1⇌4ℙ) (3fb) ⠙ in area of dining room ⠙ in 1
lounge CTV in all bedrooms ⓡ T sB&B⇌ℙ£19.50-£35
dB&B⇌ℙ£38-£59.50 WB&B£140-£160 WBDi£199-£225 Lunch
£3.50-£16alc High tea £3.50-£12.95alc Dinner £12.50&alc LDO
9pm
⠿ CTV
Credit Cards ☐1 ☐3 ☐5 ⓔ

MINSTER LOVELL Oxfordshire   Map **04** SP31

FH ℚℚℚ Mrs Katherine Brown **Hill Grove** *(SP314115)*
OX8 5NA (off B4047) ☎Witney(0993) 703124 FAX (0993) 700528
Closed Xmas
A modern Cotswold farmhouse with views over the Windrush
valley, Hill Grove is conveniently situated just off the B4047
towards Crawley. Comfortable bedrooms are equipped with colour
TV, and guests are invited to join the Browns in their sitting room.
Breakfast is served around one large dining table.
2⇌ℙ ⠙ CTV in all bedrooms ⓡ ⠳ (ex guide dogs) ⠙
dB&B£36-£38 dB&B⇌ℙ£42-£44
⠿ CTV 300 acres arable beef mixed
ⓔ

MISTLEY Essex   Map **05** TM13

INN ℚℚℚ Thorn Hotel Mr T Newman, High Street CO11 1HE
☎(0206) 392821 FAX (0206) 392133
4ℙ CTV in all bedrooms ⓡ ⠳ ⠙ sB&Bℙ£30 dB&Bℙ£45 Lunch
£4-£6&alc Dinner £8-£12&alc LDO 9.30pm
⠿ CTV nc5yrs
Credit Cards ☐1 ☐3

MOFFAT Dumfries & Galloway *Dumfriesshire*   Map **11** NT00
See also Beattock

GH ℚℚ Barnhill Springs Country DG10 9QS (.5m E of A74)
☎(0683) 20580
Standing in its own grounds with fine views of the Annan valley,
this early Victorian house is accessible from the southbound
carriageway of the A74 immediately to the south of the junction
for Moffat. It offers comfortable accommodation, a friendly
atmosphere, and dinner by prior arrangement.
5rm(1ℙ) (1fb) ⠙ in dining room ⓡ ⠳ sB&B£18.50-£19.50
dB&B£37-£39 WB&B£129.50-£136.50 WBDi£206.50-£223.50
LDO 9am
Lic ⠿ CTV
ⓔ

SELECTED

GH ℚℚℚℚ Gilbert House Beechgrove DG10 9RS (from
A74 go through town & turn right after school)
☎(0683) 20050
This lovely detached white stone Victorian house is not far
from the town centre, yet enjoys a peaceful setting in a quiet
residential area with views of the surrounding hills. Modern
fabrics have been used to good effect in the individually

---

decorated bedrooms which are comfortably furnished and
maintained to a high standard. Smoking is not permitted in the
public areas, which include a comfortable lounge and smart
dining room, where a delicious home-cooked set dinner is
offered. The hotel provides superior accommodation at
competitive prices, with personal attention from the
enthusiastic owners.
6rm(4ℙ) (2fb) ⠙ in dining room ⠙ in lounges ⓡ ⠳
sB&B£16-£18 dB&B£32-£35 dB&Bℙ£34-£37 WB&B£101-
£114 WBDi£164-£177 LDO 5pm
Lic ⠿ CTV
Credit Cards ☐1 ☐3

GH ℚℚ St Olaf Eastgate, Off Dickson Street DG10 9AE
☎(0683) 20001
Apr-Oct
Quietly situated in a side street off the High Street, the house
offers pleasant and reliable accommodation which includes bright,
cheerful bedrooms and an inviting first-floor lounge.
7rm(1ℙ) (2fb) ⠙ in dining room ⠙ in lounges ⓡ ⠳ sB&B£15-
£16 dB&B£29 dB&Bℙ£31 WB&B£100
⠿ CTV
ⓔ

MOLD Clwyd   Map **07** SJ26

FH ℚℚ Mrs A Brown **Hill** *(SJ263265)* Llong CH7 4JP (on A5118
between Chester and Mold) ☎Buckley(0244) 550415
Situated alongside the A5118 Chester road with good views over
the surrounding countryside, this attractively creeper-clad listed
house fronted by pretty lawns and gardens offers bed and
breakfast accommodation. Good-sized bedrooms decorated to a
floral theme include some suitable for family occupation, and
guests also have the use of two lounges.   ▶

Main Street, Cosgrove,
Nr. Milton Keynes
Tel: 01908 262255/263103
Fax: 01908 263620

The Old Bakery offers a variety of
accommodation ranging from elegant
executive rooms to the old world charm of
the original bakehouse.
All rooms are ensuite, & include colour TV
with Sky, direct dial telephone, & tea/coffee
making facilities
AA QQQQ Selected

3rm (1fb) 🚭 in bedrooms 🚭 in dining room [R] 🐕 (ex guide dogs) * sB&Bfr£16 dB&Bfr£28
♨ CTV 300 acres dairy mixed

MOLESWORTH Cambridgeshire Map **04** TL07

INN[Q][Q] ***Cross Keys*** PE18 0QF (turn off A14 follow signs to Molesworth) ☎Bythorn(08014) 283 due to change to (0832) 710283

A whitewashed village pub just off the A14 offers accommodation both in the main house and in an annexe block; rooms in the original building are more modest in appointment and less up-to-date, all have en suite facilities and are equipped with TV and tea trays. Home-made meals are served in an open-plan bar area where the comprehensive list is displayed on a large blackboard.

4rm(1🛁3🚿) Annexe 5rm(2🛁3🚿) (1fb) CTV in all bedrooms [R] LDO 10.30pm
♨
Credit Cards [1][3]

MONMOUTH Gwent Map **03** SO51

GH [Q][Q] **Church Farm** Mitchel Troy NP5 4HZ ☎(0600) 712176
6rm(4🚿) (1fb) 🚭 [R] * sB&B£16 dB&B£32 dB&B🚿£37 WB&B£105-£122.50 WBDi£171.50-£189 LDO noon
♨ CTV

MONTGOMERY Powys Map **07** SO29

SELECTED

FH [Q][Q][Q][Q] Mrs G M Bright **Little Brompton** *(SO244941)* SY15 6HY (2m E on B4385) ☎(0686) 668371

Oak beams and exposed timbers abound in this delightful early 17th-century stone farmhouse standing near Offa's Dyke, east of the town off the B4385. Bedrooms are cosy and some have kept their original stone fireplaces. Real farm food is served here with an emphasis on organic produce. Robert and Gaynor Bright have been welcoming guests for over 20 years, and their hospitality has never failed.

3rm(2🚿) (1fb) 🚭 CTV in all bedrooms [R] * sB&B🚿£18-£20 dB&B🚿£34-£38 LDO 5pm
♨ CTV shooting in season 100 acres arable beef mixed sheep
[£]

MONTROSE Tayside *Angus* Map **15** NO75

GH [Q][Q][Q] **Murray Lodge** 2-8 Murray Street DD10 8LB ☎(0674) 678880 (0674) 678877

This tasteful conversion of an old stone building offers modern, well equipped bedrooms with quality furnishings and fabrics. There is a comfortable lounge and a bright, cheery dining room where snacks are available throughout the day.

12🚿 🚭 in 9 bedrooms 🚭 in dining room CTV in all bedrooms [R] **T** 🐕 (ex guide dogs) * sB&B🚿£25-£42 dB&B🚿£45-£60 LDO 6.30pm
Lic ♨ CTV
Credit Cards [1][2][3][£]

GH [Q][Q][Q] **Oaklands** 10 Rossie Island Road DD10 9NN (on A92) ☎(0674) 672018 FAX (0674) 672018
7🚿 (1fb) 🚭 in dining room CTV in all bedrooms [R] sB&B🚿£18-£20 dB&B🚿£32
♨ CTV 🚗
Credit Cards [1][3][£]

Telephone national area codes are due to change by 16th April 1995. Please see the note under 'How to Use this Guide' at the front of the book.

MORCHARD BISHOP Devon Map **03** SS70

PREMIER SELECTED

FH [Q][Q][Q][Q][Q] Mr & Mrs S Chilcott **Wigham** *(SS757087)* EX17 6RJ (1.5m NW of Morchard Bishop in the direction of Chulmleigh) ☎(0363) 877350

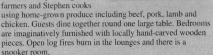

In a rural area with views over farmland this 16th-century thatched Devon longhouse is run by Stephen and Dawn Chilcott. They are organic farmers and Stephen cooks using home-grown produce including beef, pork, lamb and chicken. Guests dine together round one large table. Bedrooms are imaginatively furnished with locally hand-carved wooden pieces. Open log fires burn in the lounges and there is a snooker room.

5🛁🚿 (1fb) 🚭 CTV in all bedrooms [R] 🐕 * dB&B🛁🚿fr£80 (incl dinner)
Lic ♨ nc10yrs 🏊(heated) 🐎 7ft snooker table 31 acres cattle sheep hay
Credit Cards [1][2][3]

MORECAMBE Lancashire Map **07** SD46

GH [Q][Q][Q] **Ashley Private Hotel** 371 Marine Road Promenade East LA4 5AH ☎(0524) 412034
Apr-Oct

There are superb views over the bay from the first floor dining room and from several of the bedrooms of this hotel, which are furnished in modern style. Family owned and run, the hotel offers good value for money.

13rm(3🛁8🚿) (3fb)CTV in all bedrooms [R] 🐕 * sB&B£13-£15 sB&B🛁🚿£17-£19 dB&B🛁🚿£34-£38 WB&B£116-£124 WBDi£150-£160 LDO 3pm
Lic ♨
[£]

GH [Q][Q][Q] **Beach Mount** 395 Marine Road East LA4 5AN ☎(0524) 420753
mid Mar-Oct

This well established private hotel has excellent views over Morecambe Bay. The public areas are comfortably furnished, bedrooms are in modern style, with pretty coordinated fabrics and everywhere is freshly decorated and well cared for.

26rm(23🛁🚿) (4fb)CTV in 23 bedrooms [R] * sB&B£17-£17.50 sB&B🛁🚿£20-£20.75 dB&B£31-£32 dB&B🛁🚿£37-£38.50 WB&B£96.50-£116.75 WBDi£136.50-£157.50 LDO 7pm
Lic ♨ CTV
Credit Cards [1][2][3][5][£]

GH [Q] **Ellesmere Private Hotel** 44 Westminster Road LA4 4JD ☎(0524) 411881

A small Victorian terraced house stands in a side road not far from the promenade. It provides adequate, compact bedrooms and a pleasant lounge, with a stair lift to both floors.

6rm (2fb) 🚭 in bedrooms 🚭 in dining room CTV in all bedrooms [R] 🐕 (ex guide dogs) * sB&B£11.50-£14 dB&B£23-£28 WB&Bfr£80.50 WBDifr£105 LDO 3pm
♨ CTV 🚫🅿
[£]

GH [Q][Q] ***New Hazelmere Hotel*** 391 Promenade East LA4 5AN ☎(0524) 417876 FAX (0524) 414488
May-29 Nov

This large seafront hotel, in the same family ownership for many years, has fine views over the bay. The public areas have a

nautical theme, and though the bedrooms are simply furnished, they are well equipped.
50rm(17🛁23🚿) (23fb) CTV in all bedrooms [R] LDO 5.30pm
Lic CTV
Credit Cards [1] [2] [3]

GH [Q][Q][Q] Hotel Prospect 363 Marine Road East LA4 5AQ
☎(0524) 417819
Etr-Nov
This family owned and run hotel has splendid views over Morecambe Bay. It provides modern bedrooms and comfortable lounges.
14🛁 (9fb) 🚭 in 8 bedrooms 🚭 in dining room CTV in all bedrooms [R] sB&B🛁fr£17.50 dB&B🛁fr£35 WB&Bfr£105 WBDifr£151 LDO 3pm
Lic ♨ CTV
Credit Cards [1] [2] [3] [5] [£]

GH [Q][Q][Q] Wimslow Private Hotel 374 Marine Road East LA4 5AW ☎(0524) 417804
This very pleasant private hotel stands on a quiet corner of the promenade, at the eastern end, with lovely views of the Cumbrian Hills. Freshly decorated bedrooms have en suite facilities, and the quiet lounge provides an alternative to a bar which - like the first-floor dining room -takes advantage of seafront views. New proprietors bring with them years of experience in the hospitality business.
14rm(1🛁13🚿) (2fb) 🚭 in dining room 🚭 in lounges CTV in 13 bedrooms [R] 🐕 (ex guide dogs) * sB&B🛁🚿£19-£20 dB&B🛁🚿£38-£40 WB&B£120-£124 WBDi£158-£168 LDO 4.30pm
Lic ♨ CTV
Credit Cards [1] [3] [£]

MORETONHAMPSTEAD Devon Map **03** SX78

PREMIER SELECTED

GH [Q][Q][Q][Q][Q] Blackaller Hotel & Restaurant North Bovey TQ13 8QY
☎Chagford(0647) 40322 due to change to 440322
Closed Jan & Feb

This former 17th-century wool mill situated on the banks of the River Bovey has been converted into a charming small hotel. Bedrooms are individually furnished and decorated; public areas are a delight, with comfortable easy chairs and plenty of reading material in the spacious sitting room, a well stocked bar, and a small restaurant. Hazel Phillips and Peter Hunt offer a choice of menu at dinner, and the hotel prides itself justifiably for its excellent home cooking using local fresh produce, including Devon lamb and beef, and fish fresh from Brixham or the rivers Dart and Teign.
5rm(4🛁1🚿) 🚭 in bedrooms 🚭 in dining room CTV in all bedrooms [R] * sB&B🛁🚿£25-£27 dB&B🛁🚿£54-£60 LDO 8pm
Lic ♨ nc2-12yrs 🎣 U
[£]

GH [Q][Q][Q] Cookshayes 33 Court Street TQ13 8LG
☎(0647) 40374 due to change to 440374
mid Mar-Oct

▶

Wigham

Stephen & Dawn Chilcott,

Morchard Bishop, Nr. Crediton, Devon, EX17 6RJ *Telephone: 01363 877350*

A 16th century thatched Longhouse within a 30 acre smallholding in a delightful rural setting with views over peaceful farming valley. Situated 1½ miles out of the village of Morchard Bishop with Exeter, Tiverton, Barnstaple, Dartmoor, Exmoor and beaches both north and south all easy car rides. Delicious freshly cooked food using own produce, free range eggs, soft and pressed cheeses, cream, fruit and organically grown vegetables, also an excellent wine list and Devon farm cider. Five guest rooms including one family suite and one delightful 4-poster honeymoon suite, all with colour TV, **VHS Video** and luxury private bathrooms.

Stock includes poultry, pigs, calves, sheep and house cow.

Heated outdoor pool. 2 sitting rooms, snooker lounge, full central heating, guest kitchen.

Sorry NO SMOKERS, CASUAL CALLERS or SMALL CHILDREN. Open all year.

FULL COLOUR BROCHURE AA Premier Selected QQQQQ Licensed

Topsy Harding's love of antiques is evident throughout this guest house, which is situated on the edge of the moorland town. It is filled with many small collectable items along with some fine pieces of furniture. The majority of the rooms have en suite facilities and one has a four-poster bed. There is a comfortable lounge with bay windows overlooking the garden, and set home cooked meals are available each evening in the dining room. A cosy bar is also provided.

8rm(6🏠)(1fb) ⊁ in dining room ⊁ in lounges CTV in all bedrooms Ⓡ sB&B£22 sB&B🏠£34 dB&B£36 dB&B🏠£38-£42 WB&B£119-£140 WBDi£224-£252 LDO 5.30pm
Lic 🅟. CTV nc7yrs putting green
Credit Cards ①②③ⓔ

SELECTED

GH 🔲🔲🔲🔲 *Gate House* North Bovey TQ13 8RB
☎(0647) 40479 due to change to 440479
Gate House, a fine medieval thatched property, is set in a classic Dartmoor village. Bedrooms are individually furnished and each has a zip-and-link bed. Vegetarian and traditional meals are served on request, using organically grown produce where available. Meals are served at one large table, candlelit at night, and guests may bring their own wine with no charge for corkage. A comfortable sitting room features a massive granite fireplace.

3⇉🏠 CTV in all bedrooms Ⓡ LDO 6pm
🅟. CTV nc15yrs ⅞(heated)

GH 🔲🔲🔲 *Moorcote* TQ13 8LS ☎(0647) 40966 due to change to 440966
Apr-Oct
A Victorian house of character is set back off the road, with a small garden. Bedrooms are cosy, comfortable, individually decorated and nicely furnished, combining modern facilities with charm and character. Hearty breakfasts are popular with the numerous Dartmoor National Park walkers and tourists.

6rm(4🏠) ⊁ in 2 bedrooms CTV in all bedrooms Ⓡ 🐾 ✳
sB&B🏠£26-£28 dB&B£34 dB&B🏠£38
🅟. CTV nc12yrs

SELECTED

GH 🔲🔲🔲🔲🔲 *Slate Cottage* The Green TQ13 8RB (take A383 to Moretonhampstead and turn left at first crossroads and then left at newsagent. Follow road into North Bovey and located near pub) ☎(0647) 40060 due to change to 440060
Slate Cottage stands on the Green in the picturesque thatched village of North Bovey, in the middle of the Dartmoor National Park. The Umney-Greys have set out to provide a quiet haven in which to relax, the bedrooms with plain white decor, stripped pine furniture and dried flowers all enhance the simple country appeal. There is a cosy sitting room with comfortable sofas and an open fireplace for chilly evenings. Breakfast is served in the kitchen around the communal family dining table, and there is a 13th century thatched pub close by where guests may take an evening meal.

2rm ⊁ CTV in all bedrooms Ⓡ 🐾 sB&Bfr£26 dB&Bfr£42
🅟. nc12yrs

SELECTED

FH 🔲🔲🔲🔲 Mrs T Merchant **Great Sloncombe** *(SX737864)* TQ13 8QF (from Moretonhampstead take A382 towards Chagford for 1.5m. At sharp double bend take left turning and farm is 0.5m up lane) ☎(0647) 40595 due to

change to 440595
3🏠 ⊁ CTV in all bedrooms Ⓡ ✳ dB&B🏠£18-£20
🅟. nc8yrs 170 acres dairy

FH 🔲🔲🔲 Mrs M Cuming **Wooston** *(SX764890)* TQ13 8QA
☎(0647) 40367 due to change to 440367
Closed Xmas
A 280-acre mixed farm is peacefully situated high above the Teign valley, with glorious open views across the moors. Fine, tastefully decorated bedrooms are comfortably furnished, with many thoughtful extras provided; smoking is not permitted in the bedrooms. There are two attractive lounges, one for non-smokers, and home cooked farmhouse fare is served around a large table in the dining room.

3rm(2🏠) ⊁ in bedrooms ⊁ in dining room ⊁ in 1 lounge CTV in all bedrooms Ⓡ ✳ dB&B£32-£38 dB&B🏠£36-£42 LDO 5pm
CTV ⚘ 280 acres mixed

MORETON-IN-MARSH Gloucestershire   Map **04** SP13

GH 🔲🔲 **Acacia** 2 New Road GL56 0AS ☎(0608) 650130
Closed 25-26 Dec
4rm (1fb) ⊁ in bedrooms CTV in all bedrooms Ⓡ sB&B£18-£20 dB&B£32-£36 WB&B£90-£110
🅟.

GH 🔲🔲 **Moreton House** High Street GL56 0LQ ☎(0608) 650747
There is a delicious smell of baking bread at this friendly guest house and tea shop which is open for coffees, lunches, teas and dinner for residents. Bedrooms are simple with a small lounge area and bar next to the tea shop.

12rm(5⇉🏠) ⊁ in area of dining room CTV in all bedrooms Ⓡ sB&B£21.50 dB&B£40 dB&B⇉🏠£46 LDO 8pm
Lic 🅟.
Credit Cards ①③ⓔ

MORLEY West Yorkshire   Map **08** SE22

GH 🔲🔲🔲 **The Old Vicarage** Bruntcliffe Road LS27 0JZ
☎Leeds(0532) 532174 FAX (0532) 533549
Next to the church and offering an interesting style of accommodation, this guest house has bedrooms that are modern and have thoughtful extras. The lounge and dining room are decorated in Victorian furnishings. Overall, this is a pleasant place to stay.

17⇉🏠 ⊁ in 5 bedrooms ⊁ in dining room ⊁ in 1 lounge CTV in all bedrooms Ⓡ T 🐾 (ex guide dogs) ✳ sB&B⇉🏠£32-£45 dB&B⇉🏠£53-£62 WB&B£276 WBDi£345.65 LDO 8pm
Lic 🅟. CTV
Credit Cards ①②③

MORPETH Northumberland   Map **12** NZ18

INN 🔲🔲🔲 **Granary Hotel** Links Road, Amble NE65 0SD (off A1068) ☎(0665) 710872 FAX (0665) 710681
13🏠 (1fb) ⊁ in 1 bedrooms CTV in all bedrooms Ⓡ T
sB&B🏠£39.95-£42 dB&B🏠£55-£60 WBDi£225-£255 Lunch £9-£12/alc High tea £3.95-£4.50 LDO 9.30pm
🅟.
Credit Cards ①②③

MORTEHOE Devon   Map **02** SS44
See also Woolacombe

SELECTED

GH 🔲🔲🔲🔲 **Sunnycliffe Hotel** EX34 7EB
☎Woolacombe(0271) 870597
Feb-Nov

This small hotel is delightfully situated on a hillside overlooking the sea. Bedrooms are very comfortable with lots of thoughtful extras, including quite a range of books, and the lounge bar and restaurant are bright, inviting rooms. Mr Bassett personally prepares all the dishes fresh on the day, even the pudding, and Mrs Bassett ensures that guests are happy and comfortable.

8rm(4⇌4♠) ⊁ in 4 bedrooms ⊁ in dining room ⊁ in 1 lounge CTV in all bedrooms ® 🦃 sB&B⇌♠£25-£32 dB&B⇌♠£50-£64 WB&B£150-£175 WBDi£245-£275 LDO 6pm
Lic ▥ nc
£

MUCH WENLOCK Shropshire   Map **07** SO69

INN🆀🆀🆀 **The Plume of Feathers Inn** Harley SY5 6LP (on A458, 1.5m SE of Shrewsbury) ☎(0952) 727360
4⇌♠ (2fb)CTV in all bedrooms ® 🦃 (ex guide dogs) dB&B⇌♠£36-£38 Lunch £7.65-£11.95alc Dinner £8.55-£17.85alc LDO 9.30pm
▥
Credit Cards ①③

MUIR OF ORD Highland *Ross & Cromarty*   Map **14** NH55

P R E M I E R 🏵 S E L E C T E D

GH 🆀🆀🆀🆀🆀 **The Dower House** Highfield IV6 7XN (off A862) ☎(0463) 870090 FAX (0463) 870090

Closed 1 wk Nov & 2 wks Feb/Mar

Nestling in three acres of lawns and wooded grounds, this captivating cottage-style house is a haven of peace and quiet. Superior appointments, combined with excellent and welcoming hospitality add to the appeal of this guesthouse, which is personally run by resident owners Robyn and Mena Aitchison. Individual bedrooms are prettily decorated, fitted with period furnishings and provide a good standard of amenities. One room has a separate sitting area and another has a brass bedstead - all have conventional bathrooms fitted with cast iron baths. The day rooms are limited but quite pleasing, including a cosy sitting room with its welcoming open fire, well filled bookshelves and chintzy seating that invites relaxation. Robyn is a gifted chef and the elegant, period style dining room is the ideal setting to enjoy his imaginative creations, produced from the best fresh ingredients available. The set price menu changes daily and is supported by an extensive and well chosen wine list.

5rm(4⇌1♠) (1fb) ⊁ in 3 bedrooms ⊁ in dining room CTV in all bedrooms T sB&B⇌♠£45-£75 dB&B⇌♠£90-£100 WB&B£315-£350 WBDi£463.75-£493.50 LDO 8.30pm
Lic ▥ ⚬ ⌡
Credit Cards ①③

MULL, ISLE OF Strathclyde *Argyllshire*   Map **10**

DERVAIG   Map **13** NM45

GH 🆀🆀 **Ardbeg House** PA75 6QT ☎(06884) 254
Good-value holiday accommodation is provided at this small country house, which stands in its own grounds on the edge of the village. Public areas are full of character and include a choice of lounges, a small bar, and an attractive restaurant with a carte dinner menu. Bar meals are also available. Some of the bedrooms

have four-poster beds.
7rm(3⇌♠) (1fb) ⊁ in 1 bedrooms ⊁ in dining room ® ☀
sB&Bfr£19 dB&B⇌♠fr£38 LDO 6pm
Lic ▥ ⌡
£

TOBERMORY   Map **13** NM55

S E L E C T E D

GH 🆀🆀🆀🆀 **Fairways Lodge** PA75 6PS ☎(0688) 2238 FAX (0688) 2238
The lodge stands on a prime site near the fourth green of Tobermory golf course with uninterrupted views down to the Sound of Mull are outstanding. Offering bed and breakfast accommodation only, the emphasis is on providing the highest standard of accommodation: bedrooms are well furnished, tastefully decorated and thoughtfully equipped with several extra touches. There is a small conservatory and an upstairs lounge for guests. Breakfasts are cooked to order with a good choice offered, including porridge and kippers. Those seeking dinner are encouraged to dine at Strongarbh House (see separate entry), also owned by the McAdam family, within 15 minutes' walk.

5⇌♠ (1fb) ⊁ in dining room CTV in all bedrooms ® ☀
sB&B⇌♠£25-£29.50 dB&B⇌♠£50-£59 WB&B£175-£185
▥ CTV ▶9
£

P R E M I E R ❦ S E L E C T E D

GH ⓠⓠⓠⓠⓠ **Strongarbh House** PA75 6PR ☎(0688) 2328 FAX (0688) 2238

A sturdy Victorian mansion stands in its own grounds on a hillside above the town, overlooking the bay. Sympathetically renovated and converted by the McAdam family, it now provides comfortable tourist accommodation together with a seafood restaurant and grill. The four bedrooms are comfortably furnished and equipped, with private bathrooms, TV and tea trays; some have views of the bay. Chef Ian McAdam uses fresh island produce to create an interesting range of seafood and char-grilled specialities from his imaginative à la carte menu, for which we have awarded two rosettes. The comfortable lounge overlooks the bay and has a bar and cosy fire.

4♨ CTV in all bedrooms ⓡ ✳ sB&B⇨♨fr£58.50 dB&B⇨♨£67-£75 WBDi£319-£347 LDO 9.45pm Lic 🍺 Credit Cards ①③ⓔ

MUMBLES West Glamorgan — Map **02** SS68

See also Bishopston & Langland Bay

GH ⓠⓠⓠ **The Shoreline Hotel** 648 Mumbles Road, Southend SA3 4EA ☎Swansea(0792) 366233

Situated directly opposite the pretty harbour with commanding views over the bay, this small and friendly guest house is personally run by the resident owners. The clean, compact bedrooms are equipped to a good standard to suit both the tourist and business guest, and rooms on the front benefit from the view. There is an attractive little restaurant with an open-plan bar and lounge.

14rm(8♨) (1fb) CTV in 13 bedrooms ⓡ LDO 9.30pm Lic 🍺 CTV ✗nc3yrs Credit Cards ①

MUNDESLEY Norfolk — Map **09** TG33

GH ⓠⓠⓠ **Manor Hotel** NR11 8BG ☎(0263) 720309 FAX (0263) 721731

Closed 2-13 Jan

The Manor Hotel is a large Victorian building perched on the cliff top with direct access to the sea. It is popular with a regular clientele who enjoy the wide range of public areas and simply appointed but comfortable bedrooms.

26rm(9⇨17♨) Annexe 4⇨ (2fb) ✗ in dining room CTV in all bedrooms ⓡ sB&B⇨♨£25-£32 dB&B⇨♨£49.50-£52 WBDi£150-£210 LDO 9pm Lic 🍺 CTV ✗(heated)

MUNGRISDALE Cumbria — Map **11** NY33

FH ⓠⓠⓠ Mr G Weightman **Near Howe** *(NY286373)* CA11 0SH (1.5m from the A66) ☎Threlkeld(07687) 79678 FAX (07687) 79678

Mar-Nov

A traditional Cumbrian farmhouse stands in 300 acres of beautiful, peaceful moorland just a mile from the A66. The bedrooms are modern and pleasantly decorated. There is a comfortable lounge and a bar, with good home cooking and friendly service provided by the owners, Mr and Mrs Weightman.

7rm(5♨) (3fb) ✗ in bedrooms ✗ in dining room ⓡ 🐾 (ex guide dogs) sB&B£18-£20 dB&B£36-£40 dB&B♨£40-£42

WB&B£126-£140 WBDi£189-£203 LDO 5pm Lic 🍺 CTV snooker 350 acres beef sheep ⓔ

INN ⓠⓠⓠ **The Mill Inn** CA11 0XR (2m N of A66 signposted midway between Keswick & Penrith) ☎Keswick(07687) 79632

Closed 25 Dec

With its impressive backdrop of fellside and nearby fast flowing river, this attractive 16th-century inn continues its appeal. The bars are full of character and the bedrooms nicely furnished and thoughtfully equipped. A good range of food is available both in the bar and the intimate restaurant.

6rm(5⇨♨) ✗ in dining room CTV in all bedrooms ⓡ ✳ sB&B£24.50-£27 sB&B⇨♨£29.50-£32 dB&B⇨♨£49-£54 Lunch fr£5alc Dinner £6-£12alc LDO 9pm 🍺 pool table

See advertisement under KESWICK

NAILSWORTH Gloucestershire — Map **03** ST89

GH ⓠⓠⓠ **Apple Orchard House** Springhill GL6 0LX ☎(0453) 832503 FAX (0453) 836213

In a pleasant situation with views across the town, this imposing modern house offers three warmly decorated bedrooms, including one ground floor room. There is a lounge, overlooking the garden, and breakfast and evening meals are served in the adjacent dining room.

3⇨♨ ✗ in 2 bedrooms ✗ in dining room ✗ in lounges CTV in all bedrooms ⓡ T sB&B⇨♨£18-£26 dB&B⇨♨£32-£38 WB&B£100.80-£119.70 WBDi£177.80-£196.70 LDO 10am 🍺 CTV Credit Cards ①②ⓔ

NAIRN Highland *Nairnshire* — Map **14** NH85

S E L E C T E D

GH ⓠⓠⓠⓠ **Greenlawns** 13 Seafield Street IV12 4HG ☎(0667) 452738

Enthusiastic owners Isabel and Bill Caldwell extend a warm welcome to guests at this charming Victorian house. The comfortable bedrooms are very individual in style and there is a quiet lounge with books and board games, a sun lounge displaying the work of local artists, including Isabel Caldwell's, and an attractive breakfast room.

6rm(4⇨♨) CTV in all bedrooms ⓡ ✳ sB&B£20-£25 sB&B⇨♨£25-£30 dB&B£32-£34 dB&B⇨♨£40-£42 🍺 CTV Credit Cards ①③ⓔ

INN ⓠⓠⓠ **Covenanters** High Street, Auldearn IV12 5TG ☎(0667) 452456 FAX (0667) 453583

8rm(2⇨6♨) (2fb) ✗ in dining room ✗ in 1 lounge CTV in all bedrooms ⓡ T ✳ sB&B⇨♨£35-£39 dB&B⇨♨£39-£42 Lunch £8.74-£18alc High tea fr£6.50alc Dinner £8.74-£18alc LDO 9.30pm 🍺 snooker Credit Cards ①③ⓔ

NANTWICH Cheshire — Map **07** SJ65

S E L E C T E D

GH ⓠⓠⓠⓠ **Oakland House** 252 Newcastle Road, Blakelow, Shavington CW5 7ET (on A500) ☎(0270) 67134

3⇨♨ (1fb) ✗ CTV in all bedrooms ⓡ sB&Bfr£20 sB&B⇨♨£25 dB&B⇨♨£32 🍺 CTV

NEAR SAWREY Cumbria Map **07** SD39

GH [Q][Q][Q] Buckle Yeat LA22 0LF ☎Hawkshead(05394) 36446 & 36538 FAX (05394) 36446

Illustrated in Beatrix Potter's 'Tale of Tom Kitten', this 200-year-old-cottage is situated in the centre of the village and is full of charm and character with its log fires and old beams. The bedrooms are prettily furnished and decorated each complete with TV and tea-making facilities. A very pleasant lounge and a spacious dining room is provided along with warm and friendly service.

7rm(4🛁3🚿) 🚭 in dining room CTV in all bedrooms [R] ✱ sB&B🛁🚿£20 dB&B🛁🚿£40 WB&Bfr£133

🅿 CTV

Credit Cards [1] [3] [£]

P R E M I E R SELECTED

GH [Q][Q][Q][Q][Q] Ees Wyke Country House LA22 0JZ (1.5m outside Hawkeshead on B5285) ☎Hawkshead(05394) 36393 FAX (05394) 36393

Mar-Dec

Boasting one of the finest views in all of lakeland over Esthwaite Water, this delightful Georgian country house is set in its own grounds, and offers honest, warm hospitality from the resident owners Mr and Mrs Williams. The bedrooms have individual colour schemes and are prettily furnished with modern style furniture. A recently completed extension includes a spacious restaurant and 2 lounges which are decorated and furnished in Georgian style, with open log fires and lots of reading material provided.

8🛁🚿 🚭 in dining room CTV in all bedrooms [R] sB&B🛁🚿£36-£48 dB&B🛁🚿£72-£76 WBDi£320-£330 LDO 7.15pm

Lic 🅿 nc10yrs

[£]

See advertisement under HAWKSHEAD

SELECTED

GH [Q][Q][Q][Q] ***The Garth*** LA22 0JZ ☎Hawkshead(05394) 36373

Closed Dec & Jan

This fine Victorian house stands in its own grounds overlooking Esthwaite Water and the Langdale mountains. There is a very comfortable lounge with an open fire and lots of family items around. Dinner, freshly cooked and English-style, is taken in the charming dining room. Bedrooms, three with four-poster beds, are individually decorated and furnished and some have colour TV.

7rm(4🚿) (1fb) CTV in 4 bedrooms [R] LDO 4pm

Lic 🅿 CTV nc5yrs

GH [Q][Q] High Green Gate LA22 0LF (on B5285 between Bowness & Hawkshead via ferry) ☎Hawkshead(05394) 36296

Apr-Oct

An 18th-century converted farmhouse standing in a cottage garden in the centre of the hamlet is famous for its Beatrix Potter connections. Bedrooms are pleasantly furnished and there are two cosy lounges - one with TV.

5rm(1🛁2🚿) (4fb) 🚭 in dining room ✱ sB&B£21 sB&B🛁🚿£24 dB&B£36 dB&B🛁🚿£42 WB&B£126-£147 WBDi£170-£190 LDO 6pm

🅿 CTV [£]

NEATH West Glamorgan Map **03** SS79

SELECTED

GH [Q][Q][Q][Q] Cwmbach Cottages Cwmbach Road, Cadoxton SA10 8AH ☎(0639) 639825 641436

These delightful 17th-century cottages offer modern comforts but have kept their character. Furnishings are of high quality and rooms are spotlessly maintained.

5rm(4🛁🚿) (1fb) 🚭 in bedrooms 🚭 in dining room CTV in all bedrooms [R] 🐕 (ex guide dogs) sB&B🛁🚿£20-£25 dB&B🛁🚿£35-£40 WB&B£122-£140

🅿 CTV

NEATISHEAD Norfolk Map **09** TG32

GH [Q][Q][Q] Regency The Street NR12 8AD ☎Horning(0692) 630233

A 17th century house is situated in a popular and picturesque village, ideal for touring the coast or the Broads. Bedrooms are prettily decorated, comfortable and well maintained; some en suite facilities are available.

5rm(1🛁1🚿) (1fb) 🚭 in dining room 🚭 in lounges CTV in all bedrooms [R] sB&Bfr£20 sB&B🛁🚿fr£28 dB&Bfr£36 dB&B🛁🚿fr£38

Credit Cards [5] [£]

NEEDHAM MARKET Suffolk Map **05** TM05

SELECTED

GH [Q][Q][Q][Q] Pipps Ford Norwich Rd Rdbt IP6 8LJ (entrance off rdbt junct A45/A140) ☎Coddenham(0449) 760208 FAX (0449) 760561

Closed Xmas & New Year

Pipps Ford is a large white, timbered Tudor farmhouse. The accommodation is divided between the main house and a nearby converted outbuilding. The named bedrooms are individual in character as well as decor, ranging from modern country to charming antiquity. There is a cosy lounge with a large open fireplace, and breakfast and dinner are served in a conservatory filled with a riot of vines and plumbago.

3🛁🚿 Annexe 4🛁🚿 🚭 in bedrooms 🚭 in dining room [R] 🐕 (ex guide dogs) sB&Bfr£17 sB&B🛁🚿£22.50-£37.50 dB&B🛁🚿£45-£65 WB&B£150-£220 WBDi£261-£331 LDO 5pm

Lic 🅿 CTV nc5yrs 🎾(hard)🎣

NETHER BROUGHTON Leicestershire Map **08** SK62

GH [Q][Q][Q] Cherry Trees Farmhouse 26 Middle Lane LE14 3HD ☎Melton Mowbray(0664) 822491

This well restored, comfortable farmhouse is in the heart of the village. All the rooms are spacious and well maintained and there is a large lounge with colour TV. There is one communal table in the breakfast room and evening meals are provided by prior arrangement.

3🛁 CTV in all bedrooms [R] ✱ sB&B🛁£22 dB&B£35

🅿 CTV

[£]

NETHY BRIDGE Highland *Inverness-shire* Map **14** NJ02

SELECTED

GH [Q][Q][Q][Q] Aultmore House PH25 3ED (turn right 0.5m N of Nethybridge, off the B970 and then 1st left) ☎(0479) 821473 FAX (0479) 821709

▶

Etr-Oct rs 26 Dec-5 Jan
3⇆® sB&B⇆£16.50-£17.50 dB&B⇆£20-£25
WBDi£150-£201 LDO 11.30pm
⊞, nc12yrs 🏊 snooker croquet piano
Credit Cards ①③

NETLEY Hampshire   Map **04** SU40

GH 🆀🆀🆀 **La Casa Blanca** SO3 5DQ
☎Southampton(0703) 453718
Closed 2 wks after Xmas

A small, family run private hotel situated close to the village centre, with views of Southampton Water. The accommodation has been extensively improved by proprietors Jane and Nigel Poole, and many en suite facilities are being provided. All rooms have direct-dial telephones, clock radios and TV; some have shower units, and the others are en suite. There is a well stocked bar and home-cooked food is served in the attractive dining room. Forecourt car parking is provided.

9rm(3⇆6ᴎ) (3fb)CTV in all bedrooms ® **T** ✠ (ex guide dogs)
sB&B⇆ᴎ£26 dB&B⇆ᴎ£44 WB&B£154-£182 WBDi£189-£231 LDO 9.30pm
Lic ⊞, CTV
Credit Cards ①②③£

NETTLECOMBE Dorset   Map **03** SY59

INN 🆀🆀🆀 **Marquis of Lorne** DT6 3SY
☎(0308) 485236 FAX (0308) 485666

Filled with character, this quiet 16th-century inn is complemented by its peaceful, rural setting. The cosy bars are complete with log fires, where a lengthy menu is available. A spacious, nicely furnished dining room offers a more extensive menu, including tempting dishes prepared with skill by Mr Bone. The bedrooms are simply furnished, freshly decorated and offer good value for money.

7rm(4ᴎ) (1fb)CTV in all bedrooms ® **T** ✠ (ex guide dogs)
sB&Bfr£22 dB&B£44 dB&Bᴎ£50 WB&B£154-£175 Bar Lunch
£7.50-£17.15alc Dinner £7.50-£17.15alc LDO 9.30pm
⊞,
Credit Cards ①③

NETTLETON Wiltshire   Map **03** ST87

SELECTED

GH 🆀🆀🆀🆀 **Fosse Farmhouse Country Hotel** Nettleton
Shrub SN14 7NJ (off B4039) ☎Castle Combe(0249) 782286
FAX (0249) 783066

An 18th-century farmhouse of Cotswold stone, this hotel stands in a pretty garden, where afternoon teas are served when weather permits (at other times they are taken in the barn dining room). Most bedrooms are in the original house and are traditional in style. There is a comfortable lounge, and a set evening meal of first class home cooking is served.

2⇆Annexe 3ᴎ ⊬ in dining room CTV in all bedrooms ® sB&B⇆ᴎ£40-£55 dB&B⇆ᴎ£70-£98 LDO 8.30pm
Lic ⊞, ♨▶18
Credit Cards ①②③£

NEWARK-ON-TRENT Nottinghamshire   Map **08** SK75

See also Kirton

INN 🆀🆀 **Willow Tree** Front Street, Barnby in the Willows
NG24 2SA (take A17 to Sleaford and turn by Newark Golf Club signposted Barnby) ☎(0636) 626613 FAX (0636) 626613
rs 25 Dec

---

5 (2fb)CTV in all bedrooms ® ✠ (ex guide dogs) sB&Bfr£20
dB&B£28-£36 dB&Bᴎ£30-£40 Lunch £5.60-£12.50alc Dinner
£5.60-£12.50alc LDO 10.30pm
Credit Cards ①②③

NEWBIGGIN Cumbria   Map **11** NY42

GH 🆀🆀🆀 **Tymparon Hall** Newbiggin, Stainton CA11 0HS (exit M6 at junct 40 and take A66 towards Keswick for approx 3m, then take right turn for village) ☎Greystoke(07684) 83236
Closed Nov-Etr

This is an early 18th-century manor with a large garden on a sheep farm at the end of the village of Newbiggin. Bedrooms are traditionally furnished and double rooms are particularly large. There is a sitting room with an open fire and a dining room where three-course dinners are served.

4rm(2⇆ᴎ) (2fb) ⊬ ® ✠ ✳ dB&B⇆ᴎ£38-£40 WB&B£105-£110 WBDi£180 LDO 4pm
⊞, CTV
£

NEWBOLD ON STOUR Warwickshire   Map **04** SP24

FH 🆀🆀 Mrs J M Everett **Newbold Nurseries** *(SP253455)*
CV37 8DP ☎(0789) 450285 FAX (0789) 450285
Mar-29 Oct

A modern farmhouse on a holding which produces hydroponically grown tomatoes and cucumbers. There is one very large bedroom for families, a twin-bedded room, a large, comfy lounge and a breakfast room where guests share a table.

2rm(1⇆ᴎ) (1fb)CTV in all bedrooms ® dB&Bfr£29
dB&B⇆ᴎfr£35
⊞, CTV 25 acres arable tomato nursery
£

NEWBURY Berkshire

See**Lambourn**

NEWBY BRIDGE Cumbria   Map **07** SD38

GH 🆀🆀 **Furness Fells** LA12 8ND (on A590 in Newby Bridge)
☎(05395) 31260
Mar-Oct

A small family-owned and run guesthouse is situated near the outfall of Lake Windermere. Built of Lakeland stone and standing in well-tended gardens, it offers pleasant accommodation and warm, friendly service.

3rm ⊬ in dining room ® ✠ ✳ dB&B£30-£34
Lic ⊞, CTV nc3yrs
£

SELECTED

GH 🆀🆀🆀🆀 **Hill Crest** Brow Edge LA12 8QP
☎(05395) 31766
Mar-Oct
2ᴎ (1fb) ⊬ CTV in all bedrooms ® ✠ dB&Bᴎ£34-£40
WB&B£105-£120
⊞, CTV

NEWCASTLE-UNDER-LYME Staffordshire   Map **07** SJ84

GH 🆀🆀🆀 **Clayton Farmhouse** The Green, Clayton ST5 4AA
☎(0782) 620401

This immaculately maintained former farmhouse stands beside Clayton village green, just half a mile from junction 15 of the M6 (via the A519); though most of the building is Victorian, parts date back to the eighteenth century. Bedrooms equipped to modern standards include family-bedded accommodation as well as one room at ground floor level. The pleasant dining room is furnished in cottage style and there is a comfortable, homely lounge. A

private car park is situated to the rear of the house.
4rm(2🚿) (1fb) 🚭 in dining room 🚭 in lounges CTV in all bedrooms [R] 🐕 (ex guide dogs) sB&B£25 sB&B🚿£25 dB&B£35 dB&B🚿£35
▥ CTV
Credit Cards [1] [2] [3] [£]

GH [Q] [Q] Durlston Kimberley Road, Cross Heath ST5 9EG (on north side of town on A34 opposite the Hanging Gate pub)
☎Stoke-On-Trent(0782) 611708
Visitors to this guest house on the A34 just north of the town centre are assured of a friendly welcome; simple but soundly maintained accommodation furnished in modern style includes some family-bedded rooms, and, since the house is licensed, drinks can be served in the comfortable lounge. There is no car park, but street parking should not present a problem.
7rm (2fb) 🚭 in bedrooms 🚭 in dining room CTV in all bedrooms [R] * sB&B£19 dB&B£34
Lic ▥ CTV
Credit Cards [1] [3] [£]

NEWCASTLE UPON TYNE Tyne & Wear Map **12** NZ26

GH [Q] [Q] [Q] Chirton House Hotel 46 Clifton Road NE4 6XH (turn right at General Hospital) ☎091-273 0407
A large semidetached Victorian property in its own grounds in a residential area west of the city centre, Chirton House is reached by turning off the A186 opposite the General Hospital. Bedrooms are individually styled and vary in size, some being suitable for family use. Two comfortable lounges are provided along with a pleasant dining room and a cosy bar.
11rm(2🛁3🚿) (3fb) 🚭 in 1 lounge CTV in all bedrooms [R] sB&B£23-£25 sB&B🛁🚿£30-£33 dB&B£30-£34 dB&B🛁🚿£40-£44 WB&B£100-£130 WBDi£150-£180 LDO 5.30pm
Lic ▥ CTV
Credit Cards [1] [3] [£]

GH [Q] [Q] The George Hotel 88 Osborne Road, Jesmond NE2 2AP (on B1600 off A1058) ☎091-281 4442 FAX 091-281 8300
A large Victorian house, in a popular area within easy reach of the city centre, the George offers well equipped traditional bedrooms. It has a large lounge bar, an attractive dining room and a comfortable lounge.
14rm(10🛁🚿) (4fb) CTV in all bedrooms [R] **T** * sB&B£25-£29 sB&B🛁🚿£25-£31 dB&B£32-£37 dB&B🛁🚿£35-£41 LDO 4pm
▥ CTV
Credit Cards [1] [2] [3] [5] [£]

NEWHAVEN East Sussex Map **05** TQ40

GH [Q] [Q] *Harbour View* 22 Mount Road BN9 0LS
☎Brighton(0273) 512096
Harbour View is a small bungalow in a quiet residential area close to the port. There are three guest bedrooms, all modern and nicely kept, and a shared bathroom. Len and Margaret Bailey are friendly hosts who happily provide early breakfasts for guests catching the morning ferry.
3rm (2fb) CTV in all bedrooms [R] 🐕 (ex guide dogs)
▥

GH [Q] [Q] [Q] Newhaven Marina Yacht Club Hotel Fort Gate, Fort Road BN9 9DR ☎(0273) 513976
Situated on the banks of the River Ouse, this popular yacht club has a range of modern bedrooms on the first floor. Many are compact but have pleasant coordinated fabrics and furniture. Guests have full use of the club bar and restaurant which offer fine views of the marina.
7rm(1🚿) CTV in all bedrooms [R] 🐕 (ex guide dogs) sB&B£22-£25 sB&B🛁🚿£25-£28 dB&B£25-£28 dB&B🛁🚿£28-£30 LDO 9.30pm/10.30pm
▥ marina facilities
Credit Cards [1] [3]

NEWMARKET Suffolk Map **05** TL66

See also Kirtling and advertisement on p.299.

GH [Q] [Q] [Q] *Live & Let Live* 76 High Street, Stetchworth CB8 9TJ
☎(0638) 508153
Closed 20 Dec-3 Jan
The Live & Let Live is less than a mile south of Newmarket in a central village location, and the whitewashed flintstone walls of the original inn are easily spotted. Mr and Mrs Human have furnished each of the bedrooms with great care and attention to detail. The decor and fabrics are colour coordinated down to the towels, and the rooms are strikingly fresh and clean. Guests take breakfast in the small dining room with a dark wood polished table and cottage-style walls, and smoking is permitted only in the first-floor lounge.
7rm(2🛁🚿) (1fb) [R] 🐕
▥ CTV nc10yrs
Credit Cards [1] [3]

NEW MILTON Hampshire Map **04** SZ29

GH [Q] [Q] [Q] St Ursula 30 Hobart Road BH25 6EG
☎(0425) 613515
Located in a residential area, this 1930s house has good accommodation including a ground floor garden room suitable for a disabled person. The sitting room is full of ornaments and family mementoes giving a friendly feeling. Full English breakfast is served and in sunny weather you may be able to enjoy a barbecue.
4rm(2🚿) 🚭 in bedrooms 🚭 in dining room CTV in 1 bedroom [R] * sB&B£15-£17 sB&B🚿£16.50-£18 dB&B£30-£32 dB&B🚿£33-£35 WB&Bfr£95 WBDifr£138
▥ CTV
[£]

AA QQQQ Selected

Lodge Down

English Tourist Board COMMENDED

Lambourn, Newbury, Berkshire RG16 7BJ
Telephone: Marlborough (01672) 540304

A Country House with luxury accommodation, en-suite bathrooms. Set in lovely grounds and gardens with views of the downs and gallops. Excellent and varied dining in surrounding villages.
Easy access to M4 Motorway Junctions 14 & 15
One hour or less from Heathrow (60 miles) London, Bath (43 miles) Oxford (26 miles) and the Cotswolds.
Proprietors: John & Sally Cook

NEWPORT Gwent   Map **03** ST38

GH Q Q **Caerleon House Hotel** Caerau Road NP9 4HJ (1m from junct 27 M4, 0.5m from town centre close to Civic Centre)
☎(0633) 264869
A friendly, well established guesthouse, personally run by the Powell family. Situated in an elevated position within walking distance of the town centre, it is a convenient base for both tourists and business guests. Bedrooms are modern and bright, and all have private bathrooms.
7rm➡🏠 (1fb) ⊬ in 1 bedrooms ⊬ in dining room CTV in all bedrooms ⓇD ✳ sB&B➡🏠fr£20 dB&B➡🏠fr£35 WB&Bfr£100 LDO 9pm
Lic ⬛
ⓔ

GH Q Q Q **Kepe Lodge** 46a Caerau Road NP9 4HH
☎(0633) 262351
Closed 22-31 Dec
This very well maintained personally run guesthouse is set back from the road within its own grounds with a tree-lined private drive, just a short walk from the town centre. Housekeeping standards are high, with bright, well equipped bedrooms prettily decorated in pastel shades with coordinating colours and fabrics. Three of the rooms have good quality en suite bathrooms, and there is a comfortable residents' lounge.
8rm(3🏠) ⊬ in dining room ⊬ in lounges CTV in all bedrooms ⓇD 🐾 (ex guide dogs) ✳ sB&Bfr£18 sB&B🏠fr£21 dB&B🏠fr£32
⬛
ⓔ

GH Q Q *Knoll* 145 Stow Hill NP9 4FZ ☎(0633) 263557
Situated near the main shopping centre on Stow Hill, this large Victorian house retains many of its original features. It offers comfortable and well-equipped bedrooms and a spacious, relaxing guest lounge.
9rm(7➡🏠) (2fb) CTV in all bedrooms ⓇD T LDO 5.30pm
⬛

GH Q Q **West Usk Lighthouse** Lighthouse Road, St Brides Wentlooge NP1 9SF (A48 then B4239 for 2m then turn left)
☎(0633) 810126 & 815860 FAX (0633) 815582
If you are looking for something distinctly different then this early 19th-century lighthouse fits the bill. It overlooks the Bristol Channel and has been transformed into a unique small guesthouse, complete with its own `flotation tank' for relaxation. Shaped like a wedding cake and perched on reclaimed land, it is reached by a long, winding, bumpy lane and is personally owned and run by Frank and Danielle Sheahan, who painstakingly restored and converted it. The wedge-shaped bedrooms, set around the central stone spiral staircase, are furnished in country pine and well equipped with today's creature comforts. Guests may not smoke anywhere in the house. They can enjoy a dinner-party atmosphere by gas lamp in the cosy dining room.
3🏠 ⊬ CTV in all bedrooms ⓇD sB&B🏠£30-£35 dB&B🏠£44-£58 LDO 8pm
⬛ CTV flotation tank
Credit Cards 1 2 3

NEWPORT Shropshire   Map **07** SJ71

INN Q Q **Fox & Duck** Pave Lane TF10 9LQ (1.5m S)
☎Telford(0952) 825580
This small family-run inn lies just off the bypass near the National Sports Centre. It is set in pleasant lawns and gardens which include a children's play area. Bedrooms are in an extension and in the older part of the inn are two traditional bars with panelled walls and open fires. Guests can choose between a bar meal and something more substantial in the separate panelled restaurant.
9rm(7➡🏠) (2fb) CTV in all bedrooms ⓇD 🐾 (ex guide dogs) ✳ sB&B£17.50-£22.50 sB&B➡🏠£20-£27.50 dB&B£30-£40

dB&B➡🏠£40-£45 Lunch £2-£5&alc High tea £2-£4 Dinner £4-£7&alc LDO 10pm
⬛
Credit Cards 1 3

NEWQUAY Cornwall & Isles of Scilly   Map **02** SW86

📖 ⚫ **GH** Q Q **Aloha** 124 Henver Road TR7 3EQ (located on the A3058, on the northern side of Newquay) ☎(0637) 878366
This well maintained guesthouse offers bright, fresh accommodation in the modern style. There is a comfortable lounge area with TV and video and a separate games room with pool and darts. Home-cooked food is served in the dining room.
13rm(6🏠) (6fb) ⊬ in dining room ⊬ in lounges CTV in all bedrooms ⓇD sB&B£11-£16 sB&B🏠£17-£22 dB&B£22-£32 dB&B🏠£28-£38 WB&B£70-£140 WBDi£90-£175 LDO 6pm
Lic ⬛ CTV games room/pool table/darts
Credit Cards 1 2 3 5 ⓔ

GH Q Q Q *Arundell Hotel* Mount Wise TR7 2BS
☎(0637) 872481
This family-run hotel is situated close to the town and offers a wide variety of leisure facilities. Accommodation is bright and nicely equipped. Most rooms are quite spacious, with en suite facilities; there is a lift to all floors. The varied public areas include a large bar/lounge where evening entertainment takes place six nights a week during the season. There is an excellent leisure complex which includes a large indoor heated pool, together with sauna, solarium and whirlpool. There is also a popular sun terrace and ample car parking.
36➡🏠 (8fb) CTV in all bedrooms ⓇD T LDO 6pm
Lic lift ⬛ CTV ꩜ (heated) snooker sauna solarium gymnasium
Credit Cards 1 2 3

GH Q Q Q **Bon-Ami Hotel** 3 Trenance Lane TR7 2HX
☎(0637) 874009
Apr-Sep
Enjoying a fine location overlooking the park and boating lake, this very friendly small hotel provides modern, bright and very well maintained bedooms, all with private shower, WC and heated towel rails. The spacious dining room offers a varied menu (special diets can be catered for on request), whilst light refreshments and cream teas are served throughout the day on the sun terrace. There is a separate bar and service is friendly and helpful.
9🏠 ⊬ in dining room ⓇD 🐾 sB&B🏠£15.50-£18.50 dB&B🏠£31-£37 WB&B£105.50-£126.50 WBDi£126.50-£144 LDO 8pm
Lic ⬛ CTV nc
Credit Cards 1 3 ⓔ

GH Q Q Q **Copper Beech Hotel** 70 Edgcumbe Avenue TR7 2NN
☎(0637) 873376
Etr-mid Oct & Xmas & New Year
This family-run hotel is situated in its own grounds in a quiet area of town opposite Trenance Gardens, and has been owned by the Lenter family for the past 20 years. Continued improvements now provide comfortable accommodation with bright, pretty coordinating decor; there are 16 bedrooms, some on the ground floor, most with private bathrooms. Public areas are well furnished and smartly decorated and include a TV lounge, spacious lounge bar opening on to a patio area and an attractive dining room.
14rm(3➡11🏠) (3fb) ⊬ in dining room CTV in all bedrooms ⓇD 🐾 ✳ sB&B➡🏠fr£18.80 dB&B➡🏠fr£37.60 WBDi£155.10-£186.78 LDO 6pm
Lic ⬛ CTV

📖 ⚫ **GH** Q Q Q **Hotel Trevalsa** Whipsiderry Beach, Porth TR7 3LX ☎(0637) 873336 FAX (0637) 878843
mid May-mid Oct rs Etr-mid May
24rm(20➡🏠) (7fb) ⊬ in dining room CTV in all bedrooms ⓇD sB&B£10-£19 sB&B➡🏠£13-£22 dB&B£20-£38 dB&B➡🏠£26-

£44 (incl dinner) WB&B£109-£159 WBDi£139-£199 LDO 7pm
Lic ⬛ CTV
Credit Cards [1] [3] (£)

GH [Q][Q][Q] *Kellsboro Hotel* 12 Henver Road TR7 3BJ
☎(0637) 874620
Etr-Oct
There is an indoor heated swimming pool with a sun terrace at this hotel. Above is a large bar with dance floor and pool table with live entertainment twice a week. Bedrooms are simply decorated. In the newly decorated dining room a choice is offered at both breakfast and dinner.
14rm(10⇆3♪) (8fb) CTV in all bedrooms ⓡ LDO 7pm
Lic ⬛ ☆ (heated) pool table
Credit Cards [1] [3]

GH [Q][Q][Q] *Links Hotel* Headland Road TR7 1HN
☎(0637) 873211
Apr-Oct
A long-established hotel conveniently situated on the Towan Headland next to the golf course and just a short walk from the beaches, harbour and town centre. Bedrooms are currently being upgraded, all have satellite TV and tea making facilities and most enjoy views of either the golf course or sea. The small bar, pool room and friendly service are added attractions.
15rm(10⇆3♪) (3fb) CTV in all bedrooms ⓡ LDO 4pm
Lic ⬛ CTV ✗

SELECTED

GH [Q][Q][Q][Q][Q] **Pendeen Hotel** Alexandra Road, Porth
TR7 3ND ☎(0637) 873521 FAX (0637) 873521
Closed Nov & Xmas

▶

CAERLEON HOUSE — HOTEL —

Welsh Tourist Board

AA QQ

Caerau Road, Newport, Gwent NP9 4HJ
Telephone: 010633 264869

A family run hotel convenient for the M4 and close to the centre of Newport, the ideal base for touring Wales. All bedrooms are en suite and have colour TV and tea & coffee making facilities. Evening meals available. Licensed bar. Ample off-road parking. Whether your visit is for business or pleasure, you are guaranteed a warm and friendly welcome.

ℋill ℱarm

Kirtling, Nr Newmarket, Suffolk CB8 9HQ
Telephone: (01638) 730253

A 400 year old farmhouse which commands superb views, offers spacious well appointed accommodation. All rooms have tea/coffee facilities and some en suite. Full central heating. Access at all times – own key. Choice of menu with home cooking and special diets catered for by prior arrangement. Fully licensed. Open all year.

PENDEEN HOTEL

Alexandra Road, Porth, Newquay
Cornwall TR7 3ND
Telephone: (01637) 873521

Beautifully located hotel 2 mins from Porth Beach. Tastefully furnished and a high standard of cuisine assured. A friendly personal and efficient service is our aim. Fully centrally heated. All bedrooms en suite with colour T.V. and tea/coffee making facilities. Private car park. Mid-week bookings accepted. Open all year. Our location is ideal for the Cornwall Coastal Path Walks.

Proprietors – Diana & Derek Woodfinden.

Many of the bedrooms have fine views over Porth Beach at a hotel which has a reputation for high standards of comfort and friendliness. A choice of menus is available at breakfast and dinner, and snacks and light lunches can be had throughout the day in the bar or on the sun terrace.

15rm(6⇔9↰) (5fb) ⊁ in 3 bedrooms ⊁ in dining room CTV in all bedrooms ℝ ⋔ (ex guide dogs) ✳ sB&B⇔↰£17-£25 dB&B⇔↰£33-£50 WB&B£116-£150 WBDi£135-£188 LDO 6pm
Lic ▦
Credit Cards ①②③ⓔ

SELECTED

GH ⓠⓠⓠⓠ **Porth Enodoc** 4 Esplanade Road, Pentire TR7 1PY ☎(0637) 872372
Mar-Oct
Well located overlooking Fistral beach, this elegant property is very well managed by professional proprietors Mr and Mrs Lawson, who took it over last year. Carefully extended over the years, the accommodation is very neat, clean and well turned out, with spotless en suites in every room. There is a comfortable lounge and a cosy bar, plus the pretty dining room where evening meals are appreciated by guests. A cheerful and relaxed atmosphere prevails throughout this friendly hotel.
15↰ (3fb) ⊁ in dining room CTV in all bedrooms ℝ ⋔ sB&B↰£19.50-£23.50 dB&B↰£39-£47 WB&B£105-£155 WBDi£129-£180.70 LDO 6.45pm
Lic ▦ CTV nc2yrs
ⓔ

SELECTED

GH ⓠⓠⓠⓠ **Priory Lodge Hotel** Mount Wise TR7 2BH (turn left at traffic lights in town centre on to the one way system & Berry Rd, right on to Mount Wise B3282 hotel is approx 0.5m on right) ☎(0637) 874111
Mar-Nov & Xmas rs Mar & Nov
This well renovated hotel stands in its own grounds close to the town centre, harbour and local beaches and offers well presented, nicely furnished accommodation. Bedrooms are well equipped, neat and bright; some have the benefit of balconies and four are located around the outdoor pool. Public areas include a comfortable dining room, a TV lounge which overlooks the swimming pool and a bar with another lounge. Lunchtime snacks and drinks can be served by the pool or in the bar, and other facilities include a sauna, solarium and games room; live entertainment is also provided, together with discos and party nights. The hotel is well run by the Pocklington family and their team of cheerful staff. There is ample car parking.
22rm(7⇔13↰) Annexe 4↰ (17fb) ⊁ in dining room CTV in all bedrooms ℝ T ⋔ (ex guide dogs) sB&B£25-£28 dB&B⇔↰£50-£56 (incl dinner) WB&B£120-£180 WBDi£150-£210 LDO 7.30pm
Lic ▦ ⚓(heated) sauna solarium pool table video machines
Credit Cards ①②③ⓔ

GH ⓠⓠⓠ **Rolling Waves** Alexandra Road, Porth TR7 3NB (off A30 & join A3059 then onto B3276 into Porth) ☎(0637) 873236
Etr-Nov Closed 2 days Xmas rs Dec-Etr
Above Whipsiderry and Porth beaches this small attractive guesthouse has panormaic views with an easy way to the sandy beach. Bedrooms are attractive and there is a small bar looking out on the bay. Dinner is available.

9rm(8↰) (2fb) CTV in all bedrooms ℝ LDO 6.30pm
Lic CTV
Credit Cards ①③

GH ⓠⓠⓠ **Tir Chonaill Lodge** 106 Mount Wise TR7 1QP ☎(0637) 876492
Guests are well looked after at this friendly guesthouse, which is personally run by Mr and Mrs Watts and family. Bedrooms are brightly decorated and simply furnished, and there is a small lounge, well stocked bar and front-facing dining room.
20rm(8⇔12↰) (9fb) CTV in all bedrooms ℝ LDO 5pm
Lic ▦ CTV darts pool

SELECTED

GH ⓠⓠⓠⓠ **Towan Beach Hotel** 7 Trebarwith Crescent TR7 1DX ☎(0637) 872093
rs Oct-1 Apr
This delightful small terraced guesthouse has been completely renovated and redecorated and is situated in the town centre in a quiet position. Bedrooms vary in size and are light, bright and modern; three rooms have private bathrooms and they all have showers, TV, tea-making facilities and clock radios. There is an elegant, well-furnished drawing room with an open fire, and a small conservatory bar. The resident chef/proprietor Andrew Medhurst, who has worked on the QE2, provides a good choice of menu, and meals are served in the candlelit dining room. His partner Tony Baker ensures that guests are well looked after. Barbecues are also provided on the patio on warm summer evenings. Limited car parking can be arranged and the house is very conveniently situated within walking distance of the shops, beach, buses and railway station. The personal attention to details and excellent service provide outstanding value for money.
6rm(3↰) (1fb) ⊁ in dining room CTV in all bedrooms ℝ ⋔ (ex guide dogs) sB&B£18-£20 sB&B↰£20-£23 dB&B£36-£40 dB&B↰£42-£46 (incl dinner) WB&B£108-£140 WBDi£150-£182 LDO 4.30pm
Lic ▦ CTV nc8yrs
Credit Cards ①②③ⓔ

GH ⓠⓠⓠ **Trewerry Mill** Trerice, St Newlyn East TR8 5HS ☎Mitchell(0872) 510345
Good Friday-Oct
Quietly located in seven acres of land, displaying beautiful, well tended gardens filled with pretty and unusual plants, this attractive property dates back to 1639 and was originally a water-powered mill. The comfortable bedrooms are nicely coordinated and many enjoy attractive garden views. There are cosy, comfortable public areas with lots of character and charm, where home-cooked meals are served, prepared with fresh, organically grown fruit and vegetables whenever possible. This no-smoking establishment has a friendly atmosphere and upholds very thorough standards of housekeeping.
6rm (1fb) ⋔ LDO 9am
Lic ▦ CTV nc7yrs

GH ⓠⓠⓠ **Wheal Treasure Hotel** 72 Edgcumbe Avenue TR7 2NN ☎(0637) 874136
Apr-mid Oct
Standing in its own grounds overlooking Trenance Gardens and boating lake, this elegant, well maintained detached house has been tastefully furnished to a good standard throughout. The bar and lounge have been extended with a new conservatory, and the attractive dining room is kept a 'no smoking' area. There are several family bedrooms available, and good car parking facilities are provided. Mr Franks does the cooking, and service is friendly and very helpful.
12rm(3⇔8↰) (3fb) ℝ ⋔ LDO 5pm
Lic ▦ CTV nc3yrs

SELECTED

🏠 🍴 GH 🔲🔲🔲🔲 **Windward Hotel** Alexandra Road, Porth TR7 3NB (approaching Newquay on the A3508, turn right onto B3276 Padstow road, hotel in 1m on right) ☎(0637) 873185
This hotel, 200 yards from Porth beach, was built only a few years ago and so benefits from many modern luxuries. There are panoramic views from the lounge, bar and many of the bedrooms and the latter are decorated using pretty borders with matching curtains and bedspreads while the modern free-standing furniture provides plenty of space for holiday luggage. Besides the lounge there is a smaller TV lounge and in the attractive dining room there is a choice of menu for breakfast and dinner. Mr and Mrs Sparrow are very good hosts and guests return year after year.
14⇌🅵 (3fb) 🗶 in 2 bedrooms 🗶 in dining room CTV in all bedrooms ® 🗶 (ex guide dogs) sB&B⇌🅵£15-£21 dB&B⇌🅵£30-£42 WB&B£105-£147 WBDi£105-£195 LDO 6.30pm
Lic 🖪 CTV
Credit Cards ① ② ③ ⑤

SELECTED

FH 🔲🔲🔲🔲 Mrs K Woodley **Degembris** *(SW852568)* Newlyn East TR8 5HY ☎Mitchell(0872) 510555
FAX (0872) 510230
Closed Xmas
This attractive 18th-century slate-hung farmhouse stands in the depths of the countryside on an arable working farm, only five miles from Newquay. Bedrooms are individually decorated, each with a pretty coordinating theme; there is a general bathroom and shower room and standards of housekeeping are high. Public areas include a comfortable lounge with TV and a cosy dining room where home-cooked evening meals are served at separate tables. The attractive, well kept grounds include a country trail, and there is parking close to the house. To find the house, turn right at the traffic lights in Summercourt to Newquay A3058. Take the third turning on the left to Newlyn East, about two miles from Summercourt, then take the second farm lane on the left.
5rm(2⇌🅵) (2fb) CTV in all bedrooms ® 🗶 sB&B£16-£18 dB&B£32-£36 dB&B⇌🅵£36-£38 WB&B£112-£126 WBDi£171.50-£185.50 LDO 10am
🖪 CTV 165 acres arable

SELECTED

FH 🔲🔲🔲🔲 J C Wilson **Manuels** *(SW839601)* Quintrell Downs TR8 4NY (signposted on the A392, 3m from Newquay) ☎(0637) 873577
Closed 23 Dec-1 Jan
This farmhouse is found along a single-track lane in a wooded valley. The bedrooms and bathrooms have recently been completely refurbished and are very attractive, enjoying rural views. Each of the three rooms is individually decorated and there is a general bath/shower room. Public areas include two comfortable lounges and a beamed dining room with a handsome antique table where guests can enjoy a home-cooked evening meal and hearty breakfast. Children are very welcome, and the atmosphere is relaxed.
4rm(1🅵) (2fb) 🗶 ® 🗶 (ex guide dogs) ✳ sB&B£18-£20 dB&B£36-£40 dB&B⇌🅵£36-£40 WB&B£126-£140 WBDi£185-£200 LDO 4pm
🖪 CTV ♨ 100 acres mixed
£

SELECTED

GH 🔲🔲🔲🔲 *Park Hall Hotel* Cwmtydu SA44 6LG (MIN) ☎(0545) 560306
Once a Victorian gentleman's residence, Park Hall is set amidst 4.5 acres of lawns and woodlands in the picturesque valley of Cwmtydu. The attractive conservatory restaurant looks out over these lawns with views down to a small cove. There is a fixed price, set menu available, augmented with a small à la carte, featuring such dishes as poached salmon in smoked salmon sauce or kebab of Welsh lamb with cranberry sauce, and Welsh cheeses are much in evidence. As well as the comfortable sitting room, a bar furnished with Chesterfields and antique armchairs provides ample space to relax. The bedrooms all have en suite bathrooms, with many still retaining the original fireplace and one featuring an antique four poster. A warm welcome is extended to all guests by the very friendly McDonnell family.
5⇌🅵 CTV in all bedrooms ® LDO 7.30pm
Lic 🖪 CTV ♪ ∪
Credit Cards ① ② ③ ⑤

FH 🔲🔲🔲 Mr M Kelly **Ty Hen** *(SN365553)* Llwyndafydd SA44 6BZ (from Llwyndafydd with phone box on left go up hill for approx 1m, after sharp right bend take `no thro road' on your right, entrance 100yds) (Logis) ☎(0545) 560346
mid Feb-mid Nov
This old farmhouse is situated two miles west of the A487. Modern bedrooms have been created in the old house and in adjoining outbuildings. A separate complex houses the bar and restaurant facilities, and this now includes a fully equipped leisure centre.
▶

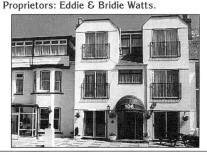

Tir Chonaill Lodge
106 Mount Wise, Newquay, Cornwall, TR7 1QP
Telephone 01637 876492
Our delightful long established, licensed Hotel is centrally located for beaches, golf-course, town centre and all amenities. We offer our guests a high standard of cuisine, comfort and personal service. 20 en-suite bedrooms with colour TV, tea/coffee making facilities and hair dryers. FREE child offer early, late season. Senior Citizens reduced rates. Large car park. OPEN ALL YEAR.
Proprietors: Eddie & Bridie Watts.

5🐾 Annexe 2🐾 (2fb) ⊬ in bedrooms ⊬ in dining room CTV in all bedrooms Ⓡ ✳ sB&B🐾£20-£29 dB&B🐾£40-£58 WB&B£120-£190 LDO 6pm
Lic ▥ CTV ⌇ (heated) sauna solarium gymnasium bowls skittles pool table tennis 40 acres sheep
Credit Cards 1 3 £

NEWTON Northumberland   Map 12 NZ06

FH Q Mrs C M Leech **Crookhill** *(NZ056654)* NE43 7UX
☎Stocksfield(0661) 843117
rs Nov-Mar
This stone-built house stands in an elevated position off the A69 overlooking open countryside, and is reached via the B6309 to the east of Newton. Bedrooms are simply appointed and there is a pleasant combined lounge/breakfast room overlooking the garden.
3rm (1fb) ⊬ Ⓡ 🏃 (ex guide dogs) ✳ sB&B£15-£17 dB&B£30-£34 WB&B£90
▥ CTV 23 acres beef mixed sheep
£

NEWTON ABBOT Devon   Map 03 SX87

GH Q Q *Lamorna* Ideford Combe TQ13 0AR (3m N A380)
☎(0626) 65627
A compact, cosy, modern guesthouse offers bed and breakfast accommodation. There are attractive rural views and pleasant gardens available to guests. Smoking is not permitted in the dining room. To find the house, follow signs for Ideford Combe off the A380 Exeter-Torquay dual carriageway, about three miles from Newton Abbot.
8rm(1🐾🐾) (2fb) CTV in 1 bedroom Ⓡ 🏃 (ex guide dogs) LDO 6pm
Lic ▥ CTV ⌇ (heated)

FH Q Q Mrs A Dallyn **Bulleigh Park** *(SX860660)* Ipplepen TQ12 5UA (take left turn from A381 at Parkhill Service Station and follow for 1m. Signposted) ☎(0803) 872254
2rm(1🐾🐾) CTV in all bedrooms Ⓡ 🏃 (ex guide dogs) ✳ sB&B£14-£15 sB&B🐾£16-£17 dB&B£28-£30 dB&B🐾£32-£34 WB&B£98-£105
▥ CTV 40 acres beef sheep

SELECTED

INN Q Q Q Q **The Barn Owl** Aller Mills, Kingskerswell TQ12 5AN (turn off A380 at signpost for Aller Mills)
☎Torquay(0803) 872130 & 872968
Closed 25-27 Dec
This 16th-century farmhouse has been lovingly restored by Derek and Margaret Warner and the characterful interior features old beams, flagstoned floors and rough exposed stone walls. The six recently created bedrooms are cottage style, with black beams, white plaster walls, locally made, dark-stained pine furniture, and individual floral decor. The rooms are well equipped with TV, hair dryers, direct-dial telephones and tea trays, together with extra touches such as fresh fruit and flowers. The three interconnecting bars have log fires, an inglenook fireplace, black leaded range and the largest bar has oak panelling and ornate plaster work. An extensive range of bar meals includes grills, salads, sandwiches and a blackboard with daily special dishes. A separate restaurant in a converted barn provides dinner six nights a week and Sunday lunch, with an à la carte menu and seasonal local specialities.
6🐾🐾 CTV in all bedrooms Ⓡ T 🏃 sB&B🐾£47.50 dB&B🐾£60 Dinner £16.50-£21alc LDO 9.30pm
▥ nc14yrs
Credit Cards 1 2 3 5 £

NEWTON FERRERS Devon   Map 02 SX54

GH Q Q Q **Maywood Cottage** Bridgend PL8 1AW (off A379 at Yealmpton onto B3186) ☎Plymouth(0752) 872372
Newton Ferrers and Noss Mayo are delightful riverside villages opposite each other on the River Yealm estuary. Maywood Cottage is equidistant between the two and is a well positioned base for touring the South Hams. One of the two guest bedrooms has its own shower room. The first-floor sitting room is traditionally furnished, and breakfast and dinner are taken in the dining room on the ground floor which features exposed stone walls.
2rm(1🐾) (2fb) ⊬ in bedrooms CTV in all bedrooms Ⓡ sB&B£17.50-£20 sB&B🐾£20-£22.50 dB&B£30-£35 dB&B🐾£35-£45 WB&B£210-£240 WBDi£260-£290 LDO 7pm
▥ CTV
£

NEWTOWN Powys   Map 06 SO19

SELECTED

FH Q Q Q Q David & Sue Jones **Dyffryn** *(SO052954)* Dyffryn, Aberhafesp SY16 3JD (from town take B4568 to Aberhafesp, turn right to Bwlchyffridd, bear left at next jct, left twice then right at X roads & farm is down hill on right)
☎(0686) 688817 & (0585) 206412
This lovingly restored half timbered barn is located in a rural haven which is ideal for most outdoor pursuits. The accommodation is furnished in a modern rustic fashion and an air of hospitality pervades the building. The owners farm 100 acres of grassland with sheep and a few cows. It is advisable to ask for directions in advance.
3🐾 (3fb) ⊬ CTV in all bedrooms Ⓡ 🏃 (ex guide dogs) sB&B🐾£20-£23 dB&B🐾£40-£46 WB&B£140-£160 WBDi£210-£230 LDO 5pm
▥ CTV ⥁ 100 acres beef sheep
£

NITON See WIGHT, ISLE OF

NORTHALLERTON North Yorkshire   Map 08 SE39

GH Q Q Q **Alverton** 26 South Parade DL7 8SG (on A684)
☎(0609) 776207
Part of a Victorian terrace, convenient for both the town centre and railway station, this well furnished guest house offers good all-round standards of accommodation and service; comfortable bedrooms are attractively decorated and the spacious lounge is very pleasant.
5rm(3🐾) (1fb) ⊬ in bedrooms ⊬ in dining room CTV in all bedrooms Ⓡ 🏃 (ex guide dogs) ✳ sB&B£17-£18 sB&B🐾£23 dB&B🐾£35-£38 WB&B£113.40 WBDi£183 LDO 1pm
▥ CTV
£

GH Q Q Q **Windsor** 56 South Parade DL7 8SL ☎(0609) 774100
Closed 24 Dec-2 Jan
This very well maintained Victorian terraced house is in easy reach both of the town centre and the railway station. The bedrooms are attractive and comfortably furnished. Fresh flowers brighten the attractive dining room with its elegantly laid tables; there is also a lounge and a neat, well tended garden at the rear.
6rm(2🐾) (1fb) ⊬ in bedrooms CTV in all bedrooms Ⓡ ✳ sB&B£20 sB&B🐾£25 dB&B£30 dB&B🐾£36 WB&B£105-£126 WBDi£161-£182 LDO 3pm
▥ CTV
Credit Cards 1 3

NORTHAMPTON Northamptonshire　　Map **04** SP76

GH Ⓠ **Hollington** 22 Abington Grove NN1 4QW ☎(0604) 32584
This friendly guest house is located on the inner A43, a mile from
the city centre and close to the county cricket ground. It offers
good-value bed and breakfast and the owners make guests feel
very welcome and will happily advise on local restaurants for
evening meals. There is limited off-street parking.
7rm (2fb) ⊬ in dining room CTV in all bedrooms Ⓡ ✳
sB&B£16-£18 dB&B£25-£30
▥
ⓔ

GH ⓆⓆⓆ **Poplars Hotel** Cross Street, Moulton NN3 1RZ
☎(0604) 643983 FAX (0604) 643985
Closed Xmas wk
A small, well kept hotel tucked away in a quiet village four miles
from Northampton offers comfortable bedrooms equipped with a
good range of modern amenities. Public rooms include a pleasant
lounge with satellite TV and a cosy dining room where home
cooking is willingly provided. Smoking is only permitted in the
TV lounge.
21rm(16⇌⤶ℝ) (4fb) ⊬ in 17 bedrooms CTV in all bedrooms Ⓡ
sB&B£15.75-£25 sB&B⇌ℝℝ£25-£35 dB&B⇌ℝℝ£40-£50 LDO
6pm
Lic ▥ CTV
Credit Cards ①②③ⓔ

SELECTED

FH ⓆⓆⓆⓆ Mr M A Turney **Quinton Green** *(SP783532)*
Quinton NN7 2EU (turn off A508 S of town, continue past
Quinton village and farm is 1m on right) ☎(0604) 863685
FAX (0604) 862230
Closed Xmas
3rm(2ℝ) CTV in all bedrooms Ⓡ ✳ sB&Bℝℝ£18-£20
dB&Bfr£35 dB&Bℝℝ£40 WB&B£119-£126
1200 acres dairy arable

NORTH BERWICK Lothian *East Lothian*　　Map **12** NT58

GH Ⓠ **Cragside** 16 Marine Parade EH39 4LD ☎(0620) 892879
Lying on the East Bay, with a fine sandy beach just over the road,
this friendly guest house has a pleasant dining room and a large
lounge. Breakfast is served at individual tables.
3rm ⊬ in dining room Ⓡ ✸ sB&B£17-£18.50 dB&B£34-£37
WB&Bfr£105
▥ CTV ✗
ⓔ

NORTH ELMHAM Norfolk　　Map **09** TF92

INN ⓆⓆⓆ *Kings Head Hotel* Crossroads NR20 5JE
☎(0362) 668856
A former 18th-century coaching inn is situated at the junction of
the B1145 and B1140 in the heart of the Norfolk countryside. Its
two guest bedrooms are spacious and equipped with every modern
facility. Nicely cooked bar meals are served in the comfortable
bars, and one displays an interesting collection of hats and
helmets. For those wishing to dine more formally, there is an
attractive restaurant. Other facilities include a beer garden and an
excellent bowling green.
2⇌ℝ (1fb) CTV in all bedrooms Ⓡ ✸ (ex guide dogs) LDO
9.30pm
▥
Credit Cards ①②③

NORTH MOLTON Devon　　Map **03** SS72

[◧▣] **GH** ⓆⓆⓆ **Homedale** EX36 3HL (off A361)
☎(05984) 206 due to change to (0598) 740206
An attractive Victorian house in the centre of this historic village

on the edge of the Exmoor National Park has bright, comfortable
bedrooms, a cosy lounge with its original cooking range, and a
dining room with a communal table.
4rm(1ℝ) ⊬ in bedrooms CTV in all bedrooms Ⓡ sB&Bfr£14
dB&Bfr£28 dB&Bℝfr£32 WB&B£73.50-£75.50 WBDi£126-
£128 LDO 5.30pm
▥ CTV
ⓔ

NORTH NIBLEY Gloucestershire　　Map **03** ST79

GH ⓆⓆⓆ **Burrows Court Hotel** Nibley Green, Dursley
GL11 6AZ (off A38) ☎Dursley(0453) 546230
Set in a quiet rural location, this stone built converted mill house
offers well equipped, prettily decorated bedrooms with modern
facilities and yet retains many original features. On reaching North
Nibley, follow signs to Berkley and the house is just past the
crossroads, set back from the road in its own grounds.
10rm(6⇌4ℝ) ⊬ in dining room CTV in all bedrooms Ⓡ ✸
sB&B⇌ℝℝ£28.50-£32.50 dB&B⇌ℝℝ£39-£45 WB&B£98-£112
WBDi£168-£182 LDO 8pm
Lic ▥ nc5yrs ✷
Credit Cards ①②③

NORTH PERROTT Somerset　　Map **03** ST40

INN ⓆⓆⓆ **The Manor Arms** TA18 7SG (on A3066, signposted
Bridport) ☎Crewkerne(0460) 72901
Visitors are sure of a warm welcome to this delightful sixteenth-
century inn in picturesque North Perrott. Olde worlde bars display
tempting menus to suit all tastes and pockets, their home-cooked
dishes representing excellent value for money. Small but well
equipped and pleasantly furnished non-smoking bedrooms are
located in the Coach House, away from the hubbub of the main
building, and there is both a garden and car park at the rear of the
pub.　　　　　　　　　　　　　　　　　　　　　▶

The Poplars Hotel
MOULTON, NORTHAMPTON NN3 1RZ
Tel: Northampton (01604) 643983
Follow signs for Moulton Village from A43

There is a small country hotel of
character, situated in a quiet village only
four miles from the centre of Northampton.
We welcome families, and children of
all ages can be catered for.
There is a large car park and garden.
**Personal attention is given to guests
by the Proprietors:
Peter and Rosemary Gillies**

5🚿 🚭 in bedrooms 🚭 in dining room 🚭 in 1 lounge CTV in all bedrooms Ⓡ 🐕 (ex guide dogs) sB&B🚿£29-£32 dB&B🚿£45-£50 Lunch £9-£13alc Dinner £9-£13alc LDO 9.45pm
♨
Credit Cards [1][3][£]

NORTH STAINLEY North Yorkshire Map **08** SE27

INN[Q][Q][Q] Staveley Arms (turn off A61 onto A6108, 3.25m on right beyond Lightwater Valley Theme Park) ☎(0765) 635439 FAX (0765) 635359
4🛁 CTV in all bedrooms Ⓡ 🐕 (ex guide dogs) LDO 9.30pm
♨
Credit Cards [1][3]

NORTH WALSHAM Norfolk Map **09** TG23

GH [Q][Q][Q] Beechwood Hotel 20 Cromer Road NR28 0HD (B1150 out of Norwich turn left at first set of traffic lights and right second) ☎(0692) 403231 FAX (0692) 407284
A delightful Georgian building close to the town centre, Beechwood Hotel provides parking spaces on the gravel driveway, and the immaculately kept lawns at the front and the back reflect the high standards throughout. The accommodation is simply furnished and most bedrooms have en suite facilities. There are two lounges and a dining room where residents can sample Mrs Townsend's home cooked food.
9rm(3🛁6🚿) (4fb) 🚭 in 5 bedrooms 🚭 in dining room CTV in all bedrooms Ⓡ **T** sB&B🛁🚿£25-£29 dB&B🛁🚿£50-£52 WB&B£175-£182 WBDi£210-£252 LDO 9pm
Lic ♨ nc10yrs games room
Credit Cards [1][2][3][£]

NORTH WARNBOROUGH Hampshire Map **04** SU75

INN[Q][Q][Q] The Jolly Miller Hook Road RG25 1ET ☎Odiham(0256) 702085 FAX (0256) 704030
8rm(4🛁🚿) (1fb)CTV in all bedrooms Ⓡ **T** sB&B£30-£40 sB&B🛁🚿£40 dB&B£39-£49 dB&B🛁🚿£49 Lunch £4.95-£10.50alc High tea fr£3.75alc Dinner £4.95-£10.50alc LDO 10.30pm
♨ CTV 🛝 pool room skittles bar
Credit Cards [1][2][3]

NORTH WHEATLEY Nottinghamshire Map **08** SK78

PREMIER SELECTED

GH [Q][Q][Q][Q][Q] The Old Plough Country Guest House Top Street, North Wheatley DN22 9DB ☎Gainsborough (0427) 880916

This delightful grade II listed building has been lovingly refurbished by its friendly owners and accommodation throughout combines comfort with quality. There is a no-smoking rule in the bedrooms and in the dining room where Mrs Pasley serves imaginative four-course dinners at a communal table. The house, in a quiet village midway between Retford and Gainsborough, is not considered suitable for young children.
3🛁🚿 🚭 in bedrooms 🚭 in dining room CTV in all bedrooms Ⓡ 🐕 (ex guide dogs) ✱ sB&B🛁🚿£25 dB&B🛁🚿£50 WB&B£175 WBDi£262.50 LDO 8.30pm
Lic ♨ CTV nc15yrs
[£]
See advertisement under RETFORD

NORTHWOOD Greater London Map **04** TQ09

GH [Q] Frithwood House 31 Frithwood Avenue HA6 3LY ☎(0923) 827864 FAX (0923) 771899
Simple and fairly basic accommodation is provided in this detached Edwardian house in a pleasant suburban road, though the friendly proprietors are gradually making improvements. There is a comfortable lounge and breakfast is served at shared tables in the kitchen.
7rm (4fb) 🚭 in bedrooms 🚭 in dining room CTV in 2 bedrooms 🐕 (ex guide dogs) sB&B£25-£27 dB&B£38-£42 WB&Bfr£175
♨ CTV
[£]

NORTH WOOTTON Somerset Map **03** ST54

🏠 **FH [Q][Q][Q]** Mrs M White **Barrow Farm** *(ST553416)* BA4 4HL ☎Pilton(0749) 890245
Closed Dec-Jan
The proprietors of this 15th-century farmhouse, three miles from the city of Wells, extend a warm welcome to their guests. The four bedrooms are comfortable and made bright with attractive soft furnishings. There is a choice of lounges, one with a log fire, and dinner is available at separate tables in the dining room.
3rm (1fb) 🚭 in dining room 🚭 in 1 lounge CTV in all bedrooms Ⓡ 🐕 sB&B£15-£16 dB&B£30 WB&B£98 WBDi£150 LDO 9am
CTV 150 acres working dairy
[£]

NORTON FITZWARREN Somerset Map **03** ST12

GH [Q][Q][Q] Old Manor Farmhouse TA2 6RZ (Logis) ☎Taunton(0823) 289801 FAX (0823) 289801
This large detached house stands on the B3227 three miles west of Taunton, with an orchard garden at the rear. The neat bedrooms are mainly on the first floor and vary in size, but all have a host of facilities. Downstairs there is a small bar lounge and a cheerful dining room with a grandfather clock and a log-burning stove. Home-cooked evening meals are available and vegetarians are welcome.
7🛁🚿 🚭 in dining room CTV in all bedrooms Ⓡ **T** 🐕 (ex guide dogs) sB&B🛁🚿£36 dB&B🛁🚿£48 WB&B£161 WBDi£266 LDO 4pm
Lic ♨
Credit Cards [1][2][3][5][£]

NORTON ST PHILIP Somerset Map **03** ST75

PREMIER SELECTED

GH [Q][Q][Q][Q][Q] Monmouth Lodge BA3 6LH (on B3110) ☎Frome(0373) 834367
Closed 15 Dec-15 Jan

This is the charming home of Mr and Mrs Graham who go out of their way to make guests feel welcome. The three ground-floor bedrooms, all prettily furnished with good quality fabrics and thoughtful touches, offer space and comfort; two of the rooms open out onto a patio. In the imaginatively furnished lounge and stylish dining room there is the same attention to detail and quality. Well kept gardens and views across to the hills of Somerset, with the village church in the foreground, add to the considerable appeal of Monmouth Lodge.

3rm(1🛁2🚿) (1fb) 🚭 CTV in all bedrooms [R] 🐕 ✱
dB&B🛁🚿£42-£50
🅿 nc5yrs
Credit Cards [1] [2] [3] [£]

SELECTED

GH [Q] [Q] [Q] [Q] The Plaine BA3 6LE ☎Frome(0373) 834723 FAX (0373) 834101

Closed 21 Dec-2 Jan

Many of the original features of this 16th-century house have been thoughtfully preserved to give it an air of great charm and individuality. There are natural stone walls, intriguing fireplaces and a flagstone entrance hall, plus a large dining room. The bedrooms all have beautifully trimmed four-poster beds and luxurious bathrooms.

3🛁🚿 🚭 CTV in all bedrooms [R] 🐕 (ex guide dogs)
dB&B🛁🚿£39-£50
🅿 CTV
Credit Cards [1] [2] [3] [5]

NORWICH Norfolk — Map **05** TG20

GH [Q] [Q] [Q] Earlham 147 Earlham Road NR2 3RG (from northern by-pass A47 take B1108 and follow signs City Centre. over 2 rbts for guesthouse on left after Earlham House Shopping Centre) ☎(0603) 54169 due to change to 454169 FAX (0603) 454169

Run by friendly and enthusiastic proprietors, this Victorian terraced property remains popular, enjoying a good deal of repeat business. There is a small guests' lounge, and enjoyable breakfasts are served in the dining room, with vegetarian choices on request.

7rm(2🚿) (1fb) 🚭 in 4 bedrooms 🚭 in dining room 🚭 in lounges CTV in all bedrooms [R] 🐕 ✱ sB&B£19-£22 dB&B£34 dB&B🚿£40
🅿 CTV P̸
[£]

GH [Q] [Q] Grange Hotel 230 Thorpe Road NR1 1TJ ☎(0603) 34734 FAX (0603) 34734

Closed Xmas wk

A large hotel on the Great Yarmouth road, the Grange has attractive public areas, including a bar, pretty restaurant and formal reception area. Accommodation is serviceable and offers a good range of facilities.

35rm(4🛁31🚿) (1fb) 🚭 in dining room CTV in all bedrooms [R] **T** 🐕 (ex guide dogs) sB&B🛁🚿£35-£37.50 dB&B🛁🚿£50-£55 LDO 9.30pm
Lic 🅿 sauna solarium pool room
Credit Cards [1] [2] [3] [5] [£]

GH [Q] [Q] Marlborough House Hotel 22 Stracey Road, Thorpe Road NR1 1EZ ☎(0603) 628005 FAX (0603) 628005

A proudly kept private hotel with some compact bedrooms, Marlborough House is conveniently located for the railway station and football ground. A cosy lounge and a breakfast room are provided.

12🛁🚿 (2fb) 🚭 in 3 bedrooms 🚭 in area of dining room 🚭 in 1 lounge CTV in all bedrooms [R] ✱ sB&Bfr£18 sB&B🛁🚿fr£28 dB&B🛁🚿fr£38 WB&Bfr£126 WBDifr£182 LDO 4.30pm
Lic 🅿 CTV
[£]

NOTTINGHAM Nottinghamshire — Map **08** SK54

In addition to the national changes to dialling codes on 16 April 1995 (ie the insertion of '1' after the first '0') the codes for certain cities are changing completely - The code for Nottingham will be '0115' with each individual number prefixed by '9'.

GH [Q] [Q] *Crantock Hotel* 480 Mansfield Road NG5 2EL ☎(0602) 623294

Located north-east of the city centre, this large white house is set back from the road, well signed, with ample parking. Bedroom styles vary between the more traditional accommodation in the main house and the modern annexe rooms. There is a small lounge bar for residents, and a meeting room for business guests.

10rm(1🛁🚿) Annexe 10rm(7🛁🚿) (5fb) CTV in all bedrooms [R] LDO 9pm
Lic 🅿 CTV pool table
Credit Cards [1] [3]

GH [Q] [Q] [Q] Grantham Commercial Hotel 24-26 Radcliffe Road, West Bridgford NG2 5FW (follow signs for Nottingham South/Trent Bridge/National Water Sports Centre, hotel is 0.75m from E end of ring road A52) ☎(0602) 811373 FAX (0602) 818567

A commercial guesthouse stands very close to the Trent Bridge cricket ground. The rooms are neat and well equipped, and some have en suite facilities.

22rm(14🛁🚿) (2fb) 🚭 in dining room CTV in all bedrooms [R] ✱ sB&B£20-£26 sB&B🛁🚿£25-£27 dB&B£34-£36 dB&B🛁🚿£37-£39 WB&B£120-£150 WBDi£156-£186 LDO 7.15pm
Lic 🅿 CTV nc3yrs
Credit Cards [1] [2] [3] [£]

GH [Q] [Q] P & J Hotel 277-279 Derby Road, Lenton NG7 2DP (on main Derby Rd A52, 0.75m from city centre) ☎(0602) 783998 FAX (0602) 783998

rs 24-29 Dec

This predominantly commercial establishment near the University offers a range of modestly appointed bedrooms. There is a lounge bar with pool table, and light snacks are available. Breakfast and dinner are served in the dining room which features a large collection of ornamental dinner plates and teapots.

▶

Marlborough House Hotel

Stracey Road, Norwich NR1 1EZ
Tel & Fax: (01603) 628005

A cheerful and clean family owned hotel situated just off the Great Yarmouth road, within easy distance of the station and city centre.
All double/twin and family rooms have private showers and toilets.
Licensed bar, lounge and car park.
Full central heating.
All bedrooms have colour TV and tea & coffee making facilities.

19rm(9🚿) (8fb) 🚭 in area of dining room 🚭 in lounges CTV in all bedrooms Ⓡ ✳ sB&B£23 sB&B🚿£30-£35 dB&B£30-£35 dB&B🚿£35-£40 WB&B£100-£150 WBDi£125-£185 LDO 9.30pm
Lic ♨ CTV
Credit Cards [1] [2] [3] [5]

GH [Q] [Q] [Q] ***Royston Hotel*** 326 Mansfield Road, Sherwood NG6 2EF ☎(0602) 622947
A detached Victorian house with off-street parking and a rear terraced garden, the Royston has pleasantly decorated, individually furnished bedrooms, most with en suite facilities. Guests have the use of a comfortable shared lounge with satellite TV.
8rm(6🚿) Annexe 4🚿 (2fb) CTV in all bedrooms Ⓡ 🐕 (ex guide dogs)
♨ CTV
Credit Cards [1] [2] [3] [5]

GH [Q] [Q] [Q] St Andrews Private Hotel 310 Queens Road, Beeston NG9 1JA ☎(0602) 254902 FAX (0602) 254902
10rm(3🚿) (1fb) 🚭 in 5 bedrooms 🚭 in dining room CTV in 7 bedrooms Ⓡ sB&B£18.50 sB&B🚿£28 dB&B£30 dB&B🚿£36 WB&B£125.50-£196 WBDi£178.15-£244.65 LDO 1pm
♨ CTV
[£]

SELECTED

GH [Q] [Q] [Q] [Q] Windsor Lodge Hotel 116 Radcliffe Road, West Bridgford NG2 5HG (0.5m from Trent Bridge cricket ground on A6011 to Grantham) ☎(0602) 528528 & 813773 FAX (0602) 520020
A family-run establishment with very good all-round facilities, Hotel Windsor is close to Trent Bridge Cricket Ground and offers good service and varied menus.
48🛁🚿 (8fb)CTV in all bedrooms Ⓡ T 🐕 ✳ sB&B🛁🚿£25-£39 dB&B🛁🚿£35-£50 LDO 8.30pm
Lic ♨ CTV snooker solarium
Credit Cards [1] [2] [3] [5]

SELECTED

FH [Q] [Q] [Q] [Q] Mr & Mrs R C Smith ***Hall Farm House*** *(SK679475)* Gonalston NG14 7JA ☎(0602) 663112
FAX (0602) 664844
Closed 17 Dec-6 Jan
Located in the village of Gonalston, north-east of Nottingham, this attractive 18th-century farmhouse is surrounded by lovely gardens. Guests are treated very much as family friends, and meals are taken with the proprietors at a communal table in the traditional farmhouse kitchen. There is a comfortable beamed lounge with an open fire and deep seating, and a heated outdoor swimming pool, tennis courts and table tennis are provided.
3rm(1🛁🚿) (1fb) Ⓡ 🐕 LDO 5pm
♨ CTV 🌳 🏊(heated) 🎾(hard)playroom with piano, table tennis 22 acres sheep/poultry

NUNEATON Warwickshire — Map **04** SP39

GH [Q] [Q] [Q] Drachenfels Hotel 25 Attleborough Road CV11 4HZ ☎(0203) 383030
Now a personally run guesthouse, this large Edwardian property stands on the B4114 about quarter of a mile south-east of the town centre. It provides soundly maintained accommodation, popular with business guests. Facilities include a small bar and an attractive dining room with separate tables.
8rm(2🚿) (2fb) CTV in all bedrooms Ⓡ sB&Bfr£21 sB&B🚿fr£25 dB&Bfr£31 dB&B🚿fr£35 LDO 8pm
Lic ♨
Credit Cards [1] [3] [£]

GH [Q] [Q] La Tavola Calda 68 & 70 Midland Road CV11 5DY ☎(0203) 383195 & 381816 FAX (0203) 383195
8🛁🚿 (2fb)CTV in all bedrooms Ⓡ 🐕 (ex guide dogs) sB&B🛁🚿£18-£20 dB&B🛁🚿£32 WB&Bfr£126 WBDifr£196 LDO 9.45pm
Lic ♨ CTV
Credit Cards [1] [2] [3] [5]

OAKAMOOR Staffordshire — Map **07** SK04

GH [Q] [Q] [Q] Admiral Jervis Country Hotel Mill Road ST10 3AG (on B5417, 1.5m from Alton Towers, 3.5m from Cheadle) ☎(0538) 702187
20 Mar-5 Nov
6🛁🚿 (4fb) 🚭 in bedrooms 🚭 in dining room CTV in all bedrooms Ⓡ 🐕 ✳ dB&B🛁🚿fr£39 LDO 8pm
Lic ♨
Credit Cards [1] [3] [£]

PREMIER SELECTED

GH [Q] [Q] [Q] [Q] [Q] Bank House Farley Lane ST10 3BD ☎(0538) 702810

Bank House stands behind sandstone walls and heavy iron gates just a few hundred yards out of the village centre. The original farmhouse has been considerably extended, creating an imaginative and high quality family home where John and Muriel Orme make guests very welcome. It has a fine setting, high above the steep wooded slopes of the Churnet Valley, and close to many places of interest. Dinner is in true family style, the menu fixed after discussion with the guests, and everyone sitting together at the beautifully laid table. A typical meal could consist of chilled creme vichyssoise, poached salmon, trout, new potatoes, a selection of vegetables, several English cheeses, then a choice of home-made praline ice-cream, lemon sorbet or Bakewell tart. Not all the cooking skills are Muriel's, the breads are made by John, including excellent brioche and croissants served at breakfast. The bedrooms are lovely big old rooms with antique furniture. Extras include bottled water and fresh fruit. Apart from the maple floored drawing room, there is a separate library and a terrace for fine weather.
3🛁🚿 🚭 in bedrooms 🚭 in dining room 🚭 in 1 lounge CTV in all bedrooms Ⓡ 🐕 (ex guide dogs) sB&B🛁🚿£33 dB&B🛁🚿£50-£70 WB&B£140-£196 WBDi£240-£297 LDO 11am
Lic ♨ CTV
Credit Cards [1] [3] [£]

SELECTED

FH [Q] [Q] [Q] [Q] Mrs Christine Shaw **Ribden Farm** Three Lows, Oakamoor ST10 3BW (on B5417 Cheadle/Ashbourne road, on right 0.5m before junction with A52) ☎(0538) 702830 & 702153
Mar-Nov
This nicely preserved and tastefully modernised stone-built farmhouse dates back to 1748. Part of a 100-acre sheep farm in the picturesque surroundings of the Staffordshire moors, it lies north-east of Oakamoor, on the B5417 road to Ashbourne,

before its junction with the A52 and within easy reach of the Peak District National Park and Alton Towers. Bedrooms are attractively decorated, with coordinating soft furnishings and modern furniture and there is a family room available. Smoking is not permitted in the bedrooms. At the time of our inspection there was a cosy lounge/breakfast room, but work was in hand to provide a separate breakfast room.

3rm(2♪) (1fb) ⊬ in bedrooms ⊬ in dining room CTV in all bedrooms ⓑ ⋒ ＊ dB&B♪£33-£37 WB&B£112-£119 ▥ CTV 100 acres sheep

---

OAKFORD Devon   Map **03** SS92

SELECTED

FH ⓠⓠⓠⓠ Anne Boldry **Newhouse** *(SS892228)* EX16 9JE (on B3227) ☎(03985) 347 due to change to (01398) 351347 Closed Xmas

Set back off the old South Molton road in 40 acres within a peaceful valley and bordered by a trout stream, this 17th-century farmhouse retains much of its charm and character whilst providing modern comfort. Two en suites have recently been installed. Home-made soups, patés, bread and preserves, as well as home-produced vegetables can be enjoyed here. The farmhouse is well sited for touring Devon, together with access to Somerset and the coast.

3⇆ (1fb) CTV in all bedrooms ⓑ ⋒ ＊ sB&B⇆£18-£20 dB&B⇆£32-£36 WB&B£105-£110 WBDi£165-£170 LDO 4pm

▥ CTV nc10yrs ✔ 42 acres beef sheep ⑥

OBAN Strathclyde *Argyllshire*   Map **10** NM83

GH ⓠⓠⓠ **Ardblair** Dalriach Road PA34 5JB ☎(0631) 62668 due to change to 562668 May-Sep rs Etr

From its elevated position, Ardblair offers fine views across the town and bay from many of its bedrooms and the sun lounge. In addition to facilities in the bedrooms, the vending arrangement for snacks and drinks proves popular with children. Access to and from the car park can be awkward.

14rm(13⇆♪) (4fb) ⊬ in dining room ⊬ in lounges CTV in all bedrooms ⓑ ⋒ sB&B⇆♪£18.50-£21 dB&B⇆♪£37-£42 WB&B£127-£135 WBDi£175-£185 LDO 5.30pm

▥ ⑥

➤◨ **GH** ⓠⓠⓠ **Briarbank** Glencruitten Road PA34 4DN ☎(0631) 66549 due to change to 566549

4rm(2⇆♪) CTV in all bedrooms ⓑ sB&Bfr£15 sB&B⇆♪£18-£20 dB&Bfr£30 dB&B⇆♪£36-£40 WB&B£85-£126 LDO 6pm ▥ CTV nc12yrs

GH ⓠⓠⓠ **Drumriggend** Drummore Road PA34 4JL ☎(0631) 63330 due to change to 563330

Good-value tourist accommodation is offered at this smartly furnished family-run guesthouse, in compact but tastefully decorated bedrooms. Public areas include a bright lounge and a neat dining room where enjoyable home cooking is served.

3⇆♪ (1fb) ⊬ in dining room CTV in all bedrooms ⓑ dB&B⇆♪£32-£36 WB&B£110-£120 WBDi£159-£169 ▥ CTV ⑥

GH ⓠⓠⓠ *Glenburnie Private Hotel* The Esplanade PA34 5AQ ☎(0631) 62089 due to change to 562089 Apr-Oct

A nice, solid, spacious period house on the Esplanade looks out across the West Bay. Bedrooms vary in size but all are ▶

comfortable.
14rm(10♪) (2fb) CTV in all bedrooms ® ⅍ (ex guide dogs)
▥ CTV nc4yrs
Credit Cards ①③

GH ⓠⓠⓠ *Glenrigh* Esplanade PA34 5AQ ☎(0631) 62991 due to change to 562991
mid Feb-mid Nov
Spotless and well maintained throughout, this substantial semidetached Victorian villa sits on the Esplanade and looks out across the bay to the Isle of Mull. Bedrooms of various sizes are all brightly decorated. There is a lounge and a cheerful breakfast room where guests might be asked to share a table.
14♪ (6fb) CTV in all bedrooms ®
▥
Credit Cards ①③

🛏🖥 **GH** ⓠⓠ **Glenroy** Rockfield Road PA34 5DQ
☎(0631) 62585 due to change to 562585
The Glenroy is a family-run semidetached Victorian villa set on a hillside above the town with views over the bay. It offers good value bed and breakfast accommodation in well decorated bedrooms. A relaxing lounge and a separate breakfast room are provided.
7rm(3♪) ⅍ in dining room CTV in all bedrooms ® ⅍ (ex guide dogs) sB&B£15-£16 dB&B£29-£30 dB&B♪£33-£35
▥ CTV
£

SELECTED

GH ⓠⓠⓠⓠ **Rhumor** Drummore Road PA34 4JL
☎(0631) 63544 due to change to 563544
Apr-Oct
Secluded in its own garden, this detached house is in a residential street and gives fine views across the town from the south. Bedrooms - a double and a twin on the ground floor and a neat single upstairs - are bright and modern. There is a cosy lounge, and breakfast is taken at one oval table in the attractive little dining room. This is a no-smoking establishment.
3rm(2⇆♪) ⅍ in bedrooms CTV in all bedrooms ® ⅍ (ex guide dogs) ✱ sB&B£17-£19 dB&B⇆♪£32-£36
▥ CTV
£

🛏🖥 **GH** ⓠⓠⓠ **Roseneath** Dalriach Road PA34 5EQ (turn left off A85 beyond Kings Knoll Hotel and follow signs for Maternity Hospital) ☎(0631) 62929 due to change to 562929
Closed 24-26 Dec
In an elevated position overlooking the town and bay, this friendly guest house offers attractively decorated accommodation. A guests' lounge is provided, and there is a compact dining room where table sharing may be necessary.
10rm(5♪) ⅍ CTV in 7 bedrooms ® ⅍ (ex guide dogs) sB&B£14-£17 dB&B£30-£38 dB&B♪£30-£36
▥ CTV

🛏🖥 **GH** ⓠⓠⓠ **Sgeir Mhaol** Soroba Road PA34 4JF (on A816)
☎(0631) 62650 due to change to 562650
This spotlessly clean and well maintained bungalow lies on the southern side of the town. It has a cosy little lounge and an attractive dining room, and while the bedrooms are compact, they are bright and airy.
7rm(5♪) (3fb) ⅍ in dining room CTV in all bedrooms ® ⅍ (ex guide dogs) sB&B£14-£20 sB&B♪£16-£26 dB&B£28-£32 dB&B♪£30-£40 LDO 4pm
▥ CTV
£

GH ⓠⓠⓠ *Thornloe* Albert Road PA34 5JA (from A85, turn left at King's Knoll Hotel and pass swimming pool, last house on right hand side) ☎(0631) 62879 due to change to 562879
Mar-Dec
A house of character, Thornloe has been tastefully refurbished to highlight its period features, with the liberal use of attractive fabrics and objets d'art. Bedrooms vary in size and two have four-poster beds. There is a cosy guests' lounge and attractive dining room. Parking may prove difficult.
8rm(6♪) (2fb) ⅍ in 4 bedrooms ⅍ in dining room ⅍ in lounges CTV in all bedrooms ® ⅍ (ex guide dogs)
▥ CTV
£

GH ⓠⓠⓠ **Verulam** Drummore Rd PA34 4JL ☎(0631) 66115 due to change to 566115
Mar-Oct
Situated in a residential cul-de-sac on the south side of town, this bungalow offers good-value accommodation in bedrooms which, though compact, are well decorated and comfortable. Hearty breakfasts are served at the communal table in the combined lounge-dining room.
2♪ CTV in all bedrooms ® ✱ dB&B♪£30
▥ CTV
£

GH ⓠⓠⓠ **Wellpark Hotel** Esplanade PA34 5AQ
☎(0631) 62948 due to change to 562948 FAX (0631) 65808
May-Oct rs Etr
On the esplanade overlooking West Bay, this substantial period mansion offers well equipped and plainly decorated modern bedrooms of varying size, and a first-floor lounge from which to enjoy the views.
17♪ ⅍ in 8 bedrooms ⅍ in dining room ⅍ in lounges CTV in all bedrooms ® T ✱ sB&B♪£24-£29 dB&B♪£40-£58
▥
Credit Cards ①③

ODDINGTON Gloucestershire   Map **04** SP22

INN ⓠⓠⓠ **Horse & Groom** Upper Oddington GL56 0XH
☎Cotswold(0451) 830584
8⇆♪ (2fb)CTV in all bedrooms ® ⅍ (ex guide dogs)
sB&B⇆♪£33 dB&B⇆♪£50 Bar Lunch £8.25-£10.35 Dinner £8.25-£10.35&alc LDO 9.30pm
▥
Credit Cards ①③

OFFTON Suffolk   Map **05** TM04

FH ⓠⓠⓠ **Mrs P M Redman Mount Pleasant** *(SS066495)*
IP8 4RP (on A1100) ☎(0473) 658896 FAX (0473) 658896
Tucked away behind the church, this 16th-century farmhouse has been extended and renovated to provide three bedrooms, each with a good range of facilities and prettily decorated using Laura Ashley fabrics. Guests are welcome to view the variety of farm animals roaming the eight acres, and, by arrangement, to sample the local and home-grown produce at dinner.
3rm(1⇆2♪) ⅍ in all bedrooms ® ⅍ (ex guide dogs) sB&B£16.50 dB&B⇆♪£28 WB&B£98-£115.50 WBDi£154-£171.50 LDO 9am
Lic ▥ nc14yrs 8 acres mixed
£

OKEHAMPTON Devon   Map **02** SX59

See also Holsworthy

FH ⓠⓠ **Mrs K C Heard** *Hughslade (SX561932)* EX20 4LR
☎(0837) 52883
Closed Xmas
Hughslade is a comfortable farmhouse close to the A30, offering easy access by road to many places of interest in Devon and

Cornwall. The accommodation has a home-from-home atmosphere and a warm welcome from the Heard family is assured.

4rm (3fb) ⓡ LDO 6pm
CTV ∪ snooker games room horse riding 600 acres beef sheep

OLD DALBY Leicestershire   Map 08 SK62

GH Ⓠ Ⓠ Ⓠ **Home Farm** Church Lane LE14 3LB (6m NW of Melton Mowbray) ☎Melton Mowbray(0664) 822622
An 18th century farm with a delightful cottage garden in the middle of a typically rural English village. The inside of the house is furnished with antiques, oak floors and rich coloured rugs and upholstery. All the bedrooms have modern tiled bathrooms and breakfast is served around a refectory table.

3rm(2🐾) Annexe 2🐾 (1fb) CTV in 2 bedrooms ⓡ 🐾 (ex guide dogs) ✳ sB&B£21-£25 sB&B🐾fr£25 dB&B🐾£37.50-£40 WB&B£118-£150
📺 CTV
Credit Cards ① ③ ⓔ

OLD SODBURY Avon   Map 03 ST78

SELECTED

GH Ⓠ Ⓠ Ⓠ Ⓠ **The Sodbury House Hotel** Badminton Road BS17 6LU ☎Chipping Sodbury(0454) 312847
FAX (0454) 273105
Closed 24 Dec-4 Jan
This popular hotel, close to the M4, M5, Bristol and Bath, is set in attractive grounds. Bedrooms in the main house are particularly comfortable while those in the stable block and coach house (where there is also a new conference facility) are

▶

The Horse and Groom Inn ★★ 72%

Upper Oddington, Moreton-in-Marsh, Gloucestershire GL56 0XH
Telephone: (01451) 830584
Ideally situated for exploring all the picturesque Cotswold villages and within easy reach of the many places of interest in the area. This XVIth century Cotswold stone Inn of great character is family run and offers seven en suite bedrooms. There are two delightful olde worlde bars and cheery Inglenook fireplace where reals ales can be enjoyed. The small, cosy dining room is renowned for its high standard of cuisine using mostly local produce with daily home made specialities. A large beer garden with stream, fishponds and aviary are interesting features.

HUGHSLADE FARM
Okehampton, Devon

See how a real Devonshire working farm is run, guests and children are made welcome. Situated on the B3260 with A30 nearby. The farmhouse overlooks Dartmoor which offers excellent walking and horse riding facilities, EXMOOR & CORNWALL are also within easy reach. The farmhouse is comfortably furnished with TV and central heating on the ground floor. Bedrooms have heating, wash basins and tea and coffee making facilities. A large dining room with separate tables serves farmhouse cooking using home produced meals. Large games room with full sized snooker table. Bed & Breakfast or Dinner, Bed & Breakfast weekly or nightly. Okehampton town is just 2 miles from the farm and has a superb golf course, tennis courts and a covered swimming pool. Our farmhouse has been offering homely accommodation for a long while with many guests returning.

Terms from MRS K C HEARD, HUGHSLADE FARM, OKEHAMPTON, DEVON EX20 4LR. TELEPHONE: 01837 52883

Week Farm
Bridestowe, Okehampton, Devon EX20 4HZ

ETB
💗💗 Telephone: (0183 786) 1221
COMMENDED   AA QQQ

A warm welcome awaits you at our 17th century farmhouse situated in beautiful countryside convenient for the A30. Ideal for a walking or touring holiday central for Dartmoor, North and South Coasts – 10 miles from Cornish border. National Trust properties plus many places of local interest in the area. All bedrooms have en suite, tea/coffee facilities and heating. A ground floor room is available for disabled guests. Many guests return annually for the delicious home cooking – roast beef, chicken, pavlova, trifles and pies.

Come and spoil yourselves.

Proprietress: Margaret Hockridge

more compact, but pleasantly decorated. Lounge and dining room are richly furnished.
6🛁🚿 Annexe 7🚿 (3fb) 🚭 in dining room CTV in all bedrooms [R] T sB&B🛁🚿£40-£45 dB&B🛁🚿£55-£70
Lic 🅿 croquet boule
Credit Cards [1] [2] [3] [£]

OLNEY Buckinghamshire Map **04** SP°5

GH [Q] [Q] [Q] Queen Hotel 40 Dartmouth Road MK46 4BH (on A509) ☎(0234) 711924
4rm(3🚿) CTV in all bedrooms [R] 🐕 (ex guide dogs) ✳ sB&B£22.50 sB&B🚿£27.50 dB&B£32.50 dB&B🚿£37.50 WB&B£100-£120
Lic 🅿 CTV
Credit Cards [1] [2] [3]

ONICH Highland *Inverness-shire* Map **14** NN06

GH [Q] [Q] [Q] ***Cuilcheanna House Hotel*** PH33 6SD ☎(08553) 226
Etr-6 Oct
A single track road off the A82 leads to this small family-run hotel, which stands in its own grounds close to the shore of Loch Linnhe. The traditionally furnished bedrooms are well decorated and public areas include a lounge bar, comfortable lounge and attractive dining room. The fixed-price menu offers a choice at each course.
8🛁 (2fb) [R] LDO 7.30pm
Lic 🅿 CTV

GH [Q] [Q] ***Tigh-A-Righ*** PH33 6SE ☎(08553) 255
Closed 22 Dec-7 Jan
A genuine Highland welcome is shown at this small family run guesthouse which stands beside the A82 just north of the village, eight miles south of Fort William. Bedrooms, though compact, are comfortable and modern, some with en suite facilities, and are equipped with useful extras. Public rooms include a reading lounge and a spacious dining room where good home cooking is served. The White Corries ski run in Glencoe is within 30 minutes of the guesthouse, and the area also offers hill-walking and climbing, fishing, yachting and canoeing.
6rm(1🛁1🚿) (3fb) [R] LDO 9pm
Lic 🅿 CTV

ORFORD Suffolk Map **05** TM44

INN [Q] [Q] ***Kings Head*** Front Street IP12 2LW (turn off A12 on outskirts of Woodbridge onto the B1084, follow signs to Orford Castle, Inn is in Market Sq) ☎(0394) 450271
This inn dates back to the late 13th-century and has a reputation as a sumgglers' haunt. Bedrooms are simply furnished and all used shared bathrooms. The bar, with its snug nautical atmosphere, low beams and open fire offers a variety of snacks. The adjoining retaurant specialises in locally caught fish, cooked by the proprietor Alistair Shaw.
6rm (1fb) CTV in all bedrooms [R] LDO 9pm
🅿 nc8yrs
Credit Cards [5]

OTTERY ST MARY Devon Map **03** SY19

GH [Q] Fluxton Farm Hotel Fluxton EX11 1RJ ☎(0404) 812818
Apr-Oct & Xmas rs Nov-Mar
Situated next to a working farm, this house is a 16th-century Grade II listed Devon longhouse. The proprietor is a great cat lover and keeps at least 20 cats. Bedrooms are well equipped and simply furnished. The home-cooked dinners are popular with guests.
12rm(6🛁4🚿) (2fb) 🚭 in dining room 🚭 in 1 lounge CTV in 11 bedrooms [R] sB&B£19.50-£22 sB&B🛁🚿£22.50-£25 dB&B🛁🚿£45-£50 WB&B£130-£170 WBDi£195-£220 LDO 5.30pm
Lic 🅿 CTV 🎣 putting garden railway
[£]

OUNDLE Northamptonshire Map **04** TL08

INN [Q] [Q] The Ship Inn 18-20 West Street PE8 4EF ☎(0832) 273918
This old world inn is situated at the heart of the picturesque market town. Guest accommodation is provided in two stone-built annexes, the coach and boat houses. Rooms have a good range of facilities and most have pine furniture and striking coordinated fabrics. Books, dried flowers and china all help to personalise the decor. Further rooms are available in the cottage, but the accommodation provided was not up to AA standard when inspected; and this annexe also houses a small dining room/lounge. There is a cosy bar with an inglenook fireplace in the inn, where a range of bar meals and real ales is served.
11rm(1🛁10🚿) (1fb) 🚭 in area of dining room CTV in all bedrooms [R] ✳ sB&B£15-£20 sB&B🛁🚿£22.50-£27.50 dB&B🛁🚿£40-£45 Lunch £2.25-£7.50 Dinner £4.25-£8.50 LDO 10pm
🅿 CTV
Credit Cards [1] [3]

OXFORD Oxfordshire Map **04** SP50

See also Yarnton

GH [Q] Acorn 260 Iffley Road OX4 1SE (From ring-road take A4158 north for 1m. On left opposite Toyota garage) ☎(0865) 247998
Closed Xmas-New Year
A Victorian semidetached property on the Iffley road offers basic facilities and services. It is professionally run and well kept by the cheerful resident proprietor, and breakfast is served in the small, modestly appointed dining room.
6rm (3fb) 🚭 in 1 bedrooms 🚭 in dining room CTV in all bedrooms [R] 🐕 ✳ sB&B£24-£26 dB&B£34-£38
🅿
Credit Cards [1] [3] [£]

GH [Q] [Q] [Q] All Seasons 63 Windmill Road, Headington OX3 7BP ☎(0865) 742215
Closed 24-26 Dec, 31 Dec & 1 Jan
A small friendly guesthouse within easy walking distance of the shops in Headington and the regular bus service to the city centre. Three of the bedrooms are furnished to a high standard with private bathrooms, and rooms on the first floor share a shower room. The small breakfast room is freshly decorated, and there is ample car parking at the rear of the property. This establishment is totally no smoking.
6rm(3🚿) 🚭 CTV in all bedrooms [R] 🐕 ✳ sB&Bfr£25 dB&B£35-£40 dB&B🚿£45-£50
🅿 nc12yrs
[£]

GH [Q] [Q] Bravalla 242 Iffley Road OX4 1SE ☎(0865) 241326 & 250511
This semidetached guest house stands on the Iffley road, which has a regular bus service to the city centre. Small and informal, it provides neat, well equipped bedrooms, with breakfast served in a modest conservatory at the rear of the property.
6rm(4🚿) (2fb) 🚭 in dining room CTV in all bedrooms [R] sB&B£20-£24 sB&B🚿£30 dB&B🚿£38
🅿 CTV
Credit Cards [1] [3] [5] [£]

GH [Q] [Q] ***Bronte*** 282 Iffley Road OX4 4AA ☎(0865) 244594
A red brick Victorian semidetached house situated within walking distance of the city centre. Bedrooms on two upper floors are neatly furnished and cheerfully decorated, with good modern beds. There is a pleasant TV lounge, and the dining room opens out

through French windows into a pretty, well tended garden.
5rm(1⊁) (1fb) CTV in all bedrooms Ⓡ ⊁ (ex guide dogs)
🛏 CTV
Credit Cards ①③

GH Ⓠ Ⓠ *Brown's* 281 Iffley Road OX4 4AQ ☎(0865) 246822
A fine detached Victorian brick-built villa stands on the Iffley road, one mile from the city centre. Bedrooms are compact but offer good facilities and are well equipped. The experienced proprietor is very friendly. Smoking is not permitted in the breakfast room.
6rm(2⊁) (1fb) CTV in all bedrooms Ⓡ
🛏 CTV
Credit Cards ①③

GH Ⓠ Ⓠ **Casa Villa** 388 Banbury Road OX2 7PW
☎(0865) 512642 FAX (0865) 512642
7rm(5⊁) (1fb) ⚲ CTV in all bedrooms ⊁ ✳ sB&B£25-£30
sB&B⊁£35-£40 dB&B£45-£50 dB&B⊁£50-£55
🛏 CTV
Credit Cards ①②③

SELECTED

GH Ⓠ Ⓠ Ⓠ Ⓠ **Chestnuts** 45 Davenant Road, off Woodstock Road OX2 8BU ☎(0865) 53375
Closed 22 Dec-4 Jan
A regular bus service can provide transport to the city-centre from this well presented, modern guest house two miles to its north. Attractively furnished and coordinated bedrooms - all of them no-smoking - are equipped with a hot-drinks tray, colour televisions and hair dryers, while the breakfast served in a bright conservatory overlooking a secluded flower-filled patio

▶

Brontë Guest House
282 Iffley Road, Oxford
Telephone: 01865 244594

Bridie and John welcome you to their family run guesthouse providing a warm and friendly atmosphere. Within walking distance of the university and City centre. Situated close to the river Thames. Bus stop outside entrance with frequent services. Ideal location for touring the Cotswolds but also convenient for major routes to London, Stratford and Birmingham. Parking facilities available. Open all year.

offers a choice ranging from fresh fruit and yoghurt to a hearty traditional spread.
4🚿 (1fb) 🚭 in bedrooms 🚭 in dining room CTV in all bedrooms Ⓡ 🐕 (ex guide dogs) sB&B🚿£30-£33 dB&B🚿£46-£50
🅿 nc12yrs
[£]

GH [Q][Q] Combermere 11 Polstead Road OX2 6TW (from jct with A40 proceed S down A4144 for 1.5m then turn right into Polstead road) ☎(0865) 56971

This small red brick Edwardian house is situated in a quiet residential area off the Woodstock road, 15 minutes' walk from the city centre, with a regular bus service available. A good choice is offered at breakfast, which is served in the small breakfast room, where smoking is not permitted.

9🚿 (2fb) 🚭 in dining room CTV in all bedrooms Ⓡ sB&B🚿£20-£30 dB&B🚿£34-£50
🅿
Credit Cards [1][2][3][5]

GH [Q][Q][Q] Conifer 116 The Slade, Headington OX3 7DX ☎(0865) 63055

This family run guesthouse is situated west of the city centre in Headington and offers spotlessly clean, well maintained simple bed and breakfast accommodation. Bedrooms are reasonable in size with neat decor, and there is a small lounge/breakfast room. Guests can make use of the outdoor heated swimming pool in the summer months.

8rm(1🛁2🚿) (1fb) 🚭 in dining room 🚭 in lounges CTV in all bedrooms Ⓡ 🐕 ✳ sB&B£21-£30 dB&B£35-£38 dB&B🛁🚿£45-£48
🅿 🏊(heated)
Credit Cards [1][3]

PREMIER SELECTED

GH [Q][Q][Q][Q][Q] Cotswold House 363 Banbury Road OX2 7PL (off A40) ☎(0865) 310558 FAX (0865) 310558

Situated two miles north of the city centre, Jim and Anne O'Kane's stone-built house was constructed relatively recently to high standards. Bedrooms vary in size but each features good quality, comfortable furnishings and good equipment; one ground-floor room is available. A choice is offered at breakfast which includes the traditional cooked meal, vegetarian with fresh fruit or home-made muesli. This is a no-smoking establishment.

7🚿 (2fb) 🚭 CTV in all bedrooms Ⓡ 🐕 ✳ sB&B🚿£34-£36 dB&B🚿£50-£54
🅿 nc6yrs

GH [Q][Q][Q] Courtfield Private Hotel 367 Iffley Road OX4 4DP (on A4158) ☎(0865) 242991 FAX (0865) 242991

An attractive detached 1930s house is located on the Iffley Road, within easy access of the city centre. The accommodation is spotless, with all rooms double glazed to combat traffic noise; most of them are en suite. Personal service is provided by the resident proprietors, and breakfast is served in a comfortable dining room which also has a lounge area.

6rm(4🛁🚿) (1fb) 🚭 in dining room 🚭 in lounges 🐕 sB&B£26-£30 sB&B🛁🚿£28-£34 dB&B£36-£38 dB&B🛁🚿£42-£45
WB&B£133-£140
🅿 CTV nc3yrs
Credit Cards [1][2][3][5] [£]

SELECTED

GH [Q][Q][Q][Q] Dial House 25 London Road, Headington OX3 7RE ☎(0865) 69944

Closed Xmas & New Year

An elegant detached half-timbered building set in well tended gardens within a mile and a half of the town, this friendly guest house offers accommodation in spacious centrally heated non-smoking bedrooms. There is a quiet lounge where guests can read or plan their next day's activities from the literature on display, and the area provides a good choice of restaurants and eating places. Off-street parking is available - and buses stop only a few steps from the front door.

8🛁🚿 (2fb) 🚭 in bedrooms 🚭 in dining room CTV in all bedrooms Ⓡ ✳ dB&B🛁🚿£48-£50
🅿 nc6yrs
[£]

GH [Q][Q][Q] *Earlmont* 322-324 Cowley Road OX4 2AF ☎(0865) 240236

Closed 24 Dec-1 Jan

A double-fronted terraced property situated on the busy Cowley road on the eastern side of the city. There are eight bedrooms in the main building, the majority furnished in pine, with private bathrooms; the remaining rooms are situated across the road in a small annexe. Public rooms are nicely furnished and decorated, although fairly small. Smoking is not permited in the main building.

8rm(1🛁6🚿) Annexe 7rm (2fb) CTV in all bedrooms Ⓡ 🐕
🅿 CTV nc5yrs
Credit Cards [1][2][3][5]

GH [Q][Q][Q] Falcon Private Hotel 88-90 Abingdon Road OX1 4PX ☎(0865) 722995

Situated along the Abingdon road just east of the city, this guesthouse has been created by the conversion of two Victorian houses and carefully refurbished by the new proprietors. Bedrooms are particularly well equipped and comfortable, with excellent en suite facilities. Public areas are comfortable, if a little limited in space. The owners are friendly, helpful and eager to provide for their guests' comfort.

11🚿 (4fb) 🚭 in bedrooms 🚭 in dining room CTV in all bedrooms Ⓡ T 🐕 (ex guide dogs) ✳ sB&B🚿£26-£28 dB&B🚿£42-£45 LDO 5pm
🅿 CTV jacuzzi
Credit Cards [1][2][3] [£]

GH [Q][Q][Q] *Gables* 6 Cumnor Hill OX2 9HA (off A420) ☎(0865) 862153

Closed 24-31 Dec

A very attractive white Victorian gabled house is set in a small garden, just off the A34. Completely gutted and refurbished some years ago, it offers modern well furnished accommodation with good facilities, crisp linens and coordinating colour schemes. All the en suite bathrooms are smart, modern and fully tiled.

6rm(1🛁4🚿) (1fb) CTV in all bedrooms Ⓡ 🐕
🅿
Credit Cards [1][3]

SELECTED

GH [Q][Q][Q][Q] *Galaxie Private Hotel* 180 Banbury Road OX2 7BT ☎(0865) 515688

A popular, privately run commercial hotel is to be found in the Summertown area just north of the city, surrounded by shops ▶

COMBERMERE HOUSE
11 Polstead Road, Oxford OX2 6TW
Telephone: Oxford (01865) 56971

Family run guest-house in quiet tree-lined road off Woodstock Road, North Oxford, 15 minutes walk from City Centre and Colleges. Frequent bus services. Parking. All rooms have television, tea and coffee-making facilities and are en suite. Full English breakfast. Open all year. Central heating. All major credit cards accepted.

COURTFIELD PRIVATE HOTEL

367 Iffley Road, Oxford OX4 4DP
Tel: Oxford (01865) 242991

An individually designed house situated in tree-lined road; with modern spacious bedrooms, majority are **en suite.** Close to picturesque Iffley Village and River Thames yet easily accessible to Oxford's historic city centre and Colleges.

PRIVATE CAR PARK

25 LONDON ROAD, OXFORD
Tel: (01865) 69944

THE DIAL is just 1.5 miles from the city centre. There is off-street parking, and for the pedestrian, bus stops only a few steps from the door.

All bedrooms have private facilities, colour TV and beverages. Smoking in guest lounge only. The proprietors, in providing the atmosphere of an elegant half-timbered house, offer a high standard of comfort to guests who prefer friendly personal service and attention.

AA   Kindly note we do not
QQQQ   have facilities for
Selected children under 6 years.

Galaxie Private Hotel
180 BANBURY ROAD, OXFORD
Telephone: (01865) 515688
Fax: (01865) 56824

This is a small, select, family hotel, recently refurbished to a very high standard. It is situated 1 mile from the City Centre. All 30 bedrooms are fully equipped with colour TV, telephone and the majority have private facilities. There is ample car parking. Terms include full English breakfast.

The hotel is open all year round and enjoys international patronage.

AA QQQQ

313

and restaurants. Recent refurbishment has added an attractive reception area and lounge/dining room housed in a modern conservatory. The bedrooms have also received attention and have furnishings of an equivalent standard, with excellent facilities.

34rm(21⇔↑) (3fb) CTV in all bedrooms T
lift ▥ CTV
Credit Cards [1] [3]

GH [Q][Q] **Green Gables** 326 Abingdon Road OX1 4TE (on A4144)
☎(0865) 725870 FAX (0865) 725870
Closed 24-28 Dec
Situated about a mile south of the city centre, this Edwardian house is set in a mature garden and offers friendly service, personally supervised by the owner. The accommodation is comfortable, with some good-sized bedrooms, and one on the ground floor suitable for disabled visitors.

9rm(1⇔5↑) (3fb) ⊁ in dining room ⊁ in lounges CTV in all bedrooms ⓡ ⋇ (ex guide dogs) sB&B£23-£25 sB&B⇔↑£27-£32 dB&B£36 dB&B⇔↑£42-£46
▥
Credit Cards [1] [3]

GH [Q][Q][Q] **Highfield** 91 Rose Hill OX4 4HT (on A4158)
☎(0865) 774083 & 718524
Doreen and Bertram Edwards provide a warm welcome at their smart and very well run guesthouse, which is just off the ring road to the east of the city. The bright and freshly decorated dining room is appealing, and there is a pleasant lounge with thick rugs and comfortable sofas. The modern bedrooms are of a high standard, making this a popular choice with the local business community.

7rm(5↑) (2fb) ⊁ in 3 bedrooms ⊁ in dining room ⊁ in lounges CTV in all bedrooms ⓡ ⋇ ⋇ sB&B£18-£20 dB&B£32-£36 dB&B↑£38-£45 WB&B£126-£154
▥ CTV
Credit Cards [1] [3]

GH [Q][Q][Q] **Homelea** 356 Abingdon Road OX1 4TQ
☎(0865) 245150
Peggy and John Hogan have created a warm and welcoming home here where generally spacious bedrooms are especially comfortable because of the excellent quality of the beds. Homelea is obviously placed on Abingdon Road and has its own parking and small garden.

6↑ (3fb) ⊁ in 2 bedrooms CTV in all bedrooms ⓡ ⋇ (ex guide dogs) ⋇ sB&B£20-£25 dB&B↑£38-£40
▥ CTV
ⓔ

GH [Q][Q][Q][Q] **Marlborough House** 321 Woodstock Road
OX2 7NY ☎(0865) 311321 FAX (0865) 515329
Closed 23 Dec-2 Jan
No meals are served to guests at this purpose-built hotel where every room has its own 'mini-kitchen' with fridge, microwave, kettle and sink. Pre-packed continental style breakfasts are delivered to the rooms in the evening which guests make up in the morning, and there are restaurants in the neighbourhood for evening meals. Drinks are available from Reception, and free tea and coffee in the Coffee Lounge. There is also concessionary membership at reasonable rates at a local Leisure Centre. Smoking in bedrooms is discouraged.

12⇔↑ (2fb) ⊁ in bedrooms CTV in all bedrooms ⓡ T ⋇
sB&B⇔↑fr£53 dB&B⇔↑fr£63
Lic ▥ nc8yrs concessionary membership of nearby leisure club
Credit Cards [1] [3] ⓔ

GH [Q][Q][Q] **Pickwicks** 17 London Road, Headington OX3 7SP
☎(0865) 750487 FAX (0865) 742208
Two Victorian properties have been joined by a lounge/bar area to create this family-run hotel conveniently situated about one and a half miles from the city centre. Bedrooms vary in size, but all are well equipped and the majority have en suite facilities; ground-floor rooms are available. A set evening meal is served by arrangement and, again by arrangement, cars may be left in the car park. Frequent buses pass the hotel.

13rm(3⇔6↑) (3fb) CTV in all bedrooms ⓡ T LDO 1pm
Lic ▥ CTV
Credit Cards [1] [2] [3] [5]

GH [Q][Q][Q] **Pine Castle Hotel** 290 Iffley Road OX4 4AE
☎(0865) 241497 & 728887
Closed Xmas
A small Edwardian semidetached house on the Iffley road, just east of the city, stands in a popular central location. The four attractive cottage-style bedrooms feature carefully chosen coordinating decor and furnishings, with pretty patchwork quilts complementing the pine furniture. Public rooms are well decorated and comfortably furnished, and include a small licensed bar and reception desk.

8rm(4⇔↑) (2fb) ⊁ in 4 bedrooms ⊁ in dining room CTV in all bedrooms ⓡ T ⋇ (ex guide dogs) ⋇ dB&B£38-£44 dB&B⇔↑£48-£60 WB&Bfr£124 LDO 8.30am
Lic ▥ CTV
Credit Cards [1] [3] ⓔ

GH [Q][Q][Q][Q] **Tilbury Lodge Private Hotel** 5 Tilbury Lane, Eynsham Road, Botley OX2 9NB (off the B4044)
☎(0865) 862138 FAX (0865) 863700
Just two miles west of the city centre, this guesthouse in a residential lane is run by Mr and Mrs Trafford and offers bed and breakfast accommodation only. Bright modern bedrooms are very well equipped and include extras like telephones and hair dryers. One bedroom features a romantic four-poster bed, and there is a ground floor room for guests unable to use the stairs. A spa bath is available for guests' use between 11am and 6pm. Breakfast is served at 8.30am in the informal breakfast room, and guests can relax in the well appointed lounge which is well stocked with tourist information.

9⇔↑ (2fb) ⊁ in dining room ⊁ in lounges CTV in all bedrooms ⓡ T ⋇ sB&B⇔↑£35-£40 dB&B⇔↑£50-£61
▥ CTV jacuzzi
Credit Cards [1] [3] ⓔ

GH [Q][Q][Q] **Westwood Country Hotel** Hinksey Hill Top
OX1 5BG (MIN) ☎(0865) 735408 FAX (0865) 736536
Closed 22 Dec-9 Jan
Situated on top of Hinksey Hill, this small family-run hotel stands in four acres of lovely woodland, now designated a nature reserve Bedrooms are mostly spacious and well equipped with modern facilities. The restaurant and bar area have recently been refurbished: the bar now has a full licence, allowing less restricted drinking hours. There is a good range of leisure facilities, including a jacuzzi, sauna and mini-gym.

22⇔↑ (5fb) ⊁ in dining room CTV in all bedrooms ⓡ T ⋇ (ex guide dogs) sB&B⇔↑£55-£60 dB&B⇔↑£80-£99 WBDifr£266 LDO 8pm
Lic ▥ CTV ⊷ sauna jacuzzi wildlife nature garden & trail
Credit Cards [1] [2] [3] [5] ⓔ

GH [Q][Q] **White House** 315 Iffley Road OX4 4AG
☎(0865) 244524 FAX (0865) 244524
8rm(5⇔↑) (1fb) ⊁ in bedrooms ⊁ in dining room CTV in all bedrooms ⓡ sB&B£20-£30 sB&B⇔↑£30-£40 dB&B£30-£40

dB&B🛁🚿£40-£55 LDO 8pm
▥ CTV
Credit Cards [1][2][3][£]

GH [Q][Q][Q] ***Willow Reaches Hotel*** 1 Wytham Street OX1 4SU
☎(0865) 721545 FAX (0865) 251139

A small hotel tucked away in a quiet cul-de-sac off the Abingdon road, within easy walking distance of the city centre. The modern comfortable bedrooms are well equipped, with clock radios and satellite TV, and some have private bathrooms. A comfortable lounge with TV and a bar adjoins the dining room. A good choice is offered at breakfast, and both English and Indian meals are available at dinner, which is served by arrangement. There is adequate parking, some covered.

9rm(3🛁6🚿) (1fb) CTV in all bedrooms [R] ✱ LDO 6pm
Lic ▥ CTV
Credit Cards [1][2][3][5]
See advertisement on p.317.

OXHILL Warwickshire Map **04** SP34

SELECTED

FH [Q][Q][Q][Q] Mrs S Hutsby **Nolands Farm** *(SP312470)*
CV35 0RJ (1m E of Pillarton Priors on A422)
☎Kineton(0926) 640309 FAX (0926) 641662
Closed 15-30 Dec

This farm is situated in a tranquil valley. Guest rooms are located in carefully restored stables, totally separate from the owner's accommodation. The comfortable bedrooms are generally spacious: two have four-poster beds and they offer a good range of facilities including private bathrooms. Public areas include a cosy dining room and a small comfortable bar

▶

Green Gables

326 Abingdon Road, Oxford
Telephone: Oxford (01865) 725870

- Characterful, secluded and detached Edwardian house, set in mature gardens.
- Bright, spacious rooms with TV and tea/coffee making facilities. The majority have en suite shower and W.C. One room is on the ground floor, with facilities for the disabled.
- Off street, secluded parking is guaranteed.
- Full English breakfast with real coffee.
- One mile to the first of the colleges. Bus stop 20 yds away with buses every 10 minutes.
- On the A4144, ½ mile from the ring road. Easy access, therefore, to sights and countryside, including Blenheim, the Cotswolds, Stratford upon Avon.

VISA Access

TILBURY LODGE

PRIVATE HOTEL

TEL: (01865) 862138
FAX: (01865) 863700

Tilbury Lodge is situated in a quiet country lane just two miles west of the city centre and one mile from the railway station. Good bus service available. Botley shopping centre is a few minutes walk away with restaurants, shops, banks, pubs etc.

All rooms en suite with direct dial telephone colour TV, radio, hair dryer and tea/coffee facilities. Jacuzzi. Four poster. Ground floor bedrooms. Central heating, double glazing. Ample parking.

TILBURY LODGE PRIVATE HOTEL
5 TILBURY LANE, EYNSHAM ROAD,
BOTLEY, OXFORD OX2 9NB

Oxford Oxfordshire
Westwood Country Hotel
E.T.B. ♛♛♛

MINOTELS Gt Britain

Hinksey Hill Top, OX1 5BG
Tel: **Oxford (01865) 735408**
Fax: **(01865) 736536**
Proprietor: **Mr and Mrs A.J. and M. Parker**

WINNER OF DAILY MAIL HOTEL AWARD 1991

A family run hotel with 23 bedrooms, all with private facilities, radio, intercom, colour TV, hairdryer, video and tea/coffee making facilities. Three acres of gardens and woodlands. Excellent food. Intimate bar. For Hotel guests, jacuzzi, sauna and mini gym available. Catering for up to 130 for weddings and 60 for conferences.

area. There is a well stocked trout lake and clay pigeon shooting and riding can be arranged nearby.
Annexe 9rm(2⇌7↱) (2fb) ⊬ in dining room ⊬ in 1 lounge CTV in all bedrooms Ⓡ ✗ (ex guide dogs) sB&B⇌↱fr£20 dB&B⇌↱fr£30
Lic ▥ nc7yrs ⚲ clay pigeon shooting bicycle hire 200 acres arable
Credit Cards [1][3] £
See advertisement under STRATFORD-UPON-AVON

PADSTOW Cornwall & Isles of Scilly — Map **02** SW97

See also Little Petherick, St Merryn and Trevone

GH QQ ***Alexandra*** 30 Dennis Road PL28 8DE ☎(0841) 532503
Etr-Oct
The Alexandra overlooks the beautiful Camel Estuary from an elevated, quiet residential position. Built in 1906, this fine Victorian house is the family home of proprietor Maureen Williams and offers a relaxing, informal atmosphere. The bedrooms are furnished in a traditional style with a TV and tea/coffee making facilities provided. A comfortable sitting room augments a small dining room, and unrestricted parking is available.
6rm (2fb) CTV in all bedrooms Ⓡ ✗ LDO noon
nc5yrs

PAIGNTON Devon — Map **03** SX86

GH QQQ ***Beresford*** 5 Adelphi Road TQ4 6AW
☎(0803) 551560
Situated between the town centre, seafront and Festival Hall, this family run guest house is within walking distance of all the major local attractions. The pleasantly decorated bedrooms all have private shower rooms, and breakfast and dinner are available in the dining room which has a small informal bar area. There is also a comfortable sitting room.
8↱ (1fb) CTV in all bedrooms Ⓡ ✗ LDO 10am
Lic ▥ CTV

GH QQQ Channel View Hotel 8 Marine Parade TQ3 2NU ☎(0803) 522432 FAX (0803) 522323
This guest house is located in a quiet cul-de-sac on the esplanade, not far from the centre of town. Owned by Margaret and David Teague for over 14 years, the friendly, cheerful atmosphere draws guests back time after time. Bedrooms are light and airy, some rooms having a sea view, and all are well equipped; there is a ground-floor room available. The front-facing dining room with a bar has superb sea views, and there is a patio for guests.
12⇌↱ (3fb) CTV in all bedrooms Ⓡ ✗ (ex guide dogs) sB&B⇌↱£15-£30 dB&B⇌↱£30-£60 WBDi£95-£210 LDO noon
Lic ▥ CTV
Credit Cards [1][3] £

GH QQ Cherra Hotel 15 Roundham Road TQ4 6DN
☎(0803) 550723
Mar-Nov
A small private hotel in a quiet residential area a short distance from the town centre, beaches and harbour. The bedrooms are comfortable though some are compact; all have TV. A colourful garden surrounds the property.
14rm(9↱) (7fb) ⊬ in dining room CTV in all bedrooms Ⓡ sB&B£11-£16 sB&B↱£14-£20 dB&B£22-£32 dB&B↱£28-£40 WB&B£75-£110 WBDi£100-£135 LDO 5.30pm
Lic ▥ CTV
£

GH QQQ Clennon Valley Hotel 1 Clennon Rise TQ4 5HG
☎(0803) 550304 FAX (0803) 552197
10rm(1⇌7↱) (2fb) ⊬ in bedrooms ⊬ in lounges CTV in all bedrooms Ⓡ **T** ✗ (ex guide dogs) sB&B£19 sB&B⇌↱£19 dB&B⇌↱£38 WB&Bfr£125 WBDifr£160 LDO 10am
Lic ▥ CTV
Credit Cards [1][3] £

GH QQQ ***Danethorpe Hotel*** 23 St Andrews Road TQ4 6HA
☎(0803) 551251
Away from the hustle and bustle of town but only a short walk to the seafront and harbour, this family-run hotel continues to be steadily upgraded and improved. The bedrooms are a little compact but each is very nicely equipped; most of them have en suite showers and all are neatly presented with pretty coordinated decor. The public areas are comfortable and include a lively, popular bar, a cosy TV lounge and a more spacious lounge. A choice of evening meal is offered from either the table d'hôte or small à la carte menu and proprietors Mr and Mrs Chillcott are amiable, cheery hosts.
10rm(6↱) (2fb) CTV in all bedrooms Ⓡ ✗
Lic ▥
Credit Cards [1][2][3]

GH QQQ Oldway Links Hotel 21 Southfield Road TQ3 2LZ
☎(0803) 559332 FAX (0803) 526071
13rm(11⇌↱) (2fb)CTV in all bedrooms Ⓡ ✗ (ex guide dogs) ✳ sB&B⇌↱£23.25-£25.25 dB&B£42-£45 dB&B⇌↱£46.50-£51 WB&B£141-£151.50 WBDi£198-£216 LDO 7.30pm
Lic ▥ CTV ⛳
Credit Cards [1][3]

GH QQQ Redcliffe Lodge Hotel 1 Marine Drive TQ3 2NL
☎(0803) 551394
Apr-mid Nov
This hotel enjoys a corner plot on Marine Drive, beside the safe, sandy beach and green, and a level walk to the town centre, pier and Festival Theatre. The bedrooms are all en suite with colour TV, and the lounge and dining room are cosy and comfortable. The menu offers simple dishes, and a happy, relaxed atmosphere is created by the friendly resident proprietors.
17rm(10⇌7↱) (2fb) ⊬ in dining room CTV in all bedrooms Ⓡ ✗ ✳ sB&B⇌↱£20-£40 dB&B⇌↱£40-£50 WBDi£180-£230 LDO 6.30pm
Lic ▥ CTV
Credit Cards [1][3]

GH QQ ***Hotel Retreat*** 43 Marine Drive TQ3 2NS
☎(0803) 550596
Etr-Sep
This comfortable private hotel is family owned and set in pleasant grounds in a secluded position on the seafront. The accommodation is comfortable with cosy, bright and well equipped bedrooms.
13rm(5⇌) (1fb) CTV in all bedrooms Ⓡ LDO 6pm
Lic CTV
Credit Cards [1][3]

GH QQQ St Weonard's Private Hotel 12 Kernou Road TQ4 6BA ☎(0803) 558842
A small, well maintained terraced house is close to the seafront, the shops and the Festival Hall. Bedrooms are comfortable and there is a television lounge and a dining room where snacks are available between breakfast and supper.
8rm(5↱) (2fb) Ⓡ ✗ ✳ sB&B£13-£15 sB&B↱£16-£18 dB&B£26-£30 dB&B↱£32-£36 WB&B£85-£100 WBDi£134-£149 LDO 3.30pm
Lic CTV
Credit Cards [1][3]

GH QQQ Sattva Hotel 29 Esplanade TQ4 6BL
☎(0803) 557820
Mar-Oct
Terry and Margaret Nadin welcome guests to their seafront hotel just a level two-minute walk to the beach. Virtually all the bedrooms are en suite, some have private balconies and a lift is provided to all floors. Entertainment is provided in the bar-lounge during the season, and the atmosphere is lively.

20⇥ (2fb) ⊁ in dining room CTV in all bedrooms Ⓡ 🔥
B&B⇥£18-£25 dB&B⇥£36-£50 WBDi£165-£198 LDO
5pm
.ic lift ⬛ CTV
Credit Cards 1 3

GH QQQ **The Sealawn Hotel** Sea Front, 20 Esplanade Rd
TQ4 6BE ☎(0803) 559031
A semidetached Victorian house stands on the seafront close to the
pier. Bedrooms are well equipped, some having stunning views.
Home-cooked dinner is available and there is a large lounge where
an organist plays on some evenings.
2rm(6⇥6⋒) (3fb) ⊁ in dining room CTV in all bedrooms Ⓡ T
🔥 sB&B⇥£16-£27 dB&B⇥£32-£44 WB&B£105-£182
WBDi£147-£224 LDO 5.30pm
.ic ⬛ CTV ◔ solarium
©

GH QQQ **Sea Verge Hotel** Marine Drive, Preston TQ3 2NJ
☎(0803) 557795
Closed 3wks Jan
Situated on Preston Green, this modern hotel is a stone's throw
from the beach, with plenty of safe bathing. Bedroom are nicely
decorated, well equipped and comfortable; three rooms benefit
from balconies, and a ground-floor room is available. Jack and
Pauline Birchall with their family provide friendly service, and a
choice of fresh, home-made courses is offered at dinner, which is
ordered at breakfast time.
1rm(9⋒) (2fb) ⊁ in dining room CTV in all bedrooms Ⓡ 🔥 ✳
B&B£32 dB&BⱤ£32-£38 WB&B£112-£133 WBDi£162-£184
LDO 6pm
.ic ⬛ CTV nc9yrs
Credit Cards 1 3 ©

Redcliffe Lodge

**1 Marine Drive,
Paignton TQ3 2NJ**
Reception (01803) 551394
Visitors (01803) 525643

RIGHT BY THE BEACH . . . The Hotel is situated
in one of Paignton's finest sea front positions in its
own grounds with an easy level walk to most
facilities including two safe sandy beaches,
harbour, theatre, shops and town centre.

DINE IN STYLE . . . Sea air sharpens appetites
remarkably. Meals in our sunny dining room
overlooking the sea front are to be lingered over
and savoured. We are proud of our cuisine, the
result of careful thought to give pleasure, variety
and interest.

All principal rooms and most of the bedrooms have
extensive seaviews. All bedrooms en-suite with
colour TV, radio and intercom to reception, tea
making facilities.

Ground floor bedrooms available. Hotel is heated
throughout making it ideal for late holidays, mid-
week bookings accepted. Large car park – perfect
touring centre. Colour brochure on request from
resident proprietors Allan & Hilary Carr.

Willow Reaches Hotel
1 Wytham St., Oxford
Tel: Oxford (01865) 721545 Fax: (01865) 251139

👑 👑 👑
English Tourist Board Commended

A private hotel with a high standard of
comfort, in a quiet location just a mile
south of Oxford city centre.

The hotel is near a fishing lake and a
public park with swimming pools and
children's boating lake.

Every bedroom has a direct dial
telephone, colour television, radio and
tea/coffee-making facility; all bathrooms
en suite. Bridal suite.

Central Heating throughout. Residents'
lounge with teletext TV. Bar, restaurant
serving English and Indian meals. A large
garden. Children welcome.

Parking facilities.

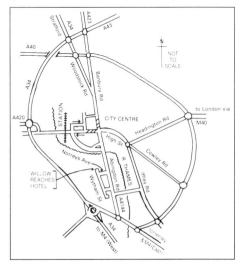

GH 🇶🇶 **Toad Hall** 49 Dartmouth Road TQ4 5AE
☎(0803) 558638
Built in the late 19th century from Devon sandstone, this semidetached house is within walking distance of Paignton Sands. Not called Toad Hall for nothing, those familiar with Kenneth Grahame's 'Wind in the Willows' will feel at home here. Attractive French windows lead from the drawing room to a covered verandah and home-cooked traditional fare with house specialities is served in the dining room.
5rm(2ⁿ) (2fb) ⊬ in dining room ⊁ sB&B£18 dB&B£30 dB&B£37 WB&B£100 WBDi£156 LDO 10am
Lic ▥ CTV nc10yrs
£

GH 🇶🇶🇶 **Torbay Sands Hotel** 16 Marine Parade, Preston Sea Front TQ3 2NU ☎(0803) 525568
Vera and Eddie Hennequin have created a hospitable atmosphere at their modern hotel which has panoramic views of the bay. The bright, cosy bedrooms are complemented by comfortable and tasteful public rooms.
13rm(11ⁿ) (4fb) ⊬ in dining room CTV in all bedrooms ® ✳ sB&Bfr£12.50 sB&B£12.50-£17 dB&B£25-£34 WB&B£90-£100 WBDi£120-£150
Lic ▥ CTV
Credit Cards ① ③ £

GH 🇶🇶🇶 **Waterleat House** 22 Waterleat Road TQ3 3UQ
☎(0803) 550001 FAX (0803) 550001
A Spanish-style villa is situated in an elevated position overlooking Paignton Zoo, away from the hustle and bustle of the town. Bedrooms are all well equipped, and most have private bathrooms. A small bar lounge is available for guests, and evening bar meals are served until 9.30pm.
6⇔ⁿ (1fb) ⊬ in dining room CTV in 5 bedrooms ® ⊁ (ex guide dogs) ✳ sB&B£14-£16 sB&B£25-£27.50 dB&B£36-£40 WB&B£108-£120 LDO 9.30pm
Lic ▥ ◐(hard)∪
£

PARKHAM Devon   Map 02 SS32

PREMIER SELECTED
GH 🇶🇶🇶🇶🇶 **The Old Rectory** EX39 5PL
☎Horns Cross(0237) 451443
Closed 11 Dec-14 Jan
Situated in the quiet village of Parkham near Horns Cross, this extended Georgian house has been restored by Jean and Jack Langton who treat their guests as family friends. Bedrooms are spacious and beautifully decorated, with many personal touches. Each has either an en suite or private bathroom. Deep, comfortable sofas furnish the drawing room, which is brightened by displays of ornaments, pictures and fresh flowers. Jean Langton is a talented cook and our inspector praised highly a meal which began with a creamed mushroom tartlet with brandy sauce, continued with local venison accompanied by excellent vegetables, and finished with a selection of delicious 'melt in the mouth' desserts.
3rm(2⇔ⁿ) ⊬ ⊁ (ex guide dogs) sB&B£50-£55 dB&B£70-£78 WB&B£220.50-£245 WBDi£395.50-£420 LDO 6pm
Lic ▥ CTV nc12yrs
£

PARKMILL (NEAR SWANSEA) West Glamorgan
                                                  Map 02 SS58

FH 🇶🇶 Mrs O Edwards *Parc-le-Breos House* (*SS529896*)
SA3 2HA ☎Swansea(0792) 371636
Formerly the shooting lodge of Lord Swansea, this 19th-century house, deep in the Gower, provides family and school party country holidays. It has full stables and riding on site. Mr and Mrs Edwards offer Welsh hospitality and friendly service.
10 ⊁ (ex guide dogs)
▥ CTV ∪ snooker 55 acres mixed

PATELEY BRIDGE North Yorkshire   Map 07 SE16

FH 🇶🇶 Mrs C E Nelson **Nidderdale Lodge** (*SE183654*)
Felbeck HG3 5DR ☎Harrogate(0423) 711677
Etr-Oct
Part of a working farm, this large bungalow is in an elevated position overlooking beautiful Nidderdale. The bedrooms are brightly decorated and comfortably furnished. There is a spacious guests' lounge with TV and a good sized breakfast room.
3rm(1⇔ⁿ) (1fb) ® ⊁ (ex guide dogs) ✳ sB&Bfr£18 dB&Bfr£30 dB&B⇔ⁿfr£36
▥ CTV 30 acres mixed
£

PATRICK BROMPTON North Yorkshire   Map 08 SE29

SELECTED

GH 🇶🇶🇶🇶 **Elmfield House** Arrathorne DL8 1NE (2m N unclass towards Catterick Camp) ☎Bedale(0677) 450558 FAX (0677) 450557
This large and attractive house enjoys delightful all-round views of open countryside from a setting in carefully tended gardens complete with a well stocked pond. Furnished along modern lines, it offers thoughtfully equipped bedrooms (including two on the ground floor which are suitable for disabled persons) and a comfortable, spacious dining room in which to enjoy quality home-cooked meals. Guests also have the use of a games room and solarium.
9rm(4⇔5ⁿ) (2fb) ⊬ in dining room CTV in all bedrooms ® T ⊁ (ex guide dogs) sB&B⇔ⁿ£27-£29.50 dB&B⇔ⁿ£39-£44 WB&B£129-£206 WBDi£217-£280 LDO before noon
Lic ▥ ◢ solarium
Credit Cards ③ £

FH 🇶🇶🇶 Mrs P Knox **Mill Close** (*SE232922*) DL8 1JY (leave A684 at Crakehall turning right to Catterick and Hackforth. After 1m turn first left, first farm on right) ☎(0677) 450257 FAX (0677) 450585
Mar-Nov
Dating in part from the 16th century, this attractive farmhouse is i a delightful rural setting. The two guest bedrooms are spacious and well furnished, and each has its own bath or shower room across the landing. A cosy lounge is provided and breakfast is served in the pleasant dining room.
2⇔ⁿ (1fb) ⊬ in bedrooms ® ⊁ sB&B⇔ⁿ£20 dB&B⇔ⁿ£34 WB&B£119 WBDi£182 LDO 9am
▥ CTV 230 acres arable/beef
£

PAWLETT Somerset   Map 03 ST2

FH 🇶🇶🇶 Mrs Worgan **Brickyard** (*ST298421*) River Road TA6 4SE ☎Puriton(0278) 683381
Over 450 years old, and recently modernised, this attractive farmhouse is situated down a long unmade road within a mile of Pawlett village, close to junctions 23 and 22 of the M5. Evening meals, with plenty of simple choices, are available and there is a cosy lounge with a small dispense bar.

3rm (1fb) ⚹ in bedrooms ® ➤ ⚹ sB&B£16-£18 dB&B£35-£37
WB&B£112-£126 WBDi£154-£168 LDO 6pm
Lic ▥ CTV ◢ 2 acres non working
£

PEEBLES Borders *Peebleshire*　　　　　　　Map **11** NT24

GH Q̲Q̲Q̲ **Whitestone House** Innerleithen Road EH45 8BD (on
A72, 100yds W of junct with A703) ☎(0721) 720337
Standing in its own garden on the eastern approach to the town,
and enjoying fine views of the hills, this stone-built former manse
offers good bed and breakfast accommodation in a friendly
atmosphere. The comfortable bedrooms are mostly in traditional
style, and hearty breakfasts are served in the lounge/breakfast
room.
5rm (1fb) ⚹ in dining room ® ➤ (ex guide dogs) ⚹ sB&B£16-
£16.50 dB&B£29-£30
▥ CTV
£

SELECTED

FH Q̲Q̲Q̲Q̲ Mrs S Goldstraw **Venlaw Farm** EH45 8QG
☎(0721) 722040
Apr-Oct
This modern bungalow occupies a quiet hillside position, but
is less than a mile from the Edinburgh road on the northern
edge of the town. There is a very comfortable lounge leading
onto a patio, and breakfast is taken around one table in the
breakfast room. Bedrooms are nicely decorated.
3rm(2⇌↑) (1fb) ⚹ ® ➤ sB&B£20 dB&B£28
dB&B⇌↑£32 WB&B£112
▥ CTV 100 acres beef sheep
Credit Cards ①②③

GH Q̲Q̲Q̲ Mrs J M Haydock **Winkston** *(NT244433)* Edinburgh
Road EH45 8PH ☎(0721) 721264
Etr-Oct
Situated in an elevated position beside the A703, 1.5 miles north
of the town, this listed Georgian farmhouse offers cosy, well
maintained accommodation and a friendly atmosphere. Bedrooms
are prettily decorated, and furnished with good beds. There is also
a comfortable lounge and a neat dining room.
3rm ⚹ in bedrooms ⚹ in dining room ® ➤ (ex guide dogs) ⚹
sB&B£30-£32
▥ CTV 40 acres sheep

PEMBROKE Dyfed　　　　　　　　　　　Map **02** SM90

SELECTED

FH Q̲Q̲Q̲Q̲ Mrs S Lewis **Poyerston** *(SM027025)*
Cosheston SA72 4SJ ☎(0646) 651347
2⇌↑ (1fb) ⚹ ® ➤ (ex guide dogs) ⚹ dB&B⇌↑£33-£37
WB&B£115.50-£129.50 WBDi£178.50-£219.50 LDO noon
▥ CTV nc4yrs 200 acres arable beef dairy
£

PENARTH South Glamorgan　　　　　　　Map **03** ST17

H Q̲Q̲ **Albany Hotel** 14 Victoria Road CF64 3EF
☎Cardiff(0222) 701598 & 701242 FAX (0222) 701598
This small, friendly, personally run guesthouse is just a short walk
from the town centre and railway station. The simply styled and
furnished bedrooms are well equipped with satellite TV, direct-
dial telephones and private bathrooms. Public rooms include a
comfortable lounge and cosy bar.
3rm(7⇌↑) (4fb) ⚹ in bedrooms CTV in all bedrooms ® T ⚹
sB&B£23.50 sB&B⇌↑£29.50 dB&B£35-£39.50 dB&B⇌↑£40-
£45 LDO 8.30pm

Lic ▥ CTV
Credit Cards ①②③ £
See advertisement under CARDIFF

PENMACHNO Gwynedd　　　　　　　　　Map **06** SH75

SELECTED

GH Q̲Q̲Q̲Q̲ **Penmachno Hall** LL24 0PU (turn off A5 2m S
of Betws-y-Coed on to B4406. Signposted at village)
☎(0690) 760207
Closed 21 Dec-14 Jan
Modwena and Ian Cutler took over this 19th-century rectory
just four years ago. It has since been transformed into an
elegant country guest house where a house-party atmosphere
is encouraged and guests dine together. All bedrooms have
modern facilities and mostly locally made furniture. Four
sitting rooms are available for guests, including a TV lounge,
library and conservatory. Modwena's cooking has already
achieved local acclaim and she sometimes organises
residential cookery courses. Art exhibitions are also held and
many works are displayed in the house for sale. The house is
set in large gardens, which extend to the river.
4rm(2⇌2↑) ⚹ in bedrooms ⚹ in dining room ⚹ in 1 lounge
➤ sB&B⇌↑£30 dB&B⇌↑£50 WBDi£235
Lic ▥ CTV
Credit Cards ③ £

PENRHYNDEUDRAETH Gwynedd　　　　　Map **06** SH63

FH Q̲Q̲ Mrs P Bayley **Y Wern** *(SH620421)* LLanfrothen
LL48 6LX (2m N off B4410) ☎(0766) 770556 FAX (0766) 770356
At the foot of the Moelwyn mountains, this attractive, creeper-clad
stone farmhouse dates back to the 17th century. The lounge has a
lovely inglenook fireplace with a wood-burning stove, and good,
honest food is served in the farmhouse kitchen/dining room.
Children are especially welcome, and there is a tumbling rocky
stream, ducks and other livestock to keep them amused.
5rm(2↑) (4fb) ® ➤ dB&B£30-£34 dB&B↑£36-£40 WB&B£95-
£114 WBDi£158-£177
▥ CTV 110 acres beef,sheep
£

PENRITH Cumbria　　　　　　　　　　Map **12** NY53

See also Penruddock & Newbiggin

GH Q̲Q̲Q̲ **Brandelhow** 1 Portland Place CA11 7QN (in town
centre) ☎(0768) 64470 due to change to 864470
Closed 24-26 Dec & 31 Dec
A friendly guest house, situated at the end of a Victorian terrace
just a short walk from the town centre, offers spacious bedrooms
made attractive by the use of co-ordinated fabrics and a
particularly comfortable lounge which echoes the Victorian theme;
there is also a small breakfast room at the rear.
6 (3fb) ⚹ in 2 bedrooms ⚹ in dining room CTV in all bedrooms
® ⚹ sB&B£16-£18 dB&B£30-£32 WB&B£101.50-£105
▥ CTV
£

GH Q̲Q̲Q̲ **Croft House** Newton Reigny CA11 0AY
☎(0768) 65435 due to change to 865435
Closed Xmas week
An attractive, Georgian Grade II listed property in its own grounds
and with lovely views from the back of the house, Croft House is
on the edge of Newton Reigny, three miles from Penrith. It is a no-
smoking establishment and has a country feel, with interestingly
shaped bedrooms and a comfortable lounge and conservatory with
a venerable vine.
3rm(2⇌↑) (1fb) ⚹ CTV in all bedrooms ® ➤ (ex guide dogs)

▶

✴ sB&B£18-£25 sB&B⇄♠£25-£30 dB&B£36 dB&B⇄♠£43 LDO day before
▥ CTV free membership to local Country Leisure Club

GH Ⓠ Ⓠ **Limes Country Hotel** Redhills, Stainton CA11 0DT (2m W A66 turn left immediately before Little Chef and follow road for 0.25 miles "The Limes" is on the right) ☎(0768) 63343 due to change to 863343
Surrounded by open fields and yet only a short distance from Penrith, this charming Victorian house provides a good standard of accommodation. There is a comfortable lounge, and service is very friendly. Leave the M6 at junction 40, turn left at the Little Chef and follow signs for the hotel.
6rm(1⇄5♠) (2fb) ✄ in dining room CTV in all bedrooms Ⓡ ⅄ (ex guide dogs) sB&B⇄♠£22-£24 dB&B⇄♠£36-£40 WB&B£115-£160 WBDi£180-£240 LDO 3pm
Lic ▥
Credit Cards 1 3 £

GH Ⓠ Ⓠ Ⓠ **Woodland House Hotel** Wordsworth Street CA11 7QY (at foot of Beacon Hill, close to Town Hall) ☎(0768) 64177 due to change to 864177 FAX (0768) 890152
This very pleasant small hotel, run by the Davies family, does not permit smoking anywhere in the building which is situated in a side road close to the town centre. Bedrooms are attractively decorated and have good facilities. Public areas include a cosy lounge with a bar and lots of wildlife books to read.
8⇄♠ (2fb) ✄ CTV in all bedrooms Ⓡ ⅄ sB&B⇄♠£23 dB&B⇄♠£39 WB&B£152 LDO 4.30pm
Lic ▥ CTV
£

PENRUDDOCK Cumbria   Map 12 NY42

SELECTED

FH Ⓠ Ⓠ Ⓠ Ⓠ Mrs S M Smith *Highgate* (NY444275) CA11 0SE (on the A66 Penrith/Keswick road) ☎Greystoke(07684) 83339
Conveniently situated near to junction 40 of the M6 this lovely old Cumbrian farmhouse contains a fascinating collection of Victoriana but also provides modern amenities. Mrs Smith offers a friendly welcome and cooks a satisfying Cumbrian breakfast.
3rm CTV in all bedrooms Ⓡ ⅄
▥ nc5yrs 400 acres mixed

PENRYN Cornwall & Isles of Scilly   Map 02 SW73

P R E M I E R 🏆 **S E L E C T E D**

GH Ⓠ Ⓠ Ⓠ Ⓠ Ⓠ **Prospect House** 1 Church Road TR10 8DA (on B3292 opposite Kessell's Volvo showroom do not follow town centre signs) ☎Falmouth(0326) 373198 FAX (0326) 373198
Barry Sheppard and Cliff Paul offer gracious living and a house-party atmosphere at their detached guest house dating from 1830. Many original features have been retained, including flagstone floors and open fires, and the comfortable bedrooms are furnished with antiques, not to mention such extras as chocolates and teddy bears. There is a pantry on the first floor, where guests can help themselves to tea, coffee, orange juice and chilled water.
3⇄♠ ✄ in dining room TV available Ⓡ sB&B⇄♠£36-£32

dB&B⇄♠£47-£52 WB&B£145-£160 WBDi£264-£279 LDO 10am
▥ CTV nc12yrs
£

PENSHURST Kent   Map 05 TQ54

P R E M I E R 🏆 **S E L E C T E D**

GH Ⓠ Ⓠ Ⓠ Ⓠ Ⓠ **Swale Cottage** Old Swaylands Lane, Off Poundsbridge Lane TN11 8AH (off A26 onto B2176 after 2.75m turn left onto Poundsbridge Lane) ☎(0892) 870738
In a superb and peaceful rural setting, this delightful guest house offers accommodation of a very high standard. The spacious, well equipped bedrooms are not only very comfortable, but are full of charm. The attractive lounge is relaxing, too, and all round the house are paintings by the owner, an accomplished artist. A traditional English breakfast is served in the elegant dining room.
3⇄♠ ✄ CTV in all bedrooms Ⓡ ⅄ sB&B⇄♠£32-£42 dB&B⇄♠£50-£58
▥ nc10yrs
£

PENYBONT Powys   Map 03 SO16

P R E M I E R 🏆 **S E L E C T E D**

GH Ⓠ Ⓠ Ⓠ Ⓠ Ⓠ **Ffaldau Country House & Restaurant** LD1 5UD (2m E A44) ☎(0597) 851421
Hospitality, comfort and good food are assured at this picturesque rural guesthouse with pretty gardens in the Radnor Hills. A listed cruck-built long house dating from 1500, it has timbered bedrooms which may not be

spacious, but are prettily decorated and furnished with assorted period pieces and an abundance of Victoriana. Our inspector particularly praised the first class beds and linen. There is one very comfortable small lounge on the first floor, squeezed beneath the beamed ceiling, and another with an open fire and a bar on the ground floor. Sylvia Knott's cooking is commendable and makes good use of own-grown and quality local produce. The freshly prepared dinners are served in the charming, flag-stoned dining room, again full of original Victorian objets d'art, and nicely set off with classical china, glassware and country embroidered napery.
3⇄♠ ✄ in bedrooms ✄ in dining room ✄ in 1 lounge CTV in 2 bedrooms Ⓡ ⅄ (ex guide dogs) ✴ dB&B⇄♠£40-£45 LDO 7.30pm
Lic ▥ CTV nc10yrs
Credit Cards 1 3 £

SELECTED

FH ⓆⓆ Mrs J Longley **Neuadd** *(SO091618)* LD1 5SW
(A44 from Kington/Rhayader to Penybont and take 1st left
after Severn Arms, then 1st right and straight on along 'no
through road') ☎(0597) 822571
Feb-Nov
3rm(1⇌2♪) (3fb) ⊁ in bedrooms Ⓡ ✗ (ex guide dogs) ✱
dB&B⇌♪£35 WB&B£110 WBDi£155 LDO noon
▥ CTV nc12yrs ✔ 92 acres sheep

PENZANCE Cornwall & Isles of Scilly　　Map **02** SW43

See also St Hilary

GH ⒬⒬⒬ **Blue Seas Hotel** 13 Regent Terrace TR18 4DW
☎(0736) 64744 FAX (0736) 330701
An early Victorian terrace house overlooking the Promenade.
Many of the bedrooms have sea views and are simply decorated.
There is a large lounge and a cheerful dining room. The
Davenports provide a warm welcome and home-cooked meals,
including freshly baked bread.
10⇌♪ (3fb) ⊁ in bedrooms ⊁ in dining room CTV in all
bedrooms Ⓡ ✗ ✱ sB&B⇌♪fr£17.50 dB&B⇌♪fr£35
WB&Bfr£245 WBDifr£392 LDO 6.30pm
Lic ▥ CTV nc5yrs
Credit Cards ① ③ ⓔ

GH ⒬⒬⒬ **Camilla Hotel** Regent Terrace TR18 4DW (take
seafront road to Promenade, Regent Terrace is at eastern end)
☎(0736) 63771
Closed Xmas
Forming part of a Regency terrace, the Camilla Hotel is in a quiet
position overlooking the seafront, and convenient for the town
centre and parks. The comfortable bedrooms are attractively
decorated and well equipped. Dinner is a set meal and special diets
can be catered for by prior arrangement.
8rm(1⇌3♪) (3fb) ⊁ in dining room ⊁ in 1 lounge CTV in all
bedrooms Ⓡ ✗ (ex guide dogs) ✱ sB&B£16.50-£19 dB&B£31-
£35 dB&B⇌♪£35-£40 WB&B£110-£125 WBDi£180-£195 LDO
noon
Lic ▥ CTV
Credit Cards ① ③ ⓔ

GH ⒬⒬⒬ **Carlton Private Hotel** Promenade TR18 4NW
☎(0736) 62081
mid Mar-mid Oct
There are uninterrupted views from all the rooms at the front out
across the beach to the sea and St Michael's Mount in the distance.
The lounge has some interesting pieces of furniture brought back
from Java and many original paintings. The dining room looks
over the small garden which is a blaze of colour in the summer
and has won several awards in Penzance. Bedrooms are simply
decorated and provide all modern comforts.
10rm(8♪) ⊁ in dining room ⊁ in lounges CTV in all bedrooms
Ⓡ ✗ (ex guide dogs) ✱ sB&Bfr£16.50 sB&B♪£20-£25
dB&Bfr£33 dB&B♪£36-£40 WB&B£115-£150
Lic CTV nc12yrs
ⓔ

SELECTED

GH Ⓠ⒬⒬⒬ **Chy-an-Mor** 15 Regent Terrace TR18 4DW
☎(0736) 63441
Closed Dec-Jan
Mr and Mrs Russell took over this charming Georgian hotel
overlooking the sea in the spring of 1993 and they have done
much to modernise the facilities but have also taken care to
respect the original character of the building. Bedrooms are of
a good size and attractively decorated. Lounge and dining

▶

Blue Seas Hotel

**Regent Terrace, Penzance
Cornwall TR18 4DW
Telephone: (01736) 64744
Fax: (01736) 330701**

Access　　　　　　　　　Visa

Blue Seas offers a high standard
of comfort and friendly service.
All bright attractive bedrooms are
en-suite with colour TV
central heating.
Tea making facilities. Crisp cotton
bed linen.
Set in a quiet terrace overlooking
the sea.
Ample private parking.
Bus, rail and boat to Isles of Scilly
within easy walking distance.

**Resident Proprietors:
Pat and Derek Davenport**

Camilla Hotel

**Regent Terrace,
Penzance,
Cornwall
TR18 4DW
Tel: Penzance
(01736) 63771**

Camilla is a delightful building of the Regency period
ideally situated in a quiet terrace overlooking the
seafront promenade within easy reach of the rail and
coach termini. The shopping centre, parks and
harbour departure for the Isles of Scilly are very close
at hand. The Hotel is licensed and offers private
parking, central heating, en suite facilities. There are
colour televisions, tea/coffee making facilities in all
bedrooms. Several European languages are spoken
by the resident proprietors Brian and Annette
Gooding.

B & B from £16.00　Evening meal optional

OPEN ALL YEAR

 Payment in European
currency accepted

room are inviting, with comfortable seating and furnished in keeping with the style of the house.

8♠ (1fb) ⊁ CTV in all bedrooms ⑧ 🛏 sB&B♠£18.50-£20 dB&B♠£37-£40 WB&B£129.50-£140 WBDi£217-£227.50 LDO breakfast
Lic ⬛ CTV nc10yrs
Credit Cards [1] [3]

📧 ✉ **GH** ⓠⓠⓠ **Dunedin** Alexandra Road TR18 4LZ (follow sea front along to mini roundabout, turn right into Alexandra road 500yds up on right) ☎(0736) 62652
Closed Xmas rs Jan-Etr
Situated on the tree-lined road not far from the town centre and the Promenade, this Victorian terrace house is larger than it appears. The bar/dining room is at garden level with polished tables and cheerful decor and bedrooms have all the usual facilities.

9rm(1⇄8♠) (4fb) ⊁ in dining room CTV in all bedrooms ⑧ sB&B⇄♠£12.50-£15 dB&B⇄♠£25-£30 WB&B£84-£99 LDO 5pm
Lic ⬛ CTV ⊬nc3yrs

GH ⓠⓠⓠ **Georgian House** 20 Chapel Street TR18 4AW
☎(0736) 65664
Closed Xmas rs Nov-Apr
Situated in the town centre, convenient for the seafront and the Isles of Scilly ferry, this family-run hotel provides comfortable, well equipped accommodation; as well as the bar with its nautical theme there is a reading lounge, and the dining room offers a varied menu. There is limited car parking behind the building.

12rm(4⇄2♠) (4fb) ⊁ in 2 bedrooms ⊁ in area of dining room CTV in all bedrooms ⑧ 🛏 (ex guide dogs) ✳ sB&Bfr£18.50 sB&B⇄♠fr£25 dB&Bfr£34 dB&B⇄♠fr£42 WB&B£110.50-£136.50 WBDi£180.50-£206.50 LDO 8pm
Lic ⬛ CTV
Credit Cards [1] [2] [3] ⓔ

GH ⓠⓠ **Kimberley House** 10 Morrab Road TR18 4EZ (take Promenade road, pass Harbour and turn right into Morrab Road) ☎(0736) 62727
Closed Dec
Set midway between town centre and seafront, this solid Cornish granite house provides accommodation in simply appointed bedrooms; less active guests should note that the stairs to the second floor are rather narrow. Dinner - served by arrangement - offers a choice of menu.

9rm (2fb) ⊁ in dining room CTV in all bedrooms ⑧ 🛏 (ex guide dogs) ✳ sB&B£13-£15 dB&B£26-£30 WB&B£86-£98 WBDi£140-£164 LDO 5pm
Lic ⬛ CTV nc5yrs
Credit Cards [1] [3]

GH ⓠⓠⓠ *Hotel Minalto* Alexandra Road TR18 4LZ
☎(0736) 62923
Standing close to the quieter end of the promenade, this spacious Victorian house forms the end of a terrace and offers very comfortable, well modernised accommodation. Public rooms include two lounges, one with a bar, and the house has a light and friendly atmosphere.

12rm(8♠) (2fb) CTV in all bedrooms ⑧ LDO 5.30pm
Lic CTV
Credit Cards [1] [3]

GH ⓠ **Mount Royal Hotel** Chyandour Cliff TR18 3LQ (on the old A30 entering Penzance) ☎(0736) 62233
Mar-Oct
Situated on the edge of the town overlooking Mounts Bay, this solid Victorian house offers modestly furnished bedrooms, a spacious dining room with period features and a simple lounge.

9rm(5⇄) (3fb) ⊁ in dining room CTV in 3 bedrooms ⑧ ✳ sB&B£17-£19 sB&B⇄£21-£25 dB&B£34-£38 dB&B⇄£42-£50

WB&B£105-£161
⬛ CTV
ⓔ

GH ⓠⓠⓠ **Penalva** Alexandra Road TR18 4LZ ☎(0736) 69060
A haven for non-smokers, this well modernised Victorian house situated within easy walking distance of seafront and town centre offers accommodation in attractively decorated and furnished bedrooms. Guests have the use of a spacious lounge, and traditionally cooked evening meals are available by arrangement.

5rm(4♠) (3fb) ⊁ CTV in all bedrooms ⑧ 🛏 ✳ sB&Bfr£10 sB&B♠£14 dB&Bfr£26 dB&B♠£32 WB&B£84-£104 WBDi£154-£174 LDO 6.30pm
⬛ CTV ⊬nc3yrs
ⓔ

GH ⓠⓠⓠ **Penmorvah Hotel** Alexandra Road TR18 4LZ
☎(0736) 63711
This personally managed hotel stands in a tree-lined road, conveniently positioned for both town centre and seafront. Simply furnished but well equipped bedrooms include one on the ground floor, a choice of menu is offered at both breakfast and dinner, and street parking is unrestricted.

8rm(4⇄4♠) (4fb) ⊁ in dining room CTV in all bedrooms ⑧ ✳ sB&B⇄♠£13-£20 dB&B⇄♠£26-£40 WB&B£85-£135 WBDi£135-£180 LDO 6pm
Lic ⬛
Credit Cards [1] [2] [3] ⓔ

📧 ✉ **GH** ⓠⓠⓠ **Trenant Private Hotel** Alexandra Road TR18 4LX (from A30 at Penzance Station follow road by harbour for about 1m, turn right into Alexandra Road) ☎(0736) 62005
Mar-Oct
A spacious double fronted Victorian mid-terrace house with comfortable public rooms stands in a tree-lined area within easy walking distance of both town centre and seafront. Dinner features plain, traditional Cornish home cooking, and bedrooms - some of them with stylish bed drapes - vary in size.

10rm(5♠) (3fb) ⊁ in dining room ⊁ in lounges CTV in all bedrooms ⑧ sB&B£14-£16 dB&B£28-£32 dB&B♠£36-£40 WB&B£90-£135 WBDi£145-£180 LDO noon
Lic ⬛ CTV ⊬nc5yrs

GH ⓠⓠ **Trevelyan Hotel** 16 Chapel Street TR18 4AW (turn left at the top of the town centre into Chapel St hotel halfway along on left) ☎(0736) 62494
Closed 24-26 Dec
This restored terraced house dates back to the 18th century and stands in the older part of the town close to the main shopping areas. Bedrooms are furnished in keeping, but have modern standards of comfort. Lounge and dining room (with its small bar) are attractively furnished.

9rm(4♠) (4fb) ⊁ in 4 bedrooms ⊁ in dining room CTV in 8 bedrooms ⑧ 🛏 (ex guide dogs) ✳ sB&B£14-£16 sB&B♠£14-£16 dB&B£28-£32 dB&B♠£30-£35 WB&B£90-£110 LDO am
Lic ⬛ CTV

📧 ✉ **GH** ⓠⓠⓠ **Trewella** 18 Mennaye Road TR18 4NG
☎(0736) 63818
Mar-Oct
Television sets have recently been installed in the neat bedrooms of this bright, cheerful guesthouse near the seafront and football ground. Proprietors proud of their reputation for traditional home-cooked food are happy to cater for special diets by prior arrangement. Smoking is not allowed in any public area, including the comfortable residents' lounge with bar.

8rm(4♠) (2fb) ⊁ in 1 bedrooms ⊁ in dining room ⊁ in lounges CTV in all bedrooms ⑧ ✳ sB&B£12-£13 dB&B£24-£26 dB&B♠£28-£30 WB&B£77-£84 WBDifr£122 LDO noon
Lic ⬛ CTV ⊬nc5yrs
ⓔ

SELECTED

FH Ⓠ Ⓠ Ⓠ Ⓠ Mrs P Lally **Rose Farm** *(SW446290)* Chyanhal, Buryas Bridge TR19 6AN (take A30 to Land's End, at Drift turn left (behind phone box), 0.75m down lane on left) ☎(0736) 731808
Closed 24-27 Dec
2♐ (1fb) ⊁ in bedrooms ⊁ in dining room CTV in all bedrooms Ⓡ ♉ (ex guide dogs) sB&Bⓕ£20-£25 dB&Bⓕ£35-£38
⊞ 23 acres beef

SELECTED

INN Ⓠ Ⓠ Ⓠ Ⓠ **The Yacht** The Promenade TR18 4AU ☎(0736) 62787
Situated on the seafront, this popular pub was built in the 1930s in an eye-catching design. Recent refurbishment has created a spacious lounge bar, where an extensive range of bar meals is served. The well equipped bedrooms are on the first floor, most having splendid sea views.
7⊸♐ (1fb) CTV in 6 bedrooms Ⓡ ♉ (ex guide dogs) LDO 9pm
⊞.
Credit Cards ① ② ③

PERRANUTHNOE Cornwall & Isles of Scilly   Map **02** SW52

GH Ⓠ Ⓠ Ⓠ **Ednovean House** TR20 9LZ (turn off A394 at Perran x-rds, then take first lane on the left and continue to very end of the lane) ☎Penzance(0736) 711071
Arthur and Val Compton are welcoming hosts at this small, relaxing hotel, quietly situated in an acre of lawns and gardens with magnificent views across Mounts Bay. A safe sandy beach is just a short walk away. Bedrooms are neat and tidy, the majority sharing the superb view. A varied table d'hôte menu and a vegetarian menu are offered each evening.
9rm(6♐) (1fb) ⊁ in dining room Ⓡ sB&B£18-£20 sB&Bⓕ£20-£22 dB&B£36-£38 dB&Bⓕ£40-£44 WB&B£114-£139 WBDi£199-£224 LDO 6pm
Lic ⊞ CTV nc7yrs 9 hole putting green
Credit Cards ① ② ③ Ⓔ

FH Ⓠ Ⓠ Ⓠ Mr & Mrs C Taylor **Ednovean** *(SW912299)* TR20 9LZ ☎Penzance(0736) 711883
Dating back to the 17th century, this granite barn has been lovingly converted to a comfortable home. It now comprises a small working farm of 22 acres and is situated above the village, with views to Mount's Bay and St Michael's Mount. Bedrooms are located on the ground floor, furnished and decorated in country style with pretty chintz fabrics and fresh fruit and flowers. Guests take breakfast around a communal table, and dinner is available by arrangement, but there are many small restaurants in the area.
3rm(1⊸) ⊁ CTV in 2 bedrooms Ⓡ ✻ sB&B£15-£30 dB&B£30-£32 dB&B⊸£40-£50 WB&B£210-£280 WBDi£280-£350
⊞ CTV nc9yrs 22 acres
Ⓔ

PERTH Tayside *Perthshire*   Map **11** NO12

See also Luncarty

SELECTED

GH Ⓠ Ⓠ Ⓠ Ⓠ **Ardfern House** 15 Pitcullen Crescent PH2 7HT ☎(0738) 622259
This fine Victorian house offers well proportioned bedrooms with extra touches including fresh fruit, flowers and magazines. Two of the single rooms have four foot wide beds.

Standards of housekeeping and maintenance are high, and guests are welcome to use the owners' elegant lounge. There is a small nine-hole putting green on the rear lawn of the immaculate garden.
3rm(1♐) CTV in all bedrooms Ⓡ LDO noon
⊞ CTV nc5yrs putting green

GH Ⓠ Ⓠ Ⓠ **Castleview** 166 Glasgow Rd PH2 0LY ☎(0738) 626415
Closed 25th Dec - Feb
Popular with both tourists and business people, this substantial detached Victorian house is set in its own gardens, midway between the by-pass and the town centre. Bedrooms are not large, but are attractively decorated, with pleasing soft furnishings. Dinner is available by arrangement, and is taken (as is breakfast) around a fine antique table in the elegant dining room.
3⊸♐ (1fb) ⊁ in 2 bedrooms ⊁ in dining room ⊁ in lounges CTV in all bedrooms Ⓡ ♉ (ex guide dogs) dB&B⊸♐£34-£36 LDO 5pm
⊞ sauna solarium

GH Ⓠ Ⓠ Ⓠ **Clark Kimberley** 57-59 Dunkeld Road PH1 5RP (0.5m N on A9) ☎(0738) 637406 FAX (0738) 643983
Two adjacent houses form this beautifully maintained guest house on the Inverness road on the northern side of the town, with convenient access to the city bypass. The bright, attractive bedrooms are furnished in a modern style, and public rooms comprise a lounge and two dining rooms - one in each house - both displaying an interesting collection of china teapots.
8rm(6♐) (4fb) ⊁ in 4 bedrooms ⊁ in dining room CTV in all bedrooms Ⓡ ♉ sB&B£16-£18 dB&Bⓕ£32-£36 WB&B£105-£119 ⊞ CTV
Ⓔ

'ENNYS'

St. Hilary, Penzance, Cornwall.

AA   **Tel: (01736) 740262**
SELECTED   **Mrs. N. J. White**

"CREAM OF CORNWALL"
Beautiful 16th century Manor Farm in idyllically peaceful surroundings. Candlelit suppers from our own produce. Comfort guaranteed in tastefully decorated surroundings. Overlooking walled garden, tennis court and heated swimming pool. Within easy reach of many lovely beaches and coves. Log fires. Bread baked daily. Three double bedrooms with *en suite* facilities, two with romantic 4-poster bed. Family suite available.
Bed & Breakfast from £20 per person.
Evening dinner from £15.00 per person.
Winter Farmhouse Breaks.
As featured in *Country Living*,
Sunday Times (1994)/Daily Telegraph
O/S Ref. SW 555328
Write or phone, brochure available.

GH Q Q Q **Clunie** 12 Pitcullen Crescent PH2 7HT (on A94 opposite side of river from town) ☎(0738) 623625
An attractively decorated semidetached Victorian house standing beside the A94 offers bedrooms which, though they vary in size, are well equipped (all containing trouser presses); the comfortable lounge leads into a small dining room where guests may be asked to share a table.
7⇌ (3fb) CTV in all bedrooms ® ✳ sB&Bfr£18
dB&B⇌fr£36 WB&Bfr£126 WBDifr£189 LDO noon
⊞ CTV
Credit Cards ① ③

GH Q Q **The Gables** 24 Dunkeld Road PH1 5RW (take A912 towards Perth guesthouse approx one and a half miles on right just beyond 3rd rdbt) ☎(0738) 624717
A cheerful and informal family guesthouse, The Gables sits by the junction of the Inverness and Crieff roads on the north side of town. Marjorie Tucker's high teas and home baking are popular, as are her hot snacks, all reasonably priced and served between 6 and 7.30pm. There is a small residents' bar in the dining room, and in the lounge a selection of board and computer games.
7rm(5⇌) (2fb) ✘ in bedrooms ✘ in dining room CTV in all bedrooms ® sB&Bfr£17 sB&B⇌fr£19.50 dB&Bfr£32 dB&B⇌fr£37 WB&B£102-£117 WBDi£144-£173 LDO midday
Lic ⊞ CTV
Credit Cards ① ③ £

✉ 💺 **GH** Q Q **The Heidl** 43 York Place PH2 8EH
☎(0738) 635031
Within walking distance of the town centre, this commercial guesthouse offers bright, well maintained bedrooms - some in the original house and some in a small modern wing. Parking can be difficult if the guesthouse's own parking spaces are full.
10rm(1⏺) (2fb) CTV in all bedrooms ® sB&B£14-£16 sB&B⏺£22-£26 dB&B£24-£30 dB&B⏺£32-£36
⊞

✉ 💺 **GH** Q Q Q **Iona** 2 Pitcullen Crescent PH2 7HT (approx 300yds along A94 from junct A94/A93) ☎(0738) 627261
Featuring an attractive little dining room with lace tablecloths and nice, modern bedrooms equipped with good en suite shower rooms, this well looked after Victorian house provides a small parking area at the front.
5rm(2⏺) (1fb) ✘ in bedrooms ✘ in dining room CTV in all bedrooms ® sB&B£15-£17 sB&B⏺£15-£18 dB&B£30-£34 dB&B⏺£30-£36 WB&B£100-£125 WBDi£140-£175 LDO 4.30pm
⊞ CTV
Credit Cards ① ③ £

GH Q Q Q **Kinnaird** 5 Marshall Place PH2 8AH
☎(0738) 628021 FAX (0738) 444056
An attractive Georgian town house overlooking South Inch Park, conveniently situated for visitors entering Perth from the south, is efficiently managed by its friendly owners. Small but bright and modern bedrooms are equipped with clock radios and hair dryers, there is a peaceful first-floor lounge and the elegant period dining room has well spaced tables. Private car parking is provided at the rear of the building.
7⇌ ✘ in dining room CTV in all bedrooms ® ✘ (ex guide dogs) ✳ sB&B⇌fr£18 dB&B⇌fr£36 LDO 4pm
⊞ nc12yrs
Credit Cards ① ③ £

✉ 💺 **GH** Q Q Q **Ochil View** 7 Kings Place PH2 8AA (on Inner Ring Rd overlooking the South Inch Park) ☎(0738) 625708 FAX (0738) 625708
Occupying the first and second floors of a semidetached Victorian house, Ochil View overlooks the park and is convenient for the town centre and station. Cheerfully decorated throughout, the bedrooms have modern furnishings and the dining room and lounge share a first-floor room with a bay window.

5rm(1⏺) (2fb) ✘ in dining room CTV in all bedrooms ®
sB&B£13-£15 dB&B£26-£30 dB&B⏺£28-£34
⊞ CTV
£

GH Q Q Q **Park Lane** 17 Marshall Place PH2 8AG (enter town on A912 and turn left at first set of lights, on right hand side opposite park) ☎(0738) 637218 FAX (0738) 643519
Closed Dec-20 Jan
Part of a Georgian terrace, this guesthouse looks out on to South Inch Park and is within walking distance of the town centre. Bedrooms are individually decorated and several are spacious, including a fine family room. There is a period lounge where breakfast is also taken.
6⇌⏺ (1fb) ✘ in 3 bedrooms ✘ in dining room ✘ in lounges CTV in all bedrooms ® ✘ (ex guide dogs) ✳ sB&B⇌⏺£18-£21 dB&B⇌⏺£36-£42 WB&Bfr£126
⊞ CTV
Credit Cards ① ③ £

GH Q Q Q **Pitcullen** 17 Pitcullen Crescent PH2 7HT (on A94)
☎(0738) 626506 FAX (0738) 628265
A semidetached house with an eye-catching garden, Pitcullen is the last guesthouse on the left on the A94 leading out of town. It is spotlessly maintained and provides an attractive lounge, dining room and two en suite bedrooms on the ground floor.
6rm(3⏺) (1fb) ✘ in 2 bedrooms ✘ in dining room CTV in all bedrooms ® ✘ ✳ sB&Bfr£18.50 sB&B⏺fr£20 dB&Bfr£34 dB&B⏺fr£36 LDO 6pm
⊞
Credit Cards ① ③

GH Q Q Q **Strathcona** 45 Dunkeld Road PH1 5RP
☎(0738) 626701 & 628773
3rm(2⏺) (1fb) ✘ in dining room ✘ in lounges CTV in all bedrooms ® ✘ (ex guide dogs) sB&B⏺£18-£22 dB&B⏺£34-£36 WB&B£105-£112
⊞ nc3yrs
£

PETERBOROUGH Cambridgeshire   Map **04** TL19

GH Q Q **Aaron Park Hotel** 109 Park Road PE1 2TR
☎(0733) 64849 FAX (0733) 64849
8⇌⏺ (2fb) CTV in all bedrooms ® sB&B⇌⏺£36-£39 dB&B⇌⏺£40-£42 LDO 6.30pm
Lic ⊞ CTV

GH Q Q Q **Hawthorn House Hotel** 89 Thorpe Road PE3 6JQ
☎(0733) 340608
This well preserved Victorian house is located near the hospital on the A1179, south of the centre. The bedrooms are generally well equipped and individually furnished. There is a conservatory lounge and a dining room with a corner bar.
8rm(2⇌6⏺) (2fb) CTV in all bedrooms ® ✘
Lic ⊞ CTV
Credit Cards ① ③

GH Q Q Q **Lodge Hotel** 130 Lincoln Road PE1 2NR
☎(0733) 341489 FAX (0733) 52072
9⏺ ✘ in dining room CTV in all bedrooms ® sB&B⏺£35-£45 dB&B⏺£45-£55 WB&B£160-£200 WBDi£200-£250 LDO 8.30pm
Lic ⊞ nc10yrs
Credit Cards ① ② ③ £

PETERSFIELD Hampshire   Map **04** SU72

See also **Rogate**

INN Q Q Q **The Master Robert** Buriton GU31 5SW (S on A3, signposted for Buriton) ☎(0730) 267275 FAX (0730) 231817
This busy, popular inn stands in the village of Buriton, two miles from Petersfield on the A3. Parts of the main building date back to

the 15th century, but the bedrooms are a more recent addition, and are well furnished and very well equipped with every modern convenience for both business and leisure guests. An extensive range of blackboard meals and snacks is offered, together with a selection of real ales. Staff are friendly and helpful.
6rm CTV in all bedrooms ® T sB&B⇌£30-£32.50 dB&B⇌£40-£45 Lunch £8-£14&alc Dinner £8-£14&alc LDO 10pm
Credit Cards 1 2 3 £

PETHAM Kent — Map 05 TR15

SELECTED
GH The Old Poor House Kake Street CT4 5RY (1.5m through village towards Waltham)
Canterbury(0227) 700413 FAX (0227) 700413
This is a spacious, red-brick Georgian building quietly set in three acres of grounds midway between Petham and Waltham. Originally it housed 30 of the parish poor, hence its name. An informal reception area with comfortable sofas doubles as a bar and there is a large country-house style restaurant plus a cocktail bar. The four bedrooms are bright and cheerful, individually decorated in pale shades of pink and blue with solid pine furniture. Each has a smart modern bathroom suite.
4rm(2⇌2) (1fb) CTV in all bedrooms ® LDO 9.45pm Lic CTV
Credit Cards 1 3

FH Mr & Mrs R D Linch **Upper Ansdore** Duckpit Lane CT4 5QB (from Canterbury take B2068 and turn right through village. Take left hand fork and after 1.5m turn right to Upper Ansdore) (0227) 700672
Closed Xmas & New Year
3 (1fb) ® (ex guide dogs) sB&B£30 dB&B£36-£38 WB&B£245-£252

PEVENSEY East Sussex — Map 05 TQ60
GH Napier The Promenade BN24 6HD
Eastbourne(0323) 768875
A modern guest house superbly positioned on the beach combines tranquility of setting with easy access to the amenities of Eastbourne, only a short drive away. Two of its simply styled bedrooms have balconies, there is a sun lounge decorated with fishing tackle, and a small bar adjoins the breakfast room.
10rm(5) (3fb) CTV in all bedrooms ® sB&B£16-£18 sB&B£16-£18 dB&B£32-£36 dB&B£32-£36 WB&B£108-£112 LDO 4pm
Lic CTV
£

PEWSEY Wiltshire — Map 04 SU16
INN Woodbridge North Newnton SN9 6JZ (2.5m SW on A345) Stonehenge(0980) 630266
Closed 25 Dec
This inn of character is situated beside the A345 in a rural location. Lou and Terry Vertessy have renovated the bars, and extensive blackboard menus offer a range of dishes including many Mexican specialities. The bedrooms are very comfortable and thoughtful extras such as bottled waters and reading materials are provided.
3rm(1) CTV in all bedrooms ® (ex guide dogs) LDO 10.30pm
CTV pentanque bar billiards darts
Credit Cards 1 2 3 5

PICKERING North Yorkshire — Map 08 SE88
GH Bramwood 19 Hallgarth YO18 7AW (off A169) (0751) 474066
A grey stone Georgian listed house close to the town centre and well cared for by Mr and Mrs Lane. Bedrooms are quite large and pleasantly decorated, and there is a snug lounge with an open fire.
6rm (1fb) ® (ex guide dogs) sB&B£14-£15 dB&B£28-£34 WB&B£84-£96 WBDi£147-£159 LDO 2.30pm
CTV nc3yrs
Credit Cards 1 3 £

SELECTED
FH Eddie & Shiela Ducat **Rawcliffe House Farm** Stape YO18 8JA (0751) 473292
Feb-Oct
This luxurious accommodation is situated at Snape, about six miles from Pickering, in a beautiful location amidst 40 acres of pasture and meadows. The bedrooms are housed in converted barns and set round a south-facing courtyard. Meals are served at a large communal table in the farmhouse, where there is also a spacious, comfortable guests' lounge. Owners Eddy and Shaila Ducat are congenial hosts providing excellent accommodation in a delightful setting.
Annexe 3 in bedrooms in dining room CTV in all bedrooms ® dB&B£34-£40 WB&B£119-£140 WBDi£182-£203 LDO 24hrs prior
CTV 40 acres non-working
£

The Master Robert
Buriton, Petersfield, Hampshire
Telephone: 01730 267275

Situated on Buriton village crossroads, this hotel offers superbly appointed overnight and conference accommodation, with full à la carte restaurant seating 40 and large bar area with open fireplace offering an extensive menu.
Facilities include 6 en-suite bedrooms, family garden, large patio area, skittle alley and Satellite Television.
Please telephone for bookings.

PIDDLETRENTHIDE Dorset   Map **03** SY79

INNQQQ **The Poachers** DT2 7QX (on B3143 from Dorchester)
☎(0300) 348358

The atmosphere is warm and friendly at this family run inn. In the attractive dining room, guests can choose from either à la carte or 'specials of the day' menus. The accommodation is in a modern annexe with spacious, attractive bedrooms, all of them well-equipped.

2⇌♠ Annexe 9⇌♠ (2fb)CTV in all bedrooms ® **T**
dB&B⇌♠£42-£50 WB&B£133-£145 WBDi£196-£208 Lunch £5-£10alc Dinner £7.50-£13alc LDO 9pm
▦ CTV ⚡(heated)
Credit Cards 1 3 ⓔ

PITLOCHRY Tayside *Perthshire*   Map **14** NN95

GH QQ **Arrandale House** Knockfarrie Road PH16 5DN
☎(0796) 472987
Nov-Mar

Enjoying fine views down the valley from its elevated position, this large, detached Victorian house is in a quiet lane off the main road on the south side of the town. There is no guests' lounge, but bedrooms are mostly quite spacious.

6rm(4♠) (2fb) CTV in all bedrooms ® ⍏
▦

GH QQQ **Comar House** Strathview Terrace PH16 5AT
☎(0796) 473531 FAX (0796) 473811
Etr-Oct

Spectacular views across the valley are a feature of this imposing stone house which dates back to 1910 and sits in a delightful position high above the town. Most of the bedrooms are well proportioned and the spacious turreted double room is particularly sought after. Public areas are tastefully decorated, and the lounge with its large bay window is specially pleasant.

6rm(1⇌2♠) ⍏ CTV in all bedrooms ® ✳ sB&B£16-£18
dB&Bfr£30 dB&B⇌♠£40
▦ CTV
Credit Cards 1 3

S E L E C T E D

GH QQQQ **Craigroyston House** 2 Lower Oakfield
PH16 5HQ ☎(0796) 472053

A warm welcome awaits you at this comfortable, family-run Victorian house which is set in its own grounds overlooking the town and surrounding hills. The bedrooms are comfortably furnished in Victorian style and most feature Laura Ashley decor and coordinating fabrics. There is a comfortable, quiet lounge and hearty breakfasts are served in the attractive dining room.

8⇌♠ (1fb)CTV in all bedrooms ® ⍏ (ex guide dogs)
sB&B⇌♠£16-£25 dB&B⇌♠£32-£50 WB&B£112-£175
WBDi£196-£273 LDO 6pm
Lic ▦
ⓔ

S E L E C T E D

GH QQQQ **Dundarave House** Strathview Terrace
PH16 5AT (from Pitlochry main street turn into West Moulin Rd second left into Strathview Terrace) ☎(0796) 473109
Mar-Oct

Mae and Bob Collier continue to run their detached Victorian house with enthusiasm. Mae has built up a reputation for her cooking, and presents an impressive dinner menu. The bright, attractive bedrooms are mostly well proportioned and all are thoughtfully equipped with fresh fruit, shortbread or home

made cake and hairdryers. The comfortable bay windowed lounge has a fine black marble fireplace and the dining room is small, but resplendent with fine china, linen and period furniture.

7rm(5⇌♠) (1fb) ⍏ in dining room CTV in all bedrooms ®
sB&B£22-£28 dB&B⇌♠£44-£56 WB&B£140-£182
WBDi£237.65-£279.65 LDO 5pm
▦
ⓔ

GH QQQ **Duntrune** 22 East Moulin Road PH16 5HY
☎(0796) 472172
Feb-Oct

Secluded in its own gardens, this large detached Victorian house enjoys fine views across the town and valley from its elevated position. The neat bedrooms are spotlessly clean.

7rm(5♠) (1fb) ⍏ in bedrooms ⍏ in dining room CTV in all bedrooms ® ⍏ sB&B£18-£20 dB&B♠£36-£40 WB&B£119-£133 WBDi£196-£210 LDO 10am
▦ nc5yrs
ⓔ

S E L E C T E D

GH QQQQ **Torrdarach Hotel** Golf Course Road
PH16 5AU ☎(0796) 472136
Etr-mid Oct

A relaxed, friendly atmosphere prevails at Richard and Vivienne Cale's fine Edwardian house, which is set in beautiful wooded gardens close to the golf course. Bright and airy bedrooms with mixed, modern furnishings offer the normal range of amenities. The quiet lounge with comfortable settees and easy chairs, invites peaceful relaxation and a Scottish menu is offered in the neat dining room, overlooking the garden.

7♠ ⍏ CTV in all bedrooms ® ⍏ (ex guide dogs)
sB&B♠£20-£27 dB&B♠£40-£54 LDO 5.45pm
Lic ▦ nc12yrs
ⓔ

GH QQQ **Well House Private Hotel** 11 Toberargan Road
PH16 5HG ☎(0796) 472239
Mar-Nov

This pleasant, well run private hotel sits in a residential area above the town centre. Bedrooms are comfortably furnished and well equipped, with extra touches such as fresh fruit and biscuits.

6♠ (1fb) ⍏ in 1 bedrooms CTV in all bedrooms ® dB&B♠£34-£42 WB&B£107-£132 LDO 5.30pm
Lic ▦
Credit Cards 1 2 3 ⓔ

PLUCKLEY Kent   Map **05** TQ94

S E L E C T E D

FH QQQQ Mr & Mrs V Harris **Elvey Farm Country Hotel** *(TQ916457)* TN27 0SU ☎(0233) 840442
FAX (02384) 840726

Standing in the peaceful Kent countryside on the outskirts of the village, Elvey farm offers accomodation in three buildings. The en suite bedrooms are furnished and decorated in keeping with the style of the farm and are well-equipped. Guests can also use a small, comfortable bar lounge and a large dining room with wooden tables which serves an evening meal on request.

10rm(7🛁3🚿) (6fb)CTV in all bedrooms Ⓡ
dB&B🛁🚿£49.50-£59.50
Lic 🍽 75 acres mixed
[£]

PLYMOUTH Devon Map **02** SX45

GH [Q][Q][Q] ***Athenaeum Lodge*** 4 Athenaeum Street, The Hoe PL1 2RH ☎(0752) 665005
Closed 24 Dec-2 Jan
Situated in the residential part of the city, close to shops, the Hoe and the Barbican, this Victorian terrace property has modernised, colour coordinated bedrooms. Breakfast is in an attractive dining room and attentive service is provided by the owners.
10rm(5🚿) (1fb) CTV in all bedrooms Ⓡ 🐕 (ex guide dogs)
🍽 nc3yrs
Credit Cards [5]

SELECTED

GH [Q][Q][Q][Q] **Bowling Green Hotel** 9-10 Osborne Place, Lockyer Street, The Hoe PL1 2PU ☎(0752) 667485
FAX (0752) 255150
Closed 25-30 Dec
Overlooking Drake's Bowling Green and close to Plymouth Hoe, this Georgian terrace house has well equipped and comfortable bedrooms. Breakfast is in an attractive open-plan dining room, at one end of which is the lounge.
12rm(8🛁🚿) (3fb)CTV in all bedrooms Ⓡ **T** * sB&Bfr£28

▶

DALNASGADH HOUSE

Killiecrankie, Pitlochry, Perthshire PH16 5LN
Telephone: (01796) 473237

Set amidst magnificent scenery and ideally situated to enjoy all the beauty of Highland Perthshire. This attractive building stands in 2 acres of its own grounds and offers the highest quality of welcome, accommodation and attention throughout your stay. Fire certificate. For details of Bed & Breakfast contact the proprietor by writing, telephoning or just calling in. ***Sorry no pets and no smoking.***

Open Easter to October

Mrs R. Macpherson-McDougall

DUNDARAVE HOUSE

Strathview Terrace, Pitlochry PH16 5AT

For those requiring Quality with Comfort Bed and Breakfast, with freedom of choice for evening meal, Dundarave must be your answer, being situated in one of the most enviable areas of Pitlochry in its own formal grounds of ½ acre. All double/twin bedded rooms with bathrooms en suite, colour TV, tea/coffee making facilities, fully heated. We invite you to write or phone for full particulars.

Telephone: 01796 473109

SPECIAL AA QUALITY AWARD
SCOTTISH TOURIST BOARD ♛♛♛
COMMENDED – ACCOMMODATION AWARD

Elvey Farm Country Hotel

Pluckley, Nr. Ashford, Kent
Tel: Pluckley (01233) 840442
Fax/Guest Tel: (01233) 840726

Situated right in the heart of 'Darling Buds of May Country', we offer delux accommodation in our Oast House converted stables and old Kent barn, giving traditional charm and comfort with modern luxury and convenience. Traditional English breakfast is served in our unique dining room, fully licensed. Double and family bedrooms, all with private bath/shower rooms and colour TV.
Children and pets are welcome on our family working farm for a happy homely holiday.

sB&B🛁🚿fr£34 dB&Bfr£36 dB&B🛁🚿fr£46
🅿 CTV
Credit Cards [1] [2] [3] [5] [£]

GH [Q][Q][Q] Caraneal 12/14 Pier Street, West Hoe PL1 3BS
☎(0752) 663589
A two-minute walk from the seafront, and conveniently positioned for the ferry terminal, city centre and Hoe, this neat mid-terrace house provides a friendly and relaxed atmosphere. Limited private parking is available and there is ample pay and display parking nearby. A range of bar meals is served during the evening.
9🛁🚿 (1fb) 🚭 in dining room CTV in all bedrooms [R] 🐕 (ex guide dogs) dB&B🛁🚿£30-£35 WB&B£100-£120 LDO 8pm
Lic 🅿 CTV
Credit Cards [1] [3] [5] [£]

GH [Q][Q] Cranbourne Hotel 282 Citadel Road,The Hoe PL1 2PZ
☎(0752) 263858 FAX (0752) 263858
An end-of-terrace Georgian hotel near to the Hoe, the Barbican and city centre. Bedrooms are simply furnished and breakfast is served in a bright dining room.
14rm(6🚿) (3fb) 🚭 in dining room CTV in all bedrooms [R] * sB&B£15-£25 sB&B🚿£25-£35 dB&B£30-£35 dB&B🚿£35-£40
Lic 🅿 CTV hairdressing salon
Credit Cards [1] [2] [3] [£]

GH [Q][Q] Devonshire 22 Lockyer Road, Mannamead PL3 4RL
☎(0752) 220726 FAX (0752) 220766
A period, double-fronted, stone-built, terraced property situated in a quiet residential road very close to the Mutley Plain shopping area. The comfortable bedrooms are bright and airy and all have TV and tea-making facilities; there are 3 bedrooms available on the ground floor. A set dinner is served at 6pm in the basement dining room. The lounge bar has a cosy atmosphere, and the guesthouse is personally run by the owners Mary and Phil Collins in a friendly and relaxed style.
10rm(3🚿) (4fb) 🚭 in dining room CTV in all bedrooms [R] 🐕 * sB&B£15-£18 sB&B🚿£24 dB&B£30 dB&B🚿£34 WB&B£105-£136 WBDi£160-£192 LDO 2pm
Lic 🅿 CTV
Credit Cards [1] [3] [£]

GH [Q][Q][Q] Dudley 42 Sutherland Road, Mutley PL4 6BN
☎(0752) 668322 FAX (0752) 673763
rs Xmas
The Dudley is a family-run guest house close to the railway station in a quiet residential area. The seven bedrooms are cheerfully decorated and most have en suite facilities as well as colour TVs and tea-making equipment. There is a comfortable lounge with ample seating and a newly decorated dining room.
7rm(5🚿) (2fb) 🚭 in dining room CTV in all bedrooms [R] * sB&B£16-£20 sB&B🚿£20-£22 dB&B🚿£30-£32 LDO 9am
🅿 CTV
Credit Cards [1] [3] [£]

🛏 ▼ **GH [Q] Elizabethan** 223 Citadel Road East, The Hoe PL1 2NG ☎(0752) 661672
Close to both the city centre and the Hoe, this mid-terrace guesthouse offers simply furnished bedrooms and a dining room for breakfast.
6rm 🚭 in dining room 🚭 in lounges CTV in all bedrooms [R] 🐕 (ex guide dogs) sB&B£15 dB&B£24
🅿 🚫

GH [Q][Q] Georgian House Hotel 51 Citadel Road, The Hoe PL1 3AU ☎(0752) 663237 FAX (0752) 253953
rs Sun
This terraced Georgian hotel is convenient for the Hoe, Barbican and city centre. Bedrooms are decorated in a modern style but will benefit from the planned improvements. Downstairs is an intimate dining room where an a la carte menu includes some imaginative dishes.
10rm(4🛁6🚿) (1fb)CTV in all bedrooms [R] T 🐕 (ex guide dogs) * sB&B🛁🚿£20-£29 dB&B🛁🚿£34-£41 LDO 9pm
Lic 🅿 CTV
Credit Cards [1] [2] [3] [5]

🛏 ▼ **GH [Q][Q][Q] Grosvenor Park Hotel** 114-116 North Road East PL4 6AH ☎(0752) 229312 FAX (0752) 252777
Comfortable, well modernised accommodation is provided at this hotel which is conveniently situated near the railway station. Public areas comprise a residents' lounge, a small bar and a dining room where half the space is reserved for non-smokers. Breakfast and dinner menus offer a choice of dishes.
18rm(9🚿) 🚭 in 3 bedrooms 🚭 in area of dining room CTV in all bedrooms [R] 🐕 (ex guide dogs) sB&B£15 dB&B£30 dB&B🚿£35 LDO 9pm
Lic 🅿 CTV
Credit Cards [1] [3] [£]

GH [Q][Q][Q] The Lamplighter Hotel 103 Citadel Road, The Hoe PL1 2RN ☎(0752) 663855
Closed 23 Dec-6 Jan
Situated on the historic Hoe, this small family-run hotel is within easy walking distance of the city centre and the Barbican. There are cheerfully decorated bedrooms with en suite or private facilities, and breakfast is served in the sunny dining room which combines with a small lounge area.
9🚿 (2fb) 🚭 in dining room CTV in all bedrooms [R] 🐕 (ex guide dogs) sB&B🚿£20-£25 dB&B🚿£30-£36
🅿 CTV sauna
Credit Cards [1] [2] [3] [£]

GH [Q][Q] *Oliver's Hotel & Restaurant* 33 Sutherland Road PL4 6BN ☎(0752) 663923
Olivers is an end-of-terrace Victorian house situated close to the city centre and the main railway station. The dining room is open to non-residents for dinner on a bookings only basis, and prides itself on its interesting cuisine. A small bar and a large sitting room are also provided for guests.
6rm(4🚿) (1fb) CTV in all bedrooms [R] 🐕 LDO 8pm
Lic 🅿 nc11yrs
Credit Cards [1] [2] [3] [5]

GH [Q][Q][Q] Rosaland Hotel 32 Houndiscombe Road, Mutley PL4 6HQ ☎(0752) 664749 FAX (0752) 256984
Set close to the city centre, the Rosaland is in a quiet residential area close to the railway station. The hotel's simple decor looks well with the stripped pine furniture, and the dried flowers and pretty borders create a country feel. There is a small bar for guests in the dining room, and leather sofas in the comfortable large sitting room.
8rm(3🚿) (2fb) 🚭 in dining room 🚭 in lounges CTV in all bedrooms [R] T 🐕 (ex guide dogs) * sB&B£16-£23 sB&B🚿£22-£23 dB&B£32 dB&B🚿£34 WB&Bfr£112 WBDifr£160 LDO noon
Lic 🅿 CTV
Credit Cards [1] [3] [5] [£]

GH [Q][Q][Q] *St James Hotel* 49 Citadel Road, The Hoe PL1 3AU
☎(0752) 661950
Closed Xmas
A family-run guest house upon the Hoe, the St James is within easy walking distance of all the city's attractions. The bedrooms are particularly well decorated and offer many extras including en suite shower rooms. An evening meal is available by arrangement in the pretty dining room, which leads through to the comfortable bar-lounge.
10🚿 (2fb) CTV in all bedrooms [R] 🐕 (ex guide dogs) LDO 9pm
Lic 🅿 🚫
Credit Cards [1] [3]

|◢ ■| **GH** Q Q **The White House Hotel** 12 Athenaeum Street
PL1 2RH ☎(0752) 662356
Athenaeum Street, the location of this small family-run
establishment, has been selected by English Heritage for
restoration. Being on the Hoe, the house is within walking
distance of the city centre and Barbican area. Bedrooms are
simply furnished and decorated and breakfast is served in the
cheerful dining room.
6rm(2♠) (1fb) CTV in all bedrooms ℝ sB&B£15-£20
dB&B£25-£30 dB&B♠£30-£35 WB&B£100-£200
▥
£

FH Q Q Q **Mrs L Brunning Netton** *(SX552464)* Noss Mayo
PL8 1HA ☎(0752) 873080 FAX (0752) 873080
Built from traditional materials about 100 years ago, and
subsequently sympathetically restored, Netton Farmhouse is
located about a mile from the village of Noss Mayo and two
minutes by car from the South Devon Coastal Path. Bedrooms are
comfortable and provided with thoughtful extras such as toiletries
and mineral water. The friendly owner, Lesley Ann Brunning, is
delighted to prepare dinner for guests, which may take the form of
a barbecue on balmy summer evenings. An indoor pool, hard
tennis court and a games room with pool, table tennis and darts are
available.
3rm(1⇔) (2fb) ⊬ ℝ ⋔ (ex guide dogs) sB&B£25 sB&B⇔£33
dB&B£35 dB&B⇔£35 WB&Bfr£100
▥ CTV ⚬ ⌁ (heated) ⚭(hard)
£

POCKLINGTON Humberside   Map **08 SE74**

FH Q **Mr & Mrs Pearson Meltonby Hall** *(SE800524)* Meltonby
YO4 2PW (2m N unclass) ☎(0759) 303214
Etr-Oct

Located in the tiny hamlet of Meltonby at the foot of the Wolds,
this friendly farm offers simple accommodation in a peaceful
location. Guests have their own comfortable lounge and evening
meals can be served with advance notice.
2rm (1fb) ℝ ⋔
▥ CTV 118 acres mixed
£

PODIMORE Somerset   Map **03 ST52**

FH Q Q Q **Mrs S Crang Cary Fitzpaine** *(ST549270)* BA22 8JB
(from A303/A37 jct take A37 signed Bristol/Shepton Mallet for
1m) ☎Charlton Mackrell(0458) 223250 FAX (0458) 223250
Closed 23-26 Dec
The ideal area from which to explore an area encompassing Wells,
Glastonbury and Bath as well as several National Trust houses and
places of historic interest, this attractive Georgian farmhouse
provides accommodation in three spacious, well furnished
bedrooms which have a refreshing country charm. Breakfast (the
only meal served) is taken in a delightful dining room with
separate tables, and the log fire which burns in the cosy lounge on
winter evenings is a welcoming sight.
3rm(1⇔♠) (1fb) ⊬ in dining room ⊬ in lounges CTV in all
bedrooms ℝ sB&B£16-£18 sB&B⇔♠fr£18 dB&Bfr£31
dB&B⇔♠fr£36 WB&B£96-£108
▥ CTV ✈ 600 acres arable beef horses sheep
£

POLBATHIC Cornwall & Isles of Scilly   Map **02 SX35**

|◢ ■| **GH** Q Q **The Old Mill** PL11 3HA (on A374)
☎St Germans(0503) 30569
This establishment dates back over 300 years and is in a peaceful
village setting, providing a convenient resting place close to the
main A roads to and from Plymouth. Bedrooms are compact, but
neatly presented, and the public areas include a small, well
stocked bar and comfortable lounge/dining area.
    ▶

Bowling Green Hotel

9-10 Osborne Place,
Lockyer St.,
The Hoe,
Plymouth,
Devon PL1 2PU

Telephone
(01752) 667485

 Selected
QQQQ

*Rebuilt Victorian property with views
of Dartmoor on the horizon.
Overlooking Sir Francis Drake's
Bowling Green on beautiful
PLYMOUTH HOE*

English Tourist Board
Highly Commended

*All rooms with bath or shower, colour TV &
satellite, direct dial telephone, radio, hairdryer,
C.H. and tea & coffee making facilities.
All en-suite rooms with pocket sprung beds.*

Harrabeer Country House Hotel

See gazetteer entry under Yelverton

Harrowbeer Lane, Yelverton, Devon PL20 6EA

Peacefully located on edge of Dartmoor yet only 9
miles from Plymouth this small friendly licensed
hotel caters all year for those on business or on
holiday. Comfortable bedrooms with en-suite
facilities, colour television, telephone, tea/coffee
makers. Laundry service available. Superb freshly
prepared food. Secluded gardens, moorland
views. Golf, walking, fishing and riding all
nearby. Bargain breaks. Visa – Access – Amex

Telephone: Yelverton (01822) 853302

10rm (3fb) ⌀ in area of dining room ⌀ in 1 lounge ®
sB&B£12.50-£15 dB&B£25-£30 WB&B£80-£95 WBDi£135-
£150 LDO 6pm
Lic CTV canoeing
Credit Cards [1] [3] [5] ⓔ

POLMASSICK Cornwall & Isles of Scilly   Map **02** SW94

GH Q Q Q **Kilbol House Country Hotel** PL26 6HA
☎Mevagissey(0726) 842481
Acres of natural grounds and well kept gardens surround this 18th-
century house which enjoys a lovely, peaceful location close to a
vineyard. A programme of refurbishment will ensure that all the
bedrooms are eventually furnished in keeping with the period.
Public rooms are spacious, well appointed and meals are
most enjoyable, tempting guests to choose something suitable
from the well thought out wine list.
8rm(4⇌) (2fb) ⌀ in bedrooms ⌀ in dining room CTV in 1
bedroom ® T ✳ sB&B£30-£37 dB&B£60-£74 dB&B⇌🐾£60-
£74 (incl dinner) WB&B£163-£185 WBDi£212-£234 LDO noon
Lic ▥ CTV ⵂ(heated)
Credit Cards [1] [2] [3]

POLPERRO Cornwall & Isles of Scilly   Map **02** SX25

SELECTED
GH Q Q Q Q **Landaviddy Manor** Landaviddy Lane
PL13 2RT (follow road through Polperro until Landaviddy is
reached on west side of village) ☎(0503) 72210
Closed Nov-Jan
Dating back over 200 years, this lovely manor house sits
within two acres of well tended gardens on a quiet lane just
above the centre of the fishing village, enjoying lovely rural
and sea views. Bedrooms are decorated in a feminine style,
with coordinated soft fabrics and a mixture of modern and
antique furniture. All are nicely equipped, some have en suite
facilities and some have four-poster beds. Public areas are
attractive and comfortable, and a relaxed atmosphere pervades
throughout, cultivated by the warm and friendly proprietors.
7rm(4🐾) ⌀ in bedrooms ⌀ in dining room CTV in all
bedrooms ® 🐾 dB&B£40-£44 dB&B🐾£48-£56
WB&B£130-£180 LDO breakfast
Lic ▥ CTV nc10yrs
Credit Cards [1] [3] ⓔ

SELECTED
GH Q Q Q Q **Lanhael House** PL13 2PW (on entering
Polperro turn right at small roundabout guesthouse 75yds on
right) ☎(0503) 72428 FAX (0503) 72428
Apr-Oct
Mrs Taylor is very welcoming and guests return on a regular
basis to stay in this attractive and appealing guest house, parts
of which date back to the 17th century. Some of the bedrooms
open directly onto the terrace garden, and all have such extras
as good toiletries, antique furniture and a selection of books.
A full English breakfast, or a variation of it, is still popular
with guests, but a large number now choose the vegetarian
alternative of fresh fruit salad, waffles and maple syrup.
4rm(1⇌1🐾) Annexe 1🐾 CTV in all bedrooms ® 🐾 (ex
guide dogs) sB&B£25-£27 sB&B⇌🐾£25-£27 dB&B£37
dB&B⇌🐾£39
▥ CTV nc14yrs ⵂ(heated)

FH Q Q Q Q Q **Mrs L
Tuckett Trenderway**
(SX214533) Pelynt PL13 2LY
(from Looe take A387 to
Polperro, farm is signposted
on main road) ☎(0503) 72214
rs Xmas
Built in the late 16th century,
the Cornish stone buildings of
this working farm are
set in peaceful, beautiful

countryside at the head of
Polperro Valley. Bedrooms here are truly superb: the two
rooms in the main farmhouse are pretty and nicely furnished,
each with an individual, stylish theme and decor; there is
another room in a recently converted adjacent barn and a
fourth room has recently been created with a four-poster bed,
beautiful furniture and attractive colour scheme. A hearty
farmhouse breakfast is served in the sunny conservatory,
which has lovely views out across the valley. Lynn Tuckett
and her family are welcoming, caring hosts, and early
reservations are advised as the farmhouse is very popular.
2⇌🐾 Annexe 3⇌🐾 ⌀ CTV in all bedrooms ® 🐾 ✳
dB&B⇌🐾£44-£52 WB&B£140-£168
▥ nc400 acres arable mixed sheep cattle
ⓔ

PONTRHYDFENDIGAID Dyfed   Map **06** SN76

GH Q Q Q **Llysteg** SY25 6BB (at the junction of B4343/B4340 at
northern side of Pontrhydfendigaid) ☎(0974) 831697
In the midst of magnificent scenery, this family-run guest house is
in an area famous for its breeding red kites, and is close to the
Cors Caron Nature Reserve. The house is pleasantly furnished and
decorated and offers a good all round style of service and
accommodation.
6⇌🐾 ⌀ in bedrooms ⌀ in dining room ® ✳
sB&B⇌🐾£18.75 dB&B⇌🐾£37.50 WB&B£108.50
WBDi£176.75 LDO 8.30pm
Lic ▥ CTV

POOLE Dorset   Map **04** SZ09
See also Bournemouth

SELECTED
GH Q Q Q Q **Acorns** 264 Wimborne Road, Oakdale
BH15 3EF (on A35 1m from town centre) ☎(0202) 672901
FAX (0202) 672901
5rm(4🐾) CTV in all bedrooms ® 🐾 sB&B🐾£17-£18
dB&B🐾£34-£38 LDO noon
Lic ▥ CTV nc
Credit Cards [1] [2] [3]

GH Q Q **Avoncourt Private Hotel** 245 Bournemouth Road,
Parkstone BH14 9HX (on A35 between Poole & Bournemouth)
☎(0202) 732025 FAX (0202) 732025
This small private hotel has a small car park at the rear. The style
of accommodation is cosy, neat and well presented. Some
bedrooms have private shower cubicles in the rooms, and another
now has en suite facilities. There is a bright, comfortable and well
decorated combined bar/breakfast room, and resident proprietors
Mr and Mrs Jones take great pride in their home and work hard to
maintain high housekeeping standards.
6rm(1⇌1🐾) (3fb) CTV in all bedrooms ® 🐾 sB&B£16-£25
dB&B£32-£38 dB&B⇌🐾£36-£44 WB&B£100-£130

WBDi£140-£182.50 LDO 10am
Lic ▥ CTV
Credit Cards 1 2 3 5 ⓔ

GH QQQ **Seacourt** 249 Blandford Road, Hamworthy BH15 4AZ
(on A350 between Upton and Poole Bridge) ☎(0202) 674995
Located close to the cross channel ferry terminal, this guesthouse
has recently been taken over by the Hewitt family, who have
implemented a programme of redecoration and improvements
since their arrival. All bedrooms now have en suite facilities, and
overall the standard of accommodation is high. Bedrooms are neat
and bright, with pretty coordinating decor, and three are
conveniently located on the ground floor. There is a cosy lounge
and bright, front-facing breakfast room. Car parking is available,
and the atmosphere is relaxed and friendly.
5rm(2⇌3♪) (1fb) ⊁ in 1 bedrooms CTV in all bedrooms ® ✳
sB&B⇌♪£20-£25 dB&B⇌♪£36 WB&B£112
▥ CTV
ⓔ

GH QQ **Sheldon Lodge** 22 Forest Road, Branksome Park
BH13 6DH (turn off A35 at Frizzel rdbt & take B3065 to traffic
lights turn right & first left) ☎(0202) 761186
This well maintained guesthouse is situated in a quiet residential
area of Branksome Park and offers bright, simply furnished
bedrooms with pleasant decor. An evening meal is served if
required and the comfortable public areas include a snooker room
with three-quarter size table. Mr and Mrs Smart's friendly
welcome means many guests return year after year.
14rm(8⇌6♪) (1fb) ⊁ in dining room CTV in all bedrooms ®
sB&B⇌♪£21-£26 dB&B⇌♪£42-£46 WBDi£185-£195 LDO
7pm
Lic ▥ solarium
Credit Cards 1 ⓔ

PORLOCK Somerset   Map 03 SS84

GH QQQ **Lorna Doone Hotel** High Street TA24 8PS (on A39)
☎(0643) 862404
Closed 24-26 Dec
Conveniently located in the centre of the village, this 19th-century
hotel has recently been upgraded and improved to provide modern
bedrooms. An attractive and well appointed no-smoking restaurant
is open all day, serving blackboard specials, light and full meals,
snacks and cream teas; the well stocked bar offers a short selected
wine list, and the comfortable lounge's log-burning fire adds to the
warm, friendly and informal atmosphere. Some car parking space
is available in the courtyard.
10rm(3⇌7♪) Annexe 1♪ ⊁ in dining room CTV in 12 bedrooms
® ✳ sB&B⇌♪£21 dB&B⇌♪£37-£48 WB&B£122.50-£161
LDO 8.45pm
Lic ▥ CTV
Credit Cards 1 3 ⓔ

GH QQQ **Seapoint** Upway TA24 8QE (behind Ship Inn)
☎(0643) 862289
This small Edwardian house is just a stone's throw from the centre
of Porlock and has views across the bay and over Exmoor. The
tastefully furnished bedrooms are well equipped and in the dining
room traditional meals are offered. Christine and Stephen
Fitzgerald specialise in vegetarian, wholefood and special diets,
and their vegetarian breakfast is becoming renowned.
3⇌♪ ⊁ CTV in all bedrooms ® ✳ sB&B⇌♪£20.50
dB&B⇌♪£41 WB&B£135.50 WBDi£190.50 LDO 3pm
Lic ▥ CTV
ⓔ

PORTHCAWL Mid Glamorgan   Map 03 SS87

GH QQQ **Heritage** 24 Mary Street CF36 3YA ☎(0656) 771881
Conveniently situated close to the promenade and pavillion, this
small, friendy hotel provides compact but comfortable, nicely
equipped bedrooms, that have bright en suites and a TV with

satellite channels. There is a cosy bar and an attractively furnished
restaurant, with worthy standards of imaginative cuisine from
chef/patron John Miller, who has established a firm reputation.
8rm(6♪) CTV in all bedrooms ® ✶ LDO 9pm
Lic ▥ ♪
Credit Cards 1 3

GH QQ **Minerva Hotel** 52 Esplanade Avenue CF36 3YU (turn
right from esplanade at Grand Pavillion) ☎(0656) 782428
Conveniently positioned just off the promenade and only a short
walk from the town centre, this small, family-run guesthouse
provides modestly furnished bedrooms which are well equipped.
The public rooms consist of a cosy, inviting lounge, a small
breakfast room and a bar for residents' use only. The proprietors
Mr and Mrs Giblett provide a personal service.
8rm(2⇌2♪) (3fb) ⊁ in dining room CTV in all bedrooms ® ✶
(ex guide dogs) ✳ sB&B£14-£16 sB&B⇌♪£22-£25 dB&B£28-
£32 dB&B⇌♪£38-£42 LDO 6pm
Lic ▥ CTV

PORTHCOTHAN BAY Cornwall &
Isles of Scilly   Map 02 SW87

GH QQ **Bay House** PL28 8LW ☎Padstow(0841) 520472
8 Apr-28 Oct
The accommodation in this guesthouse offers a choice of bright
basic bedrooms: the best have front-facing balconies, and rooms
on the second floor afford the best sea views. Generous public
rooms include sun and TV lounges and a very popular well
stocked bar, together with a dining room offering a daily menu.
There are also 3 self-catering holiday flats available, and adequate
parking.
16rm(5♪) (1fb) ⊁ in dining room ® ✶ (ex guide dogs) ✳
sB&B£15-£22 dB&B£30-£44 WBfr£95 LDO 4.30pm
Lic CTV

PORTHCURNO Cornwall & Isles of Scilly   Map **02** SW32

[🖼 ▼] **GH** [Q][Q] **Corniche** Trebehor TR19 6LX (at Sennen turn left off the A30 at the Wreckers Inn on to B3315, establishment 1m on left) ☎Sennen(0736) 871685

Closed 21-31 Dec

Near the hamlet of Porthcurno with its popular open air Minack Theatre, this spacious detached house offers clean, well equipped modern bedrooms and bright attractive public rooms. There are magnificent views over the surrounding countryside.

6rm (1fb) ⊁ ® 🏌 sB&B£12-£13 dB&B£24-£26 WB&B£80-£87.50 WBDi£122-£129.50 LDO 3.30pm

Lic ▥ CTV
£

PORTHMADOG Gwynedd   Map **06** SH53

GH [Q] *Oakleys* The Harbour LL49 9AS ☎(0766) 512482

Apr-Oct

This large early 19th-century stone-built house is situated right on the harbour and within easy walking distance of the local shops. Bedrooms are rather dated by modern day standards but provide good value for money; family rooms are available and there is a bedroom on the ground floor. Guests have the use of a small TV lounge and there is a large car park.

8rm(1⇌2ⁿ) (3fb) 🏌 (ex guide dogs) LDO 5pm

CTV nc5yrs

GH [Q][Q] **Owen's Hotel** 71 High Street LL49 9EU (on A487) ☎(0766) 512098

This small, friendly guesthouse dates back to 1840, when it was known as the Royal Commercial Hotel. It is in the High Street over the proprietor's coffee shop/confectionery business, and a small private car park is located a few yards away. The bedrooms are not modern but are soundly maintained, and equipped to satisfy the needs of both tourists and business people requiring bed and breakfast accommodation.

10rm(3⇌4ⁿ) (3fb) ⊁ in dining room ⊁ in lounges CTV in all bedrooms ® sB&B£18-£25 sB&B⇌ⁿ£20-£30 dB&B£30-£35 dB&B⇌ⁿ£38-£43 WB&Bfr£133

Lic ▥ CTV

Credit Cards [1][3] £

FH [Q][Q][Q] Mrs P Williams **Tyddyn Du** *(SH691398)* Gellilydan, Ffestiniog LL41 4RB (1st farmhouse on left after junct of A487/A470 near village of Gellilydan) ☎(0766) 590281

FAX (0766) 590281

Closed 24-31 Dec

3rm(1ⁿ) (2fb) ⊁ in bedrooms CTV in all bedrooms ® dB&Bfr£32 dB&Bⁿ£34-£38 WB&B£100-£121 WBDi£151-£171

250 acres sheep poultry

PORT ISAAC Cornwall & Isles of Scilly   Map **02** SW98

SELECTED

GH [Q][Q][Q][Q] **Archer Farm Hotel** Trewetha PL29 3RU (on B3267) ☎Bodmin(0208) 880522

Etr-Oct

This rambling Cornish farmhouse has been lovingly converted to provide a choice of modern and old bedrooms, some with full en suite facilities; several of the rooms have lovely rural views and a balcony. There is a small TV lounge on the ground floor, and a very comfortable well appointed bar lounge and dining room on the first floor. The atmosphere is very friendly and informal, with the proprietor Vickie Welton personally supervising the service and cooking. A four-course Cordon Bleu dinner is served using fresh local produce, which is ordered when confirming the booking. Ample car parking and a garden are also available.

5⇌ⁿ (2fb) ⊁ in dining room ⊁ in 1 lounge CTV in 4 bedrooms T ✱ sB&B⇌ⁿ£24-£25.50 dB&B⇌ⁿ£48-£57

WB&B£162-£172 WBDi£252-£262 LDO 8pm

Lic ▥ CTV
£

GH [Q][Q] **Bay Hotel** 1 The Terrace PL29 3SG (turn off A39 onto B3314 then onto B3267) ☎Bodmin(0208) 880380

Etr-Oct

Enjoying a good position overlooking the sea, this long-established hotel has been run by Mary and Jim Andrews for over 13 years. The bedrooms are furnished to a satisfactory standard in a conventional style and several are suitable for families. There is a comfortable lounge facing the sea, with a separate bar and a plain but practical dining room where an à la carte menu is usually available. Parking can be a little difficult at times but there is a pay and display car park opposite.

10rm(4⇌ⁿ) (5fb) ⊁ in dining room ® sB&B£17-£20.50 dB&B£34-£42 dB&B⇌ⁿ£42-£49 WB&B£103-£125.50 WBDi£164-£213 LDO 7pm

Lic ▥ CTV

PORTLAND Dorset   Map **03** SY67

GH [Q][Q][Q] **Alessandria Hotel & Italian Restaurant** 71 Wakeham Easton DT5 1HW ☎(0305) 820108 & 822270

FAX (0305) 820561

This bright Portland stone house stands towards the southern tip of Portland Bill. It is well-maintained throughout with clean, comfortable accomodation, including a small lounge with welcoming seating and a nicely appointed restaurant serving the well-prepared Italian menu of propietor Giovanni Bisogno.

15rm(1⇌10ⁿ) Annexe 1⇌ⁿ (3fb)CTV in all bedrooms ® 🏌 (ex guide dogs) ✱ sB&B£25-£35 sB&B⇌ⁿ£35-£45 dB&B£40-£50 dB&B⇌ⁿ£45-£60 WB&B£125-£175 WBDi£175-£275 LDO 9pm

Lic ▥ CTV

Credit Cards [1][2][3][5] £

PORTNANCON Highland *Sutherland*   Map **14** NC46

GH [Q][Q] **Port-Na-Con House** IV27 4UN (0.25m off A838, on shore of loch) ☎Durness(0971) 511367

Mar-Oct

Quietly situated by the picturesque shore of Loch Erribol, this former custom house and harbour store has been converted and modernised to create a comfortable, family-run guesthouse. The bedrooms have modern furniture and all enjoy loch views, as does the inviting first-floor lounge which also offers access to the adjoining balcony.

4rm(1ⁿ) (1fb) ⊁ ® sB&Bfr£22.50 dB&Bfr£33 dB&Bⁿfr£36 LDO 5pm

Lic ▥ air available for divers

Credit Cards [1][3]

PORTPATRICK Dumfries & Galloway *Wigtownshire*   Map **10** NX05

GH [Q][Q][Q] **Blinkbonnie** School Brae DG9 8LG ☎(0776) 810282

Closed Dec

Situated some distance from the seafront - though the harbour is only five minutes' walk away - this detached house is nevertheless set high enough to give sea views across the town. Compact bedrooms are well maintained, a pleasant lounge looks out onto the garden, and the cheerful proprietor is an enthusiastic hostess.

6rm(3ⁿ) ⊁ CTV in all bedrooms ® 🏌 LDO 6.30pm
▥ CTV

PORTREATH Cornwall & Isles of Scilly Map **02** SW64

SELECTED

GH [Q][Q][Q][Q] Benson's 1 Hillside TR16 4LL (off B3300)
☎(0209) 842534

A recently built modern guest house is situated in an elevated position with beautiful views over the village, harbour and coastline. Bedrooms are all located on the ground floor and are very well equipped. Self-service breakfast is taken in the conservatory, which offers spectacular views. Much of the coastline and surrounding countryside are owned by the National Trust, and there are marvellous clifftop walks and secluded coves to explore.

4🚿 🚭 in dining room 🚭 in lounges CTV in all bedrooms [R] 🐕 sB&B🚿£25-£35 dB&B🚿£35 WB&B£119
🅿 nc
[£]

PORTREE See **SKYE, ISLE OF**

PORTSMOUTH & SOUTHSEA Hampshire Map **04** SZ69

GH [Q][Q] Abbey Lodge 30 Waverley Road PO5 2PW (follow sea front signs towards pier turn left into Granada, Clarendon or Burgoyne Rd to rdbt for Waverley Rd) ☎(0705) 828285 FAX (0705) 872943

A terraced property with an informal relaxed atmosphere, personally run by friendly proprietors Linda and Michael Forbes. The accommodation is being progressively upgraded, and well equipped bedrooms include satellite TV. There is a cosy lounge also with TV, and a separate well appointed breakfast room. An evening meal can be provided by prior arrangement, making this a useful stop-over for the cross-channel ferries.

9rm(1🛁2🚿) (2fb)CTV in all bedrooms [R] 🐕 (ex guide dogs) LDO 9am
🅿 CTV P̸
Credit Cards [1][2][3][5]

GH [Q][Q][Q] Ashwood 10 St Davids Road PO5 1QN
☎(0705) 816228 FAX (0705) 753955
Closed 23 Dec-1 Jan

A Victorian property set in a quiet residential area between the shops and seafront, this friendly guesthouse is both charming and cosy. One bedroom has a four-poster, many have coronet beds, and all are made attractive with coordinating decor. Bright public areas include a comfortable lounge and a smart dining room.

7rm 🚭 in dining room 🚭 in lounges CTV in all bedrooms [R] 🐕 (ex guide dogs) ✳ sB&B£15-£17 dB&B£30-£34 WB&B£105-£119 LDO 4pm
🅿 CTV P̸nc5yrs

GH [Q][Q][Q] Bembell Court Hotel 69 Festing Road PO4 0NQ (road opposite Natural History Museum)
☎Portsmouth(0705) 735915 & 750497

Good value accommodation within easy reach of all the local attractions is available at this family-run, licensed hotel. Bedrooms, though rather compact, are very well equipped with direct-dial telephone and satellite TV, with some rooms on the ground floor. Public areas inclue a traditional lounge, a well-stocked bar and a basement dining room which serves freshly prepared tempting meals and a choice of wines. There is ample car parking.

13rm(7🛁🚿) (4fb) 🚭 in 4 bedrooms 🚭 in dining room 🚭 in 1 lounge CTV in all bedrooms [R] T 🐕 (ex guide dogs) ✳ sB&B£19-£25 sB&B🛁🚿£28-£35 dB&B£38-£44 dB&B🛁🚿£40-£48 WB&B£140-£155 WBDi£195-£220 LDO 4pm
Lic 🅿 CTV
Credit Cards [1][2][3][5][£]

THE OAKLEYS GUEST HOUSE

The Harbour, Porthmadog.
Telephone Porthmadog (01766) 512482

Proprietors: Mr & Mrs A. H. Biddle

H&C in bedrooms, electric shaver points. Spacious free car park. No undue restrictions. Informal atmosphere. Personal attention.

Comfortable lounge. Interior sprung beds. Tea and snacks obtainable during the day. Excellent facilities for salmon and trout fishing. Also some excellent sea fishing. Comparatively close to an excellent golf course.

BEMBELL COURT HOTEL

69 Festing Road, Southsea, Portsmouth, Hampshire PO4 0NQ
Tel: (01705) 735915 (Reservations)
(01705) 750497 (Guests)
Resident Proprietors: Elaine & Keith Irwin

A friendly family run, licensed hotel. Ideally situated in Portsmouth & Southsea's prime holiday area, with an excellent selection of shops, pubs and restaurants nearby. Centrally heated bedrooms with tea and coffee making facilities, telephone, CTV with satellite channel, hair dryers. Most rooms have private en-suite facilities.

- **Early breakfast for ferry passengers**
- **Hotel Car Park**
- **Single night and midweek booking accepted**
- **Ground floor rooms available**
- **Children stay free in family rooms**
- **Off season bargain breaks**
- **Well stocked cosy licensed bar**

GH [Q][Q] Birchwood 44 Waverley Road PO5 2PP (keeping South Parade Pier on left take 1st right onto rdbt leave at 3rd exit into Waverley Rd) ☎(0705) 811337

This Victorian terraced house is situated five minutes' walk from the seafront and has a welcoming, informal atmosphere. Bedrooms offer modern facilities and there is a comfortable lounge and an attractive breakfast room.

6rm(3🚿) (2fb) 🚭 in 2 bedrooms 🚭 in dining room CTV in all bedrooms Ⓡ 🐕 (ex guide dogs) ✻ sB&B£14.50-£20 dB&B£29-£33 dB&B🚿£33-£37 WB&B£90-£130 WBDi£120-£165 LDO 3pm

Lic 🅿 CTV Ᵽ

Credit Cards [1][2][3][5][£]

🛏 ☕ GH [Q][Q] Collingham 89 St Ronans Road PO4 0PR ☎(0705) 821549

Closed 24-26 Dec

The resident Cole family offer a friendly, personal welcome to this small comfortable guesthouse in a quiet residential road north of the seafront. Bedrooms are comfortable and modern and there is a combined lounge and breakfast room downstairs.

6rm (3fb) 🚭 in 4 bedrooms 🚭 in dining room 🚭 in lounges CTV in all bedrooms Ⓡ sB&B£14-£15 dB&B£28-£30 WB&B£85-£87

🅿 CTV Ᵽ

[£]

🛏 ☕ GH [Q] The Elms 48 Victoria Road South PO5 2BT (left at rdbt at end of M275, straight ahead at next 3 rdbts & traffic lights guesthouse 300yds on right) ☎Portsmouth(0705) 823924

Conveniently located close to the shops and seafront, this Victorian property offers simply furnished, clean, reasonably equipped bedrooms particularly aimed at families, with several bunk beds. The front-facing lounge is shared with the Erskine family, and the atmosphere is informal. There is a small bar, and breakfast is served downstairs, with early breakfasts available for those catching ferries.

6rm (3fb) 🚭 in dining room CTV in all bedrooms Ⓡ 🐕 (ex guide dogs) sB&B£15 dB&B£30 WB&B£98

Lic 🅿 CTV

[£]

GH [Q][Q][Q] Fortitude Cottage 51 Broad Street, Old Portsmouth PO1 2JD ☎(0705) 823748

Closed 25 & 26 Dec

This pretty house - overlooking the quayside at Old Portsmouth with views of the ferries and fish markets - has much to recommend it. Each of the three charming bedrooms is attractively decorated in pastel shades, and a choice of English or Continental breakfast is served in an attractive pine-furnished dining room with beams and wood panelling. A good variety of restaurants nearby provides a choice of cuisines at dinner time.

3rm(1🚿) CTV in all bedrooms Ⓡ 🐕

🅿 Ᵽnc

Credit Cards [1][3]

GH [Q][Q] Gainsborough House 9 Malvern Road PO5 2LZ ☎(0705) 822604

Closed Xmas

Many guests return time and time again to this friendly guesthouse which is quietly situated in a residential area fairly close to the shops and seafront. Neat, tidy bedrooms are well kept, while the lounge and dining room are both attractive and comfortable.

7rm (2fb) 🚭 in dining room 🚭 in lounges CTV in all bedrooms Ⓡ 🐕 ✻ sB&B£14-£15 dB&B£28-£30

🅿 CTV Ᵽnc3yrs

[£]

GH [Q][Q] Glencoe 64 Whitwell Road PO4 0QS ☎(0705) 737413

Just a short walk from both sea and shops, this well presented hotel offers bright, clean and comfortable accommodation in a friendly atmosphere. The breakfast room and lounge, freshly decorated and well furnished, overlook the patio.

7rm(3🚿) (1fb) 🚭 CTV in all bedrooms Ⓡ 🐕 ✻ sB&Bfr£16.50 sB&B🚿fr£20 dB&Bfr£30 dB&B🚿fr£35

🅿 CTV Ᵽnc8yrs

Credit Cards [1][3][5][£]

GH [Q][Q][Q] Hamilton House 95 Victoria Road North PO5 1PS ☎(0705) 823502 FAX (0705) 823502

A deceptively spacious Victorian property in a central residential area, only five minutes from the ferry terminal, which has been skilfully renovated over recent years to provide comfortable, well decorated and attractively coordinated bedrooms (three of them with bright, modern en suite facilities). Welcoming proprietors, Graham and Sandra Tubb, create a warm atmosphere, and there is a well furnished lounge in which guests can relax.

8rm(3🚿) (3fb) 🚭 in 1 bedrooms 🚭 in dining room 🚭 in lounges CTV in all bedrooms Ⓡ 🐕 ✻ sB&B£16-£18 sB&B🚿£19-£21.50 dB&B£32-£36 dB&B🚿£39-£43 WB&B£109-£148 WBDi£144-£182 LDO noon

🅿 CTV Ᵽ

[£]

GH [Q][Q][Q] Upper Mount House Hotel The Vale, Clarendon Road PO5 2EQ ☎(0705) 820456

Standing in a quiet road between the town centre and seafront, this large Victorian house designed by Thomas Owen has been renovated by its owners, Mr and Mrs Moth, to create a hotel that offers modern comfort while preserving the building's original character. There is a cosy lounge and an interesting collection of glass ornaments is displayed in the spacious dining room.

12rm(11🛁🚿) (3fb) CTV in all bedrooms Ⓡ 🐕 (ex guide dogs) ✻ sB&Bfr£20 sB&B🛁🚿£25 dB&B🛁🚿£34-£46 WBDi£169-£190 LDO 6pm

Lic 🅿 CTV

Credit Cards [1][3][£]

GH [Q][Q][Q] Victoria Court 29 Victoria Road North PO5 1PL ☎(0705) 820305

Located in a residential area, this semidetached Victorian property continues to be upgraded and improved by resident proprietors Mr and Mrs Johnson. The comfortable bedrooms are well furnished and equipped, with bright decor and modern en suite shower rooms. There is a small first floor lounge, and a set home-cooked evening meal is offered in the dining room, where there is also a tiny bar.

7🚿 (3fb) 🚭 in dining room CTV in all bedrooms Ⓡ T 🐕 (ex guide dogs) ✻ sB&B🚿£21.50-£35 dB&B🚿£28-£42 LDO am

Lic 🅿

Credit Cards [1][3][5][£]

PORT WILLIAM Dumfries & Galloway *Wigtownshire*

Map **10** NX34

FH [Q][Q][Q] Mrs Mary McMuldroch ***Jacobs Ladder*** *(NX364502)* Whauphill DG8 9BD ☎Mochrum(098886) 227

Jacob's Ladder is a charming country house standing in eight acres of woodland and gardens. It offers well equipped bedrooms and spacious public areas including a comfortable lounge. Mr McMuldroch provides a warm welcome and friendly service.

3rm(2🚿) (1fb) CTV in all bedrooms Ⓡ LDO 3pm

🅿 8 acres beef & sheep

POUNDSGATE Devon

Map **03** SX77

FH [Q][Q][Q] Mrs Margaret Phipps **New Cott Farm** *(SX703727)* TQ13 7PD (approx 4m NW of Ashburton through Poundsgate village then 1st left & follow farm signs) ☎(03643) 421 due to change to 631421

Margaret and Terry Phipp's farm bungalow is situated in a large garden on the southern slopes of Dartmoor, and there are two private trout ponds for guests' use. Enjoyable farmhouse cooking is served in the lounge/dining room, including fresh locally produced meat and vegetables followed by traditional puddings and clotted cream. Partially disabled guests are welcomed and

help is readily available. This is a no-smoking house.
4⇆🛏 ⚹ ® 🐾 (ex guide dogs) ✻ dB&B⇆🛏£33-£35
WBDi£160-£170 LDO 5pm
▥ CTV nc3yrs ✔ 130 acres cattle, sheep
£

PRESTATYN Clwyd   Map **06** SJ08

🖛 ▆ **GH** **Q Q** **Roughsedge House** 26-28 Marine Road
LL19 7HD (on A548, coast road, opposite fire station & Llys Nant
Day Care Centre) ☎(0745) 887359 FAX (0745) 887359
A small guest house with a friendly atmosphere, Roughsedge is
situated a short walk from the town centre on the eastern side. The
rooms are equipped with tea trays and TVs and the heating is fully
controllable. There is a dining room complete with its own small bar
and a modern residents' lounge. Easy street parking is available.
10rm(2⇆1🛏) (2fb) ⚹ in 5 bedrooms ⚹ in dining room CTV in
all bedrooms ® 🐾 sB&B£14-£16 dB&B£28-£30
dB&B⇆🛏£35-£40 LDO 4pm
Lic ▥ CTV
Credit Cards ① ② ③ ⑤ £

INN **Q Q Q** **Sophies** 17 Gronant Road LL19 9DT (leave A548 at
Drivers Garage into Nant Dr continue along this road for half a
mile) ☎(0745) 852442
Closed 24 Dec-1 Jan
This black and white inn is situated near the town centre and is a
short distance from the start of Offa's Dyke. Popular locally for
the good-value bar meals, it has a very cosy, comfortable bar with
a wood burning stove. The pretty restaurant overlooks the garden,
and local produce is served whenever possible. Bedrooms are
smart and modern; one situated on the ground floor has an extra
single room attached.
5🛏 (1fb) ⚹ in bedrooms ⚹ in dining room ⚹ in 1 lounge CTV in
all bedrooms ® ✻ sB&B🛏fr£24 dB&B🛏fr£36 WB&Bfr£140
WBDifr£200 Lunch £7-£12&alc High tea £4.35 Dinner £7-
£12&alc LDO 9pm
▥
Credit Cards ① ③ £

PRESTON Lancashire   Map **07** SD52
See also Longridge

GH **Q Q Q** **Tulketh Hotel** 209 Tulketh Road, Ashton PR2 1ES
(leave M6 junct 31 or M55 junct 1 towards Blackpool on A5085,
turn left onto A5072 at St Andrews Church) ☎(0772) 726250 &
728096 FAX (0772) 723743
Closed Xmas-New Year
Situated in the residential area of Ashton, north-west of the town
centre, this detached, extended Edwardian property stands in its
own gardens. It is a pleasant family run private hotel with a
friendly and relaxed atmosphere. Bedrooms are all well equipped
with modern amenities, the best being in a new wing. There is a
cosy bar lounge and an attractive dining room where an à la carte
menu is offered at dinner.
12rm(11⇆🛏) (1fb) ⚹ in dining room CTV in all bedrooms ® T
🐾 (ex guide dogs) ✻ sB&B£30-£35 sB&B⇆🛏£35-£40
dB&B£42-£46 dB&B⇆🛏£46-£48 LDO 7.30pm
Lic ▥ CTV
Credit Cards ① ② ③ ⑤ £

GH **Q** **Withy Trees** 175 Garstang Road, Fulwood PR2 4LL (2m N
on A6) ☎(0772) 717693 FAX (0772) 726483
This privately owned guesthouse offers an improving standard of
accommodation, the best rooms now having modern en suite
shower rooms. There is a comfortable guest lounge and a separate
dining room where breakfast and evening meals are served.
11rm(5🛏) (2fb) ⚹ in 7 bedrooms ⚹ in dining room CTV in all
bedrooms ® ✻ sB&B£20 sB&B🛏£27 dB&B£30 dB&B🛏£37
LDO 2pm
▥ CTV
£

"Hamilton House"

95 VICTORIA ROAD NORTH, SOUTHSEA
PORTSMOUTH, HANTS PO5 1PS
TELEPHONE & FAX: (01705) 823502

Delightful family-run guest house, centrally located
just 5 mins by car, to continental ferry terminal,
Guildhall/City Centre and main Tourist attractions of
Portsmouth/Southsea. Ideal touring base.
The bright, modern bedrooms have heating, colour
TVs and tea/coffee making facilities.
Some en suite rooms available.
Traditional English, Vegetarian or Continental
breakfast is served from 6.00 a.m.
Holidaymakers, business people & travellers are
assured a warm welcome & pleasant stay
at any time of the year.
For brochure please send SAE to
Graham & Sandra Tubb & quote ref AA.

VICTORIA COURT
29 Victoria Road North, Southsea,
Hampshire PO5 1PL
Telephone: (01705) 820305

Victoria Court offers the warmth of a comfortable
licensed Victorian house representing value and
the kind of facilities demanded by todays business
traveller combined with a friendly service for the
holiday maker.

All rooms have: en suite facilities, colour TV. clock,
radio, tea/coffee making facilities, direct dial
telephone, hair dryer and individual temperature
control. Breakfasts available for ferry travellers
from 6am.

INN[Q][Q][Q] **Birley Arms Motel** Bryning Lane, Warton PR4 1TN (leave M55 at junct 3 then A585 to Kirkham, follow signs to Wrea Green & Warton, Birley Arms between the two) ☎(0722) 679988 FAX (0772) 679435

This extended country inn offers a good standard of modern accommodation. Pleasantly appointed bedrooms are furnished in Victorian pine and are well equipped with extras such as telephones and trouser presses An extensive range of bar meals is offered at both lunch and dinner.

16🚿 CTV in all bedrooms [R] 🐕 (ex guide dogs) ✱ sB&B🚿£27-£39.50 dB&B🚿£40-£49 Lunch £7-£13.50alc Dinner £7.95-£8.95&alc LDO 9.15pm

🅿

Credit Cards [1] [2] [3] [5] [£]

PRESTWICK Strathclyde *Ayrshire* Map **10** NS32

SELECTED

GH [Q][Q][Q][Q] **Fairways Hotel** 19 Links Road KA9 1QG ☎(0292) 70396 FAX (0292) 70396

This fine house built around the turn of the century overlooks the golf course and caters well for devotees of the game. Bedrooms are attractively furnished, with extra touches provided. There is a comfortable first-floor lounge and the dining room features a fine antique sideboard, with well spaced tables. The breakfast menu offers a good choice.

5rm(4🚿) (1fb) 🚭 in dining room CTV in all bedrooms [R] ✱ sB&B🚿£22-£23 dB&B🚿£42-£44

Lic 🅿 CTV

Credit Cards [2] [£]

GH [Q][Q][Q] **Fernbank** 213 Main Street KA9 1SU ☎(0292) 75027

Fernbank is a red sandstone house set beside the main road on the southern side of town. It is immaculately maintained and offers a range of bedrooms with quality fabrics and linen. There is a cosy lounge and a lovely pine-furnished breakfast room. Wood strip panelling has been used to great effect throughout and paintings and photographs by the owner and her daughter are displayed.

7rm(4🚿) (1fb) CTV in all bedrooms [R] 🐕 ✱ sB&B£15-£16 dB&B🚿£34-£36

🅿 CTV nc5yrs

[£]

SELECTED

GH [Q][Q][Q][Q] **Golf View Hotel** 17 Links Road KA9 1QG (take road to for Prestwick Airport/Ayr turn at Prestwick Cross & follow signs for golf club guesthouse opposite) ☎(0292) 671234 FAX (0292) 671244

Graham and Isobel McKerrigan's semidetached red sandstone house is situated 5 minutes' walk from the town centre and overlooks Prestwick Golf Club, home of the first Open Championship in 1806. It offers a high standard of accommodation, with well appointed bedrooms, equipped with several extra touches. The comfortable first floor lounge overlooks the 14th green, as does the attractive ground floor dining room, where freshly cooked breakfasts are served.

6rm(5🛁🚿) (2fb) 🚭 in 2 bedrooms 🚭 in dining room 🚭 in lounges CTV in all bedrooms [R] 🐕 (ex guide dogs) sB&Bfr£23 dB&B🛁🚿fr£46

Lic 🅿 CTV ⛳

Credit Cards [1] [3] [£]

GH [Q][Q][Q] ***Kincraig Private Hotel*** 39 Ayr Road KA9 1SY ☎(0292) 79480

Set on the main road on the Ayr side of town, this detached red sandstone house offers well proportioned bedrooms, a comfortable lounge and an attractive dining room. A ground-floor bedroom is contained in its own small building to the rear of the house, looking out onto the garden.

6rm(3🚿) (1fb) CTV in all bedrooms [R] LDO 5pm

Lic 🅿 CTV nc3yrs

SELECTED

GH [Q][Q][Q][Q] **Redlands** Redlands, 38 Monkton Rd KA9 1AR (going S on A77 pass airport, take 3rd exit off rdbt towards Prestwick, Redlands on left in 100yds) ☎(0292) 79479

This sturdy detached red sandstone house, immaculately maintained and efficiently run by its friendly owners, offers easy access to the airport from a position beside the main road. Airy, attractively decorated bedrooms are comfortably furnished, and public areas include a delightful lounge and a separate dining room where it may sometimes be necessary to share tables. Guests should note that this is a non-smoking establishment.

3rm(1🚿) (1fb) 🚭 CTV in all bedrooms [R] 🐕 (ex guide dogs) ✱ sB&B£15-£20 sB&B🚿£20 dB&B£30-£32 dB&B🚿£37-£40

🅿

RAMSGATE Kent Map **05** TR36

GH [Q][Q] **Eastwood** 28 Augusta Road CT11 8JS (east side of harbour near Granville Theatre) ☎Thanet(0843) 591505 FAX (0843) 591505

This well-maintained establishment provides accomodation in two houses. Each has its own brightly decorated dining room serving a set evening meal. A small sitting room is also available for guests' use. Some bedrooms are small but all have colourful soft furnishings.

7rm(2🛁🚿) (4fb) CTV in all bedrooms [R] ✱ sB&B£20-£28 sB&B🛁🚿£25-£30 dB&B£35-£40 dB&B🛁🚿£35-£40 WB&B£120-£150 WBDi£150-£170 LDO 6pm

🅿 CTV

[£]

GH [Q] **St Hilary Private Hotel** 21 Crescent Road CT11 9QU (follow A253 to B2054 at small roundabout turn into Westcliff road, take second left into Crescent Road) ☎Thanet(0843) 591427

rs 25-26 Dec

A modest, traditional and professionally run guest house, St Hilary is located in a Victorian residential district. It provides a lounge with a TV and video recorder, and a bar-cum-breakfast room. Some of the bedrooms have shower cubicles.

7rm (4fb) 🚭 in 2 bedrooms 🚭 in dining room 🚭 in lounges [R] 🐕 ✱ sB&B£16-£18 dB&B£30-£32 WB&B£84 WBDi£91-£98 LDO 3.30pm

Lic CTV 🅿̸ nc4yrs

Credit Cards [1] [2] [3] [£]

RASKELF North Yorkshire Map **08** SE47

SELECTED

GH [Q][Q][Q][Q] **Old Farmhouse Country Hotel** YO6 3LF (Logis) ☎Easingwold(0347) 821971 FAX (0347) 822392

Closed 22 Dec-Jan

Originally the farmhouse for the village farm, this lovely old building is now a well furnished and comfortable hotel with a reputation for hospitality and good food. It is ideal for exploring the North York Moors and the Hambleton Hills. The beamed bedrooms, which include two family rooms and one room with a four-poster bed, are decorated in a mixture of styles and are well equipped. Two very comfortable lounges are available, one smaller with a TV, and the very popular restaurant offers a wide choice of home-cooked dishes.

10rm(6🛁4🚿) (2fb) 🚭 in dining room CTV in all bedrooms [R] T sB&B🛁🚿£25-£29 dB&B🛁🚿£40-£50 LDO 7pm
Lic 🔥

RAVENSCAR North Yorkshire — Map **08** NZ90

GH [Q][Q][Q] The Smugglers Rock Country YO13 0ER
☎Scarborough(0723) 870044
Mar-Nov
Once a coaching inn, this delightful stone-built house has links with the many smuggling activities that flourished along this coast. Now a guesthouse, it offers a high standard of accommodation with all en suite rooms. The beamed guests' lounge is particularly comfortable, and there is a games room with snooker, pool or table tennis, as well as a cosy bar. Home cooked meals are served in the attractive dining room.
9🛁🚿 (2fb) 🚭 in dining room 🚭 in lounges CTV in all bedrooms [R] * sB&B🛁🚿£19-£21 dB&B🛁🚿£38-£42 WB&B£125-£135 WBDi£169-£179 LDO 4.30pm
Lic 🔥 CTV nc3yrs snooker games room
[£]

RAVENSTONEDALE Cumbria — Map **12** NY70

🛏☕ **INN [Q][Q][Q] Kings Head** Coldbeck CA17 4NH
☎Newbiggin-on-Lune(05396) 23284 FAX (05396) 23604
Standing on the approach to the village, and next to a fast flowing beck, this delightful old inn offers pleasantly furnished bedrooms. The bar and restaurant have old-world appeal and offer a good range of well produced food.
4rm(2🛁) (1fb) 🚭 in area of dining room CTV in all bedrooms [R] T sB&Bfr£15 sB&B🛁£20 dB&B🛁£40 WB&B£120 WBDi£130 Lunch £4-£8&alc High tea £1.50-£4 Dinner £8-£12&alc LDO 9.30pm
🔥 CTV 🎣
[£]

READING Berkshire — Map **04** SU77

GH [Q][Q][Q] Abbey House Hotel 118 Connaught Road RG3 2UF (take A329 towards Tilehurst after Reading West Railway bridge take 3rd left) (MIN) ☎(0734) 590549 FAX (0734) 569299
Situated in a quiet residential road off the A329 and convenient for Reading West Station and the town centre, this friendly family-run hotel provides a sound standard of accommodation. Bedrooms vary in size and style from the relatively modest to some with three-star comfort and extras such as trouser presses and telephone computer terminals. There is a comfortable lounge and a small bar adjoins the dining room serving an extensive range of meals each evening.
18rm(9🛁🚿) (1fb) 🚭 in dining room CTV in all bedrooms [R] T 🐕 (ex guide dogs) * sB&B£25-£29 sB&B🛁🚿£35-£45.50 dB&B£40-£48.50 dB&B🛁🚿£44-£58 LDO 8.30pm
Lic 🔥 CTV
Credit Cards [1][2][3][5] [£]

GH [Q][Q][Q] Aeron Private Hotel 191-193 Kentwood Hill, Tilehurst RG3 6JE (3m W off A329) ☎(0734) 424119
FAX (0734) 451953
This family run hotel is in Tilehurst on the North West edge of Reading. It has been extensively upgraded to offer bedrooms in two adjacent houses in a variety of styles to suit all pockets. All the rooms are well maintained and equipped with direct dial telephone and TV but en suite rooms have been more recently refurbished and provide such extras as writing desks and hairdryers. There is a smartly decorated lounge and dinner is served Monday to Thursday in the licensed dining room and includes dishes such as lasagne or chicken kiev and home made spotted dick or treacle sponge. A large car park is available for guests' use.

▶

[AA]
QQ
EASTWOOD GUEST HOUSE
R·H·A

28 Augusta Road, Ramsgate, Kent CT11 8JS
Tel/Fax: Thanet (01843) 591505

- The house is situated in a lovely position adjacent to the beach, the Ferry port and the town centre.
- 13 Comfortable rooms with satellite TV and hot drink making facilities. 8 En suite rooms available.
- Good food and any special diets happily catered for.

This house is appraised for its unique friendly atmosphere

OPEN ALL YEAR

GARAGE PARKING AND AMPLE SAFE PARKING

B & B from £15.00 nightly. Evening meal £5.00
Reduced weekly terms
Send for colour brochure
Proprietor: Mrs Carole Gunnell

THE KINGS HEAD HOTEL

Ravenstonedale, Kirkby Stephen, Cumbria CA17 4NH
Telephone No. 015396 23284
AA LISTED

A Charming Village Inn within an area of outstanding natural beauty.

The Kings Head Hotel is a quaint village Inn offering comfortable accommodation in en-suite bedrooms, all with excellent outlooks, and good food served either as a bar snack in the Lounge bar or beer garden beside the beck, or taken at leisure in the cosy restaurant. There is a pool table, darts board and dominoes in the games room and for the really energetic our residents have use of the village tennis court or bowling green.
Nearby there is excellent fishing.
Ravenstonedale is a superb base for fell-walkers and ramblers alike and mountain bikes can be hired in nearby Kirkby Stephen. Scotland, the Lake District and the Yorkshire Dales National Park are all within easy motoring distance.

14rm(7♠) Annexe 11rm (1fb) ⚥ in area of dining room CTV in all bedrooms ® T ✳ sB&B£25-£28 sB&B♠£26-£41 dB&B£33-£43 dB&B♠£44-£54 LDO 8.15pm
Lic ▥ CTV
Credit Cards ① ② ③

REDCAR Cleveland   Map 08 NZ62

GH ◖◗◖◗◖◗ Claxton Hotel 196 High Street TS10 3AW
☎(0642) 486745 FAX (0642) 486522
Situated at the end of the High Street, this well established hotel provides well appointed accommodation, with both the business and leisure guest in mind. The spacious, attractive open-plan bar and restaurant are popular, and there is a cosy TV lounge; some rooms enjoy sea views.
27rm(21♠) (3fb) ⚥ in dining room CTV in all bedrooms ® ✳ sB&B£19-£22 sB&B♠£22 dB&B£34.50 dB&B♠£38 LDO 7pm
Lic ▥ CTV
£

REDHILL Surrey   Map 04 TQ25

GH ◖◗◖◗◖◗ Ashleigh House Hotel 39 Redstone Hill RH1 4BG
☎(0737) 764763 FAX (0737) 780308
Closed Xmas
This attractive detached Edwardian house stands on the hill to the east of the town and is ideally located for the town centre and station. Hospitable owners Jill and Michael Warren are committed to a programme of improvements, and half the bedrooms have been smartly refurbished; they are now all equipped with TV and hair dryers. There is a cosy guests' lounge, and hearty English breakfasts are served. Summer weather permits use of the garden and access to an outdoor swimming pool at specific times of the day.
8rm(1⇆5♠) (2fb)CTV in all bedrooms ® ✗ (ex guide dogs) sB&B£25-£30 sB&B⇆♠£35-£40 dB&B£38-£40 dB&B⇆♠£45-£50
▥ ⭍(heated)
Credit Cards ① ③

GH ◖◗◖◗ Lynwood House 50 London Road RH1 1LN
☎(0737) 766894 & 778253
An ivy-clad semidetached house situated close to the town centre and only a short distance from the airport provides accommodation in freshly decorated but relatively simply furnished bedrooms. Guests have the use of a small lounge as well as the dining room, and car parking space is available at the rear of the building.
9rm(2♠) (4fb) ⚥ in dining room CTV in all bedrooms ® ✗ (ex guide dogs) ✳ sB&B£22-£28 dB&B£38-£42 dB&B♠£40-£45
▥
Credit Cards ① ③ £

REDMILE Leicestershire   Map 08 SK73

GH ◖◗◖◗◖◗ Peacock Farm Guest House & Restaurant
NG13 0GQ ☎Bottesford(0949) 42475 due to change to 842475 FAX (0949) 43127
There are clear signs to this roadside building, located to the north of Redmile. The restaurant provides generous meals to overnight guests as well as encouraging local and passing trade. Five of the individually furnished bedrooms are in the main building, while the remainder are in an extension with separate entrances.
4rm Annexe 6⇆♠ ⚥ in dining room CTV in 4 bedrooms ® ✗ (ex guide dogs) ✳ sB&B£26 sB&B⇆♠£30 dB&B£36 dB&B⇆♠£44 LDO 8.30pm
Lic ▥ CTV ⭍ snooker solarium table tennis croquet
Credit Cards ① ② ③ £

REDWICK Gwent   Map 03 ST48

GH ◖◗◖◗◖◗ Brickhouse NP6 3DX ☎Magor(0633) 880230
FAX (0633) 880230

This delightful large Georgian style original farmhouse is situated on the edge of the village near Newport, in a quiet peaceful location, yet only three miles from Junction 23 of the M4. Although part of a working farm, the guesthouse is run separately and provides spotlessly clean, comfortable and spacious no smoking bedrooms with good quality furnishings and decor, the majority with excellent private bathrooms. Home-cooked meals and handsome breakfasts are served in the pleasant dining room.
7rm(5⇆♠) (1fb) ✗ ✳ sB&Bfr£24 sB&B⇆♠£29 dB&B⇆♠£39 LDO 6pm
Lic ▥ CTV
£

REEDHAM Norfolk   Map 05 TG40

GH ◖◗◖◗◖◗ Briars 10 Riverside NR13 3TF (approach on B1140, turn right at Reedham railway station, 0.5m to war memorial and fork right) ☎Great Yarmouth(0493) 700054
This small, welcoming home has a wonderful location overlooking the River Yare and Broads, in a quiet village. The ground floor is taken up by a tea shop and hair salon by day, and on certain nights a dinner menu is offered. The three comfortable bedrooms are furnished in pine; there is also a lounge and conservatory with sweeping views over the Broads.
3rm(2♠) ⚥ in dining room CTV in all bedrooms ® ✗ (ex guide dogs) sB&B£24 sB&B♠£28 dB&B£30 dB&B♠£35 LDO 9pm
▥ CTV ✔
£

REETH North Yorkshire   Map 07 SE09

P R E M I E R   ❦   S E L E C T E D

GH ◖◗◖◗◖◗◖◗◖◗ Arkleside Hotel DL11 6SG
☎Richmond(0748) 84200
Mar-Oct rs Nov-Dec
There are fine views along the dale from the rear of this delightful, friendly and enthusiastically run little hotel - originally a row of cottages dating back to the 1600s. Attractively decorated bedrooms offer many thoughtful extras, while both the comfortable sitting room and a separate bar lounge provide an abundance of books and magazines. The well produced four-course dinner is served in a dining room featuring natural stonework and enjoying a delightful outlook.
9rm(1⇆7♠) CTV in all bedrooms ® LDO 7.30pm
Lic ▥ nc10yrs ✛(hard)✔
Credit Cards ① ③

INN ◖◗◖◗◖◗ Buck Hotel DL11 6SW ☎(0748) 884210
FAX (0748) 884802
10⇆♠ (2fb)CTV in all bedrooms ® sB&B⇆♠£25 dB&B⇆♠£49 Bar Lunch £9 LDO 9pm
▥ CTV
Credit Cards ① ③

REIGATE Surrey   Map 04 TQ25

S E L E C T E D

GH ◖◗◖◗◖◗◖◗ Cranleigh Hotel 41 West Street RH2 9BL (on A25 at end of High St heading towards Dorking) (MIN)
☎(0737) 223417 FAX (0737) 223734
Closed 24-26 Dec
Situated just beyond the end of the High Street, en route for

Dorking, this small, privately owned and personally run hotel offers bedrooms well suited to the needs of business travellers; spacious public areas include a comfortable lounge with some original features, a small bar and an attractive dining room with an adjoining conservatory which is available for small meetings and private dinners. A popular range of pasta dishes supplements the short, weekly-changing menu available from Monday to Thursday (meals being by request at other times). The delightful garden includes a small orchard and heated swimming pool.
9rm(6🛁) (1fb)CTV in all bedrooms [R] T 🐕 (ex guide dogs)
sB&B£36-£39 sB&B🛁£49.95-£52 dB&B🛁£59.95-£64
LDO 9pm
Lic ▦ CTV 🏊(heated) 🎾(hard&grass)
Credit Cards [1][2][3][5][£]

RETFORD Nottinghamshire

See **North Wheatley**

RHANDIRMWYN Dyfed — Map **03** SN74

INN[Q][Q] The Royal Oak SA20 0NY (follow signs to Rhandirmwyn from A40 at Llandovery) ☎(05506) 201
FAX (05506) 332
Reached by a picturesque drive through a wooded valley along the A48 north of Llandovey, this secluded inn has pretty, well equipped bedrooms and a warm, welcoming bar.
5rm(2🛁1🚿) (1fb)CTV in 3 bedrooms [R] ✳ sB&B£18-£20.50
dB&B🛁🚿£45-£50 LDO 9.30pm
pool table clay pigeon wknds
Credit Cards [1][3][£]

The Aeron Private Hotel

191 Kentwood Hill, Tilehurst, Reading.
Tel: (01734) 424119 Fax: (01734) 451953

25 bedrooms, standard & en suite, all with colour TV, direct dial telephone, tea & coffee making facilities. Full English breakfast. Dinner served Mon-Thurs inclusive, except weekends & Bank Holidays. Excellent accommodation at very competitive rates.

WEEKEND DISCOUNT

2 miles M4 exit 12. 45 minutes London Airport via M4. 25 minutes London Paddington via BR.

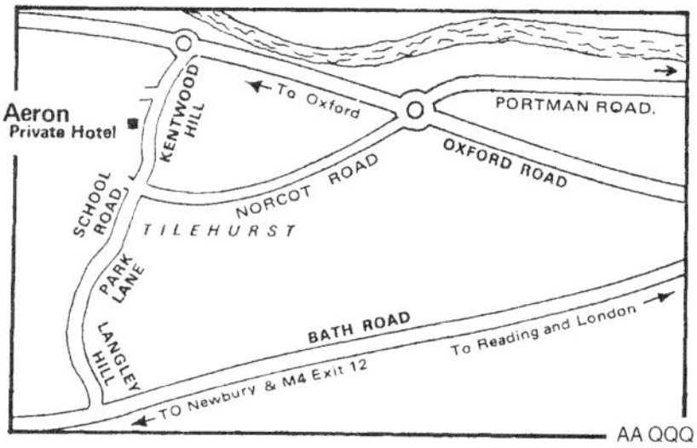

Aeron Private Hotel
KENTWOOD HILL
To Oxford
PORTMAN ROAD
OXFORD ROAD
NORCOT ROAD
SCHOOL ROAD
TILEHURST
PARK LANE
LANGLEY HILL
BATH ROAD
To Reading and London
TO Newbury & M4 Exit 12

AA QQQ

Guests using Airports and Ferries may leave their cars here free of charge.

English Tourist Board COMMENDED

Ashleigh House Hotel

39 Redstone Hill, Redhill, Surrey RH1 4BG
Tel: (01737) 764763 Fax: (01737) 780308

This fine Edwardian residence now run as a family hotel offers a genuine friendly atmosphere with the personal attention of the owners at all times. Ideally located for visiting London and houses and gardens of historic interest.
★ Hair dryer, tea/coffee & colour television in all rooms ★ Many en suite
★ Exit junction 6 & 8 M25
Gatwick by car 15 minutes, by train 10 minutes
London by train 30 minutes

Awarded AA QQQQQ Premier Selected for 1993/94

The Old Plough

Country Guest House
Top Street, North Wheatley, Retford, Nottingham DN22 9DB
Tel: (01427) 880916

Situated in a quiet unspoiled rural village, The Old Plough has, in only three years been acclaimed by the AA as best newcomer in the Midlands for 1992-93, and graded 👑👑 De Luxe by the ETB. Its elegant and comfortable accommodation leaves nothing to be desired and is complemented by superb cuisine. Fully licensed for a relaxing and peaceful stay.

Colour brochure on request.

RHAYADER Powys   Map **06** SN96

INNQ̲ *Lamb & Flag Inn* North Street LD6 5BU ☎(0597) 810819
This old inn is at the heart of the busy market town. The bar, with
exposed timers and an inglenook fireplace, is full of character and
there is a separate restaurant where meals are served. Four
bedrooms are available in the main building and there are two
more in a nearby annexe. One of these is a two-bedroomed family
suite.
4♠ Annexe 3rm(1⇄2♠) (3fb) CTV in 2 bedrooms ℝ ⅋ (ex
guide dogs) LDO 9.30pm
▥

RHOSCOLYN See **ANGLESEY, ISLE OF**

RHOS-ON-SEA Clwyd
See **Colwyn Bay**

RHYL Clwyd   Map **06** SJ08

GH Q̲Q̲Q̲ **Pier Hotel** 23 East Parade LL18 3AL (on promenade
between Sea Life and bowling greens) ☎(0745) 350280
Closed 22-31 Dec
Standing on the promenade near to the leisure Sun Centre and the
shops, this terraced house has both well equipped bedrooms and
family suites - many with sea views. There is also a TV lounge, a
cosy bar and spacious dining room. The car park is limited but
there is ample public parking nearby.
8rm(3⇄4♠) (3fb)CTV in all bedrooms ℝ ✳ sB&B£14-£15
dB&B⇄♠£32-£36 WB&B£95-£110 WBDi£145-£155 LDO 3pm
Lic ▥ CTV
Credit Cards ①③ⓛ

RICHMOND North Yorkshire   Map **07** NZ10

See also Low Row, Reeth and Thwaite

GH Q̲Q̲Q̲ **Pottergate** 4 Pottergate DL10 4AB ☎(0748) 823826
This Georgian terraced house is just a short walk from the town
centre. The bedrooms, although compact, are well equipped and
family rooms are available. A small bar, lounge, and an attractive
breakfast room are located on the ground floor.
6rm (2fb) CTV in all bedrooms ℝ ⅋ sB&B£22-£24 dB&B£34-
£36 WB&B£110-£160
Lic ▥ CTV nc2yrs

FH Q̲Q̲Q̲ Mr & Mrs P Chilton **Mount Pleasant** *(NZ149058)*
Whashton DL11 7JP ☎(0748) 822784
Closed 20-28 Dec
This 19th-century family farm specialising in sheep and beef cattle
has belonged to the Chilton family for more than 100 years. It is
situated in delightful countryside and provides very comfortable
accommodation. Four of the rooms are in a convertyed
outbuilding and have names such as The Piggery and The Bull
Pen. One room has facilities for disabled guests. In the farmhouse
itself are two cosy lounges and an attractive dining room with
individual tables. Evening meals are served at 7pm.
6rm(4⇄4♠) (2fb) CTV in all bedrooms ℝ ✳ sB&B£18.50-
£19.50 sB&B⇄♠£18.50-£19.50 dB&B£34-£36 dB&B⇄♠£34-
£36 WB&B£119-£126 WBDi£182-£189 LDO 6pm
Lic ▥ CTV 280 acres sheep/beef

Telephone national area codes are due
to change by 16th April 1995. Please
see the note under 'How to Use this
Guide' at the front of the book.

PREMIER 🏅 **SELECTED**

FH Q̲Q̲Q̲Q̲Q̲ Mrs M F
Turnbull **Whashton Springs**
(NZ149046) DL11 7JS (in
Richmond turn left at traffic
lights towards Ravensworth,
3m down steep hill farm at
bottom on left)
☎(0748) 822884
Closed late Dec-Jan

Very warm and friendly
service is provided by the
family who own this charming
Georgian farmhouse set in delightful countryside to the north
of Richmond. Wholesome Yorkshire breakfasts and well
prepared dinners are served in the cosy dining room, and
guests can relax in a comfortable lounge (warmed by a log fire
during the colder months) which has lovely views over the
garden. Bedrooms in the garden annexe are modern in style
whilst those in the main house are more traditional, but all are
thoughtfully equipped as well as attractively furnished and
decorated. Guests are encouraged to explore the farm or to
wander down to the stream through well tended grounds.
3rm(2⇄1♠) Annexe 5rm(2⇄3♠) (2fb) ⅋ in 3 bedrooms ⅋
in dining room CTV in all bedrooms ℝ T ⅋ (ex guide dogs)
sB&B⇄♠£26-£28 dB&B⇄♠£40-£44 WB&B£137-£144
WBDi£200-£220 LDO am
Lic ▥ nc5yrs 600 acres arable beef mixed sheep
ⓛ

RINGWOOD Hampshire   Map **04** SU10

PREMIER 🏅 **SELECTED**

GH Q̲Q̲Q̲Q̲Q̲ **Little
Forest Lodge Hotel** Poulner
Hill BH24 3HS (1.5m E on A31)
☎(0425) 478848
Just a mile from Ringwood,
surrounded by the New Forest,
this attractive, personally run
hotel has much to offer. Its
period is Edwardian and its
style very much that of a
country house, with attentive
service throughout. Eric
Martin is the convivial host, and his wife Jane presides over
the kitchen, offering an imaginative menu of home cooked
meals. Bedrooms, individually decorated and very pretty, are
equipped with a host of extras to ensure a comfortable stay.
There is a lounge with a small bar at one end and a snooker
table at the other.
5rm(2⇄3♠) (2fb) ⅋ in 3 bedrooms CTV in all bedrooms ℝ
sB&B⇄♠£27.50-£45 dB&B⇄♠£39-£65 WB&B£113-£225
LDO 4pm
Lic ▥
Credit Cards ①③ⓛ

SELECTED

GH Q̲Q̲Q̲Q̲ **The Nest** 10 Middle Lane BH24 1LE (off A31
into B3347 at 2nd pedestrian lights turn sharp left into School
Lane then left again) ☎(0425) 476724
Watch out for the B&B sign on the wooden fence and follow
directions to find this delightful, family-run former
schoolhouse, which is within walking distance of the town
centre. The pretty bedrooms are all individually furnished and

the standard of housekeeping is particularly high. Full English breakfast is served in the conservatory dining room overlooking the neat rear garden. This is a no-smoking establishment.
3rm ⊁ CTV in all bedrooms ⓡ ✳ sB&B£18-£25 dB&B£32-£36 WB&B£105-£119 ▥ ⓕ

RIPON North Yorkshire　　　　　　Map **08** SE37

FH ⓠⓠⓠ Mrs V Leeming **Bay Tree** *(SE263685)* Aldfield
HG4 3BE (approx 4m W, take unclass road S off B6265)
☎(0765) 620394
6rm(2⇌2↿) (1fb) ⊁ in bedrooms CTV in all bedrooms ⓡ ✳ sB&B⇌↿£18 dB&B⇌↿£36 LDO 10am
▥ ⚭ 400 acres dairy beef arable
Credit Cards ①③

ROADWATER Somerset　　　　　　Map **03** ST03

SELECTED

FH ⓠⓠⓠⓠ Mr & Mrs Brewer **Wood Advent** *(ST037374)*
TA23 0RR ☎Washford(0984) 40920 due to change to 640920
FAX (0984) 40920
Part of a working 360-acre mixed farm, this secluded 19th-century farmhouse nestles at the foot of the Brendon hills in the beautiful Exmoor National Park. The no-smoking bedrooms are spacious, comfortable, and beautifully furnished, with delightful views over the large garden, woods and fields. A set five-course dinner cooked by Mrs Brewer is served at separate tables in the dining room. Possible leisure pursuits include walking, riding, clay-pigeon shooting and golf.
5rm(1⇌3↿) (3fb) ⊁ in bedrooms ⊁ in dining room ⊁ in lounges ⓡ ⊁ ✳ sB&B⇌↿£17.50-£23.50 dB&B⇌↿£35-£47 (incl dinner) WBDi£170-£200 LDO 9.30am
Lic ▥ CTV ⚭ ⭍(heated) ⬚(grass)clay pigeon shooting 350 acres arable beef sheep

ROCHDALE Greater Manchester　　　　Map **07** SD81

FH ⓠⓠ Mrs J Neave **Leaches** *(SD837139)* Ashworth Valley
OL11 5UN ☎(0706) 41116 & 228520
Closed 22 Dec-2 Jan
The Neaves have improved the farm track that leads to this 17th-century farmhouse, situated between the A680 and the B6222, enjoying breathtaking views over the Manchester plain. Bedrooms are simple but pleasantly furnished, though the single room is extremely small. There is a comfortable lounge in which to relax and the Neaves are a mine of local information.
3rm (2fb) ⊁ in bedrooms ⊁ in dining room CTV in all bedrooms ⓡ ✳ sB&Bfr£18 dB&Bfr£34
▥ CTV ⏺ 140 acres beef sheep
ⓕ

ROCHE Cornwall & Isles of Scilly　　　Map **02** SW96

GH ⓠⓠⓠ **Asterisk** Mount Pleasant PL26 8LH
☎St Austell(0726) 890863
This detached stone house stands back from the A30 east of Roche in its own grounds, which contain cows, horses, goats and Shetland ponies. Proprietors Mr and Mrs Zola are steadily improving the accommodation, with a restaurant and smart lounge/bar new additions this year. The bedrooms are bright and fresh, two have private bathrooms, another two have showers. Some of the bedrooms have rural views. There is a comfortable TV lounge with TV, books and a log fire, and a cosy bar.

7rm(2↿) (2fb) ⓡ
Lic ▥ CTV
Credit Cards ①③

ROCHESTER Northumberland　　　　Map **12** NY89

[⇤▪] FH ⓠⓠ Mrs J M Chapman **Woolaw** *(NY821984)*
NE19 1TB ☎Otterburn(0830) 520686
This traditional farmhouse offers charmingly unpretentious bed and breakfast accommodation in lovely rural surroundings. The ground-floor en suite bedrooms are compact and modestly furnished; the first-floor room offers greater comfort, but shares a bathroom with the owners.
3rm(2↿) (1fb) TV available ⛨ (ex guide dogs) sB&B↿£13.50-£15 dB&B↿£27-£30 LDO 5.30pm
▥ CTV ⏺ 740 acres beef horses sheep

ROCK Cornwall & Isles of Scilly　　　Map **02** SW97

GH ⓠⓠ **Roskarnon House Hotel** PL27 6LD
☎Trebetherick(0208) 862329
Mar-Nov
Set in an acre of mature grounds, this detached Edwardian house has been owned by the same family for over 35 years. Standing in an elevated position, it has spectacular panoramic views over the Camel Estuary, and offers peaceful relaxation at an affordable price. Two of the bedrooms have a private shower, some have TV and two are conveniently located on the ground floor; most have sea views. The lounge and dining room overlook the lawns and beach. A table d'hôte menu is served, using home-grown produce, and the friendly service is personally supervised by the proprietor Ian Veall. Table tennis is available in the games room, and local sports including sailing, golf, tennis, riding, water skiing, surfing and fishing can be arranged.

▶

Mount Pleasant Farm

This is a PLEASANT place to stay and we give our visitors a real Yorkshire welcome

Mount Pleasant Farm

Situated in the heart of lovely rolling countryside 3 miles from the market town of Richmond and just outside the peaceful town of Whashton. Built in 1850 this stone farmhouse has been in the same family since the 1880's. It is a working farm with sheep and beef cows and you are welcome to walk round and see the animals, there is also a farm walk. All rooms are en suite and all have good heating, colour TV and tea/coffee facilities. Noted for its good food, start your day with a farmers breakfast and end your day with a drink before a 3 course dinner – all home-made and lots of it! An ideal base to visit the many attractions and beautiful countryside of the Yorkshire Dales.

Whashton, Richmond, North Yorkshire DL11 7JP
Telephone: (01748) 822784

12rm(9⇄🟊) (5fb) ⚹ in dining room CTV in all bedrooms ® 🍴 (ex guide dogs) ✳ sB&Bfr£20 sB&B⇄🟊fr£20 dB&Bfr£40 dB&B⇄🟊fr£45 WB&Bfr£160 WBDifr£180 LDO 8pm
Lic CTV
Credit Cards ② £

RODE Somerset   Map **03** ST85

GH 🅀🅀🅀🅀🅀 **Irondale**
67 High Street BA3 6PB
☎(0373) 830730
Closed 24-27 Dec

Situated in the High street of
the village of Rode, this
elegant three-storey family
home is convenient for the
city of Bath and many places
of interest. A warm welcome
awaits guests, and they are
treated as part of the Holder
family, sharing the two delightful lounges and taking breakfast
at one large table in the attractive dining room. The bedrooms
have been tastefully decorated and furnished with beautiful
floral drapes, and each has its own bathroom across the
landing.
2⇄🟊 ⚹ in bedrooms ⚹ in 1 lounge CTV in all bedrooms ®
✳ sB&B⇄🟊£35-£40 dB&B⇄🟊£40-£45
🛏 CTV nc8yrs
£
See advertisement under BATH

ROEWEN Gwynedd   Map **06** SH77

S E L E C T E D
GH 🅀🅀🅀🅀 **Gwern Borter Country Manor** Barkers
Lane LL32 8YL (take B5106 for half a mile turn right take left
fork Gwern Borter just up on left)
☎Tyn-y-Groes(0492) 650360
Closed 23 Dec-2 Jan
A 19th-century manor house and former mink farm, Gwern
Borter is situated in ten acres of landscaped grounds with
farmyard birds, pets and a duck pond. Notable features are the
oak panelled entrance hall and staircase, and the oak fireplace
in the dining room. Bedrooms all have en suite or private
facilities and the beds are attractively canopied. A self-catering
apartment is available in the courtyard.
3rm(1⇄2🟊) (1fb) ⚹ in dining room CTV in all bedrooms ®
✳ sB&B⇄🟊£35-£40 dB&B⇄🟊£36-£48 WB&B£120-£160
WBDi£160-£198 LDO 4pm
Lic 🛏 CTV ⚲ ∪ cycle hire
Credit Cards ① ③ £

ROGART Highland *Sutherland*   Map **14** NC70

S E L E C T E D
FH 🅀🅀🅀🅀 Mrs J S R Moodie **Rovie** *(NC716023)*
IV28 3TZ (A838 into village of Rogart then take first right over
railway crossing and follow sign to guesthouse)
☎(0408) 641209
mid Mar-Nov
Guests return year after year to sample the welcoming
hospitality and enjoyable home cooking offered by Christine
Moodie, at her delightful lodge-style farmhouse in the
picturesque valley of Streathfleet. The comfortable bedrooms

are spacious with individual decor and furniture of various
styles. The main lounge with its welcoming peat-burning fire
is comfortable and pleasantly furnished, inviting peaceful
relaxation, and a TV is provided in the cosy timber-lined sun
lounge. Hearty breakfasts and enjoyable home-cooked dinners
are served at separate tables in the attractive dining room,
though at peak times it may be necessary to share a table with
other guests. A genuine home-from-home atmosphere prevails
and home baking is personally served with morning and
evening teas. Fishing and shooting can be arranged.
6rm (1fb) ⚹ in 4 bedrooms ⚹ in dining room ⚹ in lounges ✳
sB&Bfr£17 dB&Bfr£34 WB&Bfr£119 WBDifr£196 LDO
6.30pm
CTV ⚲ ►9 ⏩ rough shooting 120 acres beef sheep
£

ROGATE West Sussex   Map **04** SU82

FH 🅀🅀🅀🅀🅀 Mrs J C
Francis **Mizzards** *(SU803228)*
GU31 5HS (from x-rds in Rogate
go S for 0.50m cross river
continue for 300yds then turn
right signed Mizzards Farm)
☎(0730) 821656
FAX (0730) 821655
Closed Xmas

This delightful 16th-century
farmhouse is set in 13 acres of
landscaped gardens, which
include a swimming pool and lake, with the river Rother
forming a boundary on one side. Attractively furnished
bedrooms are individually decorated, the most impressive
being the 'Glitter Room' with its raised, canopied bed, and
marble-tiled, mirrored bathroom. The elegant drawing room is
comfortable, with a log fire in winter and the spectacular
breakfast room is galleried and beamed, with a huge
inglenook fireplace. No evening meals are served but there are
many good local pubs and restaurants nearby and the huge
farmhouse breakfast may include Manx kippers and home-
produced honey. Mrs Francis does not allow smoking in the
house.
3⇄🟊 ⚹ CTV in all bedrooms ® 🍴 sB&B⇄🟊£30-£36
dB&B⇄🟊£46-£54
🛏 nc9yrs ⚹(heated) croquet 13 acres sheep non-working
£

FH 🅀🅀🅀 Mrs J Baigent **Trotton** *(SU835225)* GU31 5EN (on
A272 between Midhurst and Petersfield)
☎Midhurst(0730) 813618 FAX (0730) 816093
A busy working farm well located off the A272 between
Petersfield and Midhurst, offers well presented, modern
accommodation in a converted barn. A third bedroom has been
added recently, conveniently sited on the ground floor, and all
bedrooms have smart, modern en suite shower rooms. The sitting
room offers a good supply of games and books, including table
tennis and darts, and children are welcome. The farm is situated in
an area of outstanding natural beauty with good fishing.
3🟊 ⚹ ® 🍴 (ex guide dogs) sB&B🟊£25-£30 dB&B🟊£35-£40
🛏 CTV ⏩ table tennis darts 230 acres arable beef mixed

ROMFORD Greater London   Map **05** TQ58

GH 🅀🅀 **Maylands View** 7 Johns Terrace, Colchester Road,
Harold Park RM3 0AW ☎(0708) 345234
2🟊 (1fb) ⚹ in dining room CTV in all bedrooms ®

dB&Bↁfr£35 WB&B£120
▥
£

GH Ⓠ *The Orchard Guest House* 81 Eastern Road RM1 3PB
☎(0708) 744099
Closed Xmas
Set in a quiet residential road, close to the town centre, this red brick Edwardian house retains many of its original features and offers simply appointed bedrooms of varying styles and a good combined lounge/dining room. Mrs Thomas has also created an attractive secluded garden for guests to enjoy during the warmer months.
5rm(1f≈) (2fb) CTV in all bedrooms ✠ (ex guide dogs) LDO am
▥ CTV

ROMSEY Hampshire   Map **04** SU32

ROSLIN Lothian *Midlothian*   Map **11** NT26

INN Ⓠ Ⓠ *Olde Original Rosslyn* 4 Main Street EH25 9LD
☎031-440 2384
This friendly village inn is just seven miles south of Edinburgh, conveniently located at the end of the village street. Attractively furnished bedrooms vary in size and some have four-posters. The bars have kept their traditional character and there is a delightful Victorian-style restaurant where prime Scottish steaks are something of a speciality.
6⇌f≈ CTV in all bedrooms Ⓡ LDO 10pm
▥
Credit Cards ① ② ③

ROSS-ON-WYE Hereford & Worcester   Map **03** SO52

See also St Owen's Cross

GH Ⓠ Ⓠ **The Arches Country House** Walford Road HR9 5PT
☎(0989) 563348
Closed Xmas
Set beside the B4234 on the outskirts of the town, this guesthouse provides neat accommodation in bedrooms which, although not very large, have been made attractive by the effective use of coordinating decor and soft furnishings. A pleasant conservatory at the entrance overlooks the well maintained garden. Personally run by welcoming hosts, this establishment is equally suited to business and leisure guests.
8rm(2⇌2f≈) (2fb) CTV in all bedrooms Ⓡ ✠ (ex guide dogs)
sB&B£17-£22 sB&Bↁf≈£22 dB&B£32 dB&Bↁf≈£42
WB&B£108-£143 WBDi£178-£213 LDO 5pm
Lic ▥ CTV
£

GH [Q] Brookfield House Ledbury Road HR9 7AT
☎(0989) 562188
Closed 3 days Xmas rs Nov-Jan
This popular guesthouse within walking distance of the town centre has modestly furnished bedrooms of varying size, a traditional lounge and small dining room where breakfasts are served.
8rm(1🛁2🚿) 🚭 in dining room CTV in all bedrooms Ⓡ ✳ sB&B£17-£19 dB&B£34-£36 dB&B🛁🚿£38-£40 WB&B£115-£129.50
Lic 🅿 nc5yrs
Credit Cards [1][2][3][£]

SELECTED

GH [Q][Q][Q][Q] Edde Cross House Edde Cross Street HR9 7BZ ☎(0989) 565088
Feb-Nov
An attractively refurbished Grade II listed Georgian town house is just a short walk from the town centre. It gives the impression of a well-cared-for house offering light bedrooms pleasantly decorated and well equipped with some thoughtful extras; some rooms have lovely views over the River Wye and most are furnished in old pine. There is a small comfortable lounge bar and a cosy dining room where a good choice is offered for breakfast, including a vegetarian menu. Guests also have the use of the delightful rear walled garden which offers fine views. Smoking is not permitted.
4🛁🚿 🚭 CTV in all bedrooms Ⓡ 🐕 ✳ sB&B£35-£40 dB&B🛁🚿£42-£46 WB&B£133-£147
🅿 🚸 nc10yrs

GH [Q][Q][Q] *Ryefield House Hotel* Gloucester Road HR9 5NA
☎(0989) 563030
A charming family-run hotel which has received awards for its decorative gardens, situated on the Gloucester road a short distance from the town centre. Mr and Mrs Edwards are enthusiastic owners, creating a welcoming atmosphere in comfortable public rooms which have been attractively furnished. Bedrooms vary in size and are well equipped, together with many thoughtful touches such as fresh flowers, fudge and books. Carefully produced home-cooked evening meals are available on advance request.
8rm(5🛁🚿) (4fb) CTV in all bedrooms Ⓡ **T** LDO 5pm
Lic 🅿 CTV

GH [Q][Q] The Skakes Glewstone HR9 6AZ (3m SW)
☎Llangarron(0989) 770456
8rm(1🛁1🚿) 🚭 in dining room CTV in all bedrooms Ⓡ sB&Bfr£20 dB&Bfr£30 dB&B🛁🚿fr£40 WB&B£105-£140 WBDi£157.50-£189 LDO 10am
Lic 🅿 nc10yrs
Credit Cards [1][3]

GH [Q][Q] Sunnymount Hotel Ryefield Road HR9 5LU
☎(0989) 563880
rs 21-31 Dec
This licensed hotel is located in a quiet residential area close to the town centre, with its own parking. Bedrooms vary in size and style and there are two lounges offering TV, books and games: one is no-smoking. Mr and Mrs Williams are welcoming hosts and provide enjoyable home-cooked meals.
9rm(7🛁🚿) 🚭 in dining room 🚭 in 1 lounge Ⓡ 🐕 (ex guide dogs) sB&B£18 sB&B🛁🚿£26-£29 dB&B🛁🚿£46-£50 WB&B£154-£175 WBDi£215-£250 LDO 6.30pm
Lic 🅿 CTV
Credit Cards [1][2][3][£]

ROTHBURY Northumberland — Map **12** NU00

SELECTED

GH [Q][Q][Q][Q] Orchard High Street NE65 7TL
☎(0669) 20684
Mar-Nov
A friendly welcome is assured at this family-run main-street guesthouse. Bedrooms are comfortable and well equipped, and there is a lounge with an honesty bar and a range of books and magazines. Each floor has an 'essential kit', including hairdryers, scissors, plasters and sewing materials. A good dinner is served each evening.
6rm(4🚿) (1fb) 🚭 in dining room CTV in all bedrooms Ⓡ 🐕 sB&B£20-£22 dB&B£40-£42 dB&B🚿£44-£46 WB&B£140-£154 WBDi£217-£231 LDO 7pm
Lic 🅿 🚸
[£]

ROTHERHAM South Yorkshire — Map **08** SK49

SELECTED

GH [Q][Q][Q][Q] Stonecroft Main Street, Bramley S66 0SF (4m E of Rotherham) ☎(0709) 540922
The owners offer a friendly welcome at this 17th-century former farmhouse which lies off the A631, conveniently near junction 1 of the M18. Accommodation is divided between the main house and the converted mews and stables in the gardens. All the bedrooms are well equipped and nicely decorated, but those in the main house are larger. There is a comfortable lounge, with satellite television, and there are plans to add a bar. Breakfast is served in the pleasant dining room and a wide choice of dishes is available.
3🛁🚿 Annexe 5🚿 (1fb) 🚭 in bedrooms 🚭 in dining room 🚭 in 1 lounge CTV in all bedrooms Ⓡ ✳ sB&B🛁🚿fr£29 dB&B🛁🚿fr£39
Lic 🅿 CTV
Credit Cards [1][3][£]

ROTTINGDEAN East Sussex — Map **05** TQ30

🛏 ☕ **GH [Q][Q] Braemar House** Steyning Road BN2 7GA
☎Brighton(0273) 304263
Peacefully situated close to the village shops and the seafront, this family-run guesthouse offers simple but particularly well kept accommodation. A cosy lounge is provided for residents in addition to the breakfast room.
15rm (2fb) 🚭 in dining room sB&Bfr£15 dB&Bfr£30
🅿 CTV 🚸
[£]

ROWSLEY Derbyshire — Map **08** SK26

INN[Q][Q][Q] Grouse and Claret Station Road DE4 2EL (on A6 between Matlock and Bakewell) ☎Darley Dale(0629) 733233
This extensively refurbished inn is just outside the village. The public areas are smart and comfortable, including public and lounge bars, and separate eating areas offer an extensive range of meals and snacks. Bedrooms are attractive and well furnished with matching coordinated soft furnishings and decor. Anglers can arrange to fish on the adjacent River Derwent.
5rm 🚭 in area of dining room 🚭 in 1 lounge CTV in all bedrooms Ⓡ 🐕 (ex guide dogs) ✳ sB&Bfr£20 dB&Bfr£35 Lunch £4.50-£10 Dinner fr£4.50 LDO 9.30pm
🅿
Credit Cards [1][3][£]

ROXTON Bedfordshire   Map **04** TL15

FH Q Q Q Mrs J Must **Church** *(TL153545)* 41 High Street
MK44 3EB (from A428 turn into Roxton village, at crossroads go
south down High St, Church Farm is second house on left after
Parish Hall) ☎Bedford(0234) 870234 FAX (0234) 871576
Set in the middle of a quiet village, this welcoming farm house is
bounded by arable fields. The two bedrooms it offers are fresh and
spacious, and there is a lounge with colour television; breakfast is
served round a large wooden table.
2rm (1fb) ⊬ Ⓡ sB&B£17-£22 dB&B£30-£36
🞉 CTV 66 acres arable

RUCKHALL Hereford & Worcester   Map **03** SO43

SELECTED

INN Q Q Q Q **The Ancient Camp** HR2 9QX
☎Golden Valley(0981) 250449 FAX (0981) 251581
rs Sun evening & Mon
At the edge of an Iron-Age camp from which it takes its name,
this well established inn is four miles south-west of Hereford
and is well signed. The view over the River Wye and Golden
Valley is a feast for the eyes, and the food and beer have quite
a local reputation as well. All the bedrooms are immaculately
kept, and the two overlooking the valley are the most
attractive. The inn has fishing rights on the river.
5rm(2⇆3♠) CTV in all bedrooms Ⓡ **T** 🐾 (ex guide dogs) ✳
sB&B⇆♠£35-£45 dB&B⇆♠£48-£58 Bar Lunch
£1.75-£8alc Dinner £8.50-£15alc LDO 9.30pm
🞉 nc10yrs ✍
Credit Cards 1 3 ①

RUFFORTH North Yorkshire   Map **08** SE55

GH Q Q **Wellgarth House** Wetherby Road YO2 3QB (turn off
A64 onto A1237, at 2nd roundabout turn left onto B1224
signposted Wetherby, 1st house on left entering village)
☎(0904) 738592 & 738595
Closed 25-26 Dec
Wellgarth is a modern house on the edge of the village four miles
west of York. The bedrooms, including one on the ground floor,
are well furnished and the majority now have en suite facilities.
There is an attractive dining room and a cosy guests' lounge.
8rm(6♠) (1fb) ⊬ in 5 bedrooms ⊬ in dining room CTV in all
bedrooms Ⓡ ✳ sB&Bfr£17 dB&Bfr£32 dB&B♠£34-£50
🞉 CTV
Credit Cards 1 3 ①

RUGBY Warwickshire   Map **04** SP57

GH Q Q **Avondale** 16 Elsee Road CV21 3BA ☎(0788) 578639
This semidetached house is situated in a quiet cul-de-sac reached
from Church Street via Moultrie Road, within easy reach of the
town centre. Bedrooms vary in size and style. Evening meals are
not served, but breakfast is provided in a combined
lounge/breakfast room with separate tables.
4rm (1♠) CTV in all bedrooms Ⓡ 🐾 sB&B£20 sB&B♠£25
dB&B£35 dB&B♠£39
🞉 CTV
①

RUGELEY Staffordshire   Map **07** SK01

GH Q Q **Ewart House** 66 Chaseley Road, Etchinghill WS15 2LG
(N on A51, turn left at lights into Hagley Road. At Chase Inn turn
right into Chaseley road) ☎(0889) 582289
♠ (1fb)CTV in all bedrooms Ⓡ **T** sB&B♠£25 dB&B♠£35
🞉
Credit Cards 1 3 ①

RUSHTON SPENCER Staffordshire   Map **07** SJ96

FH Q Q Mrs J Brown **Barnswood** *(SJ945606)* SK11 0RA (on
A523, 5m from Leek) ☎(0260) 226261
Closed 24 Dec-5 Jan
This 300-year-old stone-built farmhouse overlooks Rudyard Lake
from its setting on a dairy farm beside the A523
Leek/Macclesfield road. Simple, soundly maintained and
traditionally furnished bedrooms (served by a large shared
bathroom) include one suitable for family use, and television is
provided in the cosy lounge/dining room.
4rm (2fb) ⊬ in bedrooms Ⓡ 🐾 ✳ sB&Bfr£15 dB&Bfr£27
🞉 CTV 100 acres dairy
①

RUSTINGTON West Sussex   Map **04** TQ00

SELECTED

GH Q Q Q Q **Kenmore** Claigmar Road BN16 2NL
☎(0903) 784634
Quietly situated in a residential area just off the main shopping
street, this well run and attractively furnished guesthouse
continues to be improved. The bedrooms offer good levels of
comfort and several are ideal for families. There is a small
lounge, and a freshly prepared set three-course meal is served
in the sunny dining room every day if arranged in advance.
7rm(1⇆5♠) (2fb) CTV in all bedrooms Ⓡ ✳ sB&B£16.50-
£18 sB&B⇆♠£22.50-£25 dB&B⇆♠£45-£50 WB&B£145-
£160 LDO noon
🞉 CTV
Credit Cards 1 2 3 ①

Ryefield House Hotel

Gloucester Road, Ross-on-Wye,
AA LISTED   **Herefordshire HR9 5NA**
    Telephone: 01989 563030

Our lovely hotel is efficiently run with warmth and
humour – a most relaxing base from which to tour the
Wye Valley, Forest of Dean, Malvern Hills and Welsh
Mountains. Altenatively, forget all that and simply
wander around our little town and stroll along the
river bank.
All bedrooms have television, direct dial telephone,
fresh flowers and fudge and you may breakfast as
early or late as you wish.
We will happily guide you on your choice of
restaurant, cafe or 'pub at which to dine each evening.
You may just about be hungry again by then having
sampled one of our renowned gargantuan breakfasts
earlier in the day. *Proprietors: The Edwards family*

RUTHIN Clwyd   Map **06** SJ15

SELECTED

GH QQQQ **Eyarth Station** Llanfair Dyffryn Clwyd
LL15 2EE (A525 1m S) ☎(0824) 703643 FAX (0824) 707464
Until the Beeching axe this little hotel was a country railway
station. It is set in the Vale of Clwyd and offers magnificent
views of the area. An elegant lounge stands where the railway
line once ran and this is warmed by a cheery wood-burning
stove. Bedrooms, including two in the old station master's
house, are individually styled and most have pretty canopied
beds. There is an attractive garden with a swimming pool for
the better weather.
4♠ Annexe 2♠ (2fb) ⊁ in bedrooms ⊁ in dining room ⊁ in 1
lounge CTV in 1 bedroom ® sB&B♠£25-£40 dB&B♠£40-
£44 WB&Bfr£280 LDO 7pm
Lic ⅲ CTV ⅍(heated) ♪9
Credit Cards 1 3 ⓒ

RYDAL Cumbria

See **Ambleside**

RYDE See **WIGHT, ISLE OF**

RYE East Sussex   Map **05** TQ92

P R E M I E R 🌢 **S E L E C T E D**

GH QQQQQ **Green
Hedges** Hilly Fields, Rye Hill
TN31 7NH (on A268, look for
'Private Road' signs on left)
☎(0797) 222185
Closed Xmas
A substantial Edwardian
red-brick house with a
no-smoking policy throughout
is set in a residential area six
minutes' walk from the town.
Bedrooms are individually and

stylishly decorated, featuring pretty wallpaper and chintz
curtains. A three-course dinner is available by arrangement
and served in the dining room which looks south over the
garden. Sheila Luck can cater for a Vegan diet if forewarned.
Guests gather in the lounge for sherry before dinner. The
house is unlicensed but guests are welcome to bring their own
wine. Breakfast is a sumptuous affair, with a choice of the
traditional English menu or, for example, freshly made
American-style pancakes with maple syrup and Greek
The house is set in spacious gardens, including a terrace and
outdoor swimming pool. Parking in the private road is
unrestricted.
3♠ ⊁ CTV in all bedrooms ® 🏃 ✳ dB&B♠£46-£56
ⅲ nc12yrs ⅍(heated)

SELECTED

GH QQQQ **Holloway House** High Street TN31 7JF
☎(0797) 224748
Built in the Tudor period on a medieval vaulted cellar in the
busy High Street, Holloway House has many interesting
architectural features. Bedrooms are mainly spacious and are
individually designed, furnished with antiques and have either
brass or four-poster beds. The residents' parlour has preserved
its Elizabethan panelling and fire place, and the hall is beamed.
Dinner is served during the summer months, and the full
English breakfast is enormous. Snacks and drinks are available

from the lounge menu. The hotel is fully licensed, and Sheila
Brown and her family offer an exceptionally warm welcome.
6rm(4⇌2♠) (2fb) ⊁ in area of dining room CTV in all
bedrooms ® 🏃 (ex guide dogs) sB&B⇌♠£39-£85
dB&B⇌♠£50-£90 LDO 8pm
Lic ⅲ ⅙
Credit Cards 1 3

P R E M I E R 🌢 **S E L E C T E D**

GH QQQQQ **Jeakes
House** Mermaid Street TN31 7ET
☎(0797) 222828
FAX (0797) 222623
Jeake's House, and Quaker's
House next door, have a well
documented history dating
from c1690. The houses were
converted into a school by the
Baptists in 1853, and were
later divided again. Now they
are happily reunited to provide

stunning bed and breakfast accommodation, refurbished and
equipped to the highest standard. The breakfast room is an
18th-century galleried chapel, and here vegetarian as well as
traditional cooked breakfasts are served. There is also a bar-
lounge with fresh flowers and complimentary newspapers.
12rm(8⇌2♠) (2fb) ⊁ in dining room CTV in all bedrooms
® T sB&B£22.50 sB&B⇌♠£35-£50 dB&B£39
dB&B⇌♠£57 WB&B£136.50-£199.50
Lic ⅲ ⅙
Credit Cards 1 2 3 ⓒ

GH QQQ **Little Saltcote** 22 Military Road TN31 7NY
☎(0797) 223210
This charming house, built in 1901, nestles under the cliff,
overlooking the river Rother and the marshes and surrounded by
an attractive garden. The five rooms are individually furnished and
decorated in a pretty cottage style and equipped with TV and tea
trays. Two of the rooms have en suite showers, including one on
the ground floor. Guests are offered a choice of menu including
vegetarian in the cosy breakfast room. Forecourt parking is
available, and the town centre is only a few minutes' walk away.
Lydd airport is nearby, from where the flight to France is only 12
minutes, or an hour from Dover via a cross-channel ferry or
hovercraft.
5rm(2♠) (2fb)CTV in all bedrooms ® 🏃 sB&B£20-£25
dB&Bfr£32 dB&B♠fr£38
ⅲ

SELECTED

GH QQQQ **Mint Lodge** 38 The Mint TN31 7EN
(☎(0797) 223268 FAX (0797) 223268
3rm(1⇌2♠) (1fb)CTV in all bedrooms ® 🏃 (ex guide dogs)
✳ dB&B⇌♠£36-£40
ⅲ ⅙
Credit Cards 1 3

SELECTED

GH QQQQ **Old Borough Arms** The Strand TN31 7DB
(off A259) ☎(0797) 222128 FAX (0797) 222128
Partially built into the medieval town wall at the foot of the
famous Mermaid Street, this guesthouse has an appealing
dining room combined with a bar on the first floor. Its aged

floorboards, beams, and log fire add to the 18th-century charm. Bedrooms are all bright and modern with assorted floral fabrics, comfortable cane seating and smart tiled en suite shower rooms. Proprietors Terry and Jane Cox and daughter Vanessa offer an informal friendly atmosphere.

9🐾 (3fb)CTV in all bedrooms ® sB&B🐾£25-£30 dB&B🐾£40-£60 WB&B£140-£175 LDO 8pm
Lic 🏫 CTV
Credit Cards 1 3 £

SELECTED

GH Q Q Q Q **The Old Vicarage Guesthouse** 66 Church Square TN31 7HF (follow Town Centre signs from A259, enter town via Landgate Arch, 3rd left in High St into West St, by St Mary's Church footpath leads to Vicarage) ☎(0797) 222119 FAX (0797) 227466
Closed 22-26 Dec

This 400-year-old listed building has many interesting features, with a Georgian façade painted pink. It stands directly opposite St Mary's church and graveyard in a picturesque square, and should not be confused with the private hotel of the same name! The bedrooms have been very prettily decorated and furnished with Laura Ashley fabrics and reproduction pine furniture; two rooms have four-poster beds and all have private bathrooms due to recent modernisation. There is an attractive lounge where guests can help themselves to a glass of sherry, and a smart dining room with a log fire overlooks the pretty walled garden. A choice of breakfast is offered, including free range eggs, home-made marmalade and freshly baked scones, and Julia and Paul Masters are charming, unobtrusive hosts. Smoking is not permitted in bedrooms.

6rm(5🐾🐾) (1fb) ✗ in bedrooms ✗ in dining room CTV in all bedrooms ® 🐾 (ex guide dogs) sB&B£28-£37 sB&B🐾🐾£40-£48 dB&B£33-£39 dB&B🐾🐾£46-£58 WB&B£116-£183
🏫 nc10yrs
£

SELECTED

GH Q Q Q Q **The Old Vicarage Hotel & Restaurant** 15 East Street TN31 7JY (Logis) ☎(0797) 225131 FAX (0797) 225131
Closed Jan

Situated just off the High Street, this listed building dates from 1706 and was originally a family home; the American author Henry James lived here briefly. It is now run as a small private hotel by proprietors Mr and Mrs Foster. Each of the bedrooms has its own character and is furnished in period style, with private bathrooms, every modern facility and thoughtful extras; some rooms have tester beds with curtains. An à la carte menu is served in the elegant restaurant which overlooks the River Rother and Romney Marsh, with local lamb and fish featuring when available. There is also an attractive cocktail bar.

4🐾🐾 (2fb)CTV in all bedrooms ® T dB&B🐾🐾£56-£84 WB&B£168-£252 WBDi£234-£318 LDO 9pm
Lic 🏫 ✗
Credit Cards 1 2 3 5

SELECTED

GH Q Q Q Q **Playden Cottage** Military Road TN31 7NY ☎(0797) 222234

In a peaceful setting just a short walk from the centre of Rye, this pretty cottage was supposedly written about in Bensons's

novels about Mapp and Lucia, where he called it 'Grebe'. The cottage dates back to the 1700s, the bedrooms are comfortable and airy and two have views across the country garden, which in summer is flower-filled and drenched in sunshine; the other room look over woodland. The lounge has a well tuned piano, TV, books and guides to local attractions. A tray of sherry is left out for guests and supper trays are available by prior arrangement. Mrs Fox, the charming hostess, produces a menu of simple home-cooked dishes, but most guests prefer to take pot luck. Breakfast is taken around a communal table and the choice is wide, including fresh fruits and huge black mushrooms cooked in butter, as well as the traditional breakfast dishes.

3🐾 (1fb) ✗ in dining room ® 🐾 (ex guide dogs) dB&B🐾£50-£60 WB&B£157.50-£189 WBDi£227.50-£259 LDO by arrangement
🏫 CTV nc12yrs
Credit Cards 1 3 £

FH Q Q Mrs P Sullivin **Cliff** *(TQ933237)* Iden Lock TN31 7QE (2m along the Military Road to Appledore turn left at hanging milk churn) ☎Iden(0797) 280331
Mar-Oct

This attractive Sussex peg tile hung farmhouse looks out over Romney Marsh. The rooms are simple in style with a floral decor and traditional furniture. A full English breakfast is served at separate tables in the small dining room and there is an adjoining cosy sitting room with TV and a wood burning stove. The patio in the front garden has lovely views over the Marsh and the River Rother which flows in front of the house.

3rm (1fb) ✗ in bedrooms ® ✳ dB&B£27-£29
🏫 CTV 6 acres smallholding
£

Mermaid Street, Rye, East Sussex TN31 7ET Tel: Rye (01797) 222828 Fax: (01797) 222623 Beautiful listed building built in 1689. Set in medieval cobblestoned street, renowned for its smuggling associations. Breakfast – served in eighteenth century galleried former chapel – is traditional or vegetarian. Oak-beamed and panelled bedrooms overlook the marsh and roof-tops to the sea. Brass, mahogany or four-poster beds, linen sheets and lace. En-suite bathrooms, hot drink trays, direct dial telephones and televisions. Honeymoon suite and family rooms available. Residential licence.

Write or telephone for further details to the proprietors: Mr & Mrs F Hadfield

SAFFRON WALDEN Essex   Map **05** TL53

GH 🔲🔲 **Rowley Hill Lodge** Little Walden CB10 1UZ (1.5m north of town centre on B1052. On left of road) ☎(0799) 525975 FAX (0799) 516622

Situated on the Linton road, this Lodge comprises a pair of extended farm-workers' cottages. The bedrooms have attractive period furnishings and there is a modern bathroom. Breakfast is served family-style around a large table and guests are welcome to use Mr and Mrs Haslem's comfortable lounge.

2⇔🐾 ⌦ in bedrooms CTV in all bedrooms Ⓡ 🏋 (ex guide dogs) sB&B⇔🐾£19.50 dB&B⇔🐾£35 WB&B£110 ▦ CTV
Ⓔ

ST AGNES Cornwall & Isles of Scilly   Map **02** SW75

GH 🔲🔲 **Penkerris** Penwinnick Road TR5 0PA ☎(0872) 552262

Designed by the Cornish architect Sylvanus Trevail, this Edwardian residence is on the outskirts of the village with views over glorious countryside. The owner is able to recommend many walks and places to visit. Bedrooms are simply decorated and the dining room and sitting room are large and look out over the garden.

6rm(2🐾) (2fb) CTV in all bedrooms Ⓡ ✻ sB&B£15-£20 dB&B£27-£35 dB&B🐾£30-£40 WB&B£80-£115 LDO 10am
Lic CTV
Credit Cards ①③ Ⓔ

GH 🔲🔲🔲 **Porthvean Hotel** Churchtown TR5 0QP ☎(0872) 552581 FAX (0872) 553773
Closed Xmas & Jan

Right at the centre of the village this is a good spot to watch the Flora Dances Carnival and Victorian Street Fayre. Parts of the building date back some 400 years and many original features still exist. There is a good local clientele as well as residents for the bar and the restaurant. Bedrooms have attractive antique pine furniture with modern comforts.

7🐾 (2fb) ⌦ in dining room CTV in all bedrooms Ⓡ T 🏋 (ex guide dogs) sB&B🐾£35-£45 dB&B🐾£50-£65 LDO 9pm
Lic ▦
Credit Cards ①③ Ⓔ

ST ALBANS Hertfordshire   Map **04** TL10

SELECTED

GH 🔲🔲🔲🔲 **Ardmore House** 54 Lemsford Road AL1 3PR (Logis) ☎(0727) 859313 & 861411 FAX (0727) 859313

Close to the town centre, in a peaceful residential area, this small, welcoming, family-run hotel has been considerably improved over recent years. All the rooms now offer the expected modern comforts, with those in the new wing being the most spacious. The lounge bar is elegant with attractive soft furnishings and decorative fireplaces, and evening meals and snacks can be served here, or in the dining room which overlooks the garden.

26⇔🐾 (3fb) ⌦ in dining room CTV in all bedrooms Ⓡ T sB&B⇔🐾£47-£51.70 dB&B⇔🐾£51.70-£56.40 LDO 8.30pm
Lic ▦ CTV
Credit Cards ①②③

GH 🔲🔲 **Melford** 24 Woodstock Road North AL1 4QQ ☎(0727) 853642 & 830486 FAX (0727) 853642

Friendly owners are justifiably proud of their simply furnished but well maintained home, a large detached house with both garden and car parking space. The television lounge has an honesty bar, and guests share several large tables at breakfast.

12rm(4🐾) (3fb) ⌦ in dining room Ⓡ ✻ sB&Bfr£24 sB&B🐾£38-

£42 dB&Bfr£38 dB&B🐾£45-£47
Lic ▦ CTV
Ⓔ

ST ANDREWS Fife   Map **12** NO51

GH 🔲🔲 **Albany Private Hotel** 56 North Street KY16 9AH ☎(0334) 477737 FAX (0334) 477737

Near the town centre, this friendly family-run guest house in a row of terraced houses has bedrooms in varying sizes and there is a comfortable lounge with plenty of books.

12rm(6🐾) (2fb) ⌦ in bedrooms ⌦ in dining room CTV in all bedrooms Ⓡ T 🏋 (ex guide dogs) ✻ sB&B£24-£28 sB&B🐾£28-£32 dB&B£46-£50 dB&B🐾£54-£58 LDO 5pm
Lic ▦
Credit Cards ①③

GH 🔲🔲 **Amberside** 4 Murray Pk KY16 9AW ☎(0334) 474644

Conveniently situated for all the town's amenities, Amberside has well kept bedrooms and there is a combined lounge/breakfast room on the ground floor.

6rm(5🐾) (2fb) ⌦ in dining room ⌦ in lounges CTV in all bedrooms Ⓡ sB&B🐾£19-£27 dB&B🐾£38-£54 WB&B£126-£168
▦ CTV ⌦
Credit Cards ②Ⓔ

GH 🔲🔲🔲 **Arran House** 5 Murray Park KY16 9AW ☎(0334) 474724 FAX (0334) 472072
Feb-Nov

Situated in a terraced row leading from the town centre to the sea, this small guesthouse offers bright and cheery accommodation in well equipped bedrooms. There is a neat breakfast room but no lounge.

4rm(3🐾) (2fb) CTV in all bedrooms Ⓡ 🏋
▦ CTV ⌦
Credit Cards ①③ Ⓔ

GH 🔲🔲 **Beachway House** 6 Murray Park KY16 9AW ☎(0334) 473319
Closed Jan

Situated in a side street between the town centre and the seafront, this guesthouse offers neat bed and breakfast accommodation. Bedrooms generally have small en suite shower rooms. There is a combined lounge/breakfast room on the ground floor.

6rm(5🐾) (2fb) CTV in all bedrooms Ⓡ ✻ dB&B🐾£36-£50
▦ ⌦

GH 🔲🔲 **Bell Craig** 8 Murray Park KY16 9AW ☎(0334) 472962 FAX (0334) 472962

Handily situated between the town centre and the seafront, this friendly guest house has nicely decorated bedrooms and offers a good choice at breakfast which is served in the spacious lounge/dining room.

5rm(3🐾) (3fb) ⌦ in dining room CTV in all bedrooms Ⓡ ✻ sB&B£20-£30 sB&B🐾£30 dB&B£40-£55 dB&B🐾£40-£45 WB&B£140-£210
▦ CTV ⌦
Credit Cards ①③ Ⓔ

GH 🔲🔲 **Burness House** Murray Park KY16 9AW ☎(0334) 7431⁴

Situated on a corner and convenient for the town centre, this neatly maintained house offers generally compact accommodation which, apart from a combined lounge and breakfast room, is contained at second floor level.

5🐾 (1fb) CTV in all bedrooms Ⓡ
▦ CTV ⌦

🛏 **GH** 🔲🔲 **Cleveden House** 3 Murray Place KY16 9AP ☎(0334) 474212

Quietly situated close to the seafront, this friendly bed and breakfast establishment offers compact but well maintained accommodation. Bedrooms are pleasantly furnished, and there is a

cosy lounge in addition to the breakfast room.
6rm(4♠) (2fb) ⊁ in bedrooms ⊁ in dining room CTV in all
bedrooms ⋔ (ex guide dogs) sB&B£15-£22 dB&B♠£30-£48
▥ CTV
①

GH ◗◗◗ Craigmore 3 Murray Park KY16 9AW
☎(0334) 472142 FAX (0334) 477963
A very well maintained and decorated guest house has attractive
modern bedrooms furnished with pine. Breakfast is served in the
dining room, which also has a small lounge area. It is convenient
for both the town centre and the seafront.
5rm(1⇄4♠) (4fb) ⊁ in dining room CTV in all bedrooms ⓡ ⋔
dB&B⇄♠£34-£48 WB&B£107-£152
▥ CTV
Credit Cards ① ③ ①

GH ◗◗◗ Doune 5 Murray Place KY16 9AP (A91 into St
Andrews, straight over 2 roundabouts and take 2nd road on left)
☎(0334) 75195
Set in a side street between the town centre and the sea, this
terraced house has been completely renovated by the present
owner. The bright modern bedrooms are not large but are well
equipped and feature smart en suite bathrooms. There is a neat
dining room, and guests are invited to use the owners' attractive
period-style lounge.
4♠ CTV in all bedrooms ⓡ ⋔
▥ CTV ⊬

GH ◗◗◗ Edenside House Edenside KY16 9SQ (on A91)
☎Leuchars(0334) 838108 FAX (0334) 838493
End March-Oct
This modernised 18th-century farmhouse is set back from the A91
about two miles North West of the town overlooking the Eden
estuary nature reserve and bird sanctuary. Bedrooms are either in
the main house or the adjoining single storey extension where they
have their own entrances; all have en suite facilities and attractive
pine furniture and fabrics. There is a cosy lounge in the main
house and an attractive dining room with four pine tables where
guests meet and chat at breakfast. Ample car parking is available
and the house is totally non-smoking.
4♠ Annexe 6♠ ⊁ CTV in all bedrooms ⓡ sB&B♠£22-£40
dB&B♠£40-£50 LDO 7pm
☐ nc10yrs located on bird sanctuary
Credit Cards ① ③ ①

GH ◗◗◗ Glenderran 9 Murray Park KY16 9AW
☎(0334) 477951 FAX (0334) 477908
This stylishly restored house offers thoughtfully equipped
accommodation in small but attractive bedrooms. Breakfasts are
chosen the night before from a comprehensive menu. Smoking is
not permitted.
rm(3♠) ⊁ CTV in all bedrooms ⓡ ⋔ sB&B♠£19-£26
dB&B♠£38-£52
☐ nc12yrs
Credit Cards ① ③

GH ◗◗◗ Hazlebank Private Hotel 28 The Scores KY16 9AS
☎(0334) 472466 FAX (0334) 472466
Enjoying fine views over St Andrews Bay, but convenient for the
town centre and University, this family run private hotel offers
generally spacious accommodation. Bedrooms vary in size and the
best have sea views. There is a small lounge and pleasant
breakfast room which at certain times of the year doubles as a
coffee shop.
⇄♠ (6fb) ⊁ in dining room CTV in all bedrooms ⓡ
sB&B⇄♠£30-£60 dB&B⇄♠£55-£80 LDO 6.45pm
c ▥ CTV ⊬
Credit Cards ① ③ ①

PENKERRIS

Penwinnick Road, St. Agnes, Cornwall TR5 0PA
Telephone: 01872 552262
OPEN ALL YEAR

Enchanting Edwardian residence with garden. Very easy
to find on B3277 road just inside this unspoilt Cornish
village. Beautiful rooms. Piano, log fires in winter.
Superb home cooking. Dramatic cliff walks and beaches
nearby. Bedrooms with colour TV, kettle, clock radio,
H & C and shaver points.
Shower room as well as bathrooms.
Large lawn with garden tables, swings and badminton
court. Bed & Breakfast, dinner if required. Delicious
meals including English traditional roasts and home
made fruit tarts.

AA

Apply resident proprietor: Dorothy Gill-Carey

Edenside House

STB ♥♥♥ AA
COMMENDED QQQ

Edenside, St Andrews, KY16 9SQ
Tel: 01334 838108   Fax: 01334 838493
Pre 1775 former Scottish farmhouse in superb
waterfront setting on estuary bird sanctuary.
St Andrews and Old Course within 2½ miles
(5 mins. by car on A91).
All nine modernised double/twin rooms
(some ground floor) have en suite facilities,
colour TV, beverage tray and guaranteed
parking space.
Golf club hire & golf booking advice.
Riding stables nearby.
Quality accommodation at realistic prices in
an exclusively non smoking house.

GH [Q][Q][Q] Lorimer House 19 Murray Park KY16 9AW
☎(0334) 476599 FAX (0334) 476599
This attractively decorated and well kept house is handy for the town and the seafront. Bedrooms, each with satellite TV, vary in size; one is on the ground floor. There is also a combined lounge and breakfast room.
5rm(4🛁🚿) (2fb) 🚭 in bedrooms CTV in all bedrooms Ⓡ sB&B£16-£25 dB&B🛁🚿£32-£50
♨ CTV 🚫🅿
[£]

GH [Q][Q][Q] Romar 45 Main Street, Strathkinness KY16 9RZ
☎Strathkinness(0334) 850308 FAX (0334) 850308
Situated on the edge of Strathkinness, this modern chalet style bungalow offers comfortable accommodation. Bedrooms have good beds and many thoughtful extras such as books, toiletries and large towels and the first floor rooms are particularly spacious. Public areas are limited to a small breakfast room with pine tables where hearty breakfasts are served.
4rm(2🚿) (1fb) 🚭 in bedrooms 🚭 in dining room 🚭 in 1 lounge CTV in all bedrooms Ⓡ 🐕 (ex guide dogs) sB&B£16-£20 dB&B🚿£32-£40
♨
[£]

GH [Q][Q][Q] West Park House 5 St Mary's Place KY16 9UY
☎(0334) 475933
Closed Jan
Located just out of the town centre, this is a relaxing place to stay. There are two bedrooms on the ground floor, and two on the second floor - one of which is a spacious family room. The cosy lounge overlooks the back garden, and breakfast is served in the elegant dining room dominated by a fine marble fireplace. Smoking is not permitted.
5rm(4🚿) (1fb) CTV in all bedrooms Ⓡ 🐕 (ex guide dogs) ✱ dB&B£36-£42 dB&B🚿£40-£46
♨ 🚫🅿

GH [Q][Q][Q] Yorkston House 68 & 70 Argyle Street KY16 9BU
☎(0334) 472019 FAX (0334) 72019
rs Xmas & New Year
Traditional standards are offered at this long-established guesthouse lying west of the town centre. The bedrooms are spacious and comfortable and there is a pleasant lounge and a large dining room with well spaced tables.
10rm(1🛁5🚿) (2fb) 🚭 in dining room 🚭 in lounges CTV in all bedrooms Ⓡ 🐕 (ex guide dogs) sB&B£20-£26 dB&B£38-£44 dB&B🛁🚿£40-£60 WB&B£133-£210 LDO 4pm
Lic ♨ 🚫🅿

FH [Q][Q][Q] Mrs A E Duncan **Spinks Town** *(NO541144)* KY16 8PN (2m E on A917 coast rd) ☎(0334) 473475
Surrounded by rolling countryside, this modern house provides pleasant and comfortable accommodation. The spacious bedrooms are plainly decorated but have good beds, period furniture and modern bathrooms while the attractively furnished public areas include a most inviting lounge and small dining room where enjoyable breakfasts are served around a communal table.
3rm(2🛁🚿) 🚭 🐕 dB&Bfr£30 dB&B🛁🚿fr£34
♨ CTV 250 acres arable cattle

ST ASAPH Clwyd — Map **06** SJ07

SELECTED

FH [Q][Q][Q][Q] Mrs A Roberts **Bach-Y-Graig** *(SJ075713)* Tremeirchion LL17 0UH ☎Trefnant(0745) 730627
Closed Xmas & New Year
The first brick house to be built in Wales, a carefully modernised 16th-century farmhouse retaining much of its original charm provides both a genuine Welsh welcome and honest home-cooked meals based on fresh produce. Bedrooms furnished with some fine antique pieces also offer TV sets and tea-making equipment, while the traditional sitting room with its impressive inglenook fireplace is supplemented by an additional lounge for guests' use. The River Clwyd runs through farmland which also includes 40-acre woods where a trail has been opened for interested visitors.
3🛁🚿 (1fb) 🚭 CTV in all bedrooms Ⓡ 🐕 ✱ sB&B🛁🚿fr£23 dB&B🛁🚿fr£36
♨ CTV 🎣 woodland trail 200 acres dairy
[£]

ST AUBIN See JERSEY under CHANNEL ISLANDS

ST AUSTELL Cornwall & Isles of Scilly — Map **02** SX05

GH [Q][Q] Alexandra Hotel 52-54 Alexandra Road PL25 4QN
☎(0726) 74242
A neat, well presented private hotel near the railway station, is run by enthusiastic, friendly owners. The bedrooms, which vary in size, are bright and well maintained, some having en suite showers. There is a comfortable front-facing lounge, a well stocked bar and a nicely appointed dining room, where home-cooked evening meals and an ample breakfast are served. Parking is available at both the front and rear.
14rm(4🚿) (6fb) 🚭 in dining room CTV in all bedrooms Ⓡ sB&Bfr£24 sB&B🚿fr£29 dB&Bfr£42 dB&B🚿fr£52 WB&B£138-£170 WBDi£180-£212 LDO 5.30pm
Lic ♨ CTV
Credit Cards [1] [2] [3] [5] [£]

SELECTED

FH [Q][Q][Q][Q] Mrs J Nancarrow ***Poltarrow*** *(SW998518)* PL26 7DR (off A390 turn right at St Mewan School entrance to farmhouse within 0.25m on left) ☎(0726) 67111
Closed 16 Dec-5 Jan
Situated in the scattered hamlet of St Mewen, with views over rolling farmland, this wisteria-clad farmhouse is a wonderful base for touring. The high quality bedrooms are individually furnished and decorated with lots of flair. Judith Nancarrow's set three-course dinners, made using local produce, are very popular, with farmhouse cookery being the order of the day. A cosy lounge is provided for guests, with a log fire burning on chilly evenings. There are three large, attractive self-catering cottages also available to let.
5rm(3🛁🚿) (1fb) CTV in all bedrooms Ⓡ 🐕 (ex guide dogs) LDO noon
Lic ♨ CTV pool table 45 acres mixed
Credit Cards [1] [3]

INN [Q][Q][Q] Rashleigh Arms Quay Road, Charlestown PL25 3NJ (A390, signposted on St Austell roundabout) ☎(0726) 73635 FAX (0726) 69246
Situated on the approach to the harbour in the village of Charlestown, this friendly inn offers comfortable bedrooms. Spacious public areas include two attractive bars and a restaurant. There is also a children's room and plenty of parking.
5🚿 CTV in all bedrooms Ⓡ 🐕 (ex guide dogs) ✱ sB&B🚿fr£24 dB&B🚿fr£48 WB&Bfr£336 Lunch £8.50-£21.90 Dinner £8.71-£24.50 LDO 10pm
♨
Credit Cards [1] [3]

ST BLAZEY Cornwall & Isles of Scilly Map **02** SX05

PREMIER SELECTED

GH [Q][Q][Q][Q][Q] ***Nanscawen House*** Prideaux Road PL24 2SR
☎Par(0726) 814488
FAX (0726) 814488
Closed 22-27 Dec

This very fine granite-built Georgian house beautifully set in the Luxulyan Valley is owned and run by the Martin family who strive to provide guests with the utmost in quality and comfort. The three bedrooms are decorated and furnished to a luxurious standard, each with their own spa bath and teddy bear. A spacious drawing room, comfortably furnished with matching chairs and sofas, leads into the conservatory where breakfast and dinner is served. All the food is home-cooked, using as much home-grown produce as possible and reviving many long-forgotten recipes. Five acres of mature south-facing gardens surround the house and an outdoor swimming pool is heated between April and September. There is also an outdoor whirlpool bath. Smoking is not permitted in the house.
3🛁🚿 CTV in all bedrooms [R] T 🐕 LDO 9.30am
Lic ▦ nc12yrs ⛱(heated) putting jacuzzi whirlpool
Credit Cards [1][3]

T CATHERINE'S Strathclyde *Argyllshire* Map **10** NN10

;H [Q][Q][Q] Arnish Cottage, Christian Guest House. Poll Bay
\25 8BA ☎Inveraray(0499) 2405 due to change to 302405
ill and Maisie Mercer's beautifully restored stone-built cottage
:ands in a carefully landscaped garden, in a delightful position on
ie picturesque shores of Loch Fyne. Bedrooms are compact but
nartly decorated and comfortably furnished, while public rooms
iclude an inviting split-level lounge and dining room where
laisie serves home-cooked dinners, based largely on fresh local
oduce and seafood. A delightful small conservatory offers fine
ews of the loch, and standards of housekeeping throughout are
npeccable. Smoking is not permitted.
🚿 🚭 [R] 🐕 (ex guide dogs) sB&B🚿£23-£27 dB&B🚿£38-£50
'B&B£120-£160 WBDi£205-£245
▦ CTV nc16yrs

SELECTED

GH [Q][Q][Q][Q] Thistle House PA25 8AZ
☎Inveraray(0499) 2209 due to change to 302209
Etr-Oct
Set in its own gardens just south of the village, this imposing stone house enjoys splendid views across Loch Fyne to Inverary. The house is spotlessly maintained throughout and the beautiful lounge is a particular feature. Bedrooms are well proportioned and there is a family room with a single room off.
5rm(3🚿) (1fb) 🚭 in dining room [R] dB&Bfr£37
dB&B🚿fr£42 WB&Bfr£125
▦
Credit Cards [1] [£]

'DAVID'S Dyfed Map **02** SM72

H [Q][Q][Q] The Ramsey Lower Moor SA62 6RP (from A487 bear
't in front of Midland bank signposted Porthclais, establishment
n on left) ☎(0437) 720321 & 720332
ɪis bright, cosy guesthouse is situated at the edge of the city,
thin easy walking distance of the shops and cathedral. Run by the
friendly Thompson family, it has recently been extended, and bedrooms are attractively fitted with full-length mirrored wardrobes, together with new en suite facilities of excellent quality. The open plan lounge/dining room and bar look out onto a neat lawn.
7rm(6🛁🚿) 🚭 [R] dB&B£30.50-£33.50 dB&B🛁🚿£33.50-£36.50 (incl dinner) WBDi£183-£219 LDO 7pm
Lic ▦ CTV nc12yrs
[£]

GH [Q][Q][Q] Y Glennydd 51 Nun Street SA62 6NU
☎(0437) 720576 FAX (0437) 720576
Closed Jan
Conveniently situated for the cathedral and the shops, this guesthouse offers comfortable accommodation and friendly service by the Foster family. Bedrooms are well maintained and attractively decorated, using some very pretty fabrics, and some have sofabeds for extra guests. The small lounge features an electric organ, and there is a bar at one end of the stone-walled restaurant. Open to non-residents, the restaurant offers a wide selection of dishes, many featuring locally caught lobster, trout and halibut.
10rm(6🛁🚿) (4fb) 🚭 in dining room CTV in all bedrooms [R] 🐕 (ex guide dogs) sB&B£18.50-£28 sB&B🛁🚿£18.50-£28 dB&B£30-£36 dB&B🛁🚿£36 WB&Bfr£113 WBDifr£197 LDO 9pm
Lic ▦ CTV ⛳
Credit Cards [1][3][5] [£]

ST ERME Cornwall & Isles of Scilly Map **02** SW84

SELECTED

FH [Q][Q][Q][Q] Mr & Mrs E Dymond **Trevispian Vean** *(SW850502)* TR4 9BL (from A30 take A3076 for Truro, in 2.5m in Trispen village take 2nd left in 0.5m bear sharp left farm entrance 500yds on left) ☎Truro(0872) 79514
Mar-Oct
The establishment manages to combine life as a working farm and as a guesthouse. The Dymonds attend to all guests' needs. There are several sitting rooms, one no-smoking, and a bright dining room with individual tables where, as well as breakfast, a four-course dinner is served. Bedrooms are all attractively decorated and a small kitchen with a fridge is provided for guests wishing to make up picnics or extra tea or coffee.
12rm(2🛁8🚿) (7fb) 🚭 in dining room 🚭 in 1 lounge [R] 🐕 (ex guide dogs) sB&B£19-£21 sB&B🛁🚿fr£21 dB&B£34 dB&B🛁🚿£38 WB&B£96-£110 WBDi£132-£146 LDO 4.30pm
Lic ▦ CTV 🎣 games room 300 acres arable pigs sheep
[£]

ST HELIER See **JERSEY under CHANNEL ISLANDS**

ST HILARY Cornwall & Isles of Scilly Map **02** SW53

PREMIER SELECTED

FH [Q][Q][Q][Q][Q] S L White **Ennys** *(SW559328)*
Goldsithney TR20 9BZ
☎Penzance(0736) 740262
Closed 25-26 Dec

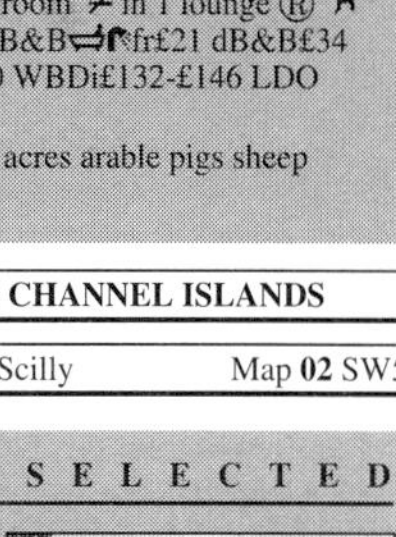

This delightful 17th-century stone manor house on a small working farm stands at the end of a tree-lined drive surrounded by well maintained gardens which include a tennis court and heated pool that guests can use at stated hours. Two bedrooms are contained in a

▶

converted barn, and two of the three contained in the main
house have four-poster beds; all of them are individually
furnished and decorated, with attractive soft furnishings. A log
fire burns in the comfortable sitting room on chilly evenings,
and the commendable home-cooked dinners served in a
candlelit dining room bring guests back year after year; home-
grown vegetables, as well as local fish and meat, are used
whenever possible, and bread is freshly made on the premises
each morning. The establishment is unlicensed but diners are
encouraged to bring in their own wine.

3rm(1⇄2ᐦ) Annexe 2⇄ᐦ (1fb) ⊬ in bedrooms ⊬ in dining
room CTV in all bedrooms ℞ ⊁ sB&Bfr£30
dB&B⇄ᐦ£45-£50 LDO 7.30pm
▥ CTV ᐟ(heated) ᐞ(grass)50 acres arable
See advertisement under PENZANCE

ST IVES Cornwall & Isles of Scilly   Map 02 SW54

GH ℚℚℚ **Bay View** Headland Road, Carbis Bay TR26 2NX
☎Penzance(0736) 796469
Mar-Oct
This family-run hotel is located in a residential area close to the
beach at Carbis Bay, within easy access of St Ives. It offers
modern, bright, comfortable bedrooms which are well appointed.
Public areas are cosy and inviting, with ornaments, books and
plants, and there is a TV lounge and bar. An evening meal is
offered, cooked by Mrs Beaver.
9rm(8ᐦ) (3fb) ⊬ in bedrooms CTV in all bedrooms ℞ ⊁ (ex
guide dogs) ✳ sB&Bfr£14.50 sB&Bᐦ£20 dB&Bfr£29
dB&Bᐦ£40 WB&B£96-£156 WBDi£155-£205 LDO 6pm
Lic ▥ CTV nc5yrs
£

GH ℚℚℚ **Blue Mist** The Warren TR26 2EA
☎Penzance(0736) 795209
Etr-Oct
This is a homely, friendly guesthouse, close to the seafront and the
town centre. Well-equipped bedrooms are attractively decorated
and have modern furnishings. The bar is small but comfortable
and a choice of breakfasts is offered in the open-plan dining room.
8ᐦ CTV in all bedrooms ℞ T ⊁ (ex guide dogs) ✳
sB&Bᐦ£20.75-£23.75 dB&Bᐦ£40.50-£47 WB&B£140.75-
£161.75
▥ nc4yrs
Credit Cards ①②③£

GH ℚℚℚ **Channings Hotel** 3 Talland Road TR26 2DF
☎Penzance(0736) 795681 FAX (0736) 797863
Closed 25 & 26 Dec
The focal point of this friendly, family-run private hotel is its
bar/lounge, though there is also a small, cosy TV lounge. The
hotel continues to improve and the bedrooms are well equipped. A
set dinner is served in the attractive dining room.
12rm(1⇄9ᐦ) (5fb) ⊬ in 6 bedrooms ⊬ in dining room ℞ ⊁ ✳
sB&B£13-£20 sB&B⇄ᐦ£15-£22 dB&B£26-£40 dB&B⇄ᐦ£30-
£44 WB&B£105-£154 WBDi£140-£210 LDO 4pm
Lic ▥ CTV
Credit Cards ①③£

▱ ▣ GH ℚℚℚ **Chy-an-Creet Private Hotel** Higher
Stennack TR26 2HA (on main road into harbour, opposite Leach
Pottery) ☎Penzance(0736) 796559 FAX (0736) 796559
On the edge of town and just a short walk from the beaches is this
family run small hotel. The bedrooms are all en suite, and public
areas are cosy and attractive. Dinner is served in the pretty dining
room and guests have a choice of dishes. Guests will enjoy their
holiday at this welcoming guesthouse.
10⇄ᐦ (4fb) ⊬ in bedrooms ⊬ in dining room ℞
sB&B⇄ᐦ£14-£21 dB&B⇄ᐦ£28-£42 WB&B£98-£147

WBDi£147-£189 LDO 4pm
Lic ▥ CTV
Credit Cards ①③£

GH ℚℚℚℚ **Dean Court Hotel** Trelyon Avenue TR26 2AD
☎Penzance(0736) 796023
Mar-Oct
Joy and Ian Alford provide accommodation of the highest
standard. There are two comfortable lounges with sea views,
and picture windows in the attractive restaurant take full
advantage of the vista. The bedrooms are comfortable and
well-equipped, and those that do not have sea views overlook
woodland.
12⇄ᐦ (2fb) ⊬ in dining room ⊬ in 1 lounge CTV in all
bedrooms ℞ ⊁ sB&B⇄ᐦ£27-£35 dB&B⇄ᐦ£52-£70
WB&B£175-£210 WBDi£210-£245 LDO 6pm
Lic ▥ nc14yrs
Credit Cards ①③

GH ℚℚℚ **The Hollies Hotel** 4 Talland Road TR26 2DF
☎Penzance(0736) 796605
A friendly family run guesthouse is situated in a quiet residential
area. The bedrooms are comfortable and well-equipped. There is a
welcoming lounge and a good size dining room.
10⇄ᐦ (4fb) CTV in all bedrooms ℞ ⊁ LDO 9am
Lic ▥ CTV

GH ℚℚ **Island View** 2 Park Avenue TR26 2DN
☎Penzance(0736) 795111
Mar-Oct
In an elevated position above the town, this pleasant hotel offers
basic, clean and comfortable accommodation in nicely decorated
bedrooms. A set dinner menu is offered and served in the small
dining room.
10rm(2ᐦ) (4fb) CTV in all bedrooms ℞ LDO 6.30pm
▥ ⊬

GH ℚℚℚ **Kandahar** 11 The Warren TR26 2EA
☎Penzance(0736) 796183
Closed Xmas, New Year & owners hols
Standing on a quaint, narrow street close to the sea, Kandahar
offers clean, comfortable accomodation in spacious, well-
maintained bedrooms, some with sea views. A small dining room
also looks out over the sea where guests can relax and enjoy a
sound English breakfast.
5rm(2ᐦ) (1fb) ⊬ in dining room CTV in all bedrooms ℞ ⊁ ✳
sB&B£16-£18 dB&B£32-£37 dB&Bᐦ£38-£46
▥ CTV
£

GH ℚℚℚℚ **Kynance** The Warren TR26 2EA (take A3074
into town centre taking sharp right hand turn before bus/coach
terminus, into railway station approach road. Kynance 20yds
on left) ☎(0736) 796636
Closed Xmas
In a convenient location, within sight and sound of the ocean,
and close to the town centre, this charming former tin miner's
cottage is full of character. The owners, Mr and Mrs Norris
have tastefully decorated and furnished the house throughout,
and bedrooms are attractive, comfortable and well-equipped.
Public areas are small and cosy. There is an attractive dining
room and a choice of English and Continental breakfast is
offered.
8rm(5⇄ᐦ) (2fb) ⊬ in dining room ⊬ in lounges CTV in all
bedrooms ℞ ⊁ ✳ sB&B£17.50-£23 sB&B⇄ᐦ£19.50-£24

Db&B£32-£34 Db&B➪£34-£39 WB&B£112-£168
🏨 CTV nc7yrs
£

GH Q Q Q **Longships Hotel** Talland Road TR26 2DF
☎Penzance(0736) 798180 FAX (0736) 798180
At the end of a terrace of small hotels, a short hilly walk from the
shops and harbour, the Longships offers a lively bar, comfortable
public areas and simply furnished bedrooms.
25rm(4➪21🛏) (7fb) ⚥ in dining room ⚥ in 1 lounge CTV in all
bedrooms ® sB&B➪£17-£25 dB&B➪£34-£50
WB&B£119-£176 WBDi£150-£208 LDO 7pm
Lic 🏨 CTV

SELECTED

GH Q Q Q Q **Lyonesse Hotel** 5 Talland Road TR26 2DF
☎Penzance(0736) 796315
Closed Dec-Jan
Set high above the town centre and harbour in a terrace of
family-run hotels, the Lyonesse provides well appointed
bedrooms and attractive public areas where entertainment is
provided on some evenings during the season in a cosy bar.
Home-cooked dishes are featured on the menu.
15🛏 (4fb) ⚥ in bedrooms ⚥ in dining room ⚥ in lounges
CTV in all bedrooms ® ⚬ ✳ sB&B£15-£22 dB&B£30-
£44 WB&B£105-£154 WBDi£160-£205 LDO 6.30pm
Lic 🏨 CTV
Credit Cards 1 3 £

SELECTED

GH Q Q Q Q **Monowai Private Hotel** Headland Road,
Carbis Bay TR26 2NR (on entering Carbis Bay turn right off
A3074 into Porthrepta Rd, Headland Rd is on the right after
300yds) ☎Penzance(0736) 795733
Mar-Sep
A family-run, character establishment stands in an elevated
position commanding glorious views across the bay. The
brightly decorated bedrooms have been furnished in a cottage
style, and a cosy atmosphere is a feature of the bar and lounge.
A choice of home-cooked dishes is offered on the table d'hôte
menu with vegetarian specialities. A friendly welcome awaits
guests.
8🛏 (3fb) ⚥ ® ✳ sB&B£16-£30 dB&B£32-£60
WB&B£112-£210 WBDi£182-£290 LDO 6.30pm
Lic 🏨 CTV nc5yrs ✤(heated) pool table darts
£

GH Q Q Q **The Old Vicarage Hotel** Parc-An-Creet TR26 2ET
☎Penzance(0736) 796124
Etr-Oct
A lovely mellowed stone 1850s vicarage which positively gleams
with polish. Public areas are furnished in keeping with the period
and one WC is reputedly the oldest in town - a Delft style
metropolitan ceramic. Bedrooms are decorated with matching soft
furnishings and there is a well stocked bar.
8rm(4➪9🛏) (3fb) ⚥ in bedrooms ⚥ in dining room CTV in 7
bedrooms ® sB&B£20-£22 dB&B£36-£40 dB&B➪£40-£46
WB&B£112-£147
Lic 🏨 CTV putting green
Credit Cards 1 2 3 £

GH Q Q Q **Pondarosa Hotel** 10 Porthminster Terrace TR26 2DQ
(approach town by A3074, fork left at Porthminster Hotel and
follow road to left hand bend) ☎Penzance(0736) 795875
This family-owned guesthouse is located at one end of a terrace in

an elevated position above the town. Mr and Mrs Richards offer
an excellent standard of accommodation of which they are justly
proud; rooms are bright and fresh and a home-cooked set evening
meal is offered in the cosy dining room.
10rm(1➪7🛏) (4fb) ⚥ in 2 bedrooms ⚥ in dining room ⚥ in 1
lounge CTV in all bedrooms ® ⚬ (ex guide dogs) ✳ sB&B£13-
£16 dB&B£30-£32 dB&B➪£34-£40 WBDi£140-£188 LDO
4pm
Lic 🏨 CTV
Credit Cards 1 2 3 5 £

SELECTED

GH Q Q Q Q **Regent Hotel** Fernlea Terrace TR26 2BH
☎Penzance(0736) 796195 FAX (0736) 794641
rs mid Sep-mid May
This friendly, family-run hotel is on the edge of town, close to
the bus and railway stations and with easy access to the
beaches. Most of the bedrooms have breathtaking views of the
harbour and St Ives Bay, all are tastefully decorated and
furnished, and several offer en suite shower rooms.
9rm(7🛏) ⚥ in 4 bedrooms ⚥ in area of dining room CTV in
all bedrooms ® ⚬ sB&B£24-£26 sB&B£32.50 dB&B£54-
£60 WB&B£178-£210 WBDi£238-£270 LDO 7pm
Lic 🏨 CTV nc7yrs
Credit Cards 1 2 3 5 £
See advertisement on p.355.

GH Q Q Q **St Merryn Hotel** Trelyon TR26 2PN
☎Penzance(0736) 795767 FAX (0736) 797248
Mar-Nov
A detached property on the main St Ives road offers well equipped
bedrooms and comfortable public areas. The hotel is about 15 ▶

KANDAHAR
"The House that thinks it's a ship"
The Warren, St. Ives. (01736) 796183

Unique location, literally lapped by the Atlantic, yet
Town Centre. All bedrooms, dining-room and
lounge, have superb views directly onto harbour and
coast line. Some rooms "en-suite" or with private
facilities, others with excellent shared bathroom
facilities, and all with colour TV and tea/coffee
making supplies. Full central heating.
BR, the National Coach Terminus, and reserved car
spaces are within 150 yards, as are the Tourist
Information Centre and all amenities of Town
Centre, harbour, beaches, and many restaurants.
The Barbara Hepworth Museum and Tate Gallery
are within 4 mins and 8 mins respectively, level
walking. Full English, vegetarian and Continental
breakfast served.

minutes' walk from the harbour and town centre.
19🛁 (8fb) 🚭 in dining room CTV in all bedrooms Ⓡ **T** 🐕 ✻ sB&B🛁£16-£22.75 dB&B🛁£32-£40 LDO 6pm
Lic ▥ CTV nc4yrs
Credit Cards [1] [3]

GH [Q][Q][Q] Sunrise 22 The Warren TR26 2AT
☎Penzance(0736) 795407
Jan-Oct
This terraced cottage in the town centre has glorious views of the harbour from the top-floor bedrooms. The attractive bedrooms are comfortably furnished, with spotless en suite facilities. Traditional English breakfasts are a speciality, and complement the warm welcome offered by Vicki Mason and her daughter.
7rm(5🛁🚿) (2fb)CTV in all bedrooms Ⓡ ✻ sB&Bfr£18 dB&B£30-£32 dB&B🛁🚿£34-£36
▥ CTV
[£]

GH [Q][Q][Q] Tregorran Hotel Headland Bay, Carbis Bay TR26 2NU ☎Penzance(0736) 795889
Apr-Oct
Catering particularly well for the family on holiday, this Spanish-looking hotel close to the sea has an excellent range of facilities and is professionally managed by the owners. Games room and bar overlook the patio and swimming pool. The menu changes daily and no dish ever appears more than once in a fortnight.
15rm(13🚿) (5fb) 🚭 in dining room CTV in all bedrooms Ⓡ ✻ sB&B£14-£28 sB&B🚿£14-£28 dB&B£28-£56 dB&B🚿£28-£56 WB&B£98-£196 WBDi£147-£245 LDO 3pm
Lic ▥ CTV 🏊(heated) solarium gymnasium pool table games room
Credit Cards [1] [2] [3] [£]

GH [Q][Q][Q] Trewinnard 4 Parc Avenue TR26 2DN (A3074 to St Ives, on entering town turn left at Nat West bank and then turn left at mini roundabout. Go past car park and house 150yds on right)
☎(0736) 794168
Apr-Oct
This three-storey terraced house overlooking the harbour has been tastefully upgraded throughout. Bedrooms have modern furnishings and are well-equipped, the lounge is comfortable and attractively decorated and the bar is small and cosy. A bright dining room serves good English dishes at dinner and a choice of English or Continental breakfast.
7rm(5🚿) (1fb) 🚭 CTV in all bedrooms Ⓡ 🐕 sB&B£18-£20.50 dB&B£26-£31 dB&B🚿£29-£35 WB&B£84-£116 WBDi£129.50-£165 LDO noon
Lic ▥ nc7yrs
Credit Cards [1] [3] [£]

INN[Q][Q][Q] ***Queens Tavern*** High Street TR26 1RR (St Austell Brewery) ☎(0736) 796468
This popular inn situated in the town centre offers well-equipped bedrooms. There is a small dining room on the first floor where a selection of meals and snacks are available and a choice of breakfasts is served.
5🚿 (3fb) CTV in all bedrooms Ⓡ 🐕 (ex guide dogs) LDO 8.15pm
▥ CTV
Credit Cards [1]

ST JUST (NEAR LAND'S END) Cornwall & Isles of Scilly
Map **02** SW33

INN[Q][Q][Q] Wellington Hotel Market Square TR19 7HL
☎Penzance(0736) 787319 FAX (0736) 787906
This historic old inn in the town's Market Square traces its history back to the mid 14th century. Its cosy bars are warm and hospitable, inviting guests to try the good range of local beers and the home-cooked bar food. Bedrooms are modern, and in the converted former stables.

Annexe 6🛁🚿 (4fb)CTV in all bedrooms Ⓡ **T** sB&B🛁🚿£25-£28 dB&B🛁🚿£35-£40 Lunch £7-£13&alc Dinner £7-£13&alc LDO 9pm
▥ CTV 🚫
Credit Cards [1] [2] [3] [5] [£]

ST JUST-IN-ROSELAND Cornwall & Isles of Scilly
Map **02** SW83

SELECTED

GH [Q][Q][Q][Q] Rose-Da-Mar Hotel TR2 5JB (turn off A390 onto B3287 to Tregony and then A3078 to St Just-in-Roseland, turn right at Crossroads along B3289,hotel 500yds on left)
☎St Mawes(0326) 270450
mid Mar-mid Oct
This attractive hotel is midway between St Mawes and the King Harry ferry on the Roseland peninsula, and stands on a quiet country lane with splendid views over the river Fal and the creeks of Carrick Roads. Attractive bedrooms all have magnificent views, there is a spacious drawing room, a cosy bar and a bright dining room, where Mrs Brown's unusual five-course dinners are served: menus are displayed during the afternoon and there is always a choice of three starters and two main courses. Early booking for the Rose-Da-Mar is advisable as many guests return regularly.
8rm(4🛁1🚿) (1fb) 🚭 in dining room Ⓡ ✻ sB&B£27 dB&B£47.50-£49.50 dB&B🛁🚿£54.50-£61 WB&B£169.25-£205 WBDi£271.30-£310.50 LDO 6.30pm
Lic ▥ CTV nc11yrs
[£]

ST KEYNE Cornwall & Isles of Scilly Map **02** SX26

FH [Q][Q][Q] Mrs B N Light ***Penbugle Farm (SX228602)*** PL14 4RS (establishment is approximately 3 miles along B3243 past Dobwalls) ☎Liskeard(0579) 20288
Mar-Oct
This small farmhouse is situated along the Looe-Duloe road and offers spacious rooms, simply presented, with smart modern shower rooms. There is a comfortable lounge with a fire, TV and video. Breakfast is served at a communal table. Part of the Duchy of Cornwall, it is a mixed farm with 287 acres of farmland, in the heart of this pretty area.
2🚿 (2fb) Ⓡ 🐕 (ex guide dogs)
▥ CTV 287 acres arable beef sheep
See advertisement under LOOE

ST MARTIN See **GUERNSEY under CHANNEL ISLANDS**

ST MARY'S See **SCILLY, ISLES OF**

ST MARY'S LOCH Borders *Selkirkshire* Map **11** NT22

INN[Q][Q][Q] Tibbie Shiels TD7 5NE ☎Capercleuch(0750) 42231
rs Mon Nov-Feb
A long tradition of hospitality is part of this inn, it has been welcoming guests since the early 19th-century. On the shore of St Mary's Loch and midway between Moffat and Selkirk. Because of its idyllic position it is very popular with bird watchers, walkers and fishermen. It is full of charm and character. The beamed bar known as Tibbie's room serves a good range of bar meals. High teas are also a speciality. In the winter, the inn is closed on Mondays.
5rm(4🚿) (2fb)Ⓡ 🐕 (ex guide dogs) sB&B🚿£26 dB&B🚿£46 Lunch £2.50-£5.50alc Dinner £7-£12alc LDO 8.30pm
▥ CTV 🎣
Credit Cards [1] [3]

ST MAWGAN Cornwall & Isles of Scilly Map **02** SW86

INN[Q][Q] The Falcon TR8 4EP (from A30 follow signs RAF St Mawgan, then St Mawgan village. Pub at bottom of hill in village centre) ☎Newquay(0637) 860225

Award winning gardens make an inviting setting for this magnolia-and wisteria-clad inn. The bar is no less inviting with pine furniture and a log fire during the winter months. There is also a pleasing lack of juke boxes and games machines. St Austell Brewery provide the house beer and there is a small, separate, no-smoking dining/breakfast room. The bedrooms are well-equipped. During the summer months a barbecue is held in the garden every evening.

3rm(2🚿) 🚭 in dining room CTV in all bedrooms [R] **T** 🐕 (ex guide dogs) sB&B£18 sB&B🚿£26 dB&Bfr£36 dB&B🚿£50 Lunch £5-£9alc Dinner £7.50-£16alc LDO 10pm

♨

Credit Cards [1] [3]

ST MERRYN Cornwall & Isles of Scilly Map **02** SW87

INN[Q][Q][Q] *Farmers Arms* PL28 8NP (St Austell Brewery) ☎Padstow(0841) 520303

A lively and informal atmosphere prevails at this old village inn, which has kept much of its original character. The bars are heavily beamed, and there are slate floors and open fireplaces. A wide selection of dishes is offered along with a range of real ales. Bedrooms are well equipped with modern creature comforts.

4🚿 (2fb) CTV in all bedrooms [R] LDO 9.30pm

♨

Credit Cards [1] [2] [3] [5]

ST OWEN'S CROSS Hereford & Worcester Map **03** SO52

FH [Q][Q] Mrs F Davies **Aberhall** *(SO529242)* HR2 8LL ☎Harewood End(0989) 730256 ▶

Closed Dec

This 16th-century farmhouse is off the B4521. Accommodation is comfortable, the views are panoramic and the owner Freda Davis is full of energy and hospitality. Guests have the use of a modern and comfortable lounge and there is a games room and an outdoor tennis court. It is a mixed working farm, with livestock, trees and turkeys. No evening meals are served.

3rm(1🚿) 🚭 [R] 🐕 (ex guide dogs) dB&B£31-£32 dB&B🚿£33-£34

▦ CTV nc10yrs 🎾(hard)pool & table tennis 132 acres arable beef mixed

[£]

ST PETER PORT See **GUERNSEY under CHANNEL ISLANDS**

ST SAMPSON See **GUERNSEY under CHANNEL ISLANDS**

ST WENN Cornwall & Isles of Scilly — Map **02** SW96

SELECTED

GH [Q][Q][Q][Q] ***Wenn Manor*** PL30 5PS

☎St Austell(0726) 890240 FAX (0726) 890680

This attractive old manor house stands in its own grounds. The three bedrooms are individually decorated and furnished with fine old furniture, and they all have excellent modern en suite bathrooms. Wood panelling, flag-stone floors and antique furniture lend character and charm to the public areas, and a recently discovered well in the cosy bar has been made into an attractive feature, together with a wood-burning fire. An array of tempting fresh dishes is offered in the restaurant, and a relaxed and friendly atmosphere prevails throughout.

3🛁 CTV in all bedrooms [R] 🐕 (ex guide dogs)

Lic ▦ nc12yrs 🏊(heated) croquet lawn

Credit Cards [1][3]

SALCOMBE Devon — Map **03** SX73

SELECTED

GH [Q][Q][Q][Q] Devon Tor Hotel Devon Road TQ8 8HJ

☎(0548) 843106

Closed 10 Dec-10 Jan rs 28 Sep-1 Nov

A small private hotel in a fine position commands magnificent views of the estuary from many of the bedrooms. Rooms are cosily decorated, each with its own colour scheme, and there is a sunny dining room and a small but comfortable guests' lounge.

7rm(6🛁🚿) (2fb) 🚭 CTV in 6 bedrooms [R] 🐕 ✱ sB&B£20-£25 dB&B🛁🚿£40-£52 WB&B£140-£169 WBDi£205-£245 LDO 4.30pm

Lic ▦ CTV nc9yrs

[£]

GH [Q][Q][Q] Lyndhurst Hotel Bonaventure Road TQ8 8BG

☎(0548) 842481

Jan-Oct

Situated in a residential area, this hotel offers wonderful views over the town and estuary. Attractively coordinated bedrooms provide modern facilities with effective showers and all rooms are equipped with TV, radio and tea-making equipment. Geoff and Sheila Sharp have built a good reputation for their four-course dinners, with a choice always available, and the selection of sweets is notable. Sheila Sharp's cooking has proved so popular that she has published her own cookery book. A comfortable bar lounge is always available for guests. This establishment is totally no smoking.

8🚿 (1fb) 🚭 CTV in all bedrooms [R] 🐕 sB&B🚿£20-£27 dB&B🚿£40-£54 (incl dinner) WB&B£138-£175 WBDi£203-£255 LDO 4.30pm

Lic ▦ nc7yrs

GH [Q][Q][Q] Torre View Hotel Devon Road TQ8 8HJ

☎(0548) 842633

6 Feb-4 Nov

Friendly and enthusiastic proprietors, Julie and Arthur Bouttle, run this small hotel, which boasts superb views of the Salcombe estuary. Rooms are mainly en suite and are decorated in a light and airy style. There is a no-smoking lounge, a residents' bar with darts and skittles, and a spacious dining room where the choice for dinner is displayed on a blackboard menu.

8🛁🚿 (2fb) 🚭 in dining room CTV in all bedrooms [R] 🐕 sB&B🛁🚿£25-£29 dB&B🛁🚿£46-£52 WB&B£145-£166 WBDi£220-£244 LDO 6pm

Lic ▦ CTV nc4yrs

Credit Cards [1][3][£]

GH [Q][Q][Q] Trennels Hotel Herbert Road TQ8 8HR (take A381 to Salcombe, from main road turn left into Devon Road then left again into Herbert road, hotel is 50yds on right) ☎(0548) 842500

Mar-Nov

A private, licensed hotel conveniently situated for the town centre and harbour in a residential area has superb views over the town, estuary and National Trust land. Bedrooms are all comfortable and simply furnished, the majority having estuary views. Home-cooked meals are served in the dining room, with a set four-course table d'hôte menu. Smoking is not permitted here.

7rm(5🚿) (1fb) 🚭 CTV in 5 bedrooms [R] 🐕 ✱ sB&B🚿£17.50-£18.50 dB&B£35-£37 dB&B🚿£37-£42 WB&Bfr£120

Lic ▦ CTV nc4yrs

[£]

SALFORD Greater Manchester — Map **07** SJ89

GH [Q][Q][Q] Hazeldean Hotel 467 Bury New Road M7 3NE (on A56) ☎061-792 6667 & 061-792 2079 FAX 061-792 6668

Closed 4 days Xmas

Sound standards of accommodation and friendly service are offered at this well established hotel, 2.5 miles from the centre of Manchester. Bedrooms are both comfortable and attractive and there is a pleasant lounge, bar and small restaurant.

21rm(17🛁🚿) Annexe 3rm(2🛁🚿) (2fb) 🚭 in dining room CTV in all bedrooms [R] **T** ✱ sB&B£29-£34 sB&B🛁🚿£35-£44 dB&B£38-£50 dB&B🛁🚿£44-£55 LDO 8.30pm

Lic ▦ CTV

Credit Cards [1][2][3][5][£]

SALISBURY Wiltshire — Map **04** SU12

See also Downton (6.5m S off A338), Whiteparish & Winterbourne Stoke

GH [Q][Q][Q] Byways House 31 Fowlers Road SP1 2QP

☎(0722) 328364 FAX (0722) 322146

Closed 24 Dec-2 Jan

An extended Victorian property with an adjoining coach house is located in a quiet residential area, a short hilly walk from the city centre. The bedrooms are brightly decorated and comfortable, equipped with TV, hairdryers and tea trays; most have en suite facilities. There is a small residents' lounge offering a host of local information. Breakfast is served at separate tables in the modern dining room. Outside, the house has a pleasant garden and car park.

23rm(19🛁🚿) (5fb) 🚭 in dining room 🚭 in lounges CTV in all bedrooms [R] ✱ sB&B£22 sB&B🛁🚿£28-£30.50 dB&B£39 dB&B🛁🚿£39-£56

Lic ▦

Credit Cards [1][3][£]

GH Q Q Q **Cricket Field Cottage** Skew Bridge, Wilton Road
SP2 7NS ☎(0722) 322595
A modernised old gamekeeper's cottage with views of Salisbury
racecourse, the village church and the South Wiltshire cricket
ground. Bedrooms are spotless. Breakfast is served at one large
table.
5rm(1⇌4♠) (2fb) CTV in all bedrooms ® ⅍ (ex guide dogs)
sB&B⇌♠£25 dB&B⇌♠£38
⬛

GH Q Q Q **The Edwardian Lodge** 59 Castle Road SP1 3RH
☎(0722) 413329
This fine Edwardian house has spacious rooms which have been
recently refurbished and tastefully decorated. Situated within easy
walking distance of the city centre and cathedral.
7♠ (2fb) ✗ in 3 bedrooms ✗ in dining room CTV in all bedrooms
® ✷ sB&B♠£22.50-£26 dB&B♠£35-£40 LDO 9pm
⬛ CTV
£

GH Q Q Q **Glen Lyn** 6 Bellamy Lane, Milford Hill SP1 2SP
☎(0722) 327880
A substantial Victorian property with its own well kept gardens in
a quiet cul-de-sac, is a few minutes' walk from the city centre. The
bedrooms are comfortable, and the public areas elegantly
furnished. The house is no smoking throughout, and offers bed
and breakfast only.
9rm(2⇌2♠) (1fb) ✗ CTV in all bedrooms ® ⅍ (ex guide dogs)
✷ sB&B£19-£21 dB&B£34-£36 dB&B⇌♠£38-£40
WB&B£120-£130 WBDi£170-£185 LDO 7pm
Lic ⬛ CTV nc12yrs
£

SELECTED

GH Q Q Q Q **Grasmere House** 70 Harnham Road SP2 8JN
☎(0722) 338388 FAX (0722) 333710
An elegant example of late Victorian architecture, Grasmere
House is set back off the Harnham Road in well kept grounds
with views across fields and river to the cathedral. The
comfortable lounge has two open fireplaces and a grand piano,
drinks are served in the small bar-lounge and guests have
access through the kitchen to the conservatory dining room,
where a choice of dishes is offered. All bedrooms are well
equipped.
5⇌♠ (1fb) ✗ in 2 bedrooms ✗ in area of dining room CTV
in all bedrooms ® T ✷ sB&B⇌♠£45-£55 dB&B⇌♠£75-
£85 WB&B£250-£300 WBDi£350-£395 LDO 9.30pm
Lic ⬛ CTV ♩ croquet badminton
Credit Cards ①②③ £

GH Q Q **Hayburn Wyke** 72 Castle Road SP1 3RL (.5m N on
A345) ☎(0722) 412627
This Victorian brick-built guesthouse on the Amesbury road is in
walking distance of the city centre and has the advantage of some
parking spaces. The bedrooms are well equipped, and breakfast is
served in an attractive dining room.
6rm(2♠) (2fb) ✗ in dining room ✗ in lounges CTV in all
bedrooms ® ⅍ (ex guide dogs) sB&B£20-£30 sB&B♠£26-£35
dB&B£32-£34 dB&B♠£37-£39
⬛ CTV ∞

GH Q **Holmhurst** Downton Road SP2 8AR (follow ring rd around
city taking south coast route) ☎(0722) 410407
Karen and Trevor Hayward's family home is on the Ringwood
road, close to the city centre and cathedral. Bedrooms are well
equipped and comfortable, and breakfast is served at separate
tables in a pleasant dining room.

6rm(4♠) (2fb) ✗ in dining room ✗ in lounges CTV in all
bedrooms ® ⅍ (ex guide dogs) ✷ sB&B£18-£20 dB&B£28-£32
dB&B♠£34-£36
⬛
£

GH Q Q **Leena's** 50 Castle Road SP1 3RL ☎(0722) 335419
This family-run establishment in walking distance of the centre
has parking space and a garden. There is an attractive breakfast
room and a comfortable lounge.
6rm(4♠) (1fb) ✗ in bedrooms CTV in all bedrooms ® ⅍ (ex
guide dogs) ✷ sB&Bfr£17 dB&B£29-£33 dB&B♠£32-£37
⬛ CTV
£

SELECTED

GH Q Q Q Q **The Old House** 161 Wilton Road SP2 7JQ (on
the A30 between Wilton and Salisbury, close to the police
station) ☎(0722) 333433
Full of character, this attractive brick house is set in its own
large gardens, within easy reach of the city and railway station.
The en suite bedrooms are brightly decorated, each furnished
in its own individual style and all are equipped with remote-
control TV and tea-making facilities. A comfortable lounge,
featuring exposed beams and brick walls, is available to
guests, and home-cooked English breakfasts are served in the
tasteful dining room, furnished and decorated in a country-
cottage style with china plates on the walls and a Welsh
dresser in one corner. Smoking is only permitted in the lounge.
6⇌♠ (2fb) ✗ in bedrooms ✗ in dining room CTV in all
bedrooms ® ⅍ (ex guide dogs) ✷ sB&B⇌♠£20-£25

▶

Grasmere House

70 Harnham Road, Salisbury, Wiltshire SP2 8JN
Telephone: 01722 338388   Fax: 01722 333710

A large, late Victorian house situated in 1½ acres of colourful
and mature grounds. Built as a family residence for
prosperous Salisbury merchants it has been delightfully
converted whilst retaining all the features and atmosphere
of a comfortable family home. The luxurious five bedrooms,
all of distinctive character have en suite facilities and
beautiful views. The Conservatory Restaurant serves freshly
cooked English food with a French flavour. Centrally
situated for the town with a regular bus service or either, an
8 minute walk via the Cathedral Close or a 20 minute walk
via the Old Mill and town path. Enjoy a unique experience
staying with us at Grasmere where comfort and attentive
service go hand in hand

dB&B⇌♠♠£30-£36 WB&B£140-£175 WBDi£210-£245 LDO 3.30pm
▥ CTV games room table tennis darts
£

SELECTED

GH ❑❑❑❑ **Stratford Lodge** 4 Park Lane, Off Castle Road SP1 3NP ☎(0722) 325177 FAX (0722) 412699
Closed 23 Dec-31 Jan
8⇌♠ (2fb) ⊁ CTV in all bedrooms ⓡ T ⋇ sB&B⇌♠£30-£35 dB&B⇌♠£50-£60 WB&B£160-£196 WBDi£282-£318 LDO 8.30pm
Lic ▥ nc8yrs ♀ (heated) small gymnasium
Credit Cards ❑❑£

FH ❑❑ A Shering **Swaynes Firs** *(SU068221)* Grimsdyke, Coombe Bissett SP5 5RF (7m SW Salisbury & 3m SW of Coombe Bissett on A354 Blandford road) ☎Martin Cross(0725) 519240
This friendly farmhouse offers accommodation in bright bedrooms with modern facilities. The guests' lounge is comfortable, and the proprietors' personal pieces create a home-from-home feel. Breakfast is served in the relaxed atmosphere of the dining room.
3♠ (1fb) ⊁ in dining room CTV in all bedrooms ⓡ dB&B£36-£40
▥ CTV 11 acres beef horses poultry
£

INN ❑❑ **Old Bell** 2 Saint Ann Street SP1 2DN ☎(0722) 327958 FAX (0722) 411485
This 14th-century inn is opposite St Anne's gate, close to the cathedral. Two bedrooms have four-poster beds and are furnished in period style: others are more simply furnished. The bar has timber beams and a log fire burning in winter.
7rm(1⇌6♠) ⓡ ⋇ dB&B⇌♠£60 Bar Lunch £3-£5
▥ CTV nc12yrs
Credit Cards ❑❑❑❑

SALTASH Cornwall & Isles of Scilly   Map **02** SX45

SELECTED

INN ❑❑❑❑ **The Crooked Inn** Stoketon Cross, Trematon PL12 4RZ ☎Plymouth(0752) 848177 FAX (0752) 843203
A friendly, family-run freehouse situated six miles from Plymouth, above a peaceful unspoilt valley. Proprietors Tony and Sandra Arnold provide an excellent standard of accommodation in an adjacent annexe across the road from the inn, and rooms are all equipped with TV, clock radio alarms and tea trays, together with good quality private bathrooms. An extensive range of meals cooked using local produce is served in the timber-beamed bar, and there is a well stocked cellar with a good choice of real ales. Children's meals may be taken in the family room upstairs, and there is an outdoor heated pool and children's play area in the garden.
Annexe 12rm(9⇌♠) (2fb)CTV in 8 bedrooms ⓡ
sB&B⇌♠fr£35 dB&B⇌♠fr£50 LDO 9.30pm
▥ CTV ♀(heated) childrens play area
Credit Cards ❑❑

SANDBACH Cheshire   Map **07** SJ76

GH ❑❑ **Poplar Mount** 2 Station Road, Elworth CW11 9JG
☎Crewe(0270) 761268
Small but well maintained and fronted by its own car park, this guesthouse stands just off the A533, opposite the railway station. Guests eat at separate tables, and there is a small lounge where handicrafts made by the owner and her daughter are displayed for

sale.
7rm(2⇌2♠) (1fb) ⓡ LDO 7.45pm
▥ CTV
Credit Cards ❑❑

SANDOWN See **WIGHT, ISLE OF**

SANDWICH Kent   Map **05** TR35

INN ❑❑❑ **St Crispin** The Street CT14 0DF
☎Dover(0304) 612081
Set in the peaceful small village of Worth, this friendly inn is particularly popular in summer with a busy bar meal trade and a well-maintained garden. Bedrooms in the main building are well-appointed with old pine and attractive soft furnishings; there are also bedrooms in an outhouse. Full meals and breakfasts are served in the pleasant dining room.
4rm(2⇌2♠) Annexe 3⇌ (2fb) CTV in all bedrooms ⓡ LDO 9.30pm
▥
Credit Cards ❑❑

SANDY Bedfordshire   Map **04** TL14

FH ❑❑❑ Mrs M Codd **Highfield Farm** *(TL515166)*
Tempsford Road SG19 2AQ (1.5m N on A1) ☎(0767) 682332
Closed Xmas
This sizeable whitewashed farm stands amid arable fields to the north of the village, off the A1. A friendly hostess takes pride in the maintenance of high standards, and bedrooms containing some fine pieces of furniture provide both peace and comfort; guests eat at the dining room's one large table and relax in a cosy television lounge.
6rm(1⇌3♠) (1fb) ⊁ CTV in 3 bedrooms ⓡ ⋇ sB&B£19-£20 sB&B⇌♠£25 dB&B£32-£35 dB&B⇌♠£35-£40 WB&B£112-£175
▥ CTV 300 acres arable
£

SARISBURY GREEN Hampshire   Map **04** SU50

SELECTED

GH ❑❑❑❑ **Dormy House Hotel** 21 Barnes Lane SO31 7DA (Take A27 towards Fareham, turn right at Warsash) ☎Locks Heath(0489) 572626
A delightful small family-run hotel, Dormy House offers a real 'home from home' atmosphere. The accommodation is tastefully furnished in the modern style, with lots of little extras, and there are several ground-floor bedrooms with direct garden access. Farmhouse-style cooking is served including a three-course evening meal with a wine list (Sunday to Thursday), a full English breakfast and vegetarian dishes.
12⇌♠ (1fb) ⊁ in 3 bedrooms CTV in all bedrooms ⓡ
sB&B⇌♠£29.50-£36.50 dB&B£40 dB&B⇌♠£45 LDO 5pm
Lic ▥ CTV
Credit Cards ❑❑❑£

SARK See **CHANNEL ISLANDS**

SAUNDERSFOOT Dyfed   Map **02** SN10

GH ❑❑❑ **Jalna Hotel** Stammers Road SA69 9HH
☎(0834) 812282
Mar-Oct rs Jan & Feb
Just above the harbour and seafront, this family-run hotel provides modern, quite spacious accommodation. The well equipped bedrooms are all en suite, there is a comfortable lounge and a large bar in the basement.

▶

14⇄ℝ (8fb) CTV in all bedrooms ℝ ✳ sB&B⇄ℝ£20-£23 dB&B⇄ℝ£36-£40 WB&B£120-£139 WBDi£160-£189 LDO 6.30pm
Lic ▥ CTV solarium
Credit Cards ① ③

GH ▢▢▢▢ The Sandy Hill Sandy Hill Road/Tenby Road
SA69 9DR ☎(0834) 813165
Mar-Oct
Owners Mr and Mrs Edwards improve this pleasing little guesthouse with every season. The cosy bedrooms have a good range of equipment. There is a comfortable lounge with patio doors leading to a secluded garden complete with outdoor swimming pool. A residents' bar is provided, and good home-cooked dishes feature daily in the dining room.
5rm(3⇄ℝ) (3fb) ⚹ in dining room CTV in all bedrooms ℝ ✳ sB&B£14-£17 sB&B⇄ℝ£17 dB&B£28-£34 dB&B⇄ℝ£34 WB&B£98-£119 WBDi£147-£168
Lic ▥ nc3yrs ⟡
£

GH ▢▢▢▢ Vine Farm The Ridgeway SA69 9LA
☎(0834) 813543
Apr-Oct
This old farmhouse, dating back in parts to the early 19th century, is now a very pleasant family-run guesthouse, set in well kept lawns and gardens. There is an attractive timbered dining room, a spacious lounge with an open fire, and pretty, well furnished and equipped bedrooms.
5⇄ℝ (1fb)CTV in all bedrooms ℝ sB&B⇄ℝ£20-£21.50 dB&B⇄ℝ£40-£43 WB&B£140-£150.50 WBDi£180-£195 LDO 6pm
Lic ▥

SAXELBY Leicestershire   Map **08** SK62

FH ▢▢▢ Mrs M A Morris **Manor House** *(SK701208)*
LE14 3PA (1.5m off A6006, the Manor is at the bottom of Church Lane) ☎Melton Mowbray(0664) 812269
Etr-Oct
Part Elizabethan, this lovely old building is in a cul-de-sac past the church in the hamlet of Saxelby. There is a snug breakfast room where dinner is also provided by the friendly hostess.
3rm(1ℝ) (1fb) ⚹ in dining room CTV in all bedrooms ℝ ✻ (ex guide dogs) sB&Bfr£25 dB&Bfr£37 dB&Bℝfr£42 WB&Bfr£120 WBDifr£178 LDO noon
▥ CTV 125 acres dairy sheep

SCARBOROUGH North Yorkshire   Map **08** TA08

GH ▢▢ Alga Court 5 Alga Terrace, off St Martins Square
YO11 2DF ☎(0723) 366078
A small terraced house situated in a quiet side street on the South Cliff offers well equipped bedrooms ranging from smallish singles to family rooms. There is a comfortable lounge and a dining area downstairs.
6rm(3⇄ℝ) (3fb) ⚹ in dining room ⚹ in lounges CTV in all bedrooms ℝ ✳ sB&B£13-£15 dB&B£26-£30 dB&B⇄ℝ£32-£38 (incl dinner) WB&B£91-£112 WBDi£105-£133 LDO 3pm
▥ CTV
£

GH ▢▢ Avoncroft Hotel 5-7 Crown Terrace YO11 2BL
☎(0723) 372737
This small hotel in the centre of a Georgian terrace is convenient for both the seafront and the town centre. Bedrooms are simply furnished and decorated. There is a comfortable lounge for residents, a spacious dining room and an adjoining lounge bar.
34rm(1⇄20ℝ) (13fb)CTV in all bedrooms ℝ sB&B£18.50-£20.50 sB&B⇄ℝ£22.50-£24.50 dB&B£37-£41 dB&B⇄ℝ£45-

£49 WB&B£129.50-£143.50 WBDi£162.50-£175.50 LDO 6.15pm
Lic ▥ CTV games room pool table
£

GH ▢▢▢▢ Burghcliffe Hotel 28 Esplanade, South Cliff
YO11 2AQ ☎(0723) 361524 FAX (0723) 361578
Closed 18 Dec-8 Jan
This friendly family run hotel enjoys splendid sea views from it's lofty position on the Esplanade of the South Bay within easy reach of the beach and Spa conference centre. Bedrooms, though varying in size, are comfortable with modern appointments, while public areas include a relaxing lounge, small snug bar, and a dining room.
11rm(3⇄8ℝ) (6fb) ⚹ in dining room CTV in all bedrooms ℝ ⚼ sB&B⇄ℝ£25-£30 dB&B⇄ℝ£50-£58 WB&B£161-£189 WBDi£234.50-£262.50 LDO 4pm
Lic ▥ CTV ⚹sauna
Credit Cards ① ③ £

GH ▢▢▢▢ Dolphin Hotel 151 Columbus Ravine YO12 7QZ
☎(0723) 374217
A small terraced house close to North Bay, the cricket ground and Peasholm Park. Bedrooms are particularly well equipped, with private bathrooms, and home-cooked dinners and breakfasts with a good choice of menu are served by the friendly resident owners.
5ℝ (2fb) CTV in all bedrooms ℝ **T ⚼** LDO 8.30pm
Lic ▥ CTV nc5yrs
Credit Cards ① ② ③

GH ▢▢▢▢ Geldenhuis Hotel 145-147 Queens Parade YO12 7HU
☎(0723) 361677
Etr-early Oct
Distinguished by the gold-coloured canopies over its lower windows, the Geldenhuis overlooks North Bay and has a large car park at the front. Public rooms are spacious, bright and airy, and several of the variably sized bedrooms have views over the sea.
30rm(3⇄6ℝ) (6fb) ℝ ⚼ (ex guide dogs) LDO 6pm
Lic ▥ CTV nc5yrs

GH ▢▢▢ Manor Heath Hotel 67 Northstead Manor Drive
YO12 6AF (establishment overlooks Peasholm Park and the sea)
☎(0723) 365720
Closed 19 Nov-5 Dec & 24-25 Dec
This family run holiday guesthouse is situated on the North Bay beside Peasholm Park, within easy reach of central amenities. Public areas are cosy, with a small lounge, a bar and a bright modern dining room. Bedrooms are in various sizes with practical appointments.
15rm(2⇄10ℝ) (6fb) ⚹ in dining room CTV in all bedrooms ℝ ⚼ sB&B£17-£19 sB&B⇄ℝ£19-£21 dB&B£34-£38 dB&B⇄ℝ£38-£42 WB&B£119-£147 WBDi£149-£175 LDO 4.30pm
Lic ▥ CTV
£

⟦⚀ ⚁⟧ GH ▢ Meadow Court Queens Terrace YO12 7HJ
☎(0723) 360839
Meadow Court is a friendly family-run guesthouse with neat bedrooms, a small bar, pleasant lounge and well appointed dining room. It is close to North Bay and the town centre; Peasholm Park and the cricket ground are also nearby.
10rm (2fb) ℝ sB&B£12-£15 dB&B£24-£30 WB&B£84-£105 WBDi£112-£133 LDO 2pm
Lic ▥ CTV

GH ▢▢▢ Mount House Hotel 33 Trinity Road, South Cliff
YO11 2TD ☎(0723) 362967
Mar-Oct
A delightful semidetached Victorian house is situated in a quiet residential area on the south side of the town. Bedrooms are very well maintained and there are two very comfortable lounges, one designated a quiet lounge. Both are furnished and decorated to a very high standard. There is also a cosy bar which features

humorous golfing prints and a conservatory. In the attractive dining room four-course dinners are served. The hotel is owned and managed by Audrey and Alf Dawson, who pride themselves on good service and value for money. Their attention to detail is evident throughout the hotel.

7rm(1⇌6♠) (3fb)CTV in all bedrooms ⓡ 🖤 (ex guide dogs) sB&B⇌♠£20 dB&B⇌♠£40 WB&B£133 WBDi£189 LDO 4pm
Lic ▥ CTV
Credit Cards ①③ⓔ

SELECTED

GH ⓠⓠⓠⓠ **Paragon Hotel** 123 Queens Parade YO12 7HU (on A64) ☎(0723) 372676
2 Jan-Oct
This delightful hotel overlooks the North Bay and Scarborough Castle and is also close to the cricket ground. The modern bedrooms are individually decorated, with many enjoying fine sea views. The very comfortable bar lounge features a large picture window, and a telescope for viewing passing ships. A choice of menu is offered at dinner which is served in the attractively appointed dining room. The hotel's car park takes up most of the front garden, but there is a patio.
15rm(3⇌12♠) (2fb) ⅄ in 6 bedrooms ⅄ in dining room CTV in 14 bedrooms ⓡ ✳ sB&B⇌♠£20-£22 dB&B⇌♠£40-£44 WB&B£140-£154 WBDi£176-£196 LDO 7pm
Lic ▥
Credit Cards ①③

GH ⓠⓠⓠ *Parmelia Hotel* 17 West Street YO11 2QN
☎(0723) 361914
Mar-Oct
This very comfortable private hotel is situated on the South Cliff only a short distance from the Esplanade and Cliff tramway. Bedrooms are modern and tastefully furnished with attractive coordinated fabrics. There is an elegant and relaxing guests lounge and also a spacious lounge bar. Five-course evening meals are served in the bright and attractive dining room. The standards of hospitality and maintenance are very high.
15rm(1⇌10♠) (4fb) CTV in all bedrooms ⓡ 🖤 (ex guide dogs) LDO 4pm
Lic ▥ CTV ⅄

GH ⓠⓠⓠ **Premier Hotel** 66 Esplanade, South Cliff YO11 2UZ
☎(0723) 501038 & 501062 FAX (0723) 501062
Mar-Nov
Large Victorian property with fine views of the sea and coastline. The hotel has a very comfortable lounge and spacious dining room and several of the well equipped and nicely decorated bedrooms also have sea views. Many of the original features of the building have been retained, and their Victorian elegance is enhanced by the friendly and relaxed atmosphere.
19⇌♠ (2fb) ⅄ in dining room CTV in all bedrooms ⓡ sB&B⇌♠fr£30 dB&B⇌♠£54-£70 WBDi£245-£300 LDO 6pm
Lic lift ▥
Credit Cards ①③ⓔ

🛏 🖵 GH ⓠⓠ **The Ramleh** 135 Queens Parade YO12 7HY
☎(0723) 365745
rs Dec-Feb
This friendly family run establishment forms part of a terraced row overlooking the North Bay close to Peasholm Park. The comfortable residents' lounge has recently been refurbished, and further improvements are planned for the front facing dining room and bar. Bedrooms are also gradually being upgraded to offer comfortable modern standards.
9rm(1⇌6♠) (4fb) ⅄ in dining room CTV in all bedrooms ⓡ 🖤 (ex guide dogs) sB&B£15-£16 sB&B⇌♠£21-£22 dB&B⇌♠£36-

£38 WB&B£119-£126 WBDi£154-£161 LDO 2pm
Lic ▥ CTV
Credit Cards ①③ⓔ

🛏 🖵 GH ⓠⓠ **Rayvil Hotel** 133 Queens Parade YO12 7HU
☎(0723) 364901
Closed Xmas & New Year
10rm(2♠) (2fb) ⅄ in dining room CTV in all bedrooms ⓡ 🖤 sB&B£15-£16.50 dB&B£30-£33 dB&B♠£36-£40 WB&B£112-£122.50 WBDi£147-£161 LDO 1pm
Lic ▥ CTV nc4yrs
Credit Cards ①③ⓔ

GH ⓠⓠⓠ **Riviera Hotel** St Nicholas Cliff YO11 2ES
☎(0723) 372277
This charmingly elegant hotel occupies a prime position close to the south beach and the town centre. The lounges reflect not only contemporary styles, but also the elegance of the Victorian era to which the building belongs. Public rooms and half of the bedrooms have recently been extensively modernised and re-furbished. Five course evening meals are served in the attractive dining room with its tented ceiling.
20rm(15⇌5♠) (3fb)CTV in all bedrooms ⓡ T 🖤 (ex guide dogs) ✳ sB&B⇌♠£24-£40 dB&B⇌♠£48-£60 LDO 7pm
Lic lift ▥ ⅄
Credit Cards ①③ⓔ

GH ⓠⓠ **Sefton Hotel** 18 Prince of Wales Terrace YO11 2AL
☎(0723) 372310
Mar-Oct
This Victorian terraced house which lies near the South Cliff and Spa Conference complex has spacious traditionally styled bedrooms and an automatic lift serving every floor. There is a small bar, extensive dining room and a comfortable television lounge on the first floor.
14rm(7⇌) ⅄ in 8 bedrooms ⅄ in dining room ⅄ in 1 lounge 🖤 (ex guide dogs) sB&B£20-£22 sB&B⇌£22-£24 dB&B£40-£44 dB&B⇌£44-£48 (incl dinner) WB&B£126-£130 WBDi£160-£165 LDO 6pm
Lic lift ▥ CTV nc12yrs
ⓔ

GH ⓠⓠ *West Lodge Private Hotel* 38 West Street, South Cliff YO11 2QP ☎(0723) 500754
Feb-Nov
This Victorian house is close to the South Cliff and within easy reach of the town centre. Spacious bedrooms are a feature, and there is a comfortable guests' lounge and a nicely appointed dining room which also incorporates a small bar.
7rm(3♠) (4fb) CTV in all bedrooms ⓡ 🖤 (ex guide dogs) LDO 10am
Lic ▥ CTV nc3yrs

GH ⓠⓠⓠ **The Whiteley Hotel** 99/101 Queens Parade YO12 7HY ☎(0723) 373514
Closed Dec-Jan
14rm(10♠) ⅄ in 1 bedrooms ⅄ in dining room ⅄ in 1 lounge CTV in all bedrooms ⓡ sB&B£17.50-£19.50 dB&B£39-£43 dB&B♠£43-£46 WB&B£135-£145 WBDi£175-£185 LDO 4.15pm
Lic ▥ CTV nc12yrs
Credit Cards ①③ⓔ

FH ⓠⓠ Mrs M A Edmondson **Plane Tree Cottage Farm** *(SE999984)* Staintondale YO13 0EY (7m N) ☎(0723) 870796
May-Oct
2rm ⓡ ✳ dB&Bfr£30 WB&Bfr£100 WBDifr£150 LDO am
▥ CTV nc60 acres rare breed sheep pigs hens
ⓔ

INN ⓠⓠⓠ **Pickwick** Huntriss Row YO11 2ED ☎(0723) 375787 FAX (0723) 374284
Closed 25 Dec

▶

10🛁🚿 CTV in all bedrooms [R] **T** 🐕 (ex guide dogs) sB&B🛁🚿£22.50-£27 dB&B🛁🚿£35-£55 WB&B£112-£133 Bar Lunch £1.75-£4.70
lift ♨ nc10yrs
Credit Cards [1] [2] [3] [5]

SCILLY, ISLES OF Map **02**

ST MARY'S Map **02**

SELECTED

GH [Q] [Q] [Q] [Q] Carnwethers Country House Carnwethers, Pelistry Bay TR21 0NX ☎Scillonia(0720) 422415
8 Apr-8 Oct
A secluded former farmhouse which has been welcoming guests for 21 years now offers comfortable, well equipped accommodation which includes five bedrooms situated on the ground floor and accessed from the garden. Rooms in a variety of sizes are all similar in style - though one is notable for its lovely views and an impressive four-poster bed. The dining room provides a choice of menus and all dishes are freshly prepared; nothing is pre-cooked or reheated, and even the marmalade at breakfast is made on the premises to an old Scillonian recipe. Secluded, sheltered gardens contain many interesting plants, and a solar-heated swimming pool is available for guests' use.
9rm(8🛁🚿) Annexe 1🚿 (2fb) 🚭 in bedrooms 🚭 in dining room 🚭 in lounges CTV in all bedrooms [R] 🐕 (ex guide dogs) sB&B🛁🚿£38-£54 dB&B🛁🚿£60-£92 (incl dinner) LDO 6.30pm
Lic ♨ CTV nc7yrs 🏊(heated) sauna

SCOTCH CORNER North Yorkshire Map **08** NZ20

SELECTED

INN [Q] [Q] [Q] [Q] Vintage Hotel DL10 6NP (leave A1 at Scotch Corner and take A66 towards Penrith, hotel is 200yds on left) ☎Richmond(0748) 824424 & 822961
Closed 25 Dec & 1 Jan rs Nov-Mar
A roadside hotel just short of Scotch Corner. There are good public areas and an extensive range of food is available at lunch and dinner in the restaurant or at the bar. The bedrooms are modern and well equipped and furnished. Service is friendly and courteous. A supplementary charge is made for a cooked or Continental breakfast.
8rm(5🛁🚿) 🚭 in dining room CTV in all bedrooms [R] **T** 🐕 (ex guide dogs) ✳ sB&B£23.50-£29.50 sB&B🛁🚿£29.50-£35.50 dB&B£29.50 dB&B🛁🚿£35.50-£37.50 Lunch £9.75-£11.75 Dinner £12.75-£20.25alc LDO 9.15pm
♨ CTV
Credit Cards [1] [2] [3] [£]

SEAFORD East Sussex Map **05** TV49

SELECTED

GH [Q] [Q] [Q] [Q] ***Avondale Hotel*** 4-5 Avondale Road BN25 1RJ (on A259 edge of town) ☎(0323) 890008 (0323) 490598
High standards of maintenance, and the easygoing manner of the owners make this a popular guesthouse with long-stay residents. Stairlifts make it easy to reach the upper floors and although some bedrooms are not over-large, there are modern amenities including satellite television. The hotel operates a no-smoking policy throughout.
16rm(4🚿) (8fb) CTV in all bedrooms [R] 🐕 (ex guide dogs) LDO 2pm
lift ♨ CTV
Credit Cards [1] [2] [3] [5]

🛏 ☕ **GH [Q] [Q] Silverdale** 21 Sutton Park Road BN25 1RH (on A259 in the centre of Seaford, close to War Memorial) ☎(0323) 491849 FAX (0323) 891131
This very friendly guest house is close to the town centre. There is a small bar and a dining area where the owners will happily cater for any special dietary requirements.
4rm(2🛁🚿) (3fb) 🚭 in 2 bedrooms 🚭 in area of dining room 🚭 in lounges CTV in all bedrooms [R] **T** 🐕 (ex guide dogs) sB&B£13.50-£18.50 sB&B🛁🚿£18.50-£23.50 dB&B£25-£32 dB&B🛁🚿£30-£38 WB&B£87.50-£155 WBDi£129.50-£220 LDO 9pm
Lic ♨ CTV
Credit Cards [1] [2] [3] [£]

SEATON Devon Map **03** SY29

GH [Q] [Q] ***Harbourside*** 2 Trevelyan Road EX12 2NL ☎(0297) 20085
Mar-Oct
This small, family-run guesthouse is situated in a quiet residential area close to the town centre and overlooking the harbour. Bedrooms are comfortable and clean, and set home-cooked meals are served in the lounge/dining area.
4rm(1🛁1🚿) (2fb) CTV in all bedrooms [R] LDO 9pm
Lic ♨ CTV

GH [Q] [Q] [Q] Mariners Hotel Esplanade EX12 2NP ☎(0297) 20560
This small, private hotel, personally run by the proprietors, has a superb seafront position overlooking Lyme Bay. Bedrooms are all en suite and a ground-floor room is available. There is a residents' lounge and an additional spacious sun lounge, and a varied choice of menu is offered at dinner.
10🛁🚿 (1fb) 🚭 in dining room CTV in all bedrooms [R] ✳ sB&B🛁🚿£23-£27.50 dB&B🛁🚿£38-£41.50 LDO 6pm
Lic ♨ CTV
Credit Cards [1] [2] [3]

SEAVIEW See **WIGHT, ISLE OF**

SEDBERGH Cumbria Map **07** SD69

GH [Q] [Q] Cross Keys Hotel LA10 5NE (4.5m from Sedbergh on A683) ☎(05396) 20284
24 Mar-6 Jan
A small 18th-century stone-built house situated on the A683 to the northeast of the town, in beautiful countryside. Owned by the National Trust, this old inn offers good accommodation combined with charm and character, with low ceilings, beams, flagged floors and open fires. Although it is unlicensed, with no TV, bedrooms have modern facilities and a good standard of home cooking is provided. Smoking is not permitted.
5 🚭 [R] 🐕 (ex guide dogs) sB&B£24 dB&B£48 dB&B£58 WB&Bfr£168 WBDifr£280 LDO 24hr notice
[£]

SEDGEFIELD Co Durham Map **08** NZ32

INN [Q] [Q] [Q] ***Dun Cow*** High Street TS21 3AT ☎(0740) 20894
This is a popular town-centre pub with a long history. The bars are attractive and the food has a high reputation. Bedrooms are comfortable and well furnished, many with exposed beams.
6rm CTV in all bedrooms [R] **T** LDO 10pm
♨
Credit Cards [1] [2] [3] [5]

SELBY North Yorkshire Map **08** SE63

GH [Q] Hazeldene 32-34 Brook Street, Doncaster Road YO8 0AR (A19) ☎(0757) 704809 FAX (0757) 709300

Closed Xmas wk

Hazeldene is a Victorian villa on the A19 just south of the town centre, with private car parking at the rear. The bedrooms are generally sizeable and traditionally furnished, and downstairs there is a comfortable guests' lounge and a large dining room with individual tables.

7rm(1🚿) (2fb) 🚭 CTV in 3 bedrooms Ⓡ 🐕 * sB&B£15-£17 dB&B£28-£30 dB&B🚿£36-£40

CTV nc2yrs

[£]

SELKIRK Borders *Selkirkshire* Map **12** NT42

GH [Q][Q][Q] Hillholm 36 Hillside Terrace TD7 4ND (S on A7) ☎(0750) 21293

Mar-Nov

This semidetached Victorian house stands beside the main road to the south of the town; attractively decorated throughout, it offers a stylish lounge and dining room, breakfasts being taken round the latter's communal table. Bedrooms are furnished in a pleasing blend of period and modern styles.

3rm(2🚿) Ⓡ 🐕 sB&Bfr£20 dB&B🚿fr£34

🅿 CTV nc10yrs

SELECTED

GH [Q][Q][Q][Q] ***Sunnybrae House*** 75 Tower Street TD7 4LS ☎(0750) 21156

A cosy little detached house south of the town centre, but within easy walking distance, offers two compact bedrooms - each of them having its own lobby and sitting area and being provided with such extras as magazines, toiletries and biscuits. Meals are taken at attractively set individual tables in the downstairs lounge.

2🛁 CTV in all bedrooms Ⓡ LDO 5pm

🅿 CTV

SEMLEY Wiltshire Map **03** ST82

INN[Q][Q] Benett Arms SP7 9AS ☎East Knoyle(0747) 830221 FAX (0747) 830152

Closed 25 & 26 Dec

Friendly proprietors, Joseph and Annie Duthie, run this country inn situated in a quiet village between Tisbury and East Knoyle. The well equipped bedrooms are simply furnished and comfortable; three rooms are located in a rear annexe on ground-floor level. The friendly informal bar is split level, with an open fire in the bar area. There is an extensive range of bar meals, and a more formal restaurant is available.

2🛁🚿 Annexe 3🚿 CTV in all bedrooms Ⓡ **T** sB&B🛁🚿£29-£33 dB&B🛁🚿£44-£48 WB&B£140-£210 Lunch £12.25-£25alc Dinner £12.25-£25alc LDO 9.45pm

🅿 👪

Credit Cards [1] [2] [3] [5] [£]

SENNEN Cornwall & Isles of Scilly Map **02** SW32

GH [Q][Q] The Old Manor Hotel TR19 7AD (on A30, opposite St Sennens Church) ☎(0736) 871280 FAX (0736) 871280

Closed 23-28 Dec

A friendly guesthouse offering comfortable bedrooms, some with private shower, and all with open views. There is a separate TV lounge/library with a video, and outside guests have the use of the walled garden and putting green. A wide choice of meals is available all day, ranging from snacks and quick orders to table d'hôte menus featuring locally caught fish; Cornish cream teas are served in the garden. Holiday cottages are also available to rent.

8rm(5🚿) (3fb) 🚭 in 1 bedrooms CTV in 7 bedrooms Ⓡ **T** 🐕 dB&B£24-£34 dB&B🚿£30-£44 WB&B£133-£168 WBDi£157.50-£192.50 LDO 5.30pm

Lic 🅿 CTV putting green

Credit Cards [1] [2] [3] [£]

GH [Q][Q] Sunny Bank Hotel Sea View Hill TR19 7AR (on A30, 8m W of Penzance just after sign for Sennen) ☎(0736) 871278

Closed Dec

This large, detached house stands in acres of gardens on the outskirts of the town. Part of the gardens are maintained in a natural state and are home to many kinds of birds as well as squirrels and badgers. There are two lounges and bedrooms vary in size and decor. Hospitality and good food are provided by the owners, Ralph and Valerie Comber.

11rm (2fb) Ⓡ 🐕 (ex guide dogs) * sB&B£13-£15 dB&B£26-£34 WB&B£91-£105 WBDi£120-£144 LDO 7pm

Lic 🅿 CTV

SENNYBRIDGE Powys Map **03** SN92

SELECTED

FH [Q][Q][Q][Q] Mrs M C Adams **Brynfedwen** *(SN963297)* Trallong Common LD3 8HW ☎(0874) 636505

With superb views across the Usk Valley and the Brecon Beacons, and set in 150 acres, this establishment is very much a working farm, and during the spring guests are welcome to help bottle feed the numerous lambs. There are two en suite bedrooms in the main house, furnished in pine with pretty duvet covers. The separate annexe flat, ideal for disabled guests, can also be used for self catering and includes a small, private sitting room overlooking the lawn. There is a modern lounge with an open fire, and proprietor Mary Adams offers genuine, warm hospitality as well as good home cooking. Brynfedwen Farm stands high above the A40 in the village of Trallong, which is signposted off the A40 just two miles east of Sennybridge.

2🛁🚿 Annexe 1🚿 (2fb) 🚭 CTV in 1 bedroom Ⓡ 🐕 (ex guide dogs) * sB&B🛁🚿fr£16 dB&B🛁🚿fr£32 WB&Bfr£112 WBDifr£175 LDO 6.30pm

🅿 CTV 150 acres sheep cattle horses

[£]

FH [Q][Q][Q] Mr & Mrs H F Mayo **Maeswalter** *(SN932237)* Heol Senni LD3 8SU ☎Brecon(0874) 636629

Set in the picturesque sheep-farming valley of Heol Senni, this 17th-century farmhouse offers a warm welcome and guests return again and again. There are just three bedrooms, including one family room, all attractively decorated. The beamed lounge also serves as a dining room.

3rm(1🛁🚿) (1fb) 🚭 in bedrooms CTV in all bedrooms Ⓡ 🐕 (ex guide dogs) sB&B£17 sB&B🛁🚿£18 dB&B£29 dB&B🛁🚿£33 WB&B£98 WBDi£161

🅿 CTV nc2yrs 1 acres

See advertisement under BRECON

SETTLE North Yorkshire Map **07** SD86

GH [Q][Q] Liverpool House Chapel Square BD24 9HR (turn off B6480 by side of police station (Chapel Street) and take 2nd turning on right) ☎(0729) 822247

Closed 21 Dec-Jan

This mid 18th-century house was originally the gatehouse for the Leeds-Liverpool canal extension. Bedrooms are well maintained and there are two cosy lounges. Light lunches are served in the dining room which is filled with interesting Victoriana. This is a no-smoking establishment.

7rm 🚭 Ⓡ 🐕 sB&B£17.50-£18 dB&B£35-£36 WB&B£122.50-

▶

£126 WBDi£200-£210 LDO 10am
Lic CTV nc12yrs
Credit Cards 1 3 £

GH Q Q The Oast Guest House 5 Pen-y-Ghent View, Church
Street BD24 9JJ ☎(0729) 822989
A family-run guest house to the north side of town, The Oast
provides a pleasant standard of accommodation and service, with a
comfortable lounge and attractively furnished bedrooms.
6rm(2⇌🛏) ⊁ in bedrooms CTV in 5 bedrooms ® 🏊 (ex guide
dogs) ✳ sB&B£14.50-£16 dB&B£30-£35 dB&B⇌🛏£36-£40
WB&B£101.50-£140 WBDi£157.50-£175 LDO noon
Lic 🏧 CTV nc5yrs
£

GH Q Q *Whitefriars Country Guesthouse* Church Street
BD24 9JD ☎(0729) 823753
Closed Xmas Day
A charming old house with monastic origins, Whitefriars stands in
its own grounds close to the town centre. It retains many original
features, including beams and marble fireplaces. This is a totally
no-smoking establishment.
9rm(3🛏) (3fb) CTV in 3 bedrooms ® 🏊 (ex guide dogs) LDO
5pm
Lic 🏧 CTV

INN Q Q *Golden Lion* 5 Duke Street BD24 9DU ☎(0729) 822203
rs 25 Dec
The Golden Lion is a pleasantly furnished pub-style hotel in the
main street, currently undergoing extensive refurbishment by new
owners. Public areas include a cosy bar and a well appointed
restaurant, both of which serve a good range of food.
11rm CTV in 1 bedroom ® 🏊 (ex guide dogs) LDO 10pm
🏧 CTV
Credit Cards 1 3

SEVENOAKS Kent
See **Wrotham**

SHALDON Devon
See **Teignmouth**

SHANKLIN See **WIGHT, ISLE OF**

SHAP Cumbria   Map **12** NY51

GH Q Q Q Brookfield CA10 3PZ (junct 39 of M6)
☎(0931) 716397
Closed 21 Dec-Jan
A detached house set in its own gardens on the A6 to the south of
the village. The bedrooms are well furnished with bright, fresh
decor, and home cooking is served in the pretty dining room
which also has a small bar. The resident owners provide friendly
and helpful service.
6rm (3fb)CTV in all bedrooms ® 🏊 ✳ sB&B£16-£17.50
dB&B£32-£34 LDO 8.15pm
Lic 🏧 CTV
£

🛏 💺 FH Q E & S Hodgson **Green Farm** *(NY565143)* CA10 3PW
(on A6 in Shap village) ☎(0931) 716619
Etr-Sep
This typical 18th-century Cumbrian farmhouse to the south of the
town offers good value for money; there are three simply
furnished bedrooms, and guests have the use of a comfortable
lounge.
3 (2fb) ® 🏊 sB&Bfr£15 dB&Bfr£30
CTV 200 acres mixed

SHEARSBY Leicestershire   Map **04** SP69

SELECTED

FH Q Q Q Q Mrs A T Hutchinson **Knaptoft House Farm
& The Greenway** *(SP619894)* Bruntingthorpe Road LE17 6PR
☎Leicester(0533) 478388 due to change to (0116) 2478388
FAX (0533) 478388 due to change to (0116) 2478388
Closed Xmas
Good accommodation is offered at this traditional mixed farm
in the original farmhouse and adjoining modern bungalow, run
by mother and daughter. Bedrooms in each establishment are
attractively decorated and very well maintained. Each house
has a comfortable lounge with a log burning stove, games and
books. The breakfast rooms are light and appealing, and for
other meals information on local restaurants is to hand. Guests
are welcome to fish, by arrangement, in the restored medieval
fishpond.
3rm(2🛏) Annexe 3rm(1🛏) (1fb) ⊁ in 1 bedrooms ⊁ in dining
room ® 🏊 ✳ sB&Bfr£20 sB&B🛏fr£25 dB&Bfr£35
dB&B🛏fr£42
🏧 CTV nc3yrs 🐾 stabling 145 acres mixed
£

SHEFFIELD South Yorkshire   Map **08** SK38

In addition to the national changes to dialling codes on 16 April
1995 (ie the insertion of `1' after the first `0') the codes for certain
cities are changing completely - the code for Sheffield will be
`0114' with each individual number prefixed by `2'.

GH Q Q Q *Hunter House Hotel* 685 Ecclesall Road, Hunters
Bar S11 8TG (on A625 overlooking Endcliffe Park)
☎(0742) 662709 FAX (0742) 686370
23rm(10⇌🛏) (9fb) CTV in all bedrooms ® T LDO 8.45pm
Lic 🏧

GH Q Q Q *Lindrick Hotel* 226 Chippinghouse Road S7 1DR
(1.5m from city centre) ☎(0742) 585041 FAX (0742) 554758
Closed 24 Dec-first Sat in Jan
A small hotel in a quiet, tree-lined, residential area of Nether
Edge, a short distance from the city centre. Friendly proprietors
provide a warm welcome and high standards throughout.
Bedrooms are pleasantly decorated, with the more compact,
cheaper rooms being mostly on the second floor. Public rooms are
inviting and include a small cosy bar and separate lounge.
Breakfast, with its good selection of dishes, is the only meal
served at weekends; a supper menu of home-made bar snacks is
available Monday - Thursday. Smoking is not permitted in the
breakfast room and lounge. There is both on-site and unlimited
on-street parking.
23rm(15🛏) (1fb) ⊁ in dining room ⊁ in 1 lounge CTV in all
bedrooms ® T sB&B£18-£25.50 sB&B🛏£26-£36.95
dB&B🛏£38-£42 LDO 8.45pm
Lic 🏧 CTV
Credit Cards 1 2 3 £

GH Q Q Q *Lindum Hotel* 91 Montgomery Road S7 1LP (city
centre take A6134 St Mary Road, follow sign A625 Eccles)
☎(0742) 552356
Closed Xmas
This stone-built Edwardian house sits in a quiet residential area in
the district of Nether Edge, two miles from the city centre. Over
recent years bedroom accommodation has been upgraded to offer
modern facilities, but room sizes vary. Guests have the use of a
ground-floor lounge, a small dining room and small car park; on-
street parking is also available.
11rm(4⇌) (1fb) CTV in all bedrooms ®
Lic 🏧 CTV

GH Q Q Q *Millingtons* 70 Broomgrove Road S10 2NA (off A625
Ecceshall Rd) ☎(0742) 669549
Friendly proprietors provide good levels of maintenance at this

small guest house in a quiet tree-lined road off the A625 south-west of the city, close to the universities and Hallamshire hospital. Guests dine at a communal table for breakfast. There is a small car park at the front of the house.
6rm(3⇆ſ⬩) ⚡ in dining room CTV in all bedrooms ® 🅇 (ex guide dogs) ✳ sB&Bfr£23 sB&B⇆ſ⬩fr£23 dB&Bfr£39 dB&B⇆ſ⬩fr£42
▥ CTV nc12yrs
£

SHENINGTON Oxfordshire   Map **04** SP34

SELECTED
GH ⓠⓠⓠⓠ **Cotman House** Shenington OX15 6NH (6m W of Banbury) ☎Edge Hill(0295) 670642
3rm(2⇆ſ⬩) ⚡ in bedrooms ® 🅇 (ex guide dogs) ✳ dB&Bfr£45 dB&B⇆ſ⬩fr£55 LDO 24hrs
▥ CTV nc8yrs snooker

SHEPTON MALLET Somerset   Map **03** ST64
INNⓠⓠ **Kings Arms** Leg Square BA4 5LN ☎(0749) 343781
Closed Xmas rs Sat lunch
Set in the old, quieter part of the town, this 17th-century inn affectionately known as The Dusthole, is well managed and popular with locals and visitors alike. The three bedrooms are well equipped, and the bars are full of character and charm, offering a choice of real ales. An extensive range of home-cooked dishes is offered including a Big Steak menu, and the pub enjoys strong local support, popular for its skittle alley, pool table and meeting room.
3ſ⬩ ⚡ in area of dining room ⚡ in 1 lounge CTV in all bedrooms ® 🅇 (ex guide dogs) ✳ sB&Bſ⬩fr£25 dB&Bſ⬩fr£33 Bar Lunch £12.50 Dinner £12.50 LDO 9.30pm
▥ nc10yrs games room
Credit Cards 1

INNⓠⓠ **The Portman** Pylle BA4 6TA (3m S)
☎Evercreech(0749) 830150
This is a busy roadside inn offering a warm welcome in a cosy traditional bar, furnished in an appealing style to suit the character of the pub. The menu of the day with tempting home-made specialities is displayed on blackboards around the bar. The bedrooms are comfortable, with en suite bathrooms and fine views across Somerset farmland.
2⇆ſ⬩ (1fb) CTV in all bedrooms ® LDO 10pm
▥
Credit Cards 1 3

SHERBORNE Dorset   Map **03** ST61
See also **Halstock.**

SELECTED
GH ⓠⓠⓠⓠ **The Alders** Sandford Orcas DT9 4SB (from town take B3148 towards Marston Magna, after 2.5m take signposted turning to Sandford Orcas. 1m after entering village turn left at T-junct) ☎(0963) 220666
2⇆ſ⬩ CTV in all bedrooms ® 🅇 (ex guide dogs) ✳ sB&B⇆ſ⬩£18.50-£26 dB&B⇆ſ⬩£37-£42
▥ CTV arrangement with Sherborne Golf Club

FH ⓠⓠⓠ Mrs J Mayo **Almshouse Farm** (ST651082)
Hermitage, Holnest DT9 6HA ☎(0963) 210296
3rm (1fb)® 🅇 ✳ sB&B£16-£18 sB&B£18-£20 dB&Bfr£32 dB&B£36-£40
CTV 160 acres dairy

FH ⓠⓠ Mrs P T Tizzard **Venn** (ST684183) Milborne Port DT9 5RA (on the A30 3m E of Sherborne, on edge of village of Milborne Port) ☎Milborne Port(0963) 250598
Neat, bright and well presented, this dairy farm stands beside the A30 only three miles from the famous abbey town. Pretty bedrooms now offer TV sets as well as tea-making facilities, and there are excellent views across the fields from the comfortable lounge where a log fire burns on cooler days; breakfast menus offer a lighter option as well as the traditional hearty meal. Cheerful hosts, a warm welcome and a relaxed atmosphere attract many guests back time and time again.
3rm (1fb) CTV in all bedrooms ® 🅇 (ex guide dogs) ✳ sB&Bfr£14 dB&Bfr£26
▥ CTV 375 acres dairy/beef

SHERIFF HUTTON North Yorkshire   Map **08** SE66
GH ⓠⓠⓠ **Rangers House** Sheriff Hutton Park YO6 1RH ☎(0347) 878397
Built in 1639 as a brewhouse and stable for the royal hunting lodge, this attractive guesthouse is situated in Sheriff Hutton Park. Adjacent to the hall, its name is derived from the rangers who looked after the park. This friendly, comfortable house contains much period style furniture and although the bedrooms have been modernised, beams and leaded windows help to retain its character. The main hall with its comfortable seating, open fire, TV and lots of literature has a gallery and an 18th-century staircase. The dining room with its yellow painted walls, also contains antique furniture, including spacious, individual tables. The hotel is fully licensed, and children are always welcome.
6rm(2⇆2ſ⬩) (1fb) ⚡ in area of dining room ® 🅇 sB&B⇆ſ⬩£35 dB&B£64 dB&B⇆ſ⬩£70 WB&B£201.60-£220 WBDi£315-£365 LDO 9.30pm
Lic ▥ CTV multigym
£

SHERINGHAM Norfolk   Map **09** TG14
GH ⓠⓠⓠ **Beacon Hotel** Nelson Road NR26 8BT ☎(0263) 822019
May-Sep
Beacon Hotel is a large black and white house, with spacious gardens, set at the top of Beeston Hill and a short distance from the sea. It is a well cared for establishment and offers comfortable accommodation with light, fresh furnishings and decor.
6rm(3ſ⬩) ⚡ in bedrooms ⚡ in dining room ® 🅇 sB&Bſ⬩fr£22 dB&Bſ⬩fr£44 WB&Bfr£140 WBDifr£196
Lic ▥ CTV nc14yrs
Credit Cards 1 3 £

SELECTED
GH ⓠⓠⓠⓠ **Fairlawns** 26 Hooks Hill Road NR26 8NL ☎(0263) 824717 FAX (0263) 824717
Etr-Oct
This large Victorian house has been sympathetically converted to provide fresh and inviting accommodation. Set in its own spacious grounds, it is located in a quiet and secluded residential cul-de-sac just a few minutes from the town centre. The bedrooms are all of a comfortable size, with spotless modern en suite bathrooms, TV and tea trays. Mrs McGill is a charming and enthusiastic hostess who prides herself on providing good quality food, including Sunday `brunch'.
5⇆ſ⬩ ⚡ in dining room CTV in all bedrooms ® 🅇 (ex guide dogs) ✳ dB&B⇆ſ⬩£40-£44 WB&Bfr£128 LDO noon
Lic ▥ nc12yrs croquet

SHETLAND Map **16**

LERWICK Map **16** HU44

GH Q Q Q **Glen Orchy House** 20 Knab Road ZE1 0AX (adjct to coastguard station) ☎Shetland(0595) 2031
Ongoing improvements are being made at this sturdy, detached house on the south side of town. Bedrooms, all well equipped, are bright and airy with attractive fabrics and modern furnishings. The public areas include a small, cosy lounge where there are books and board games and a refurbished dining room where home-cooking is much enjoyed by regular guests.
8rm(1🟢) (2fb) ⊱ in dining room CTV in all bedrooms ⓡ ✳
sB&Bfr£25.50 sB&B🟢fr£34 dB&Bfr£48 dB&B🟢fr£56
WB&B£168-£238 WBDi£241.50-£311.50 LDO 2pm
Lic 📖 ▶9
ⓔ

SHIFNAL Shropshire Map **07** SJ70

GH Q Q Q **Village Farm Lodge** Sheriffhales TF11 8RD (on B4379) ☎Telford(0952) 462763 FAX (0952) 677912
Former farm buildings have been cleverly converted to provide modern bedrooms at this pleasant little guest house in the village of Sheriffhales. Beams, exposed brickwork and pine furniture are features of the accommodation, and there is cottage-style dining room with individual tables, and a cosy conservatory lounge. Several bedrooms are at ground-floor level, some with external access from the car park.
8🟢 (3fb) ⊱ in 4 bedrooms CTV in all bedrooms ⓡ ✝ (ex guide dogs) sB&B🟢£25-£28.50 dB&B🟢£35-£39
Lic 📖 CTV
Credit Cards ① ② ③ ⓔ

SHILLINGFORD Devon Map **03** SS92

SELECTED

GH Q Q Q Q **The Old Mill** EX16 9BW (on B3227)
☎Bampton(0398) 331064
A carefully restored stone-built mill is set in pretty gardens by a stream on the edge of the village. The spacious well equipped bedrooms are furnished in pine, and two are arranged in suites with private lounges. The lounge in the main house is reserved for guests taking dinner. Proprietor Di Burnell offers a set menu of home-cooked food with fresh local vegetables; special dietary needs are provided for by arrangement. The wine list features about 25 wines all very reasonably priced. Smoking is not permitted.
2🟢🟢 Annexe 2🟢 (2fb) ⊱ CTV in all bedrooms ⓡ ✝ LDO noon
Lic 📖 CTV nc5yrs ♪
ⓔ

SHIPBOURNE Kent Map **05** TQ55

SELECTED

INN Q Q Q Q **The Chaser** Stumble Hill TN11 9PE
☎Plaxtol(0732) 810360 FAX (0732) 810941
The front part of this imposing Victorian building is a rustic inn, but to the rear there is a popular restaurant with a high, vaulted ceiling. Here, freshly made dishes drawn from local produce are served. The well equipped accommodation is divided between the main building and the converted stable block.
15🟢🟢 (1fb)CTV in all bedrooms ⓡ T ✳ sB&B🟢🟢fr£45
dB&B🟢🟢fr£55 Lunch £12.50 Dinner £19.95 LDO 9.30pm
📖
Credit Cards ① ② ③ ⓔ

SHIPSTON ON STOUR Warwickshire Map **04** SP24

GH Q Q Q **The Manor** Main Street, Long Compton CV36 5JJ (centre of Long Compton village on A3400 50yds S of St Peter & St Pauls church) ☎Long Compton(0608) 684218
The Manor House built of Cotswold stone dates back to 1710 and stands in the centre of Long Compton. The bedrooms are roomy with traditional furnishings. There are no less than three sitting rooms: one with inglenook fireplace and bar, a TV room and a quiet reading room. The dining room has separate tables. June and Colin Empson, the owners, provide friendly service.
5rm(3🟢) (1fb) ⊱ in dining room ⓡ ✝ (ex guide dogs) ✳
sB&B£24-£34 dB&B£36-£70 dB&B🟢£40-£74 WB&B£126-£140 WBDi£176-£190 LDO 6.45pm
Lic 📖 CTV
ⓔ

SHOTTLE Derbyshire Map **08** SK34

GH Q Q **Shottle Hall Farm** DE5 2EB (leave A517 at crossroads with B5023, 200yds towards Wirksworth then turn right & proceed for 0.5m) ☎Cowers Lane(0773) 550276 & 550203
Closed Nov & Xmas
Guests are assured of a warm welcome at this large family home. Surrounded by three acres of grounds and a large farm, this is ideal spot for a relaxing holiday.
11rm(1🟢) (3fb) CTV in 1 bedroom ⓡ LDO 6pm
Lic 📖 CTV
See advertisement under BELPER

P R E M I E R 🏅 S E L E C T E D

FH Q Q Q Q Q Mrs J L
Slack **Dannah** *(SK314502)*
Bowmans Lane DE56 2DR
☎Cowers Lane(0773) 550273
& 550630 FAX (0773) 550590
Closed Xmas
A genuine welcome from proprietors Joan and Martin Slack is assured at this delightful Georgian farmhouse set in open countryside high above Ecclesbourne valley.
Guests are encouraged to relax and enjoy the comfortable public rooms, and the bedrooms are delightfully decorated in individual styles. In 1992 Joan won a national award for farm catering. Good quality fresh produce is carefully prepared and presented, with set menus for the first half of the week then a choice of menus on the other days.
8rm(7🟢🟢) (1fb) ⊱ in bedrooms ⊱ in dining room ⊱ in 1 lounge CTV in all bedrooms ⓡ ✝ (ex guide dogs)
sB&B🟢🟢£35-£55 dB&B🟢🟢£54-£70 WB&B£165-£250
LDO 6.15pm
Lic 📖 128 acres mixed
Credit Cards ① ③ ⓔ
See advertisement under DERBY

SHREWSBURY Shropshire Map **07** SJ41

SELECTED

GH Q Q Q Q **Fieldside** 38 London Road SY2 5NX
☎(0743) 353143
Closed 18 Dec-18 Jan
Fieldside is a beautifully preserved and impeccably maintained Victorian house close to the Shire Hall. It provides tastefully decorated bedrooms with a good array of modern equipment. There is an attractive breakfast room with period-style furniture, and other facilities include a large rear garden

and a private car park. The whole house is no-smoking.
9rm(6🐾) 🦵 CTV in 7 bedrooms ⓇⓉ🎯 ✳ sB&Bfⓡ£28-£30
dB&B£36-£38 dB&Bfⓡ£40-£45
⊞ nc9yrs
Credit Cards ⑴⑵⑶

SELECTED
GH ⓆⓆⓆⓆ *Mytton Hall* Montford Bridge SY4 1EU
☎(0743) 850264
A very large house dating from 1790, Mytton Hall has been
extended at various times over the centuries. It is quietly
situated in its own extensive grounds on the edge of the village
of Mytton. There are three double rooms, two of which are
very spacious, and all have antique furnishings and modern en
suite facilities. Welcoming fires burn in both the cosy sitting
room and the lovely breakfast room, where guests eat at a
communal table.
3🛏 🎯
⊞ CTV nc14yrs 🏌

GH ⓆⓆ **Restawhile** 36 Coton Crescent SY1 2NZ
☎(0743) 240969
The Restawhile is a cosy, family-run guest house just off the A528
Ellesmere road, north of the town centre. Bedrooms all have en
suite bath or shower rooms, and are well equipped with extras
such as televisions and tea trays. There is a comfortable residents'
lounge and easy street parking available.
4🛏fⓡ 🦵 in dining room CTV in all bedrooms ⓇⓉ🎯
sB&B🛁fⓡ£25-£28 dB&B🛁fⓡ£35-£39 WB&B£175-£196

▶

GLEN ORCHY HOUSE
20 Knab Road, Lerwick, Shetland ZE1 0AX
Telephone: 01595 2031

AA LISTED, QQQ & STB CROWN COMMENDED

Situated on the south side of Lerwick
adjoining 9 hole golf course free to the
public. Close to the town centre and
harbour. Licensed, excellent cuisine, TV and
tea & coffee making facilities in all
bedrooms.

Rooms:- 2 single 2 Family 3 Twin 1 En-suite
Prices:- Single from £20.50
Twin/Double from £19.50 per person
Dinner B&B from £30.00 per person
Terms on application

Central for the Cotswolds
Excellent catering with meal choices
Large comfortable bedrooms with
tea/coffee facilities

THE MANOR HOUSE
Long Compton, Warks CV36 5JJ
Tel: 01608 684 218

Spacious manor house of Cotswold
stone dating back to 1710 and standing
in a picturesque garden. Comfortable TV
lounge. Small reading room. Small
lounge/bar with inglenook fireplace.
Spacious dining room

Fieldside
38 London Road, Shrewsbury SY2 6NX
Tel: (01743) 353143

A lovely Victorian house with attractive
gardens. Centrally heated bedrooms have
shower en-suite, colour television, direct line
telephone and tea/coffee making facilities. The
hotel is situated 1½ miles from town centre of
Shrewsbury, famous for its floral displays,
ancient buildings and interesting museums.
Adjacent to Fieldside is St Giles church visited
by 'Brother Cadfel' the medieval sleuth in Ellis
Peters novels.
NON SMOKING
Enclosed parking. S.A.E. for details.
Resident proprietors: Pat & Ian Fraser

WBDi£245-£266 LDO 6pm
🔥 CTV nc11yrs Credit Cards [1][2][3] [£]

[🛏] GH [Q][Q][Q] **Roseville** 12 Berwick Road SY1 2LN (on B5067) ☎(0743) 236470
Closed 20 Dec-31 Jan
Now a small, no-smoking guesthouse, this well maintained Victorian property is situated north of the town centre, conveniently close to the Agricultural Show ground. Attractively decorated modern bedrooms are provided with extras like mineral water, razors and toiletries as well as a good selection of books; there are a cosy lounge and a separate dining room with individual tables, and some car parking space is available.
3rm(2🚿) 🚭 🐕 sB&B£15-£17 dB&B🚿£36-£40 WB&B£120-£140 WBDi£160-£200 LDO noon
🔥 CTV nc12yrs [£]

SELECTED

GH [Q][Q][Q][Q] Sandford House Hotel St Julians Friars SY1 1XL (cross River Severn over 'English Bridge' and take first sharp left) ☎(0743) 343829
A small hotel close to English bridge and river walks, is located on a narrow road off the main route into the town centre. There is no parking at the hotel, but there is a public car park nearby. The elegant lounge overlooks a well tended rear garden, and the owners make every effort to ensure a pleasant stay.
11rm(9🛁🚿) (3fb) 🚭 in dining room CTV in all bedrooms Ⓡ sB&Bfr£23 sB&B🛁🚿fr£31 dB&Bfr£38 dB&B🛁🚿fr£43.50
Lic 🔥 CTV
Credit Cards [1][3][5] [£]

GH [Q][Q][Q] Sydney House Hotel Coton Crescent, Coton Hill SY1 2LJ (jct of A528/B5067) ☎(0743) 354681 & Freecall 0500 130243 FAX (0743) 354681
Closed 24-31 Dec
A smart, friendly and well run Victorian house with facilities that benefit both the tourist and the business person. It is situated on the northern edge of town.
7rm(4🚿) (1fb) 🚭 in dining room 🚭 in lounges CTV in all bedrooms Ⓡ T 🐕 (ex guide dogs) * sB&B£32-£35 sB&B🚿£42-£45 dB&B£42-£46 dB&B🚿£55-£60 WB&B£135-£290 WBDi£207.50-£360 LDO 8.30pm
Lic 🔥 Credit Cards [1][2][3] [£]

GH [Q][Q][Q] Tudor House 2 Fish Street SY1 1UR (enter town by crossing English Bridge, ascend Wyle Cop after 50yds first right) ☎(0743) 351735
Closed 24-26 Dec
Dating from 1460, this beautifully preserved house stands in the town centre opposite St Alkmund's Church. The bedrooms are traditionally furnished but have modern facilities and equipment. The cosy lounge contains a small bar, and separate tables are provided in the pleasant dining room. A warm welcome from Mair Harris awaits all her guests, many of whom are regular visitors.
3rm(2🚿) 🚭 in 2 bedrooms 🚭 in dining room CTV in all bedrooms 🐕 sB&B£25-£34 sB&B🚿£30-£34 dB&B£38-£40 dB&B🚿£40-£44 WB&Bfr£150
Lic 🔥 CTV 🚫 [£]

FH [Q][Q][Q] Mrs P A Roberts **The Day House** *(SJ465104)* Nobold SY5 8NL (2.5m SW between A488 & A49) ☎(0743) 860212
Closed Xmas & New Year
Farmland and gardens surround this large farmhouse which dates back in parts to the 18th century. The spacious bedrooms have preserved their original fireplaces. Deep settees and armchairs make the lounge a comfortable chatting place, and although no evening meal is served there are many restaurants in the neighbourhood, Shrewsbury being only four miles away.
3rm(1🛁1🚿) (3fb)CTV in all bedrooms Ⓡ 🐕 (ex guide dogs) * dB&B🛁🚿£40-£44
🔥 CTV 🎣 rough & game shooting 400 acres arable dairy [£]

FH [Q][Q][Q] Mrs J M Jones ***Grove*** *(SJ537249)* Preston Brockhurst SY4 5QA (5m N on A49) ☎Clive(093928) 223
Closed Xmas & New Year
This 17th-century farmhouse has cosy guest rooms and a comfortable lounge that doubles as a dining room. Children are especially welcome, but smoking is banned in the house.
3rm (1fb) CTV in 1 bedroom Ⓡ 🐕 (ex guide dogs)
🔥 CTV 320 acres arable mixed

FH [Q][Q][Q] Mrs C Yates **Upper Brompton** *(SJ548078)* Cross Houses SY5 6LE (from town take A452 to Cross Houses and turn first left after Fox public house, past houses and down lane for 0.5m) ☎(0743) 761629
3rm(2🛁1🚿) (1fb) 🚭 CTV in all bedrooms Ⓡ sB&B🛁🚿£25-£30 dB&B🛁🚿£36-£40 WB&B£113-£140 WBDi£200-£227.50 LDO 10am
🚜 315 acres arable

SIDMOUTH Devon — Map 03 SY18

See also Harpford

PREMIER SELECTED

GH [Q][Q][Q][Q][Q] Broad Oak Sid Road EX10 8QP (from A3052) ☎(0395) 513713
Feb-Nov

This beautifully restored Victorian house stands near the river and is only five minutes from the town centre. The well equipped bedrooms are furnished to a high standard, there is a cosy sitting room and attractive breakfast room.
3rm(2🚿) 🚭 CTV in all bedrooms Ⓡ 🐕 (ex guide dogs) sB&B£20 dB&B🚿£46-£50 WB&B£144.90-£157.50
🔥 nc

GH [Q][Q][Q] Canterbury Salcombe Road EX10 8PR (200yds from central Sidmouth, next to River Sid hump back bridge) ☎(0395) 513373
Mar-Nov
Small and homely, this is a well-maintained guest house. Bedrooms vary in size but are reasonably equipped, all with en suite facilities. Public rooms are small yet comfortable with a set price menu available at dinner. Parking is limited.
8rm(7🛁🚿) (4fb)CTV in all bedrooms Ⓡ sB&B£16-£18 sB&B🛁🚿£18-£21 dB&B£30-£32 dB&B🛁🚿£34-£36 WB&B£104-£124 WBDi£155-£172 LDO 4.30pm
Lic CTV
Credit Cards [1][2][3] [£]

GH [Q][Q][Q] ***Mariners*** 69 Sidford High Street EX10 9SH ☎(0395) 515876
Closed Nov & Dec
The family home of the resident proprietors, is set in well kept grounds in the small village of Sidford, just 1.5 miles from the seafront. The bedrooms are modern and brightly decorated and the lounge cosy. Evening meals are available in the relaxed atmosphere of the dining room.
8🚿 (2fb) CTV in all bedrooms Ⓡ LDO 10am
🔥 CTV

GH QQQ The Old Farmhouse Hillside Road EX10 8JG
☎(0395) 512284
Feb-15 Nov
This delightful thatched 16th-century farmhouse is in a residential area, within easy walking distance of the sea and shops. Bedrooms, some in a small cottage across the patio, are decorated with pretty floral papers and soft furnishings. The lounge and dining room are full of character with exposed beams and original fireplaces. The dinner menu offers a choice at each course, and features home-made soups and pates and lovely old-fashioned puddings. Smoking is not permitted in the bedrooms or dining room.
4rm(1⇌) Annexe 4rm(3⇌1↱) (2fb) ✗ in bedrooms ✗ in dining room Ⓡ ✳ sB&Bfr£19 sB&B⇌↱fr£23 dB&Bfr£38 dB&B⇌↱fr£46 WB&B£120-£145 WBDi£170-£195
Lic 🅿 CTV
Credit Cards 1 3

GH Q Ryton House 52-54 Winslade Road EX10 9EX
☎(0395) 513981
Feb-Oct
Set in a quiet residential area about a mile from the seafront, Ryton House offers bright and clean bedrooms, some with en suite facilities. There is a TV lounge and a licensed dining room where a traditional set dinner is served.
9rm(2⇌4↱) (4fb) ✗ in dining room ✗ in lounges Ⓡ sB&B⇌↱£16-£20 dB&B£30-£32 dB&B⇌↱£32-£38 WB&B£99-£130 WBDi£120-£180 LDO 4.30pm
Lic 🅿 CTV
£

SILLOTH Cumbria — Map **11** NY15

GH QQQ Nith View 1 Pine Terrace CA5 4DT (on the sea front)
☎(06973) 31542
▶

RESTAWHILE

Guest House, 36 Coton Crescent, SHREWSBURY SY1 2NZ
Telephone: (01743) 240969

Restawhile Guest House is situated just North of the Town off the Junction of the **A528 Ellesmere Road** and the **B5067 Baschurch Road** in a quiet one-way street. 10 min's walk from town centre. **All** rooms are **En-Suite** and include **Colour Television, Tea and Coffee** facilities.

*Prices from £17.50 per person Double or Twin Room, £25.00 for Single Room and include **Full English Breakfast.***

Direct Dial Telephone. Hair Dryer and Iron/board are available on request. A pleasant welcome awaits you.

AA 2Q Listed
Lock Up Garage
Car Parking

English Tourist Board COMMENDED — VISA

SYDNEY HOUSE HOTEL

Coton Crescent • Coton Hill
Shrewsbury • Shropshire • SY1 2LJ
Tel:/Fax: Shrewsbury (01743) 354681
FREECALL: 0500 130243
Resident Proprietors: T. S. & P. A. Hyde

THE HOTEL OFFERS:
• Free Car Park
• Lounge Bar and Home Cooking

All rooms have direct dial Telephone, Radio and TV etc. Most rooms en-suite.
Please write or phone for Brochure and Rates.

LES ROUTIERS — AA LISTED — LICENSED — VISA — English Tourist Board COMMENDED

The Old Farmhouse

Sidmouth

Quietly situated in residential area on the edge of the Byes and only a few minutes walk from both sea and shops. A delightful 16th century farmhouse with an adjoining cottage which once housed the local cider mill. Whilst all modern amenities have been provided the originality has been preserved with no two rooms the same but all sharing the pretty decor and homely feel. Relax in the cosy, low beamed lounge or the intimate Inglenook bar with a pre dinner drink. Delicious old fashioned recipes form the basis of the menus with the same meal never served twice in a fortnight. Car parking space available.

Hillside Road, Sidmouth, Devon EX10 8JG
Telephone: 01395 512284

Nith View is a family-run licensed guesthouse, situated at the end of a terrace overlooking the Solway Firth. Bedrooms are comfortably furnished and most have en suite facilities. There is also a guests' lounge, a small bar and an attractive dining room. All groups are catered for and those playing golf on the nearby Championship Course will find it particularly convenient.
8rm(5♠) (4fb) ⊁ in 2 bedrooms ⊁ in 1 lounge CTV in 5 bedrooms ® ✻ sB&B£16.50 sB&B♠£19.50 dB&B£29 dB&B♠£33.50 WB&B£96-£110
Lic ▥ CTV
Credit Cards [1][3] ⓔ

SILVERDALE Lancashire   Map **07** SD47

SELECTED

GH Ⓠ Ⓠ Ⓠ Ⓠ **Lindeth House** Lindeth Road LA5 0TX (junct 35 of M6) ☎(0524)701238
Mar-Dec
In a village setting surrounded by woodland trails, this former gentleman's residence offers inviting accommodation with a friendly and relaxing atmosphere. The pleasantly decorated bedrooms are not large, but are comfortably furnished with pine units and have smart en suite bathrooms and many thoughtful extras. There is a lounge and a spacious dining room where imaginatively prepared home cooked meals are served.
3rm(1⇋2♠) ⊁ in bedrooms ⊁ in dining room ⊁ in 1 lounge CTV in all bedrooms ® ✻ (ex guide dogs) sB&B⇋♠£30 dB&B⇋♠£43-£46 LDO 2pm
Lic ▥ nc11yrs
ⓔ

SILVERSTONE Northamptonshire   Map **04** SP64

FH Ⓠ Ⓠ Ⓠ Mr & Mrs Branch *Silverthorpe (SP661456)*
Silverthorpe Farm, Abthorpe Road NN12 8TW
☎Towcester(0327) 858020
This modern farm building with five acres of land is on the road between Abthorpe and Silverstone, less than two miles from the racetrack. The accommodation benefits from its modern decor, and if guests are interested, the owners will show them round their mushroom farm.
3 CTV in all bedrooms ®

SITTINGBOURNE Kent   Map **05** TQ96

P R E M I E R ✿ **S E L E C T E D**

GH Ⓠ Ⓠ Ⓠ Ⓠ Ⓠ **Hempstead House** London Road, Bapchild ME9 9PP (on A2, 1.5m E opposite turning to Tonge)
☎(0795) 428020
FAX (0795) 428020
Surrounded by beautiful countryside, this Victorian family house stands in three acres of gardens that include a kitchen garden. The Holdstock family treat guests
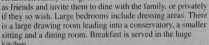
as friends and invite them to dine with the family, or privately if they so wish. Large bedrooms include dressing areas. There is a large drawing room leading into a conservatory, a smaller sitting and a dining room. Breakfast is served in the huge kitchen.
7⇋♠ (1fb) ⊁ in bedrooms ⊁ in area of dining room ⊁ in 1 lounge CTV in all bedrooms ® sB&B⇋♠£50-£55

dB&B⇋♠£62 WB&B£180-£195 WBDi£278 LDO 9pm
Lic ▥ CTV ♨ ⍋(heated) play area croquet pitch & putt
Credit Cards [1][2][3][5] ⓔ

SELECTED

FH Ⓠ Ⓠ Ⓠ Ⓠ Mrs Y P Carter **Saywell Farmhouse** *(TQ874575)* Bedmonton, Wormshill ME9 0EH (take B2163 S from Sittingbourne after approx 5m turn e onto unclassified road towards Wormshill) ☎Wormshill(0622) 884444
FAX (0622) 884444
Closed Xmas
Dating back in part to the 13th century, this property stands in a quiet, rural area, though convenient for major roads. The bedrooms are attractive and the house has a congenial feeling about it. Mrs Carter's home-cooked meals are much appreciated by her guests. This is a no-smoking house.
3⇋♠ ⊁ CTV in all bedrooms ® ✻ sB&B⇋♠£25-£35 dB&B⇋♠£45-£55 WB&B£150-£185 WBDi£265.50-£300.50 ▥ nc12yrs 5 acres
ⓔ

SKEGNESS Lincolnshire   Map **09** TF56

GH Ⓠ Ⓠ Ⓠ *Crawford Hotel* South Parade PE25 3HR
☎(0754) 764215
Located at the quieter south end of the promenade, this hotel overlooks the foreshore gardens and beach. It offers particularly good public areas and amenities, with a comfortable lounge bar, indoor heated swimmimg pool and games room. Home-cooked food is served in the dining room and snacks and refreshments in the lounge. The neat bedrooms each have en suite facilities and satellite TV.
20rm(10⇋7♠) (8fb) CTV in all bedrooms ® ✱ LDO 5pm
Lic lift ▥ CTV ♥♨ (heated) sauna jacuzzi games room
Credit Cards [1][3]

GH Ⓠ Ⓠ Ⓠ *Northdale* 12 Firbeck Avenue PE25 3JY
☎(0754) 610554
This small, friendly hotel is situated in a quiet residential area south of the town near the seafront. Bedrooms are bright and inviting, with white walls and furniture and contrasting bold coloured fabrics. Public areas are very comfortable, featuring plenty of seating, and there is a choice of menu for the home-cooked dinners served in the dining room.
12rm(2⇋7♠) (3fb) ⊁ in dining room ⊁ in lounges CTV in 8 bedrooms ® ✻ sB&B£15-£17 sB&B⇋♠£17-£19 dB&B£30-£34 dB&B⇋♠£34-£38 WB&B£90 WBDi£110 LDO 5.30pm
Lic ▥ CTV

SKIPTON North Yorkshire   Map **07** SD95

SELECTED

GH Ⓠ Ⓠ Ⓠ Ⓠ *Bridge House* Chapel Hill BD23 1NL
☎(0756) 796676 FAX (0756) 796725
Closed 1-8 Jan
5⇋♠ CTV in all bedrooms ® T ✱ (ex guide dogs) ✻ sB&B⇋♠£48-£58 dB&B⇋♠£58-£68 LDO 10pm
Lic ▥ nc
Credit Cards [1][3] ⓔ

GH Ⓠ Ⓠ *Craven House* 56 Keighley Road BD23 2NB
☎(0756) 794657
Closed 24-31 Dec
This double-fronted Victorian house stands beside the A629 Keighley road only a short walk from the town centre. Family owned and run, it provides good all-round standards of

accommodation and service; individually furnished bedrooms offer good facilities, and there is an attractive breakfast room.
7rm(2🛁1🚿) CTV in all bedrooms Ⓡ
Lic ♨
Credit Cards [1] [2] [3]

GH [Q][Q][Q] Highfield Hotel 58 Keighley Road BD23 2NB (on A629 heading towards Keighley, 0.25m from town centre)
☎(0756) 793182
Closed 28 Dec-1 Feb rs 24-30 Dec
An attractive Victorian house on a corner site offers pleasantly furnished bedrooms with good facilities and a comfortable bar lounge and dining room at lower ground level; resident owners provide friendly service.
10rm(3🛁6🚿) (2fb) 🚭 in dining room CTV in all bedrooms Ⓡ
sB&B£18.50-£19.50 sB&B🛁🚿£21-£28 dB&B🛁🚿£37-£39
WB&B£122.50-£129.50 LDO 8pm
Lic ♨ CTV 🚫🅿
Credit Cards [1] [2] [3] [5] [£]

INN [Q][Q] *Red Lion Hotel* High Street BD23 1DT (WB)
☎(0756) 790718
Situated in the High Street, this pleasant old inn is said to be the oldest in Skipton and dates back to 1205. The bedrooms are comfortably furnished and well equipped. The bars have been refurbished and are spacious and full of charm and character; home-made bar meals are served at lunchtime.
3🛁🚿 (2fb) CTV in all bedrooms Ⓡ 🐕
♨
Credit Cards [1] [3]

SKYE, ISLE OF Highland *Inverness-shire* Map **13**

DUNVEGAN Map **13** NG24

GH [Q][Q][Q] Roskhill Roskhill IV55 8ZD (2m S A863)
☎(0470) 521317
Mar-Nov
This comfortable guesthouse, is a former croft dating from 1900. Bedrooms, though small, are bright and airy, and there is a cosy lounge with colour TV, books and board games. The beamed, stone-walled restaurant is open all day for teas, coffees and light snacks, and in the evening a small à la carte menu is offered. Smoking is not permitted.
5rm(3🚿) (1fb) 🚭 Ⓡ ✱ dB&B£31-£33 dB&B🚿£37-£39
WB&B£102-£130 WBDi£172-£250 LDO 7pm
Lic ♨ CTV
Credit Cards [1] [3]

PORTREE Map **13** NG44

GH [Q][Q][Q] *Craiglockhart* Beaumont Crescent IV51 9DF
☎(0478) 612233
Closed Dec
Two adjoining houses have been linked to create this comfortable holiday house which is right on the waterfront overlooking the bay and harbour. Bedrooms vary in size but are well decorated and comfortably furnished. Public areas include a cosy lounge with lovely views and an attractive dining room where hearty breakfasts are served at shared tables. Dogs are not permitted.
10rm(3🚿) CTV in 9 bedrooms Ⓡ 🐕
♨ CTV

SELECTED

GH [Q][Q][Q][Q] Quiraing Viewfield Road IV51 9ES (on A850)
☎(0478) 612870 FAX (0478) 612870
This smart modern bungalow stands beside the main road on the southern edge of town and offers good value accommodation. Bedrooms, although compact, are cheerful and adequately furnished. There is a comfortable lounge and ▶

Bridge House Hotel Restaurant

Chapel Hill, Skipton, BD23 1NL
Tel: 01756 796676 Fax: 01756 796725
An 18th century town house in a quiet corner of Skipton's picturesque, historic centre, near the Castle and street market. The hotel combines period charm with modern comfort to provide five en suite double bedrooms. Each bedroom is luxuriously decorated and furnished, all have colour TV, telephone, bar and tea tray etc.
The Restaurant provides gourmet food, Northern European in style and modestly priced. Private parking.

ROSKHILL GUEST HOUSE

Roskhill By Dunvegan Isle of Skye
Telephone: 01470 521317
AA Guest House STB 👑👑
Mr and Mrs Suckling

This traditional Croft house is in an ideal position for touring this lovely island. Dinner is served in the old stone walled dining room with cosy log fires. There is a choice of menu and a good selection of French wines.

A true Highland welcome awaits you

nicely cooked breakfasts are served at individual tables in the adjacent spacious dining room.
6🚿 (2fb) 🚭 in bedrooms CTV in all bedrooms [R] 🐕 (ex guide dogs) ✱ sB&B🚿fr£20 dB&B🚿fr£42
♨ CTV

SLAIDBURN Lancashire — Map **07** SD75

PREMIER SELECTED

GH [Q][Q][Q][Q][Q] Parrock Head Farm House Hotel Woodhouse Lane BB7 3AH (1m NW, up Back Lane to Newton on left) (Logis)
☎(0200) 446614 & 446313

Picturesquely surrounded by sheep and rolling countryside, this very comfortable seventeenth-century farmhouse stands in the beautiful Forest of Bowland. It has been considerably extended over the years to provide good accommodation, the three bedrooms in the main house (which include a suite suitable for family use) featuring a wealth of exposed timbers, while modern but equally comfortable annexe rooms are pine furnished. There are two elegant sitting rooms, one with a library and a collection of local guidebooks, the other - in what was the old hay loft - looking down over a cane-furnished restaurant that began life as the milking parlour. A daily-changing dinner menu which offers some four choices is made up of totally fresh and attractively presented dishes; a full lunch is served only on Sundays, though snacks are available on other days.
3🛁🚿 Annexe 6🛁🚿 (1fb) CTV in all bedrooms [R] T LDO 8.30pm
Lic ♨ 🏡
Credit Cards [1][2][3][5][£]

SLEAFORD Lincolnshire — Map **08** TF04

See also Aswarby

SELECTED

INN[Q][Q][Q][Q] Carre Arms Hotel Mareham Lane NG34 7JP
☎(0529) 303156 FAX (0529) 303139
A large Victorian coaching inn is situated half a mile from the town centre, close to the railway station. It has been refurbished to a good standard to offer well equipped bedrooms and spacious comfortable public areas which include an · la carte restaurant.
13🛁🚿 (2fb) 🚭 in area of dining room CTV in all bedrooms [R] T 🐕 (ex guide dogs) ✱ sB&B🛁🚿£30-£35 dB&B🛁🚿£55 Lunch £9.50&alc Dinner £16-£20alc LDO 9.45pm
♨
Credit Cards [1][3]

SLEDMERE Humberside — Map **08** SE96

INN[Q][Q] Triton YO25 0XQ ☎Driffield(0377) 236644
This 18th-century inn, with its cream-washed walls, nestles in the picturesque wolds, and while simple is fastidiously clean and well kept. The bar is oak panelled with a warm open fire and offers hand-pumped real ales and interesting bar meals, hence its popularity with the locals. There is a separate dining room with deep brown dralon banquettes and light pink flock wallpaper. The bedroom furniture is solid, with floral duvets, plain carpets and light wallpaper - gradually fabrics are being coordinated more fashionably.
7rm(3🛁2🚿) (1fb) CTV in all bedrooms [R] ✱ sB&Bfr£17.50 sB&B🛁🚿£19.50 dB&B£35 dB&B🛁🚿£39 WB&B£120 Lunch £1.85-£9.95alc Dinner £2.95-£9.95alc LDO 9pm
♨ CTV
Credit Cards [1][3][5][£]

SLOUGH Berkshire — Map **04** SU97

GH [Q][Q] Colnbrook Lodge Bath Road, Colnbrook SL3 0NZ (3m E A4) ☎(0753) 685958 FAX (0753) 685958
Closed 24-25 Dec
Situated east of Colnbrook, just under two miles from junction 5 of the M4, this detached Edwardian house offers simple, cosy accommodation which is constantly being updated. Dinner is available at several nearby pubs.
8rm(3🛁🚿) (2fb) 🚭 in dining room CTV in all bedrooms [R] 🐕 (ex guide dogs) sB&B£28-£32 sB&B🛁🚿£35-£38 dB&B£33-£35 dB&B🛁🚿£35-£42 WB&B£168-£180 WBDi£200-£220 LDO 7pm
Lic ♨ CTV 🏡
Credit Cards [1][3][£]

SOLIHULL West Midlands — Map **07** SP17

GH [Q][Q][Q] The Gate House Barston Lane, Barston B92 0JN
☎(0675) 443274
A Victorian property on the edge of the pretty village, the Gate House offers particularly spacious bedrooms with modern bathrooms. It retains much of its period charm and is set in three acres of grounds where guests are welcome to wander.
3rm(2🛁🚿) 🚭 CTV in all bedrooms [R] 🐕 (ex guide dogs) ✱ sB&B£20-£25 sB&B🛁🚿£25 dB&B🛁🚿£40
♨ CTV

SOLVA Dyfed — Map **02** SM82

SELECTED

FH [Q][Q][Q][Q] Mrs M Jones **Lochmeyler** *(SM855275)* SA62 6LL (4m N on unclass rd) ☎Croesgoch(0348) 837724
A 16th-century farmhouse is set in 220 acres of a busy dairy farm. Six miles from St Davids, near the little hamlet of Llandeloy, it provides farm trails, duck ponds and an abundance of wildlife. Bedrooms are large, comfortably furnished and contain every modern facility including videos and free films. Two relaxing lounges are available, and good home cooking is provided by the very hospitable Mrs Jones.
10🛁🚿 (9fb) 🚭 in bedrooms 🚭 in dining room 🚭 in 1 lounge CTV in all bedrooms [R] T ✱ sB&B🛁🚿£20-£30 dB&B🛁🚿£40 WB&B£140 WBDi£200 LDO 6pm
Lic ♨ CTV nc10yrs 220 acres dairy
Credit Cards [1][3][£]

SOMERTON Somerset — Map **03** ST42

GH [Q][Q][Q] Church Farm Compton Dundon TA11 6PE
☎(0458) 272927
Closed 20 Dec-7 Jan
Guests are assured of a warm welcome at this quietly located Somerset cottage with its pretty garden. Four of the well presented bedrooms are in an old stable block. Each room has its own spotless bathroom, and there are thoughtful extras such as hot water bottles and brolleys. Dinner is served in the attractive beamed dining room, where a collection of china and paintings is displayed.
1🛁🚿 Annexe 5🛁🚿 (2fb) 🚭 in dining room 🚭 in lounges CTV in all bedrooms [R] sB&B🛁🚿£20 dB&B🛁🚿£35 LDO 10am
Lic ♨ nc5yrs 🎣

PREMIER SELECTED

GH [Q][Q][Q][Q][Q] The Lynch Country House 4 Behind Berry TA11 7PD
☎(0458) 272316
FAX (0458) 272590

A delightful Georgian Grade II listed property, the hotel stands on the edge of this medieval market town, surrounded by beautiful well kept grounds which include a lake with black swans, exotic ducks and fish. The interior has been lovingly restored and furnished with antiques, and the atmosphere is relaxed and comfortable. Bedrooms are pleasantly decorated. There is a small sitting area downstairs, and the elegant breakfast room overlooks the grounds and lake. Hearty English breakfasts are one of owner Mr Roy Copeland's specialities: another being the naturally friendly, relaxing manner in which he cares for his guests. Two self-catering cottages are also available.

5⇌🚿 CTV in all bedrooms [R] **T** 🐕 (ex guide dogs) ✻ sB&B⇌🚿£35-£50 dB&B⇌🚿£45-£65

Lic ▦

Credit Cards [1] [3]

SOUTHAMPTON Hampshire — Map **04** SU41

GH [Q][Q] Banister House Hotel Banister Road SO15 2JJ ☎(0703) 221279 & 225753 FAX (0703) 221279

Closed 25-27 Dec

This modernised hotel, standing just off The Avenue, offers good-value, well equipped accommodation under the personal supervision of owners David and Jackie Parkinson. A wide range of very reasonably priced meals is available in the bar/dining room.

23rm(13⇌🚿) (3fb)CTV in all bedrooms [R] **T** ✻ sB&Bfr£21.50 sB&B⇌🚿fr£25.50 dB&Bfr£29.50 dB&B⇌🚿fr£34 LDO 7.45pm

Lic ▦ CTV

Credit Cards [1] [2] [3] [£]

GH [Q][Q][Q] Capri 52 Archers Road SO1 2LU ☎(0703) 632800

This Mediterranean-inspired house offers attractive bedrooms, decorated with imagination, one of which is distinctly luxurious and equipped with a water bed, corner bath and steam room. The dining room is cheerful and informal and the lounge, furnished with comfortable sofas, retains its fine original marble fireplace.

15rm(11⇌🚿) (2fb) 🚭 in 1 bedrooms 🚭 in 1 lounge CTV in all bedrooms [R] **T** 🐕 (ex guide dogs) sB&B⇌🚿£21 dB&B⇌🚿£38 WB&B£120 LDO 1pm

Lic ▦

Credit Cards [1] [3] [£]

GH [Q][Q][Q] Dodwell Cottage Dodwell Lane, Bursledon SO31 1AD ☎Bursledon(0703) 406074 FAX (0489) 578659

Closed 23 Dec-30 Jan

Mr and Mrs Howard welcome guests warmly into their home, with evening meals being taken en famille, by arrangement. Breakfast is served at a communal table. Each of the bedrooms is individually decorated and well equipped and the public areas have a warm, cosy feel to them. Smoking is not permitted.

3rm(1⇌🚿) (1fb) 🚭 [R] 🐕 (ex guide dogs) sB&B£23-£24.50 sB&B⇌🚿fr£27.50 dB&B£36-£39 dB&B⇌🚿fr£45 WB&B£108-£135 LDO 6pm

▦ CTV nc5yrs ⛳

[£]

GH [Q][Q][Q] Edgecombe House 188 Regents Park Road, Shirley SO1 3NY ☎(0703) 773760

West of the city centre in a quiet residential area, this handsome, ivy-clad, red-brick house still has much of its original character, from the Victorian tiles and stained-glass windows to the fine antiques in the entrance hall. The friendly atmosphere is particularly encouraged in the dining room where guests eat at one of the two large tables and families are welcomed. Berdrooms are mostly of a good size and have modern facilities.

12rm(1⇌5🚿) (1fb)CTV in all bedrooms [R] **T** 🐕 (ex guide dogs) sB&Bfr£19 sB&B⇌🚿fr£24 dB&Bfr£32 dB&B⇌🚿fr£38 LDO 1pm

L.c ▦ CTV

Credit Cards [1] [2] [3]

SELECTED

GH [Q][Q][Q][Q] Hunters Lodge Hotel 25 Landguard Road, Shirley SO1 5DL ☎(0703) 227919 FAX (0703) 230913

Closed 17 Dec-7 Jan

This neatly presented family-run hotel offers a choice of bedrooms furnished in the modern style. The TV lounge bar, which serves draught beer, is comfortable and relaxing. Full English breakfast is included in the good-value room tariff, and a three-course set evening meal is available Monday to Thursday.

18rm(8⇌4🚿) (2fb) 🚭 in 4 bedrooms 🚭 in area of dining room 🚭 in 1 lounge CTV in all bedrooms [R] **T** ✻ sB&B£23.50-£25 sB&B⇌🚿£33.50-£38 dB&Bfr£44.06 dB&B⇌🚿fr£53.46 LDO 6pm

Lic ▦ CTV

Credit Cards [1] [2] [3]

GH [Q][Q][Q] Landguard Lodge 21 Landguard Road SO1 5DL ☎(0703) 636904 FAX (0703) 636904

An Edwardian house in a residential neighbourhood has been extended and converted into a small hotel with a range of pretty, well equipped bedrooms. The breakfast room is particularly bright and fresh, decorated with potted plants and pictures and furnished with marble-topped Victorian tables.

13rm(4🚿) (1fb) 🚭 in dining room 🚭 in lounges CTV in all bedrooms [R] 🐕 (ex guide dogs) ✻ sB&B£16 sB&B🚿£19 dB&B£30 dB&B🚿£32 LDO 9am

▦ CTV nc5yrs

Credit Cards [1] [2] [3] [5] [£]

GH [Q][Q] Linden 51-53 The Polygon SO1 2BP ☎(0703) 225653

Closed Xmas

Set in a quiet residential area in walking distance of the shopping centre, this long established and personally run guesthouse offers well maintained value-for-money accommodation. The lounge is comfortable, there is an attractive front-facing breakfast room and some forecourt car parking. The atmosphere throughout is cheery, relaxed and informal.

12rm (4fb) 🚭 in dining room 🚭 in lounges CTV in all bedrooms [R] 🐕 ✻ sB&B£13-£15 dB&B£26-£30

▦ CTV

[£]

GH [Q][Q][Q] Lodge 1 Winn Road, The Avenue SO2 1EH ☎(0703) 557537

Closed 23 Dec-1 Jan

Situated close to the university, this very well maintained, personally managed Victorian hotel is a busy and popular one. Bedrooms are well equipped and a good choice of meals is offered in the evening. There is a lounge area and a licensed bar.

14rm(1⇌7🚿) (2fb) 🚭 in dining room CTV in all bedrooms [R] **T** ✻ sB&Bfr£22.50 sB&B⇌🚿fr£30.50 dB&B⇌🚿fr£42.50 LDO 9pm

Lic ▦ CTV

Credit Cards [1] [2] [3] [£]

GH 🆀🆀 **Madison House** 137 Hill Lane SO1 5AF (A33 then A35, at next roundabout turn left, straight over mini-roundabout into Hill Ln, 0.75m on left) ☎(0703) 333374 FAX (0703) 322264

This simple detached house is located in a busy residential area, with easy access to the city centre and docks. Bedrooms are all on the first floor, and there is a piano in the lounge.

9rm(3⇌🝿) (1fb) ⊬ in dining room CTV in all bedrooms ⓡ ⊁ (ex guide dogs) sB&Bfr£15 sB&B⇌🝿fr£22 dB&Bfr£32 dB&B⇌🝿fr£38

📺 CTV

Credit Cards 🔢 £

GH 🆀 **Wayside Lodge** 2 Midanbury Lane, Bitterne SO18 4HP ☎(0703) 228780

Located on the east carriageway of the Bitterne road, not far from Northam Bridge, this very friendly guesthouse is personally run by resident proprietors Bob and Ingrid Tyley. Bedrooms are reasonably well furnished, with plans for further upgrading. There is a well appointed breakfast room and guests can also use the family lounge. Evening meals can be provided by prior arrangement.

8rm (2fb)CTV in all bedrooms ⓡ ✳ sB&B£14.50 dB&B£29 LDO 8.30pm

📺 CTV

£

SOUTHEND-ON-SEA Essex Map **05** TQ88

GH 🆀🆀 **Argyle Hotel** 12 Clifftown Parade SS1 1DP ☎(0702) 339483

Closed Xmas

Overlooking the sea and the bandstand, this terraced house offers comfortable bedrooms with shared bathrooms. The hotel is licensed and the breakfast room/restaurant serves good value home cooking. The restaurant is open at lunchtime only.

11rm (3fb) CTV in all bedrooms ⓡ ⊁ ✳ sB&B£18-£19 dB&B£36-£38

Lic 📺 CTV ✗nc5yrs

GH 🆀🆀 **Marine View** 4 Trinity Avenue, Westcliff on Sea SS0 7PU ☎(0702) 344104

As its name suggests, this semidetached guesthouse is close to the seafront. It is situated in an attractive tree lined avenue. The bedrooms are furnished in a traditional style and a small lounge adjoins the ground floor dining room.

6rm (1fb) ⊬ in dining room CTV in all bedrooms ⓡ ⊁ (ex guide dogs) ✳ sB&B£15-£17.50 dB&B£28-£30 WB&B£150-£175 📺 CTV ✗nc3yrs

GH 🆀🆀 *Mayflower Hotel* 5-6 Royal Terrace SS1 1DY ☎(0702) 340489

Closed Xmas

A Grade II listed Georgian building is situated in the historic Royal Terrace, in a fine position overlooking gardens and the sea, and convenient for the beach and shops. The simply furnished bedrooms are on four floors and all have TV and radios; some rooms have private bathrooms. There is a lounge on the first floor with TV, a pool table, drinks machine and an attractive balcony. The Powell family are resident proprietors and a generous breakfast is served in the basement dining room.

23rm(4🝿) (3fb) CTV in all bedrooms ⓡ

📺 CTV pool table

GH 🆀🆀 **Terrace Hotel** 8 Royal Terrace SS1 1DY (Royal Terrace can only be approached from Southend seafront, via Pier Hill, opposite the pier) ☎(0702) 348143

Part of an attractive listed terrace above the cliffs and overlooking the sea, this small hotel looks particularly appealing in the summer with its many colourful hanging baskets. Bedrooms are simply furnished and two have their own balcony. Downstairs there are three small public rooms: a TV lounge, bar and breakfast room.

9rm(3🝿) (3fb) ⊬ in lounges CTV in all bedrooms ⓡ sB&B£20-

£29 sB&B🝿£29 dB&B£30 dB&B🝿£36 WB&B£105-£140 Lic 📺 CTV ✗

£

GH 🆀🆀🆀 **Tower Hotel** 146 Alexandra Road SS1 1HE ☎(0702) 348635 FAX (0702) 433044

Built in 1901, this attractive hotel is situated in the conservation area, not far from the seafront. The bedrooms in the main building and the adjacent annexe are furnished in the modern style with unit furniture - all are en suite and are equipped very adequately, but some are rather compact. There is a smart Victorian style lounge bar on the ground floor and the basement restaurant `Basils' offers a short table d'hôte menu in elegant surroundings.

16rm(14⇌🝿) Annexe 17rm(4⇌13🝿) (6fb) ⊬ in area of dining room CTV in all bedrooms ⓡ T ✳ sB&B⇌🝿£29-£39.50 dB&B⇌🝿£40-£55 WB&B£180-£250 WBDi£230-£300 LDO 9pm

Lic 📺 CTV residents membership of nearby sports club

Credit Cards 🔢 £

SOUTH MOLTON Devon Map **03** SS72

P R E M I E R 🏵 **S E L E C T E D**

FH 🆀🆀🆀🆀🆀 Mrs Theresa Sampson **Kerscott** (SS793255) Bishopsnympton EX36 4QG (6m E on B3227) ☎(1769) 550262

Closed mid Dec-mid Jan

3rm(2🝿) ⊬ ⓡ ⊁ sB&B£14.50-£15 sB&B🝿£16.50-£18 dB&B£29-£30 dB&B🝿£32-£33 WB&B£101.50-£126 WBDi£147-£171.50 LDO 4pm

📺 nc8yrs 72 acres beef sheep

SOUTH PETHERTON Somerset Map **03** ST41

P R E M I E R 🏵 **S E L E C T E D**

GH 🆀🆀🆀🆀🆀 **Oaklands** 8 Palmer Street TA13 5DB (enter village from A303 and follow directions for Shepton, establishment on right 200mtrs after Methodist church) ☎(0460) 240272 & 241998

mid Jan-mid Nov rs Mon

A beautiful Georgian house on the fringe of the village centre has been tastefully refurbished. Public areas include three lounges, small but elegant with fine paintings and period furniture, a dining room with panelled and primrose-painted walls and a popular restaurant offering a style of food influenced by the French chef and French owners. Bedrooms are spacious, comfortable and well-equipped and there is a small, well-kept garden and ample parking facilities. A Continental breakfast is served.

5rm(3⇌2🝿) ⓡ T ✳ sB&B⇌🝿£40-£50 dB&B⇌🝿£60-£75 LDO 9.30pm

Lic 📺 ⵀ(heated)

Credit Cards 🔢

SOUTHPORT Merseyside Map **07** SD31

GH 🆀🆀🆀 **Ambassador Private Hotel** 13 Bath Street PR9 0DP ☎(0704) 543998 & 530459 FAX (0704) 536269

Closed 20 Dec-7 Jan

This small privately owned hotel is centrally situated adjacent to Lord Street and close to the promenade, providing easy access to the town centre. The accommodation is impeccably maintained throughout. Bedrooms include family rooms and one on the ground floor. They vary in size but have modern furnishings and a good array of equipment. There is a small, quiet lounge as well as a cosy bar.

8🚿 (4fb) 🚭 in 4 bedrooms 🚭 in dining room CTV in all bedrooms [R] ✳ sB&B🚿£29 dB&B🚿£46 WB&Bfr£140 WBDifr£180 LDO 7pm

Lic 🅿 nc5yrs

Credit Cards [1] [3]

GH [Q] [Q] Lake Hotel 55-56 The Promenade PR9 0DY ☎(0704) 530996 & 501900

Close to the Marine Lake on the Promenade, this large end of terrace house offers simple, modern accommodation, including two bedrooms on the ground floor. In addition to the TV lounge, there is a simple lounge bar.

20🚿 (5fb) 🚭 in dining room 🚭 in lounges CTV in all bedrooms [R] **T** sB&B🚿£23-£25.50 dB&B🚿£39-£45 WB&B£126-£160 WBDi£170-£208 LDO 4.30pm

Lic 🅿 CTV nc6yrs

Credit Cards [1] [3] [£]

GH [Q] Lyndhurst 101 King Street PR8 1LQ ☎(0704) 537520

This small guesthouse is situated in a terrace in a side street close to the town centre. The compact bedrooms have modern furnishings and equipment, and family rooms are available. There is a small, pleasant lounge/dining room on the ground floor, and limited car parking at the front.

7rm CTV in all bedrooms [R] 🐕 (ex guide dogs) ✳ sB&B£14 dB&B£28 WB&Bfr£91 WBDifr£126 LDO noon

Lic 🅿 CTV nc5yrs

GH [Q] [Q] [Q] Oakwood Private Hotel 7 Portland Street PR8 1LJ ☎(0704) 531858

Etr-Nov

Two semidetached houses have been combined to form this sound guesthouse, just a short walk from Lord Street. Some of the bedrooms, which have modern and traditional furniture, are quite spacious, and one is on the ground floor. There is a quiet lounge as well as a TV lounge and an attractive dining room.

7rm(4🚿) 🚭 CTV in all bedrooms [R] 🐕 ✳ dB&B🚿£36-£42

Lic 🅿 CTV nc5yrs

GH [Q] [Q] Rosedale Hotel 11 Talbot Street PR8 1HP ☎(0704) 530604

This large semidetached house is centrally located and within easy reach of all amenities. The well maintained bedrooms vary in size and style and include family rooms. There is a small bar in addition to the pleasant lounge and modern dining room.

10rm(7🚿) (2fb) 🚭 in bedrooms 🚭 in dining room CTV in all bedrooms [R] 🐕 (ex guide dogs) ✳ sB&B£18-£22 sB&B🚿£18.50-£24 dB&B£36-£44 dB&B🚿£37-£48 LDO 4pm

Lic 🅿

Credit Cards [1] [2] [3] [5]

GH [Q] [Q] The White Lodge Private Hotel 12 Talbot Street PR8 1HP ☎(0704) 536320

Within a short walk of Lord Street, this large detached house has a comfortable lounge and a traditional-style dining room. Bedrooms, which include one on the ground floor, have a mixture of modern and older furniture, but all have modern equipment.

8rm(1🛁4🚿) (3fb) 🚭 in dining room CTV in 7 bedrooms [R] 🐕 (ex guide dogs) sB&B£16-£20 sB&B🛁🚿£17-£22 dB&B£32-£40 dB&B🛁🚿£34-£44 WB&B£99-£135 WBDi£110-£170 LDO 6pm

Lic CTV 🏠

[£]

INN [Q] [Q] *The Herald Hotel* 16 Portland Street PR8 1LT ☎(0704) 534424

Located close to the town centre, this friendly public house is attractively decorated and offers a sound standard of bedroom accommodation. Rooms without en suite facilities have shower cabinets.

12rm(4🚿) (1fb) CTV in all bedrooms [R] LDO 8pm

🅿

SOUTHSEA Hampshire

See **Portsmouth & Southsea**

SOUTHWELL Nottinghamshire Map **08** SK65

INN [Q] [Q] [Q] *Crown Hotel* 11 Market Place NG25 0HE ☎(0636) 812120

The Crown is an attractive Georgian inn located in the town centre. The refurbished public areas are effectively a pleasant open-plan pub, in which breakfast and bar snack lunches are taken. The bedrooms are nicely appointed, with light wood furniture and pretty fabrics. More en suite facilities are to be added during 1994.

7rm(1🚿) CTV in all bedrooms [R] 🐕 (ex guide dogs) LDO 9.30pm

🅿

Credit Cards [1] [3]

SOUTHWOLD Suffolk Map **05** TM57

GH [Q] [Q] [Q] Oldhurst 24 High Street IP18 6AD ☎(0502) 723829

A well maintained whitewashed Victorian house located at the western end of the High Street. There are three large bedrooms, mostly furnished with old pieces of wooden furniture, and the breakfast room on the ground floor also has a few armchairs for extra comfort. ▶

TOWER
HOTEL & RESTAURANT
ENGLISH TOURIST BOARD RATING
AA QQQ recommended
146 Alexandra Road, Southend-on-Sea, Essex SS1 1HE
Telephone: Southend-on-Sea (01702) 348635
Fax: No: (01702) 433044

The award winning Tower Hotel is situated in Southend's historic conservation area less than ten minutes' walk from the cliffs, the sea, the pier, Southend High Street, Southend Central station (London – 45 minutes), plus many restaurants, nightclubs, art galleries and leisure centres. Public golf courses, parks and bowling greens are a short drive away as is the beautiful Essex countryside.

VISA AMERICAN EXPRESS Access
Luncheon Vouchers & Travellers Cheques

3⇥♪ ⵏ in dining room CTV in all bedrooms ® ✳
sB&B⇥♪£25-£30 dB&B⇥♪£40-£45
▥ ♪
£

GH Q Q Saxon House 86 Pier Avenue IP18 6BL (from A12 take
A1095 to village and cross Mights Bridge. Take second turning on
left) ☎(0502) 723651
4rm(2♪) (1fb) ⵏ ® ✳ sB&B£25 sB&B♪£30 dB&B£40
dB&B♪£44
▥. CTV
Credit Cards ①③

INN Q Q Kings Head Hotel High Street IP18 6AD (300yds past
police station on right of main road on entering Southwold)
☎(0502) 724517
This cosy 17th-century inn has been attractively furnished by the
friendly proprietors Mr and Mrs Atkins. The open-plan bar with
its Victorian style furniture provides ample room for guests to
enjoy the freshly prepared bar meals. The bright bedrooms on the
first floor are modestly furnished but equipped with modern
facilities.
3rm CTV in all bedrooms ® ✳ sB&B£20-£35 dB&B£40-£45
Lunch £2.50-£6.50 Dinner £2-£12 LDO 9.30pm
▥ ♪

SOUTH ZEAL Devon   Map 03 SX69

GH Q Q Q Poltimore EX20 2PD (leave A30 at Whidden Down
towards South Zeal and turn left after Rising Sun public house)
☎Okehampton(0837) 840209
A peacefully situated cottage offering character accommodation
with easy access to the A30. Bedrooms are compact but clean and
comfortable, and there are two lounges with exposed timbers and
feature fireplaces. A choice of food is served in the informal
dining room.
7rm(2⇥2♪) ⵏ in dining room CTV in all bedrooms ®
sB&B£19-£23 sB&B⇥♪£21-£25 dB&B£38-£46 dB&B⇥♪£42-
£50 WB&B£125.50-£139.50 WBDi£206-£220 LDO 9pm
Lic ▥. CTV nc8yrs
Credit Cards ①②③ £

SPAXTON Somerset   Map 03 ST23

SELECTED
GH Q Q Q Q Gatesmoor Hawkridge TA5 1AL
☎(0278) 671353
Gatesmoor is a white painted 17th-century cottage set in a
beautiful garden bordering a scenic reservoir, close to the
Quantocks and within easy driving distance of Taunton. The
bedrooms are attractively furnished, and share a bathroom.
Many extras are provided for the comfort of guests who also
have their own sitting room with colour TV. A four-course
dinner is served in the beamed dining room.
3rm(1⇥♪) ⵏ ® 🐾 (ex guide dogs) ✳ dB&B£32-£36
dB&B⇥♪£40 WB&B£112-£140 WBDi£199.50-£227.50
LDO 6.30pm
▥. CTV nc10yrs
£

SPEAN BRIDGE Highland *Inverness-shire*   Map 14 NN28

↩▉ **GH Q Q Coire Glas** PH34 4EU (on A86) ☎(0397) 712272
Jan-Oct
This friendly family run tourist guesthouse, looking across to the
Ben Nevis mountain range from a setting in its own garden on the
eastern edge of the village, provides good value accommodation in
practically appointed rooms of various sizes; public areas include
a spacious lounge where refreshments are available. A la carte
menus offer a good choice of dishes at dinner, but, on occasions,
guests may have to share tables.

14rm(8♪) (2fb) ⵏ in bedrooms ⵏ in dining room ® 🐾 (ex guide
dogs) sB&B£14-£18 dB&B£27-£28 dB&B♪£33-£35 LDO 8pm
Lic CTV
£

SELECTED
GH Q Q Q Q Distant Hills PH34 4EU (on A86)
☎(0397) 712452
Friendly owners Meg and Ian McCluskey have recently
completed a major extension to their comfortable detached
bungalow, which stands in its own large grounds to the east of
the village. Bedrooms are small but bright and comfortably
furnished and a spacious lounge is provided. Enjoyable home
cooking is offered at individual tables in the dining room.
7♪ ⵏ in 2 bedrooms ⵏ in dining room CTV in all bedrooms
® sB&B♪£21 dB&B♪£32 WB&B£112 WBDi£175 LDO
5pm
▥. CTV ⚓
See advertisement under INVERNESS

↩▉ **GH Q Q Q Inverour** PH34 4EU ☎(0397) 712218
rs Jan
Conveniently situated at the junction of the A82/A86, this friendly
family-run guesthouse is an ideal touring base. It has a
comfortable lounge, and hearty breakfasts are served in the
beamed dining room. Bedrooms, with fitted units, are warm and
comfortable, though some are compact.
7rm(3♪) (1fb) ⵏ in bedrooms ⵏ in dining room CTV in 1
bedroom ® sB&B£15-£17 dB&B£30-£34 dB&B♪£34-£38
▥. CTV
£

STAFFORD Staffordshire   Map 07 SJ92

GH Q Q Bailey Hotel 63 Lichfield Road ST17 4LL
☎(0785) 214133
Closed Xmas
This large detached house stands on the A34, south of the town
centre, opposite the GEC works. It provides well maintained
accommodation with well equipped bedrooms. The pleasant
dining room has cottage-style furniture, and there is a comfortable
lounge.
11rm(3♪) (1fb) ⵏ in dining room CTV in all bedrooms ® T
sB&B£16.50-£19.50 sB&B♪£24.50-£26.50 dB&B£30-£32
dB&B♪£36-£38 LDO 6.45pm
Lic ▥. CTV
Credit Cards ①③ £

GH Q Q Q Leonards Croft Hotel 80 Lichfield Road ST17 4LP
(A34, on right after railway bridge) ☎(0785) 223676
Closed Xmas
Fronted by its own car park and set in delightful gardens, this
large gabled house stands beside the A34, south of the town centre
and opposite the GEC works. Soundly maintained, it provides
comfortable accommodation which includes two ground-floor
bedrooms and two that have recently been equipped with new en
suite shower and toilet facilities. Other amenities include a
spacious lounge and small bar.
12rm (2fb) ® LDO 9pm
Lic ▥. CTV

STAMFORD Lincolnshire Map 04 TF00

SELECTED
GH Q Q Q Q The Priory Church Road, Ketton PE9 3RD
☎(0780) 720215 FAX (0780) 721881
The Priory is an impressive stone-built house with gardens

running down to the River Chater. Enthusiastic hosts Moya
and John Acton work continually to upgrade the amenities,
and have recently put telephones into the bedrooms and had
showers fitted to the baths. The bedrooms (all no-smoking) are
quite spacious and imaginatively decorated using designer
fabrics. Public areas are enhanced by colourful flower
arrangements and numerous paintings. There is a lounge, a
conservatory where meals are served in summer, and a richly
decorated dining room used in the winter months. Evening
meals, including vegetarian dishes, are available by prior
arrangement.
3rm(2⇌3ⁿ) ⊁ in bedrooms ⊁ in dining room CTV in all
bedrooms Ⓡ T ✻ (ex guide dogs) sB&B£28-£35
sB&B⇌ⁿ£30-£35 dB&B£38-£55 dB&B⇌ⁿ£48-£55
WB&B£135-£220 WBDi£220-£315 LDO 7pm
Lic ▥ CTV ◑ ♪ croquet
Credit Cards [1][3]Ⓔ

STAMFORD BRIDGE Humberside
See **Low Catton & High Catton**

STANLEY Co Durham   Map **12** NZ15
INNⓆⓆⓆ **Oaktree** Tantobie DH9 9RF (1.75m NE)
☎(0207) 235445
This typical pub lies in the village of Tantobie, near Stanley. There
is a Victorian-style dining room where good home-produced food
is served. Bedrooms are well equipped, some being located in a
separate building.
2rm(1⇌) Annexe 3rm(1⇌2ⁿ) (1fb)CTV in all bedrooms Ⓡ ✶
sB&B⇌ⁿ£20.50-£26 dB&B£38 dB&B⇌ⁿ£40-£50
WB&B£126-£138.60 WBDi£179.50-£192 Bar Lunch £1-£8&alc
Dinner £8.50-£9.50&alc LDO 10.30pm
▥, snooker
Credit Cards [1][2][3][5]Ⓔ

STANLEY Tayside *Perthshire*   Map **11** NO13

SELECTED

FH ⓆⓆⓆⓆ Mrs D A Dow **Tophead** *(NO080321)*
Tullybelton PH1 4PT ☎(0738) 828259
Apr-Oct
In well tended gardens in a peaceful, elevated position, this
attractive modern farmhouse enjoys glorious views. Bedrooms
are very spacious and comfortable and there is also a lovely
sitting room and a sun lounge. Breakfasts are served round the
large communal table.
3rm(1ⁿ) (1fb) ⊁ Ⓡ ✻ (ex guide dogs) ✶ dB&B£30-£32
dB&Bⁿ£36-£38
▥ CTV 400 acres arable dairy beef
Ⓔ

STANSTED Essex   Map **05** TL52
GH ⓆⓆⓆ **The Laurels** 84 St Johns Road CM24 8JS
☎(0279) 813023 FAX (0279) 813023
This welcoming guest house stands at the centre of the village, six
miles from the airport. Bedrooms are well equipped, a bright
ground-floor lounge is comfortable and there is a combined
residents' bar/dining room; evening meals are provided on
request.
6rm(5⇌2ⁿ) (2fb) ⊁ in bedrooms CTV in all bedrooms Ⓡ ✶
sB&B⇌ⁿ£24-£29 dB&B⇌ⁿ£40-£45 LDO 10pm
Lic ▥ CTV
Ⓔ

Abbey House

Though mainly Georgian in appearance, the house
dates in part from 1190AD having been formerly
owned by Thornley Abbey and Peterborough
Minster before its later use as a Rectory. Set in
pleasant gardens in a quiet village between
Stamford and Market Deeping, and offering 7 rooms
with private facilities. Abbey House provides an
ideal base for touring the Eastern Shires with their
abundance of stately homes, abbeys, cathedrals
and delightful stone villages and market towns.

AA QQQ
Proprietors: Mr and Mrs A B Fitton
Abbey House, West End Road, Maxey, PE6 9EJ
Telephone: Market Deeping (01778) 344642

THE PRIORY
· CHURCH ROAD ·
· KETTON · STAMFORD · LINCOLNSHIRE ·

Historic 16ᵗʰ Century Country House near
Stamford – "England's finest stone town". Quiet
setting in picturesque village. Luxury ensuite
bedrooms overlook delightful gardens.
Colour TVs, phones, tea and coffee and teddy
bears in all rooms. Private parking. Convenient
for A1. Near Rutland Water, Burghley House and
forest walks. Colour brochure available.

AA QQQQ
SELECTED

**HIGHLY
COMMENDED**

Tel: 01780 720 215 Fax: 01780 721 881

STARBOTTON North Yorkshire   Map **07** SD97

P R E M I E R 🏵 **S E L E C T E D**

GH Q Q Q Q Q **Hilltop Country** BD23 5HY (on B6160) ☎Kettlewell(0756) 760321 mid Mar-mid Nov

Dating back to the 17th century, this charming farmhouse is situated in the pretty hamlet of Starbotton, on the road between Kettlewell and Buckden. Standing in an elevated position, the house has fine views of the surrounding hills, and the grounds slope down to Cam Gill Beck. Tasteful use of modern fabrics has ensured that the house has retained much of its character. Bedrooms are spacious and comfortable, although one in the converted barn is more compact. The drawing room is comfortable and relaxing, with a log fire for cooler evenings and a small bar for pre-dinner drinks. Excellent meals are taken in the former parlour where guests enjoy superb meals at antique tables. The owners, Mr and Mrs Rathmell, have written a book containing Hilltop recipes, on sale to guests. A typical meal might include smoked fillet of Kilnsey trout, breast of Nidderdale chicken stuffed with mushroom pâté, served with sherry sauce, and followed by lemon meringues and local cheeses.

4rm(1⇄3♠) Annexe 1♠ (1fb) ⊁ in bedrooms ⊁ in dining room ⊁ in lounges CTV in all bedrooms ® 🖈 (ex guide dogs) dB&B⇄♠£58 LDO 6pm Lic ▥ ⓔ

STARCROSS Devon   Map **03** SX98

INN Q Q **The Galleon** The Strand EX6 8PR ☎(0626) 890412 The Galleon Inn is situated at the centre of the village opposite Brunels' Museum, overlooking the Exe estuary. Bedrooms, which have an entrance from the car park, are simply appointed, though several have full en suite facilities. An à la carte menu is offered in the oak-beamed restaurant, and an extensive range of home-made dishes is also available in the bar. Fresh local fish is usually on offer. 9rm(1⇄) (3fb) CTV in all bedrooms ® 🖈 (ex guide dogs) LDO 9.30pm ▥ CTV pool darts

STEEPLE ASTON Oxfordshire   Map **04** SP42

GH Q Q Q **Westfield Farm Motel** The Fenway OX5 3SS (off A4260, 0.5m from junction with B4030) ☎(0869) 40591 & 47594 Situated on the edge of a pretty Cotswold village, this motel was converted from farm buildings and offers six bedrooms with direct access from a central car park. The cottage-style rooms provide modern, tiled shower rooms with larger than average showers and all bedrooms are well equipped with most modern facilities. There is a small breakfast room and a lounge with a counter selling soft drinks. 7♠ (1fb) ⊁ in 2 bedrooms CTV in all bedrooms ® T ✶ sB&B♠£32-£36 dB&B♠£45-£50 LDO 7pm Lic ▥ CTV U Credit Cards [1][3] ⓔ

STEPASIDE Dyfed   Map **02** SN10

GH Q Q **Bay View Hotel** Pleasant Valley SA67 8LR (behind the chapel) ☎Saundersfoot(0834) 813417 Apr-Sep

A modern hotel is situated in a secluded position in a lovely wooded valley convenient for many fine beaches. Accommodation is simple but clean and bright: there is a large residents' bar, a small TV lounge and an outdoor pool for the summer. 11rm(8♠) (5fb)® 🖈 (ex guide dogs) sB&B£20-£22.85 dB&B£40-£45.70 dB&B♠£42.90-£48.60 (incl dinner) WBDif140-£170 LDO 5pm Lic ▥ CTV ᐅ(heated)

STEWARTON Strathclyde *Ayrshire*

See **Dunlop**

STEYNING West Sussex   Map **04** TQ11

GH Q Q Q **Nash Hotel** Horsham Road BN4 3AA ☎(0903) 814988 An attractive Elizabethan manor house, with more recent additions, stands in peaceful countryside overlooking the South Downs. The formerly bumpy drive has recently been much improved. Bedrooms are spacious and furnished in traditional style. There is a large comfortable lounge with TV, books and a paino. The hotel owns the Steyning Vineyard and serves their wines at dinner; tastings are arranged occasionally in the special tasting room. Facilities include an all-weather tennis court and outdoor swimming pool. There are also three self-catering cottages to let. 5rm(1⇄) (2fb) ⊁ in 3 bedrooms ⊁ in dining room ⊁ in lounges CTV in all bedrooms ® ✶ sB&B£30 sB&B⇄£45 dB&B£40-£45 dB&B⇄£43-£52 LDO 8pm Lic ▥ CTV ᐅ❄(hard) ⓔ

S E L E C T E D

GH Q Q Q Q **Springwells Hotel** 9 High Street BN44 3GG ☎(0903) 812446 & 812043 Closed 24 Dec-1 Jan Conveniently situated close to the village centre, this fine Georgian merchant's house has been sympathetically converted to provide a range of individually furnished bedrooms, including four-poster and family rooms. Among the attractive features are the walled garden with its 300-year-old yew trees, the outdoor heated pool, the new conservatory and the elegantly furnished TV lounge. A generous English breakfast including whisky porridge and fish alternatives is served. 10rm(8⇄♠) (1fb) CTV in all bedrooms ® T LDO 8.45pm Lic ▥ CTV ᐅ(heated) sauna Credit Cards [1][2][3][5]

STIPERSTONES Shropshire   Map **07** SJ3⬦

GH Q Q **Tankerville Lodge** SY5 0NB ☎Shrewsbury(0743) 791401 A well hidden house in a rural setting is reached by turning off the A488 Shrewsbury to Bishops Castle road, signed to Snailbeach, and passing through Stiperstones; in three quarters of a mile there is a bed and breakfast sign on a bend in the road. The rooms are neat, there is a lounge full of touring information, and a daily weather chart is posted in the country-style dining room. A self-catering cottage is also available. 4rm ⊁ in dining room ® sB&B£15.75-£18.25 dB&B£31.50 WB&B£99.23-£116.73 WBDif160.48-£177.98 Lic ▥ CTV nc5yrs ⓔ

STIRLING Central *Stirlingshire*   Map **11** NS7⬦

See also **Denny**

GH [Q][Q][Q] Castlecroft Ballengeich Road FK8 1TN (leave M9 junct10 toward Stirling turn right at fire station turn left at Back'O'Hill then immediatley right) ☎(0786) 474933
Closed Xmas & New Year
Built in the late 1970s, this detached villa sits in an elevated position in the shadow of Stirling Castle and offers breathtaking views. The bright modern bedrooms are located on three levels, and a feature of the house is the comfortable first-floor lounge and balcony. Breakfast is served downstairs around two tables.
6🚿 (1fb) 🚭 in dining room CTV in all bedrooms [R] *
sB&B🚿£25-£35 dB&B🚿£35-£40
lift ♨
[£]

STOCKBRIDGE Hampshire — Map **04** SU33

GH [Q][Q][Q] Carbery Salisbury Hill SO20 6EZ (on A30)
☎Andover(0264) 810771 FAX (0264) 811022
Closed 2 wks Xmas
A fine, cream painted Georgian house in an acre of well kept gardens, Carbery Guest House has been run by Ann and Philip Hooper for over 27 years. They offer a warm welcome to guests, many of whom have become friends. Bedrooms are freshly decorated and comfortably equipped, and there is an elegant lounge and a games room for children. A set dinner is available at 7pm each evening.
11rm(2🛁6🚿) (2fb) CTV in all bedrooms [R] 🐕 sB&B£22
sB&B🛁🚿£29.50 dB&B£44 dB&B🛁🚿£48 WB&B£150-£200
WBDi£223-£275 LDO 6pm
Lic ♨ 🏊(heated) pool table

GH [Q][Q][Q] ***Old Three Cups Private Hotel*** High St SO20 6HB
☎Andover(0264) 810527
24 Dec-early Jan rs Jan
A 15th-century inn, now run as a private hotel with a restaurant and residential license, the Old Three Cups is situated on the main street of the charming village. Public areas include a bar and restaurant with exposed beams and low ceilings. The bedrooms are attractively decorated.
8rm(4🛁🚿) (2fb) CTV in all bedrooms 🐕 (ex guide dogs) LDO 9.30pm
Lic ♨
Credit Cards [1] [3]

STOCKTON-ON-TEES Cleveland — Map **08** NZ41

SELECTED

GH [Q][Q][Q][Q] ***The Edwardian Hotel*** 72 Yarm Road TS18 3PQ
☎(0642) 615655
Conveniently located for the town centre and the A66, this pleasant house has been carefully furnished, with some particularly nice touches in the bedrooms. A comfortable lounge is provided and dinner is available by prior arrangement.
6rm(4🚿) (3fb) CTV in all bedrooms [R] 🐕 (ex guide dogs) LDO 7pm
Lic ♨ CTV
Credit Cards [1]

STOGUMBER Somerset — Map **03** ST03

GH [Q][Q][Q] ***Chandlers House*** TA4 3TA ☎(0984) 56580
Apr-Oct
A white-painted, listed property with a pretty walled garden, Chandlers House is in the conservation village of Stogumber. Guest rooms are tastefully decorated, one with an en suite shower, the other with a private bathroom across the landing. The elegant lounge is in the Georgian part of the house, while the breakfast room is more cottagey with a wood-burning stove in an inglenook fireplace. Here guests share one large table for traditional English breakfast.
2rm(1🚿) CTV in all bedrooms [R]
♨ CTV

STOKE-BY-NAYLAND Suffolk — Map **05** TL93

SELECTED

INN [Q][Q][Q][Q] The Angel Inn Polstead Street CO6 4SA (on B1068) ☎Nayland(0206) 263245 FAX (0206) 337324
Closed 25-26 Dec
A popular and at times very busy inn dating from the 16th-century, situated in one of Suffolk's most interesting villages and surrounded by lovely countryside, has been totally restored and refurbished whilst retaining such original features as exposed brickwork, beams, two large open fireplaces in the bars and a gallery overlooking the high-ceilinged dining room. Individually decorated and furnished bedrooms of a high standard are provided with good modern en suite facilities. The restaurant serves the same dishes as are listed on the daily blackboard bar-meals menu - both bars and restaurant being much frequented by local customers.
5🛁🚿 Annexe 1🛁🚿 CTV in all bedrooms [R] **T** 🐕 (ex guide dogs) sB&B🛁🚿£44 dB&B🛁🚿£57.50 Lunch £10.90-£22alc Dinner £18.95-£23alc LDO 9pm
♨ nc8yrs
Credit Cards [1] [2] [3] [5] [£]

STOKE HOLY CROSS Norfolk — Map **05** TG20

FH [Q][Q] Mrs Harrold **Salamanca** *(TG235022)* NR14 8QJ (at A47/A140 intersection take minor road to Caistor St Edmunds, then first left, farm approx 1m on left)
☎Framingham Earl(0508) 492322

►

Springwells Hotel

STEYNING, WEST SUSSEX (Nr. Brighton)
Telephone: 01903-812446
Once a Georgian merchant's town house now an elegant ten-bedroomed bed & breakfast hotel. All rooms have telephones & colour TV and most have private facilities.
Tea/coffee making facilities if required.
Some four-poster beds. Lovely walled gardens, outdoor swimming pool. Victorian style conservatory. Half hour from Gatwick/Newhaven.
£25-£68 per room

Closed 15 Dec-15 Jan & Etr
This large farmhouse is set in the heart of a picturesque village and dates back to the 16th century. Surrounded by well tended gardens, it offers traditional, comfortable accommodation and a pleasant lounge.
3rm(1⇌2🏠) Annexe 1⇌ ⊬ CTV in 1 bedroom 🏿 ✳
sB&B⇌🏿£17-£19 dB&B⇌🏿£32-£38
💾 CTV nc6yrs 165 acres beef mixed
Credit Cards 5 ⓔ

STOKE-ON-TRENT Staffordshire   Map **07** SJ84

SELECTED

GH Ⓠ Ⓠ Ⓠ Ⓠ **Old Dairy House** Trentham Park ST4 8AE (from M6 junct 15 turn right at 1st roundabout, left at lights and then 3rd turning right, following signs for Trentham Park Golf Club) ☎(0782) 641209 FAX (0782) 712904
3rm(1⇌3🏿) CTV in all bedrooms ⓇT 🏿 (ex guide dogs) ✳
sB&B⇌🏿£30 dB&B⇌🏿£40 WB&B£120 WBDi£150-£170
LDO 3pm
💾 nc7yrs ℺(hard)

GH Ⓠ Ⓠ Ⓠ **White Gables Hotel** Trentham Road, Blurton ST3 3DT (establishment 2 miles past Trentham Gardens, off A34) ☎(0782) 324882 FAX (0782) 598302
This small privately owned hotel stands on the A5035, close to both Trentham Gardens and the Wedgwood factory. It is also within easy reach of Junction 15 of the M6, and is convenient for access to the city centre. Bedrooms vary in size and style, but all are very well equipped and one has a four-poster bed. Recreational facilities include a hard-surface tennis court and a games room with snooker, pool and darts.
9rm(3⇌3🏿) (2fb) ⊬ in dining room ⊬ in lounges CTV in all bedrooms ⓇT 🏿 (ex guide dogs) sB&B£20-£25 sB&B⇌🏿£30-£40 dB&B£34-£40 dB&B⇌🏿£40-£50 LDO 7.30pm
Lic 💾 CTV ℺(hard)games room
Credit Cards 1 2 3 5 ⓔ

GH Ⓠ Ⓠ Ⓠ **The White House Hotel** 94 Stone Road, Trent Vale ST4 6SP (1.5m from junct 15 of M6 at crossroads of A500 and A34) ☎(0782) 642460 FAX (0782) 657189
Conveniently situated on the A34 close to its junction with the A500, this small family-run hotel is well positioned for access to Trentham Gardens as well as the city centre and other local amenities. Junction 15 of the M6 is only a mile away. Recent improvements include the building of extra bedrooms. Ground-floor rooms are available, and two are situated in a separate annexe building. There is a small lounge, and a dining room where dinner and breakfast are available during the week, but only breakfast is served at weekends.
10rm(3🏿) Annexe 2🏿 (2fb) ⊬ in bedrooms ⊬ in dining room CTV in all bedrooms ⓇT 🏿 (ex guide dogs) sB&B£20-£23 sB&B⇌🏿£30-£35 dB&B£32-£38 dB&B🏿£40-£46 WB&B£150-£300
Lic 💾 CTV
Credit Cards 1 2 3 5 ⓔ

STONE Staffordshire   Map **07** SJ93

SELECTED

GH Ⓠ Ⓠ Ⓠ Ⓠ **Whitgreave Manor** Whitgreave ST18 9SP (3m N off A34) ☎(0785) 51767 FAX (0785) 51767
4🏿 (1fb) ⊬ in bedrooms ⊬ in dining room ⊬ in 1 lounge CTV in all bedrooms ⓇT 🏿 sB&B⇌🏿£25-£27.50 dB&B⇌🏿£40-£45
💾 CTV ⋈ 🏿℺(grass)table tennis fishing by arrangement ⓔ

STONEHOUSE Gloucestershire   Map **03** SO80

INN Ⓠ Ⓠ Ⓠ **Rose & Crown Inn** Nympsfield GL10 3TU (turn off B4066 at Coaley Peak, 0.75m to village) ☎(0453) 860240 FAX (0453) 860240
4rm(3⇌🏿) (3fb)CTV in all bedrooms Ⓡ 🏿 (ex guide dogs) ✳
sB&B£24 sB&B⇌🏿£28 dB&B£39 dB&B⇌🏿£48 Bar Lunch £2.95-£10.50 Dinner £2.95-£10.50 LDO 9.30pm
💾 CTV
Credit Cards 1 2 3

STORNOWAY See **LEWIS, ISLE OF**

STOURBRIDGE West Midlands   Map **07** SO98

GH Ⓠ Ⓠ **Limes Hotel** 260 Hagley Road, Pedmore DY9 0RW (on A491, 1.5m from Stourbridge) ☎Hagley(0562) 882689
A popular commercial guesthouse is situated 1.5 miles from the town, close to the business centres. Bedrooms are modestly furnished and some are compact, but they offer a good range of facilities including direct-dial telephones. The combined lounge/dining room has a small corner bar, and a set three-course evening meal is offered.
11rm(2⇌3🏿) (1fb) ⊬ in 1 bedrooms ⊬ in area of dining room CTV in all bedrooms ⓇT ✳ sB&Bfr£24.50 sB&B⇌🏿fr£32.50 dB&Bfr£32 dB&B⇌🏿fr£40 LDO 7.30pm
Lic 💾 CTV
Credit Cards 1 2 3 5 ⓔ

STOW-ON-THE-WOLD Gloucestershire   Map **04** SP12

SELECTED

GH Ⓠ Ⓠ Ⓠ Ⓠ **Cotswold Cottage** Chapel Street, Bledington OX7 6XA (4m SE off B4450) ☎(0608) 658996 FAX (0608) 658978
This charming listed cottage with its own garden stands in a picturesque village. Bedrooms are decorated with floral designs, one has a spa bath. There is a small sitting area on the first floor and breakfast is served round a large table in the dining room. This is a no-smoking guesthouse.
2⇌🏿 (2fb) ⊬ CTV in all bedrooms Ⓡ 🏿 sB&B⇌🏿£28-£30 dB&B⇌🏿£40-£46 WB&B£133-£150
💾 nc16yrs

GH Ⓠ Ⓠ **Cotswold View** Nether Westcote OX7 6SD (4m E, signed from A424) ☎Shipton under Wychwood(0993) 830699
This guesthouse is situated in the village of Nether Westcote, four miles from Bourton-on-the-Water. Some bedrooms in the main house are rather compact, but two recently converted rooms called The Hayloft and The Granary are more spacious. The dining room has a conservatory extension and doubles as a tea room in the summer. There is a guests' lounge with TV, and art and craftwork are available for sale.
6rm(3🏿) Annexe 2⇌🏿 ⊬ CTV in all bedrooms Ⓡ ✳
sB&Bfr£20 dB&Bfr£34 dB&B⇌🏿£36-£42 LDO 4pm
CTV

GH Ⓠ Ⓠ **Limes** Evesham Road GL54 1EJ
☎Cotswold(0451) 830034
Closed 23 Dec-1 Jan
Built in 1926, this mellow brick guesthouse reflects the comfort and hospitality that any visitor would wish to receive. Mr and Mrs Keyte provide well equipped bedrooms, one with an impressive four-poster bed, and a warm atmosphere prevails throughout. The dining room looks out on a well tended garden with a pond and an aviary buzzing with cockatiels and budgerigars. The lounge windows look out across rolling countryside to Lower Swell and beyond. This is an excellent base for touring the Cotswolds and is in walking distance of the town.

2rm(1↱) Annexe 1↱ (1fb)CTV in all bedrooms Ⓡ dB&B£31-£33 dB&B↱£36-£39
▥ CTV

GH QQQ Oddington Lodge GL56 0UR
☎Cotswold(0451) 830655
A beautiful Regency house built in 1827 of Cotswold stone, is situated in a quiet hamlet close to the town. Owned by Mr and Mrs Barrington, this is essentially a private home welcoming guests, and is set in two acres of formal gardens with a tennis court and outdoor swimming pool. The four bedrooms vary in size and style, but all benefit from Mrs Barrington's design skill with good quality antiques and beautiful soft furnishings. Elegant, comfortable public rooms include a drawing room opening onto a covered terrace, a sunny breakfast room off the kitchen, and meals are taken 'dinner party' style around the large table in the dining room.
4rm(1⇆) (4fb) ⊁ in bedrooms Ⓡ ✱ sB&Bfr£29 dB&Bfr£50 dB&B⇆fr£50 LDO 6pm
▥ CTV ⌇(heated) ♒(hard)snooker

FH QQ Mr R Smith **Corsham Field** *(SP217249)*
Bledington Road GL54 1JH ☎Cotswold(0451) 831750
Standing one and a half miles from Stow, this modern, stone-built farmhouse enjoys views of rolling farmland. Three comfortable bedrooms are well equipped and there is a spacious lounge/dining area with an open fire where breakfast is served. Meals are available at a good pub within walking distance.
3rm(1⇆) (1fb) CTV in all bedrooms Ⓡ sB&B£15-£25 dB&B£25-£35 dB&B⇆£30-£35
▥ CTV 100 acres arable beef sheep

INN QQQ Kings Head Inn & Restaurant The Green, Bledington OX7 6HD (4m SE off B4450) ☎Kingham(0608) 658365 FAX (0608) 658365
Closed Xmas day
This delightful inn stands by the village green with its brook and resident ducks. The bedrooms, which vary in size, have attractive coordinated fabrics, pine furniture and many thoughtful extras, including telephones and fresh flowers, but beware of the low beams! Guests can play pool or darts in the snug public bar, and the charming lounge bar offers comfortable seating, flagstone floors and an open fire. Bar meals are available and imaginative à la carte menus are presented in the pleasant restaurant with its smoking and non-smoking areas.
⇆ Annexe 6⇆↱ (4fb) ⊁ in bedrooms ⊁ in area of dining room CTV in all bedrooms Ⓡ T ✱ (ex guide dogs) ✱ sB&B⇆↱£32-£40 dB&B⇆↱£55-£65 Bar Lunch £2.95-£6.95 Dinner £4.95-£12.95alc LDO 9.45pm
▥ CTV
Credit Cards [1][3]£

SELECTED

INN QQQQ Royalist Hotel Digbeth Street GL54 1BN (turn off A429 onto A436) ☎Cotswold(0451) 830670 FAX (0451) 870048
Said to be the oldest building in Stow, the Royalist Hotel dates from 947AD. The present owners have provided modern bedrooms with attractive decor. The bar has a log fireplace and there is a coffee shop which serves breakfast and is open all day for snacks and light meals, but dinner is not served.
12⇆↱ (2fb)CTV in all bedrooms Ⓡ T ✱ sB&B⇆↱£35-£55 dB&B⇆↱£45-£75 Bar Lunch £2.25-£5.25
▥
Credit Cards [1][3]£

STRACHUR Strathclyde *Argyllshire* Map **10** NN00

INN QQQ *Glendale* PA27 8BX ☎(036986) 630
Glendale is a Victorian house set in its own gardens beside the A815 overlooking Loch Fyne. It is family run and has a friendly and informal atmosphere. Meals and snacks are available throughout the day in the comfortable bar and dinner is served in the cosy little dining room. The small, brightly decorated bedrooms offer modern facilities.
3↱ (1fb) CTV in 2 bedrooms Ⓡ ✱
▥ games room

STRATFORD-UPON-AVON Warwickshire Map **04** SP25

See also Newbold on Stour

GH QQQ Aberfoyle 3 Evesham Place CV37 6HT
☎(0789) 295703
An impeccably kept, tiny guesthouse stands near the town centre. There is a cosy combined lounge and breakfast room.
2↱ (1fb) ⊁ CTV in all bedrooms Ⓡ ✱ sB&B↱£20-£24 dB&B↱£38-£42 WB&B£90-£100
▥ nc5yrs

GH QQQ Ambleside 41 Grove Road CV37 6PB (turn off A3400 onto B439, through traffic lights, guesthouse on right)
☎(0789) 297239 & 295670 FAX (0789) 295670
Closed Xmas
There are family rooms and rooms reserved for non-smokers - all well furnished - in this soundly maintained guest house. Lounge and dining room are combined which is rather limiting. It is within easy walking distance of the town centre and has a large car park.
7rm(3↱) (3fb) ⊁ in 4 bedrooms ⊁ in dining room CTV in all bedrooms Ⓡ sB&B£17-£20 dB&B£36-£40 dB&B↱£40-£44
▥ CTV
Credit Cards [1][3]£

GH QQQ Brook Lodge 192 Alcester Road CV37 9DR (W on A422) ☎(0789) 295988 FAX (0789) 295988
Closed Xmas

▶

Mr and Mrs Charlette provide a welcoming atmosphere at Brook Lodge, a charming establishment just half a mile from Anne Hathaway's cottage. The house is sparklingly maintained and the bedrooms prettily decorated, well furnished and equipped with modern amenities. Breakfast is served in the split-level lounge/breakfast room.

7🚿 (1fb) 🚭 in dining room 🚭 in lounges CTV in all bedrooms Ⓡ 🐕 (ex guide dogs) sB&B🚿£25-£38 dB&B🚿£38-£48

♨ CTV

Credit Cards [1] [2] [3] [£]

GH [Q] [Q] Courtland Hotel 12 Guild Street CV37 6RE (on A3400) ☎(0789) 292401

Conveniently positioned close to the town centre, this Georgian house provides simple accommodation with some modern but mostly older furniture. The bedrooms all have modern equipment, and a small lounge and traditionally furnished breakfast room are provided.

7rm(3🛁🚿) (1fb) 🚭 in dining room 🚭 in 1 lounge CTV in all bedrooms Ⓡ 🐕 (ex guide dogs) ✱ sB&B£16-£18 sB&B🛁🚿£25-£35 dB&B£33-£35 dB&B🛁🚿£36-£45

♨ CTV

Credit Cards [1] [2] [3] [£]

GH [Q] [Q] [Q] *Craig Cleeve House* 67-69 Shipston Road CV37 7LW ☎(0789) 296573 FAX (0789) 299452

Five minutes' walk south of the town centre is this nicely maintained guesthouse. Bedrooms have modern equipment. There is a bright breakfast room and a small lounge bar.

15rm(9🚿) CTV in all bedrooms Ⓡ

Lic ♨

Credit Cards [1] [2] [3] [5]

GH [Q] [Q] [Q] The Croft 49 Shipston Road CV37 7LN (on A3400, 400 yds from Clopton Bridge) ☎(0789) 293419 FAX (0789) 293419

Five minutes' walk south of the town centre, this large semidetached Victorian house offers well equipped bedrooms, most of which have been redecorated and upgraded. This good work is programmed for the remainder of the rooms. Family rooms and a ground-floor room are also available. There is a comfortable residents' lounge and a small dining room, where evening meals are available by prior arrangement. The large rear garden includes a heated swimming pool.

9rm(4🚿) (5fb) 🚭 in 2 bedrooms 🚭 in dining room CTV in all bedrooms Ⓡ sB&B£19-£19.50 dB&B£34-£49 dB&B🚿£42-£49 WB&B£119-£171.50 WBDi£185.50-£238 LDO noon

Lic ♨ CTV 🏊(heated)

Credit Cards [1] [3] [5] [£]

GH [Q] [Q] Curtain Call 142 Alcester Road CV37 9DR ☎Stratford(0789) 267734

Curtain Call is a simple little guesthouse, conveniently situated for the town centre and amenities, with modest bedrooms and a cosy breakfast room.

4rm(3🚿) (2fb) 🚭 in 2 bedrooms 🚭 in dining room 🚭 in lounges CTV in all bedrooms Ⓡ ✱ sB&B£15-£18 sB&B🚿£18-£25 dB&B£30-£38 LDO 8pm

♨

[£]

GH [Q] [Q] [Q] The Dylan 10 Evesham Place CV37 6HT ☎(0789) 204819

A friendly family guesthouse is centrally located with bright, comfortable and well equipped bedrooms, some featuring stylish Victorian fireplaces. There is a pleasant breakfast room complete with an old Wurlitzer juke box for nostalgic entertainment.

5🚿 (1fb) CTV in all bedrooms Ⓡ ✱ sB&B🚿£18-£24 dB&B🚿£36-£42

♨

GH Ⓠ Ⓠ **East Bank House** 19 Warwick Road CV37 6YW (Take A439 into town and turn 1st right at St Gregory's church)
☎(0798) 292758 FAX (0798) 292758
11rm(6⇌�) (2fb) ✗ in bedrooms ✗ in dining room CTV in all bedrooms Ⓡ ✗ (ex guide dogs) ✳ sB&B£19.50-£24.50 dB&B£31-£41 dB&B⇌↫£39-£49
≋

Credit Cards ① ③

GH Ⓠ Ⓠ Ⓠ **Eastnor House Hotel** Shipston Road CV37 7LN (on A3400) ☎(0789) 268115
Closed Xmas
Very handy for the theatre, this large, detached Victorian house has attractively decorated bedrooms with mostly reproduction furniture. Two rooms are on the ground floor. There is a small lounge and a breakfast room.
↫↫ (3fb) ✗ in bedrooms ✗ in dining room CTV in all bedrooms Ⓡ dB&B⇌↫£40-£57
Lic ≋
Credit Cards ① ② ③ ⓒ

GH Ⓠ Ⓠ **Eversley Bears** 37 Grove Road CV37 6PB
☎(0789) 292334
This small, friendly guest house, well maintained by the owners Clive and Judy Thomas, lies within easy walking distance of the town centre. Accommodation is not luxurious but is well cared for and there is a pleasant lounge and dining room. The hotel's name comes from the Thomas' collection of teddy bears.
5rm(2↫) (2fb) Ⓡ ✗ (ex guide dogs) ✳ sB&B£20-£22 dB&B£40-44 dB&B↫£44-£48
Lic CTV nc14yrs

CRAIG CLEEVE HOUSE
Private Hotel

67-69 Shipston Road, Stratford upon Avon,
Warwickshire CV37 7LW
Telephone: 0189 296573 Fax: 01789 299452

Good friendly service, family atmosphere and comfortable rooms of a high standard plus a breakfast where no one is left feeling hungry! These are just four reasons for staying at the centrally situated CRAIG CLEEVE HOUSE. Just five minutes walk to the town centre with all it's amenities. Ideal for visiting Shakespeare Country and the Cotswolds. All rooms have tea/coffee making facilities and colour TV. Most have en suite facilities and there are 4 rooms available on the ground floor.

"Our sole aim is to make our guests feel comfortable and welcome."

Courtland Hotel
12 Guild Street, Stratford-on-Avon
CV37 6RE

Bed and Breakfast
From/to £15-£26
En suite facilities available.
Personal attention in well appointed Georgian House. Full English & Continental breakfast with home made preserves. All rooms with H&C, central heating, double glazing, colour television, tea & coffee making facilities. Antique furniture. Town centre situation. 3 minutes' level walk to theatre.

AA **Tel: (01789) 292401**
Mrs. Bridget Johnson
LISTED *Recommended by Arthur Frommer*

The Dylan
10 Evesham Place, Stratford upon Avon CV37 6HT
Telephone: (01789) 204819

A spacious Victorian house with original fireplaces. Centrally situated in the town only five minutes from the shops and the Royal Shakespeare Theatre. Comfortable, friendly accommodation, all rooms are tastefully furnished and decorated with en suite facilities, colour television, tea/coffee making facilities and central heating. Ground floor bedroom available. Car parking. An ideal base for touring the Heart of the Midlands.

SELECTED

GH [Q][Q][Q][Q] Gravelside Barn Binton CV37 9TU ☎(0789) 750502 & 297000 Telex no 311827 FAX (0789) 298056

A gem of a B&B, this stone-built barn has been cleverly converted by proprietors Denise and Guy Belchambers to provide good quality modern accommodation in a delightful rural setting. Each of the attractive bedrooms has a spectacular view. One room is conveniently located on the ground floor and another has its own external entrance reached by a spiral staircase. There is a comfortable open plan lounge area and a dining room offering a good choice at breakfast. Smoking is not permitted in the bedrooms or dining room.

3🚿 🚭 CTV in all bedrooms Ⓡ T 🚫🐕 (ex guide dogs) sB&B🚿£30-£40 dB&B🚿£40-£60

▦ nc12yrs ⚑18 🎾(hard)

Credit Cards [1][3][£]

GH [Q][Q][Q] Hardwick House 1 Avenue Road CV37 6UY (off A439) ☎(0789) 204307 FAX (0789) 296760

Closed Xmas

An elegant Victorian property stands in a tree-lined avenue, set back within mature gardens and grounds yet within walking distance of the town centre. Owned by the Coulson family for over 20 years, it provides generally spacious, bright comfortable and well equipped bedrooms. Breakfast is served in the attractive dining room, and there is a pleasant lounge.

14rm(7🛁🚿) (3fb) 🚭 in bedrooms 🚭 in dining room CTV in all bedrooms Ⓡ 🚫🐕 (ex guide dogs) sB&B£19-£24 dB&B£38-£48 dB&B🛁🚿£46-£62

▦ CTV

Credit Cards [1][2][3][5][£]

GH [Q][Q][Q] Highcroft Banbury Road CV37 7NF (on A422 out of town, 2m from river bridge on left) ☎(0789) 296293 FAX (0789) 415236

A friendly family house with extensive gardens, Highcroft is situated next to the main Banbury road, two miles from the town centre, with an attractive rural backdrop. Period-style furniture is combined with modern equipment in the bedrooms, and one room in the ground floor extension has its own entrance. There is a lounge/breakfast room with lots of comfortable seating, and a tennis court is provided in the grounds.

1🛁🚿 Annexe 1🛁🚿 (1fb) 🚭 CTV in all bedrooms Ⓡ ∗ dB&B🛁🚿£33

▦ CTV 🎾(hard)

[£]

GH [Q][Q][Q] Hollies 'The Hollies', 16 Evesham Place CV37 6HQ ☎(0789) 266857

This well maintained guesthouse is privately owned and personally run by a mother and daughter partnership, and is well positioned a few minutes' walk west of the town centre. The fresh bedrooms have modern furnishings and equipment, and family rooms are available. There is no lounge, but TV's are provided in the bedrooms.

6rm(3🛁🚿) (3fb) 🚭 CTV in all bedrooms Ⓡ ∗ dB&B£30-£36 dB&B🛁🚿£40-£45

▦ CTV

[£]

GH [Q][Q][Q] Hunters Moon 150 Alcester Road CV37 9DR (on A422) ☎(0789) 292888

Proprietors Rosemary and David Austin have made a lot of improvements to this small guest house since acquiring it in 1992 The bedrooms are attractively decorated and have modern furnishings and equipment. Family bedrooms are available, one ir a garden chalet, and there is a single ground-floor room. An

GRAVELSIDE BARN

Offers the discerning traveller all the modern conveniences and comforts of today in a stunning and tranquil setting.

Serenely situated on a hilltop in the middle of rolling Warwickshire farmland, with magnificent views of the countryside and Cotswold Hills.

A great base for exploring Shakespeare's Country and the Heart of England, or somewhere to relax and feel the cares and stresses slip away.

3½ miles from Stratford and 10 minutes from Junction 15 of the M40.

Please ring or fax for a brochure.

"Your place in the country"

GRAVELSIDE BARN

Denise & Guy Belchambers
Gravelside Barn, Binton, Stratford-upon-Avon, Warwickshire CV37 9TU
Tel: 01789 750502/293122 Fax: 01789 298056

English Tourist Board HIGHLY COMMENDED

AA Selected QQQQ

attractive breakfast room is provided and a small lounge for smokers to use.
7🚿 (3fb) 🚭 in 1 lounge CTV in all bedrooms Ⓡ sB&B🚿£17-£26 dB&B🚿£32-£44
♨ CTV
Credit Cards [1] [2] [3] [5]

GH [Q][Q] Marlyn 3 Chestnut Walk CV37 6HG (from Evesham Road A439 towards town centre, second right after roundabout) ☎(0789) 293752
Closed Xmas
Conveniently positioned for the town centre, theatre and amenities, this Victorian terraced property is in a tree-lined street just west of the town. The simple accommodation is clean and well maintained, if rather dated in parts with limited facilities; one room is located on the ground floor with a shower nearby. Cosy public areas include a TV lounge and small dining room.
8rm (1fb) Ⓡ 🐕 (ex guide dogs) ✳ sB&B£18 dB&B£34
♨ CTV 🚫P

GH [Q][Q][Q] Melita Private Hotel 37 Shipston Road CV37 7LN (on A3400, 200yds from Clopton Bridge) ☎(0789) 292432 FAX (0789) 204867
Closed Xmas
This large, well maintained Victorian house is close to the town centre and the theatre. Bedrooms are attractive with mostly period style furniture. Some rooms are on the ground floor. There is a comfortable lounge with a bar and a pleasant breakfast room.
12⇌🚿 (3fb) 🚭 in bedrooms 🚭 in dining room CTV in all bedrooms Ⓡ T ✳ sB&B⇌🚿£29-£40 dB&B⇌🚿£45-£66
Lic ♨ CTV
Credit Cards [1] [2] [3] [£]
See advertisement on p.387.

HARDWICK HOUSE

STRATFORD-UPON-AVON

A delightful Victorian Building dating from 1887 situated at the bottom of Avenue Road, in a quiet mature area. Only a few minutes walk to the Shakespearian properties and Royal Shakespeare Theatre. Ideal position for Warwick Castle, Birmingham Arena and the National Exhibition Centre.
Large comfortable rooms. Ensuite and standard available. All with colour T.V., Tea/Coffee making facilities, hot & cold water, full central heating, ample car parking.

RESIDENT PROPRIETORS
DRENAGH AND SIMON WOOTTON
Hardwick House, 1 Avenue Road,
Stratford-upon-Avon, Warwickshire. CV37 6UY

LES ROUTIERS — AA QQQ — English Tourist Board ACCLAIMED

TELEPHONE
RESERVATIONS **01789 204307** — GUESTS **01789 296174**
FAX: 01789 296760 — Credit Cards accepted

HUNTERS MOON
GUEST HOUSE

150 ALCESTER ROAD
STRATFORD-UPON-AVON
WARWICKSHIRE
CV37 9DR

English Tourist Board

RESERVATIONS:
(01789) 292888

AA
QQQ

All rooms are en-suite and are comfortably furnished also with colour television, clock radio, tea and coffee making facilities and fitted hairdryer. Single, double, twin and family rooms are available.
Hunters Moon is close to Anne Hathaway's cottage, and is an ideal base for visiting the Cotswold villages, Warwick Castle and all the other Shakespearian properties.

Guest telephone available.
Private car parking for guest's use and also a garden patio and ornamental fountain and pond to relax by.
An excellent English breakfast is served by resident hosts Stratfordians
ROSEMARY and DAVE AUSTIN.

Visa, Access and American Express cards accepted.
Recommended by Arthur Frommer

GH [Q][Q][Q] Moonraker House 40 Alcester Road CV37 9DB (on A422, 900yds NW of town centre) (MIN) ☎(0789) 299346 267115 FAX (0789) 295504

This popular, personally owned and run guesthouse is rather unusual, comprising four different properties within the same street. This makes for very varied accommodation, with some bedrooms being more luxurious than others, but all are well furnished and equipped with modern comforts and facilities; some rooms are on the ground floor. Continued improvements include a range of good quality bedrooms and an appealing new sun lounge.

6🚿 Annexe 9🛁🚿 (1fb) 🚭 in 7 bedrooms 🚭 in dining room 🚭 in lounges CTV in all bedrooms Ⓡ dB&B🛁🚿£41-£60 WB&B£140-£210

🅿

Credit Cards [1][3]

GH [Q][Q][Q] Nando's 18-19 Evesham Place CV37 6HT (on A439) ☎(0789) 204907 FAX (0789) 204907

Conveniently positioned close to the town centre and amenities, this friendly little hotel offers well equipped bedrooms and congenial public areas.

21rm(1🛁6🚿) (10fb) 🚭 in dining room CTV in all bedrooms ✱ sB&B£17-£20 sB&B🛁🚿£25-£29 dB&B£26-£34 dB&B🛁🚿£36-£42

🅿 CTV

Credit Cards [1][2][3][5][£]

GH [Q][Q] Parkfield 3 Broad Walk CV37 6HS ☎(0789) 293313

A semidetached Victorian house within walking distance of the town centre, offers a mixture of bedrooms furnished in modern and traditional styles. All the rooms are adequately equipped, and recent improvements have increased the number of en suite showers. There is no lounge, and only bed and breakfast is available.

7rm(5🚿) (1fb) 🚭 CTV in all bedrooms Ⓡ ✱ sB&B£17-£19 dB&B£34-£38 dB&B🚿£39-£44

🅿 nc7yrs

Credit Cards [1][2][3][5]

GH [Q][Q][Q] *The Payton Hotel* 6 John Street CV37 6UB (follow A439 from town centre towards Warwick and M40, then first left) ☎(0789) 266442

Closed 25-26 Dec

Close to the town centre, this late Georgian house is very well maintained, with a particularly high standard of cleanliness. Bedrooms are attractive and modern, though one has a restored antique brass bedstead, and there is a pleasant traditional-style breakfast room. There is a small lounge area in the entrance hall.

5rm(4🚿) (1fb) CTV in all bedrooms Ⓡ 🐕 (ex guide dogs)

🅿 🚫

Credit Cards [1][2][3]

🛏 ☕ **GH [Q][Q][Q] Penryn House** 126 Alcester Road CV37 9DP (0.5m past railway station, right hand side of A422) ☎(0789) 293718

Well positioned on the A422 Alcester road, this detached house is also convenient for the railway station. Recent improvements now provide comfortable, well equipped and furnished bedrooms and family rooms are available with one on the ground floor. There is a pleasant combined lounge/dining room, with individual tables.

7rm(5🚿) Annexe 1🚿 (3fb) 🚭 in dining room 🚭 in lounges CTV in all bedrooms Ⓡ sB&B£15-£21 sB&B🚿£25-£35 dB&B£30-£37 dB&B🚿£35-£46 WB&B£105-£140

🅿

Credit Cards [1][2][3][5][£]

See advertisement on p.388.

GH [Q][Q] Ravenhurst 2 Broad Walk CV37 6HS ☎(0789) 292515

Closed Xmas

Well positioned for the town centre and amenities, this large semidetached Victorian house offers bright, modern, well equipped accommodation. There is a combined lounge/breakfast room on the ground floor.

5🛁🚿 (1fb) 🚭 CTV in all bedrooms Ⓡ 🐕 ✱ dB&B🛁🚿£38-£45 WB&Bfr£122

🅿

Credit Cards [1][2][3][5]

GH [Q] Salamander 40 Grove Road CV37 6PB (on A439 towards Evesham, just behind the police station) ☎(0789) 205728 FAX (0789) 205728

Conveniently positioned close to the town centre, this semidetached house provides simple but sound accommodation. Bedrooms are furnished with a mixture of old and new and some have TV.

6rm(4🚿) (3fb) 🚭 in dining room CTV in all bedrooms Ⓡ ✱ sB&B£16-£20 dB&B£32-£44 dB&B🚿£35-£44 WB&B£105-£112 WBDi£157.50-£165 LDO 6.30pm

🅿 CTV

Credit Cards [1]

SELECTED

GH [Q][Q][Q][Q] Sequoia House Private Hotel 51-53 Shipston Road CV37 7LN (on A3400 close to Clopton Bridge) ☎(0789) 268852 FAX (0789) 414559

Closed 22-27 Dec

A very pleasing little hotel, this extended Victorian house stands close to the river and town centre (guests can walk into town via the rear garden). Bedrooms vary in size and some are more opulent than others but all are well equipped and brightly decorated. Five rooms are located in a converted cottage, and no-smoking rooms are available. There is also a lounge bar and a large air-conditioned conference/function room.

20rm(16🛁🚿) Annexe 5🚿 (4fb) 🚭 in 6 bedrooms 🚭 in area of dining room 🚭 in 1 lounge CTV in all bedrooms Ⓡ **T** 🐕 ✱ sB&B£29 sB&B🛁🚿£39-£49 dB&B£39-£45 dB&B🛁🚿£49-£72

Lic 🅿 CTV nc5yrs

Credit Cards [1][2][3][5][£]

See advertisement on p.389.

GH [Q][Q][Q] Stretton House Hotel 38 Grove Road CV37 6PB ☎(0789) 268647

A well kept semidetached house stands near the town centre. Bedrooms have modern furniture and include family rooms. There is a combined breakfast room and lounge.

6rm(4🚿) (2fb) 🚭 CTV in all bedrooms Ⓡ 🐕 (ex guide dogs) ✱ sB&B£15-£20 dB&B£30-£34 dB&B🚿£30-£44 LDO 4pm

🅿 nc8yrs

SELECTED

GH [Q][Q][Q][Q] Twelfth Night Evesham Place CV37 6HT (on A439) ☎(0789) 414595

A late Victorian villa situated west of the town centre provides convenient access to most amenities. Now a privately owned, personally run hotel, it offers tastefully decorated bedrooms recently restored with good use of pleasant colour and bold fabrics, together with good quality modern facilities, with some welcome extra touches. There is a comfortable lounge and an attractive dining room featuring period furniture complemented by good quality linen and crockery. Smoking is not permitted.

7🚿 🚭 CTV in all bedrooms Ⓡ 🐕 sB&B🚿£23-£27 dB&B🚿£44-£56

🅿 nc12yrs

Credit Cards [1][3]

MELITA
PRIVATE HOTEL
**37 Shipston Road,
Stratford-upon-Avon,
Warwickshire
CV37 7LN
Tel: (01789) 292432
Fax: (01789) 204867**

"The Melita has over many years established itself as one of the premier private hotels in Stratford upon Avon."

Commended by the ETB and 3 Q's by the AA.

This beautifully appointed Victorian house offers its guests a friendly welcome, cheerful service and a high standard of accommodation.

With ample car parking and only 5 minutes walk to the theatre and town centre, the Melita with its ideal location is a must for those seeking a relaxing atmosphere and warm hospitality.

PARKFIELD GUEST HOUSE

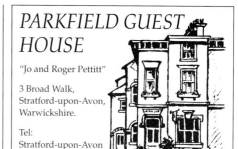

"Jo and Roger Pettitt"

3 Broad Walk,
Stratford-upon-Avon,
Warwickshire.

Tel:
Stratford-upon-Avon
(01789) 293313

A most attractive Victorian house in a quiet but central location, only 6 minutes' walk to the Town, Royal Shakespeare Theatre and places of interest. Spacious accommodation. Excellent choice of breakfast. Central heating throughout. Colour TV and tea and coffee making facilities in all rooms. Most rooms en-suite. Unrestricted access. Fire Certificate. Large private car park. Tourist and Theatre information available.

Member of Hotel & Caterers' Association.

Highly recommended by Arthur Frommer.

ETB rating: 2 crowns.   A no smoking house

Moonraker House

★ **ALL** rooms have en-suite bathrooms, tea & coffee making facilities, colour TV, clock radios and fitted hairdryers.

★ There are also extra special rooms with **four poster beds,** lounge area and garden patio (non-smoking).

★ Enjoy an excellent English breakfast prepared with care by the resident proprietors Mauveen and Mike Spencer.

★ **ALL** rooms are elegantly decorated and designed with your comfort in mind.

★ 5 minutes walk from town centre.

★ CAR PARK (open and garage).

★ Ideal centre for exploring the Cotswolds, Shakespeare's countryside, Warwick Castles and Shakespeare Theatres.

**40 Alcester Road, Stratford-upon-Avon CV37 9DB
Tel: (01789) 299346 or 267115 Fax: (01789) 295504**

SELECTED

GH Ⓠ Ⓠ Ⓠ Ⓠ **Victoria Spa Lodge** Bishopton Lane CV37 9QY ☎(0789) 267985 & 204728 FAX (0789) 204728
In recent times Paul and Doreen Tozer have transformed their early Victorian house with significant upgrading to the bedrooms. These are now prettily decorated and comfortable with quality furnishings, efficient en suite showers and a good range of modern equipment. The attractive lounge/dining room is similarly well furnished in period style, and handsome English or vegetarian breakfasts start the day. This is a no-smoking establishment.
7↑ (3fb) ⊁ CTV in all bedrooms Ⓡ ↑ ✳ sB&Bↆ£33-£38 dB&Bↆ£39-£50
▥.
Credit Cards ①③

GH Ⓠ Ⓠ Ⓠ **Virginia Lodge** 12 Evesham Place CV37 6HT ☎(0789) 292157
Near the town centre, this guesthouse provides stylishly furnished bedrooms. There is a welcoming lounge and guests have their own tables in the dining room. It is non-smoking.
7↑ (1fb) ⊁ in bedrooms ⊁ in dining room CTV in all bedrooms Ⓡ sB&B£18-£20 dB&Bↆ£36-£46
Lic ▥. CTV

GH Ⓠ Ⓠ Ⓠ **Willicote House** Willicote, Clifford Chambers CV37 8LN ☎(0789) 294456
May-Oct
In a rural location two miles south of the village of Clifford Chambers, this Georgian house is set in four acres of grounds amid a scattering of farm out-buildings. Following recent renovation, the house offers spacious bedrooms of charm and quality, traditionally furnished yet with a good range of modern

facilities. A comfortable period-style dining room is also provided.
3rm(1⇌2↑) (2fb)CTV in all bedrooms ↑ (ex guide dogs) sB&B⇌↑£18 dB&B⇌↑£35
▥. ⁊ (heated)
Ⓔ

GH Ⓠ Ⓠ **Winterbourne** 2 St Gregory's Road CV37 6UH (from A439 Warwick to Stratford road turn right by church) ☎Stratford-uopon-Avon(0789) 292207
Closed 23-27 Dec
A house of character, personally owned and run on friendly lines offers bright comfortable bedrooms and homely public areas. Quietly located yet within easy walking distance of the town and all amenities, it has the added advantage of an attractive enclosed garden to the rear.
5rm(2↑) (1fb) ⊁ CTV in all bedrooms Ⓡ ↑ ✳ sB&B£20-£35 sB&Bↆ£25-£40 dB&B£35-£45 dB&Bↆ£40-£50
▥.
Ⓔ

FH Ⓠ Ⓠ Mrs R M Meadows **Monk's Barn** *(SP206516)* Shipston Road CV37 8NA (on A3400 approx 1.25m S) ☎(0789) 293714
Closed 25-26 Dec
Monk's Barn Farm, two miles south of the centre of Stratford, has its origins in the 16th century, though the pretty house is more recent. It offers a split-level lounge/dining room, so smoking is not permitted while meals are in progress, though there are plans to add a separate lounge. Bedrooms include cosy main house rooms and two new rooms in a converted milking parlour.
4rm(2↑) (1fb) ⊁ in 2 bedrooms ⊁ in dining room ⊁ in lounges CTV in all bedrooms Ⓡ ↑ (ex guide dogs) sB&B£15.50-£16 sB&Bↆ£17.50-£18 dB&B£28-£29 dB&Bↆ£32-£33
▥. CTV ⋌ 75 acres mixed

STRATHAVEN Strathclyde *Lanarkshire* Map **11** NS74

GH 🅀🅀 **Springvale Hotel** 18 Letham Road ML10 6AD
☎(0357) 21131 FAX (0357) 21131
Closed 26-27 Dec & 1-3 Jan
Friendly and family-run, this guest house is situated in a quiet residential area some 300 yards from central amenities. Compact bedrooms with mixed practical appointments offer the expected facilities, while public areas include a homely lounge as well as the large rear dining room where enjoyable high teas are served to residents and non-residents alike. Some long-stay guests are also accommodated.
14rm(1⇌10🟕) (1fb)CTV in all bedrooms ⓇＲ ✻ sB&Bfr£28 sB&B⇌🟕£30 dB&Bfr£38 dB&B⇌🟕£40 LDO 6.45pm
Lic 🎞 CTV

STRATHPEFFER Highland *Ross & Cromarty* Map **14** NH45

GH 🅀🅀🅀 **Inver Lodge** IV14 9DL ☎(0997) 421392
Mar-mid Dec
2rm (1fb) ⨾ CTV in all bedrooms ⓇＲ ✷ sB&B£18-£22 dB&B£29-£31 WB&B£100-£108 WBDi£170-£178 LDO 4pm
🎞 ๏ fishing and riding can be arranged
Credit Cards 1 3

STRATHTAY Tayside *Perthshire* Map **14** NN95

GH 🅀🅀🅀 **Bendarroch House** PH9 0PG ☎(0887) 840420
FAX (0887) 840438
This substantial period mansion lies in its own grounds in a quiet part of the village close to the northern bank of the River Tay. Its bedrooms, with just one exception, are elegant and spacious and all are very comfortable and well equipped. There are two lounges, one for television, and both invite relaxation. Home-cooked meals are served in the attractive dining room. This is an ideal base for people who love country pursuits. ▶

5🚿 (1fb) 🚭 in dining room 🚭 in 1 lounge CTV in 2 bedrooms [R] T 🐕 (ex guide dogs) ✱ sB&B🚿£25 dB&B🚿£40-£50 LDO 5.30pm
Lic ♨ CTV 🅿 croquet

STRATHYRE Central *Perthshire* — Map **11** NN51

SELECTED

GH [Q][Q][Q][Q] Creagan House FK18 8ND (0.25m N of Strathyre on A84) ☎(0877) 384638 FAX (0877) 384638
Closed 29 Jan-3 Mar
5rm(3🛁🚿) (1fb) 🚭 in bedrooms [R] sB&B£34.25 sB&B🛁🚿£42.50 dB&B£49 dB&B🛁🚿£61 WB&B£154.35-£192.15 WBDi£301.35-£339.15 LDO 8.30pm
Lic ♨
Credit Cards [1][2][3]

STREFFORD Shropshire — Map **07** SO48

FH [Q][Q][Q] Mrs C Morgan **Strefford Hall** *(SO444856)* Strefford SY7 8DE ☎Craven Arms(0588) 672383
Closed Xmas & New Year
In the spring this imposing Victorian farmhouse is surrounded by colourful yellow fields, and the 360-acre farm also has sheep and cattle. There are three spacious bedrooms with solid older style furniture, two of which have en suite shower rooms and the third has a private bathroom. The comfortable residents' lounge is furnished with modern three-piece suites and has a log-burning stove. Strefford Hall Farm is set in its own pretty lawns and gardens, and is situated just off the A49.
3rm(2🚿) 🚭 [R] dB&B🚿£36-£38
CTV 350 acres arable beef sheep

STROUD Gloucestershire — Map **03** SO80

GH [Q][Q][Q] Downfield Hotel 134 Cainscross Road GL5 4HN (2m W on A419) ☎(0453) 764496 FAX (0453) 753150
Closed 2 wks from 25 Dec
Situated only half a mile from Stroud, this hospitable hotel offers comfortable accommodation in well equipped bedrooms, including ground floor rooms with en suite facilities. The spacious bar with its open plan seating area provides a warm welcome to guests on arrival. An extensive menu is available for dinner, and vegetarians can be catered for.
21rm(11🛁🚿) (4fb)CTV in 17 bedrooms [R] T ✱ sB&B£20-£23 sB&B🛁🚿£29 dB&B£29 dB&B🛁🚿£35 WB&B£101.50-£203 WBDi£175-£203 LDO 8pm
Lic ♨ CTV
Credit Cards [1][3]

STUDLEY Warwickshire — Map **04** SP06

FH [Q][Q][Q] Miss S A Walters ***Bug In The Blanket*** *(SP089643)* Castle Farm B80 7AH ☎(0527) 854275 & 852254
FAX (0527) 854897
Do not be put off by the name; this reflects the quirky but pleasing nature of this farmhouse. Set in the grounds of a 500-acre estate, the majority of accommodation is offered in `The Wing', converted from old garden buildings. These modern rooms have a good range of facilities including a kitchenette and en suite. Two rooms are situated in the 15th-century black and white cottage, `The Bug'; these rooms have access to shower facilities only via public areas. `The Bug' also contains the dining room where appetising meals are served around a commual table, helping to maintain the convivial and fun atmosphere of the place. Continental breakfast can be left in room refrigerators, alternatively, a cooked breakfast is available in the cottage. There is also a cosy lounge and the restaurant is licensed.
2rm (1fb) CTV in 6 bedrooms [R] 🐕 (ex guide dogs) LDO 2pm
Lic ♨ CTV 🏊(heated) sauna 500 acres arable beef sheep

STURMINSTER NEWTON Dorset — Map **03** ST71

FH [Q][Q][Q] Mrs S Wingate-Saul **Holebrook** *(ST743117)* Lydlinch DT10 2JB ☎Hazelbury Bryan(0258) 817348
rs 25 Dec-1 Jan
Standing in a quiet rural setting at the end of a long, narrow track to the west of the town, this charming 18th-century farmhouse features comfortable lounges and well-appointed bedrooms in its converted outbuildings. Breakfast and dinner are served at a communal table in the spacious kitchen of the main house. Other facilities include an outdoor swimming pool and a large games room which can also be used for small conferences.
2rm Annexe 4rm(3🚿) 🚭 in dining room 🚭 in 1 lounge CTV in 4 bedrooms [R] 🐕 (ex guide dogs) ✱ sB&B£21-£23 dB&B🚿£36-£46 WB&B£126-£154 WBDi£203-£258 LDO 4pm
Lic ♨ CTV 🏊games room mini-gym 126 acres mixed
[£]

STURTON BY STOW Lincolnshire — Map **08** SK88

SELECTED

FH [Q][Q][Q][Q] Mrs Brenda Williams **Gallows Dale Farm** *(SK874809)* Stow Park Road LN1 2AH (1m W on A1500) ☎Gainsborough(0427) 788387
An attractive 18th-century red-brick farmhouse, Gallows Dale has been sympathetically extended and modernised to provide individually styled bedrooms with attractive fabrics. Public rooms comprise a cosy lounge with TV, books and local information, and an inviting dining room where a substantial breakfast is served. This is a no-smoking establishment.
3 (1fb) 🚭 [R] 🐕 ✱ sB&B£14-£15 dB&B£28-£30 WB&B£90
♨ CTV 33 acres cattle
[£]

SUDBURY Suffolk — Map **05** TL84

GH [Q][Q] ***Hill Lodge Private Hotel*** 8 Newton Road CO10 6RL ☎(0787) 377568
17rm(7🚿) CTV in all bedrooms 🐕 (ex guide dogs)
Lic ♨ CTV
Credit Cards [5]

GH [Q][Q] Old Bull And Trivets Church Street CO10 6BL ☎(0787) 374120 FAX (0787) 379044
A pink-washed timbered building dating from the 16th century, this guest house has a restaurant specialising in pizzas. En suite bedrooms, some in a nearby annexe, are individually decorated. Situated a short walk from the town centre, you reach the Bull & Trivets by following Friar Street from the market place to the T-junction.
7rm(4🛁🚿) Annexe 3🛁🚿 (5fb)CTV in all bedrooms [R] T ✱ sB&B£23-£32 sB&B🛁🚿£36-£40 dB&B£36-£48 dB&B🛁🚿£49-£54 LDO 10pm
Lic ♨
Credit Cards [1][2][3][5]

SURBITON Greater London — Map **04** TQ16

GH [Q][Q] Warwick 321 Ewell Road KT6 7BX (on A240) ☎081-399 5837 & 2405
This small guesthouse, convenient for the A3, is run by a cheerful proprietress. Bedrooms are clean, simply furnished and best suited for single guests. Public areas are limited.
9rm(1🛁🚿) (1fb)CTV in all bedrooms [R] T sB&B£28-£30 sB&B🛁🚿£30-£34 dB&B£38-£40 dB&B🛁🚿£40-£44 WB&B£160-£175 WBDi£195-£210 LDO 2pm
♨ CTV
Credit Cards [1][3][£]

SUTTON Greater London   Map **04** TQ26

GH Ⓠ Ⓠ Ⓠ **Ashling Tara Hotel** 50 Rosehill SM1 3EU
☎081-641 6142 FAX 081-644 7872
Located opposite the Rose Hill tennis centre and sports complex
and only a mile from the nearest tube to central
London, this hotel is ideal for business and pleasure. The
accommodation is slowly being upgraded: Ashling House
comprising reception, bar, restaurant, lounge and function room,
while most of the bedrooms, which have every modern facility, are
in the Ashling Tara Annexe.
10⇌🎄 Annexe 6rm(4🎄) (2fb) 🍴 in bedrooms 🍴 in dining room
🍴 in lounges CTV in all bedrooms Ⓡ T 🎄 ✳ sB&B⇌🎄£30-£52
dB&B£40-£65 dB&B⇌🎄£45-£56 WB&B£240-£300
WBDi£300-£360 LDO 9.30pm
Lic ▥ CTV
Credit Cards ① ② ③ Ⓔ

GH Ⓠ **Dene Hotel** 39 Cheam Road SM1 2AT (W on A232)
☎081-642 3170 FAX 081-642 3170
The Dene has been personally run as a bed and breakfast hotel for
many years, in a very friendly manner. It is a pair of linked houses,
very close to the town centre, opposite the Holiday Inn, offering
bedrooms in a variety of sizes, some with garden views.
28rm(12⇌🎄) (3fb)CTV in all bedrooms Ⓡ T 🎄 (ex guide dogs)
✳ sB&B£19.98-£27.03 sB&B⇌🎄£27.03-£37.60 dB&B£39.95
dB&B⇌🎄£39.95-£49.35
▥,
Ⓔ

GH Ⓠ Ⓠ Ⓠ **Thatched House Hotel** 135 Cheam Road SM1 2BN
☎081-642 3131 FAX 081-770 0684
Full of old-world charm, this well managed and very popular hotel
offers a good range of accommodation including ground floor and
four-poster rooms. All rooms are well equipped with extras such
as intercom child listening. The restaurant provides a three-course,
set-price dinner (with specials) Monday to Friday. There is a
licensed bar, with beer on draught, and a quiet lounge.
26rm(21⇌🎄) CTV in all bedrooms Ⓡ T ✳ sB&B£39.50-£42.50
sB&B⇌🎄£50-£55 dB&B£45-£49.50 dB&B⇌🎄£59.50-£77.50
LDO 8.45pm
Lic ▥ CTV
Credit Cards ① ③

SUTTON West Sussex   Map **04** SU91

P R E M I E R 🦌 **S E L E C T E D**

INN Ⓠ Ⓠ Ⓠ Ⓠ Ⓠ **The White**
Horse RH20 1PS ☎(07987) 221
(07987) 291
Recently restored and
completely refurbished, this
privately owned inn has
offered comfort and
sustenance to travellers and
locals alike since 1746.
Bedrooms vary in shape and
size, but all have been
thoughtfully equipped and
attractively refurnished in modern style; should you wish to
get away from it all, the Cottage Annexe with its quiet garden
setting and absence of telephone provides the ideal opportunity.
The bar is double-sided - the 'public' featuring a
comprehensive range of real ales, the other complementing a
more sophisticated choice of drinks by a blackboard menu of
meals and snacks. There is also a slightly more formal eating
area, and the beer garden and patio add a further dimension
during the warmer months.
5⇌ CTV in all bedrooms Ⓡ T 🎄 ✳ sB&B⇌£48

▶

dB&B🛁£58 WB&B£134-£218 WBDi£206-£290 Lunch £12&alc High tea fr£3 Dinner £12&alc LDO 9.30pm
🅿
Credit Cards [1][2][3][5] [£]

SUTTON COLDFIELD West Midlands Map **07** SP19

GH [Q][Q] Standbridge Hotel 138 Birmingham Road B72 1LY (1m S on A5127) ☎021-354 3007

A well established guesthouse, conveniently situated for access to Birmingham, Sutton Coldfield and the motorway network, provides well kept bedrooms of varying sizes. Although rooms are not en suite, the majority do have private shower facilities.

8rm 🚭 in 4 bedrooms 🚭 in dining room 🚭 in lounges CTV in all bedrooms [R] * sB&B£20 sB&B£25 dB&B£35-£39.50 LDO 6pm
Lic 🅿 CTV nc5yrs jacuzzi spa bath
Credit Cards [1][3]
See advertisement under BIRMINGHAM

SWAFFHAM Norfolk Map **05** TF80

SELECTED

GH [Q][Q][Q][Q] Corfield House Sporle PE32 2EA (on S edge of village, 0.5m from A47) ☎(0760) 723636

mid Mar-mid Dec

Corfield is an immaculately kept house dating from 1820 with a 1950s extension. The bedrooms are neat and attractively furnished and there is a small lounge with plenty of useful leaflets (the owner works in a local tourist information centre). The set dinner is discussed at the start of the day, enthusiastically prepared, and served in the cosy dining room. Smoking is not permitted in the house.

5rm(2🛁3🚿) 🚭 CTV in all bedrooms [R] sB&B🛁🚿£23 dB&B🛁🚿£37-£43 WB&B£129.50-£150.50 WBDi£205-£230 LDO 5.30pm
Lic 🅿
Credit Cards [1][3]

SWANAGE Dorset Map **04** SZ07

GH [Q][Q][Q] Bella Vista Hotel 14 Burlington Road BH19 1LS ☎(0929) 422873

Feb-Nov

This small, friendly guesthouse continues to provide a high standard of accommodation. The bedrooms are attractive and reasonably equipped. There is a comfortable lounge and a choice of breakfasts is served in the dining room.

6rm(5🚿) (4fb) 🚭 [R] 🐕
Lic 🅿 CTV nc4yrs

GH [Q][Q][Q] *Burlington House Hotel* 7 Highcliffe Road BH19 1LW ☎(0929) 422422

26 Mar-5 Nov

This small private hotel provides comfortable and well-equipped accommodation. There is a relaxing lounge and separate bar. Dinner and breakfast are served in the dining room.

9rm(7🛁🚿) (5fb) CTV in 8 bedrooms [R] 🐕 LDO 5pm
Lic 🅿 CTV musical evenings

GH [Q][Q][Q] Chines Hotel 9 Burlington Road BH19 1LR ☎(0929) 422457

24 Apr-Sep rs Mar-Oct

This family run guesthouse has a warm friendly atmosphere and is clean and well maintained. The bedrooms are bright, and well-equipped. with modern shower rooms. Public areas include a comfortable lounge and bar and evening meals are served in the light and airy dining room.

12rm(8🚿) (3fb) 🚭 in bedrooms 🚭 in dining room CTV in all bedrooms [R] 🐕 * sB&Bfr£16 dB&Bfr£32 dB&B🚿fr£37 WB&Bfr£112 WBDifr£182 LDO 4pm
Lic 🅿 CTV
[£]

🛏 🍷 **GH [Q][Q][Q] Crowthorne Hotel** 24 Cluny Crescent BH19 2BT ☎(0929) 422108

Closed Jan

In a quiet residential area, this Victorian villa-style house provides a high standard of accommodation and friendly service. There is a choice of dishes at dinner and the cooking is a good balance of English dishes.

8rm(2🛁2🚿) (2fb) 🚭 [R] 🐕 sB&B£15-£18 dB&B£30-£36 dB&B🛁🚿£36-£44 (incl dinner) WB&B£90-£130 WBDi£155-£195 LDO 5pm
Lic 🅿 CTV
Credit Cards [1][3] [£]

GH [Q][Q] Eversden Private Hotel Victoria Road BH19 1LY ☎(0929) 423276

Mar-Nov

A small comfortable family-run hotel is pleasantly situated in New Swanage, with fine open views, convenient for the Isle of Purbeck golf club and the sandy beach. Public areas include a small TV lounge, a lounge bar for residents and a light, spacious dining room where a set-price dinner is served at separate tables. There is ample private parking.

12rm(2🛁3🚿) (3fb) 🚭 in 5 bedrooms 🚭 in dining room CTV in 10 bedrooms [R] 🐕 LDO 6pm
Lic 🅿 CTV

SELECTED

GH [Q][Q][Q][Q] Fernlea Acton, Langton Matravers BH19 3JS (3m W) ☎Worth Matravers(0929) 439104 & 439105

Mar-Oct

A warm and friendly atmosphere prevails at this charming, late Victorian house, and children are made particularly welcome. In peaceful, rural surroundings, the house is large and comfortable, its bedrooms attractively furnished in pine, with modern tiled bathrooms. In the relaxing lounge an open coal fire burns in winter, and in the bright, well appointed dining room dinner is available from Easter onwards. A superb English breakfast is always available.

7🛁🚿 🚭 in dining room 🚭 in 1 lounge CTV in all bedrooms [R] T sB&B🛁🚿£24-£29 dB&B🛁🚿£44-£52
Lic 🅿 CTV
[£]

🛏 🍷 **GH [Q][Q][Q] Firswood Hotel** 29 Kings Road BH19 1HF ☎(0929) 422306

Closed Xmas rs Jan-Mar & Nov-Dec

Conveniently located in a central position close to the shops and steam railway, this small friendly run guesthouse offers neat well presented bedrooms with bright, fresh decor. The first floor lounge has comfortable sofas and TV, and the dining room is nicely furnished and smartly decorated. Mrs Baker and her family are very welcoming and friendly, and the atmosphere is relaxed.

6rm(2🛁2🚿) (2fb) 🚭 in dining room CTV in all bedrooms [R] 🐕 sB&B£15-£16 dB&B£30-£32 dB&B🛁🚿£32-£33 WB&Bfr£105 LDO 4.30pm
🅿 CTV nc5yrs

GH [Q][Q][Q] Gillan Hotel 5 Northbrook Road BH19 1PN ☎(0929) 424548

A programme of improvements is continuing at this small, family run private hotel. The bedrooms, which are of various sizes, are well equipped and comfortable. Breakfast and dinner are served in the bright and spacious dining room.

11rm(3🛁6🚿) (4fb) 🚭 in bedrooms 🚭 in dining room CTV in all bedrooms Ⓡ 🐕 * sB&B🛁🚿fr£34 dB&Bfr£34 LDO 5.30pm
Lic CTV 🏊(heated)
Credit Cards [1] [3]

GH [Q] [Q] [Q] Havenhurst Hotel 3 Cranbourne Road BH19 1EA
☎(0929) 424224

In a quiet residential area, this family run private hotel continues to improve. A number of bedrooms have been upgraded and new modern showers installed. Public areas include a comfortable bar and a small television lounge. A choice of menus is available at lunch and dinner, which include a good selection of home made desserts.

17rm(7🛁10🚿) (4fb) 🚭 in dining room Ⓡ 🐕 (ex guide dogs) * sB&B🛁🚿£15-£28 dB&B🛁🚿£30-£56 WB&B£105-£196 WBDi£170-£235 LDO 7pm
Lic 🅿 CTV
[£]

GH [Q] [Q] Kingsley Hall Hotel 8 Ulwell Road BH19 1LT
☎(0929) 422872 FAX (0929) 421194

Situated a short distance from the beach with uninterrupted views across bay.

7rm(6🛁) (2fb) CTV in all bedrooms Ⓡ * sB&B🛁£17.50-£20 dB&B🛁£35-£50 WB&B£120-£160
Lic 🅿
Credit Cards [1] [3]

GH [Q] [Q] [Q] ***Oxford Hotel*** 3/5 Park Road BH19 2AA
☎(0929) 422247

In a pleasant location on the edge of the town and close to the seafront, this comfortable guesthouse offers attractive and well equipped bedrooms. There is a good sized lounge and bar as well as a dining room.

14rm(7🛁🚿) (4fb) CTV in 12 bedrooms Ⓡ 🐕 LDO 4.30pm
Lic 🅿 CTV

GH [Q] [Q] [Q] St Michael Hotel 31 Kings Road BH19 1HF
☎(0929) 422064
Feb-Nov

Centrally situated near the steam railway and shopping area, this guesthouse offers neat, bright and nicely presented bedrooms. The lounge area is cosy and attractively furnished, with a piano in one corner. Home-cooked evening meals can be served, and proprietors Mr and Mrs Large are a helpful, friendly couple. There is a small car park in addition to the public car park and on-street parking nearby.

5rm(3🚿) (4fb) CTV in all bedrooms Ⓡ * dB&B£29-£30 dB&B🚿£31-£35 WB&B£85-£115 WBDi£137.50-£167.50 LDO 2pm
Lic 🅿 CTV nc5yrs
[£]

GH [Q] [Q] [Q] Sandringham Hotel 20 Durlston Road BH19 2HX (Follow signs for 'Durlston Country Park) ☎(0929) 423076

Mr and Mrs Sill are the new owners of this well maintained and comfortable guest house. Situated in a quiet residential area, it offers well appointed bedrooms and restful public areas.

11rm(9🚿) (5fb) 🚭 in dining room Ⓡ 🐕 (ex guide dogs) sB&Bfr£22 sB&B🚿£26 dB&Bfr£44 dB&B🚿£52 WB&B£150-£175 WBDi£192-£216 LDO 6.30pm
Lic 🅿 CTV
Credit Cards [1] [3]

GH [Q] [Q] [Q] White Lodge Hotel Grosvenor Road BH19 2DD
☎(0929) 422696 & 425510
rs Dec & Feb

Improvements have recently been made to this small but comfortable guesthouse. The bedrooms are nicely furnished and equipped with the usual facilities. Public areas are compact and a choice of breakfasts is available in the dining room.

14rm(13🛁🚿) (4fb) 🚭 in 10 bedrooms 🚭 in dining room 🚭 in 1 lounge CTV in all bedrooms Ⓡ * sB&B🛁🚿£17-£25 dB&B🛁🚿£34-£44 (incl dinner) WB&B£120-£140 WBDi£180-£205 LDO 6pm
Lic 🅿 CTV nc2yrs
Credit Cards [1] [2] [3] [£]

SWANSEA West Glamorgan — Map 03 SS69

See also Bishopston, Langland Bay and Mumbles

GH [Q] [Q] [Q] Alexander Hotel 3 Sketty Road, Uplands, Sketty SA2 0EU (on A4118, 1m from city centre on road to Gower Peninsula) ☎(0792) 470045 & 476012 FAX (0792) 476012
Closed Xmas

Well positioned for the city centre and the Uplands shopping centre, this established family-run hotel offers comfortable accommodation. Bedrooms are equipped with the usual facilities and also offer satellite TV.

7rm(6🛁🚿) (4fb) 🚭 in dining room CTV in all bedrooms Ⓡ T 🐕 (ex guide dogs) * sB&B£20 sB&B🛁🚿£30 dB&B£42-£45 dB&B🛁🚿£42-£45 WB&B£120 WBDi£190
Lic 🅿 🚫nc2yrs pool table weights exercise bike
Credit Cards [1] [2] [3] [5] [£]

SELECTED

GH [Q] [Q] [Q] [Q] Cefn Bryn 6 Uplands Crescent SA2 0PB (on A4118, 1m from Swansea Railway Station) ☎(0792) 466687
Closed Xmas

Top marks are gained for exceptional standards at this very well maintained, family-run guesthouse conveniently located near the Uplands shopping centre and not far from the city centre. Cosy bedrooms are furnished with a good range of modern facilities. Public rooms are spacious and full of character, with many Victorian features including ornate interior plasterwork and large fireplaces. There is an attractive lawned front garden.

6🚿 (2fb) 🚭 in dining room CTV in all bedrooms Ⓡ 🐕 * sB&B🚿£20 dB&B🚿£40 WB&Bfr£110
CTV 🚫

GH [Q] [Q] [Q] Crescent 132 Eaton Crescent,Uplands SA1 4QR
☎(0792) 466814
Closed 24 Dec-1 Jan

A friendly, family owned and run guesthouse is neatly tucked away in a quiet residential area, yet in a very convenient position for the Uplands shopping centre and not far from the city centre and seafront. Bedrooms are bright and well equipped and there is a comfortable lounge and breakfast room.

6🛁🚿 (1fb) 🚭 in 2 bedrooms CTV in all bedrooms Ⓡ sB&B🛁🚿£25 dB&B🛁🚿£40 LDO noon
🅿 CTV
[£]

GH [Q] [Q] [Q] The Guest House 2/4 Bryn Road SA2 0AR
☎(0792) 466947

This friendly little hotel is conveniently positioned for the city centre, beach and cricket/rugby ground which is just across the road. Well managed by the Tough family, it offers good value for money, with a range of modern bedrooms and some simpler rooms, together with a cosy bar and a choice of comfortable lounges.

14rm(6🚿) (2fb) 🚭 in bedrooms 🚭 in dining room 🚭 in 1 lounge CTV in 8 bedrooms Ⓡ * sB&B£14-£20 dB&B£28-£40 dB&B🚿£32-£40 WB&Bfr£90 WBDifr£150 LDO 1pm
Lic 🅿 CTV 🚫nc9yrs
Credit Cards [1] [2] [3] [£]

SELECTED

GH [Q][Q][Q][Q] Tredilion House Hotel 26 Uplands Crescent, Uplands SA2 0PB (on A4118) ☎(0792) 470766
FAX (0792) 456044
rs Xmas
This charming Victorian house has been thoughtfully converted by the owners Mr and Mrs Mesner, and retains much of the original distinctive character, with attractive interior plasterwork and cornices, an open staircase and polished wooden floors. With top marks for sparkling cleanliness throughout, the bedrooms are furnished in keeping with the period and have all the expected modern comforts. There is a pleasant lounge and the small breakfast room has a dispense bar. Outside there is a pretty little front garden, and the house is well positioned for the city centre and beaches or as a touring base for the Gower coast.
7🛁🚿 (1fb) 🚭 in dining room CTV in all bedrooms [R] **T** ✻ sB&B🛁🚿£31-£38 dB&B🛁🚿£41-£48 WB&B£145-£240 WBDi£220-£315 LDO noon
Lic ♨ CTV
Credit Cards [1][2][3][5][£]

SWAY Hampshire Map **04** SZ29

PREMIER SELECTED

GH [Q][Q][Q][Q][Q] The Nurse's Cottage Station Road SO41 6BA (off B3055 in village next to post office)
☎Lymington(0590) 683402
FAX (0590) 683402

This delightful little cottage next to the village shop and post office was the former residence of the district nurse for more than 50 years. Since the present owner, Tony Barnfield, took it over, the accommodation has been completely refurbished with admirable attention to detail. All the bedrooms have TV, radio alarm, tea and coffee making facilities and two rooms have their own modular shower room and WC. Plans were afoot last year to extend the dining room where Tony Barnfield offers a monthly changing, three-course menu for dinner, served between 6 and 9pm, at a very reasonable price.There is also an excellent wine list. Short break holidays and leisure pursuits can be arranged, and car parking can be provided.
3🚿 🚭 CTV in all bedrooms [R] sB&B🚿£25 dB&B🚿£45 WB&B£157.50-£175 WBDi£200 LDO 8pm
Lic ♨ nc5yrs
Credit Cards [1][2][3][£]

SWINDERBY Lincolnshire Map **08** SK86

GH [Q][Q][Q] ***Halfway Farm Motel & Guest House*** A46 LN6 9HN (8m N of Newark on A46, 8m SW Lincoln) ☎(0522) 868749
FAX (0522) 868082
Standing beside the A46 midway between Lincoln and Newark, this 18th-century farmhouse and stable complex has been cleverly converted into a modern motel, with some main house accommodation. The motel rooms all have modern en suite shower rooms, and all the bedrooms have a good range of facilities. The farmhouse retains much of its original character, offering a beamed lounge and an attractive dining room.
7rm(3🚿) Annexe 10🚿 (3fb) CTV in all bedrooms [R] **T**
♨ CTV
Credit Cards [1][2][3][5]
See advertisement under LINCOLN

SWINDON Wiltshire Map **04** SU18

GH [Q][Q][Q] Fir Tree Lodge 17 Highworth Road, Stratton St Margaret SN3 4QL (opposite 'The Rat Trap' public house)
☎(0793) 822372
Hosts Mr and Mrs Duggan are concerned to make guests feel welcome at their large modern house. Bedrooms may not be particularly large, but the decor, furnishings and facilities are all fresh.
11🚿 🚭 in bedrooms CTV in all bedrooms [R] 🐕 (ex guide dogs) ✻ sB&B🚿£23-£29 dB&B🚿£35-£40
♨ CTV
[£]

FH [Q][Q][Q] Mrs J Hussey **Weir Farm** *(SU114772)* Broad Hinton SN4 9NE (6m SW of Swindon) ☎(0793) 731207
FAX (0793) 731207
Closed 24 Dec-2 Jan
In the village of Broad Hinton between Swindon and Devizes, this elegant 18th-century farmhouse offers spacious bedrooms with many thoughtful extras, such as sewing kits, tissues and writing paper. There is a lounge for guests' use and breakfast is served at one large table in the dining room. This is a no-smoking establishment.
3rm 🚭 [R] 🐕 ✻ sB&B£18-£22 dB&B£30-£36
♨ CTV nc8yrs 🎾(hard)U 1000 acres arable beef dairy
[£]

SWINTON Borders *Berwickshire* Map **12** NT84

INN[Q][Q][Q] Wheatsheaf Hotel TD11 3JJ (6m N of Duns on A6112) ☎(0890) 860257 FAX (0890) 860257
Closed last wk Oct & last 2 wks Feb rs Mon
4rm(3🛁🚿) (1fb) 🚭 in 2 bedrooms CTV in all bedrooms [R] sB&B£28-£30 sB&B🛁🚿£42-£45 dB&B£40-£42 dB&B🛁🚿£58-£60 WB&B£174-£180 Lunch £12-£20alc Dinner £15-£25alc LDO 9.30pm
♨ 🏠
Credit Cards [1][3]

SYMONDS YAT (EAST) Hereford & Worcester Map **03** SO51

GH [Q][Q][Q] Garth Cottage Hotel HR9 6JL ☎(0600) 890364
This well maintained cottage is set on the banks of the river Wye and is popular with anglers, walkers and tourists. The Eden family offer genuine hospitality and immaculate bedrooms supplied with welcoming extras and decorated with pretty fabrics. There is a comfortable TV lounge, dinner is served by prior arrangement, and the cosy bar has a residents' licence.
4🚿 🚭 in dining room [R] 🐕 (ex guide dogs) dB&B🚿£44 WB&B£140 WBDi£241 LDO 3pm
Lic ♨ CTV nc12yrs 🎣

INN[Q][Q] ***Saracens Head*** HR9 6JL ☎(0600) 890435
Once a cider mill, this friendly family-run half-timbered inn lies alongside the River Wye at this lovely beauty spot. Many rooms overlook the river and they are all attractively decorated; several have en suite shower rooms. There is an upstairs lounge, again overlooking the river, with books, games and satellite TV. The public bar is long and narrow and features a red GPO box in working order; another lounge bar has a central fireplace. A good choice of menus is available in the restaurant, with bistro meals as well as à la carte and table d'hôte; fresh Wye salmon is a speciality, and there is an extensive seafood menu.
10rm(7🚿) (1fb) [R] 🐕 LDO 9.30pm
♨ CTV 🎣
Credit Cards [1][2][3][5]

SYMONDS YAT (WEST) (NEAR ROSS-ON-WYE)
Hereford & Worcester Map **03** SO51

GH [Q][Q][Q] Woodlea Hotel HR9 6BL (on B4164, 1.5m from junct with A40) ☎Symonds Yat(0600) 890206 FAX (0600) 890206
A family-run hotel dating back to the 16th century is idyllically

situated overlooking the River Wye on wooded slopes with views onto this famous beauty spot. Bedrooms are simply furnished and most have fine views. There are attractive public areas including two lounges and a cosy cottage-style bar. The gardens contain terraced lawns and a patio.

9rm(6⇄♪) (2fb) ⚥ in dining room ⓡ T sB&Bfr£22 dB&Bfr£44 dB&B⇄♪fr£53 WBDi£210-£245 LDO 6.30pm

Lic ▦ CTV

Credit Cards ① ③ ⓔ

TADCASTER North Yorkshire — Map 08 SE44

GH ⓠⓠ **Shann House** 47 Kirkgate LS24 9AQ ☎(0937) 833931

An imposing Georgian town house stands in the centre of the town. The bedrooms are spacious: there are plans to refurbish them soon. There is a guests' lounge and small dining room. Parking is over the road.

8⇄♪ (1fb) ⚥ in dining room CTV in all bedrooms ⓡ ✳ sB&B⇄♪£20.50-£23 dB&B⇄♪£36-£41 WB&B£126-£161 Lic ▦ ✗

Credit Cards ① ③ ⓔ

TALGARTH Powys — Map 03 SO13

FH ⓠⓠⓠ Mrs B Prosser **Upper Genffordd** (SO171304) LD3 0EN ☎(0874) 711360

Many guests return year after year to this guest house at the heart of the Black Mountains. Mrs. Bronwen Prosser takes delight in sharing her home - and in cooking the special Welsh cakes which her visitors so much enjoy! Each of the two pretty bedrooms has en suite facilities, TV and extra heating when required, while a traditional family lounge with exposed oak beams displays an abundance of personal bric-a-brac.

2⇄♪ (1fb) CTV in all bedrooms ⓡ ✳ sB&B⇄♪£15-£16 dB&B⇄♪£30-£32

▦ CTV 200 acres dairy mixed sheep

ⓔ

INN ⓠⓠ **Castle Inn** Pengenffordd LD3 0EP (4m S, off A479) ☎(0874) 711353

Once a hill farm, situated at the heart of the Black Mountains over 1,000 feet above sea level, an inn which is understandably popular with those who love the great outdoors also provides a suitable stop-off for tourists in the area. Modern bedrooms - two of which now have en suite facilities - are equipped with extras like televisions and hair dryers, and there are two bars: one is used for breakfast and bar meals and contains a pool table at one end while the other features a cheerful log fire and an interesting collection of bank notes.

5rm(2⇄♪) (1fb) ⚥ in bedrooms CTV in all bedrooms ⓡ ⅍ (ex guide dogs) ✳ sB&Bfr£18 dB&Bfr£36 dB&B⇄♪fr£42 WB&Bfr£120 WBDifr£150 Lunch £3-£8alc Dinner £3-£8.50alc LDO 9.30pm

▦

ⓔ

See advertisement on p.397.

TAL-Y-LLYN Gwynedd — Map 06 SH70

SELECTED

GH ⓠⓠⓠⓠ **Dolffanog Fawr** LL36 9AJ ☎Corris(0654) 761247

Surrounded by attractive gardens, this 17th-century former farmhouse is situated at one end of Tal-y-Llyn Lake, at the foot of Cader Idris Mountain and commands magnificent views of the lake and valley. The new owners Pam and Alan Coulter have made extensive improvements to the house and bedrooms, including the provision of en suite facilities and central heating. The brightly decorated rooms have solid pine furniture with pretty coordinated soft furnishings and extra

▶

thoughtful touches include a wide variety of toiletry items. A choice of lounges is available for smokers or non-smokers, and a traditionally furnished dining room with a feature stone fireplace seats six people at a communal table.
4rm(3⇌⌐) CTV in all bedrooms Ⓡ ✘ (ex guide dogs) ✳ dB&B⇌⌐£38-£42 WB&B£133 WBDi£220 LDO 5pm
▦ CTV nc10yrs

TARRANT MONKTON Dorset Map **03** ST90

INNQQQ **Langton Arms** DT11 8RX ☎(0258) 830225 FAX (0258) 480053

In the middle of a tiny village, this inn offers six chalet-style bedrooms in a modern annexe complete with courtyard where guests may enjoy the sunshine. The rooms are all very well equipped and each has a useful lobby area and very smart en suite bath/shower rooms. The inn itself has plenty of character and charm. There is a lounge and public bar where an extensive range of bar snacks is served. If more formal dining is preferrred, there is a cosy restaurant with tempting table d'hôte and à la carte menus. Breakfast is served in a sunny conservatory and the atmosphere throughout is relaxed, cheerful and friendly, with locals mingling easily with guests.
Annexe 6⇌⌐ (2fb) ⊬ in area of dining room CTV in all bedrooms Ⓡ **T** ✳ sB&B⇌⌐£35 dB&B⇌⌐£49 Lunch £7.50-£12.50 Dinner £7.50-£12.50 LDO 9.45pm
skittles
Credit Cards [1][2][3] (£)

TAUNTON Somerset Map **03** ST22

See also Churchingford

GH QQ **Brookfield** 16 Wellington Road TA1 4EQ (just out of town on A38) ☎(0823) 272786

This small family-run hotel continues to be steadily upgraded. The bedrooms whilst simply furnished, are reasonably equipped, have bright carpeting, a fresh decor and are generally nicely presented. All public rooms are comfortable with a warm, relaxed feel about them. Dinner is occasionally offered, depending on guests' requirements, and smoking is not permitted in the dining room. A small front forecourt parking area is provided.
8rm (2fb) ⊬ in dining room CTV in all bedrooms Ⓡ ✳ sB&B£15-£18 dB&B£25-£30 WB&B£105-£126
Lic ▦ CTV
(£)

SELECTED

GH QQQQ ***Meryan House Hotel*** Bishop's Hull TA1 5EG (take A38 out of town) ☎(0823) 337445 FAX (0823) 322355

This charming period residence is located in a village just one mile from the centre of Taunton. The house has been carefully modernised and features original inglenook fireplaces, exposed beams and also a working well that dates back some 300 years. The bedrooms are simply decorated which sets off the attractive coordinating fabrics and pieces of antique furniture. All rooms are en suite and amenities include direct dial telephones, colour TV and thoughtful extras such as baskets of fruit and quality toiletries. There is a comfortable lounge, separate bar lounge and at dinner a selection of dishes is offered, carefully prepared using local produce. The Clark family enjoy welcoming guests and all requests are catered for in a relaxed and friendly manner.
12⇌⌐ (3fb) CTV in all bedrooms Ⓡ **T** LDO 6.30pm
Lic ▦ CTV
Credit Cards [1][3]

SELECTED

FH QQQQ Mrs M Fewings **Higher Dipford** *(ST216205)* Trull TA3 7NU ☎(0823) 275770 & 257916
Closed Feb

An attractive Somerset long house in a farmyard setting at the foot of the Blagdon Hills, this hotel affords easy access to the M5 and the centre of Taunton. The interior reflects good taste, quality and charm. A choice of beamed lounges includes one with an inglenook fireplace and a small bar. Farmhouse cooking based on local ingredients is served at separate tables in the dining room.
3⇌⌐ ⊬ in 2 bedrooms ⊬ in dining room ⊬ in 1 lounge CTV in all bedrooms Ⓡ ✘ (ex guide dogs) sB&B⇌⌐£25-£30 dB&B⇌⌐£46-£54 LDO 8pm
Lic ▦ CTV ⌂ 120 acres beef dairy
Credit Cards [2] (£)

FH QQ Mrs Weatherill **Webb Hill** *(ST146269)* Heathfield TA4 1DP (take B3227 out of Taunton towards Barnstaple. 2m past Norton Fitzwarren take right turn signposted Heathfield, past the church to crossroads) ☎(0823) 433815
3rm (1fb) ⊬ in dining room ⊬ in lounges Ⓡ ✘ (ex guide dogs) ✳ sB&B£12-£15 dB&B£15-£18
CTV 73 acres mixed
(£)

TAVISTOCK Devon Map **02** SX47

See also Mary Tavy

SELECTED

GH QQQQ **Old Coach House Hotel** Ottery PL19 8NS (2m W) ☎(0822) 617515

Originally built for the Duke of Bedford in 1857, this former farm coach house is situated in the hamlet of Ottery. Sympathetically renovated in 1989, it has been converted into a small hotel of character with well equipped bedrooms, of which three are conveniently on the ground floor. Both the cosy lounge and the intimate restaurant have access to the patio and south-facing rear garden. A set meal or an à la carte menu is offered.
6rm(4⇌2⌐) (1fb) ⊬ in dining room CTV in all bedrooms Ⓡ **T** sB&B⇌⌐£22-£30 dB&B⇌⌐£40-£56 WB&B£117.50-£168 WBDi£139.50-£198 LDO 10pm
Lic ▦ CTV
Credit Cards [1][2][3] (£)

TEBAY Cumbria Map **07** NY60

GH QQQ ***Carmel House*** Mount Pleasant CA10 3TH ☎Orton(05874) 651
Closed 23 Dec-3 Jan

A charming little guesthouse stands in the village centre next to the Post Office. Bedrooms are attractively furnished with pretty bedcovers and curtains and quality pine furniture, and have lots of little extras. There is a small cosy lounge and attentive service is provided by resident owners.
5⌐ (1fb) CTV in all bedrooms Ⓡ ✘ (ex guide dogs)
▦ CTV
Credit Cards [1][3]

TEIGNMOUTH Devon Map **03** SX97

SELECTED

GH QQQQ **Fonthill** Torquay Road, Shaldon TQ14 0AX (on B3199) ☎Shaldon(0626) 872344 FAX (0626) 872344

This Georgian manor house has been owned by the Graeme family for over 120 years, and is set in 25 acres of gardens and grounds overlooking the River Teign. Two of the three delightful bedrooms in the west wing have en suite bathrooms and there is also a combined breakfast and sitting room. Breakfast is attractively served, with a good choice of starters and hot dishes available. Mrs Graeme is happy to advise guests of local inns and restaurants for dinner. Smoking is not permitted.

3rm(2⊸♠) ⊬ ® ⊁ dB&B⊸♠£44-£50 WB&B£147-£168 ▦ CTV ९(hard)

▷▼ GH Ⓠ Ⓠ Ⓠ **Hill Rise Hotel** Winterbourne Road TQ14 8JT
☎(0626) 773108

In a quiet residential cul-de-sac, this red-brick Edwardian house offers light, airy accommodation. There is a comfortable guests' lounge with television, and home-made bar snacks are available in the evening. Smoking is not allowed in the hotel except in the bar.

8rm(3♠) (2fb) ⊬ in bedrooms ⊬ in dining room ⊬ in 1 lounge CTV in all bedrooms ® ⊁ (ex guide dogs) sB&B£12-£15 dB&B£24-£28 dB&B♠£28-£32 WB&B£84-£96
Lic ▦ CTV
£

GH Ⓠ Ⓠ Ⓠ *Lyme Bay House Hotel* Den Promenade TQ14 8SZ
☎(0626) 772953
Apr-Oct

A large Victorian house overlooking the sea on Den Promenade, next to the church, is situated close to the town's amenities. Three of the bedrooms have private bathrooms, and TVs are available in rooms on request. A lift serves all floors.

9rm(3♠) (1fb) ®
Lic lift ▦ CTV ⊬

Castle Inn
Pengenffordd, Nr Talgarth,
Powys LD3 0EP
Telephone: (01874) 711353

The Castle Inn lies at the top of an unspoilt valley in a peaceful part of southern Powys. Grass covered mountains ascend on all sides. It has its own spring water drinking supply. All rooms are in a pine and white theme with colour TV, central heating, easy chairs and tea & coffee facilities. The Inn offers home cooked food, real ales and both en suite and non en suite accommodation in a quiet rural location.

MERYAN HOUSE HOTEL

BISHOPS HULL
TAUNTON
SOMERSET TA1 5EG

★ Comfortable Country House Hotel
★ Full En Suite Facilities
★ Close to Town Centre
★ Peaceful Village Surroundings

English Tourist Board
COMMENDED
♛♛♛♛

TAUNTON (01823) 337445

THE ROCK INN
WATERROW, TAUNTON, SOMERSET
Tel: Wiveliscombe (01984) 623293

Situated 14 miles along the B3227 (ex A361) Taunton to Barnstaple road, nestling in the Brendon foothills making places like Exmoor, Clatworthy Reservoir and the North and South coasts very accessible. Fully centrally heated, with comfortable residents' lounge. All bedrooms have private bath, wc, colour TV and direct dial telephone. Breakfast, Luncheon & Dinner are served in addition to food at the bar all year round. B & B prices from £21.00 inc VAT Per Person Per Night. Full English Breakfast. Dogs Allowed £1.25 Per Night. Accommodation is closed Xmas Eve, Xmas Day and Boxing Day.

GH Q Q **Rathlin House Hotel** Upper Hermosa Road TQ14 9JW
☎(0626) 774473
Closed Xmas rs Nov-Mar
This attractive Victorian villa is set in a quiet residential area a
little way from the town centre and seafront. Several of the rooms
are designed for families; some rooms have views over the large
gardens. The sitting room and dining room both have attractive
bay windows looking onto the south-facing gardens and sunny
terrace.
7⇌↾ (4fb) ⊁ in dining room CTV in all bedrooms ® ✱
sB&B⇌↾£16.50-£18.50 dB&B⇌↾£33-£37 WB&B£110-£124
WBDi£150-£165 LDO 6.15pm
Lic CTV
£

GH Q Q Q Q Q **Thomas
Luny House** Teign Street
TQ14 8EG ☎(0626) 772976
Closed Jan
Thomas Luny, the marine
artist, built this beautifully
proportioned house in the late
18th century. It is situated in
the old quarter of Teignmouth,
approached through an
archway into a courtyard.
Inside there is an elegant

drawing room with French windows leading into a walled
garden. Guests gather round a large table in the dining room
for dinner, a set meal skilfully prepared from fresh produce.
John and Alison Allan spare no effort in attending to every
detail. Bedrooms are well decorated and comfortably
furnished with many antique pieces and you can also enjoy the
flowers, bottled water and other extras that are provided.
4rm(3⇌1↾) ⊁ in dining room CTV in all bedrooms **T** ✶ (ex
guide dogs) sB&B⇌↾£28-£30 dB&B⇌↾£56-£60
WB&B£196 WBDi£280 LDO 8pm
Lic 🎱 nc12yrs
£

TELFORD Shropshire   Map **07** SJ60

GH Q Q Q Q **Church Farm** Wrockwardine, Wellington
TF6 5DG (in centre of village, opposite church)
☎(0952) 244917
A large brick-built farmhouse dating from 1750, Church Farm
stands opposite the church in Wrockwardine village. Much of
the original character has been preserved and there is an
inglenook fireplace and exposed beams. The dining room is
furnished with antiques and guests share one large table.
Bedrooms have a mixture of furnishings from antique to
modern. One ground-floor room is available in the house and
there is another room in a single-storey converted outbuilding.
5rm(2⇌↾) Annexe 1↾ (1fb) ⊁ in dining room CTV in all
bedrooms ® ✱ sB&Bfr£25 sB&B⇌↾fr£30 dB&Bfr£40
dB&B⇌↾£44-£48 WB&B£126-£189 WBDi£224-£308 LDO
9am
🎱 CTV
Credit Cards 1 3 £

INN Q Q *Cock Hotel* 148 Holyhead Road, Wellington TF1 2ED
☎(0952) 244954
This traditional town inn is situated at the busy junction of the
B5061 and the A5 close to junction 7 of the M54. Clean, simply
furnished bedrooms are available, together with ample parking

facilities.
7rm (1fb) CTV in all bedrooms ® ✕ LDO 9pm
🎱

INN Q Q Q **Swan Hotel** Watling Street, Wellington TF1 2NH
☎(0952) 223781 FAX (0952) 223781
Since purchasing the hotel from the brewery, the proprietors have
made great improvements to the accommodation; the rooms are
now smart and modern, and the meal choices vary from an à la
carte menu to lighter bar snacks.
12rm(7⇌↾) (2fb) CTV in all bedrooms ® ✱ sB&B£20-£25
sB&B⇌↾£30-£35 dB&B£35-£40 dB&B⇌↾£40-£45 Lunch £5-
£10&alc Dinner £5-£10&alc LDO 10pm
🎱
Credit Cards 1 2 3 £

TEMPLE CLOUD Avon   Map **03** ST65

FH Q Q Q Mr & Mrs Wyatt **Temple Bridge** *(ST627575)*
BS18 5AA (0.5m S of village, on A37 towards Wells)
☎Mendip(0761) 452377
Closed 25-26 Dec
A 17th-century white-washed farmhouse is situated at the end of a
short drive set back from the A37. Accommodation is provided in
neat bedrooms, and there is a cosy guests' lounge. Features
include mullioned windows and oak beams, and there is a large
garden. Breakfast is served in a pleasant dining room, and there is
a good variety of places to eat nearby. Bath, Bristol and Wells are
within an easy drive.
2rm (2fb) ⊁ in bedrooms ® ✕ ✱ sB&B£16-£17 dB&B£30-£32
🎱 CTV nc2yrs 150 acres arable
£

TENBY Dyfed   Map **02** SN10

GH Q Q Q **Buckingham** Esplanade SA70 7DU ☎(0834) 842622
Apr-Oct
8⇌↾ (1fb) ⊁ in 4 bedrooms ⊁ in dining room CTV in all
bedrooms ® sB&B⇌↾£20-£24 dB&B⇌↾£34-£40
WB&B£100-£120 WBDi£160-£180 LDO 5pm
Lic 🎱 ⊀nc5yrs
Credit Cards 1 3 £

⊠ 🎱 **GH** Q Q **Castle View Private Hotel** The Norton SA70 8AA
☎(0834) 842666
A family-run hotel ideally situated overlooking the harbour and
North Beach. The first-floor lounge and several bedrooms have
lovely views of the beach and harbour, and all the rooms are well
equipped.
12rm(7⇌3↾) (4fb) ⊁ in dining room CTV in all bedrooms ®
sB&B£14-£18.50 sB&B⇌↾£15-£20 dB&B⇌↾£30-£40 LDO
6.30pm
Lic CTV
Credit Cards 3 £

GH Q Q **Clarence House Hotel** Esplanade SA70 7DU
☎(0834) 844371 FAX (0834) 844372
Apr-Sep
A large Victorian hotel overlooks the sandy south beach, with
good sea views from some rooms and views of the garden from
others. Bedrooms are all en suite and well equipped, and there is a
bar and a choice of two lounges for residents.
68⇌↾ ⊁ in 30 bedrooms ⊁ in dining room ⊁ in 1 lounge CTV
in all bedrooms ® sB&B⇌↾£17-£40 dB&B⇌↾£28-£68 LDO
7.30pm
Lic lift 🎱 CTV ⊀nc3yrs in house entertainment
Credit Cards 1 3 £

GH Q Q **Gumfreston Private Hotel** Culver Park SA70 7ED
☎(0834) 842871
Closed Nov
Just a short stroll from the south beach you will find this cosy
guesthouse, run by the friendly owners, Bill and Dot Tovey. The

individually decorated bedrooms have recently been updated with clever use of bed canopies, satin bed covers and matching fabrics. A comfortable residents' lounge and cosy basement bar provide adequate facilities.

11rm(1⇌10♠) (5fb) ⓡ ✻ LDO 4pm
Lic ▥ CTV ⨍
Credit Cards ③

GH ⓠⓠⓠ **Hildebrand Hotel** Victoria Street SA70 7DY
☎(0834) 842403
Apr-Oct rs Jan-Mar & Nov
Veronica and Jim Martin have run this small hotel for two decades and make every effort to ensure their guests feel at home. It is situated a short walk from the walled town and just 200yds from the golden South Beach. There is an excellent first-floor lounge, a cosy basement bar and the hotel features award-winning floral displays, which are on show in season.

7⇌♠ (4fb) ✻ in 4 bedrooms ✶ in dining room CTV in all bedrooms ⓡ ✻ ✶ sB&B⇌♠£17-£20 dB&B⇌♠£29-£38 WB&B£95-£125 WBDi£145-£175 LDO 4pm
Lic ▥ CTV nc3yrs
Credit Cards ① ② ③ ⑤ ⓔ

GH ⓠⓠ **Ripley St Marys Hotel** Saint Mary's Street SA70 7HN
☎(0834) 842837
Apr-Sep rs Feb-Mar & Oct-Nov
Situated within the town walls and less than 100 yards from the sea, this guesthouse offers cosy bedrooms, a comfortable, traditional lounge, and a small bar. It has been run by the same friendly family for over 20 years.

14rm(8⇌♠) (6fb) ✶ in dining room CTV in all bedrooms ⓡ sB&B£17-£18 sB&B⇌♠£19-£20 dB&B£34-£36 dB&B⇌♠£38-£40 WB&B£125-£130 WBDi£180-£185 LDO 5.30pm
Lic CTV ⨍
Credit Cards ① ③ ⓔ

GH ⓠⓠ *Sea Breezes Hotel* 18 The Norton SA70 8AA
☎(0834) 842753
Jun-Sep rs Mar-May & Oct-Nov
This small, family-run guesthouse stands a few yards from the sandy North Beach and harbour, two minutes from the town centre. Bedrooms are modestly appointed, but all have TV and tea-making facilities. There is a comfortable combined lounge/bar on the first floor.

11rm(5⇌1♠) (3fb) CTV in 6 bedrooms ⓡ ✻ (ex guide dogs) LDO 4.30pm
Lic ▥ CTV ⨍

GH ⓠⓠⓠ **Tall Ships Hotel** 34 Victoria Street SA70 7DY
☎(0834) 842055
Mar-Oct
The sandy South Beach, town centre and bowling green are all within easy walking distance of this guesthouse where a warm welcome is extended by Marianne and Dilwyn Richards. Bedrooms are neat and warm, with attractive flower baskets complementing the pretty duvets. Some have en suite shower rooms. Public areas include a cosy basement 'nautical' bar and a comfortable modern lounge.

8rm(5♠) (6fb) ✶ in dining room CTV in all bedrooms ⓡ ✻ (ex guide dogs) ✶ sB&B£15.50-£18.50 sB&B♠£17.50-£21 dB&B£27-£33 dB&B♠£32-£38 WB&B£90-£127.50 WBDi£130-£170.50 LDO 5pm
Lic CTV ⨍
Credit Cards ① ③ ⓔ

Telephone national area codes are due to change by 16th April 1995. Please see the note under 'How to Use this Guide' at the front of the book.

TETBURY Gloucestershire — Map **03** ST89

P R E M I E R ⚜ **S E L E C T E D**

GH ⓠⓠⓠⓠ **Tavern House** Willesley GL8 8QU (3m SW on A433) 
☎Westonbirt(0666) 880444
Dating back to the 17th century, this delightful stone-built property is situated in the hamlet of Willesley, about four miles west of Tetbury beside the A433. The property has been sympathetically restored over the last few years by owners Tim and Janet Tremellen, and the well equipped bedrooms are tastefully decorated and furnished with country antiques; two have a separate shower cubicle as well as a bath. There is a comfortable guests' lounge, and breakfast is served in the cosy well appointed dining room, or in the secluded south-facing walled garden during summer months. Mr Tremellen is very happy to recommend one of the many local restaurants or inns for dinner. Smoking is not permitted in the bedrooms or dining room.

4⇌♠ ✶ in bedrooms ✶ in dining room CTV in all bedrooms ⓡ T ✻ sB&B⇌♠£37.50-£47.50 dB&B⇌♠£55-£63 WB&B£192.50-£220.50
▥ nc10yrs
Credit Cards ① ③

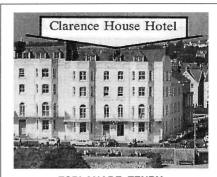

ESPLANADE, TENBY, PEMBROKESHIRE SA70 7DU
TEL: 01834 844371 & FAX: 01834 844372
South seafront near old walled town. Superb coastal views to Caldy Island. Residents only bar-patio rose garden. Seaview restaurant, excellent cuisine. Auto-safety Otis lift to all floors. All bedrooms WC/Shower, Col. TV, T/C inc. Groups welcome, Free brochure/Tariff. Quiet old world comfort offering modern amenities at reasonable cost.

TEWKESBURY Gloucestershire Map **03** SO83

GH [Q][Q] The Abbey Hotel 67 Church Street GL20 5RX
☎(0684) 294247 FAX (0684) 297208
Closed 24 Dec-New Year

This fine Georgian terraced town house has been converted into a family-run hotel of character. Situated opposite the Abbey gardens, it has a private car park at the rear. Bedrooms are modestly decorated and furnished in a variety of styles, but all offer good facilities including telephones and trouser presses. There is a small residents' bar and an attractive Edwardian-style restaurant where meals are served on weekdays.

16rm(7🛁7🚿) (3fb) 🚭 in 8 bedrooms CTV in all bedrooms Ⓡ ✳ sB&B£25-£30 sB&B🛁🚿£30-£42 dB&B🛁🚿£44-£50 LDO 9.30pm
Lic 🅿
Credit Cards [1] [2] [3] [£]

THAME Oxfordshire Map **04** SP70

GH [Q][Q] Essex House Chinnor Road OX9 3LS ☎(0844) 217567 FAX (0844) 216420

Built in 1870, this detached red brick property with a walled garden is situated in a residential area of the town. The majority of the rooms are very well equipped. Smoking is not permitted in the annexe nor the second floor bedrooms. There is a cosy bar, and an à la carte restaurant.

7rm(5🚿) Annexe 6rm(3🛁3🚿) (1fb) 🚭 in 11 bedrooms 🚭 in dining room 🚭 in lounges CTV in all bedrooms Ⓡ **T** 🐕 (ex guide dogs) ✳ sB&B🛁🚿fr£41 dB&B🛁🚿fr£56 LDO 7pm
Lic 🅿
Credit Cards [1] [2] [3] [5]

PREMIER SELECTED

FH [Q][Q][Q][Q][Q] Mrs M Aitken **Upper Green** *(SP736053)* Manor Road, Towersey OX9 3QR (1.5m E unclass rd) ☎(01844) 212496 FAX (01844) 260399

An attractive 15th-century listed thatched farmhouse is quietly situated down a No Through Road in the village of Towersley, just east of Thame. The cosy bedrooms are located in the farmhouse, with more rooms in the timber-framed Paradise Barn, each named after royalty and furnished with antiques and objets d'art. Breakfast is served in the barn, and the farm is set in seven acres of sheep pasture, with ducks and geese on the pond. Smoking is not permitted.

2rm(1🛁1🚿) Annexe 6🛁🚿 🚭 CTV in 7 bedrooms Ⓡ 🐕 sB&B🛁🚿£28-£37 dB&B🛁🚿£38-£50
🅿 CTV nc13yrs 6 hole pitch & putt croquet lawn 7 acres poultry sheep

THAXTED Essex Map **05** TL63

GH [Q][Q][Q] Folly House Watling Lane CM6 2QY
☎(0371) 830618

Quietly situated in a lane just off the centre of the village, this modern house offers three comfortably furnished bedrooms, one being en suite and the other two sharing a spacious bathroom. Downstairs, guests have their own smart lounge, furnished with some antique pieces and with a real coal fire. Breakfast is served in the small dining room on a communal oak table (separate tables can be set up if preferred) and French doors lead to the patio and garden which overlook the Chelmer Valley. Hosts Mr and Mrs King will happily transport guests to and from Stansted Airport which is just twelve minutes away.

3rm(1🚿) (3fb) CTV in all bedrooms Ⓡ 🐕 LDO 9.30pm
🅿 CTV nc3yrs

SELECTED

FH [Q][Q][Q][Q] Mr & Mrs Hingston **Piggot's Mill** *(TL608314)* Watling Lane CM6 2QY ☎(0371) 830379
rs Xmas

Great care has been taken to preserve the character of this converted barn and stable which forms the attractive and welcoming nucleus of an 850-acre arable farm run by Richard and Gillian Hingston. The bedrooms are well equipped and furnished, and the large lounge has comfortable seating, a log-burning stove, a piano, and good views, shared with the bedrooms, over the neat garden. Good breakfasts are served at a shared table in the airy breakfast room which has a heated flagstone floor and timbered roof.

2🛁🚿 🚭 in bedrooms 🚭 in dining room CTV in all bedrooms Ⓡ 🐕 sB&B🛁🚿£28-£30 dB&B🛁🚿£42-£45 WB&B£126-£180
🅿 nc12yrs 850 acres arable
[£]

THIRLMERE Cumbria Map **11** NY31

FH [Q][Q] Mr & Mrs J Hodgson **Stybeck** *(NY319188)* CA12 4TN (on A591 near junct B5322) ☎Keswick(07687) 73232
Closed 25 Dec

A Victorian Lakeland stone farmhouse, on a dairy cattle, beef and sheep farm, Stybeck is set back from the A591 Ambleside to Keswick road with an impressive backdrop of fells and crags. Bedrooms are comfortably furnished and attractively decorated, and a guests' lounge is provided. Smoking is not permitted.

3rm(1🚿) (1fb) 🚭 Ⓡ 🐕 sB&B£16 dB&B£30 dB&B🚿£32-£34 LDO 3.30pm
🅿 CTV nc5yrs 200 acres dairy mixed sheep working

THORNEY Cambridgeshire Map **04** TF20

FH [Q][Q] Mrs Y G Baker ***Oversley Lodge*** *(TF269041)* The Causeway PE6 0QH ☎Peterborough(0733) 270321

The friendly owners of this fenland farmhouse offer guests a warm welcome and, by arrangement, will provide traditional farmhouse food in the evenings. Bedrooms, which share a general bathroom, are clean and comfortable and the open plan public area serves both as a dining room and pleasant lounge.

3rm (1fb) CTV in all bedrooms Ⓡ LDO 7pm
🅿 CTV 260 acres arable

THORNHILL Central *Stirlingshire* Map **11** NN60

SELECTED

GH [Q][Q][Q][Q] Corshill By Thornhill FK8 3QD
☎(0786) 850270
Apr-Oct
3🚿 🚭 Ⓡ ✳ dB&B🚿£36-£40 LDO 10am
🅿 CTV
[£]

Telephone national area codes are due to change by 16th April 1995. Please see the note under 'How to Use this Guide' at the front of the book.

THORNTON Lancashire Map **07** SD34

GH Ⓠ Ⓠ Ⓠ Ⓠ Ⓠ The
Victorian House Trunnah
Road FY5 4HF (take A585 in
direction of Fleetwood and
exit at Thornton. Pass the
Gardener's Arms on right and
turn right at church)
☎Blackpool(0253) 860619
FAX (0253) 865350

Standing in its own pleasant
garden close to the B5268, this
delightful house is, as its name
suggests, full of Victorian charm and character. Essentially a
restaurant with rooms, it has been decorated and furnished
with care by the proprietors Louise and Didier Guerin, and
offers high standards throughout. There is an authentic period
parlour crammed with objects d'art, prints, paintings and fresh
flowers, together with a selection of comfortable chairs and a
cosy fire. Aperitifs are available in the snug bar, and dinner is
served by long-skirted waitresses in the elegant, well appointed
restaurant (lunches are taken in the attractive modern
conservatory) where chef patron Didier Guerin offers a French
menu with a wide choice of dishes. The three individual
bedrooms are most comfortable and equipped with modern
facilities and thoughtful extras; one has a four-poster bed, and
they are all sumptuously furnished and decorated in Victorian
style.
3⇌↑ CTV in all bedrooms Ⓡ T sB&B£49.50
sB&B⇌↑£49 dB&B⇌↑£75 LDO 9.30pm
Lic ⬛ nc6yrs
Credit Cards ①③

THORNTON DALE North Yorkshire Map **08** SE88

INNⓆ The New Inn YO18 7LF ☎Pickering(0751) 474226
6rm(1⇌↑) (1fb)Ⓡ ✖ (ex guide dogs) sB&B£21 dB&B£34-£38
dB&B⇌↑£40-£45 Lunch £4.10-£10alc Dinner £4.10-£10alc
LDO 8.30pm
CTV

THORPE BAY Essex

See **Southend-on-Sea**

THREE COCKS Powys Map **03** SO13

GH Ⓠ Ⓠ Ⓠ *Old Gwernyfed Country Manor* Felindre LD3 0SU
☎Glasbury(04974) 376
mid Mar-mid Nov
This Elizabethan manor house lies in several acres of parkland,
and has many notable features including a minstrel's gallery, an
oak-panelled banqueting hall, a mast from the Spanish Armada, a
secret code carved by Shakespeare and a priest's hole. The
accommodation is comfortable, with most of the bedrooms en
suite, and there is a good range of home-cooked meals.
11rm(7⇌2↑) (4fb) LDO 7.30pm
Lic croquet

THREE LEGGED CROSS Dorset Map **04** SU00

FH Ⓠ Ⓠ Mr & Mrs B Gent **Homeacres** *(SU096054)* Homeacres
Farm BH21 6QZ ☎Verwood(0202) 822422 FAX (0202) 822422
Parking facilities are available at this modern farmhouse near the
industrial park. Popular with both business and leisure users, it
offers a relaxed, friendly atmosphere and comfortable
accommodation in homely bedrooms made attractive with pretty
soft fabrics; most rooms have en suite facilities. There are two
lounge areas - one next to the breakfast room and the other (which

is equipped with books and games) on the first floor.
6rm(4⇌↑) (3fb) ✖ Ⓡ ✳ sB&B£17-£19.50 dB&B£28-£32
dB&B⇌↑£34-£38 WB&B£98-£119
⬛ CTV games room 270 acres beef sheep
£

THURNING Norfolk Map **09** TG02

FH Ⓠ Ⓠ Mrs A M Fisher **Rookery** *(TG078307)* NR24 2JP
☎Melton Constable(0263) 860357
Closed Dec-Jan
This idyllic rural retreat is quite hard to find, as the old redbrick
house hides behind a flint wall and is surrounded by outbuildings
and lawns. The lounge doubles as a breakfast room and, if an
evening meal has been requested, it is also served here.
2rm(1↑) (1fb) Ⓡ ✖ ✳ dB&B↑fr£28
CTV 400 acres arable

THURSBY Cumbria Map **11** NY35

FH Ⓠ Ⓠ Ⓠ Mrs M G Swainson **How End** *(NY316497)* CA5 6PX
(7m W of Carlisle) ☎Wigton(06973) 42487
Dating from 1764, this farmhouse offers attractively decorated
accommodation overlooking meadowland towards the Lakeland
hills. None of the rooms has en suite facilities, but there are two
separate bathrooms. The beamed lounge leads out to the garden,
and in the dining room breakfast is served at one large table. How
End is a working dairy farm of 200 acres.
2rm (1fb) ✖ in bedrooms ✖ in dining room Ⓡ ✖ (ex guide dogs)
✳ sB&B£14-£15 dB&B£28-£30
⬛ CTV 200 acres dairy mixed

THE ABBEY HOTEL

Centrally situated in a conservation area.

**This warm family run hotel offers private and
business accommodation at reasonable cost.**

**The hotel has a residents car park and all rooms
have a colour TV and Telephone.**

**There is a Resident's Bar and the restaurant is
open Monday to Friday.**

67 Church Street, Tewkesbury, Glos GL20 5RX
Telephone: (01684) 294247 & 294097

THWAITE North Yorkshire Map **07** SD89

GH [Q][Q] Kearton DL11 5DR
☎Richmond (North Yorks)(0748) 886277 FAX (0748) 886590
Mar-Dec

This attractive guesthouse, tea room and restaurant enjoys a small village setting. It features modern style bedrooms, a comfortable lounge, a snug bar and a large, well appointed dining room in which good old fashioned Yorkshire home cooking is the speciality.

13rm (2fb) 🚭 in dining room [R] 🐕 (ex guide dogs) * sB&B£23.50-£25 dB&B£47-£50 (incl dinner) WB&B£133 WBDi£164.50 LDO 6.30pm
Lic 🅿
Credit Cards [1][3][£]

TIDEFORD Cornwall & Isles of Scilly Map **02** SX35

FH [Q][Q] Mrs B A Turner **Kilna House** *(SX353600)* PL12 5AD (on A38, 5m W of Tamar Bridge) ☎Landrake(0752) 851236
Closed Xmas & New Year

This small, stone-built farmhouse is set in a large pleasant garden and overlooks the River Tiddy Valley; it is situated between Liskeard and Plymouth, just outside the village. Bedrooms are well appointed and comfortable and the public areas simple but neat, with a relaxed atmosphere. The proprietors have run it for the past twenty years and, having made gradual improvments, now enjoy a returning clientele.

5rm (2fb) 🚭 in dining room CTV in all bedrooms [R] * sB&B£16-£18 dB&B£30-£32 WB&B£90-£96
🅿 CTV 12 acres arable pasture
[£]

TIMSBURY Avon Map **03** ST65

GH [Q][Q][Q] ***Old Malt House Hotel & Licensed Restaurant*** Radford BA3 1QF (from A367 turn onto B3115 & follow signs for Radford Farm) (MIN) ☎Mendip(0761) 470106
FAX (0761) 472616
Closed Xmas

On the outskirts of the village. This former malting house has been renovated to provide spacious public areas and well equipped bedrooms which all have en suite facilities. The Horler family also operate a shire horse stud adjacent to the house.

10🛁🚿 (2fb) CTV in all bedrooms [R] **T** 🐕 LDO 8.30pm
Lic 🅿
Credit Cards [1][2][3][5]

TINTAGEL Cornwall & Isles of Scilly Map **02** SX08

[🛏☕] **GH [Q][Q][Q] Castle Villa** Molesworth Street PL34 0BZ (on entering Tintagel on B3263 turn left by Nat. West Bank signposted Camelford/Trebarwith, Castle Villa is 150yds on left)
☎Camelford(0840) 770373 & 770203

Built of Cornish stone in the early 1800s, Castle Villa is situated close to the 14th-century post office and the legendary Castle of King Arthur. The house has been carefully modernised by the resident proprietors and the bedrooms are brightly decorated. There is a cosy lounge, a small bar and a selection of bar meals is readily available in the attractive dining room. Three-course dinners can be served by arrangement.

5rm(1🚿) 🚭 in bedrooms 🚭 in area of dining room CTV in all bedrooms [R] sB&B£14.50-£15.50 dB&B£29-£31 dB&B🚿£34-£36 WB&B£91.35-£97.65 LDO 9pm
Lic 🅿 CTV
Credit Cards [1][3][£]

P R E M I E R S E L E C T E D

GH [Q][Q][Q][Q][Q] Trebrea Lodge Trenale PL34 0HR (turn off A30 on to the B395 after Launceston at A39 junct take sign to Tintagel, 1.5m before Tintagel turn left to Trenale)
☎Camelford(0840) 770410

Built of stone in the 14th century, this handsome, listed building stands in 4.5 acres of wooded hillside with breathtaking views across the village to the north Cornish coast. Enlarged in the 18th century, the house is now a graceful Georgian-style residence, where quality is evident throughout the public areas and bedrooms. The elegant drawing room is a complete contrast to the cosy snug, where there is an honesty bar, and a set four-course dinner is served in the oak panelled dining room.

6🛁🚿 Annexe 1🚿 (1fb) 🚭 in bedrooms 🚭 in dining room 🚭 in 1 lounge CTV in all bedrooms [R] **T** * sB&B🛁🚿£45-£50 dB&B🛁🚿£58-£72 WB&B£192.85-£239.40 WBDi£284.55-£326.20 LDO 8pm
Lic 🅿 nc5yrs
Credit Cards [1][2][3][£]

GH [Q][Q][Q] Trewarmett Lodge PL34 0ET (from A39 take B3314 then B3263 to centre of village) ☎Camelford(0840) 770460
Closed Nov rs Dec-1 Mar

A former public house located between Tintagel and Trebarwith Strand, this property has been carefully altered to retain its old world charm, and now offers six letting rooms and a popular bistro restaurant. The bedrooms are simply furnished and decorated and have fine country views. A cosy lounge and a cellar bar are also provided.

6rm(1🚿) (2fb) 🚭 in bedrooms 🚭 in dining room [R] sB&B£17-£20 dB&B£34-£40 dB&B🚿£39-£45 WB&B£110-£119 WBDi£164-£179 LDO 9pm
Lic 🅿 CTV
Credit Cards [1][3]

INN[Q][Q][Q] Tintagel Arms Hotel Fore Street PL34 0DB
☎Camelford(0840) 770780

Centrally situated in the village, this family-run, fully licensed free house has tastefully decorated bedrooms. There is an attractive bar with small lounge and dining areas. An extensive choice of dishes is offered from the blackboard menus, which always include several Greek dishes. The resident proprietors are well known for their friendliness.

7🛁🚿 CTV in all bedrooms [R] 🐕 (ex guide dogs) * sB&B🛁🚿£25 dB&B🛁🚿£35 Bar Lunch £1.50-£10.50 Dinner £5.50-£10.50 LDO 9.30pm
🅿
Credit Cards [1][3][£]

TINTERN Gwent Map **03** SO50

GH [Q][Q][Q] Valley House Raglan Road NP6 6TH (take A466 from Chepstow and turn left at Raglan Road, passing Cherry Tree Inn after 800 yds and Valley House after another 100 yds) ☎(0291) 689652

In a lovely position in a wooded valley just above Tintern on the Raglan road, Peter and Ann Howe's stylish, tall, Georgian house offers bright, spotless and comfortable bedrooms furnished with antiques, stripped pine and coordinating fabrics. The bedrooms are well equipped and have good en suite facilities.

3🛁🚿 🚭 CTV in all bedrooms [R] **T** * sB&B🛁🚿£26-£30 dB&B🛁🚿£36-£38 LDO by arrangement
🅿
Credit Cards [2][£]

INN|Q| **Fountain** Trellech Grange NP6 6QW ☎(0291) 689303
In an attractive wooded valley just outside Tintern, on the old
Raglan road, this rustic inn offers modest but clean
accommodation. The bars are popular with both locals and tourists
and there is also a restaurant where good value food is served.
5rm(1♠) (2fb)CTV in 4 bedrooms ⓡ ✳ sB&Bfr£17 dB&Bfr£34
LDO 10.30pm
▥
Credit Cards ① ② ③ ⓔ

TISSINGTON Derbyshire   Map **07** SK15

FH |Q||Q||Q| Mrs B Herridge **Bent** *(SK187523)* DE6 1RD
☎Parwich(0335) 390214
Etr-Oct
Part of a country estate within the Peak District National Park, this
stone-built house is part of a working farm. Guests will enjoy
comfortable accommodation and a charming country garden.
4rm(2⇄) (1fb) ⓡ ♪ (ex guide dogs) ✳ dB&Bfr£31
dB&B⇄fr£33 WB&Bfr£200
▥ CTV nc5yrs 280 acres beef dairy mixed sheep

TIVERTON Devon   Map **03** SS91

GH |Q||Q||Q| **Bridge** 23 Angel Hill EX16 6PE ☎(0884) 252804
A family-run guesthouse near the centre of town enjoys an
enviable position beside the river with its own small garden. The
bedrooms are well decorated and some now have en suite
showers. There is a cosy guests' lounge and home-cooked dinners
are served in the lower ground floor dining room.
9rm(5♠) (2fb) ✗ in dining room CTV in all bedrooms ⓡ ✳
sB&B£18 sB&B♠£23 dB&B£34 dB&B♠£36-£42 WB&B£115-
£145 WBDi£165-£190 LDO 7pm
Lic ▥ CTV ♪
ⓔ

FH |Q||Q||Q||Q||Q| Mrs B
Pugsley **Hornhill** *(SS965117)*
Exeter Hill EX16 4PL (follow
signs to Grand Western Canal,
take right fork up Exeter Hill
farmhouse on left at top of hill)
☎(0884) 253352
Situated at the top of the hill,
with panoramic views over the
Exe valley, parts of Hornhill
Farm date back to the 18th
century and it has been the
home of the Pugsley family for over 100 years. Bedrooms are
comfortable with attractively co-ordinating soft furnishings
and many thoughtful extras such as bottled water, herbal tea
and locally produced toiletries. The ground floor bedroom has
an ensuite shower room and is suitable for the partially
disabled. The remaining bedrooms have private bathrooms
across the corridor. Breakfast is served around one large table;
dinner is available by prior arrangement, a set meal using local
produce wherever possible. The hospitality is natural and
abundant.
3rm(1♠) ✗ CTV in all bedrooms ⓡ ♪ sB&B♠fr£18
dB&B♠fr£35 WBDifr£180 LDO 24hr in advance
nc12yrs 75 acres beef sheep

FH |Q| Rita & Brian Reader **Lodge Hill** *(SS945112)* EX16 5PA
☎(0884) 252907 FAX (0884) 242090
Just one mile south of the town on the road to Bickleigh, the
farmhouse occupies a quiet and elevated rural location set back
from the road. It is popular with people touring the area and
cyclists, children and pets are all made welcome. As no evening

meal is provided, there is a small kitchen available to guests to
prepare drinks and snacks.
7♠ (2fb) ✗ in dining room CTV in all bedrooms ⓡ sB&B♠£18
dB&B♠£34 WB&B£110 WBDi£180
Lic ▥ CTV 10 acres poultry sheep horses
Credit Cards ① ② ③ ⓔ

FH |Q||Q||Q||Q| Mrs R Olive **Lower Collipriest** *(SS953117)*
EX16 4PT (1m from town hall) ☎(0884) 252321
Etr-Oct
Mrs Linda Olive welcomes guests to her 17th-century
farmhouse in the beautiful Exe Valley. The spacious bedrooms
have many thoughtful extras, and the bathrooms are also of a
good size. In the comfortable lounge a fire burns in the
inglenook fireplace on cooler evenings, and there is plenty of
tourist information. Guests eat at a communal table and a good
set dinner is available.
3⇄♠ ✗ ⓡ ♪ (ex guide dogs) sB&B♠⇄£28-£30
dB&B⇄♠£56-£60 (incl dinner) WB&B£136-£142
WBDi£186-£190 LDO noon
▥ CTV nc16yrs ♪ 220 acres beef dairy
ⓔ

TIVETSHALL ST MARY Norfolk   Map **05** TM18

INN|Q||Q||Q||Q| **Old Ram Coaching Inn** Ipswich Road
NR15 2DE ☎Pulham Market(0379) 676794 FAX (0379) 608399
Closed 25-26 Dec

▶

Ṯḥe Ṯintagel Arms

Tintagel

AA Listed
QQQ

A charming free house, fully licensed, within
walking distance of King Arthur's legendary
countryside. Excellent centrally heated
accommodation. 7 en suite bedrooms, tastefully
furnished. Delightful Taverna, highly commended
for its delicious meals and
extensive wine list.
George & Margaret Hunter.
For further details please telephone:
01840 770780
Tintagel, North Cornwall PL34 0DB

Located four miles north of Scole, this widely popular 300-
year-old inn provides hearty home-produced fare in a
convivial setting, with log fires, rustic furniture and old beams.
Rooms and suites on the second floor are furnished in lavish
style .
5⇒↿ (1fb) ⊬ in area of dining room CTV in all bedrooms Ⓡ
T 💥 (ex guide dogs) sB&B⇒↿£40-£45 dB&B⇒↿£55-£60
WB&B£285 Lunch £5.25-£16alc High tea £3.45-£3.70alc
Dinner £8.20-£17.95alc LDO 10pm
🛗

Credit Cards 1 3

TOBERMORY See **MULL, ISLE OF**

TONBRIDGE Kent   Map **05** TQ54
See also Penshurst & Shipbourne

P R E M I E R ⚜ S E L E C T E D

GH Ⓠ Ⓠ Ⓠ Ⓠ Ⓠ **Goldhill
Mill** Golden Green TN11 0BA
☎Hadlow(0732) 851626
FAX (0732) 851881
Closed 16 Jul-Aug &
24-26 Dec
This beautiful house offers
warm hospitality. The
Millhouse was mentioned in
the Domesday Book and has
been restored by Mr and Mrs
Cole. One bedroom has a
four-poster bed, another a Louis XVth bed with silk
furnishings, and many extras are provided. Breakfast is served
in the huge kitchen at a large table with the mill machinery on
display behind glass. There is a sitting room set aside for the
guests, furnished with some fine antique furniture. We are
pleased to award Goldhill Mill the title 'Guesthouse of the
Year' 1995 for England.
3⇒↿ ⊬ CTV in all bedrooms Ⓡ T 💥 (ex guide dogs) ✳
sB&B⇒↿£55-£60 dB&B⇒↿£67.50-£72.50
🛗 CTV nc8yrs ꝃ(hard)croquet
Credit Cards 1 3 ©

TORBAY Devon

See **Brixham, Paignton and Torquay**

TORQUAY Devon   Map **03** SX96

GH Ⓠ Ⓠ Ⓠ *Atlantis Hotel* 68 Belgrave Road TQ2 5HY
☎(0803) 292917
11rm(9⇒↿) (6fb) CTV in all bedrooms Ⓡ LDO 5pm
Lic 🛗 CTV
Credit Cards 1 3

GH Ⓠ Ⓠ *Avron Hotel* 70 Windsor Road TQ1 1SZ (from A3022
follow signs to Plainmoor for Windsor Rd) ☎(0803) 294182
May-Sep
In a quiet residential area between the town centre and
Babbacombe, this family-run guesthouse has a friendly, relaxing
and informal atmosphere. Bedrooms are well equipped and there
is a traditional TV lounge and separate dining room. Audrey Auld
offers a daily four-course menu which includes home made breads
and patisserie, while husband Len supervises the service.
14rm(6↿) (1fb)CTV in 6 bedrooms Ⓡ sB&B£16-£22
sB&B↿£18-£25 dB&B£32-£50 dB&B↿£34-£60 (incl dinner)
WB&B£90-£120 WBDi£115-£160
CTV

S E L E C T E D

GH Ⓠ Ⓠ Ⓠ Ⓠ **Barn Hayes Country Hotel** Brim Hill,
Maidencombe TQ1 4TR ☎(0803) 327980
rs Nov-Feb
There are stunning views out to sea from this 1920s country-
house hotel and the well kept gardens, outdoor swimming pool
and terrace are added attractions. The bedrooms in the house
are very attractively coordinated and provide many extras, and
the two garden chalet suites are ideal for families. Good public
rooms include a large sun-lounge, a separate bar for pre-dinner
drinks, a television snug and a main drawing room. A choice
of menus is available in the dining room where a collection of
local Watcombe pottery takes pride of place on the dresser.
10rm(8↿) Annexe 2⇒↿ (4fb) ⊬ in dining room ⊬ in 1 lounge
CTV in all bedrooms Ⓡ sB&B⇒↿£24-£27 dB&B⇒↿£48-
£54 WB&B£160-£175 WBDi£224-£252 LDO 7pm
Lic 🛗 CTV ꝁ
Credit Cards 1 3 ©

🚭 🅿 GH Ⓠ Ⓠ **Beauly** 503 Babbacombe Road TQ1 1HL
☎(0803) 296993 FAX (0803) 296993
Proprietor Wilma Farrell offers a warm and friendly welcome to
her charming, flower decked guesthouse. The atmosphere is
informal and relaxing and bedrooms are comfortable and
individually furnished. The lounge is combined with the breakfast
room, where a choice of fish is a feature of the breakfast menu,
alongside the more traditional fare.
5⇒↿ (3fb) ⊬ in dining room ⊬ in lounges CTV in all bedrooms
Ⓡ sB&B⇒↿£15-£19 dB&B⇒↿£30-£38 WB&B£98-£126
🛗 CTV
©

S E L E C T E D

GH Ⓠ Ⓠ Ⓠ Ⓠ **The Berburry Hotel** 64 Bampfylde Road
TQ2 5AY (at Torre Railway Station bear right into Avenue Rd
signposted Seafront hotel 50yds before2nd set of lights)
☎(0803) 297494
Closed 3 wks during Dec-Jan
Standing in its own terraced gardens, the Berburry offers
tastefully furnished and individually decorated bedrooms
which have lots of extra facilities. There is a drawing room, a
bar lounge and an attractive dining room, where professionally
trained chef/proprietor Rosemary Sellick provides a four-
course daily menu which demonstrates her flair and has earned
a good local reputation. Bernard Sellick supervises the service,
helping to generate the relaxing and informal atmosphere.
Smoking is not allowed.
10⇒↿ (2fb) CTV in all bedrooms Ⓡ 💥 sB&B⇒↿£20.80-
£27.50 dB&B⇒↿£41.60-£55 WB&B£145.60-£175
WBDi£180-£230 LDO 5pm
Lic 🛗 CTV nc8yrs
Credit Cards 1 3 ©

GH Ⓠ Ⓠ Ⓠ **Braddon Hall Hotel** Braddons Hill Road East
TQ1 1HF ☎(0803) 293908
Facing south, this elevated hotel is conveniently located for easy
access to the town centre and harbour. Personally run by owners
Peter and Carol White, good standards of service and facilities are
offered. The bedrooms are comfortably furnished, with one on the
ground floor. A good choice of dished is offered for the evening
meal, which is served in an attractive dining room , which has an
adjacent bar. There is also a small sun lounge.
12⇒↿ (3fb) ⊬ in dining room CTV in all bedrooms Ⓡ 💥
sB&B⇒↿£16-£20 dB&B⇒↿£32-£40 WB&B£99-£129
WBDi£148-£178 LDO 5pm
Lic 🛗 nc5yrs
Credit Cards 1 3 ©

GH Ⓠ Ⓠ Ⓠ **Burleigh House** 25 Newton Road TQ2 5DB
☎(0803) 291557
Closed Xmas & New Year
A Tudor-style guest house situated on the main route into Torquay is within walking distance of the town centre. The bedrooms are pleasantly decorated with matching fabrics and there is pine furniture throughout the house. There is a beamed dining room where breakfast and dinner are served, plus a combined lounge and entrance hall.
9rm(4⇌fl) CTV in all bedrooms Ⓡ ⅋ (ex guide dogs) ✳
sB&B£13-£15 sB&B⇌fl£18-£25 dB&B£26-£30 dB&B⇌fl£30-£36 LDO 5pm
⬛ CTV
£

GH Ⓠ Ⓠ Ⓠ **Burley Court Hotel** Wheatridge Lane, Livermead TQ2 6RA ☎(0803) 607879
mid Mar-mid Nov
Quietly situated in an acre of grounds, Burley Court offers traditional style accommodation in well equipped bedrooms. There is a bar in the dining room, where a four-course dinner menu is offered, and the lounge overlooks the swimming pool.
11fl (5fb) ⅋ in dining room CTV in all bedrooms Ⓡ T ⅋ (ex guide dogs) sB&Bfl£23-£28 dB&Bfl£46-£56 (incl dinner) WB&B£90-£140 WBDi£140-£190 LDO 6.30pm
Lic ⬛ ❦ (heated) ❦(heated) solarium gymnasium table tennis pool darts
Credit Cards 1 £

🚗 ▼ **GH** Ⓠ Ⓠ Ⓠ **Chesterfield Hotel** 62 Belgrave Road
TQ2 5HY ☎(0803) 292318
In a popular road close to the main shopping areas and the seafront, this Victorian terraced hotel offers neat, en suite accommodation. Rooms vary in size and some are suitable for family occupation. The sitting room has floor to ceiling windows and ample comfortable seating. Traditional set evening meals are served in the attractive dining room.
12rm(11fl) (5fb) ⅋ in dining room CTV in all bedrooms Ⓡ
sB&B£12-£19 dB&Bfl£28-£42 WB&B£88-£135 WBDi£118-£176 LDO 4pm
Lic ⬛ CTV
Credit Cards 1 3 £

GH Ⓠ Ⓠ **Clevedon Hotel** Meadfoot Sea Road TQ1 2LQ
☎(0803) 294260
12⇌fl (4fb)CTV in all bedrooms Ⓡ sB&B⇌fl£18.50-£27.50 dB&B⇌fl£37-£46 WB&B£115-£173 WBDi£167-£225 LDO 5.30pm
Lic CTV 🏓 table tennis
Credit Cards 1 3

🚗 ▼ **GH** Ⓠ **Clovelly** 91 Avenue Road TQ2 5LH (at Torre Station take right hand lane into Avenue Rd guesthouse 100yds on left)
☎(0803) 292286
A real home from home atmosphere is created at this friendly guesthouse, and many of its customers return time and time again. The bedrooms are simply decorated and all are provided with colour and satellite TV and tea-making facilities. There is a spacious lounge with numerous pot plants and a separate dining room where a choice is offered at breakfast and dinner.
6rm (2fb) ⅋ in 3 bedrooms ⅋ in dining room CTV in all bedrooms Ⓡ sB&B£12-£14 dB&B£24-£28 WB&B£84-£98 WBDi£126-£140 LDO 5pm
⬛ CTV
Credit Cards 1 3 5 £

GH Ⓠ Ⓠ Ⓠ *Hotel Concorde* 26 Newton Road TQ2 5BZ
☎(0803) 292330
Standing on the outskirts of town, this guesthouse has been well modernised and offers spacious public areas, well equipped bedrooms and a sheltered sun-trap garden area with an outdoor heated pool.

22rm(14⇌fl) (7fb) CTV in all bedrooms Ⓡ LDO 6pm
Lic ⬛ CTV ❦(heated)
Credit Cards 1 3

GH Ⓠ Ⓠ Ⓠ **Craig Court Hotel** 10 Ash Hill Road, Castle Circus TQ1 3HZ (from Castle Circus (town hall) take St Mary Church Road (left by Baptist Church) first on right is Ash Hill Road)
☎(0803) 294400
Etr-Oct
Craig Court is a large detached Victorian house in a residential area of Torquay, with splendid views over the town to the sea. Bedrooms are well proportioned and carefully maintained, and several have en suite shower rooms. A choice is offered at breakfast and dinner in the spacious dining room. There is a comfortable sitting room and separate bar overlooking the neat garden, where David Anning's model narrow gauge railway is laid out. Visitors are invited to bring their own models to run on the line.
10rm(5fl) (2fb) ⅋ in dining room Ⓡ ⅋ (ex guide dogs)
sB&B£16.50-£19.50 sB&Bfl£19.50-£22.50 dB&B£33-£39 dB&Bfl£39-£45 WB&B£115.50-£157.50 WBDi£154-£196 LDO noon
Lic CTV model railway in garden
£

🚗 ▼ **GH** Ⓠ Ⓠ Ⓠ **Cranborne Hotel** 58 Belgrave Road TQ2 5HY
☎(0803) 298046
Closed Dec
This Victorian mid-terrace house, with its pretty and colourful display of flowers in the front garden is a regular winner of the Torquay in Bloom competition. Bedrooms are all nicely furnished. There is a comfortable lounge area and a cosy dining room where puddings are a notable feature.
12rm(11fl) (6fb) ⅋ in dining room CTV in all bedrooms Ⓡ ⅋
sB&B£14-£21 sB&B⇌fl£16-£23 dB&B⇌fl£32-£46 WB&B£95-£147 WBDi£115-£172 LDO 3pm
Lic ⬛ CTV
Credit Cards 1 3 £

GH Ⓠ Ⓠ Ⓠ **Cranmore** 89 Avenue Road TQ2 5LH (on A3022)
☎(0803) 298488
The Cranmore is a large semidetached house on one of the main routes into town, close to the shops and seafront. Friendly owners provide attractive accommodation with mostly en suite facilities and one four-poster room. A convivial atmosphere prevails in the Tudor-style sitting room and ajoining dining room, where host Ken Silver's watercolours are displayed.
8⇌fl (2fb) ⅋ in dining room ⅋ in lounges CTV in all bedrooms Ⓡ ⅋ (ex guide dogs) dB&B⇌fl£28-£34 WB&B£98-£119 WBDi£143.50-£162.50 LDO 3.30pm
⬛ CTV
Credit Cards 1 2 3 5 £

GH Ⓠ Ⓠ *Devon Court Hotel* Croft Road TQ2 5UE
☎(0803) 293603
Etr-Oct
In a quiet but central location the hotel is within easy walking distance of Torre Abbey Gardens, Abbey Sands and all the town's facilities. Some ground-floor bedrooms are available, and there is an outdoor heated swimming pool set in sheltered gardens. Varied home cooking is prepared by the family partnership.
13rm(8fl) (3fb) CTV in all bedrooms Ⓡ ⅋ LDO 4.30pm
Lic ⬛ CTV ❦(heated)
Credit Cards 1 3

GH Ⓠ Ⓠ Ⓠ **Elmdene Hotel** Rathmore Road TQ2 6NZ
☎(0803) 294940
Mar-Oct
Elmdene is conveniently situated near the railway station and the cricket ground, and within easy walking distance of Abbey Sands. Spacious public areas include a bar lounge and separate sun lounge. Five-course table d'hôte meals are offered with additional dishes carrying a supplementary charge. Many of the comfortable

▶

bedrooms have en suite facilities.
11rm(2🛁5🚿) (3fb) CTV in all bedrooms [R] sB&B£16-£20 sB&B🛁🚿£25-£30 dB&B£32-£40 dB&B🛁🚿£38-£46 LDO 5pm
Lic ♨ CTV nc5yrs
Credit Cards [1] [3]

GH [Q] [Q] [Q] Exmouth View Hotel St Albans Road, Babbacombe Down TQ1 3LG (from St Marychurch town centre follow Babbacombe Rd towards Torquay after 500yds turn left into St Albans Rd) ☎(0803) 327307 FAX (0803) 329967
Live entertainment, including Party Nights and dancing, is provided every evening at this friendly and informal hotel. The accommodation is gradually being upgraded and some bedrooms have sea views. There is a popular bar and a large dining room where chef/proprietor John Larkin offers a daily four-course set menu. There is a small TV lounge and facilities include a chair lift on the stairs.
30rm(24🛁🚿) (8fb) 🚭 in dining room 🚭 in 1 lounge CTV in all bedrooms [R] 🐕 (ex guide dogs) ✱ sB&B£14-£24 sB&B🛁🚿£16-£26 dB&B£28-£48 dB&B🛁🚿£32-£52 (incl dinner) WB&B£110-£180 WBDi£125-£220 LDO 6.30pm
Lic ♨ CTV
Credit Cards [1] [3] [5] [£]

GH [Q] [Q] [Q] Fairways Hotel 72 Avenue Road TQ2 5LF ☎(0803) 298471
Fairways hotel is on one of the main approach routes to the seafont, central for both the town centre and beaches. Four of the bedrooms have en suite showers and the provision of an ironing room is a useful extra. Breakfast, and supper if desired, is served in the dining room, and a comfortable lounge is also available.
6rm(4🚿) (2fb) 🚭 in dining room CTV in all bedrooms [R] ✱ sB&Bfr£14 dB&Bfr£28 dB&B🚿fr£32 WB&Bfr£107 WBDifr£156 LDO 4pm
♨
Credit Cards [1] [3] [5] [£]

🛏☕ **GH [Q] [Q] Fircroft** 69 Avenue Road TQ2 5LG (turn off A380 onto A3022. At Torre railway station take right fork and establishment 300/400 yds on left) ☎(0803) 211634
Situated about half a mile from the seafront, this small family-run guesthouse offers comfortable bedrooms, the majority with en suite facilities. Mostly home-made traditional set menus are served in the attractive blue-and-white painted dining room. There is a comfortable guests' lounge with TV.
6rm(4🚿) (2fb) 🚭 in dining room CTV in all bedrooms [R] 🐕 sB&B£13-£16 sB&B🚿£15.50-£18.50 dB&B£22-£28 dB&B🚿£27-£33 WB&B£70-£106 WBDi£98-£141 LDO 10am
♨ CTV
Credit Cards [1] [3] [5] [£]

🛏☕ **GH [Q] [Q] Gainsborough Hotel** 22 Rathmore Road TQ2 6NY ☎(0803) 292032 FAX (0803) 292032
Mar-Oct
7rm(3🚿) (1fb)CTV in 3 bedrooms [R] 🐕 sB&B£10-£14 dB&B£20-£28 dB&B🚿£24-£32 WB&B£70-£95
♨ CTV nc6yrs
Credit Cards [1] [3]

SELECTED

GH [Q] [Q] [Q] [Q] Glenorleigh Hotel 26 Cleveland Road TQ2 5BE (follow A3022 Newton Abbot/Torquay road until traffic lights at Torre Station, bear right into Avenue Road A379 and Cleveland Road is first left) ☎(0803) 292135 FAX (0803) 292135
6 Jan-14 Oct
Plenty of holiday facilities are provided at this special family hotel, including a beautiful outdoor pool, games room, solarium, darts and video games, plus live entertainment two evenings a week. It is quietly situated in a residential area away from the bustle of the town and seafront, and has a Spanish-style patio overlooking the lovely garden - a frequent winner of the Torbay in Bloom award. Bedrooms are very attractive and there is an elegant lounge with TV. A choice of menus is available in the dining room, and there is a bar-lounge complete with a small dance floor.
16rm(9🚿) (5fb) 🚭 in dining room [R] 🐕 (ex guide dogs) sB&B£18-£22 sB&B🚿£20-£24 dB&B£36-£44 dB&B🚿£40-£48 WB&B£110-£150 WBDi£150-£240 LDO 6pm
Lic ♨ CTV 🏊(heated) solarium pool table
Credit Cards [1] [3]
See advertisement under Colour Section

GH [Q] [Q] [Q] *Grosvenor House Hotel* Falkland Road TQ2 5JP ☎(0803) 294110
A well placed property close to the seafront and the main shopping area. Ten bedrooms provide good facilities, including satellite television. Guests can relax in the friendly bar or the large lounge, which is a no-smoking room, and breakfast and dinner are served in the dining room. Lighter snacks are available from the bar.
10🚿 (4fb) CTV in all bedrooms [R] 🐕 (ex guide dogs) LDO 4.30pm
Lic ♨ CTV
Credit Cards [1] [3]

GH [Q] [Q] [Q] *Heritage Hotel* Shedden Hill TQ2 5TY ☎(0803) 299332
Situated just a stone's throw from the seafront, this former gentleman's residence has been sympathetically re-modelled into a comfortable hotel with excellent leisure facilities. Most bedrooms have sea views and can inter-connect to form private suites. One spacious room has a four-poster bed. Carriages Restaurant offers a choice of menus and there is also a good choice of breakfast dishes - or room service of Continental breakfast. There is a lounge with television and a bar lounge for light meals.
20🛁🚿
See advertisement under Colour Section

GH [Q] [Q] [Q] *Hotel Trelawney* 48 Belgrave Road TQ2 5HS ☎(0803) 296049
Positioned within easy walking distance of most of Torquay's main attractions, this family-run hotel provides all en suite bedrooms. There is a comfortable sitting room, a separate bar and a dining room where traditional cooking is served.
14rm(13🛁🚿) (2fb) CTV in all bedrooms [R] **T** 🐕 (ex guide dogs) LDO 2pm
Lic ♨ CTV
Credit Cards [1] [3] [5]

GH [Q] [Q] [Q] *Ingoldsby Hotel* 1 Chelston Road TQ2 6PT ☎(0803) 607497
This quietly situated guesthouse has lovely views over the bay, yet is only 200yds from the beach. The majority of bedrooms have private bathrooms, and four of the rooms are on the ground floor. The spacious public areas are simple but comfortable, and a choice of menus is offered at dinner. The hotel is run by a friendly team of proprietors in a relaxed atmosphere.
15rm(3🛁9🚿) (5fb) [R] 🐕 (ex guide dogs) LDO 7pm
Lic ♨ CTV
Credit Cards [1] [3]

🛏☕ **GH [Q] Jesmond Dene Private Hotel** 85 Abbey Road TQ2 5NN (take last exit from rdbt at bottom of Union St, hotel opposite R.C church) ☎(0803) 293062
An attractive listed building with a balustrade balcony stands within walking distance of the town centre. Bedrooms are adequately furnished and there is a sunny breakfast room where a full breakfast is served, as well as a TV lounge.
10rm (3fb) 🚭 in dining room [R] sB&B£12-£15 dB&B£24-£30 WB&B£80-£90
♨ CTV
[£]

SELECTED

GH Q Q Q Q **Kingston House** 75 Avenue Road TQ2 5LL (from A3022 to Torquay turn right at Torre Station down Avenue Rd, Kingston House approx a quarter of a mile on left) ☎(0803) 212760

Apr-Oct

Friendly owners at Kingston House make all their guests feel instantly welcome. The bedrooms are prettily decorated and all have en suite or private shower and bathrooms. A choice of dinner menus is offered at individual tables laid with linen cloths and silver cutlery. The ample sitting room has comfortable sofas, a piano, lots of pictures and a warm, friendly atmosphere.

6rm⇌ŕ (3fb) ⊁ in dining room ⊁ in lounges CTV in all bedrooms ® sB&B⇌ŕ£19-£22.50 dB&B⇌ŕ£27-£35 WB&B£89-£119 WBDi£135-£159 LDO noon

▥ nc8yrs

Credit Cards 1 3 5

GH Q Q **Lindum** Abbey Road TQ2 5NP ☎(0803) 292795

Etr-Oct

A long-established family-run hotel centrally situated within easy access of the main shopping centre and the Abbey sands. Bedrooms are well equipped and include some on the ground floor. There is a comfortable lounge, a cosy bar, and a variety of interesting dishes is served in the dining room, which is supervised by the resident proprietor.

20rm(14⇌ŕ) (2fb)CTV in all bedrooms ® ✳ sB&B£12-£17.70 sB&B⇌ŕ£15.50-£20 dB&B£24-£35.40 dB&B⇌ŕ£31-£40 WB&B£84-£140 WBDi£125.50-£185 LDO 7.15pm

Lic ▥ CTV

£

GH Q Q Q **Millbrook House** Old Mill Road, Chelston TQ2 6AP (800yds from seafront) ☎(0803) 297394 FAX (0803) 297394

A small, neatly furnished hotel personally run by Lesley and Brian James is located a level 800-yard walk from the seafront. Bedrooms are well equipped, with de luxe rooms featuring dramatic soft furnishings and mini bars. The lounge has a small conservatory extension, and guests can meet in the White Rose Cellar Bar for a drink and a game of pool or darts. A three-course set dinner is served every day except Sunday. Smoking is not permitted in the hotel except in the Cellar Bar.

9rm(8⇌ŕ) CTV in all bedrooms ® ✶ ✳ sB&B£20 sB&B⇌ŕ£22.50-£24.50 dB&B⇌ŕ£45-£55 WB&B£138-£174 LDO 7pm

Lic ▥ mini-gym pool table

Credit Cards 1 3 £

GH Q Q Q **Newton House** 31 Newton Road, Torre TQ2 5DB ☎(0803) 297520

Closed 21 Dec-1 Jan

On the main road into Torquay, this detached Tudor-style house has ample private parking and is only a few minutes' stroll from the seafront and shops. The attractively decorated bedrooms offer many little extras, such as ironing facilities, sweets and hot water bottles. There is a large sitting room with family photos, and a separate dining room for breakfast. Guests are asked to refrain from smoking in the bedrooms and dining room.

8rm(6ŕ) (2fb) CTV in all bedrooms ® ✶

▥ nc5yrs

SELECTED

GH Q Q Q Q **Olivia Court** Upper Braddons Hill Road TQ1 1HD ☎(0803) 292595

A Grade II listed Victorian villa is set in a quiet residential area close to the town centre, with a secluded garden. The owners Malcolm and Althea Carr took over in 1991 and have

made improvements to the hotel, creating a new reception area, lounge and small dispense bar. The bedrooms are furnished to a high standard and are attractively coordinated; most are en suite. A four-course table d'hôte menu is served in the attractive dining room.

13rm(12⇌ŕ) (2fb) ⊁ in 4 bedrooms ⊁ in dining room ⊁ in 1 lounge CTV in all bedrooms ® sB&B⇌ŕ£17.50-£20.50 dB&B⇌ŕ£35-£41 WB&B£107-£128 WBDi£151-£171 LDO 4pm

Lic ▥ CTV

Credit Cards 1 2 3

GH Q Q **The Pines** 19 Newton Road, Torre TQ2 5DB ☎(0803) 292882

Apr-Dec

A small, no-smoking guesthouse has a colourful display of flowers in the terraced gardens. Bedrooms are freshly decorated and adequately equipped.

3rm(2ŕ) ⊁ CTV in all bedrooms ® ✶ ✳ dB&B£20-£32 dB&Bŕ£24-£32 WB&B£70-£126

▥

Credit Cards 3

GH Q Q **The Porthcressa Hotel** 28 Perinville Road,Babbacombe TQ1 3NZ (follow A380 turn let at Torbay Hospital & follow signs to Babbacombe, hotel 200yds from Babacombe Theatre) ☎(0803) 327268

In a quiet residential part of the town, this family-run, licensed hotel with a terrace provides attractive bedrooms plus a popular bar and dining room. A three-course evening is served at 6pm if required.

13rm(2ŕ) (3fb)® sB&B£16 dB&B£32 dB&Bŕ£36 WB&B£75-£95 WBDi£90-£135 LDO 8pm

Lic ▥ CTV

GH Q Q Q *Seaway Hotel* Chelston Road TQ2 6PU ☎(0803) 605320

A large Victorian residence is quietly situated in its own garden with glimpses of the sea. Bedrooms have recently been improved and the lounge, dining room and bar are all bright and well furnished. Dinner is available.

14rm(1⇌6ŕ) (3fb) ® LDO 6.30pm

Lic ▥ CTV

Credit Cards 1 3

GH Q Q Q *Sevens Hotel* 27 Morgan Avenue TQ2 5RR ☎(0803) 293523

This small hotel is situated in a quiet avenue within easy walking distance of the town centre. It is supervised by the friendly proprietors, Mr and Mrs Stephens, who create a relaxed, informal atmosphere. There are simple, comfortably furnished bedrooms and a lower ground floor bar lounge where guests can play pool and darts.

12rm(3ŕ) (3fb) ® LDO 4.30pm

Lic ▥ CTV

GH Q Q Q **Silverlands Hotel** 27 Newton Road TQ2 5DB (on A3022 after Torre Station traffic lights) ☎(0803) 292013

A well maintained Tudor-style house stands close to the centre of town and the seafront. There are prettily decorated bedrooms and breakfast is served at pine tables in the airy dining room. Lots of tourist information is available in the entrance hall-cum-sitting room

11rm(7ŕ) (2fb) ⊁ in dining room CTV in all bedrooms ® ✳ sB&B£13 sB&Bŕ£16-£18 dB&B£24-£28 dB&Bŕ£28-£36 ▥

GH Q Q **Skerries Private Hotel** 25 Morgan Avenue TQ2 5RR ☎(0803) 293618

The Skerries is situated in a residential area not far from the town centre. All the bedrooms are comfortably furnished and have

▶

videos as well as televisions. Breakfast and dinner are served in the dining room and there is a licensed bar where snacks are available, plus a homely sitting room.
12rm(3🚿) (3fb) 🚭 in dining room CTV in all bedrooms [R] ✳ sB&B£12.50-£15 dB&B£25-£30 dB&B🚿£33-£35 WB&B£84.50-£115.50 WBDi£115.50-£149.50 LDO 2pm
Lic 🌡 CTV
Credit Cards [5] [£]

SELECTED

GH [Q][Q][Q][Q] Suite Dreams Steep Hill, Maidencombe TQ1 4TS (2m from St Marychurch on B3199, turn right at Maidencombe garage) ☎(0803) 313900 FAX (0803) 313841
Located away from the hurly burly of Torquay and surrounded by countryside, this purpose built hotel provides spacious and elegantly furnished bedrooms. All of them are exceedingly well equipped and half of them seaward facing. A good value fixed price dinner menu is offered at the Thatched Tavern next door, under the same ownership as the hotel, and an extensive range of bar meals is offered.
14🛁🚿 (3fb) 🚭 in 4 bedrooms 🚭 in dining room CTV in all bedrooms [R] **T** ✳ sB&B🛁🚿£27.50-£40 dB&B🛁🚿£35-£60 WB&B£122.50-£280
🌡 golfing tuition breaks
Credit Cards [1] [3] [£]

GH [Q][Q] Sunnymead 501 Babbacombe Road TQ1 1HL
☎(0803) 296938
A single-fronted period property, situated some 600 yards from the town centre and Torquay's unique harbour, offers a relaxed atmosphere and comfortable accommodation in soundly furnished and decorated bedrooms equipped with tea-making facilities and television. An evening meal can be served in the combined lounge/dining room by prior arrangement.
5rm(2🚿) (3fb)CTV in all bedrooms [R] ✳ sB&B£10-£15 dB&B£20-£32 dB&B🚿£36 WB&B£70-£112 WBDi£99-£154 LDO 6pm
🌡 CTV

GH [Q][Q] *Torbay Rise* Old Mill Road TQ2 6HL ☎(0803) 605541
Apr-Oct
There are panoramic views of the bay and the harbour from the terrace and bar-lounge of this Victorian house. Vivian and Alan Plewes run their guest house in a relaxed and informal way, providing a four-course dinner (orders by 12 noon). Bedrooms are comfortable with one having a four-poster bed.
15rm(9🛁6🚿) (2fb) CTV in all bedrooms [R] LDO 11am
Lic 🌡 nc3yrs 🏊(heated)
Credit Cards [1] [3]

GH [Q][Q][Q] Westgate Hotel Falkland Road TQ2 5JP
☎(0803) 295350
The Westgate is a large semidetached house in a tree-lined road. The bedrooms all have en suite showers or bathrooms, and there is a lounge with bay windows and comfortable seating as well as a large separate bar. A choice of meals is available at breakfast and dinner in the dining room, which extends into a sun room with french doors, and special diets can be catered for by arrangement. A huge games room, with darts, table tennis and a pool table, opens onto the terrace.
13🚿 (2fb) 🚭 in 3 bedrooms 🚭 in dining room 🚭 in lounges CTV in all bedrooms [R] 🐕 ✳ sB&B🚿£20-£24 dB&B🚿£40-£48 WB&B£126-£147 WBDi£187.25-£208.25 LDO 8pm
Lic CTV nc5yrs games room pool table
Credit Cards [1] [3]

TOTLAND BAY See **WIGHT, ISLE OF**

TOTNES Devon Map **03** SX86

SELECTED

GH [Q][Q][Q][Q] The Old Forge Seymour Place TQ9 5AY
☎(0803) 862174
rs Xmas wk
The Old Forge dates back to the 14th century and is unusual in that it still has a working forge, complete with its own prison cell. The bedrooms are individually decorated and furnished in a cottage style. Some rooms have direct access on to the garden, and the most recent, self-contained unit is suitable for disabled guests. Breakfast is special, with a wide choice including a vegetarian option. This is served in the Tudor-style dining room, where cream teas, home-made cakes and jams can also be enjoyed. This is a no smoking house.
10rm(8🛁🚿) (4fb) 🚭 CTV in all bedrooms [R] **T** 🐕 (ex guide dogs) sB&Bfr£30 sB&B🛁🚿£40-£44 dB&Bfr£40 dB&B🛁🚿£50-£60
Lic 🌡 CTV ⛳ putting
Credit Cards [1] [3] [£]

SELECTED

GH [Q][Q][Q][Q] Red Slipper Stoke Gabriel TQ9 6RU
☎(0803) 782315
mid Mar-Oct
5rm(3🚿) (1fb) 🚭 in bedrooms CTV in 4 bedrooms [R] sB&B🚿fr£27 dB&B🚿£42-£44 WB&B£136-£142 LDO 8.30pm
Lic 🌡 CTV

INN [Q][Q] Steam Packet St Peter's Quay TQ9 5EW
☎(0803) 863880 FAX (0803) 868484
The Steam Packet Inn is an imposing Georgian building on the edge of the town, with a lawn leading down to a private quay on the River Dart. The bedrooms are simply furnished and some have en suite shower rooms. The attractive bar, with exposed brick work, stone walls and beams, is open-plan, but split into a dining area with blackboard menus, a music room and a children's lounge.
9rm(6🚿) (1fb)CTV in all bedrooms [R] ✳ sB&B£15-£20 sB&B🚿£18-£22 dB&B🚿£36-£45 WB&B£105-£140 WBDi£145-£190 Lunch £6-£9alc Dinner £8-£14alc
🌡 🎣 squash 🐎
Credit Cards [1] [3] [5]

PREMIER SELECTED

INN [Q][Q][Q][Q][Q] The Watermans Arms Bow Bridge, Ashprington TQ9 7EG (CON)
☎Harbertonford(0803) 732214 FAX (0803) 732214

Situated by the River Dart, next to Bow Bridge, this famous country inn has a long and colourful history. The character bars, with exposed beams and open fires, offer an extensive selection of dishes, while a more sophisticated table d'hôte menu is available in the informal restaurant. Bedrooms are tastefully decorated and furnished, and each has an en suite shower room and a range of modern facilities.

TOTTENHILL Norfolk　　　　　　　　Map **09** TF61

GH ⓠⓠ **Oakwood House Private Hotel** PE33 0RH (6m S on
A10) ☎Kings Lynn(0553) 810256
This elegant Georgian house of mellow brick with a slate roof is
set in its own well tended gardens. The bedrooms have been
professionally fitted with good rattan-faced laminated furniture,
with white woven bed covers, fresh decor and matching pastel
headboards and curtains. Good framed prints relieve the plainness
of the annexe room walls and enhance the pleasant blue and cream
colour scheme. Bathrooms are all tiled and have modern suites. A
six-course à la carte menu is offered in the dining room, which has
an attractive Victorian fireplace with a mirrored mantel, shuttered
windows and white linen covered tables.
7rm(5⇋ſ) Annexe 3⇋ſ CTV in all bedrooms ⓡ ✳
sB&B⇋Bſ£30 dB&B⇋Bſ£40 LDO 8.30pm
Lic ⊞
Credit Cards ① ③

TREARDDUR BAY See **ANGLESEY, ISLE OF**

TREGARON Dyfed　　　　　　　　Map **03** SN65

FH ⓠⓠⓠ Mrs M J Cutter **Neuadd Las Country Guest House**
(*SN663620*) SY25 6LJ (from Tregaron take A485 north towards
Aberystwyth, Neuaddlas is on approx 0.75m on left just over
bridge) ☎(0974) 298905 & 298965
This well maintained guesthouse is situated just a mile from town
off the A485 on the Aberystwyth side. Bedrooms are
brightly decorated, there is a comfortable TV lounge for guests,
with a cheerful log fire, and good traditional evening meals can be
provided. Private fishing is also available.
4rm(3⇋) (2fb) ⓡ ✸ (ex guide dogs) sB&B£16.50-£19.50
sB&B⇋£17.50-£19.50 dB&B£33-£39 dB&B⇋£35-£39
WB&B£115.50-£136.50 WBDi£171.50-£192.50 LDO 9pm
⊞ CTV ⅃ 25 acres mixed
£

TREVONE Cornwall & Isles of Scilly　　　　Map **02** SW87

GH ⓠⓠⓠ *Green Waves Private Hotel* PL28 8RD
☎Padstow(0841) 520114 & 521069
Etr-Oct
Green Waves is a family-run hotel in a quiet residential area just a
few minutes from two beaches, one of which has a natural bathing
pool. The bedrooms are mostly en suite and many have superb
views of Trevone Bay. There is an attractive lounge, a small bar
and a billiard room. Mrs Chellew supervises the kitchen, which
has gained the hotel a good reputation for its home-cooked food.
20rm(17⇋ſ) (3fb) CTV in all bedrooms ⓡ LDO 7pm
Lic ⊞ nc4yrs half size snooker table
Credit Cards ① ③
See advertisement under **PADSTOW**

TROON Cornwall & Isles of Scilly　　　　Map **02** SW63

🚪 ⚑ **GH** ⓠⓠ **Sea View** TR14 9JH ☎Praze(0209) 831260
Closed Dec
This spacious detached house on the southern outskirts of the
village has good sized, cosy bedrooms and a spacious,
comfortable lounge from which there is a splendid outlook over
the surrounding countryside. The well kept gardens include a
swimming pool.

7rm (3fb) ⓡ sB&B£11.50-£13.50 dB&B£23-£27 WB&B£70-
£85 WBDi£115.50-£130.50 LDO 6pm
Lic ⊞ CTV ✲(heated)
£

TROUTBECK (NEAR KESWICK) Cumbria　　Map **11** NY32

GH ⓠⓠⓠ *Netherdene* CA11 0SJ (off A66, on A5091)
☎(07684) 83475
Closed 25 Dec
4rm(2ſ) (1fb) ⅛ in bedrooms CTV in all bedrooms ⓡ ✶ LDO
4pm
⊞ CTV nc7yrs

TROUTBECK (NEAR WINDERMERE) Cumbria
　　　　　　　　　　　　　　　Map **07** NY40

GH ⓠⓠⓠ **High Green Lodge** High Green LA23 1PN
☎(05394) 33005
3⇋ſ ⅛ in bedrooms CTV in all bedrooms ⓡ ✳
sB&B⇋ſfr£25 dB&B⇋ſ£40-£50
⊞ nc⅃ ∪ use of nearby leisure centre

TRURO Cornwall & Isles of Scilly   Map **02** SW84

SELECTED

GH 🆀🆀🆀🆀 **Bissick Old Mill** Ladock TR2 4PG (7m NE on
A39) ☎(0726) 882557
Closed 24 Dec-1 Jan
Owners of some three years' standing have carefully
refurbished Blissick Old Mill without sacrificing its original
character and charm - but beware low beams and doorways if
you are tall! Neatly furnished and well decorated bedrooms are
equipped with a good range of facilities, and real fires burn in
the spacious lounge's large fireplace in winter. Fresh local
produce is the basis of set dinner menus which include many
French dishes, kitchen staff also creating the home-made cakes
and pastries served in a tearoom open to the public.
5rm(3♠) ⊁ in bedrooms ⊁ in dining room CTV in all
bedrooms ⓡ ✻ sB&B£25 sB&B♠£30 dB&B♠£50-£54
WB&B£150-£180 WBDi£227-£278 LDO 5pm
Lic ⅏ nc10yrs
Credit Cards ①③

GH 🆀🆀🆀 **Conifers** 36 Tregolls Road TR1 1LA (on A39)
☎(0872) 79925
An elegant Victorian property, this guesthouse is set in its own
garden, elevated off the A39 St Austell road, within easy walking
distance of the city centre. The lounge and breakfast room have
been tastefully redecorated and comfortably furnished. The
bedrooms, too, are well presented.
4rm ⊁ in dining room CTV in all bedrooms ⓡ ✻ (ex guide
dogs) sB&B£17 dB&B£34 WB&B£119
⅏ CTV
£

SELECTED

🛏💷 **GH** 🆀🆀🆀🆀 **Lands Vue** Lands Vue, Three
Burrows TR4 8JA ☎(0872) 560242
Closed Xmas & New Year
Lands Vue is a country home set in two acres of peaceful
gardens with croquet and a swimming pool. Home cooked
food using home grown produce and free range eggs is served
in the large dining room, which has panoramic views over the
Cornish countryside, and there is a cosy lounge with TV and
an open fire.
2rm(1♠) Annexe 1♠ ⊁ in bedrooms ⊁ in dining room CTV
in 2 bedrooms ⓡ ✻ (ex guide dogs) sB&B£15-£16
dB&B£30-£32 dB&B♠£34-£40 WB&B£105-£112 LDO 4pm
⅏ CTV nc12yrs ⋉croquet
£

SELECTED

GH 🆀🆀🆀🆀 **Rock Cottage** Blackwater TR4 8EU
☎(0872) 560252
An 18th-century beamed cottage located in the village of
Blackwater on the old A30. Bedrooms are compact and
tastefully furnished; one is located on the ground floor. There
are two charming sitting rooms, both very comfortable, with
beams and original stone walls. Dinner is available by prior
arrangement from a varied à la carte menu, and as Rock
Cottage is unlicensed, guests are encouraged to bring their
own wine. A good choice of dishes is offered at breakfast, and
Shirley and Brian Wakeling ensure guests friendly, personal

service in a relaxed, informal atmosphere. Smoking is not
permitted.
3♠ ⓡ ✻ ✻ dB&B♠fr£37
⅏ CTV nc

TUNBRIDGE WELLS (ROYAL) Kent   Map **05** TQ53
See also **Frant**

SELECTED

GH 🆀🆀🆀🆀 **Danehurst House** 41 Lower Green Road,
Rusthall TN4 8TW ☎(0892) 527739 FAX (0892) 514804
An immaculately kept Victorian home in a quiet, residential
area, with patio, garden and fish pond. Proprietor Angela
Godbold has furnished each bedroom individually with
several extra thoughtful touches. There is a cosy lounge with
books and an honesty bar. Breakfast is served in the
conservatory and a three-course dinner in the dining room. A
snack menu is also available.
6rm(4⇔♠) (1fb) CTV in all bedrooms ⓡ ✻ ✻ sB&B£25-
£29.50 sB&B⇔♠£45 dB&B£39.50 dB&B⇔♠£55
WB&B£206.50-£315 WBDi£339-£472.50 LDO 6pm
Lic ⅏ CTV
Credit Cards ①③

SELECTED

GH 🆀🆀🆀🆀 **St Martins** 31 Broadwater Down TN2 5NL
☎Tunbridge Wells(0892) 536857
Closed Xmas & New Year
In a peaceful residential within easy walking distance of the
town centre, this large Victorian house has three bedrooms, all
tastefully decorated and provided with personal touches. In the
dining room, tables are attractivly laid and there is an informal
guest lounge with TV and video. Mrs Henderson assures you
of a hospitable welcome.
3⇔♠ (1fb) ⊁ CTV in all bedrooms ⓡ ✻ (ex guide dogs) ✻
sB&B⇔♠£27.50-£36.50 dB&B⇔♠£42.50-£52.50
⅏ CTV
Credit Cards ①③

TWO BRIDGES Devon   Map **02** SX67

GH 🆀🆀🆀 *Cherrybrook Hotel* PL20 6SP
☎Tavistock(0822) 88260
Closed 20 Dec-4 Jan
Originally a farmhouse, this small family run hotel is located in
the heart of Dartmoor, set in three and a half acres of grounds.
Bedrooms are comfortable and decorated in attractive colours. The
cosy lounge/bar features beams and a slate floor. The table d'hôte
dinner menus offer fresh local produce, and owners Andy and
Margaret Duncan are members of Taste of the West, ensuring
standards are high.
7rm(6♠) (2fb) CTV in all bedrooms ⓡ LDO 7.15pm
Lic ⅏

TWYNHOLM Dumfries & Galloway *Kirkcudbrightshire*
          Map **11** NX65

SELECTED

GH 🆀🆀🆀🆀 **Fresh Fields** DG6 4PB ☎(05576) 221
FAX (05576) 221
Mar-Oct
Conveniently situated, just minutes from the A75, in this
relatively undiscovered region of Scotland, is Len and Ivy
Stanley's attractive home, where they successfully create a

relaxed, informal atmosphere. It is a distinctive, three-gabled detached house with a pleasant garden, which is tastefully decorated and furnished throughout. Nowhere is over spacious but it is all most comfortable and spotlessly maintained. The thoughtfully equipped bedrooms are delightful with their striking fabrics, and all have private facilities. There is a comfortable sitting room and dining room, where a five-course dinner is served. The menu features sound home cooking and is changed every day.
5🚿 🚭 in 2 bedrooms 🚭 in lounges [R] * sB&B🚿£39-£40 dB&B🚿£78-£80 (incl dinner) LDO 5.30pm
Lic 🅿 CTV nc5yrs
[£]

TYNEMOUTH Tyne & Wear Map **12** NZ36

SELECTED

GH [Q][Q][Q][Q] Hope House 47 Percy Gardens NE30 4HH
☎091-257 1989 FAX 091-257 1989
An elegant Victorian house which overlooks the sea and coastline, yet is situated within 20 minutes' drive of the city centre. Owned by Anna and Pascal Delin, it is opulently furnished and decorated throughout, in a style reminiscent of the luxury of the period. The three bedrooms are very spacious and two have sea views; a stair chair lift operates to all floors. The beautifully furnished and decorated dining room features a handsome oval Georgian table, and the drawing room enjoys sea views and fine period furnishings.
3rm(1🛁2🚿) (1fb)CTV in all bedrooms [R] 🐕 (ex guide dogs) * sB&B🛁🚿£35-£42.50 dB&B🛁🚿£37.50-£47.50 LDO 9pm
Lic 🅿
Credit Cards [1][2][3][5] [£]

TYWARDREATH Cornwall & Isles of Scilly Map **02** SX05

SELECTED

GH [Q][Q][Q][Q] Elmswood Tehidy Road PL24 2QD (situated in village centre , opposite St Marys church)
☎Par(0726) 814221
This very attractive hotel offers excellent standards, a friendly atmosphere and good value. Bedrooms are individually decorated, and furnished with pretty coordinated fabrics and modern en suite facilities. One or two also offer a flower-filled balcony to add to guests' enjoyment of the lovely rural views. Public areas are comfortable and have a fresh, pretty decor, and there is a colourful garden with tables and chairs set out for guests in good weather.
7rm(1🛁4🚿) (1fb) 🚭 in dining room CTV in all bedrooms [R] 🐕 (ex guide dogs) * sB&B£17-£21 sB&B🛁🚿£25 dB&B£34 dB&B🛁🚿£38-£40 WB&B£119-£175 WBDi£175-£231 LDO noon
Lic 🅿 CTV

UCKFIELD East Sussex Map **05** TQ42

SELECTED

GH [Q][Q][Q][Q] Hooke Hall 250 High Street TN22 1EN
☎(0825) 761578 FAX (0825) 768025
Closed 25-31 Dec
This elegant Queen Anne house stands at the top of the High Street of this small Sussex town and has been transformed by owners Mr and Mrs Percy into a tastefully appointed, yet friendly and relaxing place to stay. Bedrooms are named after historic pairs of lovers, and all have en suite bathrooms and are individually furnished and decorated to offer a high standard of comfort. In the attractive restaurant, the short à la carte menu may include dishes such as the marinated herrings, roast rack of lamb and chocolate marquise enjoyed by our inspector. Although the restaurant is open to non-residents, the atmosphere here is that of a family home, with rooms full of comfortable sofas, antique furniture and open fires.
9rm(7🛁1🚿) 🚭 in dining room CTV in all bedrooms [R] T 🐕 sB&B🛁🚿£40-£70 dB&B🛁🚿£60-£110 LDO 9pm
Lic 🅿 nc10yrs
Credit Cards [1][2][3]

SELECTED

GH [Q][Q][Q][Q] South Paddock Maresfield Park TN22 2HA
☎(0825) 762335
This delightful country house is set in 3.5 acres of landscaped gardens, found down a peaceful private road opposite the church in the centre of Maresfield village. There are two bedrooms, both facing south, attractively furnished and decorated, and sharing the large bathroom across the hall. They are twin-bedded rooms, but other beds are available to accommodate families. There is a comfortable lounge with a real log fire, and breakfasts, featuring home-made preserves, are taken around the large antique dining table. Major and Mrs Allt are friendly hosts and always available to provide local information and anything else guests might need.
3rm CTV in all bedrooms [R] 🐕 (ex guide dogs) sB&B£32-£36 dB&B£48-£53 WB&B£144-£220
🅿 CTV nc5yrs croquet
[£]

CHERRYBROOK HOTEL
TWO BRIDGES
YELVERTON
DEVON PL20 6SP
Telephone: (01822) 880260

Set in the heart of the National Park, this early 19th century, family run hotel has a splendidly central position for a Dartmoor holiday. All bedrooms have own private facilities and the views from the front are magnificent.
There is good quality home cooked food, where possible using fresh local produce, including fresh herbs from the garden. There is always a choice on the menu.

FH Q Q Q Mr & Mrs D Salmon **Sliders Farm** *(TQ404257)*
Furners Green TN22 3RT (1m S of Danehill village on A275,
signposted at small crossroads) 🕿Danehill(0825) 790258
FAX (0825) 790125
Closed 21 Dec-1 Jan
There are plenty of outdoor pursuits at this quiet farmhouse,
located south of the small village of Danehill. The building is
surrounded by 30 acres of land with some animals and a trout
lake. The accommodation and public areas are spacious and the
hosts are keen to make their guests feel at home.
3⇌🛏 (1fb) ⊬ in dining room CTV in all
bedrooms ® 🛏 sB&B⇌🛏£25 dB&B⇌🛏£38-£50 WB&B£133-
£175 WBDi£220-£260 LDO 24hrs prior
🅫 ⚡(heated) ⚲(hard)🛇 30 acres non working
£

UFFCULME Devon   Map **03** ST01

GH Q Q Q **Gaddon Leaze** Smithincott EX15 3DL
🕿(0884) 840267
Closed Xmas
2rm(1⇌1🛏) (1fb) ⊬ in bedrooms CTV in all bedrooms ® LDO
24hrs
CTV nc6yrs

FH Q Q Mrs S R Farley **Houndaller** *(ST058138)* EX15 3ET
(0.25m from junct 27 of M5) 🕿Craddock(0884) 840246
This 16th-century Devonshire longhouse is situated only a quarter
of a mile from the M5 at junction 27, and is part of a 600-acre
mixed farm. There are two spacious family bedrooms and a
lounge/dining room where guests can enjoy their home-cooked
breakfasts seated around the large communal table, well looked
after by the Farleys.
3rm (2fb)CTV in 2 bedrooms ® ✳ sB&B£16-£17 dB&B£32-£34
🅫 CTV 176 acres arable beef sheep
Credit Cards ② ③ £

ULLAPOOL Highland *Ross & Cromarty*   Map **14** NH19

SELECTED

GH Q Q Q Q **Ardvreck** Morefield Brae IV26 2TH (N on
A835) 🕿(0854) 612028 FAX (0854) 612028
10🛏 (2fb) ⊬ CTV in all bedrooms ® ✳ sB&B🛏£18-£24
dB&B🛏£34-£44 WB&B£119-£147
🅫 ♨
£

SELECTED

GH Q Q Q Q **The Sheiling** Garve Road IV26 2SX
🕿(085461) 2947
Closed Xmas & New Year
Owners Duncan and Mhairi MacKenzie give guests a warm
welcome to their delightful home which stands in its own
garden beside the picturesque shore of Loch Broom.
Bedrooms are bright and airy, and public areas include a
comfortable lounge and neat split-level dining room where
hearty breakfasts are served at separate tables. This is a no-
smoking establishment.
7rm(2⇌5🛏) ⊬ ® 🛏 (ex guide dogs) sB&B⇌🛏£18-£25
dB&B⇌🛏£36-£40 WB&B£126-£140
🅫 CTV 🛇 sauna
£

UNDERBARROW Cumbria   Map **07** SD49

SELECTED

FH Q Q Q Q Mrs D M Swindlehurst **Tranthwaite Hall**
(SD469930) LA8 8HG 🕿Crosthwaite(05395) 68285
A charming Cumbrian farmhouse full of character and
lovingly cared for by Mr & Mrs Swindlehurst who offer a
friendly welcome to their guests. There are two well furnished
bedrooms, a comfortable lounge with a range of books and a
cosy dining room. From the centre of Underbarrow follow the
Kendal road for about 300 yards then turn left into a lane
which leads to the farmhouse.
2⇌🛏 (1fb) ⊬ ® 🛏 (ex guide dogs) ✳ dB&B⇌🛏£32-£36
WB&Bfr£112
🅫 CTV 200 acres dairy sheep
£

UPPINGHAM Leicestershire   Map **04** SP89

SELECTED

GH Q Q Q Q **Rutland House** 61 High Street East LE15 9PY
🕿(0572) 822497 FAX (0572) 822497
This comfortable house is located at the quieter end of High
Street East, with a small car parking area to the rear. The
spacious bedrooms, including one ground floor room, have
been comfortably furnished to compensate for the lack of
lounge area. Each room has en suite facilities, most now with
showers over the baths. Breakfast is taken in the strictly no-
smoking dining room.
4⇌🛏 (1fb) ⊬ in dining room CTV in all bedrooms ® ✳
sB&B⇌🛏£29 dB&B⇌🛏£39
🅫
Credit Cards ① ③ £

UPTON UPON SEVERN Hereford & Worcester   Map **03** SO84

GH Q Q Q **Pool House** WR8 0PA 🕿(0684) 592151
Closed Xmas
A substantial Queen Anne country house is situated a short
distance from the town, on the banks of the river Severn. The
comfortable bedrooms are generally well proportioned, with
individual decor and furnishings; most have private bathrooms
and views of the garden, and one room has a four-poster bed. The
comfortable sitting room has an open fire, and there is also a
smaller TV lounge. Breakfast is served in the dining room, which
overlooks the lawns sweeping down to the river. Proprietors Brian
and Jill Webb provide a personal service to guests in their
attractive country house hotel. Smoking is not permitted in
bedrooms or the dining room.
9rm(3⇌3🛏) (2fb) ⊬ in bedrooms ⊬ in dining room CTV in 1
bedroom ® 🛏 ✳ sB&B£22-£24 sB&B⇌🛏£31.50-£34
dB&B£35-£40 dB&B⇌🛏£46-£50 WB&B£105-£186
Lic CTV 🛇
Credit Cards ① ③ £

UTTOXETER Staffordshire   Map **07** SK03

GH Q Q Q *Hillcrest* 3 Leighton Road ST14 8BL 🕿(0889) 564627
Closed Xmas Day
A considerably modernised, well maintained detached Victorian
house with very friendly proprietors who are regularly making
improvements. It is located in a residential area close to the town
centre, and offers attractively decorated bedrooms with modern
equipment and facilities; family rooms are available, and one
room is located on the ground floor; all bedrooms are no smoking.
There is a spacious lounge, and separate tables are provided in the
dining room.

7🛁🚿 (6fb) CTV in all bedrooms [R] 🐕 (ex guide dogs) LDO 4pm
Lic ♨ CTV
Credit Cards [1][2][3]

VENN OTTERY Devon Map **03** SY09

GH [Q][Q][Q] **Venn Ottery Barton Country Hotel** EX11 1RZ ☎Ottery St Mary(0404) 812733

Built in 1530 this former farmhouse has many original features; there are inglenook fireplaces, beamed ceilings, bible attics and a bread oven in one of the ground floor bedrooms. Two and a half acres of country gardens and several cobbled courtyards also contribute to the unique setting. The bedrooms are tastefully decorated, and several are situated in a ground floor wing which was once a hay barn. A choice of meals is available at breakfast and dinner and local produce is used wherever possible.

16rm(5🛁6🚿) (3fb)[R] ✳ sB&B£23 sB&B🛁🚿£27 dB&B£42 dB&B🛁🚿£50 WBDi£213-£262 LDO 7.30pm
Lic ♨ CTV large games room
Credit Cards [1][3][£]
See advertisement under OTTERY ST MARY

VENTNOR See **WIGHT, ISLE OF**

WADEBRIDGE Cornwall & Isles of Scilly Map **02** SW97

INN[Q][Q][Q] **Swan Hotel** Molesworth Street PL27 7DD (St Austell Brewery) ☎(0208) 812526

A character inn at the centre of this riverside town extends a traditional Cornish welcome to guests. Modern bedrooms are well equipped, meals are served in bars as well as the restaurant, and there is a spacious function room on the first floor.

6🛁 (1fb)CTV in all bedrooms [R] 🐕 (ex guide dogs) LDO 9pm
♨
Credit Cards [1][2][3][5][£]

WAKEFIELD West Yorkshire Map **08** SE32

SELECTED

GH [Q][Q][Q][Q] **Stanley View** 226 / 228 Stanley Road WF1 4AE ☎(0924) 376803 FAX (0924) 369123

A large, attractive mid-terrace house situated on the A642 with easy access to the city, M62 and M1. The modern bedrooms are bright and cosy, and the traditional dining room has a restful atmosphere. There is car parking at the rear.

9rm(7🚿) (5fb) 🚭 in bedrooms CTV in all bedrooms [R] **T** 🐕 (ex guide dogs) ✳ sB&B£18-£34 sB&B🚿£26-£34 dB&B£30-£34 dB&B🚿£34 LDO 8.30pm
Lic ♨ CTV
Credit Cards [1][3][£]

WALSTON Strathclyde *Lanarkshire* Map **11** NT04

FH [Q][Q][Q] Mrs Margaret Kirby **Walston Mansions Farmhouse** *(NT060456)* ML11 8NF ☎Dunsyre(089981) 338

From its elevated position in the village, this farmhouse enjoys sweeping views across open moorland. With its play area, duck pond, aviary, chipmunks and pet rabbits, it will be of particular appeal to families. Guest pets are also welcomed. Of the two comfortable en suite rooms, one has a four-poster and a single bed, and the other a double and a set of full-sized bunks. The smaller twin room has exclusive use of the nearby bathroom.

3rm(2🛁🚿) (1fb) 🚭 in 1 bedrooms 🚭 in dining room CTV in all bedrooms [R] ✳ sB&B£12.50-£14.50 dB&Bfr£25 dB&B🛁🚿fr£29 WB&B£87.50-£101.50 WBDi£136-£150 LDO 5pm
♨ CTV 🐄 2000 acres sheep/cattle

WAREHAM Dorset Map **03** SY98

FH [Q][Q] L S Barnes **Luckford Wood** *(SY873865)* East Stoke BH20 6AW ☎Bindon Abbey(0929) 463098 FAX (0929) 463098

This modern farmhouse stands in a field, just across from the original farmhouse and yard. There is a friendly, informal atmosphere and the Barnes family welcome guests to their home. Bedrooms are neat and comfortable, with bright coordinating decor. Telephone reservations are adviseable in order to ensure a booking. To find the hotel; take the A352 from Wareham, after two miles turn left at the church, cross the manually-operated level crossing, and the house is half-a-mile along the lane on the right hand side. The farm, predominantly dairy, still belongs to the Barns family, and trips are easily arranged.

4rm(2🚿) (3fb) 🚭 in dining room 🚭 in lounges CTV in all bedrooms [R] ✳ sB&B£18-£22 sB&B🚿£20-£24 dB&B£30-£36 dB&B🚿£36-£44
♨ CTV 167 acres dairy
[£]

SELECTED

FH [Q][Q][Q][Q] Mrs J Barnes **Redcliffe** *(SY932866)* BH20 5BE ☎(0929) 552225
Closed Xmas

A warm, friendly welcome and hearty breakfasts eaten around a large communal table are traditional features of a farmhouse and at Redcliffe Mr and Mrs Baines provide both. The farmhouse itself is modern; the bedrooms share a bathroom with shower and guests are welcome to relax in the spacious family sitting room. As well as the friendly atmosphere, the farmhouse also offers a beautiful countryside setting on the banks of the Frome, and many guests have become faithful return visitors.

4rm(1🛁1🚿) 🚭 in bedrooms 🚭 in dining room 🚭 in lounges 🐕 (ex guide dogs)
♨ CTV 250 acres dairy mixed
[£]

WARKWORTH Northumberland Map **12** NU20

GH [Q][Q][Q] **North Cottage** Birling NE65 0XS ☎Alnwick(0665) 711263
Closed Xmas & 2wks Nov

An attractive 300-year-old house situated to the north of the town, North Cottage offers thoughtfully equipped bedrooms and a good lounge. Guests are very well cared for by Mrs Howilston; the house is fully no-smoking.

4rm(3🚿) CTV in all bedrooms [R] 🐕 ✳ sB&Bfr£17 dB&B🚿fr£34 WB&Bfr£112
♨ CTV nc14yrs

WARREN STREET (NEAR LENHAM) Kent Map **05** TQ95

INN[Q][Q][Q] **Harrow** Hubbards Hill ME17 2ED ☎Maidstone(0622) 858727 FAX (0622) 850026
Closed 25 & 26 Dec

Originally the forge and resthouse for travellers on the Pilgrims' Way to Canterbury, this is now an inn, high on the North Downs. It has modern, spacious bedrooms furnished in cottage style. The restaurant is in a conservatory and there is a large choice of bar meals. In summer, guests can sit on the patio that is complete with wishing well and fish pond.

15🛁🚿 (6fb)CTV in all bedrooms [R] **T** 🐕 (ex guide dogs) sB&B🛁🚿£45 dB&B🛁🚿£58 LDO 10pm
♨ CTV
Credit Cards [1][2][3]

WARSASH Hampshire — Map **04** SU40

SELECTED

GH [Q][Q][Q][Q] ***Solent View Private Hotel*** 33-35 Newtown Road SO3 9FY ☎Locks Heath(0489) 572300

Personally run by Mrs Anne Mills, this modern guesthouse is close to the village centre and within walking distance of the River Hamble. The accommodation has recently been upgraded and a new lounge and dining room have been added. Ground-floor rooms and a bar-lounge are also available. A generous full English breakfast is included in the tariff and the four-course dinner menu is recommended.

8rm(1🛁7🚿) (1fb) CTV in all bedrooms [R] **T** LDO noon
Lic 🅿 CTV
Credit Cards [1] [3]

WARWICK Warwickshire — Map **04** SP26

See also Haseley Knob & Lighthorne

GH [Q][Q][Q] **Austin House** 96 Emscote Road CV34 5QJ (on A445 Warwick to Leamington Spa) ☎(0926) 493583

A large semidetached house to the east of the town centre. Bedrooms vary in size, and one of the family bedrooms is on the ground floor. The lounge has TV.

7rm(5🚿) (3fb) CTV in 6 bedrooms [R] ✱ sB&B🚿£16-£18 dB&B🚿£32-£36
🅿 CTV
Credit Cards [1] [2] [3] [5]

GH [Q][Q] **Avon** 7 Emscote Road CV34 4PH (on A445 opposite entrance to St Nicholas Park) ☎(0926) 491367

The Avon is an early Victorian house on the main road to Leamington opposite St Nicholas Park. The accommodation is well maintained. Some bedrooms have en suite showers but not toilets, and three of these are located in a coach-house annexe. Main-house bedrooms are more traditionally furnished, and no-smoking and family rooms are available. There is a cosy lounge with TV and a dining room with individual tables.

7rm Annexe 3rm (4fb) 🚭 in 6 bedrooms 🚭 in dining room CTV in all bedrooms [R] 🐕 ✱ sB&B£15-£17 sB&B£16-£18 dB&B£30-£32 dB&B£32-£36 WB&B£105-£119 WBDi£135-£149 LDO 6pm
Lic 🅿 CTV
[£]

SELECTED

GH [Q][Q][Q][Q] **The Old Rectory** Vicarage Lane, Sherbourne CV35 8AB (off A46 2m SW)
☎Barford (Warwicks)(0926) 624562 FAX (0926) 624562
Closed 24-27 Dec

A delightful Grade II listed Georgian house, complete with cellars and an underground passage, dates back to 1700, when it was known as the White Horse Inn. Many of the original features have been retained, including flagstone floors, beamed ceilings and inglenook fireplaces. The bedrooms, some with direct dial telephone, are individual in style and furnishings and all have modern facilities. Some are housed in tastefully converted cottages and outbuildings adjacent to the attractive walled garden to the rear of the house. The charming dining room has antique oak furniture, and a log fire burns in the large fireplace in the cosy sitting room, which also houses an honesty bar.

7🛁🚿 Annexe 7🛁🚿 (2fb)CTV in all bedrooms [R] **T** ✱ sB&B🛁🚿£31.50-£37.50 dB&B🛁🚿£39.50-£50 LDO 8pm
Lic 🅿 CTV
Credit Cards [1] [3] [£]

PREMIER SELECTED

GH [Q][Q][Q][Q][Q] **Shrewley House** Shrewley CV35 7AT (5m NW of Warwick on B4439) ☎Claverdon(0926) 842549 FAX (0926) 842216

Quietly situated by the village of Shrewley, this charming listed Georgian farmhouse is a welcoming retreat. Mr and Mrs Green provide an exceptionally wide range of services together with some thoughtful extras. In the main house there are three beautifully decorated rooms in Victorian pine, two with king sized, draped, four-poster beds, sumptuous en suites, fluffy towels and excellent linen. Smaller self-catering rooms are offered in the converted stables. There is a cosy sitting room with a piano, and an elegant drawing room opening onto the garden. Generous breakfasts are served in the dining room, and suppers by arrangement. This is a no-smoking establishment.

4🛁🚿 Annexe 6🛁🚿 (1fb) 🚭 CTV in 5 bedrooms [R] **T** ✱ sB&B🛁🚿fr£43 dB&B🛁🚿fr£62 LDO 2pm
🅿 CTV ⛳
Credit Cards [1] [3]

INN [Q][Q][Q] **Tudor House** West Street CV34 6AW (on A46, opposite entrance to castle) ☎(0926) 495447 FAX (0926) 492948

Built in 1472, this is one of the few buildings to survive the Great Fire of Warwick in 1694. It has a wealth of character with exposed timbers and an abundance of bric-à-brac in both the bars. The style of bedrooms furniture varies, but the rooms are all equipped with direct-dial telephones, TV and radio. A variety of menus is offered, including freshly cooked bar meals and an à la carte menu served in the small restaurant.

11rm(8🛁🚿) (1fb)CTV in all bedrooms [R] **T** 🐕 (ex guide dogs) ✱ sB&Bfr£24 sB&B🛁🚿fr£38 dB&B🛁🚿fr£54 Lunch fr£9.95&alc Dinner fr£12&alc LDO 10.30pm
🅿
Credit Cards [1] [2] [3] [5] [£]

WASHFORD Somerset — Map **03** ST04

SELECTED

INN [Q][Q][Q][Q] ***Washford*** TA23 0PP (on A39) ☎(0984) 40256 FAX (0984) 41288

A popular Somerset country inn stands on the A39 beside the local steam railway station. Accommodation is in well maintained bedrooms, each with a shower room. There is a large, convivial bar and the pleasant dining room has an adjacent patio for use in the summer. An extensive menu offers a good choice, which might include game pie, home-made steak and kidney pie or locally-caught trout. The inn is ideally situated for an overnight stop en route to or from the west country.

8🚿 CTV in all bedrooms [R] **T** 🐕 (ex guide dogs) LDO 9pm
🅿 nc12yrs
Credit Cards [1] [2] [3] [5]

Telephone national area codes are due to change by 16th April 1995. Please see the note under 'How to Use this Guide' at the front of the book.

415

WATCHET Somerset   Map **03** ST04

P R E M I E R 🌸 **S E L E C T E D**

FH 🇶🇶🇶🇶🇶 Mrs L C Lewis **Chidgley Hill**
(ST047365) Chidgley TA23 0LS
☎Washford(0984) 40403
Closed 21 Dec-1 Jan

This thatched 15th-century cottage has been lovingly restored in perfect style by Mrs Lewis, featuring good quality fabrics, furniture and family possessions. The surrounding countryside is real Somerset, with rolling hills, rich green fields and an abundance of wild flowers, and bedrooms enjoy fine views to the woods and even the Quantock Hills.

2rm(1⇔🛏) ⚡ in bedrooms ⚡ in 1 lounge CTV in 1 bedroom
® 🐾 sB&B£18-£19.50 dB&B⇔🛏£36-£39 WB&Bfr£110
🏠 CTV 🐾 8 acres non-working

WATERHOUSES Staffordshire   Map **07** SK05

GH 🇶🇶 **Croft House Farm** Waterfall ST10 3HZ (1m NW unclass) ☎(0538) 308553

This stone-built farmhouse is about a mile north of the A523 at the hamlet of Waterfall. Partly dating from 1520, it now provides neat bedrooms, a small residents' lounge and a cosy bar.

6rm (2fb) ⚡ in dining room CTV in all bedrooms ® 🐾
sB&B£17-£23 dB&Bfr£34 WB&B£95-£120 WBDi£132.50-£157.50 LDO 8pm
Lic 🏠 CTV

INN 🇶🇶 **Ye Olde Crown** ST10 3HL ☎(0538) 308204

Set in the village centre, beside the main road, this old stone-built inn offers simple but sound accommodation with modern furnishings and equipment; four rooms are contained in adjacent former cottages. There are two characterful bars, both of which serve meals.

7rm(5⇔🛏) (1fb)CTV in all bedrooms ® 🐾 (ex guide dogs) ✳
sB&B£15 sB&B⇔🛏£22.50 dB&B£30 dB&B⇔🛏£35
WB&B£105-£157 Lunch £6-£14alc Dinner £6-£14alc LDO 10pm
🏠

WATERMILLOCK Cumbria   Map **12** NY42

P R E M I E R 🌸 **S E L E C T E D**

GH 🇶🇶🇶🇶🇶 **The Old Church Hotel** CA11 0JN (on A592)
☎Pooley Bridge(07684) 86204 FAX (07684) 86368
Apr-Oct rs Sun eve

Built on the site of a 12th-century church, this charming Georgian house is situated on the shore of Ullswater with lawns running down to the water's edge. Bedrooms are individually designed and beautifully furnished. Many have spectacular views, which can also be enjoyed from the comfortable lounges and the attractive dining room.

10⇔ CTV in all bedrooms ® T 🐾 (ex guide dogs)
sB&B⇔£45-£75 dB&B⇔£90-£150 LDO 7pm
Lic 🏠 🚣 boating

GH 🇶🇶🇶 **Waterside House** CA11 0JH (on A592)
☎Pooley Bridge(07684) 86038
Closed 24-26 Dec

This charming house dates back to 1771 and retains much of its original character. Old beams abound, and there are two lounge areas, one with a piano for musical guests. Bedrooms are bright and fresh. Smoking is not permitted in the house. A good Cumbrian breakfast is provided, and the owner Mrs Jenner is always on hand to chat. The grounds extend to ten acres and go down to the shores of Lake Ullswater.

7rm(3⇔🛏) (1fb) ⚡ ® dB&B£40-£50 dB&B⇔🛏£40-£70 LDO 8.30pm
Lic 🏠 CTV
Credit Cards 1️⃣ 3️⃣ ©

WATERROW Somerset   Map **03** ST0

INN🇶🇶🇶 *The Rock* TA4 2AX ☎Wiveliscombe(0984) 623293
rs 25-26 Dec

An attractive roadside pub built on a rock face in the delightful Tone Valley. Accommodation is in pleasant bedrooms provided with thoughtful extras such as fresh fruit, telephone, radio and TV. On the first floor there is a cosy residents' lounge. The recently refurbished bar retains much of its original charm and a welcoming log fire burns on chilly days. An interesting menu is offered and the restaurant looks out over the valley.

7rm(6⇔🛏) (1fb) CTV in all bedrooms T LDO 10pm
🏠 CTV
Credit Cards 1️⃣ 3️⃣
See advertisement under TAUNTON

WATFORD Hertfordshire   Map **04** TQ1

GH 🇶🇶🇶 **Upton Lodge** 26-28 Upton Road WO1 2EL (Logis)
☎(0923) 237316 FAX (0923) 233109
rs Xmas

(1fb) ⚡ in 5 bedrooms ⚡ in 1 lounge CTV in all bedrooms ® T
sB&B⇔🛏£35-£45 dB&B⇔🛏£45-£55 WBDi£259-£359 LDO 9.45pm
Lic 🏠 CTV
Credit Cards 1️⃣ 2️⃣ 3️⃣ 5️⃣ ©

WEETON Lancashire   Map **07** SD3

FH 🇶 Mr & Mrs J Colligan **High Moor** *(SD388365)* PR4 3JJ
☎Blackpool(0253) 836273 FAX (0253) 836273
Closed mid Jan-mid Feb, Xmas & New Year

In open countryside, near Weeton Barracks, this former farmhouse provides comfortable and simple accommodation.

2rm (1fb) CTV in all bedrooms ® 🐾 ✳ dB&Bfr£25
🏠 CTV 7 acres non-working

WELLINGBOROUGH Northamptonshire   Map **04** SP8

GH 🇶🇶🇶 **Oak House Private Hotel** 8-11 Broad Green NN8 4LE (turn off A45 & head towards Kettering on A509, hotel on edge of town near cenotaph) ☎(0933) 271133
FAX (0933) 271133
Closed Xmas

This well established, professionally run guesthouse is situated in the older part of Wellingborough on the former village green, is convenient for the town centre. Rooms can be compact, but accommodation is functional and all rooms have private showers. Home-cooked meals are served in the split-level dining room and a comfortable guests' lounge is available.

16rm(15🛏) (1fb)CTV in all bedrooms ® ✳ sB&B🛏£28-£32
dB&B🛏£36-£42 LDO noon
Lic 🏠 CTV
Credit Cards 1️⃣ 2️⃣ 3️⃣ ©

WELLINGTON Shropshire   Map **07** SJ61

See also Telford

GH QQQ **Shray Hill** Shray Hill, Crudgington TF6 6JR (Turn off A442 at Crudgington cross roads onto B5062 towards Newport. Shray Hill House on left) ☎(0952) 541260 FAX (0952) 541512
Closed 21 Dec-2 Jan
3♠ (1fb)CTV in all bedrooms Ⓡ ⁾ᶜ ✳ sB&B♠£17.50-£25 dB&B♠£30-£50 LDO 9pm
▥ CTV

WELLINGTON Somerset   Map **03** ST12

SELECTED

FH QQQQ Mrs N Ash **Pinksmoor Mill House**
(ST109198) Pinksmoor TA21 0HD (2m W off A38 at Beam Bridge Hotel) ☎Greenham(0823) 672361
Closed 23-29 Dec
Pinksmoor Farm has been worked by members of the Ash family since the turn of the century. It is rich in wildlife and offers the rare chance to see heron, mallard, kingfisher and snipe. The farm is believed to date back to the 13th century; and though the mill stones have not been used since the 1940s the mill leat and pond remain. There is a spacious lounge with a log burning fire and colour TV and a separate no smoking lounge. A good value four-course dinner is served, by arrangement, at a communal table.
3rm(2⇻♠) (1fb) ⁾ᶜ CTV in all bedrooms Ⓡ ⁾ᶜ (ex guide dogs) sB&B♠£21 dB&B♠£36
dB&B⇻♠£37 WB&B£112-£132.50 WBDi£192.50-£213 LDO 4pm
▥ CTV 98 acres dairy sheep
ⓔ

WELLS Somerset   Map **03** ST54

See also Chewton Mendip

GH QQQ **Bekynton House** 7 St Thomas Street BA5 2UU (on B3139) ☎(0749) 672222 FAX (0749) 672222
Closed 24-26 Dec
Well positioned for the Cathedral and Bishop's Palace, this period house, with furnishings that are all in keeping with the style of the house, has good sized bedrooms, all well equipped. There is also a comfortable lounge and dining room with separate tables.
8rm(6⇻♠) (2fb) ⁾ᶜ CTV in all bedrooms Ⓡ ⁾ᶜ sB&B£22-£24 dB&B£38-£40 dB&B⇻♠£40-£47
▥ nc5yrs
Credit Cards ①③ⓔ

SELECTED

GH QQQQ **Infield House** 36 Portway BA5 2BN (from city centre, on right hand side of A371) ☎(0749) 670989 FAX (0749) 679093
3⇻♠ ⁾ᶜ CTV in all bedrooms Ⓡ ⁾ᶜ (ex guide dogs) dB&B£32 dB&B⇻♠£42 LDO 8.30pm
▥ nc16yrs
Credit Cards ①③

Telephone national area codes are due to change by 16th April 1995. Please see the note under 'How to Use this Guide' at the front of the book.

P R E M I E R   🏆   S E L E C T E D

GH QQQQQ **Littlewell Farm** Coxley BA5 1QP (1m from centre on A39 towards Glastonbury)
☎(0749) 677914
Mr and Mrs Gnoyke's charming 18th-century white-painted farmhouse nestles in a pretty garden just off the A39, about a mile from the city, and enjoys extensive views across the rolling Somerset countryside. The cosy bedrooms are well equipped, and each has an immaculate bath or shower room. Rooms are individual in style, furnished with some beautiful pictures and pieces of furniture, with the decor and soft furnishings complementing the age and style of the house. An excellent three-course dinner is available by arrangement; Mr Gnoyke prepares both traditional and original dishes using fresh local produce.
5rm(2⇻3♠) CTV in all bedrooms Ⓡ ⁾ᶜ (ex guide dogs) ✳ sB&B⇻♠£21-£23 dB&B⇻♠£39-£44 LDO 3pm
Lic ▥ nc10yrs ◡

SELECTED

GH QQQQ **Tor** 20 Tor Street BA5 2US ☎(0749) 672322 FAX (0749) 672322
The Tor is a charming 17th-century family home set in attractive grounds overlooking the Bishop's Palace and the cathedral, and bordering on National Trust land. It offers

▶

BEKYNTON HOUSE

7 ST THOMAS STREET
WELLS, SOMERSET
BA5 2UU

A delightful setting close to the Cathedral and Bishop's Palace makes our period home an ideal choice for a special holiday.

Comfortable pretty bedrooms with en-suite facilities, colour TV and complimentary hot drinks trays. An attractive sitting room and pleasant dining room for your chosen breakfast add to your pleasure.

An ideal touring centre and walkers' paradise.

Desmond & Rosaleen Gripper
Wells (01749) 672222

beautifully furnished and well equipped bedrooms and a comfortable lounge with a selection of books. There are two spacious dining rooms where Mrs Horne offers traditional, continental or vegetarian breakfasts, and a delightful garden with a patio area is available to guests. This is a no-smoking household.

8rm(2⇔3ℝ) (2fb) ⊬ CTV in all bedrooms ⓡ ⊁ ✳
sB&B£25-£35 sB&B⇔ℝ£30-£40 dB&B£35-£40
dB&B⇔ℝ£40-£50 WB&B£175-£245
▥ CTV nc5yrs
Credit Cards ①③

FH ⓠⓠ Mrs P Higgs **Home** *(ST538442)* Stoppers Lane, Upper Coxley BA5 1QS (2m SW off A39) ☎(0749) 672434
Closed 1wk Xmas
At this Somerset farmhouse, just outside the city, with marvellous views to the Mendip Hills, Mrs Higgs takes trouble to ensure comfort and relaxation for her guests. Bedrooms are fresh and dainty and there is a lounge and dining room where Mrs Higgs serves hearty breakfasts.

7rm(2⇔) (1fb) ⓡ ✳ sB&B£16.50-£17.50 dB&B£33-£35
dB&B⇔£37-£39
Lic ▥ CTV nc5yrs 15 acres pigs

FH ⓠⓠⓠ Mrs J Gould **Manor** *(ST546474)* Old Bristol Road, Upper Milton BA5 3AH (1m W A39 towards Bristol,200 yds beyond rdbt) ☎(0749) 673394
Closed Xmas
In the hamlet of Upper Milton, this gracious Elizabethan farmhouse is set on a 130-acre farm with glorious views to Brent Knoll, and the whole surrounding area is one of oustanding natural beauty. The three cosy guest rooms are pleasantly furnished and breakfast is taken in the panelled dining room, which also serves as a lounge. The garden is a delight, and guests are welcome to sit out and enjoy its tranquillity.

3rm (1fb) ⊬ ⓡ ⊁ (ex guide dogs) sB&B£16-£17 dB&B£28-£30
WB&Bfr£90
▥ CTV 130 acres beef

SELECTED

FH ⓠⓠⓠⓠ Mr & Mrs Frost **Southway** *(ST516423)* Polsham BA5 1RW (3m SW off A39) ☎(0749) 673396
Feb-Nov
A pleasant farmhouse where bedrooms, with views over the Pennard hills, are a good size and thoughtfully furnished. There is a garden and the interest of a working farm. Breakfast is served round a large mahogany table.

3rm(1⇔ℝ) ⊬ in bedrooms ⊬ in dining room CTV in 1
bedroom ⓡ ⊁ (ex guide dogs) sB&B£20-£22
sB&B⇔ℝ£22-£25 dB&B£32-£34 dB&B⇔ℝ£35-£40
▥ CTV 170 acres dairy
Ⓛ

WELSHPOOL Powys   Map **07** SJ20

SELECTED

FH ⓠⓠⓠⓠ Mrs E Jones **Gungrog House** *(SJ235089)* Rhallt SY21 9HS (1m NE off A458) ☎(0938) 553381
Apr-Oct
Providing good quality bedrooms and public rooms this guesthouse has superb views from its elevated position over the Severn Valley.

3rm(2ℝ) ⊬ ⓡ ⊁ ✳ sB&Bℝfr£20 dB&Bℝfr£36 LDO 5pm
▥ CTV 21 acres mixed
Ⓛ

FH ⓠⓠⓠ Mr & Mrs M C Payne **Heath Cottage** *(SJ239023)* Kingswood, Forden SY21 8LX (next to Forden P.O. on the A490 Welshpool/Churchstoke road) ☎Forden(0938) 580453
Etr-Oct
This creeper-clad farmhouse was once a pub and dates back to 1715. It is off the A490, south-east of the town at Forden, near Offa's Dyke, and it has sheep, poultry and other domestic animals. Comfortable bedrooms all have modern facilities, and there is a lounge for residents. Evening meals are available by arrangement.

3⇔ℝ (1fb) ⊬ ⓡ ⊁ ✳ sB&B⇔ℝ£17 dB&B⇔ℝ£34
WB&B£110 WBDi£180
▥ CTV 6 acres poultry sheep
Ⓛ

SELECTED

FH ⓠⓠⓠⓠ Mr & Mrs G Jones **Lower Trelydan** *(SJ225105)* Lower Trelydan, Guilsfield SY21 9PH (3.5m N off A490) ☎(0938) 553105
This 16th-century black and white timbered farmhouse is set in pleasant lawns and gardens. The accommodation is spacious and comfortable with a panelled lounge and a dining room still with its original butler's pantry. An unusual feature of the house is the licensed bar which has been built into the 400-year-old inglenook fireplace. The house is located at Guilsfield.

3rm(2⇔1ℝ) (1fb) ⊬ in bedrooms CTV in 2 bedrooms ⓡ ⊁
✳ sB&B£21 sB&B⇔ℝ£25 dB&B⇔ℝ£36 WB&B£126
WBDi£203 LDO 5pm
Lic CTV 108 acres beef dairy sheep

SELECTED

FH ⓠⓠⓠⓠ Mr & Mrs W Jones **Moat** *(SJ214042)* SY21 8SE (on A483, 0.5m from junct with A490) ☎(0938) 553179
Apr-Oct rs Feb, Mar & Nov
One mile south of Welshpool, this working farm dates back to the 16th century and provides comfortable accommodation. The Jones family are welcoming and a tennis court and pool table are available. The River Severn runs through the grounds.

3⇔ℝ (1fb) ⊬ in dining room ⊬ in lounges CTV in all
bedrooms ⓡ ⊁ ✳ sB&B⇔ℝ£20-£22 dB&B⇔ℝ£36-£38
WB&B£126-£133 WBDi£190-£200 LDO 2pm
▥ ✎(grass)260 acres dairy
Ⓛ

FH ⓠⓠⓠ Mrs F Emberton **Tynllwyn** *(SJ215085)* SY21 9BW
☎(0938) 553175
Providing good comfortable bedrooms and a spacious lounge this large 18th-century farmhouse is situated off the A490 North of Welshpool with good rural views.

6rm (3fb) CTV in all bedrooms ⓡ ⊁ ✳ sB&Bfr£14.50
dB&Bfr£29 WB&Bfr£98 WBDifr£140 LDO 6.30pm
Lic ▥ CTV 150 acres mixed
Ⓛ

WEM Shropshire   Map **07** SJ5☐

SELECTED

FH ⓠⓠⓠⓠ Mrs A P Ashton **Soulton Hall** *(SJ543303)* Soulton SY4 5RS ☎(0939) 232786
This historic manor house retains great character in its exposed timbers, uneven floors and original fireplaces, and it provides large and well furnished bedrooms. Guests are invited to join in the farming activities, and there are ponies available

for riding. Fifty acres of oak woodland and miles of riverside will tempt walkers.
3rm(2🛁) Annexe 2🛁🚿 (2fb) CTV in all bedrooms [R] LDO 9pm
Lic 📺 🏠 🎣 U 560 acres mixed
Credit Cards [1] [3]
See advertisement under Colour Section

WEMBLEY Greater London — Map **04** TQ18

GH [Q][Q][Q] Adelphi Hotel 4 Forty Lane HA9 9EB
☎081-904 5629 FAX 081-908 5314
A family-run guesthouse catering for business travellers, is conveniently located about two miles from the M1, off the A406 North Circular road. Recently refurbished, it is furnished throughout in a modern style, and offers a range of neat bedrooms. There is a combined lounge and bright dining room, where a full cooked English breakfast is available. Ample forecourt car parking is provided.
11rm(7🚿) (2fb) 🚭 in dining room CTV in all bedrooms [R] 🐕 ✳ sB&B£25-£28 sB&B🚿£30-£35 dB&B£35-£38 dB&B🚿£38-£45 WB&B£155-£175
CTV
Credit Cards [1] [2] [3] [5] [£]

GH [Q][Q][Q] Arena Hotel 6 Forty Lane HA9 9EB
☎081-908 0670 & 081-908 2007 FAX 081-908 2007
This extended late Edwardian hotel is convenient for Wembley Park station and the Stadium. It offers well equipped modernised bedrooms, small TV lounge and pleasant breakfast room where light meals can be provided in the evening by arrangement with the friendly owners Amarjit and Sarjit Paul.

▶

10rm(3🛁4🚿) (1fb) 🚭 in dining room CTV in all bedrooms [R] 🐕 (ex guide dogs) * sB&B£25-£28 sB&B🛁🚿£30-£35 dB&B£35-£38 dB&B🛁🚿£40-£45 LDO 10.30pm
📺 CTV
Credit Cards [1] [2] [3] [£]

WEOBLEY Hereford & Worcester Map **03** SO45

SELECTED

INN [Q] [Q] [Q] [Q] Ye Olde Salutation Market Pitch HR4 8SJ
☎(0544) 318443 FAX (0544) 318216

Created from the combination of a former ale and cider house, this black and white English inn with misshapen walls and timbers, has been a feature of this area for about 500 years. The present hosts Christopher and Frances Anthony have added to its already substantial reputation; oak beams, chintzy soft furnishings, armchairs and comforts like tea-making equipment, TV and hair dryer are standard in all bedrooms, and some have excellent en suite bathrooms. Humourous names are given to the bedrooms, such as the four-poster room favoured by honeymooners, called after Richard Tonkins, a local character who fathered thirty children. While ales and beer are the usual attractions, the imaginative bar food is well worth a visit with such treats as roast lamb with honey and rosemary or a French stick stuffed with hot roast beef; vegetarian meals are also available. The restaurant has a lengthy menu with hearty portions and local produce is used whenever possible.

3🛁🚿 🚭 in bedrooms 🚭 in dining room CTV in all bedrooms [R] * sB&B🛁🚿£32.50 dB&B🛁🚿£55-£60 Lunch £15.60-£25.20alc Dinner £15.60-£25.20alc LDO 9.30pm
📺 CTV nc14yrs
Credit Cards [1] [2] [3] [5] [£]

WEST BAGBOROUGH Somerset Map **03** ST13

GH [Q] [Q] [Q] *Higher House* TA4 3EF
☎Bishops Lydeard(0823) 432996 FAX (0823) 433568
Closed Xmas rs Dec-Mar

Originally dating back to 1661, Higher House stands at one end of the village, nestling at the foot of the Quantock Hills and enjoying superb views. The comfortable bedrooms are pretty and nicely coordinated and offer good facilities. There is a choice of spacious and charming lounge areas, consisting of a drawing room, complete with snooker table and a cosy morning room, with a log fire and pretty garden views. Evening meals are served on a long polished communal table and a dinner-party atmosphere is promoted by the proprietors, who remain charming and helpful throughout their guests' stay. A heated outdoor swimming pool is an added bonus.

3🛁 (1fb) CTV in all bedrooms [R] **T** 🐕
Lic 📺 nc13yrs 🏊(heated) 🎾(hard)tennis coaching available
Credit Cards [1]

INN [Q] [Q] [Q] *Rising Sun* TA 4 3EF
☎Bishops Lydeard(0823) 432575 Telex no 94013345

Set in the quaint village of West Bagborough and surrounded by the natural beauty of the Quantocks, this sixteenth-century inn offers three attractive, colour coordinated bedrooms with en suite facilities; each of them also has tea-making facilities and colour TV. A varied selection of snacks and meals is served both in the evening and at lunchtime in the cosy bar, and breakfast is taken in a comfortable room nearby.

Annexe 4🚿 (1fb) CTV in all bedrooms [R] 🐕 LDO 9.30pm
📺

WEST CHILTINGTON West Sussex Map **04** TQ01

FH [Q] [Q] [Q] Mrs A M Steele ***New House*** *(TQ091185)* Broadford Bridge Road RH20 2LA (leave A29 for B2133 after 2m turn right, signposted West Chiltington, farmhouse on left as you approach village) ☎(0798) 812215
Closed Dec

Despite its name, this stone-built farmhouse dates from about 1450, and the beamed interior combines original charm with a friendly, relaxed atmosphere. The two large bedrooms contained in the main building are augmented by The Dairy, a modern annexe. All are thoughtfully equipped, and smoking is prohibited. Generous breakfasts - perhaps including free-range eggs and home-made marmalade - are served in a cosy lounge/breakfast room warmed by a log fire. The atmosphere is relaxed and friendly, gardens are well kept and there is ample car parking space.

2🛁🚿 (2fb) CTV in all bedrooms [R] 🐕 (ex guide dogs)
CTV nc10yrs 50 acres mixed

WESTCLIFF-ON-SEA Essex

See **Southend-on-Sea**

WEST DOWN Devon Map **02** SS54

PREMIER SELECTED

GH [Q] [Q] [Q] [Q] [Q] The Long House EX34 8NF
☎Ilfracombe(0271) 863242
FAX (0271) 863242
early Mar-early Nov

In a peaceful village on the fringes of Exmoor, and within easy reach of the sandy beaches, this converted village smithy has comfortable, individually designed bedrooms with many thoughtful little extras as well as good facilities. The quaint teashop is transformed into an attractive dining room at night offering inspired home-cooked dinners, and there is also a cosy lounge where guests can relax over coffee. Friendly and attentive service is provided by the resident proprietors Pauline and Rob Hart.

4🛁🚿 CTV in all bedrooms [R] 🐕 (ex guide dogs)
dB&B🛁🚿fr£53 WBDifr£255 LDO 8pm
Lic 📺 CTV
Credit Cards [1] [3] [£]

GH [Q] [Q] [Q] *Sunnymeade Country House Hotel* Dean Cross EX34 8NT (1m W on A361) ☎Ilfracombe(0271) 863668
Apr-Nov

Set back from the road, with gardens to the front, this family-run guesthouse is conveniently situated for access to Ilfracombe and Braunton. The friendly and courteous proprietors offer neat and well maintained accommodation.

10rm(8🚿) (2fb) CTV in all bedrooms [R] 🐕 LDO 6pm
Lic 📺 CTV
Credit Cards [1] [2] [3] [5]

WEST DRAYTON Greater London

For accommodation details see **Heathrow Airport**

WESTGATE ON SEA Kent Map **05** TR37

GH [Q] [Q] White Lodge 12 Domneva Road CT8 8PE
☎Thanet(0843) 831828

White Lodge is a friendly guesthouse located close to the beach and just a five-minute walk from the railway station. Most of the bedrooms have their own facilities. There is a wood-panelled lounge with an honesty bar and a bright breakfast room.

7rm(5🛁🚿) (2fb) 🚭 in 3 bedrooms 🚭 in dining room 🚭 in lounges CTV in all bedrooms [R] * sB&B£18 sB&B🛁🚿£24

dB&B£36 dB&B⇌ſ⁀£40 WB&B£114-£151 WBDi£170-£207 LDO 7pm Lic ▥ CTV
(£)

WEST GRAFTON Wiltshire   Map **04** SU26

P R E M I E R ⬧ S E L E C T E D

FH ⓆⓆ Ⓠ Ⓠ Ⓠ Mrs A
Orssich **Mayfield** *(SU246598)*
SN8 3BY
☎Marlborough(0672) 810339
FAX (0672) 811158
Closed Xmas

A delightful thatched farmhouse is surrounded by well kept grounds and gardens in a rural area. The property has been carefully extended by the present proprietors to provide three comfortably sized bedrooms and two bathrooms. There is a choice of lounges and guests share a single table in the breakfast room. Mayfield is decorated with taste and style, and furnished with antiques. Chris and Angie Orssich welcome guests with open arms, and the family kitchen, where there is a relaxed party atmosphere, is the heart of the place.
3rm ⊬ in bedrooms CTV in all bedrooms Ⓡ T sB&B£25-£30 dB&B£39-£42
▥ CTV ↖(heated) ۹(hard)table tennis play area 8 acres non-working
(£)

WEST MALLING Kent   Map **05** TQ65

S E L E C T E D
GH Ⓠ Ⓠ Ⓠ Ⓠ **Scott House** High Street ME19 6QH (on A228)
☎(0732) 841380 FAX (0732) 870025
Closed 24 Dec-1 Jan
This attractive Georgian building in the village centre now doubles as a guesthouse and an antique and furniture restoration shop. Individually and well furnished bedrooms are all on the first floor. Breakfast is served in a large, bright room overlooking the street and there is a lounge area with comfortable seating.
3ſ⁀ ⊬ CTV in all bedrooms Ⓡ ⅋ (ex guide dogs) ✳
sB&Bſ⁀£39 dB&Bſ⁀£49
▥ ⋌nc
Credit Cards ①③

S E L E C T E D
GH Ⓠ Ⓠ Ⓠ Ⓠ **Woodgate** Birling Road, Leybourne ME19 5HT
☎(0732) 843201
This attractive 18th-century cottage stands in well kept gardens in peaceful rural surroundings. Bedrooms are individually furnished and decorated and there is a comfortable lounge. Breakfasts are served in the dining room round an unusual table made from railway sleepers.
3rm(1⇌ſ⁀) (1fb) ⊬ CTV in 2 bedrooms Ⓡ ✳ sB&B£18-£20
dB&B⇌ſ⁀£36-£40 WB&Bfr£126 WBDifr£210 LDO 9.30pm
▥ CTV

WEST MERSEA Essex   Map **05** TM01

GH Ⓠ Ⓠ Ⓠ **Blackwater Hotel** 20-22 Church Road CO5 8QH
☎Colchester(0206) 383338 & 383038

Closed 8 Jan-5 Feb rs Tue & Sun
Situated in the heart of the village and close to West Mersea beach, this late-Victorian building with its attractive ivy-clad faáade was previously a coaching inn. Comfortable bedrooms are simply furnished but freshly decorated, and most have private bathrooms adjacent. The Champenois restaurant offers genuine French cooking in an authentic and friendly atmosphere, and there is a cosy bar and a comfortable lounge. Ample car parking is available at the rear.
7rm(2ſ⁀) CTV in all bedrooms Ⓡ ⅋ (ex guide dogs) sB&Bfr£25
sB&Bſ⁀£30-£48 dB&Bfr£40 dB&Bſ⁀£50-£62 LDO 10pm
Lic ▥
Credit Cards ① ② ③ (£)

WESTON-SUPER-MARE Avon   Map **03** ST36

S E L E C T E D
GH Ⓠ Ⓠ Ⓠ Ⓠ **Ashcombe Court** 17 Milton Road BS23 2SH
(follow signs for 'Seafront North' and 'Milton')
☎(0934) 625104
Sian and Tom Bisdee's delightful Victorian house, with pretty little gardens and flowering tubs, is a personally run guesthouse with an air of genuine hospitality. The charm and character of the building have not been lost in the installation of comfortable, modern facilities. Individually styled and decorated bedrooms feature a good combination of rich colours, with coordinating fabrics and soft furnishings. There is a comfortable lounge and appealing dining room, where home-cooked breakfasts make a good start to the day.
6rm(1⇌5ſ⁀) (1fb) ⊬ in bedrooms ⊬ in dining room CTV in all bedrooms Ⓡ ⅋ ✳ dB&B⇌ſ⁀£39 WB&B£115.50-£123

▶

WOODGATE
Birling Road, Leybourne, West Malling, Kent ME19 5HT
AA
Selected
Telephone: 01732 843201

Pretty 17th Century Cottage in rural location surrounded by woodland, furnished with antiques from many countries. Bedrooms are attractively furnished, two with ensuite facilities, all with tea and coffee makers and TV. One overlooks garden and the others overlook woodland. Bantams wander free in the garden, and tropical birds are housed in spacious planted aviaries. Meals are interestingly different, all bread is home baked.
Prices £18 per person B & B.
Dinner by prior arrangement £12.50. No smoking.
Dogs and children welcome.

421

WBDi£145.50-£155.50 LDO 6pm
♨ CTV
Credit Cards [2] [£]

GH [Q][Q][Q] Baymead Hotel Longton Grove Road BS23 1LS
☎(0934) 622951 FAX (0934) 628110
Closed Jan & Feb
A popular, family-run holiday hotel stands in a central location close to the town centre and all amenities. It offers bright, well equipped bedrooms with private bathrooms and modern facilities. The lively bars provide entertainment three nights a week.
33rm(30🛁🚿) (3fb) 🚭 in dining room CTV in all bedrooms Ⓡ *
sB&B£15-£18 sB&B🛁🚿£20-£22.50 dB&B🛁🚿£35-£40 WB&B£115-£140 WBDi£150-£195 LDO 7pm
Lic lift ♨ CTV half size snooker table

GH [Q][Q][Q] Beverley 11 Whitecross Road BS23 1EP
☎(0934) 622956
5🚿 (3fb)CTV in all bedrooms Ⓡ 🐕 (ex guide dogs) *
sB&B🚿£15-£18 dB&B🚿£30-£34 WB&B£90-£105 WBDi£115-£130 LDO 4pm
♨ 🚭

SELECTED

GH [Q][Q][Q][Q] Braeside 2 Victoria Park BS23 2HZ
☎(0934) 626642
This delightful family-run hotel has views over Weston Bay to Brean Down, and is just a short walk from the seafront. Bedrooms vary in size, are well maintained and have all modern facilities. At 6.30pm a gong summons guests to the set four-course dinner and the comfortable lounge houses an electronic organ, which proprietor Hugh Wallington plays if requested. There is unrestricted street parking nearby.
9🛁🚿 (3fb) 🚭 in dining room CTV in all bedrooms Ⓡ
sB&B🛁🚿£22.50 dB&B🛁🚿£45 WB&B£135 WBDi£186 LDO 6pm
Lic ♨

GH [Q][Q] *Clifton Lodge* 48 Clifton Road BS23 1BN
☎(0934) 629357
A small friendly guesthouse which is situated in a residential area close to the seafront, Tropicana leisure centre and within walking distance of the shops. The compact, attractively decorated bedrooms are well suited to shorter stay guests.
5rm(1🛁🚿) (3fb) CTV in all bedrooms Ⓡ 🐕 (ex guide dogs) LDO noon
♨ CTV

GH [Q][Q] Conifers 63 Milton Road BS23 2SP (turn off M5 at junct 21 and follow A370) ☎(0934) 624404
Closed 22-31 Dec
A spotlessly clean and bright little bed and breakfast guesthouse close to the town centre and all amenities. Bedrooms are comfortable and well decorated, and there is a small cosy breakfast room. There is a pretty garden adjacent, and the house is located with good access to the M5.
3rm(1🛁🚿) 🚭 in dining room CTV in all bedrooms Ⓡ 🐕
sB&B£17 sB&B🛁🚿£20 dB&B£30 dB&B🛁🚿£36 WB&B£100-£120
♨ nc14yrs
[£]

GH [Q][Q][Q] *Lewinsdale Lodge Hotel* 5-7 Clevedon Road BS23 1DA ☎(0934) 632501
May-Sep rs Mar-Apr & Oct-Nov
Well positioned close to the seafront and opposite the Tropicana leisure centre, this small hotel provides comfortable accommodation. The original building dates back 150 years and retains much of its former character, and its facilities have recently been enhanced by the addition of new bedrooms and a function suite. Owners Valerie and Thomas Farmer are conscientious hoteliers and the hotel provides good value for money.
10🚿 CTV in all bedrooms Ⓡ 🐕 (ex guide dogs) LDO noon
Lic ♨ nc12yrs

SELECTED

GH [Q][Q][Q][Q] Milton Lodge 15 Milton Road BS23 2SH
☎(0934) 623161
Apr-Sep rs Oct-Mar
Milton Lodge is a comfortable Victorian house on the outskirts of town, yet convenient for the parks, shops and town's amenities. The house has been sympathetically restored to retain its original character and incorporate modern facilities. Bedrooms are individually styled and decorated in soft shades. Standards of furnishing and equipment are high and the rooms are sparklingly clean. Hospitable service is provided by owners Adrienne and Les Cox.
6rm(3🛁3🚿) 🚭 in dining room CTV in all bedrooms Ⓡ 🐕
sB&B🛁🚿£18-£21 dB&B🛁🚿£30-£36 WB&B£95-£120 WBDi£130-£155 LDO 10am
♨ CTV nc9yrs
[£]

GH [Q][Q] *Saxonia* 95 Locking Road BS23 3EW
☎(0934) 633856 FAX (0934) 623141
Well equipped bedrooms are offered at this small guesthouse, which is in a central location with limited but useful car parking. A cosy dining room and a bar are provided.
8rm(5🚿) (4fb) CTV in all bedrooms Ⓡ 🐕 LDO 2pm
Lic ♨ CTV
Credit Cards [1] [2] [3] [5]

GH [Q][Q][Q] *Shire Elms* 71 Locking Road BS23 3DQ
☎(0934) 628605
Closed 23 Dec-2 Jan
This is a family-owned and run guesthouse close to the town centre. Bedrooms are bright and equipped with the usual modern comforts. There are spacious public areas with a choice of lounges including a comfortable bar/lounge. A friendly welcoming atmosphere has been created by the Bartlett family. There is on site car park for guests.
11rm Annexe 2rm (3fb) CTV in all bedrooms 🐕 LDO 3pm
Lic ♨ CTV

GH [Q][Q][Q] Wychwood Hotel 148 Milton Road BS23 2UZ
☎(0934) 627793
Closed 23 Dec-2 Jan
Owned and enthusiastically run by experienced hoteliers, Mr and Mrs Whitehouse, this spacious Victorian house is conveniently positioned on the outskirts of the town, with good access to the M5 and the town centre. Spotlessly clean and bright throughout, it provides comfortable and well furnished bedrooms with modern facilities. There is a pleasant dining room and a cosy little bar lounge.
9🛁🚿 (3fb)CTV in all bedrooms Ⓡ 🐕 (ex guide dogs) *
sB&B🛁🚿£25-£27 dB&B🛁🚿£42 WB&B£150-£160 WBDi£213-£223 LDO 6.30pm
Lic ♨ 🏊(heated)
Credit Cards [1] [3] [£]

FH [Q][Q][Q] Mrs T G Moore **Purn House** *(ST331571)* Bleadon BS24 0QE ☎Bleadon(0934) 812324
Feb-Nov
An attractive creeper-clad 17th-century farmhouse is situated three miles from Weston in the peaceful village of Bleadon, close to the A370. Bedrooms are bright and mostly spacious, and have TV, clock radios and modern fittings, yet retain some of the original character and charm of the period. There is also a cosy

comfortable lounge, a panelled breakfast room and a pretty lawned garden full of colour.

6rm(4⇄♪♒)(3fb) ⊬ in bedrooms ⊬ in dining room CTV in 4 bedrooms ® ⅄ (ex guide dogs) dB&Bfr£32 dB&B⇄♪♒fr£40 WB&B£90-£110 WBDi£135-£155 LDO 10am
▦ CTV ♪ childrens playroom snooker table tennis 700 acres arable dairy
£

WESTON UNDERWOOD Derbyshire — Map 08 SK24

FH ⓆⓆⓆⓆ Mrs L Adams **Parkview Farm** *(SK293425)* DE6 4PA (6m NW of Derby, 0.5m from Kedleston Hall National Trust property) ☎Ashbourne(0335) 360352
Closed 24 & 25 Dec
Linda and Michael Adams are the enthusiastic hosts at this delightful Victorian farmhouse, which overlooks the parkland of the National Trust's Kedleston Hall. The splendid accommodation includes beautifully furnished bedrooms, two with antique four-poster beds. Guests have their own lounge full of books, games and local information. A carefully presented breakfast is served from a good choice in the small dining room at polished wood tables. This is a no-smoking establishment.
3rm ® ⅄ ✳ sB&B£20-£25 dB&B£37-£38
▦ CTV nc2yrs 375 acres mixed

WEST STOUR Dorset — Map 03 ST72

INNⓆⓆⓆ **The Ship** SP8 5RP (on A30 between Shaftesbury & Sherborne) ☎East Stour(0747) 838640
A family run, cosy inn offers accommodation of a very good standard. The bedrooms are thoughtfully and comfortably appointed; all are of a good size and well equipped. In the two small dining rooms guests can choose from either a dinner or bar menu. The cooking is good, honest and uncomplicated.
6⇄♪♒(2fb) ✳ in area of dining room CTV in all bedrooms ® ⅄ (ex guide dogs) ✳ sB&B⇄♪♒£28 dB&B⇄♪♒£38-£42 WB&B£114-£168 LDO 9.30pm
▦ CTV ♪
Credit Cards ①③£

WESTWARD HO! Devon — Map 02 SS42

GH ⓆⓆⓆ **The Buckleigh Lodge** 135 Bayview Road EX39 1BJ ☎Bideford(0237) 475988
An elegant Victorian property in its own well kept gardens, Buckleigh Lodge is just a few minutes' steep walk from the sea and a beautiful sandy beach. It offers a choice of attractive lounges and a dining room where a set menu is available for dinner. Bedrooms vary in size and several have en suite facilities.
6rm(3⇄♪♒)(1fb) ⊬ in dining room CTV in all bedrooms ® ⅄ (ex guide dogs) sB&Bfr£16 sB&B⇄♪♒fr£18 dB&B£32-£36 dB&B⇄♪♒fr£36 WB&B£105-£120 WBDi£158-£172 LDO 4pm
Lic ▦ CTV ⚬⚬

WETHERBY West Yorkshire — Map 08 SE44

GH ⓆⓆ **Prospect House** 8 Caxton Street LS22 4RU ☎(0937) 582428
Friendly service is provided by the resident owners at Prospect House, which occupies a corner site close to the town centre. Bedrooms are well cared for, and there is a combined breakfast room and sitting area.
6rm (1fb)CTV in 1 bedroom ® sB&B£16-£16.50 dB&B£32-£33 WB&B£112-£115.50
▦ CTV
£

WEYBRIDGE Surrey — Map 04 TQ06

GH ⓆⓆ **Warbeck House Hotel** 46 Queens Road KT13 0AR ☎(0932) 848764 FAX (0932) 847290
An atractive Edwardian house is situated on the A317, close to the town centre, with forecourt parking. Bedrooms are modestly furnished; one has en suite facilities and others have shower cubicles, though they all have TV. There is a small bar, and many of the original features of the house have been retained, including the original fireplaces and mahogony doors. Breakfast is served in the spacious Barclay Room which has a conservatory extension leading to the patio and garden, making it an ideal venue for functions and weddings.
10rm(5♪♒) (1fb) ⊬ in dining room CTV in all bedrooms ® ✳ sB&B£35-£45 sB&B♪♒fr£45 dB&Bfr£45 dB&B♪♒fr£60 Lic ▦ CTV

WEYMOUTH Dorset — Map 03 SY67

See also Portland

GH ⓆⓆⓆⓆ **Bay Lodge** 27 Greenhill DT4 7SW (on A353, near Lodmoor Country Park) ☎(0305) 782419 FAX (0305) 782828
rs Nov
An attractive and interesting property built around 1929 stands in an elevated position, set back from the main road, with glorious views overlook the sea. Propietors Graham and Barbara Dubben are continually implementing improvements; their personal involvement and cheerful presence ensures guests of a warm welcome. Bedrooms are very nicely presented, with pretty coordinating decor and smartly tiled en

▶

suite facilities. They are all equipped to a high standard, and have comfortable beds. Public areas are very cosy and inviting, with many original features retained including open fires and a central glass dome over the staircase. There is a comfortable bar/lounge and a snug, quiet day lounge. An evening meal cooked by Mrs Dubben is offered in the pretty dining room where a selection of good value wines is available. Reservations are advisable for visits during the winter months.
7🛁🚿 Annexe 5🛁🚿 🚭 in dining room 🚭 in 1 lounge CTV in all bedrooms [R] T sB&B🛁🚿£23-£38 dB&B🛁🚿£44-£59 WBDi£215-£284 LDO 5pm
Lic ♨ CTV
Credit Cards [1][2][3][5]

GH [Q][Q] Birchfields 22 Abbotsbury Road DT4 0AE
☎(0305) 773255
Mar-Oct
A family run guesthouse stands on a corner site, part of a terraced row not far from the town centre. The accommodation is clean and bright and is ideally suited to those seeking a budget holiday yet well situated for the fun of Weymouth. There is a cosy lounge/dining room with TV, and an imaginative set menu is offered for the evening meal.
9rm(3🚿) (4fb) 🚭 in dining room CTV in all bedrooms [R] * sB&B£15-£20 dB&B£30-£38 dB&B🚿£34-£42 WB&B£73-£100 WBDi£113-£150 LDO 3pm
Lic ♨ CTV
[£]

SELECTED

GH [Q][Q][Q][Q] Channel View 10 Brunswick Terrace, The Esplanade DT4 7RW ☎(0305) 782527
A delightful, immaculate small guesthouse situated yards from the promenade and beach, along a 'no through road' where parking is restricted. Bedrooms are thoughtfully decorated with extra personal touches, and front rooms have sea views. The dining room also looks out to sea and there is a very well stocked bar. Home-cooked five-course evening meals feature meat, fish and vegetables in season, delivered fresh daily. Car parking from June 1st - September 30th can be arranged at a reasonable charge.
7rm(5🚿) (2fb) 🚭 CTV in all bedrooms [R] 🐕 (ex guide dogs) sB&B£17-£24 sB&B🚿£21-£25 dB&B£30-£35 dB&B🚿£34-£48 WB&B£119-£168 WBDi£175-£224 LDO 4pm
Lic ♨ CTV nc12yrs
Credit Cards [1][3]

GH [Q][Q][Q] *Cumberland Hotel* 95 Esplanade DT4 7BA
☎(0305) 785644
The owners of this small private hotel continue to improve the facilities offered to guests. The brightly decorated bedrooms are nicely furnished and well-equipped. Public areas include a lounge and dining room. A high standard of cleanliness is apparent throughout the hotel.
12rm(2🛁10🚿) (4fb) CTV in all bedrooms [R] 🐕
Lic nc8yrs

GH [Q][Q][Q] Ferndown 47 Walpole Street DT4 7HQ
☎(0305) 775228
Closed 25 Dec-7 Jan
A neat little guesthouse situated in a quiet residential area, close to the seafront and town centre. It offers pretty, individually decorated bedrooms with some welcoming extra touches. Public areas are compact, but offer a comfortable and friendly atmosphere. A home-cooked evening meal is provided by Mrs Waddell using good quality fresh produce. The whole Waddell family are involved in running this guesthouse, and the atmosphere is friendly and relaxed.
8rm 🚭 in area of dining room CTV in 6 bedrooms [R] * sB&B£12-£15 dB&B£24-£30 WB&B£82-£90 WBDi£110-£120
CTV
[£]

GH [Q][Q] *Hazeldene* 16 Abbotsbury Road, Westham DT4 0AE
☎(0305) 782579
This cosy seaside guesthouse is located a short distance from the centre of town and the seafront. The bedrooms are compact but spotlessly clean and neat, with bright, cheerful decor. Public areas include a comfortable lounge area with TV and a small dining room.
7rm (4fb) [R] 🐕 LDO noon
Lic ♨ CTV nc5yrs

GH [Q][Q][Q] Hotel Malta 141 The Esplanade DT4 7NJ
☎(0305) 783129
Apr-Sep rs Apr
This family run hotel stands along the Esplanade, just a short walk for the centre of town. Personally run by Kathy Paul and her family, the bedrooms are very pretty with co-ordinated fabrics and fresh bright decor. Those at the front of the house enjoy good sea views and are bright and sunny. The property dates from 1835 and has much character with all rooms located above ground level. The rear car-park is a bonus during the busy summer months
12rm (4fb) 🚭 in dining room CTV in all bedrooms [R] 🐕 * sB&B£16.50-£18.50 dB&B£33-£37 WB&B£105-£119 WBDi£150-£167 LDO 5pm
Lic CTV
[£]

GH [Q][Q][Q] Kenora 5 Stavordale Road DT4 0AB
☎(0305) 771215
Etr & 7 May-1 Oct
This handsome Victorian property is located in a quiet residential area on the edge of town, with views of the harbour from the rear. Bedrooms are neat, clean and well presented, most with modern en suite facilities. There is a comfortable bar/lounge and pretty dining room where a limited menu is served. Mrs Lamb's award-winning garden includes a summer house and children's play area, and ample car parking is provided.
15rm(4🛁9🚿) (5fb) 🚭 in dining room CTV in all bedrooms [R] 🐕 (ex guide dogs) sB&B🛁🚿£26-£30 dB&B🛁🚿£42-£48.50 WB&B£139-£164 WBDi£160-£186 LDO 4.30pm
Lic ♨
Credit Cards [1][3]

GH [Q][Q][Q] Kings Acre Hotel 140 The Esplanade DT4 7NH
☎(0305) 782534
Closed 15 Dec-5 Jan rs Oct, Nov & Dec
Dating back to the 1850's, this family run guesthouse enjoys a superb location on the Esplanade. Bedrooms are spacious, clean and bright, several with new en suite facilities. There is a cosy lounge and the pleasantly furnished dining room has views across the Channel. Mrs Mears is happy to cater for special diets and she offers a choice for breakfast. There is some off road parking to the rear of the hotel.
12rm(8🚿) (4fb) 🚭 in dining room CTV in all bedrooms [R] 🐕 * sB&B£20-£40 sB&B🚿£20-£40 dB&B£34-£38 dB&B🚿£38-£50 LDO 4.30pm
Lic ♨ CTV
Credit Cards [1][3][£]

GH [Q][Q][Q] New Salsudas Hotel 22 Lennox St DT4 7HE (left of clock on esplanade and turn left at traffic lights, 300yds down Lennox Street) ☎(0305) 771903
7🛁🚿 (3fb)CTV in 6 bedrooms [R] sB&B🛁🚿£17-£20 dB&B🛁🚿£28-£36 WB&B£93-£112 WBDi£135-£160 LDO 3.30pm
Lic ♨
Credit Cards [1][3]

GH [Q][Q][Q] Sou'west Lodge Hotel Rodwell Road DT4 8QT
☎(0305) 783749
Closed 21 Dec-1 Jan
Family owned, this welcoming hotel stands above the Old Quay on the main route to Portland, a short distance from the bustling town centre. Bedrooms are well decorated and appointed, while comfortable public areas provide a traditional lounge area and bar as well as the dining room where a home-cooked evening meal is served.
8🛁🚿 (2fb) 🚭 in dining room CTV in all bedrooms [R] ✳ sB&B🛁🚿£21-£22.50 dB&B🛁🚿£42-£45 WB&B£125-£145 WBDi£147-£190 LDO 3pm
Lic 🌡 CTV
[£]

GH [Q][Q][Q] Sunningdale Private Hotel 52 Preston Road, Overcombe DT3 6QD (on A353 2m E of town centre)
☎(0305) 832179
Mar-Oct
Families are made especially welcome at this private hotel, where good, comfortable accommodation is provided. The bedrooms, which are in various sizes, are well equipped. Public areas include a spacious lounge, a dining room, a small bar and a games room.
18rm(11🛁2🚿) (8fb)CTV in all bedrooms [R] sB&B£19.50-£25 sB&B🛁🚿£24.50-£30 dB&B£39-£50 dB&B🛁🚿£44-£55 WB&B£126-£158 WBDi£158-£199 LDO 6.30pm
Lic CTV 🏊(heated) putting green table tennis games room
Credit Cards [1][3][5][£]

GH [Q][Q][Q] Tamarisk Hotel 12 Stavordale Road, Westham DT4 0AB ☎(0305) 786514
Mar-Oct
This house offers simple, comfortable accomodation in well-decorated, well-equipped bedrooms. There is a bright dining room
▶

Channel View
Guest House
10 Brunswick Terrace, Weymouth
Tel: (01305) 782527

Cleanliness & comfort assured.
H&C and shaver points in all bedrooms.
Avoid disappointment. Book early.
No main roads to cross to beach.
Non smoking house.
En-suite in some rooms.
Licensed residents' bar.

WEYMOUTH

Visa and Access cards accepted.
10 yards from the beach.
Electric radiators in all rooms.
Walking distance to shops.

English Tourist Board COMMENDED

Good home cooking & fresh vegetables in season.
Unrestricted entry - own keys.
Even towels & bathrobes provided.
Separate tables in dining room.
TV and tea & coffee bars in all rooms.

AA RECOMMENDED QQQQ

Hairdryer and iron facilities.
Open all year.
Unspoilt sea views from front rooms.
Sorry no children under 12, or pets.
Enjoy your stay with us.

Bed and Breakfast according to season £17-£24
Four Course Evening Meal £9.00 per person
Full Fire Certificate. Food hygiene certificate
Send SAE for brochure.

AA QQQ
Cumberland Hotel
95 The Esplanade
Weymouth
Dorset DT4 7BA
Telephone: 01305 785644

SEA FRONT HOTEL

The Cumberland is centrally situated with superb views of the Bay.

We are close to the town centre, bus and railway station and only a few minutes from the Harbour ferry and Pavilion Theatre.
All twelve bedrooms are en-suite and have colour TV, tea tray and radio also full central heating, most have sea views.
Open all year including Christmas.
The hotel is noted for its home cooked food, friendly service and cleanliness.
We offer a choice of menu at breakfast and dinner.

English Tourist Board

Brochure on request.

WEYMOUTH

Sunningdale Hotel
Preston Road, Weymouth.

Set in 1¼ acres of gardens we offer you good food, good company and good service. A heated swimming pool, 6 hole putting green, games room, large free car park and lounge bar are just some of the facilities. Rooms with private bathroom or shower are available. 'Live music' nights in the summer are particularly enjoyable.

Telephone: (01305) 832179 for attractive brochure & tariff.

serving a set menu at dinner and special dishes by arrangement and a welcoming bar and lounge.

16rm(4⇔8♠) (7fb) ⊁ in dining room CTV in 6 bedrooms ® ⊀ sB&B£18-£21 sB&B⇔♠£20-£23 dB&B£36-£42 dB&B⇔♠£40-£46 WB&B£100-£130 WBDi£135-£165 LDO 2pm
Lic ▥ CTV
£

GH Q Q *Trelawney Hotel* 1 Old Castle Road DT4 8QB
☎(0305) 783188
A small, family-run hotel close to the town centre offers basic but adequate accomodation. There is a comfortable lounge with a small bar and a bright, attractive dining room serving plain English cooking made with fresh produce.
10⇔♠ CTV in all bedrooms ® LDO 7pm
Lic ▥ CTV putting green
Credit Cards 3

GH Q Q *The Westwey* 62 Abbotsbury Road DT4 0BJ
☎(0305) 784564
The Westwey is a cheery establishment standing away from the centre of town. The bedrooms, which vary in size, are neatly presented, simply furnished and mostly en suite. A car park is provided at the rear.
11rm(1⇔8♠) (2fb) CTV in all bedrooms ® ⊀ LDO 6.30pm
Lic ▥ CTV nc6yrs

WHADDON Buckinghamshire   Map 04 SP83
INN Q Q *Lowndes Arms & Motel* 4 High Street MK17 0NA
☎Milton Keynes(0908) 501706 FAX (0908) 504185
Well suited to the needs of the business guest, this small friendly inn located at the centre of a peaceful village offers well equipped bedrooms in a converted stable block.
Annexe 11♠ CTV in all bedrooms ® ⊀ (ex guide dogs) LDO 9.30pm
▥ nc14yrs
Credit Cards 1 3 5

WHALEY BRIDGE Derbyshire   Map 07 SK08
GH Q Q *Old Bakery* 80 Buxton Road SK12 7JE (on A5004, N of junction with A5470) ☎(0663) 732359
3rm CTV in all bedrooms ® ⊀ (ex guide dogs) ✳ sB&B£15-£19.50 dB&B£32 WB&B£100-£110 WBDi£160 LDO 10pm
▥ CTV

WHITBY North Yorkshire   Map 08 NZ81
GH Q Q Q **Corra Lynn Hotel** 28 Crescent Avenue YO21 3EW
☎(0947) 602214
Mar-Oct rs Nov & Feb
The Corra Lynn is a small, friendly hotel conveniently situated for Whitby's West Cliff, the harbour and the town. Bedrooms are immaculately decorated and equipped with modern comfort. Guests have a comfortable lounge, and dinner is served by prior arrangement - the hotel is licensed, so wine is available at table.
6⇔♠ (1fb) ⊁ in dining room CTV in all bedrooms ® ✳ sB&B⇔♠£20-£22 dB&B⇔♠£40-£48 WB&B£130-£145 WBDi£217-£231 LDO 1pm
Lic ▥ CTV nc5yrs
£

Telephone national area codes are due to change by 16th April 1995. Please see the note under 'How to Use this Guide' at the front of the book.

GH Q Q Q Q Q Q *Dunsley Hall* Dunsley YO21 3TL
☎(0947) 83437
FAX (0947) 83505
Closed 25-26 Dec
Built at the turn of the century, this lovely old house is set in four acres of grounds in the village of Dunsley. Oak panelling is a feature of the hotel, but the original panelled billiard room with its exquisitely carved fireplace and stained glass window is unique. Spacious bedrooms are attractively decorated and furnished and several have sea views. There is a cosy bar and lounge, and four-course meals are served in the charming dining room.
7⇔♠ (2fb) CTV in all bedrooms ® T LDO 6.30pm
Lic ▥ ⤜ (heated) ⚑(hard)snooker croquet putting green
Credit Cards 1 3

GH Q Q Q **Europa Private Hotel** 20 Hudson Street YO21 3EP (A169 from Pickering to Whitby, turn right at A171 follow signs to West Cliff, turn right at Royal Crescent then first left Hudson Street) ☎(0947) 602251
Feb-Oct
In a quiet road close to West Cliff, this small, friendly hotel offers attractively decorated accommodation, retaining some of its Victorian character. Public rooms comprise a well appointed dining room and a comfortable guests' lounge.
10rm(2♠) (1fb) ⊁ in dining room CTV in all bedrooms ® ⊀ ✳ sB&Bfr£18 dB&Bfr£30 dB&B♠fr£36 WB&Bfr£105 WBDifr£168 LDO 11am
▥ CTV nc3yrs

GH Q Q Q **Glendale** 16 Crescent Avenue YO21 3ED
☎(0947) 604242
Apr-Oct
Glendale is a very comfortable and friendly guesthouse with neat bedrooms. It offers very good value for money.
6rm(5♠) (3fb) ⊁ in dining room CTV in all bedrooms ® ✳ sB&B£15-£16 dB&B♠£36-£38 WB&B£145-£147 WBDi£160 LDO 4.15pm
Lic CTV
£

GH Q Q Q Q Q **Grantley House** 26 Hudson Street YO21 3EP
☎(0947) 600895
Feb-Nov
A black canopied entrance and attractive flower tubs and boxes distinguish this Victorian terraced house from a row of similar properties, just a few minutes from the seafront on Whitby's West Cliff. Bedrooms are attractively styled with much use of modern coordinated fabrics. Good home cooking is provided at separate tables in the dining room, after which guests can relax in the comfortable TV lounge.
8rm(4♠) (1fb) CTV in all bedrooms ® ⊀ (ex guide dogs) dB&Bfr£30 dB&B♠fr£36
Lic ▥ CTV

GH Q Q Q **Haven** 4 East Crescent YO21 3HD ☎(0947) 603842
rs Nov-Jan
This friendly, comfortable guesthouse is in an early Victorian crescent high on the West Cliff, with fine views over the harbour

and sea. Bedrooms are well equipped and those at the front have splendid sea views. There is a comfortable guests' lounge and an attractively decorated dining room where substantial home-cooked dinners and breakfasts are provided.
8rm(5🛁🚿) (1fb) 🚭 in dining room CTV in all bedrooms Ⓡ 🐕 sB&B£18-£20 dB&B£32-£34 dB&B🛁🚿£36-£42
Lic ♨ CTV nc5yrs
[£]

GH [Q][Q][Q] ***Sandbeck Hotel*** 2 Crescent Terrace, Westcliff YO21 3EL ☎(0947) 604012
Etr-Oct
15🛁🚿 (5fb) CTV in all bedrooms Ⓡ 🐕 (ex guide dogs)
Lic ♨ CTV nc6yrs
Credit Cards [1] [3]

SELECTED

GH [Q][Q][Q][Q] Seacliffe Hotel North Promenade, West Cliff YO21 3JX ☎(0947) 603139 FAX (0947) 603139
A friendly, family-run private hotel is situated in a prime location high on Whitby's West Cliff overlooking the sea, yet within easy reach of the town and golf course. Bedrooms are well equipped, with every modern facility, and many have fine sea views. Downstairs there is a comfortable lounge and a cosy bar, with a patio at the rear. The Candlelight Restaurant offers an extensive menu including a very good choice of vegetarian dishes.
19🛁🚿 (4fb) 🚭 in 1 bedrooms 🚭 in dining room CTV in all bedrooms Ⓡ T sB&B🛁🚿£29.50-£37.50 dB&B🛁🚿£46-£57 WB&B£178.50-£199.50 LDO 8.45pm
Lic ♨ CTV
Credit Cards [1] [2] [3] [5] [£]

SELECTED

GH [Q][Q][Q][Q] Waverley Private Hotel 17 Crescent Avenue YO21 3ED (follow signs to West Cliff, hotel 200yds from Crescent Gardens) ☎(0947) 604389
Mar-Oct
A large Victorian terraced house is situated on the West Cliff, only a few minutes' walk from the promenade. The spacious bedrooms are very comfortable and freshly decorated. There is a first-floor guests' lounge, a large dining room with separate tables and a cosy bar. The hotel is particularly well maintained, with friendly service.
6rm(5🚿) (4fb) 🚭 in dining room CTV in all bedrooms Ⓡ 🐕 sB&B£16.50-£17.50 dB&B🚿£37-£39 WB&B£107-£122 WBDi£145-£160 LDO 5pm
Lic ♨ CTV nc3yrs
[£]

WHITCHURCH Hereford & Worcester Map **03** SO51

INN[Q] ***Crown Hotel*** HR9 6DB ☎Symonds Yat(0600) 890234
Closed 25-26 Dec
A 16th-century inn situated beside the A40 between Ross and Monmouth offers well equipped, comfortable bedrooms reached via narrow corridors. There is a first-floor lounge, and downstairs a characterful bar with a separate dining room to one side serves as a popular meeting place.
5rm(1🛁4🚿) (3fb) CTV in all bedrooms Ⓡ LDO 9pm
♨ CTV skittle alley pool room
Credit Cards [1] [2] [3] [5]

WHITCHURCH Shropshire Map **07** SJ54

FH [Q][Q][Q] Mrs M H Mulliner **Bradeley Green** *(SJ537449)* Waterfowl Sanctuary, Tarporley Road SY13 4HD (2m N on A49) ☎(0948) 663442
Closed Xmas
This spacious farmhouse is part of a working dairy farm two miles from Tarporley, in an unusual setting in water gardens where there is a waterfowl collection and a farm nature trail. A feature of the large bedrooms is their exposed timbers and all are comfortably furnished. There is a TV lounge with a fine tiled fireplace burning logs in colder weather. Guests receive a warm welcome from Mrs. Ruth Mulliner, who provides evening meals with advance notice.
3rm(2🛁🚿) 🚭 Ⓡ * dB&B🛁🚿fr£40 WB&Bfr£130 WBDifr£190 LDO 9am
♨ CTV water gardens 180 acres dairy waterfowl fish farming
[£]

WHITEPARISH Wiltshire Map **04** SU22

GH [Q][Q][Q] Newton Farmhouse Southampton Road SP5 2QL ☎(0794) 884416
8rm(2🛁6🚿) CTV in all bedrooms Ⓡ sB&B🛁🚿fr£22.50 dB&B🛁🚿£35-£40 LDO noon
♨ 🏊
See advertisement under Salisbury.

WHITESTONE Devon Map **03** SX89

🛏 ☕ **FH [Q][Q]** Mrs S K Lee **Rowhorne House** *(SX880948)* EX4 2LQ ☎Exeter(0392) 74675
Rowhorne House is a real away-from-it-all farmhouse. Mrs Lee has a naturally welcoming manner. Bedrooms are large with marvellous views from every window to the Exe estuary. Dinner is available if arranged beforehand.
3rm (2fb) CTV in 1 bedroom 🐕 sB&B£14 dB&B£28 WB&B£98
CTV 103 acres dairy
Credit Cards [1] [2] [3] [5] [£]

WHITEWELL Lancashire   Map **07** SD64

INNQQQ **The Inn at Whitewell** BB7 3AT
☎Dunsop Bridge(0200) 448222 FAX (0200) 448298
This charming country inn, situated in the picturesque Forest of
Bowland, is full of character. Bedrooms have been tastefully
refurbished in Victorian style, and are generally well proportioned.
They feature fine fabrics, paintings and antiques (including
telescopes, binoculars and old telephones); sophisticated hi-fi
equipment and TV provide a contrasting modern touch.
Bathrooms are well lit and equipped with Victorian sanitary wear.
Bedrooms can also have peat fires and early morning tea provided
as extras. Oak beams, wood panelled walls and blazing log fires
distinguish the bars, which offer a wide choice of menu. The
restaurant overlooking the river provides a more formal setting for
breakfast and evening meals. Two further dining rooms double as
a small but interesting art gallery.
10⇌ſ (4fb)CTV in all bedrooms T ✳ sB&B⇌ſ£45-£49.50
dB&B⇌ſ£59.50-£67 Bar Lunch £6.50-£10.50alc Dinner £13.70-
£20.90alc LDO 9.30pm
▥ CTV ⌁ clay pigeon shooting by arrangement
Credit Cards ①②③⑤

WHITING BAY See **ARRAN, ISLE OF**

WHITLAND Dyfed   Map **02** SN21

FH QQQ C M & I A Lewis *Cilpost (SN191184)* SA34 0RP
☎(0994) 240280
Apr-Sep
Personally run by the friendly Lewis family, this busy working
farm provides bright, modern bedrooms. Comfortable public areas
include a cosy lounge and spacious dining room where
imaginative and enjoyable home cooking is served. There is an
attractive garden which includes an indoor swimming pool and
excellent snooker room. The farmhouse is north of the village
signposted off the Henllan Amgoed road.
7rm(3⇌3ſ) (3fb) ✻
Lic ▥ ₹ (heated) ⌁ snooker 160 acres dairy mixed

WHITLEY BAY Tyne & Wear   Map **12** NZ37

GH QQ **Cherrytree House** 35 Brook Street NE26 1AF
☎091-251 4306
A large, double-fronted Edwardian town house situated close to
both seafront and town centre offers homely accommodation,
most of its well furnished bedrooms now having en suite facilities.
The comfortable residents' lounge is provided with books and
magazines, and good home-cooked meals are served in a
pleasantly appointed dining room. Unrestricted parking is allowed
on the road outside.
4rm(3ſ) ⊬ in dining room CTV in all bedrooms ® ✳
sB&B£15-£20 sB&Bſ£20-£25 dB&B£25-£27 dB&Bſ£32-£36
LDO 9.30am
▥ CTV
⑤

GH QQ *Lindisfarne Hotel* 11 Holly Avenue NE26 1EB
☎091-251 3954 & 091-297 0579
A friendly family run hotel, stands a few minutes' walk from both
the seafront and town. The hotel holds a residential licence and
there is a comfortable and spacious lounge bar. One of the
bedrooms has a four-poster bed, and a number of rooms and
public areas have modern wall coverings.
14rm(9⇌ſ) (2fb) CTV in all bedrooms ® LDO 9pm
Lic ▥ CTV ⥮pool table
Credit Cards ①③

GH QQQ **Marlborough Hotel** 20-21 East Parade, Central
Promenade NE26 1AP ☎091-251 3628 FAX 091-251 3628
A family-owned double-fronted private hotel is situated on the
seafront. The spacious accommodation includes two comfortable
lounges with sea views. Bedrooms vary in size and standard of

furnishings, but are gradually being improved. Home-cooked
evening meals are available on request, and private parking is
provided in front of the hotel.
15rm(11⇌ſ) (4fb) ⊬ in bedrooms ⊬ in dining room CTV in all
bedrooms ® T ✻ (ex guide dogs) ✳ sB&Bfr£20
sB&B⇌ſfr£32 dB&B⇌ſ£43-£48 LDO noon
Lic CTV
Credit Cards ①②③ ⑤

GH QQ **White Surf** 8 South Parade NE26 2RG ☎091-253 0103
This neatly maintained terraced house is situated between the
seafront and the town centre. It offers bright and fresh, plainly
decorated and furnished accommodation, with generally compact
bedrooms, all with TV. The attractive dining room has a
continental atmosphere, with white walls and a tiled floor, and the
lounge has comfortable leather seating and a small pool table.
9rm (2fb) ⊬ in bedrooms ⊬ in dining room CTV in all bedrooms
® ✻ (ex guide dogs) sB&B£16.50 dB&B£33 WB&B£115.50
WBDi£161 LDO 6pm
▥ CTV

GH QQQ **York House Hotel** 30 Park Parade NE26 1DX
☎091-252 8313 & 091-251 3953
Small, friendly and family run, this guest house stands in a
Victorian terrace within easy reach of both town centre and sea
front. Bedrooms (all but one with en suite facilities) are equipped
with television sets, radios and telephones; a comfortable lounge is
provided for guests' use, and the attractive dining room offers a
short wine list with dinner menus which include seafood
specialities. A room on the ground floor provides convenient
accommodation for visitors unable to climb stair
8rm(7⇌ſ) (3fb) ⊬ in dining room CTV in all bedrooms ® T ✳
sB&B£22 sB&B⇌ſ£26.50-£28 WB&B£154-£190 WBDi£200-
£260 LDO 8pm
Lic ▥ CTV
Credit Cards ①②③ ⑤

WHITNEY-ON-WYE Hereford & Worcester   Map **03** SO24

P R E M I E R 🏆 S E L E C T E D

INN QQQQQ *The
Rhydspence* HR3 6EU (2m W
A438) ☎Hay(0497) 831262
This attractive black and white
timbered inn - parts of which
date back to the 14th century -
stands beside the A438 a mile
west of the village. Much of
its original charm survives in
the beamed ceilings and stone
walls of the cosy public areas,
while bedrooms offer a high

standard of modern facilities as well as comfort and a rich
decor with coordinating soft furnishings; guests are welcomed
by roaring fires in winter, and in summer they can enjoy a
delightful garden running down to the stream that forms the
English/Welsh border. The bar's range of real ales and
interesting dishes provides an alternative to equally good but
more formal restaurant meals.
5rm(4⇌1ſ) CTV in all bedrooms ® ✻ (ex guide dogs)
LDO 9.30pm
▥
Credit Cards ①②③

WHIXLEY North Yorkshire   Map **08** SE45

GH QQQ **Princes Lodge** YO5 8EE
☎Boroughbridge(0423) 330168 FAX (0423) 331458
Bright, en suite accommodation is offered at this modernised
Victorian farmhouse, situated on the A59 between York and

Harrogate. It has an attractive guests' lounge and a separate dining room with period-style tables. Outside, there is a heated swimming pool and several self-catering units.
3rm(1🛁2🚿) 🚭 in dining room 🚭 in lounges CTV in all bedrooms [R] 🐕 (ex guide dogs) dB&B🛁🚿£34-£36 WB&B£112-£119
Lic 🅿 CTV 🏊(heated)
[£]

WIGAN Greater Manchester — Map **07** SD50

GH [Q][Q] ***Aalton Court*** 23 Upper Dicconson Street WN1 2AG
☎(0942) 322220
This Victorian terraced house is conveniently located close to the town centre and rugby league ground. Privately owned and personally run, it provides simple but soundly maintained accommodation. The attractively decorated bedrooms have modern furnishings and equipment: some are rather compact. The guesthouse has a private car park at the rear.
6rm(2🛁4🚿) (1fb) CTV in all bedrooms [R] 🐕 LDO 2pm
Lic 🅿 CTV

WIGHT, ISLE OF — Map **04**

BRADING — Map **04** SZ68

GH [Q][Q][Q] ***Red Lion Inn*** 10 High Street ☎(0983) 407307
This quaint restaurant dates back in parts to the 1760's and has much character and charm. There are three nicely presented bedrooms located in the adjacent 'sun deck' annexe, each of which is well equipped and nicely decorated to complement the beams and low ceilings. Extensive menus are served at lunch and dinner in the popular restaurant, and ample car parking is provided at the rear.
3🛁🚿 CTV in all bedrooms [R] LDO 10.30pm
Lic 🅿
Credit Cards [1][2][3]

FRESHWATER — Map **04** SZ38

GH [Q][Q][Q] **Blenheim House Hotel** Gate Lane PO40 9QD (on main road out of Freshwater & 3m from Yarmouth Ferry Terminal) ☎(0983) 752858
May-Sep
A real 'home from home' is provided in the traditional atmosphere of this long-established guesthouse. The accommodation is impressively well maintained, and there is a particularly comfortable lounge. In the bright dining room, a very reasonably priced four-course evening meal is available by arrangement. A well furnished bar is also provided.
8🚿 (3fb) CTV in all bedrooms [R] 🐕 * sB&B🚿fr£21 dB&B🚿fr£42 WB&Bfr£147 WBDifr£203 LDO noon
Lic 🅿 nc10yrs 🏊(heated) table tennis billiards darts

NITON — Map **04** SZ57

GH [Q][Q][Q] **Pine Ridge Country House** Niton Undercliff PO38 2LY ☎(0983) 730802 FAX (0983) 731001
Quietly situated in three and a half acres of mature, well kept grounds, this extended country house has an established air and this is borne out inside: large bedrooms are made even more comfortable by a generous provision of facilities; the public rooms are attractive, and the lounge bar is warmed by an open fire on chillier evenings. There are wonderful views from all sides of the building.
9rm(6🛁🚿) (2fb) 🚭 in 2 bedrooms 🚭 in dining room CTV in all bedrooms [R] T * sB&B£20-£35 sB&B🛁🚿£30-£35 dB&B£40-£50 dB&B🛁🚿£50-£60 WB&B£160-£195 LDO 9pm
Lic 🅿 CTV
Credit Cards [1][3][£]

RYDE — Map **04** SZ59

GH [Q][Q][Q] **Teneriffe Hotel** 36 The Strand PO33 1JF
☎(0983) 563841 FAX (0983) 615692
Closed Jan-Feb
Personally run by the Brown family for over 29 years, this popular hotel has been furnished in the modern style and offers a lift to most levels. There is live entertainment in season, and the newly refurbished lounge bar provides good function facilities. Other public rooms include a TV lounge and a dining room where home-cooked food is served. Coaches and parties are very welcome.
50🛁🚿 (7fb) 🚭 in dining room CTV in all bedrooms [R] 🐕 (ex guide dogs) * sB&B🛁🚿£17.65-£18.65 dB&B🛁🚿£35.65-£36.65 WB&B£123.55-£130.55 WBDi£130-£179 LDO 7pm
Lic lift 🅿 CTV
Credit Cards [1][2][3][£]

SANDOWN — Map **04** SZ58

GH [Q][Q][Q] **Bertram Lodge** 3 Leed Street PO36 9DA
☎(0983) 402551
Closed Xmas
In a quiet residential area, this 19th-century house has a warm friendly atmosphere. Bedrooms are nicely decorated and comfortable and the lounge promotes relaxation. Breakfast and dinner are served in the bright, fresh dining room.
9rm(8🚿) (3fb) 🚭 in 5 bedrooms 🚭 in dining room 🚭 in 1 lounge CTV in all bedrooms [R] 🐕 * sB&B🚿£17-£18.50 dB&B🚿£34-£37 WB&B£99-£122 WBDi£125-£145 LDO 3.30pm
🅿 CTV nc3yrs

🛏☕ **GH [Q][Q]** **Chester Lodge Hotel** Beachfield Road PO36 8NA
☎(0983) 402773
mid Mar-mid Oct
The Hayward family have run this guesthouse for many years and continue to make it a cosy and relaxing place to stay. The bedrooms are furnished in a bright and homely style and they all have modern facilities; the majority of them are en suite. The spacious public areas have a happy, relaxed atmosphere about them. Guests are offered a choice of evening meal and the hotel is busy and popular.
18rm(2🛁12🚿) (5fb) CTV in all bedrooms [R] sB&B£13-£14 sB&B🛁🚿£18-£20 dB&B£26-£30 dB&B🛁🚿£36-£40
Lic 🅿 CTV
Credit Cards [1][3][£]

GH [Q][Q][Q] **Culver Lodge Hotel** Albert Road PO36 8AW
☎(0983) 403819 & 402902
Mar-Nov
Culver Lodge is a large Victorian property a short walk from the centre of town. It offers attractively presented bedrooms in a bright modern style. Public rooms include a smart dining room, where a home-cooked evening meal is served, a comfortable lounge and a well stocked bar.
21🛁🚿 (4fb) 🚭 in dining room CTV in all bedrooms [R] 🐕 sB&B🛁🚿£19-£22.50 dB&B🛁🚿£38-£45 WB&B£125-£150 WBDi£150-£196 LDO 10pm
Lic 🅿 CTV pool room darts video games
Credit Cards [1][2][3][5][£]

GH [Q][Q][Q] **Cygnet Hotel** 58 Carter Street PO36 8DQ
☎Isle of Wight(0983) 402930 FAX (0983) 405112
This large hotel offers lots of facilities to holiday-makers. It is lively, with a large bar lounge and live entertainment on some evenings, but there is a choice of quiet lounges too. Bedrooms, including some on the ground floor, are neat and nicely furnished with a reasonable array of facilities. The dining room is pretty and bright and the staff are pleasant.
50rm(36🛁🚿) (8fb) 🚭 in dining room CTV in 30 bedrooms [R] 🐕 (ex guide dogs) sB&B£20-£25 sB&B🛁🚿£24-£28 dB&B£40-£50 dB&B🛁🚿£50-£63 (incl dinner) WB&B£150-£185 WBDi£180-£220 LDO 6.30pm
▶

Lic lift ▥ CTV ❦ (heated) ⊀(heated) sauna solarium gymnasium spa pool
Credit Cards 1 2 3 ⓔ

GH Q Q Q *Norton Lodge* 22 Victoria Road PO36 8AL
☎Isle of Wight(0983) 402423
Mar-Oct
9rm(5ᐟ❀) (4fb) CTV in all bedrooms ® ⅋ (ex guide dogs)
Lic ▥ CTV nc5yrs

SEAVIEW   Map **04** SZ69

GH Q *Northbank Hotel* Circular Road PO34 5ET
☎(0983) 612227
Etr-Sep
Northbank is an old Victorian house with a garden sloping down to the seashore. Splendid views are enjoyed from the traditional lounge, the cosy bar crammed with memorabilia, and many of the bedrooms. The latter vary in size, some have fine old furniture, but most are fairly simple.
18rm (6fb) CTV in 2 bedrooms ® LDO 8pm
Lic CTV ⚿ ✎ snooker

SHANKLIN   Map **04** SZ58

GH Q Q Q **Aqua Hotel** The Esplanade PO37 6BN
☎(0983) 863024 FAX (0983) 864841
Etr-5 Nov
Personally managed by Mr and Mrs Blanchett, this good-value hotel continues to be improved. It stands on the esplanade offering fine sea views, and there is a terrace where guests can sit and enjoy the sunshine. A good choice of dishes is offered in Boaters restaurant, and lunches are also available in the smartly refurbished bar. Bedrooms vary in size but all have comfortable modern furniture and en suite facilities.
22⇆❀ (4fb) ⅌ in dining room CTV in all bedrooms ® ⅋
sB&B⇆ᐟ❀£18-£24 dB&B⇆ᐟ❀£36-£48 WB&B£126-£168
WBDi£168-£210 LDO 4.30pm
Lic ▥ darts pool table
Credit Cards 1 2 3 5

GH Q Q Q **Culham Lodge** 31 Landguard Manor Road PO37 7HZ
☎(0983) 862880 FAX (0983) 865858
Mar-Oct
Away from the bustle of the town centre, this attractive Victorian property offers comfortable, bright accommodation. Some of the bedrooms are on the ground floor and the majority have en suite facilities. There is a well furnished lounge and a dining room leading into another conservatory-style lounge, which overlooks the garden and outdoor swimming pool. A choice of dishes is offered each evening from the table d'hôte menu.
10rm(1⇆7❀) ⅌ in dining room ⅌ in lounges CTV in all bedrooms ® ⅋ (ex guide dogs) ✳ sB&B£16-£17.50
sB&B⇆ᐟ❀£19-£20.50 dB&B£32-£35 dB&B⇆ᐟ❀£38-£41
WB&B£104-£135 WBDi£139-£175 LDO 4pm
▥ CTV nc12yrs ⊀(heated) solarium
Credit Cards 1 3 ⓔ

GH Q Q **Curraghmore Hotel** 22 Hope Road PO37 6EA
☎(0983) 862605
Mar-Oct
This licensed hotel occupies an elevated position overlooking the beach, only 150 yards away. Most of the bedrooms have en suite facilities and there are some ground-floor rooms, although disabled guests should know that there are steps up to the main entrance. Spacious public areas include a popular bar and ballroom that offers entertainment every other night during the season. There is also a small roof-top sun lounge. The atmosphere here is very relaxed and informal, making it an ideal base for family holidays.
24rm(10⇆14❀) (9fb)CTV in all bedrooms ® sB&B⇆ᐟ❀£20-£22 dB&B⇆ᐟ❀£40-£44 WB&B£140-£154 WBDi£179-£199 LDO 6pm
Lic putting
ⓔ

GH Q Q Q **Edgecliffe Hotel** Clarence Gardens PO37 6HA (first left down Arthurs Hill) ☎(0983) 866199 FAX (0983) 404812
Mar-Sep
A quietly located establishment just off Arthur's Hill, this hotel is a haven for non-smokers and has recently received a no-smoking award from the Isle of Wight authorities. Public areas offer a comfortable lounge and a bright dining room where home-cooked evening meals are served, including vegetarian fare. Bedrooms are comfortably furnished and traditionally styled.
9rm(2⇆4❀) (2fb) ⅌ CTV in all bedrooms ® ⅋ sB&B£16-£18.50 dB&B£32-£37 dB&B⇆ᐟ❀£44-£59 WB&B£96-£145
WBDi£135-£194 LDO 6.30pm
Lic ▥ nc3yrs cycles for hire
Credit Cards 1 2 3 5 ⓔ

GH [Q][Q][Q] Hambledon Hotel Queens Road PO37 6AW (off A3055) ☎(0983) 862403 & 863651 FAX (0983) 867894

Closed 2 wks Nov

Personally run by cheery proprietors Norman and Beryl Birch, this private hotel offers comfortable bedrooms, a smart dining room, two lounges, one no smoking, and a cosy bar with a host of teddies and cuddly toys which are donated to charity at the end of every season.

11🚿 (4fb) 🚭 in dining room 🚭 in 1 lounge CTV in all bedrooms Ⓡ T 🐕 (ex guide dogs) sB&B🚿£17-£20 WB&B£115-£159 WBDi£139-£189 LDO 6pm

Lic 🅿 CTV 🏠

Credit Cards [1] [3] [£]

GH [Q][Q][Q] Kenbury Private Hotel Clarence Road PO37 7BH ☎(0983) 862085

Etr-Oct

Quietly positioned in its own mature gardens on the outskirts of town, this small family-owned hotel offrs traditional guesthouse hospitality in comfortable surroundings. The dining room is particularly cosy, with its wood panelling, oak furniture and lace tablecloths. The bedrooms are modern, bright and functional, and public rooms include a comfortable lounge, a separate bar with dance floor and pool table.

18rm(16🛁🚿) (3fb) CTV in all bedrooms Ⓡ 🐕 (ex guide dogs) * sB&Bfr£17 sB&B🛁🚿£22 LDO 6.30pm

Lic 🅿 CTV nc3yrs

Credit Cards [1] [3] [£]

GH [Q][Q][Q] *Mount House Hotel* 20 Arthurs Hill PO37 6EE ☎(0983) 862556

Mount House is a family owned hotel on Arthur's Hill, convenient for the sea and shops. The bedrooms are nicely decorated and all but one have modern en suite shower rooms. The traditionally styled public areas are comfortably furnished and include a small, well stocked bar. A home cooked evening meal is available.

10🚿 (2fb) CTV in all bedrooms Ⓡ 🐕 (ex guide dogs) LDO 4pm

Lic 🅿 CTV

Credit Cards [1] [3]

SELECTED

GH [Q][Q][Q][Q] Osborne House Esplanade PO37 6BN ☎(0983) 862501 FAX (0983) 862501

Jan-18 Oct

Osborne House is an attractive property in a slightly elevated position with lovely sea views, and it has a pretty garden where guests may sit and watch the world go by. The bedrooms are fresh and bright and well equipped with plenty of extras. There are two comfortable lounges, one serving snacks and meals in addition to the restaurant's enjoyable home-cooked dishes.

12🛁🚿 🚭 in dining room CTV in all bedrooms Ⓡ 🐕 * sB&B🛁🚿fr£30 dB&B🛁🚿fr£60 LDO 8pm

Lic 🅿 nc13yrs

Credit Cards [1] [3]

GH [Q][Q][Q] Rowborough Hotel 32 Arthurs Hill PO37 6EX (1m S of Lake at junct of A3055/A3056) ☎(0983) 866072 FAX (0983) 864000

Mar-28 Oct

A convivial, well stocked bar and candlelit dinners are features of this friendly family-run hotel. Bedrooms are furnished in the modern style, and there is a residents' lounge in addition to the banquet seating in the reception lobby. A well kept garden overlooks the main road, and the hotel has its own side car park. Good home cooking is provided by members of the proprietor's family.

8rm(3🛁4🚿) (3fb)CTV in all bedrooms Ⓡ 🐕 sB&B£15.50-£19.50 sB&B🛁🚿£17-£21 dB&B🛁🚿£34-£42 WB&B£116-£136 WBDi£146-£185 LDO 8pm

Lic 🅿 CTV nc5yrs

Credit Cards [1] [3] [5] [£]

🛏 ☕ **GH [Q][Q][Q] Soraba Private Hotel** 2 Paddock Road PO37 6NZ ☎(0983) 862367

Mar-Nov

This attractive detached Victorian house is located in a quiet but central area of the town, convenient for the beach, shops and theatre. It is well run by resident proprietors Mr and Mrs Wynn Davies, and many guests return regularly to enjoy the care and attention offered. The simply furnished bedrooms are bright and fresh with tastefully coordinating decor.

7rm(4🛁🚿) 🚭 in 1 bedrooms 🚭 in dining room CTV in 4 bedrooms sB&B£14.50-£17 dB&B£29-£32 dB&B🛁🚿£32-£37 WB&B£91-£130 WBDi£118-£154 LDO 3pm

Lic 🅿 CTV nc3yrs

Credit Cards [1] [3] [£]

GH [Q][Q][Q] White House Hotel Eastcliff Promenade PO37 6AY ☎(0983) 862776 & 867904 FAX (0983) 865980

6 Jan-Oct & Xmas

11rm(2🛁9🚿) (1fb) 🚭 in 9 bedrooms CTV in all bedrooms Ⓡ T 🐕 (ex guide dogs) sB&B🛁🚿£22-£26 dB&B🛁🚿£44-£52 WB&B£150-£180 WBDi£195-£235 LDO 7pm

Lic 🅿 CTV

Credit Cards [1] [2] [3] [5]

TOTLAND BAY

Map **04** SZ38

GH [Q][Q] *Frenchman's Cove Country Hotel* Alum Bay Old Road PO39 0HZ ☎(0983) 752227

rs May-Jun

Recently purchased by Mr and Mrs Boatfield, this hotel is located in a country lane with glorious views across fields and meadows.

▶

St. Catherine's Hotel

1 Winchester Park Road
(off The Broadway) Sandown
Tel & Fax: 01983 402392

Holiday and business hotel open all year, except Christmas and New Year. Your bedroom has private en suite facilities, and telephone, colour television, radio and free tea/coffee making facilities. Tastefully decorated. Five course evening meal and full English breakfast with excellent friendly service. Car parking and ground floor rooms available. Licensed bar and restful lounge with Sky television. Only 5 minutes walk to shops, seafront, pier complex and new modern leisure centre.

Please phone for brochure.

English Tourist Board COMMENDED

The bedrooms vary in size and shape, and those on the ground and first floors offer more comfort than the few at the top of the house. Public rooms include a cosy bar, spacious dining room and a small lounge. This is a no-smoking establishment.
13rm(2⇄7♪) (11fb) CTV in all bedrooms ® ⅍ (ex guide dogs) LDO 8pm
Lic ▥ CTV badminton net play equipment
Credit Cards 1 3

GH ◖Q◗◖Q◗ Littledene Lodge Granville Road PO39 0AX
☎(0983) 752411
Feb-Nov
A very well presented friendly guesthouse is located in a quiet residential area, conveniently close to the Yarmouth ferry. Bedrooms are well equipped and very attractive, with well coordinated, fresh, bright decor and pretty soft fabrics; the en suite facilities are smart and well maintained. The house is efficiently run by the charming Mrs Wright, who enjoys cooking the fresh five-course evening meal and who will also offer advice on places of interest. Public rooms are comfortable and cosy and include a TV lounge and a spacious dining room with a small bar.
6rm(2⇄3♪) (3fb) ® LDO 4.30pm
Lic ▥ CTV nc3yrs
Credit Cards 3

GH ◖Q◗◖Q◗◖Q◗ The Nodes Country Hotel Alum Bay Old Road
PO39 0HZ ☎(0983) 752859 FAX (0705) 201621
In rural surroundings along a country lane, yet fairly close to both Alum Bay and Totland, this well managed establishment offers a good standard of accommodation with brightly decorated, mostly en suite bedrooms, some in an annexe building. There is a comfortable, traditionally furnished lounge, and in the dining room guests are offered home-cooked meals prepared by the amiable host, Mr Sanchis.
11rm(3⇄6♪) (5fb) ⅍ in 6 bedrooms ⅍ in dining room CTV in all bedrooms ® ✴ sB&B£28-£31 sB&B⇄♪£31.50-£36.50 dB&B⇄♪£63-£73 (incl dinner) WB&B£132.50-£186 WBDi£185-£238.50 LDO 3pm
Lic ▥ CTV ⚬⚬ badminton table tennis
Credit Cards 1 3

GH ◖Q◗◖Q◗◖Q◗ Sandford Lodge Hotel 61 The Avenue PO39 0DN
☎(0983) 753478
Mar-Oct rs Jan-Feb
Attractive accommodation is offered at this family-run establishment in a residential area of Totland Bay. A comfortable lounge is provided and a pretty dining room where home cooked meals are available. Smoking is not permitted anywhere in the hotel.
6rm(3⇄2♪) (2fb) ⅍ ® ⅍ (ex guide dogs) sB&Bfr£18 sB&B⇄♪£21 dB&B£30-£32 dB&B⇄♪£34-£38 WB&B£98-£127 WBDi£160-£187 LDO 4pm
Lic ▥ CTV
Credit Cards 3 £

VENTNOR   Map 04 SZ57

GH ◖Q◗◖Q◗ Channel View Hotel Hambrough Road PO38 1SQ
☎(0983) 852230
Apr-19 Oct rs Mar
There are fine channel views from the Russell family's hotel which stands in a prominent position overlooking the sea front. This late Victorian house still has many of its original attractive features, particularly in the comfortable first-floor sitting room and the large dining room which looks out to sea. Bedrooms are spacious and comfortable.
14rm(2♪) (6fb) ® ⅍ (ex guide dogs) LDO 8pm
Lic CTV ⅌
Credit Cards 1 3

GH ◖Q◗◖Q◗◖Q◗ Glen Islay Hotel St Boniface Road PO38 1NP
☎(0983) 854095
Mar-Oct
In a quiet residential area with views towards St Boniface Downs, the Glen Islay offers nicely presented, mostly en suite bedrooms. Public rooms include an attractive dining room, where evening meals are available, a comfortable lounge, and a spacious bar complete with pool, darts and books. The dining room and bar lead out onto a sunny patio area, which is popular in summer.
10rm(1⇄8♪) (8fb)CTV in all bedrooms ® ⅍ (ex guide dogs) ✴ sB&Bfr£17 dB&B⇄♪fr£34 WB&Bfr£119 WBDi£170
Lic ▥ CTV
£

GH ◖Q◗◖Q◗◖Q◗ Hillside Private Hotel Mitchell Avenue PO38 1DR
☎(0983) 852271
An attractive 18th-century three-storey thatched house is set in three acres of mature grounds and garden, with glorious views. Bedrooms are pretty and well equipped with attractive soft fabrics; some have recently been redecorated, others enjoy sea views over the garden and one room is conveniently located on the ground floor. Public rooms include a comfortable no-smoking lounge and a separate bar with a sunny conservatory. The menu is served in the pleasant dining room, and light refreshments are available throughout the day.
11rm(4⇄7♪) (2fb) ⅍ in dining room ⅍ in lounges CTV in all bedrooms ® sB&B⇄♪£18.50-£21.50 dB&B⇄♪£37-£43 WB&B£129.50-£150.50 WBDi£189-£210 LDO 6.30pm
Lic ▥ nc5yrs
Credit Cards 1 2 3 £

GH ◖Q◗◖Q◗◖Q◗ Lake Hotel Shore Road, Bonchurch PO38 1RF
☎(0983) 852613 FAX (0983) 852613
Mar-Oct
This family-run hotel is quietly situated in over an acre of lovely terraced gardens in the village of Bonchurch. Bedrooms are prettily and tastefully decorated in coordinated Laura Ashley prints, and many have en suite facilities. The public areas include two sunny conservatory-style lounges, a TV lounge and a comfortably appointed larger seating area; there is also a cosy bar area with a range of bar games.
11rm(10⇄♪) Annexe 10⇄♪ (7fb) ⅍ in dining room ⅍ in 1 lounge ® sB&Bfr£29.50 sB&B⇄♪£20-£31.50 dB&Bfr£59 dB&B⇄♪£63 (incl dinner) WB&B£127.50-£157.50 WBDi£169.75-£185.50 LDO 6.30pm
Lic ▥ CTV nc3yrs
£

GH ◖Q◗◖Q◗◖Q◗ Llynfi Hotel 23 Spring Hill PO38 1PF
☎(0983) 852202
Etr-Oct
Standing on the edge of the town centre, this early Victorian house has been converted into a comfortble and well equipped modern hotel. Bedrooms, in a range of sizes, are all attractively decorated. Guests are welcome to relax in the comfortable lounge or cosy bar and the dining room makes a pleasant setting in which to enjoy Mrs Fisher's cooking skills.
10rm(7♪) (2fb) ⅍ in dining room CTV in all bedrooms ® ⅍ (ex guide dogs) sB&B£16-£18.50 sB&B♪£19-£21 dB&B£32-£37 dB&B♪£38-£42 WBDi£145-£180 LDO 7pm
Lic CTV
Credit Cards 1 3 £

SELECTED

GH ◖Q◗◖Q◗◖Q◗◖Q◗ Madeira Hall Country House Trinity Road, Bonchurch PO38 1NS (turn off main Ventnor to Shanklin road by Trinity Church towards Bonchurch. 100yds on right hand side) ☎Isle of Wight(0983) 852624 FAX (0983) 854906
8⇄♪ (1fb) ⅍ CTV in 7 bedrooms ® T ⅍ (ex guide dogs)

sB&B🛁🚿£25-£35 dB&B🛁🚿£50-£70 WB&B£175-£210
🅿 nc5yrs 🏊(heated) putting green croquet lawn
Credit Cards [1] [3] [£]

GH [Q][Q] Medina House Hotel Alma Road PO38 1JU
☎(0983) 852424
Closed 1 wk Xmas

Close to the esplanade at the top of a steep hill, this personally managed small hotel offers freshly decorated accommodation. Some of the front-facing bedrooms have sunny balconies and a number of the rooms enjoy sea views. There is a cosy TV lounge and a bar area with TV and a pool table. A good choice is offered at breakfast and an extensive range of bar meals is available. The patio, leading out from the bar is a new addition.

10rm(2🛁3🚿) 🚭 in dining room 🚭 in lounges CTV in 8 bedrooms [R] 🐕 (ex guide dogs) * sB&Bfr£15 sB&B🛁🚿fr£18 dB&B£30-£32 dB&B🛁🚿£34-£36 WB&B£105-£126 WBDi£157.50-£178.50
Lic 🅿 CTV nc10yrs
Credit Cards [1] [2] [3] [£]

GH [Q][Q][Q] Hotel Picardie Esplanade PO38 1JX ☎(0983) 852647
Mar-Oct

Situated on the esplanade, just yards from the beach, this well kept hotel is personally run by friendly proprietors, Mr and Mrs Sparkes, who create a warm and cheerful atmosphere. Bedrooms vary in size but all have en suite or private facilities. There is a comfortable lounge and an attractive dining room where home cooked food is served, including delicious home-baked bread. The bar is a sunny room at the front of the hotel, where guests can enjoy a drink and watch the world go by.

10🛁🚿 (3fb) 🚭 CTV in all bedrooms [R] sB&B🛁🚿£17.25 dB&B🛁🚿£34.50 WB&B£120 WBDi£175 LDO 4.30pm
Lic CTV
Credit Cards [1] [3] [£]

GH [Q][Q][Q] St Maur Hotel Castle Road PO38 1LG
☎(0983) 852570 FAX (0983) 852306
Closed Dec-Jan

Peacefully situated on a hillside, overlooking the park, this private hotel offers bright and freshly decorated bedrooms with simple, modern furniture. The public rooms are comfortable and traditional in style, with a cosy bar area complementing the spacious lounge and dining room. The well managed service is personally supervised by the proprietor.

14rm(13🛁🚿) (4fb) 🚭 in dining room [R] 🐕 * sB&B🛁🚿£24 dB&B🛁🚿£48 (incl dinner) WB&B£168 WBDi£210 LDO 7pm
Lic 🅿 CTV nc3yrs
Credit Cards [1] [2] [3] [5] [£]

WIGMORE Hereford & Worcester — Map 07 SO46

INN[Q] ***Compasses Hotel*** HR6 9UN ☎(056886) 203

Reputedly dating back to around 1700, this ivy-clad village inn was once a bakery and farmhouse. The two bars and separate dining area display an abundance of ceiling beams and wall timbers.

3rm (1fb) CTV in all bedrooms [R] LDO 9.30pm
🅿
Credit Cards [1] [2] [3] [5]

WILBERFOSS Humberside — Map 08 SE75

FH [Q][Q] Mrs J M Liversidge **Cuckoo Nest** *(SE717510)* YO4 5NL
☎(0759) 380365

This traditional 200-year-old farmhouse is set back from the road, close to the village. A non smoking policy has been adopted in the neat fresh bedrooms. Recently extended, the lounge is both spacious and comfortable, and is equipped with board games and television. Breakfast can be served in sittings at a communal table in the small, traditional dining room.

3rm (1fb) 🚭 in bedrooms [R] 🐕 * sB&B£16-£18 dB&B£30-£32
🅿 CTV nc2yrs 150 acres arable beef dairy mixed sheep
[£]

WILLERSEY Gloucestershire — Map 04 SP13

P R E M I E R S E L E C T E D

GH [Q][Q][Q][Q][Q] Old Rectory Church Street WR12 7PN (from Broadway take B4632 Stratford Rd for one and a half miles turn right into Church St at Bell Inn)
☎Broadway(0386) 853729
Closed Xmas

As we went to press we learned that this delightful 17th-century house has new owners.Individually furnished and immaculate no-smoking bedrooms - two in the coach house - offer an excellent range of modern facilities. The comfortable lounge, with an open fire and plentiful reading material, overlooks the pretty garden. Handsome breakfasts are served in the oak-beamed dining room.

6🛁🚿 Annexe 2🛁🚿 🚭 in bedrooms 🚭 in dining room 🚭 in 1 lounge CTV in all bedrooms [R] **T** 🐕 (ex guide dogs)
🅿 CTV nc9yrs
Credit Cards [1] [3]
See advertisement under BROADWAY

WILLEY Warwickshire — Map 04 SP48

FH [Q][Q][Q] Mrs Helen Sharpe ***Manor*** *(SP496849)* Willey CV23 0SH ☎Lutterworth(0455) 553143

This brick-built farmhouse on a 93-acre stock rearing farm is situated on the edge of the village close to the A5, from which it is signed, and five miles from the M6. It provides three comfortable, attractively decorated bedrooms: one double, one twin and one family. Each is individually styled and overlooks the garden and open farmland beyond. There is a comfortable lounge with TV and a library, and the breakfast room seats eight people at two tables, with period and antique furniture. Breakfast, snacks and super can be provided: the latter needs to be pre-ordered. Smoking is not permitted.

3rm(1🚿) CTV in 1 bedroom [R] 🐕 (ex guide dogs)
🅿 CTV nc93 acres sheep

WILMCOTE Warwickshire — Map 04 SP15

GH [Q][Q][Q] Dosthill Cottage The Green CV37 9XJ
☎Stratford-Upon-Avon(0789) 266480

This little house in the centre of the village dates back some 300 years and is full of character with flagstone floors. It offers comfortable and well equipped accommodation with a hospitable atmosphere.

2🚿 Annexe 1🚿 🚭 in dining room 🚭 in lounges CTV in all bedrooms [R] 🐕 (ex guide dogs) * dB&B🚿£36-£40 WB&Bfr£120
🅿 CTV
[£]

WILMINGTON East Sussex — Map 05 TQ50

SELECTED

GH [Q][Q][Q][Q] Crossways Hotel Lewes Road BN26 5SG (on A27 between Lewes and Polegate, 2m E of Alfriston roundabout) ☎(0323) 482455 FAX (0323) 487811

▶

Closed 24 Dec-23 Jan
This delightful restaurant with rooms, set in two acres of attractive grounds beside the A27 some seven miles from Eastbourne, provides well appointed accommodation, each of its bright, modern, individually styled bedrooms being equipped with thoughtful extras as well as a mini-bar, TV set, telephone and hairdryer. Some rooms overlook the lawned garden, and one of the best has its own balcony. The restaurant offers lunches and dinners of a high enough quality to have earned it two rosettes and locally produced, organically grown ingredients are also used to create the excellent breakfast - including home-made bread rolls and marmalades - which is served in a bright, sunny breakfast room. Service is particularly attentive and helpful.
7🛁🚿 CTV in all bedrooms [R] **T** 🐕 (ex guide dogs) sB&B🛁🚿£36-£40 dB&B🛁🚿£60-£68 LDO 8.45pm
Lic ♨ nc12yrs
Credit Cards [1][2][3][5]

WILMSLOW Cheshire — Map **07** SJ88

GH [Q][Q][Q] Fernbank 188 Wilmslow Road, Handforth SK9 3JX (2m N on A34) ☎(0625) 523729
Closed Xmas-New Year
A large detached house in an ideal location for the airport. Rooms are spacious and well equipped and residential ceramic courses are held periodically.
3🛁🚿 (1fb) CTV in all bedrooms [R] sB&B🛁🚿£25-£33 dB&B🛁🚿£35-£44 WB&B£107-£117 WBDi£122-£175
♨ CTV china restoration and weekend leisure courses
[£]

GH [Q][Q][Q] Rylands Farm Altrincham Road SK9 4LT (leave M56 junct 6 take A358 towards Wilmslow guesthouse in 1m on left just past Wilmslow Moat House) ☎(0625) 535646
FAX (0625) 535646
Rylands is a tastefully modernised old farmhouse on the A538 north of Wilmslow, convenient for Manchester Airport and the M56. All six bedrooms are located in a purpose built annexe, half on ground floor level. Some are rather small but all have modern facilities. The cottage-style dining room is in the main house and guests eat at a communal table. Self-catering units are also available.
Annexe 6🚿 🚭 in 3 bedrooms 🚭 in dining room 🚭 in 1 lounge CTV in all bedrooms [R] **T** * sB&B🚿£25-£33 dB&B🚿£30-£38 WB&B£165 WBDi£217 LDO 7pm
♨ CTV
Credit Cards [1][3][£]

WIMBORNE MINSTER Dorset — Map **04** SZ09

GH [Q] Riversdale 33 Poole Road BH21 1QB (on B349) ☎(0202) 884528
Closed Xmas rs Nov-Feb
Mr and Mrs Topham have been running this popular guesthouse for nearly 20 years, and they enjoy a loyal following of regular returning guests. Parts of the house date back 350 years, and some of the bedrooms at the top of the house have quaint features including sloping ceilings and winding staircases; though simply furnished, they are clean and nicely presented, with bright decor. Public areas include a pleasant breakfast room and cosy lounge area, and the house features a collection of antique artefacts and utensils from a bygone era.
8rm(1🚿) (3fb) 🚭 in bedrooms 🚭 in dining room CTV in all bedrooms [R] * sB&B£15-£25 dB&B🚿£30-£44 LDO 10am
♨ CTV nc3yrs
[£]

GH [Q][Q][Q] Stour Lodge 21 Julian's Road BH21 1EF (near town centre) ☎(0202) 888003
Closed 20 Dec-5 Jan
Located just five minutes from the minster and the centre of town, this attractive Victorian property enjoys lovely rural views from the rear of the house. There is a comfortable lounge and a dining room, where breakfast is served and evening meals are available by arrangement. Leading off the dining room is a sunny conservatory filled with colourful plants. There are three guest bedrooms, one with en suite facilities.
3rm(1🛁) (2fb)CTV in all bedrooms [R] sB&B£25-£30 sB&B🛁£25-£30 dB&B£45-£50 dB&B🛁£45-£50 WB&B£150-£175 WBDi£200-£220 LDO 9pm
Lic ♨ CTV motor boat trips can be arranged
[£]

WIMPSTONE Warwickshire — Map **04** SP24

🛏 ▼ **FH [Q][Q]** Mrs J E James **Whitchurch** *(SP222485)* CV37 8NS (take A3400 out of Stratford towards Oxford,in 4m turn right to Wimpstone, at telephone box bear left and keep straight on for 0.25m to farm) ☎Alderminster(0789) 450275
An enormous Georgian house built in 1725 in a quiet stretch of the Stour valley, this farmhouse has outstanding views. Part of a working farm of 220 acres of sheep and cereals, it offers spacious bedrooms including a family room. There is a residents' lounge and a pleasant dining room with antique furniture.
3🚿 (2fb) CTV in 1 bedroom [R] 🐕 sB&B🚿£15-£17 dB&B🚿£30-£34 LDO 6.30pm
♨ CTV 220 acres arable beef sheep
[£]

WINCANTON Somerset — Map **03** ST72

SELECTED

FH [Q][Q][Q][Q] Mrs A Teague **Lower Church** *(ST721302)* Rectory Lane, Charlton Musgrove BA9 8ES (from Wincanton take B3081 Bruton Rd. 1m turn right into Rectory Lane opposite the racecourse, first farm on left) ☎(0963) 32307
Closed Xmas & New Year
This small 18th-century farmhouse retains many original features including exposed beams and brickwork and a large inglenook fireplace in the lounge. The cosy bedrooms are freshly decorated and very pretty, with comfortable beds and several extra touches. The breakfast room has one large table and carved wooden chairs, and outside the small garden includes a new terrace.
3rm(2🚿) 🚭 [R] dB&B🚿£30 WB&B£95
♨ CTV nc6yrs 60 acres beef sheep

WINCHCOMBE Gloucestershire — Map **04** SP02

GH [Q][Q][Q] The Homestead Footbridge, Broadway Road GL54 5JG ☎Cheltenham(0242) 602536
Closed Xmas & New Year
A farmhouse of 1750s construction, Alan and Maureen Brooker's delightful house provides spotlessly clean accommodation. An attractive flagstoned entrance leads into a comfortable lounge and pretty breakfast room, where the hearty meal is taken at a communal table. The boldly decorated bedrooms have good divans and linen. One room is en suite and the other two share a large, well appointed bathroom. This is a no-smoking establishment.
3rm(1🚿) 🚭 CTV in all bedrooms * sB&B£22-£25 dB&B£32-£35 dB&B🚿£38-£40
♨ CTV ♣
[£]

GH [Q][Q][Q] ***Pilgrims Bistro*** 6 North Street GL54 5LH ☎Cheltenham(0242) 603544 & 604194
Closed Xmas rs Sun (Etr-Oct)
This cosy, friendly little bistro is situated in the centre of the village and has comfortable, individually styled and decorated bedrooms on the first floor. Downstairs the popular bistro serves

enjoyable dishes like Jerusalem artichoke soup, seafood pancakes, guinea fowl with a red-wine sauce, or venison with chocolate. The wine list is reasonably priced.

3♪ (1fb) CTV in all bedrooms ℝ LDO 9.30pm
Lic ▥.⋒⊁18 ᴗ
Credit Cards ⊡⊡

SELECTED

GH ⚅⚅⚅⚅ **Wesley House** High Street GL54 5LJ
☎Cheltenham(0242) 602366 FAX (0242) 602405
Closed 17 Jan- 9 Feb
5♪ ⊁ in bedrooms ⊁ in area of dining room CTV in all bedrooms ℝ T ⋔ (ex guide dogs) sB&Bfr£25-£55 dB&Bfr£45-£65 LDO 10pm
Lic ▥.⋒
Credit Cards ⊡⊡⊡⊕

WINCHELSEA East Sussex　　　　Map **05** TQ91

SELECTED

GH ⚅⚅⚅⚅ **The Country House at Winchelsea** Hastings Road TN36 4AD (off A259, Hastings side of town)
☎Rye(0797) 226669
Closed Xmas
Set in an old walled garden, this 17th-century Sussex-tiled house has a paved terrace giving views of the rolling countryside. The well equipped, individually named bedrooms are tastefully decorated and have matching fabrics. Local produce and home-made ice-cream feature on the dinner menu, which is cooked by the friendly owner, Mrs Carmichael, and served in the elegant dining room by her son Alex.
4rm(3⇨♪) ⊁ in dining room CTV in all bedrooms ℝ T ⋔
sB&Bfr£30 dB&Bfr£45 LDO 7.30pm
Lic ▥. nc9yrs
Credit Cards ⊡⊡⊡

WINCHESTER Hampshire　　　　Map **04** SU52

GH ⚅⚅⚅ **Camellias** 24 Ranelagh Road SO23 9TA
☎(0962) 878223 & 0831-804 381
Standing in a good residential area, this lovely 1860's house offers well proportioned bedrooms which provide modern facilities such as colour TV, tea/coffee making equipment and neatly fitted showers whilst retaining original features such as marbled fireplaces. A light and sunny lounge in green and pink looks out onto the flower-filled walled garden, while the foyer and stairs have art nouveau wallpaper to match the various pieces of 20's and 30's furniture in the house. Fabrics are Rene Mackintosh designs. The open plan, split level breakfast room and kitchen are divided by shelves carrying a display of glassware and serve an English or Continental breakfast.
2♪ (1fb) ⊁ CTV in all bedrooms ℝ ✳ dB&Bfr£30-£36
▥.

GH ⚅⚅⚅ *Harestock Lodge Hotel* Harestock Road SO22 6NX (situated 2m N of the city on the B3420) ☎(0962) 881870
Closed 24 Dec-3 Jan
Harestock Lodge is a peacefully located Victorian property two miles north of the city centre between the Stockbridge and Andover Roads. It stands in its own grounds complete with an outdoor pool. Bedrooms are plainly furnished but well equipped, and public areas are spacious and comfortable. The restaurant, also open to non-residents, offers home-cooked food from a choice of menus.

20rm(9♪) (5fb) CTV in all bedrooms ℝ ⋔ (ex guide dogs) LDO 9.15pm
Lic ▥.CTV ⋌spa pool
Credit Cards ⊡⊡⊡

SELECTED

GH ⚅⚅⚅⚅ **Leckhampton** 62 Kilham Lane SO22 5QD
☎(0962) 852831
Mar-Sep
Leckhampton is an attractive property located in a rural lane one and a half miles from the centre of town. It has the feel of a comfortable home, with family photographs and ornaments about the house. Mrs Regan takes great care of her guests, many of whom return regularly. Breakfast is the only meal served (and very good it is too), but menus for local restaurants are to hand. Bedrooms, including two ground-floor rooms, are pretty and bright, and there is a sunny conservatory, breakfast room and a comfortable lounge.
3rm(1⇨♪) ⊁ CTV in all bedrooms ℝ ⋔ ✳ dB&Bfr£34 dB&B⇨♪£36
▥.

GH ⚅⚅⚅ **Markland** 44 St Cross Street SO23 9PS
☎(0962) 854901
The Markland is a pretty Victorian property situated in the residential area of St Cross on the south side of the city. The neat bedrooms offer good quality beds and modern en suite shower rooms, and there is also a ground floor room suitable for disabled guests. In sunny weather guests can sit out in the garden.

▶

NORTHILL HOUSE
Horton • Wimborne • Dorset • BH21 7HL
Telephone Witchampton (01258) 840407
AA Premier Selected ⚅⚅⚅⚅⚅

Six miles north of Wimborne. Peaceful rural situation, mid-19th century farmhouse providing spacious reception rooms and all bedrooms en-suite with TV and tea/coffee making facilities. Within easy reach of Kingston Lacy, Cranborne Chase, Blackmore Vale, New Forest and Salisbury. Traditional English breakfasts with home-made bread and preserves. Excellent evening meals from local produce. One room equipped for disabled guests (Category 1)

Recommended in "The Good Hotel Guide 1994"

4↝ (1fb) ⌘ in dining room ⌘ in lounges CTV in all bedrooms ®
sB&B↰£35 dB&B↰£45
▥ CTV
Credit Cards ① ③

SELECTED

GH ⓠⓠⓠⓠ **Shawlands** 46 Kilham Lane SO22 5QD (take
A3090 from Winchester, straight over roundabout and turn
right at second set of traffic lights) ☎(0962) 861166
FAX (0962) 861166
Standing in a peaceful rural setting on the Eastern side of
town, Shawlands offers comfortable bedrooms, attractively
decorated and well-equipped. There is a cosy sitting room
with modern furnishings and a dining room with one large
table for communal dining.
4rm(1⇉↰) (2fb) ⌘ CTV in all bedrooms ® ⌗ (ex guide
dogs) sB&B£20-£22 dB&B£34-£36 dB&B⇉↰£36-£38
WB&Bfr£112
▥ CTV
£

PREMIER ✿ **SELECTED**

INN ⓠⓠⓠⓠⓠ **The
Wykeham Arms** 73 Kingsgate
Street SO23 9PE (immediately
south of the Cathedral, by
Kingsgate and opposite
Winchester College)
☎(0962) 853834
FAX (0962) 854411
Centrally located in the oldest
part of the city between the

cathedral and the college, this
250-year-old inn is one of the
most popular in Winchester and the surrounding area, so
booking for its above-average meals is definitely to be
recommended. Full of character, the bars are divided into a
series of small eating and drinking areas, some of them no-
smoking. The attractive bedrooms are all en suite and well
equipped for comfort. Breakfast is served to residents in the
first-floor breakfast room.
7⇉↰ CTV in all bedrooms ® T ✳ sB&B⇉↰£65
dB&B⇉↰£75 Lunch £11-£15alc Dinner £15-£20alc LDO
8.45pm
▥ nc14yrs sauna
Credit Cards ① ② ③

WINDERMERE Cumbria   Map **07** SD49

⊨ ▣ **GH** ⓠⓠ **Aaron Slack** 48 Ellerthwaite Road LA23 2BS
☎(05394) 44649
Part of a Victorian terrace, this small friendly guesthouse provides
clean, freshly decorated accommodation combined with personal
service. The three bedrooms are prettily furnished, each with TV
and tea-making facilities, and two are now en suite. There is a
small lounge and a separate breakfast room. Smoking is not
permitted and pets are not accepted.
3rm(2⇉↰) ⌘ CTV in all bedrooms ® ⌗ sB&B⇉↰£13-£22
dB&B⇉↰£26-£38
▥ ⌘nc12yrs
Credit Cards ① ② ③ £

SELECTED

GH ⓠⓠⓠⓠ **Applegarth Hotel** College Road LA23 1BU
☎(05394) 43206

A Victorian lakeland stone hotel is situated in an elevated
position yet close to the town centre and railway station. The
modern bedrooms are very spacious, all with private
bathrooms and TV; four have four-poster beds and several
have fine views towards the lake and fells. The lounge/bar and
restaurant are all elegantly furnished and comfortable, and
there is a notable stained glass window over the original oak
staircase. Bed and breakfast accommodation only is provided,
but there are ample restaurants nearby open for dinner.
15↰ (4fb) ⌘ in dining room CTV in all bedrooms ® T
sB&B£20-£35 dB&B↰£36-£70 WB&Bfr£133 WBDifr£231
LDO 5pm
Lic ▥ CTV
Credit Cards ① ② ③

SELECTED

GH ⓠⓠⓠⓠ **Archway** College Road LA23 1BU
☎(05394) 45613
Situated in an attracive terrace close to the village centre this
small Victoiran guesthouse is full of charm and character.
There are open fires, fresh flowers and lots of books and
paintings; the bedrooms have patchwork quilts, direct dial
telephones and homemade biscuits are provided for guests.
The fine English cooking uses the best available produce and
breakfast is also very special.
5↰ ⌘ CTV in all bedrooms ® ⌗ sB&B↰£21-£25
dB&B↰£42-£50 LDO 3pm
Lic ▥ nc10yrs
Credit Cards ① ② ③ £

SELECTED

GH ⓠⓠⓠⓠ **The Beaumont Hotel** Holly Rd LA23 2AF
(follow town centre signs through one-way system then 2nd
left into Ellerthwaite Rd then 1st left into Holly Rd)
☎(05394) 47075
Closed Dec-Jan
A delightfully furnished Victorian house close to the village
centre, the Beaumont prohibits smoking and has been
beautifully redecorated and offers pretty, en suite bedrooms.
Home-cooked dinners are served in the charming dining room.
11rm(3⇉8↰) (4fb) ⌘ CTV in all bedrooms ® ⌗ (ex guide
dogs) sB&B£35-£40 dB&B⇉↰£42-£52 WB&B£140-£175
▥ CTV nc6yrs
Credit Cards ① ② ③ £

GH ⓠⓠⓠ **Belgrave** 2 Ellerthwaite Road LA23 2AH
☎(05394) 43335
3rm(2↰) ⌘ in bedrooms CTV in all bedrooms ® ⌗ (ex guide
dogs) ✳ sB&B£18-£20 dB&B↰£37-£45 WB&Bfr£112
nc
Credit Cards ① ③

GH ⓠⓠⓠ **Belsfield House** 4 Belsfield Terrace LA23 3EQ (from
A592 in Bowness, take first left after mini-roundabout onto
Kendal road) ☎(05394) 45823
This is a charming, friendly black and white Victorian house in the
centre of Bowness. Bedrooms are attractively furnished and some
are large enough for families. The sitting room and dining room
have lovely, original fireplaces.
9↰ (4fb) ⌘ in dining room CTV in all bedrooms ⌗ (ex guide
dogs) ✳ sB&B↰£20-£24 dB&B↰£36-£44
▥
£

SELECTED

GH Ⓠ Ⓠ Ⓠ Ⓠ **Blenheim Lodge** Brantfell Rd, Bowness on Windermere LA23 3AE (A592 to Bowness village, across mini-roundabout, turn first left and left again) ☎(05394) 43440 FAX (05394) 43440

Blenheim Lodge occupies an elevated position in well kept gardens and has superb views of Lake Windermere. The bedrooms are furnished in different styles and are spotlessly clean. All have colour TV. The residents' lounge is cosy and very relaxing. A well produced home cooked dinner is served in the pretty dining room. Mr and Mrs Sanderson, the friendly owners, make their guests very welcome.

11⇌⋔ (1fb) ✗ in bedrooms ✗ in dining room CTV in all bedrooms Ⓡ ⅓ * sB&B⇌⋔£26-£28 dB&B⇌⋔£45-£60 WB&B£150-£195 WBDi£245-£290 LDO 7pm
Lic ▥ CTV nc6yrs membership of country club
Credit Cards ①②③ⓔ
See advertisement on p.438 and in colour section.

GH Ⓠ Ⓠ Ⓠ **Brendan Chase** 1 & 3 College Road LA23 1BU ☎(05394) 45638 FAX (05394) 45638
A delightful Edwardian house, close to Windermere village with attractively decorated bedrooms, sitting room and dining room. It also has a games room with full-sized snooker table.
8rm(4⋔) (4fb) ✗ in bedrooms ✗ in dining room ✗ in 1 lounge CTV in all bedrooms Ⓡ * sB&B£15-£18 sB&B⋔£18-£22 dB&B£26-£30 dB&B⋔£32-£44 WB&B£85-£145
▥ CTV ☉
ⓔ

Applegarth Hotel

AA Selected   QQQQ

College Road, Windermere, Cumbria LA23 3AE
Tel: 015394 43206
Proprietors: Mr & Mrs D C Himlin

A comfortable Victorian mansion house situated in its own grounds close to the village centre and lake.

Offering individually designed bedrooms and four poster suites. Lounge bar, dining room, extensive menus. Large car park. Free use of private leisure club. Special breaks available.

All rooms have private facilities, colour TV, radio, telephone, tea/coffee making facilities and hair dryers. Dogs accepted.

THE BEAUMONT

Holly Rd. Windermere, Cumbria LA23 2AF   Telephone: (015394) 47075

👑👑
HIGHLY COMMENDED

AA QQQQ
Selected

Opened Easter 1992
The Beaumont has very quickly gained a reputation for quality.
Ideally situated for Windermere and Bowness and a perfect central location for touring the lakes. This elegant Victorian house lends itself to all the grace and charm of this era combined with all the comforts of today.
All 10 luxury bedrooms are en-suite with tea making facilities, TV and hair dryer. Four poster rooms are available for that special occasion and a 'Romantic Presentation' of wine, chocolates, fruit and flowers may be ordered. The breakfasts are hearty, the standards are high and the hospitality is warm and sincere. Private parking and some ground floor rooms. Prices from £20.00 per person.
Leisure facilities available nearby

GH Ⓠ Ⓠ **Broadlands** 19 Broad Street LA23 2AB ☎(05394) 46532 FAX (05394) 46532

Broadlands is a compact guesthouse situated in a side road not far from the village centre. The small bedrooms are bright and fresh, and a cosy residents' lounge is provided.

5rm(3🏠) (1fb) ⚹ in dining room ⚹ in lounges CTV in all bedrooms Ⓡ dB&B£26-£30 dB&B🏠£30-£40 🏛, CTV 🚲 mountain bike hire

Credit Cards ①③ Ⓔ

GH Ⓠ Ⓠ Ⓠ **Brooklands** Ferry View, Bowness LA23 3JB (from Windermere enter Bowness, follow Kendal/Lancaster road A5074 in 0.75m establishment on left) ☎(05394) 42344

A delightful small family-owned and run guesthouse stands in a lovely rural setting, south of Bowness on the Kendal road at the top of Longtail Hill. Bedrooms have individual colour schemes, with pretty prints and TV; most are now en suite. A good lakeland breakfast is provided in the cosy dining room, and there is a comfortable lounge. Parking is available alongside the house.

6rm(5🏠) (3fb) CTV in all bedrooms Ⓡ ✳ sB&B£16-£20 dB&B🏠£32-£38 WB&B£112-£140 🏛, CTV Ⓔ

GH Ⓠ Ⓠ Ⓠ **Eastbourne Hotel** Biskey Howe Road LA23 2JR (from A591 turn left into town and proceed towards Bowness and lake. Take 2nd left after police station) ☎(05394) 43525

A comfortable Victorian house in a quiet location just off the Windermere to Bowness road, this family-run establishment offers sizeable bedrooms, nicely furnished in pine. There is a comfortable lounge and an attractive dining room with individual tables.

8rm(5🏠) (1fb) ⚹ in 3 bedrooms ⚹ in dining room CTV in all bedrooms Ⓡ 🍴 sB&B£18-£25 sB&B🏠£20-£26 dB&B£33-£37 dB&B🏠£38-£50 WB&B£120-£170

Lic 🏛, nc5yrs

Credit Cards ①③

GH Ⓠ Ⓠ Ⓠ **Fairfield Country House Hotel** Brantfell Road, Bowness LA23 3AE ☎Ambleside(05394) 46565 FAX (05394) 46565

This spacious, well furnished house stands in its own grounds in a quiet backwater close to the centre of Bowness village. It provides modern, prettily decorated bedrooms and comfortable public rooms. Friendly service is provided by the resident owners, Mr and Mrs Hood.

9rm(8🏠) (3fb) ⚹ CTV in all bedrooms Ⓡ sB&B£22-£28 dB&B🏠£44-£56 WB&B£150-£175 WBDi£255-£280 LDO breakfast

Lic 🏛, CTV

Credit Cards ①③ Ⓔ

bedrooms Ⓡ T sB&B🏠£35-£55 dB&B🏠£45-£80 LDO 8pm

Lic 🏛, ✳(grass)

Credit Cards ①②③ Ⓔ

GH Ⓠ Ⓠ Ⓠ **Glencree Private Hotel** Lake Road LA23 2EQ (0.5m from town centre) ☎(05394) 45822

Mar-Dec rs Feb

This very well maintained house built of Lakeland stone stands opposite the Catholic church on the main road from Windermere village to Bowness. All the particularly well appointed en suite ▶

bedrooms offer colour television, and several have pleasant views over a wooded valley and stream. The lounge is very comfortable, the breakfast room attractive, and there is a small private car park.
5rm(3⇌2↱) (1fb) ⊁ in 2 bedrooms ⊁ in dining room ⊁ in lounges CTV in all bedrooms ® ✗ (ex guide dogs) ✻ sB&B⇌↱£29-£45 dB&B⇌↱£45-£60
Lic ▥ nc9yrs
Credit Cards [1] [3] £

GH QQQ ***Glenville Hotel*** Lake Road LA23 2EQ (turn left off A591 into Windermere Village, follow main road for 0.5m, Glenville is on the right next to St Johns Church)
☎(05394) 43371
Feb-Nov
Well positioned between Bowness and Windermere, this stone house is well furnished and stands in its own grounds. The atmosphere is friendly and there are two lounges - one for non-smokers. The attractive bedrooms have colour TV and tea-making facilities. Hearty breakfasts are a speciality.
9rm(1⇌8↱) (1fb) CTV in all bedrooms ® ✗ LDO 2pm
Lic ▥

GH QQQ Green Gables 37 Broad Street LA23 2AB
☎(05394) 43886
Closed Xmas & New Year
Green Gables is an attractive double-fronted house in a Victorian terrace facing Elleray Gardens, a short walk from the village centre. Recently considerably refurbished, the house offers comfortable and reasonably priced accommodation. Guests will appreciate the tastefully decorated lounge and the bright bedrooms.
7rm(3↱) (2fb) ⊁ in bedrooms ⊁ in dining room CTV in all bedrooms ® ✗ (ex guide dogs) sB&B£13-£17 sB&B↱£16-£20 dB&B£26-£32 dB&B↱£30-£40 WB&B£90-£135
▥ CTV golf can be arranged
£

GH QQQ Haisthorpe Holly Road LA23 2AF (turn off A591, onto A5074 and after 0.25m turn left into Ellerthwaite Road and then 1st left) ☎(05394) 43445
A comfortable and well furnished guesthouse, family owned and run, offering good hospitality.
6rm(4↱) (2fb) ⊁ in bedrooms CTV in all bedrooms ® sB&B£15-£18 dB&B£26-£30 dB&B↱£32-£36 WB&B£85-£110 WBDi£130-£155 LDO 5pm
▥ CTV
Credit Cards [1] [2] [3]

SELECTED

GH QQQQ The Hawksmoor Lake Road LA23 2EQ (follow Windermere town centre one-way system for approximately half a mile and establishment can be found opposite the church) ☎(05394) 42110
11 Feb-24 Nov & 27 Dec-7 Jan
The owners, Barbara and Bob Tyson are very friendly hosts who have created a delightfully comfortable small hotel between Bowness and Windermere. Bedrooms are en suite, and are attractively appointed with matching fabric and wallpaper, and each has colour TV and tea-making facilities. Home cooking is of a good standard and served in a well furnished and comfortable dining room matched by an elegant lounge.
10⇌↱ (3fb) ⊁ in 5 bedrooms ⊁ in dining room CTV in all bedrooms ® ✗ (ex guide dogs) ✻ sB&B⇌↱£21-£35 dB&B⇌↱£40-£62 WB&B£149-£195 WBDi£216-£262 LDO 5pm
Lic ▥ nc6yrs
Credit Cards [1] [3] £
See advertisement also in Colour Section

GH QQQ Hazel Bank Hazel Street LA23 1EL ☎(05394) 45486
Mr and Mrs Matthews, the owners of this attractive detached Victorian house, are keen walkers and love to offer advice on walking the lakeland fells; Mr Matthews also leads walking tours. The house stands in a quiet side road close to the village centre, has its own car park and good-sized bedrooms with comfortable beds and good quality furniture. There is a pleasant lounge with a log fire and a good range of walking guides and books. Evening meals can be provided by arrangement, and there are plenty of restaurants in the village. This establishment is totally no smoking.
3⇌↱ ⊁ ® ✗ dB&B⇌↱£32-£38 WB&B£110-£130 LDO 10am
▥ CTV nc7yrs
£

GH QQQ Holly Lodge 6 College Road LA23 1BX (from the A591 opposite Windermere Hotel follow the road downhill towards Bowness through the village turn right into College Rd)
☎(05394) 43873 FAX (05394) 43873
Standing in a side road close to Windermere village, this mid-Victorian house has been vastly improved by the present owners, who offer guests friendly and attentive service. The attractively decorated bedrooms have mixed styles of furnishing and all are equipped with colour TV and tea-making facilities. There is a comfortable lounge and meals are served in the intimate dining room.
10rm(4↱) (3fb) ⊁ in bedrooms ⊁ in dining room CTV in all bedrooms ® ✗ (ex guide dogs) sB&B£16-£18 dB&B£32-£36 dB&B↱£38-£40 WB&B£112-£126 WBDi£182-£196 LDO 10am
Lic ▥
£

GH QQQ Holly Park House 1 Park Road LA23 2AW
☎(05394) 42107
Mar-Oct
This attractive Lakeland stone house is in a quiet side road close to Windermere village. Bedrooms are very well furnished and there is a comfortable lounge. Friendly service is provided by the resident owners.
6⇌↱ (4fb) ⊁ in 4 bedrooms ⊁ in dining room CTV in all bedrooms ® ✗ (ex guide dogs) ✻ sB&B⇌↱£25-£30 dB&B⇌↱£32-£45 WB&B£105-£123
Lic ▥
£

GH QQQ Kenilworth Holly Road LA23 2AF
☎(05394) 44004
A pleasant little guesthouse set in a quiet side road, with limited parking, is owned and run by the charming, friendly owners Mr and Mrs Gosling. Bedrooms are modern, bright and freshly decorated, with pretty soft furnishings.
6rm(3↱) (1fb) ⊁ ® ✗ (ex guide dogs) sB&B£14.50-£16 dB&B£29-£32 dB&B↱£34-£38 WB&B£98-£125
▥ CTV
£

GH QQQ Kirkwood Prince's Road LA23 2DD ☎(05394) 43907
This attractive Lakeland stone house is in a quiet side road close to both Windermere and Bowness. Public areas are Victorian in style and comprise a comfortable lounge and a pleasant dining room. Bedrooms are well equipped.
7⇌↱ (4fb) CTV in all bedrooms ® dB&B⇌↱£38-£50 WB&B£126-£170
▥ CTV
Credit Cards [1] [3] £

GH QQ Latimer House Lake Road LA23 2JJ ☎(05394) 46888
A Lakeland stone building close to the centre of Bowness village offers well equipped, pretty bedrooms with attractive coronets above the beds together with matching drapes. Cooked breakfasts are served to the bedrooms. The car park is adjacent. The house is exclusively non smoking.
►

GLENVILLE

Lake Road, Windermere LA23 2EQ
Tel (015394) 43371

Glenville stands comfortably within its own grounds, perfectly positioned for access to all amenities and in walking distance of the lake. Retaining a host of original features, full of character with a friendly country house atmosphere and high standards of comfort and cleanliness. En-suite bedrooms with colour TV and tea/coffee making facilities, licensed, with comfortable lounges. Superb car park. Mid week and short stays welcome.   **AA QQQ**

Please telephone for room availability.
Proprietor: Paul Whitton.

ℭreen ℭables
ℭuest ℌouse
37 Broad Street, Windermere, Cumbria LA23 2AB
Telephone: Windermere (015394) 43886

Family run guest house situated in a pleasant position. Shops, restaurant, bus and railway stations are all nearby. TV lounge, separate dining room, central heating, first class bathrooms, toilets and showers. All our cosy bedrooms have colour TV, hair dryers and tea/coffee making facilities. Most rooms en suite. Single and family rooms available.

Cleanliness, friendliness and a good hearty breakfast is the key to our success

A warm welcome awaits you from Sheila and Joe Lawless.

HAWKSMOOR

Lake Road, Windermere, Cumbria LA23 2EQ
Telephone: (015394) 42110

Large ivy-clad house with every modern facility and superb private car park. Ideally situated between Windermere and Bowness. All rooms en-suite, some ground floor rooms. All rooms have colour TV and tea/coffee facilities.

See colour advertisement in colour section.

Kirkwood
Guest House
Prince's Road, Windermere
Cumbria LA23 2DD
Tel: (0153 94) 43907)
3 Crown Commended

AA QQQ
Recommended

Kirkwood is a large Victorian stone house, ideally positioned for exploring the lakeland area, situated on a quiet corner betwixt Windermere and Bowness. All our rooms are en-suite with radio, TV and tea/coffee making facilities. Some rooms have four poster beds, ideal as honeymoon, anniversary, or just a special treat, and our lounge is cosy and comfortable in which to relax. For breakfast there is a large choice of menu including vegetarian or special diets with prior notice. Help with planning your walk, drive or choosing your mini-bus tour is all part of our individual personal service, all to help make your stay in the most beautiful part of England one to remember.

6rm(4♠) (1fb) ⊁ CTV in all bedrooms ® ✝ dB&B£30-£42
dB&B♠£40-£54 WB&B£139-£159
▥ CTV nc8yrs
Credit Cards ① ③ ⓔ

SELECTED

GH ⓆⓆⓆⓆ Laurel Cottage Saint Martins Square
LA23 3EF (from A592 turn right at St Martins church onto
A5074 then first cottage on left) ☎(05394) 45594
FAX (05394) 45594
Converted from an early 17th-century grammar school, this
charming cottage with neat garden is just a few steps from the
Lakeshore Promenade. It has kept its character, not only with
oak beams, but in the bedroom decorations. Full English
breakfast is served in the oak-beamed dining room and there is
a comfy lounge.
15rm(10♠) (2fb) ⊁ in dining room ⊁ in lounges CTV in 10
bedrooms ® ✝ (ex guide dogs) sB&B£21-£23 dB&B£34-
£38 dB&B♠£44-£52 WB&B£95-£150
▥ CTV
ⓔ

◄ ▣ **GH ⓆⓆⓆ Lynwood** Broad Street LA23 2AB
☎(05394) 42550 FAX (05394) 42550
Improvements have been made to this quietly located corner house
over the last year. The bedrooms, now mostly en suite, have
attractive decorations and good facilities. There is a cosy lounge
and friendly, attentive service is provided.
9♠ (4fb) ⊁ CTV in all bedrooms ® ✝ (ex guide dogs)
sB&B♠£14-£20 dB&B♠£26-£36
▥ nc5yrs
ⓔ

GH ⓆⓆⓆ Meadfoot New Road LA23 2LA ☎(05394) 42610
Feb-Nov & Xmas
Built in the late sixties, this two-storey house is just below the
level of the main road, which shields it from traffic noise. A
tastefully furnished lounge has French windows leading to the
secluded gardens, whilst most of the bedrooms also enjoy this
peaceful outlook.
8rm(4♠) (1fb) CTV in all bedrooms ® ✝ (ex guide dogs)
▥ nc3yrs

GH ⓆⓆⓆ Mylne Bridge House Brookside, Lake Road
LA23 2BX (at the top of Lake Road behind New Road adjacent to
the Carver Church) ☎(05394) 43314
Just a short distance from Windermere village centre, this
attractive house is set in a quiet side road. It offers fresh, bright
bedrooms, a combined lounge and breakfast room, and good
parking facilities.
9rm(7♠) (1fb) ⊁ in dining room ⊁ in lounges CTV in all
bedrooms ® ✳ sB&B£16-£19 sB&B♠£18-£22 dB&B£32-£38
dB&B♠£36-£44 WB&B£105-£140
Lic ▥ nc2yrs
Credit Cards ① ③ ⓔ

GH ⓆⓆⓆ Oldfield House Oldfield Road LA23 2BY
☎(05394) 88445 FAX (05394) 43250
Closed 6-31 Jan
Quietly located close to Windermere village and within easy reach
of Bowness, this delightful Lakeland house offers particularly well
appointed accommodation featuring pretty coordinated fabrics.
Books and magazines are provided in the guests' lounge and there
are individual tables in the pleasant dining room.
8rm(1⇄4♠) (2fb) ⊁ in 5 bedrooms ⊁ in dining room ⊁ in
lounges CTV in all bedrooms ® T ✝ (ex guide dogs)
sB&B⇄♠£19-£27 dB&B£34-£46 dB&B⇄♠£38-£50

WB&B£107.10-£170.10
▥ CTV nc2yrs free membership to leisure club
Credit Cards ① ② ③ ⓔ

GH ⓆⓆⓆ Orrest Close 3 The Terrace LA23 1AJ
☎(05394) 43325
6rm(4♠) (2fb) ⊁ CTV in all bedrooms ® ✝ (ex guide dogs)
dB&B£30-£35 dB&B♠£36-£44 WB&B£100-£120 WBDi£160-
£195 LDO 3.30pm
▥ CTV
Credit Cards ① ③ ⓔ

SELECTED

GH ⓆⓆⓆⓆ Parson Wyke Country House Glebe Road
LA23 3HB (400 metres from Tourist Information Centre)
☎(05394) 42837
Formerly the rectory to St Martins church, this Grade II listed
building, which stands in 1.5 acres of lovely grounds close to
the lake, is now the house of Jean and David Cockburn. Parts
of the house date back to the 15th century and it has the style
of a medieval cottage. There are three spacious bedrooms
furnished in antique pieces and old bedsteads, with
coordinated decor and soft furnishings, all equipped with TV
and en suite facilities. A comfortable lounge, decorated in red,
overlooks the garden, and breakfast is served in the delightful
dining room, complete with beams and a lovely old fireplace.
Considerate and attentive service is provided at all times.
3rm(2⇄1♠) (1fb) ⊁ in 1 bedrooms ⊁ in dining room CTV
in all bedrooms ® ✝ (ex guide dogs) ✳ sB&B⇄♠£36
dB&B⇄♠£50-£60 WB&B£300
▥ CTV nc4yrs
ⓔ

GH ⓆⓆⓆ Rocklea Brookside, Lake Road LA23 2BX (proceed
through village towards Bowness and after approx 0.5m turn sharp
left at monument into Lake Road) ☎(05394) 45326
7rm(5♠) CTV in all bedrooms ® sB&B♠£17-£19 dB&B£30-
£34 dB&B♠£34-£38
▥ nc3yrs

GH ⓆⓆⓆ Rosemount Lake Road LA23 2EQ ☎(05394) 43739
Feb-Nov
This bright, well maintained and freshly looking semidetached
house lies on the main road on the northern outskirts of Bowness.
There is a small lounge and a dining room with a dispense bar,
whilst the modern bedrooms are thoughtfully furnished.
Rosemount is a non-smoking guesthouse.
8rm(5♠) ⊁ CTV in all bedrooms ® ✝ sB&B£17.50-£24
sB&B♠£17.50-£24 dB&B♠£35-£48 WB&B£115-£160
Lic ▥ nc8yrs
Credit Cards ① ③ ⓔ

GH ⓆⓆⓆ St Johns Lodge Lake Road LA23 2EQ
☎(05394) 43078
Feb-Nov
The hotel, built of Lakeland stone, is situated on the main road
between Bowness and Windermere. Good quality furnishings and
decor feature throughout; bedrooms are bright and fresh, with
coordinating fabrics: beds all have coronets above and there are
two four-poster beds. Public areas include a comfortable lounge
and a pleasant dining room with bar.
14rm(1⇄13♠) (3fb) CTV in all bedrooms ® ✝ (ex guide dogs)
sB&B⇄♠£18.50-£25 dB&B⇄♠£35-£50 WB&B£128-£138
WBDi£189-£210 LDO 6pm
Lic ▥ nc3yrs
Credit Cards ① ③ ⓔ

GH ⓆⓆⓆ Thornleigh Thornbarrow Road LA23 2EW (turn off
A591 into Windermere, approx 1m down main road to Bowness,
Thornburrow Road is on left) ☎(05394) 44203
Feb-Nov

▶

Laurel Cottage

St Martins Square
Bowness-on-Windermere
Cumbria LA23 3EF
Telephone: 015394 45594

AA
QQQQ

Charming early 17th century oak beamed cottage with pretty front garden in village centre and close to lake. Excellent selection of restaurants, shops and pubs nearby. Membership of Leisure Club available. Family run business with 30 years experience and enviable reputation for value. Choice of tasteful rooms to suit all requirements. Ideal centre for touring Lake District. Private parking.

Oldfield House

BED & BREAKFAST

We would like to welcome you to Oldfield House, which has a friendly, informal atmosphere within a traditionally-built Lakeland residence.

7 Bedrooms, most en-suite, four poster room, all with Colour TV & Telephone • Quiet central location • Leisure Club facilities • Car Park

Bob and Maureen Theobald,
Oldfield House, Oldfield Road,
Windermere, Cumbria LA23 2BY

AA
LISTED
QQQ
COMMENDED

(015394) 88445

Rosemount

PRIVATE HOTEL

NON SMOKING

**Lake Road, Windermere,
Cumbria LA23 2EQ**
Telephone: Windermere (015394) 43739

Delightful guest house built in traditional Lakeland style, ideally situated between Windermere village and the Lake, offering warm and comfortable accommodation. Bedrooms are immaculate and attractively furnished, all with private facilities, colour television and tea trays. Scrumptious sizzling breakfasts (or refreshing fruit alternative) – above all else, friendly and personal attention from the resident owners, Alan and Dorothy Fielding. Licensed Bar. Car Parking. Recommended by all major guides.

St John's Lodge

Lake Road, Windermere LA23 2EQ
Telephone: (015394) 43078

COMMENDED

Ideally situated mid way between Windermere and Bowness. Comfortable private hotel managed by resident chef proprietor. All rooms are en suite and include a colour TV and tea/coffee making facilities. Residents' lounge plus dining room and bar. Four poster beds. Excellent cuisine and wine list. Reduced off season rates. Facilities of private sports/leisure club available to guests.

Send for brochure to: Doreen and Ray Gregory.

A small family-run guesthouse stands in a quiet side road between Bowness and Windermere. Bedrooms are bright, fresh and modern and provided with good facilities. There is a combined lounge/dining room.
6rm(2🚿) (4fb) 🚭 in dining room CTV in 5 bedrooms [R] 🐕 * sB&B£17-£22.60 dB&B£32-£36 dB&B🚿£36-£40
🅿 CTV
Credit Cards [1] [3] [£]

GH [Q] [Q] [Q] Westbury House 27 Broad Street LA23 2AB
☎(05394) 46839 & 44575 FAX (05394) 44575
4rm(2🚿) (2fb)CTV in all bedrooms [R] 🐕 (ex guide dogs) * sB&B£13-£15 sB&B🚿£15-£20 dB&B£26-£31 dB&B🚿£30-£40 WB&B£88-£123 WBDi£151-£186 LDO 9am
🅿 ✗nc2yrs
Credit Cards [3]

GH [Q] [Q] [Q] Westlake Lake Road LA23 2EQ ☎(05394) 43020
Comfortable and nicely coordinated bedrooms are a feature of this friendly family-run guesthouse, situated midway between Windermere and Bowness. All the rooms have en suite facilities and colour TV and one has a four-poster bed. Downstairs there is a lounge and dining room.
7🛁🚿 (2fb) 🚭 in 2 bedrooms 🚭 in dining room CTV in all bedrooms [R] 🐕 sB&B🛁🚿£18-£25 dB&B🛁🚿£36-£50 WB&B£126-£160 LDO 3.30am
Lic 🅿 CTV nc5yrs
Credit Cards [1] [3] [£]

GH [Q] [Q] [Q] *Westwood* 4 Ellerthwaite Road LA23 2AH
☎(05394) 43514
5🚿 CTV in all bedrooms [R] 🐕 (ex guide dogs)
🅿 CTV nc12yrs

GH [Q] [Q] [Q] White Lodge Hotel Lake Road LA23 2JJ
☎(05394) 43624
Mar-Nov
This comfortable and well furnished hotel is situated on the main road just to the north of Bowness village. Bedrooms are modern, well designed and mainly spacious. There is a cosy lounge, an elegant dining room and a coffee shop in summer months. A car park is also available.
12🛁🚿 (3fb) CTV in all bedrooms [R] 🐕 (ex guide dogs) sB&B🛁🚿£22-£28 dB&B🛁🚿£44-£54 WB&B£155-£185 WBDi£210-£250 LDO 6.30pm
Lic 🅿 CTV membership of leisure club
Credit Cards [1] [3]

SELECTED

GH [Q] [Q] [Q] [Q] Woodlands New Road LA23 2EE
☎(05394) 43915
Closed telephone for details
A very comfortable small hotel, family owned and run, offers friendly, attentive service. Bedrooms are well equipped, there is a delightful lounge and good home cooking is provided.
15rm(1🛁14🚿) (2fb) 🚭 in 8 bedrooms 🚭 in dining room CTV in all bedrooms [R] 🐕 (ex guide dogs) * sB&B🛁🚿£19-£28 dB&B🛁🚿£38-£56 WB&B£130-£170 WBDi£210-£275 LDO 4pm
Lic 🅿 nc5yrs
Credit Cards [1] [3]

INN [Q] *Oakthorpe Hotel* High Street LA23 1HF ☎(05394) 43547
Closed 25 Dec-24 Jan
16rm(4🛁3🚿) (3fb) CTV in all bedrooms [R] LDO 8.30pm
🅿 ⛳
Credit Cards [1] [3]

WINDSOR Berkshire — Map **04** SU97

GH [Q] [Q] Clarence Hotel 9 Clarence Road SL4 5AE
☎(0753) 864436 FAX (0753) 857060
This attractive detached Victorian villa, located within walking distance of the town centre and castle, attracts predominantly business trade during the week. Professionally run, it offers regularly upgraded bedrooms and a comfortable bar/lounge well stocked with draught lager; dinner can be provided on request.
21🛁🚿 (6fb)CTV in all bedrooms [R] sB&B🛁🚿£33-£37 dB&B🛁🚿£45-£52
Lic 🅿 CTV
Credit Cards [1] [2] [3] [5] [£]

SELECTED

GH [Q] [Q] [Q] [Q] Melrose House 53 Frances Road SL4 3AQ
☎(0753) 865328
This elegant, detached Victorian house lies in a residential street some 10 minutes' walk from the town centre. Bedrooms, decorated in pinks and greens, are bright, clean and very well equipped. Downstairs is a spacious breakfast room, a mirrored reception hall and a cosy TV lounge. Mrs Daniel, the manageress, offers a warm and cheery welcome.
9🛁🚿 (2fb) 🚭 in 3 bedrooms 🚭 in dining room CTV in all bedrooms [R] **T** * sB&B🛁🚿£28-£30 dB&B🛁🚿£42-£45
🅿 CTV
Credit Cards [1] [3] [£]

GH [Q] [Q] [Q] Netherton Hotel 96 Leonards Road SL4 5DA
☎(0753) 855508
11rm(7🛁4🚿) (5fb)CTV in all bedrooms [R] 🐕 * sB&B🛁🚿£30-£35 dB&B🛁🚿£40-£55
🅿 CTV
Credit Cards [1] [3]

WINKLEIGH Devon — Map **03** SS60

GH [Q] [Q] [Q] London House Dining Room EX19 8HQ ((on B3220)
☎(0837) 83202
London House is a listed property dating from 1750, situated in the centre of a quaint Devonshire village. Two rooms, furnished in keeping with the ancient building, are let to one family or party. Downstairs there is an attractive dining room where Barbara Jameson offers a predominantly set menu of good home cooking, while Peter Jameson provides old English service. A comfortable lounge with an open fire is also available, and there is plenty of on street parking outside.
1🛁 [R] * sB&B🛁£40 dB&B🛁£80 (incl dinner) LDO 9pm
Lic CTV ✗nc14yrs
Credit Cards [1] [3] [£]

WINSTER Derbyshire — Map **08** SK26

SELECTED

GH [Q] [Q] [Q] [Q] The Dower House Main Street DE4 2DH
☎(0629) 650213 FAX (0629) 650894
Mar-Oct
This Elizabethan country house with its walled garden stands in the heart of the Peak District village. It has spacious bedrooms and a lounge with a log fire. Breakfast is served `en famille'.
3rm(1🚿) 🚭 in bedrooms 🚭 in dining room CTV in all bedrooms [R] 🐕 sB&B🚿£20-£35 dB&B🚿£36-£55 WB&B£140-£245
Lic 🅿 nc10yrs
[£]

WINTERBOURNE ABBAS Dorset   Map 03 SY69

GH Ⓠ Ⓠ Ⓠ **Churchview** DT2 9LS ☎Martinstown(0305) 889296
rs Nov-Feb
Conveniently situated on the main A35 road West of Dorchester,
this is a house of some character. Its comfortable bedrooms are
attractively decorated and well-equipped, and the dining room
(made up of two parts with a central fire place) is cosy. The
lounges, one for non-smokers, are small but welcoming, and the
atmosphere throughout is warm and friendly.
9rm(7⇄↑) (1fb) ⊁ in dining room ⊁ in 1 lounge Ⓡ sB&B£17-
£22 sB&B⇄↑£21-£26 dB&B£34-£38 dB&B⇄↑£42-£48
WB&B£110-£158 WBDi£200-£240 LDO 7pm
Lic ▥ CTV nc3yrs
Credit Cards ①③ⓔ
See advertisement under DORCHESTER

WINTERBOURNE STOKE Wiltshire   Map 04 SU04

SELECTED

GH Ⓠ Ⓠ Ⓠ Ⓠ **Scotland Lodge** SP3 4TF (on A303 0.25m W
of village beyond turning to Berwick St James)
☎(0980) 620943 FAX (0980) 620943
This family home is set in its own grounds and offers three
tastefully furnished bedrooms. Breakfast is served around a
large table in the dining room and there is a comfortable sitting
room for guests. Jane Armfelt and John Singleton make guests
very welcome.
3⇄↑ (1fb) ⊁ CTV in all bedrooms Ⓡ ⊁ (ex guide dogs) ⊁
sB&B⇄↑£25-£30 dB&B⇄↑£35-£45 WB&B£100-£125
▥
ⓔ

THORNLEIGH
GUEST HOUSE

AA QQQ
Thornbarrow Road,
Bowness-on-Windermere, Cumbria LA23 2EW
Tel: (015394) 44203
A small, friendly guest house, offering bed and breakfast
at very reasonable rates. Comfortable, well appointed
bedrooms, with colour TV and tea/coffee making
facilities. Rooms with private shower and en suite
available. Fully centrally heated, private parking,
colour TV lounge. Pleasantly situated in good
residential area, just off the main road, and close to
Bowness and Windermere.

WHITE LODGE HOTEL
Lake Road, Bowness-on-Windermere, Cumbria LA23 2JJ
Tel: Windermere (015394) 43624

👑 👑 👑
COMMENDED

'Welcome'
'Welkon'
'Willkommen'
'Bienvenido'
'Bienvenue'
'Benvenuti'

White Lodge Hotel, a Victorian country house, is situated on the road to the Lake and only a
short walk from Bowness Bay. Its spacious rooms are all centrally heated and have their
own private bathroom and colour television. Four posters and lake views on request. All
have complimentary tea and coffee making facilities.
Membership to Lakeland's premier leisure club.
We are a small, friendly, family owned hotel with high standards and good home cooked
cuisine. We serve a traditional full English breakfast.
In addition to our licensed residents dining room we also run a small coffee house 'Plants'.
The residents lounge has a colour television. We have our own car park.
Featured on TV holiday programme 'Wish you were here.'

WISBECH Cambridgeshire   Map **05** TF40

FH Q Q Q Mrs S M King **Stratton** *(TF495144)* West Drove
North, Walton Highway PE14 7DP (leave A47 at Little Chef onto
B198, then right into Walton Highway. After 1m turn left into
West Drove North and continue for 0.5m) ☎(0945) 880162
Lying in 22 acres of peaceful countryside, this ranch-style
bungalow offers good facilities, thoughtful extras and some
superior non-smoking accommodation. Hearty breakfasts are
taken at a large communal table.
3⇄🛏 ⊱ CTV in all bedrooms ® 🐾 (ex guide dogs)
sB&B⇄🛏£21 dB&B⇄🛏£42 WB&B£132.30
Ⓜ CTV nc7yrs 🕯 (heated) ✈ 22 acres beef
£

WITHERIDGE Devon   Map **03** SS81

INN Q Q Q **Thelbridge Cross** Thelbridge, Witheridge EX17 4SQ
(2m W on the B3042) ☎Tiverton(0884) 860316
FAX (0884) 860316
rs 25 & 26 Dec
Thelbridge Inn, recently renovated, welcomes guests to stay in
freshly decorated, comfortable bedrooms. Log fires burn in
lounge/bar areas where guests can select their meals either from an
extensive menu or from the blackboard with its range of house
specials.
8⇄🛏 (1fb) CTV in all bedrooms ® 🐾 (ex guide dogs) ✳
sB&B⇄🛏fr£35 dB&B⇄🛏£60 WB&B£150-£175 WBDi£220-
£250 Lunch £10-£20alc Dinner £12.50-£20alc LDO 9pm
Ⓜ CTV
Credit Cards 1 2 3 5 £

WITNEY Oxfordshire   Map **04** SP30

GH Q Q Q **The Close** Witney Road, Long Hanborough OX8 8HF
☎Freeland(0993) 882485 FAX (0993) 883819
This detached pebble-dashed property is set in its own gardens
three miles west of Woodstock, on the outskirts of Long
Hanborough, well screened from the A4095 Witney road. Two of
the spacious bedrooms are on the ground floor, whilst the other
bedroom and guests' sitting room are on the first floor. Dinner is
not served, but there is a good selection of local inns, eating
houses and restaurants.
Annexe 3🛏 (3fb) ⊱ CTV in all bedrooms ® dB&B🛏£30-£35
WB&B£105-£175
Ⓜ
£

GH Q Q Q **Greystones Lodge Hotel** 34 Tower Hill OX8 5ES
☎(0993) 771898
Closed 2wks Xmas
An attractive 1930s house is set amongst neat flowerbeds.
Bedrooms are generally of a good size and the new owners have
already begun to redecorate. Evening meals are available. French
windows at the rear overlook the garden and swimming pool.
12🛏 (1fb) CTV in all bedrooms ® ✳ sB&Bfr£23.80
sB&B🛏fr£27.60 dB&Bfr£36.95 dB&B🛏fr£42 LDO 8.30pm
Lic Ⓜ CTV 🕯(heated)
Credit Cards 1 2 3 5 £

WIX Essex   Map **05** TM12

FH Q Q Q Mrs H P Mitchell **New Farm House** *(TM165289)*
CO11 2UJ (turn off A120 into Wix, at village crossroads take
Bradfield road, under A120 to top of hill turn right farmhouse
200yds on left) ☎(0255) 870365 FAX (0255) 870837
This modern farmhouse stands in a peaceful rural position with a
50-acre working arable farm, landscaped garden and childrens'
playground. The majority of bedrooms in the main house share
bathroom facilities but are equipped with wash basins, radio
alarms, TV and tea trays; rooms in the ground floor annexe all
have private bathrooms and two are equipped for disabled guests.
All the rooms are maintained to a very high standard, with regular

improvements being made. Two bedrooms are available for guests
who smoke; the rest are strictly no smoking. The farmhouse is run
in a friendly but professional manner by the Mitchell family, who
cater for families, the partially disabled and those with special
dietary requirements. Children are welcome, and free baby sitting
is provided. An evening meal is available if requested and the
breakfast menu is translated into seven different languages! There
is a small no-smoking lounge with a mini kitchenette, and a
second, larger, lounge has TV and an open fire.
6rm(1🛏) Annexe 6🛏 (5fb) ⊱ in 10 bedrooms ⊱ in dining room
⊱ in 1 lounge CTV in all bedrooms ® ✳ sB&Bfr£19
sB&B🛏fr£23 dB&Bfr£37 dB&B🛏fr£42 WB&B£116.55-£132.30
WBDi£193.55-£209.30 LDO 5.30pm
Lic Ⓜ CTV ♨ 42 acres arable non-working
Credit Cards 1 3 £

WOKING Surrey   Map **04** TQ05

GH Q Q Q *Glen Court* St Johns Hill Road GU21 1RQ
☎(0483) 764154 FAX (0483) 764154
An attractive Edwardian house is set in an acre of secluded
gardens to the rear, with ample car parking at the front. Bedrooms
in the main house have retained their original generous
proportions, and are furnished with a mixture of period pieces and
mahogany; all the rooms have private bathrooms although some
are old-fashioned. There are three modern annexe rooms in the
house next door, located above the Fountain restaurant, which
offers a lengthy continental menu. There is also a separate
breakfast room which overlooks the garden.
9rm(6⇄3🛏) Annexe 3⇄🛏 (1fb) CTV in all bedrooms ® LDO
11pm
Lic Ⓜ table tennis
Credit Cards 1 3

WOODBRIDGE Suffolk   Map **05** TM24

GH Q Q **Grove House** 39 Grove Road IP12 4LG (on A12, 400yds
beyond junct with B1079) ☎(0394) 382202
A modern bungalow is located on the northbound section of the
A12 on the outskirts of town. Bedrooms are well maintained and
adequately equipped, with rooms on the ground floor suitable for
partially disabled guests. There is a lounge with an honesty bar,
and small business parties and meetings can be accommodated.
Reasonably priced evening meals can be served in the small
breakfast room, cooked by the cheerful owner Mrs Kelly.
9rm(5🛏) (1fb) ⊱ in dining room CTV in all bedrooms ®
sB&B£19-£20 sB&B🛏£25-£30 dB&B£36-£38 dB&B🛏£39.50-
£42 WB&B£120-£140 WBDi£160-£198 LDO 6pm
Lic Ⓜ CTV
Credit Cards 1 3 £

WOODBURY Devon   Map **03** SY0?

FH Q Q Q Mrs S Glanvill **Rydon** *(SX999871)* Woodbury
EX5 1LB (B3179 to village and on entering village turn right 10 yds
before 30mph sign. Signposted) ☎(0395) 232341
3rm(2⇄) (1fb)® ✳ sB&B£16-£20 sB&B⇄£18-£22 dB&B£32-
£36 dB&B⇄£36-£44
Ⓜ CTV 280 acres dairy

Telephone national area codes are due
to change by 16th April 1995. Please
see the note under 'How to Use this
Guide' at the front of the book.

WOODFALLS Hampshire   Map **04** SU12

WOODHALL SPA Lincolnshire   Map **08** TF16

GH Q Q **Claremont** 9/11 Witham Road LN10 6RW
☎(0526) 352000
8rm(2ฅ) (1fb)CTV in all bedrooms Ⓡ ✳ sB&B£15-£17.50
sB&B✧ฅ£20-£24 dB&B£30-£32 dB&B✧ฅ£35 WB&B£90-£150

GH Q Q **Duns** The Broadway LN10 6SQ ☎(0526) 352969
A well established guesthouse situated on the B1191 in this
Victorian spa town. Accommodation is clean and comfortable
with an attractive lounge and a warm welcome from proprietor Mr
Griffin.
7rm(1✧ฅ) (2fb) ✕ in 3 bedrooms ✕ in dining room CTV in all
bedrooms Ⓡ ✻ ✳ sB&B£15-£17 sB&B✧ฅ£18 dB&B£30-£32
dB&B✧ฅ£36 WB&Bfr£105 WBDifr£147 LDO 5.30pm
▥ CTV ♨
ⓔ

WOODSTOCK Oxfordshire   Map **04** SP41

GH 🔲🔲🔲 **The Ridings** 32 Banbury Road OX20 1LQ
☎(0993) 811269
rs Dec-1 Mar
This 1930's detached house, peacefully set away from the noise
and bustle of the town, offers comfortable no-smoking
accommodation. Well decorated bedrooms are soundly furnished,
the sitting/dining room opens on to a large colourful garden, and
enjoyable breakfasts include home-made muesli and marmalade.
3rm(1⇌📷) (1fb) ⠜ CTV in all bedrooms ® ⋔ (ex guide dogs)
✳ sB&B£18-£25 sB&B⇌𝒓£30 dB&B£36 dB&B⇌𝒓£40
WB&B£126-£175
▥. CTV

WOOL Dorset   Map **03** SY88

GH 🔲🔲 **Fingle Bridge** Duck Street BH20 6DE
☎Bindon Abbey(0929) 462739
Convenient for many of Dorset's beauty spots, this family house,
alongside a stream, offers good value for money. Guests are very
much en famille here, and there is a relaxed and cheery
atmosphere about the house. Breakfast is served at a communal
table.
3rm(1⇌📷) (1fb) ⠜ CTV in all bedrooms ® ⋔ (ex guide dogs)
sB&Bfr£16 dB&Bfr£32 dB&B⇌𝒓fr£35
▥. CTV

WOOLACOMBE Devon   Map **02** SS44
See also Mortehoe

GH 🔲🔲🔲 **Camberley Hotel** Beach Road EX34 7AA (from A361
Barnstaple to Ilfracombe, turn left at Mullacott roundabout, after
3m establishment is on right) ☎(0271) 870231
FAX (0271) 870231
This family run small hotel on the edge of town has fine views
across the valley to the sea. The bright bedrooms are all en suite
and offer good family accommodation. The cosy bar has a darts
board and there is a separate and comfortable TV lounge.
6⇌𝒓 (2fb) ⠜ in dining room CTV in all bedrooms ® ✳
dB&B⇌𝒓£30-£40 WB&B£105-£125 WBDi£150-£171 LDO
5.30pm
Lic ▥. CTV ⌖
Credit Cards [1] [3] (£)

GH 🔲🔲🔲 **The Castle** The Esplanade EX34 7DJ
☎(0271) 870788
Apr-Oct
Built in 1897 by Colonel Pickering, this castle-style building has
views over Woolacombe Sands, and the lounge benefits from the
dramatic position. Its ceiling features an unusual cedar wood
design and the walls are adorned with brass panels. Bedrooms are
comfortable and pleasantly furnished, and service is friendly and
relaxed.
8𝒓 (2fb) ⠜ in dining room CTV in all bedrooms ® ⋔ (ex guide
dogs) ✳ sB&B𝒓£19-£22 dB&B𝒓£38-£44 WB&B£129.50-£147
WBDi£178.50-£198.50 LDO 6pm
Lic ▥. CTV nc5yrs

GH 🔲🔲🔲 **Holmesdale Hotel** Bay View Road EX34 7DQ
☎(0271) 870335
Closed Feb
This well managed guesthouse centres round the interesting, good
value restaurant menu, provided by cheerful, friendly proprietors
who are also responsible for the unpretentious and very nicely
maintained accommodation.
15𝒓 (10fb) ⠜ in bedrooms ⠜ in dining room ⠜ in 1 lounge CTV
in all bedrooms ® ✳ (incl dinner) WBDi£176-£528 LDO
8.30pm
Lic ▥. CTV
Credit Cards [1] [3] (£)

WOOLHOPE Hereford & Worcester   Map **03** SO6?

INN 🔲🔲 **Butchers Arms** HR1 4RF (from the village of Fownhope
on the B4224, turn towards Woolhope, inn is approx 3m on right
hand side) ☎Fownhope(0432) 860281
This half-timbered building dating back to the 14th century lies on
the Ross-on-Wye side of the village. Its rooms are modestly
furnished but provide a good range of facilities. The inn has a
good reputation for its food, which is served in the informal
atmosphere of the bar.
3rm CTV in all bedrooms ® T ⋔ (ex guide dogs) LDO 9.30pm
▥.

WOOLSTONE Oxfordshire   Map **04** SU28

SELECTED

INN 🔲🔲🔲 **The White Horse** SN7 7QL
☎Farringdon(0367) 820566 & 820726 FAX (0367) 7820566
Tucked away amid rolling countryside, Woolstone is a
charming village near the White Horse chalk hill, from which
the 16th-century inn takes its name. Chef Ian Lovering serves
good food either as snacks in the beamed bar or as full meals
in the more comfortable restaurant. In the annexe, bedrooms
are mostly on the ground floor with their bathrooms reached
by a staircase.
Annexe 6⇌𝒓 ⠜ in 2 bedrooms CTV in all bedrooms ® T
⋔ (ex guide dogs) sB&B⇌𝒓£35-£40 dB&B⇌𝒓£45-£50
Lunch fr£14.95&alc LDO 10pm
▥.
Credit Cards [1] [2] [3] [5] (£)

WORCESTER Hereford & Worcester   Map **03** SO8?

GH 🔲🔲 **Farthingale** 324 Bath Road WR5 3ET ☎(0905) 359169
Bright, modern bedrooms and breakfast room are provided by this
small, value-for-money guesthouse which is conveniently located
beside the main road.
3rm

GH 🔲🔲 **Wyatt** 40 Barbourne Road WR1 1HU (im N on A38)
☎(0905) 26311
This well-run guesthouse is a short distance to the north of the
town centre on the A38. Bedrooms vary in size but are well
decorated and there is a large comfortable lounge. Dinner can be
served by prior arrangement in the breakfast room.
8rm(4𝒓) (4fb) ⠜ in dining room CTV in all bedrooms ®
sB&B£18-£20 dB&B𝒓£32-£34 LDO 5pm
▥. CTV ✗ Credit Cards [1] [3] (£)

WORKINGTON Cumbria   Map **11** NX9?

GH 🔲🔲🔲 **Morven Hotel** Siddick Road CA14 1LE (on A596)
☎(0900) 602118 & 602002
The Morven is a large Victorian house offering a good all round
standard of accommodation and service. Bedrooms are modern
and well equipped and there are two lounges, one of which is no
smoking.
6rm(4⇌𝒓) (1fb) ⠜ in dining room ⠜ in 1 lounge CTV in all
bedrooms ® sB&B£18-£20 sB&B⇌£20-£30 dB&B£30-£35
dB&B⇌£36-£40 LDO 4pm
Lic ▥. CTV

WORTHING West Sussex   Map **04** TQ1?

SELECTED

GH 🔲🔲🔲🔲 **Aspen House** 13 Winchester Road BN11 4DJ
☎(0903) 230584
Closed 23 Dec-5 Jan
An elegant Edwardian house dating back to 1902 but

modernised to a high standard offers particularly bright and comfortable bedrooms, all individually furnished and equipped with a good range of extras. Breakfast is taken in the lounge/dining room, and there are a wide variety of restaurants within walking distance for dinner; both town centre and seafront are also just a short walk away. Extra car parking is now being provided on the forecourt.
3rm(1🛁2🚿) CTV in all bedrooms [R] 🚫🐕 * dB&B🛁🚿fr£40 🅿 nc13yrs
[£]

GH [Q][Q][Q] Blair House 11 St Georges Road BN11 2DS (half a mile E of town centre on A259) ☎(0903) 234071
A long-established, family-run guesthouse is located near the seafront and town centre. There is a good choice of attractive bedrooms, most with private bathrooms and all having TV and tea trays. There is a comfortable lounge with a bar, and service is personally supervised by Mrs Grace Taylor. Chef/proprietor Malcolm Taylor provides a good choice of dishes which are served at separate tables in the dining room. Car parking is generally available at the roadside.
7rm(2🛁5🚿) 🚭 in dining room CTV in all bedrooms [R] 🚫🐕 (ex guide dogs) * sB&B🛁🚿£20-£25 dB&B🛁🚿£35-£40 WB&B£122.50-£140 WBDi£182-£199.50 LDO 4.30pm
Lic 🅿
Credit Cards [1] [3] [£]

GH [Q][Q][Q] Delmar Hotel 1-2 New Parade BN11 2BQ (off A259 adjoining Aquarena Swimming Pool) ☎(0903) 211834
FAX (0903) 219052
This seafront hotel offers comfortable, well equipped, well maintained bedrooms with a host of additional amenities. There is a smart, well furnished lounge and a small bar, and Jenny Elms provides a home-cooked, four-course evening meal of essentially English dishes. During summer months a weekly barbecue is held in the roof garden which also features a sun lounge and aviary.
13🛁🚿 (4fb) 🚭 in bedrooms 🚭 in dining room 🚭 in 1 lounge CTV in all bedrooms [R] T 🚫🐕 (ex guide dogs) sB&B🛁🚿£27.50 dB&B🛁🚿£50 WB&B£173.25 WBDi£269.75 LDO noon
Lic 🅿 CTV
Credit Cards [1] [2] [3] [5] [£]

SELECTED

GH [Q][Q][Q][Q] Moorings 4 Selden Road BN11 2LL (on A259 towards Brighton, pass indoor swimming pool on right and hotel opposite garage) ☎(0903) 208882 & 236878
This is a comfortable and welcoming guesthouse, with well-appointed bedrooms. There is a very pleasing lounge and attractive dining room where a good selection of home cooking is offered. The restaurant is open to non-residents by prior arrangement.
9🛁🚿 (3fb)CTV in all bedrooms [R] T * sB&B🛁🚿£20-£24 dB&B🛁🚿£37-£44 WB&B£126-£154 WBDi£193-£221 LDO 6.30pm
Lic 🅿
Credit Cards [1] [2] [3]

GH [Q][Q] *Wolsey Hotel* 179-181 Brighton Road BN11 2EX ☎(0903) 236149
Closed mid-end Dec
This long-established family-run guesthouse is ideally located on the seafront, convenient for all local leisure facilities and town centre shopping precincts. Run by proprietor Mrs Brenda Price for over 30 years, many regualar guests return to enjoy reliable and consistent standards of comfort and cooking. All bedrooms have satellite TV, radio and tea trays, and some rooms have en suite showers. There is a comfortable lounge, residents' bar and an attractive dining room.
▶

13rm(3🚿) (2fb) CTV in all bedrooms [R] LDO 6.30pm
Lic ♨ CTV 🚫🅿
Credit Cards [1] [2] [3]

GH [Q] [Q] [Q] Woodlands 20-22 Warwick Gardens BN11 1PF
☎(0903) 233557
Woodlands is located in an Edwardian conservation area, a few minutes from the town centre and seafront. There are bright bedrooms with modern furnishings and a comfortable lounge for guests' use. A freshly prepared set four-course evening meal is served every day, and the breads, desserts, pies and preserves are all home made. Vegetarian dishes are also available.
11rm(6🛁🚿) (3fb) 🚭 in 6 bedrooms 🚭 in dining room CTV in all bedrooms [R] sB&B£17-£24 dB&B£32-£38 dB&B🛁🚿£40-£46 WB&B£110-£160 WBDi£160-£215 LDO 6pm
Lic ♨ CTV
Credit Cards [1] [3] [£]

WROTHAM Kent — Map **05** TQ65

INN [Q] [Q] The Bull Hotel Bull Lane TN15 7RF (off A20)
☎Borough Green(0732) 885522 FAX (0732) 886288
Dating back to the 14th century, this former coaching inn is right in the centre of this small village. Full of character, it provides simple but adequate accommodation. A nicely appointed restaurant offers lunch and dinner with a selection of dishes. Bar meals are also available.
10rm(6🛁🚿) (1fb)CTV in all bedrooms [R] **T** ✱ sB&B£35-£40 sB&B🛁🚿£40 dB&B£45 dB&B🛁🚿£50 LDO 10pm
♨
Credit Cards [1] [2] [3] [5] [£]

WYBUNBURY Cheshire — Map **07** SJ64

FH [Q] [Q] Mrs Jean E Callwood **Lea** *(SJ717489)* Wrinehill Road CW5 7NS ☎Crewe(0270) 841429
Peacocks roam in the attractive gardens which surround this large house situated on a dairy farm between Wybunbury village and Wrinehill. Three bedrooms (two of them suitable for family occupation) are furnished in a mixture of styles, a large modern bathroom serving the only one that does not have en suite facilities. The spacious lounge contains a small snooker table, and an evening meal can be provided, by prior arrangement, round the single table of a traditionally furnished breakfast room overlooking the garden.
3rm(2🚿) (1fb) 🚭 in area of dining room CTV in all bedrooms [R] ✱ sB&Bfr£17 sB&B🚿fr£19 dB&Bfr£27 dB&B🚿fr£29 WB&Bfr£90 WBDifr£140 LDO 5pm
CTV 🎣 pool table 150 acres dairy
[£]

YARMOUTH, GREAT Norfolk — Map **05** TG50

GH [Q] [Q] *Balmoral Private Hotel* 65 Avondale Road NR31 6DJ
☎(0493) 662538
Close to the seafront, this small, well maintained, family-run guesthouse offers pleasant compact rooms with light decor and furnishings. There is a comfortable TV lounge and evening meals are provided by prior arrangement.
7rm(4🚿) (3fb) CTV in all bedrooms [R] LDO 4pm
Lic ♨ CTV 🚫🅿

GH [Q] [Q] Frandor 120 Lowertoft Road NR31 6ND (2m S off A12)
☎(0493) 662112
Situated close to Gorleston town centre this small, family-run guesthouse provides simply furnished accommodation with a comfortable lounge and bar.
6rm(3🚿) (2fb) CTV in all bedrooms [R] ✱ sB&B🚿£15-£17.50 dB&B£29-£31 dB&B🚿£30-£35 WB&B£95-£105 WBDi£130-£149 LDO 6.30pm
Lic ♨ CTV
Credit Cards [3] [£]

GH [Q] [Q] Georgian House 16-17 North Drive NR30 4EW (on seafront, N of Britannia pier) ☎Great Yarmouth(0493) 842623
Closed Xmas-Feb rs Nov-Etr
A popular, family-run guesthouse located in the quieter northern end of town, on the seafront. Gradual improvements to the decor will further enhance this immaculately kept establishment.
19rm(11🛁6🚿) (1fb) 🚭 in dining room CTV in all bedrooms [R] 🐕 dB&B£32-£36 dB&B🛁🚿£35-£45 WB&B£100-£130
Lic ♨ nc5yrs

GH [Q] [Q] *Jennis Lodge* 63 Avondale Road NR31 6DJ (2m S off A12) ☎(0493) 662840
A personally run guesthouse lies within easy access of a sandy beach and the centre of Gorleston town. There is some emphasis on hospitality and ready service at the bar and restaurant.
11rm (4fb) CTV in all bedrooms [R] LDO 4pm
Lic ♨ CTV 🚫🅿

🛏 ☕ **GH [Q] [Q] Spindrift** 36 Wellesley Road NR30 1EU
☎Great Yarmouth(0493) 858674
Closed 25 & 26 Dec
A well maintained guesthouse is set in a tree-lined avenue running parallel to the seafront, to the north of the town centre. Resident owner Mrs Wells maintains a high standard of cleanliness and bedrooms are very satisfactory, if a little compact. There is a pleasant lounge with comfortable seating and TV.
8rm(5🛁🚿) (3fb)CTV in all bedrooms [R] 🐕 (ex guide dogs) sB&B£15-£20 sB&B🛁🚿£20-£25 dB&B£25-£28 dB&B🛁🚿£30-£40 WB&B£80-£120
Lic ♨ CTV nc3yrs
Credit Cards [1] [2] [3] [£]

GH [Q] [Q] [Q] Squirrels Nest 71 Avondale Road NR31 6DJ
☎Great Yarmouth(0493) 662746 FAX (0493) 662746
Located near the seafront, this guesthouse provides well kept accommodation. Bedrooms are neatly furnished and well equipped. Public areas include a comfortable lounge, a small bar and a dining room, where a good range of meals and snacks is available.
9rm(1🛁8🚿) (1fb) 🚭 in dining room CTV in all bedrooms [R] ✱ sB&B🛁🚿£15-£32 dB&B🛁🚿£30-£64 WB&B£90-£180 WBDi£145-£220 LDO 8.30pm
Lic ♨ CTV
Credit Cards [1] [2] [3] [£]

YARNTON Oxfordshire — Map **04** SP41

GH [Q] [Q] [Q] Eltham Villa 148 Woodstock Road OX5 1PW (on A44) ☎Kidlington(0865) 376037 FAX (0865) 376037
An attractive cottage guesthouse, set in its own garden beside the road to Woodstock a few miles north of Oxford, offers comfortable bedrooms named after local rivers - all of them well equipped. Breakfast is taken in a sunny pine-furnished breakfast room, and a set evening meal can be served by arrangement; there is also a cosy lounge.
7🛁🚿 (2fb) 🚭 in bedrooms 🚭 in dining room CTV in all bedrooms [R] **T** 🐕 ✱ sB&B🛁🚿£20-£25 dB&B🛁🚿£30-£35 WB&B£140-£150 WBDi£190-£220 LDO 10am
♨ CTV
[£]
See advertisement under WOODSTOCK

YATTON Avon — Map **03** ST46

INN [Q] [Q] Prince of Orange High Street BS19 4JD (on B3133)
☎(0934) 832193
8rm(5🚿) 🚭 in bedrooms CTV in 7 bedrooms [R] 🐕 (ex guide dogs) ✱ sB&Bfr£25 sB&B🚿fr£25 dB&Bfr£37 dB&B🚿fr£37 WB&B£126-£175 WBDi£161-£210 LDO 9pm
♨ skittle alley pool
Credit Cards [1] [3]

YEALAND CONYERS Lancashire — Map **07** SD57

SELECTED

GH [Q][Q][Q][Q] The Bower LA5 9SF (follow A6 towards Milnthorpe for 0.75m, after passing under narrow bridge, take next left and bear left at end) ☎Carnforth(0524) 734585

Easily reached via the A6 from junction 35 of the M6, this delightful 18th-century house stands in its own attractive grounds overlooking the surrounding countryside. The comfortable bedrooms are tastefully decorated and have smart modern bathrooms. The ground-floor rooms are equally elegant, and the young owners' interest in music is evident in the presence of various musical instruments.

2🛁🚿 (1fb) 🚭 CTV in all bedrooms 🐕 (ex guide dogs) sB&B🛁🚿£29.50-£34 dB&B🛁🚿£44-£53 WB&B£140-£165 WBDi£245-£270 LDO noon

♨ CTV nc12yrs croquet lawn

[£]

YELVERTON Devon — Map **02** SX56

GH [Q][Q][Q] Harrabeer Country House Hotel Harrowbeer Lane PL20 6EA (at roundabout stay on A386, after 200yds turn right into Grange rd, at bottom of hill turn right to hotel) ☎(0822) 853302

Closed Xmas & New Year

Mr and Mrs Back welcome guests to their home which stands on a quiet, winding country lane (request directions when booking). Public areas are cosy, with blazing log fires to keep the nip out of the air. In the dining room, Patsy Back serves wholesome and enjoyable home cooked food, with a small choice of starter and dessert and a set main course (though she is always flexible). Bedrooms are well presented, with good-quality, comfortable beds and a good range of facilities.

7rm(4🛁🚿) (1fb) 🚭 in 2 bedrooms 🚭 in dining room CTV in all bedrooms [R] **T** ✳ sB&B£22-£24 dB&B🛁🚿£48-£51 WB&B£140-£150.50 WBDi£210-£238 LDO 6pm

Lic ♨ CTV

Credit Cards [1][2][3][£]

See advertisement under PLYMOUTH

FH [Q][Q][Q] Mrs B Cole **Greenwell** *(SX536659)* Meavy PL20 6PY (leave A386 and follow signs for Meavy, continue for approx 2m farm a further 100yds after cattle grid) ☎(0822) 853563 FAX (0822) 853563

Closed Xmas

Greenwell Farm is situated two miles from Yelverton on the Cadover Bridge road on the edge of Dartmoor and has parts dating from the 15th century. The bedrooms are attractively coordinated and there are books and games for children on the landing. Traditional farmhouse cooking is provided and a set menu is served by arrangement only.

3🛁🚿 (1fb) 🚭 in bedrooms CTV in 2 bedrooms [R] 🐕 ✳ sB&B🛁🚿fr£20 dB&B🛁🚿£38-£44 WB&B£130-£140 WBDi£195-£205 LDO 4pm

Lic ♨ CTV stabling for guests horses clay shooting 220 acres beef sheep

[£]

YEOVIL Somerset — Map **03** ST51

See also Crewkerne & Halstock

FH [Q][Q][Q] Mrs M Tucker **Carents** *(ST546188)* Yeovil Marsh BA21 3QE (2m N of Yeovil off A37 half a mile into village on left) ☎(0935) 76622

Feb-Nov

This beautiful Somerset farmhouse enjoys a peaceful location, yet is only about two miles from Yeovil. Although the main part of the house was built in the 17th century, there is evidence that parts date back even earlier. Mrs Tucker pays particular attention to furnishing her home with good quality fabrics and furniture, and bedrooms are comfortable and well equipped. The sitting room features a wonderful fireplace, and breakfast is taken in the attractive breakfast room at a shared table.

3rm 🚭 in bedrooms [R] 🐕 ✳ sB&B£15-£16 dB&B£30-£32 CTV 350 acres arable beef

[£]

INN[Q][Q][Q] The Half Moon Main Street, Mudford BA21 5TF (leave A303 at Sparkford, onto A359 continus for approx 4 miles) (MIN) ☎Marston Magna(0935) 850289 FAX (0935) 850842

This 17th-century inn situated three miles north of Yeovil offers two bars and two restaurants (one of the latter designated non-smoking) as well as eleven small but well organised ground-floor bedrooms equipped with telephones, television sets and tea-making facilities. South Somerset has many attractions, including several National Trust properties.

Annexe 11rm(1🛁10🚿) 🚭 in 6 bedrooms 🚭 in dining room CTV in all bedrooms [R] **T** ✳ sB&B🛁🚿£30 dB&B🛁🚿£40 WB&B£186 Lunch £3.95-£7.50 Dinner £6.50-£12.50alc LDO 9.30pm

♨

Credit Cards [1][2][3][5][£]

YORK North Yorkshire — Map **08** SE65

See also Acaster Malbis, Copmanthorpe & Rufforth

GH [Q][Q][Q] Abbeyfields 19 Bootham Terrace YO3 7DH (3rd turning on left of A19 from city walls) ☎(0904) 636471

This immaculate Victorian terraced house stands in the popular Bootham area, within easy walking distance of the city centre. Bedrooms furnished in good quality pine have many modern features, a comfortable lounge is provided for guests' use and the small, neat breakfast room has individual tables; smoking is not permitted anywhere on the premises. Limited parking is available at the rear of the building (access via Queen Anne's Road).

9rm(8🚿) 🚭 CTV in all bedrooms [R] 🐕 ✳ sB&B£16-£18 sB&B🚿£22.50-£26 dB&B🚿£35-£44

♨ nc

[£]

GH [Q][Q] Aberford Hotel 35 East Mount Road YO2 2BD ☎(0904) 622694

An attractive terraced house set in a quiet side road within easy walking distance of the town centre offers accommodation in adequately furnished and decorated bedrooms; public rooms include a lounge area and cellar bar, and there are parking facilities to the rear of the hotel.

12rm(3🛁🚿) (1fb) 🚭 in 6 bedrooms 🚭 in dining room CTV in all bedrooms [R] 🐕 (ex guide dogs) sB&B£19-£24 sB&B🛁🚿£22-£27 dB&B£34-£38 dB&B🛁🚿£44-£52 WB&B£100-£120

Lic ♨ CTV

Credit Cards [1][2][3][£]

See advertisement on p.452.

GH [Q][Q][Q] Acer Hotel 52 Scarcroft Hill, The Mount YO2 1DE ☎(0904) 653839 & 628046

A comfortable house offers compact but well appointed bedrooms, a very good value dinner menu with a good choice of dishes and friendly service from the proprietors.

6rm(2🛁4🚿) (1fb) 🚭 in 3 bedrooms 🚭 in dining room 🚭 in lounges CTV in all bedrooms [R] **T** ✳ sB&B🛁🚿£27.50 dB&B🛁🚿£44-£55 WB&B£145 WBDi£205 LDO 6.30pm

Lic ♨ CTV

Credit Cards [1][2][3][£]

See advertisement on p.453.

[🛏☕] **GH [Q][Q][Q] Acorn** 1 Southlands Road, Bishopthorpe Road YO2 1NP ☎(0904) 620081

This late 19th-century house is about ten minutes' walk from the city centre. The bedrooms are neat and nicely decorated, some have en suite facilities and all have television and a beverage tray. There is a small lounge with television and an attractive dining room at the front of the house.

▶

6rm(3↺) (3fb)CTV in all bedrooms ® ⊀ (ex guide dogs)
sB&B£13-£17.50 dB&B£24-£33 dB&B↺£28-£37 LDO 10am
▥ CTV
Credit Cards ①②③ ⓔ

GH ⓠⓠⓠ **Adams House Hotel** 5 Main Street, Fulford YO1 4HJ
☎(0904) 655413
This Tudor-style house is conveniently situated on the A19, south
of the city and within easy reach of the A64. Family owned and
run, it offers spacious and comfortable bedrooms, with family
rooms also available. There is a large dining room with separate
tables, and a private car park.
7rm(2⇄4↺) (2fb) ⊬ in dining room CTV in all bedrooms ®
sB&B£16-£25 sB&B⇄↺£25-£40 dB&B⇄↺£32-£48
WB&B£90-£140 WBDi£157.50-£217.50 LDO 6.30pm
Lic ▥.
ⓔ

GH ⓠⓠⓠ **Alcuin Lodge** 15 Sycamore Place, Bootham
YO3 7DW ☎(0904) 632222
Closed 24-26 Dec & mid 2wks Jan
An Edwardian terrace guesthouse lies in a quiet cul-de-sac with a
footpath leading to the city centre. Bedrooms are thoughtfully
furnished. There is no lounge, but guests may use their rooms at
all times. Smoking is not allowed.
5rm(4↺) (1fb) ⊬ CTV in all bedrooms ® ⊀ (ex guide dogs)
dB&B£30-£33 dB&B↺£33-£40 WB&B£100-£200
▥ nc8yrs
Credit Cards ①③ ⓔ

GH ⓠⓠⓠ **Alfreda** 61 Heslington Lane, Fulford YO1 4HN
☎(0904) 631698
A large Edwardian house is situated in spacious grounds and
gardens off the A19, not far from York University and Fulford
Golf Course. Bedrooms, including some family rooms and some
ground-floor rooms, are modern in style and well equipped; two
have four-poster beds. Meals are taken round a large communal
table in the attractive dining room, which features an impressive
antique dresser.
10rm(8⇄↺) (4fb) ⊬ in dining room ⊬ in lounges CTV in all
bedrooms ® T dB&B£30-£40 dB&B⇄↺£30-£50
▥ CTV
Credit Cards ①②③ ⓔ

GH ⓠⓠⓠ **Ambleside** 62 Bootham Crescent YO3 7AH
☎(0904) 637165
Closed Jan
A friendly guest house with good standards a short walk from the
city walls. The lounge is comfortable with an attractive fireplace
and television with Sky channels and video. Bedrooms are fresh
and vary in size.
8rm(6↺) (1fb) ⊬ CTV in all bedrooms ® ⊀ dB&B£28-£34
dB&B↺£32-£42
▥ CTV ⊬nc9yrs

PREMIER ♣ SELECTED

GH ⓠⓠⓠⓠⓠ **Arndale
Hotel** 290 Tadcaster Road
YO2 2ET (turn off A64 on to
A1036 towards city centre for
2m, on left overlooking
racecourse) ☎(0904) 702424
Closed Xmas & New Year
This delightful hotel stands in
an acre of secluded walled
gardens on the outskirts of the
city, overlooking the famous
racecourse. Built as a private
residence in 1888, it has been extensively restored,
successfully combining the character of the house with the

comforts of today. Many of the spacious bedrooms have large
antique four-poster and half tester beds, and two rooms are on
the ground floor. Bathrooms feature Victorian-style wash
basins and brassware, complete with whirlpool baths. There is
a particularly large, elegant lounge overlooking the garden,
with a cosy bar which looks out onto the racecourse. Breakfast
is served in the very pretty dining room at lace-clothed tables
with fresh flowers.
10⇄↺ (1fb) ⊬ in dining room CTV in all bedrooms ® ⊀
(ex guide dogs) sB&B⇄↺£29-£45 dB&B⇄↺£39-£57
WB&B£129.50-£161
Lic ▥ nc5yrs
ⓔ

GH ⓠⓠ **Arnot House** 17 Grosvenor Terrace, Bootham YO3 7AG
(from Bootham Bar drive along Bootham the A19 towards Thirsk,
Grosvenor terrace is second on right) ☎(0904) 641966
Feb-Nov
In a row of Victorian terrace houses, Arnot House overlooks
Bootham Park towards the Minster. Bedrooms are furnished in
traditional style, and breakfast is served at individual tables in the
bay-windowed dining room. Evening meals can be arranged.
6rm (2fb) CTV in all bedrooms ® ⊀ ∗ sB&B£16-£17.50
dB&B£32-£35 WB&B£112-£122.50 WBDi£180.25-£190.75
LDO 1pm
Lic ▥ nc5yrs
ⓔ

GH ⓠⓠⓠ **Ascot House** 80 East Parade, Heworth YO3 7YH
☎(0904) 426826 FAX (0904) 431077
Conveniently situated about 15 minutes' walk from the city
centre, this Victorian house has a beautiful pine staircase and a
rare curved stained glass oriel window. Bedrooms are comfortable
with some antiques and two have four-poster beds. ▶

*Aberford House
Hotel*

35 – 36 East Mount Road, York YO2 2BD
Telephone: (01904) 622694

Splendid Victorian property situated within
easy walking distance of the city centre.
Offering a wide variety of accommodation to
suit both preference and pocket. All rooms
have colour television, wash basins and tea
making facilities. Some ensuite. Guests can
relax in our cosy cellar bar.
Car park available.

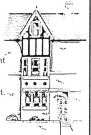

15rm(5🛁7🚿) (3fb) 🚭 in dining room CTV in all bedrooms [R] sB&B£18-£20 dB&B£34-£38 dB&B🛁🚿£34-£40 WB&B£115-£130
♨ CTV sauna
Credit Cards [1][3][£]

SELECTED

GH [Q][Q][Q][Q] Ashbourne House 139 Fulford Road YO1 4HG ☎(0904) 639912 FAX (0904) 631332

Efficiently run by enthusiastic owners Aileen and David Minns, this comfortable and well maintained semidetached Victorian house is situated in a residential area south of the city centre. Relaxing public areas include a no smoking lounge which has a comfortable leather suite, a piano and a dispense bar, while the dining room, with its locally made elm tables, provides the setting for Aileen's enjoyable home cooking. Bedrooms with modern fitted units, attractive bright soft furnishings and all the expected amenities.

6rm(1🛁5🚿) (1fb) 🚭 in 3 bedrooms 🚭 in dining room 🚭 in lounges CTV in all bedrooms [R] **T** ✱ sB&B🛁🚿£30-£34 dB&B🛁🚿£40-£48 WB&B£126-£151.20 WBDi£213.50-£238.70 LDO 6pm
Lic ♨ CTV
Credit Cards [1][2][3][5][£]

SELECTED

GH [Q][Q][Q][Q] *Ashbury Hotel* 103 The Mount YO2 2AX (from A64 take A1036 signposted 'York West') ☎(0904) 647339

Closed Xmas

A Victorian town house has a distinctive blue canopied entrance, situated on the A1036 which leads to The Mount, within a short walk of the city centre. Elegantly furnished and decorated in a modern style, the hotel provides comfortable accommodation. There is a pleasant lounge and an elegant dining room, with a small garden at the side of the house.

5🚿 CTV in all bedrooms [R] 🐕
Lic ♨ CTV 🅿

🛏☕ **GH [Q] Avenue** 6 The Avenue, Clifton YO3 6AS ☎(0904) 620575

This pantiled, late-Victorian mid-terrace house is situated in a quiet tree-lined avenue just off the A19 at Clifton, about 10 minutes' walk from the city centre. It has a combined lounge and dining room, and simple bedrooms - all with colour TV and one with an en suite shower. Unrestricted kerbside parking is allowed in the avenue.

7rm(2🚿) (4fb) 🚭 [R] 🐕 (ex guide dogs) sB&B£15-£18 sB&B🚿£18-£24 dB&B£26-£36 dB&B🚿£30-£44
♨ CTV 🅿

GH [Q][Q][Q] Barclay Lodge 19/21 Gillygate YO3 7EA (Gillygate is part of the Inner Ring Rd closest to the Minster entrance to the city) ☎(0904) 633274

An attractive Georgian town house, retaining much of its original character, is situated close to the Minster and only a short walk from York's many other attractions. Some of the attractive, cosy bedrooms have their original fireplaces and, although only two have en suite facilities, there are modern bathrooms close to all the other rooms. The pretty dining room has individual tables and there is also a comfortable guest lounge.

10rm(2🛁🚿) (3fb) 🚭 in dining room CTV in all bedrooms [R] 🐕 (ex guide dogs) sB&B£20 dB&B£38 dB&B🛁🚿£45
Lic ♨ CTV 🅿 🏠
Credit Cards [3][£]

🛏☕ **GH [Q][Q][Q] The Beckett** 58 Bootham Crescent YO3 7AH (take A19 past traffic lights at Clifton) ☎(0904) 644728

A terraced house is situated in a residential road at Bootham just a few minutes' walk from the city centre. The attractively decorated bedrooms have many modern features and most have en suite facilities. There is a comfortable guest lounge and also a small breakfast room at the rear.

7rm(5🚿) (2fb) 🚭 in 2 bedrooms 🚭 in dining room CTV in all bedrooms [R] 🐕 (ex guide dogs) sB&B£15-£17 sB&B🚿£25 dB&B£32-£36 dB&B🚿£34-£38 WB&B£112-£126
♨ CTV
[£]

GH [Q][Q][Q] Bedford 108/110 Bootham YO3 7DG (a few hundred yards N of the Minster) ☎(0904) 624412

In this private hotel a short walk from the railway museum and the city centre, everything is kept in good order. Bedrooms are fresh and light and the lounge has local information, Sky channels, a video of the Minster fire, and a bar. Guests can have dinner by arrangement.

14rm(3🛁11🚿) (3fb) 🚭 in lounges CTV in all bedrooms [R] 🐕 (ex guide dogs) sB&B🛁🚿£28-£34 dB&B🛁🚿£44-£50 LDO 1pm
Lic ♨ CTV
Credit Cards [1][3][£]

GH [Q][Q][Q] Beech House 6-7 Longfield Terrace, Bootham YO3 7DJ ☎(0904) 634581 & 630951

Closed Xmas & New Year

Situated in a quiet street, this small terraced house is within easy walking distance of the city centre. Bedrooms are bright, modern and well-equipped, whilst there is a cosy little lounge and attractive dining room.

9🚿 🚭 in dining room 🚭 in lounges CTV in all bedrooms [R] **T** 🐕 sB&B🚿£22-£27 dB&B🚿£36-£40 LDO breakfast
♨ nc10yrs
[£]

GH [Q][Q][Q] Bloomsbury Hotel 127 Clifton YO3 6BL ☎(0904) 634031

Just a brisk twenty minutes' walk from the Bootham Bar (one of the city's gates), this end-terrace brick-faced house is on the A19 northern approach to the town, opposite the parish church. Bedrooms vary in size, some furnished in traditional style, and most have comfortable seating. Proprietor Jaqueline Jessop keeps a cosy house with personal touches such as potted plants and fresh flowers throughout. Car parking is provided behind the house.

7rm(1🛁2🚿) (4fb) 🚭 CTV in all bedrooms [R] 🐕 (ex guide dogs) ✱ sB&B£18-£24 sB&B🛁🚿£25-£30 dB&B£30-£34 dB&B🛁🚿£34-£40 LDO noon
♨ CTV
[£]

GH [Q][Q] Bootham Bar Hotel 4 High Petergate YO1 2EH (100yds from Minster) (CON) ☎(0904) 658516

Closed 22-27 Dec & 9-19 Jan

Set in a narrow lane of shops, next to one of the fortified gateways to the old town, this Georgian house offers modern well equipped bedrooms of varying size, with cream coloured furniture and attractive coordinated fabrics. Breakfast and light meals are served in the adjoining Parlour Tea Room, which is under the same ownership. Secure private parking can be arranged nearby with prior notice.

9🛁🚿 (2fb) 🚭 in area of dining room CTV in all bedrooms [R] 🐕 (ex guide dogs) dB&B🛁🚿£52-£65
Lic ♨
Credit Cards [1][3][£]
See advertisement on p.457.

GH [Q][Q] Brönte House 22 Grosvenor Terrace, Bootham YO3 7AG ☎(0904) 621066

Just off the A19 coming from the north, this Victorian terrace house overlooks Bootham Park in the Minister direction. Bedrooms are cheerful and breakfast is served in a general purpose room which is a quiet room with limited seating out of meal hours.

▶

Ascot House

80 East Parade, Heworth, York YO3 7YH
Tel: 01904 426826 Fax: 01904 431077

A most attractive family run Victorian Villa, 15 minutes walk from City Centre. All double rooms are en-suite, some have four-poster or canopy beds. Large private car park.
Write or phone Mrs June Wood for a brochure.

AA QQQ

ASHBURY HOTEL

103 The Mount, York YO2 2AX
Telephone: 01904 647339

An elegant Victorian town house built in the 19th century that has been tastefully refurbished to a very high standard. The Hotel is personally supervised by the resident proprietors whose aim is to provide a personal service completing the feeling of luxury. Start the day with a hearty breakfast served in the elegant dining room, with a choice of full English or Continental. All bedrooms are en suite and tastefully decorated. A delightful garden and ample parking both at the front and side of the hotel are also available for guests.

Barclay Lodge

19 Gillygate, York YO3 7EA
Telephone: (01904) 633274

A pair of Georgian town houses that have been extensively refurbished and modernised to provide accommodation of the highest standard. Situated close to York Minster, Barclay Lodge is the ideal base from which to explore the historic city of York. Comfortable lounge where you can relax after an enjoyable day sightseeing.
All bedrooms are equipped with tea and coffee making facilities, colour TV and clock radio alarm some include bathroom-shower.

Beech House

6-7 Longfield Terrace, Bootham, York
Tel: (01904) 634581

Beech house is family run and situated in a quiet tree lined street, just over five minutes' walk to York Minster and the city centre.

- All rooms have ensuite shower and toilet
- Colour TV and clock radio in all rooms
- Direct dial telephone
- Tea & coffee making facilities
- Central heating & double glazing in all bedrooms
- Full English breakfast

Bed & breakfast, ensuite £17-24
Special Winter Breaks

Proprietors: Bill and Sheila Stratton

6rm(4🚿) (1fb) 🚭 in dining room 🚭 in lounges CTV in all bedrooms Ⓡ 🐕 (ex guide dogs) ✻ sB&B£13-£17 dB&B£24-£34 dB&B🚿£28-£40
♨ CTV
Credit Cards [1] [3]

GH [Q] [Q] [Q] Burton Villa 22 Haxby Road YO3 7JX (take ring rd A1237, leave on B1363, past hospital then sharp left)
☎(0904) 626364
Only a short walk from the city walls, and close to the Minster, this Victorian end-of-terrace house has individually furnished rooms which include some family rooms. The breakfast room is well appointed, with individual tables and attractive place settings. Off-street parking is available.
11rm(1🛁7🚿) (3fb) 🚭 in dining room CTV in all bedrooms Ⓡ ✻ sB&B£15-£18 sB&B🛁🚿£20-£35 dB&B£30-£36 dB&B🛁🚿£33-£43
♨
[£]
See advertisement on p.458.

GH [Q] [Q] [Q] Byron House Hotel 7 Driffield Terrace, The Mount YO2 2DD ☎(0904) 632525 FAX (0904) 639424
Closed 24-26 Dec
This elegant late Regency-style end-of-terrace house has particularly lofty and spacious bedrooms of a modern design which will please both business and leisure guests. There is also a comfortable lounge and bar combined, with a number of dralon upholstered chesterfields, where one can enjoy pre and post-dinner drinks. The restaurant is a well proportioned room with french windows looking out onto a terrace. Private parking is provided at the front, and the hotel is conveniently situated west of the city centre, standing back from the A1036.
10rm(7🛁🚿) (4fb) 🚭 in 4 bedrooms 🚭 in dining room CTV in all bedrooms Ⓡ T 🐕 (ex guide dogs) sB&B£22-£25 sB&B🛁🚿£35-£40 dB&B🛁🚿£45-£70 LDO noon
Lic ♨
Credit Cards [1] [2] [3] [5] [£]
See advertisement on p.458.

GH [Q] [Q] Carousel 83 Eldon Street, off Stanley St, Haxby Road YO3 7NH ☎(0904) 646709
A former dairy built partly around a small courtyard, this neat guesthouse is tricky to find and is best approached by Huxby Road and then Stanley Street. The well equipped bedrooms all have en suite facilities, and there is an attractive panelled lounge and dining room in which full English breakfast is served.
9🚿 (2fb) 🚭 in dining room 🚭 in lounges CTV in all bedrooms Ⓡ 🐕 ✻ sB&B🚿£15-£18 dB&B🚿£30-£34 WB&B£100-£115 WBDi£150-£170 LDO 9.30am
Lic ♨ CTV
[£]

GH [Q] [Q] [Q] *Cavalier Private Hotel* 39 Monkgate YO3 7PB (situated on the A1036 (A64) York to Malton Road, 250mtrs from York Inner Ring road and City Wall (Monkgate))
☎(0904) 636615 & 640769
An early Georgian listed building close to the city walls and the Minster, this hotel has been furnished and decorated to a high standard throughout, the bedrooms being particularly attractive and comfortable. There is a spacious lounge and a large dining room with individual tables. Car parking can be arranged.
10rm(2🛁5🚿) (4fb) CTV in all bedrooms Ⓡ 🐕 (ex guide dogs)
Lic ♨ CTV sauna
Credit Cards [1] [3]
See advertisement on p.459.

GH [Q] [Q] [Q] City 68 Monkgate YO3 7PF ☎(0904) 622483
This charming family-run guesthouse stands close to the city walls within five minutes' walk of the Minster. The attractively decorated en suite bedrooms are all well equipped to modern standards and public areas include a small lounge and a dining room.
8rm(1🛁5🚿) (4fb) 🚭 CTV in all bedrooms Ⓡ 🐕 ✻ sB&B£15-£20 sB&B🛁🚿£15-£25 dB&B£32-£40 dB&B🛁🚿£36-£48 WB&B£105-£168
♨ nc5yrs
Credit Cards [1] [3] [£]
See advertisement on p.459.

GH [Q] [Q] [Q] *Clifton Green Hotel* 8 Clifton Green, Clifton YO3 6LH (on A19) ☎(0904) 623597
This attractive Victorian property overlooks the old village green in what is now a suburb of York, just north-west of the city centre. The immaculate bedrooms are bright and modern, and there is a separate dining room with individual tables and a cosy little residents' bar where bar meals are served. The bar, along with the rear garden, patio and car park, are shared with guests at Inglewood.
8rm(2🚿) CTV in all bedrooms Ⓡ 🐕 (ex guide dogs)
Lic ♨ CTV

GH [Q] [Q] [Q] Collingwood Hotel 163 Holgate Road YO2 4DF (Holgate Rd is a continuation of the A59) ☎(0904) 783333
This listed Georgian house within walking distance of the city, set in its own grounds beside the A59, provides very good standards of both accommodation and service. All its en suite bedrooms are well furnished - one with a four poster bed - whilst public areas are spacious and comfortable.
10rm(20🛁🚿) (2fb) 🚭 in 1 bedrooms 🚭 in dining room CTV in all bedrooms Ⓡ 🐕 (ex guide dogs) sB&B🛁🚿£25-£35 dB&B🛁🚿£48-£52 WB&B£168-£182 LDO 8.30pm
Lic ♨ CTV
Credit Cards [1] [2] [3] [5] [£]

GH [Q] Coppers Lodge 15 Alma Terrace, Fulford Road YO1 4DQ
☎(0904) 639871
This hotel, once a police station, is now a comfortable guesthouse. The bedrooms are basically furnished but there is an attractive, small breakfast room and lounge.
8rm(1🛁🚿) (5fb) 🚭 in dining room CTV in all bedrooms Ⓡ ✻ sB&B£16-£18 dB&B£26-£30 dB&B🛁🚿£30-£36 LDO 2pm
♨ CTV
[£]
See advertisement of p.459.

GH [Q] [Q] [Q] Crescent 77 Bootham YO3 7DQ (approach city on A19 city centre road, hotel 5mins for centre) ☎(0904) 623216 FAX (0904) 623216
This Georgian-style house is situated on the A19 on the north side of the city and is only a short walk from the centre. Bedrooms are particularly well equipped and most have en suite facilities. There is a small lounge downstairs and an attractive dining room in which breakfast is served; evening meals are available on request.
10rm(8🛁🚿) (5fb) 🚭 in dining room CTV in all bedrooms Ⓡ T 🐕 ✻ sB&Bfr£18.50 sB&B🛁🚿£26 dB&B£29-£39 dB&B🛁🚿£37-£52 WB&B£129-£182 WBDi£199-£251 LDO noon
Lic ♨
Credit Cards [1] [2] [3] [5] [£]

GH [Q] [Q] [Q] Crook Lodge 26 St Marys, Bootham YO3 7DD
☎(0904) 655614
Closed Dec
This attractive early Victorian house forms the end of a terrace in a very pleasant area of the city only a few minutes' walk from the centre. Bedrooms are attractive, well equipped and furnished in keeping with the character of the house. Private parking is available.
7rm(3🛁4🚿) 🚭 in 1 bedrooms 🚭 in dining room 🚭 in lounges CTV in all bedrooms Ⓡ 🐕 ✻ sB&B🛁🚿£21.50-£24.50 dB&B🛁🚿£39-£45 LDO 10am
Lic ♨ nc

Bootham Bar Hotel

4 High Petergate
York YO1 2EH
Tel. (01904) 658516

One of the best locations in York. This 18th century building is situated only 100 yards from York Minster, adjacent to the city walls.

All York's other tourist attractions, shopping streets, restaurants and the theatre are within easy walking distance.

All our bedrooms are very comfortably furnished. Each room has private facilities, colour TV, radio with alarm and tea making facilities.

Our Victorian tearoom is open from Monday to Saturday for light refreshments 10.30 a.m. – 5.30 p.m.

Telephone or write to the resident proprietors:
Mr. & Mrs. J. Dearnley for further details.

GH Q Q **Crossways** 23 Wiggington Road YO3 7HJ (opposite York District Hospital) ☎(0904) 637250
A small Edwardian townhouse with a long narrow front garden, is situated a brisk 15 minutes' walk north of the city centre. Bedrooms are compact but have pretty decor and cheerful soft furnishings; one room is located on the ground floor. There is no lounge, but breakfast is taken in the attractive little dining room at individual tables.
6♠ CTV in all bedrooms ® ⅋ (ex guide dogs) ✳ dB&B♠£32-£38 WB&B£210-£220
▥,
Credit Cards ③

GH Q Q Q **Cumbria House** 2 Vyner Street, Haxby Road YO3 7HS ☎(0904) 636817
Only ten minutes' walk from the city centre, this end of terrace house has bedrooms attractively decorated with modern fabrics. A choice of menu is served at breakfast. Smoking is not permitted.
5rm(3♠) (2fb) ⅋ in dining room CTV in all bedrooms ® ⅋ (ex guide dogs) sB&Bfr£20 dB&Bfr£30 dB&B♠fr£36 WB&B£105-£140
▥,
ⓔ

SELECTED

GH Q Q Q Q **Curzon Lodge and Stable Cottages** 23 Tadcaster Road, Dringhouses YO2 2QG (follow signs for "park & ride" from A64, between Forte Posthouse & Swallow Hotel) ☎(0904) 703157
Closed Xmas-New Year
This attractive early 17th-century house is situated in colourful gardens on the A1036, close to the famous Knavesmire racecourse. All bedrooms are of a very high standard; some

are in the Lodge and others are in a wisteria-clad former coach house and stable block at the rear. Original oak beams are a feature of the coach house while antique furniture, Victorian brass bedsteads and a four-poster bed adorn the Lodge which also houses a delightful drawing room and a small dining room. Family-run and welcoming, the guesthouse is within easy reach of the city centre and the A64.
5rm(3⇆2♠) Annexe 5rm(3⇆2♠) (1fb) ⅋ in dining room ⅋ in lounges CTV in all bedrooms ® T ⅋ sB&B⇆♠£29.50-£38 dB&B⇆♠£45-£56
▥, nc7yrs
Credit Cards ① ③ ⓔ
See advertisement on p.460

GH Q Q Q **Field House Hotel** 2 St George's Place, Tadcaster Road YO2 2DR (turn off A64 onto A1036, 1m on left) ☎(0904) 639572
Closed Xmas
Conveniently situated for both the racecourse and the town centre, this impressive house provides spacious bedrooms, a comfortable lounge and an attractive dining room.
17rm(1⇆16♠) ⅋ in dining room CTV in all bedrooms ® T ⅋ (ex guide dogs) sB&B⇆♠£23-£31 dB&B£38 dB&B⇆♠£54-£59 LDO 7pm
Lic ▥,
Credit Cards ① ② ③ ⓔ

GH Q Q Q **Four Poster Lodge Hotel** 68-70 Heslington Road, off Barbican Road YO1 5AU ☎(0904) 651170
Closed 25-26 Dec
This Victorian villa has been tastefully restored by hosts Peter and Judith Jones; it is situated in a residential area of the city, yet within a short walk of the city's tourist attractions and shops.

▶

A small Private Hotel open all year and offering every modern comfort in a beautiful old building only a 100 yards from the ancient city walls and five minutes from the Minster and City centre.

Bed and Breakfast – colour TV's, coffee and tea facilities in all rooms – Central Heating – Sauna, most rooms with en-suite facilities.

JOHN and MARJORIE POTTS
The Cavalier Private Hotel,
39 Monkgate, York YO3 7PB
Telephone: (01904) 636615

CHURCH COTTAGE

Family run, licensed guest house on the A19 at Escrick, convenient for York & Selby. Standing in two acres of lawn and woodland, with large private car park. Local bus service available directly into York.
At Church Cottage we have first class en suite accommodation with tea & coffee making facilities and remote control TV in all rooms.
Contact: The Robinson Family, Church Cottage, Escrick, York YO4 6EX
Telephone: 01904 728462
Fax: 01904 728896
AA QQQ

Simply a stone's throw from York Minster. Leave your car in our car park and enjoy all the convenience of a city centre Guest House. We can offer a choice of cosy comfortable rooms, fully en-suite or shower only. All rooms have a colour T.V., tea trays, and central heating, some overlooking our large garden. Breakfasts are served in our elegant Victorian dining room with a choice of English, continental or vegetarian.
The entire Guest House is of a no smoking standard.
City Guest House,
68 Monkgate, York YO3 7PF
Telephone: York (01904) 622483

Coppers Lodge Guest House

15 Alma Terrace, Fulford Road,
York YO1 4DQ
Telephone: (01904) 639871

Quietly situated off the main road just two minutes walk from the River Ouse and five minutes to the City Walls. Coppers Lodge is open all year round offering bed & breakfast with evening meal available on request.
All rooms are tastefully decorated and have colour TV, tea & coffee facilities, hot & cold and central heating.
Comfortable lounge with TV is also available.

Many of the bedrooms have four-poster beds and are very attractively decorated, some rooms have private bathrooms, TV, radio alarms, hair dryers and tea and coffee-making facilities, and a few feature antique fireplaces. Downstairs there is a very comfortable bar/lounge, and hearty English breakfasts are served in the dining room. There is a private car park at the rear of the guesthouse.

10🛏️📞 (2fb) ⊁ in 5 bedrooms ⊁ in dining room ⊁ in lounges CTV in all bedrooms ® ✳ sB&B🛏️📞£30-£36 dB&B🛏️📞£49-£52 WB&Bfr£152 WBDifr£229 LDO 6pm
Lic ▥.
Credit Cards ① ② ③

SELECTED

GH Q Q Q Q **Four Seasons Hotel** 7 St Peters Grove, Bootham YO3 6AQ ☎(0904) 622621 FAX (0904) 430565
Closed 24 Dec-1 Jan
A detached red brick Victorian house enjoys a peaceful location in a quiet avenue off the A19, about five minutes' walk from the town centre. The bedrooms are comfortable and well equipped and all of them have en suite facilities. There is also a relaxing guest lounge and parking facilities at the rear of the hotel. A warm and friendly welcome is extended by the owners.

5🛏️📞 (2fb) ⊁ in 2 bedrooms ⊁ in dining room CTV in all bedrooms ® ✳ dB&B🛏️📞£44-£50
Lic ▥ CTV
Credit Cards ① ③ £

GH Q Q **Freshney's Hotel** 54 Low Petergate YO1 2HZ ☎(0904) 622478 FAX (0904) 426931
10rm(5📞) (1fb) ⊁ in dining room CTV in all bedrooms ® T ✳ sB&Bfr£23 dB&B£40-£42 dB&B📞£44-£52 LDO 9.30pm
Lic ▥.
Credit Cards ① ③ £

SELECTED

GH Q Q Q Q **Grasmead House Hotel** 1 Scarcroft Hill, The Mount YO2 1DF ☎(0904) 629996 FAX (0904) 629996
Closed 25-26 Dec
A delightful small, family run hotel is situated just south of the city centre. Bedrooms feature antique furniture and four-poster beds, the oldest dating back to 1730; they also have comfortable seating and good bathrooms. There is a comfortable lounge with a small bar in the corner, and an attractive dining room.

6🛏️📞 (2fb) ⊁ in 3 bedrooms ⊁ in dining room CTV in all bedrooms ® 🐾 (ex guide dogs) ✳ dB&B🛏️📞£54-£58 WB&B£189-£203
Lic ▥ CTV
Credit Cards ① ③

GH Q Q **Greenside** 124 Clifton YO3 6BQ ☎(0904) 623631
This attractive detached conservation house is situated on the A19, north of the city centre overlooking Clifton Green. The good sized bedrooms, all with central heating and colour TV, are mostly on the first floor, but there is one on the ground floor at the rear with an en suite shower and WC. The pretty dining room features separate tables with lace cloths and wheelback chairs, and there is a comfortable guests' lounge with TV. Private parking facilities are available at the rear.

6rm(3📞) (2fb) ⊁ in dining room ⊁ in lounges CTV in all bedrooms ® sB&Bfr£16 dB&Bfr£24 dB&B📞fr£30 LDO 6pm
Lic ▥ CTV ⚓
£

SELECTED

GH Q Q Q Q **The Heathers** 54 Shipton Rd, Clifton - Without YO3 6RQ (mid-way between A1237 and town centre) ☎(0904) 640989
Closed Xmas
In this 1930's detached house the bedrooms have been expensively furnished and decorated with much use of designer fabrics and antique furniture. Those at the rear overlook a large garden and those at the front have views over meadow land and a distant cricket ground. It is a comfortable and friendly house with many thoughtful touches and lots of books everywhere.

6rm(2📞) (1fb) ⊁ CTV in 3 bedrooms ® 🐾 dB&B£28-£38 dB&B📞£36-£60
▥ CTV nc8yrs
Credit Cards ②

GH Q Q **Heworth** 126 East Parade YO3 7YG ☎(0904) 426384
Situated in a quiet area in walking distance of the city, this small Victorian end-of-terrace house has attractive bedrooms including one with en suite facilities on the ground floor. There is a small breakfast room downstairs which can double as a lounge.
7rm CTV in all bedrooms ®
▥.

GH Q Q **Hillcrest** 110 Bishopthorpe Road YO2 1JX ☎(0904) 653160
This Victorian terraced house has high ceilings and large windows, making the freshly decorated bedrooms appear more spacious. They are well equipped with TV and beverage trays, and seven have en suite showers. There is a large, comfortable lounge, an attractive dining room and a private car park at the rear.

Four Poster Lodge Hotel

A Victorian villa lovingly restored and furnished, situated between the University and York's historic centre. Enjoy our relaxing atmosphere, good food, (English breakfast a speciality) and quality service.

Our amenities include a residents licence and private car park. The four poster bedrooms have private facilities and are fully equipped for your comfort.

Your hosts, Peter & Judith Jones.
70 Heslington Road, off Barbican Road, York, YO1 5AU.
Telephone: 01904 651170

Four Seasons Hotel

7 St Peters Grove
York YO3 6AQ

| AA |
| QQQQ |

Tel: 01904 622621
Fax: 01904 430565

An elegant detached Victorian residence ideally situated in a peaceful cul-de-sac only five minutes walk from the Minster and York's many historic attractions.

Private car parking. Residential licence. All rooms en suite and with courtesy tray and colour TV. Full English breakfast served.

A warm and friendly reception awaits you from Julie and Adrian Brown.

Access   *Barclaycard*

Grasmead House Hotel

A small family owned and run hotel situated within easy walking distance of the City Centre. Restful nights are assured in our luxurious centrally heated bedrooms, all with antique four-poster beds. All bedrooms have private bathroom, tea and coffee making facilities, colour TV.
The resident proprietors, Sue and Stan Long ensure that a real welcome and personal service awaits each and every guest.

GRASMEAD HOUSE HOTEL
1 Scarcroft Hill
York YO2 1DF

Tel/Fax: York (01904) 629996

Greenside

124 Clifton, York. Tel: York (01904) 623631
Martyn & Lynne Tattersall

Greenside is a charming detached conservation house fronting on to Clifton Green. Situated in a most convenient location just outside the city walls, close to the many attractions that York has to offer.
Spacious fully equipped large bedrooms are all situated on ground or first floor, all have tea/coffee facilities, colour TV and central heating. En suite rooms available but there are also ample bath, shower and WC facilities. Enclosed car park. First class English breakfast and evening meals. Licensed. Fire certificate.
Winter Break Specials.
Registered with English Tourist Board.

13rm(7🚿) (4fb) 🚭 in 9 bedrooms 🚭 in dining room CTV in all bedrooms [R] ✱ sB&B£13-£18 dB&B£24-£34 dB&B🚿£28-£38 LDO noon
📺 CTV
Credit Cards [1] [3] [£]

GH [Q] [Q] The Hollies 141 Fulford Road YO1 4HG
☎(0904) 634279
Closed Xmas
This comfortable family-run guesthouse is situated on the A19 about a mile from the city centre and a similar distance from the southern bypass, convenient for the univeristy. All rooms have colour TV and tea-making facilities and two have en suite showers. There is also a spacious guests' lounge.
5rm(2🚿) (3fb) 🚭 in 2 bedrooms 🚭 in dining room CTV in all bedrooms [R] 🐕 ✱ sB&B£18-£25 sB&B🚿£25-£30 dB&B£30-£38 dB&B🚿£34-£42
📺 CTV nc3yrs
Credit Cards [1] [3]

SELECTED

GH [Q] [Q] [Q] [Q] *Holmwood House Hotel* 112-114 Holgate Road YO2 4BB (on A59) ☎(0904) 626183 FAX (0904) 670899
Two elegant early Victorian houses form this pleasant guesthouse close to the city centre. The bedrooms are all decorated with attractive coordinated fabrics and equipped with many nice extra touches. One has a spa bath. The small, cosy sitting room looks out over the neat front garden and in the dining room excellent breakfasts are served.
12🛁🚿 (1fb) CTV in all bedrooms [R] **T**
Lic 📺 nc8yrs
Credit Cards [1] [2] [3]

GH [Q] [Q] [Q] *Inglewood* 7 Clifton Green YO3 6LH (turn off A1237 onto A19) ☎(0904) 653523
This charming Victorian terraced house looks out over Clifton Green, just north-west of the city centre. Spotlessly clean and immaculately maintained, it offers bright modern bedrooms and an attractive small dining room. Situated next door to the Clifton Green, the hotels share a cosy residents' bar and a secluded patio and garden.
7rm(3🚿) (2fb) CTV in all bedrooms 🐕
📺 CTV

🛏 📺 **GH [Q] [Q] [Q] Jubilee** 120 Haxby Road YO3 7JP
☎(0904) 620566
Closed 16 Dec-4 Jan
Conveniently situated about ten minutes' walk from the city centre, this pleasantly appointed Victorian terraced property provides friendly service and accommodation in bright, fresh bedrooms equipped with colour television sets and tea-making facilities. There is car parking space at the rear of the house.
5rm(3🚿) (1fb) 🚭 in dining room 🚭 in 1 lounge CTV in all bedrooms [R] 🐕 (ex guide dogs) sB&B£15-£19 dB&B£28-£34 dB&B🚿£30-£38
📺 CTV nc4yrs
[£]

GH [Q] [Q] [Q] Linden Lodge Hotel Nunthorpe Avenue, Scarcroft Rd YO2 1PF ☎(0904) 620107
Closed 23 Dec-9 Jan
This comfortable Victorian town house, in a quiet cul-de-sac not far from the city centre, is proud of its award-winning floral displays which are a feature of the faáade in summer. Bedrooms vary in size, but include some family rooms and a good number with en suite facilities. There are two cosy lounges and a nicely appointed dining room.
12rm(9🚿) (2fb) 🚭 in bedrooms 🚭 in dining room CTV in 9 bedrooms [R] 🐕 ✱ sB&B£17-£20 sB&B🚿£20-£25 dB&B£34-£40 dB&B🚿£40-£50
Lic 📺 CTV
Credit Cards [1] [2] [3] [£]

SELECTED

GH [Q] [Q] [Q] [Q] Midway House Hotel 145 Fulford Road YO1 4HG (S side on A19) ☎(0904) 659272
This Victorian gabled house stands in its own grounds on the A19, not far from its junction with the A64. Bedrooms are generously sized, comfortable and thoughtfully furnished throughout. Public areas include a very comfortable lounge and a spacious dining room where enjoyable home cooking is served at individual tables. There is a walled garden and patio where drinks and snacks are served in summer months, and ample car parking.
12rm(11🚿) (2fb) 🚭 in bedrooms 🚭 in dining room CTV in all bedrooms [R] 🐕 (ex guide dogs) sB&B🚿£27-£46 dB&Bfr£38 dB&B🚿£50 WB&B£133-£175 LDO 5pm
Lic 📺
Credit Cards [1] [2] [3] [5] [£]

GH [Q] [Q] Minster View 2 Grosvenor Terrace YO3 7AG
☎(0904) 655034
With the advantage of its own car park, this tall Victorian terrace house faces Bootham Park towards the Minster. Bedrooms are mostly of a good size - some have striking wallpaper. Breakfast is served in a pleasant dining room.
9rm(5🛁🚿) (4fb) 🚭 in dining room 🚭 in lounges CTV in all bedrooms [R] ✱ sB&B£14-£16 dB&B£28-£32 dB&B🛁🚿£30-£38 WB&B£98-£112 WBDi£161-£175 LDO 10am
Lic 📺 CTV
[£]

GH [Q] [Q] Moat Hotel Nunnery Lane YO2 1AA
☎(0904) 652926 FAX (0904) 652926
Situated beside the inner ring road, close to the railway station, this hotel with the advantage of its own car park provides good all round standards of service and accommodation. Smoking is not permitted anywhere on the premises.
8🛁🚿 (1fb) 🚭 CTV in all bedrooms [R] 🐕 (ex guide dogs) ✱ dB&B🛁🚿fr£36
Lic 📺 CTV ⛳
Credit Cards [1] [2] [3] [5]

GH [Q] [Q] Monkgate Lodge 51 Monkgate YO3 7PB (turn of A64 at Hopegrove Rdbt follow signs for city centre Monkgate at 3rd rdbt) ☎(0904) 631501
Mar-mid Dec
An attractive little guest house offers friendly service and accommodation in two comfortable bedrooms (both of them now equipped with en suite facilities); there is no lounge, but meals are served in a bright, fresh breakfast room.
2🛁🚿 (1fb) 🚭 CTV in all bedrooms [R] 🐕 ✱ dB&B🛁🚿£40-£45 WB&B£135-£150
📺 CTV nc5yrs
[£]

GH [Q] [Q] [Q] Nunmill House 85 Bishopthorpe Road YO2 1NX
☎(0904) 634047
Closed Dec-Jan
9rm(2🛁2🚿) (2fb) 🚭 CTV in all bedrooms [R] 🐕 ✱ sB&B£16-£18 dB&B£30-£32 dB&B🛁🚿£36-£44
📺 CTV

GH [Q] [Q] [Q] Orchard Court Hotel 4 St Peters Grove YO3 6AQ
☎(0904) 653964
This detached Victorian house dates back to 1881 and is situated in a quiet cul-de-sac at Bootham, just off the A19 and within walking distance of the city. Double bedrooms are particularly spacious, and ground-floor rooms are also available. There is a

very comfortable lounge with a small bar overlooking the garden, and enjoyable home-cooked meals are a feature of the attractive dining room.

11rm(8⇌♠ℜ) (4fb) CTV in all bedrooms ® ↑ (ex guide dogs) sB&B£20-£25 sB&B⇌♠ℜ£28-£35 dB&B⇌♠ℜ£46-£60 LDO 7.30pm
Lic ▥ CTV
Credit Cards [1] [3] ⓒ

SELECTED

GH [Q][Q][Q][Q] St Denys Hotel St Denys Road YO1 1QD
☎(0904) 622207 FAX (0904) 624800
Closed 2wks Xmas
A former vicarage offers comfortable spacious accommodation and a cosy lounge.
10🛁🚿 (4fb) CTV in all bedrooms Ⓡ ✻ sB&B🛁🚿£25-£35 dB&B🛁🚿£40-£50 LDO noon
Lic ▥ CTV
Credit Cards [1][3][£]

GH [Q][Q][Q] ***St Georges House Hotel*** 6 St Georges Place, Tadcaster Road YO2 2DR ☎(0904) 625056
This large and attractive Victorian house stands in a quiet side road just off the A64, close to the racecourse. Well furnished throughout, it offers a cosy lounge and a restaurant (now open to the public) featuring a short but interesting carte.
10rm(1🛁7🚿) (5fb) CTV in all bedrooms Ⓡ LDO 7pm
Lic ▥ CTV
Credit Cards [1][2][3]

GH [Q][Q] St Raphael 44 Queen Anne's Road, Bootham YO3 7AF
☎(0904) 645028
Limited kerbside parking is available outside this semidetached house which stands in a quiet side road not far from the city centre, just off Bootham. Friendly service is provided by the resident owner and, though there is no lounge, bedrooms are comfortably furnished and adequately equipped.
8rm(3🚿) (2fb) 🚭 in dining room 🚭 in lounges CTV in all bedrooms Ⓡ ✻ sB&B£14-£19 dB&B£28-£34 dB&B🚿£30-£36 LDO 4pm
▥ CTV ✗
Credit Cards [1][3]

🛏☕ **GH [Q][Q][Q] Staymor** 2 Southlands Road YO2 1NP
☎(0904) 626935
Feb-Nov
A Victorian house is situated in a residential area just off Bishopthorpe Road, south of the city. Bedrooms are attractively decorated in a modern style. There is a comfortable guests' lounge as well as a small dining room with individual tables. Guests are asked not to smoke in the bedrooms.
4🛁🚿 (2fb) 🚭 in bedrooms 🚭 in dining room CTV in all bedrooms Ⓡ sB&B🛁🚿£15-£20 dB&B🛁🚿£24-£32 WB&B£84-£112
▥
[£]

GH [Q][Q][Q] Sycamore 19 Sycamore Place, Bootham YO3 7DW
☎(0904) 624712
Closed 18-31 Dec
Only a short walk from the city centre, an attractive front garden and an old street gas lamp show the way to this delightful little guesthouse situated in a quiet cul-de-sac. Bedrooms have been totally redecorated and new carpets fitted. There is no lounge, but guests may use their rooms at all times. The breakfast room has individual tables.
6rm(2🚿) (1fb) 🚭 in dining room 🚭 in lounges CTV in all bedrooms Ⓡ 🐕 dB&B£30-£34 dB&B🚿£32-£40 WB&B£105-£130
▥ nc5yrs
See advertisement on p.466.

GH [Q][Q][Q] Tower 2 Feversham Crescent, Wigginton Road YO3 7HQ (on B1363 adjacent to district hospital) ☎(0904) 655571 & 635924
Distinguished by its blue window canopies, this Edwardian house is within easy walking distance of the city centre. The bedrooms provide contemporary comforts and have been tastefully modernised with white furniture, bright wall coverings and attractive curtains. A spacious dining room is provided, enhanced by small flower arrangements and paintings. Private parking is available at the front of the hotel.
5rm(1🛁4🚿) (3fb) CTV in all bedrooms Ⓡ 🐕 ✻ dB&B🛁🚿£32-£40
▥
Credit Cards [1][3][£]

GH [Q][Q][Q] Turnberry House 143 Fulford Road YO1 4HG
☎(0904) 658435
Closed 25-26 Dec
This attractive and well cared for Edwardian house, set beside the A19 to the south of the city, has the advantage of on site parking. Spacious, comfortable bedrooms provide good facilities, service is friendly and the atmosphere warm.
4🚿 (2fb) 🚭 CTV in all bedrooms Ⓡ 🐕 (ex guide dogs) ✻ sB&B🚿£20-£30 dB&B🚿£30-£40
▥
[£]
See advertisement on p.466.

INN[Q][Q][Q] Jacobean Lodge Hotel Plainville Lane YO3 8RG (take B1363 from York towards Helmsley for approx 3m and turn left after the right turn for Wigginton. After 1.5m turn right at crossroads) ☎(0904) 762749 FAX (0904) 762749
A 17th-century converted farmhouse is situated in open countryside and its own well tended gardens. Bedrooms have modern facilities and several are en suite. Substantial bar meals are served at lunch time and in the evening, and the main restaurant is open nightly for more formal dining.
8rm(2🛁6🚿) (2fb)CTV in all bedrooms Ⓡ **T** sB&B🛁🚿£28-£32 dB&B🛁🚿£39-£52 Lunch £4.80-£14alc Dinner £7.50-£20alc LDO 9.30pm
▥ CTV 🏠
Credit Cards [1][3][£]
See advertisement on p.466.

Telephone national area codes are due to change by 16th April 1995. Please see the note under 'How to Use this Guide' at the front of the book.

Telephone national area codes are due to change by 16th April 1995. Please see the note under 'How to Use this Guide' at the front of the book.

The Priory Hotel, York

The Priory offers comfortable accommodation with full English breakfast, and is situated 600 yards south of York's medieval city walls, within easy direct reach of the nearby inner and outer ring roads. The city centre can be reached by a pleasant riverside walk.

The 20 bedrooms, all equipped with colour TV and tea/coffee making facilities, include single, double and family accommodation, all with en suite shower and toilet facilities.

The hotel is AA listed, and has full central heating, a licensed bar and restaurant. The pleasant garden leads to the large private car-park. Reductions are available for children sharing accommodation with their parents. Please send for brochure and tariff.

Proprietors:
George and Barbara Jackson
The Priory Hotel
Fulford Road
York YO1 4BE
Telephone York (01904) 625280

NORTHERN IRELAND AND THE REPUBLIC OF IRELAND

USEFUL INFORMATION

In most instances, the details for establishments in the Irish Directory are as outlined in the sections at the front of the book headed AA Inspections and Classification and How to Use this Guide. See also the explanation of Symbols and Abbreviations.

TOWN & COUNTRY

In the Republic of Ireland, establishments classified as Town & Country Houses are indicated by the abbreviation T & C. Because of statutory regulations, these properties cannot be officially classified as Guest Houses, although their facilities are similar.

MAP REFERENCES

In the Irish Directory, the six-figure map references shown against establishments have been taken from the Irish National Grid.

PRICES

In the Republic, prices are quoted in Punts, indicated by the symbol IR£. Please consult your bank or the daily paper for the current exchange rate.
Hotels must display tariffs, either in the bedrooms or at reception.

Application of VAT and service charges varies, but all prices quoted must be inclusive of VAT.

TELEPHONE NUMBERS

Area codes shown against the numbers in the Republic of Ireland are applicable only within the Republic. If dialling from outside, you will need to check with the telephone directory. The area codes shown for hotels in Britain and Northern Ireland cannot be used directly from the Republic.

FIRE PRECAUTIONS

The Fire Services (NI) Order 1984 covers establishments accommodating more than 6 persons, and they must have a fire certificate issued by the Northern Ireland Fire Authority. Places accommodating fewer than 6 persons must have adequate exits.
Republic of Ireland: safety regulations are a matter for local authority regulations, but AA

officials inspect emergency notices, fire-fighting equipment and fire exits.
For your own and others' safety, you must read the emergency notices displayed and be sure you understand them.

LICENSING REGULATIONS

Northern Ireland: public houses open from 11.30-23.00, and on Sun 12.30-14.30 and 19.00-22.00. Hotels can serve residents without restriction. Non-residents can be served from 12.30-22.00 on Christmas Day. Children under 18 are not allowed in the bar area and may neither buy nor consume liquor in hotels.

Republic of Ireland
General licensing hours at present are 10.30-23.00 (23.30 in summer), Mon - Sat. On Sun and St Patrick's Day (17th March), 12.30-14.00 and 16.00-23.00. There is no service on Christmas Day or Good Friday.

ACHILL ISLAND Co Mayo — Map **01** A4

SELECTED

GH [Q][Q][Q][Q] ***Gray's*** Dugort ☎(098) 43244 & 43315
Mar-7 Oct
Gray's offers comfortable accommodation in a quiet location with ample lounge space and is especially suitable for family holidays.
8rm Annexe 7rm(5🚿) 🐕 LDO 6pm
▥ CTV table tennis pool table

T&C[Q][Q] **West Coast House** School Rd, Dooagh ☎(098) 43317 FAX (098) 43317
This smart new house is in an elevated position giving superb views over Dooagh to the sea. It is furnished to a high standard, and no effort is spared to make guests comfortable.
4rm(2🚿) (1fb) 🚭 🐕 (ex guide dogs) ✳ sB&BIR£14-IR£18 sB&B🚿IR£15-IR£20 dB&B🚿IR£28-IR£30 WB&BIR£85-IR£95 WBDiIR£150-IR£175 LDO 6pm
▥ CTV

ADARE Co Limerick — Map **01** B3

SELECTED

T&C[Q][Q][Q][Q] **Adare Lodge** Kildimo Road (in village turn right at bank) ☎(061) 396629
6🚿 (3fb) 🚭 in bedrooms 🚭 in dining room 🚭 in 1 lounge CTV in all bedrooms Ⓡ 🐕 dB&B🚿IR£34
▥ CTV
Credit Cards [1] [2] [3] [5]

GH [Q][Q][Q] **Carrabawn House** Killarney Road (on N21) ☎(061) 396067 FAX (061) 396925
This friendly guest house stands on the main Killanney road just a few minutes from the pretty village of Adare. A dining room and cosy sun lounge overlook picturesque gardens including a fish pond. Bedrooms have good-sized en suite showers, are bright and cheerful and are equipped with TVs and tea/coffee making facilities. The Lohan family are attentive hosts.
7🚿 (2fb) 🚭 in bedrooms CTV in all bedrooms Ⓡ **T** sB&B🚿IR£22-IR£26 dB&B🚿IR£32-IR£37 LDO noon
▥ CTV
Credit Cards [1] [3]

SELECTED

T&C[Q][Q][Q][Q] **Coatesland House** Killarney Road, Graigue (from Adare village follow Killarney road N21 for less than 0.5m, Coatesland House is on left) ☎Limerick(061) 396372 FAX (061) 396833
Closed 25 Dec
Coatesland House, situated on the main Killarney road (N21) five minutes from Adare village, is a very well appointed house featuring attractive bedrooms, all with en suite facilities. Proprietors Florence and Donal Hogan are welcoming and friendly and give superb attention to detail. Dinner is available. Nearby activities include hunting, fishing, golf and there is also an equestrian centre.
6🚿 (3fb) 🚭 in 2 bedrooms 🚭 in dining room CTV in 3 bedrooms Ⓡ **T** ✳ sB&B🚿IR£18-IR£23 dB&B🚿IR£30-IR£34
▥ CTV
Credit Cards [1] [2] [3]

ANNAMOE Co Wicklow — Map **01** D3

T&C[Q][Q] **Carmel's** ☎(0404) 45297
Etr-Oct
This modern bungalow with nice gardens is situated in a scenic touring area of Co Wicklow on the R755 giving easy access to all areas of local interest.
4rm(3🚿) (2fb) 🐕 ✳ sB&BfrIR£18 dB&BfrIR£30 dB&B🚿frIR£30 LDO noon
▥ CTV P̸

ARDARA Co Donegal — Map **01** B5

T&C[Q][Q][Q] **Bay View Country House** Portnoo Road (half a mile outside Ardara, on the Portnoo road) ☎(075) 41145
Mar-5 Nov
This large, modern bungalow, on the outskirts of a small town, overlooks the sea.
6🚿 (2fb) 🚭 🐕 ✳ sB&B🚿IR£19.50 dB&B🚿frIR£29 WB&BfrIR£100 LDO noon
▥ CTV
Credit Cards [1]

ARDEE Co Louth — Map **01** D4

SELECTED

GH [Q][Q][Q][Q] ***The Gables House*** Dundalk Road ☎Drogheda(041) 53789
Closed first 2wks in Jun & Nov
This smart, comfortable house has a historic past and offers very fully equipped bedrooms and a popular restaurant serving excellent food.
5rm(2🛁1🚿) (2fb) CTV in all bedrooms Ⓡ 🐕 (ex guide dogs) LDO 9.30pm
Lic ▥
Credit Cards [1] [2] [3] [5]

ARKLOW Co Wicklow — Map **01** D3

FH [Q][Q] M T Bourke ***Killinskyduff*** *(T254731)* (1m N, off N11) ☎(0402) 32185
Jun-Sep
This large, modern farmhouse has well tended lawns and a well kept garden, set in peaceful surroundings, convenient for the sea.
3rm (3fb) 🐕 LDO 4pm
▥ CTV nc12yrs 165 acres hens tillage
Credit Cards [1] [2] [3] [5]

ASHFORD Co Wicklow — Map **01** D3

T&C[Q][Q] **Gorsehaven** Annagolan ☎(0404) 40398
May-Sep
4rm(2🚿) 🚭 in dining room Ⓡ 🐕 (ex guide dogs) ✳ sB&BfrIR£19 dB&BfrIR£28 dB&B🚿frIR£33
▥ CTV nc4yrs

ATHY Co Kildare — Map **01** C3

FH [Q][Q] Mrs V Gorman **Ballindrum** *(S7747968)* Ballindrum ☎(0507) 26294 FAX (0507) 26294
Apr-Oct
This white house stands in meticulously-kept farmland at the end of a tree-lined avenue. Accommodation is comfortable with all new appointments. Hospitable owners Mary and Vincent Gorman bake their own bread and cook with fresh farm produce. Golf, fishing, horseriding and forest walks are available locally.
4rm(1🚿) (1fb) 🚭 in bedrooms 🐕 ✳ sB&BIR£13.50 dB&BIR£27 dB&B🚿IR£29 WB&BIR£84 WBDiIR£155 LDO 3pm
▥ CTV 🏠 guided farm tours 75 acres dairy tillage

AVOCA Co Wicklow   Map **01** D3

T&CQQ *Ashdene* Knockanree Lower ☎Arklow(0402) 35327
Apr-Oct
Set two miles from Avoca, Ashdene represents an ideal centre for
touring Co Wicklow. Mrs Burne is very enthusiastic in her care of
guests, and takes pride in her breakfast menu.
5rm(4♠) (2fb) � LDO noon
🎢 CTV ℺(grass)

T&CQQQ *Old Coach House* ☎(0402) 35408
This black and white coaching inn set in the picturesque Vale of
Avoca has been tastefully restored by the friendly Susan and Aidan
Dempsey. A warmly invitng atmosphere pervades the restful lounge
and smart restaurant. Charming en suite bedrooms feature stripped
pine furnishings, pretty decor and tea/coffee making facilities.
6♠ (2fb) ✰ in 2 bedrooms ✰ in area of dining room Ⓡ ✰ (ex
guide dogs) ✳ sB&B♠IR£20-IR£25 dB&B♠IR£32-IR£36
WB&BIR£110-IR£115 WBDiIR£200-IR£225 LDO 9pm
Lic 🎢 CTV ♨
Credit Cards 1 3

BALLINA Co Mayo   Map **01** B4

T&CQQQ *Whitestream House* (N57) Foxford Road
☎(096) 21582
This spacious new house stands within walking distance of the
bus/train station. It has extensive gardens with a stream adjoining;
fishing routes are planned and fishing tackle (and bicycles) can be
stored in the basement. All rooms have hairdryers and tea/coffee
making facilities and a breakfast menu is served.
6rm(5♠) (2fb) Ⓡ ✰ LDO 4pm
🎢 CTV
Credit Cards 3

BALLINADEE Co Cork   Map **01** B2

SELECTED
T&CQQQQ *Glebe House* ☎(021) 778294
FAX (021) 778456
Closed 2wks Xmas
This lovely old house stands in well kept gardens. Beautifully
furnished rooms have many antiques and the proprietors are
always looking for ways to spoil guests.
4rm(2⇆2♠) (2fb) ✰ in area of dining room ✰ in 1 lounge
TV available Ⓡ ✰ T ✰ (ex guide dogs) sB&B⇆♠frIR£30
dB&B⇆♠frIR£45 LDO noon
🎢 croquet
Credit Cards 1 3

BALLINHASSIG Co Cork   Map **01** B2

T&CQQ *Blanchfield House* Rigsdale (main Cork/Bandon Rd
N71) ☎Cork(021) 885167 FAX (021) 885167
Mar-Nov rs Dec-Feb
This guesthouse is in a quiet, but convenient location within easy
reach of the airport and ferry. Proprietor Patricia Blanchfield
offers good home cooking, and private salmon and trout fishing
are available.
6rm(2⇆2♠) (2fb) ✰ (ex guide dogs) LDO 9pm
Lic 🎢 CTV
Credit Cards 1 2 3 5

BALLYCASTLE Co Antrim   Map **01** D6

GH Q *Hilsea* 28 Quay Hill BT54 6BH ☎(02657) 62385
Occupying a grand position on the hill overlooking the bay, this
hotel offers good-value holiday accommodation. Appetising
breakfast with home-backed breads is served in a bright, airy
dining room. The well-decorated bedrooms vary in size and there
is a cosy lounge.

19rm (4fb) ✰ in dining room ✳ sB&Bfr£15 dB&Bfr£30
WB&Bfr£100 LDO 7.30pm
🎢 CTV
Credit Cards 1 2 3 £

BALLYHACK Co Wexford   Map **01** C2

SELECTED
⇆ ✰ **T&C** QQQQ *Marsh Mere Lodge*
☎(051) 389186
This charming shell-pink house is situated a few minutes'
walk from the Ballyhack ferry overlooking Waterford harbour.
Mrs Mcnamara is a friendly host and the house is full of her
personal touches. Bedrooms are delightful and a fine tea is
served on the verandah. This is a lovely place to stay.
5⇆♠ ✰ ✰ sB&B⇆♠IR£15-IR£20 dB&B⇆♠IR£30-
IR£35
CTV

BALLYMACARBRY Co Waterford   Map **01** C2

GH QQQ *Clonanav Farm* Nire Valley ☎Clonmel(052) 36141
FAX (052) 36141
Feb-Nov
Lenny and Eileen Ryan have created a friendly atmosphere and
comfortable en suite accommodation at this charming hotel. The
couple specialise in fishing and walking holidays, their son
Andrew offering advice to those guests who try the hotel's own
salmon and trout fishing.
10♠ (1fb) ✰ in bedrooms ✰ in dining room ✰ (ex guide dogs)
sB&B♠IR£20-IR£27 dB&B♠IR£36-IR£40 WB&BIR£126-
IR£130 WBDiIR£210-IR£214
Lic 🎢 CTV ♪ ∪
Credit Cards 1 2 3

BALLYMOTE Co Sligo   Map **01** B4

T&CQQQ *Corran House* Sligo Road (last house on right
leaving Ballymote on R293 to Collooney) ☎(071) 83074
A comfortable, well-maintained house stands in attractive gardens
just around the corner from the village. En suite bedrooms have
attractive decor and are equipped with televisions and tea/coffee
making facilities. The area is well-known as an angling centre.
5♠ (1fb) ✰ in dining room CTV in all bedrooms
Ⓡ ✰ (ex guide dogs) sB&B♠IR£18.50 dB&B♠IR£27
WB&BfrIR£85 WBDifrIR£155 LDO 5pm
🎢 CTV
Credit Cards 1 3

BALLYVAUGHAN Co Clare   Map **01** B3

SELECTED
T&CQQQQ *Rusheen Lodge* (on N67) ☎(065) 77092
FAX (065) 77152
Closed 17 Dec-Jan
A charming house nestles in the valley of the Burren
Limestone mountains, an area famous for its Arctic and
Alpine plants in spring and summer. The McGann family were
founders of the famous Aillwee Caves and have a fund of local
folklore. The bedrooms are excellent, large and well equipped
with attractive decor and extras that ensure a comfortable visit.
The cosy dining room has patio gardens leading from it. Car
parking is available.
6⇆♠ (3fb) ✰ in 3 bedrooms ✰ in dining room ✰ in lounges
CTV in all bedrooms Ⓡ T ✰ (ex guide dogs)
dB&B⇆♠IR£36-IR£40
🎢 CTV
Credit Cards 1 2 3

BALLYVOURNEY Co Cork   Map **01** B2

GH [Q][Q][Q] **The Mills Inn** (on main Cork/Killarney road N22)
☎(026) 45237 FAX (026) 45454
Closed 24-25 Dec
This charming inn dates back to the mid 18th century and stands
in extensive gardens including a vintage car and folk museum as
well as a shop. Bedrooms are comfortable and licensees Donal
and Mary Seannell are welcoming hosts. The bar offers hot food
all day and there is also a cosy restaurant. The inn is nine miles
from Macroom and twenty miles from Killarney.
9➜﨔 (4fb) CTV in all bedrooms Ⓡ T ✳ sB&BIR£25-IR£30
dB&BIR£36-IR£45 WB&BIR£140 WBDiIR£260 LDO 9pm
Lic ⊞ CTV
Credit Cards [1][2][3][5]

BANSHA Co Tipperary   Map **01** C3

T&C[Q][Q][Q] **Bansha Castle** (5m S of Tipperary on N24)
☎(062) 54187 FAX (062) 54187
Teresa and John Russell have spent the last few years restoring the
castle which stands on the edge of the magnificent Glen of
Akerlow and was once the residence of the painter Lady Elizabeth
Butler. An informal atmosphere pervades the hotel and a genuine
warmth is extended to guests. Rooms are spacious, there is a fine
walled garden and good car parking. Walking, golf, fishing,
hunting and horseriding are all available in the area.
5rm(3﨔) (3fb)﨔 (ex guide dogs) ✳ sB&BfrIR£21 sB&B﨔frIR£24
dB&BfrIR£32 dB&B﨔frIR£38 WB&BIR£112-IR£133
WBDiIR£215-IR£235 LDO 4pm
Lic ⊞
Credit Cards [1][2][3]

BANTRY Co Cork   Map **01** B2

T&C[Q][Q][Q] **Shangri-La** Glengarriff Road (on N71, near Bantry
Golf Course) ☎(027) 50244
Closed Xmas
This bungalow overlooks Bantry Bay with spacious gardens and is
an ideal centre for touring Cork and Kerry.
7rm(4➜﨔) (1fb) ⍲ in area of dining room ⍲ in 1 lounge Ⓡ 﨔
✳ sB&BIR£20 dB&BIR£30 dB&B➜﨔IR£34 WB&BIR£100
⊞ CTV
Credit Cards [1][3]

BELFAST   Map **01** D5

GH [Q][Q] **Camera** 44 Wellington Park BT9 6DP ☎(0232) 660026
& 667856
Situated in a tree-lined avenue close to the University, this end-of-
terrace Victorian house offers good-value bed and breakfast.
Bedrooms range from singles to large family rooms. There is a
comfortable lounge and a breakfast room.
11rm(2﨔) (2fb) ⍲ in dining room CTV in all bedrooms 﨔 (ex guide

dogs) sB&Bfr£17 sB&B﨔£30 dB&Bfr£35 dB&B﨔£45 LDO 9am
⊞ CTV ⍩
Credit Cards [1][2][3] ⓔ

GH [Q][Q][Q] **Malone** 79 Malone Rd BT9 6SH ☎(0232) 669565
Closed 2wks Jul & 2wks Xmas
On the south side of the town and close to the University, this
detached red brick Victorian villa is kept in a spotless condition
with bright and airy bedrooms, a comfortable lounge and breakfast
room with separate tables.
8﨔 CTV in all bedrooms Ⓡ 﨔 sB&B﨔£24-£31 dB&B﨔£38-£46
WB&B£149-£196
⊞ nc12yrs
ⓔ

BUSHMILLS Co Antrim   Map **01** C6

CAHERDANIEL Co Kerry   Map **01** A2

T&C[Q][Q] *O'Sullivan's Country House* ☎(066) 75124
This house is situated on the Ring of Kerry and provides a country
house welcome, with home cooking a feature of Mrs O'Sullivan's
hospitality. Sandy beaches, fishing, golf and boat trips can be
found nearby, and it is possible to arrange hill walking holidays.
6rm(1➜﨔) (3fb)
CTV

CAHIRCIVEEN Co Kerry   Map **01** A2

FH [Q][Q][Q] T Sugrue **Valentia View** (*V457773)* ☎(066) 72227
Mar-Oct
This fine old country farmhouse on The Ring of Kerry has a warm
and hospitable atmosphere. Rooms overlook Valentia island and
bay.
6rm(5﨔) (2fb) ⍲ in dining room Ⓡ ✳ sB&B﨔frIR£20
dB&B﨔frIR£30 WB&BfrIR£105 WBDifrIR£175 LDO 7pm
⊞ CTV nc2mths 38 acres beef

CAPPOQUIN Co Waterford   Map **01** C2

10🛁🚿 (2fb) 🚭 in area of dining room [R] T 🐕
sB&B🛁🚿IR£25-IR£30 dB&B🛁🚿IR£46-IR£50
WB&BIR£142-IR£155 WBDiIR£260-IR£280 LDO 8pm
Lic ▦ CTV 🚲
Credit Cards [1] [2] [3] [5]

CARLOW Co Carlow Map **01** C3

SELECTED

GH [Q] [Q] [Q] [Q] Barrowville Town House Kilkenny Road (on N9) ☎(0503) 43324 FAX (0503) 41953
This lovely Georgian house, situated on the edge of town, offers a high standard of comfort and convenience in well furnished accommodation.
7🛁🚿 (2fb) 🚭 in bedrooms 🚭 in dining room CTV in all bedrooms [R] T 🐕 (ex guide dogs) * sB&B🛁🚿IR£17.50-IR£25 dB&B🛁🚿IR£35-IR£40
Lic ▦ CTV nc12yrs

CARRICK-ON-SHANNON Co Leitrim & Roscommon Map **01** C4

FH [Q] [Q] [Q] Mr & Mrs P Harrington **Glencarne House** *(G867003)* Ardcarne (on N4 between Carrick-on-Shannon and Boyle) ☎(079) 67013
Mar-Oct
This charming period house stands in 100 acres of grazing farmlands between Boyle and Carrick-on-Shannon. Hospitable owners Agnes and Patrick Hamilton offer comfortable accommodation with antique furnishings; four of the bedrooms are en suite. Dinner is a special experience, served every evening in country house style using farm produce including organically grown vegetables.
4🛁🚿 (4fb) 🚭 in bedrooms 🐕 sB&B🛁🚿frIR£22 dB&B🛁🚿frIR£40 WB&BfrIR£119 WBDifrIR£185 LDO 8pm
▦ CTV 100 acres mixed

CARRIGALINE Co Cork Map **01** B2

T&C [Q] [Q] ***Beaver Lodge*** ☎(021) 372595
Closed Xmas
An old ivy-clad house stands in its own grounds off the main street.
6rm(2🛁2🚿) (5fb) CTV in all bedrooms [R] 🐕 (ex guide dogs) LDO 4pm
▦ CTV
Credit Cards [1] [2] [3]

CARRIGANS Co Donegal Map **01** C5

SELECTED

T&C [Q] [Q] [Q] [Q] Mount Royd Country Home (postal address is Carrigans, Lifford P.O.) ☎Letterkenny(074) 40163
Situated off N13, N14 and A40 a large, attractive creeper-clad house is surrounded by a well tended garden. Very well appointed bedrooms and excellent home cooking make it popular with both tourist and business guests.
4🚿 (3fb) 🚭 in dining room CTV in 2 bedrooms [R] 🐕 (ex guide dogs) sB&B🚿IR£18.50 dB&B🚿IR£30 LDO noon
▦ CTV

CASHEL Co Tipperary Map **01** C3

SELECTED

GH [Q] [Q] [Q] [Q] Legends The Kiln ☎(062) 61292
This distinctive house has been purpose built to blend in with its dramatic surroundings beneath the Rock of Cashel. The restaurant in particular enjoys mystical floodlit views of this historic site (as well as the cooking of chef/proprietor Phil Delaney). Other facilities include two lounges, one with a TV and a wine bar. Decor throughout is refined and the furnishings are attractive. The well-equipped bedrooms are all en suite. The surrounding area is home to a public car park, a golf course, good fishing and various hill walks.
5🚿 (3fb)CTV in all bedrooms [R] T 🐕 * sB&B🚿IR£20-IR£25 dB&B🚿IR£37-IR£45 WB&BIR£115-IR£120 WBDiIR£220-IR£240 LDO 9.30pm
Lic ▦
Credit Cards [1] [2] [3]

FH [Q] [Q] E O'Brien ***Knock-Saint-Lour House*** *(S074390)*
☎(062) 61172
Apr-Oct
8rm(4🛁🚿) (2fb) CTV in 1 bedroom 🐕 (ex guide dogs)
▦ CTV 30 acres mixed

CASTLEGREGORY Co Kerry Map **01** A2

FH [Q] Mrs C Griffin ***Griffin's*** *(Q525085)* Goulane
☎(066) 39147
Apr-Oct

▶

Richmond House

Cappoquin Co Waterford
Tel: (00 353) 58 54278
Fax: (00 353) 58 54988

Award winning eighteenth century Georgian country house, standing in timbered parkland, ½ mile from the picturesque town of Cappoquin. Old world charm and character, log fires and central heating. All bedrooms en-suite, tea/coffee making facilities and direct dial telephone. Top class fully licensed restaurant. Listed in most International guides. Ideal centre for golfing, fishing, horse-riding, sightseeing and mountain walking.

This is a two-storey farmhouse situated on the Dingle Peninsula.
8rm(4⇌4♒) (3fb) LDO 5pm
📖 CTV 150 acres dairy sheep

CAVAN Co Cavan   Map **01** C4

T&CⓆⓆ **Halcyon** Drumalee (turn right off N3 immediately after the cathedral, signposted 'Cootehill'. Turn right at X-roads, 'Halcyon' 100yds on left) ☎(049) 31809
7 Jan-22 Dec
This lovely modern bungalow on the edge of town offers peace and quiet in attractive, comfortable accommodation. It is very popular with anglers as there is good coarse fishing in the many local lakes.
5rm(4♒) (4fb) ⌦ in dining room 🍴 (ex guide dogs) ✳
sB&BIR£18.50 sB&B♒IR£30 dB&B♒IR£30 LDO noon
📖 CTV nc2yrs

CHEEKPOINT Co Waterford   Map **01** C2

SELECTED

GH ⓆⓆⓆⓆ **Three Rivers** ☎(051) 382520
FAX (051) 382542
This charming house is superbly located overlooking the rivers Barrow, Noire and Suir, within sight of the twinkling lights of passage east where a ferry provides quick access to Rosslare port. There are well appointed bedrooms, attractive gardens and a sunny balcony, and the lounge and dining room are sited to take full advantage of the magnificent views. The house stands within five minutes of Faithlegg golf course.
14♒ (4fb) ⌦ in bedrooms ⌦ in dining room ⌦ in 1 lounge CTV in 5 bedrooms T 🍴 (ex guide dogs) ✳ sB&B♒IR£18-IR£25 dB&B♒IR£34-IR£54 WB&BIR£100-IR£150
📖 CTV
Credit Cards ①③

CLIFDEN Co Galway   Map **01** A4

✉ ☎ **T&C**ⓆⓆ **Ben View House** Bridge Street (entering town on N59, opposite Esso petrol station) ☎(095) 21256
This town-centre house offers good quality accommodation at a moderate cost making it an ideal touring base.
8rm(7♒) (3fb) ⌦ in dining room 🍴 (ex guide dogs)
sB&B♒IR£13-IR£20 dB&B♒IR£26-IR£33 WB&BIR£84-IR£105
📖 CTV ⌦

T&CⓆⓆⓆ **Connemara Country Lodge** Westport Road ☎(095) 21122
This is a very comfortable house, purpose built to a high standard, on the main Clifden/Westport road. Charming and hospitable owners provide a warm welcome and home cooking. French and German are spoken here.
6♒ (4fb) CTV in 3 bedrooms LDO noon
📖 CTV ⚑
Credit Cards ②③

✉ ☎ **T&C** ⓆⓆⓆ **Failte** Ardbear, Ballyconneely Road ☎(095) 21159
Apr-Sep
A modern bungalow in scenic location on edge of Clifden features excellent standards of comfort and welcoming hosts and is an ideal touring centre.
5rm(2♒) (2fb) ⌦ in dining room ⌦ in 1 lounge 🍴 (ex guide dogs)
sB&BIR£13 dB&BIR£24-IR£26 dB&B♒IR£28-IR£30
WB&BIR£70-IR£77
📖 CTV
Credit Cards ①②③

T&CⓆⓆ **Kingstown House** Bridge Street ☎(095) 21470
Closed 23-28 Dec
Situated just off Clifden's main street and centrally located close

to all amenities, this pleasant guesthouse offers a warm welcome from the friendly proprietors Mary and Joe King, who provide comfortable accommodation.
8rm(6♒) (3fb) ⌦ in area of dining room 🍴 (ex guide dogs) ✳
sB&B♒frIR£20 dB&BfrIR£28 dB&B♒frIR£30
📖 CTV ⌦
Credit Cards ①③

SELECTED

GH ⓆⓆⓆⓆ **Maldua** Galway Road (on N59)
☎(095) 21171 & 21739 FAX (095) 21739
Closed Dec
This guesthouse is situated on the main Galway/Clifden road, just before the entrance to this cosmopolitan village in the heart of Connemara; it is easily distinguished by its conservatory entrance and balcony. The excellent bedrooms are attractive and well appointed, with good facilities. Outside there is a patio, garden and ample car parking.
9♒ (2fb) ⌦ in bedrooms CTV in all bedrooms Ⓡ T 🍴 (ex guide dogs) ✳ sB&B♒IR£18-IR£21 dB&B♒IR£30-IR£44
📖
Credit Cards ①③

SELECTED

T&CⓆⓆⓆⓆ **Mallmore House** Ballyconneely Road
☎(095) 21460
Mar-1 Nov
A charming Georgian-style house set in 35 acres of woodland overlooking Clifden Bay, is situated one mile from Clifden on the Ballyconneely road, close to the Rock Glen Hotel. Alan and Kathy Hardman have tastefully restored the house, with parquet flooring and some favourite antiques, together with turf fires providing warmth and atmosphere.
6♒ (2fb) ⌦ in dining room ⌦ in lounges 🍴 (ex guide dogs)
dB&B♒IR£30
📖 CTV

FH ⓆⓆⓆ Mrs K Conneely **Faul House** (*L6650475*)
Ballyconneely Road (1m from town, turn right at Connemara Pottery and follow signs) ☎(095) 21239 FAX (095) 21998
15 Mar-Oct
A fine modern farmhouse stands on a quiet and secluded road overlooking Clifden Bay. It is smart and comfortable with large en suite bedrooms, all well furnished and with good views on all sides.
6♒ (3fb) ⌦ in 3 bedrooms ⌦ in dining room ⌦ in 1 lounge 🍴 dB&B♒IR£31
📖 CTV 28 acres sheep

CLIFFONY Co Sligo   Map **01** B5

GH ⓆⓆ **Villa Rosa** Donegal Road, Bunduff (1m N)
☎Sligo(071) 66173
May-Oct rs Nov & Mar-Apr
This comfortable house is situated on the main Sligo/Donegal route and has good parking facilities to the rear. The surrounding area is famous for its historic folklore, walks and beautiful scenery.
6rm(2♒) (2fb) ⌦ in 3 bedrooms ⌦ in dining room ⌦ in lounges 🍴 (ex guide dogs) ✳ sB&BfrIR£13.50 dB&BfrIR£27 dB&B♒frIR£30 WB&BIR£84 WBDifrIR£160 LDO noon
📖 CTV
Credit Cards ①②③

CLONAKILTY Co Cork   Map **01** B2

FH Ⓠ D Jennings **Desert House** (*W390411)* Ring Road
(signposted on N71, 1km E of Clonakilty) ☎Bandon(023) 33331
FAX (023) 33048

This Georgian farmhouse, overlooking Clonakilty Bay, is an ideal
centre for touring West Cork and Kerry.

5rm(4♠) (3fb)CTV in 4 bedrooms Ⓡ ✳ sB&BIR£18
sB&B♠IR£20 dB&BIR£26 dB&B♠IR£30 WB&BIR£91
WBDiIR£169.75 LDO 5pm

▥ CTV 100 acres dairy mixed

Credit Cards [1] [2] [3]

CLONBUR Co Galway   Map **01** B4

GH Ⓠ *Fairhill* ☎Galway(092) 46176

Etr-19 Oct

Owned and run by Mrs Lynch, who offers a most hospitable
service, this village guesthouse is presently being refurbished and
boasts a cosy bar which serves food throughout the day.

11rm(2♠) (1fb) CTV in 1 bedroom Ⓡ ✻ (ex guide dogs) LDO
9pm

Lic CTV outdoor pursuit centre pitch & putt

COLERAINE Co Londonderry   Map **01** C6

SELECTED

GH ⓆⓆⓆⓆ **Greenhill House** 24 Greenhill Road,
Aghadowey BT51 4EU (take A29 for 7m turn onto B66 for
approx 300yds house on right) ☎Aghadowey(0265) 868241
Mar-Oct

This is a lovely Georgian house standing in its own well-
tended garden in the Bann Valley with views of the Antrim
Hills. It is efficiently run by Elizabeth and James Hegarty:
bedrooms are spotless and there are many thoughtful extras.
There is also a comfortable sitting room and dining room
where good home-cooked meals are served.

6rm(2⇔4♠) (2fb) CTV in all bedrooms Ⓡ ✻ (ex guide
dogs) ✳ sB&B⇔♠fr£26 dB&B⇔♠fr£42 LDO noon

▥ CTV

Credit Cards [1] [3]

CORK Co Cork   Map **01** B2

T&C ⓆⓆⓆ **Antoine House** Western Road (1m from city centre
on the Cork-Macroom-Killarney road) ☎(021) 273494
FAX (021) 273092

This converted four-storey house is close to the University and
caters for both tourist and commercial clientele.

7♠ CTV in all bedrooms Ⓡ T ✻ (ex guide dogs) sB&BIR£20-
IR£28 dB&B♠IR£36

▥ CTV

Credit Cards [1] [3] [5]

GH ⓆⓆⓆ *Garnish House* 1 Aldergrove, Western Road
☎(021) 275111 FAX (021) 273872

This is a three-storey house opposite the University on the main
Cork/Killarney road.

15rm(10♠) (1fb) CTV in all bedrooms Ⓡ T ✻ (ex guide dogs)
▥ CTV

Credit Cards [1] [2] [3] [5]

GH ⓆⓆⓆ *Killarney House* Western Road ☎(021) 270290 &
270179 FAX (021) 271010

Closed 25-26 Dec

Mrs O'Leary is the welcoming owner of this newly decorated,
well equipped guesthouse near Cork University on the N22 road.
Behind the house is a large car park.

19rm(14♠) (3fb) CTV in all bedrooms Ⓡ T ✻ (ex guide dogs)
▥ CTV

Credit Cards [1] [2] [3] [5]

GH ⓆⓆⓆ **Roserie Villa** Mardyke Walk, off Western Road
☎(021) 272958 FAX (021) 274087

This bright new guesthouse is conveniently situated for the city
centre and offers good car parking facilities.

16♠ (4fb) CTV in dining room CTV in all bedrooms Ⓡ T ✻ (ex
guide dogs) sB&B♠IR£22.50-IR£35 dB&B♠IR£35-IR£48
WB&BIR£120-IR£200

▥ CTV nc5yrs

Credit Cards [1] [2] [3] [5]

GH ⓆⓆⓆ *St Kilda's* Western Road ☎(021) 273095 & 275374
FAX (021) 275015

Approached via the city centre on the N22 route, this comfortable
guesthouse is situated opposite University College. Under the
personal supervision of the hospitable owners, Pat and Pauline
Hickey, St Kilda's offers pleasant, nicely appointed
accommodation.

13rm(12⇔♠) (1fb) CTV in all bedrooms T ✻ (ex guide dogs)
▥ CTV

Credit Cards [1] [3]

COROFIN Co Clare   Map **01** B3

FH ⓆⓆⓆ Mary Kelleher **Fergus View** (*R265919)* Kilnaboy (2
miles north of Corofin en route to Kilfenora, past the ruins of
Kilnaboy Church) ☎Limerick(065) 37606 FAX (065) 37192
Etr-Sep

Sensitively renovated to provide an excellent standard of comfort,
this fourth generation family home is at an attractive farmhouse,
centrally located for touring the Burren area. Mary Kelleher
enjoys cooking and wherever possible uses all home-grown
vegetables to prepare the meals.

6rm(5♠) (4fb) ✬ in bedrooms ✬ in dining room ✻
sB&BIR£20.50 sB&B♠IR£22.50 dB&BIR£29 dB&B♠IR£33
WB&BIR£110.50-IR£115.50 WBDiIR£196-IR£210.50 LDO
noon

Lic ▥ CTV 17 acres non-working

FH ⓆⓆⓆ Mrs B Kelleher **Inchiquin View** (*R270916)*
Kilnaboy ☎(065) 37731

Apr-Sep

This comfortable modern farmhouse overlooks the River Fergus,
two miles north of Corofin on L53 road. Owners Betty and John
Kelleher provide evening meals by arrangement. Angling and golf
are available in the neighbourhood and Shannon is only 23 miles
away.

5♠ (2fb) ✬ in 3 bedrooms ✻ (ex guide dogs) ✳ sB&BIR£15
sB&B♠IR£16 dB&BIR£30 dB&B♠IR£32 WB&BIR£105 LDO
5pm

▥ CTV 15 acres beef mixed

CROSSHAVEN Co Cork   Map **01** B2

GH ⓆⓆⓆ **Whispering Pines** ☎Cork(021) 831843 & 831448
FAX (021) 831679

There is something particularly inviting about this comfortable
guesthouse with its sun lounge and bar overlooking the river. The
Twomey family are most hospitable and cater well for all guests,
particularly anglers, for whom a fishing boat and equipment is
available for hire. Transfer from Cork Airport can be arranged if
required.

15rm(11⇔4♠) (6fb)T ✻ (ex guide dogs) ✳ sB&B⇔♠IR£23-
IR£28 dB&B⇔♠IR£40-IR£50 WB&BIR£133-IR£154
WBDiIR£210-IR£231 LDO 9.30pm

Lic ▥ CTV own angling boats fish daily

Credit Cards [1] [2] [3] [5]

CRUSHEEN Co Clare   Map 01 B3

FH Ⓠ Ⓠ Ⓠ Dilly Griffey **Lahardan** (*R397889)* Lahardan
☎Ennis(065) 27128 FAX (065) 27319
rs Nov-Apr
This sensitively restored farmhouse stands on 300 acres of land off
the Galway to Limerick road near Ennis. It is a charming old
building with spacious rooms that invite relaxation. Guests will
experience true hospitality from the welcoming Griffey family,
and evening meals are served.
8rm(6⇌2♠) (4fb) ✔ in bedrooms ♈ LDO 3pm
Lic ▥ CTV 230 acres beef
Credit Cards [1] [3]

DINGLE Co Kerry   Map 01 A2

GH Ⓠ Ⓠ Ⓠ *Alpine* Mail Road ☎(066) 51250
Feb-Nov
On the edge of Dingle, this large, three-storey guesthouse is run
by the O'Shea family, who maintain excellent standards.
14♠ (4fb) CTV in all bedrooms ♈
▥ CTV
Credit Cards [1] [3]

T&CⓆ Ⓠ Ⓠ Ⓠ **Ard-na-Greine House** Spa Road
☎(066) 51113 & 51898
This modern bungalow is situated on the edge of town towards
Connor Pass. All the rooms are en suite and offer an unrivalled
range of facilities.
4♠ (2fb) CTV in all bedrooms Ⓡ T ♈ (ex guide dogs) ✱
dB&B♠IR£32-IR£34
▥ CTV nc7yrs
Credit Cards [1] [2] [3]

T&CⓆ Ⓠ Ⓠ Ⓠ **Ard-Na-Mara** Ballymore, Ventry ☎(066) 59072
Etr-Oct
This comfortable country house overlooks Ventry harbour two
miles out of Dingle. The bedrooms are en suite with tea/coffee
facilities. There is a very good breakfast menu and warm
hospitality from the Murphy family.
4♠ (1fb) ✔ in dining room Ⓡ ♈ ✱ sB&B♠IR£20 dB&B♠IR£29
LDO day before
▥ CTV

S E L E C T E D

T&CⓆ Ⓠ Ⓠ Ⓠ *Bambury's* Mail Road ☎(066) 51244
Set on the edge of Dingle, this pink house is eyecatching on
the outside and attractive on the inside with pretty decor and
comfortable appointments. There is a cosy lounge and a
spacious dining room. En suite bedrooms are excellent with
pine furnishings, pottery lamps, tea/coffee trays and big
showers. The friendly Mrs Bainbury is very helpful.
12♠ CTV in all bedrooms T

S E L E C T E D

GH Ⓠ Ⓠ Ⓠ Ⓠ **Barnagh Bridge Country House** Camp
☎Tralee(066) 30145 FAX (066) 30299
Closed Dec
This is an eyecatching cream-coloured house set back from the
road. Its interior is well-designed and offers every comfort.
The cosy lounge has an open fire, the dining room overlooks
nearby beaches and the well-appointed, en suite bedrooms
have scenic views.
5♠ in bedrooms ✔ in dining room T ♈ (ex guide dogs) ✱
sB&B♠IR£16-IR£22 dB&B♠IR£32-IR£40
▥ CTV
Credit Cards [1] [3]

T&CⓆ Ⓠ Ⓠ Ⓠ **Cleevaun** Lady's Cross, Milltown ☎(066) 51108
mid Jan-mid Dec
Luxury bungalow on a one-acre site with superb views of Dingle
Bay and surrounding mountains.
9⇌♠ (2fb) ✔ in bedrooms CTV in 4 bedrooms Ⓡ T ♈ (ex guide
dogs) ✱ dB&B♠IR£35-IR£39
▥ CTV nc3yrs
Credit Cards [1] [3]

T&CⓆ Ⓠ Ⓠ **Dingle Heights** Ballinaboola (proceed up Main Street
for 0.5m until hospital, house 3rd on right after further 200yds)
☎(066) 51543
Etr-Nov
Set high overlooking Dingle Bay, this house features comfortable,
well-appointed accommodation and the hospitality of owner Mrs
Fitzgerald.
4rm(3⇌♠) (4fb)♈ ✱ sB&BIR£15-IR£18 dB&B♠IR£32
WB&BIR£100
▥ CTV

S E L E C T E D

GH Ⓠ Ⓠ Ⓠ Ⓠ **Doyles Town House** 4 John Street
☎Tralee(066) 51174 FAX (066) 51816
mid Mar-mid Nov
Stella and John Doyle are the warm and friendly owners of
this charming town house. Bedrooms are spacious, well
equipped and tasteful, with period furnishings and marble tiled
bathrooms. Adjoining the house is their award-winning and
very popular seafood restaurant, where the chat flows easily as
guests make selections from the lobster tank or try the catch of
the day specials.
8⇌♠ ✔ in area of dining room CTV in all bedrooms T ♈ (ex
guide dogs) ✱ sB&B♠IR£39 dB&B♠IR£62 LDO 9pm
Lic ▥
Credit Cards [1] [3] [5]

S E L E C T E D

T&CⓆ Ⓠ Ⓠ Ⓠ **Greenmount House** (on entering town turn
right at roundabout & next right at T jct) ☎(066) 51414
FAX (066) 51974
Closed 20-29 Dec
Set on a hillside overlooking Dingle Harbour, Greenmount is
run with great dedication and warm hospitality by Mary and
John Curran. The accommodation is very comfortable, and
Mary's award-winning breakfasts are served in the charming
dining room. Car parking facilities are good.
6⇌♠ ✔ in dining room CTV in all bedrooms
T ♈ (ex guide dogs) ✱ dB&B♠IR£30-IR£40
▥ CTV nc8yrs
Credit Cards [1] [3]

S E L E C T E D

GH Ⓠ Ⓠ Ⓠ Ⓠ **Milltown House** Milltown
☎Tralee(066) 51372 FAX (066) 51095
Situated on a sea channel to the west of town, the house has
been elegantly refurbished and has a warm inviting
atmosphere, Mr and Mrs Gill making guests feel really
welcome. Bedrooms are all en suite, have attractive decor and
are well equipped. There is also a cosy sitting room leading to
a conservatory.
7rm(4⇌3♠) (3fb) ✔ in dining room ✔ in 1 lounge CTV in
all bedrooms Ⓡ T ♈ (ex guide dogs) ✱ sB&B♠IR£25-

IR£44 dB&B🛁🚿IR£32-IR£44
♨ nc5yrs mini golf
Credit Cards [1] [3]

FH [Q][Q][Q] Mr M Hurley **Hurleys** An Dooneen, Kilcooley ☎(066) 55112
Etr-Oct
Despite its sombre exterior Hurleys farm is a welcoming and comfortable house featuring relaxing bedrooms, some with large shower rooms. An evening meal is available by arrangement.
4🚿 🚭 in 1 lounge 🐕 (ex guide dogs) sB&B🚿IR£18 dB&B🚿IR£28 WB&BIR£98
♨ CTV 32 acres mixed

DONEGAL Co Donegal Map **01** B5

T&C[Q][Q] **Ardeevin** Lough Eske, Barnesmore ☎(073) 21790 FAX (073) 21790
Apr-Oct
This comfortable homely house enjoys a lovely location on a height above Lough Eske and with superb views of lake and mountain. Well appointed bedrooms have en suite facilities.
5🛁🚿 (2fb) 🚭 in dining room 🚭 in lounges CTV in 1 bedroom Ⓡ 🐕 sB&B🛁🚿IR£18 dB&B🛁🚿IR£30 LDO noon
♨ CTV nc9yrs

DOOLIN Co Clare Map **01** B3

T&C[Q][Q][Q] ***Churchfield*** (in Doolin village) ☎(065) 74209 FAX (065) 74622
Closed 20-27 Dec
6rm(5🚿) (3fb)
♨ CTV
Credit Cards [1] [3]

T&C[Q][Q][Q] ***Doonmacfelim House*** ☎Ennistymon(065) 74503 FAX (065) 74421
This large new two-storey house is on the edge of the tiny west coast village. It offers comfortable, well planned accommodation, car parking and a friendly welcome from the owners Frank and Majella Moloney.
6🚿 **T** 🐕 (ex guide dogs) LDO 2pm
♨ CTV
Credit Cards [1] [3]

FH [Q][Q][Q] J Moloney ***Horse Shoe*** *(R073971)* (on N67) ☎(065) 74006 FAX (065) 74421
Closed Nov-Dec
This comfortable farmhouse is the home of the hospitable Moloney family and overlooks a village famous for traditional Irish music. They have a tennis court in the pleasant gardens, and can lend racquets to their guests, and there are bicycles for hire and a bureau de change service.
5🚿 🐕 (ex guide dogs)
♨ CTV 🎾(hard)boat trips rent-a-bike 20 acres dairy
Credit Cards [3]

DOWNPATRICK Co Down Map **01** D5

FH [Q][Q] Mrs Macauley ***Havine*** 51 Bally Donnel Road BT30 8EP ☎Ballykinlar(0396) 85242
Closed Xmas wk
Palm trees grow in the garden of this modernised 18th-century farmhouse. Mrs McAuley is a genial host and many guests return regularly for the genuine home-from-home atmosphere. Bedrooms are small but comfortable, and there is a choice of lounges, one of which has a communal table where enjoyable home cooking is served.
4rm (1fb) Ⓡ LDO 4.40pm
♨ CTV 125 acres arable

DROGHEDA Co Louth Map **01** D4

SELECTED

T&C[Q][Q][Q][Q] **Tullyesker House** Monasterboice (3m N on Dublin/Belfast road N1) ☎(041) 30430 & 32624
Closed 25-27 Dec
This large family-run house occupies a spectacular site on Tullyesker Hill, overlooking the Boyne Valley and Drogheda. Many of the well equipped and beautifully decorated rooms look out over the lovely gardens and wooded grounds. Historic and archaeological sites abound in the area.
5🚿 (2fb) 🚭 in dining room CTV in all bedrooms Ⓡ 🐕 (ex guide dogs) * dB&B🚿IR£36
♨ CTV 🎾(hard)

DUBLIN Co Dublin Map **01** D4

SELECTED

GH [Q][Q][Q][Q] **Aaron House** 152 Merrion Road, Ballsbridge ☎(01) 2601644 & 2601650 FAX (01) 2601651
Closed 24-26 Dec
6🚿 (1fb) 🚭 in 3 bedrooms 🚭 in dining room Ⓡ 🐕 (ex guide dogs) sB&B🚿IR£25-IR£30 dB&B🚿IR£50-IR£60
♨ CTV
Credit Cards [1] [3]

T&C[Q][Q][Q] **Aaronmor House** 1c Sandymount Avenue, Ballsbridge ☎(01) 6687972 FAX (01) 6682377
This family run house is comfortably furnished and decorated and is situated close to the Royal Dublin Society Showgrounds and Lansdowne rugby ground.
6🚿 (2fb) CTV in 1 bedroom Ⓡ 🐕 (ex guide dogs) LDO 10am
♨ CTV nc5yrs
Credit Cards [1] [3]

PREMIER SELECTED

GH [Q][Q][Q][Q][Q] ***Aberdeen Lodge*** 53/55 Park Avenue ☎(01) 2838155 FAX (01) 2837877

This particularly fine early Edwardian house stands on one of Dublin's most prestigious roads near to the main hotel and embassy suburb in Dublin. Bedrooms are fully equipped and there are suites with air spa baths. It has its own car park and is only minutes away from the centre by DART or bus, as well as being easily accessible from the airport and car ferries. Dinner is served and a Christmas Programme is available.
16🛁🚿 (8fb) CTV in all bedrooms **T** 🐕 LDO 9pm
Lic ♨ CTV
Credit Cards [1] [2] [3] [5]

PREMIER SELECTED

GH [Q][Q][Q][Q][Q] Ariel House 52 Lansdowne Road (turn off at Irish Bank Ballsbridge on left before Lansdowne Rugby Stadium) ☎(01) 6685512 FAX (01) 6685845

Closed 23 Dec-14 Jan

A luxurious Victorian mansion built in 1850 is situated beside Lansdowne Rugby grounds. Charming proprietors ensure guests every comfort in attractive bedrooms with authentic period antiques.

28🛁🚿 🚭 in bedrooms 🚭 in dining room 🚭 in 1 lounge CTV in all bedrooms **T** 🐕 ✱ sB&B🛁🚿IR£45-IR£120 dB&B🛁🚿IR£68-IR£120

Lic 🅿 CTV nc5yrs

Credit Cards [1][2][3]

GH [Q][Q][Q] Beddington 181 Rathgar Road ☎(01) 4978047 FAX (01) 4978275

Closed 23 Dec-13 Jan

At the city end of Rathgar Road, near Rathinines, this comfortable, well maintained house offers beds made up with crisp linen sheets in its attractive bedrooms. There is a residents' lounge, and the premises are licensed. There is secure car parking at the rear, and the hotel stands on a direct bus route to the city centre, three kilometres away.

14🚿 (1fb) 🚭 in dining room 🚭 in lounges CTV in all bedrooms [R] **T** sB&B🚿IR£27.50-IR£30 dB&B🚿IR£50-IR£55

Lic 🅿 CTV nc7yrs

Credit Cards [1][2][3]

GH [Q][Q][Q] Charleville Lodge 268/272 North Circular Road ☎(01) 8386633 FAX (01) 8385854

Closed 19-26 Dec

Situated close to the city centre near Phoenix Park, this elegant terrace of Victorian houses has been tastefully restored to a high standard. The two interconnecting lounges are welcoming and the smart dining room offers a choice of breakfasts. Bedrooms are very comfortable with pleasant decor and there is a secure car park for guests' use.

20rm(17🚿) (2fb) 🚭 in bedrooms CTV in all bedrooms **T** 🐕 (ex guide dogs) ✱ sB&BIR£23-IR£30 sB&B🚿IR£25-IR£35 dB&BIR£36-IR£56 dB&B🚿IR£40-IR£60 WB&BIR£126-IR£196

🅿 CTV

Credit Cards [1][2][3]

T&C[Q][Q] Clifden 32 Gardiner Place ☎(01) 8746364 FAX (01) 8746122

10🚿 (4fb) 🚭 in dining room 🚭 in lounges CTV in all bedrooms [R] **T** 🐕 sB&B🚿IR£17-IR£30 dB&B🚿IR£32-IR£56 WB&BIR£90-IR£158 WBDiIR£168-IR£294

🅿 CTV

Credit Cards [1][3]

GH [Q][Q][Q] Egan's 7/9 Iona Park, Glasnevin ☎(01) 8303611 & 8305283 FAX (01) 8303312

Situated in a quiet suburb on the north side of the city, this Victorian, red-brick, streetside house has large, comfortable bedrooms, relaxing lounges and good gardens at the rear. It is a family-run house renowned for its friendly and cheerful atmosphere and is conveniently located for the National Botanic Gardens and airport.

25🚿 (4fb) 🚭 in dining room CTV in all bedrooms [R] **T** ✱ sB&B🚿IR£28.60-IR£35.20 dB&B🚿IR£50.60-IR£59.40 WB&BIR£170-IR£199 WBDiIR£230-IR£270 LDO 8pm

Lic 🅿

Credit Cards [1][3]

GH [Q][Q][Q] *The Fitzwilliam* 41 Upper Fitzwilliam Street ☎(01) 6600199 FAX (01) 6767488

5 Jan-15 Dec

Situated in the heart of Georgian Dublin, this house has been newly renovated to a very high standard. Ideal for business people and tourists it is close to the National Concert Hall.

12rm(2🛁10🚿) (1fb) CTV in all bedrooms LDO 10.30pm

Lic 🅿 CTV

Credit Cards [1][2][3][5]

SELECTED

GH [Q][Q][Q][Q] Glenogra 64 Merrion Road, Ballsbridge (opposite Royal Dublin's Showgrounds) ☎(01) 6683661 & 6683698

7 Jan-23 Dec

This fine gabled house run by Cherry and Seamus McNamee is only 2.5 miles from the centre of Dublin and stands in a pleasant suburb opposite the RDS Centre. The house offers comfort with more than a touch of elegance, and the atmosphere is exceptionally welcoming.

9🛁🚿 (1fb) 🚭 in dining room CTV in all bedrooms [R] **T** 🐕 (ex guide dogs) ✱ sB&B🛁🚿IR£40-IR£50 dB&B🛁🚿IR£55-IR£65

🅿 CTV

Credit Cards [1][3]

PREMIER SELECTED

GH [Q][Q][Q][Q][Q] The Grey Door 22/23 Upper Pembroke Street (city centre, close to St Stephens Green and Grafton Street) ☎(01) 6763286 FAX (01) 6763287

rs Bank Hols

This elegant, tastefully restored town house is a jewel in the heart of Georgian Dublin. The extremely attractive bedrooms have a warm, pleasing appearance, with comfort a priority, and each has a luxurious bathroom. There is a delightful upstairs sitting room, a residents' lounge on the first floor and a spacious private dining room. Guests have a choice of two restaurants, the formal 'Grey Door' and the informal rendezvous 'Blushers'.

7🛁🚿 (2fb) 🚭 in 1 bedrooms 🚭 in area of dining room 🚭 in lounges CTV in all bedrooms [R] **T** 🐕 (ex guide dogs) ✱ sB&B🛁🚿IR£65 dB&B🛁🚿IR£85-IR£95 LDO 11.30pm

Lic 🅿 🚫

Credit Cards [1][2][3][5]

GH [Q][Q][Q] Iona House 5 Iona Park ☎(01) 8306217 & 8306855 FAX (01) 8306742

Closed Dec-Jan

Situated in a quiet residential suburb on the north side of the city, this family-run Victorian red-brick house has large modern bedrooms, a comfortable lounge and a small garden for exclusive use of guests. It is conveniently located for National Botanic Gardens and airport.

14rm(12🚿) (1fb) 🚭 in area of dining room CTV in 11 bedrooms **T**

✳ sB&BIR£23-IR£28.50 sB&BℛIR£31-IR£36.50 dB&BIR£53 dB&BℛIR£46-IR£57

🛏 nc3yrs

Credit Cards ① ③

GH Ⓠ Ⓠ Ⓠ **Kingswood Country House** Old Kingswood, Naas Road, Clondalkin D22 ☎(01) 4592428 & 4592207
FAX (01) 4592428

Closed 25-28 Dec & Good Fri rs Sat & Sun

Situated off the N7, turn left past Newlands Cross en route from Dublin. This Georgian house offers attractive en suite bedrooms, a cosy sitting room and an intimate restaurant specialising in good home cooking. The proprietors make guests feel very welcome here and there are also well maintained gardens and ample car parking facilities.

7⇆ℛ (2fb)CTV in all bedrooms T 🛉 (ex guide dogs) ✳
sB&B⇆ℛIR£39.38-IR£50.63 dB&B⇆ℛIR£61.88-IR£78.75
LDO 10.30pm

Lic 🛏

Credit Cards ① ② ③

T&C Ⓠ Ⓠ Ⓠ **Marelle** 92 Rathfarnham Road, Terenure
☎(01) 4904690

This attractive house, recently refurbished, is set back from the road in its own gardens. It has good parking facilities.

6rm(5ℛ) (1fb) CTV in 5 bedrooms 🛉 ✳ sB&BℛfrIR£28
dB&BℛfrIR£44 LDO 10am

🛏 CTV nc5yrs

Credit Cards ① ③

T&C Ⓠ Ⓠ Ⓠ **Morehampton Lodge** 113 Morehampton Road, Donnybrook ☎(01) 2837499 FAX (01) 2837595

Totally restored to a high standard, this Victorian house is very conveniently situated near the city centre and good bus routes. Excellent bedrooms are provided, and off-street parking is available.

5⇆ℛ (3fb) ⌇ CTV in all bedrooms Ⓡ T 🛉 ✳
sB&B⇆ℛIR£35-IR£40 dB&B⇆ℛIR£50-IR£65

🛏

Credit Cards ① ③

▶

ᴛʜᴇFitzwilliam

41 UPPER FITZWILLIAM STREET, DUBLIN 2.
TELEPHONE: (00 3531) 6600448/6600199

Located in the heart of elegant Georgian Dublin, a very comfortable friendly establishment offering centrally heated rooms, ensuite facilities, TV, telephone, hair dryer, and clock radio. Tea making facilities also available. Enjoy Dublin in a relaxed atmosphere. Within walking distance of shopping areas, museums, Trinity College and St Stephen's Green.

Marelle

92 Rathfarnham Road, Terenure, Dublin
Telephone: (00 3531) 4904690

Old style residence, beautifully appointed. Just 15 minutes from city centre. Linked to N4, N7 and N81 routes from car ferry. Plenty of private car space. All rooms are en suite and have TV, tea making facilities available. Golf courses and parks nearby.

dogs) LDO 9.30pm
Lic lift ▦ CTV ൭ sauna solarium
Credit Cards [1] [2] [3] [5]

T&C[Q][Q][Q][Q] *Northumberland Lodge* 68 Northumberland
Road, Ballsbridge (beside US Embassy) ☎(01) 6605270
FAX (01) 6688679
This gracious Georgian house stands in a convenient location,
close to the city centre and the Lansdowne road rugby ground
and a few minutes from the public transport systems. Bridget
and Tony Brady enjoy welcoming guests to their charming
home. The large, well equipped bedrooms are all en suite and
there are attractive gardens.
6rm(1⇌5♠) CTV in all bedrooms ® T ✹ (ex guide dogs)
▦ CTV
Credit Cards [1] [3]

GH [Q] *Phoenix Park House* 38-39 Parkgate Street (beside main
gates of Phoenix Park) ☎(01) 6772870 FAX (01) 6799769
Freshly decorated, well equipped bedrooms now have double-
glazing to ensure peace and quiet at this comfortable guesthouse
near Heuston Station, Phoenix Park and Dublin Zoo.
13rm(4♠) (3fb) CTV in all bedrooms ✹ (ex guide dogs)
▦ CTV
Credit Cards [1] [2] [3]

GH [Q][Q][Q][Q] *Raglan Lodge* 10 Raglan Road, Ballsbridge
☎(01) 6606697 FAX (01) 6606781
Closed 22-31 Dec
This charming restored Victorian Lodge stands on a tree-lined
road close to the US embassy, the RDS showground and
within easy reach of the city centre. En suite bedrooms are
comfortable with good facilities and antique furnishings, and
a fine dining room serves a breakfast that received the Irish
Breakfast Award for 1993. Guests also have use of a garden
and secure car parking.
7⇌♠ (4fb) ✹ in 2 bedrooms CTV in all bedrooms ® T
sB&B⇌♠IR£43-IR£48 dB&B⇌♠IR£67-IR£85
▦ CTV
Credit Cards [1] [2] [3]

T&C[Q][Q][Q][Q][Q] *No 66* Northumberland Road, Ballsbridge
☎(01) 6600333 & 6600471 FAX (01) 6601051
This imposing house has six comfortable bedrooms all fully
equipped to a very high standard. Attractive public areas
include a dining room and two comfortable lounges, one in a
lovely conservatory. It is very convenient the City,
Landsdowne Road and the RDS showgrounds.
6♠ (2fb) ✹ in dining room ✹ in lounges CTV in all bedrooms
® T ✹ (ex guide dogs) ✳ sB&B♠IR£35-IR£40
dB&B♠IR£55-IR£60 WB&BfrIR£175
▦ CTV
Credit Cards [1] [3]

GH [Q][Q][Q] *St Aiden's* 32 Brighton Road, Rathgar
☎(01) 4902011 & 4906178 FAX (01) 4920234
10rm(2⇌5♠) (3fb) ✹ in 3 bedrooms ✹ in area of dining room
CTV in all bedrooms T ✹ ✳ sB&BIR£20-IR£22

---

sB&B⇌♠IR£27.50-IR£35 dB&B⇌♠IR£46-IR£60
Lic ▦ CTV
Credit Cards [1] [2] [3]

DUNGANNON Co Tyrone | Map **01 C5**

GH [Q][Q][Q][Q][Q] **Grange
Lodge** 7 Grange Road BT71 7EJ
(1m from M1 junct 15 on A29
Armagh)
☎Moy(08687) 84212
FAX (08687) 23891
Closed 20 Dec-1 Jan
Many guests return year after
year to Ralph and Norah
Brown's charming country
house, set in 20 acres of well
laid gardens. Bedrooms are
small, but individually styled and provided with many
thoughtful extras. Fine paintings, fresh flowers and antiques
adorn the drawing room, and the separate small lounge offers
a selection of books and board games as well as TV. Enjoyable
home cooking is served at individual tables in the elegant
dining room.
5⇌♠ ✹ in bedrooms ✹ in dining room ✹ in 1 lounge CTV
in all bedrooms ® ✹ (ex guide dogs) sB&B⇌♠£35-£40
dB&B⇌♠£55-£60 LDO 1pm
▦ CTV nc12yrs ⚲(hard)
Credit Cards [1] [3] £

DUNGARVAN Co Waterford | Map **01 C2**

FH [Q][Q] Miss B Lynch **Killineen House** (*X302963*) Waterford
Road (off N25, 4.5m E) ☎Waterford(051) 91294
This attractive house with well-tended gardens and views of
Comeragh mountains is situated four miles east of town on
Waterford road.
5rm(3♠) (3fb) ✹ in bedrooms ® ✳ sB&BIR£13-IR£15
sB&B♠IR£15-IR£20 dB&BfrIR£26 dB&B♠frIR£30
WB&BIR£90 WBDifrIR£165 LDO 5pm
▦ CTV 50 acres grass

DUN LAOGHAIRE Co Dublin | Map **01 D4**

T&C[Q][Q] **Ferry House** 15 Clarinda Park North ☎(01) 2808301
FAX (01) 2846530
Closed Xmas & holidays
Large Victorian house overlooking People's Park.
6rm(3♠) (2fb) CTV in all bedrooms ✹ (ex guide dogs) ✳
dB&BIR£32-IR£35 dB&B♠IR£37-IR£38
▦ CTV ✗nc5yrs
Credit Cards [1] [3]

T&C[Q] **Tara Hall** 24 Sandycove Road, Sandycove
☎(01) 2805120 FAX (01) 2805120
New owners have recently acquired this large Victorian house and
a refurbishment programme is pending. The house is situated on a
main road a few minutes south of Ferryport and has its own car
park at the rear.
6rm(4♠) (3fb)CTV in all bedrooms ® sB&BfrIR£20
sB&B♠IR£28-IR£32 dB&BIR£30-IR£34 dB&B♠IR£36-IR£40
▦ CTV
Credit Cards [1] [3]

DUNMORE EAST Co Waterford   Map **01** C2

SELECTED

T&C Q Q Q Q **Hillfield House** Ballymabin
☎(051) 383565
Closed Dec & Jan
This luxury new dormer bungalow is set back from the
Waterford road in its own grounds. It offers lovely bedrooms
and public rooms with a strong emphasis on comfort.
4⇌ℝ (2fb) ⊁ CTV in all bedrooms ⊀ sB&B⇌ℝIR£20-
IR£25 dB&B⇌ℝIR£30-IR£35 WB&BIR£100-IR£110
⊞ CTV 18 hole pitch & putt adjacent

ENNIS Co Clare   Map **01** B3

T&C Q Q Q **Carraig Mhuire** Barefield ☎(065) 27106
FAX (065) 27375
This attractive and comfortable bungalow is set back from the
main Galway road in well-tended gardens. Well-equipped
bedrooms are welcoming and nothing is too much trouble for
charming hosts Mr and Mrs Morris.
5rm(3ℝ) (1fb) ⊁ in bedrooms ⊁ in dining room ℝ ⊀ (ex guide
dogs) ✳ sB&BfrIR£13.50 sB&BℝIR£18 dB&BℝIR£27 LDO
noon
⊞ CTV
Credit Cards ①②③

SELECTED

GH Q Q Q Q **Cill Eoin House** Killadysert Cross, Clare
Road (on N18) ☎(065) 41668 FAX (065) 20224
Closed 22 Dec-9 Jan
This smart purpose-built house stands a short distnce from the
town centre. It is attractively furnished and comfortable with
well-equipped en suite bedrooms. A hospitable owner is
always available to attend to guests needs.
14ℝ (2fb) ⊁ CTV in all bedrooms ℝ T ⊀ ✳ sB&BℝIR£20
dB&BℝIR£32
⊞ CTV ℺(hard)
Credit Cards ①②

ENNISCORTHY Co Wexford   Map **01** D3

SELECTED

FH Q Q Q Q Mr & Mrs J Maher **Ballinkeele House**
(T0030334) Ballymurn ☎(053) 38105 FAX (053) 38468
Mar-12 Nov rs 13 Nov-Feb
This classical house designed by Daniel Robertson and built in
1840, stands in 360 acres. It has been lovingly restored by
owners John and Margaret Maher, completely retaining its
ambience while providing today's comforts. There is a lovely
drawing and dining room and very comfortable bedrooms with
a decanter of sherry to welcome guests.
5rm(4ℝ) ⊁ in 2 bedrooms ⊁ in lounges ⊀ (ex guide dogs) ✳
sB&BℝIR£33-IR£35 dB&BℝIR£56-IR£60 WB&BfrIR£180
WBDifrIR£300 LDO noon
Lic ⊞ ℺(hard)snooker croquet 350 acres arable
Credit Cards ①③

ᴹᴴ

ᴹᴼᵁᴺᵀ ᴴᴱᴿᴮᴱᴿᵀ

Herbert Rd, Lansdowne Rd Ballsbridge DUBLIN 4
TEL: (00 3531) 668 4321 Fax: (00 3531) 660 7077

140 en suite bedrooms with TV, Phone etc.
★ Security Controlled Parking
★ A La Carte Restaurant ★ Gift Shop
★ Sauna/Sunbed ★ Conference Rooms
★ Picturesque Gardens ★ Childrens' Play Area
★ City centre 5 mins. by Dart electric rail

● 66 ●

T O W N H O U S E

66 Northumberland Road, Ballsbridge,
Dublin 4, Ireland
Tel: 00 3531 6600333
Fax: 00 3531 6601051
Ideally situated in Dublin's most
elegant suburb, 1 mile from the city
centre and 5 miles from Dun Laoghaire
Ferry. Convenient for buses and Dart
rail station. This Victorian residence
has been recently completely
refurbished to provide all rooms with
full facilities including en suite.
Parking available.

FERNS Co Wexford   Map **01** D3

SELECTED

FH Q Q Q Q Mrs B Breen **Clone House** *(T0022484)* (2m
SE off N11) ☎Enniscorthy(054) 66113 FAX (054) 66113
Mar-Oct
The hospitable Mrs Breen takes great pride in her farmhouse.
Fine furniture from past generations enhances the modern day
comforts and the prize-winning gardens are a delight.
5rm(4⇔♠) (4fb) ⌘ in bedrooms ⌘ in dining room CTV in 1
bedroom ✗ (ex guide dogs) ✳ sB&BIR£20-IR£23
sB&B⇔♠IR£22 dB&B⇔♠IR£30-IR£36 WB&BfrIR£105
WBDiIR£190 LDO 4pm
▥ CTV ໒ ℺(hard)✦ 280 acres mixed

FOULKESMILL Co Wexford   Map **01** C2

FH Q Q Ivor Young **Horetown House** *(S870189)*
☎Waterford(051) 63771 FAX (051) 63633
Mar-Jan (ex Xmas day)
An 18th-century manor house stands in 214 acres of farmland with
its own equestrian centre and cellar restaurant. The Young family
are hospitable hosts and the farmhouse makes an ideal touring
centre.
12rm (10fb) LDO 9pm
Lic ▥ CTV ∪ all weather indoor riding arena outdoor riding 214
acres beef dairy mixed
Credit Cards ①③

GALWAY Co Galway   Map **01** B4

SELECTED

T&C Q Q Q Q Q **Ardawn House** 31 College Road (from N6
into Galway take first left at roundabout near Huntsman public
house. At lights take right hand fork) ☎(091) 68833 & 64551
FAX (091) 68833
Closed 21-29 Dec
6⇔♠ (2fb) CTV in all bedrooms T ✗ (ex guide dogs) ✳
sB&B⇔♠IR£20-IR£27.50 dB&B⇔♠IR£32-IR£46
WB&BIR£105-IR£150
Credit Cards ①③

T&C Q Q **Bay View** Gentian Hill, Upper Salthill ☎(091) 22116
& 26140
17 Mar-Nov
Modern house situated on edge of Salthill. Ideal touring centre.
6rm(5♠) (2fb) ⌘ CTV in all bedrooms T ✗ sB&B♠IR£18.50
dB&B♠IR£29
▥ CTV nc5yrs

T&C Q Q Q Q **Corrib Haven** 107 Upper Newcastle (on N59)
☎(091) 24171
A new, purpose-built guesthouse stands on the N9 route to
Connemara, close to the university. The excellent bedrooms all
have private bathrooms, and ample car parking is provided.
6♠ (3fb) ⌘ in bedrooms ⌘ in dining room CTV in all bedrooms
✗ (ex guide dogs) ✳ sB&B♠IR£20-IR£25 dB&B♠IR£32-IR£40
WB&BIR£105-IR£112
▥ CTV
Credit Cards ①③

T&C Q Q Q **Flannery's** 54 Dalysfort Road, Salthill (R338 to
Salthill then first left from Threadneedle Road to Dr Mannix Road
and second left) ☎(091) 22048 FAX (01) 6683023
4rm(3♠) (2fb) ⌘ in dining room sB&BIR£18.50-IR£20

---

sB&B♠IR£20-IR£22 dB&BIR£27-IR£32 dB&B♠IR£29-IR£32
▥ CTV
Credit Cards ①③

SELECTED

T&C Q Q Q Q Q **Killeen House** Killeen, Bushypark (on N59
Galway/Oughterard road) ☎(091) 24179 FAX (091) 28065
Closed 22-31 Dec
4⇔♠ (1fb)CTV in all bedrooms ® **T** ✗ sB&B⇔♠IR£35-
IR£45 dB&B⇔♠IR£50-IR£70
lift ▥ nc7yrs
Credit Cards ①③

T&C Q Q Q Q **Roncalli House** 24 Whitestrand Avenue, Lower
Salthill ☎(091) 584159
Mr and Mrs O'Halloran are the hospitable owners of this modern
corner house hear the beach and in walking distance of the city
centre. Bedrooms are all equipped with TV and shower rooms,
there is good lounge space and, outside, a patio and well tended
garden.
6 (1fb) ⌘ in dining room ⌘ in 1 lounge CTV in all bedrooms ✗
✳ sB&B♠IR£18.50-IR£20 dB&B♠frIR£30
▥ CTV

GLENDALOUGH Co Wicklow   Map **01** D3

SELECTED

T&C Q Q Q Q **Laragh Trekking Centre** ☎(0404) 45282
FAX (0404) 45204
This hotel is run by husband and wife team David and Noreen
McCallion whose joint skills (Noreen's experience in the hotel
industry and David's love and knowledge of horses) combine
to make a holiday spent with them a memorable occasion.
David personally leads the rides around 600 acres of
mountains and forests of Co Wicklow.
6rm(4fb) (1fb) ✗ in 4 bedrooms ✗ in dining room CTV in all
bedrooms ® **T** ✳ sB&BIR£20-IR£25 sB&B♠IR£25-IR£30
dB&BIR£30-IR£32 dB&B♠IR£35-IR£38 WB&BfrIR£129.50
WBDifrIR£224 LDO noon
▥ CTV
Credit Cards ①②③

GLENEALY Co Wicklow   Map **01** D3

FH Q Q Mrs Mary Byrne **Ballyknocken House** *(T246925)* (turn
right after Jet garage in Ashford) ☎Wicklow(0404) 44627 &
44614 FAX (0404) 44627
Closed 1 Dec-1 Feb
This comfortable farmhouse stands one mile from Glenealy
offering pleasant en suite accommodation. Its hospitable owner
Mrs Byrne organizes walking and cycling tours. Dinner is also
provided.
8♠ (1fb) ✗ LDO 5pm
Lic ▥ CTV ℺(hard)200 acres dairy sheep

GOREY Co Wexford   Map **01** D3

SELECTED

FH Q Q Q Q Q P O'Sullivan **Woodlands** *(T1163648)*
Killinierin ☎Arklow(0402) 37125 & 37133
Closed Dec-Jan
This Georgian-style residence, 1.5 kilometres off the N11,
offers excellent accommodation, three of its rooms having
balconies. A charming dining room is run by chef Gara,
daughter of the proprietor. Mrs O'Sullivan and only uses fresh

---

produce. Award-winning gardens enhance a house in which relaxation is assured.
6🚿 (3fb) 🚭 in bedrooms 🚭 in dining room CTV in all bedrooms 🐕 (ex guide dogs) * sB&BIR£18-IR£19 sB&B🚿IR£23-IR£24 dB&B🚿IR£36-IR£38 WB&BfrIR£126 WBDiIR£230-IR£235 LDO 8pm
Lic ♨ CTV 🎾(hard)pool table pony rides 8 acres beef (non-working)
Credit Cards [1]

KANTURK Co Cork — Map **01** B2

PREMIER SELECTED

GH [Q][Q][Q][Q][Q] Assolas Country House (3.5m NE, off N72) ☎(029) 50015
FAX (029) 50795
15 Mar-1 Nov

This 17th-century manor house enjoys a sylvan setting on a tributary of the River Blackwater, surrounded by prize-winning gardens, parkland and rolling country. Magnificent public rooms have log fires and fresh garden and local produce is creatively presented in the restaurant.
6🛁🚿 Annexe 3🛁🚿 (3fb)T 🐕 (ex guide dogs) * sB&B🛁🚿IR£50-IR£75 dB&B🛁🚿IR£80-IR£150 WB&BfrIR£250 WBDifrIR£425 LDO 8.30pm
Lic ♨ 🎾(grass)🎣 croquet boating
Credit Cards [1][2][3][5]

KENMARE Co Kerry — Map **01** B2

GH [Q][Q][Q] Foleys Shamrock Henry Street ☎(064) 41361 FAX (064) 41799
This is a town-centre guesthouse over a pub/restaurant. All bedrooms have been recently refurbished and are very comfortable. A good food service is available via the bar and restaurant.
10🛁🚿 CTV in all bedrooms Ⓡ T 🐕 (ex guide dogs) * sB&B🛁🚿IR£15-IR£20 dB&B🛁🚿IR£30-IR£40 LDO 10pm
Lic ♨ CTV 🅿
Credit Cards [1][3]

FH [Q][Q] M P O'Sullivan ***Sea Shore*** *(V899705)* Tubrid
☎(064) 41270
May-Sep
A modern bungalow stands in its own grounds on the edge of town overlooking Kenmare Bay.
4🚿 (3fb) 🐕 (ex guide dogs) LDO 3pm
♨ CTV 32 acres dairy

FH [Q][Q] Mrs R Doran **Templenoe House** *(V840693)* Greenane (on N70) ☎(064) 41538
Etr-Oct
This two-storey farmhouse reputed to be about 200 years old is situated on the Ring of Kerry about four miles west of Kenmare.
5rm(2🚿) 🚭 in bedrooms 🚭 in dining room Ⓡ 🐕 (ex guide dogs) dB&BIR£30 dB&B🚿IR£34
♨ CTV 50 acres mixed

KILCULLEN Co Kildare — Map **01** C3

FH [Q][Q][Q] B O'Sullivan ***Chapel View*** *(N856055)*
Gormanstown ☎Curragh(045) 81325
May-Dec
6🚿 (2fb) LDO 4pm
♨ CTV 22 acres beef
Credit Cards [1][3]

KILKENNY Co Kilkenny — Map **01** C3

T&C[Q][Q][Q] Launard House 2 Maiden Hill, Kells Road
☎(056) 51889
Mar-Nov
Conveniently situated a mile from the city centre, this purpose-built house is very comfortable. Owners Sandra and John Cahill offer a warm welcome.
4🛁🚿 (2fb) 🚭 Ⓡ 🐕 * sB&B🛁🚿frIR£20 dB&B🛁🚿frIR£30
♨ CTV nc12yrs
Credit Cards [1][3]

SELECTED

T&C[Q][Q][Q][Q] ***Shillogher House*** Callan Road
☎(056) 63249
Closed 20-31 Dec
A lovely new house stands in its own gardens on the road to Clonmel. It is tastefully furnished and decorated and Mrs Kennedy has a keen eye to her guests' comfort.
5🛁🚿 (1fb) CTV in 1 bedroom Ⓡ 🐕 LDO 2pm
♨ CTV
Credit Cards [1][3]

KILLARNEY Co Kerry — Map **01** A2

T&C[Q][Q][Q] Avondale House Tralee Road (on N22)
☎(064) 35579
17 Mar-7 Nov
This is a distinctive pink house surrounded by attractive gardens five minutes' drive from Killarney. There is a comfortable lounge and en suite bedrooms equipped with TVs and tea/coffee making facilities. A golf course and riding stables are available nearby.
5rm (4fb)CTV in all bedrooms Ⓡ 🐕 (ex guide dogs) sB&BIR£18-IR£18.50 dB&BIR£28-IR£30 WB&BIR£95-IR£100 WBDiIR£170-IR£177 LDO 3pm
♨ CTV

GH [Q][Q][Q] ***Beaufield House*** Cork Road (on N22)
☎(064) 34440 FAX (064) 34663
Closed 15-26 Dec
A purpose-built guesthouse is located less than a mile from the town centre on the Cork road. The spacious, bright bedrooms are all well equipped, with generous-sized showers or bathrooms. Hosts Danny and Moya Bowe place a high priority on hospitality, and they have a wine licence. Good car parking is provided.
14🛁🚿 Ⓡ 🐕
♨ CTV
Credit Cards [1][2][3]

T&C[Q][Q] Dirreen House Tralee Road (on N22) ☎(064) 31676
Mar-Nov
This large purpose-built house stands in attractive lawns and flower beds on the Tralee road. The en suite bedrooms are all well-equipped and well-furnished and have good views over the surrounding countryside.
4🚿 (2fb) 🚭 in 2 bedrooms 🚭 in dining room 🚭 in lounges CTV in all bedrooms Ⓡ 🐕 * sB&B🚿IR£18-IR£20 dB&B🚿IR£28-IR£30 WB&BIR£98-IR£105 WBDiIR£161-IR£165
♨ CTV

SELECTED

GH [Q][Q][Q][Q] Foleys Town House 22/23 High Street
☎(064) 31217 FAX (064) 34683
Apr-Oct
Charming bedrooms with stripped pine furniture and coordinated colour schemes are a feature of this delightful town house, which also offers a cosy lounge, a bar and private car park. It is run by Carol Hartnett who is also head chef at her popular adjoining seafood restaurant.
12🛁🚿 🚭 in 2 bedrooms 🚭 in area of dining room CTV in all bedrooms Ⓡ **T** 🐕 ✳ sB&B🛁🚿IR£38.50-IR£41.80 dB&B🛁🚿IR£55-IR£77 LDO 10.30pm
Lic 🅿 CTV
Credit Cards [1][2][3]

GH [Q][Q][Q] Gleann Fia Deerpark ☎(064) 35035
FAX (064) 35000
14 Mar-Oct
Gleann Fia means 'Glen of the Deer', and it is certainly appropriate, for this guesthouse enjoys a tranquil setting among mature woodlands. The owner, Mora Galvin, takes a real interest in her guests.
8🚿 (2fb) 🚭 in 2 bedrooms 🚭 in dining room 🚭 in 1 lounge Ⓡ **T** 🐕 (ex guide dogs) ✳ sB&B🚿IR£20-IR£23 dB&B🚿IR£34-IR£36 WB&BfrIR£119
🅿 CTV playground
Credit Cards [1][2][3]

GH [Q][Q][Q] *Glena House* Muckross Road ☎(064) 32705
FAX (064) 34033
Closed Xmas
A large, comfortable house close to town offers en suite accomodation and on-site parking.
18rm(3🛁15🚿) (3fb) **T** LDO 8.30pm
Lic 🅿 CTV
Credit Cards [1][2][3][5]

T&C[Q][Q][Q] Gorman's Tralee Road ☎(064) 33149
A large and attractive bungalow is set in well cultivated gardens and 3.5 miles from Killarney on the Tralee road. It offers comfortable en suite bedrooms.
5🛁🚿 (2fb) CTV in all bedrooms Ⓡ ✳ sB&BIR£13.50-IR£18 dB&BIR£26-IR£28 dB&B🛁🚿IR£26-IR£29 WBDiIR£152-IR£169 LDO 6pm
🅿 CTV P̸

T&C[Q][Q] *Green Acres* Fossa ☎(064) 31454
Closed Xmas
This modern house is situated on the Ring of Kerry 1.5 miles outside town.
8rm(6🚿) (2fb) 🐕
🅿 CTV

SELECTED

GH [Q][Q][Q][Q] Kathleen's Country House Tralee Road (on N22 3km N) ☎(064) 32810 FAX (064) 32340
17 Mar-5 Nov
An exclusive, modern, purpose-built guesthouse is set in its own lovely gardens one mile from town centre on Tralee road. Family-run, luxury accommodation in scenic countryside makes this an ideal touring centre.
16🛁🚿 (2fb) 🚭 in 9 bedrooms 🚭 in dining room 🚭 in lounges CTV in all bedrooms Ⓡ **T** 🐕 dB&B🛁🚿IR£40-IR£70 WB&BIR£130.50-IR£210 LDO 6pm
Lic 🅿 nc5yrs lawn croquet
Credit Cards [1][2]

T&C[Q][Q][Q] Killarney Villa Cork-Waterford Road (N72)
☎(064) 31878
Apr-Oct
This purpose-built country home run by a family is equipped with all modern comforts and makes an ideal holiday destination.
11🛁🚿 🚭 in 5 bedrooms 🚭 in dining room 🚭 in lounges Ⓡ 🐕 (ex guide dogs) sB&B🛁🚿IR£16-IR£20 dB&B🛁🚿IR£30-IR£34 WB&BIR£100-IR£115 WBDiIR£180-IR£195 LDO 6.30pm
🅿 CTV nc6yrs
Credit Cards [1][2][3]

GH [Q][Q][Q] Lime Court Muckross Road ☎(064) 34547
FAX (064) 34121
A large modern house has spacious public rooms and well equipped bedrooms with private bathrooms. Many of the rooms have fine views. High standards are maintained throughout, and evening meals can be provided to groups.
12🛁🚿 (4fb) 🚭 in 6 bedrooms 🚭 in area of dining room 🚭 in 1 lounge CTV in all bedrooms **T** 🐕 (ex guide dogs) ✳ dB&B🛁🚿IR£42-IR£50 WB&BIR£144-IR£170
Lic 🅿 CTV
Credit Cards [1][3]

GH [Q][Q][Q] Lissivigeen House Cork Road (1m from Killarney, on Cork/Killarney N22) ☎(064) 35522
May-Oct
This attractive yellow house with its grey slate roof has been purpose-built with the comfort of guests in mind. Bedrooms are attractively furnished in pine and have all modern comforts. The house is on the N22 about a mile from the centre of town. Car parking is good.
8🚿 🚭 in bedrooms 🚭 in dining room CTV in all bedrooms **T** 🐕 ✳ sB&B🚿IR£22-IR£28 dB&B🚿IR£40-IR£50 WB&BIR£110
🅿 CTV
Credit Cards [1][2][3][5]

GH [Q][Q][Q] *Loch Lein* Golf Course Road, Fossa (on R562)
☎(064) 31260
17 Mar-Sep
A single-storey bungalow stands in a quiet and peaceful loction on the shores of the Lower Lake with well maintained lawns and flower beds.
15rm(2🛁10🚿) (5fb) 🐕
🅿 CTV

T&C[Q][Q][Q] Lohan's Lodge Tralee Road (on N22)
☎(064) 33871
Proprietors Cathy and Mike Lohan are hospitable and caring hosts, who keep their house in pristine condition. The bedrooms are cosy and attractive and the comfortable lounge has a turf fire in cooler weather.
5🚿 (1fb) 🚭 in 2 bedrooms 🚭 in area of dining room 🚭 in 1 lounge CTV in all bedrooms Ⓡ 🐕 ✳ dB&B🚿IR£27-IR£30 WB&BIR£91-IR£98 WBDiIR£150-IR£170 LDO noon
🅿 CTV nc7yrs

T&C[Q][Q] *Nashville* Tralee Road (2m from Killarney on main Dublin/Limerick road, N22) ☎(064) 32924
15 Mar-Nov
This white, double-fronted house on the main N22 road is about two miles from Killarney and very easy to find. The large bedrooms are bright, cheerful, and well equipped. David Nash and his family are very welcoming hosts.
6🚿 (2fb) Ⓡ 🐕 (ex guide dogs)
🅿 CTV

T&C[Q][Q] The Purple Heather Glencar Road, Gap of Dunloe
☎(064) 44266
Mar-Oct
This modern bungalow stands by the roadside among spectacular mountain scenery and is an ideal touring centre.
5rm(4🚿) (1fb) 🚭 in 3 bedrooms 🚭 in dining room 🚭 in 1 lounge

Ⓡ ✶ ✱ sB&BIR£15 sB&BſIR£18.50 dB&BſIR£24-IR£26.50 WB&BIR£84-IR£94.50 WBDiIR£160-IR£170 LDO 7pm ▥ CTV ℁(hard)pool room
Credit Cards ① ③

T&C Ⓠ Ⓠ St Anthonys Villas Cork Road ☎(064) 31534
Mar-Nov
This pleasant house stands on the Cork road. It is well appointed, its en suite bedrooms having good equipment and furnishings. Evening meals are available at a local hotel by arrangement.
4ſ (2fb) ✱ in bedrooms ✱ in dining room CTV in 2 bedrooms Ⓡ ✶ (ex guide dogs) ✱ sB&BſIR£18-IR£20 dB&BſIR£30-IR£32 WB&BIR£105-IR£108 WBDiIR£166-IR£172 LDO noon ▥ CTV
Credit Cards ① ② ③

T&C Ⓠ Ⓠ Shraheen House Ballycasheen ☎(064) 31286
Closed Xmas & New Year
In a peaceful, scenic area, this modern and comfortable house has well equipped bedrooms and a patio lounge.
6rm(2⇌4ſ) (2fb) ✱ in bedrooms ✱ in dining room CTV in all bedrooms ✶ ✱ sB&B⇌ſfrIR£22 dB&B⇌ſIR£31-IR£35 ▥ CTV

⨇ ▆ FH Ⓠ Mrs B O'Connor **Glebe** Off Tralee Road ☎(064) 32179
Mar-Dec
In a peaceful location on a side road, but convenient for the N22, this charming guesthouse contains an interesting display of farm memorabilia which has been collected by the owner, Mrs O'Connor.
4⇌ſ (1fb) ✱ in dining room ✶ (ex guide dogs) sB&B⇌ſfrIR£15 dB&B⇌ſIR£24 WB&BIR£80 WBDiIR£156 LDO 1pm CTV

KILLEAGH Co Cork ⎯ Map **01 C2**
T&C Ⓠ Ⓠ Tattans Main Street (on N8, between Midleton and Youghal) ☎(024) 95173
Mar-Oct
Very comfortable bedrooms are a feature of Tattans Town House on the main Cork-Rosslare road, N25. There is a TV room, large attractive gardens, a hard tennis court and an adjoining bar where snacks are available all day. Evening meals are served to residents. Mrs Tattan takes pride in running the hotel, is very welcoming and serves good food.
5rm(4ſ) (3fb)✶ ✱ sB&BIR£18 sB&BſIR£18 dB&BIR£32 dB&BſIR£32 WB&BIR£112 WBDiIR£220 LDO 10pm Lic ▥ CTV ℁(hard)

SELECTED
FH Ⓠ Ⓠ Ⓠ Mrs Browne **Ballymakeigh House** *(X0005765)* ☎Youghal(024) 95184 FAX (024) 95370
Hospitable Margaret Browne, winner of many awards, makes guests feel very much at home in her delightful, 250-year-old farmhouse. The cheerful bedrooms are attractively decorated and an elegant dining room provides the setting for a five-course dinner served every evening.
5⇌ſ (5fb) ✱ in dining room ✶ (ex guide dogs) ✱ sB&B⇌ſfrIR£20-IR£25 dB&B⇌ſfrIR£40 WB&BfrIR£136 WBDifrIR£250 LDO 6pm
Lic ▥ CTV ℁(hard)snooker games room 180 acres dairy

KILMALLOCK Co Limerick ⎯ Map **01 B3**
FH Ⓠ Ⓠ Mrs Imelda Sheedy-King **Flemingstown House** *(R629255)* (on R512) ☎(063) 98093 FAX (063) 98546
Mar-Oct
This 18th-century farmhouse has been modernised to provide attractive, well equipped accommodation with all the comforts today's holiday maker expects. Imelda Sheedy-King has good

reason to be proud of her cooking, and much of the produce comes from her own farm. She will provide dinner for her guests by arrangement. The farm is on the Limerick/Mitchelstown road, has good car parking and the countryside is excellent for walkers, riders, anglers and golfers.
6rm(5ſ) (2fb) ✱ in dining room Ⓡ ✶ (ex guide dogs) ✱ sB&BIR£15 dB&BIR£30 LDO 3pm ▥ CTV ◡ 102 acres dairy

KILRANE Co Wexford ⎯ Map **01 D2**
FH Ⓠ Ⓠ K O'Leary *O'Leary's (T132101)* Killilane, St Helen's Bay ☎(053) 33134
This farmhouse is located in a quiet and peaceful setting overlooking St George's Channel.
10rm(7ſ) (3fb) ✱ LDO noon
▥ CTV 97 acres arable

KINSALE Co Cork ⎯ Map **01 B2**
T&C Ⓠ Ⓠ Ⓠ *Kieran's Folkhouse Inn* Guardwell ☎(021) 772382 FAX (021) 774380
An 18th-century house with a bar and public restaurant is situated in the town centre. It offers excellent accommodation of a uniformly high standard and good food service throughout the day.
19⇌ſ (3fb) CTV in all bedrooms T ✶ (ex guide dogs) LDO 10pm
Lic ▥ CTV
Credit Cards ① ③

SELECTED
GH Ⓠ Ⓠ Ⓠ **The Moorings** Scilly ☎(021) 772376 FAX (021) 772675
Entering from the Cork road (R600) take the sharp left turn for Scilly, and there nestling on the hillside is this superbly appointed guesthouse. Owner Pat Jones' keen interest in interior decoration has resulted in very comfortable, individually styled and colour coordinated bedrooms all with en suite facilities. Guests can enjoy peace and tranquility in the inviting surroundings which encirlces the house.
8⇌ſ CTV in all bedrooms Ⓡ T sB&B⇌ſfrIR£50 dB&B⇌ſIR£60-IR£90
▥ CTV nc16yrs
Credit Cards ① ③

SELECTED
GH Ⓠ Ⓠ Ⓠ **Old Bank House** 11 Pearse Street ☎(021) 774075 FAX (021) 774296
Closed 23-25 Dec
Under the personal supervision of Marie and Michael Riese, this delightful Georgian house - once a bank house - has been restored to its former elegance. The en suite bedrooms, with period furniture and attractive decor, combine charm with modern comforts. Dinner is offered in the owners' restaurant.
9⇌ſ (2fb) ✱ in dining room ✱ in 1 lounge CTV in all bedrooms T ✶ (ex guide dogs) sB&B⇌ſfrIR£35-IR£50 dB&B⇌ſfrIR£70-IR£110 WB&BIR£210-IR£350 LDO 10pm
Lic ▥ ✗nc12yrs
Credit Cards ① ② ③

KNOCKFERRY Co Galway ⎯ Map **01 B4**
FH Ⓠ Ⓠ D & M Moran **Knockferry Lodge** *(M238412)* ☎Galway(091) 80122 FAX (091) 80328
2 May-1 Oct
Situated on the shores of Lough Corrib, this farmhouse offers good food, cosy turf fires and a welcome that is warm and sincere.
▶

Fishing is available outside the door.
10🛁🚿 (1fb) 🚭 in dining room 🚭 in lounges 🐕 (ex guide dogs) sB&B🛁🚿IR£27 dB&B🛁🚿IR£40 WB&BIR£140 WBDiIR£200 LDO 8pm
Lic ▥ CTV boats for hire 35 acres mixed
Credit Cards [1][2][3][5]

LARNE Co Antrim — Map **01** D5

GH [Q][Q][Q] Derrin 2 Prince's Gardens BT40 1RQ (access via A2) ☎(0574) 273269 & 273762

A substantial property dating from 1912, this guesthouse is just off the A2 Coast Road close to the town centre and within easy reach of the ferry terminal. Impeccably maintained, it provides well equipped accommodation with modern furnishings. There is a spacious lounge and an attractive breakfast room with individual tables.
7rm(4🚿) (2fb) 🚭 in dining room CTV in all bedrooms Ⓡ ✱ sB&Bfr£16 sB&B🚿fr£18 dB&Bfr£27 dB&B🚿fr£32
▥ CTV
Credit Cards [1][2][3][£]

LIMERICK Co Limerick — Map **01** B3

GH [Q][Q][Q] Clifton House Ennis Road (on direct route to Shannon airport N18, opposite Woodfield House Hotel) ☎(061) 451166 FAX (061) 451224
Closed 18 Dec-4 Jan
Providing well equipped, attractive and very comfortable bedrooms has been the aim of the refurbishment of Michael and Mary Powell's guesthouse. Complimentary tea and coffee are available in the spacious, relaxing lounge and there is an excellent car park.
16🛁🚿 CTV in all bedrooms **T** 🐕 (ex guide dogs) ✱ sB&B🛁🚿IR£20-IR£22 dB&B🛁🚿IR£30-IR£32
▥

LISBURN Co Antrim — Map **01** D5

SELECTED

FH [Q][Q][Q][Q] Mrs D Moore **Brook Lodge** *(J3315608)* 79 Old Ballynahinch Road, Cargacroy BT27 6TH ☎Bailliesmills(0846) 638454
A modern bungalow in rural surroundings, Brook Lodge Farmhouse offers a warm welcome and cosy accommodation at very reasonable rates. The bedrooms, some with small shower rooms, are compact and attractively furnished. The comfortable lounge has a splendid outlook and home-cooked meals are served in a small dining room.
6rm(4🚿) 🚭 in dining room 🚭 in lounges CTV in 1 bedroom 🐕 (ex guide dogs) ✱ sB&B£17 dB&B£34 WB&B£119 WBDi£175
▥ CTV 65 acres mixed

LISDOONVARNA Co Clare — Map **01** B3

T&C[Q] Sunville off Doolin Road (situated 200yds from town centre, off N67) ☎(065) 74065 FAX (065) 74065
This modern house in pleasant gardens reaching to roadway makes an ideal touring centre.
5🛁🚿 (3fb) 🚭 in bedrooms 🚭 in area of dining room Ⓡ 🐕 (ex guide dogs) sB&BfrIR£18.50 dB&B🛁🚿frIR£28 WB&BfrIR£95 WBDifrIR£175 LDO noon
▥ CTV
Credit Cards [1][3]

LISTOWEL Co Kerry — Map **01** B3

T&C[Q][Q] North County 67 Church Street ☎(068) 21238
This comfortable streetside house in the centre of the market town is conveniently situated for Shannon car ferry and all amenities.
8rm(2🚿) (2fb) 🚭 in 2 bedrooms 🚭 in dining room 🐕 (ex guide dogs) ✱ sB&BIR£13.50-IR£18.50 dB&BIR£27-IR£35 dB&B🚿IR£30-IR£38 LDO noon
▥ CTV 🚫🏠

LUSK Co Dublin — Map **01** D4

T&C[Q][Q][Q] Carriage House ☎8438857 FAX 8438933
This attractive bungalow is set in well tended gardens, just off the N1 main Dublin/Belfast road. The Curtin family are very hospitable and nothing is too much trouble. The well equipped bedrooms are all en suite. The house is convenient for both tourists and business guests with office facilities and an information centre. There is an outdoor heated swimming pool and good car parking.
5🚿 CTV in all bedrooms Ⓡ **T** 🐕 (ex guide dogs) ✱ sB&B🚿IR£25 dB&B🚿IR£34
▥ CTV 🏊 (heated) sauna gymnasium 9 hole putting
Credit Cards [1][2][3][5]

MILFORD Co Carlow — Map **01** C3

SELECTED

T&C[Q][Q][Q][Q] Goleen Country House (on N9) ☎(0503) 46132 FAX (0503) 42861
Closed Dec-1 Jan
This is a lovely house, tree-screened from the Carlow/Waterford road (N9) and with substantial well tended gardens to the front. The Mulveys have done everything possible to make guests comfortable and the bedrooms especially reflect this concern - being very fully and comfortably equipped. Mrs Mulvey is a charming hostess.
6rm(4🚿) 🚭 in bedrooms 🚭 in dining room CTV in all bedrooms Ⓡ **T** 🐕 ✱ sB&BIR£15-IR£18 dB&B🚿IR£30-IR£36
▥ CTV
Credit Cards [1][2][3]

MOUNTRATH Co Laois — Map **01** C3

T&C[Q][Q][Q] Roundwood House ☎(0502) 32120 FAX (0502) 32711
Closed 25 Dec
This Palladian villa, in a secluded woodland setting, transports one back in time to an era of grace and leisure. Excellent hospitality and good food are offered by hosts Frank and Rosemarie Keenan.
6🛁 (2fb) 🚭 in bedrooms 🐕 (ex guide dogs) sB&B🛁IR£32-IR£41 dB&B🛁IR£64-IR£70 WB&BIR£200-IR£220 WBDiIR£340-IR£360 LDO 5pm
Lic ▥ 🏠
Credit Cards [1][2][3][5]

MOYARD Co Galway — Map **01** A4

FH [Q][Q][Q] Mrs M O'Toole **Rose Cottage** *(L673565)* Rockfield ☎(095) 41082
May-Sep
This is a comfortable farm bungalow on the Clifden/Leenane road (N59), near the new National Park.
6🚿 (2fb) Ⓡ 🐕 (ex guide dogs) ✱ dB&B🚿IR£30-IR£32
▥ CTV 36 acres mixed

NAAS Co Kildare — Map **01** D4

FH [Q][Q][Q] Mrs J McLoughlin **Setanta** *(N857230)* Castlekeely, Caragh ☎(045) 76481
Mar-Oct
This modern farm bungalow stands in a quiet, peaceful area.

rm(3🚿) (4fb) 🚭 in bedrooms 🚭 in dining room Ⓡ 🐕 (ex guide
ogs) ✱ sB&BIR£14 dB&B🚿IR£30 LDO noon
♨ CTV 43 acres dry stock

H [Q][Q] M & E Nolan **Westown** *(N9921214)* Johnstown (off
7) ☎(045) 97006
losed 16 Dec-Jan
1odern two-storey house 0.5m off N7.
rm (3fb) 🐕 ✱ sB&BIR£15-IR£17 dB&BfrIR£30 LDO noon
♨ CTV 92 acres arable mixed tillage

EWBAWN Co Wexford Map **01** C3

'&C[Q][Q] **Woodlands House** Carrickbyrne (on N25
osslare/Cork rd) ☎(051) 28287
1rs Susan Halpin, the hospitable and charming owner of
Voodlands, is an experienced apiarist and offers guests the
pportunity of seeing the interesting honey-processing tower. The
stablishment, which is about twenty miles from Rosslare ferry,
as nearby forest walks, bird watching, horse riding and golf.
rm(3🚿) (1fb) 🐕 (ex guide dogs) ✱ sB&BIR£13 dB&B🚿IR£28
VB&BIR£84-IR£88
♨ CTV games room
'redit Cards [1][3]

EW ROSS Co Wexford Map **01** C3

T&C[Q] **Millfield House** The Maudlins ☎(051) 21734
1ar-Oct
riendly owner Mrs Rosa Ronan offers clean accommodation and
ieals by arrangement at this pleasant house set in the Maudlins.
rm (5fb) 🚭 in bedrooms 🚭 in dining room 🐕 sB&BIR£15
B&BIR£27 WB&BIR£91 WBDiIR£150 LDO 6pm
♨ CTV

INE MILE HOUSE Co Tipperary Map **01** C3

'&C[Q][Q] **Grand Inn** (situated on the main Clonmel/Kilkenny
1, N76) ☎(051) 647035
7th-century historic Bianconi Inn is situated in the scenic Valley
f Slievenamon, on the N76.
rm(3🚿) (3fb)✱ sB&BfrIR£16 sB&B🚿frIR£18 dB&BfrIR£27
B&B🚿frIR£31 WB&BfrIR£94.50 WBDifrIR£150 LDO 7pm
♨ CTV

GONNELLOE Co Clare Map **01** B3

&C[Q][Q][Q] **Lantern House** ☎(061) 923034 & 923123
AX (061) 923139
iid Feb-Oct
ituated overlooking Lough Derg, in a very scenic setting on the
436 route, this comfortable house offers nicely furnished and
ecorated bedrooms, together with a popular restaurant. The well
nded gardens provide a marvellous view of the lake.
🚿 (2fb)CTV in all bedrooms **T** 🐕 (ex guide dogs) ✱
3&B🚿IR£20-IR£24 dB&B🚿IR£36 WB&BfrIR£112
VBDifrIR£210 LDO 9.30pm
ic ♨ CTV
redit Cards [1][2][3][5]

RANMORE Co Galway Map **01** B4

&C[Q][Q][Q] **Ashbrook House** Dublin Road ☎(091) 94196
losed 22 Dec-1 Jan
shbrook House is set in an acre of grounds on the N6 opposite a
ellow water tower, six minutes' drive from Galway. It is
tractively decorated throughout and has cosy, en suite bedrooms
id good car parking.
🚿 (4fb) 🚭 CTV in all bedrooms Ⓡ 🐕 (ex guide dogs)
♨ CTV

OUGHTERARD Co Galway Map **01** B4

GH [Q][Q][Q] **The Boat** The Square (on N59) ☎(091) 82196
FAX (091) 82694
The Boat Inn has recently been refurbished to a very high standard, with attractive and comfortable bedrooms. Hosts Anne and Tom Little provide a friendly welcome and are sure to make a visit a memorable one.
11rm(6🛁5🚿) (4fb) 🚭 in area of dining room CTV in all bedrooms Ⓡ **T** ✱ sB&B🛁🚿IR£24-IR£28 dB&B🛁🚿IR£38-IR£46 WB&BIR£119-IR£139 WBDiIR£195-IR£215 LDO 10pm
Lic ♨ CTV 🅿
Credit Cards [1][2][3][5]

OVENS Co Cork Map **01** B2

T&C[Q][Q] **Milestone** Ballincollig (on N22) ☎(021) 872562
This large, modern, detached roadside residence enjoys a quiet and peaceful setting and well-maintained lawns and gardens.
5🛁🚿 (1fb) 🚭 in 2 bedrooms 🚭 in dining room 🚭 in lounges Ⓡ 🐕 ✱ sB&B🛁🚿IR£18.50-IR£20 dB&B🛁🚿IR£30-IR£32 LDO noon
♨ CTV

PORTLAOISE Co Laoise Map **01** C3

T&C[Q][Q] ***O'Sullivan*** 8 Kelly Ville Park ☎(0502) 22774
Situated on the outskirts of town, this family-run, two-storey, semidetached house has a homely atmosphere.
6🚿 (1fb) 🐕 (ex guide dogs)
♨ CTV

T&C[Q][Q] **Vicarstown Inn** Vicarstown ☎(0502) 25189
FAX (0502) 25544
Mar-Dec
This 200-year-old roadside village inn, has well appointed bedrooms and public rooms and is situted on the banks of the Grand Canal, making it an ideal centre for coarse fishing.
6rm(2🛁🚿) Annexe 3rm (3fb) 🚭 in 1 bedrooms 🚭 in dining room 🐕 (ex guide dogs) LDO noon
Lic ♨ CTV
Credit Cards [3]

RATHDRUM Co Wicklow Map **01** D3

GH [Q][Q] ***Avonbrae House*** ☎Wicklow(0404) 46198
15 Mar-15 Nov
This small, exclusively run guesthouse nestles in the Wicklow Hills amid mountains, rivers and forests. Situated on the Glendalough road from Rathdrum, it is an ideal touring base, and walking holidays are a speciality. The Avonbrae has a heated indoor swimming pool.
6🚿 (2fb) Ⓡ LDO noon
Lic ♨ CTV 🏊 (heated) 🎾(grass)solarium games room
Credit Cards [1][2][3]

SELECTED

T&C[Q][Q][Q][Q] **Whaley Abbey Country House**
Ballinaclash (between Rathdrum & Aughrim) ☎(0404) 46529
FAX (0404) 46793
Mar-Oct
A fine old country house built in 1760, this was the shooting lodge of the famous adventurer Buck Whaley. Situated in 200 acres of farm and parkland Whaley Abbey has been sympathetically restored and offers comfort and hospitality in beautiful surroundings.
7🛁🚿 🐕 (ex guide dogs) ✱ sB&B🛁🚿frIR£30 dB&B🛁🚿frIR£50 LDO 4pm
Lic ♨ CTV nc16yrs 🎾(hard)croquet
Credit Cards [1][2][3]

ROSSLARE Co Wexford Map **01** D2

SELECTED

GH [Q][Q][Q][Q] Churchtown House Tagoat ☎(053) 32555 FAX (053) 32555
15 Mar-15 Nov
A charming period house is set in mature grounds on a link road between Rosslare Harbour and Rosslare Strand, just a short distance from the ferry port. Recently refurbished it has spacious, comfortable bedrooms, one of which is suitable for wheelchair users. Dinner is served by arrangement only.
8🛁🚿 (2fb) CTV in 2 bedrooms sB&B🛁🚿IR£22-IR£29.50 dB&B🛁🚿IR£43-IR£55 LDO noon previous day
♨ CTV
Credit Cards [1] [3]

ROSSLARE HARBOUR Co Wexford Map **01** D2

T&C[Q] Kilrane House (on N25) ☎(053) 33135
This period house situated a short distance from Rosslare Harbour in the village of Kilrane, has been restored and all bedrooms now have private bathrooms. There are many original features, open fires and a superb guest lounge. Ample car parking is provided and early breakfasts can be served if required.
(2fb) 🚭 in dining room CTV in 2 bedrooms [R] 🐕 (ex guide dogs) * sB&B🚿IR£20-IR£25 dB&B🚿frIR£30
♨ CTV
Credit Cards [1] [2] [3]

ROSSNOWLAGH Co Donegal Map **01** B5

T&C[Q][Q][Q] ***Smugglers Creek*** ☎(072) 52366
With probably the best view in Ireland from its hilltop position overlooking Donegal Bay, this delightful inn has been lovingly restored in traditional country style. All the bedrooms are attractive and offer a high standard of comfort; one has a balcony. A bar with superb views serves a wide range of bar food, and the restaurant, open in the evenings, has a good choice of fresh fish.
5🛁🚿 **T** LDO 9.30pm
Lic ♨ CTV
Credit Cards [1] [3]

SHANAGARRY Co Cork Map **01** C2

SELECTED

GH [Q][Q][Q][Q] ***Ballymaloe House*** ☎Cork(021) 652531 Telex no 75208 FAX (021) 652021
Closed 24-26 Dec
This comfortable house situated within a 400-acre farm was part of Old Geraldine Castle and has been rebuilt and modernised. Run by the Allen family, the individually decorated bedrooms have antique furnishings and modern bathrooms. The award-winning restaurant is under the personal supervision of Myrtle Allen, and the drawing room boasts huge welcoming log fires. There is a heated outdoor pool and the Ballymaloe Shop to explore. To find the house, turn off the main Cork/Wexford N25 road at Middleton roundabout and follow the signs.
19rm(18🛁🚿) Annexe 11🛁🚿 (1fb) **T** 🐕 (ex guide dogs) LDO 9pm
Lic ♨ CTV 🏊(heated) ⛳7 🎾(hard)
Credit Cards [1] [3] [5]

SKERRIES Co Dublin Map **01** D4

T&C[Q] ***Teresa's*** 9 Thomas Hand Street ☎(01) 491411
Mar-Sep
Located in a seaside village in the north of Co Dublin, this house offers pleasant accomodation in bright, clean bedrooms and a cos sitting room. Mes Boylan, the popular owner, also runs the adjacent Coffee Shop which is a meeting point for tourists and local inhabitants who enjoy the home-cooking on offer.
4rm 🐕
♨ CTV

SLIGO Co Sligo Map **01** B

T&C[Q][Q][Q] ***Aisling*** Cairns Hill ☎(071) 60704
Closed 24-28 Dec
Bungalow overlooking Sligo Bay and near Lough Gill.
6rm(3🚿) (2fb) 🐕
♨ CTV nc6yrs

T&C[Q][Q][Q] Tree Tops Cleveragh Road (on N4) ☎(071) 6016(FAX (071) 62301
Closed 16 Dec-14 Jan
This modern home stands in a woodland setting on the Dublin edge of Sligo town, off the N4 Sligo to Dublin road. En suite bedrooms are very well appointed, with colour TVs and telephones, and attractively decorated.
5rm(4🚿) (2fb) 🚭 CTV in all bedrooms **T** 🐕 * sB&B🚿IR£19 dB&BIR£27 dB&B🚿IR£31
♨ CTV
Credit Cards [1] [3]

FH [Q][Q] Mrs E Stuart **Hillside** *(G720394)* Enniskillen Rd (on N16) ☎(071) 42808
Apr-Oct
Situated in the heart of Yeats Country on the Sligo/Enniskillen road (N16) offering comfortable accommodation. Pony and donkey for children.
4rm(2🚿) (4fb) 🚭 in bedrooms 🚭 in dining room * sB&BIR£16-IR£18.50 sB&B🚿IR£19.50 dB&BIR£28-IR£31 dB&B🚿IR£31 WB&BfrIR£90 WBDifrIR£185 LDO 3pm
♨ CTV 65 acres beef dairy
Credit Cards [3]

SPIDDAL Co Galway Map **01** B

T&C[Q][Q] Ard Aoibhinn Cnocan-Glas ☎Galway(091) 83179
Modern bungalow set back from road in lovely garden. Fine view over Galway Bay and Aran Islands.
6🚿 (3fb) 🚭 in 3 bedrooms 🚭 in area of dining room 🚭 in 1 lounge 🐕 (ex guide dogs) * sB&BIR£12.50-IR£15 dB&B🚿IR£25-IR£30 WB&BIR£87.50-IR£100 WBDiIR£152.50 IR£165 LDO noon
♨ CTV
Credit Cards [1] [3]

T&C[Q][Q][Q] Ardmor Country House Greenhill ☎Galway(091) 83145 FAX (091) 83145
Luxury, split-level bungalow on edge of village. Bright, comfortable rooms and lounge. Sun balcony and fine views over Galway Bay and Aran Islands.
8rm(2🛁6🚿) (4fb) 🚭 in dining room 🚭 in lounges 🐕 (ex guide dogs) * dB&B🛁🚿IR£30-IR£31
♨ CTV
Credit Cards [1] [3]

STRADBALLY Co Waterford Map **01** C

SELECTED

T&C[Q][Q][Q][Q] Carrigahilla House and Gardens Carrighilla ☎(051) 93127
This unusual building was once a convent and many fine original features remain including heavy wooden doors and wide corridors. These have been renovated and enhanced by modern facilities that have been subtly introduced. The old chapel with its stained glass windows and secret garden is

popular with visitors as are the other magnificent gardens. There is also the cheerful Willow room where guests dine (booking is requested), and an elegant sitting room for relaxation. Bedrooms are en suite and are all very comfortable. There is good parking and a sandy beach, a golf course, horse riding and walking are all to be found nearby.
5✿ CTV in 2 bedrooms ✳ sB&B✿frIR£40 dB&B✿frIR£40 LDO 4pm
⊞ CTV

STREAMSTOWN Co Westmeath   Map **01** C4

FH Q|Q Mrs M Maxwell *Woodlands* (N2286426)
☎Mullinngar(044) 26414
Mar-Oct
Large, attractive house in a sylvan setting off Mullingar/Athlone road.
6rm(2✿) (2fb) LDO 3pm
⊞ CTV 120 acres mixed
Credit Cards 3

TAGOAT Co Wexford   Map **01** D2

FH Q|Q Mrs E Doyle **Orchard Park** (T101120) Rosslare (turn left at Cushens pub in village on to R736) ☎Wexford(053) 32182
Enlarged farm bungalow in a quiet location, convenient to beach and Rosslare car ferry.
8rm(3✿) (2fb) ✍ in bedrooms ✍ in area of dining room ✍ in 1 lounge ✳ sB&BIR£15-IR£20 dB&B✿IR£30-IR£40
WB&BfrIR£95 LDO noon
CTV ℀(hard)✈ trampoline 80 acres arable

TAHILLA Co Kerry   Map **01** A2

SELECTED

GH Q|Q|Q|Q **Tahilla Cove** ☎Killarney(064) 45204
Etr-Oct
Family-run, split-level bungalow in idyllic setting on a sandy cove on Kenmare Bay.
3✿✿ Annexe 6✿✿ (4fb)T ✳ sB&B✿✿IR£40-IR£45
dB&B✿✿IR£60-IR£66 WBDiIR£280-IR£290 LDO 10am
Lic ⊞ CTV
Credit Cards 1|2|3|5

THE ROWER Co Kilkenny   Map **01** C3

FH Q|Q Mrs J Prendergast **Garranavabby House** (S7708346) on L18A) ☎Waterford(051) 23613
Apr-Oct
Two-storey, old-style farmhouse situated in scenic setting between Rivers Nore and Barrow.
5rm (2fb) ✳ dB&BfrIR£35 LDO noon
⊞ CTV 84 acres sheep & dairy

TIPPERARY Co Tipperary   Map **01** C3

GH Q|Q|Q **Ach-na-Sheen** Clonmel Road ☎(062) 51298
Closed 23-31 Dec
Large, modern bungalow, five minutes' walk from main street.
10rm(5✿✿) (2fb) ✍ in 8 bedrooms ✍ in dining room ✍ in 1 lounge ✳ sB&BIR£15-IR£16 sB&B✿✿IR£17.50-IR£18.50
dB&BIR£27-IR£29 dB&B✿✿IR£31-IR£33
⊞ CTV
Credit Cards 1|2|3|5

TOBERCURRY Co Sligo   Map **01** B4

&CQ|Q|Q|Q **Cruckawn House** Ballymote/Boyle Road ☎Sligo(071) 85188 FAX (071) 85239

The Walsh family offer a warm welcome at this guesthouse on the outskirts of town, in a scenic area which offers good fishing, horse riding and pony trekking.
5✿✿ (1fb)CTV in all bedrooms ✿ (ex guide dogs)
sB&B✿✿IR£16-IR£18 dB&B✿✿IR£30 LDO 6pm
⊞ CTV ▶9 ℀(hard)squash snooker sauna gymnasium
Credit Cards 1|3

TRALEE Co Kerry   Map **01** A2

T&CQ **Cnoc Mhuire** Oakpark Road (on N69) ☎(066) 26027
Closed Xmas
Modern home on the Listowel road backed by a pleasant park. Convenient for Shannon car ferry.
5rm(3✿✿) (5fb) ✍ in 2 bedrooms ✍ in area of dining room Ⓡ ✳
sB&BfrIR£15 sB&B✿frIR£18 dB&BfrIR£27 dB&B✿frIR£28
LDO noon
⊞ CTV
Credit Cards 1|2|3

TRAMORE Co Waterford   Map **01** C2

T&CQ|Q **Rushmere House** Branch Rd
☎Waterford(051) 381041
Closed Xmas & New Year
Three-storey, 100-year-old semi-detached house situated on main road overlooking sea, with well-tended gardens.
6rm(3✿) (2fb) ✍ in dining room Ⓡ ✿ (ex guide dogs) ✳
sB&BfrIR£18 dB&BfrIR£27 dB&B✿frIR£31
⊞ CTV ♪
Credit Cards 1|2|3|5

WATERFORD Co Waterford   Map **01** C2

GH Q|Q|Q **Diamond Hill** Diamond Hill, Slieverue
☎(051) 32855 & 32254 FAX (051) 32254 ▶

A two-storey house in its own well maintained grounds with well tended flower beds and lawns. Situated on Waterford/Wexford Road.
10⇆🐾 (2fb) ✗ in 4 bedrooms ✗ in dining room Ⓡ 🐾 (ex guide dogs) ✳ dB&B⇆🐾IR£25-IR£34
📷 CTV
Credit Cards ① ③

T&CQ̲Q̲ Villa Eildon Belmont Road, Ferrybank (situated on N25 2km from Waterford City) ☎(051) 32174
Jun-Oct
Excellent house situated on New Ross/Waterford road. Beautifully furnished and decorated with a nice outlook from bedrooms.
4rm(2🐾) ✗ in 2 bedrooms ✗ in dining room 🐾 ✳ dB&BIR£30 dB&B🐾IR£36
📷 CTV nc7yrs

FH Q̲Q̲ Mrs A Forrest *Ashbourne House (S6631140)* Slieverue (2.5m E of Waterford, off N25 Waterford/Wexford Rd, signposted) ☎(051) 32037
Apr-Oct
A comfortable ivy-clad house on the main N25 Waterford/Wexford road. Turn off at the Slieverue sign 2 miles from Waterford. Hospitality is guaranteed from the charming owner Mrs Forrest.
7rm(6🐾) (5fb) LDO 3pm
CTV ∪ 20 acres beef

WATERVILLE Co Kerry   Map **01** A2

T&CQ̲Q̲ Golf Links View Murreigh ☎(066) 74623
Apr-Oct
A new house stands in developing gardens outside the town. Bedrooms are well appointed and have good views.
4⇆🐾 🐾 ✳ sB&B⇆🐾IR£15-IR£18.50 dB&B⇆🐾IR£27-IR£30 WB&BfrIR£85 WBDifrIR£155
📷 CTV

T&CQ̲Q̲Q̲ Klondyke House New Line Road (on N70) ☎(066) 74119 FAX (066) 74666
An attractive house at the western end of the village. Recently extended and refurbished to high standards. A nice sun lounge to the front has views over Waterville Bay. Bedrooms are comfortable with semi-orthopaedic beds and large showers en-suite. Breakfast features an excellent choice including an attractive fruit plate, fresh fruit yoghurts and homebaked breads.
6🐾 (1fb) Ⓡ 🐾 (ex guide dogs)
📷 CTV ò̸ Q̧(hard)
Credit Cards ① ③

T&CQ̲Q̲Q̲ O'Gradys Spunkane ☎(066) 74350
6🐾 (2fb) ✗ in dining room Ⓡ 🐾 ✳ sB&B🐾IR£20 dB&B🐾IR£28
📷 CTV
Credit Cards ① ③

WESTPORT Co Mayo   Map **01** B4

FH Q̲Q̲Q̲ Mrs M O'Brien **Rath-a-Rosa** *(L953822)* Rossbeg ☎(098) 25348
Mar-Oct
A modern bungalow on R335, overlooking Clew Bay.
6rm(4⇆🐾) (2fb) ✗ in bedrooms ✗ in dining room 🐾 (ex guide dogs) ✳ sB&BIR£16-IR£18 sB&B⇆🐾IR£20-IR£25 dB&BIR£28 dB&B⇆🐾IR£30-IR£32
📷 CTV 20 acres beef sheep
Credit Cards ① ③

FH Q̲Q̲Q̲ M O'Malley **Seapoint House** *(L972897)* Kilmeena ☎(098) 41254
Apr-Oct
Large and luxurious modern, two-storey farmhouse set in 40 acres on Clew Bay.

6⇆🐾 (4fb) ✗ in 2 bedrooms ✗ in dining room ✗ in lounges CTV in 2 bedrooms Ⓡ 🐾 sB&B⇆🐾frIR£20 dB&B⇆🐾frIR£30 WB&BfrIR£100 WBDifrIR£182 LDO 1pm
📷 CTV sea angling 40 acres mixed

WEXFORD Co Wexford   Map **01** D3

SELECTED

T&CQ̲Q̲Q̲Q̲ Ardruagh Spawell Road ☎(053) 23194
Closed 17 Dec-7 Jan
A former Vicarage, this magnificent house on the edge of Wexford looks out over the roofs of houses to the estuary in Wexford. The bedrooms and public rooms are spacious and luxurious and the Corish family take a particular pride in looking after their guests.
5🐾 (2fb) ✗ in dining room CTV in all bedrooms Ⓡ 🐾 (ex guide dogs) ✳ sB&B🐾IR£20 dB&B🐾IR£33
📷 CTV
Credit Cards ① ③

T&CQ̲Q̲Q̲ Auburn House 2 Auburn Terrace, Redmond Road ☎(053) 23605
Closed 23 Dec-2 Jan
Auburn House is the second in a terrace of three houses near the station and should not be confused with the similarly named house next-door. Bedrooms are attractive and the public rooms are comfortable.
5rm(4🐾) (4fb) ✗ in dining room CTV in 4 bedrooms Ⓡ 🐾 (ex guide dogs) ✳ sB&BfrIR£18 sB&B🐾frIR£18 dB&B🐾frIR£30 WB&BfrIR£100
📷 CTV
Credit Cards ① ③

GH Q̲Q̲ Faythe Swan View ☎(053) 22249
This fine old house is centrally situated in a quiet part of the town. A new owner has upgraded the bedrooms which are now very comfortable with new bathrooms. Evening meals are available by arrangement and there is ample car parking.
10⇆🐾 (4fb) CTV in all bedrooms Ⓡ T 🐾 (ex guide dogs) ✳ dB&B⇆🐾IR£32-IR£39 LDO 7.30pm
Lic 📷 CTV
Credit Cards ① ③

T&CQ̲Q̲Q̲ Rathaspeck Manor Rathaspeck ☎(053) 42661 & 45148
Jun-Oct
Standing in its own grounds, which feature an 18-hole par-3 golf course, this 300-year-old restored Georgian country house is situated half a mile from Johnstone Castle. The comfortable, spacious bedrooms are en suite and the public rooms are appointed with period furnishings. Hospitable Mrs Cuddihy will provide dinner by arrangement and the guesthouse holds a wine licence. Good parking is available.
7⇆🐾 (3fb)CTV in all bedrooms Ⓡ 🐾 ✳ dB&B⇆🐾IR£40 WB&BfrIR£130 LDO noon
📷 nc10yrs ▶18 Q̧(hard)

T&CQ̲Q̲Q̲ Tara Villa Larkins Cross, Barntown (on main Wexford/New Ross route) ☎(053) 45119 FAX (053) 45119
Mar-Nov
Situated on main Wexford/New Ross route (N25) go past the sign for Barntown, continue on main road until a large pink house is reached where a warm welcome awaits the traveller from proprietors Mr and Mrs Whitty.
6🐾 (3fb) ✗ in 1 bedrooms CTV in all bedrooms Ⓡ 🐾 (ex guide dogs) ✳ dB&B🐾IR£30-IR£35 LDO 8pm
Lic 📷 CTV pool table
Credit Cards ① ③

WICKLOW Co Wicklow   Map **01** D3

SELECTED

GH Ⓠ Ⓠ Ⓠ Ⓠ **The Old Rectory Country House & Restaurant** (on R750, 1m S of Rathnew) ☎(0404) 67048 FAX (0404) 69181

Apr-Oct

A charming Victorian rectory has been converted into a very attractive guesthouse on the outskirts of Wicklow town. Paul and Linda Saunders are the hospitable owners, to whom all credit is due for the relaxing atmosphere and the standard of the accommodation. The well equipped bedrooms are all individually styled, with period furniture, while the public rooms have marble fireplaces and high, corniced ceilings. The popular Orangery Restaurant is the showcase for Linda's innovative cooking. It is for these reasons that The Old Rectory has been designated 'Guesthouse of the Year' 1995 for Ireland.

5⇨🅟 (1fb) ⊬ in dining room ⊬ in 1 lounge CTV in all bedrooms Ⓡ T 🕇 sB&B⇦🅟IR£45-IR£67 dB&B⇦🅟IR£90 WB&BIR£236-IR£252 WBDiIR£373-IR£398 LDO 6pm Lic ▥

Credit Cards [1] [2] [3] [5]

H Ⓠ Ⓠ Ⓠ Mrs P Klaue **Lissadell House** (*T3302925*) Ashtown Lane ☎(0404) 67458

Mar-Dec

This two-storey modern house stands in its own grounds in scenic location on the outskirts of town.

4rm(1⇨1🅟) (1fb) ⊬ in bedrooms ⊬ in dining room 🕇 (ex guide dogs) ✶ sB&BIR£19 sB&B⇦🅟IR£21 dB&BIR£28 dB&B⇦🅟IR£32 LDO noon

▥ CTV 285 acres mixed

YOUGHAL Co Cork   Map **01** C2

SELECTED

GH Ⓠ Ⓠ Ⓠ Ⓠ **Ahernes** 163 North Main Street (on N25) ☎(024) 92424 FAX (024) 93633

Closed Xmas & Good Friday

Offering accommodation in spacious bedrooms, furnished to the highest standard with antiques and modern facilities, this pleasant guesthouse boasts an award-winning restaurant, well known for its seafood specialities. There is a cosy drawing room provided for guests and parking is available.

10⇨🅟 ⊬ in area of dining room CTV in all bedrooms T 🕇 (ex guide dogs) ✶ sB&B⇦🅟IR£50-IR£60 dB&B⇦🅟IR£35-IR£50 LDO 9.30pm

Lic ▥

Credit Cards [1] [2] [3] [5]

FH Ⓠ Mrs E Long **Cherrymount** (*X0071823*) ☎(024) 97110

This 500-year-old farmhouse is situated on high ground off the main N25 road near Youghal. Simple in style, a friendly welcome is offered by owner Mrs Long.

5rm (2fb) LDO 5pm

▥ CTV ▶18 ⚲(hard)70 acres dairy

Credit Cards [1] [2] [3]

BUDGET BED & BREAKFAST

Establishments offering bed and breakfast for £15 or less per person per night are listed below. Please note that the fact that a room and breakfast are available at this bargain rate does not mean that every room in the establishment is available at this price. For example, it may be that rooms with en suite bath or shower are more expensive.

ENGLAND

AVON
KEYNSHAM
Uplands

CHESHIRE
CHESTER
Egerton Lodge

CORNWALL
BOSCASTLE
Old Coach House
BOSCASTLE
Trerosewill
BUDE
Pencarrol
FALMOUTH
Dolvean Hotel
Treggenna
Trelawney
GRAMPOUND
Perran House
NEWQUAY
Aloha
Hotel Trevalsa
Windward Hotel
PENZANCE
Dunedin
Trenant Private
  Hotel
Trewella
POLBATHIC
The Old Mill
PORTHCURNO
Corniche

ST IVES
Chy-an-Creet Private
  Hotel
TINTAGEL
Castle Villa
TROON
Sea View
Land's Vue

CUMBRIA
CARLISLE
Blackwell
Howard House
Kenilworth
Warren
CASTLE CARROCK
Gelt Hall
KESWICK
Avondale
Goodwin House
RAVENSTONEDALE
Kings Head
SHAP
Green Farm
WINDERMERE
Aaron Slack
Green Gables
Haisthorpe
Kenilworth
Lynwood

DEVON
BEER
Bay View
CHERITON FITZPAINE
Brindiwell

HOLSWORTHY
Woodlands
HONITON
Roebuck
ILFRACOMBE
Southcliffe Hotel
LYNTON
Retreat
MARY TAVY
Wringworthy
NORTH MOLTON
Homedale
PAIGNTON
Channel View Hotel
Cherra Hotel
PLYMOUTH
Elizabethan
Grosvenor Park
  Hotel
White House Hotel
SOUTH MOLTON
Kerscott
TEIGNMOUTH
Hill Rise Hotel
TORQUAY
Beauly
Chesterfield Hotel
Clovelly
Cranborne Hotel
Fircroft
Gainsborough
  Hotel
Jesmond Dene
  Private Hotel
WHITESTONE
Rowhorne House

DORSET
BOURNEMOUTH
Amitie
Cransley Private Hotel
Hotel Sorrento
Mayfield Private Hotel
Thanet Private Hotel
Tudor Grange Hotel
SWANAGE
Crowthorne Hotel
Firswood Hotel

GLOUCESTERSHIRE
CHELTENHAM
Manor Barn
STOW-ON-THE-WOLD
Corsham Field

HAMPSHIRE
PORTSMOUTH &
SOUTHSEA
Collingham
Elms
SOUTHAMPTON
Madison House

KENT
CANTERBURY
Cathedral Gate Hotel
DYMCHURCH
Waterside

LANCASHIRE
BLACKPOOL
Ashcroft Private Hotel
Colby Hotel

Lynwood
North Mount
  Private Hotel
Sunny Cliff
Surrey House Hotel
Woodleigh
  Private Hotel

LINCOLNSHIRE
ANCASTER
Woodlands
HAINTON
Old Vicarage

NORFOLK
YARMOUTH, GREAT
Spindrift

NORTHUMBERLAND
BERWICK-UPON-
TWEED
Old Vicarage
ROCHESTER
Woolaw

SHROPSHIRE
SHREWSBURY
Roseville

SOMERSET
MINEHEAD
Avill House
NORTH WOOTTON
Barrow Farm

SUSSEX, EAST
ROTTINGDEAN
Braemar House
SEAFORD
Silverdale

WARWICKSHIRE
ETTINGTON
Whitfield
LEAMINGTON SPA
(ROYAL)
Charnwood
STRATFORD-UPON-
AVON
Penryn House

WIMPSTONE
Whitchurch

WIGHT, ISLE OF
SANDOWN
Chester Lodge Hotel
SHANKLIN
Soraba Private Hotel

WILTSHIRE
MALMESBURY
Stonehill

YORKSHIRE, NORTH
PICKERING
Bramwood
SCARBOROUGH
Meadow Court
Ramleh
Rayvil Hotel
YORK
Acorn
Avenue
Beckett
Jubilee
Staymor

BORDERS
BURNMOUTH
Greystonelees

DUMFRIES &
GALLOWAY
DALBEATTIE
Pheasant Hotel

FIFE
DUNFERMLINE
Hopetoun Lodge
ST ANDREWS
Cleveden House

HIGHLAND
AVIEMORE
Craiglea
DRUMNADROCHIT
Linne Dhuinn

FORT WILLIAM
Benview
GRANTOWN-ON-SPEY
Brooklynn
SPEAN BRIDGE
Coire Glas
SPEAN BRIDGE
Inverour

STRATHCLYDE
AYR
Langley Bank
CONNEL
Ronebhal
KILMARNOCK
Eriskay
OBAN
Briarbank
Glenroy
Roseneath
Sgeir Mhaol

TAYSIDE
BLAIR ATHOLL
Dalgreine
BLAIRGOWRIE
Norwood House
COMRIE
Mossgiel
PERTH
Heidl
Iona
Ochil View

ANGLESEY, ISLE OF
HOLYHEAD
Offaly
Wavecrest
TREARDDUR BAY
Moranedd

CLWYD
CORWEN
Corwen Court
  Private Hotel
MARFORD
Brackenwood

PRESTATYN
Roughsedge House

DYFED
CARDIGAN
Brynhyfryd
CWMDUAD
Neuadd-Wen
TENBY
Castle View
  Private Hotel

GWYNEDD
BALA
Eirianfa
Erw Feurig
CONWY
Glan Heulog
DOLGELLAU
Glyn
LLANDUDNO
Bryn Rosa
Rosaire Private Hotel

POWYS
LLANDRINDOD WELLS
Kincoed
LLANGURIG
Old Vicarage

CO GALWAY
CLIFDEN
Ben View House

CO GALWAY
CLIFDEN
Failte

CO KERRY
KILLARNEY
Glebe

CO WEXFORD
BALLYHACK
Marsh Mere Lodge

CO WEXFORD
NEW ROSS
Millfield House

AA

ONE-STAR CLASSIFIED HOTELS

Although there are no star-rated hotels in the directory of this guide, the following quick-reference list, in country and county order, gives the telephone number to call for further details. All the hotels listed will be found in the 1995 edition of the AA HOTELS guide.

C. ISLANDS

SARK
Stocks Island Hotel
(0481) 832001

ENGLAND

CAMBRIDGESHIRE
CHATTERIS
Cross Keys Hotel
(0354) 693036
ELY
Nyton Hotel
(0353) 662459
MARCH
Olde Griffin Hotel
(0354) 52517

CHESHIRE
CHESTER
Leahurst Court Hotel
(0244) 327542
CHESTER
The Weston Hotel
(0244) 326735
ELLESMERE PORT
Woodcore Hotel and
Restaurant
051-327 1542
MACCLESFIELD
Moorhayes House Hotel
(0625) 433228
WARRINGTON
Kenilworth Hotel
(0925) 262323

CLEVELAND
MIDDLESBROUGH

Grey House Hotel
(0642) 817485

CORNWALL & ISLES OF SCILLY
BUDE
Meva Gwin Hotel
(0288) 352347
HARLYN BAY
Polmark Hotel
(0841) 520206
MOUNT HAWKE
Tregarthen Country
Cottage Hotel
(0209) 890399
NEWQUAY
Trevone Hotel
(0637) 873039
PENZANCE
Estoril Hotel
(0736) 62468
Tarbert Hotel
(0736) 63758
PERRANPORTH
Beach Dunes Hotel
(0872) 572263
POLPERRO
Claremont Hotel
(0503) 72241
ST AGNES
Sunholme Hotel
(0872) 552318
ST AUSTELL
Selwood House Hotel
(0726) 65707
ST IVES
Dunmar Hotel
(0736) 796117
Hotel Rotorua
(0736) 795419

TALLAND BAY
Allhays Country House
(0503) 72434

CUMBRIA
AMBLESIDE
Gables Hotel
(05394) 33272
APPLEBY-IN-WESTMORLAND
Courtfield Hotel
(07683) 51394
BEETHAM
Wheatsheaf Hotel
(05395) 62123
BROUGHTON IN FURNESS
Old King's Head Hotel
(0229) 716293
CARLISLE
Vallum House
Garden Hotel
(0228) 21860
CONISTON
The Old Rectory Hotel
(05394) 41353
GRANGE-OVER-SANDS
Clare House
(05395) 33026 &
GRASMERE
White Moss House
(05394) 35295
KESWICK
Highfield Hotel
(07687) 72508
Linnett Hill Hotel
(07687) 73109
Priorholme Hotel
(07687) 72745
Swinside Lodge
(07687) 72948

LOWESWATER
Grange Country House
Hotel
(0946) 861211
MARYPORT
Waverley Hotel
(0900) 812115
MUNGRISDALE
The Mill Hotel
(07687) 79659
PENRITH
Glen Cottage Hotel
(0768) 62221
WINDERMERE
Willowsmere Hotel
(05394) 43575
WITHERSLACK
Old Vicarage
Country House Hotel
(05395) 52381

DERBYSHIRE
BUXTON
Hartington Hotel
(0298) 22638

DEVON
BARNSTAPLE
Halmpstone Manor
(0271) 830321
BIGBURY-ON-SEA
Henley Hotel
(0548) 810240
BRIXHAM
Smuggler's Haunt
Hotel & Restaurant
(0803) 853050
CLOVELLY
Red Lion Hotel
(0237) 431237

492

XMOUTH
liston House Hotel
0395) 274119
FRACOMBE
orrs Hotel
0271) 862334
IFTON
hatched Cottage
ountry Hotel
0566) 784224
YNMOUTH
elephone numbers are
ue to change during the
urrency of this guide)
ock House Hotel
0598) 53508
YNTON
elephone numbers are
ue to change during the
urrency of this guide)
hough's Nest Hotel
0598) 53315
ombe Park Hotel
0598) 52356
airholme Hotel
0598) 52263
orth Cliff Hotel
0598) 52357
ockvale Hotel
0598) 52279
53343
eawood Hotel
0598) 52272
EWTON ABBOT
azelwood Hotel
0626) 66130
AIGNTON
outh Sands Hotel
0803) 557231
LYMOUTH
rake Hotel
0752) 229730
nperial Hotel
0752) 227311
ictoria Court Hotel
0752) 668133
ALCOMBE
unny Cliff Hotel
0548) 842207
Voodgrange Hotel
0548) 42439
TAVERTON
ea Trout Inn
0803) 762274

TEIGNMOUTH
Belvedere Hotel
(0626) 774561
Glenside Hotel
(0626) 872448
TORCROSS
Grey Homes Hotel
(0548) 580220
TORQUAY
Ashley Rise Hotel
(0803) 327282
Fairmount House
Hotel
(0803) 605446
Hotel Fluela
(0803) 297512
Rawlyn House
(0803) 605208
Shelley Court Hotel
(0803) 295642
Sunleigh Hotel
(0803) 607137
Westwood Hotel
(0803) 293818
WOOLACOMBE
Crossways Hotel
(0271) 870395

DORSET
BOURNEMOUTH
Lynden Court Hotel
(0202) 553894
Montague Hotel
(0202) 551074
Taurus Park
(0202) 557374
BRIDPORT
Bridge House Hotel
(0308) 423371
Bridport Arms Hotel
(0308) 422994
LYME REGIS
Tudor House Hotel
(0297) 442472
POOLE
Fairlight Hotel
(0202) 694316
WEST LULWORTH
Shirley Hotel
(0929) 400358
WEYMOUTH
Alexandra Hotel
(0305) 785767

ESSEX
CLACTON-ON-SEA
Chudleigh Hotel
(0255) 425407
FRINTON-ON-SEA
Rock Hotel
(0255) 677194
SOUTHEND-ON-SEA
Balmoral Hotel
(0702) 342947

GLOUCESTERSHIRE
CHELTENHAM
Regency House Hotel
(0242) 582718
GLOUCESTER
Rotherfield House
Hotel
(0452) 410500

GREATER
MANCHESTER
ALTRINCHAM
The Unicorn Hotel
061-980 4347
ASHTON-UNDER-LYNE
Welbeck House Hotel
061-344 0751
BURY
Woolfield House Hotel
061-797 9775
MARPLE
Springfield Hotel
061-449 0721
SALFORD
Beaucliffe Hotel
061-789 5092

HAMPSHIRE
LYNDHURST
Knightwood Lodge
(0703) 282502

HEREFORD &
WORCESTER
LEOMINSTER
Marsh Country Hotel
(0568) 613952
MALVERN
Bredon House
(0684) 566990
WORCESTER
Park House Hotel
(0905) 21816

HUMBERSIDE
FLAMBOROUGH
Flaneburg Hotel
(0262) 850284
POCKLINGTON
Yorkway Motel
(0759) 303071

LANCASHIRE
BLACKPOOL
Kimberley Hotel
(0253) 341184
LYTHAM ST ANNES
Ennes Court Hotel
(0253) 723731
Lindum Hotel
(0253) 721534

LEICESTERSHIRE
UPPINGHAM
Crown Hotel
(0572) 822302

MERSEYSIDE
RAINHILL
Rockland Hotel
051-426 4603

NORFOLK
CAWSTON
Grey Gables Hotel
(0603) 871259
DOWNHAM MARKET
Crosskeys
Riverside Hotel
(0366) 387777
EAST DEREHAM
George Hotel
(0362) 696801
HUNSTANTON
Wash & Tope Hotel
(0485) 532250
THETFORD
Wereham House Hotel
(0842) 761956
WELLS-NEXT-THE-SEA
Scarborough House
Hotel
(0328) 710309

NORTHUMBERLAND
BAMBURGH
Mizen Head Hotel
(0668) 214254

Sunningdale Hotel
(0668) 214334
BARDON MILL
Vallum Lodge Hotel
(0434) 344248
BERWICK-UPON-TWEED
Queens Head
(0289) 307852

OXFORDSHIRE
OXFORD
River Hotel
(0865) 727627

SHROPSHIRE
SHREWSBURY
Abbots Mead Hotel
(0743) 235281
WHITTINGTON
Ye Olde Boot Inn
(0691) 662250

SOMERSET
WELLS
Ancient Gate House
Hotel
(0749) 672029
WILLITON
Curdon Mill
(0984) 56522
YEOVIL
Little Barwick House
(0935) 23902
Preston Hotel
(0935) 74400

SUFFOLK
CLARE
The Clare Hotel
(0787) 277449
LAVENHAM
Angel Hotel
(0787) 247388
LEISTON
White Horse Hotel
(0728) 830694
SAXMUNDHAM
Bell Hotel
(0728) 602331

SUSSEX, EAST
EASTBOURNE
Lathom Hotel
(0323) 720985

TYNE & WEAR
WHITLEY BAY
Cavendish Hotel
091-253 3010

WARWICKSHIRE
LEAMINGTON SPA
Lansdowne Hotel
(0926) 450505
Milverton House
Hotel
(0926) 428335
WARWICK
Penderrick Hotel
(0926) 499399

WILTSHIRE
MERE
Talbot Hotel
(0747) 860427
TROWBRIDGE
Hilbury Court Hotel
(0225) 752949

YORKSHIRE, NORTH
GOATHLAND
Whitfield House
Hotel
(0947) 896215
GRASSINGTON
Black Horse Hotel
(0756) 752770
HARROGATE
Alvera Court Hotel
(0423) 505735
Britannia Lodge Hotel
(0423) 508482
Croft Hotel
(0423) 563326
Duchy Hotel
(0423) 565818
Gables Hotel
(0423) 505625
Grafton Hotel
(0423) 508491
Scotia House Hotel
(0423) 504361
LEYBURN
Golden Lion Hotel
(0969) 22161
MALTON
Newstead Grange
(0653) 692502

Wentworth Arms
(0653) 692618
ROBIN HOOD'S BAY
Grosvenor Hotel
(0947) 880320
THIRSK
Old Red House
(0845) 524383
THORNTON WATLASS
Buck Inn Hotel
(0677) 422461

YORKSHIRE, WEST
BRADFORD
Park Grove
(0274) 543444
ILKLEY
Grove Hotel
(0943) 600298
Moorview House Hotel
(0943) 600156
LEEDS
Aragon Hotel
(0532) 759306

SCOTLAND

CENTRAL
CALLANDER
Highland House Hotel
(0877) 330269
LOCHEARNHEAD
Lochearnhead Hotel
(0567) 830229
Mansewood
Country House Hotel
(0567) 830213
ROWARDENNAN
Rowardennan Hotel
Loch Lomond
(036087) 273

DUMFRIES & GALLOWAY
CROCKETFORD
Lochview Motel
(0556) 690281
LOCKERBIE
Ravenshill House Hotel
(0576) 202882
MOFFAT
Well View Hotel
(0683) 20184

PORTPATRICK
Mount Stewart Hotel
(0776) 810291

FIFE
CRAIL
Croma Hotel
(0333) 450239

GRAMPIAN
BRIDGE OF MARNOCH
Old Manse of Marnoch
(0466) 780873
OLDMELDRUM
Meldrum Arms Hotel
(0651) 872238

HIGHLAND
ARDELVE
Loch Duich Hotel
(059985) 213
FORT WILLIAM
Factor's House
(0397) 705767
GRANTOWN-ON-SPEY
Tyree House
(0479) 872615
HARLOSH
Harlosh House
(0470) 521367
INVERNESS
Redcliffe Hotel
(0463) 232767
ISLE ORNSAY
Hotel Eilean Iarmain
(04713) 332
(telephone number due to change during the currency of this guide)
KINGUSSIE
Osprey Hotel
(0540) 661510
PORTREE
Isles Hotel
(0478) 612129
UIG
Ferry Inn
(0470) 542242

LOTHIAN
DUNBAR
Courtyard
Hotel & Restaurant
(0368) 864169

STRATHCLYDE
AYR
Aftongrange Hotel
(0292) 265679
Almont Hotel
(0292) 263814
BUNESSAN
Assapol
Country House Hotel
(06817) 258
DERVAIG
Druimard
Country House Hotel
(06884) 345
DUNOON
Lyall Cliff Hotel
(0369) 2041
INVERARAY
Fernpoint Hotel
(0499) 2170
SCALASAIG
Colonsay Hotel
(09512) 316
TOBERMORY
*(telephone numbers are
due to change during the
currency of this guide)*
Mishnish Hotel
(0688) 2009
Ulva House Hotel
(0688) 2044

TAYSIDE
ABERFELDY
Guinach House Hotel
(0887) 820251
BRIDGE OF CALLY
Bridge of Cally Hotel
(0250) 886231
CARNOUSTIE
Station Hotel
(0241) 852447
CRIEFF
Locke's Acre Hotel
(0764) 652526
FEARNAN
Tigh-an-Loan
(0887) 830249
PERTH
Woodlea Hotel
(0738) 621744
PITLOCHRY
Fasganeoin Hotel
(0796) 472387

WALES

CLWYD
COLWYN BAY
Glyndwr Private Hotel
(0492) 533254
Marine Hotel
(0492) 530295

DYFED
ABERPORTH
Glandwr Manor Hotel
(0239) 810197
FISHGUARD
Abergwaun Hotel
(0348) 872077

GLAMORGAN, SOUTH
PENARTH
Walton House Hotel
(0222) 707782

GLAMORGAN, WEST
MUMBLES
St Anne's Hotel
(0792) 369147
PORT EINON
Culver House Hotel
(0792) 390755
SWANSEA
Parkway Hotel
(0792) 201632
Windsor Lodge Hotel
(0792) 642158

GWYNEDD
ABERDOVEY
Maybank Hotel &
Restaurant
(0654) 767500
BARMOUTH
Bryn Melyn Hotel
(0341) 280556
Llwyndu Farmhouse
(0341) 280144
BEDDGELERT
*(telephone numbers are
due to change during the
currency of this guide)*
Sygun Fawr
Country House Hotel
(076686) 258

Tanronen Hotel
(076686) 347
BETWS-Y-COED
Fairy Glen Hotel
(0690) 710269
CONWY
Old Rectory
Country House
(0492) 580611
CRICCIETH
Abereistedd Hotel
(0766) 522710
Caerwylan Hotel
(0766) 522547
DOLGELLAU
Clifton House Hotel
(0341) 422554
HARLECH
Noddfa Hotel
(0766) 780043
LLANBERIS
Gallt-y-Glyn Hotel
(0286) 870370
LLANDUDNO
Banham House
Hotel & Restaurant
(0492) 875680
Brigstock Hotel
(0492) 876416
Bryn-y-Mor Hotel
(0492) 876790
Clontarf Hotel
(0492) 877621
Concord Hotel
(0492) 875504
Crickleigh Hotel
(0492) 875926
Epperstone Hotel
(0492) 878746
Gwesty Leamore
Hotel
(0492) 875552
Heath House Hotel
(0492) 876538
Hilbre Court Hotel
(0492) 876632
Min-y-Don Hotel
(0492) 876511
Oak Alyn Hotel
(0492) 860320
Quinton Hotel
(0492) 876879
Ravenhurst Hotel
(0492) 875525

Stratford Hotel
(0492) 877962
Tan-y-Marian Private
Hotel
(0492) 877727
MALLWYD
Brigand's Inn
(0650) 531208
PWLLHELI
The Seahaven Hotel
(0758) 612572
TAL-Y-LLYN
Minffordd Hotel
(0654) 761665
TYWYN
Greenfield Hotel
(0654) 710354

POWYS
ABERCRAF
Maes-Y-Gwernen
(0639) 730218
BRECON
Lansdowne
Hotel & Restaurant
(0874) 623321
LLANWRTYD WELLS
Carlton House Hotel
(0591) 610248

N. IRELAND

CO ANTRIM
CARRICKFERGUS
Dobbins Inn
(0960) 351905

CO FERMANAGH
ENNISKILLEN
Railway Hotel
(0365) 22084

REP. OF IRELAND

CO DONEGAL
RATHMULLAN
Pier Hotel
(074) 58178

CO TIPPERARY
TIPPERARY
Royal Hotel
(062) 51204

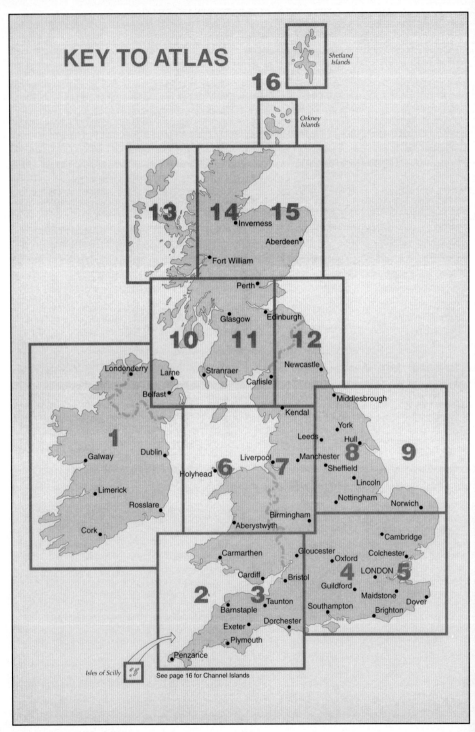

KEY TO ATLAS

Shetland Islands

16

Orkney Islands

13 **14** **15**

Inverness

Aberdeen

Fort William

Perth

Glasgow Edinburgh

10 **11** **12**

Londonderry Larne Stranraer Newcastle

Belfast Carlisle

1 Kendal Middlesbrough

York

Leeds Hull

Galway Dublin Liverpool **7** Manchester **8** **9**

Holyhead **6** Sheffield

Limerick Lincoln

Rosslare Nottingham Norwich

Cork Birmingham

Aberystwyth

Cambridge

Carmarthen Gloucester Colchester

Oxford

Cardiff Bristol **4** LONDON **5**

2 **3** Guildford

Taunton Maidstone Dover

Barnstaple Southampton

Dorchester Brighton

Exeter

Plymouth

Penzance

Isles of Scilly See page 16 for Channel Islands

© The Automobile Association 1994

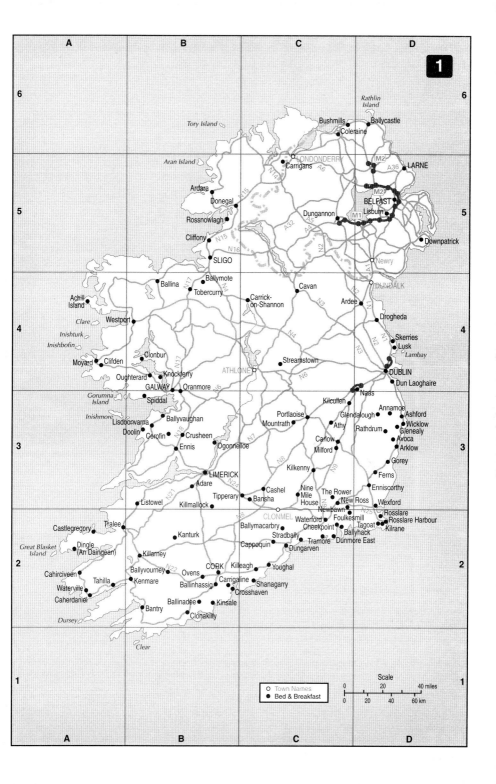

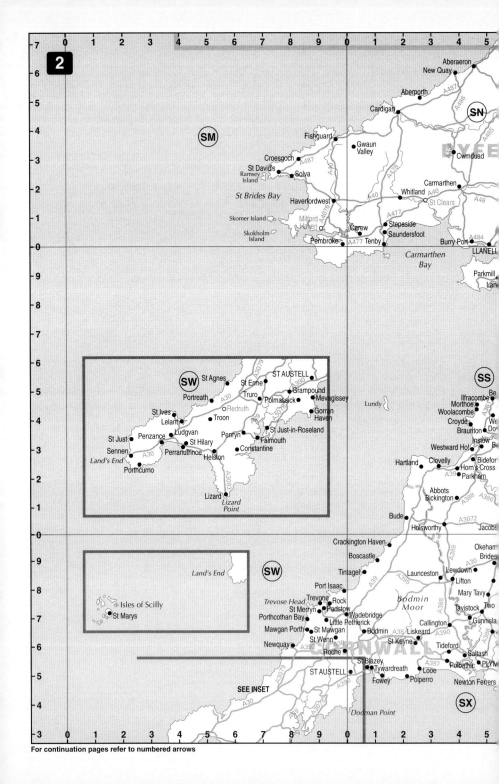

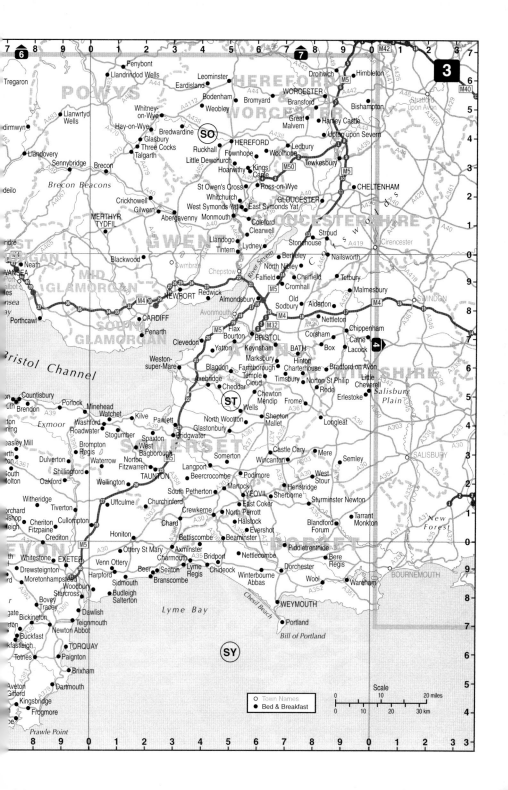

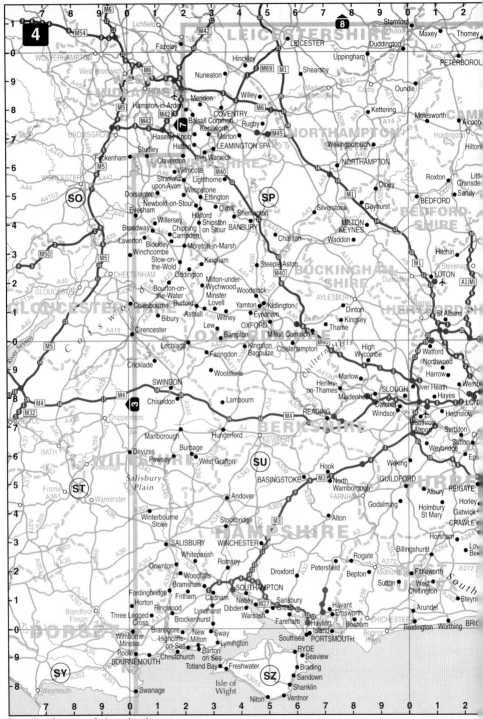

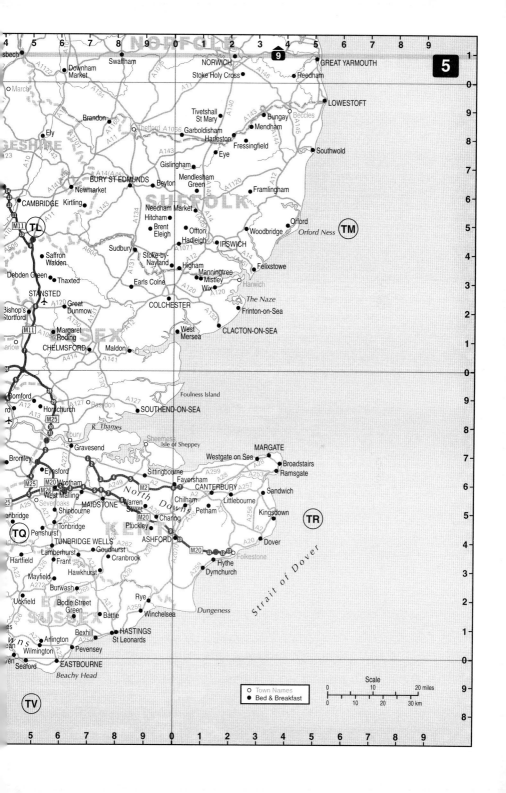

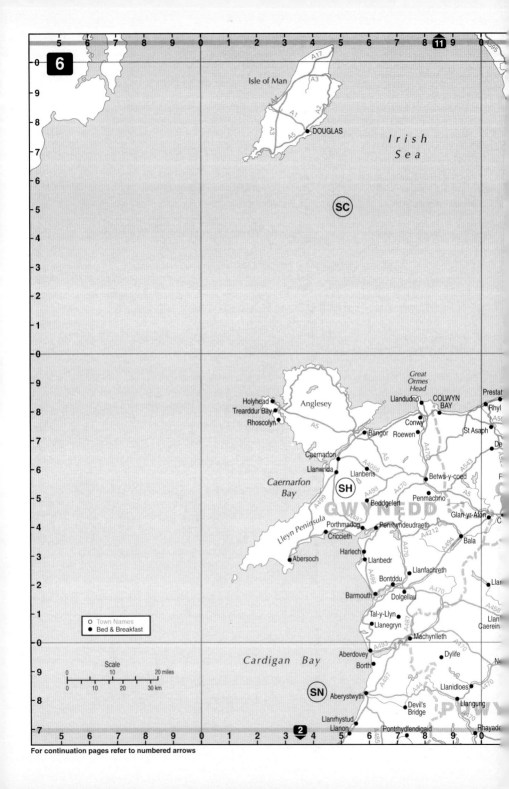

Isle of Man

A17

A3

A1

A2

A3

A5

DOUGLAS

Irish Sea

SC

Great Ormes Head

Holyhead
Trearddur Bay
Rhoscolyn

Anglesey

A5

Llandudno

COLWYN BAY

Prestat

Rhyl

A55

Conwy
Roewen

St Asaph

De

Bangor

Caernarfon

Caernarfon Bay

Llanwnda

Llanberis

A4086

A5

Betws-y-coed

F

SH

A543

GWYNEDD

A493

A470

A5

Beddgelert

Penmachno

Glan-yr-Afon

C

Lleyn Peninsula

A499

A487

Porthmadog

Penrhyndeudraeth

A4212

Bala

A494

Criccieth

Abersoch

Harlech

Llanbedr

Llanfachreth

Lla

A496

Bontddu

A470

Barmouth

Dolgellau

A458

Tal-y-Llyn

Llanegryn

A487

Machynlleth

A493

Llan
Caerein

Cardigan Bay

Aberdovey
Borth

Dylife

N

A44

Llanidloes

A470

Llangurig

SN

Aberystwyth

A487

Devil's Bridge

POWY

○ Town Names
● Bed & Breakfast

Scale
0   10   20 miles
0   10   20   30 km

Llanrhystud

Llanon

2

Pontrhydfendigaid

Rhayade

A485

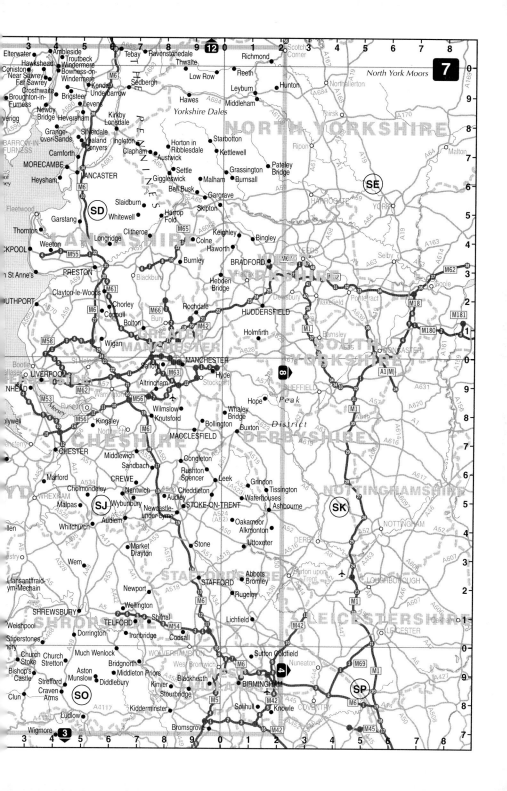

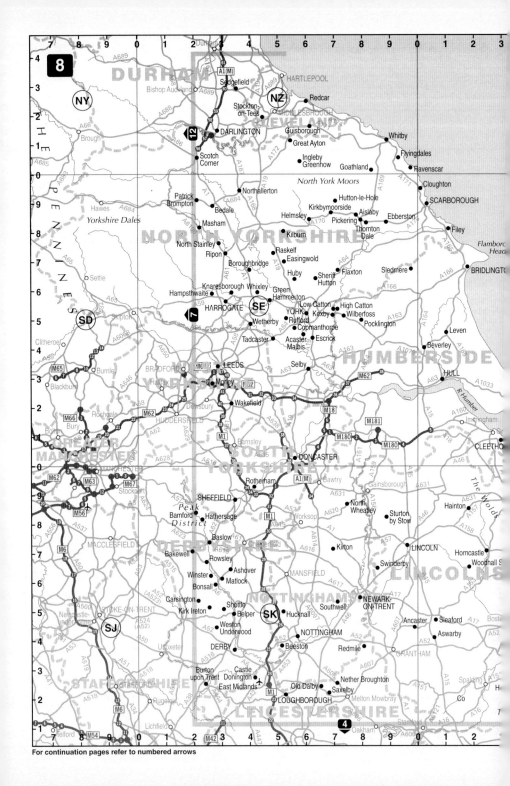

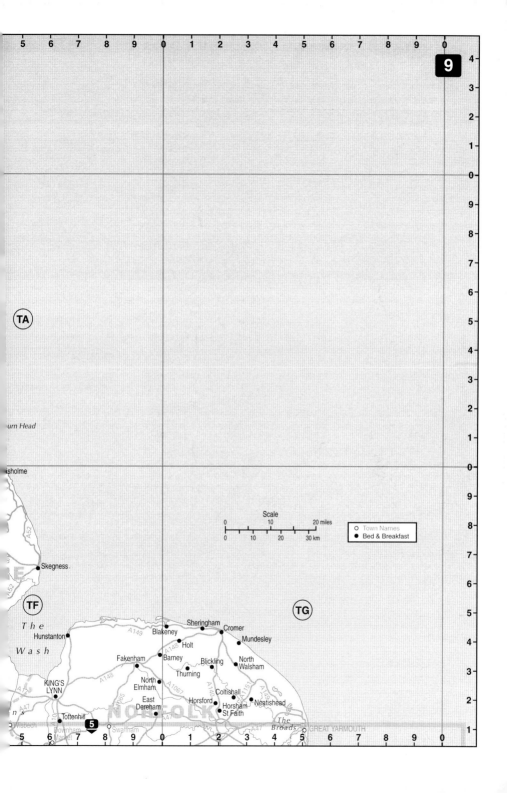

9

5 6 7 8 9 0 1 2 3 4 5 6 7 8 9 0

4
3
2
1
0
9
8
7
6
5
4
3
2
1
0
9
8
7
6
5
4
3
2
1

(TA)

urn Head

isholme

Scale
0   10   20 miles
0   10   20   30 km

○ Town Names
● Bed & Breakfast

Skegness

(TF)

(TG)

The
Hunstanton   Sheringham   Cromer
Blakeney   Mundesley
W a s h   Holt
              Barney   North
Fakenham   Blickling   Walsham
                  Thurning
KING'S   North   Coltishall
LYNN   Elmham   Horsford   Neatishead
              East   Horsham
n s   Dereham   Horsford   St Faith   *The*
Tottenhill   *Broads*   GREAT YARMOUTH
Wisbech Downham   A47
         Market Swaffham

5 6 7 8 9 0 1 2 3 4 5 6 7 8 9 0

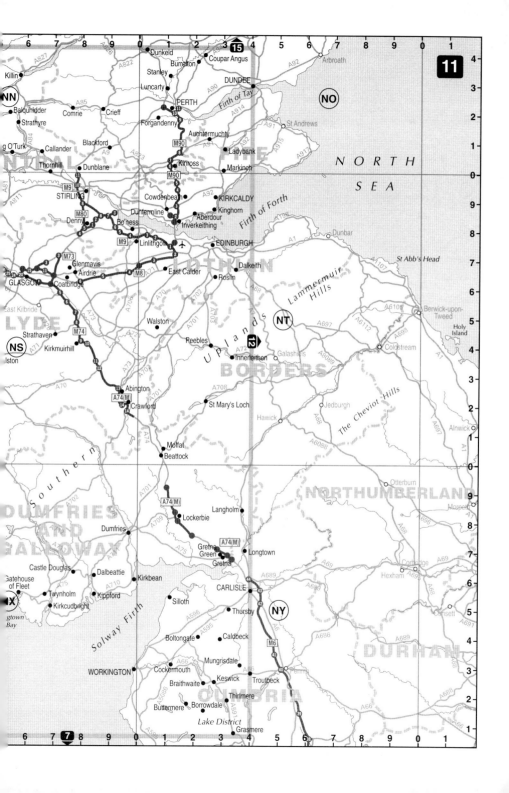

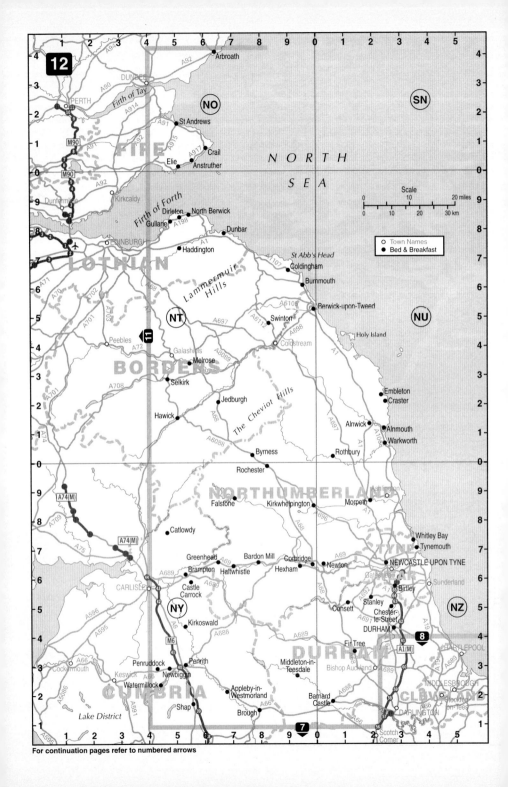

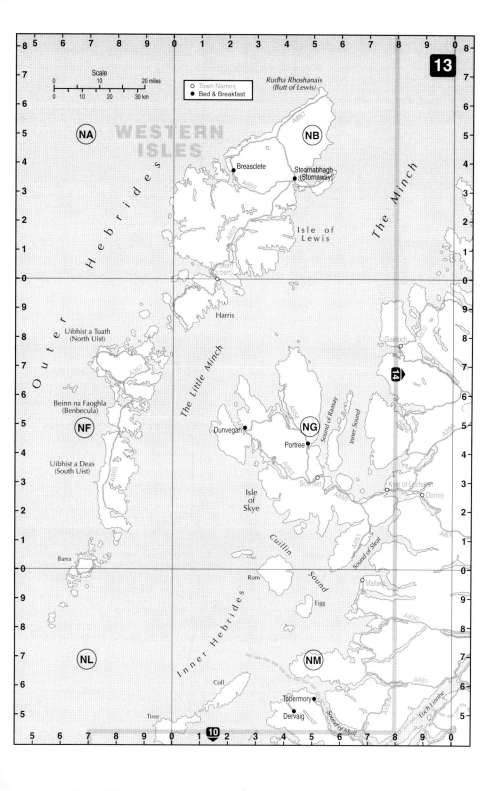

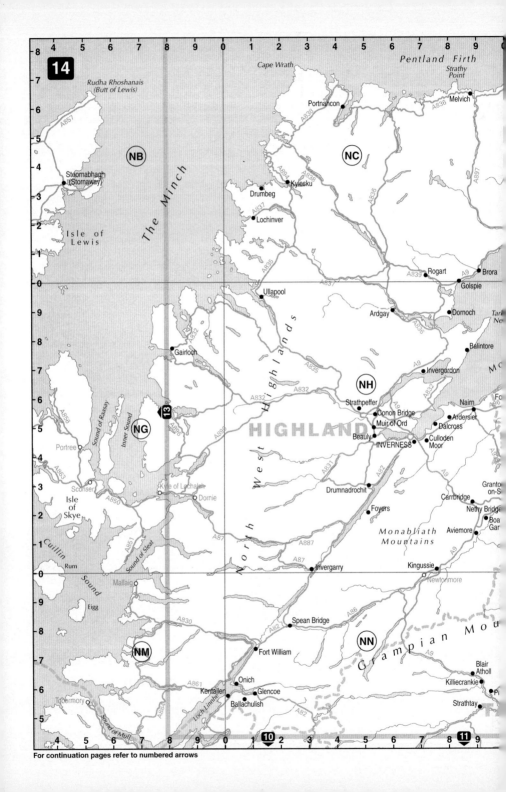

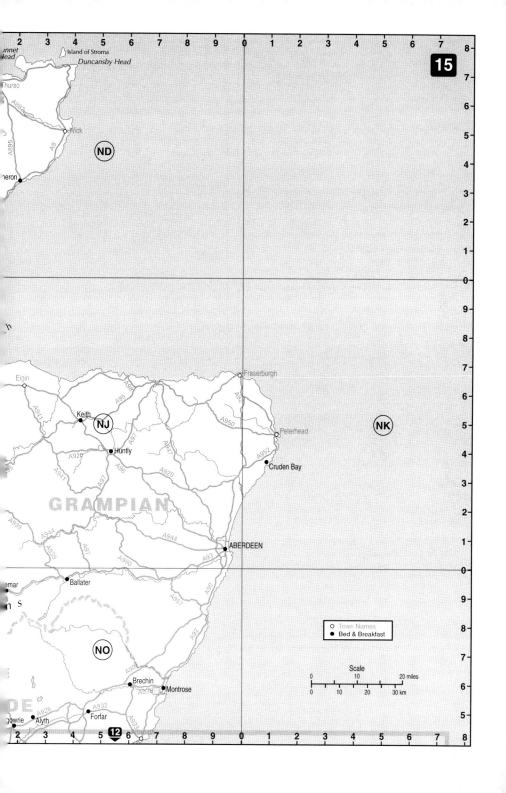

2 3 4 5 6 7 8 9 0 1 2 3 4 5 6 7

8
7
6
5
4
3
2
1
0
9
8
7
6
5
4
3
2
1
0
9
8
7
6
5

unnet
Head
Island of Stroma
Duncansby Head

Thurso

A882

A895

A9

Wick

neron

ND

h

Elgin

A96

A98

A95

A941

Keith

NJ

A97

A96

A920

Fraserburgh

A92

A950

Peterhead

A952

Cruden Bay

NK

A947

A941

A97

A96

Huntly

A926

GRAMPIAN

A939

A944

A97

A944

A93

ABERDEEN

A939

A950

A93

emar

Ballater

A957

S

NO

A92

A90

Brechin

A926

Montrose

DE

A926

gowrie

Alyth

A932

Forfar

A933

12

| Town Names |
| Bed & Breakfast |

Scale
0   10   20 miles
0   10   20   30 km

2 3 4 5 6 7 8 9 0 1 2 3 4 5 6 7

8

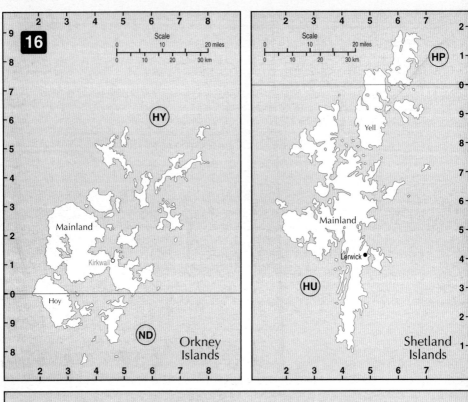

16

Orkney Islands

Scale
0 — 10 — 20 miles
0 — 10 — 20 — 30 km

HY

Mainland

Kirkwall

Hoy

ND

Shetland Islands

Scale
0 — 10 — 20 miles
0 — 10 — 20 — 30 km

HP

Yell

Mainland

Lerwick

HU

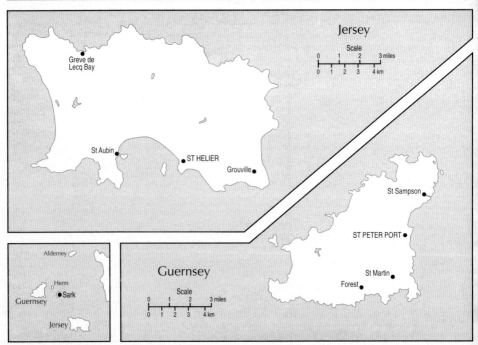

Jersey

Scale
0 — 1 — 2 — 3 miles
0 — 1 — 2 — 3 — 4 km

Greve de Lecq Bay

St Aubin

ST HELIER

Grouville

St Sampson

ST PETER PORT

St Martin

Forest

Alderney

Herm

Sark

Guernsey

Jersey

Guernsey

Scale
0 — 1 — 2 — 3 miles
0 — 1 — 2 — 3 — 4 km